ARCHAEOLOGY OF ANCIENT MEXICO AND CENTRAL AMERICA

Archaeology of Ancient Mexico and Central America
An Encyclopedia

Susan Toby Evans
David L. Webster

Editors

Garland Publishing, Inc.
New York & London
2001

This volume is dedicated to its contributors for their inestimable work in reconstructing the ancient lifeways of Mexico and Central America.

Published in 2001 by
Garland Publishing, Inc.
29 West 35th Street
New York, NY 10001

Garland is an imprint of the Taylor & Francis Group.

Production Editor:	Alexis Skinner
Copyeditor:	Jane McGary
Indexer:	Cynthia Crippen
Composition:	Publisher's Studio/Stratford Publishing Services
Development Manager:	Richard Steins
Publishing Director, Reference:	Sylvia K. Miller

Library of Congress Cataloging-in-Publication Data

Archaeology of ancient Mexico and Central America : an encyclopedia / Susan Toby
Evans, David L. Webster, editors.
    p. cm.
  Includes bibliographical references and index.
  ISBN 0-8153-0887-6 (alk. paper)
    1. Indians of Mexico—Antiquities—Encyclopedias. 2. Indians of Central
America—Antiquities—Encyclopedias. 3. Archaeology—Mexico—Encyclopedias.
4. Archaeology—Central America—Encyclopedias. 5. Mexico—Antiquities—
Encyclopedias. 6. Central America—Antiquities—Encyclopedias. I. Evans, Susan
Toby, 1945– II. Webster, David L., 1943–

F1218.6 .A73 2000
972'01—dc21
                              00-056155

CONTENTS

PREFACE

This volume includes more than 500 articles that together provide basic information about the ancient past of Middle America, that geographical area that includes the modern nations of Mexico, Guatemala, Belize, Honduras, El Salvador, Nicaragua, Costa Rica, and Panama. As an indigenous culture area, it was first inhabited well over 10,000 years ago, and by 4,000 years ago its peoples had begun to farm and live in villages. Complex societies emerged in the subsequent millennia in the region's core area, known as Mesoamerica. This culture history culminated in the Aztec empire, the last great indigenous Mesoamerican polity, which was absorbed by Spain in A.D. 1521. Indigenous cultural traits have survived strongly, and some Mesoamerican traits have spread throughout the world, but the subject of this book is, by and large, Mesoamerica before contact with European culture.

Selecting the topics for articles for the encyclopedia was a daunting task. Thousands of books and articles have been written about the cultures of ancient Mexico and Central America, but the goal of producing a single-volume encyclopedia on the subject, the first such encyclopedia in the English language, was made easier by my fine advisory panel: Elizabeth Hill Boone, Norman Hammond, Linda Manzanilla, Joyce Marcus, William Sanders, and George Stuart. Together we devised a topic list that combined balanced coverage with trends in scholarly and public interest. Many of the best-known archaeological sites, for example, are those of the Maya, and it would have been easy to devote much of the volume to them, but Mesoamerican culture encompasses many regions and time periods, and all have been covered herein.

Several scholars impressed upon me the importance of orthography, that is, providing the correct spelling of native words and place names. However, "orthography" is a very difficult thing to achieve because of how quickly orthographers change standards and the lack of consensus among them. A good example is the recent vogue in replacing "c"s in Maya words with "k"s, "ua"s with "w." Thus the site name traditionally spelled "Uaxactun" is now, in some sources, "Waxaktun." In others, it appears as "Waxactun." Because a good encyclopedia can only function properly if readers can find the subject, this volume emphasizes more traditional spellings. After all, the writing systems of the ancient Mesoamericans were not alphabetical, so any transliteration into alphabet is an arbitrary decision on the part of the recorder, as, to some extent, is the decision to include accents.

In the course of producing this encyclopedia, I have had the enormous good fortune to find hundreds of scholars who enthusiastically shared their hard-won knowledge. Because this has been a cooperative project, I dedicate this volume to its authors: without their work in the field and archives, our understanding of the ancient past of Middle America would be dim indeed. Some scholars were particularly generous with their time. Fred Lange and Jeff Wilkerson, each concerned that somewhat neglected regions receive balanced coverage, provided much-needed information about the Intermediate Area and the Gulf Lowlands. Other scholars who provided particularly timely advice were John Clark, Michael Coe, David Grove, Steve Houston, Patricia Plunket Nagoda, Helen Perlstein Pollard, Karl Taube, and Eduardo Williams. Many thanks to Dorie Reents-Budet for guiding the choice of cover art.

At Garland Publishing, Richard Steins has ably guided this volume through its development from manuscript to published book, and it has been my good fortune to benefit from his editorial expertise and great sense of humor. Sylvia Miller, Garland's Publishing Director for Reference, has provided essential help in insuring a high quality production. Other editors at Garland have been generous with help: thanks to Alexis Skinner, Joanne Daniels, Marianne Lown, and Kennie Lyman. Our copy-editor, Jane McGary, caught and dispatched innumerable problems, and we appreciate the efforts of Lara Stelmaszyk, for troubleshooting the master proofs, and Cynthia Crippen, our indexer.

This project was facilitated by support from the Pennsylvania State University, and especially by the backing of Dean Snow, head of the Department of Anthropology.

Penn State's Paterno-Pattee Library has been an important resource, as was the Pre-Columbian Studies library at Dumbarton Oaks. Special thanks to Jeffrey Quilter, director of Pre-Columbian Studies, and Bridget Gazzo, librarian. Important help was provided by Penn State students who drafted preliminary maps—Amy Kovak, Erin Falconer, David Reed, and Will Hemler.

Finally, a project that takes years to complete is grim, indeed, without the interest (and hospitality) of dear friends and family. I wish especially to thank Leena Scholten, Jon Toby and Cheryl Cross, and Mike Davis for their lively curiosity about this project.

Susan Toby Evans
Pine Grove Mills, Pennsylvania

INTRODUCTION

In 1492 Christopher Columbus set sail from Europe, seeking a route to China and Japan, the great civilizations of eastern Asia. He expected to encounter densely settled agricultural landscapes, populous cities, great kings and lords, skilled artisans, and wealthy merchants—in short, societies similar to those of Europe. The islands of the West Indies, which Columbus and later explorers first found and colonized, were certainly populated, but they displayed little of this hoped-for wealth and complexity. For twenty years the Spanish occupied themselves in the Caribbean and Panama, unaware that a few days' sail to the west and north there in fact existed a great civilization in the mainland region that we today call Mesoamerica. It is this pre-Columbian civilization, along with cultures extending to the U.S. Southwest in the north and to northern Ecuador in the south, that we explore in this encyclopedia.

We distinguish between "Middle America" and "Mesoamerica." Middle America is the geographical region consisting of modern Mexico and Central America, which consists of the nations of Guatemala, Belize (formerly British Honduras), Honduras, El Salvador, Nicaragua, Costa Rica, and Panama. Mesoamerica is a somewhat smaller region within Middle America where many pre-Columbian societies shared common cultural characteristics. In geographical terms, Mesoamerica encompasses about 912,500 square kilometers, including all but the northernmost parts of Mexico, all of Guatemala, Belize, and El Salvador, and the western zones of Honduras. Some scholars would also include Pacific coastal Nicaragua and Costa Rica, because Mesoamerican migrants, languages, and artifacts were intermittently present in those areas.

Although the boundaries of Mesoamerica are often represented by lines on a map, they are not determined by any modern national borders or well-defined topographic features, but rather by the distribution of a distinctive mix of pre-Columbian culture area traits that defined this particular part of the world as opposed to neighboring regions. In 1943, Paul Kirchhoff introduced a long list of such traits, including specific ways of farming and preparing foods, particular kinds of dress, tools, and weapons, the ball game, stepped pyramids, specialized markets, hieroglyphic writing, several different calendars, and a distinctive set of deities and associated religious beliefs and rituals, many of which featured human heart sacrifice. Some of these things, such as the ball game, were not restricted to Mesoamerica, but were found in neighboring regions as well, albeit in slightly different forms. Collectively, however, this set of cultural characteristics, along with many others noted by Kirchhoff, occurred only within Mesoamerica and was not present in the other culture areas to the north and south. There were no hard and fast barriers to migration, trade, or transmission of information. Exactly where one would draw the boundaries of Mesoamerica thus depends upon specific historical processes, and their locations would vary with time.

Several other characteristics strongly distinguished pre-Columbian Mesoamerica from regions to the north and south: Except on its northern frontiers, there were no hunting-gathering societies in Mesoamerica in the sixteenth century A.D. Wild resources certainly contributed to the Mesoamerican diet, but everywhere people were overwhelmingly dependent on agriculture. In fact, as we shall see, Mesoamerica is one of several parts of the world where effective plant and animal domestication independently developed. Its complex of domesticated native foods is as distinctive of the region as the other culture traits defined by Kirchhoff, and their use eventually spread far to the north and south.

Mesoamerica had a long tradition of urbanism that began when the first great cities appeared around 500 B.C., a process dependent on productive agricultural economies. In A.D. 1519 the Aztec capital, Tenochtitlán, was one of the most impressive and populous of the world's cities. Nowhere else in the New World, except in the Central Andes, was there a comparable development of urban life.

Mesoamerica has more time-depth as a culture area than neighboring regions, with many of its characteristic features distinguishable before 1200 B.C.

Much of Mesoamerica was periodically affected by influences emanating from particular subregions or urban centers. Archaeologists call such episodes "horizons," and they are traced by widely shared art styles and evidence of widespread trade, commerce, migrations, and perhaps military conquests.

It cannot be too strongly emphasized that a culture area does not necessarily encompass ethnic, linguistic, or political unity. Certainly no pre-Columbian peoples ever thought of themselves as Mesoamericans in any general sense. Ethnic identification instead focused on the local community or polity, each of which had its own traditional leaders, customs, resources, and conceptions of origins and history. Although warfare and conquest were common, no empires, states, or other kinds of political systems ever unified all of Mesoamerica. Within each political empire, in fact, were many different ethnic and linguistic groups, and many independent polities. Even when great empires, such as that of the Aztecs, succeeded in subordinating other autonomous polities or peoples, these tended to retain their own identities to a surprising degree. Some language families even straddled culture area boundaries. For example, the language of the Aztecs, Nahuatl, is part of a larger Uto-Aztecan language family that extends north into the southwestern United States and includes Shoshone, Paiute, and Hopi languages. Enclaves of Nahuatl dialects also have discontinuous distribution as far south as Costa Rica. What is significant is that within culture areas, centuries of intense social and economic interaction, along with broadly similar adaptations, promoted the widespread sharing of cultural characteristics despite diverse linguistic, ethic, and political affiliations.

Anthropologists and historians today use the word civilization to refer to a particular kind of cultural tradition that dominates large regions of the world for centuries or even millennia. Societies that made up preindustrial civilizations had stratified forms of social organization and the complex, highly centralized, political institutions of true states. Large, dense populations were supported by effective agrarian economies. Specialized artisans and merchants engaged in long-distance trade and commerce. Great cities or ruling centers appeared, dominated by temples, palaces, and other impressive architectural complexes. In addition to all these very tangible things, civilizations had impressive aesthetic and intellectual achievements manifested in art, writing, mathematics, astronomy, philosophy, ethical codes, and world views. Such qualitative achievements were expressed very differently from one civilization to another, giving to each a distinctive "Great Tradition," or cultural style. Fundamental ideological, intellectual, and symbolic components were reproduced over very long periods of time, giving to each civilization an enduring and very distinctive character that is shared by many interacting societies over hundreds or thousands of years. Mesoamerica is commonly recognized as a hearth of civilization in these terms.

Civilizations, of course, are dynamic. Although in any long historical tradition there may be periods of little change, there are also times of extraordinary innovation and expansion. Such changes often emanate from cities, one reason why urbanism and civilization are so closely related. Because of such dynamism, civilizations, for better or worse, tend to dominate, destroy, or absorb other kinds of societies. Whether or not we choose to regard civilizations as desirable, superior, and progressive sociocultural forms, as early anthropologists did, or simply as particularly vigorous, complex, and long-lasting cultural traditions, they are certainly competitive and often expansionistic.

When Hernán Cortes and his tiny army made their way inland from the Gulf Coast of Mexico in 1519, European and Mesoamerican civilizations confronted one another for the first time. The Spanish saw much that was very familiar in the Mesoamerican societies they encountered. Rulers and nobles lived in palaces in large towns and cities, and officials and judges kept order in their kingdoms, which had well-defined laws and territories. Most people were peasants who worked on the land and supported their lords with taxes and labor, and in many places subject peoples paid tribute to imperial capitals. Temples were staffed by professional priests who served state religions. Thousands of people exchanged goods and services in huge marketplaces. All this, the underlying infrastructure of Mesoamerican civilization, was not in principle very different from life in Spain, or from what Columbus had hoped to find in China or Japan.

On the other hand, there was much that the Spanish found utterly strange, even inexplicable. The crops Mesoamerican farmers grew—maize, beans, tomatoes, chocolate, tobacco, and a host of others—were not those of the Old World. In the temples were images of alien gods who demanded sacrifice and blood, and the sacred books told stories very different from those of the Bible. The Spanish were also perplexed by what they did not see. There were no large domestic animals to carry loads or pull plows, no iron tools or weapons, no sails, wheeled vehicles, or other labor-saving devices. Most work had to be done by human muscle power. Commerce, surprisingly, thrived in the absence of many of the standardized systems of coinage or weights and measures deemed essential by Europeans.

This combination of the familiar and the strange fascinates modern scholars just as it did the Spaniards, but for different reasons. We now know that ancient civilizations, as defined above, emerged in at least five regions of the world in addition to Mesoamerica—Egypt, Mesopotamia, the Indus Valley, China, and the Central Andes. All shared basic organizational features, but there was strong variation in subsistence economies, technologies, and Great Tradition elements from civilization to civilization. Such variation, plus the fact that each tradition of civilization emerged at a different time and had a highly distinctive historical trajectory, tells us that each case represents a process of development largely or wholly independent of the others. Each, in a sense, is a separate experiment in long-term culture change. The shared basic organizational features show not only that cultures and societies change, but that they evolve, and that there are regular processes, or principles, that govern cultural evolution.

Although anthropologists debate the nature and mechanisms of these evolutionary processes, the information presented in this volume demonstrates a series of broad, unfolding patterns of cultural development in Mesoamerica and adjacent culture areas. Such patterns include the origins and spread of agricultural economies out of earlier collecting or foraging ways of life and the emergence of large, dense populations, impressive sedentary settlements, and hierarchically organized political systems.

Central to our understanding of such regular changes is the idea that human cultural behavior is, in part, an adaptive response to environmental challenges and opportunities, with environment understood here to include features of landscape and climate, biota, and other human groups. This perspective is called cultural ecology, and many of the entries in this encyclopedia have implicit or explicit ecological themes. As we shall see, both natural and cultural landscapes have changed—sometimes dramatically—during the thousands of years that humans have inhabited them.

The Land

Mesoamerica. Middle America is environmentally diverse, united by great mountain systems that form the western "spine" of the North and South American continents in the Northern Arid Zone, the coastal and Sierra ranges of California that extend down into Baja California and along the western edge of the continent. The Rocky Mountains extend south, becoming the Sierra Madre Oriental on the west and, on the eastern side of Middle America, the Sierra Madre Occidental. The two ranges enclose an extensive high plateau and coalesce around the Basin of Mexico, where Tenochtitlán, the Aztec capital, was located and overlaid by modern Mexico City. Looming over Mexico City are majestic snow-covered mountains: Ixtaccíhuatl and Popocateptl, nearly 18,000 feet high. They are part of the Neovolcanic Axis, a series of volcanic peaks running from east to west at this latitude.

Other highland systems at lesser elevations continue down to the Isthmus of Tehuantepec, a low-lying region that has long provided a corridor between the Pacific and Atlantic coasts of Mesoamerica. Still farther south rise the mountains of southeastern Mexico and Guatemala, the Sierra Madre del Sur, dominated by impressive volcanic cones, some over 14,000 feet high. Many of these are active today, and eruptions and earthquakes pose situational threats to human populations. Yet eruptions bring to the surface fresh mineral deposits that in the long run weather into fertile soils and also produce volcanic glass (obsidian), the premier cutting tool material in pre-Columbian Mesoamerica. Impressive chains of mountains extend through southern Central America and eventually join the foothills of the northern Andes in Colombia, where long river valleys and mountain basins lead south, in ramplike fashion, to Ecuador and the Central Andes, the heart of the Inka empire in the early sixteenth century A.D.

All but the most northerly parts of Mesoamerica lie in the tropics, but the region is characterized by striking variations in temperature, rainfall, and biota that are controlled as much by altitude as by latitude. Mesoamerica encompasses within its boundaries alpine peaks, temperate plateaus, hot and humid lowlands, and even desert-like regions. One can now travel by car in a single day from the high, semiarid Basin of Mexico, at an elevation of 7,800 feet (2,400 meters) to the humid tropical lowlands of the Gulf Coast. Other lowland zones are found along the Pacific coast, but the largest expanse of landscape below 1,000 meters in elevation is in southeastern Mexico, Belize, and northern Guatemala, where ancient Maya civilization flourished. Distinctive assemblages of flora and fauna characterize different elevation zones, and resources such as obsidian, basalt, and metals had discontinuous geological distributions.

High, rugged topography influences the amount and seasonality of rainfall, and climate tends to be marked by strong wet-season/dry-season fluctuations. Rain generally is heaviest in the warm months from May to December, but exactly when it falls, and in what amounts, are conditioned locally by altitude and exposure. Northern and western parts of Mesoamerica are usually drier than its southern and eastern portions because so much of the precipitation comes from westward-moving summer storms originating in the Caribbean and Gulf of Mexico.

Mesoamerica's ethnic and linguistic groups' diversity is partly due to the compartmentalization of the landscape into separate valleys and basins. Although the Mesoamerican highlands are drained by many rivers, most are not navigable for great distances. No river system serves to unite the whole culture area, as the Tigris-Euphrates did in the Near East, or the Yellow River in north China. Mesoamerica is consequently not a riverine civilization focused on a great artery of travel and commerce or a single source of irrigation water, as were most of those in the Old World. Nevertheless, many valued items, including obsidian for cutting tools, salt, cotton, precious skins and feathers, gold, jade, and cacao (chocolate), were obtained in restricted locales and then moved great distances by human porters as trade goods or tribute. There was also extensive maritime trade using huge dugout canoes along the Pacific, Atlantic, and Gulf coasts. Some prized goods, such as polychrome pottery, turquoise, copper bells, weapons, and gold, were exchanged with peoples far beyond the borders of Mesoamerica both to the north and south. Several subregions within Mesoamerica, sometimes called nuclear areas, are of particular cultural-historical significance. Of these, the Basin of Mexico and the Valley of Oaxaca are especially important because of their long traditions of urban civilization and expansive states. Other dynamic regions are the Gulf Lowlands, where the Olmec created one of Mesoamerica's first complex societies, and the Maya Lowlands, where architecture, writing, calendrics, and art all achieved great sophistication from about A.D. 300 to 900.

Chronological and Evolutionary Overview

Archaeologists and ethnohistorians have developed many chronological frameworks for Mesoamerica and its neighboring culture areas. Some of these, such as local ceramic sequences, are very detailed and specific to particular regions or even single sites. Here we present instead a very broad, introductory overview briefly summarizing what we know about the earliest human populations, the emergence and spread of food production, and the rise of complex societies. First, however, we should consider the kinds of evidence used to date events in the past or changes through time.

Cultures throughout the Northern Arid Zone, the Intermediate Area, and Mesoamerica each had distinctive traditions concerning their origins and their own known or imagined pasts. For the most part, such information was passed down orally, although to some degree it was also symbolically expressed in art. All these cultures, in other words, had native histories that helped them to conceive and make sense of their own pasts. Of the three great regions under consideration here, only in Mesoamerica were there pre-Columbian historical records in our Western sense of the word—information preserved in the form of written documents. Screen-fold books of bark paper or deerskin were repositories of esoteric religious, ritual, and divinitory information. More practically, books also recorded historical events, migration stories, royal genealogies, and probably much detailed economic information concerning taxes, tribute, and land holdings. Most significantly for our purposes, many such texts included dates recorded in complex native systems of calendrical notations. Regrettably, only a handful of pre-Columbian books from the highlands of Mexico and northern Yucatán survived the Spanish conquest and the subsequent Colonial period. Many books written after the conquest, however, preserved native scribal and literary conventions and information, and the Spaniards themselves recorded many of the ancient oral traditions, often in cooperation with Indian informants.

Fortunately, many pre-Columbian inscriptions and texts were also carved or painted in more durable form on wood, bone, shell, and stone. The oldest known calendrical glyphs are over 2,000 years old, but the largest corpus of written material comes from the Maya Lowlands, particularly after about A.D. 300, when the Maya began to write copiously and also to use a system of calendrical reckoning called the Long Count. Scholars decoded the Long Count almost a century ago, so we can directly express Long Count dates in terms of our own calendar, often with such precision that the specific day of a particular ancient event is known. Using all these historical sources, we can piece together quite a detailed story about what happened in pre-Columbian times—i.e., we have a real historical record to work with, directly or indirectly produced by ancient Mesoamerican peoples themselves.

Even for Mesoamerica, however, such historical information is rare, patchy in its distribution, sometimes hard to understand, and uninformative about the earliest times. The introductory framework presented below, as well as the more detailed chronological information provided by many of the entries, are thus based on standard archaeological methods of dating past events and processes. These include stratigraphic relationships, changes in pottery styles, archeomagnetism, and obsidian hydration dating. By far the most important, however, is radiocarbon (14C) dating, which everywhere is essential in determining prehistoric chronology. None of these methods is extremely precise, however, and archaeologists usually can reliably date past events only within 50-100 years. An exception is when tree-ring dating (dendrochronology) is possible, as it is in some parts of the Northern Arid Zone. This method allows precision comparable to that provided by calendrical dates, but unfortunately it has not been widely applied in either Mesoamerica or the Intermediate Area.

The Earliest Peoples: Paleoindians. New World populations predating the end of the Pleistocene are called Paleoindians. Archaeologists agree that the earliest human inhabitants of the New World came from northeast Asia in one or several migrations, crossing a vast land bridge that connected Alaska and Siberia during periods of Pleistocene glacial advance, or moving along the shoreline in simple boats. Until very recently, however, there were spirited debates about how early the first migrations occurred. Everyone has long agreed that hunting-gathering peoples using distinctive Clovis projectile points were widespread in the western United States by 11,500 to 11,000 B.P. Artifacts of these Clovis people, and their Folsom successors, were long ago found with extinct Pleistocene mammoths and bison at kill sites in New Mexico, on the fringes of the Northern Arid Zone. Similar artifacts have since been unearthed by archaeologists in northern Mexico, and surface finds of these distinctive tools occur as far south as Panama.

Environmental conditions many thousands of years ago, of course, were very different than those described above for historical times. Extinct Pleistocene elephants roamed cold grasslands in the Basin of Mexico, as revealed at Santa Isabel Iztapan, where people killed and dismembered mammoth sometime around 11,000 B.P. Northern Yucatán was dominated by temperate, thorn-scrub vegetation prior to about 14,000 years ago, instead of tropical forest.

But what about traces of earlier humans? In 1997 a consensus was reached among Paleoindian scholars that human settlements as far south as central Chile date to at least 13,500 years ago, and to possibly as much as 33,000 years ago. These dates have obvious implications for the regions we are concerned with here. Middle America served as a huge funnel through which expanding human populations moved from North America to South America, and they must have done so thousands of years before the Chilean settlements were established. Archaeological sites that might date from these early times are very rare in the regions we examine in this encyclopedia, however, and present, at best, equivocal evidence for the presence of humans before 13,500 B.P.

Two examples are the sites of Valsequillo and Tlapacoya in the Central Highlands of Mexico. Each has yielded what may be human-made tools in possible association with remains of extinct Pleistocene mammals, and both have produced radiocarbon dates in excess of 21,000 years old. At both sites, however, associations of bones, tools, and dated samples are questionable, and so are the human origins of the artifacts themselves. Much further south, at El Bosque, Nicaragua, similar problems surround the discovery of sloth bones, possible implements, and signs of burning in a bog deposit. At best, archaeologists will now have to regard such finds as more plausible, given the antiquity of humans in South America, but solid evidence for early humans in our regions predating the very end of the Pleistocene remains to be found.

What we can say for certain is that hunter-gatherers were widespread throughout Middle America well before the end of the Pleistocene. Small communities of such people ranged widely across environments very different from those of today. Although their artifacts are often associated with large game animals, plants and small animals probably contributed as much or more to their diets. As conditions changed after the end of the Pleistocene, it was some of these populations that very gradually pioneered the new agricultural ways of life we consider next.

The Origins and Spread of Food Production

Archaeological evidence of hunting and gathering peoples who made the transition from Pleistocene to Holocene (recent) environments is widespread in the Northern Arid Zone and Mesoamerica. The interval between the last glacial episode, which ended by about 8000 B.C, and 2000 B.C. is Mesoamerica's Archaic period, which was the time of one of the most momentous evolutionary processes that has ever affected ancient humans—the origins of agriculture.

Hunter-gatherer people the world over have cleverly and flexibly used a wide range of resources and also directly manipulated plant and animal populations to increase their productivity or reliability. Such manipulation has sometimes resulted in varieties of plants and animals whose ranges, morphologies, and reproductive habits have been altered by human interference and selection. We may properly regard these as domestic plants or animals. In a few regions of the world, commonly called "hearths" of food production, integrated complexes of domesticates gradually became available over hundreds or thousands of years. They were so productive that they stimulated the widespread appearance of settled farming societies, one of the most fundamental transformations in human cultural evolution.

Each of these agricultural complexes was dominated by one or several staples that contributed heavily to the diet, along with a host of other useful domesticates. Parts or all of these complexes spread to people in adjacent regions outside the original hearths, many of whom had carried on their own local experiments with domestication that made them receptive to such borrowing. Mesoamerica is one such world agricultural hearth. Although animal domesticates were rare (mainly dogs, turkeys, and varieties of ducks), Mesoamerican farmers developed a wealth of cultivated plants that were eaten or otherwise useful. These included, in addition to the three staples already mentioned, chocolate, tomatoes, chile peppers, cotton, avocados, gourds, and tobacco, to name only the most familiar. By far the most important native staple was maize (Zea mays)—what we in the United States call corn—which, along with other domesticated plants, spread widely throughout both the Northern Arid Zone and the Intermediate Area. In 1948, finds of well-preserved early maize in New Mexico stimulated a series of research projects that attempted to trace the origins of maize, beans, squash, and other important New World plants and to determine whether domestication in Mesoamerica was independent of similar processes in the Old World.

Research by archaeologists, botanists, and plant geneticists, aided by recent advances in radiocarbon dating, now provides a general picture of the origins of Mesoamerican agriculture. Most of the direct archaeological evidence comes from dry caves in the valleys of Tehuacán and Oaxaca in Mesoamerica, and Tamaulipas on the southern fringe of the Northern Arid Zone.

Domestic maize was developed from a closely related wild grass called teosinte, which grows in the uplands of west-central Mexico. Although directly dated samples are no older than 4,700 years, it seems likely that maize was first domesticated sometime between 4000 and 3000 B.C. Between 4,000 and 3,500 years ago maize, probably accompanied by a suite of other plants, spread widely throughout highland and lowland Mesoamerica. At first, such plants were adjuncts to diets based on wild resources, but because they were predictable and storable they became increasingly important, and after 2000 B.C. many Mesoamericans became settled, pottery-using agriculturalists.

Complex Societies and the Spanish Conquest

Mesoamerica. Shortly after 2000 B.C., during the Mesoamerican Formative period (2500 B.C. to A.D. 300), some societies began to develop complex forms of hierarchical social and political organization. Although our understanding of the beginnings of this process of political evolution is poor, the evidence indicates that some individuals or families became highly ranked and enjoyed greater inherited prestige, authority, and wealth than others. By 1200–800 B.C. powerful chiefs in the Gulf Coast, the Valley of Oaxaca, and elsewhere dominated small, multicommunity polities from impressive capitals. These ruling centers had monumental civic structures, houses of particularly fine quality, and in some places large stone monuments carved with complex and highly distinctive symbols that projected rulership, ritual authority, and world view. Raw materials such as jade and finely worked objects of high value were exchanged over long distances, and distinctively Mesoamerican symbols, along with the belief systems they reflect, were widely shared as well. Such widespread communication contributed to the formation of the first Mesoamerican cultural horizon.

By mid-to-late Formative times (after 800 B.C.) regional chiefdoms or incipient states were common in much of Mesoamerica, and populations grew rapidly, perhaps because staple crops were more productive than ever before. Writing, calendars, and many other characteristic Mesoamerican cultural features are evident by Late Formative times. About 500–300 B.C. the first great urban state, centered on the city of Monte Albán, was founded in the Valley of Oaxaca. Shortly thereafter an even larger city, Teotihuacán, developed in the Basin of Mexico, and the cultural, political and economic influence of this great metropolis permeated much of Mesoamerica during the first part of the Classic period (A.D. 300–900), forming a second great horizon. Other impressive Classic cultures emerged on the Gulf Coast, in the highlands of Guatemala. Scores of Lowland Maya polities, each centered on a ruling dynasty and capital, warred and traded with one another.

Teotihuacán's power had declined by A.D. 700, and many Classic Maya centers declined between A.D. 700 and 900, but other thriving Postclassic (A.D. 900–1519) cultures replaced them. In the early fifteenth century the Aztecs began their career of conquest, and by 1519 they had created the largest city and political system ever known in pre-Columbian Mesoamerica.

The Spanish Conquest. Spanish and allied Indian forces led by Hernán Cortes captured the Aztec capital of Tenochtitlán in 1521. During the next thirty years most of the rest of Mesoamerica fell under Spanish colonial control, although some native polities, such as the Maya Itza kingdom in northern Guatemala, held out until as late as 1697. Spanish expeditions pushed north from their Mexican bases and established a colonial presence in the Northern Arid Zone in the mid-to-late sixteenth century, and by about the same time much of the Intermediate Area was subjugated. Although the sixteenth century brought to an end the independent evolution of native cultures in Mesoamerica and adjacent regions, many populations today are direct descendants of pre-Columbian peoples and vigorously maintain many ancient cultural practices, reminding us of the durability of pre-Columbian traditions.

FURTHER READINGS

Adams, R. E. W. 1991. *Prehistoric Mesoamerica.* Norman: University of Oklahoma Press.

Blanton, R. E., S. A. Kowalewski, G. M. Feinman, and L. A. Finsten. 1993. *Ancient Mesoamerica: A Comparison of Change in Three Regions.* Cambridge: Cambridge University Press.

Carmack, R. J., J. Gasco, and G. H. Gossen. 1996. *The Legacy of Mesoamerica.* New York: Prentice-Hall.

Helms, M. W. 1982. *Middle America: A Culture History of Heartland and Frontiers.* Lanham, Md.: University Press of America.

Kirchhoff, P. 1981 [1943]. Mesoamerica: Its Geographic Limits, Ethnic Composition and Cultural Characteristics. In J. Graham (ed.), *Ancient Mesoamerica,* pp. 1–10. (Reprinted from *Acta Americana* 1:92–107.) Palo Alto, Calif: Peek Publications.

Sanders, W. T., and B. Price. 1968. *Mesoamerica: The Evolution of a Civilization.* New York: Random House.

Weaver, M. P. 1993. *The Aztecs, Maya, and their Predecessors.* San Diego: Academic Press.

West, R. C., and J. P. Augelli. 1989. *Middle America: Its Lands and Peoples.* Englewood Cliffs, N.J.: Prentice-Hall.

Willey, G. R. 1966. *An Introduction to American Archaeology.* Vol. 1, *North and Middle America.* Englewood Cliffs, N.J.: Prentice-Hall.

David L. Webster and Susan Toby Evans

SUBJECT GUIDE

Laguna de los Cerros
Laguna Zope
Lamanai
Lambityeco
La Libertad
Loma Torremote
Los Angeles
Machomoncobe
El Manatí
Matacapan and the Tuxtla Region
Maya: Motagua Region
Maya Culture and History
Maya Lowlands: North
Maya Lowlands: South
Mazatan Region
El Mesak
Mezcala Lapidary Style
Michoacán Region
Mirador
El Mirador
Mixtec History, Culture, and Religion
La Mojarra
Monagrillo
Monte Albán
Monte Negro
Morelos Region
Morett
Nacascolo
Naco
Nadzcaan
Naj Tunich
Naranjal and Environs
Los Naranjos
Nicaragua: North Central and Pacific Regions
Nicoya, Greater, and Guanacaste Region
Nohmul
Northern Arid Zone
Northwestern Frontier
Nosara
Oaxaca and Tehuantepec Region
Olmec Culture
Olmec-Guerrero Style
El Opeño
El Ostional
Oxkintok
La Pachona
Pánuco
Paso de la Amada
Pavón

Peñoles Region
Petexbatun Region
Piedras Negras
El Pital
Playa de los Muertos
Puebla-Tlaxcala Region
Puerto Escondido
Pulltrouser Swamp
Purrón Dam
Quachilco
Remojadas
Río Azul
Río Verde Region
Río Viejo
Salinas la Blanca
San Antonio Nogalar
San Cristóbal
San Isidro and Environs
San José Mogote
San Lorenzo Tenochtitlán
Santa Catarina
Santa Leticia
Santa Luisa
Santa Marta Cave
Santa Rita Corozal
Seibal
Shaft Tombs
La Sierra
Siteia
Soconusco–South Pacific Coast and Piedmont Region
South America, Interaction of Mesoamerica with
Southeast Mesoamerica
Stann Creek District
Stela Cult
Tabachines
El Tajín
Tancol
Tayasal
Tehuacán Region
Temesco
Teopantecuanitlán
Teotihuacán
Tepeapulco
El Terremote
Tetimpa Region
Teuchitlan Tradition
El Teúl
Tibas, Talamanca de
Ticoman

Tikal
Tilantongo
Tlacozotitlán
Tlalancaleca
Tlapacoya
Tlatilco
Toluca Region
Tonalá
Toniná
Tres Zapotes
Tula Region
Tututepec del Sur
Uaxactun
Uxmal
La Venta
Las Victorias
Vidor
El Viejón
Villa Tiscapa
West Mexico
Xico
Xochipala Style
Xochitécatl
Yagul
Yarumela
Yaxhá
Yaxuna
Yohualinchan
Zacatenco
Zapotec Culture and Religion
Zapotitan Region
Zempoala

Classic Period (A.D. 300–900)
Abaj Takalik
Acahualinca
Acámbaro-Cerro el Chivo
Acanceh
Ahualulco
Alta Vista de Chalchihuites
Altar de Sacrificios
Altun Ha
Amalucan
Amapa
Apatzingán Region
Asuncion Mita
Atemajac Region
Atzompa
Ayala

Azcapotzalco
Aztatlan Complex
Bajío Region
Balamkú
Balcón de Montezuma
Basin of Mexico
Becan
Bonampak
Buenavista Huaxcama and the Río Verde Region
Bugambilias
Cacaxtla
El Cajón
Calakmul
Cantona
Caracol
La Ceiba
Cerén
Cerro de las Mesas
Cerro Encantado
Cerro Palenque
Cerro Portezuelo
Cerro Zapotecas
Cerros
Chahuite Escondido
Chalchihuites Culture
Chalchuapa
Chiapa de Corzo
Chichén Itzá
Chihuahua, West Central
Cholula
Cobá
Colha
Comala
Comalcalco
La Conchita
Copán
Copán Region
Corralitos
Cotzumalhuapa Sites: Bilbao, El Baúl, and El Castillo
Coyotlatelco
Cozumel Island
Cuello
Cuicatlán Canyon
Dainzú
Dos Pilas
Dzibilchaltún
Edzna
Etlatongo
Fonseca, Gulf of

Maya: Motagua Region
Chalchuapa
Copán
Los Naranjos
Quiriguá
Salitron Viejo
Santa Leticia
Tenampua
Las Victorias
Yarumela

Maya Lowlands: North
Acanceh
Becan
Chichén Itzá
Cobá
Cozumel Island
Dzibilchaltún
Edzna
Hochob
Izamal
Jaina
Kabah
Labna
Mayapan
Naranjal and Environs
Oxkintok
Putun
Sayil and Chac
Tulum
Uxmal
Yaxuna

Maya Lowlands: South
Altar de Sacrificios
Altun Ha
Balamkú
Belize River Region
Bonampak
Calakmul
Caracol
Cerros
Colha
Comalcalco
Cuello
Dos Pilas
Holmul
Itzan
Lacandón Maya

Lamanai
Lubaantún
El Mirador
Nadzcaan
Naj Tunich
Naranjo
Nohmul
Palenque
Petexbatun Region
Piedras Negras
Planchón de las Figuras
Pulltrouser Swamp
Río Azul
Santa Rita Corozal
Seibal
Stann Creek District
Tayasal
Tikal
Uaxactun
Xicalango
Xunantunich
Yaxchilan
Yaxhá

Michoacán Region
Apatzingán Region
Chupícuaro
Huandacareo
Ihuatzio
Tarascan Culture and Religion
Tingambato
Tzintzuntzan
Zinapécuaro

Morelos Region
Chalcatzingo
Chalcatzingo: Ritual Appropriation of the Sacred
   Landscape
Cuauhnahuac and Teopanzolco
Gualupita
Huaxtepec
Tepoztlán
Xochicalco
Yautépec

Northern Arid Zone
Acámbaro-Cerro el Chivo
Bajío Region
Buenavista Huaxcama and Río Verde Region

Casas Grandes
Cerro de Trincheras
Chaco Canyon
Chihuahua, West Central
Corralitos
Machomoncobe
Pala Chica Cave
Playa de los Muertos
Snaketown

Northwestern Frontier
Alta Vista de Chalchihuites
Amapa
Aztatlan Complex
Cerro Encantado
Chalchihuites Culture
Guasave and Related Sites
Huistle, Cerro del
La Quemada
Schroeder Site
El Teúl

Oaxaca and Tehuantepec Region
Atzompa
Coixtlahuaca
Coyotera, La
Cueva Blanca
Cuicatlán Canyon
Dainzú
Etlatongo
Fábrica San José
Gheo-Shih
Guiengola
Guila Naquitz
Huitzo
Jalieza
Laguna Zope
Lambityeco
Mitla
Mixtec History, Culture, and Religion
Monte Albán
Monte Negro
Peñoles Region
Río Verde
Río Viejo
San José Mogote
Tilantongo
Tututepec del Sur
Yagul

Zapotec Culture and Religion
Zapotec Mortuary Practices

Puebla-Tlaxcala Region
Amalucan
Las Bocas
Cacaxtla
Cantona
Cerro Zapotecas
Cholula
Gualupita Las Dalias
Tepexi el Viejo
Tetimpa Region
Tizatlán
Tlalancaleca
Xochitécatl

Soconusco–Pacific Coast and Piedmont Region
Abaj Takalik
El Bálsamo
Cotzumalhuapa Sites: Bilbao, El Baul, and El Castillo
Cotzumalhuapa Style
Izapa
Izapa Style
Mazatan Region
El Mesak
Paso de la Amada
Salinas la Blanca
Tonalá

Southeast Mesoamerica
El Cajón
Cerén
Cerro Palenque
Cihuatán and Santa María
Cuyamel Caves
Fonseca, Gulf of
Gualjoquito
Naco
Playa de los Muertos
Puerto Escondido
La Sierra
Travesía
Zapotitan Region

Tehuacán Region
Cuayucatepec
Purrón Dam
Quachilco

CONTRIBUTORS

Elliot M. Abrams
Ohio University
Architecture: Vernacular-Mundane
Lime and Limestone

Karen R. Adams
Crow Canyon Archaeological Center
Chihuahua, West Central

R. E. W. Adams
University of Texas
Río Azul

Ana María Alvarez P.
Instituto Nacional de Antropología e Historia, Mexico
Machomoncobe

Patricia Rieff Anawalt
University of California, Los Angeles
Clothing
Weaving and Textiles

Anthony P. Andrews
New College, University of South Florida
Mayapan
Salt

E. Wyllys Andrews V
Tulane University
Doris Zemurray Stone

George Andrews
University of Oregon
Comalcalco
Hochob

Wendy Ashmore
University of Pennsylvania
Gualjoquito
Xunantunich

Ivonne Athie
Instituto Nacional de Antropología e Historia, Mexico
Obsidian: Properties and Sources

Joseph W. Ball
California State University, San Diego
Maya Lowlands: North
Naranjo

Christopher S. Beekman
Vanderbilt University
Atemajac Region
Bugambilias
El Grillo
El Ixtépete
Ixtlan del Río
Tabachines

Frances F. Berdan
California State University, San Bernardino
Aztec Culture and History
Cotton
Tribute

Ronald L. Bishop
Smithsonian Institution
Jade

Michael Blake
University of British Columbia
Canajasté
Mazatan Region
Paso de la Amada

Richard E. Blanton
Purdue University
Exchange Media
Monte Albán

Jeffrey P. Blomster
Yale University
Etlatongo

Frederick J. Bové
University of California, Santa Barbara
Abaj Takalik
Cotzumalhuapa Sites: Bilbao, El Baúl, and El Castillo
Tonalá

James Brady
George Washington University
Caves
Cuyamel Caves

Rosa Brambila Paz
Instituto Nacional de Antropología e Historia, Mexico
Bajío Region

Juergen K. Brueggemann
Instituto Nacional de Antropología e Historia, Mexico
El Tajín

Karen Olsen Bruhns
San Francisco State University
South America, Interaction of Mesoamerica with

Elizabeth M. Brumfiel
Albion College
Huexotla
Xaltocan
Xico

Ellen S. Brush
Independent Scholar
Barnard Site

Robert Bye
Universidad Autónoma de México
Flowers

Edward Calnek
University of Rochester
Tenochtitlán-Tlatelolco

John B. Carlson
The Center for Archaeoastronomy
Astronomy, Archaeoastronomy, and Astrology

Robert M. Carmack
State University of New York, Albany
Utatlán

Davíd Carrasco
Princeton University
Central Mexican Religion
Sacrifice

Pedro Carrasco
Brandeis University and State University of New York, Stony Brook
Otomí Cultural Tradition

Maria Tereza Cavazos Perez
The Pennsylvania State University
Geography and Climate

John K. Chance
Arizona State University
Ethnicity

Thomas H. Charlton
University of Iowa
Otumba
Tepeapulco

Arlen F. Chase
University of Central Florida
Caracol
Tayasal

Diane Z. Chase
University of Central Florida
Caracol
Santa Rita Corozal

Oswaldo Chinchilla Mazariegos
Universidad de San Carlos de Guatemala, Escuela de Historia
Cotzumalhuapa Style
Iximché
Mixco Viejo
Zaculeu

John E. Clark
Brigham Young University
Chiapas Interior Plateau
Formative Period
Gulf Lowlands: South Region
Izapa
La Libertad
Mirador
Obsidian: Tools, Techniques, and Products
Tenam Rosario and Environs

Robert H. Cobean
Instituto Nacional de Antropología e Historia, Mexico
Coyotlatelco
Toltec Culture
Tula Region

Michael Coe
Yale University
Chocolate and Cacao
Food and Cuisine

Sophie Coe
Yale University
Food and Cuisine

Clemency Chase Coggins
Boston University
Chichén Itzá

George L. Cowgill
Arizona State University
Teotihuacán

Ann Cyphers
Universidad Autónoma de México
San Lorenzo Tenochtitlán

Annick Daneels
Belgian Archaeological Mission
Isla de Sacrificios

J. Andrew Darling
Independent Scholar
Huistle, Cerro del
El Teúl

Beatriz de la Fuente
Universidad Autónoma de México
Mural Painting

Arthur Demarest
Vanderbilt University
Dos Pilas
El Mesak
Petexbatun Region
Santa Leticia
Las Victorias

Richard A. Diehl
University of Alabama
Arroyo Pesquero
La Mojarra

Boyd Dixon
International Archaeological Research Institute
Los Naranjos
Tenampua
Yarumela

Keith A. Dixon
California State University, Long Beach
Pala Chica Cave
Temesco

Robert D. Drennan
University of Pittsburgh
Cuayucatepec
Fábrica San José
Quachilco

Peter S. Dunham
Cleveland State University
Minerals, Ores, and Mining

Munro S. Edmonson
Tulane University
Bernardino de Sahagún

Kitty Emery
Cornell University
Fauna

Deborah Erdman-Cornavaca
Independent Scholar
León Viejo

Francisco Estrada Belli
Boston University
Holmul
Lubaantún
Nohmul

Susan Toby Evans
The Pennsylvania State University
Alta Verapaz Region
Asunción Mita
Chiconautla
Cihuatecpan
Coixtlahuaca
Cuicuilco
Family and Household
Gardens
Huaxtepec
Jaina
El Manatí
Sweat Baths
Tenochtitlán: Palaces

Scott L. Fedick
University of California, Riverside
Agriculture and Domestication
Naranjal and Environs

Gary M. Feinman
University of Wisconsin, Madison
Crafts and Craft Specialization
Economic Organization

Laura Finsten
McMaster University
Jalieza
Peñoles Region

Kent V. Flannery
University of Michigan
Ignacio Bernal
Cueva Blanca
Dog
Gheo-Shih
Guila Naquitz
Huitzo
Salinas la Blanca
San José Mogote
Turkeys

Laraine Fletcher
Adelphi University
Nicaragua: North Central and Pacific Regions
La Pachona
San Jacinto
Las Tapias

William Folan
Universidad Autónoma de Campeche
Calakmul

Anabel Ford
University of California, Santa Barbara
Belize River Region

Michael Foster
Independent Scholar
Cerro Encantado
Chalchihuites Culture
Guasave and Related Sites
Schroeder Site
Shaft Tombs

Melvin Fowler
University of Wisconsin
Amalucan

William Fowler
Vanderbilt University
Cihuatán and Santa María

David A. Freidel
Southern Methodist University
Cerros
Yaxuna

Ann Corinne Freter
Ohio University
Dating Methods

Peter T. Furst
State University of New York, Albany
Intoxicants and Intoxication

Luís Javier Galván Villegas
Instituto Nacional de Antropología e Historia, Mexico
Atemajac Region
Bugambilias
El Grillo
Tabachines

James F. Garber
Southwest Texas State University
Ground Stone Tools

Angel García Cook
Instituto Nacional de Antropología e Historia, Mexico
Cacaxtla
Cantona
Gualupita Las Dalias
Tizatlán
Tlalancaleca

Florentino García Cruz
Instituto Nacional de Antropología e Historia, Mexico
Balamkú
Nadzcaan

Joaquin García-Bárcena
Instituto Nacional de Antropología e Historia, Mexico
Santa Marta Cave

Janine Gasco
California State University, Dominguez Hills
Calendrics
Colonial Period

Susan D. Gillespie
University of Illinois at Urbana-Champaign
Archaeology: Research Design and Field Methods

Mary Glowacki
Florida State University
Bernal Díaz del Castillo

Nancy Gonlin
Bellevue Community College
Family and Household
Museums, Archives, and Libraries

Rebecca González Lauck
Instituto Nacional de Antropología e Historia, Mexico
La Venta

Ernesto González Licón
Instituto Nacional de Antropología e Historia, Mexico
Atzompa
Dainzú

Shirley Gorenstein
Rensselaer Polytechnic Institute
Acámbaro-Cerro el Chivo
Tepexi el Viejo

Elizabeth Graham
York University
Stann Creek District

Ian Graham
Harvard University
Alfred Percival Maudslay
Sylvanus Griswold Morley
Herbert Joseph Spinden

Merle Greene Robertson
Pre-Columbian Art Research Institute
Palenque

David C. Grove
University of Illinois at Urbana-Champaign
Las Bocas
Caves of Guerrero
Chalcatzingo
Gualupita
Laguna de los Cerros
Olmec Culture

Juan Vicente Guerrero
Independent Scholar
Nicoya, Greater, and Guanacaste Region

María de la Luz Gutiérrez
Instituto Nacional de Antropología e Historia, Mexico
Corralitos

Norman Hammond
Boston University
Cuello
La Milpa
J. Eric S. Thompson

Peter D. Harrison
Maxwell Museum of Anthropology
Tikal

Herbert Harvey
University of Wisconsin
Mathematics

George Hasemann
Instituto Hondureño de Antropología e Historia
Los Naranjos

Ross Hassig
University of Oklahoma
Famine
Militarism and Conflict
Transport
Weaponry

Marion Popenoe de Hatch
Universidad del Valle de Guatemala
Kaminaljuyu
Uaxactun

Dan M. Healan
Tulane University
Tollan
Tula de Hidalgo

Paul Healy
Trent University
Río Claro

John S. Henderson
Cornell University
Naco
Puerto Escondido

Thomas R. Hester
University of Texas
Chipped Stone Tool Production and Products
Colha
Paleoindian Period
Silex

Doris Heyden
Instituto Nacional de Antropología e Historia, Mexico
Diego Durán

Frederic Hicks
University of Louisville
Azcapotzalco
Texcoco
Texcotzingo

Kenneth G. Hirth
The Pennsylvania State University
El Cajón
Morelos Region
Salitron Viejo
Xochicalco

Mary G. Hodge
University of Houston Clear Lake
Chalco
Charles Gibson
Market Systems

John Hoopes
University of Kansas
Guayabo de Turrialba
Monagrillo

Dorothy Hosler
Massachusetts Institute of Technology
Metal: Tools, Techniques, and Products

Stephen D. Houston
Brigham Young University
Civic-Ceremonial Center
Maya Lowlands: South
Piedras Negras
Stelae
Sweat Baths

Justin R. Hyland
University of Capetown
Corralitos

Kevin J. Johnston
Ohio State University
Itzan

Christopher Jones
University of Pennsylvania
Caches

Arthur A. Joyce
Vanderbilt University
Río Verde Region
Río Viejo
Tututepec del Sur

Rosemary Joyce
University of California, Berkeley
Cerro Palenque
Cuyamel Caves
Playa de los Muertos
Travesía

Ellen Abbott Kelley
Southern Illinois University
Alta Vista de Chalchihuites

J. Charles Kelley
Southern Illinois University
Alta Vista de Chalchihuites

Jane H. Kelley
University of Calgary
Chihuahua, West Central

Susan Kellogg
University of Houston
Ethnohistorical Sources and Methods

Edward B. Kurjack
Western Illinois University
Dzibilchaltún

Frederick W. Lange
University of Colorado
Acahualinca
Ayala
Carlos Balser
Barrio Las Torres
La Ceiba
Chahuite Escondido
Gulf of Fonseca
Hector Gamboa
La Guinéa
Herramientas
Las Huacas
Los Innocentes
Intermediate Area: Overview
Isla [del] Caño
Isla Solentiname
Isla Zapatera
Laguna Moyua
Los Angeles
Samuel K. Lothrop
Las Marías
Nacascolo
Nicoya, Greater, and Guanacaste Region
Nosara
El Ostional
Papagayo
San Cristóbal
Siteia

Doris Zemurray Stone
Tibas, Talamanca de
Vidor
Villa Tiscapa

Dana Leibsohn
Smith College
Painting

Richard Leventhal
University of California, Los Angeles
Xunantunich

Edelmira Linares
Universidad Nacional Autónoma de Mexico
Flowers

Michael Lind
Independent Scholar
Lambityeco

Leonardo López Luján
Instituto Nacional de Antropología e Historia, Mexico
Tenochtitlán: Ceremonial Center

Gareth W. Lowe
New World Archaeological Foundation
Chiapa de Corzo
Mirador
San Isidro and Environs

Richard S. MacNeish
Andover Foundation for Archaeological Research
Archaic Period
Pavón
Tehuacán Region

A. C. MacWilliams
University of Arizona
Chihuahua, West Central

Linda Manzanilla
Universidad Nacional Autónoma de Mexico
Cobá
Manuel Gamio
Underworld

Joyce Marcus
University of Michigan
Blood and Bloodletting
Cosmology

Huitzo
Leadership and Rulership
Lightning and Thunder
Monte Negro
Names and Titles
Tatiana Proskouriakoff
San José Mogote
Writing
Zapotec Culture and Religion

Alejandro Martínez Muriel
Instituto Nacional de Antropología e Historia, Mexico
Don Martín

Alba Guadalupe Mastache Flores
Instituto Nacional de Antropología e Historia, Mexico
Coyotlatelco
Toltec Culture
Tula Region

Ray T. Matheny
Brigham Young University
Edzna
El Mirador
Putun
Xicalango

Peter Mathews
University of Calgary
Toniná

Judith M. Maxwell
Tulane University
Languages at the Time of Contact

Patricia A. McAnany
Boston University
Ancestor Veneration

Geoffrey G. McCafferty
Brown University
Cholula
Gender Roles

Emily McClung Heumann de Tapia
Universidad Autónoma de México
Maize

Randall H. McGuire
Binghamton University
Chaco Canyon
Northern Arid Zone
Snaketown

Heather McKillop
Louisiana State University
Ports of Trade

Clement Meighan
University of California, Los Angeles
Amapa
Ixtlan del Río
Morett

Mary Ellen Miller
Yale University
Bonampak

Virginia E. Miller
University of Illinois at Chicago
Acanceh

Leah Minc
University of Michigan
Ceramics
Pottery

Paul E. Minnis
University of Oklahoma
Casas Grandes

John Monaghan
Vanderbilt University
Mixtec History, Culture, and Religion
Soul and Spirit Companion

Joseph B. Mountjoy
University of North Carolina at Greensboro
Aztatlan Complex
Capacha
Cerro Zapotecas
Ixtapa
Matanchén
La Peña Pintada
Rock Art

Barbara E. Mundy
Fordham University
Maps and Place-Names

Hector Neff
University of Missouri
Plumbate Ware

Loy C. Neff
University of Calgary
Chihuahua, West Central

Ben A. Nelson
Arizona State University
Northwestern Frontier
La Quemada

Elizabeth Newsome
University of Wisconsin, Eau Claire
Stela Cult

Deborah L. Nichols
Dartmouth College
Tlapacoya

H. B. Nicholson
University of California, Los Angeles
Cerro Portezuelo

Bernard R. Ortiz de Montellano
Wayne State University
Disease, Illness, and Curing

Joel W. Palka
Vanderbilt University
Lacandón Maya

Louise I. Paradis
Université de Montréal
Guerrero Region

Jeffrey R. Parsons
University of Michigan
Agave
Basin of Mexico

Alejandro Pastrana
Instituto Nacional de Antropología e Historia, Mexico
Obsidian: Properties and Sources

David M. Pendergast
Royal Ontario Museum
Altun Ha
Cinnabar and Hematite
Lamanai

David A. Phillips
SWCA, Inc.
Chihuahua, West Central

Sophia Pincemin Deliberos
Universidad de Ciencias y Artes del Estado de Chiapas
Music, Dance, Theater, and Poetry

Patricia Plunket Nagoda
Universidad de las Américas, Puebla
Puebla-Tlaxcala Region
Tetimpa Region

John M. D. Pohl
University of California, Los Angeles
Coixtlahuaca
Tilantongo
Yanhuitlán

Mary Pohl
Florida State University
Pulltrouser Swamp

Helen Perlstein Pollard
Michigan State University
Michoacán Region
Tarascan Culture and Religion
Tzintzuntzan

Christopher A. Pool
University of Kentucky
Tres Zapotes

Kevin Pope
Geo Eco Arc Research
Pulltrouser Swamp

Marion Stirling Pugh
Independent Scholar
Matthew Williams Stirling

Mary Pye
Independent Scholar
Balcón de Montezuma
Buenavista Huaxcama and the Río Verde Region
Wood: Tools and Products

Jeffrey Quilter
Dumbarton Oaks
Rivas

Evelyn Rattray
Universidad Autónoma de México
Thin Orange Ware

Elsa M. Redmond
American Museum of Natural History
Cannibalism
La Coyotera
Cuicatlán Canyon
Purrón Dam

David M. Reed
University of Michigan
Diet and Nutrition

F. Kent Reilly III
Southwest Texas State University
Mezcala Lapidary Style
Olmec-Guerrero Style
Teopantecuanitlán
Tlacozotitlán
Xochipala Style

Don S. Rice
Southern Illinois University
Yaxhá

Miguel Rivera Dorado
Universidad Complutense de Madrid
Oxkintok

Sonia Rivero Torres
Instituto Nacional de Antropología e Historia, Mexico
Lagartero and Environs

Nelly M. Robles García
Instituto Nacional de Antropología e Historia, Mexico
Mitla
Yagul

Octavio Rocha Herrera
Universidad Autónoma de México
Huaxtepec
Tepoztlán

Teresa Rojas Rabiela
Instituto Nacional de Antropología e Historia, Mexico
Angel Palerm

Jeremy A. Sabloff
University of Pennsylvania
Cozumel Island

Alan R. Sandstrom
Indiana University and Purdue University, Fort Wayne
Paper

Pamela Effrein Sandstrom
Indiana University and Purdue University, Fort Wayne
Paper

Robert S. Santley
University of New Mexico
Classic Period
Loma Torremote
Matacapan and the Tuxtla Region

Patricia J. Sarro
Youngstown State University
El Tajín: Architecture and Murals

Frank P. Saul
Medical College of Ohio
Cosmetic Alterations of the Face and Body

Julie Mather Saul
Lucas County Coroner's Office
Cosmetic Alterations of the Face and Body

Nicholas J. Saunders
University College, London
Feathered Serpent
Jaguars

Vernon Scarborough
University of Cincinnati
Ball Game
Hydrology

Edward Schortman
Kenyon College
Interregional Interactions
Maya: Motagua Region
La Sierra
Southeast Mesoamerica

Sue Scott
Independent Scholar
Figurines, Terracotta

Marí Carmen Serra
Instituto Nacional de Antropología e Historia, Mexico
Xochitécatl

Harry J. Shafer
University of Texas
Chipped Stone Tool Production and Products
Colha
Silex

Robert J. Sharer
University of Pennsylvania
Chalchuapa
Quiriguá

Payson Sheets
University of Colorado, Boulder
Cerén
Zapotitan Region

Jay Silverstein
The Pennsylvania State University
Fortifications
Guiengola

Andrew Sluyter
The Pennsylvania State University
Geography and Climate

Michael E. Smith
State University of New York at Albany
Cuauhnahuac and Teopanzolco
Mixteca-Puebla Style
Morelos Region
Postclassic Period
Yautépec

Virginia G. Smith
Kentucky Humanities Council
Izapa Style

Michael Smyth
University of Pennsylvania
Kabah
Labna
Sayil and Chac
Uxmal

Charles S. Spencer
American Museum of Natural History
La Coyotera
Cuicatlán Canyon
Purrón Dam

Leticia Staines Cicero
Universidad Autónoma de México
Mural Painting

Barbara L. Stark
Arizona State University
El Bálsamo
Cerro de las Mesas
Ethnicity
Gulf Lowlands: South Central Region

Joe D. Stewart
Lakehead University
Chihuahua, West Central

Andrea J. Stone
University of Wisconsin, Milwaukee
Naj Tunich

Rebecca Storey
University of Houston
Demographic Trends
Skeletal Analysis

David Stuart
Harvard University
Bundles
Emblem Glyphs
Scribes

George Stuart
National Geographic Society
Diego de Landa
Planchón de las Figuras
John Lloyd Stephens and Frederick Catherwood
Tuxtla Statuette

Yoko Sugiura
Instituto Nacional de Antropología e Historia, Mexico
Toluca Region

Carolyn Tate
Texas Tech University
Art
Yaxchilan

Karl Taube
University of California, Riverside
Maya Deities
Mirrors
Teotihuacán Religion and Deities

Barbara Tedlock
State University of New York, Buffalo
Divination

Paul Tolstoy
Université de Montréal
El Arbolillo
Ayotla-Zohapilco
Coapexco
Santa Catarina
El Terremote
Ticoman
Tlatilco
Zacatenco

Richard F. Townsend
The Art Institute of Chicago
Chalcatzingo: Ritual Appropriation of the Sacred Landscape
Malinalco
Sacred Places and Natural Phenomena
Teotihuacán: Sacred Landscape

Marta Turok Wallace
Asociación Mexicana de Arte y Cultura Popular
Dyes and Colors for Cloth

Emily Umberger
Arizona State University
Castillo de Teayo
Huatusco
Sculpture

Patricia Urban
Kenyon College
Interregional Interactions
Maya: Motagua Region
La Sierra
Southeast Mesoamerica

Javier Urcid
Brandeis University
Zapotec Mortuary Practices

Gabriela Uruñela
Universidad de las Américas, Puebla
Puebla-Tlaxcala Region
Tetimpa Region

Fred Valdez
University of Texas
Río Azul

Ralph H. Vigil
University of Nebraska
Alonso de Zorita

Elisa Villalpando
Instituto Nacional de Antropología e Historia, Mexico
Cerro de Trincheras

Barbara Voorhies
University of California at Santa Barbara
Soconusco–South Pacific Coast and Piedmont Region

Martin Wasserman
Adirondack Community College
Games and Gambling

David L. Webster
The Pennsylvania State University
Becan
Copán
Copán Region
Fortifications

Introduction
Maya Culture and History
Maya Religion
Seibal
Thrones and Benches
Tulum
Warfare

John M. Weeks
University of Pennsylvania
Guatemala Highlands Region

Phil C. Weigand
Colegio de Michoacán
Ahualulco
Chupícuaro
Comala
Etzatlán
Teuchitlan Tradition
West Mexico

Michael E. Whalen
University of Tulsa
Casas Grandes

Randolph Widmer
University of Houston
Activity Areas and Assemblages
Archaeology: Analytical Methods
Artifacts and Industries
Lapidary Industry

S. Jeffrey K. Wilkerson
Institute for Cultural Ecology of the Tropics
La Conchita
Gulf Lowlands
Gulf Lowlands: North Central Region
Gulf Lowlands: North Region
Las Higueras
Pánuco
Paxil
El Pital
Quiahuiztlan
Remojadas
San Antonio Nogalar
Santa Luisa
Smiling Face Figurines
El Tajín: Art and Artifacts

El Tajín: Chronology
El Tajín: Religion and Ideology
Tamuín-Tantoc
Tancol
Usumacinta River Dams Project
Vega de la Peña and Cuajilotes
El Viejón
Villa Rica de Veracruz
Yohualinchan
Zempoala

Gordon R. Willey
Harvard University
Altar de Sacrificios
Settlement Patterns and Settlement Systems
George Clapp Vaillant

Eduardo Williams
El Colégio de Michoacán
Apatzingán Region
Huandacareo
Huitzilapa
Ihuatzio
El Opeño
Tingambato
Zinapécuaro

Lorraine Williams
Universidad Autónoma de Campeche
Architecture: Civic-Ceremonial

Eric R. Wolf
City University of New York
Pedro Armillas

Robert N. Zeitlin
Brandeis University
Laguna Zope
Oaxaca and Tehuantepec Region

Beatriz Zúñiga Bárcenas
Instituto Nacional de Antropología e Historia, Mexico
Calixtlahuaca
Tenayuca

A

Abaj Takalik (Retalhuleu, Guatemala)

Noted for its large sculptural corpus in three or more different art styles, possibly including Olmec, Abaj Takalik is a multi-component site consisting of about seventy structures aligned on nine north–south oriented plazas at an elevation of 600 meters. It is situated within the agriculturally rich upper piedmont of the Guatemala Pacific Slope, on an ancient route between the Guatemala Highlands and the Pacific Coast.

No adequate chronology exists for the site, except one based on severely eroded ceramics and changing art styles. Many believe the majority of these sculptures represent a locally derived Abaj Takalik style of the Middle Formative, a potbelly style of the Late Formative, along with Terminal Formative-Early Classic proto-Maya or early Maya, and Late Classic Maya.

Abaj Takalik has several early monuments with long-count dates from the several centuries before and after A.D. 1. These monuments, their stratigraphic placement, and the architectural sequence at Structure 12 suggest that an intrusive Maya group entered the area of Abaj Takalik from the adjacent highlands around the beginning of the Terminal Formative, in a movement perhaps similar to the presumed temporary intrusive move suggested in the Cotzumalhuapa zone at the same time (Chocolá, a nearby site, also has early Maya Terminal Formative sculpture).

FURTHER READINGS

Graham, J. A., R. F. Heizer, and E. M. Shook. 1978. Abaj Takalik 1976: Exploratory Investigations. *Contributions of the University of California Archaeological Research Facility* 36: 85–109.

Miles, S. W. 1965. Sculpture of the Guatemala-Chiapas Highlands and Pacific Slopes, and Associated Hieroglyphs. In *Handbook of Middle American Indians,* vol. 2, pp. 237–275. Austin: University of Texas Press.

Parsons, L. A. 1986. *The Origins of Maya Art: Monumental Stone Sculpture of Kaminaljuyú, Guatemala, and the Southern Pacific Coast.* Studies in Pre-Columbian Art & Archaeology, 28. Washington, D.C.: Dumbarton Oaks.

Sharer, R. J., and D. C. Grove (eds.). 1989. *Regional Perspectives on the Olmec.* Cambridge: Cambridge University Press.

Frederick J. Bové

SEE ALSO

Soconusco–South Pacific Coast and Piedmont Region

Acahualinca (Managua, Nicaragua)

Situated less than 0.5 km from the shore of Lake Managua in the Greater Nicoya region, this site bears the earliest firm evidence for human occupation in Nicaragua, with a total span of occupation from 6000 B.C. to A.D. 1520. Evidence for earliest occupation includes no artifacts; it consists of a trail of human and animal footprints preserved in mud, similar to footprints found at San Rafael on the Pacific Coast. Much later occupations (600 B.C. to A.D. 1520) left ceramics similar to those found at other sites around the southern shore of Lake Managua and the Pacific Coast/Isthmus of Rivas.

FURTHER READINGS

Bryan, A. L. 1973. New light on ancient Nicaraguan footprints. *Archaeology* 26(2): 146–147.

A

Lange, F. W., P. Sheets, A. Martinez, and S. Abel-Vidor. 1992. *The Archaeology of Pacific Nicaragua.* Albuquerque: University of New Mexico Press.

Frederick W. Lange

SEE ALSO
Nicoya, Greater, and Guanacaste Region

Acámbaro-Cerro el Chivo (Guanajuato, Mexico)

Acámbaro-Cerro el Chivo was occupied from Formative (Chupícuaro phase, 650 B.C.–A.D. 100) to Postclassic times, when it was under Tarascan control. It lies in the Acámbaro Valley, within the tropical highlands in the Mesa Central in an area of volcanic tablelands. Cerro el Chivo, the main archaeological site, is a low hill on a flat-floored valley; its summit is 150 meters above the valley floor. Eight major structures have been discovered on the summit of the hill. About seventy petroglyphs, made by carving and pecking/abrading rock outcrops, have been identified. Lithic artifacts are primarily of obsidian from the nearby Zinepécuaro and Ucareo sources. Four ceramic complexes are chronologically associated: Chupícuaro, Mixtlan (A.D. 100–475), Lerma (475–1450, including three periods not fully identified), and Acámbaro (1450–1520). The Lerma River, a major landscape feature of the archaeological zone, separated the Acámbaro Valley from the Aztecs on the east and from other ethnic groups on the north during the Acámbaro period, when the site served as an administrative and military outpost for the Tarascan state, whose core was in the Lake Pátzcuaro Basin. It defended the state against both Aztec and Chichimec attacks and played a role in Tarascan government-administered exchange.

FURTHER READINGS

Gorenstein, S. 1985. *Acámbaro: Frontier Settlement on the Tarascan Aztec Border.* Nashville: Vanderbilt University Publications in Anthropology, 32.

Shirley Gorenstein

SEE ALSO
Bajío Region; Michoacán Region; Tarascan Culture and Religion

Acanceh (Yucatán, Mexico)

The modern town of Acanceh overlies an extensive but little-known, multi-component pre-Hispanic settlement.

Still visible are the large radial Formative pyramid on the north side of Acanceh's main plaza and, 300 meters to the southeast, a massive acropolis surmounted by the remains of several buildings. The best-preserved of these, the Palace of the Stuccoes, is a small, four-chambered structure of uncertain date, uncovered in 1906. At that time, its upper façade displayed two rows of polychrome birds and animals modeled in stucco, each contained within a stepped frame. The frieze, which belongs stylistically to the period A.D. 600–700 or slightly earlier, displayed twenty-one anthropomorphized creatures, including a bat, snakes, frogs, a gopher, monkeys, and a feline seated before a severed human head, and a single human figure. Certain details of this unusual relief (speech scrolls, ringed eyes, and feathered water drops) recall the art of Teotihuacán, but the overall style and iconography are Maya. Although not presented as a narrative, the imagery encompasses themes of sacrifice, death, and the underworld.

Opposite the Palace of the Stuccoes and contemporaneous with it, Structure 2 apparently once contained Late Classic-style murals and hieroglyphs. Both buildings were filled in to serve as the base for Pure Florescent (A.D. 800–1000) buildings, of which only a few scattered stones are visible now. Mexican archaeologists have recently undertaken excavations and conservation at Acanceh, discovering an intrusive vaulted tomb with offerings beneath the floor of one of the rooms of the Palace of the Stuccoes.

FURTHER READINGS

Breton, A. 1908. Archaeology in Mexico. *Man* 8: 34–37.

Miller, V. E. 1991. *The Frieze of the Palace of the Stuccoes, Acanceh, Yucatan, Mexico.* Washington, D.C.: Dumbarton Oaks.

von Winning, H. 1985. *Two Maya Monuments in Yucatan: The Palace of the Stuccoes at Acanceh and the Temple of the Owls at Chichen Itza.* Los Angeles: Southwest Museum.

Virginia E. Miller

SEE ALSO
Dzibilchaltún; Maya Lowlands: North

Activity Areas and Assemblages

At archaeological sites, particular functions and activities are associated with particular structures and areas. Archaeologists try to identify these "activity areas" and associated tasks so that past lifeways at these sites can be reconstructed. The various tools and other artifacts used in a particular activity together are called an "assemblage." Activity areas are often found within rooms or structures, and also in open areas, adjacent to habitations or isolated from settlements. Archaeologists identify the function of artifacts and then discern a pattern in which functionally related items discretely correlate with space to form distinctive activity areas. This can be challenging, because many artifacts have multiple functions and a number of different activities can take place in the same location.

Archaeologists differentiate two general types of activity areas—*domestic* and *specialized.* Domestic activities are those associated with everyday maintenance of the basic social unit, a nuclear or extended family living and working together as a household. These activities would include sleeping, food preparation, eating, heating, clothing production and maintenance, and other tool and utensil production and maintenance.

Specialized activities, on the other hand, are those that are more focused on a single or limited activity: one whose intensity indicates that it involves behavior which exceeds that associated with the maintenance of the basic social unit, or else one that is not spatially associated with residential habitation. Examples of both domestic and specialized activity areas and assemblages follow.

Activity areas and assemblages at Mesoamerican archaeological sites vary depending on region and time period, because the level of sociocultural integration influences the nature of the assemblages and activity areas. Specialized kill and butchering sites are associated with Pleistocene hunters during the Paleoindian period. Tepexpan in the Basin of Mexico, where a mastodon was killed and butchered, represents such a site. Other specialized food-collection-activity assemblages can be quite extensive, such as the large shrimp-collecting and drying sites in the Soconusco area of the western Mexico coast, or they may be as ephemeral as a stick for knocking fruit off cactus that has been left near the cactus, or heavy mortars left in groves of nut-bearing trees rather than being hauled back to the campsite.

Open-air fire hearths are associated with ephemeral residential campsites of nomadic bands from the Paleoindian period through the Archaic period. These hearths form the nuclei of domestic activities, but domestic artifact refuse is relatively sparse at these temporary sites because their populations were low. These mobile groups had very streamlined tool kits which were carefully preserved; frequent movement inhibited the development of an extensive, bulky assemblage of artifacts. However, there is evidence of cooking and food-consumption activities, and also of the production and maintenance of stone tools from the debitage near the hearths, and of clothing production and maintenance from bone needles and awls, and hide-scraping tools.

With the establishment of sedentary communities with denser habitation in Formative and later times, a wider range of other activity areas can be identified because there are more different types of artifacts, which can include bulky items, and also because architecture and its partitioning into distinctive units of space can be associated with different tasks. Often activities were differentiated into distinct activity areas. The single most commonly encountered activity area is the trash heap, or midden. With sedentary habitation, population size, density, and intensity of consumption increased, resulting in a greater accumulation of refuse to be removed from domestic space or from the specialized activity areas where it was produced. This removal is called "secondary refuse disposal" and results in middens, which can occur as deep piles or accumulations of refuse behind buildings or in abandoned rooms, or as thin scatters of refuse ("sheet middens") that accumulate in the cleared area around buildings. These middens provide a complete inventory of the inorganic material refuse produced by domestic or specialized activities. Unfortunately, these assemblages are always spatially disassociated from the primary activity areas, and so waste streams must be established to link middens back to the original activity area.

Because Mesoamerican sedentary communities relied on stored agricultural products, storage facilities were required. These may have simply been rooms containing large ceramic vessels or, often, subterranean pits, such as the *chultun* storage pits found in the Maya area. The *chultun*'s primary function was to store water during the dry season, but it could also be used to store seeds and nuts, and it might be filled with refuse when abandoned. Elsewhere, such as in the Valley of Oaxaca, bottle-shaped storage pits were sometimes reused as burial places.

Specialized burial facilities are widely found, including the Shaft Tomb complexes of western Mexico. Styles of interment vary regionally, through time, and by socioeconomic class.

Important diagnostic features include the orientation of human remains, their form (e.g., bundles, ashes, disarticulated skeletons), the nature of associated grave goods (e.g., personal tools and adornments, signs of office,

A

portable art), the cause of death, and the presence of remains of other humans or animals, possibly sacrificed to provide companionship.

Food-processing areas can be identified by the location of maize-grinding stones, called "manos" and "metates." Kitchens can be identified by the occurrence of hearths and cooking vessels such as *comal* griddles. Cooking hearths often consist of three triangularly spaced stones over which a *comal* or another cooking vessel is placed. Portable braziers were used in many Mesoamerican cultures to warm food in areas other than the kitchen.

Many Classic Maya buildings contain rooms with masonry benches. These are thought to have been loci of domestic activities such as sleeping, socializing, and crafts. Conversely, rooms that do not contain benches are thought to have non-dormitory functions, although still domestic in nature. Some benchless rooms, however, have have been found containing assemblages of artifacts clearly representing a specialized craft workshop. Classic Maya buildings often contain niches, recessed into both interior and exterior walls, which hold ceramic vessels and so represent storage areas.

In the Central Highlands, specialized areas producing chipped stone tools, ceramics, and lapidary items are associated with open patios adjacent to residences. Such workshops are identified primarily by the waste debris associated with the manufacture of the various items. In all cases, the amount of debris dramatically underrepresents the actual rate of production. In a dense urban context, the excess waste from specialized production needs to be removed periodically, or the residence will literally be buried in waste. The rate of production, therefore, is determined by a comparison of the amount of debris at various locations. This represents a static snapshot of the actual dynamic process of material moving through the waste stream of any community.

Quarries and mines are activity areas not directly associated with residences. These were specialized extraction areas for the raw materials used for stone tools and lapidary items; examples include obsidian mines and the solitary Mesoamerican source of jadeite, the quarries on the Montagua River. The artifact assemblages at these sites are quite distinctive, including tailings and broken tools from the quarrying activities, as well as debitage and debris from the reduction of the raw materials into more easily transportable and workable units.

Another distinctive activity area in Mesoamerican sites is the dedication cache. This is typically an offering made of useful artifacts, rather than refuse, in locations associated with architecture. Assemblages associated with these activity areas can range from mundane items, such as freshly struck obsidian blades, to fancy, valuable artifacts made from precious stones and shell. These caches are often placed within the fill of platforms and under the floors of rooms. It is thought that they functioned ritually to inaugurate the structure.

In another type of ritual activity, a special altar, shrine, or ritual vessel received offerings on a continuing basis. Often the assemblages associated with these activity areas are identical with those in dedication caches; in many areas, however, particularly the Maya Lowlands, a distinct assemblage of greenstone perforators, obsidian blades, and/or stingray spines occurs, indicating an assemblage for the ritual propitiatory activity of bloodletting. These altars and shrines are often situated in public areas and buildings. These areas signal temples and other religious activity areas, as well as providing some understanding of the content of the ritual behavior. For example, at Tlajinga 33, a Teotihuacan apartment compound, juvenile burials were found within one altar, while a ceramic theater censer and five adult burials were found in a tomb under another altar. It is suggested that the latter tomb represents a lineage shrine, with the censer being used to burn incense as a continuation ritual for the ancestors of the compound. In the Maya area, altars and dedication caches are often found in front of stelae, which provide a means for making offerings to important ancestors and lineage members.

FURTHER READINGS

Flannery, K. V. (ed.). 1976. *The Mesoamerican Village.* New York: Academic Press.

Hirth, K. G., and R. S. Santley (eds.). 1993. *Prehispanic Domestic Units in Western Mesoamerica.* Boca Raton, Fla.: CRC Press.

Wilk, R. R., and W. Ashmore (eds.). 1988. *Household and Community in the Mesoamerican Past.* Albuquerque: University of New Mexico Press.

Randolph Widmer

Agave

The genus *Agave* (also called "maguey," or "century plant") is diverse and widely distributed in North and Middle America. Gentry distinguishes two subgenera, twenty "generic groups," 136 species, and 197 total taxa in the huge region between Utah and Costa Rica. Agave is also widely distributed in South America, although much less is known about its characteristics and pre-Columbian significance there. Agave plants are adapted to an extremely wide range of environmental conditions and occur in almost every conceivable niche between arid, cool highlands and humid, tropical lowland zones.

The archaeological record indicates that agave fiber and cooked agave flesh (recognized in ancient trash deposits by the presence of roasting pits and numerous fibrous quids spat out by people who had masticated succulent mouthfuls of the cooked plant) were being used by pre-agricultural peoples and incipient cultivators in highland Mexico several thousand years ago. The abundant presence in archaeological deposits of distinctive stone and ceramic tools associated with scraping agave plants and spinning their fiber indicate that agave flesh, fiber, and sap continued to be exploited by agriculturalists throughout the entire pre-Hispanic period. In the southwestern United States, archaeological studies reveal similar kinds of agave use as early as a thousand years ago.

Except for agave species utilized for the commercial production of henequen fiber in Yucatán and distilled alcohol (tequila and mescal) in southern and western Mexico (neither product having pre-Hispanic antecedents), it appears that the only fully effective domestication of agave in Middle America during historic times has been restricted to a half dozen species of very large plants in the Mexican highlands: *Agave salmiana, A. mapisaga, A. atrovirens, A. ferox, A. hookeri,* and *A. americana.* Individual plants of these species typically attain heights of 1.5 to 2.5 meters, and each plant is comprised of 20 to 40 large leaves *(pencas)* that typically weigh 3 to 8 kg apiece and contain a rich store of both fiber and sap (individual plants produce up to 1,000 liters of sap, and several kilograms of dried fiber). These are the agave species that are usually referred to nowadays as "maguey" or "pulque maguey" in the highlands of central and north central Mexico, and it is to these species that we direct our attention.

The central Mexican maguey flourishes at elevations higher than about 1,800 meters. Its most important product in historic times has been pulque, a mildly alcoholic beverage formed by the natural fermentation of the plant's sugary sap *(aguamiel).* Other uses of the plant include non-alcoholic sap products (fresh sap, syrup, and sugar), fiber *(ixtle)* for spinning and weaving textiles, cooked edible flesh, and the employment of the plant's stalk *(quiote),* trunk, and leaves as construction materials, household utensils, domestic fuel, and even beehives.

Commercial pulque production has dominated maguey utilization in general for several centuries. Nevertheless, maguey has long been a staple component of subsistence agriculture in highland Mexico, and archaeological and ethnohistoric information indicate that this importance as an agricultural staple extends far back into pre-Hispanic times. These same ethnohistoric sources also inform us about the significance of maguey in pre-Hispanic cosmology: the goddess Mayahuel was closely identified with the maguey plant and its products, and the consumption of pulque often accompanied important ceremonies and rituals.

Maguey can withstand extended drought, cold temperatures, and hailstorms, and it is capable of thriving on impoverished soils—all common problems for ancient highland agriculturalists, particularly before the introduction of European domestic grazing animals (sheep, goats, and cattle) made it possible to extend productive landscapes by means of pastoralism. Individual maguey plants mature over a cycle of six to twenty years (depending mainly on local conditions of soil fertility and moisture availability), and virtually all reproduction is vegetative—i.e., by means of young plants that appear naturally as offshoots around the base of parent plants and are transplanted from there to new locations.

With its nonseasonal growth cycle and hardy character, maguey has long provided an ideal complement to the seed-based agriculture in highland Mexico. It can be interplanted with seed crops to expand the overall productive capacity of good agricultural land and extend its productivity over an entire annual cycle (seed crops produce only one harvest per year above 1,800 meters elevation, whereas with proper management a maguey orchard can remain in production year round). Such interplanting also reduces sheet wash and conserves the land through the holding and stabilizing action of the massive maguey plant and its extensive root system. Since maguey will grow on land too dry or cold, and on soils too thin, for dependable production of maize, amaranth, beans, or squash, its cultivation substantially extends the range of agricultural land all over highland Mexico.

Maguey sap and cooked flesh are rich in both calories and nutrients and supply significant proportions of both in the diets of rural Mexican farmers. It has been estimated, for example, that in many cases interplanting maguey with seed crops can double the potential caloric yield of a given unit of agricultural land. In addition to its edible sap and flesh, maguey provided a major source of fiber for making cordage and clothing in highland

Mexico, where it is usually too cold for local cotton production (cotton was the only other major source of fiber for clothing in ancient Mesoamerica). Furthermore, in treeless or deforested areas, maguey could be a significant, even predominant, source of fuel and construction material; ethnohistoric sources describe the sale for household fuel of dried maguey leaves and stumps in sixteenth-century urban marketplaces.

Ethnographic accounts describe a typical rural settlement pattern throughout highland Mexico of domestic residences surrounded by intensively cultivated gardens, fertilized by domestic wastes, in which maize, beans, squash, maguey, and a wide variety of other domesticated plants are intimately associated. These agricultural "in-fields" are, in turn, surrounded by more extensively cultivated "out-fields" where interplanted seed crops and maguey predominate. Fields are also often maintained in more marginal terrain, in higher, drier zones of thinner soil at greater distances from residences, and in such localities maguey is often the sole crop. In some cases, agriculturalists living in marginal regions have come to be maguey specialists, exchanging their surplus of maguey products, through village and urban marketplaces, for materials like maize and beans provided by their counterparts cultivating more fertile lands.

Archaeological surveys and excavations suggest that these historically known patterns and associations are deeply rooted in the pre-Hispanic past. Nevertheless, because of archaeologists' longstanding preoccupation with seed-based agriculture, it has remained difficult to assess properly the significance of maguey in the pre-Hispanic economy: the physical remains of the plants themselves are generally much less well preserved than those of seed crops, and the technological apparatus associated with maguey cultivation, fiber extraction, spinning and weaving, sap extraction and fermentation have not generally been well understood. The remainder of this discussion will focus on the archaeological implications of recent ethnoarchaeological studies of maguey sap and fiber processing.

Sap Extraction and Fermentation

If the maguey plant is left alone at maturity, a woody, seed-bearing stalk forms, and over the next eight to twelve weeks it grows to a height of 4 to 8 meters. This phenomenal growth is fed by a tremendous flow of sap (500–1,000 liters per plant); after a few months the seeds at the top of the stalk have been widely distributed by the wind and the plant itself is dead. In order to acquire this sap for human use, it is necessary to interrupt the natural process at the critical point just before the stalk begins to form. This is accomplished by cutting out the heart of the nascent stalk and preparing a hollow cavity at the center of the plant into which the sap drains and collects, and from which the liquid is removed twice a day, a few liters at a time, over the course of the subsequent four or five months. Sap flow is facilitated by means of daily scraping the interior surface of the plant cavity with a fine-edged, circular scraper, and the accumulated sap in the cavity is daily sucked out into a large, hollow bottle gourd container. The sap is then transported to a place where it is poured into a large ceramic or wood container, in which it ferments to form pulque, or from which it is removed for immediate consumption in a non-alcoholic state.

The archaeological correlates of pre-Hispanic sap extraction, fermentation, and storage are likely to include (1) large, jagged-edged knives (made of either obsidian or flint) suitable for cutting out the heart of the plant; (2) obsidian plano-convex scrapers, circular in form and with handles and finely retouched edges suitable for the daily scraping of the interior cavity surface; and (3) a variety of ceramic vessels for transporting and fermenting the liquid. All these implements are abundant in known archaeological deposits, although to date the only definitive association with maguey sap extraction has been for the plano-convex scrapers that appear to have been highly specialized tools, used exclusively for scraping the interior cavity walls of the mature maguey plant.

Fiber Extraction, Spinning, and Weaving

It is important to realize that once a maguey plant has been prepared for sap production, it will produce sap continuously for three to six months. If it produces for over four months, the whole plant becomes dry and leathery, fit only for fuel (i.e., it is so rigid that it is impossible to extract the fiber). However, if sap production continues for less than approximately four months, the leaves remain green and relatively pliable. Thus, it is possible to obtain both sap and fiber from the same plant, but this requires proper management. There is some reason to suspect that there was a selective development, probably during the later first millennium A.D., of different varieties of maguey for specific types of products (e.g., fiber vs. sap, etc.). This selective process, still almost completely unstudied, may have produced the numerous maguey subspecies that exist today throughout rural Mexico—a botanical diversity that is apparently nonfunctional at the present time.

Each maguey leaf contains abundant fiber, whose great length, strength, and fineness make it ideal for spinning thread and weaving cloth. However, this fiber is firmly encased in compact flesh that must be softened and removed before the fiber is available for human use. Softening is typically accomplished today by heating the detached leaves in an open-air hearth and burying them in an underground pit for several days. This results in a rotting and softening of the encasing flesh, which is subsequently removed by scraping it away from the fiber, using a thick, dull-edged and even-edged metal scraper that is pressed firmly against the rotted maguey leaf with strong, downward movements along a backing board that supports the leaf and resists the scraping pressure.

The archaeological correlates of these activities would be the rotting pits associated with large hearths and distinctive ground-stone (usually fine basalt) scrapers (sometimes called *azadas*) of trapezoidal form. These occur in two distinct sizes, the smaller of which seems to have been intended for one-handed operation, while the larger was manipulated with two hands. It is also possible that in some cases the encasing flesh was removed by using a more generalized scraper—a large, plano-convex tool often referred to as a "scraper-plane," or "turtleback scraper." It appears that the latter tool may have been largely replaced by the more specialized ground-stone trapezoidal scraper at some point in the late first millennium A.D.

Once the removed fiber has been dried, cleaned, and carded (usually with a thick maguey thorn), it is then spun into thread of varying diameter. This is accomplished by drop spinning, using a wooden spindle weighted at one end with a distinctive ceramic spindle whorl. An experienced spinner employs whorls of different weights to make threads of different thicknesses: smaller whorls, typically weighing 11 to 25 grams, for making fine thread, and progressively heavier whorls, weighing 35 to 75 grams or more, for progressively thicker thread. Archaeologists now believe that it should be possible to distinguish workshops where fine thread was produced from those in which spinners prepared thicker thread, or multiple grades of thread.

Once the thread has been spun, it is woven on simple back-strap looms into large, square carrying cloths (*ayates*), typically measuring slightly over a meter on a side, which are employed today for back-packing burdens ranging from babies to firewood. Ethnohistoric sources inform us that in pre-Hispanic times maguey-fiber textiles were also used for making a wide variety of clothing,

especially for highland commoners who lacked access to scarce, imported cotton cloth. To date there has been little systematic archaeological investigation of pre-Hispanic maguey-fiber weaving, but probable material correlates would include bone implements associated with packing and separating the threads within wooden frames.

FURTHER READINGS

Gentry, H. 1982. *Agaves of Continental North America.* Tucson: University of Arizona Press.

Parsons, J. R., and M. H. Parsons. 1990. *Maguey Utilization in Highland Central Mexico.* Anthropological Papers, Museum of Anthropology, University of Michigan, 82. Ann Arbor.

Jeffrey R. Parsons

SEE ALSO

Agriculture and Domestication; Food and Cuisine; Paper; Weaving and Textiles

Agriculture and Domestication

The term "domestication" refers to genetic changes in a population that are the result of human selection, either conscious or unconscious. "Cultivation" denotes the act of encouraging the growth of certain plants through improving the soil, eliminating competing plants, transplanting, watering, fertilizing, and so on. Thus, a cultivated plant can be either a domesticated or nondomesticated form.

As means of obtaining subsistence from plants, foraging and agriculture represent two ends of an economic continuum. At one end of this continuum, foragers, or hunter-gatherers, might be characterized as passive collectors of natural resources, playing no active role in management or manipulation of the environment. At the other end of the continuum are agriculturalists who are wholly dependent on domesticated plants that are cultivated in artificial environments of formal fields and gardens. In reality, human subsistence systems lie at points along this continuum, with no clear dichotomy existing between foraging and agriculture.

Domestication and the development of an agricultural way of life were not inventions, but rather the result of a long history of interaction between people and plants. Although we can trace the physical changes in plants resulting from the domestication process, there is still no consensus on how or why agriculture arose as a way of life in Mesoamerica, despite considerable study. Recent research has steered away from theories of why agriculture

A

was developed and has focused instead on a more detailed examination of how the transition from foraging to agriculture occurred in various locales. This transition is now viewed as an evolutionary continuum, and scholars recognize a very long, and previously underappreciated, history of plant manipulation in both highland and lowland Mesoamerica.

Even with the recognition of an increased time depth for plant manipulation, the synchronicity of the domestication process in most centers of origin throughout the world between 12,000 and 8,000 years ago is striking and suggests the emergence of some world-scale process related to agricultural origins. The transition from the Pleistocene to the Holocene resulted in the development of strongly seasonal rainfall patterns that dramatically altered plant communities in the arid highlands of Mesoamerica; it also brought about a rise of sea level that created new ecosystems along the coast. Although these environmental changes may not provide a satisfactory explanation for plant domestication and the development of agriculture, they did present new challenges and opportunities to the early occupants of Mesoamerica.

One theoretical approach to the development of agriculture that downplays the often-cited factors of population pressure, resource stress, or climatic change has been presented by Brian Hayden, who suggests that complex hunter-gatherers living in rich environments initiated food production to gain social advantage in competitive feasting. Thus, food production should be coincident with the development of social inequity, and Hayden finds a fit between his model and available information from various areas around the world, including Mesoamerica.

A systems theory approach has been adopted by Kent Flannery to understand the process of plant domestication and the development of agriculture in the highlands of Mexico. According to Flannery's model, hunter-gatherers gradually adapted to changes in plant communities during the Pleistocene-to-Holocene transition, making increasing use of wild species which they eventually domesticated. Flannery describes highland subsistence systems as focusing initially on procurement of tree legumes (primarily mesquite), cactus fruits, maguey, white-tailed deer, and cottontail rabbits.

The procurement of these resources was regulated by two mechanisms that enabled the subsistence system to work and to suppress deviations that would upset the balance of the system: seasonality, which resulted in differential availability of resources through the year, and scheduling, the timing of the movement of hunter-gatherer bands

across the landscape in order to take advantage of these seasonal resources. The system of seasonality and scheduling would maintain equilibrium through "negative feedback," preventing the overuse of any one seasonal resource because of the disruption in the scheduled exploitation of other resources that would result. Change would occur in the system when a "positive feedback" situation amplified and supported a deviation from the set pattern, causing the whole system to readjust.

Gradual genetic changes in plants such as maize and beans made these resources slightly more productive, encouraging people to make adjustments in the scheduling of band movements. Increasing interaction with these plants produced a positive feedback situation that amplified the selection process and thereby promoted further genetic change. The increasing time spent cultivating these productive plants would eventually necessitate the rescheduling of procurement activities, resulting in decreased exploitation of resources whose timing conflicted with the cultivation and harvest of maize and beans; people would also pay more attention to other resources that did not interfere with their increasing agricultural activities.

Investigation of ancient seasonal encampments and settlements and the recovery of associated plant and animal remains have allowed the reconstruction of subsistence changes as they relate to seasonality and scheduling in the highland valleys of Oaxaca and Tehuacán, and to some degree the Basin of Mexico. In general, the cultural sequences indicate that a hunting and gathering way of life became established in the highlands between 10,000 and 7000 B.C., adjusting through that period to changes in plant and animal communities that coincided with the termination of the Pleistocene and the onset of the Holocene. This included a general shift from large-game hunting to smaller game and the increasing exploitation of plant resources. Between 7000 and 5000 B.C., plant collection increased, and there is evidence for the exploitation of species that were later domesticated.

Small varieties of domesticated maize appear in the archaeological record about 5000 B.C., and incipient forms of agriculture begin to develop as more domesticated and cultivated varieties of plants were added. The size of seasonal encampments enlarges and the duration of occupations increases, and by 1500 B.C., if not earlier, permanent settlements appear in association with full-time agriculture.

Pollen evidence suggests that maize was introduced into the humid tropics of southern Mesoamerica around

A

3000 B.C., where Archaic period people apparently practiced slash-and-burn cultivation as a supplement to a basically hunting and gathering economy. Between about 2000 and 1000 B.C., incipient agriculture, along with the exploitation of abundant coastal, estuarine, and riverine resources, allowed the earliest development of sedentary villages in the lowlands.

The interior tropical forests of Mesoamerica present interesting problems in the study of early human migration and subsistence systems of the New World. It has been suggested by some researchers that the tropical forests of the world could not have been inhabited by humans without the use of domesticated plants and animals. Although tropical forests are recognized as some of the most productive terrestrial ecosystems, it is claimed that they are unsuited to human foraging because of the extreme dispersion of food resources in space and through time, the high cost of processing many of the available plant foods, and the low incidence of resources that provide good sources of carbohydrates, protein, and calorie-rich fat. This argument has interesting bearing on the earliest occupation of tropical forests in Mesoamerica, particularly the interior Maya Lowlands. No pre-agricultural occupation has been confirmed for the interior tropical forests, and no study has yet attempted to determine if human foragers could have sustained themselves in the region without the use of domesticates.

Lines of Evidence: Physical Remains, Diversity, and Genetics

Physical evidence for the use of plants in ancient times takes the form of plant remains recovered in association with human settlements, activity areas, and trash deposits. Abundant plant remains have been recovered from sites in environments that deter the decay of organic materials, such as the dry caves of the Mesoamerican highlands, and inundated areas and wetlands of the lowlands. Carbonization also deters decay, and plant parts that were carbonized during the burning of trash or catastrophic fire are retrieved from archaeological deposits through a water separation process known as "flotation recovery." These carbonized remains, often in the form of small fragments, are identified with the assistance of comparative collections and seed identification manuals. Microscopic pollen grains preserve very well and can be recovered from archaeological deposits. The distinctive size and shape of pollen grains can generally be used to establish the taxonomic identity of the plant to at least the family level, and in some cases to genus or species. Phy-

toliths—microscopic silicate bodies that provide structural support in plant tissues—also preserve well and can be recovered from archaeological contexts and identified. Although the taxonomic level of identification for phytoliths is generally not as specific as can be obtained with pollen, some important crops, particularly maize, can be identified to the species level from phytoliths. Preserved starch grains from plant tissues, as well as chemical residues remaining on ancient cooking vessels, provide another means of identifying ancient uses of plants.

In the search for evidence of early plant use and domestication, the dating of plant remains recovered from archaeological sites has often been tenuous or debatable. Advances in radiocarbon (^{14}C) dating now allow for analysis of minute fragments of plant remains, including the organic component of pollen. These technological advances are now helping to refine our picture of the origin and spread of domesticated plants.

The relative importance of a particular plant food in the diet of an ancient individual can sometimes be determined by literal application of the old adage "You are what you eat." Certain species of plants, or groups of related species, contain distinctive combinations of trace elements as well as isotopes that are incorporated into the human skeleton in proportion to the amount of that plant in the individual's diet over an extended period of time. Of particular interest to Mesoamerican studies is the analysis of stable isotope ratios of carbon and nitrogen in prehistoric bone as a measure of the importance of maize in the ancient diet.

The geographic origin of a domesticated plant species is often reconstructed by identifying the region with the greatest amount of modern physical diversity for the species being studied. Under this approach, it is assumed that the greatest diversity of a species will be found in the area in which it has been under human selective pressure for the longest period of time. Advances in genetics now allow measurements of diversity and similarity of plants to be made at the molecular level, providing a means of tracing changes in a plant species across space and, theoretically, through time.

Domesticated and Cultivated Plants of Mesoamerica

Maize (corn) was probably the most important domesticated plant in ancient Mesoamerica. Maize remains are commonly recovered from archaeological contexts when flotation of soil samples is conducted, and pollen from the plant is nearly ubiquitous in samples taken from areas of ancient settlement. Maize figures prominently in

A

Mesoamerican art and iconography and continues to be the staff of life for traditional diets today. The earliest physical evidence for domesticated maize comes from the Mesoamerican highlands, specifically within the Tehuacán Valley and Basin of Mexico, dating back to about 5000 B.C. The identification of the wild progenitor of maize has been a source of debate among botanists for more than a century, with most current research supporting the theory that maize (*Zea mays* subs. *mays*) originated from the wild tropical highland grass teosinte (*Z. mexicana,* or *Z. mays* subsp. *parviglumis* or subsp. *mexicana*), either through gradual change or by catastrophic sexual transmutation. Genetic research suggests that the most likely geographic location for the domestication of maize is either the Basin of Mexico or the Rio Balsas region of Jalisco, Mexico.

It was not until the late nineteenth century that the New World was accepted as the origin of the common bean *(Phaseolus vulgaris),* and recent studies move toward a consensus for multiple independent domestications in Mesoamerica, South America, and the American Southwest. Although human selection may have resulted in increasing size of beans perhaps as early as 7000 B.C. in Tamaulipas, Mexico, the earliest archaeological specimens identified as domesticates date to about 5000 B.C. in the Tehuacán Valley.

Cucurbits (*Cucurbita* spp.) include the many varieties of squash and pumpkins, and some gourds, and may represent the earliest domesticated plants of the New World. Genetic research indicates that there may have been independent domestications of the oldest known cultivated species, *C. pepo,* in multiple areas of North America, including northeastern Mexico and central or southern Mexico.

Though not a staple food, chile peppers (*Capsicum* spp.) have long been an integral part of Mesoamerican cuisines, supplying a significant source of vitamins. In Mesoamerica, many varieties of chiles appear to have been independently domesticated from the wild forms of *C. frutescens* and *C. annuum.* In the highlands of Mexico, archaeological remains indicate that wild chiles were gathered before 5000 B.C., with cultivation and domestication beginning before 3500 B.C.

Roots and tubers, though not originally domesticated in Mesoamerica, constitute a significant component of traditional Mesoamerican food, and they have often been suggested as a potential staple of ancient diets. However, the difficulty of identifying these plants in the archaeological record has hindered efforts to assess their importance in prehistoric times. Pollen evidence suggests that manioc (*Manihot* spp.) may have been introduced into the Maya Lowlands around 3000 to 2500 B.C. The site of Cuello, Belize, has yielded remains of manioc (*M. esculenta*) and tissue tentatively identified as malanga (*Xanthosoma* spp.) from archaeological deposits dated to the Early to Middle Formative period (1200–400 B.C.). The ancient cultivation of manioc has also been identified from casts formed in volcanic ash deposits that buried the site of Cerén, El Salvador, around A.D. 590. Recent advances in the analysis of starch grains and chemical residues promise to increase the potential for identifying archaeological evidence of root and tuber use.

Species of amaranth (*Amaranthus* spp.) and the related goosefoot (*Chenopodium* spp.) are known to have been long utilized in Mesoamerica as an important food source; they have edible seeds, leaves, and inflorescences. Domesticated varieties of these plants produce greater numbers of seeds, although the size and morphology of the seeds differ little between wild and domesticated varieties, resulting in difficulties in distinguishing the two when they are recovered from archaeological contexts. There is a rich historical record for use of *Amaranthus* and *Chenopodium* by the Aztecs, who apparently referred to both grains as *huauhtli.* The grain served the Aztec not only as an important staple but also as a ceremonial food associated with numerous public and domestic rituals.

The cultivation of trees is a major component of subsistence in many areas of the American tropics, and there is growing evidence for the significance of tree cultivation in ancient times. It appears to have been particularly important in the Maya Lowlands. Botanist Arturo Gómez-Pompa has suggested that forest management by the ancient Maya resulted in the abundance and distribution of fruit-bearing and otherwise economically valuable trees found in the lowland forest today. Remains of at least seventeen species of economically important trees have been recovered from ancient sites in the Maya Lowlands, with numerous species of palms being commonly represented, including coyol (*Acromia mexicana*), cohune (*Orbignya cohune*), and conoboy (*Bactris major*). Other native tree species such as ramón (*Brosimum alicastrum*) have been suggested as potential subsistence alternatives for the ancient Maya. The nut of the ramón is highly nutritious and stores well because of a low moisture content, but archaeological remains are unlikely to be preserved owing to the lack of a durable shell or the need to process it in a way that might lead to carbonization. The most familiar domesticated trees of Mesoamerica are avocado *(Persea americana)* and cacao *(Theobroma cacao).* Wild avocado was utilized by humans as early as 8000 B.C. in the Tehuacán Valley, although larger seed size, indicating human selection, did not appear until about 500 B.C. Cacao is a small tropical tree, the seeds of which are used to make chocolate through a process of fermentation and roasting. Cacao was a highly valued commodity in most of Mesoamerica and was most commonly consumed as a drink mixed with maize, chile, and other ingredients. Two species of cacao are native to southern Mexico and Central America, *T. bicolor* and *T. cacao,* the latter being the more commonly cultivated.

A number of other plants were grown in Mesoamerica for food, beverages, fiber, and flavoring, as well as sources of psychoactive substances. Several species of agave *(Agave* spp.) were domesticated and cultivated for food and fiber, and as the main ingredient in the fermented, mildly alcoholic Aztec beverage pulque. In the Maya area, two domesticated species of agave, henequen *(A. fourcroydes)* and sisal *(A. sisalana),* were cultivated for their long, durable fibers. Cotton *(Gossypium* spp.), as a domesticated form of the native wild plant *G. hirsutum* of the Mexican Gulf coast, was widely cultivated in the lowlands of Mesoamerica by the time of European contact. Cotton has a history of use as fiber in Mesoamerica going back to at least 3500 B.C., as indicated by remains recovered from caves in the Tehuacán Valley.

Slash-and-Burn Cultivation

Slash-and-burn cultivation, also known as "swidden" or "shifting" cultivation, is a widespread technique in Mesoamerica, with pollen evidence suggesting its practice prior to 3000 B.C. The technique involves cutting the vegetation on a plot of land during the dry season, allowing it to dry, and then burning it; crops are planted in the burned area with the onset of seasonal rains. A field is cultivated for one or more years, then abandoned as yields decline owing to decreased fertility or competition with weeds or insects.

A new plot is then selected and the cycle begins again. After active cultivation, a particular plot of land will be left in fallow for a period of time, often from five to twenty years, before being cleared again for cultivation. It is common practice for a farming family to have several small plots under cultivation at any one time, scattering the fields among various landforms, soil types, or hydrological settings in order to maximize production and minimize the risk brought on by unpredictable fluctuations in climate. Though requiring extensive land, slash-and-burn

cultivation is highly labor efficient, and it has been practiced in areas of high vegetation density and seas rainfall patterns, particularly in semideciduous tropic forests of the lowlands. In Mesoamerica, the typical slash-and-burn plot is planted in maize, supplemented by beans and squash, with the cultivated field being referred to by the Nahuatl (Aztec) term *milpa.*

Slash-and-burn cultivation systems can be intensified by a number of strategies beyond shortening the fallow cycle. Increasing the diversity of crops planted in an individual plot can extend the growing season, make maximum use of horizontal space, and increase resistance to insect predation. Tree crops can be planted, and succession species managed, in order to maintain the productivity of the plot while in fallow.

Agricultural production under rain-fed cultivation systems was improved in ancient times through a number of field-surface management strategies that function to modify soil conditions, moisture availability, and microclimate in order to promote crop growth. Ridging and mounding of soils is a common cultivation technique, represented archaeologically in Mesoamerica by examples such as the maize ridges, with plant stubs intact, that were preserved beneath volcanic ash at the site of Cerén, El Salvador. Vestiges of maize mounds are known from the highlands of Guatemala, and the traditional raised planting beds known as *tablones* undoubtedly have pre-Hispanic origins. Narrow, rectangular enclosures defined by rock alignments are often interpreted as remnants of raised seed-beds, and circular piles of small rocks known as *chich* mounds probably functioned to retain moisture and provide support to trees in the shallow-soiled, arid Yucatán Peninsula of the northern Maya Lowlands.

Home Gardens

Home gardens are small "in-field" plots of land, generally in direct spatial association with residences, that are used for cultivating a variety of useful plants. In Mesoamerica today, the home garden is known by the Nahuatl term *calmil.* Many of the plants cultivated there are generally less amenable to cultivation in "out-fields" because of their perishability or higher care requirements, or they are needed on a regular basis in small quantities. Fruit or nut trees often dominate home gardens, forming a canopy over a complex mix of productive shrubs, perennials, and annuals. Home gardens are also commonly used for experiments with new cultigens; they serve as sources of medicinal, ceremonial, and ornamental plants, and are areas for seedling propagation under the watchful eye of the resident farmers. Gardens situated within the immediate living space of a family benefit not only from close attention and protection from predators, but also from the byproducts of everyday life, such as irrigation with household waste water and soil improvement through incorporation of organic wastes. In many areas of the world, home gardens provide the bulk of subsistence needs for the family. Tenure over house-lot gardens often represents a source of family-based wealth, even in situations where out-field lands are controlled communally.

Home gardens were apparently widespread in ancient Mesoamerica, from the arid north through the tropical lowlands. Several lines of archaeological evidence have been used to identify ancient home gardens. Ethnographically, they are usually well demarcated, and the remains of ancient house-lot walls are often interpreted as garden boundaries; thousands of such enclosures have been recorded in the northern Maya Lowlands. Where such boundary walls are not evident archaeologically, the spacing of household sites, the distribution of small artifacts from sheet midden used as fertilizer, and the enrichment of soils with nutrients such as phosphorus all suggest ancient cultivation practices. Features that indicate field-surface management are often incorporated into home gardens, and wells situated within boundary walls suggest that pot irrigation could also have been used in home-garden cultivation.

Terracing

The terracing of sloping lands to aid in the retention of soil and moisture is one of the most widespread cultivation techniques found in Mesoamerica. Terracing is used in a wide range of terrains, from extremely steep, otherwise unusable land to barely perceivable slopes, where it is a form of micromanagement to control sheet-wash. Terracing can depend solely on rainfall as a source of moisture or can be incorporated into irrigation systems. Terraces are also constructed across intermittent stream channels, where they function as retaining walls to catch water-transported soil and to preserve moisture after floods.

Terraces are constructed by modifying hillsides into sloping fields of gradients less than the natural terrain, or by sculpting the landscape into cascades of level benches. Soils may be retained by simple barricades of brush or logs, or more permanent retaining walls may be constructed of stone. Stones from field clearance activities are often used to build up terrace retaining walls incrementally over many years; in other cases, planned and highly

engineered stone constructions are evident. Living plants are also used as terrace borders that function to retain soils.

In the tropical lowlands, terracing functioned primarily to prevent erosion and to build up soils behind retaining walls. Terracing could also extend growing time by helping to retain soil moisture during the dry season. In the Maya Lowlands, extensive tracts of low-slope terraces have been identified in areas such as the Rio Bec zone; in other, more hilly regions, such as the Puuc Hills, terraces seem to be restricted to foot-slope situations. Large-scale, and perhaps centrally planned, terrace systems surround the large Maya center of Caracol, situated in highly dissected karst terrain in the foothills of the Maya Mountains of southern Belize. Elsewhere in the tropical lowlands, extensive systems of sloping-field terraces brought piedmont areas of central Veracruz under cultivation.

In the arid central highlands of Mexico, many terrace systems functioned for runoff management as well as soil retention. In runoff management, one goal is to prevent crops from being damaged by fast-moving water and transported sediments; a second goal is to slow water down and spread it out so it can be better used by crops. In the Tehuacán Valley, numerous small systems of terraces, check dams, rock alignments, and other features managed runoff on hillsides and along the floodplains of rivers and intermittent streams. In the Basin of Mexico, piedmont land was terraced using the resilient and productive agave (maguey) plant to form terrace borders.

Irrigation

Irrigation involves the artificial transport and distribution of water to otherwise dry lands. Canal irrigation in Mesoamerica was a widespread phenomenon, yet it was never developed to the scale or level of engineering sophistication seen in irrigation systems in the Old World, or New World systems such those constructed by the Moche of Andean South America or the Hohokam of southern Arizona. Some have suggested that irrigation did not reach high development in Mesoamerica because of the lack of suitable large, slow-moving rivers outside the tropical lowlands, where irrigation was not needed. Virtually all irrigation systems in Mesoamerica make use of water originating from ephemeral streams or springs.

Irrigation has a history in Mesoamerica spanning approximately 3,000 years. The beginnings of irrigation agriculture may be traced to drainage ditches excavated to move water away from habitation sites, a problem more easily solved than transporting water to a desired location. Other theories suggest that irrigation developed out of floodwater farming as a means to control flood damage after crops were planted and to distribute runoff.

Irrigation systems of Mesoamerica involve a number of technological components. Dams were constructed as diversion structures and to store water for controlled release. Natural watercourses were channelized to improve or modify flow, and canals were dug to move water from natural sources. Also constructed were aqueducts, specialized elevated canals that transported water over low-lying areas and ravines. Head gates controlled water flow from streams into canals, and sluice gates regulated flows from main canals into dendritic systems of branch canals. Various devices were constructed to control the flow of water across field surfaces, including terraces, mounded-earth bunds, and water-spreading blockades of brush, earth, or stone.

Current evidence suggests that the earliest Mesoamerican canal irrigation systems date to around 1000 B.C. The Olmec site of Teopantecuanitlán includes a storage dam and associated canal that have been interpreted as a water delivery system for agricultural fields, with the most likely date of construction being between 1200 and 1000 B.C. A more thoroughly documented early irrigation system is that of Santa Clara Coatitlán, where a channelized gully and branch canals functioned to deliver runoff waters from the east slopes of Cerro Guadalupe, ultimately discharging into Lake Texcoco in the Basin of Mexico. Construction and use of the irrigation system at Santa Clara Coatitlán is dated within the Middle Formative period (c. 1150–725 B.C.), possibly during the early Middle Formative (c. 1150–900 B.C.). Irrigation technology, and the area of lands under irrigation, reached their height during the Postclassic period, from approximately A.D. 1200 to 1520.

There are many notable and well-studied examples of Mesoamerican irrigation systems. The Río Cuautitlán irrigation works in the northern Basin of Mexico is probably the largest and most complex system in Mesoamerica. A system of canals and monumental aqueducts brought water across Lake Texcoco and into the Aztec capital of Tenochtitlán, providing water for irrigated gardens as well as for household use and the maintenance of water levels around *chinampa* fields within the shallow lake. In the Tehuacán Valley, the Purron Dam complex made a significant contribution to irrigated farming of the area. The travertine-encrusted canals of Hierve el Agua, in Oaxaca, represent a wonderfully preserved network of ancient canals and the best-documented spring-fed irrigation system in Mesoamerica. Recent work in the Maya Lowlands suggests the possibility of previously unrecognized irrigation systems associated with artificial reservoirs.

Pot irrigation, in which water is hand-carried in vessels from a source to the field, opened large areas of land to cultivation that would otherwise be of limited agricultural capability. In the Valley of Oaxaca, shallow wells excavated at intervals across the broad alluvial plain provided a significant source of agricultural production in a system known today as *riego a brazo*. Wells are the most common source of water in pot-irrigation systems; other sources include natural bodies of water, and artificial canals and reservoirs.

Wetland Cultivation

The use and manipulation of wetlands for cultivation has a long history in Mesoamerica. It accounts for one of the most famous cultivation techniques of the region, the *chinampa* system constructed by the Aztecs in the Xochimilco-Chalco Basin in the Valley of Mexico. *Chinampas* are raised planting platforms constructed within shallow freshwater swamps from transported soils and organic detritus. The raised planting beds are elevated enough to provide adequate drainage for cultivated plants, while supplying permanent moisture that is drawn up from below and from the canals that separate the beds. The water level within the shallow lakes was controlled by a dike system. Fertility of the soils was maintained by composting and by scooping organic-rich muck from the canals to spread on the planting beds. A significant proportion of *chinampa* farmers lived in dwellings constructed on artificial platforms dispersed among the planting beds. It has been estimated that *chinampa* cultivation covered approximately 120 square kilometers of reclaimed wetlands at the time of Spanish contact in the early sixteenth century. Remnants of the *chinampa* system continue to be cultivated today in the Xochimilco area.

Cultivation of wetlands was also a widespread phenomenon in the tropical lowlands of Mesoamerica, with many examples along the Gulf Coast and in the Maya Lowlands of the Yucatán Peninsula. In the Maya Lowlands, wetlands are common as backswamps along slow-moving rivers on the southeastern and southwestern margins of the Yucatán Peninsula, and in natural depressions called *bajos* that are concentrated in the southern interior. Wetlands are much less common in the northern Maya Lowlands, occurring along coastal margins, in

A

isolated inland patches, and in association with the Holbox fracture system within the Yalahau region of northern Quintana Roo. It has been suggested that wetland cultivation was a major component of ancient Maya agriculture in the southern lowlands, with the distribution of *bajos* having a significant influence on the location of political centers of power, particularly during the Classic period when regional populations were highest. There is, however, a great deal of debate over the types of wetlands that were used, the dating of Maya wetland cultivation, the construction and cultivation techniques used, and the local versus regional importance of wetland agricultural production. Wetland cultivation in the Maya Lowlands, as well as other wetland areas, involved a range of cultivation techniques that were dictated by local conditions of hydrology and soils, as well as by varying demands for production, which would have influenced the degree of labor input.

The earliest and simplest form of wetland cultivation probably involved coordinating the planting of crops to coincide with natural flooding cycles along riverine floodplains and swamp margins. Crops would be planted in moist soils as floodwaters receded and would be harvested before, or as, the waters rose with the onset of the rainy season. No manipulation of the landscape is necessary under such a water-recessional system. Channelizing or ditching the margins of riverine floodplains and swamps would extend the growing season by improving drainage at the beginning and end of the flooding cycle. The construction of raised planting platforms, similar to those used in the *chinampa* system, would represent the most labor-intensive form of wetland cultivation and would be instituted under the greatest demands for increased production. Wetland agricultural systems can also be combined with the use or management of fish, snails, and other aquatic animals, and the production of other products, such as edible algae.

The most thoroughly studied wetland sites in the Maya Lowlands are those of northern Belize, most of which are associated with the New River and Rio Hondo. These sites include Pulltrouser Swamp, Albion Island, and Douglas Swamp. The wetlands of northern Belize show evidence of agricultural use ranging from simple water-recessional cultivation, through channelization of wetland margins, and possibly construction of raised planting platforms at Pulltrouser Swamp. *Bajos* of the interior have received much less study; an exception is the examination of the ditched fields associated with the El Pedernal *bajo,* near the site of Río Azul, northern

Guatemala. The El Pedernal *bajo* is dominated by the escoba palm *(Crysophila argentea),* a vegetation association indicating a *bajo* that is transitional between the well-drained uplands and the lower or more poorly drained areas of *tintal bajo* characterized by the tinto tree *(Haematoxylon campechianum).* In the case of the El Pedernal *bajo,* landscape manipulation appears to consist of channels that run parallel to the natural drainage slope of the seasonally flooded wetland, with little or no raising of the field surface between the channels. In the northern Maya Lowlands, recent investigations in wetlands of the Yalahau region of northern Quintana Roo, Mexico, have revealed a complex of rock alignments that apparently functioned to control the movement of soil and water within the body of these seasonally flooded, thin-soiled wetlands.

Other Cultivation Techniques

A wide range of other cultivation techniques and technologies were undoubtedly used in ancient Mesoamerica, some of which are more easily discerned in the archaeological record than others. Traditional agriculture informs us of many sophisticated techniques for managing space and scheduling planting in order to gain maximum production. Growing numerous crops in the same field (intercropping) can help prevent erosion, maintain soil fertility, ward off insects, and make maximum use of vertical space by layering plants of various heights from root crops to trees. Plant remains recovered from archaeological contexts can document the range of plant species used and suggest what cropping systems might have been practiced. Outside gardens and agricultural fields, the forests themselves may have been managed—or cultivated, in a sense—to increase the numbers and productivity of food-producing and economically useful trees.

FURTHER READINGS

Coe, S. D. 1994. *America's First Cuisines.* Austin: University of Texas Press.

Donkin, R. A. 1979. *Agricultural Terracing in the Aboriginal New World.* Viking Fund Publications in Anthropology, 56. New York: Wenner-Gren Foundation for Anthropological Research.

Doolittle, W. E. 1990. *Canal Irrigation in Prehistoric Mexico: The Sequence of Technological Change.* Austin: University of Texas Press.

Fedick, S. L. (ed.). 1996. *The Managed Mosaic: Ancient Maya Agriculture and Resource Use.* Salt Lake City: University of Utah Press.

Flannery, K. V. 1968. Archaeological Systems Theory and Early Mesoamerica. In B. J. Meggers (ed.), *Anthropological Archeology in the Americas,* pp. 67–87. Washington, D.C.: Anthropological Society of Washington.

Hayden, B. 1995. An Overview of Domestication. In T. D. Price and A. B. Gebauer (eds.), *Last Hunters—First Farmers: New Perspectives on the Prehistoric Transition to Agriculture,* pp. 273–299. Santa Fe: School of American Research Press.

Killion, T. W. (ed.). 1992. *Gardens of Prehistory: The Archaeology of Settlement Agriculture in Greater Mesoamerica.* Tuscaloosa: University of Alabama Press.

Sanders, W. T. 1976. The Agricultural History of the Basin of Mexico. In E. R. Wolf (ed.), *The Valley of Mexico: Studies in Pre-Hispanic Ecology and Society,* pp. 101–159. Albuquerque: University of New Mexico Press.

Siemens, A. H., and D. E. Puleston. 1972. Ridged Fields and Associated Features in Southern Campeche: New Perspectives on the Lowland Maya. *American Antiquity* 37: 228–239.

Sluyter, A. 1994. Intensive Wetland Agriculture in Mesoamerica: Space, Time, and Form. *Annals of the Association of American Geographers* 84: 557–585.

Turner, B. L., II. 1974. Prehistoric Intensive Agriculture in the Mayan Lowlands. *Science* 185: 118–124.

Wilken, G. C. 1987. *Good Farmers: Traditional Agricultural Resource Management in Mexico and Central America.* Berkeley: University of California Press.

Scott L. Fedick

SEE ALSO
Agave; Dog; Maize; Turkeys

Ahualulco (Jalisco, Mexico)

This habitation zone covered about 500 hectares and was occupied during phases from El Arenal (300 B.C.–A.D. 200), Ahualulco (A.D. 200–400), and Teuchitlán I (400–700), as demonstrated by a 12-meter profile exposed in the largest pyramid, Pyramid A. The site, part of the larger settlement system focused on Teuchitlán, is one of the four largest concentrations of precincts in the area. The site overlooks a marshy lake zone, which had several thousand canals and drained-field farm plots. Ahualulco has five civic-ceremonial precincts; the largest comprises six separate concentric, circular buildings (Teuchitlán style), including two monumental structures, one

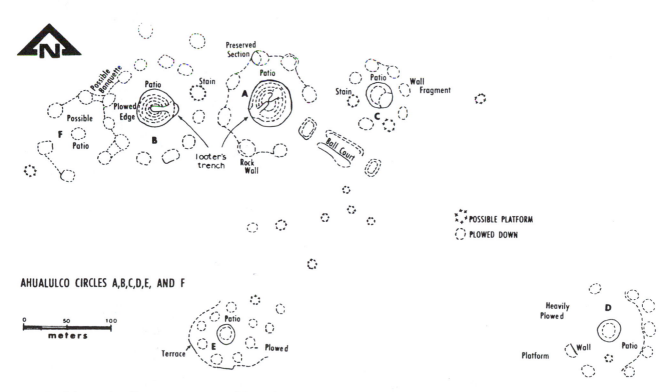

The Ahualulco circles. Illustration courtesy of the author.

A

monumental ball court, and several elite residential areas. Pyramid cores are adobe and rubble, faced with terraced rock, and were probably plastered and painted. Wattle-and-daub superstructures were also brightly painted (as inferred from architectural figurines), with thatched, gabled roofs.

The other four precincts, considerably smaller, consist of a single circular building, one small ball court, and modest elite residential structures at each. Two or possibly three tiers of ceremonial architecture are represented in this sector of the site. Residential architecture is very poorly preserved and quite dispersed. Most compounds comprise two to four low platforms facing a plazuela. The most elaborate have small altars and enclosing banquettes. Shaft tombs at the site have been looted for their hollow figurines, ceramic vessels (including pseudo-cloisonné), and carved stone materials. Trade sherds found at the site include Thin Orange, and conch shells from the Pacific are common.

FURTHER READINGS

Weigand, P. C. 1974. The Ahualulco Site and the Shaft Tomb Complex of the Etzatlán Area. In B. Bell (ed.), *The Archaeology of West Mexico,* pp. 120–131. Ajijic, Jalisco: West Mexican Society for Advanced Study.

———. 1985. Evidence for Complex Societies during the Western Mesoamerican Classic Period. In *The Archaeology of West and Northwest Mesoamerica,* edited by M. Foster and P. Weigand, pp. 47–91. Boulder, Colo.: Westview.

———. 1993. *Evolución de una civilización prehispánica: Arqueología de Jalisco, Nayarit, y Zacatecas.* Zamora: Colegio de Michoacán.

Phil C. Weigand

SEE ALSO

Shaft Tombs; Teuchitlán Tradition; West Mexico

Ahuináhuac

See Mezcala Lapidary Style

Alta Verapaz Region

In central Guatemala, this region in the high, forested Sierra de Chamá, is habitat of the quetzal bird and, in the sixteenth century, was the source of 10,000 feathers per year in trade. It was also a source of jade-type stone and fine polychrome pottery from Classic Maya Chamá (A.D. 200–800).

FURTHER READINGS

Arnauld, M. C. 1986. *Archéologie de l'Habitat en Alta Verapaz (Guatemala).* Études Américaines, 10. Mexico City: Centre d'Études Mexicaines et Centroaméricaines.

Butler, M. 1940. Study of Maya Archaeological Material, Chiefly Pottery, from Chamá, Alta Verapaz, Guatemala. *American Philosophical Society Yearbook* 1940: 133–135.

Weeks, J. M. 1993. *Maya Civilization.* New York: Garland.

Susan Toby Evans

SEE ALSO

Chiapas Interior Plateau

Alta Vista de Chalchihuites (Zacatecas, Mexico)

This ceremonial center of about 8 hectares is situated on a low ridge of the Río Colorado/Suchil Valley, near mineral sources for blue and green stones called *chalchihuitl* (true turquoise, however, was largely imported). The site was the center of a network of roads and of an archaeoastronomical assemblage based on an eastern horizon calendar and related defensible sites on high hills—Chapin to the south and Pedragoso to the north. On Chapin are two cross-circle petroglyphs, calendrical and benchmark features common at Teotihuacán: here the summer solstice sunrise appears over Cerro Picacho, as it does from Pedragoso at the winter solstice.

The probable site occupation was c. A.D. 350–950. Initial construction in the site nucleus, c. 400–450, consisted of the Hall of Columns on a massive platform faced with sloping *talud* panels, and the Great Forecourt, surrounded by banquettes, platforms, and a central altar, all with diagonals, cardinally oriented. We believe that initial construction, involving Canutillo phase labor and foreign architects, installed a shrine on the Tropic of Cancer, marking the place where "the sun turned," an important Mesoamerican astronomical, calendrical, and religious location. Settlement compound construction involved a small group from Teotihuacán (possibly a specialized group of astronomers, architects, and priests), and continuing use of village corvée labor. A new ceramic complex was initiated; its influence on local ceramics produced the Vesuvio phase pottery. Joint occupation slowly dissolved with local intermarriage.

The Compound of the Four World Quarters was constructed around A.D. 510–600, complete with banquettes, adobe rooms on platforms, and a pyramidal court altar. The basic structural plan is that of a Canutillo phase village, but with many Teotihuacán-style architectural innovations. Initial construction fills contained Canutillo phase ceramics, plus an exotic ware—pseudo-cloisonné, common in West Mexico and known at Teotihuacán. A meandering hall-like structure, the Labyrinth, runs through a Teotihuacán-style settlement compound, recording equinox sunrise over Picacho and the single zenith sun passage at summer solstice.

Decorated ceramics include Suchil Red on Brown and Michilia Red-Filled Engraved (a Teotihuacán champlevé decorative technique) (Alta Vista phase). The latter black tripod ware is decorated with *cipactli* crocodilian designs; the former includes jars, bowls, and plates with interior quadrate designs.

Late in the occupation, a three-temple complex was completed, including a central pyramidal structure with sloping *talud* sides; below were interred three sequential high-status burials. Two longbone skull racks were assembled, and the two-part Serpent Wall encloses the complex, opening on a plaza that was probably the market; cracked human bones and drilled skulls contaminate the refuse.

Buttresses were constructed on the sides of the Hall, forming colonnaded galleries, wherein a multiple sacrificial burial was made, and many offering pits were dug. Around A.D. 750–850, the compound was destroyed; walls were pushed in, the temple burned, and scattered skeletal remains littered an atrium floor. Subsequently, fill was dumped over the compound ruins. On the court floor in the northern and eastern corners there were scattered human skeletal remains, partially covered with a later floor. Both the pyramid and the Hall of Columns burned, probably c. 850; finally, the courtyard drains were sealed and the Hall was filled with Alta Vista phase refuse.

After Teotihuacán's fall, a Florescent Alta Vista phase statelet developed, involved in turquoise trade, warfare, and excessive human sacrifice. Eventually, Alta Vista fell to outsiders (possibly from Durango), or to local rebels, who temporarily reoccupied the site during the Calichal phase.

FURTHER READINGS

Aveni, A. F., H. Hartung, and J. C. Kelley. 1981. Alta Vista (Chalchihuites): Astronomical Implications of a Mesoamerican Ceremonial Outpost at the Tropic of Cancer. *American Antiquity* 47: 316–335.

Coggins, C. C. 1993. The Age of Teotihuacán and Its Mission Abroad. In K. Berrin and E. Pasztory (eds.), *Teotihuacán: Art from the City of the Gods,* pp. 141–155. London: Fine Arts Museum of San Francisco and Thames and Hudson.

Kelley, J. C., and E. A. Kelley. 1980. Sipapu and Pyramid Too: The Temple of the Crypt at Alta Vista, Chalchihuites. *Transactions of the Illinois State Academy of Science* 73.2: 62–79.

Riley, C. L., and B. C. Hedrick (eds.). 1978. *Across the Chichimec Sea: Papers in Honor of J. Charles Kelley.* Carbondale: Southern Illinois University Press.

J. Charles Kelley and Ellen Abbott Kelley

SEE ALSO

Astronomy, Archaeoastronomy, and Astrology; Northwestern Frontier

Altar de Sacrificios (Petén, Guatemala)

A major Maya center in the southern Maya lowlands, Altar de Sacrificios is known for its carved stone stelae and long hieroglyphic textual record. It was occupied from the Middle Formative through the Classic period (c. 600 B.C.–A.D. 900). The site is on the southern bank of the Río Pasión (1–2 km east and upstream from the Pasión's confluence with the Río Salinas), occupying a natural rise above the lower-lying and seasonally flooded local riverbank terrain. Vegetation is tropical rainforest on the rises, with bamboo and other shrubs forming thickets on lower ground.

The three main plaza groups at Altar de Sacrificios extend over an area of 400 square meters, and none of the pyramids or platforms therein is of great height or constructional volume. There are no standing superstructures, nor has any evidence of corbeled vaulting been found; thus, presumably, all temple or palace structures that once stood on the mounds of Altar de Sacrificios were built of perishable materials.

Dates carved on the stelae range from A.D. 455 (Stela 10) to 771 (Stela 15), and the monument sequence lists several rulers in this span. The three earliest reigns are placed in the Early Classic period, between A.D. 455 and 524. A subsequent hiatus lasted until 589, when a new ruler acceded, remaining in power until 633. He was followed by four rulers in quick succession, until 662. After this, there is no clear succession record; however, construction and ceramic sequences indicate continued occupation of the site until at least the ninth century.

A

The site is composed of three major mound groups and a nearby scattering of smaller mounds. Excavations into Structure B-I, the site's largest pyramid (13 meters high), revealed early Middle Formative period Xe phase (900–600 B.C.) small residential platforms on the original ground level. These were then overlain by the first pyramid platform, dating from the late Middle Formative San Félix Mamom phase (600–300 B.C.). New levels were added during the Late Formative Plancha phase (300 B.C.–A.D. 100), and these were finally capped by the Protoclassic–Early Classic Salinas phase (A.D. 100–450) outer construction of the pyramid. This final and outer construction layer of the B-I pyramid took the form of a series of terraces laid up in red sandstone block masonry; it can be associated with a stela dated A.D. 455, probably marking the completion of the pyramid. The three other aforementioned Early Classic stelae can be associated with subsequent use of the B-I pyramid.

Structures B-II and B-III of Group B are smaller pyramids, while Structure B-IV is a large palace-type mound with at least two levels of raised interior courts. The outer masonry of these other Group B structures is also red sandstone.

Group C is much less regular in its layout than Group B. Test excavations in Structure C-I, a palace-type mound, revealed a stratigraphic sequence of construction and ceramics ranging from Middle to Late Formative times. The masonry material, like that of Group B, is red sandstone, possibly from a sizable outcrop occurring 1 km upstream along the Río Pasión, there being no stone outcrops in the immediate vicinity of the site. The limestone used in Group A structures and monuments probably came from another Pasión outcrop, about 6 km upstream from the site.

Group A covers an area larger than that of the other two groups combined. At its northern end, Structure A-I, a large multi-level platform, has been partially destroyed by the action of the Río Pasión. Structure A-II is a long platform providing the western site of the North Plaza of Group A. Excavations into Structure A-II disclosed (among other things) a rich tomb of a noblewoman, who had among her grave goods the handsome "Altar Vase," a polychrome cylinder jar of great beauty and iconographic interest. Another long palace-type mound, Structure A-III, forms the eastern side of the North Plaza. The layout of the South Plaza of Group A is somewhat less tidy than the North, and, as can be seen from the map, it is outlined by many platform structures. Throughout, the masonry and stelae are of limestone.

Much of Group A's construction and probably all its stelae date to the Late Classic period, which spans the Chixoy and Pasión phases (A.D. 600–771). There was also some additional building and overbuilding in the succeeding Terminal Classic Boca phase (771–900) and the Jimba phase (immediately after 900).

Small residential mounds lie to the west of the large mound groups. About forty of these were mapped, and several were tested by excavation. The mounds were occupied from the Formative through Classic period and must have been the house sites for some of the sustaining population; probably more of the sustaining population lived farther away. Although no systematic surveys have been conducted along the Pasión and Salinas rivers in the area around Altar de Sacrificios, it should be noted that small residential mounds occur on high ground along the riverbanks for several kilometers in all directions.

The ceramic record at Altar de Sacrificios parallels, in general, that established elsewhere in the Petén, especially as defined at Uaxactún and Tikal. Altar de Sacrificios Middle Formative Xe-Mamom wares pertain to those spheres, as do the Late Formative Plancha phase Chicanel sphere materials. There are also some general Protoclassic characteristics in Salinas phase materials at the site. One notable difference in timing, however, is that Classic Tzakol-like pottery does not appear at Altar de Sacrificios until after A.D. 450, some 200 to 300 years after it first appears in the northeastern Petén. The subsequent Pasión phase pottery types at Altar de Sacrificios are comfortably at home in the general Tepeu sphere. Boca pottery, however, is much stronger in fine paste wares, in Fine Orange and Fine Gray, than would be the case for Tepeu assemblages farther east and north; and the Jimba pottery complex, with its abundant Fine Orange vessels and figurines, shows links to the Gulf Coast rather than the rest of the Petén.

The site was first mentioned in 1883, by Alfred Maudslay, who had visited it. Teobert Maler worked there in 1894–1895, naming the site "Altar de Sacrificios" after a large altar he found there. S. G. Morley's epigraphic surveys led him to the site in 1914 and again in 1944, and he provided the first substantial site description (Morley 1937–1938). Between 1959 and 1964, G. R. Willey and A. L. Smith led a Harvard University project of survey, mapping, and excavations, providing the most detailed account of the site to date.

FURTHER READINGS

Adams, R. E. W. 1971. *The Ceramics of Altar de Sacrificios.* Papers of the Peabody Museum of Archaeology and Ethnology, 63.1. Cambridge, Mass.: Harvard University.

Graham, J. A. 1972. *The Hieroglyphic Inscriptions and Monumental Art of Altar de Sacrificios.* Papers of the Peabody Museum of Archaeology and Ethnology, 64.2. Cambridge, Mass.: Harvard University.

Maler, T. 1908. *Explorations of the Upper Usumacinta and Adjacent Region.* Memoirs of the Peabody Museum, 4.1. Cambridge, Mass.: Harvard University.

Mathews, P., and G. R. Willey. 1991. Prehistoric Polities of the Pasión Region: Hieroglyphic Texts and Their Archaeological Settings. In T. P. Culbert (ed.), *Classic Maya Political History: Hieroglyphic and Archaeological Evidence,* pp. 30–71. New York: Cambridge University Press.

Maudslay, A. P. 1883. Explorations in Guatemala and Examination of the Newly Discovered Ruines of Quirigua, Tikal, and the Usumacinta. *Proceedings of the Royal Geographical Society* 5: 185–204.

Morley, S. G. 1937–1938. *The Inscriptions of Peten.* 5 vols. Carnegie Institution of Washington Publication 437. Washington, D.C.: Carnegie Institution.

Saul, F. P. 1972. *The Human Skeletal Remains of Altar de Sacrificios: An Osteological Analysis.* Papers of the Peabody Museum, 63.2. Cambridge, Mass.: Harvard University.

Smith, A. L. 1972. *Excavations at Altar de Sacrificios: Architecture, Settlements, Burials, and Caches.* Papers of the Peabody Museum, 62.2. Cambridge, Mass.: Harvard University.

Willey, G. R. 1972. *The Artifacts of Altar de Sacrificios.* Papers of the Peabody Museum, 64.1. Cambridge, Mass.: Harvard University.

———. 1973. *The Altar de Sacrificios Excavations: General Summary and Conclusions.* Papers of the Peabody Museum, 64.3. Cambridge, Mass.: Harvard University.

Willey, G. R., and A. L. Smith. 1969. *The Ruins of Altar de Sacrificios, Department of Peten, Guatemala: An Introduction.* Papers of the Peabody Museum, 52, part 1. Cambridge, Mass.: Harvard University.

Gordon R. Willey

SEE ALSO

Classic Period; Formative Period; Maya Lowlands: South; Petexbatun Region

Altun Ha (Belize, Belize)

This small but important site near the northern Belize coast flourished from the Middle Formative period (c. 800 B.C.) to the Terminal Classic (c. A.D. 900–925 or later), with Late Postclassic (fifteenth–early sixteenth century) reoccupation. Possibly the earliest intellectual and political, rather than economic, link between Teotihuacán and the Maya area is demonstrated by a tomb-related 258-piece offering, c. A.D. 250–300, of green obsidian from Navajas, near Teotihuacán, in Teotihuacán ritual and utilitarian forms, with Teotihuacán-related ceramics. Similar offerings at Teotihuacán are in the Adosado of the Sun Pyramid (Miccaotli phase, A.D. 150–200) and in Ofrenda 1 in the Feathered Serpent Temple-Pyramid (Miccaotli or Early Tlamimilolpa phase, A.D. 200–300). There is no other contemporaneous or later Altun Ha evidence of Teotihuacán influence, however. Twelve other royal tombs and 119 offerings in the Classic period two-plaza central precinct and surrounding residential/administrative zones yielded large quantities of carved jade objects, including a 14.9 cm high, 4.42 kg full-round head of Kinich Ahau, the sun god.

FURTHER READINGS

Pendergast, D. M. 1971. Evidence of Early Teotihuacán-Lowland Maya Contact at Altun Há. *American Antiquity* 36: 455–459.

———. 1979–1990. *Excavations at Altun Ha, Belize, 1964–1970.* 3 vols. Toronto: Royal Ontario Museum.

———. 1992. Noblesse Oblige: The Elites of Altun Ha and Lamanai, Belize. In D. Z. Chase and A. F. Chase (eds.), *Mesoamerican Elites: An Archaeological Assessment,* pp. 61–79. Norman: University of Oklahoma Press.

Spence, M. W. 1984. Craft Production and Polity in Early Teotihuacan. In K. Hirth (ed.), *Trade and Exchange in Early Mesoamerica,* pp. 87–114. Albuquerque: University of New Mexico Press.

David M. Pendergast

SEE ALSO

Maya Lowlands: South

Amalucan (Puebla, Mexico)

Large complex of Formative and Early Classic mounds located at the eastern edge of the city of Puebla. This area is largely the fossil basin of a Pleistocene lake, bounded on the south by a ridge of lower hills, on the west by a large

A

hill called Cerro Amalucan, and on the north by Malinche Mountain. The mounds are in two concentrations. The lower one, in the center of the basin, is primarily a Middle Formative occupation and is associated with a system of combined irrigation and drainage canals. This water-management system was built and primarily used during the Middle Formative period and appears to have been abandoned in the late Formative/Early Classic. The other mound concentration, on the slopes and top of Cerro Amalucan, is primarily an Early Classic occupation, and there are more than a hundred residential terraces on the slopes of Cerro Amalucan. Survey, mapping, surface collections, and excavations were conducted in the 1960s and 1970s.

Melvin Fowler

SEE ALSO
Puebla-Tlaxcala Region

Amapa (Nayarit, Mexico)

A large, mostly Postclassic site on the floodplain of the Río Grande de Santiago, consisting of multiple earth mounds up to 200 meters long and 8 meters high, extending all the way to the Pacific Coast, 12 km to the west. Borders of the site could not be determined, but there is a central concentration of mound and plaza areas, with adjacent cemeteries and a well-preserved ball court. In this alluvial area, the water table is less than 2 meters below the surface; some site features, including cemeteries, are now under water. There are numerous ponds created as borrow pits in the course of obtaining soil for the mounds. Some mounds show cut-stone staircases; the lack of native stone meant that all stone had to be imported from many kilometers upriver.

Postclassic population was probably in the thousands; the area was (and is) intensely cultivated with Mesoamerican staples—maize, beans, and squash. Chronology extends back to the beginning of the common era, but by far the dominant period of occupation is Postclassic, related to the Aztatlán complex extending into the thirteenth and fourteenth centuries A.D. Several hundred pottery vessels were recovered from a cemetery area; these comprise the largest controlled collection of Aztatlán artifacts from western Mexico. Late Postclassic polychromes resemble Mixteca-Puebla and Guasave ceramics. The collection includes a ceramic temple model, many painted and polychrome vessels, and a number of copper artifacts (mostly utilitarian awls and needles).

FURTHER READINGS
Meighan, C. W. (ed.). 1976. *The Archaeology of Amapa, Nayarit.* UCLA Institute of Archaeology, Monumenta Archaeologica, 2. Los Angeles: University of California.

Clement Meighan

SEE ALSO
Aztatlan Complex; Guasave and Related Sites; Northwestern Frontier

Ancestor Veneration

A social practice that includes ritual behavior surrounding the burial and commemoration, by name, of specific members of ascendant generations within kin groups. In ancient Mesoamerica, this practice included interment of the remains of deceased individuals within pyramids, household shrines, and central locales within residences. Certain anatomical elements (such as crania and long bones) might have been retained among the living to stress the link between them and their powerful dead ancestors. In ancient Zapotec elite tombs at Lambityeco, femora are underrepresented, and a stucco façade outside one tomb depicts an elite individual holding the femur of an ancestor. Royal ancestor veneration was an important component of Classic Maya statecraft. Elites evoked ancestors' names in hieroglyphic texts, which were sometimes carved into stone staircases (e.g., Copán), and had themselves depicted in juxtaposition to alleged ancestors on carved monuments (Copán Altar Q, Tikal Stela 31).

Through ancestor veneration, resources, privileges, and political power were transmitted between generations, with ancestors representing jural authority. This practice is thus an important indicator of the emergence of social inequality in Formative Mesoamerica, because it reinforces transgenerational economic differences. In all likelihood, ancestor veneration initially provided a vehicle for the transmission of land and other critical resources between generations; the practice appears in Mesoamerica during the first millennium B.C. and is succeeded by the development of royal ancestor veneration among many Mesoamerican groups. Today ancestor veneration has been absorbed within the Christian feasts of All Saints and All Souls (November 1 and 2), when ancestors—who cement links to resources such as land—are remembered in prayers and offerings.

FURTHER READINGS

Lind, M., and J. Urcid. 1983. The Lords of Lambityeco and Their Nearest Neighbors. *Notas Americanas* 9: 78–111.

Marcus, J. 1992. *Mesoamerican Writing Systems: Propaganda, Myth, and History in Four Ancient Civilizations.* Princeton: Princeton University Press.

McAnany, P. A. 1995. *Living with the Ancestors: Kinship and Kingship in Ancient Maya Society.* Austin: University of Texas Press.

Miller, A. G. 1995. *The Painted Tombs of Oaxaca, Mexico: Living with the Dead.* Cambridge: Cambridge University Press.

Patricia A. McAnany

SEE ALSO
Zapotec Mortuary Practices

Apatzingán Region (Michoacán, Mexico)

The Apatzingán area cannot be identified definitively as to speech or culture, but it probably was non-Tarascan linguistically and ethnically; it shows little archaeological evidence of Tarascan penetration at Apatzingán. It may have been linked with the Teco Indians, who also inhabited parts of Michoacán.

Apatzingán is situated in the Tierra Caliente (hot lands) of Michoacán, largely a parched and arid area, dotted by some oases with swamps, lush vegetation, and fertile soil. Subsistence was based on agriculture, hunting, and gathering wild plants. Some archaeological sites in the Apatzingán area appear to be exclusively mortuary, while others are both burial and occupational. Kelly excavated several sites: Capiral, identified as a burial site with few surface remains; Las Delicias, which consisted of a single low but fairly extensive artificial mound; and El Llano, which consisted of many low, platform-like mounds, associated with many cobble-outlined rectangles and circles. Chronology for this region is poorly understood, but dates associated with named phases are as follows: Chumbícuaro, A.D. 250; Delicias, A.D. 400; Apatzingán, A.D. 500; Tepetate, A.D. 700; and Chila, A.D. 1100.

Types of burial varied with time, from extended supine bodies associated with large stone slabs, to flexed or seated postures, to burials made in earth *yácatas* (Tarascan-style monumental platforms) built for that purpose. Ceramics included polychrome, incised wares, bowls, plates, jars, geometric decoration, zoomorphic vessels, figurines, and clay pipes (possibly Tarascan). Also found were shell and pyrite ornaments (anthropomorphic figurines, pendants, etc.), stone mallets and laurel-leaf blades, greenstone necklaces, and copper artifacts (rattle, figurine, bells, hoes, etc.).

FURTHER READINGS

Kelly, I. 1947. *Excavations at Apatzingán, Michoacán.* Viking Fund Publications in Anthropology, 7. New York: Viking Fund.

Eduardo Williams

SEE ALSO
Michoacán Region

Arbolillo, El (D.F., Mexico)

Small village site (c. 8 hectares) dating from 900 to 500 B.C., at the southern base of the Guadalupe Hills on the northwestern edge of modern Mexico City. Vaillant tested it in 1931, confirming his ceramic sequence from nearby Zacatenco. In 1965 tests, Tolstoy identified three principal occupations: El Arbolillo, Early La Pastora, and Early Cuautepec. Deposits of the first two phases are dense and deep (over 7 meters in places). Refuse contained maize and beans, many bones of deer, mud-turtle, and water birds, and some charred human remains. Abundant clay figurines in the refuse suggest transient use in domestic rituals. Though blades occur, nodule-smashing predominates. Obsidian is mostly from the nearby Otumba source. Burials (excavated by Vaillant) are unelaborate but suggest some differences in rank. Carinated vessels and white bowls bearing the double-line-break motif link the earliest phase with contemporaneous sites elsewhere in Mesoamerica, but the later ceramics are of local styles.

FURTHER READINGS

Boksenbaum, M. W., P. Tolstoy, G. Harbottle, J. Kimberlin, and M. Nievens. 1987. Obsidian Industries and Cultural Evolution in the Basin of Mexico before 500 B.C. *Journal of Field Archaeology* 14: 65–76.

Tolstoy, P., S. K. Fish, M. W. Boksenbaum, K. B. Vaughn, and C. E. Smith. 1977. Early Sedentary Communities of the Basin of Mexico. *Journal of Field Archaeology* 4: 91–106.

Vaillant, George. 1935. Excavations at El Arbolillo. *American Museum of Natural History, Anthropological Papers* 35.2: 199–439.

Paul Tolstoy

A

SEE ALSO
Basin of Mexico; Formative Period; Zacatenco

Archaeology: Analytical Methods

Laboratory analytic methods used by archaeologists directly parallel, and in many cases are identical to, those used by forensic scientists for solving crimes, because their goals are similar: reconstructing past events from material evidence. Selected artifacts or sedimentary samples are collected in the field and brought to the laboratory for processing and study. Each of the various analytic techniques demands different preparations of the sample, but all samples are subject to the problem of contamination. Most of these analytic techniques involve small samples—microscopic and even chemical—so any foreign substances introduced into the sample will bias the results.

Contamination can occur in two ways. Taphonomic contamination results from the site deposition process or disturbance by biotic and other natural processes that introduce materials foreign to the archaeological context. Alternatively (or additionally), extraneous foreign materials may be introduced into the sample during extraction, storage, processing, and handling. To avoid these problems, extreme care must be exercised in selecting samples for analysis in the field and in processing the samples at the site and in the lab.

Different analytic techniques used on both organic and inorganic remains include various chemical techniques, and elemental and physical analyses. These will be discussed, followed by a review of the types of analysis that are applied to organic remains, indicative generally of diet. All these techniques require specialized training and usually very specialized instruments to realize their analytic potential for understanding the past.

Soil chemistry is extremely powerful for reconstructing archaeological activity patterns. Certain natural processes and human behaviors result in a buildup of particular chemicals on the surfaces of an archaeological site. Often, surfaces of archaeological sites become buried by other sediments, but the original paleosoil can be identified by its high concentration of humic acid, indicative of plant decay. Phosphates and carbonates with low pH values are associated with organic accumulation and decay. At Oztoyahualco, a Teotihuacán apartment compound, soil chemistry was used to isolate activity areas by measuring these values for soil samples from rooms and thus defining food preparation and consumption areas, and ritual areas in patios and open areas rather than in enclosed rooms. These chemical values were spatially clustered to suggest three different families. Larger artifacts were not associated with the activity areas indicated by chemical readings, suggesting that they were being cleared away while this process of organic decay was going on.

Soil pH at an archaeological site provides a way of evaluating the preservation potential of artifacts. Highly acidic soils (low pH) cause a rapid breakdown of organic materials like hide, bone, and vegetal remains. Therefore, the absence of these artifacts might be due to poor preservation rather than cultural patterns. Sometimes natural pH conditions can be ameliorated by cultural practices. Tropical soils in Mesoamerica are typically acidic because of the high temperature, moisture, and rapid organic decomposition, which creates carbonic acid as a byproduct. In Classic Mayan elite residences, however, powdered limestone was used to plaster building surfaces. Eventually this lime dissolved in rainwater and went into solution in the soil as calcium carbonates, buffering the carbonic acid and raising pH values to near neutral or even slightly basic, creating improved taphonomic conditions for preservation. With high pH readings, even minute bone remains such as human fetal bone and fish scales are preserved.

Residues left on tool and artifact surfaces provide evidence of their function. Blood residues on lithic tools, or in shell and ceramic containers, indicate that they were used to cut flesh or otherwise came in contact with blood. Blood hemoglobins vary by species, so hemoglobin identification provides direct evidence of what types of animals were butchered or, in the case of human blood, whether a tool was used for autosacrifice or sacrifice. At Copán, human blood residues have been found inside *Spondylus* shells. If human skeletal remains retain blood residues, it is possible to determine ABO and other blood group types, indicating kinship and patterns of inheritance.

Agave plants contain distinctive crystals of calcium oxalate or calcium carbonate, and it is possible that such crystals might adhere to the stone tools that are thought to be used for processing these plant products. Similarly, salt and lime residues have been found in the interiors of ceramic vessels, indicating their use in specialized activities.

Residue analysis can also use analytic techniques like gas and liquid chromatography to determine the existence of complex molecules, such as those from lipid fat residues from specific plant and animal food remains on ceramic cooking and serving vessels. With chromatography it is possible to differentiate animal fat from vegetal fat residues.

Spectroscopic techniques identify the elements in a sample by studying how energy is reflected or absorbed. The wavelengths of the emissions from each chemical element can be measured by different techniques (e.g., optical, X-ray fluorescence). Mass spectroscopy measures the different isotopes of each element and is useful in dietary analysis. Plants metabolize carbon in two distinct pathways, referred to as the C_3 and C_4 pathways. In addition, some plants, like pineapples, can switch between the two metabolic pathways; these plants are referred to as CAM plants. C_3 plants primarily comprise shrubs, trees, and temperate grasses; C_4 plants are primarily tropical grasses, including maize. These metabolic pathways of plants leave isotopic signatures in human or animal bone in varying amounts of ^{13}C depending on the proportions of C_3 or C_4 plants in the diet. Diets rich in maize have a definite isotopic signature. Animals feeding on marine organisms have very different stable isotope ratios for carbon and nitrogen than their terrestrial counterparts. The stable isotope ^{15}N, present in bone gelatin, is greater at sites with a marine diet. The stable isotopic values of nitrogen and carbon can be studied to see how diet varies with sex, age, or social class within a population, or how it varies through time. Stable isotope values of ^{13}C and ^{15}N of skeletal samples from the Classic Maya of the Copán Valley indicate that males had higher maize signatures than females, and older females had less maize in their diet than younger females of the same high status grouping; the ^{15}N values indicated, as would be expected, that no marine animals were in the diet.

Neutron activation is a very useful laboratory technique for determining the frequencies of elements in artifact samples or bones, thus permitting samples to be classified as to source or composition. Numerous applications of neutron activation have been implemented in Mesoamerica. The initial application of the technique was to chemically identify and source obsidian, which has relatively uniform mineral composition and whose source cannot be determined by visual inspection or petrographic techniques alone. However, obsidian samples from different sources have characteristic combinations of trace elements, and it is possible to obtain the chemical signatures characteristic of each source. Most of the major and minor obsidian sources have been characterized by neutron activation, and it is now possible to source obsidian using this technique. Neutron activation has also been used to determine the trace element constituents in

ceramics to pinpoint the geographic locations or sources of certain clays, allowing ceramics to be identified as to their place of origin. This would permit study of the patterns of distribution of various wares.

Neutron activation can also be used in skeletal analysis, to identify the elemental composition of bone within and between populations. Differences in trace elements in human bone reflect different diets; for example, vegetarian diets result in increased levels of strontium, while diets high in meat leave high quantities of zinc and copper. Often, these patterns of trace element frequency vary within a population, and the differences may be attributable to age, gender, or status. This technique has several problems related to the contaminating or distorting effects of elements from the environment, which change the composition of the bone during the long time it is buried. Fortunately, these problems do not occur with ceramic or lithic samples.

Petrographic analysis can be used to identify the minerals in a sample. These minerals can in fact be artifacts, either as individual artifacts or as diverse mineral materials that make up artifacts, like ceramics. Petrographic analysis can examine thin sections under a microscope with various filters, such as a polarizing filter, or filters that measure the various angles of reflected light. The most common examples of thin sections are ceramic and soil sediments. Samples are prepared by impregnating the ceramic or soil with epoxy and then grinding the sample to a uniform thickness of 0.03 mm. The combination of angles of reflected light and color of the rays characterize the mineral. Not only can this be used to identify the minerals in ceramics, but it can also be used to identify minute residues of debitage, such as fuchsite, jadeite, and serpentine, from craft production, and the abrasives used to produce them, which are incorporated in the soil from workshop areas. This technique has been used identify lime production at the Maya site of Santa Cruz in Belize.

Petrographic analysis can also be used to study artifacts or site sediments by characterizing the grains of the individual physical constituents of an artifact or a soil sample, a technique called "granularmetrics." This is a classification of the size, shape, degree of sorting, and percentage of inclusions in the sample. The degree of roundness (angularity) and sphericity (how closely the grains approximate a spherical shape) are shape attributes, useful in determining the degree of erosion of the materials, or in ascertaining if anthropogenically crushed materials are found in otherwise highly eroded sediments, suggesting the presence of possible lapidary or other craft activity in an area. Often, it is useful to separate the fine, light grains, such as silt and clay, from heavier minerals, such as iron, chromium, and jadeite, which are associated with lapidary production or ceramic inclusions. This is accomplished by placing the pulverized sample into a liquid with a high specific gravity to float off lighter minerals such as silt and clay.

X-ray diffraction can also be used to identify the minerals in a sample. X-rays are trained into a specimen and are defracted along planes associated with the lattice planes in the mineral crystals. Each mineral has its own distinctive diffraction pattern. This technique, however, is difficult to implement because too many different minerals, and in varying quantities, will often result in a mixing or blending of intensities characteristic of specific minerals.

Macrofloral analysis is also a valuable laboratory technique for identifying plant remains that have been collected using the flotation technique of water-sorting soil samples. They are then slowly dried (to avoid cracking), and the taxa are identified under a low-power stereoscopic microscope. Usually seeds are the most diagnostic and common floral remains; however, wood charcoal from fuel remains and burned buildings is extremely common as well. It is possible with this identification to determine the plants utilized for food and the wood used for buildings, food, containers, and fuel. Plant remains too small for identification under an optical microscope are viewed with an electron microscope.

Palynology, the study of plant pollen, is used to determine which plants grew in an environment and also which plants were used in the diet. Pollen can be identified to individual taxa under a high-power microscope by the distinct shape of the grains. In the Copán Valley, pollen cores were taken to obtain a sequence of vegetation for the occupational history of the valley; the sequence showed that there was a decrease in forest pollen correlated with an increase in weed and Compositae pollen associated with cleared areas for agriculture. This trend peaked at around A.D. 800, then reversed, so that by 1200 only tree pollen remained. This pollen sample dramatically documented the increase in area of agricultural fields in the Copán Valley, and then cultivation's decline and the eventual reforestation. More important, it demonstrated that the reforestation started much later than had been thought and that the valley was still populated after 1000.

At the Maya site of Cerros, both macrobotanical and pollen data were used to reconstruct the diet for the Formative occupation. This study indicated the existence of pollen from several economic plants that were not recovered in flotation samples. Pollen data indicated that the settlement area had been cleared by 50 B.C., 300 years after the initial occupation of the site, resulting in new animal habitats and thus increasing the diversity of animals in the diet.

Unfortunately, pollen is not always preserved, particularly if the ambient environment is high in oxygen. However, other microfloral elements can be identified. Phytoliths are silica skeletal elements of plants. Like pollen, they have specific shapes that allow them to be identified to taxa, but unlike pollen, they are virtually indestructible. This can create a problem because they can be ubiquitous in soil sediments, having been eroded from geological deposits. One particular species, maize, has a very distinctive, easily recognized shape and is not subject to such problems of contamination because it is recently evolved. This means that there is great potential for identifying agricultural fields that grew maize.

Fungal spores, also identified through laboratory analysis, indicate the existence of moisture and decomposing plant remains on which fungi subsist. Concentrations of spores can indicate the existence of middens or moist enclosed rooms. This is particularly valuable in the arid highlands of Mexico, where moisture is typically lacking in open areas.

Archaeofaunal analysis is a necessary complement to the various floral laboratory analytic techniques because animals constitute a portion of most diets in Mesoamerica and are extremely important, like pollens, for reconstructing paleoenvironments. Faunal remains are most typically animal bones and mollusc shells, but they can include eggshells from birds and reptiles, and carbonized insects. Traditionally, these remains are collected as encountered in excavations, but they are also found in the heavy fraction of soil samples, which are then fine-screened to remove tiny bones and shell.

The faunal skeletal remains are sorted according to scientific taxa and to the various anatomical elements, and the side of the animal, if appropriate. The elements are also examined to see if they are burned. This is important because many small faunal remains are of small rodents, reptiles, amphibians, and insects that can be intrusive in the sediments of the site and therefore not food remains. However, if these remains are burned, it may indicate that they are food remains. Even if these animals are intrusive and not food items, they provide important environmental information based on their habitats.

The patterns of skeletal parts provide important information with respect to butchering patterns, because standardized butchering patterns can indicate a specialized meat-processing and distributing economic activity, which may be correlated with complex societies. The contribution of the animals to the diet can be determined by two techniques. One of these is referred to as "MNI" (Minimum Number of Individuals). Here, the largest number of the same skeletal element of a species—e.g., seven left humeri of deer—indicate the minimum number of these animals in an assemblage. The other technique is skeletal allometry, which calculates the weight of bone or shell of each species to determine the relationship of the bone of that species to the amount of meat it represents.

Coprolites are feces preserved in the archaeological record, and they represent the remains of complete meals; thus, the relative contributions of various food types can be directly quantified. Coprolite analysis identifies some plant species or edible parts of plants that do not produce pollen, as well as the portions consumed (e.g., roots, tubers, or fleshy stalks). Often these plant portions are not completely digested, and so it is possible to identify the species of the plant remains in the coprolites. Unfortunately, coprolites are most commonly associated with dry campsites that are only temporarily occupied by mobile foragers; human waste is generally removed from settlements. Important coprolite analysis was conducted on samples from Archaic period sites in the Tehuacán Valley. In these studies, various seeds, nuts, and fruit fragments were found, as well as fibers from agave, cactus, pochote, and manioc. The last finding is extremely important because manioc cannot grow in the Tehuacán Valley, which means that it was imported into the area. Remains of black sapote were also found, another plant not native to the area. It was also possible to determine what season the sites in the valley were occupied by identifying the fruit remains found in the coprolites. Small faunal remains—particularly fish and small rodent bones, and incidental hairs of larger animals—are also found in coprolites, as are parasites and their eggs. These last remains provide important information on the health of the ancient group.

Statistical analysis is an extremely important analytic technique for organizing the various archaeological data produced by the various laboratory techniques. These data can be analyzed using statistical techniques to infer behavior. Statistical techniques can also be used to determine if there are significant differences in the quantities of artifacts of different types across the area of a site.

FURTHER READINGS

Barba, L., and A. Ortiz. 1992. Analisis químico de pisos de ocupación: Un caso etnografico en Tlaxcala, México. *Latin American Antiquity* 3: 63–82.

Callem, E. O. 1967. Analysis of the Tehuacan Coprolites. In D. S. Byers (ed.), *The Prehistory of the Tehuacán Valley,* vol. 1, *Environment and Subsistence,* pp. 261–289. Austin: University of Texas Press.

Crane, C. J., and H. S. Carr. 1994. The Integration and Quantification of Economic Data from a Late Preclassic Maya Community in Belize. In K. D. Sobolk (ed.), *Paleonutrition: The Diet and Health of Prehistoric Americans,* pp. 66–79. Carbondale, Ill.: Center for Archaeological Investigations, Southern Illinois University, Occasional Paper 22.

Lenz, D. L. 1991. Maya Diets of the Rich and Poor: Paleoethnobotanical Evidence from Copán. *Latin American Antiquity* 2: 269–287.

Manzanilla, L., and L. Barba. 1990. The Study of Activities in Classic Households: Two Case Studies from Coba and Teotihuacán. *Ancient Mesoamerica* 1: 41–49.

Neff, H., F. J. Bove, E. J. Roboinson, and B. Arroyo L. 1994. A Ceramic Compositional Perspective on the Formative to Classic Transition in Southern Mesoamerica. *Latin American Antiquity* 5: 333–358.

Ortiz, A. B. and L. Barba. 1993. La química en el estudio de áreas de actividad. In L. Manzanilla (ed.), *Anatomía de un conjunto residencial Teotihuacano en Oztoyahualco,* vol. 2, *Los Estudios Específicos,* pp. 617–660. Mexico City: Universidad Nacional Autónoma de Mexico.

Price, T. D. (ed.). 1989. *The Chemistry of Prehistoric Human Bone.* New York: Cambridge University Press.

Reed, D. M. 1994. Ancient Maya Diet at Copán, Honduras as Determined through the Analysis of Stable Carbon and Nitrogen Isotopes. In K. D. Sobolk (ed.), *Paleonutrition: The Diet and Health of Prehistoric Americans,* pp. 210–221. Center for Archaeological Investigations, Southern Illinois University, Occasional Paper 22.

Remington, S. J., and T. H. Loy. 1994. Identifying Species of Origin from Prehistoric Blood Residues. *Science* 266: 289–296.

Rice, P. M. 1987. *Pottery Analysis: A Sourcebook.* Chicago: University of Chicago Press.

Rovner, I. 1983. Plant Opal Phytolith Analysis: Major Advances in Archaeobotanical Research. In M. B. Schiffer (ed.), *Advances in Archaeological Method and Theory*, vol. 6, pp. 225–266. New York: Academic Press.

Rue, D. 1987. Early Agriculture and Early Postclassic Maya Occupation in Western Honduras. *Nature* 326: 285–286.

Tieszen, L. L. 1991. Natural Variations in the Carbon Isotope Values of Plants: Implications for Archaeology, Ecology, and Paleoecology. *Journal of Archaeological Science* 18: 227–248.

Randolph Widmer

SEE ALSO
Archaeology: Research Design and Field Methods

Archaeology: Research Design and Field Methods

Archaeology is the study of human societies based on their surviving physical remains. Archaeological field methods are used to locate and investigate sites (loci of past human activities). The artifacts (human-made or modified objects) and other preserved remains from the sites are collected and analyzed to assess the cultural patterns, or lifeways, of the society that created and used them.

Archaeological investigations begin with a research design—a formal plan to collect or record physical evidence to answer specific questions or to provide new information on a particular society. It states the problem to be investigated, the data to be collected that bear on that problem, the specialists whose expertise is needed to assess those data, and a budget and time frame for completing the project. The extent of field work envisioned in the research design may be as large as an entire geographic region, to understand the patterned occupation of communities within a large bounded area (settlement studies), or as small as a single site or even a portion of a large and complex site, such as an urban center.

The sites and their artifacts are the patrimony of the modern countries within which they are found, so permission from national caretaker institutions (listed in Table 1), as well as from local authorities and landowners, is obtained in order to undertake fieldwork. Although these countries fund some of the archaeological work carried out within their borders, foreign archaeologists working in Mexico and Central America generally obtain funding for all or portions of their field work from their own governments or private institutions and foundations. At the completion of the project, a written report is submitted to the caretaker institutions and funding agencies, and the findings are published to disseminate that information.

The discovery of sites is referred to as "archaeological reconnaissance," and the assessment of their physical and spatial characteristics is "archaeological survey." Various systematic reconnaissance techniques (see Table 2) are used; the chosen method depends on the size of the area to be covered, the expected visibility of sites—determined in part by the modern vegetation and geography—and their characteristics (for example, whether they exhibit aboveground architecture such as mounds).

Ground reconnaissance (surface inspection) techniques are the most commonly employed. Where the area to be examined is large, time and budget constraints may permit only a portion of a region to be sampled, and

TABLE 1.

Country	Caretaker Institutions
Belize	Belize Department of Archaeology
Costa Rica	Museo Nacional de Costa Rica, San José
El Salvador	Museo Nacional, San Salvador
Guatemala	Instituto de Antropología e Historia, Guatemala City
Honduras	Instituto Hondureño de Antropología e Historia, Tegucigalpa
Mexico	Instituto de Antropología e Historia, Mexico City
Nicaragua	Museo Nacional de Nicaragua, Managua
Panama	Museo del Hombre, Panama City

TABLE 2. SITE IDENTIFICATION AND ASSESSMENT TECHNIQUES.

Technique	Description	Used to Detect
GROUND RECONNAISSANCE		
Surface Inspection	walking, riding over terrain to be examined; observing soil exposures in road and river cuts	visible artifacts, structures, human land modification
AERIAL TECHNIQUES		
aerial photography	vertical and oblique photographic views taken from aircraft	crop marks (patterned discontinuities in vegetation growth), soil marks, frost marks (differential melting of snow), shadows—all indications of low or shallow subsurface features
SLAR	side-looking airborne radar imagery	large-scale landscape patterns hidden under clouds or vegetation
satellite imagery	LANDSAT satellite transmissions	patterns of differential intensity of reflected light or infrared radiation
NONINVASIVE SUBSURFACE TECHNIQUES (INSTRUMENT-BASED TECHNIQUES)		
magnetometry	measures magnetic contrasts in soil	burned soils, rocks, bricks, humic fill in pits
soil resistivity	measures differential electrical resistivity or conductivity of soil	stone walls, foundations, compacted soil, filled pits and ditches
ground-penetrating radar	measures discontinuities in soil via "echoes" of electromagnetic pulses	house floors, compacted layers, stone walls, foundations, voids, rocks, metal
INVASIVE SUBSURFACE PROBES		
coring	removal of continuous section of sediments using hollow cylinder	features, artifacts, soil horizons
augering	drilling hole into soil to examine removed earth and hole	features, artifacts, soil horizons
shovel tests, divots	shovelful of dirt turned over and contents examined	shallow buried features, artifacts

inferences must be made as to how representative the sample is of the entire region. Probabilistic sampling using statistical techniques ensures a more representative sample.

Aerial reconnaissance is a method of remote sensing (the discovery of information at a distance from the phenomenon being investigated). Patterns in the landscape that result from human occupation and that are generally not readily apparent on the ground may be discerned from aerial photographs or satellite images. Suspected indications of human occupation discovered with the various aerial techniques must be verified by ground survey. Aerial reconnaissance is well suited for quickly locating relatively visible sites within a large region.

An adjunct reconnaissance method is to probe beneath the surface to look for buried sites. The surface to be examined is systematically covered at measured intervals, using invasive or noninvasive exploratory techniques (Table 2) in order to detect spatially patterned variations

A

in subsurface soil constituency. Noninvasive techniques require sophisticated instruments to measure the patterned discontinuities below the surface, and these findings must be verified or interpreted by excavation. Slightly invasive probing techniques using a coring tool or shovel allow for rapid examination of subsurface soil characteristics. Because of the time and expense involved, subsurface techniques are often limited to a sample of a larger area and are more frequently used to assess the characteristics of previously discovered sites—for example, to locate buried monuments or structures—rather than to find sites themselves.

Once a site is discovered, the coordinates of its geophysical location are plotted on base maps available from government and other agencies, or on aerial photographs. Hand-held Global Positional System receivers are now often used to pinpoint location via triangulation data transmitted by satellites. Site location information is increasingly being stored using Geographic Information Systems technology, a computer-assisted mapping system in which digitized locational data are entered into a computerized database that allows the storage, manipulation, and retrieval of spatial information. The resulting regional site maps allow the interpretation of settlement patterns with regard to intersite relationships, the interaction of people with their environment, and change in settlements over time.

The archaeological survey gathers information concerning a site's surface characteristics and suspected subsurface features prior to excavation. A site map is made to indicate its boundaries, associated geographic features, relief (topography), and internal characteristics, such as structures, roads, canals, and clusters of surface artifacts. Optical mapping instruments (theodolite, transit, alidade, Brunton compass) are commonly utilized to construct the map, although they are being replaced by more efficient electronic distance-measuring equipment. Photogrammetric maps of sites or regions can be made directly from aerial photographs taken in stereo pairs.

The site map is a first step in interpreting the patterned use of space by a past society. Because spatial patterning of artifacts and other remains is critical to archaeological interpretation, several techniques have been developed to efficiently record provenience (the positioning of archaeological remains in three dimensions). Using the site map as a base, the site is divided into standardized segments to facilitate the recording of horizontal provenience during survey and excavation. Most sites are divided into numbered squares following a grid pattern oriented to magnetic (or true) north. Larger sites, such as urban centers, require more complex subdivision schemes.

Although it is not part of every research design, excavation is necessary to observe and record the spatial organization of subsurface archaeological remains in three dimensions within a matrix (surrounding medium, usually soil). In addition to artifacts, these remains consist of features (non-portable human-modified phenomena that cannot be removed without disturbing their physical structure), such as burials, hearths, caches, trash dumps (middens), and pits; structures (architectural forms) such as houses, platform mounds, and raised roadways; and ecofacts (non-human-made materials) such as seeds, bones, and charcoal, which provide information on diet and environment.

The vertical and horizontal positioning of the archaeological remains relative to one another is referred to as their "association." By assessing the provenience, matrix, and association of the remains, the archaeologist makes an interpretation of their context—a hypothesized reconstruction of the behavioral processes and events that may account for their perceived patterning and characteristics. Interpretation of the context also incorporates evidence of later disturbances of the originally deposited remains by both human and natural actions. For example, mound-building often involved the collection of dirt and rubble from previously occupied areas, so that earlier artifacts were removed from their original location and deposited in a later structure.

Excavation methods and techniques vary depending on the research design and the nature of the site. Only a portion of the site area is excavated, to prevent total destruction of its remains. Surface indications usually guide the placement of excavation units, and in addition, probabilistic (statistically determined) sampling techniques help to ensure that a representative portion of the site is excavated in areas lacking surface clues.

Vertical or penetrating excavations rapidly and efficiently gauge the nature and depth of buried archaeological materials. Most often these excavations take the form of square or rectangular test pits of minimal horizontal extent (generally from 1×1 to 2×2 meters). The regular size of these units, oriented to the site's gridded subdivisions, facilitates the recording of horizontal provenience information, precisely locating the positions of artifacts and features. Vertical provenience is determined by the elevation of the remains relative to a fixed point, usually on the surface; hence, measurements taken to record locations are often referred to as depth "below surface."

Penetrating excavations also reveal the matrix as composed of sequential layered deposits (strata) that result from both human and natural processes. These include, for example, superimposed house floors, created as buildings were built and demolished on the same site over a period of time. Stratigraphy, the evaluation of these sequential deposits, is essential for interpreting contexts and for dating the various site components (discrete occupations of the site by a group of people), so provenience information must include these strata. Where strata are clearly distinguishable, archaeologists may excavate units layer by layer down to the pre-occupation level, which can be bedrock, subsoil, or soil that is sterile (devoid of cultural materials), providing a quick assessment of changes at the site over time. Until these layers are discerned, or in the absence of discrete layers, excavation is carried out in layers of a standard measured depth ("arbitrary" or "metric" strata), keeping separate the remains found in each layer.

To expand the excavation rapidly to provide more horizontal information, the test pit can be enlarged in a single direction, creating a test trench. Trenches are used especially to cross-section mounds or other large architectural forms. Excavations within very large mounds and some deeply buried sites may require the use of a tunnel. When features or structures are located, the initial exploratory pits or trenches may be further extended to reveal a wider area. These horizontal or clearing excavations maximize the horizontal dimensions of the excavation unit while minimizing its depth, in order better to assess the extent and associations of remains at a single point in time in the past.

While excavations are progressing, an ongoing task is to record all the observations made concerning the spatial relationships of the remains within their matrix, since those relationships will be destroyed by the excavation process itself. Field journals provide a daily narrative or chronological commentary on the excavation. Standardized forms ensure the comparable recording of all characteristics of provenience units and features. They also allow for easy transferral of the information into a computerized database, and portable computers are frequently taken into the field for immediate data entry.

Much of the spatial information is recorded by visual means. Scaled drawings indicating provenience and association are of two types. Plan views are horizontal ("bird's-eye view") renderings of the floor of an excavation unit at a particular depth below surface. Profile or section views depict the sidewalls of the unit or mound, providing information on stratification. In addition to these schematic representations, photographs and slides (both black-and-white and color) are indispensable for recording the progress of the excavations, the plan and profile views of the units, and the individual artifacts and features recovered. A photo board placed within the area to be photographed provides the provenience information for each picture, and a log is kept to record photographs sequentially. Video cameras are also used to provide panoramic views and to record the progress of more complex excavations.

Observations concerning the matrix and its component strata include the texture, physical composition (clay, silt, sand, rock), color, and inclusion of artifacts. Soil color is determined with a standard designating system, the Munsell Soil Color Charts. Features require special treatment and excavation depending on their type: pits and middens are often cross-sectioned to reveal their depth and shape; burials, whether simple graves or tomb interments, are complex features requiring special handling for recording the information on the grave pit, associated objects, and positioning of the body, as well as for the ultimate disposition of the human remains recovered.

Artifacts are collected and recorded by different methods, depending in large part on their context. Where the context is considered to be "primary" (relatively undisturbed since the artifacts were first deposited by their users), the spatial patterning of those remains may be significant enough to require recording the precise location of each artifact where it lies. If the context is considered to be "secondary," or disturbed, it is often sufficient to collect and separate artifacts by provenience lot, usually a single stratum or measured depth within a specific excavation unit. This is efficiently done by removing the soil from a designated layer of an excavation unit and dumping it onto a prepared screen or a layered series of screens of graduated mesh sizes. Shaking the screen or running a trowel across it causes the soil to fall through the screen, thereby separating out the larger artifacts. Screening is also done on the soil removed from primary contexts to recover any additional artifacts. Water sprayed onto the soil (water screening) speeds up the process and is helpful where the artifacts or ecofacts (such as shell and bone) are fragile and may otherwise be damaged.

Because screening and simple hand-recovery techniques are insufficient to collect the smallest artifacts and ecofacts, flotation is used to retrieve very small specimens. Soil is placed in a large container of water with one or a graduated series of very fine screens at the bottom. Light materials, such as seeds or small pieces of bone, float to

A

the surface, while heavier materials are trapped in the fine screens. Chemicals are often added to the water to increase the specific gravity, allowing heavier materials to float. Because flotation is time-consuming, usually only a sample of soil is processed in this manner.

Other ecofacts, such as microscopic pollen and plant phytoliths, are retrieved from specially selected soil samples. Chemical analysis is also performed on soil samples—for example, to detect the presence of phosphates that may indicate a burial in a suspected grave lacking preserved bone. Samples of materials that can be used for dating purposes, such as charcoal and other organic remains, are also collected using special techniques. All remains extracted from the excavation units and surface are carefully bagged and labeled to record their provenience. They are transferred to a laboratory for cleaning, processing, and analysis.

Especially where stone architecture is involved, archaeological projects are usually responsible for consolidating, or even reconstructing, affected structures to restore the integrity and appearance of the original building.

FURTHER READINGS

Breiner, S., and M. D. Coe. 1972. Magnetic Exploration of the Olmec Civilization. *American Scientist* 60: 566–575.

Carr, C. 1982. *Handbook on Soil Resistivity Surveying.* Research Series, 2. Evanston, Ill.: Center for American Archaeology.

Clark, A. 1990. *Seeing Beneath the Soil: Prospecting Methods in Archaeology.* London: Batsford.

Ebert, J. I. 1984. Remote Sensing Applications in Archaeology. In M. B. Schiffer (ed.), *Advances in Archaeological Method and Theory,* vol. 7, pp. 293–362. New York: Academic Press.

Harris, E. C. 1989. *Principles of Archaeological Stratigraphy.* 2nd ed. New York: Academic Press.

Joukowsky, M. 1980. *A Complete Manual of Field Archaeology: Tools and Techniques of Field Work for Archaeologists.* Englewood Cliffs, N.J.: Prentice-Hall.

Kvamme, K. L. 1989. Geographic Information Systems in Regional Archaeological Research and Data Management. In M. B. Schiffer (ed.), *Archaeological Method and Theory,* vol. 1, pp. 139–203. Tucson: University of Arizona Press.

McManamon, F. P. 1984. Discovering Sites Unseen. In M. B. Schiffer (ed.), *Advances in Archaeological Method and Theory,* vol. 7, pp. 223–292. New York: Academic Press.

Millon, R. 1973. *The Teotihuacán Map: Urbanization of Teotihuacán, Mexico.* Vol. 1. Austin: University of Texas Press.

Munsell Soil Color Charts. 1975. Baltimore: Munsell Color.

Scarborough, V. L., R. P. Connolly, and S. P. Ross. 1994. The Pre-Hispanic Maya Reservoir System at Kinal, Peten, Guatemala. *Ancient Mesoamerica* 5: 97–106.

Scollar, I., A. Tabbagh, A. Hesse, and I. Herzog. 1990. *Archaeological Prospecting and Remote Sensing.* Cambridge: Cambridge University Press.

Sharer, R. J., and W. Ashmore. 1993. *Archaeology: Discovering Our Past.* 2nd ed. Mountain View, Calif.: Mayfield.

Sheets, P. D. 1992. *The Ceren Site.* New York: Harcourt Brace Jovanovich.

Stein, J. K. 1986. Coring Archaeological Sites. *American Antiquity* 51: 505–527.

Weymouth, J. W. 1986. Geophysical Methods of Archaeological Site Surveying. In M. B. Schiffer (ed.), *Advances in Archaeological Method and Theory,* vol. 9, pp. 311–395. New York: Academic Press.

Susan D. Gillespie

SEE ALSO
Archaeology: Analytical Methods; Dating Methods

Archaic Period (c. 8000–2000 B.C.)

This cultural stage followed the cessation of Paleoindian hunting of now-extinct Pleistocene animals and preceded the Formative period, when agriculture, village life, and pottery began around 2000 B.C. in Mesoamerica and Central America. The Archaic consists of three substages: (1) Early Archaic or First Forager, marked by new foraging adaptations and a more seasonally scheduled subsistence system, and characterized by grinding stones, the beginning of a complex weaving industry, and extensive use of various storage facilities; (2) Middle Archaic or Incipient Agriculture, when foraging activities were supplemented by the beginnings of agriculture with stone bowls, more complex storage facilities, and various notched projectile points used to tip *atlatl* (spear-thrower) darts; and (3) Late Archaic, a "semisedentary" substage marked by expanded agriculture, use of more species of domesticated plants, and a more sedentary way of life, with pit houses and a mano-metate complex.

The Archaic was a period of adaptation to changing ecological conditions that extended far beyond Mesoamerica. Because it involved different adaptations to a series of slightly different ecozones, increasing numbers of traditions developed. With the megafauna gone, people had to turn to other food sources. During the Archaic they became increasingly efficient hunters of small game and turned more and more to the collection of plants. The limited Archaic remains in Mesoamerica point to at least three highland traditions and three to five lowland ones, in addition to three in the northern peripheries and at least one completely unrelated tradition (the Talamancan phase), which has been found in western Panama.

Early Archaic, c. 8000–5000 B.C.

This poorly defined substage is represented by four or five traditions (from north to south): the Cochise tradition of the southwestern United States and far northwestern Mexico, the Infiernillo and Big Bend traditions on the northern periphery of Mesoamerica, the Santa Marta and El Riego traditions, and the Southern Maritime tradition.

The El Riego tradition, c. 7600–5000 B.C., is found from Tecolote Cave (Hidalgo) to El Riego in the Tehuacán Valley (Puebla). It also includes Layer 24 (a summer occupation) and Layer 25 (a winter occupation) of the Playa I phase of Tlapacoya (Basin of Mexico), excavated by Niederberger, and it may include some of the lower layers from Texcal (1) Cave (Puebla). This tradition has a seasonally scheduled subsistence system and microband to macroband settlement pattern; artifacts include Hidalgo, El Riego, Flacco, and Trinidad points, large scraper planes, bifacial choppers, nets, baskets, crude blades, and mullers and milling stones.

The closely related Santa Marta tradition, c. 8000–4000 B.C., extends from Santa Marta Cave and the nearby Los Grifos site in the Ocozocoautla Valley in highland Chiapas to the Jicaras and Naquitz phases of Oaxaca. The settlement pattern and subsistence systems of Santa Marta probably were similar to El Riego, with different plants (seeds of *Cucurbita pepo,* some pollen of *Zea mays*) either collected wild or in the first stages of domestication in Oaxaca. Projectile points include Pedernales-like types, which are rare or absent in most El Riego components, and Trinidad, San Nicolas, Nogales, and La Mina points.

The undated Southern Maritime tradition of Belize is composed of the Sand Hill and Orange Walk phases. Diagnostic traits are large macroblades and Lowe points. Some tools from the Quiché Valley (Guatemala) and some points from Turrialba (Costa Rica) are similar, as are the Agua Verde materials of Cuba and the Couri complex of Haiti. In sharp contrast to the highland traditions, this lowland Archaic adaptation has no apparent evidence of attempts at plant domestication or cultivation.

The ill-defined Infiernillo tradition of northeastern Mexico, c. 7000–6000 B.C., is found in the lowest level of Romero's Cave, the three lowest levels of Valenzuela's Cave, and the lowest level of Ojo de Agua Cave in southwestern Tamaulipas. Like the Southern Maritime, it appears unconnected with the central highland tradition. Tamaulipas sites had abundant artifacts—diamond-shaped and contracting-stemmed points and scraper planes—in good contexts, abundant preserved vegetal artifacts (nets, mats, baskets), and plant remains that included pumpkins (*Cucurbita pepo),* gourds (*Lagenaria siceraria),* and possibly chile peppers. Similar lithic remains occur in units 5 and 6 (the lowest occupations) of La Calsada Cave (Nuevo León), dated c. 8640–5040 B.C.; on the surface of the San Isidro and Punta Negra sites in Nuevo León; and in Frightful, Fat Burro, and CM65 caves in Coahuila, dated c. 6025–5290 B.C. This tradition has general connections to the Clear Fork and Guadalupe complexes of central Texas and the Cochise tradition of the Southwest, characterized by its Bajada and Jay points, scraper planes, and grinding stones, but no hint of plant domestication.

Middle Archaic

The Middle Archaic is characterized by an increase in the number of sites or components, and at least seven traditions developed: Cochise, Big Bend, Chihuahua, Repelo, Tehuacán, Belize, and Cerro Mangote. In the incipient agriculture stage of the Middle Archaic, this generalized Cochise tradition, represented by the Sulphur and Gardner Spring phase, develops into two new traditions, while the Cochise tradition, represented by the earliest Chiricahua phase, continues in northwestern Mexico, characterized by new point types, scraper planes, and grinding stones.

Out of it developed, in Chihuahua and southern New Mexico, the Chihuahua tradition, with Gypsum-Almagre, Todsen, and Keystone points, one-handed manos, and metates. People began to live in pit houses. To the east, the Big Bend tradition developed, represented in Coahuila by the Middle and Late Coahuila complex, dated c. 5300–1200 B.C. The Pecos River focus of Texas is a further extension of the Big Bend tradition. This complex is characterized by Langtry stemmed, Shumla, Pedernales, Almagre, and Gary points, large scraper planes, Clear Ford-type gouges, distinctive coiled basketry, a few grinding stones, and a collecting system. Connections with the Archaic of Central Mexico are almost nonexistent, and ties with the Repelo tradition of northeastern Mexico are surprisingly weak, considering the geographic proximity of the two traditions.

The remains of the Repelo tradition, c. 5500–2400 B.C., are found in Unit 1 of La Calsada rockshelter in Nuevo León, in the Nogales and Repelo phase components from northern Tamaulipas, and in the La Perra phase sites of the Sierra de Tamaulipas. A site on Laguna Chila, just west of Tampico in the state of Veracruz, is the southernmost extension. None of the northern traditions shows the rapid increase in domesticates found at Tehuacán or the tendency toward sedentarism that appears in coastal Chiapas, Palma Sola of Veracruz, and the Cerro Mangote tradition to the south in Panama.

Most data come from the central highlands of Mexico, particularly Tehuacán, and suggest that wet-season macroband occupations were as numerous as microband occupations. The northern limits are marked by zones C and D of Cueva Blanca in Oaxaca, Texcal II near Puebla, the Tecolote phase levels of Tecolote Cave in Hidalgo, and Playa II in the Valley of Mexico. A rich variety of plant remains has been found in Tehuacán—avocado, squash (*Cucurbita mixta* and *C. moschata*), gourds, common beans, black and white zapotes, chupandilla plums, chile peppers, amaranth, and a couple of varieties of maize.

The Archaic traditions to the south appear separate; they may include one near Santa Marta Cave in Chiapas, preceramic sites of the Quiché Basin of Guatemala, the Marcala complex from La Esperanza, Honduras, and Palma Sola on the central coast of Veracruz. In the lowlands to the south, the Belize phase is somewhat better defined, and some of the Turrialba remains from Costa Rica may be part of it.

On the Pacific coast in Panama, other kinds of Archaic materials comprise the Cerro Mangote tradition, dated 4810 B.C. A rich midden reveals exploitation of sea resources and hunting of land mammals, with no signs of incipient agriculture.

Late Archaic

In the Late or semisedentary Archaic phase we began to discern the dichotomy between the highlands and the lowlands that so strongly characterizes the Formative and later stages of Middle American prehistory. The first indications appear of a true Mesoamerican culture area. Each of the major culture areas—the Greater Southwest extension, Mesoamerica, and Central America (the area from south of Honduras through Panama)—has its distinctive characteristics. Outside the scope of this discussion are the Southwest and the northern area of Mexico, as well as the Central American traditions.

The portion of the northernmost tradition that seems to fall within the Mesoamerican highland framework is the San Nicolás tradition, with materials from San Nicolás Cave near San Juan del Río in Querétaro, excavated by Cynthia Irwin-Williams. Closely related are the Abejas tradition to the south, which includes materials called Texcal II, from arbitrary levels III, IV, and perhaps V of Texcal Cave just west of the city of Puebla; materials from levels 14–17 at Zohapilco in Mexico City; the many Abejas components in the Tehuacán Valley; the Martinez complex of Oaxaca; and a component from Yuzanu near Yanhuitlán, Oaxaca. At present, Oaxaca appears to have been the southern limit of the tradition.

Putting together the limited materials, we can tentatively define the tradition. A major change in settlement patterns seems to occur. All four levels from Zohapilco seem to have been permanent settlements, and three from Tehuacán may have been pit house hamlets, while twelve were macroband camps, from which fifteen microbands spun off to perform various specialized tasks in the worst part of the dry season. The shift in settlement patterns may have been due in large part to an increased practice of incipient agriculture—specifically, growing a surplus of hybrid maize and other domesticates to last through the dry season.

Limited surface collections of stemmed points and ground-stone tools from the territory around Santa Marta Cave in the Ocozocoautla Valley of Chiapas suggest that another tradition might have existed during the Late Archaic; Catan and Matamoros points in the Quiché Valley of Guatemala may indicate that yet another tradition existed there. Stemmed and side-notched points, fine blades, and manos with metates from the Plowden Saw Mill site near Esperanza, Honduras, might indicate still another highland Mesoamerican tradition. Several distinctive highland traditions seem to contrast with those found in coastal or lowland environs. Because of their paucity, it is very difficult to determine whether these regional sites represent different traditions or are parts of one large, all-encompassing coastal tradition.

On the northern Pacific coast of Mexico is the Matanchén complex, known from a shell mound near Ceboruco, Nayarit. Near Acapulco, Guerrero, a series of levels at the bottom of a shell midden at Puerto Márquez yielded flakes, a mano fragment, and a burned clay house floor; this assemblage was dubbed the Ostiones phase.

Pacific coastal finds farther south were made around Laguna Chantuto, in Chiapas.

On the Gulf coast, we find the Palo Hueco phase of the Santa Luisa site near Zamora, Veracruz. Underlying the strata with ceramics is a distinct zone, dated c. 3250–2410 B.C., of what might be a large preceramic village. Other preceramic remains from the Gulf coast occur in northern Belize, where the Melinda phase seems to develop into the Progreso phase, characterized by straight-stemmed points and a riverine and maritime economy. Manos and metates suggest maize agriculture. Lithics include hoes, netsinkers, scraper planes, and fine, straight, keeled endscrapers and fine obsidian blades. There are hints that pyramids were being built.

The Late Archaic ought to be transitional, marking the addition of pottery, pyramid-building, figurines, and ceremonialism to the late preceramic base. Information at present is so limited, however, that there is little evidence of the Late Archaic being a transition toward anything. The Archaic is the base on which the Formative stage of Mesoamerican culture was built, when village agriculture became dominant.

FURTHER READINGS

MacNeish, R. S. 1986. The Preceramic of Mesoamerica. In *Advances in World Archaeology,* vol. 5, pp. 93–129. New York: Academic Press.

MacNeish, R. S., and A. Nelken. 1983. The Preceramic of Mesoamerica. *Journal of Field Archaeology* 10: 71–84.

Richard S. MacNeish

SEE ALSO
El Tajín: Chronology

Architecture: Civic-Ceremonial

If architecture is an attempt to create places for human activities that modify and separate us from the surrounding, "infinite" natural environment, then these "finite" and bounded spaces, and moreover those areas with great basal platforms and massive superstructures, create places where the contrasting buildings and plazas, "solid and void, or mass and plane, . . . dominate" the natural and modified landscapes, and this monumental aspect "is necessary before the full process of symbolization of detachment from nature is complete" (Andrews 1975:7). In this sense, monumental architecture is a massive, concrete expression through which nature and topography are molded into a culturally built landscape—a space that fulfills the inherent human need to organize, classify, and channel amorphous natural surroundings into more manageable pieces of reality through creating formal activity areas. Although monumental edifices originally may have had different sets of activities assigned to them in any human settlement, traditionally they are concentrated within the confines of accessible public spaces, which through time have been generally assigned specific ceremonial, ideological, and/or civic-governmental functions—hence our identification of such spaces as playing a civic and ceremonial role.

Mesoamerican monumental architecture varies geographically, chronologically, and ethnically, but certain uniformities can be identified through their formal antecedents and possible symbolic meanings, as well as their temporal and geographical origins. Formal aspects of monumental architecture, most scholars agree, comprise a conscious arrangement of structures situated in and around an open public space, in Mesoamerica called a "patio/plaza" context. Although the specific elements of civic-ceremonial or monumental architecture vary over time, they appear to form generic conceptual units that include the following basic elements: the plaza or open gathering space; the planned orientation of principal large structures along a particular directional axis, which also defines the boundaries of this public space; a program of monumental sculpture within the public area's confines; and special-purpose structures, such as ball courts, temples, and other buildings used for ritual or ceremonial purposes. Special-purpose structures may conform to a particular orientation and distribution at a site, and they may display special treatment in such features as façade and/or substructural platform, with unique building materials, sculptural stonework, molded stucco adornments, and plastered walls of carefully dressed stone. Horizontal or vertical dimorphism also sets them apart from the other architectural members of the aggregate.

The earliest examples of monumental architectural planning probably date to the Middle Formative period. Formative period architecture in Mesoamerica provided a pattern for urban planning, monumental and complexly organized civic-ceremonial precincts, and sculptural art such as portraits of individual leaders or supernatural patrons. With these elements in place at the onset of the Classic period, architecture began to express a transition from an agrarian society to a more urbanized one, with pronounced regional architectural styles that are variations on common monumental themes. Monumental structures

A

also display refined astronomical orientation, patterned distribution of structures over the civic-ceremonial precinct, reduced access to certain areas reserved for domestic and ritual activities, and more individualized or elite group patronage of artistic expression.

Middle Formative Basin of Mexico lakeshore sites—Cuicuilco, Tenayuca, Tlapacoyan, and others—display distinct formal architectural elements. Cuicuilco's pyramid is large, of packed earth and stone, a superimposed series of truncated conical platforms. Excavations around the base of this enormous platform mound have revealed several burials, indicating ritual functions. Contemporaneous monumental architectural elements similar to Cuicuilco have also been discovered in the northern Huasteca zone of the Gulf Coast region, at the Tancanhuitz site (San Luis Potosí), and in Huichapan (Hidalgo).

Tlapacoyan, however, had a monumental substructural foundation topped by a series of discrete, small platforms, some with unadorned stairs and others lined with protective *alfardas* (balustrades), leading to different levels atop this structure. Margain suggested that not only does this monumental architecture illustrate a high degree of building experimentation for such an early cultural horizon, but it and several other similar structures perhaps "prefigure the architecture at Teotihuacan, largely because of the full use of available materials" (1971: 51).

Among numerous Middle and Late Formative sites in Oaxaca, Monte Albán displays social complexity through monumental architecture during the "early urban" periods I and II. Basal platforms in the Great Plaza public areas of the site, such as structures L-sub, IV-sub, and J, as well as the Danzantes building, show monolithic block construction; the latter two also contain naturalistic and/or anthropomorphic sculptural elements, either adorning the building blocks or associated with the monumental architecture itself. The lower wall sections of many superstructures in this area also display a construction technique whereby single rows of square, dressed stones are alternated among smaller blocks penetrating from the building's fill zones into its foundations, possibly to stabilize the building against the effects of earthquakes. This technique is later modified, with double rows of smaller stones for each row of square dressed stone exterior wall foundations.

The Olmec of the Gulf lowlands have been traditionally interpreted as Mesoamerica's "mother culture," the originators of widely influential architectural and sculptural features and of settlement complexity dating to the Early and Middle Formative periods. Whether laid out atop natural plateaus (San Lorenzo Tenochtitlán), placed on elevated alluvial fans close to permanent rivers (Tres Zapotes), or on platforms made of earthen fill, surrounded by perennially wet swamplands (La Venta), all large Olmec centers share what appear to be the following precise, generic models of architectural planning: monumental molded-earth pyramids that dominate long, parallel mounds forming a large, central public plaza aligned along a directional axis of eight degrees west of true north, which are often associated with carved basalt colossal heads, monumental altars, or other sculptures quarried from resource areas in the Tuxtla Mountains.

The colossal heads provenienced from San Lorenzo, Tres Zapotes, Corbata, and La Venta sites appear to be the earliest form of portraiture for prominent leaders or their elite lineages recorded in Mesoamerica. Some of these monumental architectural elements, in conjunction with modeled ceramic figurines, carved jadeite artifacts, and other manifestations of material culture, have also been documented at distant sites, such as Tlatilco (Basin of Mexico), Chalcatzingo (Morelos), and Teopantecuanitlán (Guerrero).

Middle and Late Formative Maya culture appears to emulate portions of the earlier Olmec ceremonial center prototype in designing plazas with platforms and temples, as well as stone monuments or plaster sculptural elements associated with them. Examples of Formative monumental architecture are found at Kaminaljuyú, Uaxactun, Nakbe, Mirador, Tikal, Izapa, Aké, and Dzibilchaltún. Basal pyramids may have had permanent superstructures, using stone foundation braces to support wattle-and-daub (*bajareque*) buildings with perishable thatched roofs.

Common to many of these structures is a basal platform copiously dressed with thick coats of lime plaster, sometimes painted red, blue, green, and ochre, or modeled plaster sculptures on foundations and/or lower exterior wall zones. Burnt lime plaster and mortar are integral construction components of Maya architecture; the evolution of plaster production techniques influenced not only architectural forms but also the character of design and ornament through space and time, as Proskouriakoff has noted.

Classic period Central Mexico's most influential site is Teotihuacán, Mesoamerica's first truly urban city. By the third century A.D., the site covered 20 square kilometers and had a population of more than 100,000. Their homes were part of a massive gridded city that focused on a huge arrangement of monumental pyramids, processional causeways, and surrounding mountains. The Sun and

Moon Pyramids were Protoclassic period constructions, followed by a significant increase in urban growth and planning during the second and third centuries A.D. This involved building the sacred Avenue of the Dead, connecting the Sun and Moon Pyramids with other ceremonial spaces—known as "triple complexes"—which are characteristic of Teotihuacán's structural symmetry. Teotihuacán's most diagnostic architectural feature is the *talud-tablero* exterior wall treatment, consisting of a steeply inclined wall plane, or *talud,* as a wall base, surmounted by a vertical wall with a thick frame of rectangular moldings, the tablet or *tablero.* Lime-plastered exterior walls, polychrome-painted plastered interior wall murals, *tezontle* (pumice) stone building fill, sculpted stone pillars, and carved stepped merlons capping ceiling friezes also adorn many of these and other satellite religious structures. Multiethnic artisan neighborhoods demonstrate urban Teotihuacán's economic and ethnic diversity.

Oaxaca's close cultural ties with Teotihuacán throughout the Formative and Classic periods inspired truly localized Zapotec expressions of Central Mexican architecture at Monte Albán, through stairways with broad *alfardas* and exceptionally long *talud/tableros* with heavy geometric moldings and straight or beveled cornices, known as the "scapulary" *talud/tablero.* Perhaps the most noteworthy Zapotec expression is Oaxaca's funerary architecture, comprised of either rectangular or cruciform plans integrating interior lateral or end tomb niches, some separated with interior mural paintings, antechambers with stairs, and flat or triangular stone slab roofs; the latter roofs often carry a central keystone support.

Regional adaptation of Classic Central Mexican architectural elements also exists at El Tajín in the north central Gulf Lowlands area, where the typical *tablero* of Teotihuacán is modified into a series of recessed concentric stonework niches, all covered by thick layers of polychrome plaster, for example at El Tajín's Pyramid of the Niches. This dynamic composition is crowned by salient beveled cornices that not only invert the inclining angle of the *talud* but also create dramatic light and shadow effects over the niches below, providing an intricate design of chiaroscuro highlighting both horizontal and vertical balance.

Although a number of Central Mexican monumental architectural elements can be identified in Maya sites such as Copán, Honduras, and Tikal, Guatemala, the Classic period in general marks a distinctively regionalized evolutionary trend in Maya civic-ceremonial architecture. Large basal platforms support stone and mortar masonry superstructures with new techniques for roofing, such as the corbeled arch or vault *(bóveda).* Lacking a keystone, this is not classified as a true arch; many early vault examples utilize overlapping courses of stones that bridge the intervening room space, so that the ceiling's narrow closure may be spanned by adjoining rectangular limestone slabs, or capstones *(tapas de bóveda).* Monumental buildings' interior and exterior masonry walls also show carefully cut and dressed stones. In areas such as the Puuc, Chenes, and Northern Lowlands, these wall stones *(sillares)* display one squarely or rectangularly dressed face backed by a roughly hewn area with a tenon *(espiga),* which was inserted into the wall rubble fill, creating a splendidly flat, veneer-like surface. These walls generally carry a smooth coat of lime plaster in a natural monochrome or combined with anthropomorphic or geometric polychrome painted images.

Maya monumental architectural development during the Classic period has traditionally been classified into regional styles, whereas distinct construction techniques or decorative doorways (monster masks or zoomorphic portals), monolithic columns, sculptural dressed stone friezes, and roof crest or roof comb characteristics are grouped into particular geographical proveniences, often ignoring the nature or evolution of their structural antecedents buried below. Most Mayan scholars recognize the following stylistic areas: the Motagua (including the sites of Quiriguá and Copán), the Petén (Tikal, Uaxactun, Río Azul, and Calakmul, to name some of the larger sites), the Usumacinta (Palenque, Bonampak, Piedras Negras, and Yaxchilán), the central Yucatán (including a large number of distinctive sites in the Río Bec, Chenes and Puuc subareas), and finally northern (Dzibilchaltún, Izamal) and eastern Yucatán (Cobá, Yaxuná).

Much stylistic variation exists from one region to the next, but some fundamental similarities in monumental architecture—known as "structural replications"—can be noted throughout the Maya area. Many scholars agree that these generic concepts may have had specific correlations: temporal (Early, Late, Terminal, or Postclassic periods); functional, housing domestic, civic, or religious activities; socio-political, illustrating centralized or decentralized power schemes with corresponding individual or group architectural patronage; or ideological, emphasizing divine kingship associated with carved or painted hieroglyphic benches depicting dynastic lineage family histories.

The Postclassic period throughout Mesoamerica is characterized by significant changes in artifact assemblages, interregional exchange relationships, social organizational power schemes, and monumental architectural traditions. Many sites simply were abandoned; building activity declined, or certain subregions, such as sites in the Río Bec, Chenes, and Petén Maya areas, ceased as other areas and centers arose.

West Mexico witnesses the combination of certain earlier semicircular and rectangular stepped-pyramid monumental architectural forms, such as the Teuchitlán tradition with clusters of round buildings, and the Tarascan *yácata,* a platform with huge semicylindrical supports, found in its capital cities of Tzintzuntzan and Ihuatzio surrounding Lake Pátzcuaro in Michoacán. Other sites in Durango and Nayarit also have strong fortifications.

In Central Mexico, for example, Teotihuacán's decline accompanied a struggle to fill the political, economic, and social vacuum it left. Classic period decorative elements or construction techniques, probably patronized by a centralized or theocratic political system, gave way to group-based glorification, immense colonnade-fronted range structures, and war cult and military iconographic decorative motifs popular during the Early and Late Postclassic periods. At Xochicalco, modifications to the Classic *talud/tablero* in the Temple of the Plumed Serpent (Quetzalcóatl) include elaborate relief carvings illustrating dignitaries of diverse ethnic groups. These reliefs envelope a buried interior foundation brace structure with twin column porticos, identifying this site as the possible Central Highlands cultural link between Classic and Postclassic Mesoamerican societies. Other sites, such as Tula (Hidalgo), display monumental structures of simple truncated pyramidal bases, and superstructures with wide porticos dressed with masonry pillars or columns, similar to those found in contemporary Chichén Itzá.

With the fall of Tula, around A.D. 1200, the Late Postclassic period began, and twin temple structures became popular in Central Mexican monumental architecture. At Tenayuca, Tenochtitlán, and other sites are found temple pyramids having two staircases and surmounted by two temples, surrounded by a ritual precinct that includes semicircular temples, probably inspired by earlier local architecture. New architectural elements also make their debut: monolithic architecture with full round sculpture, at Malinalco; the fortified central monumental zone, in Huexotla near modern Texcoco; the *coatepantli,* or serpent walls, crowned with merlons delimiting sacred precincts; and *tzompantli,* or skull rack altars.

In Oaxaca, the Postclassic Zapotec site of Mitla demonstrates not only a modification of Classic period urban planning but also the scapulary *talud/tablero* architectural tradition featuring stone mosaics. Monumental buildings grouped around quadrangle open spaces or patios, much like structures in the Maya area, now carry intricately cut stone stepped frets along basal platforms or as façade frieze moldings, adorning flat beam and mortar roofs supported by solid or rectangular columns. Other sites in the Mixtec highlands became fortress citadels with commanding views of their surroundings.

In the northern Maya Lowlands during the Terminal Classic and Early Postclassic horizons, Chichén Itzá emerged as Yucatán's largest multiethnic capital city. Its central districts, formally known as "Old" and "New" Chichén, display a probably contemporaneous mixture of the following monumental architectural elements: stone monster mask-adorned vaulted structures; flat-roofed temples and sculpted door jambs atop radial pyramids accessed by steep stairways with feathered serpent *alfardas;* sculpted, three-piece, round masonry pillar colonnades dominating public plaza areas; and *tzompantli,* or skull rack stone altars, adjacent to others with Venus, jaguar, and eagle iconographic motifs, similar to those found in Tula (Hidalgo). With the fall of Chichén Itzá, Mayapán emerged as the new peninsular capital, sharing the same monumental architectural tradition.

Sites strategically located on maritime trade routes along the Caribbean coast, on the Mexican Gulf coast, and on Cozumel Island during the Postclassic period have temple shrines with flat mortar-and-beam roofs, recessed stone lintels dressed with copious layers of plaster, and interior walls with polychrome anthropomorphic or zoomorphic lime-stucco mural paintings. At many of these sites, Classic period vaulted room structures were intentionally filled with rubble to support stone foundation braces with round monolithic column porticos.

Over more than two thousand years, monumental architectural evolution in Mesoamerica demonstrates the complex diversity of human responses to modifying the natural environment in order to meet basic needs by creating specific formal activity areas. One particular problem in architectural analysis and interpretation is a priori application of functional labels to features and buildings, thus assuming different civic or ceremonial activities associated with these structures. This could be addressed by analyzing pre-Hispanic urban contexts as conjunctive units of architectural form, material and structural content, ethnohistoric documentation, and ethnographic analogues, in order to build more enduring functional interpretive foundations.

FURTHER READINGS

Andrews, G. F. 1975. *Maya Cities: Placemaking and Urbanization.* Norman: University of Oklahoma Press.

Boone, E. H. (ed.). 1985. *Painted Architecture and Polychrome Monumental Sculpture in Mesoamerica.* Washington, D.C.: Dumbarton Oaks.

Fahmel Beyer, B. 1990. *La Arquitectura de Monte Albán.* Mexico City: Instituto de Investigaciones Antropológicas, Universidad Nacional Autónoma de México.

Hardoy, J. 1973. *Pre-Columbian Cities.* New York: Walker.

Heyden, D., and P. Gendrop. 1973. *Pre-Columbian Architecture of Mesoamerica.* New York: Harry N. Abrams.

Kubler, G. 1975. *The Art and Architecture of Ancient America.* Baltimore: Penguin.

Margain, C. R. 1971. Pre-Columbian Architecture of Central Mexico. In R. Wauchope (ed.), *Handbook of Middle American Indians,* vol. 10, part 2, pp. 45–91. Austin: University of Texas Press.

Marquina, I. 1990. *Arquitectura Prehispánica.* Mexico City: Instituto Nacional de Antropología, Secretaría de Educación Pública.

Proskouriakoff, T. 1963. *An Album of Maya Architecture.* Norman: University of Oklahoma Press.

Robertson, D. 1963. *Pre-Columbian Architecture.* New York: Braziller.

Lorraine Williams

SEE ALSO
Architecture: Vernacular-Mundane

Architecture: Vernacular-Mundane

The architecture built by and for the common household in ancient Mesoamerica has been termed popular, basic, primitive, and folk, as well as vernacular. These buildings are defined on a variety of characteristics, many of them shared with elite architecture. Socially, vernacular architecture is associated with commoners. Materially, it is constructed with local raw materials, readily available to all. In terms of cost, or energy expended in construction, such buildings are very low, being built by the occupant and/or a few close kin or peers. Statistically, they are the most numerous of structures. Artistically, they are the product of nonspecialists and thus are more functional than esthetic in their conceptualization and design. In terms of engineering, these structures are relatively simple, and knowledge of their construction is quite widespread.

The primary function of most Mesoamerican vernacular buildings was as dwellings or residences of commoner households, during life and occasionally after death. The majority of other functional types of structures are those associated with these houses, including separate kitchens, work sheds, and storage facilities. Generally, shrines or altars, though associated with houses, are studied as distinct categories of architecture. This consideration of vernacular architecture discusses only the houses of commoners, because they represent the vast majority of structures within the category of vernacular architecture and are extremely powerful analytically in the archaeological study of societies.

What follows is a description of the "typical" dwellings for a variety of societies during the height of their sociopolitical complexity. The descriptions of architecture are uneven owing to the nature of the archaeological record. First, various building components offer different levels of preservation based on material type: stone is better preserved than wood. Second, lower portions of houses are better preserved than upper portions; in part, this differential preservation is a consequence of material type, but it is also due to differential exposure to destructive agents. Roofs are more exposed to rainfall and other destructive elements than are wall foundations, and thus they and upper portions of walls collapse first, often protecting lower walls. As a consequence, the description of upper walls and roofs is more tentative, guided by available archaeological data as well as by ethnohistoric and contemporary descriptions of domestic architecture.

The Southern Lowland Maya: A.D. 700
A relatively large number of sites have yielded evidence of domestic architecture; some of the most complete excavations of vernacular architecture have been conducted at Copán (Honduras) and Cerén (El Salvador). The normative template of the commoner dwelling for the southern Lowland Maya is based primarily on data from these sites. The house was built in two separate components—a substructural platform measuring about 5 by 6 meters, and a superstructural house unit measuring about 4 by 5 meters. The platform was built principally of fill, comprised of earth mixed with some stones and artifact debris. Often the earth was obtained through the process of leveling the construction site; thus, the preparation of a horizontal surface on which to build the house yielded the earth that went into the platform. This platform was enclosed by a retaining wall, usually of unworked or only slightly modified cobbles, typically limestone owing to its

abundance throughout the southern Lowlands. The platform for commoner houses was low, ranging from about 10 to 40 cm in height. The provision of a platform on which to build the superstructure was quite common in this region of Mesoamerica, which receives high rainfall.

The rectangular outline of the superstructure was built of large cobbles, either unworked or only modestly faced. Large posts were placed at the corners of this stone foundation and at strategic points such as door frames. The superstructure, the house itself, was of wattle-and-daub construction, in which a wooden frame of thin poles, intertwined with a series of horizontal strips of thin wood called wattles, was fastened to the mainposts, forming the wall frame. Daub, or mud containing an aggregate such as grass, small stones, or even small artifacts, coated the wattle from both the outside and the inside; the builder ensured that the daub fully penetrated the wattle matrix. The daub was then smoothed and, when dry, formed the walls of the house. A thin plaster wash, composed of crushed limestone and water, was applied to these mud walls for protection.

Poles lashed to the wall posts formed the frame of the roof. This roof was gabled, or pitched on two sides, with the roof extending beyond the front entrance of the house. This wooden roof structure was covered with vegetation, usually palm thatch but also local grass, depending on availability as well as personal preference. At Copán, grass was the predominant roofing material, but palm thatch is more typical of southern Lowland houses because of its availability as well as its greater strength, water repellency, and fire resistance. A porch was typically built as an extension of the front eave of the roof. Lower posts were dug into the edge of the platform to support the front of the porch.

A Maya house in the Yucatán. Photo courtesy of the author.

There are no permanent interior divisions within the southern Lowland Classic Maya house, and thus the house is essentially a one-room structure. However, perishable curtains probably partitioned some interior spaces, such as kitchens and sleeping areas. Comparing the commoner dwellings among various sites yields a relative consistency of form, with local differences augmenting but not replacing a standard formal structure. This repetition of form is evident at other Maya sites in the northern Lowlands, such as Dzibilchaltún, as well as in southern Highland Maya sites, such as Kaminaljuyú.

Although a small number of individuals occupied single houses, households lived in clusters, with houses facing onto and connected by courtyards. These courtyard units socially reflected households affiliated through lineal ties, and thus extended families were the household units associated with domestic architecture.

Teotihuacán: A.D. 600

The commoner dwelling at Teotihuacán was the apartment compound. Each rectilinear apartment building measured, on average, about 50 to 60 meters on each side, and housed between 30 and 100 individuals, or up to 20 patrilineally related families.

The apartment compound was built directly on the ground surface rather than on an elevated platform. The ground surface was first prepared by leveling (if necessary) to build a floor of tamped earth, or earth covered with a "concrete" of crushed basalt bedrock and compacted volcanic ash (tepetate) set in a mud mortar, or earth covered with a stone grouting topped by lime plaster. This floor was repeatedly raised by adding more earth or stone and plaster, and thus the interior floor became elevated above the outside surface of the street. The surrounding wall of each apartment was built of cut or uncut stone, with adobe bricks constituting the upper portion of the wall. These walls were held in place both by mud mortar placed between each of the stones or the adobe bricks, and by the concrete of crushed basalt and mud placed on the exterior and interior of each wall. A thin lime plaster was the final coating, which on occasion served as the substrate for mural decorations.

There were multiple interior dividing walls, constructed like the exterior walls, and most of these walls were weight-bearing. The large size of the apartment compound structurally necessitated these interior walls, which further served as spatial partitions for living rooms, kitchens, open courtyards, and civic spaces. Occasionally stone drains were placed at the level of the plaster floors to remove water from the interior of the structure. The entire structure was built to just one story—perhaps 3 meters high—and thus was unlike the multistory apartment buildings of contemporary cities. The roof was of beam-and-mortar construction—each wooden beam spanning several rooms, with beams secured in place by a mortar of earth, rubble, and water and coated with lime plaster. Portions of the roof were intentionally left uncovered, resulting in interior courtyards that provided light and heat to the apartments. Teotihuacán apartment roofs were sloped to provide effective drainage away from the interior of the building.

The two thousand Teotihuacán apartment compounds were closely spaced, separated by narrow alleys or streets. Commoners and elite lived in quite similar forms of structures, although the quality of the elite apartment compounds, or palaces, clearly surpassed that of the commoners. In addition, there is an individuality to each apartment compound, with no two being identical. Apartment compounds were not built in a single episode of construction; rather, various portions of the compound were constructed as they were needed to accommodate a growing population. Certainly the long history of lineage occupation and concomitant architectural modifications accounts for the uniqueness of each apartment compound, as do wealth and status distinctions inherent within an empire the scale of Teotihuacán.

Tula and the Toltecs: A.D. 1000

Vernacular architecture excavated at Tula, in northern Mesoamerica, reveals that as many as five houses formed a courtyard unit, and several of these units comprised a residential complex separated from similar domestic units by exterior house and courtyard walls. Although the exact spatial arrangement physically connecting residential structures differed from that of the single-unit Teotihuacán apartment compound, the Tula structures were built in similar fashion and housed families of similar lineal affiliation.

Each individual house was a large rectangular or square structure containing several rooms. The house was built either directly on a leveled ground surface or on a low platform of earth and rubble supported by a stone retaining wall. The floors were typically tamped earth but on occasion were built of stone and lime plaster. The exterior walls consisted of a low stone foundation topped by several courses of stones, with the upper portion of the walls consisting of adobe bricks. Interior walls were similarly built with a combination of stone and adobe brick, or, in

some cases, entirely of adobe brick. All wall stones or bricks were joined by a simple mud mortar as well as by an exterior coating of either fine mud mortar or thin lime plaster. Most interior walls helped to support the weight of a flat roof composed of beams, mortar, and plaster. This roof was probably sloped to remove and perhaps capture the scant rainfall in this northern region of Mesoamerica. The channeling of roof water is further evidenced by the recovery of ceramic tubes that would have served as drains. The presence of interior room drains suggests that some of the roof may have been open, as was the case in Teotihuacán architecture.

The Aztecs: A.D. 1450

Despite the fact that hundreds of thousands of common Aztec and Aztec-period dwellings existed in the fifteenth and sixteenth centuries, very few have been excavated. Sahagún lists and briefly describes twenty-three different types of Aztec commoner houses, although two or three may not be long-term residential structures. Combining these ethnohistoric data with those excavated from the Aztec period villages of Cihuatecpan in the Teotihuacán Valley, and Capilco and Cuexcomate in Morelos, a description of two general types of vernacular architecture can be offered.

One general type is the small, single-room structure housing the nuclear or extended family. The wall types show great variability of materials—stone, stone foundations supporting adobe brick, wattle and daub, and wood. If appropriate in maintaining structural integrity, a mud mortar or a thin plaster wash would have coated the exterior walls. The majority of floors were of tamped earth or flat cobbles, with some earthen floors capped with a layer of crushed stone. The roofs also displayed considerable variability. Some houses had gabled roofs of straw or grass, while others bore flat roofs of beam-and-mortar construction. These single-room houses were relatively small, with exterior walls measuring approximately 4 × 5 meters.

The second general type was the multi-room structure. Here the walls consisted of a stone foundation topped by courses of adobe brick. Again, exterior wall support came from a mud mortar and plaster wash. Basalt cones are often found as part of the wall. Floors were of tamped earth, with occasional fine grouting or plaster wash used as a protective and decorative element. Adobe bricks were used as floor elements to define work and sleeping areas. In multi-room houses, interior walls were constructed of stone and adobe brick to bear some of the weight of the

A

large beam-and-mortar roof. Roof and floor drains attest to the channeling of water away from the interior surfaces and, as was suggested in the Teotihuacán and Tula cases, may indicate that roofs served as means of collecting water. These houses were larger than the single-room dwellings, with exterior dimensions averaging 10 × 13 meters. Like the single-room structures, they were built directly on the prepared ground surface.

Aztec houses differed from all others in Mesoamerica in terms of variability within the commoner segment. Within that single social segment, houses varied in wall quality, size, and roof form, reflecting a considerable range of status among commoners. This marked variability among commoner houses is concomitant with the greater economic and political scale inherent in the Aztec Empire.

Labor Organization

The building of vernacular architecture in ancient Mesoamerica was a process entirely organized and effected by the actual occupants of the house or their kin. However, the number of laborers involved in the construction process, and the organization of these laborers, undoubtedly varied with the scale of construction. Since considerable work has been conducted in discerning the Classic Maya organization of labor for commoner dwellings, that organization will first be discussed.

Maya houses were built by the occupants of the house and their close kin. For example, when a new household was formed through marriage, a new structure was built by the occupants-to-be and their families. This task involved two to six people, generally but not exclusively males, the specific number depending on the laborers available and the size of the house. In general, commoner houses cost less than 100 person-days to build. That means that a house costing 80 person-days required either the input of two people for 40 days, or three people for 27 days, and so on. The entire process of construction would have taken place within a month or so during the dry, non-agricultural season.

The highest-status individual, possessing the greatest knowledge and background on house construction, assumed the role of supervisor, but no formal position existed. Roles were assumed based on pre-existing interpersonal relations established in other joint, familial economic tasks such as agricultural production. No formal specialists were required, given the common knowledge of tasks and the simplicity of manufacturing finished materials. Given the similarity in size and quality between the Classic Maya houses and the single-room dwellings of the Aztecs, it is reasonable to assume a similar organization and timing for the construction of this type of Aztec residence.

The above reconstruction was based on detailed quantification of costs of Maya architecture, guided by ethnographic observations. No such quantification has been done on stone architecture in the Basin of Mexico; however, certain similarities and differences can be proposed. In general, each Toltec house and each segment of the Teotihuacán apartment probably cost more than 100 person-days, based on the overall size, the type of roof construction, the use of adobe bricks, and the use of lime plaster. The beam-and-mortar roofs cost more than vegetal roofs in terms of procurement and transport, as well as in the use of lime plaster as a surface material. Lime plaster is a specialized product that involved considerable technical skill in manufacture and certainly required the talents of a specialist. Adobe bricks were also the product of a community specialist, with such bricks probably traded through the market system. All these factors suggest that costs were beyond those of the commoner Maya structure.

In terms of organization, it is likely that the builders of a new commoner house were the occupants-to-be and their close kin, as was the case for the Maya. However, manufacturing specialists for lime plaster and adobe bricks were involved, and the purchase of raw materials, such as beams, may have been necessary. If the number of laborers was high, a greater degree of organizational complexity would have existed, placing greater demands on the supervisor, perhaps to the degree that specialist architects may have been hired to help in the planning and orchestration of construction.

The multi-room dwellings of the Aztecs appear to be intermediate in scale of complexity between the Classic Maya and Teotihuacán dwellings. The procurement of adobe brick may have required outside involvement with non-kin, but the scale of construction is lower than at Teotihuacán, and thus some intermediate organization was likely in effect.

FURTHER READINGS

Abrams, E. 1994. *How the Maya Built Their World: Energetics and Ancient Architecture.* Austin: University of Texas Press.

Diehl, R. 1983. *Tula: The Toltec Capital of Ancient Mexico.* London: Thames and Hudson.

Evans, S. (ed.) 1988. *Excavations at Cihuatecpan.* Vanderbilt University Publications in Anthropology, 36. Nashville.

Manzanilla, L. (ed.). 1986. *Unidades habitacionales mesoamericanas y sus areas de actividad.* Mexico City: Universidad Nacional Autónoma de México, Imprenta Universitaria.

Millon, R. 1981. Teotihuacán: City, State, and Civilization. In *Handbook of Middle American Indians,* Supplement 1, pp. 198–243. Austin: University of Texas Press.

Sheets, P. 1992. *The Cerén Site.* Fort Worth, Tex.: Harcourt Brace.

Smith, M. 1992. *Archaeological Research at Aztec-Period Rural Sites in Morelos, Mexico.* Vol. 1. University of Pittsburgh Memoirs in Latin American Archaeology, 4. Pittsburgh.

Wauchope, R. 1938. *Modern Maya Houses: A Study of Their Archaeological Significance.* Washington, D.C.: Carnegie Institution.

Elliot M. Abrams

SEE ALSO

Activity Areas and Assemblages; Architecture: Civic-Ceremonial

Arithmetic

See Mathematics

Armillas, Pedro (1914–1984)

Born in Spain, Armillas lived there until the age of twenty-five. He emigrated to Mexico after serving on the Republican side in the Spanish Civil War. In Mexico, he enrolled in the Escuela Nacional de Antropología e Historia in 1940 and studied with Paul Kirchhoff, reading F. Engels and V. G. Childe, and coming to understand the practice of archaeology as "paleosociology." His perspective emphasized the behaviorial component of archaeological cultures at a time when the general thrust of most research was to recover precious objects or pyramids. Strongly influencing students at the Escuela and Mexico City College, Armillas criticized emphasis on monumental sites and advocated pedestrian surveys and aerial photography to ascertain society–environment relations and to recover information about all segments of the archaeological population. Armillas surveyed in Central Mexico, excavated at Teotihuacán, and studied fortified sites. He left Mexico to work with UNESCO in Ecuador (1956–1959) and to teach in the United States, most recently at University of Illinois (Chicago), 1972–1984.

FURTHER READINGS

Armillas, P. 1949. Notas sobre sistemas de cultivo en Mesoamérica, cultivos de riego y humedad en la cuenca del río Balsas. *Anales del Instituto Nacional de Antropología e Historia* 3:85–113.

———. 1951. Tecnología, formaciones socio-económicas y religión en Mesoamérica. In S. Tax (ed.), *The Civilizations of Ancient America: Papers of the XXIXth International Congress of Americanists,* pp. 19–30. University of Chicago Press, Chicago.

———. 1971. Gardens on Swamps. *Science* 174:653–661.

Rojas Rabiela, T. (ed.). 1991. *Pedro Armillas: Vida y obra.* 2 vols. Mexico City: CIESAS, INAH.

Eric R. Wolf

Arroyo Pesquero (Veracruz, Mexico)

Olmec Formative period site, discovered by looters who removed hundreds of objects from the riverbed. It is known for scores of exquisitely carved green-and-white stone masks, hundreds of jadeite and serpentine celts, and many fine figurines.

FURTHER READINGS

Joralemon, P. D. 1988. The Olmec. In *The Face of Ancient America: The Wally and Brenda Zollman Collection of Precolumbian Art,* by L. A. Parsons, J. B. Carlson, and P. D. Joralemon, pp. 9–50. Indianapolis: Indianapolis Museum of Art and Indiana University Press.

Richard A. Diehl

SEE ALSO

Gulf Lowlands; Olmec Culture

Art

As a preliminary definition, "art objects" are considered to be functional or decorative objects, crafted or transformed by persons to express ideas. However, this definition springs from modern thought; "art" was not a conceptual category to the peoples of ancient Mesoamerica. No Mesoamerican language contained a term corresponding to contemporary concepts of "art" as the expression of the concerns of an individual "artist."

A

Cylinder vase, Maya civilization. Ht: 21.5 × 13.2 cm (diameter). A.D. 600–900. Private collection.

The Mesoamerican terms most closely related to the Euro-American category of art are found in the *Diccionario Maya Cordemex* (a Yucatec-Spanish dictionary): *its'atil* and *miats*. The term *its'atil* has been translated as "art or science, skill, ability, wisdom, caution, industriousness, knowledge." *Ah its'at* means "an artist or ingenious, well-read, and wise person." A related word, *miats',* refers to "wisdom, philosophy, science, art, and culture." These terms denote intellectual skills and wisdom valued by the community, rather than a special category of beautiful objects. In most tradition-oriented societies, such as those of Mesoamerica, aesthetic activities make tangible certain culturally specific concepts of morality and the order of the properly functioning cosmos. For this discussion, "art" refers to objects into which persons have deliberately and skillfully encoded or infused local wisdom or spiritual forces.

Art-Making, Artists, and Patrons

In Mesoamerica, where the calendar juxtaposed synchronous identities and events into a sacred, cyclical present time, human artistic activity was necessarily a replica of primordial creative precedents. Artists employed a vocab-

ulary of familiar forms and images, recombining them in imaginative ways. They aimed to acknowledge and honor tradition by reinventing it through repetition. To most of its viewers, the iconography inscribed on objects was unambiguous. Although symbols could possess several levels of meaning—political, astronomical, or myth-historical— the forms of each symbol were sufficiently recognizable to allow communication of traditional concepts.

In some cases, both the processes of making art and the completed objects were considered sacred. For example, Archbishop Diego de Landa's account of the Maya in Yucatán after the imposition of Spanish rule indicates that one of the months of the Vague Year *(haab)*, Mol, was dedicated to renewing wooden statues, probably of ancestors, for household shrines. This enterprise was considered potentially dangerous for the sculptors because the rituals accompanying the carving process invoked powerful spiritual forces and occurred in a locale liminal to the central, civilized zone of the community. Such a spiritually charged situation was necessary to create forms that could be infused with or inhabited by the spirits of ancestors of the patrons who commissioned the works. Only after the skilled carvers received many petitions from the patrons and assurances of protection from the priests and community elders did they agree to undertake this effort. While the patron went to cut a special, fragrant tree, *Cedrela mexicana,* the elders, priests, and carvers fasted and made offerings of their own blood. In a specially built straw hut, they continued these spiritual purifications for the duration of their creative activity, probably so that the statues, which were kept under wraps in large urns when not actively being worked on, would be pure vessels for the ancestral spirits.

During Ch'en, the next month, after the statues were completed, the spiritual entities were installed during a ceremony in which they were fed incense, blessed with prayers, and then delivered to their new owners. Landa commented, "The good priest then preached a little on the excellence of the profession of making new gods, and on the danger that those who made them ran, if by chance they did not keep their abstinence or fasting" (in Tozzer 1941: 161). According to this eyewitness account, Maya woodcarvers drew on ambivalent powers and beings from outside the community as well as on local ritual expertise to effect the transformation of a living tree into vehicles for local mores and traditions.

The notion that making ancestor images was a sacred activity is corroborated in the Postclassic Maya Madrid Codex. The carvers as well as the materials were trans-

Tablet of the Cross from Palenque, central section; Maya civilization. A.D. 690. Ht: approximately 170 cm. The Tablet of the Cross illustrates part of the ritual celebrating King Chan Bahlum's accession to the throne of Palenque. The image functions on many levels. It shows the king paying homage to the sacred world tree, an aspect of the shamanic worldview of the Maya. The monument and its text are rich with astronomical references to the Milky Way, the ecliptic, a rare conjunction of Jupiter and Saturn, and the summer solstice. This display of scientific knowledge and ritual piety were intended to legitimize the rule of this son as a powerful ruler. Courtesy Museo Nacional de Antropología, Mexico.

formed by the ritual into identification with deities, especially Itzamná and the Maize God. In the Late Classic period, engaging in creative activity submerged the individuality of the artist into the primordial half-brothers of the Hero Twins, Hun Batz and Hun Chuen, who had been transformed into monkeys and were creators of song, music, and objects.

As a result of the decipherment of Maya hieroglyphs, we have considerable information about the social status of Maya artists. On some painted vessels, the scribal

Eccentric flints from the cache in the Hieroglyphic Stairway of the Maya city of Copán. Photo by William Fash, as reprinted in *Scribes, Warriors, and Kings: The City of Copán and the Ancient Maya.* New York: Thames and Hudson, 1991, figure 91.

artist's signature phrase appears, as David Stuart recognized in 1987. Although they are not common, such phrases indicate that most individuals who painted figures and glyphs were younger sons of the nobility. Among the Aztecs, education for youth of the nobility included instruction in certain crafts, although many craftsmen producing objects for temples and trade were not from elite classes.

Patrons who commissioned works of art probably came from upper social classes, and rulers commissioned art as one of their duties. Aztec rulers commissioned monumental sculptures associated with major temples from metropolitan workshops. Members of craft guilds carved smaller monuments in cities throughout the Valley of Mexico. Aztec rulers also commissioned elaborate vessels, war costumes, and jewelry for distribution to successful warriors, to accumulate the resources of the different regions of the empire, and to demonstrate control over the status and wealth of the elite in dominated cities. Monument workshops have been found at the Olmec sites of San Lorenzo and Tres Zapotes, so the association

of rulership and the creation of didactic sculpture in ceremonial cities may have been the prerogative of rulers throughout Mesoamerican history.

Functions of Art

Art objects fulfilled cultural purposes that often focused on establishing ideal patterns. They were intended to show idealized concepts of rulership and cyclic time; of relationships between humans and the ancestors; of relationships between humans and the city, or humans and cosmic forces; of distinctions among ethnic groups and social classes; or what happened when ideals were transgressed. From a Euro-American viewpoint, the intent of manifesting ideals in material form can be viewed as propaganda. In ancient Mesoamerica, although these ideal patterns were invoked for political ends by the elites, they were communicated in the language of ancestor worship and cosmic processes guiding and sacralizing the daily existence of all persons.

In the major capitals of Mesoamerica, monumental sculptures and painted reliefs defined the boundaries and

Seated female figure, Classic Veracruz culture. Ceramic, hollow; ht: 45 cm; c. A.D. 600. This figure's abstracted forms include a triangular face, cylindrical arms, square shoulders, and highly polished surfaces. Museo Nacional de Antropología, Mexico. Photo reprinted from Esther Pasztory, *Aztec Art*. New York: Abrams, 1983, plate 13.

the centers of ritual locations and recreated in miniature the spatial order of the political and/or topographic landscape. Their imagery often refers to the founding of the culture and its rulers, to dynastic legitimacy and ritual piety of rulers, and to sources of supernatural power and rituals involving it. For both the Maya and the Aztecs, the redistribution of these artworks was a source of power and legitimacy, just as the redistribution of ritual objects and spiritual offerings, a common subject of artworks, served to bolster the power and prestige of the ruler.

In addition to this didactic function, art comprised wealth and status. In Aztec society, textiles and gold jewelry functioned as currency, along with cacao beans and copper axes. The *tlatoani* demanded textiles, warrior costumes, paper, and raw materials for art (such as feathers) in tribute from various provinces. Among the Maya, elaborate pottery vessels were a prime form of "social currency" exchanged by the elite as gifts bestowing status on giver and recipient. The same vessels functioned to serve

food, especially in royal and ritual contexts, and as funerary ware.

Elaborate furnishings to accompany the deceased were not the only art objects that were taken out of economic and intellectual circulation and placed in a sacred context. Mesoamerican peoples also placed objects in dedicatory caches within ceremonial complexes. Among many instances of this practice, the massive offerings of the Olmecs of La Venta are remarkable. "Massive Offering" 2 (of three) consisted of about 1,000 tons of rough slabs of imported serpentine. Above the offering were two caches, each with nine celts and a stone mirror. Another offering above and between them consisted of 37 celts in a cruciform arrangement. Over this complex a sandstone sarcophagus and two tombs were aligned, the former made of huge basalt columns, each of which contained jade figurines and other jade objects such as beads, decorated rectangles, hands, and effigies of a clamshell and a stingray

Olmec Colossal Head (San Lorenzo Monument 1); basalt; ht: approximately 200 cm; c. 1200 B.C. These images of Olmec rulers were carved of basalt quarried 50 miles away and carried up a high plateau to be placed—with other monuments—along the north-south axis of the site. University of Jalapa Museum of Anthropology, Jalapa, Veracruz. Photo reprinted from Esther Pasztory, *Aztec Art*. New York: Abrams, 1983, plate 6.

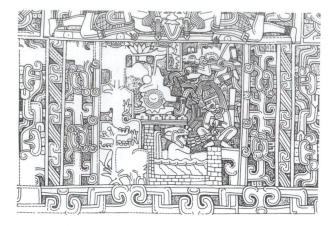

Relief panel from the South Ball Court, El Tajín, Veracruz, c. A.D. 900. In situ. In this image, one of many at El Tajín, a squatting man draws blood from his penis to replenish a deity in a poll of pulque. Photo reprinted from Michael D. Coe, *The Maya: From the Olmecs to the Aztecs,* 5th edition. New York: Thames and Hudson, 1993, figure 42.

spine, along with a stone mirror, real stingray spines, and a shark tooth. Mound A-2 covered the entire quantity of buried objects so that none of them were seen once deposited (or cached). The "Massive Offerings" of La Venta have been interpreted as effigies of the watery underworld, their reflective surfaces marked by mirrors and connected to the earth's surface by world trees symbolized by the celts in a cruciform arrangement. The tombs and their human and marine life effigies were situated above the edges of the seas, symbolically at the threshold of the underworld.

Illustrative of Maya caches is one tucked beneath a stone slab below the large zoomorphic pedestal at the foot of Copán's Hieroglyphic Stairway, excavated in 1987. A lidded ceramic censer contained two jadeite figures representing a deified ancestor and a patron of war; a flint knife; and marine material—once more, stingray and sea urchin spines and a spiny oyster shell containing red pigment—items used for or related to bloodletting rituals involved in purification for ancestor worship and other rituals. One of the jadeite figures was an heirloom from the Early Classic, an example of the widespread use of heirlooms as regalia and in caches. Next to the censer were three eccentric flints with branching stylized human heads dramatized by large negative spaces. Most eccentric flints seem to have been cached to sacralize an important structure.

Caching crafted objects and exotic traded marine items points to respect for their purity and power. Concealing

statues of the ancestors and supernatural beings continued into the Colonial period among the Quiché Maya and the Aztecs. Similarly, cave and cliff art is found in remote places throughout Mesoamerica. In a study of Maya cave painting, Andrea Stone observes that the images are often in remote areas even when more accessible sites were available. She argues for seeing the practice of sequestering images in pristine environments as establishing "a meeting ground between the human and the divine." From the Maya making of ancestor statues in secluded arbors to the Olmec underground Massive Offerings, the processes of making and using many types of objects occurred in remote locations for spiritual reasons.

A special category of art includes the screenfold books often called "codices." Made for the use of priestly elite, they frequently include tables of astronomical or calendrical information. Of fourteen surviving pre-Columbian handpainted manuscripts on deerhide or bark paper, all are either Maya (four, of astronomical content), Mixtec (historical), or Mixteca-Puebla (concerning deities and divination).

Materials

Many materials prized for their visual and conceptual qualities—especially those used for ornaments and ritual objects, such as jadeites and other green stones, obsidian, flint, shell, and tropical feathers—also indicated the knowledge and political astuteness necessary to locate and

Fresco from Tepantitla apartment complex, Teotihuacán, c. A.D. 300–600. Two profile figures dressed in female attire flank a frontal goddess whose face is nearly obscured by her mouth mask and owl headdress. Rain and seeds fall from their hands and a tree grows from the central figure. Photo reprinted from Esther Pasztory, *Aztec Art.* New York: Abrams, 1983, plate 10.

trade for them as well as the skill necessary for their crafting. Elaborate caches such as those at La Venta and the Aztec Templo Mayor should be considered in this light.

Formal Qualities

Each culture established canons of human proportion and treatment of mass and volume, distinguishing its style from all others. Subject matter also varied, but the repetition of important themes—such as glorification of rulership, warfare, rituals honoring deities or ancestors, cosmic origins of power, the ball game as a shamanic death and rebirth, the layered universe, and the organization of space and time—indicates that many fundamental concepts were shared by Mesoamerican cultures and adapted to differing political systems.

Although Mesoamerican artists made recognizable images, it is important to realize that their human and other subjects were rendered with varying degrees of abstraction. Most cultures (except the Maya) avoided the portrayal of natural bodily proportions (1:7.5), deliberately compacting it into canons of 1:4 or 1:5 (typical of Aztec sculptures) or even shorter. Freed from any mandate to use natural proportions, the artists could abstract other elements of the figure—for example, changing the shape of the face into a triangle (typical of some ceramic figurines from Classic Central Veracruz), composing the body as subtly modulated cylinders (in Aztec sculpture), or developing local conventions for the portrayal of eyes (as in West Mexican art).

Other details of the figure, such as pose, hair, and costume, carried encoded meanings. Logic indicates that portraiture, in the sense of revealing the natural physical appearance and the individual idiosyncrasies of a specific person, is suppressed in Mesoamerican art: even in the masterfully carved life-size jade masks from the Olmec locale of Río Pesquero, facial features are highly idealized and conform to a geometric conception of the face. Joyful smiles or expressions of astonishment, fear, or anger seldom enliven faces in Mesoamerican art, nor does a figure's gaze engage the viewer. The focus appears to be within, perhaps on the animating entities enlivening each being. Unnatural canons of proportion, geometricization of features, and the suppression of personal expression in figures suggest that art objects were meant to convey ideal attitudes and relationships, not to express quirks of behavior or individuality. Abstraction, then, serves to create human bodies conforming to corporate or community ideals.

Similarly, elements of the natural world were stylized into conventionalized symbols. Trees, for example, were

Variously identified as the Great Goddess or the Water Goddess Chalchihuitlicue, from Teotihuacán. Ht: 3 m; c. A.D. 150. Identified as a woman by her cape and long skirt, this woman's strong horizontal planes and cleft head suggest she is associated with the strata of the earth and underground water. Museo Nacional de Antropología e Historia, Mexico.

often rendered as crosses with a few leaves or fruit characteristic of a certain species attached to the end of each branch. Every culture developed specific ways to represent such important objects as the sun, mountains, and caves, and the surface of the earth. Landscape was never represented for its own sake, but rather to identify a cosmic locale in which an activity occurred. The "setting" for the human figure on a stela often was the ceremonial center itself. For a sequestered cave painting, which might illustrate aberrant acts, "setting" consisted of the disorderly, chaotic environment of the cave itself.

Gold pendant from Tomb 7, Monte Albán, Oaxaca. Mixtec civilization, c. A.D. 1150–1400; ht: 22 cm. A ball game, a solar disk, a flint knife, and an earth monster form the subjects of each separately cast section of this ornament. Museo Regional de Oaxaca. Photo reprinted from Michael D. Coe, *Mexico: From the Olmecs to the Aztecs,* 4th edition. New York: Thames and Hudson, 1994, figure 120.

In both public ceremonial spaces and sequestered art environments, assemblages of objects were insistently repetitive. At Yaxchilán, Tikal, and Copán, stelae with virtually identical imagery punctuated the great plaza spaces, with only the names and dates changing at the first two sites, and only the costume at the latter. In Tenochtitlán's Templo Mayor, dozens of Mezcala style masks were cached together. Accompanying the carved bones in the burial in Tikal Temple 1 were more than ninety other bones. Such visual repetition evokes the verbal repetition of Mesoamerican orations, and both establish an atmosphere charged with ritual heat or energy.

Regional Styles, Themes, and Iconographic Studies

Early and Middle Formative period village cultures produced many ceramic figurines for household ritual use. These are usually highly stylized; they often represent women and often wear complex headgear, minimal clothing, and perhaps body paint. Ceramic vessels were made in a variety of forms, including animal effigies. The preliminary typology of Central Mexican figurines was made by George Vaillant in the 1930s. Late Formative village cultures known as Shaft Tomb cultures of West Mexico also made larger, often hollow, highly stylized effigies of figures engaged in ritual actions from offering food to meditation.

Olmec art was recognized as distinct from other Mesoamerican cultural traditions only early in the twentieth century, and confirmation of its chronological priority was gained through radiocarbon dating of samples from La Venta in 1957. First identified near the Gulf Coast, objects that share the style, themes, subjects, and materials of Olmec art have been found in many locations along the upper tributaries and main branch of the Río Balsas, especially in Guerrero, and as far south as Honduras. Unlike the objects made in contemporary but less complex societies, most Olmec art is in stone. It includes many pieces of monumental scale; these portray men, not women, with the single exception of Chalcatzingo Monument 21, which portrays a woman who stands on the emblem of sacred earth or place, raising a world tree. Monumental basalt heads, high-relief thrones with replicas of male rulers emerging from caves, large, seated or kneeling shamans, and stelae with images of rulers originate primarily in the Gulf Coast. Cave paintings and cliff reliefs are found in the central and western highlands of Mexico. Most widespread are the small greenstone human figures standing or seated in meditation postures, or kneeling while transforming into animal alter egos. A variety of small items served as regalia and signified status and affiliation with specific patrons of supernatural power. Certain Olmec-related Formative period villages also created large, ceramic animal-effigy vessels; large, hollow infant figures; and figurines of males and females in certain roles, such as ballplayer or Fat God; these figurines are best documented at San Lorenzo.

After Olmec civilization declined, the Gulf Lowlands were the locus of the "Bridge Culture," known only from a dozen artifacts sharing a writing system believed to record the Proto-Mixe-Zoque language. One stela, from La Mojarra, portrays a ruler wearing massive stacked headdresses representing a bird and standing on an earth symbol, which may be a toponym. Other objects include jade sculptures.

Although no single civilization united the Gulf Lowlands in the Classic period, there was continuous cultural presence throughout Mesoamerican history. At several sites, such as Tres Zapotes and Cerro de las Mesas, stelae record rulers. Post-Olmec monuments include potbelly boulder sculptures. During the Classic period, many Gulf Lowlands villages produced ceramic figures and figurines, each in a distinct style and representing both men and women.

The ball game was a prominent cultural expression. Its paraphernalia, including U-shaped stone "yokes" *(yugos),* an axelike form *(hacha),* and a leaflike tall form *(palma),* were frequently richly carved with an iconography of creatures and humans in strange positions and often elaborated with scrolls.

The Huastecs of the northern Gulf Lowlands were related linguistically to the Mayas. Their prominent forms of monumental sculpture include freestanding slablike sculpture representing Tlazolteotl, a female deity who encompassed an array of related concepts referring to the relation between lunar and menstrual cycles and earthy fertility; a few freestanding sculptures of young males incised with complex references to sacrifice and cosmos; and figures of wizened old men with planting sticks. In mural paintings at Tamuín, about A.D. 1000, the Huastecs represented processions of warriors in proportions that speak of Mixtec influence.

Unique in Mesoamerica was the metropolis of Teotihuacán, the sixth largest city in the world in A.D. 200. Dominated by two huge, stepped pyramids (one built over a sacred cave), whose location anchored the orientation of a grid to which all construction conformed, Teotihuacán's art is devoid of recognizable representations of rulers, the worship of ancestors in human form, and written lan-

guage. Instead, a Great Goddess and Storm God dominate the murals painted in elite apartments after A.D. 300. Other subjects of polychrome murals were stylized birds, coyotes, and jaguars in somewhat human attitudes. Only a few pieces of monumental sculpture survive, the largest being the Great Goddess, designed with strong horizontal planes and a cleft head, suggesting strata of the earth. Face panels and standing figures in stone representing the corporate ideal are two types of objects that continue an Olmec tradition. In ceramics, the most characteristic object is the lidded *incensario,* shaped like a large hourglass, with frames constructed of ceramic appliqué surrounding and obscuring small human-face panels with regalia and symbols.

Evidence points to Oaxaca as the earliest crucible for the development of the Mesoamerican calendar and writing systems, but these were elaborated to a greater extent by the "Bridge Culture" and the Maya. The art of Zapotec Oaxaca was influenced by other Mesoamerican cultures throughout history. Most characteristic are modeled, molded, and appliqué effigies of seated supernaturals, such as the rain-agriculture god Cocijo, placed in multiples in tombs, which were sometimes painted with scenes of ritual processions.

The Mixtecs of Oaxaca introduced gold-working, decorated ceramics, enriched masks, shields, and knife handles with turquoise mosaic and produced deerhide books, or codices. Surviving screenfold books document the political maneuvers of dynastic leaders, focusing on the tragic rivalries of 8 Deer Jaguar Claw of Tilantongo.

Modeled stucco figures and painted decoration transformed Maya buildings into tableaux of royal ritual action in a cosmic setting. Stucco skybands soared over rulers wielding double-headed bars representing the ecliptic. Beneath the royal feet were images of the local ancestral burial ground and topography. This kind of imagery, along with rulers as successful warriors, also appeared on stela and pedestal pairs. These public art objects represented the prerequisites and duties of Maya kingship: correct genealogy, pious blood sacrifices to ancestral and cosmic deities, astronomical learning, successful warfare, and survival of the shamanic contest (in the form of a ball game) with the Lords of the Underworld. Much Maya imagery is two-dimensional and narrative in content; like their hieroglyphic writing, it concerns the deeds of kings in the waking and dreaming worlds.

From A.D. 550 to 850, one of the best-respected Maya arts was painting on simple ceramic plates and cylinders, sometimes accompanied by hieroglyphic phrases

A

Chac Mool at the top of the stairs on the Temple of the War-
riors, Chichén Itzá. Maya civilization; ht: 1.1 m; c. A.D. 900.
Supine warrior or sacrificial figures with raised shoulders and
knees are common to the Maya, Toltecs, and Aztecs in the
Postclassic Period. Photo reprinted from Michael D. Coe,
The Maya: From the Olmecs to the Aztecs, 5th edition. New
York: Thames and Hudson, 1993, figure 34.

dedicating the vessel and naming its scribal painter. These
vessels, used to serve chocolate, *atole* (gruel), and tamales
in ritual settings, illustrate palace behavior and shamanic
encounters with otherworld beings. Problems with provenience mitigate against an overview of the styles and subjects of carved jades.

The collapse of the two great cultural forces of Classic
Mesoamerica, Teotihuacán and the Maya cities, left
groups everywhere without large trading partners, moral
examples, or political affiliations. In this vacuum, several
cities, intriguing for their art styles, flourished. Cacaxtla
(Tlaxcala), Xochicalco (Morelos), El Tajín (Veracruz),
Uxmal and other Puuc cities of the northern Yucatán
peninsula, and Mitla (Oaxaca) drew inspiration from the
two great Classical civilizations as well as their local ones
to create unique fusions of Maya and Central Mexican
imagery, themes, and art forms such as stelae, architectural decoration, and murals.

Later, around A.D. 900, Tula (Hidalgo) rose to prominence. Considerable current debate centers around the
relative priority of Tula and Chichén Itzá in Maya
Yucatán. They share remarkable parallels of architectural
and sculptural forms, including Atlantean and Chac
Mool figures and royal bench reliefs.

As Aztec beliefs and its pantheon drew on those of
conquered peoples, so did the types of objects and

imagery it used. Its senses of volumetric form and proportion seem most like those of the Olmec. Like Teotihuacán, the Aztecs eschewed portraits of rulers and did
not adopt a hieroglyphic writing system, despite the fact
that they must have been aware of Mayan phonetic writing. Instead, screenfold books (of which only early post-
Conquest examples survive) communicated through
ideographs and pictographs, with some phonetic elements
as an aid to those using them to recount oral tradition.

Aztec sculpture emerged as a coherent style after 1450.
Basalt sculptures, often of massive size, combine low-
relief imagery with clearly defined volumetric forms.
Most subjects inspire awe or even terror through size and
through an insistent, rational presentation of such
imagery as fearful beings with large claws and teeth,
humans bound for sacrifice, and other themes of destructiveness. Formats include Chac Mools and bench reliefs, probably appropriated from the Postclassic Maya;
Atlantean warriors reminiscent of those at Tula; and
gigantic earth goddesses on the scale of the Chalchihuitlicue of Teotihuacán. They introduced such formats
as stone boxes, colossal jaguars, huge disks with basins
used as receptacles for sacrificial offerings of human
hearts, thrones in the form of temples, and smaller effigies
of the many cult deities of the communities tributary
to Tenochtitlán. Perhaps the most unusual sculpture represents Coatlicue, the earth mother killed by her daughter, Coyolxauhqui, whom the Aztec tribal deity,
Huitzilopochtli, son of Coatlicue, in turn killed by throwing her from the top of Snake Mountain. A 3.5-meter-tall
image of Coatlicue, who wears a skirt of intertwined
snakes and a necklace of human hearts and hands, and
whose severed head spouts blood in the form of two confronted snake heads, was found in 1790 near the heart of
Tenochtitlán. Instead of a human shape, her massive
tectonic forms and complex iconography emulate a
cliff overhanging a cavelike recess. Like other Aztec
sculptures, the bottom of the monolith is also carved, here
with a relief image of Tláloc in a birthing position.
Although it echoes the monuments of past civilizations in
scale and treatment of volumes, this combination of conventionalized iconography with geologic scale and
abstract three-dimensional form is a conception peculiar
to the Aztecs.

FURTHER READINGS

Berrin, K., and E. Pasztory (eds.). 1993. *Teotihuacán: Art
from the City of the Gods.* New York: Thames and
Hudson.

Coe, M. D., et al. 1995. *The Olmec World: Ritual and Rulership.* Princeton: The Art Museum, Princeton University.

Freidel, D. A., L. Schele, and J. Parker. 1993. *Maya Cosmos: Three Thousand Years on the Shaman's Path.* New York: William Morrow.

Kubler, G. 1975. *The Art and Architecture of Ancient America: The Mexican, Maya, and Andean Peoples.* 2nd ed. Harmondsworth: Penguin.

Pasztory, E. 1983. *Aztec Art.* New York: Abrams.

Reents-Budet, D. 1994. *Painting the Maya Universe: Royal Ceramics of the Classic Period.* Durham and London: Duke University Press.

Robertson, M. G., and V. M. Fields (eds.). 1994. *Seventh Palenque Round Table, 1989. IX.* San Francisco: Pre-Columbian Art Research Institute.

Schele, L., and M. Miller. 1986. *The Blood of Kings: Dynasty and Ritual in Maya Art.* Fort Worth, Tex.: Kimbell Art Museum.

Stone, A. J. 1995. *Images from the Underworld: Naj Tunich and the Tradition of Maya Cave Painting.* Austin: University of Texas Press.

Tate, C. E. 1992. *Yaxchilan: The Design of a Maya Ceremonial City.* Austin: University of Texas Press.

Townsend, R. F. 1992. *The Aztecs.* London and New York: Thames and Hudson.

Townsend, R. F. (ed.). 1998. *Ancient West Mexico: Art and Archaeology of the Unknown Past.* New York: Thames and Hudson.

Carolyn Tate

SEE ALSO
Architecture: Civic-Ceremonial; Painting

Artifacts and Industries

Artifacts and industries are among the most important classes of information used to reconstruct past lifeways. An "artifact" typically is anything portable that can be identified as having been made or modified by humans. This differentiates artifacts from fixed, non-movable products of human modification such as architecture and features (e.g., hearths, burials, or caches).

Artifacts can be divided into two gross categories: *tools,* which are artifacts specifically manufactured to perform a function, and *debitage,* the waste material produced during the manufacture of tools or resulting from their use. Archaeologists organize and classify artifacts in order to infer cultural patterns and temporal characteristics. The most basic of these approaches is to group artifacts into industries: similar materials and methods of manufacturing. Pre-Columbian industries include such categories as lithics, ceramics, bone, shell, and other organic material groups. Identification of raw material requires no knowledge of human social behavior because it is natural, not cultural, and can be identified by combining geological, chemical, and biological tests—which can also determine if an object was the result of natural processes—with the locus of origin of the raw material (a process called "sourcing").

Because different raw materials may require different manufacturing techniques, industries represent technological categories: the ways in which these materials were procured and manufactured into tools, and the ways these tools functioned. Archaeologists analyze artifact function according to three distinct categories of use. First, tools perform specific tasks or behaviors that are technical: for example, hunting equipment such as the atlatl spear-thrower and its chipped stone dart point, or ceramic vessels for cooking, storing, and serving food. Functional categories often cross-cut industries because the same function may be served by different materials—food containers might be wood or ceramic, or knives made from stone, shell, or bone.

Artifacts can also serve social functions, particularly if their form or design is unusual, or if they are made out of rare and valuable materials. Such artifacts might then indicate differences in social or economic status. Often the designs on ceramic vessels differentiate one group or culture from another. These stylistic differences are not necessarily intentional on the part of the original creators, but they usually represent social boundaries. Mesoamerican archaeologists rely on them to recreate prehistoric social groups and processes of change from the Formative period on. Many chronological phase names refer to time periods defined by the presence or preponderance of a particular pottery type in ceramic assemblages, and this is why such phase names are so important in the archaeological literature.

Some artifacts are found in distinctive non-utilitarian contexts associated with religion and ritual, such as in mortuary contexts. Many of these artifacts are also utilitarian, such as ceramic vessels for domestic activities; however, their placement in burials suggests very different functions associated with the funerary rite and with the ideology of death and the afterworld. Utilitarian artifacts of high value are also commonly placed as offerings and caches in buildings, altars, and shrines. Some ceramic artifacts served

A

primarily ideological purposes; they include the Classic Teotihuacán theater censers and candelarios, Classic Maya censers, and figurines of all periods and areas.

The lithic industry is usually subdivided by technique into ground stone and chipped stone artifacts. Grinding produces manos and metates, distinctive slab-shaped, flat grinding stones whose basic function is the production of flour from soaked maize kernels or other grains. Other mortars and grinding palettes of ground stone are thought to have been used for grinding minerals into paints and pigments. Some celts, adzes, and scrapers were produced by this technique, as were some lapidary items and portable sculpture.

Knapping, the process of removing chips of stone by percussion or pressure to create a tool of the desired shape, is the most distinctive form of lithic production in Mesoamerica. One such industry involved the reduction of a core of cryptocrystalline stone, such as chert, chalcedony, or obsidian, by percussion and pressure flaking into finished tools, such as projectile points. Axes, adzes, and some hoes were also produced by this core-tool reduction technique. The Maya site of Colhá in the chert-bearing zone of northern Belize specialized in the production of these tools from thick, large flakes with a triangular cross-section; the tools were then retouched, a process of systematically removing chips from a preformed tool to shape it into a form similar to that of our axe or hoe. Note that names are sometimes applied to tools without any functional basis: many basalt "hoes" in the Central Highlands are actually pre-Columbian maguey-fiber scrapers.

The most distinctive lithic industry in Mesoamerica was obsidian blade production. Obsidian is extremely fine-grained and can be worked to produce highly regularized tools known as "blades." These obsidian blades are distinctive in that each is produced by a single movement. Blades were produced from hemispherical cores, referred to as "macrocores," which were initially reduced by percussion flaking to produce a uniform cylindrical core from which the artisan produced the regularized blades. The initial series of blades driven from these cores were often retouched into scrapers. These tools were used to process animal skins and hides and to remove the pulp and fiber from from plant products such as maguey and cactus. One such specialized scraper form has an expanded T-shaped end and is thought to have been used to scrape the inside of the disbudded maguey plant to promote the production of sap for pulque production.

Once the core was prepared, hundreds of uniform blades could be removed from it by pressure flaking. These blades were used for sawing, scraping, cutting, and planing a wide range of materials, including bone, horn, skin, hides, animal flesh, plant fibers, and wood. Traces of human blood have also been found on obsidian blade sections, suggesting their use in bloodletting and autosacrifice. Blade production is an extremely efficient technique of production in that a much higher ratio of tools to debitage is achieved than by the core-tool reduction sequence, where the original core actually becomes the product.

Bone tools constitute another industry found in Mesoamerica. The most common bone artifacts are needles and awls found in domestic refuse. These are often made from deer bone. Human skeletal remains were also used: masks were made from the facial area of skulls, and a musical instrument, the bone rasp, or *omichicahuastli*, was produced from a long bone notched with incised grooves—sound was produced by rubbing a stick along the grooved length of the long bone, using a skull as a resonator. Fish spines, particularly stingray spines, have been found in ritual contexts and were possibly involved in bloodletting and autosacrifice.

Unfortunately, many industries and artifacts in Mesoamerican archaeology are less well known, particularly those industries based on organic materials such as wood, bone, plant fibers, feathers, and hides. We know that these media were used very extensively based on historic, ethnohistoric, and iconographic information; however, these materials do not preserve as well as their more durable inorganic counterparts. The textile industry is another one well known from ethnohistoric descriptions and artistic depictions, but not from archaeological materials.

FURTHER READINGS

Gaxiola G., M., and J. E. Clark (eds.). 1989. *La Obsidiana en Mesoamerica.* Coleccion Cientifica, Series Arqueología, 176. Mexico City: Instituto Nacional de Antropología e Historia.

Hester, T. R., and H. J. Shafer (eds.). 1991. *Maya Stone Tools: Selected Papers from the Second Maya Lithic Conference.* Monographs in World Archeology, 1. Madison, Wis.: Prehistory Press.

Parry, W. J. 1987. Chipped Stone Tools in Formative Oaxaca, Mexico: Their Procurement, Production and Use. In *Prehistory and Human Ecology of the Valley of Oaxaca,* vol. 8. Memoir 20. Ann Arbor: Museum of Anthropology, University of Michigan.

Parsons, J. R., and M. H. Parsons. 1990. *Maguey Utilization in Highland Central Mexico.* Anthropological

Papers, 82. Ann Arbor: Museum of Anthropology, University of Michigan.

Tolstoy, P. 1971. Utilitarian Artifacts of Central Mexico. In G. Ekholm and I. Bernal (eds.), *Handbook of Middle American Indians,* vol. 10, pp. 270–296. Austin: University of Texas Press.

Randolph Widmer

SEE ALSO

Activity Areas and Assemblages; Ceramics; Crafts and Craft Specialization; Metal: Tools, Techniques, and Products; Obsidian: Tools, Techniques, and Products; Weaving and Textiles; Wood: Tools and Products

Astronomy, Archaeoastronomy, and Astrology

Archaeoastronomy addresses the question of the role of astronomy and astronomers within their cultural and social contexts, and not merely as part of "science." As it has developed, a broad range of topics have been addressed, including Native American mathematics, counting systems, calendrics, numerology, navigation, surveying, cartography, urban planning, and orienting principles, in addition to astronomy and cosmology. The term "cosmovision" was coined to embrace this more comprehensive perspective, particularly as it relates to nonliterate societies.

The peoples of pre-Columbian America were essentially the descendents of *Homo sapiens sapiens* populations from Siberia and Asia who migrated across the Bering Straits region of the North Pacific Rim on foot and by ocean-going canoes. They brought with them certain deep, archetypal elements of cosmovision that are still alive today. These include an animistic worldview with a specific set of shamanistic practices, and the belief that humans emerged onto the surface of Earth from worlds below at a central place. The surface of the Earth stretches out into four world-quarters, which are often associated with specific colors, trees, birds, animals, mountains, and even units of time. The heavens and underworld are often seen as layered, populated by anthropomorphic celestial entities and a bicephalic dragon that may represent the ecliptic or zodiacal band. Time is cyclical, and the cosmogonies often involve a series of catastrophic destructions of the world followed by new creations. The forces of nature are seen as personified powers that require penance, sacrifice, and propitiation to maintain a precarious balance.

There is strong evidence in Mesoamerica, in particular, for a highly developed numerical and calendrical astronomy that involved maintaining long-term records of periodic celestial phenomena tied to an accurate count of days. Horizon-based, naked-eye observations were likely to have been important, including the keeping of annual star calendars by noting the heliacal rise phenomena associated with bright stars and constellations as well as various planetary bodies. Within the tropics, there is also ample evidence for careful observations of the solar zenith passage. Whether an advanced positional astronomy reminiscent of that practiced by the Babylonians was developed is still an open question.

It is now established that a fundamental system of calendrical divination existed well back into the first millennium B.C., and an elaborate dynastic calendar was certainly in place in the Late Formative period (from c. 400 B.C.). From Classic Maya inscriptions combined with the general Mesoamerican epigraphic record, ephemerides for the Sun, Moon, and Venus must have existed from Late Formative times, which provided long-term agreement with astronomical observations and served as the basis for correctable ritual almanacs. In the Maya Dresden Codex, probably dating from around the time of the Conquest but containing information reflecting a deep data base, there is an eclipse almanac that at least attests that the Maya could predict eclipse warning and safe periods. Venus almanacs are found in five of the sixteen or so surviving pre-Cortesian codices. These were used to regulate specific practices of warfare and ritual sacrifice.

The study of the ancient and contemporary indigenous astronomical practices, celestial lore, mythologies, religions, and cosmological systems of Native American peoples has become a coherent discipline only within the last three decades of the twentieth century. Prior to the development in the late 1960s of archaeoastronomy and ethnoastronomy in the Americas, there were few scientific explorations of these astronomical and cosmological systems as a whole. For example, most research in Mesoamerica focused on calendrical inscriptions on Maya monuments and on almanac tables in the few surviving pre-Columbian codices.

There would seem to have been two basic reasons, historically, for the neglect of the Americas. First, most work in the history of astronomy has concentrated on the Western tradition, has dealt largely with written sources, and has viewed astronomy narrowly as part of the history of science. Within the academic establishment, non-Western astronomical traditions were often viewed as "failed

A

sciences," along with astrology, perhaps worthy of study only by anthropologists. A new direction in interdisciplinary scholarship was required. Second, in many cases insufficient data existed on Native American astronomy. Beginning particularly with the pioneering work of the astronomer Anthony Aveni and the architect Horst Hartung, obscure source material was collected and fundamental surveys of building and site alignments were made. From this beginning, based on more than a century of pioneering scholarship—including notable studies such as Ernst Forstemann's 1880s research on the Dresden Codex, Eduard Seler's massive corpus of Mesoamerican studies, and John Teeple's 1931 "Maya Astronomy"—most of the work has concentrated on Mesoamerica (including the U. S. Southwest) and the Andean cultural zone.

The study of Native American astronomy has now reached the point that it has provided a new dimension for understanding the function of certain ancient buildings and structures. Now that astronomers, archaeologists, architects, and historians are working together on questions of ancient American cosmovision, a detailed appreciation of their astronomical sophistication has emerged that makes these indigenous astronomies and science appear second to none in the ancient world.

FURTHER READINGS

Aveni, A. F. 1980. *Skywatchers of Ancient Mexico.* Austin: University of Texas Press.

———— (ed.). 1989. *World Archaeoastronomy.* Cambridge: Cambridge University Press.

Baity, E. C. 1973. Archaeoastronomy and Ethnoastronomy So Far. *Current Anthropology* 14:389–449.

Carlson, J. B. 1990. America's Ancient Skywatchers. *National Geographic Magazine* 177(3):76–107.

Carlson, J. B., and J. W. Judge (eds.). 1987. *Astronomy and Ceremony in the Prehistoric Southwest.* Papers of the Maxwell Museum of Anthropology, 2, Albuquerque, N.M.

Ruggles, C. L. N., and N. J. Saunders (eds.). 1993. *Astronomies and Cultures.* Niwot: University Press of Colorado.

Williamson, R. A., and C. R. Farrer (eds.). 1992. *Earth and Sky: Visions of the Cosmos in Native American Folklore.* Albuquerque: University of New Mexico Press.
John B. Carlson

SEE ALSO
Calendrics

Asuncion Mita (Jutiapa, Guatemala)

Classic Maya site in the highlands, best known for the corbeled vaults found in its tombs, one of the only Maya highland manifestations of this elite architectural trait widespread among the lowland Maya.

FURTHER READINGS
Weeks, J. 1993. *Maya Civilization.* New York: Garland.
Susan Toby Evans

SEE ALSO
Architecture: Civic-Ceremonial; Guatemala Highlands Region; Maya Culture and History

Atemajac Region (Jalisco, Mexico)

The Atemajac Valley now holds Guadalajara, Mexico's second-largest city, but little attention has been paid to the region's pre-Hispanic past, and now much of archaeological value has been lost to ferocious looting and urban expansion. Nonetheless, carefully chosen salvage projects combined with intensive studies of less damaged areas offer critical data pertaining to some major issues in western Mexican prehistory. Situated in the highlands of central Jalisco, the valley covers an area of 747 square kilometers, bounded on the north and east by the great *barranca* (ravine) of the Río Grande de Santiago, a continuation of the Río Lerma. To the south, a series of low hills separates the valley from the approach to Lake Chapala, and to the west is the Sierra La Primavera, today a national park and in the past a major source of obsidian. Moderate rainfall, occurring from June to October, is quickly absorbed by the highly pumiceous and porous soils. As a result, there are only minor year-round streams, and settlement was concentrated in these areas during all periods.

Archaeological settlement surveys were made by Galván in the 1970s, extended into the La Venta Corridor to the west (which leads to the valleys ringing the Volcan de Tequila; *see* Teuchitlán Tradition), and by Beekman in the 1990s. Settlement data are still being analyzed. Several of the larger sites, such as Coyula, were independently mapped during the 1970s and 1980s by Weigand. Excavations in the valley have been few. Four sites in the La Venta Corridor have been test-pitted, and more extensive research and salvage excavations were completed at El Grillo, La Coronilla, Bugambilias, and Tabachines; larger-scale excavations and reconstruction have taken place at Ixtépete.

The current chronological sequence, based on several of the above excavations, combines elements of sequences developed by Galván and Beekman. Where the two differ, we will here use the latter system.

Ceramics have been classified into three groups—Tabachines, Colorines, and Arroyo Seco—whose combinations form the basis for the three subphases. The Tabachines phase is generally associated with the well-known shaft tombs and with the concentric circular *guachimonton* structures as surface architecture. During this phase, the Atemajac Valley was clearly peripheral to the major social and political developments taking place in the Tequila valleys to the west. The La Venta Corridor survey found a rapid increase in population between the Early (A.D. 1–200) and Middle Tabachines phases (A.D. 200–450); the series of hilltop sites from that period may have monitored traffic through the corridor. Population nucleated into those hilltop sites during the Late Tabachines phase (A.D. 450–550), but most settlements were abandoned. This may be related to the growth of political complexity in the Tequila valleys to the west, and Beekman proposed that these strategic sites marked the boundary of the core of the Teuchitlán Tradition. Most of the Atemajac Valley lay beyond this boundary, but the region shared architectural and ceramic affinities with the core region, suggesting a peripheral relationship. Tabachines phase dates in this valley are still preliminary: Galván posits 750 B.C.–A.D. 400 on the basis of obsidian hydration dates from a series of shaft tombs, while Beekman places the phase from A.D. 1–550 on the basis of comparisons with the sequences from adjoining valleys.

A major shift in material culture remains marks the succeeding El Grillo phase, probably concurrent with the Epiclassic period. New ceramic types and forms of decoration appear, and no types from the earlier phase continue. New ceramics include the first appearance of ring-based cups, molcajetes, pseudo-cloisonné, resist decoration, and other new techniques. Architectural changes include rectangular platforms, U-shaped structures that replace earlier circular structures, and box tombs that replace the shaft and chamber tombs. Most architecture in the valley is associated with this phase, probably reflecting a general population boom. On the basis of *talud-tablero* façades found at three sites and one obsidian hydration date, Galván dates the phase to c. A.D. 300–600 and sees the new complex as indicative of a Teotihuacán expansion into the region, although El Grillo, Ixtépete, and Coyula each appear to have headed separate subareas. While Beekman agrees that the complex is intrusive to the region, he sees its origins in

an expansion of southern Guanajuato societies during the Epiclassic period (A.D. 550–850). Both see the El Grillo phase as the local manifestation of extensive social changes across northern Mesoamerica that probably involved some population movement.

The Atemajac phase is defined by another complex composed of largely distinct ceramics and small sets of foundation walls without basal platforms, presumably residential in function, nicknamed *corrales*. No clear public architecture is associated with these sites, and they appear to represent a substantially less hierarchical society. This phase has less settlement in the Atemajac Valley proper, but in the La Venta Corridor, settlement frequency reaches a peak, with many hilltop communities and many dispersed sites with no clear orientation of structures. Galván hypothesizes a period of abandonment between the El Grillo and Atemajac phases and dates the latter to the Early Postclassic (A.D. 900–1200), primarily on the basis of one eleventh-century obsidian hydration date. Beekman sees sufficient shared traits between El Grillo and Atemajac artifacts and ceramic types to suggest a period of contemporaneity, and he places the Atemajac complex in the period A.D. 750–900. Both agree that the complex has its origins in northern Jalisco and southern Zacatecas, where very similar structures are found with a similar emphasis on hilltops.

Galván's final Tonalá phase is represented only by a few small aceramic sites in the hills, so assigned for lack of any better evidence. The Vaca Calderón site has possible Epiclassic to Early Postclassic remains. Weigand and Beekman have proposed two Postclassic phases, but their markers are largely imported, low-frequency ceramics, or unusual elite architectural forms. Coyula was the capital of a polity at the time of Spanish contact, and Site TN 5 (Baños de Oblatos) has a series of carved rock constructions reminiscent of Malinalco and may pertain to the Postclassic.

FURTHER READINGS

Galván Villegas, L. J. 1976. *Rescate arqueológico en el fraccionamiento Tabachines, Zapopan, Jalisco.* Cuadernos de los Centros Regionales, 28. Mexico City: Instituto Nacional de Antropología e Historia.

———. 1991. *Las Tumbas de Tiro del Valle de Atemajac, Jalisco.* Mexico City: Serie Arqueológica, Instituto Nacional de Antropología e Historia.

Schöndube Baumbach, O., and L. J. Galván Villegas. 1978. Salvage Archaeology at El Grillo-Tabachines, Zapopan, Jalisco, Mexico. In C. L. Riley and B. C.

A

Hedrick (eds.), *Across the Chichimec Sea: Papers in Honor of J. Charles Kelley,* pp. 144–164. Carbondale: Southern Illinois University Press.

Weigand, P. C. 1993. The Political Organization of the Trans-Tarascan Zone of Western Mesoamerica on the Eve of the Spanish Conquest. In A. I. Woosley and J. C. Ravesloot (eds.), *Culture and Contact: Charles C. Di Peso's Gran Chichimeca,* pp. 191–217. Albuquerque: University of New Mexico Press.

Luís Javier Galván Villegas and Christopher S. Beekman

SEE ALSO

Grillo, El; Ixtépete, El; Tabachines; Teuchitlán Tradition; West Mexico

Atlantean Figure

Architectural support in the form of a standing person, a trait found at Formative Olmec Potrero Nuevo, but best known from Early Postclassic Tula. Figures supporting stone slabs are found at Chichén Itzá.

Susan Toby Evans

SEE ALSO

Architecture: Civic-Ceremonial; Chichén Itzá; Tula de Hidalgo

Atzompa (Oaxaca, Mexico)

Situated on a hill 4 km distant from Monte Albán, Atzompa was an important and distinct barrio of the Zapotec capital during Monte Albán IIIa and IIIb periods. By the latter period it reached its maximum development, with settlement covering over 47 hectares, and a total estimated population of 2,500 to 5,000. Based on the architecture and urban layout, the elite governing Atzompa had its own political and administrative functions, with palaces and temples similar to those in Monte Albán. Its buildings are in the Monte Albán style, but the frontal *tablero* panels on buildings are decorated with *greca*-style step-fret designs like those in Yagul and Mitla.

In addition to farming, Atzompa's inhabitants specialized in ceramic production. Today local artisans continue this tradition.

FURTHER READINGS

Blanton, R. E. 1978. *Monte Albán: Settlement Patterns at the Ancient Zapotec Capital.* New York: Academic Press.

Hartung, H. 1970. Notes on the Oaxaca Tablero. *Boletín de estudios oaxaqueños,* 27. Oaxaca: Museo Frissell de Arte Zapoteca.

Kowalewski, S. A. 1982. Population and Agricultural Potential: Early I through V. In R. Blanton et al. (eds.), *Monte Albán's Hinterland Part I. The Prehispanic Settlement Patterns of the Central and Southern Part of the Valley of Oaxaca, Mexico,* pp. 149–180. Memoirs of the Museum of Anthropology, University of Michigan, 15. Ann Arbor.

———. 1983. Monte Albán IIIb-IV Settlement Patterns in the Valley of Oaxaca. In K. V. Flannery and J. Marcus (eds.), *The Cloud People: Divergent Evolution of the Zapotec and Mixtec Civilizations,* pp. 113–115. New York: Academic Press.

Sharp, R. 1970. Early Architectural Grecas in the Valley of Oaxaca. *Boletín de estudios oaxaqueños,* 32. Oaxaca: Museo Frissell de Arte Zapoteca.

Ernesto González Licón

SEE ALSO

Monte Albán; Oaxaca and Tehuantepec Region

Ayala (Granada, Nicaragua)

One of the largest sites yet identified in the Greater Nicoya region, and the site having the strongest associations with southern Honduras. Occupied from 300 B.C. to A.D. 1520, it features artificial mounds, and cultural enhancement of natural mounds, house foundations, and a cemetery. Some burials were recovered from beneath mounds (which represent postinterment constructions, not burial mounds), but no skeletal analysis has been reported. Ceramics show strong influence from southern Honduras, especially A.D. 300 to 800; obsidian was imported from southern Honduras (flakes) and Guatemala (mostly blades).

FURTHER READINGS

Healy, P. F. 1980. *The Archaeology of the Rivas Region, Nicaragua.* Waterloo, Ontario: Wilfred Laurier University Press.

Lange, F. W., P. Sheets, A. Martinez, and S. Abel-Vidor. 1992. *The Archaeology of Pacific Nicaragua.* Albuquerque: University of New Mexico Press.

Salgado G., S. 1993. Proyecto: La evolucion de la complejidad socio-política en Granada, Nicaragua. In J. E. Arellano (ed.), *30 años de arqueología en Nicaragua,* pp. 127–134. Managua: Instituto Nicaraguense de Cultura.

Salgado G., S., and J. Zambrana H. 1994. El sector norte de Gran Nicoya: Nuevos datos en la provincia de Granada, Pacífico de Nicaragua. *Vínculos* 18/19: 121–137.

Frederick W. Lange

SEE ALSO

Intermediate Area: Overview

Ayotla-Zohapilco (Mexico, Mexico)

Formative site on the north shore of Lake Chalco at the base of Cerro Tlapacoya, with Olmec-related materials dating to the Ayotla and Manantial subphases, 1100–1000 B.C. At the Ayotla locale (Tlapacoya; IX-EF-1), a 4.50-meter-deep trench was excavated in 1967. In 1969, Niederberger excavated a trench about 60 meters to the south, at the Zohapilco ("Tlapacoya IV") locale. These two excavations at the same site (which thus possibly measured about 12 hectares in extent at 1100 B.C.) revealed parallel stratigraphies. The 1967 test demonstrated that Olmec-related materials pre-date the basal levels of Zacatenco and El Arbolillo (formerly thought to yield the oldest pottery in the Basin of Mexico). Niederberger's trench extended the Tlapacoya sequence still further in time, uncovering an earlier Nevada ceramic complex and the still older preceramic Zohapilco and Playa phases. The 1100–1000 B.C. deposits from the 1967 test produced cobs of a low-yield maize and evidence of heavy dependence on lake resources.

FURTHER READINGS

Niederberger Betton, C. 1987. *Paléopaysages et archéologie pré-urbaine du Bassin de Mexico.* Études Méso-américaines 5.11, vols. 1 and 2. Mexico City: Centre d'Études Méxicaines et Centraméricaines.

Tolstoy, P., and L. I. Paradis. 1970. Early and Middle Pre-classic Cultures in the Valley of Mexico. *Science* 167:344–351.

Tolstoy, P., S. K. Fish, M. W. Boksenbaum, K. B. Vaughn, and C. E. Smith. 1977. Early Sedentary Communities of the Basin of Mexico. *Journal of Field Archaeology* 4:91–107.

Paul Tolstoy

SEE ALSO

Arbolillo, El; Basin of Mexico; Tlapacoya

Azcapotzalco

The Postclassic Tepanec capital, on the former western shore of Lake Texcoco, was situated in what is today part of northwestern Mexico City. Excavations on the hill called Coyotlatelco, in a part of Azcapotzalco called Santiago Ahuitzotla, were the first to yield abundant pottery of the Coyotlatelco type. This in turn led to the recognition of what is now generally called the Epiclassic period. Azcapotzalco appears to have been one of the few significant settlements in the Basin of Mexico outside of Teotihuacán in the Epiclassic period. A residential structure was also excavated at Coyotlatelco.

As a Tepanec capital, Azcapotzalco played a major role in the Late Postclassic history of the Basin of Mexico. Under King Tezozomoc, who ruled until the first part of the fifteenth century, the city came to dominate a large part of the Basin of Mexico, and possibly parts of the valleys of Puebla and Morelos as well. The Mexica of Tenochtitlán, who had long been subordinate allies of Azcapotzalco, finally undertook to throw off the Tepanec yoke. The long Tepanec War (1428–1430) led to the defeat of the Tepanec and the formation of the Aztec Empire.

FURTHER READINGS

Carrasco, P. 1984. The Extent of the Tepanec Empire. In J. de Durand-Forest (ed.), *The Native Sources and History of the Valley of Mexico,* pp. 73–92. BAR International Series 204. London: International Congress of Americanists.

Tozzer, A. M. 1921. *Excavations at a Site at Santiago Ahuitzotla, Mexico, D. F.* Bureau of American Ethnology, Bulletin 74. Washington, D.C.: Government Printing Office.

Frederic Hicks

SEE ALSO

Aztec Culture and History; Coyotlatelco

Aztatlan Complex

The Aztatlan (Spanish, Aztatlán) complex was part of a widespread and uniform cultural expansion with an early Postclassic time of occupation. It covered a great part of the West Mexican coast, from at least central Jalisco up to the Sinaloa/Sonora border, and extended up into the western fringe of the Mexican plateau from the Jalisco/Michoacán border area in the south to central Durango in the north. In some areas the Aztatlan complex constitutes the highest development of Mesoamerican indigenous culture in pre-Hispanic times.

The term "Astatlán" first appeared in the map atlas of Ortelius (1570), designating a large and important region of Contact-period indigenous culture along the West Mexican coast between the Santiago River (Nayarit) and the Sinaloa River (Sinaloa), extending eastward into the Sierra Madre. This ethnohistorical term was adopted by Sauer and Brand (1932) to designate a cultural complex found along the coast of Sinaloa and Nayarit within Ortelius's "Astatlán" area. Owing in part to the depth of archaeological deposits at some Aztatlan sites, Sauer and Brand suggested that the Aztatlan region attained its relatively high level of cultural development at a time corresponding to the Epiclassic Toltec culture in central highlands of Mexico, as opposed to later, Aztec cultural development. They proposed that during Toltec times central Sinaloa was colonized from somewhere to the south by the bearers of Aztatlan culture.

It now seems probable that there was at least one ceremonial-civic center of the Aztatlan complex established near the center of every large coastal river valley between central Jalisco and northern Sinaloa, as well as in strategic locations and along routes of communication and commerce in some highland valleys to the east. The locations of many Aztatlan temple town centers domi-

nated ample areas of fertile and humid river alluvium along the coast, suggesting dependence on more extensive, and possibly more intensive, floodplain agriculture than had been practiced previously. There was some cultivation of subsistence crops, such as maize, squash, beans, and chile peppers, and cotton and tobacco cultivation are evidenced by an abundance of spindle whorls and pipes in some areas of the northwestern part of the coast. In the southeastern part of the coast, cacao was probably an important non-subsistence crop. In some northwestern coastal areas, mollusks, especially oysters, were heavily exploited, probably for food but perhaps for pearls as well.

The distribution of high-quality obsidian from mines in the highlands was another important aspect of Aztatlan economy; exported items took the form of finished prismatic blades as well as cores of raw material. Metallurgy too was important, with copper products predominating, and some bronze (tin or arsenical). The ultimate origin of this metallurgical tradition was probably South America (coastal Ecuador or northern Peru), but the Aztatlan people learned to smelt metal ores, and they appear to have colonized some areas in order to secure a stable supply of ores. Other Aztatlan industries include the manufacture of shell jewelry, and carving exotic stones such as steatite.

Pottery was another important Aztatlan craft. It seems that major centers of pottery production supplied large areas of the coast and highlands with vessels of consistently fine, hard paste, decorated with design styles that are very similar if not identical over large geographical areas. Some designs are executed in elaborate polychrome, sometimes incised, and they display an iconographic system closely related to the codex iconography of Postclassic Mixteca-Puebla cultures of the central Mexican highlands. At some sites, Toltec-related Mazapan style mold-made human figurines are common, and some were locally produced. Some sites have an abundance of Plumbate pottery, suggesting long-range contacts with southern Mesoamerica.

Monumental architecture took the forms of monumental platforms of earth and stone on which major civic-ceremonial structures were built; stone stelae associated with such structures; courts for playing the ritual ball game; petroglyphic designs pecked on boulders; and community cemeteries displaying variety in the deposition of skeletal remains—extended position, flexed in a pit (seated or lying on the side), or inside a large pottery urn. Grave goods included incense burners, possibly used in burial rites.

A plate from the Aztatlan complex along the western coast of Mexico. Illustration courtesy of the author.

Chronometric dates for Aztatlan materials include radiocarbon dates from the West Mexican coast (many corrected for the Seuss Effect), ranging from A.D. 883 to 1400. Obsidian hydration dates range from A.D. 520 to 1664. Most researchers believe that the earliest manifestation of the Aztatlan complex on the West Mexican coast dates to approximately A.D. 900; however, some coastal and some highland valleys appear to have been colonized considerably later in the process of Aztatlan expansion. For example, several radiocarbon dates suggest an Aztatlan colonization of the coastal Banderas Valley on the Jalisco/Nayarit border at about 1130. The cultures in the coastal valleys encountered by Spanish explorers in the 1500s were remnants of the original Aztatlan development, or were derived in part from an earlier mixing of Aztatlan with local Classic period cultures.

FURTHER READINGS

Meighan, C. W. (ed.). 1976. *The Archaeology of Amapa, Nayarit.* Monumenta Archaeológica, 2. Los Angeles: Institute of Archaeology, University of California.

Mountjoy, J. B. 1990. El desarrollo de la cultura Aztatlán visto desde su frontera suroeste. In F. Sodi (ed.), *Mesoamerica y norte de México: Siglo XI–XII,* vol. 2, pp. 541–564. Mexico City: Instituto Nacional de Antropología e Historia.

Sauer, C., and D. Brand. 1932. *Aztatlán: Prehistoric Mexican Frontier on the Pacific Coast.* Ibero-Americana, 1. Berkeley: University of California Press.

Joseph B. Mountjoy

SEE ALSO

Guasave and Related Sites

Aztec Culture and History

"Aztec" is a term used generally to refer to Late Postclassic (c. A.D. 1200–1520) central Mexican Nahua peoples. These people, however, did not refer to themselves as "Aztecs," but rather as members of specific ethnic groups normally tied to distinct city-states. The people customarily referred to as "Aztec" were, to themselves and their neighbors, Mexica or Tenochca, residents of the dual island city of Tenochtitlán-Tlatelolco (today, Mexico City). Their neighbors to the east were the Acolhua; to the west, the Tepaneca; to the south, the Chalca, Xochimilca, Mizquic, and others. The term "Aztec" is also frequently used to designate the military alliance of three of these powerful groups; thus, the Mexica of Tenochtitlán,

the Acolhua of Texcoco, and the Tepaneca of Tlacopan comprised the Aztec Triple Alliance, which dominated much of Mexico from 1430 to 1521.

The Aztecs often serve as a starting point for studies of Mesoamerican civilizations. They were the culmination of a long and turbulent history that saw the rise and demise of complex civilizations over some three millenia. The Aztecs exhibit full-blown and extensively documented Mesoamerican cultural themes such as urbanization, warfare, imperial expansion, dynastic hierarchies, human sacrifice, and polytheism, and therefore they provide a benchmark for the investigation of the progression of earlier cultures.

The Basin of Mexico was the heartland of Aztec civilization and imperial power. By 1519 this vast lake-dominated basin was occupied by a diversity of peoples of varying backgrounds and histories. Some of them were long-term inhabitants of the region, such as the Otomí. Others (such as the citizens of Culhuacan) were associated with the Toltecs, who achieved political supremacy in central Mexico three to five centuries prior to the rise of the Aztecs.

Many others were Chichimec immigrants who, in successive waves from at least Toltec times, settled in nearly every corner of the Basin of Mexico. These included the Mexica, reportedly the last of these nomadic and semi-nomadic groups to mesh with the Basin's settled village and urban dwellers. Still others were very late arrivals from throughout Mesoamerica, attracted to the urban possibilities and potential in the Basin of Mexico; included among these were certain luxury artisan groups who hailed from southern and eastern Mexico and settled in defined sections of the Basin's cities.

Thus, on the eve of the Spanish conquest, the population of the Basin of Mexico displayed considerable variety in cultural background, historical traditions, and language. These groups were also divided from one another by intense city-state loyalties, which provided the structural basis for political hierarchies and military alliances and conflicts. City-states (sing., *altepetl*) also provided the context for economic specialization and the worship of particular patron deities.

Despite these forces for fragmentation, Central Mexico nonetheless displayed important unifying characteristics. Nahuatl was a broadly used and understood language, and it often served as the language of political administration in non-Nahuatl-speaking communities. The region was also unified, in a general sense, by similarities in social and political stratification, economic

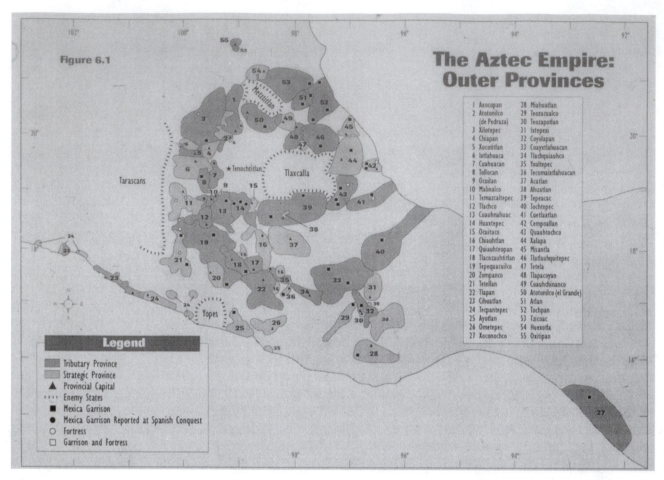

The Aztec Empire: Outer Provinces. Reproduced and used by permission from Frances Berdan, Richard Blanton, Elizabeth Boone, Mary Hodge, Michael Smith, and Emily Umberger, *Aztec Imperial Strategies,* p. 138 (figure 6.1). Washington, D.C.: Dumbarton Oaks Research Library and Collection, 1996.

specialization, religious rituals and beliefs, and more specific commonalities such as approaches toward warfare, mythologies, and types of acceptable apparel (although, for instance, the various city-states emphasized different legends and oral traditions and wore clothing designs that were hallmarks of their community and ethnic affiliations).

The Aztec (or Triple Alliance) Empire spread over much of modern-day Mexico, extending discontinuously from the Pacific to Gulf coast and from just north of the Basin of Mexico to the border of Guatemala. The imperial domain encompassed a wide range of environmental zones. The highland Basin of Mexico, at over 2,200 meters in elevation, served as the core of the empire. Its vast lake system provided a multitude of lacustrine resources, while its hillsides offered agricultural lands and forests. To the north are generally drier highlands where maize and maguey production predominated and tur-

quoise, eagles, and wild game supplemented the economy. To the east, west, and south, uplands are punctuated by gaping *barrancas* that dipped to elevations sufficiently low for the cultivation of cotton and other lowland crops. Maize, beans, chiles, and squashes provided staple sustenance for local highland and lowland populations, and surplus for trade and tribute. To the east, the descent from the highlands to the Gulf coast is relatively gradual, with an extensive lowland plain spreading to the coast—fertile ground for tropical resources from cultivated cacao and cotton to liquidambar and brilliant-feathered birds. To the west, the drop from highland to coast is more precipitous, but it nonetheless allowed space for production of valued crops such as cacao.

South of the Basin of Mexico, the landscape consists of a series of crumpled volcanic mountains and valleys: these lands were noted for agricultural productivity and the localized presence of specialized resources such as copal incense, amber, honey, and salt. The most southerly and southeasterly reaches of the empire are marked by tropical and semitropical lands and abounded in some of the most prized resources of the empire: shimmering feathers of a multitude of birds, jaguar skins, cacao, gold, amber, and jadeite. Political and military control of such extensive and diverse landscapes provided the Aztec (Triple Alliance) imperial powers with an abundance of agricultural staples and a vast array of diverse utilitarian and luxury resources. The flow of these resources into the Aztec heartland augmented the everyday sustenance of large urban populations, enriched the glamor of state and religious ceremonies, and enhanced the nobles' ability to display ostentatiously their status and wealth.

These broad regions defined the domain of the Aztec Empire in 1519, on the eve of the Spanish arrival. But it was more than four centuries earlier that the Mexica began their long and arduous road to empire. The Mexica migrated from northern regions into the Basin of Mexico like many nomadic and seminomadic groups before them. According to historic and mythic accounts, that migration lasted more than 200 years (A.D. 1110–1325). It began at an unidentified place called Aztlan ("Place of the Herons"); from there the Mexica traveled to Chicomoztoc ("Seven Caves"). This was reputedly a jumping-off point for many nomadic groups (collectively called Chichimeca), including the Tlaxcalan, Tepaneca, Chalca, Xochimilca, Tlahuica, and others, each separately journeying southward to settle in the Basin of Mexico and neighboring areas; the Mexica were reportedly the last to leave.

Although they are frequently depicted as nomadic hunters and gatherers, they had also acquired many of the trappings of settled agricultural life during their extended journey. They reportedly cultivated maize, chiles, and other crops, constructed substantial buildings (including temples for their patron god, Huitzilopochtli), measured time according to the sophisticated Mesoamerican calendar, and were well aware of prestige goods such as cacao and jadeite. The Mexica also exhibited a heterogeneous and complex social order: priests held considerable power, and rival factions developed. They were, however, generally considered "barbaric" by the sedentary peoples they encountered in their migration.

When the Mexica arrived in the Basin of Mexico, they found the area already densely populated. Intensive agriculture supported a large number of settlements characterized by complex social and political hierarchies and exhibiting a variety of economic specializations. The Basin was politically and militarily volatile, with the several city-states (*altepetl*) shifting in and out of alliances and warfare with their neighbors. The entrance of the Mexica onto this scene apparently generated ambivalent reactions: they were reputedly feared and despised for some of their customs, yet admired for their ferocity and skill as warriors. In this latter capacity, they were particularly valued by warring city-states as mercenaries.

Bouncing from settlement to settlement, they were finally chased into the lake itself, where they ended their long journey on a mid-lake island. The location had both symbolic and practical aspects. Symbolically, it was said that the fleeing Mexica saw an eagle resting on a prickly-pear cactus on that very island, signifying the destination foretold by the god Huitzilopochtli. Probably in commemoration of this, the beleaguered newcomers named their site Tenochtitlán ("Among the Stone-Cactus Fruit"), although it may have been named after their founding leader, Tenoch.

On the practical side, this island was one of the few locales still available for occupation in the Basin. It also provided abundant fish and aquatic birds and animals, was readily expandable by means of intensive *chinampa*-style drained-field cultivation, and was preeminently situated for efficient lake transportation and communication. On the problematic side, however, the small island lacked some important raw materials (such as stone and wood for building); it was beset with periodic flooding and had limited access to potable water. These problems were offset, however, as the island settlement expanded in both area and power.

The Mexica settled Tenochtitlán most probably in the year 1325. They spent the subsequent century developing their island site into a significant urban settlement, paying tribute and serving as military mercenaries to more powerful Basin city-states, and acquiring external lands and resources through this military service. Importantly, they also forged political alliances and legitimacy through strategic marriages: Acamapichtli, the first Tenochtitlán ruler (r. 1372–1391), was reportedly the son of a Mexica noble and a princess from Culhuacán. This heritage, traced through the Culhuacán dynasty, lent Acamapichtli and his successors a legitimacy derived from the highly revered and prestigious Toltecs.

Acamapichtli's son, Huitzilihuitl (r. 1391–1415), likewise used marriage to his advantage, tying the knot with a granddaughter of the powerful Tepanec ruler of neighboring Azcapotzalco. This tie eased the Mexicas' tribute load and gained them expanded economic and political perquisites in the Basin. These advantages lent greater

A

strength to the people of Tenochtitlán through the reigns of the subsequent two rulers, Chimalpopoca (r. 1415–1426) and Itzcoatl (r. 1426–1440); it was in 1428, during the latter's rule, that the Mexica, in collusion with the Acolhua of Texcoco, rebelled against powerful Azcapotzalco. While the Tepanec city of Azcapotzalco was razed (and maguey planted in its marketplace as a searing insult), the Tepanecs of nearby Tlacopan joined the Mexica and Acolhua in establishing a Triple Alliance that came to dominate central and southern Mexico over the subsequent ninety years.

The history of the Aztec Triple Alliance is a history of imperial expansion. Itzcoatl and his kingly allies scored repeated military victories within the Basin of Mexico. His successor Motecuhzoma Ilhuicamina (or Motecuhzoma I, r. 1440–1468) spread imperial domination beyond the Basin and into adjacent regions, controlling extensive lands, labor, and valuable resources. The Triple Alliance powers enlisted cooperative support from subservient city-states within the Valley of Mexico (such as Xochimilco and Culhuacán) for far-flung military ventures over the remaining history of the empire, as each successive ruler (Axayacatl, r. 1468–1481; Tizoc, r. 1481–1486) progressively broadened the bounds of the empire. Some of the most aggressive expansion took place under the rulership of Ahuitzotl (r. 1486–1502); his successor, Motecuhzoma Xocoyotzin (or Motecuhzoma II, r. 1502–1520), while extending the empire somewhat, spent a good deal of his military energies in consolidating already-conquered lands and in quelling rebellions.

This is not to suggest that the empire expanded neatly and smoothly. The Mexica and their allies suffered many setbacks in their quest for imperial rule. In the mid-1400s a serious famine debilitated the people of the Basin for four years, and in 1510 a devastating flood laid waste to much of Tenochtitlán. The Aztec armies suffered extreme losses in a campaign against the Tarascans to the west, and the Triple Alliance military forces were never able to conquer the staunch Tlaxcalans, who maintained their autonomy fully within the bounds of the Triple Alliance Empire. Especially as the empire expanded farther and farther afield, rebellions became more and more common.

Imperial goals had internal and external correlates and consequences. For the imperial capitals, especially Tenochtitlán, military expansion was associated with rapidly growing urban population, intensification in social hierarchy and economic specialization, and increasingly flamboyant religious structures and ceremonies. In addition, distant military successes increased the capacity of the ruling elite to control and display exotic sumptuary trappings such as precious jadeite and tropical feathers; they provided urban artisans with raw and semimanufactured materials for their artistry; they increased the availability of human sacrifices for religious ceremonies; they reinforced the values of warfare and a commitment to warrior training; and they enhanced the ability of these powerful rulers to display their power and intimidate recalcitrant city-state rulers.

In 1519, on the eve of Spanish contact, the Basin of Mexico as a whole may have supported as many as one million inhabitants. It was demographically dominated by the urban core of Tenochtitlán-Tlatelolco, with an estimated 150,000 to 200,000 residents; the second-largest Basin city, Texcoco, embraced only around 30,000 urban inhabitants. At the time of Tenochtitlán's settlement in 1325, the tiny island could support only small numbers of people and few religious and public buildings. As the Mexica population outgrew its island domain, the process of urban expansion was systematic and followed Mexica notions of geographic, social, and symbolic space.

The central district of the city, as with other central Mexican cities, was devoted primarily to religious structures, highlighting the prominent place of ritual and ceremony in Mexica life. Nearby were the expansive palaces of past and present rulers and other high-ranking nobles. Adjacent to Tlatelolco's ceremonial district was the greatest marketplace in the land. Over all, major religious, political, and economic functions were geographically featured in the urban core. The remainder of the city was divided into four quarters, each of which was further subdivided into residential districts usually called *calpulli* (although *tlaxilacalli* is likely a more appropriate term). These were not merely places of residence, but also significant social entities: each *calpulli* contained a temple and a school, served as a military and taxation unit, and sometimes focused on an economic specialization.

The physical growth of Tenochtitlán-Tlatelolco (and neighboring lakeside cities) was accomplished through the creation of highly productive drained field land plots in the surrounding shallow lake bed. Called *chinampas* and miscalled "floating gardens," these stable plots provided multiple crops each year and resulted in a settlement pattern woven with canals. Well-established *chinampas* also supported resident households, often of joint families and therefore providing many hands for the labor-intensive cultivation.

As the Basin cities grew in size, they also expanded in social and political complexity. The social order was fundamentally divided between nobles and commoners, based on birthright and, to a lesser extent, on extraordinary achievement. Nobles claimed high social and political positions as well as control over basic resources (land and labor) and sumptuary display of precious goods (such as tropical-feather headdresses and jadeite ornaments) and other rights (such as polygyny and two-story houses). A ruler (*tlatoani*) was selected from the ranks of the nobility, as were judges and other high-ranking officials of government. Noble boys were typically educated in *calmecac,* schools run by priests and providing an erudite, administrative, and martial curriculum. This prepared the young nobles for the more prestigious positions in the society—officials in the massive bureaucracy, priests, military officers, teachers, and similar occupations. Some noble girls were trained formally as priestesses. Commoners (sing., *macehualli*) were the primary producers in the society, and their labor and production supported not only themselves but also an elevated standard of living for the nobles. They were farmers, fishermen, artisans of utilitarian objects, porters, and similar laborers. Formal education for commoner boys focused on martial training in *telpochcalli* (*calpulli* schools), as all were expected to be available for service in the interminable imperial wars. Both boys and girls were educated in *cuicacalli* ("houses of song"), where they learned songs and dances for the many and frequent religious rituals. It appears that early in the history of the empire some commoners were successful at achieving noble or quasi-noble status through notable battlefield feats. That avenue for advancement, however, seems to have become increasingly curbed over time; the number of noble progeny competing for elite positions was expanding disproportionately as a result of polygynous unions.

While the social and political hierarchy appears to have become more complex and solidified, "intermediate positions" of luxury artisans and long distance merchants became more visible and well established. Although intense economic specialization was already well entrenched throughout Mesoamerica, these urbanites particularly focused their energies and resources on economic specializations geared toward noble and political consumption: featherwork for headgear and shields; jadeite, turquoise, and gold objects for exquisite ornamentation; and employment of merchants (*pochteca*) as spies and envoys in the service of the state. A result of the high demand and value of their artistry and services was substantial wealth, although they were not accorded the privileges and rights of noble rank.

The polytheistic religion of the Mexica and their neighbors was manifest in imposing temples and flamboyant ceremonies. The Great Temple (Templo Mayor) of Tenochtitlán housed sanctuaries for the Mexica patron god, Huitzilopochtli, and the longstanding Mesoamerican rain deity, Tláloc. This dual temple dominated Tenochtitlán's central ceremonial district, and its recent (1978–1982) excavation has revealed seven separate building periods, each progressively expanding the size of this structure. Excavations around the sacred precinct have also revealed the deposition of more than 100 offerings containing more than 7,000 material remains, ranging from stone idols to jadeite beads to human skulls. Military successes provided tribute income to the state to support expansion in religious building, priestly personnel, and ceremonial paraphernalia. Battlefield captives also served as sacrificial offerings to the many Aztec deities, and ritual sacrificial events gained in magnitude as the empire vanquished city-state after city-state.

Warfare was a way of life among the Mexica, their neighbors, and their enemies. Wars transformed into territorial conquest provided the Triple Alliance powers with lands, labor, and portable tributes to support and embellish life in the urban capitals. But the Aztecs were not always successful on the battlefield; especially formidable were the tenacious Tlaxcalans to the east of the Basin of Mexico. Repeated wars between the Triple Alliance and Tlaxcala were termed "flowery wars," ostensibly conducted on a quasi-ritual level for purposes of obtaining human sacrifices and providing novice warriors with battlefield experience. Yet the Mexica and their allies frequently fared poorly in these confrontations, and it is likely that they were trying in earnest to conquer the Tlaxcalans but were simply unable to do so.

In addition to having substantial impact on urban Aztec life, imperial expansion also had significant consequences for conquered and "annexed" peripheries. Areas subdued by military force served as tributary provinces in the imperial arrangement. But many other city-states and groups of city-states became part of the empire through more diplomatic and less violent means; these areas often served strategic functions and can be called "strategic provinces."

For most tributary provinces, Aztec conquest did little to change the political arrangements of subjugated city-states. Normally the existing ruler (*tlatoani*) was allowed to remain in local power as long as he displayed subservience and made tribute payments. One or more

A

tribute collectors were always based in conquered regions; at times an Aztec governor was installed in an especially critical area; and at times a military garrison was established in a particularly volatile region. The imperial powers did maintain certain political and social expectations: marriages along elite lines solidified conquests into stronger loyalties, and compulsory service by conquered nobles in imperial palaces symbolized subservience and allowed for their direct supervision.

Strategic provinces were valued for their geographic location along unstable borderlands or for their situation astride critical transportation routes. Many of them maintained low-level warfare with enemy city-states, holding those borders for the empire with little or no cost to the imperial armies. Their relations with the empire were subservient, to be sure, but with more elements of reciprocity in evidence: "gifts" rather than tribute were given, presents were often delivered to them by the Triple Alliance rulers as well, and kinship ties were forged.

The major impact of imperial conquest on vanquished city-states was economic. Tributary city-states were grouped into "provinces" for administrative ease, and regular payments in tribute goods were demanded of these provinces. There were thirty-eight such provinces in 1519; their tribute is recorded in the Matrícula de Tributos and Codex Mendoza. Typically a tributary province paid in goods readily available to it—food staples, clothing, utilitarian crafts, or luxury raw materials; these goods were available to the people of the province through their own local production or through longstanding trading relations.

As the imperial armies moved into more and more distant regions, a greater variety of resources came under the empire's control. As the empire grew, economic control expanded increasingly into regions well endowed with precious resources such as jadeite, gold, and especially tropical feathers. Access to these luxuries coincided well with the increase in the number of nobles and their need for elaborate, socially linked finery. The payment of large quantities of tribute channeled much economic production from the provinces to the urban imperial core. At the same time, however, it stimulated a good deal of economic specialization in the outlying areas, since much of the tribute demanded was in the form of manufactured or partially fashioned goods rather than raw materials.

These interwoven processes, affecting both imperial core and outlying peripheries, yielded varying relationships over time throughout central Mexico. An enemy one year was transformed into a conquered subject the next, to be later enlisted as an uneasy ally in further joint conquests; this was the case with many city-states in the Basin of Mexico during Aztec imperial growth. Alternatively, a distant enemy was coerced into "strategic" status and performed useful borderland functions for the empire until it was no longer a borderland; it then moved into "tributary" status while more distant city-states took on "strategic" functions. These scenarios exemplify the complex and dynamic character of this short-lived imperial enterprise.

FURTHER READINGS

Barlow, R. H. 1949. *The Extent of the Empire of the Culhua Mexica.* Ibero-Americana, 28. Berkeley and Los Angeles: University of California Press.

Berdan, F. F. 1982. *The Aztecs of Central Mexico: An Imperial Society.* New York: Holt, Rinehart and Winston.

Berdan, F. F., and P. R. Anawalt (eds.). 1992. *The Codex Mendoza.* Berkeley: University of California Press.

Berdan, F. F., R. E. Blanton, E. H. Boone, M. G. Hodge, M. E. Smith, and E. Umberger. 1996. *Aztec Imperial Strategies.* Washington, D.C.: Dumbarton Oaks.

Boone, E. H. (ed.). 1987. *The Aztec Templo Mayor.* Washington, D.C.: Dumbarton Oaks.

Bray, W. 1968. *Everyday Life of the Aztecs.* New York: G. P. Putnam.

Carrasco, P. 1971. The Peoples of Central Mexico and Their Historical Traditions. In G. F. Ekholm and I. Bernal (eds.), *Handbook of Middle American Indians,* vol. 11, pp. 459–473. Austin: University of Texas Press.

Davies, N. 1987. *The Aztec Empire: The Toltec Resurgence.* Norman: University of Oklahoma Press.

Gibson, C. 1964. *The Aztecs under Spanish Rule.* Stanford: Stanford University Press.

Hodge, M. G., and M. E. Smith (eds.). 1994. *Economies and Polities in the Aztec Realm.* Studies in Culture and Society, 6. Austin, Albany: Institute for Mesoamerican Studies, SUNY Albany, and University of Texas Press.

Lockhart, J. 1992. *Nahuas after the Conquest.* Stanford: Stanford University Press.

Smith, M. E. 1996. *The Aztecs.* Cambridge: Blackwell.

Frances F. Berdan

SEE ALSO

Central Mexican Religion; Tenochtitlán: Ceremonial Center; Tenochtitlán: Imperial Ritual Landscape; Tenochtitlán: Palaces; Tenochtitlán-Tlatelolco

B

Bajío Region (Guanajuato and Adjacent States, Mexico)

A fertile and spacious plain at about 1,600 meters elevation, with low hills and a few mountains, in the northeastern Central Highlands. It includes the central part of the modern state of Guanajuato, as well as parts of Jalisco, Querétaro, and Michoacán. Water resources are derived from the Lerma River and other watercourses, and soils are deep and fertile, of alluvial and volcanic origin. Based on ceramic typologies and settlement patterns, Castañeda and colleagues have proposed three broad pre-Hispanic periods: an initial occupation during the Formative period; depopulation during the Early Postclassic (A.D. 800 to early 1300s); and a final repopulation in the late 1300s, extending into the early 1400s.

During the first period, cultures such as the Chupícuaro were characterized by hierarchical organization, exhaustive exploitation of natural resources, and agriculture in cultivable areas. From A.D. 400 to 900, several groups experienced population growth and development of distinctive features. Settlements were scattered in hilltop, high slope, and plateau areas, with terraces for housing and cultivation. Several political units joined in a semiautonomous confederation, with a common pottery tradition of red and buff and white wares *(blanco levantado)*. With its productivity enhanced through such organization, the area became attractive to powerful neighbors, such as Teotihuacán, and Teotihuacán-style objects appear at many sites, indicating the presence of a Teotihuacán-related minority group living among the local populations.

Around A.D. 900, a period of decreasing population of the Bajío by agriculturalists began; this was completed by around 1350. During the period of declining population, communities were established in inaccessible places—some, such as La Gloria and Peralta, with defensive constructions. The architectural tradition includes round structures and the use of columns. Ceramics from this period include red wares and two-color designs, such as black on white. Ceramics shared with the Tula region do not include those from early Tula, but instead are from periods of Tula's height and decline (Corral Terminal to Tollan phase), found at southern Bajío sites such as La Magdalena, El Cerrito, and La Griega, and at the northern Bajío sites Carabino and El Cópora. Ceramic artifacts include pipes, perfuming pots, incense burners, Mazapan figurines, and Tollan phase vessels such as Polished Orange *(Naranja pulido)*, Painted Orange *(Naranja a brochazos)*, and some Plumbate. These are associated with local pottery with simple forms and finishes.

Settlements show varying degrees of Toltec influence. Carabino resembles a small Tula, with a metropolitan pattern suggesting occupation by people from the capital. In contrast, El Cerrito, which was the main center for a large local population with some elements imposed from Tula, has a smaller nucleated area. The presence of a Tula-related group in this depopulating area is puzzling; possibly some areas of the Bajío were segments of a northern and western province of the Toltec Empire, as suggested by Kirchhoff. The breakdown of the Toltec Empire coincided with the depopulation of the southern Bajío, and settlements remained only along the Lerma River. The economy was mixed (hunting-gathering and agriculture), pottery was monochromatic thick paste, and old settlements were reused.

B

After about 1359, the Bajío region drew the attention of developing political centers in Tarascan Michoacán and the Aztec Basin of Mexico. The Aztec Mexica of Tenochtitlán came to dominate the province of Xilotepec from the 1430s to about 1480, while Tarascans conquered Acámbaro and Maravatío. Documentary sources indicate a local, seminucleated population of Otomís, but as the Bajío became a buffer zone between competing Mexica and Tarascans, local populations were forced to relocate within the region.

FURTHER READINGS

Acuña, R. (ed.). 1988. Relación de la Villa de Celaya y su partido. In *Relaciones geográficas del siglo XVI: Michoacán,* vol. 5, part 9, pp. 47–72. Mexico City: Universidad Nacional Autónoma de México.

———. (ed.). 1988. Relación de Querétaro. In *Relaciones geográficas del siglo XVI: Michoacán,* vol. 5, part 9, pp. 207–248. Mexico City: Universidad Nacional Autónoma de México.

Blancas Tome, G. 1979. *Projecto atlas de arte rupestre del estado de Guanajuato.* Archivo del Centro Regional de Guanajuato, México. Mexico City: Instituto Nacional de Antropología e Historia.

Brambila Paz, R. 1988. 1993. Datos generales del Bajío. *Cuadernos de Arquitectura Mesoamericana* 25:3–10.

Brambila Paz, R., A. M. Crespo, and J. C. Saint-Charles. 1993. Juegos de pelota en el Bajío. *Cuadernos de Arquitectura Mesoamericana* 25:89–95.

Braniff, B. 1993. El norte de México. In *El Poblamiento de México, El México Prehispánico,* pp. 307–325. Mexico City: TI, Secretaría de Gobernación.

Carrasco, P. 1979 [1950]. *Los Otomies: Cultura e historia prehispánica de los pueblos mesoamericanos de habla otomiana.* Mexico City: Biblioteca Enciclopédica del Estado de México.

Crespo, A. M., and R. Brambila Paz. 1991. *Querétaro prehispánico.* Mexico City: Instituto Nacional de Antropología e Historia.

Crespo, A. M., and C. Viramentes (eds.). 1996. *Tiempo y teritorio en arqueología: El Centro-Norte de México.* Mexico City: Instituto Nacional de Antropología e Historia.

Rosa Brambila Paz

SEE ALSO
Chupícuaro

Stucco figure of a cat divinity at Balamkú. Photo courtesy of the author.

Balamkú (Campeche, Mexico)

This recently discovered site was occupied from the Late Formative period (300 B.C.), reached its peak in the Early Classic period (A.D. 300–600), and continued its development to the Terminal Classic period (A.D. 900), based on ceramic phase diagnostics. It covered about 10 square kilometers, comprising architectural groups clustered 150 to 180 meters apart. A survey located two acropolises, a ball court, a type "E" astronomical group, round stone altars, stelae, and column fragments. The most notable feature is the polychrome stucco façade of Structure B-I-A, with high-relief figures related to earth, water, underworld, and Balamkú's rulers. Balamkú was one of a chain of interacting Maya centers, beginning in Guatemala's central Petén region and continuing to Edzná.

FURTHER READINGS

Baudez, C.-F. 1996. La casa de los cuatro reyes de Balamkú. *Arqueología Mexicana* 3.18:36–41.

García Cruz, F. 1991. Balamkú: A New Archaeological Site in Campeche. *Mexicon* 13.3:42–44.

———. 1994. Balamkú. *Arqueología Mexicana* 1.5:59–60.

Florentino García Cruz

Balcón de Montezuma (Tamaulipas, Mexico)

Roughly 7 hectares in extent and lying atop a defensible hilltop with canyons running along the northern and southern sides, Balcón de Montezuma probably dates from the Late Classic and Postclassic periods; it consists of more than 90 circular stone foundations grouped around two irregularly shaped plaza areas. Each plaza contains a small altar in its center (3 meters in diameter, 50 cm in height). An archaeological and conservation project was undertaken at the site by Jesús Nárez from 1988 to 1990.

A sloped outcrop of sedimentary limestone defines the western entrance to the site, a staircase formed by removal of large stone slabs. The circular stone foundations measure between 9 and 11 meters across and vary in height from a few centimeters to 2 meters; the higher platforms have one or two steps built into the walls. These features probably formed the base for thatched-roof structures. Artifactual remains, including ceramics, spindle whorls, grinding stones, and hearths, were found on what were probably the floor surfaces of these structures, and they indicate a residential function; burials were found below the floor surfaces within the foundations.

Dating of occupation is problematic because radiocarbon dates have not yet been obtained. Ceramics resemble materials found farther south in Tamaulipas and the Huastec zone in Veracruz and San Luis Potosí, in the Late Classic through Postclassic periods. Balcón may have been settled by northern nomadic groups, or Chichimeca, and influenced by Huastec groups to the south; or it may represent the northernmost extent of Huastec occupation, and thus the northernmost edge of Mesoamerican civilization, although more archaeological work is needed better to define the concept of this northeastern frontier.

FURTHER READINGS

Michelet, D. 1995. La zona nororiental en el Clásico. In L. Manzanilla and L. López Luján (eds.), *Historia antigua de México,* vol. 2, *El horizonte clásico,* pp. 206–226. Mexico City: Instituto Nacional de Antropología e Historia.

Nárez, J. 1992. *Materiales arqueológicas de Balcón de Montezuma, Tamaulipas.* Mexico City: Instituto Nacional de Antropología e Historia.

Mary Pye

SEE ALSO

Northern Arid Zone

Ball Game

Played on a masonry court with a rubber ball by two opposing teams, the Native American ball game was widely known in Mesoamerica and Central America. Its range extended from the U.S. Southwest into the Amazon region of South America (over an area of 2,500,000 square kilometers), and it was played for at least two thousand years prior to European contact.

The object of the game, as indicated by archaeological and ethnohistoric evidence, was to score a goal by propelling the ball onto the ground of the opposing team's end of the court, or through a ring or other marker along the side of the court. As in modern soccer, players could not use their hands to propel the ball, and the game in play may have resembled soccer, with considerable action. The game is known to us from archaeological remains of courts and court markers, from artistic depictions on vases and murals or as figurines and sculpture, and from ethnohistoric accounts describing the game and its ritual and political importance. Although the game had important ideological overtones, it was also no doubt a widespread form of more casual recreation, and the outcome of a game was the focus of considerable gambling action, with bets of all sizes and bettors of all social classes.

Ethnohistoric accounts describe Aztec nobility and warrior classes playing a competitive version of the game *(tlachtli),* which gained the winners goods and prestige. The importance and popularity of the game among the Aztecs at the time of contact is indicated by the annual importation of approximately sixteen thousand rubber balls into Aztec Tenochtitlán from the tropical lowlands, where rubber trees grew. In the Maya area, the game reached a zenith of elaboration, as evidenced by the varied paraphernalia and depictions on fixed and portable art, as well as the more than two thousand masonry ball courts that have been identified.

Rules of Play

Several distinct ball games were played by various groups throughout ancient Mesoamerica, but the most widespread and important was the hip-ball game played with a rubber ball. Artistic representations indicate that players struck a fast-moving ball with their hips in returning a volley from the opposing end of an elongated court. Ethnohistoric and ethnographic accounts suggest that the ball was kept aloft as long as possible, with points scored when the ball touched the ground of the opposing team's end of the court.

Many ball courts had parallel-running benches attached to the interiors of the side playing walls defining the alleyway. These surfaces were frequently sloping, to keep the ball in the air when struck, thereby adding to the complexity and strategy of the sport. During the Postclassic period, many courts had sculpted, vertically oriented stone rings tenoned into the upper side walls of the

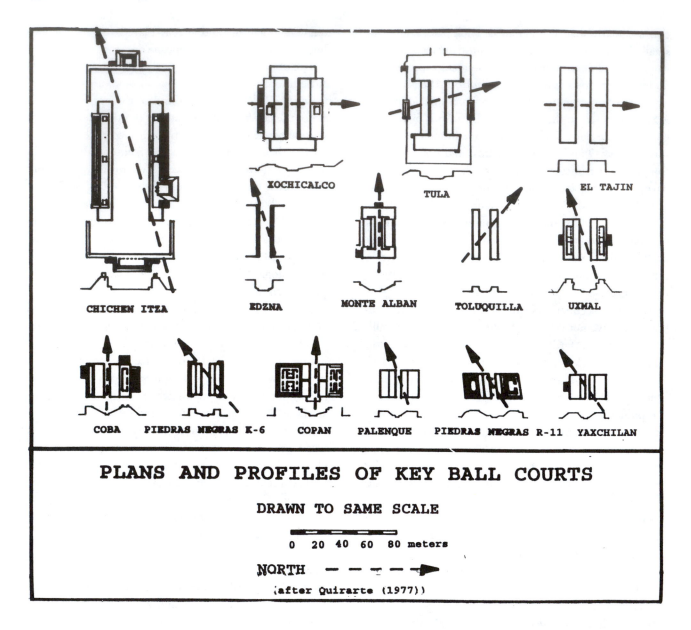

XOCHICALCO

TULA

EL TAJIN

CHICHEN ITZA

EDZNA

MONTE ALBAN

TOLUQUILLA

UXMAL

COBA

PIEDRAS NEGRAS K-6

COPAN

PALENQUE

PIEDRAS NEGRAS R-11

YAXCHILAN

PLANS AND PROFILES OF KEY BALL COURTS

DRAWN TO SAME SCALE

0   20   40   60   80 meters

NORTH — — — — →

(after Quirarte (1977))

playing alley; passing the ball through this ring must have been extremely difficult, and important to the outcome of the game.

Equipment

Most scenes of the ball game show players protected by a padded belt or girdle over the hips, sometimes extending above the abdomen. Probably made of leather and/or reed, such gear would have protected the body from the impact of the ball and from injury sustained in falls and slides. Sculpted stone replicas of these padded belts are called "yokes" *(yugos),* and examples from the Classic period, particularly from the Gulf Coast and southern Pacific Coast, are reported. Yokes or similar padded belt-like gear are seen on figurines and in painted scenes, as are depictions of knee pads worn on one or both knees.

Other ball game paraphernalia included the *hacha* (a thin stone-headed implement shaped like an axe) and the *palma* (a palmate-shaped stone), used particularly in the non-Maya lowlands of the Gulf Coast and the Soconusco. Loop-handled handstones are sometimes associated with this predominantly Middle Classic to Early Postclassic period ball game assemblage. These sculpted stone representations of the accouterments of a version of the game, together with the yoke, are found as offerings in symbolic contexts, as well as in pictorial representations of ballplayers. The latter show the *palma* and perhaps the *hacha* as elongated slablike gear secured to the inside of the yoke worn around the player's hips, and projecting upward toward the player's neck. Their function is uncertain; perhaps they serve as breastplates for additional protection from the ball, or they may represent paddles or sticks used in a significantly modified version of hip-ball, and carried in this manner. Highly stylized and frequently carved to express anthropomorphic and zoomorphic forms, stone *palmas, hachas,* and (to a lesser degree) yokes reveal aspects of ball game symbolism, especially in images of sacrifice and fertility.

Architecture: Form, Function, and Location

The basic form of the ball court was an elongated playing alley defined by parallel-running side walls, frequently identified with a low-lying, projecting bench. End zones consisted of two more open areas beyond the side walls. Masonry courts sometimes included tenoned stone rings or markers projecting from the side walls of the alley, as well as centrally placed alley-marker stones at floor level. Ball courts were situated principally in the central precinct of a community in proximity to other public buildings.

Layout and architecture varied markedly from region to region. Taladoire has reviewed ball courts and has proposed a formal typology consisting of fourteen types for Mesoamerica. His review is an important contribution, but there are difficulties in reconstructing meaningful units of analysis and defining significant architectural attributes.

Perhaps the most distinctive ball court plan is the I-shaped masonry court, with examples as far north as Casas Grandes (northern Chihuahua) and as far south as Copán (Honduras). The I-shape suggests well-defined end zones for the game. Some suggest a symbolic representation of a sacrificed human body in repose, with the severed head represented by the rubber ball.

Considerable variation from the I-shape exists. Many formal ball courts are open ended, lacking one or both end zones—a form attested from northern Mexico to the Maya Lowlands. One such style is the basin-like *palangana* ("washbasin") ball court, defined by rectangular playing alleys surrounded by walls of consistent height, but lacking end zones. *Palangana* courts occur in the Guatemalan Highlands and southern Mexican Highlands, but may have their greatest antiquity in the Gulf Lowlands. One of the earliest proposed ball courts in Mesoamerica is of the *palangana* type and is found at San Lorenzo (Veracruz), associated with late Olmec occupation.

Sunken courts associated with the I-shaped form and with variations of the open-ended form have an early origin as well. The principal courts at Cerros (Belize) and Monte Albán (Oaxaca) were constructed as sunken ball courts as early as the Late Formative period, and at Monte Albán remained that way throughout the Zapotecan occupation.

In the U.S. Southwest from around A.D. 700 to 1250, the typical Hohokam ball court consisted of a slightly concave playing field with a mounded clay surface on either side. Wilcox has carefully articulated the function of these structures, arguing convincingly against their primary use as dance plazas. Balls made from guayule, an indigenous desert plant, have been found in Hohokam towns.

In the Antilles by A.D. 700, the ball game was played on broad clay surfaces. Oviedo's eyewitness accounts indicate large teams (twenty to thirty players on a side) and heavy betting. In addition to the rubber ball (from local rubber sources), paraphernalia may have included collars (representations of which are sculpted in stone); other sculpted representations include elbow-shaped stones of uncertain function. This game resembles less the hip-ball game of mainland Mesoamerica, and probably has its origins with Taino migrations from South America into the Antilles. Stern suggests that the rubber ball game in all its later manifestations had an origin in rubber-tree-rich Amazonia.

Size of Ball Courts

Overall dimensions of ball courts vary considerably within a range of 250 × 135 meters for the largest quadrangular ball court and ceremonial plaza, reported from Pueblo Viejo (Cuba), to the narrow and diminutive ball court at Lamanai (Belize), with a playing alley of 16 × 2 meters. In the Maya Lowlands, alleys were usually between 14 and 35 meters long and between 3 and 12 meters wide. Alley size seems to have been less standardized elsewhere in Mesoamerica. The largest and perhaps the grandest of all Mesoamerican ball courts is the Great Ballcourt at Chichén Itzá, a 70 × 168 meter playing field with towering sidewall structures.

In highland Mexico, ball courts at Tula and Xochicalco seem to have been expanded during the Early Postclassic period, perhaps linking these centers with Chichén Itzá into a redefined pan-Mesoamerican ball game tradition. Nevertheless, there persists the far more common smaller court size, and the associated playing rules implied by these dimensions. At Chichén Itzá, at least twelve other

B

ball courts are of the smaller, more standardized Maya form.

Ball Court Markers

Many ball courts had stone markers centrally placed along the alleyways. Markers included rings, posts, and disk-shaped alley floor stones. The most embellished forms of the latter are from the Maya area and are short, cylindrical, altar-like stones, sometimes carved to depict the importance of the game to the elites. An unusual example of this general type is the carved, dome-shaped stone from the Great Ballcourt at Chichén Itzá, possibly used for human heart excision.

Stone staffs or marker posts have been identified in versions of the game played in the highlands of Mexico; such a marker was found at the La Ventilla compound of Teotihuacán. This marker is similar to one from Tikal (Guatemala), suggesting Teotihuacán influence at Tikal during the Early Classic period, and perhaps the presence of a version of the game as it was played in the highlands.

Multiple Ball Courts and Their Implications

Many large communities had more than one ball court within their central precincts of monumental architecture. Sometimes these courts were conjoined: double ball courts were often attached at right angles near their end zones, but some ran parallel to each other, permitting two games to be played simultaneously and viewed by the same audience. A triple court at Tikal allowed three games to be played and viewed at the same time. A few large centers contained several ball courts, among them Chichén Itzá (13), Kaminaljuyú (12), El Tajín (11), Monte Albán (8), Los Horcones (5), Rana (5), and Tikal (5). Possibly the presence of multiple courts indicates an attempt to control intragroup conflict, and some scholars associate multiple ball courts with moiety or clan divisions, suggesting that internal rivalries were settled in part by the game.

No ball court has been discovered at Teotihuacán, but murals at the Tepantitla compound there show the game being played on a formal ball court. Informal earthen playing surfaces were no doubt widely in use, but would show few archaeological manifestations except, possibly, a packed earth surface and marker posts. Formal masonry courts suggest corporate labor projects, sanctioned by community authority. Furthermore, recent interpretations of the game in the Maya Lowlands suggest that elaborate pre- and post-ball game pageantry took place on the staircases and surfaces of monumental structures, away

from the courts themselves. At sites with more than one court, some ball courts may have functioned as staging areas for a game played in a neighboring court.

Ball Game Sacrifice and Symbolism

Scholars have frequently associated the game with human blood sacrifice. Much of our understanding of the myth and significance of the ball game comes from the account of the Third Creation in the Maya epic, the *Popul Vuh*, wherein both generations of Hero Twins, avatars of the Sun and Venus, are sacrificed by decapitation and then reborn. Numerous portrayals of the game show decapitation of a ballplayer, the same image emphasized in the *Popul Vuh*. Gillespie associates this ritual death with a deeper, pan-American Rolling Head myth and its association with ball games of all types. She and other scholars see a strong fertility symbolism in this imagery, associated with seasonality and the annual—possibly diurnal—position of astronomical bodies. Blood sacrifice in many forms, though principally decapitation, is identified with the game.

Gambling

In addition to its sacred and political ceremonial functions, the game provided recreational play and chances for winning (or losing) bets, between and within villages. Betting on games was widespread, spirited, and sometimes costly. People would wager their goods, holdings of land or exchange media (such as mantles and cacao beans), slaves, and even themselves as indentured servants. One chronicler indicated that the fate of a kingdom rested on the outcome of a game in highland Mexico, but it is unlikely that such stakes were ever honored. Yet this indicates the strength of the practice of gambling, and it also suggests political overtones to the ball game. The stakes associated with these wagers were frequently high.

Conflict Resolution

The game's role in conflict resolution has received recent scholarly attention, with investigators studying the game's role in mediating disputes; the location of ball courts within a region may reveal the ball game's adjudicating function. Of the sixteen ball courts known in the Valley of Oaxaca during Monte Albán II times, eleven are situated on the valley's periphery. This was a period of significant population expansion outside the valley, thus increasing the possibility of boundary disputes and rendering peripheral populations along the interregional border more difficult to control. Establishment of ball courts and playing the ball game may have mediated disputes and kept peripheral populations in contact with central authority.

In some regions, core area and peripheral communities differed as to the location of the ball court within the community. Among the Hohokam of the U.S. Southwest, and, to a degree, in the Maya Lowlands and adjacent Southeastern Periphery, communities in the core of the culture area built courts in the central part of town, while in the hinterlands, courts were placed on the outskirts of town. These spatial arrangements suggest that formal ball courts were introduced to the hinterlands by way of the core area, perhaps as an invitation from the dominant group to participate in its domain. Ball courts would have been constructed on the outskirts if the central area of a community were already built up, and location there may also have expressed the peripheral town's wish to promote formal interaction and to reduce the intimidation effect of powerful "foreigners."

FURTHER READINGS

Alegria, R. E. 1983. *Ball Courts and Ceremonial Plazas in the West Indies*. New Haven: Yale University Press.

Gillespie, S. D. 1991. Ballgames and Boundaries. In V. L. Scarborough and D. R. Wilcox (eds.), *The Mesoamerican Ballgame*, pp. 317–345.

Leyenaar, T. J. J., and L. A. Parsons. 1988. *Ulama: The Ballgame of the Mayas and Aztecs*. Leiden: Spruyt, Van Mantgem and De Does.

Quirarte, J. 1977. The Ballcourt in Mesoamerica: Its Architectural Development. In A. Cordy-Collins (ed.), *Pre-Columbian Art History*, pp. 191–212. Palo Alto: Peek.

Scarborough, V. L., and D. R. Wilcox (eds.). 1991. *The Mesoamerican Ballgame*. Tucson: University of Arizona Press.

Stern, T. 1949. *The Rubber-Ball Game of the Americas*. Monographs of the American Ethnological Society, 17. New York: J. J. Augustin.

Taladoire, E. 1981. *Les terrains de jeu de balle (Mesoamérique et Sud-Ouest des États-Unis)*. Études Mesoaméricaines, series 2, no. 4. Mexico City: Mission Archéologique et Ethnologique Française au Mexique.

Wilcox, D. R., and C. Sternberg. 1983. *Hohokam Ballcourts and Their Interpretation*. Arizona State Museum Archaeological Series, 160. Tucson.

Vernon Scarborough

SEE ALSO
Games and Gambling

Bálsamo, El (Escuintla, Guatemala)

A large center in the Pacific Lowlands, occupied c. 500–200 B.C. Surrounding surface scatters and low mounds represent habitation. Occupation in the vicinity occurred earlier, but mounds were built at the center during the Late Formative period, although chronology has been debated because of the problem of redeposition in mound fill. Platform mounds up to 10 meters in height are aligned about 16° E of N, forming long, narrow plazas. A series of shallow ponds was constructed on Mound A, possibly for ritual use. Ten stone sculptures have been found in the area. Two large, plain slabs and a small crouching feline are definitely from Bálsamo, but there are no "pot-belly" boulder sculptures similar to those at nearby Monte Alto. Chipped stone tools are of obsidian, in the form of bipolar flakes and prismatic blades, imported from two sources in the Guatemalan highlands. Local plain or coarsely incised brown or orange pottery is common, but many rare vessels, especially white ware, came from the highlands. Coastal products sent in exchange remain unknown, but cotton, cacao, feathers, and jaguar pelts are among the possibilities.

FURTHER READINGS

Clewlow, C. W., and H. F. Wells. 1987. El Bálsamo: A Middle Preclassic Complex on the South Coast of Guatemala. In G. W. Pahl (ed.), *The Periphery of the Southeastern Classic Maya Realm*, pp. 27–40. UCLA Latin American Studies, 61. Los Angeles: UCLA Latin American Center Publications.

Heller, L., and B. L. Stark. 1989. Economic Organization and Social Context of a Preclassic Center on the Pacific Coast of Guatemala: El Bálsamo. In F. J. Bové and L. Heller (eds.), *New Frontiers in the Archaeology of the Pacific Coast of Southern Mesoamerica*, pp. 43–64. Anthropological Research Papers, 39. Tempe: Arizona State University.

Shook, E. M., and M. P. Hatch. 1978. The Ruins of El Bálsamo, Department of Escuintla, Guatemala. *Journal of New World Archaeology* 3:1–37.

Stark, B. L., L. Heller, F. W. Nelson, R. Bishop, D. M. Pearsall, D. S. Whitley, and H. Wells. 1985. El Bálsamo Residential Investigations: A Pilot Project and Research Issues. *American Anthropologist* 87:100–111.

Barbara L. Stark

B

SEE ALSO
Soconusco–South Pacific Coast and Piedmont Region

Balser, Carlos (1903–1995)

A native of San José, Costa Rica, Balser never formally trained as an archaeologist, but he nonetheless made significant contributions to the profession through his studies of prehistoric metallurgy and jade-working techniques. Trained in Europe as a painter, he worked closely with Doris Stone in the late 1940s to convert the Bellavista Fortress in San José into a new home for the National Museum of Costa Rica. He often credited his interest in pre-Columbian technology to his friendships with Samuel K. Lothrop and Doris Stone.

Frederick W. Lange

SEE ALSO
Intermediate Area: Overview; Metal: Tools, Techniques, and Products

Barnard Site (Guerrero, Mexico)

Situated on the coast of Guerrero, this large Postclassic site is known for the abundance and variety of its metalwork. Remains of domestic structures are found scattered throughout the area, but the extent of the site is not known. The central structure, a circular mound in a plaza-like area enclosed by rectangular structures, was heavily looted and had held about twenty skeletons in a chamber lined with cobblestones. Looting has also occurred in other parts of the site.

Metalwork found at the site includes open rings hooked together, bells, thin sheets of gold, a fishhook and twine, a bronze celt, and metal beads with the string cordage preserved. There is also evidence of the use of barkcloth and shreds of cloth attached to plaques of silver alloy. There are signs of deliberate alloying of bronze and of sophistication in cold working of that metal. Remains of silver, silver-copper, silver-gold, and silver-copper-gold, as well as bits of slag and metal found in situ in small stratigraphic excavations of domestic structures, suggest local manufacture.

Finely worked obsidian lip plugs and ear spools indicate ties to the Postclassic cultures of Michoacán, while polychrome pottery and solid cylindrical and bifurcated vessel supports resemble the Yestla Naranjo Complex of inland Guerrero. The polychrome also resembles Middle Polychrome period pottery from Costa Rica. The purity of some silver specimens and the techniques of bronze-working suggest possible influences from Peru.

FURTHER READINGS
Brush, C. F. 1962. Pre-Columbian Alloy Objects from Guerrero, Mexico City. *Science* 138:1336–1338.

Ellen S. Brush

SEE ALSO
Guerrero Region; Metal: Tools, Techniques, and Products

Barrio Las Torres (Managua, Nicaragua)

Situated in the modern Managua metropolitan area, this site—part of an extensive cemetery—was rescued from urban sprawl; twenty-four predominantly shoe-shaped funerary urns were recovered. The cemetery dates from the Sapoa and Ometepe periods (A.D. 800–1520), and the urns appear to have been concentrated in specific "family plots." Stone beads and other items of personal adornment were also found.

FURTHER READINGS
Ramiro Garcia, A. D., and S. Algozar. 1996. Hallazgo arqueológico en el Barrio Las Torres: Un posible cementerio con entierros multiples. In F. W. Lange (ed.), *Abundante cooperacion vecinal: La segunda temporada del proyecto "Arqueologia del la Zona Metropolitana de Managua,"* pp. 105–124. Managua: Alcaldia de Managua.

Frederick W. Lange

SEE ALSO
Intermediate Area: Overview

Basin of Mexico

One of Mesoamerica's key regions for the past two thousand years, this was the heartland of its largest pre-Hispanic states during Classic and Postclassic times; it remained the core area subsequent to European intrusion, as the ancient Aztec capital, Tenochtitlán, became Mexico City. Earlier, during the long Formative era, it provided a setting for the emergence of sedentary agricultural communities and the development of early hierarchical societies. Since the early sixteenth century, the urban capitals of colonial New Spain and republican Mexico have been located here. Since the late nineteenth century, scores of

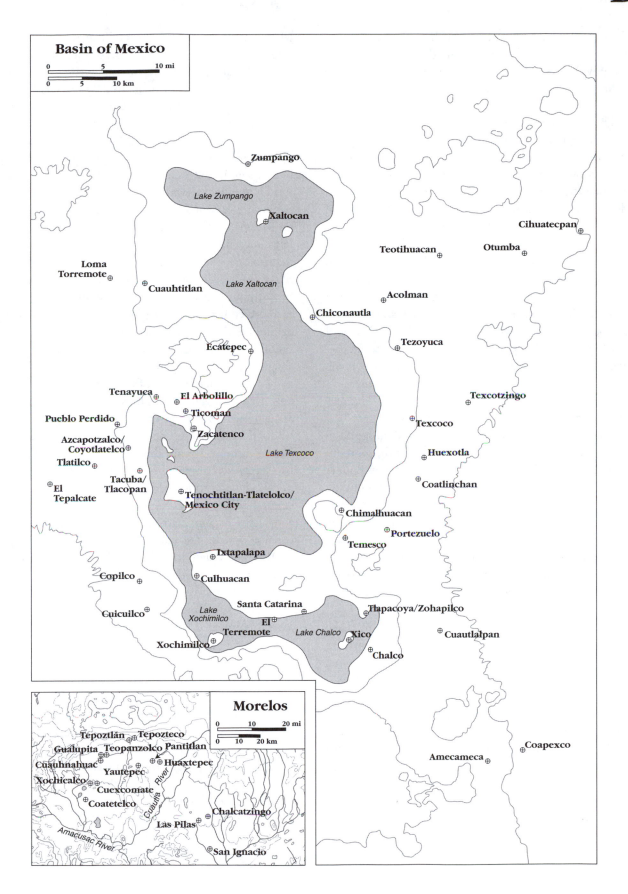

Basin of Mexico

0 5 10 mi
0 5 10 km

Zumpango

Lake Zumpango

Xaltocan

Cihuatecpan

Teotihuacan

Otumba

Loma
Torremote

Cuauhtitlan

Lake Xaltocan

Acolman

Chiconautla

Tezoyuca

Ecatepec

Tenayuca

El Arbolillo

Texcotzingo

Ticoman

Pueblo Perdido

Zacatenco

Texcoco

Azcapotzalco/
Coyotlatelco

Lake Texcoco

Huexotla

Tlatilco

Coatlinchan

Tacuba/
Tlacopan

El
Tepalcate

Tenochtitlan-Tlatelolco/
Mexico City

Chimalhuacan

Portezuelo

Ixtapalapa

Temesco

Copilco

Culhuacan

Cuicuilco

Santa Catarina

Tlapacoya/Zohapilco

*Lake
Xochimilco*

El
Terremote

Cuautlalpan

Lake Chalco

Xico

Xochimilco

Chalco

Morelos

0 10 20 mi
0 10 20 km

Tepoztlán Tepozteco

Gualupita Teopanzolco Pantitlan

Cuauhnahuac Huáxtepec

Yautepec

Xochicalco

Cuexcomate

Cuautla River

Coatetelco

Coapexco

Amecameca

Chalcatzingo

Amacusac River

Las Pilas

San Ignacio

B

archaeologists and ethnohistorians have studied its pre-Hispanic past, and for many years the Basin of Mexico has provided one of the main natural laboratories for the anthropological study of cultural evolution in the New World.

The long-term importance of the Basin of Mexico stems from two important factors: its ability to support large, dense populations and its strategic placement at the intersections of ecological diversity and of interregional transportation and communication networks in central Mexico. Large population and strategic location translated into political dominance. However, at the same time it is important to realize that the evolution of socio-political hierarchy and regional dominance in the Basin of Mexico cannot be understood simply as a product of human biology, food production, or material exchange; it also involved the complex interplay of social and religious ideologies that motivated and constrained the behavior of human actors. Although it is very difficult to do so, archaeologists must attempt to comprehend these ideologies and to discern their role in long-term cultural change.

The Basin of Mexico as a Natural Region

The Basin of Mexico comprises an internal drainage basin that covers about 7,000 square kilometers at the southern edge of the central Mexican high plateau. With its floor at 2,240 meters elevation, and the crests of surrounding mountain ranges rising to elevations between 4,000 and 5,500 meters, the Basin has a climate characterized by highly seasonal summer rainfall and strong winter frosts. Formed by intensive Pleistocene vulcanism, the Basin is centered on what was in pre-Hispanic times a large expanse of interconnected shallow lakes and swamps measuring about 1,000 square kilometers in area.

The higher, southern third of this lake system (Lake Chalco–Xochimilco) was freshwater; the lowest-lying central lake segment (Lake Texcoco) was highly saline; and the northern third (Lake Xaltocan–Zumpango) was brackish to saline. In pre-Columbian times the lake area was a highly productive zone of abundant plant and animal life, including reeds, insect larvae, several species of amphibians, turtles, several species of fish, and vast numbers of waterfowl, including both migratory and year-round species.

At approximately 2,270 meters elevation the terrain begins to steepen slightly, and from there up to about 2,500 meters one moves across well-drained lower piedmont land traversed by numerous small streams, many of which provide excellent sources of irrigation water for sizable expanses of moderately deep soil. Above 2,500 meters the land surface steepens notably up to the base of the thickly forested sierra at about 2,750 meters. In earlier pre-Hispanic times much of the piedmont terrain would also have been forested and home to deer, rabbit, and other animal species. The northern half of the basin has a significantly lower average annual rainfall than the more humid south, and everywhere rainfall tends to increase steadily at higher elevations.

Pre-Columbian agriculturalists were vitally affected by the seasonality of rainfall and frost. The onset of summer rains (normally in mid-May, but sometimes delayed until mid-June) is uncertain and unpredictable, and the quantity of rainfall can vary unpredictably over time and space; similarly, the first severe autumn frosts often occur as early as mid-October. Thus, the productivity of seed-crop agriculture based on rainfall was always uncertain. The cultivation of annual cultigens like maize, beans, squash, amaranth, and chenopodium could only yield one crop per year. Furthermore, artificial water control was the only way to ensure that crops could be planted early enough in the spring so that they would attain maturity before the onset of killing autumn frosts. Consequently, canal irrigation, swamp drainage, and the cultivation of two hardy xerophytic species—maguey (*Agave* sp.) and nopal (*Opuntia* sp.)—were essential components of agricultural subsistence. Domestic animals, mainly turkey and dog, were comparatively insignificant in terms of subsistence, agricultural cultivation, or overland transport.

Also highly significant in pre-Hispanic times were the exceptionally large outcrops of obsidian at Otumba, near Teotihuacán, and Pachuca in the northeast. For millennia these quarries, some of the largest anywhere in Mesoamerica, provided virtually inexhaustible quantities of this lithic raw material, used for making knives, scrapers, blades, and projectile points. The procurement and distribution of this restricted resource was an essential part of pre-Hispanic adaptation in central Mexico.

The Basin of Mexico thus offered both opportunities and problems for hunter-gatherers and agriculturalists. For hunter-gatherers, the circumlacustrine niche contained especially productive resources available both seasonally and year round, but the biomass at higher elevations was significantly lower. For agriculturalists, especially those living in the drier northern third of the Basin, the productivity of annual seed crops was secure only where canal irrigation or swamp drainage were feasible. Lacustrine resources (numerous species of plants and animals, plus the large quantities of salt readily available around the shoreline of saline Lake Texcoco) remained an important part of the economic base even after agriculture became fully established. The lakes were also significant as transportation and communication arteries—it was only by means of canoe or raft transport that efficient movement of bulk commodities was possible.

Pre-Agricultural Society, c. 10,000–3000 B.C.

It is still not clear when the Basin's earliest human inhabitants arrived. Deep excavations at the Zohapilco site at Tlapacoya on the northeastern shore of Lake Chalco suggest the possible presence of humans well before 10,000 B.C., and the Tlapacoya phase, with its still scanty suggestions of generalized hunting and gathering, may begin prior to 20,000 B.C. We know that some of the earliest of the Basin's human inhabitants killed and dismembered mammoth in the swamps around Lake Texcoco. However, the first really secure evidence for human occupation dates to the sixth millennium B.C. (Playa 1 phase) at Zohapilco, where there was heavy reliance throughout the sixth and fifth millennia B.C. on the same lacustrine resources that have been used by more recent peoples. Studies of ancient pollen indicate that these lakeshore people were probably experimenting with the wild ancestors of amaranth and maize, gradually transforming them into domesticates, within a subsistence mode that remained predominantly nonagricultural.

The thickness of the occupational debris at Zohapilco suggests a relatively sedentary existence in small lakeshore hamlets. Unfortunately, almost nothing is yet known about preagricultural occupation in the higher piedmont terrain, where early experiments with plant cultivation may have been more important for subsistence needs.

Transition to Fully Developed Agriculture, c. 3000–1500 B.C.

During the third millennium B.C. at Zohapilco (Zohapilco phase), there is evidence for increasing use of more productive forms of maize, amaranth, squash, and other cultivated plants, with continuing heavy reliance on lacustrine resources, and secondary use of terrestrial fauna (deer, rabbit, dog, and rodents). A more diverse kit of stone utensils, including more obsidian tools, is suggestive of the intensification of production and the expansion of social networks for procuring nonlocal resources. There is still no direct, archaeologically documented transition, even at Zohapilco, from preceramic to ceramic occupations in the Basin of Mexico. The earliest known ceramics belong to the Coapexco phase, probably beginning no earlier than c. 1400 B.C.

Development of Formative Chiefdoms, c. 1400–100 B.C.

In addition to the use of pottery, the Formative era is characterized by several long-term trends: population increased substantially; settlements became much larger; public architecture expanded in size and elaboration; occupation expanded into virtually all environmental zones; and the most florescent developments occurred in the southern half of the Basin. The unmistakable foundations for these developments are apparent during the Early and Middle Formative (c. 1400–600 B.C.), when the great bulk of permanent settlement was narrowly confined to the southern lakeshore region. The Late Formative and early Terminal Formative (c. 600–100 B.C.) witnessed some significant departures, as substantial numbers of people expanded into higher ground around the lake margins and into the northern half of the Basin. However, it was not until the late Terminal Formative (Tzacualli phase, c. 100 B.C.–A.D. 100) that these long-established trends were substantially modified.

The most important known Early Formative centers in the Basin of Mexico were established at Tlatilco and Cuicuilco. In Tlatilco, we appear to be dealing with a substantial village settlement (of uncertain size) with many burials, some of which contained moderately impressive quantities of elaborate ceramic vessels as offerings. For Cuicuilco we know even less. It is also known that Early Formative sites in the southern Basin share many attributes of ceramic style (including a number of so-called Olmec decorative motifs) with contemporary sites in adjacent Morelos, immediately to the south, and that this stylistic linkage with Morelos and other parts of central and southern Mexico continued into Middle Formative times.

By later Middle Formative times, the shoreline zone of the southern Basin was filled in, with eight or nine substantial settlements, spaced remarkably evenly at intervals of 6 to 8 km, from the southeastern corner of Lake Texcoco westward around to Cuicuilco at the western end of Lake Xochimilco. Recent excavations at one of these settlements have revealed modest public architecture in the form of rock-rubble platforms that probably supported small ritual structures. Comparable public architecture probably existed at other, still unexcavated Middle Formative lakeshore centers. There is an obvious direct correlation between the size of each Middle Formative center and the extent of its local agricultural productivity.

Three Middle Formative centers (Cuicuilco in the southwestern Basin, Cuautlalpan in the southeastern Basin, and Chimalhuacan, in the eastern Basin) are far larger (with areas of 40–50 hectares) than the others (which measure 10–15 hectares), and may have exercised some degree of regional dominance. However, given the regular site spacing, the apparent absence of monumental public architecture, and the strong direct correlation between site size and local productivity, it appears unlikely that Middle Formative regional hierarchy was based on either forceful extraction of tribute or a highly stratified socio-political order. Given the easy, direct access of each substantial Middle Formative settlement to the full range of the southern Basin's lacustrine and agricultural resources, it seems unlikely that there would have been any significant community specialization in utilitarian products or any significant exchange of utilitarian materials between these communities. The Middle Formative appears to be comparatively simple and generalized, with each substantial settlement functioning as the center of a comparatively autonomous polity.

The picture becomes notably more complex in the subsequent Late Formative and early Terminal Formative (Ticomán and Patlachique phases). Population increased markedly; many old Middle Formative centers grew substantially; many new centers were established; and there was significant movement into previously unoccupied terrain, including the sparsely settled northern Basin. During the Patlachique phase, both Cuicuilco and Teotihuacán attained unprecedented levels of population (c. 40,000 inhabitants each) and architectural elaboration. It is likely that Cuicuilco and Teotihuacán were now the capitals of two multitiered centralized polities, one in the southwestern Basin and the other in the northeast, which dominated their local areas and competed actively with each other for regional hegemony.

The development of Teotihuacán was perhaps the single most impressive change during the period 600–100 B.C. Scholars have pointed to a variety of important ideological and ecological factors in this development—e.g., the religious importance of the sacred caves beneath the Sun Pyramid, the role of irrigation agriculture in promoting population growth and political centralization, the economic and political importance of controlling access to obsidian, and the overall socio-political implications of

increasing population. Even more dramatic changes after ca. 100 B.C. produced the rapid development of a radical new Teotihuacán-centered polity.

The Teotihuacán State, 100 B.C.–A.D. 750

Three remarkable events occurred during the first century B.C.: the destruction of Cuicuilco and its sustaining heartland by a series of volcanic eruptions; the rapid expansion of Teotihuacán to a population of roughly 80,000 to 100,000 inhabitants, with a corresponding elaboration of the center's monumental public architecture, highlighted by the construction of two massive pyramidal constructions along a formal avenue nearly 2 kilometers long; and, perhaps most remarkable of all, a massive reconfiguration of the Basin's entire population, with an apparent wholesale abandonment of large areas in the southern Basin. Thus, the rapid urbanization at Teotihuacán itself must be understood in broad regional terms.

After the first century A.D., Teotihuacán moved to consolidate its position in the Basin of Mexico, and for more than 500 years it completely dominated a major portion of highland central Mexico. Archaeological surveys and excavations have provided an overwhelming impression of a very large (well over 125,000 inhabitants in an area of c. 20 square kilometers), highly centralized, highly stratified, and tightly organized Teotihuacán urban community. We know that the major avenue and massive pyramids constructed during the Tzacualli phase were incorporated into a much larger and more formally planned complex of public architecture. The construction of some of the earliest public buildings (e.g., the Temple of Quetzalcoatl in the Ciudadela Complex at the city's central hub) was associated with large-scale sacrifice of dozens of warriors, whose bodies and their associated offerings were then interred in and around the building.

During the fourth and fifth centuries A.D. there was a massive architectural reorganization, producing the pattern of walled apartment compounds and a gridded street plan. These apartment compounds apparently formed units of economic specialization and were occupied by groups of closely related people. Analyses of skeletal remains in subfloor burials suggests that for much of the urban population, mortality was high and fertility was low; the urban center may have depended on its rural hinterlands for demographic replacement. It appears that most of the inhabitants of urban Teotihuacán were farmers: there are very few rural settlements within a radius of 20 km, and beyond that distance most Classic period sites are small and widely scattered. Thus, there would have been too few rural people to produce adequate food for the city, and the only way for Teotihuacán to subsist was to feed itself.

Teotihuacán appears to have been at least ten times larger than any other known Classic settlement in the Basin of Mexico. Furthermore, overall population size and density throughout the Basin of Mexico outside of Teotihuacán is notable for being small, sparse, and rather evenly distributed. This pattern might imply tight, direct control from Teotihuacán, with a deliberate policy of maintaining a reduced (and perhaps somewhat specialized) rural population in the interests of political security, demographic replenishment of the urban community, and access to certain valued products (e.g., salt, timber, and cotton) that could not be produced at or around Teotihuacán itself.

We also know that after the third century A.D. Teotihuacán was a center of notable pan-Mesoamerican significance: for example, near the western urban border is an area with distinctive tombs, pottery, and ritual paraphernalia characteristic of Monte Albán and other Oaxacan centers; near the city's eastern periphery is an area with high concentrations of Gulf Coast and Mayan pottery, associated with unusual large circular buildings; Classic occupation throughout the city, and the entire Basin of Mexico as well, was characterized by the common use of Thin Orange ceramics, a type of pottery that we now know was produced at workshops about 150 km southeast of Teotihuacán. These material remains suggest some special linkages with distant centers like Cholula, Monte Albán, Kaminaljuyú, Matacapan, and Tikal. Architectural similarities, fancy trade pottery, and the presence of wall murals and carvings that appear to depict personages with distinctive Teotihuacán-style costumes and insignia at several of these widely scattered "foreign" sites—all these features may represent the other ends of such linkages between Teotihuacán and numerous major regional capitals throughout Mesoamerica. Whatever these linkages may represent, it is clear that Teotihuacán played a major political, economic, and ideological role in pan-Mesoamerican affairs.

By the late seventh century A.D. there are clear indications of changing circumstances at Teotihuacán. There are hints of increased militarism in iconography and suggestions that certain public areas were falling into disrepair. After the early to mid-seventh century, many public buildings along the main north–south avenue were deliberately burned, and soon thereafter the city lost roughly four-fifths of its population. Although it continued to be

a local center of some importance, by 700 Teotihuacán had begun its long and irreversible slide toward obscurity.

Collapse and Realignment During the Epiclassic and Early Postclassic, c. A.D. 750–1150

The disintegration of urban Teotihuacán and its regional settlement system appears to have occurred in two distinct stages: an earlier era (Epiclassic) when large groups of people apparently emigrated from Teotihuacán and established themselves in large, nucleated settlements throughout the Basin, and a later era (Early Postclassic) marked by notable ruralization and substantial population decline everywhere except in the northern quarter of the Basin.

The Epiclassic was an era when there were apparently no dominant urban centers in central Mexico. This was apparently a time of political fragmentation, when a series of relatively autonomous polities struggled among themselves for regional hegemony. Virtually all the major Epiclassic centers in the Basin of Mexico appear to share a fairly uniform assemblage of red/buff pottery (Coyotlatelco). Closely related variants of this pottery occur at Epiclassic sites all across central Mexico.

Some archaeologists have suggested that the stylistic similarity and spatial distribution of Coyotlatelco pottery reflect the dispersal of emigrants from Teotihuacán. Others have argued that Coyotlatelco pottery was ultimately of West Mexican origin, and that its presently known characteristics and distribution are the product of incompletely understood processes of interregional movement and exchange in the unsettled era following Teotihuacán's collapse. Whatever the case, it now appears that within the Basin of Mexico itself, the Epiclassic was clearly transitional to the population decline and settlement dispersal of the subsequent Early Postclassic.

These latter trends must be understood in the context of socio-political relationships between two new regional capitals: Tula, immediately northwest of the Basin, and Cholula, just to the southeast. These relationships were apparently such as to preclude large, dense occupation anywhere in the Basin south of Lake Xaltocan–Zumpango.

Antecedents of the Mexica State During the Middle Postclassic, A.D. 1150–1350

Just as the Early Postclassic developments in the Basin of Mexico can be understood only in relation to the rise and florescence of Tula and Cholula, so too the dramatic population growth and urbanization within the Basin during the subsequent Middle Postclassic make little sense unless

B

they are firmly linked to the larger socio-political changes that affected the whole of central Mexico during that era. Archaeological and ethnohistoric sources indicate that by the end of the twelfth century, Tula had lost its importance as a major political center. From about that point, we see remarkable population growth throughout the Basin of Mexico—within a short time, regional population exceeded the old Classic maximum and rapidly expanded to unprecedented levels. Unlike all earlier periods, this population growth was notably even in its distribution within the Basin: in all areas new urban centers developed, especially within and around the lake margins, but also in many piedmont areas from north to south. With the removal of the Tula-Cholula confrontation, the sparsely settled central and southern parts of the Basin now provided ideal places for new immigrants (some of them probably refugees produced by the collapse of Tula's regional hegemony) to relocate and reestablish themselves.

The ethnic and socio-political complexity suggested by the ethnohistorical sources is mirrored archaeologically by the extreme variability in Middle Postclassic ceramic styles within the Basin. It now appears that there are three basic spatial-stylistic divisions: a southern division, around Lake Chalco–Xochimilco, typified by Aztec I Black/Orange pottery; a central division, around Lake Texcoco, characterized by Aztec II Black/Orange; and a northern division, around Lake Xaltocan–Zumpango, apparently characterized by a still poorly known ceramic complex closely linked to the antecedent Mazapan phase. This unprecedented regional ceramic variability is highly suggestive of socio-political borders that were so impermeable that they functioned greatly to reduce the flow of material products. This archaeological pattern dovetails with ethnohistorically derived impressions of political fragmentation and intense interpolity hostility.

The Middle Postclassic was also the time of the first large-scale (and apparently successful) experiments with swamp drainage and the creation of highly productive *chinampa* agriculture in the vast swamplands of Lake Chalco–Xochimilco. However, it was not until the subsequent Late Postclassic, under the stimulus of imperial consolidation and expansion by the Aztec state centered at Tenochtitlán, that the full productive potential of this immensely productive, but highly labor-intensive, agricultural technique was fully realized.

The Late Postclassic Mexica State, A.D. 1350–1521

This final pre-Hispanic era was characterized by three principal developments: rapid population growth, to an unprecedented level of well over a million inhabitants—more than four times the Classic period maximum; rapid urbanization, with an increasing number and proportion of the total population residing in nucleated urban settlements throughout the Basin of Mexico, and especially around the lakeshore margins; and rapid political consolidation and imperial centralization, manifested by the formation of the Triple Alliance and the growing domination of Tenochtitlán, both within the Basin of Mexico and throughout broad areas of central and southern Mexico.

Ethnohistoric sources inform us about the highly stratified social order, with several different categories of nobility and commoners. They also provide details about the physical and sociological characteristics of major urban centers: the massive temples and palaces that formed the administrative and religious cores, and the importance of centrally administered artisan and craft workshops. The ethnohistoric sources describe the lively marketplaces and suggest that administered market exchange was an increasingly important and deliberate strategy to increase the dependence of all kinds of producers and consumers in the Basin of Mexico on the central administrative authority, and so to strengthen Triple Alliance control within the imperial heartland.

Ethnohistory tells us that the great majority of urban residents were non-agriculturalists, and that a great number of people in the Late Postclassic urban milieu were transients from elsewhere: messengers, diplomats, merchants and their clients, palace servants, corvée laborers involved in public maintenance and construction projects, soldiers, participants in religious festivities, etc. Ethnohistoric sources also speak about the importance of warfare and military conquest in individual social mobility and in the consolidation and expansion of the Triple Alliance and Tenochtitlán—and they provide hints that some of this activity may have been politically, rather than economically, motivated, as each new ruler strove to demonstrate and strengthen claims to power and authority by means of successful military action.

Similarly, ethnohistoric sources provide us with much of what we understand about the regional socio-political hierarchy within the Basin of Mexico. We know that Tenochtitlán, together with Texcoco and Tacuba, comprised a confederation known as the Triple Alliance, which had been formed in the early fifteenth century through large-scale warfare between major city states, and which pooled its military resources to create and maintain a far-flung tributary domain. We also know that there were numerous second- and third-order city-states within the Basin of Mexico, each of which paid some form of tribute in goods and services to the Triple Alliance centers, and each of which dominated a local area, with roots in the antecedent Middle Postclassic.

Regional archaeological surveys have demonstrated the high level of population and its comparatively even distribution throughout the Basin of Mexico. Extensive excavations at the Templo Mayor complex in Tenochtitlán have provided important insights into the growth of the religious core of the Mexica capital and the importance of religious ideology in imperial consolidation—for example, the offering caches within and around the main temple contain exotic materials and products derived from distant tributary provinces. Systematic archaeological studies of the growth and development of several smaller Middle to Late Postclassic centers—notably Huexotla, Xico, Otumba, and Xaltocan—have begun to suggest that there was considerable variability within the Basin of Mexico in the dynamics of urbanization and political centralization; for example, Huexotla may have become increasingly important as a center that administered agricultural production, whereas at Otumba there may have been more emphasis over time on certain kinds of craft production. Complementary new studies of stylistic variability in Late Postclassic decorated pottery have revealed distinct stylistic clusters suggestive of political and/or economic entities operative at middle and lower levels within the Triple Alliance hierarchy.

Summary

Pre-Hispanic cultural development in the Basin of Mexico was marked by relatively long periods of gradual change punctuated by relatively short periods of much more rapid development. The long preceramic era was succeeded by the Formative period, during which population gradually increased and agricultural subsistence gradually expanded, and when it appears that simple chiefdoms were gradually succeeded by more complex forms of hierarchical society. During a relatively short period at the very end of the Formative, c. 100 B.C.–A.D. 100, there was rapid urbanization, construction at Teotihuacán of massive public architecture on an unprecedented scale, and massive reconfiguration of regional population. Then there was another long era of comparative stability during the Classic period, c. A.D. 100–650, when Teotihuacán consolidated and maintained its position as a preeminent political, economic, and religious center in central Mexico. The succeeding Epiclassic was another era of more rapid change,

as the Teotihuacán-centered system fell apart and was replaced by a much less centralized regional organization. The Early and Middle Postclassic witnessed another gradual transformation, as the Basin of Mexico recovered its regional dominance in the wake of major geopolitical transformations that affected all of central Mexico. The rapid development of the Triple Alliance and the ascendancy of Tenochtitlán after 1350 was the final chapter in the long pre-Hispanic sequence.

FURTHER READINGS

Berlo, J. (ed.). 1992. *Art, Ideology, and the City of Teotihuacán.* Washington, D.C.: Dumbarton Oaks.

Boone, E. (ed.). 1987. *The Aztec Templo Mayor.* Washington, D.C.: Dumbarton Oaks.

Evans, S. (ed.). 1988. *Excavations at Cihuatecpan: An Aztec Village in the Teotihuacán Valley.* Vanderbilt University Publications in Anthropology, 36. Nashville.

Harvey, H. (ed.). 1991. *Land and Politics in the Valley of Mexico: A Two-Thousand-Year Perspective.* Albuquerque: University of New Mexico Press.

Hassig, R. 1988. *Aztec Warfare: Imperial Expansion and Political Control.* Norman: University of Oklahoma Press.

Hodge, M., and M. E. Smith (eds.). 1994. *Economies and Polities in the Aztec Realm.* Albany: Institute for Mesoamerican Studies, State University of New York.

Manzanilla, L. (ed.). 1993. *Anatomía de un conjunto residencial Teotihuacano en Oztoyahualco.* 2 vols. Mexico City: Instituto Nacional de Antropología e Historia.

Niederberger, C. 1987. *Paleopaysages et archéologie preurbaine du Bassin de Mexico.* 2 vols. Mexico City: Centre d'Études Mexicaines et Centraméricaines.

Ortiz de Montellano, B. 1990. *Aztec Medicine, Health, and Nutrition.* New Brunswick: Rutgers University Press.

Sanders, W., J. Parsons, and R. Santley. 1979. *The Basin of Mexico: Ecological Processes in the Evolution of a Civilization.* New York: Academic Press.

Sempowski, M., and M. Spence. 1994. *Mortuary Practices and Skeletal Remains at Teotihuacán.* Salt Lake City: University of Utah Press.

Serra Puche, M. C. 1988. *Los recursos lacustres de la Cuenca de Mexico durante el Formativo.* Mexico City: Instituto de Investigaciones Antropológicas, Universidad Nacional Autónoma de Mexico.

Wolf, E. (ed.). 1976. *The Valley of Mexico: Studies in Pre-Hispanic Ecology and Society.* Albuquerque: University of New Mexico Press.

Jeffrey R. Parsons

B

Baúl, El
See Cotzumalhuapa Sites: Bilbao, El Baúl, and El Castillo

Becan (Campeche, Mexico)

Situated in the tropical forest zone of central Yucatán, this is one of the largest centers in the Lowland Maya Río Bec region. Becan's most remarkable feature is a ditch and earthen parapet, 1,890 meters long, that encloses an area of about 19 hectares. Three major architectural groups lie within this perimeter, including one temple-pyramid over 30 meters high. Smaller outlying centers such as Xpuhil, Chicanna, and Río Bec are situated within a few kilometers of Becan and share its Río Bec architectural tradition. Along with most other sites in the Río region, Becan lacks a tradition of carved monuments with associated dates and inscriptions.

The regional ceramic chronology indicates colonization around 600 B.C., with major architectural construction at Becan beginning after A.D. 50. The ditch and parapet were a system of fortifications probably built around A.D. 150, at the end of the Late Formative period Pakluum phase, and by 250 Becan was an impressive regional center. Teotihuacán ceramic elements appeared by the mid-fifth century, but ceramic ties were strongest at that time with the Classic Maya Petén tradition to the south. Architectural activity peaked during the early Late Classic (A.D. 600–700), a period when foreign contacts declined. Buildings in the region's distinctive Río Bec architectural style proliferated at Becan and elsewhere, and were used well into the eighth century.

By the late eighth to early ninth century, striking changes in Becan's ceramics suggest a rapid and possibly militaristic influx of northen Maya. At or shortly after that time, major architectural and elite activity dramatically declined, although there is evidence for continued population in the region until about 1200.

Becan was first explored and mapped in 1934 by Carnegie Institution archaeologists. Between 1969 and 1973, a Tulane University–National Geographic Society expedition under the direction of E. Wyllys Andrews IV (and later Richard E. W. Adams) carried out a multifaceted regional research project focusing on Becan itself, on nearby Chicanna, and on smaller sites and ancient agricultural features in the surrounding countryside. Research included a regional settlement system project and innovative rural household excavations. Ancillary surveys revealed the widespread use of what appear to have been agricultural terraces and enclosed fields begin-

ning in the sixth century A.D. Several major Late Classic structures have been excavated and restored.

FURTHER READINGS

Ball, J. W. 1977. *The Archaeological Ceramics of Becan, Campeche, Mexico.* Middle American Research Institute, Tulane University, Publication 43. New Orleans.

Ball, J. W., and E. W. Andrews V. 1978. *Preclassic Architecture at Becan, Campeche, Mexico.* Middle American Research Institute, Tulane University, Occasional Paper 3. New Orleans.

Eaton, J. 1975. Ancient Agricultural Farmsteads in the Río Bec Region of Yucatán. *University of California Archaeological Research Facility Contributions* 27: 56–82.

Potter, D. F. 1977. *Maya Architecture of the Central Yucatán Peninsula, Mexico.* Middle American Research Institute, Tulane University, Publication 44. New Orleans.

Thomas, P. M. 1981. *Prehistoric Maya Settlement Patterns at Becan, Campeche, Mexico.* Middle American Research Institute, Tulane University, Publication 45. New Orleans.

Webster, D. L. 1976. *Defensive Earthworks at Becan, Campeche, Mexico: Implications for Maya Warfare.* Middle American Research Institute, Tulane University, Publication 41. New Orleans.

David L. Webster

SEE ALSO

Fortifications; Maya Lowlands: North

Belize River Region

The Belize River area Classic period Maya settlement system demonstrates that dispersed communities and settlements were hierarchically arranged with respect to agricultural resources. Zones of primary agricultural resources have settlement densities greater than 100 structures per square kilometer and are situated in the alluvial valley and western ridgelands. The secondary resource zones dominate the foothills that rise from the valley to the ridges, with settlement densities under 50 structures per square kilometer.

The proportion and distribution pattern of primary resources in the Belize River area played a major role in the density and composition of settlements and communities. The valley is one of the best agricultural zones in the Maya Lowlands. Its Classic period residents had access to a variety of valuables as measures of wealth and were probably involved in the production of specialized crops such as cacao, cotton, or tobacco. Centers of the valley are small in size, consistent with the moderate settlement density of the zone.

The Belize River area's largest center, El Pilar, is located within a substantial concentration of primary resources. Settlement density and composition are comparable to Tikal, although the largest residential units around El Pilar were only half the size of those around Tikal.

At centers like El Pilar, public monuments were used by the residential elite to symbolize control and power. Investigations of residential units of the rural community of Latón, in the ridgelands of the Belize River area, surprisingly revealed that one of the large elite units was heavily involved in an obsidian prismatic blade production industry. No excavation area at the residence yielded fewer than 3,000 obsidian pieces per square meter. One deposit of blade debitage contained more than 33,000 pieces of obsidian, and another contained 39 complete, but exhausted, prismatic blade cores. These deposits suggest provisional discard areas staged, or "stashed," for future use. In light of the distribution of debitage at centers, it seems very likely that these "stashes" were destined to be ritually employed in the monumental public setting.

FURTHER READINGS

Fedick, S. L., and A. Ford. 1990. Prehistoric Agricultural Landscape of the Central Maya Lowlands: An Examination of Local Variability in a Regional Context. *World Archaeology* 22:21–33.

Ford, A. 1986. 1990. Maya Settlement in the Belize River Area: Variations in Residence Patterns of the Central Maya Lowlands. In T. P. Culbert and D. S. Rice (eds.), *Prehistoric Population History in the Maya Lowlands*, pp. 167–181. Albuquerque: University of New Mexico Press.

Ford, A., and S. L. Fedick. 1992. Prehistoric Maya Settlement Patterns in the Upper Belize River Area: Summary Results of the Regional Survey Phase of the Belize River Archaeological Settlement Survey. *Journal of Field Archaeology* 19:35–49.

Anabel Ford

SEE ALSO

Maya Lowlands: North; Maya Lowlands: South

Bernal, Ignacio (1910–1992)

The leading authority on ancient Oaxaca, Bernal worked with Alfonso Caso and Jorge Acosta at Monte Albán, Oaxaca's greatest pre-Hispanic city, between 1942 and 1953. He was personally responsible for the definition of the periods Monte Albán I, II, and IIIa. From 1962 to 1964, he directed a large project at Teotihuacán in the Basin of Mexico. Noted for an approach that combined ethnohistoric and archaeological data, he continued to excavate and publish extensively until his death at age eighty-one.

FURTHER READINGS

Bernal, I. 1969. *The Olmec World*. Berkeley: University of California Press.

———. 1972. *Tenochtitlan en una isla*. Mexico City: Colección SEP-Setentas, 39.

———. 1980. *A History of Mexican Archaeology*. London: Thames and Hudson.

Flannery, Kent V. 1994. Ignacio Bernal: 1910–1992. *American Antiquity* 5:72–76.

Kent V. Flannery

SEE ALSO

Monte Albán; Oaxaca and Tehuantepec Region

Bilbao

See Cotzumalhuapa Sites: Bilbao, El Baúl, and El Castillo

Blood and Bloodletting

The act of shedding some of one's own blood ("autosacrifice" or "bloodletting") was often accomplished in ancient Mesoamerica by using a sharp instrument (a shark's tooth, an agave thorn, or a spine from a marine ray) to perforate a fleshy part of the body, such as the thigh, tongue, or earlobe. The flowing blood might then be allowed to drip onto a piece of cloth or paper, or a ball of copal incense; this then would be burned to produce an offering, a column of smoke rising to the sky. Mesoamerican groups such as the Zapotec, Mixtec, and Maya believed that the burning of incense or blood-spattered media was one way of communicating directly with sky-dwelling supernatural beings, such as the lightning god.

Ritual bloodletting was probably being practiced by 1200 to 1000 B.C., because at that time we start to find shark's teeth, obsidian blades, and stingray spines discarded near public buildings in Mesoamerica's earliest

B

villages. Thus, from that time onward, we can make a case that blood was an important part of Mesoamerican ritual practices. It appears that, initially, the majority of villagers were active participants in this ritual practice; later, ritual bloodletting was gradually restricted to an emerging elite, with high-status people using actual stingray spines, while low-status people used imitation stingray spines whittled from deer bone. This decreasing participation in ritual bloodletting is directly related to the growing belief that the elite were the only people in direct communication with supernatural beings. The elite were in a special position to petition Lightning to break the clouds to send rain, to beseech Earthquake to stop shaking the Earth, or to speak directly with other elite ancestors. During the period 700–500 B.C. in Oaxaca and Morelos, obsidian blades were chipped to resemble stingray spines. By A.D. 100 in the Maya area, there are examples of obsidian blades and stingray spines included in high-status graves; these implements are often found near the pelvis, probably because they were in a bag (now disintegrated) that was worn at the waist.

Still later, after A.D. 300–400, ritual bloodletting was appropriated by royalty—often royal women, as among the Maya—who invoked the image of a deceased royal ancestor. Bloodletting was also performed by members of Aztec society in many different contexts: by a diviner petitioning supernatural spirits, by a warrior before going to battle, and by a new ruler in rites associated with his inauguration. During the Classic period (A.D. 250–900), Mesoamerican peoples such as the Zapotec linked concepts of blood to royal genealogies by choosing red (the color of blood) to paint their genealogical registers.

Concepts of blood were also directly linked to the heart sacrifice, a practice that began by 600 B.C. but continued throughout Mesoamerica until A.D. 1519, when the Spaniards arrived and described it in vivid detail. The Aztecs are well known for heart sacrifice, which they usually performed on captives taken in raids. Such sacrifices often accompanied dedications of new temples and inaugurations of new rulers in the Main Plaza (Zócalo) of Tenochtitlán.

Joyce Marcus

SEE ALSO

Sacrifice

Bocas, Las (Puebla, Mexico)

Situated at the base of hills on the southeastern side of Izúcar de Matamoros Valley, near a junction with a large side valley, this small Early Formative period site is adjacent to a small stream and overlooks the humid bottomlands of the Río Nexapa. Las Bocas was intensively looted before the mid-1960s and yielded pottery and figurine types prized by collectors as "Olmec." Because of this, the site—probably only a minor hamlet in the regional site hierarchy—has gained an exaggerated importance. Looted artifacts from sites throughout the region, together with objects of unknown provenience and recent forgeries, continue to be falsely asserted to be from Las Bocas to increase their market value and claim authenticity. Excavations by Mexican government archaeologists in 1966, under the site name Caballo Pintado, encountered very few unlooted areas and remain unpublished.

FURTHER READINGS

Coe, M. D. 1965. *The Jaguar's Children.* New York: Museum of Primitive Art.

David C. Grove

SEE ALSO

Formative Period; Puebla-Tlaxcala Region

Bonampak (Chiapas, Mexico)

Brought to modern attention in 1946 by Giles Healey, a photographer and cinematographer working for the United Fruit Company, the site of Bonampak is best known for its murals in Structure 1, generally considered to be the most complete program of Maya paintings to survive from the Classic era (A.D. 250–900) in the southern lowlands. About 30 km southwest of Yaxchilán, the site seems to have been linked to nearby and larger Lacanhá throughout most of its history. Both Bonampak and Lacanhá paid fealty to Piedras Negras during the early seventh century before entering the sphere of Yaxchilán after the accession of Shield Jaguar in 681.

Although there may once have been many Maya buildings with painted interiors, only the one at Bonampak has survived more or less intact, preserved by a semitranslucent calcification that formed on top of the paintings. Upon hearing a verbal description from Healey of what he had seen inside Structure 1, Sylvanus G. Morley christened the site "Bonampak," or "painted walls" in Morley's pidgin Maya. Despite important discoveries of Maya art in the second half of the twentieth century, the Bonampak

Maya paintings from the Classic era found in Structure 1 at Bonampak. Photo courtesy of Garland Publishing, Inc.

murals continue to be thought of as the most extraordinary paintings made by the ancient Maya.

The Carnegie Institution of Washington sponsored two seasons of study, in 1947 and 1948, yielding two copies of the paintings, one by Antonio Tejeda and the other by Agustín Villagra. A life-size copy of the entire program was reconstructed by Rina Lazo at the Museo Nacional de Antropología in Mexico City, and a copy of Room 1 by Felipe Dávalos at the Florida State Museum. Despite campaigns of consolidation, the large stucco figure photographed on the western end of the structure collapsed. Efforts to consolidate the paintings culminated in a three-year cleaning in the 1980s that temporarily removed the opaque mineral deposits and salt encrustations. Some portions of the paintings were reconstructed in 1995 using both digital enhancement and infrared photography, an ongoing project.

Painted in the last decade of the eighth century and depicting more Maya lords together than in any other Maya visual work, the Bonampak paintings serve as a window on both Maya artistic production and Maya society in the period. They also portray the most specific image ever recorded of the ancient Maya sky, providing the basis for many differing points of view regarding the Maya cosmos. The text also reveals a hierarchy in which the Bonampak king, Chan Muwan, and his lords served local Lacanhá lords, with connections as well to the powerful Yaxchilán dynasty. The paintings offer a united, harmonious narration of a world that seems simultaneously fractured by war and sacrifice.

Set off by itself to the west on the main acropolis of the site, Structure 1 features three rooms, in what archaeologists usually call a "range-type" building; each is separate except for unique small openings that link the rooms laterally, perhaps for oral communication. Specific as well to Bonampak is a large built-in bench with painted riser that lines the east, south, and west walls of each room, limiting viewing for any observer not seated on the bench. The structure features a completely perpendicular façade, more common to Puuc architecture than to Usumacinta sites, with elaborate stuccos above the vault spring and paintings below.

B

With its clear Initial Series text wrapping the horizontal vault spring along the east, south, and west walls, the narration begins in Room 1: a series of lords in long white mantles (some named *ahaw*, or "lord," in east wall captions) attend a royal family assembled on a large throne. A bundle to the right of the throne bears the text 5 *PI KAKAW*, presumably identifying the contents as five 8,000-bean counts of cacao, which would have been a substantial tribute or tax payment. The text below notes an installation in office of a kinsman of the Yaxchilán royal family, possibly the child presented above. A distance number leads to the apparent dedication date of the temple, and a day for the first appearance of the evening star.

Maya painters recorded the events of the dedication in lavish detail, with rituals that continued celebrating the installation of the little child as well. Only seated observers could witness the elaborate dressing rituals featured on the north wall, where three prominent dancers—members of the royal lineage—adorn themselves in jaguar pelts, quetzal feathers, and boa constrictors, attended by lesser members of the court. So attired, these three lords then dance on the lower tier of the south wall, attended by flanking *sahals*, or regional governors, on one side, and musicians and performers on the other. Although musical bands are known from other representations, the Bonampak musical band is the most complete, depicting trumpets, three kinds of drums, and turtle shells. Costumed ball players, the Maize God, and a figure dressed like a freshwater lobster all apparently wait their turn to perform.

Wrapped around the east, south, and west walls of Room 2 from floor to ceiling, a great battle painting reveals dozens of combatants charging into battle from the east, banners and weapons held high, and converging under a large elbow of text on the south wall, where jaguar-attired warriors strike their enemy with such energy that his body almost seems to fly right out of the picture plane. The text itself offers only an enigmatic date, perhaps a few years before the Initial Series text. In the upper west vault, defenders try to protect a wooden box, perhaps the same one that then appears under the throne in Room 3. Damage along the join of the wall and bench may conceal concentrated captive-taking and dismemberment.

On the north wall, Chan Muwan, accompanied by warriors and female dynasts, including his Yaxchilán wife, receives presented captives on a staircase, the preferred locus for such an event. Elegantly drawn with sweeping,

continuous lines defining body outline, eyes, hands, and hair, these captives have long been considered among the most beautiful figures of Maya art. Captives at right reach out, as if to protest their treatment at the hands of the warrior at far left, his figure partly truncated by the crosstie holes. Bending over, this warrior grabs a captive by the wrist, and either pulls out the fingernails or cuts off the final finger joint (to put in ceramic vessels that archaeologists call "finger bowls" when they find such offerings, usually in Belize). Blood arcs and spurts from the hands of captives sitting in a row, and a single captive presented on the upper tier appeals to Chan Muwan. At his feet, a dead captive sprawls, cuts visible across his body; his foot leads to a decapitated head, gray brains dribbling from the open cranium.

Overhead, Maya painters have rendered a compelling picture of the sky, with mating peccaries at left and a swimming turtle at right. This is a clear rendering of the constellations today called Gemini and Orion, with the three stars of Orion's belt stretched across the turtle's back.

In Room 3, the lords of Bonampak don great "dancer's wings" for a final orgy of autosacrifice and captive dismemberment, all arrayed against a large pyramid that reaches around the east, south, and west walls. Whirling lords have pierced their penises, and blood collects on the white, diaper-like cloth at the groin, while captives led in from the side are slaughtered at the center of the south wall. "Microtexts" about 2 cm high are inscribed in several locations, and a particularly fine one at the center of the south wall—where it would easily be spotted—names Itzam Balam, the coeval king of Yaxchilán. A band of deformed musicans enters from the west, while in the upper east vault, the ladies of the court gather in the throne room to pierce their tongues and instruct a little child—presumably the same one featured in Room 1—who holds out a hand for piercing.

Depicted only in the first and final scenes of the program, the little heir may represent the ostensible motivation for the entire sequence of events. But the scale of warfare on this occasion may show an elite world out of control: if this battle is just one of many carried out by Bonampak, and perhaps indirectly to serve Yaxchilán as well, then the Bonampak murals reveal a world convulsed by war and chaos, beyond the reach of order and control that human sacrifice sought to reinstate.

Never finished, the Bonampak paintings are also the final work made at the site. Stelae 1, 2, and 3 celebrate earlier events in Chan Muwan's life, and Stela 2 is the only Maya monument to feature two women and a single male—in this case, the king with his mother and his wife. Archaeologists have recovered several wall panels, all belonging to the seventh and eighth centuries; the Bonampak emblem glyph occurs on looted monuments from the Early Classic, but archaeologists have not identified their specific origin. Lacanhá, on the opposite side of the Lacanhá River, may well have been a substantially larger settlement, but little is known beyond Frans Blom and Gertrude Duby's 1955–1957 report.

FURTHER READINGS

Blom, Frans, and Gertrude Duby. 1955–1957. *La selva lacandona.* 2 vols. Mexico City: Editorial Cultura.

Espinosa, A., M. Rosas, B. Sandoval, and A. Venegas. 1988. *Bonampak.* Mexico City: Citicorp.

Miller, M. 1995. Maya Masterpiece Revealed at Bonampak. *National Geographic Magazine,* February, 50–69.

Miller, M. 1997. Virtual Bonampak. *Archaeology Magazine,* May–June, 36–41.

Nájera Coronada, M. 1991. *Bonampak.* Mexico City: Edo de Chiapas.

Ruppert, K., J. Thompson, and T. Proskouriakoff. 1955. *Bonampak, Chiapas, Mexico.* Washington, D.C.: Carnegie Institution.

Villagra Caletí, A. 1949. *Bonampak, la ciudad de los muros pintados.* Mexico City: INAH.

Mary Ellen Miller

SEE ALSO
Maya Lowlands: South

Buenavista Huaxcama and the Río Verde Region (San Luis Potosí, Mexico)

Situated within the Río Verde drainage between the Sierra Madre Oriental and Sierra Gorda mountains, this site consists of mounds of varying sizes randomly placed around a small central plaza. The most interesting architectural feature is a circular stone structure consisting of two concentric rows of stone cemented with mud. Inside were eight individuals, lying in the fetal position, with no offerings except broken ceramics in the rubble that covered the burials.

Du Solier excavated there in 1941–1942 as part of a larger Huasteca regional project with Ekholm, who excavated in the Pánuco region in Veracruz. Other work done in the Río Verde region includes regional survey and preliminary excavations, and a more recent regional survey project. Given the preliminary nature of these excavations

and reliance on survey data, it is not surprising that chronologies for the sites and the region diverge, although they generally agree on a primary occupation in the Late Classic to Early Postclassic periods.

Ceramics of the Río Verde region appear to be similar to those of the Huasteca coastal plain to the east, with some minor variants noted. Ties with Tajín and the ritual ball game are indicated by the importation of carved stone artifacts, as well as the presence of numerous ball courts, yokes, and figurines in the area. Also interesting are the suggestions of trade networks with Caddoan groups of the southeastern United States, particularly in the use of red pigment rubbed into incisions on polished black ware.

FURTHER READINGS

Du Solier, W. 1945. Estudio arquitectónico de los edificios huaxtecas. *Anales del Instituto de Antropología e Historia* 1939–1940:121–146.

———. 1947. Sistema de entierros entre los Huaxtecos prehispánicos. *Journal de la Société des Américanistes* 34:195–214.

Du Solier, W., A. Krieger, and J. B. Griffin. 1947. The Archaeological Zone of Buena Vista, Huaxcama, San Luis Potosí, Mexico. *American Antiquity* 13:15–32.

Michelet, D. 1984. *Río Verde, San Luis Potosí (Mexique).* Études Mésoaméricaines, 9. México: Centre D'Études Mexicaines et Centraméricaines.

Troike, N. 1961. Archaeological Reconnaissance in the Drainage of the Río Verde, San Luis Potosí, Mexico. *Bulletin of the Texas Archaeological Society* 32:43–55.

Troike, R., N. Troike, and J. Graham. 1972. Preliminary Report on Excavations in the Archaeological Zone of Río Verde, San Luis Potosí, Mexico. *Contributions of the University of California Archaeological Research Facility* 16:69–87.

Mary Pye

SEE ALSO
Gulf Lowlands: North Region; Tajín, El

Bugambilias (Jalisco, Mexico)

Situated in the Atemajac Valley on the southwestern outskirts of Guadalajara, this site was mapped and salvage-excavated in the early 1980s, with further excavations by Galván, Deraga, and Fernandez. Some results have been published, and much of the site has since been destroyed. The "site" is actually composed of upper and lower

B

Bugambilias, dating to two different periods. On the lower piedmont next to a seasonal arroyo is a concentric circular structure of the Teuchitlán tradition, with eight structures on a circular patio, all ringing a circular pyramidal mound. It is one of the few surviving examples of this form of architecture in the valley; it points to a link with the core area of the Teuchitlán tradition to the west. No other structures have been located in the area, but Shaft Tomb BG-1 is a short distance away. Intensive clearing and surface collections indicated a Tabachines phase (A.D. 1–550) occupation of the site.

Above this section of the site is upper Bugambilias, composed of more than thirty rectangular and circular structures of a construction method and form called *corrales*. They form a dispersed pattern across the top of a volcanic dome, and only one group appears to resemble a plaza formation. Excavations identified these structures as residential, and there are no clear public buildings. Similar structures have been identified elsewhere in central and northern Jalisco and southern Zacatecas, frequently on hilltops and associated with possible defensive walls. Artifacts from this part of the site date to the Atemajac phase in the local sequence (A.D. 1200–1500).

FURTHER READINGS

Deraga, D., and R. Fernandez. 1986. Unidades habitacionales en el Occidente. In L. Manzanilla (ed.), *Unidades habitacionales mesoamericanas y sus areas de actividad,* pp. 375–398. Mexico City: Universidad Nacional Autónoma de México.

Galván Villegas, L. J. 1991. *Las tumbas de tiro del Valle de Atemajac, Jalisco.* Serie Arqueológica. Mexico City: INAH.

Luís Javier Galván Villegas and Christopher S. Beekman

SEE ALSO

Teuchitlán Tradition; West Mexico

Bundles

Bundles are wrapped packages of utilitarian, luxury, or sacred items, and they played important political, ritual, and economic roles in Mesoamerican communities. There is considerable variation in the types of bundles used. Bundles of trade goods (cloth, feathers, utilitarian items, foodstuffs) were carried throughout Mesoamerica by merchants such as the *pochteca* of Postclassic times. Tribute was sometimes gathered in bundles, as shown in scenes on Maya pots and in the Mendoza Codex.

Cloth bundles are depicted in paintings and other narrative scenes. These were considered sacred objects and contained items of great spiritual power, such as maize cobs, divining stones, sacrificial instruments, or deity images. Wrapping venerated things in cloth served to protect them from the elements and from everyday sights, and to ensure that the items retained their "heat" and spiritual essence. Thus, sacred bundles enclosing the patron gods of Quiché Maya lineages were called "wrapped heat." Unwrapping such a bundle, in the context of presentation or sacrifice, was an event of considerable ceremony.

Bundles containing emblems of office were used in connection with accession ceremonies among the Maya. In the sculpture of Palenque, unwrapped bundles containing a flint and shield—the emblems of sacred warfare—are shown being presented to new rulers. Similarly, among the modern Tzotzil Maya, outgoing officials place their medallion necklaces in cloth bundles and present them to the incoming officials. Some large cloth bundles in ancient Maya art are labeled with the glyph meaning "burden, charge," a concept related to the idea of political office throughout Mesoamerica. The symbolic meaning of similar bundles from central Mexico is "town heart," because they are invested with the essence of community identity. In some areas of Mesoamerica, deceased rulers and nobles were wrapped as bundles, adorned with masks, feathers, and paper streamers, and then venerated in the same way as other sacred bundles.

FURTHER READINGS

Stenzel, W. 1968. The Sacred Bundle in Mesoamerican Religion. In *Thirty-eighth International Congress of Americanists, Stuttgart-München, 1968,* vol. 5, part 2, pp. 347–352.

Stross, B. 1988. The Burden of Office: A Reading. *Mexicon* 10.6:118–121.

David Stuart

C

Cacaxtla (Tlaxcala, Mexico)

Fortified Late Classic–Epiclassic city (A.D. 600–900, based on radiocarbon dates and cultural features) of relatively small size but having important mural pictures. Situated on a slope in the Puebla–Tlaxcala Valley, surrounded by fertile valleys and an abundance of water, Cacaxtla based its economy on agricultural production and commerce, supporting about 10,000 people at the site at its peak. Political control is thought to have been administered by civil and military chiefs, rather than through theocratic organization. Site surveys have delimited at least nine moats and a footed wall. Only one elevated platform has been investigated; this revealed superimposed strata indicating numerous stages of construction, and one pyramid from the early phase of occupation, also contemporaneous with Cacaxtla. Besides the murals, not many cultural materials have been found—some stone or clay sculpture, and some bone artifacts. Construction materials used at the site included blocks of tepetate, adobe, and stone, surfaced with lime or mud plaster.

The murals are found throughout the construction phases. They contain symbolic and narrative elements. The most important represent strongly realistic battle scenes with ritual and anecdotal qualities, as well as activities of agriculture and commerce (Red Temple), symbolism (Temple of Venus or the Paired Scorpion), and magico-religious mysticism (Building A). Some depict aquatic animals, while others feature serpents, plumed or in jaguar skins. Depictions of humans denote two different groups, those from the Central Highlands (associated with jaguars), and Mayas; the latter are associated with birds, perhaps Tlaloc and Quetzalcoatl. Ritual life is revealed in the murals, in child burials found in the North Plaza, and in other cultural features.

Cacaxtla defeated Cholula—or contributed to its fall—and was the capital of the Puebla Valley during the Epiclassic (A.D. 650–900). It seems that Cacaxtla was occupied by the Olmeca-Xicalanca people (a triethnic group of Mixtecs, Chochopolocans, and Nahua) who gained control of the Puebla Valley as Cholula's power declined. Later, Cacaxtla too was destroyed—by Tolteca-Chichimecs—and its people migrated and contributed to the resurgence of Cholula's power in reestablishing control over the region.

Contacts with the Maya area, with Oaxaca, Xochicalco, and the Basin of Mexico are evidenced. Cacaxtla is contemporaneous with Xochicalco, with Cantona (at its second peak), and with one of the occupation phases at Teotenango.

FURTHER READINGS

García Cook, A., and B. L. Merino Carrión. 1995. *Antología de Cacaxtla*. 2 vols. Mexico City: INAH.

McVicker, D. 1985. The "Mayanized" Mexicans. *American Antiquity* 50:82–101.

Angel García Cook

SEE ALSO

Mural Painting; Puebla-Tlaxcala Region

Caches

Intentionally hidden objects or groups of objects. Those that by content, grouping, or context appear to have a votive, dedicatory, or ceremonial function have variously

C

been termed "offerings," *ofrendas,* or *esconditas.* These are found in most regions of Mesoamerica, the U.S. Southwest, Central America, and Colombia, but, strangely, not in the remainder of North or South America. The first and still the most thorough survey of Mesoamerican caches is Coe's 1959 publication, now supplemented by his 1990 summary of caches at the main group at Tikal. Caches found in the Aztec Great Temple at Tenochtitlán show surprising similarity to Tikal's in both content (jade and greenstone, chipped flint, obsidian, shells and other sea materials, and several kinds of reptiles) and location (beneath floors and stairs on axis, and at the corners of structures).

FURTHER READINGS

Coe, W. R. 1959. *Piedras Negras Archaeology: Artifacts, Caches, and Burials.* University Museum Monographs. Philadelphia: University of Pennsylvania.

———. 1962. A Summary of Excavation and Research at Tikal, Guatemala: 1956–1961. *American Antiquity* 27:479–507.

———. 1990. *Excavations in the Great Plaza, North Terrace, and North Acropolis of Tikal.* 5 vols. University Museum, Tikal Reports, 14. Philadelphia: University of Pennsylvania.

López Lujan, L. 1994. *The Offerings of the Templo Mayor of Tenochtitlán.* Niwot: University of Colorado Press.

Matos Moctezuma, E. 1994. *The Great Temple of the Aztecs: Treasures of Tenochtitlán.* Doris Heyden (trans.). London and New York: Thames and Hudson.

Stromsvik, G. 1941. Substela Caches and Stela Foundations at Copán and Quirigua. *Contributions to American Anthropology and History* 7:63–96.

Christopher Jones

SEE ALSO
Bundles

Cajón, El (Honduras)

This natural communication corridor in west central Honduras along the Sulaco and Humuya rivers connects highland areas with the northern coastal plain. It was first occupied around 400 B.C. by non-Maya groups from adjacent riverine or lacustrine areas, possibly from the Yojoa Basin or Comayagua Valley. Groups in the El Cajón region practiced a mixed economy of maize agriculture combined with hunting, fishing, and wild plant collecting. Settlements were established on or near good agricul-

tural land, most of which is concentrated in small plains along the margins of the rivers. Most prehistoric settlements were small hamlets or farmsteads of between two and ten residential structures. The largest settlements are nucleated communities of 500 to 1,500 persons, with special-purpose mounded architecture indicative of broader civic-ceremonial functions.

Population densities reached their highest level between A.D. 600 and 800, when the region supported at least one small chiefdom society centered on the site of Salitron Viejo along the Sulaco River. Socio-political development in the El Cajón region was equivalent in scale and complexity to that found among other non-Maya groups in central Honduras between A.D. 400 and 1000. The El Cajón region actively engaged in interregional exchange with areas of eastern Honduras that linked it indirectly with areas as distant as Costa Rica. The development of chiefdoms in central Honduras was based on control of limited agricultural resources in riverine settings and on interregional exchange for a variety of elite items, including jade, marble, and ceramic used by local elite. Population declined after A.D. 800, and the area was abandoned after 1000.

FURTHER READINGS

Hirth, K. G. 1988. Beyond the Maya Frontier: Cultural Interaction and Syncretism along the Central Honduran Corridor. In E. H. Boone and G. R. Willey (eds.), *The Southeast Classic Maya Zone,* pp. 297–334. Washington, D.C.: Dumbarton Oaks.

Hirth, K. G., G. Lara, and G. Hasemann. 1989. *Archaeological Research in the El Cajon Region.* Vol. 1, *Prehistoric Cultural Ecology.* University of Pittsburgh Memoirs in Latin American Archaeology, 1. Pittsburgh and Tegucigalpa: University of Pittsburgh and Instituto Hondureño de Antropología e Historia.

Kenneth G. Hirth

SEE ALSO
Salitron Viejo; Southeast Mesoamerica

Calakmul (Campeche, Mexico)

One of the largest and most powerful Maya regional capitals, Calakmul was occupied from the Late Formative to the end of the tenth century. It was a state capital surrounded by tributary sites, administering a four-tiered hierarchy with a strong Formative relationship to El Mirador and other sites such as El Guiro, Nakbe, and

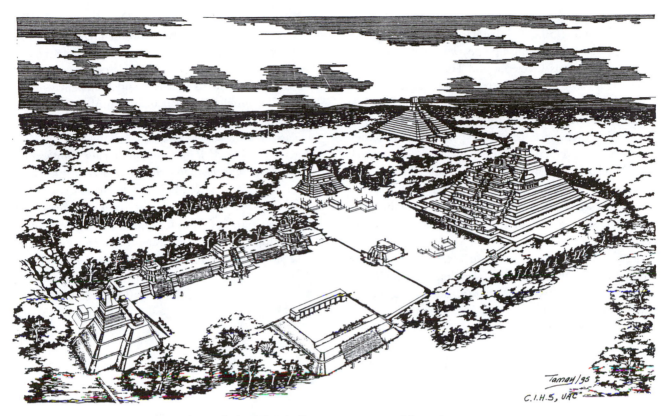

A drawing of the great Maya regional capital of Calakmul. Illustration courtesy of the author.

Tintal, all of which were linked by raised roadways around the first century A.D. Calakmul later developed into the major regional capital of a state in the northern Petén rivaled only by Tikal, persisting up to the ninth century, when Petén-related urban centers and regional states fragmented and collapsed into principalities as the result of a long-lasting severe drought from which they never recovered their former splendor.

Calakmul is linked to sites in the heavily forested Maya Lowlands by means of several long distance *sacbes* (raised roads). Sacbe 6 extended southwest 38 kilometers to El Mirador (Guatemala), and 30 kilometers farther south to Tintal and perhaps beyond that point. Sacbe #4 extended 20 kilometers northeast toward the tributary center of El Laberinto. The greater part of the 10,000 square kilometers of Calakmul's Classic period regional state is within the Petén region of the present state of Campeche (Mexico).

Little or no surface water is available in the region, so the ancient Maya of Calakmul relied on thirteen reservoirs with a capacity of up to 100 million liters. Recent analysis indicates that Calakmul thrived for a thousand years during mild, warm periods characterized by moder-ate but dependable rainfall. Partial collapses occurred in 450 and 150 B.C. and A.D. 250 owing to colder conditions, with a prolonged drought between A.D. 750 and 950 that contributed to the general Maya collapse.

The urban center of Calakmul was organized in a strongly concentric fashion along the edge of the extensive seasonal swamp of El Laberinto, inhabited and exploited by Calakmulecos for its deposits of chert as well as for farming the rich, moist soils along its edges. The 30-square-kilometer mapped area of Calakmul contains 6,250 structures and other cultural features, including a large, astronomically oriented plaza marking the equinoxes and solstices, two of the largest structures in greater Mesoamerica, and more than 116 stelae dating from the fifth to the ninth century. Calakmul's emblem glyph is found in the texts of many sites outside its realm, including Copán, Dos Pilas, Palenque, Piedras Negras, and Tikal. It is more frequent than those of other major centers, underscoring Calakmul's far-reaching importance, particularly during the reign of Jaguar Paw.

The Late Classic population of Calakmul has been estimated at 25,000 citizens, based on a detailed analysis of architectural remains within its arroyo-rimmed nucleus

C

of 22 square kilometers, with the rest of the city reaching a total of about 50,000 inhabitants. Ceramic analysis indicates a strong relationship between Calakmul and El Mirador, as well as Uaxactún and Tikal during the Preclassic (Zihnal y Takan), Early Classic (Kaynikte), and Late Classic (Ku) ceramic periods. During the Terminal Classic (Halibe), Calakmul and Río Bec sites such as Becán also exchanged ceramic types and architectural styles (but not the custom of producing dynastic texts). The Postclassic is identifiable through small quantities of Chichén Itzá and Mayapan-style wares (including a copper finger ring) present in the region just before the Spanish conquest, thus providing the term "Cehache" for this ceramic phase.

Regional survey has produced a record of nineteen large sites, including Uxul, Sasilha, Oxpemul, La Muñeca, Altamira, and Naachtun, and a number of smaller sites, as well as 362 stelae, within the 10,000 square kilometers around Calakmul. The combined population is estimated at 500,000 people. The monuments depict rulers and their spouses, as well as dynastic texts recording their names and those of their wives and children, along with information on the relationship of Calakmul with other cities identified through emblem glyphs, a register of wars fought, captives taken, and marriages of rulers and of their siblings, as well as their deaths. The records span the fifth to ninth century A.D.

Several royal tombs have been excavated, providing a vision of Maya funeral customs and afterlife. Several burials are of individuals laid out on top of several plates after being wrapped in cloth, *petates,* and other materials. Some were accompanied by masks formed of multiple jadeite plaques; one burial was accompanied by three celts with incised glyphs containing the name of the tomb occupant. Spectacular anthropomorphic and polychrome ceramic offerings were also found in these tombs.

FURTHER READINGS

Folan, W. J. 1992. Calakmul, Campeche: A Centralized Urban Administrative Center in the Northern Petén. *World Archaeology* 24:158–168.

Folan, W. J., J. M. Garcia Ortega, and M. C. Sanchez Gonzalez (eds.). 1992. *Programa de Manejo: Reserva de la Biosfera, Calakmul, Campeche, Campeche.* 4 vols. Campeche: Centro de Investigaciones Historicas y Sociales, Universidad Autónoma de Campeche, Secretario de Desarrollo Social.

Folan, W. J., J. Marcus, M. d. R. Dominguez C., S. Pincemin Deliberos, L. A. Fletcher, and A. Morales Lopez. 1995. Calakmul, New Data from an Ancient Maya Capital in Campeche, Mexico. *Latin American Antiquity* 6:310–334.

Gunn, J. D., W. J. Folan, and H. R. Robichaux. 1995. A Landscape Analysis of the Candelaria Watershed in Mexico: Insights Into Paleoclimates Affecting Upland Horticulture in the Southern Yucatan Peninsula Semi-Karst. *Geoarchaeology* 10:3–42.

Marcus, J. 1976. *Emblem and State in the Classic Maya Lowlands: An Epigraphic Approach to Territorial Organization.* Washington, D.C.: Dumbarton Oaks.

———. 1987. *The Inscriptions of Calakmul: Royal Marriage at a Maya City in Campeche, Mexico.* Museum of Anthropology, Technical Report 21. Ann Arbor: University of Michigan.

William Folan

SEE ALSO

Maya Lowlands: South

Calendrics

Mesoamerican peoples relied on a number of cyclical calendrical systems. The systematic repetition of the perceived movement of heavenly bodies was a constant reminder of order in the universe. An element of fate was embedded in the interpretation of these cycles, because it was believed that events could repeat themselves at certain points within calendrical cycles. Thus, there were calendrical specialists within Mesoamerican societies who were called on to divine the meaning of particular days and to predict the future. Although many astronomical cycles were known in ancient Mesoamerica, a basic calendrical system was used across the entire region, beginning at least several centuries before the common era; one element of this system continues to be used by Maya communities today.

At the time of the Spanish invasion, there were several versions of the basic Mesoamerican calendar in existence, but all of these calendars had the same structure: they were composed of one cycle of 260 days and a second cycle of 365 days. These two cycles ran concurrently, creating a third cycle of 52 years; only once every 52 years would a day have the same designation in both calendars. The 52-year cycle is known as the Calendar Round.

The 260-day calendar is referred to as the Sacred Round, the Ritual calendar, or the Sacred Almanac; the Aztecs called it *tonalpohualli,* and the Zapotecs called it *piye* (other groups had their own names for it). In this cycle each day was named using a number from 1 to 13 together with one of twenty day names. Among the many Mesoamerican ethnolinguistic groups, the day names varied from group to group, but all the 260-day calendars worked on the same principle. For example, among the Yucatec Maya the first five day names were Imix, Ik, Akbal, Kan, and Chicchan; thus, the first five days of the Sacred calendar were called 1 Imix, 2 Ik, 3 Akbal, 4 Kan, and 5 Chicchan. The first five day names for the Aztecs were Cipactli (Alligator), Ehécatl (Wind), Calli (House), Cuetzpallin (Lizard), and Coatl (Snake), so the first five days were called 1 Cipactli, 2 Ehecatl, 3 Calli, 4 Cuetzpallin, and 5 Coatl.

Each day in the Ritual calendar had a particular fate that could be interpreted with the help of a diviner, and the calendar was used as an almanac to make predictions. An individual's destiny was determined by the date of birth, and other social and political events, ranging from planting crops to planning marriages to waging war, were scheduled for appropriate days.

There has been a great deal of speculation about the origins and basis of the 260-day cycle. Some scholars believe it is based on some astronomical cycle or on the human gestation cycle, but it is also possible that it is simply the result of using the important numbers 13 (there are thirteen levels in the heavens) and 20 (Mesoamericans all used a vigesimal or base-20 counting system). The earliest known representation of this cycle comes from the Zapotec site of San José Mogote in the Valley of Oaxaca at around 500 B.C. It is likely that the Sacred Round was in use before this time, however. The 260-day Ritual calendar continues to be used in some Maya communities today.

The 365-day calendar is also called the "Solar cycle" or "Solar calendar"; the Yucatec Maya called it *haab*, the Aztecs *xiuitl*, and the Zapotecs *yza*. It is similar to our own 365-day annual calendar, although we add a day every four years (except for century years that are not divisible by 400) to account for the fact that the Earth's rotation actually takes 365 days, 5 hours, and 48 minutes. In the Mesoamerican Solar year there were 18 named months, each with 20 days, plus an additional 5-day period to complete the 365-day cycle.

Mesoamericans identified each day in terms of both the 260-day and 365-day calendars. Each day was named with a number and name of the day in the Sacred almanac and a number and month name from the Solar calendar. Because the two cycles were of different lengths, only once every 52 years did a day occur at the same point in both

cycles. The day that marked the beginning of both cycles was a momentous occasion that was celebrated—and sometimes feared. The significance of the 52-year cycle or the Calendar Round (called *xiuhmolpilli* by the Aztecs) is often likened to the importance we place on the turn of the century. We typically think in 100-year blocks of time; similarly, Mesoamericans had 52-year blocks of time.

We know that the Aztecs celebrated the end of one 52-year cycle and the beginning of the next with the New Fire Ceremony. As the end of a 52-year cycle approached, fear grew that the world might be destroyed. Household items were discarded and hearth fires were extinguished. Once priests had determined that the Sun would rise again, ensuring that another 52-year cycle would begin, a fire was started on the chest of a sacrificial victim. Torches were then carried throughout the Aztec realm, and hearths in all houses were rekindled with sparks from this single fire.

In addition to the basic Mesoamerican calendrical system, another way of reckoning time was through the long count. Although the long count was ultimately based on the notion of cycles—in this case, cycles of 5,128 solar years—for all practical purposes it is a measure of linear time beginning from a fixed date. Long count dates indicate the exact number of days that have passed since the beginning of the current cycle, which began in August of 3114 B.C., according to the most widely accepted correlation. As a result, a long count date can be read and converted into our own dating system, allowing us to learn the precise dates of certain events.

Unlike the Mesoamerican calendar, the long count system was not used across Mesoamerica, and it was in use for a relatively short time, between approximately 36 B.C. and A.D. 909. The earliest long count dates known come from the Olmec region, the Central Depression (Grijalva Valley) of Chiapas, and Pacific coastal Guatemala; these regions are thought to have been populated by Mixe-Zoque speakers, so it is probable that the long count originated with the Mixe-Zoque. It was the Classic Maya, however, who made the most extensive use of the long count. From around A.D. 200 until 909, long count dates appear on Maya stone monuments (stelae), buildings, pottery, and other artifacts.

The long count dating system works much like our own system. Whereas we refer to a day as Wednesday, June 3, 1998, the long count typically refers to a date using five numbers (each of which stands for a given unit of time), followed by the day names from the Sacred Round and the Solar year. Our notation of the year 1998

C

simply reflects our use of the decimal system; the date really means that since the beginning of our calendrical system (the year 0), one unit of 1,000 years, 9 units of 100 years, 9 units of 10 years, and 8 units of 1 year have passed. A five-digit long count date of 9.6.10.0.0 is read in a similar fashion: 9 *baktuns* (units of 144,000 days), 6 *katuns* (units of 7,200 days), 10 *tuns* (units of 360 days), 0 *uinals* (units of 20 days), and 0 *kins* (units of 1 day) have passed since the beginning of the current cycle (August 3114 B.C.). By adding 9 times 144,000, 6 times 7,200, and 10 times 360, we arrive at a number of days, and this figure can be converted to a date in our own calendrical system by first dividing by 365 and then adding this number to −3114 (corrections also must be made for leap years and the shift from the Julian to Gregorian calendar). The long count date of 9.6.10.0.0 converts to a date of A.D. 564 in the Gregorian calendar.

The use of the long count dating system has been a tremendous help to archaeologists studying the Classic Maya and the earlier Mixe-Zoquean peoples because of its precision. As the Classic Maya civilization collapsed, however, the long count dating system fell out of use.

FURTHER READINGS

Aveni, A. 1989. *Empires of Time: Calendars, Clocks, and Cultures.* New York: Basic Books, Inc.

Coe, M. D. 1994. *Mexico: From the Olmecs to the Aztecs.* 4th ed. New York: Thames and Hudson.

Marcus, J. 1992. *Mesoamerican Writing Systems: Propaganda, Myth, and History in Four Ancient Civilizations.* Princeton: Princeton University Press.

Sharer, R. J. 1994. *The Ancient Maya.* 5th ed. Stanford: Stanford University Press.

Janine Gasco

SEE ALSO

Astronomy, Archaeoastronomy, and Astrology; Writing

Calixtlahuaca (Toluca, Mexico)

One of the most important settlements of the Matlatzinca people, who settled in the lake region of the Valley of Toluca and lived principally on lacustrine resources (fish and waterfowl), as well as by maize farming. The archaeological site of Calixtlahuaca is characteristic of the period of local city-states and imperial metropolises, c. A.D. 900–1521. Built on Cerro Tenismó, Calixtlahuaca was explored in 1932–1934 by José García Payón.

The Matlatzincas used topography in their construction of monuments, creating systems of terraces and platforms from the summit down the sides of the hill, and one can observe seventeen large monuments erected on dispersed terraces. Some are grouped in small clusters around a plaza. Principal monuments are the Tlaloc Group, the Temple of Ehecatl, and the Calmecac. The last is in the lower part of the site, near the Tecaxic River, and consists of a group of residential and ceremonial structures situated around a rectangular patio enclosed by platforms that had room groups. Toward the southeast are groups of residential rooms with hearths. The rooms are on different levels, connected by small staircases and narrow passageways.

The Tlaloc Group is made up of three structures around a plaza. The most distinctive, the *tzompantli* (skull rack), is built of tezontle in a cruciform plan; its walls are decorated with tenons, some of which are cylindrical and some in the form of human skulls. The Temple of Tlaloc, the largest building in this group, has a square plan with a stairway delineated by balustrades. To the north is a small platform of square plan with remains of rooms on the top.

Calixtlahuaca's most imposing monument is the round Temple of Ehecatl. It was so named because ethnohistoric sources document that circular temples were dedicated to the deity Quetzalcoatl as Ehecatl, god of the wind. During excavations into this structure, a sculpture of this god was discovered, with his costume of duck-billed mask, loincloth, and sandals. García Payón's excavations found four construction phases, all with circular plans. The first was a simple platform with a staircase toward the east, built of stone faced with sloping walls (*talud* style). The second phase had straight walls, and the third had serpent-head decorations. From this, one deduces that the third phase corresponds to the epoch of Matlatzinca hegemony (A.D. 1200–1474). The fourth construction phase, after Calixtlahuaca was conquered by the Mexica in 1474, also has serpent decorations.

FURTHER READINGS

García Payón, J. 1974. *La zona arqueológica de Tecaxic-Calixtlahuaca y los Matlatzinca.* Mexico City: Biblioteca Enciclopédica del Estado de México.

———. 1979. *La zona arqueológica de Tecaxic-Calixtlahuaca y los Matlatzinca: Etnología y Arqueología.* Part 2. Mexico City: Biblioteca Enciclopédica del Estado de México.

Piña Chan, R. 1983. *El Estado de México antes de la Conquista.* Toluca: Universidad Autónoma del Estado de México.

Quezada, N. 1972. *Los Matlatzincas: Epoca prehispánica y epoca colonial.* Investigaciones Históricas, 22. Mexico City: Instituto Nacional de Antropología e Historia.

Beatriz Zúñiga Bárcenas

SEE ALSO

Toluca Region

Calón, El

See Northwestern Frontier

Canajasté (Chiapas, Mexico)

Although hundreds of ancient settlements have been discovered in the Upper Tributaries region of the Grijalva River basin, Canajasté is one of the few sites that date exclusively to the Postclassic period. Canajasté lies only 200 meters from the present Mexican-Guatemalan border in the state of Chiapas, Mexico.

Canajasté was originally settled in the 1200s by Mayan colonists, possibly Chuj speakers, from western Guatemala. They built a small fortified town perched on a bend in the Lagartero River and protected it with a 230-meter-long, 2-meter-high stone wall. Within the confines of the 2.5-hectare walled zone was a ceremonial center with several stone masonry temples, at least one of which had plastered walls painted with polychrome murals. About two hundred houses were closely clustered within the walled zone.

There were several groups of large platform structures near the ceremonial center of the site. Some may have had administrative functions, and others were probably residences of the community's nobility. One such patio group, consisting of three structures, has been excavated in its entirety. The house platforms were well preserved, and each contained a stratified sequence of building episodes and middens. The largest house platform in the group was initially built toward the end of the Early Postclassic period and was expanded in height and length six times. The majority of the house platforms were clustered in tight patio groups of between two and four buildings. The two-house groups that were completely excavated showed initial architectural styles that were smaller and less regular than the large elite house group. However, by the Late Postclassic period these non-elite houses had been rebuilt to emulate the elite houses.

The house remains provide evidence for the community's ongoing participation in both trade and warfare. Many artifacts were imported items, such as copper bells and ornaments, marine shell beads and pendants, obsidian tools, ceramic vessels, figurines, and spindle whorls. During the Late Postclassic period, as the frequency of these trade items declined, there was increasing evidence of warfare. The buildings showed traces of multiple burnings; the houses became ever more tightly packed within the town's fortifications; and larger numbers of small obsidian arrow points were recovered. Although Canajasté was not a large site, even by Postclassic standards, it gives us a fascinating glimpse of the way small-scale secondary states changed during this period. It probably started as a small colony or bud-off from a neighboring community in highland Guatemala. Throughout its history the balance between trade and warfare constantly shifted as the people of Canajasté tried to maintain control over their town and lands. By the time of the Spanish conquest, the community was abandoned, eventually to be replaced by new colonial towns such as Coneta and Coapa along the Camino Real.

FURTHER READINGS

Blake, M. 1984. The Postclassic Maya of Canajasté, Chiapas, Mexico. *Masterkey: Anthropology of the Americas* 58:9–17.

de Montmollin, O. 1989. *The Archaeology of Political Structure: Settlement Analysis in a Classic Maya Polity.* Cambridge: Cambridge University Press.

Michael Blake

SEE ALSO

Chiapas Interior Plateau

Cannibalism

In Mesoamerica, the consumption of human flesh seems to have been limited to ritual cannibalism, which is best documented for the Aztec of Central Mexico. Fray Bernardino de Sahagún described how prisoners of war were offered as sacrifices to various deities, among them the legendary Aztec hero god Huitzilopochtli, whose cult involved the reenactment of Huitzilopochtli's mythical defeat of his sister, Coyolxauhqui, in a battle that was waged atop his mother's mountaintop home, from which

C

Coyolxauhqui's dismembered body was cast down the slope. Prisoners of war were led up the steps to Huitzilopochtli's temple atop the Great Pyramid in Tenochtitlán, where they were sacrificed by having their hearts removed; their bodies were then thrown down the steps of the temple, decapitated, dismembered, and ritually consumed by the victorious Aztec warriors.

The archaeological record of Mesoamerica discloses what appear to be ritually cannibalized human remains, extending back to the Formative period at the Olmec site of San Lorenzo (and possibly back to the Archaic period at El Riego Cave and Purrón Cave in the Tehuacán Valley). These human bone remains have not yet been subjected to an intensive analysis of their skeletal parts; their breakage patterns; and their degree of butchering, burning, or cooking, which could confirm their association with the practice of cannibalism.

FURTHER READINGS

Redmond, E. M. 1994. *Tribal and Chiefly Warfare in South America.* Memoirs of the University of Michigan Museum of Anthropology, 28. Ann Arbor.

Elsa M. Redmond

SEE ALSO

Sacrifice

Cantona (Puebla, Mexico)

Fortified city of approximately 12.5 square kilometers, during the Classic period second in size only to Teotihuacán, with which it competed in the obsidian trade. It was occupied during the whole Classic period, from A.D. 100 to 900, peaking during 600–900 with a population of 80,000 to 90,000. It is situated on a badlands area, a basaltic lava flow bearing little or no sedimentary overburden, at an elevation between 2,500 and 2,600 meters, surrounded by fertile valleys. The climate is temperate, with 20 to 40 days of frost. Agriculture and exploitation and exchange of obsidian formed the basis of the economy.

The site includes twenty-four ball courts, twelve of which occur as an architectural ensemble aligned so that in those courts found in the extreme and opposite to a pyramid there are one or two walled plazas enclosed by the complex. Another highlight is the elevated and constructed street in the residential zone and sunken plaza in the civic-ceremonial area. The habitational area was densely settled, with patio groups of dwellings surrounded by high walls and intercommunicating through constructed streets and passageways; paved roads also crossed the badlands and connected the city with other towns and villages.

No mortar or cement was used in construction, nor was plaster or mud stucco used to cover the walls; everything was stone on stone, and asymmetrical. Enclosed ceremonial plazas are common, in which one high pyramid encloses the whole with its walls. The site has large workshops where obsidian was prepared for export and other crafts manufactured for local and household use.

The site is notable for its engraved stones and abundant sculpture with detailed representation of phalluses. In Cantona there are elements similar to those of the Maya area—phallic sculptures, discs in ball courts, and ceramic elements. Similarities to southern Puebla, the central Gulf Lowlands, and the Bajío are evidenced by ceramic and stone remains. Obsidian from the Oyameles-Zaragoza source has been found in places in southern Puebla, southern Veracruz, and the Maya area, apparently sent from Cantona during the Classic.

Cantona was a completely fortified city, and its setting and layout indicate an absolute control over the population and its circulation. There existed strong ceremonialism, evidenced by human remains showing decapitation; boiled, burned, and carved bones, with artifacts deposited over the bones; and offerings of human remains in the construction of altars and pyramids. Though contemporaneous with Teotihuacán and Cholula, Cantona seems to have shared few cultural elements with them, and there is no strong evidence (ceramic, lithic, or architectonic) of influence from either. In having been strongly fortified at its peak and in decline, it resembles Teotenango, Xochicalco, and Cacaxtla. Less than 1 percent of the site surface (only 9 hectares) has been investigated.

FURTHER READINGS

García Cook, Angel. 1994. Cantona. *Arqueología Mexicana* 5.2.9:79–80; 5.2.10:60–65.

———. 1994. *Cantona: Guía.* Mexico City: INAH-SALVAT.

García Cook, A., and B. L. Merino Carrión. 1998. Cantona: Urbe prehispánica en el altiplano central de México. *Latin American Antiquity* 9:191–216.

Angel García Cook

SEE ALSO

Puebla-Tlaxcala Region

C

Capacha (Colima, Mexico)

The term "Capacha" refers primarily to a set of related cultural materials found mainly in the state of Colima in West Mexico, and dated there to the early to middle Formative period. In Colima, Capacha remains consist mostly of pottery vessels and stone tools found, in association with human burials, by looters or by the archaeologist Isabel Kelly. Although some looters reported having found Capacha material in shaft-and-chamber tombs, this could not be verified by Kelly. The Capacha material she recovered accompanied burials made in simple subsoil pits. Nevertheless, some aspects of the form and decoration of Capacha pottery appear to link it to roughly contemporary material from shaft-and-chamber tombs at the site of El Opeño (highlands of northwestern Michoacán).

The Capacha archaeological culture has been defined primarily on the basis of the form and decoration of funerary pottery vessels, by Kelly in 1970. These vessels probably contained liquids or foods to sustain the spirit of the deceased on its journey to the afterworld. The most characteristic vessel form is a large jar with a constricted midsection, presumably an imitation of gourd vessels still used by many farmers in West Mexico to carry drinking water. There are other, rarer Capacha vessels that Kelly called "trifids"; instead of having a constricted midsection, they have three hollow tubes connecting the upper and lower globular sections of the vessel. This form may symbolize the connection between the world of the living and that of the spirits. A few "trifids" have only two tubes and therefore resemble a widely distributed New World vessel form, the "stirrup spout." Other Capacha vessel forms include high-necked jars, *tecomate* jars, and double- or triple-connected bowls. Also, there exist at least one bird effigy vessel and several human pottery figurines attributed by Kelly to Capacha.

The Capacha phase is generally dated early in the Formative period, but its precise dating is problematic. There is one radiocarbon date on a minute amount of carbon extracted from sherds of Capacha funerary pottery. The date was obtained in 1970, prior to the use of the much more reliable A.M.S. method for dating such small samples. The raw date falls most probably (67 percent) between 1650 and 1250 B.C., but this statistical range was eventually "corrected" by the laboratory, resulting in a calculation of 2110 to 1520 B.C. There are, however, seven radiocarbon dates on charcoal associated with pottery similar to Capacha available from shaft-and-chamber tombs at El Opeño. Their central dates range from 1280 to 891 B.C. and average 1082 B.C. ± 127 years. In addition, there are a radiocarbon date and a thermoluminescence date from Capacha deposits in other Colima sites, and they fall in the range of 1320 to 880 B.C. Several hydration measurements on obsidian from Capacha contexts in Colima suggest a somewhat later dating, between 806 and 520 B.C. To the northwest of Colima, along the coast of Jalisco and Nayarit, contexts bearing pottery sherds of Capacha-like vessel forms or bearing Capacha-like decoration have been obsidian-hydration dated in the range of 1390 to 1080 B.C. at Tomatlán (Jalisco), and radiocarbon dated in the range of 890 to 220 B.C. in deposits at Ixtapa (Jalisco) and San Blas (Nayarit).

Characteristic decoration of Capacha funerary pottery includes designs that are incised, punched, or painted in zones delimited by incised lines or narrow, raised strips of clay. Sometimes whitish pigment was rubbed into the incised designs to highlight them, but surface paint, when present, is a rose-red to purplish color. It is probable that the common (non-funerary) pottery of the Capacha people consisted primarily of plainware or solid rose-red to purplish painted vessels of simple forms, including bowls, necked jars, and *tecomates*. Such plainware and rose-red to purplish painted pottery is early and relatively widespread in Colima and other parts of West Mexico, and it is much more abundant than the highly diagnostic but rare Capacha funerary ware. Thus, Capacha culture may have been much more extensive and important in West Mexico than it would appear from the limited occurrence of the exotic funerary pottery.

The funerary offerings of pottery vessels and stone tools (including abundant mano and metate grinding stones) seem to indicate that the people responsible for the Capacha remains came into Colima from somewhere else, bringing with them a new, relatively sedentary way of life probably based on the garden-farming cultivation of plants such as maize, beans, and squash. In some areas they may have displaced hunting and gathering peoples, but in many cases they appear to have colonized previously unsettled, virgin territory. Kelly stressed the possibility that Capacha had a South American origin, perhaps derived from the Machalilla culture of coastal Ecuador. She also recognized certain similarities between Capacha pottery and the Tlatilco style in the highlands of central Mexico, but she suggested an ultimately South American origin for the Tlatilco style as well.

There are many more similarities in form and decoration of pottery between Capacha and Tlatilco than

C

between Capacha and Machalilla, but it is also important to point out certain similarities between Capacha iconography and that of the Olmec—similarities that Kelly did not recognize or accept. One of these is the "sunburst" design common on the funerary pottery. This design may be a variant of the "Saint Andrew's Cross" motif common in Olmec iconography, and very possibly used by the Olmecs to represent the sun. There are also significant similarities between Olmec and Capacha pottery figurines, especially the probable representations of forehead deformation and lip excision to expose the front teeth.

FURTHER READINGS

Kelly, I. T. 1980. *Ceramic Sequence in Colima: Capacha, an Early Phase.* Anthropological Papers of the University of Arizona, 37. Tucson.

Mountjoy, J. B. 1994. Capacha: Una cultura enigmática del Occidente de México. *Arqueología Mexicana* 2.9:39–42.

Joseph B. Mountjoy

SEE ALSO

West Mexico

Caracol (Cayo District, Belize)

A large Classic period Maya center situated away from natural water sources in extremely hilly terrain within the Vaca Plateau of Belize, Caracol was first occupied during the Late Formative period (c. 300 B.C.). Caches and epicentral building efforts dating to A.D. 1 indicate that Caracol was a participant in wider lowland Maya cultural and ritual practices at this time, and was also well connected to long-distance trade routes. Caracol achieved prominence during the Late Classic period (A.D. 550–900). At its peak of political power in A.D. 650, the city covered an area greater than 177 square kilometers, with a population of at least 115,000. Some 60 km of internal causeways radiate out from the center and connect various parts of the city. Agricultural terraces were intermixed with settlement within the site core.

Hieroglyphic texts from stone monuments, stucco buildings, and tomb walls provide substantial historic information. Caracol's ruling dynasty traced its history back to A.D. 331. Caracol was extremely warlike during several periods in its history. During the sixth and seventh centuries A.D., it records conquest in war of two Petén (Guatemala) sites—Tikal in 562, and Naranjo during a ten-year period of war from 626 to 636.

Caracol's population increased dramatically during the Late Classic period following this initial period of war. General prosperity is visible throughout the site. It is during and after the period of greatest epigraphic claims that public works such as causeways and agricultural fields were developed. Various cultural patterns indicate that the people of Caracol also developed a distinctive cultural identity during this time. Dental decoration (inlays) is far more common in the Caracol area than in neighboring sites such as Tikal, and ancestor veneration seems to have become more intense. The eastern building in each living group contains human burials and caches rather than standard household remains. There are many caches consisting of pottery vessels with human fingerbones inside them, or with modeled human faces applied to them. Tombs were increasingly used to inter the dead, and often one or more tombs occur in a single living group. Perhaps as a result of increased population, tombs frequently house the remains of more than one person. Skeletal remains in tombs and burials are often incomplete and disarticulated, suggesting that secondary burial was common.

Caracol's historic record indicates further military activity against neighboring cities during the ninth century; indications of increased warfare are found in scenes on model-carved pottery and in weapons encountered on palace floors. Nevertheless, Caracol continued to prosper in the Late to Terminal Classic period. Caana, the most massive architectural complex, was rebuilt during the ninth century, and excavations indicate that a substantial population continued to live and build in the Caracol core. Artifacts and burning encountered on building floors suggest that site abandonment, when it finally occurred, was abrupt and may be dated to just before A.D. 900 for the center. Limited occupation in the surrounding region and sporadic reoccupation of the center may have continued for an additional 200 years.

FURTHER READINGS

Beetz, C. P., and L. Satterthwaite. 1981. *The Monuments and Inscriptions of Caracol, Belize.* University Museum Monograph 45. Philadelphia: University of Pennsylvania.

Chase, A. F., and D. Z. Chase. 1987. *Investigations at the Classic Maya City of Caracol, Belize, 1985–1987.* Pre-Columbian Art Research Institute, Monograph 3. San Francisco.

Chase, A. F., and D. Z. Chase. 1994. *Studies in the Archaeology of Caracol, Belize.* Pre-Columbian Art Research Institute, Monograph 7. San Francisco.

Arlen F. Chase and Diane Z. Chase

SEE ALSO

Maya Lowlands: South

Casas Grandes (Chihuahua, Mexico)

With more than 2,000 rooms, the largest prehistoric pueblo known in the U.S. Southwest and northern Mexico is Casas Grandes, also known as Paquimé. The community was the center of one of the few complex societies to develop north of Mesoamerica. It lies in semiarid northwestern Mexico, but its population was supported by intensive farming in the valleys of rivers descending from nearby mountains. Recently revised occupation dates place it later than originally thought, at c. A.D. 1150–1450.

The site is notable for its combination of pueblo residential architecture and Mesoamerican-style ball courts and platform mounds. Large quantities of imported luxury materials were recovered here, including seashell, copper, turquoise, and many cages for parrots, which were probably kept for their plumes.

The elites of Casas Grandes presumably controlled access to these imported goods, and the site was originally interpreted as a trading outpost established by Mesoamericans to control commerce with areas to the north. Casas Grandes was also seen as the center of a large, highly integrated political system. Many of these interpretations are now being challenged. Some studies argue that mercantile activity and centralized craft production probably were not central to the Casas Grandes economy.

Proposed instead is a "prestige goods" economic model, where rising local elites competed to procure and distribute exotica as a means of building power bases in an emergent complex society. New regional survey work also suggests that the Casas Grandes polity may not have been as large or as highly centralized as once believed. Like Casas Grandes, some neighboring communities within 30 km also have ball courts and parrot cages and presumably participated in a network of ritual and prestige goods exchanges. Communities only 70 km away have none of these things, however, although their artifacts show that they interacted significantly with Casas Grandes. Despite interpretive controversies, Casas Grandes is indisputably the major late prehistoric community of the region.

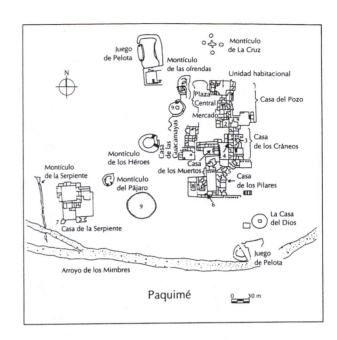

Site plan of Casas Grandes, also known as Paquimé, in northwestern Mexico. Illustration adapted from the original by Charles Di Peso.

FURTHER READINGS

Di Peso, C. C., J. B. Rinaldo, and G. J. Fenner. 1974. *Casas Grandes: A Fallen Trading Center of the Gran Chichimeca.* 8 vols. Dragoon: Amerind Foundation; Flagstaff: Northland Press.

Minnis, P. E., M. E. Whalen, J. H. Kelley, and J. D. Stewart. 1993. Prehistoric Macaw Breeding in the North American Southwest. *American Antiquity* 58:270–276.

Phillips, D. A., Jr. 1989. Prehistory of Chihuahua and Sonora, Mexico. *Journal of World Prehistory* 3:373–401.

Whalen, M. E., and P. E. Minnis. 1996. Ball Courts and Political Centralization in the Casas Grandes Region. *American Antiquity* 61: in press.

Woosley, A. I., and J. C. Ravesloot. 1993. *Culture and Contact: Charles C. Di Peso's Gran Chichimeca.* Dragoon: Amerind Foundation; Albuquerque: University of New Mexico.

Michael E. Whalen and Paul E. Minnis

SEE ALSO

Northern Arid Zone

Castillo, El

See Cotzumalhuapa Sites: Bilbao, El Baúl, and El Castillo

C

Castillo de Teayo (Veracruz, Mexico)

Castillo de Teayo, whose Postclassic period roots have been known since the foundation of the modern town there in 1872, is the only place in the Aztec Triple Alliance Empire where remains of a colony of central Mexicans can be identified. Probably first settled by immigrants who left the highlands during the great famine of 1454, the area was not incorporated into the empire until the late 1470s, when the ruler Axayacatl waged war against it. The site of Castillo may have been Tezapotitlán in the tribute province of Atlán. If so, it was reportedly one of eleven places in the empire with high Aztec officials, either a *tlacatecuhtli* or a *tlacochtecuhtli*. A well-preserved pyramid stands in the town square, surrounded by numerous freestanding sculptures, found by the nineteenth-century settlers and set into cement bases around the pyramid. Other sculptures are in the Museo Nacional de Antropología, the Metropolitan Museum of Art, and the Musée de l'Homme. The sculptures are made of local sandstone but represent distinctively Aztec standard-bearers, date reliefs, and the deities Tláloc (storm god), Chalchiuhtlicue (goddess of water), a corn goddess with a "paper house" *(amacalli)* headdress, Mixcoatl (hunting god), Quetzalcóatl (Feathered Serpent), and Xipe Totec (flayed skin god). A number can be matched as pairs by size and style or by recorded proximity on hill sites near the town. A few are in the imperial Aztec style of the Valley of Mexico, but most, which are redundant images of fertility gods, were probably made by amateurs for the different neighborhoods of commoner farmers who comprised the majority of colonists. The colony is on the southern periphery of Huastec territory, and both Huastec and Aztec ceramic sherds have been collected there.

FURTHER READINGS

Solís Olguin, F. R. 1981. *Escultura del Castillo de Teayo, Veracruz, Mexico, Catálogo.* Mexico City: Instituto de Investigaciones Estéticas, Universidad Nacional Autónoma de México.

Drawings of two Tláloc figures (two on the left) and a Xipe (right). Illustrations from Eduard Seler, "Die Alterhumer von Castillo de Teayo," in *Gesammelte Abhandlungen zur Amerikanischen Sprach- und Alterthumskunde,* vol. 3, Akademische Druck- und Verlagsanstalt, Graz, Austria, 1960–1961: 410–449 (1904).

———. 1986. La estructura pirámidal de Castillo de Teayo. *Cuaderno de Arquitectura Mesoamericana* 8:73–79.

Umberger, E. 1996. Aztec Presence and Material Remains in the Outer Provinces. In F. Berdan et al., *Aztec Imperial Strategies,* pp. 151–179. Washington, D.C.: Dumbarton Oaks.

Emily Umberger

SEE ALSO

Gulf Lowlands: North Central

Caves

It is axiomatic in archaeology that people cross-culturally do not live in the dark zone of caves. Habitation most frequently occurs in rock shelters rather than caves, even though the former are often called "caves" in the literature. There is little good evidence for cave habitation in Mesoamerica, with most sources suggesting that caves were instead places of religious importance to pre-Columbian peoples.

Caves fall into an indigenous category of holes or cavities that penetrate the earth, including grottoes, cenotes, sinkholes, many springs, places where rivers emerge from or disappear into the earth, crevices, and any number of other holes. While features such as rock shelters may at times have been recognized and used as "caves," this is not always so.

Caves as Places for Religious Ritual

The principal association of caves is with the larger concept of a sacred, animate earth. Rain in Mesoamerica is thought to be formed in caves before being released into the sky. Thus, caves represent the essence of fertility where earth and water meet. Because of the connection with fertility, caves have a strong sexual connotation, often being compared to the womb or vagina. The belief that particular groups of people emerged from a seven-chambered cave is a pan-Mesoamerican motif related to the cave as the womb of the earth.

Not surprisingly, most of the deities connected with earth, water, fertility, and crops are thought to live in caves. Caves, therefore, are the most fitting and powerful places for petitioning the earth and its deities for their bounty. When Q'eqchi' (Kekchi) Maya speak of going to one of the principal sacred mountains to make an offering, their destination is actually the caves within the mountain; there are few caves, at least in the Maya area,

that do not contain evidence of utilization. Most of the functions that Thompson has ascribed to caves stem from their use for religious ritual. Archaeological evidence of pre-Columbian ritual is often abundant. At Dos Pilas, the Petexbatún Regional Cave Survey recovered so much material that it forms a large percentage of all the artifacts recovered by the larger Petexbatún Regional Archaeological Project.

Caves as Pilgrimage Sites

Because caves represent some of the most sacred space in the community's ideational landscape, it should not be surprising that they appear frequently as pilgrimage locations—sites that epitomize the sacred on a regional level. In part this reflects the fact that most Mesoamerican pilgrimage sites are associated with water cults.

Among the better-known pilgrimage caves (some of which later became Catholic pilgrimage centers) are

Photograph: A male figure, made of limestone, at Castillo de Teayo. Courtesy of the author.

C

Chalma, Esquipulas, the Cenote of Sacrifice at Chichén Itzá, and Cozumel Island. The Speaking Cross, focus of the nineteenth-century revitalization movement associated with the Caste War of Yucatán, first appeared in a grotto. One of the few pilgrimage caves to be intensively investigated archaeologically is Naj Tunich.

Burial Caves

Caves are also associated with the underworld, and the souls of the dead are often said to enter a cave on their journey to this realm. It may be this association that accounts for the use of caves as ossuaries. Enough documented ossuaries exist to sketch tentatively the distribution of this practice. Starting from the south, ossuaries appear to be common throughout Honduras up to the border of Guatemala. Evidence is lacking for eastern Guatemala, but cave ossuaries are reported for the western Guatemala Highlands and Chiapas. Cave ossuaries have yet to be firmly identified in the Maya Lowlands. Six masonry tombs are reported from Naj Tunich, but these are, at this point, unique. A rock shelter in Belize with dozens of burials dating to the Formative period has recently come to light, which may fill in the distribution of ossuaries. Cave burial appears to have been prevalent in Oaxaca. Sparse data also suggest that the practice is found in West Mexico and is widely reported in northern Mexico. Some data also suggest that ossuary burial was practiced in central Mexico.

Caves and Mesoamerican Society

Caves appear to have been used by all strata of society, from elite to commoner. In ethnohistoric sources and modern folklore, Postclassic rulers are said to have been born in, to have emerged from, or to disappear into caves. The motif of cave emergence imparts supernatural status and marks the individual as a god/hero/king. This belief appears to be ancient and to be portrayed in Olmec sculpture. At Chalcatzingo, Monument 9, a large monster mask was set up at the front of the main plaza and would have allowed those who passed through the mouth, a cave motif, to enter and reemerge from a symbolic cave. At Utatlán, a seven-chambered cave was excavated below the main plaza to represent the place where the K'iche (Quiché) kings were granted the right to rule by the high god Tohil. The cave was then a physical symbol of the king's divine mandate. The Aztecs excavated a cave/temple into living rock at Malinalco and may have used it for the investiture of officials.

Shamanic specialists are closely identified with caves in ethnography throughout Mesoamerica. In the Maya area, stones taken from caves frequently form part of a modern shaman's bundle of power objects. Curing ceremonies often involve caves because the latter are associated with both power and disease. Witchcraft is very often said to be carried out in caves. Evidence of pre-Columbian shamanic cave activity includes the recovery of a shaman's bundle in Chiapas.

Cave ritual, especially among the peasant class, is tied to the agricultural cycle. Modern cave ceremonies are most prominent before the clearing of the fields, before planting, before the first rains, and at harvest time. Caves in rural areas are often reported to contain pre-Columbian idols associated with non-elite cave utilization, and these are most frequently identified with rain deities.

Caves as Cosmological Anchors of Communities

By combining earth and water, caves symbolize the power of the earth, a fundamental concept in Mesoamerican religion. The "earth lord" who lives in the cave is felt throughout Mesoamerica to be the "owner" of the community lands. The cave ritual validates the unwritten contract between the community and the earth lord. In the Maya highlands, groups settle around a named cave that gives its name to the community. In Yucatán, the most common place-names refer to caves, cenotes, and watering places. In Central Mexico, the prevalence of -oztoc, Nahuatl for "cave," in place-names again reflects the importance of caves in the cultural landscape.

Archaeologists are only beginning to explore the role of caves in Mesoamerican sacred landscapes. Doris Heyden first proposed a model of cave use in which architecture was constructed over caves, based on the discovery of a cave under the Pyramid of the Sun at Teotihuacán. Another well-known example was found under the Osario at Chichén Itzá. A four-year cave study at the Maya site of Dos Pilas has found that architecture was systematically located in relation to caves, from the largest public complexes down to small residential platforms.

Man-Made Caves

Mexican investigators using remote sensing have determined that the tunnel system beneath Teotihuacán is more extensive than previously thought and, very importantly, that these tunnels are artificial constructions. They fall into a category of man-made caves that have been documented elsewhere: in central Mexico at Malinalco and Xochicalco; at the Highland Maya sites of La Lagunita, Guumarcaj (Utatlán), Mixco Viejo, and Esquipulas; in the Maya Lowlands at Topoxte; and into Honduras at Tenampua and the Bay Islands. One of the caves at Guumarcaj is an elaborate multi-passage construction that appears to represent the seven-chambered cave of origin. The Teotihuacán, La Lagunita, and Guumarcaj caves are all built beneath their sites' most important public architecture.

There are also buildings that were apparently meant to represent caves. Among the best-known are the Aztec temple of Yopico, described by Sahagún as a low, dark place, and the labyrinth-like Satunsat at Oxkintok, which was partially excavated into bedrock.

These artificial constructions occur most frequently in non-karstic regions where caves do not naturally form. They are significant because they indicate that the cave cult is a fundamental aspect of Mesoamerican religion rather than simply a regional manifestation limited to karstic areas. Furthermore, many of the constructions are elaborate, large-scale affairs that occupy important political and social space at the very heart of the community. Such placement and the massive labor expenditure entailed are generally taken as evidence that here one is dealing with a central concern of the society.

FURTHER READINGS

Brady, J. E. 1997. Settlement Configuration and Cosmology: The Role of Caves at Dos Pilas. *American Anthropologist* 99:602–618.

———. 1999. *Sources for the Study of Mesoamerican Ritual Cave Use.* 2nd ed. Los Angeles: California State University, Los Angeles.

Heyden, D. 1981. Caves, Gods and Myths: World-View and Planning in Teotihuacán. In E. P. Benson (ed.), *Mesoamerican Sites and World View*, pp. 1–39. Washington, D.C.: Dumbarton Oaks.

Stone, A. J. 1995. *Images from the Underworld: Naj Tunich and the Tradition of Maya Cave Painting.* Austin: University of Texas Press.

Thompson, J. E. S. 1975. Introduction. In H. C. Mercer, *Hill-Caves of Yucatan.* Norman: University of Oklahoma Press.

James Brady

SEE ALSO

Caves of Guerrero; Naj Tunich; Underworld

C

Caves of Guerrero (Guerrero, Mexico)

The earliest sophisticated painted art known in Mesoamerica occurs in Juxtlahuaca and Oxtotitlan caves, Guerrero, in west central Mexico. Those cave murals share various motifs with Middle Formative Gulf Lowlands Olmec stone monuments and portable art and can therefore be stylistically dated to that time period.

The Juxtlahuaca paintings, known since the 1920s, were brought to worldwide scholarly attention in 1967. The art occurs at several locations deep within the lengthy cave system. One mural depicts two human characters: a standing personage wearing a multicolored, striped *huipil* (shirt) and a headdress with plumes, and a much smaller, masked individual sitting at the personage's feet. A separate mural group includes a small, jaguar-like feline and a serpent, both painted in red and black. Some simpler drawings in the cave are executed only in black.

The Oxtotitlan murals first received major notice in the late 1960s. The cave, 30 km north of Juxtlahuaca, consists of two large, shallow grottoes at the base of a large cliff face. The largest and most elaborate of the murals occurs on the cliff directly above the mouth of the south grotto. The polychrome painting portrays a personage with an "owl" headdress and feathered cape seated on a large "earth-monster" face. The small paintings within the north grotto are executed in black and include a human-jaguar "copulation" scene. The south grotto depictions are rendered in red and are generally simpler.

Several other caves with relatively simple rock art have recently been reported in central Guerrero. They include Cacahuaziqui, with a large painted face, and Texayac, with a small "Olmec style" face carved above a small grotto.

FURTHER READINGS

Gay, C. T. E. 1967. The Oldest Paintings of the New World. *Natural History* 76.4:28–35.

Grove, D. C. 1970. *The Olmec Paintings of Oxtotitlan Cave, Guerrero, Mexico.* Studies in Pre-Columbian Art and Archaeology, No. 6. Washington, D.C.: Dumbarton Oaks.

———. 1973. Olmec Altars and Myths. *Archaeology* 26:128–135.

Vilella, S. L. 1989. Nuevo testimonio rupestre Olmeca en el Oriente de Guerrero. *Arqueología* (segunda época), pp. 37–48. México.

David C. Grove

SEE ALSO

Caves; Guerrero Region; Olmec Culture

C

Caxcan or Cazcan Culture
See Teúl, El

Ceiba, La (Guanacaste, Costa Rica)

This large habitation and cemetery complex in the middle reaches of the Tempisque River Valley region of Greater Nicoya was occupied from A.D. 500 to 1350. It has large oval hearths/ovens similar to those at Nacascolo. Seventy-eight primary and multiple interments have been recovered, representing individuals between thirteen and thirty-five years of age, with associated polychrome and monochrome ceramics, bone, copper, and jadeite/greenstone pendants. The site's ceramics include white-slipped ware from Pacific Nicaragua. The subsistence base was fishing (marine and riverine), gathering and collecting, and some agriculture. Other contemporaneous and similar sites include La Guinea and Nacascolo.

FURTHER READINGS

Guerrero, M., J. V., and A. Blanco. 1987. La Ceiba: Un asentamiento del Policromo Medio en el Valle del Tempisque con actividades funerarias (G-60-LC). Licenciatura thesis, University of Costa Rica.

Guerrero, M., J. V., and F. S. Del Vecchio. 1997. Los pueblos antiguos de la zona Canas-Liberia. San José: Museo Nacional de Costa Rica and SENARA.

Obando S., P., and F. Cruz V. 1988. Análisis de restos óseos humanos: Sitio La Ceiba (G-60LC), Agua Caliente (C-35AC) and Rodríguez (UCR-34). Licenciatura thesis, University of Costa Rica.

Frederick W. Lange

SEE ALSO

Intermediate Area: Overview

Central Mexican Religion

The religions of Central Mexico developed in the ceremonial centers of numerous settlements during several millennia beginning around 1500 B.C. Sacred spaces in the form of household shrines, ball courts, local temples, burial sites, statues of deities, palace complexes, colossal pyramids, monumental ceremonial centers, or capital cities provided profound and varied forms of religious orientation and access to the gods and the powers of the cosmos. A number of major sites in central Mexico—including Teotihuacán, Cholula, Cacaxtla, Tula, Xochicalco, Tlatelolco, Tenochtitlán, and Texcoco, among others—appear in the pictorial and archaeological record as places where religious and cultural creativity was crystallized and dispersed. Each of these sites transformed ritual, mythic, and cosmic elements from the heterogeneous cultural groups who inhabited the central plateau of Mesoamerica and expressed new syntheses.

Mexico's central highlands had been the dominant cultural region of central Mesoamerica since the beginning of the common era with the establishment of the great Classic period capital, Teotihuacán ("abode of the gods"). Teotihuacán was organized into four great quarters around a massive ceremonial center, and the four-quartered city may have been a vast spatial symbol for the major cosmological conceptions that developed in many areas and ceremonial centers within central Mexican culture. In many respects, the cultural and religious patterns of Teotihuacán laid the groundwork for later developments in and around the Basin of Mexico. The mythologies of successive cultures—the Toltec and the Aztec most prominent among them—looked back to the archaeological assemblages, deities, and ritual practices of Teotihuacán as their symbolic place of origin and as the source for the legitimacy of their political authority. It appears that the cultural formations and religious ideas of communities in the Tlaxcala and Puebla regions were also compatible with the religious worldview of the Teotihuacán achievement.

Even earlier ceremonial centers played prominent roles in the history of central Mexican society. For instance, at Tlatilco, a large village established around 1200 B.C., numerous individuals were found buried with figurines and other funerary offerings. Some of these figurines, especially those with two heads or with split faces depicting attributes of both the living and the dead, represent early expressions of duality, or the combining of opposing but complementary forces, a pervasive theme in all subsequent central Mexican religions. Many Tlatilco offerings also indicated influence from the emerging Olmec civilization.

Although the Olmec heartland was in the Gulf Lowlands, the Olmecs influenced central Mexican religious development in a variety of ways. The Olmec sites of San Lorenzo (1200–900 B.C.) and La Venta (900–400 B.C.) present some of the earliest examples of symmetrically planned Mesoamerican ceremonial centers, organized around massive pyramid structures, monumental sculpture, temple platforms, and ball courts—features that would come to characterize the great cities of central Mexico. Olmec religious ideas, art styles, and trade items spread from the Gulf Coast region to sites in the central highlands, such as Tlatilco, Oxtotlán, Juxtlahuaca, and Chalcatzingo. The cosmological significance of caves, reflected at Juxtlahuaca and in an Olmec carving on Petroglyph 1 at Chalcatzingo, for example, finds later expression in the modified underground passageways beneath the Pyramid of the Sun at Teotihuacán and in the Aztec conception of Chicomoztoc (the "place of the seven caves"), where legend tells us the first Mexica ancestors emerged. And the fact that at least one Olmec object, a beautiful greenstone mask, was carefully buried among offerings at the Templo Mayor (the Great Temple of Tenochtitlán, the symbolic center and replica of the Aztec universe) suggests that the Aztecs ascribed a special cosmological significance to this ancient civilization.

Two other ceremonial centers predating Teotihuacán also deserve mention. Monte Albán, established around 500 B.C. on a prominent hilltop overlooking the Valley of Oaxaca, contains a collection of large stone-slab reliefs, known as the Danzantes, which depict slain—possibly ritually sacrificed—rulers or war captives. These and other Zapotec reliefs contain some of the earliest evidence of pictographic writing, numerical notation, and time-reckoning used in the sophisticated ritual calendar systems of Classic and Postclassic central Mexico (similar evidence exists in the late Olmec site of Tres Zapotes). Far less is known about the second site, Cuicuilco, also dating from around 500 B.C. and situated just south of Mexico City. Partially buried by ash and lava from a volcanic eruption around 100 B.C., its massive circular platform and pyramid anticipate later round temple structures in central Mexico, most notably those at Cholula, Tlatelolco, and Tenochtitlán, and may suggest an early presence of the cult dedicated to Quetzalcoatl (the "feathered serpent"). The presence of incense burners and effigies of the fire god at Cuicuilco is also significant. Undoubtedly the ceremonial center of Cuicuilco played a major role in the religious and social development of the Basin of Mexico before the rise of Teotihuacán.

The basic settlement pattern of central Mexico from the time of Teotihuacán on was the city-state, consisting of a capital city surrounded by dependent communities that provided tribute in goods and services for the elite classes in the capital. In this social context, deities were worshipped, rituals were carried out, myths were painted and sung, and the material world was reshaped by the human mind and body. These crucial elements may be understood by focusing on three topics: cosmology and mythology, the pantheon, and ritual sacrifice.

Cosmogony and Cosmology

Central Mexicans had a ritual of spatial orientation that was carried out in various places and times. At sunrise on a chosen day of the year, an experienced archer would be directed to an auspicious location in the landscape and, according to a prescribed sequence, shoot arrows in the four cardinal directions. This ritual practice reflected one of the widespread models of cosmic order, which received its most sophisticated expression in the Aztec term *cemanahuac,* meaning "land surrounded by water." At the center of this terrestrial space, known as *tlalxico,* or "navel of the earth," stood the city—in the Aztec case, Tenochtitlán—from which extended the four quadrants called *nauchampa,* the "four directions of the wind." The waters surrounding the inhabited land were called *ilhuicatl* and extended upward to merge with the lowest of thirteen celestial levels. Below the earth were nine levels of the underworld, conceived of as "hazard stations" for the souls of the dead, who, aided by magical charms buried with the bodies, were assisted in their quest for eternal peace at the lowest level, known as Mictlan, the land of the dead.

Within this cosmic theater the mythic stages of creation were carried out. The best archaeological image of this cosmic order—quadripartition around a center that extends vertically through the universe—is the famous Calendar Stone, a colossal depiction of the ages of the universe, exemplified by four concise sections arranged around a fifth, a central image of the sun god, Tonatiuh, whose tongue is a protruding sacrificial knife. H. B. Nicholson outlined the "basic cosmological sequential pattern" of central Mexican cosmogony found in the myths and historical accounts associated with the Mexica. A summary view reveals that life unfolded in a cosmic setting that was dynamic, unstable, and finally destructive. Even though the cosmic order fluctuated between periods of stability and periods of chaos, the emphasis in many myths and historical accounts is on the destructive forces that repeatedly overcame the ages of the universe, divine society, and the cities of the past.

This dynamic universe appears in the sixteenth-century prose accounts of the *Historia de los mexicanos por sus pinturas* and the *Leyenda de los soles.* In the former, the universe is arranged in a rapid, orderly fashion after the dual creative divinity, Ometeotl, dwelling in Omeyocan ("place of duality") at the thirteenth level of heaven, generates four children, the Red Tezcatlipoca ("smoking mirror"), the Black Tezcatlipoca, Quetzalcoatl ("plumed serpent"), and Huitzilopochtli ("hummingbird on the

C

left"). They all exist without movement for six hundred years, then the four children assemble "to arrange what was to be done and to establish the law to be followed." Quetzalcoatl and Huitzilopochtli arrange the universe and create fire, half of the sun ("not fully lighted but a little"), the human race, and the calendar. Then the four brothers create water and its divine beings.

Following this rapid and full arrangement, the sources focus on a series of mythic events that constitute a sacred history throughout which the dynamic instability of the Aztec universe is revealed. The universe passes through four eras, called "Suns," each presided over by one of the great gods, and each named for the day (day number and day name) within the calendrical cycle on which the age began (which is also the name of the force that destroys that Sun). The first four Suns were called, respectively, 4 Jaguar, 4 Wind, 4 Rain (or 4 Rain of Fire), and 4 Water. The name of the fifth (and last) cosmic age, 4 Movement, augured the earthquakes that would inevitably destroy the world.

The creation of this final age, the one in which the Mexicas occupied the Basin of Mexico (1325–1521 A.D.), took place around a divine fire in the darkness on the mythical plain of Teotihuacán (to be distinguished from the actual city of the same name). According to the version of this story reported in Sahagún's Florentine Codex (1540s to 1570s), an assembly of gods choose two of their group, Nanahuatzin and Tecuciztecatl, to cast themselves into the fire in order to create the new cosmic age. Following their self-sacrifice, dawn appears in all directions, but the sun does not rise above the horizon. In confusion, different deities face various directions in expectation of the sunrise. Quetzalcoatl faces east, and from there the sun blazes forth but sways from side to side without climbing in the sky. In this cosmic crisis, it is decided that all the gods must die at the sacrificial hand of Ecatl, who dispatches them by cutting their throats. Even this massive sacrifice does not move the sun until the wind god literally blows it into motion. These combined cosmogonic episodes demonstrate the fundamental Aztec conviction that the world is unstable and that it draws its energy from massive sacrifices made by or to the gods. Large-scale sacrifice became a basic pattern in Aztec religion, a ritual means of imposing or maintaining social and cosmological order.

With the creation of the Fifth Sun, the focus of the sacred history shifts from heaven to earth, where agriculture is discovered and human sacrifice is established as the proper ritual response to the requirements of the gods. In one account, Quetzalcoatl, as a black ant, travels with a red ant to Sustenance Mountain, where they acquire maize for human beings. Other accounts reveal the divine origins of cotton, sweet potatoes, different types of corn, and the intoxicating agave sap drink called *octli* or *pulque*. This mythic sequence introduces a number of other sacred entities that played major roles in the central Mexican world. For instance, maize, which was personified as the gods Centeotl or Xilonen, performed important daily material and imaginative functions in various communities. One of the most important cult of gods, the cult of pulque, takes its mythic origin in a series of mythic episodes in which the chief deity and personification of pulque, the goddess Mayahuel, joins with a group of other pulque deities known as the Centzon Tochtin ("Four Hundred Rabbits").

Other accounts tell us that warfare was established so that human beings could be captured and sacrificed to nourish the sun on its heavenly and nocturnal journey. Typically, a sky god like Mixcoatl, the Cloud Serpent, creates four hundred human beings to fight among themselves, becoming captives to be sacrificed in ceremonial centers to provide divine food—blood—for the gods who ensure cosmic life. Significantly, many images of these gods appear in architecture and ritual objects, allowing us to appreciate the symbols, costumes, and ritual accouterments utilized in various cults.

Finally, in some accounts, cosmic history culminates with the establishment of the magnificent kingdom and city of Tollan, where Quetzalcoatl, the god, and Topiltzin Quetzalcoatl, the priest-king, organize a ceremonial capital divided into five parts, with four pyramids and four sacred mountains surrounding the central temple. Aztec tradition states that "from Quetzalcoatl flowed all art and knowledge," representing the paradigmatic importance of the Toltec kingdom and its religious founders.

Pantheon

An incredible array of deities animated the ancient Mesoamerican world. H. B. Nicholson's authoritative study includes a list of more than sixty distinct and interrelated names. Scholarly analysis of these many deities suggests that virtually all aspects of existence were considered inherently sacred and that these deities were expressions of a numinous quality that permeated the "real" world. Aztec references to numinous forces, expressed in the Nahuatl word *teotl*, were always translated by Spaniards as "god," "saint," or "demon." But the Aztec *teotl* signified a sacred power manifested in natural forms (a rainstorm, a tree, a mountain), in persons of high distinction (a king, an ancestor, a warrior), or in mysterious and chaotic places. What the Spanish translated as "god" really referred to a broad spectrum of hierophanies that animated the world. While it does not appear that the various pantheons or patterns of hierophanies were organized as a whole, clusters of deities were organized around the major cult themes of cosmogonic creativity, fertility and regeneration, and war and sacrificial nourishment of the sun.

On the whole, deities were represented as anthropomorphic beings; even when they took the form of an animal (Xolotl, the divine dog) or of a ritual object (Iztli, the knife god), they often had human features like arms, torso, legs, and face. Many of these deities dwelt in the different levels of the thirteen-layered celestial sphere or the nine-layered underworld. The general structuring principle for the pantheon, derived from the cosmic pattern of a center and four quarters, resulted in the quadruple or quintuple ordering of the gods. For instance, the Codex Borgia's representation of the Tlaloques (rain gods) features the rain god, Tlaloc, in the central region of heaven, while four other Tlaloques inhabit the four regions of the sky, each dispensing a different kind of rain. A few deities—such as Huehueteotl (the ancient god) or Xiuhtecuhtli (the fire god)—characteristically occupied the central place of the home, the hearth, the pyramid, or certain ritual burials, thereby anchoring the social and ritual world in the ancient traditions of fire and wisdom. Although deities were invisible to the human eye, Mesoamerican people saw them in dreams, in visions, and in the "deity impersonators" *(teixiptlas)* who appeared at major ceremonies. These costumed impersonators, sometimes human and sometimes effigies of stone, wood, or dough, were elaborately decorated with identifying insignia such as conch shells, masks, weapons, jewelry, mantas, feathers, and a myriad of other items. They were considered the containers of the divine force, fire, or persona that entered the world through sacrifice.

One of the most widespread patterns of creative orientation was the sacred history of ethnic groups migrating from a homeland to a promised land. For example, the religions of the peoples encountered by the Spaniards in the Basin of Mexico were formed in part by integrating the myths, rites, and deities of the Chichimecs who entered the Basin and established important political and cultural alliances with long-established social centers. This process of migration and integration informed and was informed by their concept of deity. An outstanding feature of many religions was the tutelary-patron relations that specific deities had with the particular social groups whom they guided during their peregrinations. These patron deities (or *abogados,* as the Spanish chroniclers called them) were represented in the *tlaquimilolli,* or sacred bundles, that the *teomamas* ("god-bearers," or shaman-priests) carried on their backs during long journeys. The *teomama* passed on to the community the divine commandments communicated to him in visions and dreams. These sacred specialists were considered "man-gods" (Spanish, *hombres-dioses*) whose extraordinary powers of spiritual transformation, derived from their closeness with these numinous forces, enabled them to guide, govern, and organize the tribe during migrations and the settlement of new places. A familiar pattern in the sacred histories of Mesoamerican tribal groups is the erection of a shrine to the patron deity as the first act of settlement in a new region. This act represented the intimate tie among the deity, the man-god, and the integrity of the people. In reverse fashion, conquest of a community was achieved when the patron deity's shrine was burned and the *tlaquimilolli* was captured and taken away.

This pattern of migration, foundation, and conquest associated with the power of a patron deity is clearly exemplified by various warrior gods who became patrons of various communities. One outstanding case was Huitzilopochtli, patron of the wandering Mexica. According to Aztec tradition, Huitzilopochtli inspired the Mexica *teomama* to guide the tribe on a century-long migration into the Basin of Mexico, where he appeared to them as an eagle on a cactus in the lake. There they constructed a shrine to Huitzilopochtli and built their city. This shrine became the Aztec Great Temple, or Templo Mayor, the supreme political and symbolic center of the Aztec Empire. It was destroyed in 1521 by the Spaniards, who blew up the temple with cannon and carried the great image of Huitzilopochtli away. This colossal image of the Aztec god has never been found.

Creator Gods

Many communities had a supreme dual god, such as Ometeotl ("lord of duality") or Tloque-Nahuaque ("lord of the close and near"), who was the celestial, androgynous, primordial creator of the universe—the omnipotent, omniscient, omnipresent foundation of all things. In some sources she/he appears to merge with a number of her/his offspring, a sign of her/his pervasive power. Ometeotl's male aspects (Ometecuhtli and Tonacatecuhtli) and female aspects (Omecihuatl and Tonacacihuatl) in turn merged with a series of lesser deities associated with

C

generative and destructive male and female qualities. The male aspect was associated with fire and the solar and maize gods. The female aspect merged with the earth fertility goddesses, especially the corn goddesses. Ometeotl was more "being" than "action." It is significant that these supreme gods were rarely represented in material form. Most of the creative effort to organize the universe was accomplished by the divine couple's four offspring: Tezcatlipoca, Quetzalcoatl, Xiuhtecuhtli, and Tlaloc, all of whom received widespread representations in wood, stone, and pictorial manuscripts.

Tezcatlipoca ("smoking mirror") was the supreme active force of the pantheon. This powerful, virile numen had many appellations and was partially identified with the supreme numinosity of Ometeotl. Tezcatlipoca was also identified with Iztli, the knife and calendar god, and with Tepeyollotl, the jaguar-earth god known as the "Heart of the Mountain"; he was often pictured as the divine antagonist of Quetzalcoatl. On the social level, Tezcatlipoca was the arch-sorcerer whose smoking obsidian mirror revealed the powers of ultimate transformation associated with darkness, night, jaguars, and shamanic magic. There are various descriptions of Tezcatlipoca's temple in Aztec communities, and it is apparent that there was an extensive cult spread throughout central Mexico at the time of the conquest. For instance, one of the most important sacrificial ceremonies, held during the month of Toxcatl in and around the city of Tenochtitlán, involved an extensive series of public displays of the god's *ixiptla* (image) to the populace at large. It also included visits to various temples situated within and beyond the island city's limits. In this way there was a ritual integration of various architectural structures and their respective symbols through the movements, dances, musical presentations, and eventual human sacrifice of the god's representative.

Another tremendous creative power was Xiuhtecuhtli, the ancient fire god, who influenced every level of society and cosmology. Xiuhtecuhtli was represented by the perpetual "fires of existence" that were kept lit at certain temples in the ceremonial centers at all times. He was manifested in the igniting of new fires that dedicated new ceremonial buildings and ritual stones. Images of Xiuhtecuhtli have been found in excavations throughout the Basin of Mexico and in various screenfolds from the Mixtec and Oaxacan regions. Most important, perhaps, Xiuhtecuhtli was the generative force at the New Fire Ceremony, also called the Binding of the Years, held on the Hill of the Star outside Tenochtitlán. At midnight on the day that a 52-year calendar was exhausted, at the moment when the star cluster we call the Pleiades passed through the zenith, a heart sacrifice of a war captive took place. A new fire was started in the cavity of the victim's chest, symbolizing the rebirth of Xiuhtecuhtli. The new fire was carried to every city, town, and home in the empire, signaling the regeneration of the universe. On the domestic level, Xiuhtecuhtli inhabited the hearth, structuring the daily rituals associated with food, nurturance, and thanksgiving.

Fertility and Regeneration

All Mesoamerican societies depended on various forms of intensive agriculture that required well-organized planting, nurturing, and harvesting schedules, and coordination between various groups. While many female deities inspired the ritual regeneration of agriculture, the most ancient and widespread fertility-rain god was Tlaloc, who dwelt on prominent mountain peaks where clouds were thought to emerge from caves to fertilize the land with life-giving rain. Tlaloc or Tlaloc-like rain gods were widespread and very ancient in central Mexican society. Tlaloc was often accompanied by a female counterpart, sometimes known as Chalchiuhtlicue, the goddess of lakes and running water, who is represented in various forms, including precious greenstone effigies. The Aztecs held Mount Tlaloc to be the original source of the waters and of vegetation. Tlaloc's supreme importance is reflected in the location of his shrine alongside that of Huitzilopochtli at the Templo Mayor. Surprisingly, the great majority of buried offerings excavated at the temple were dedicated to Tlaloc rather than Huitzilopochtli.

The most powerful group of female fertility deities were the Teteoinnan, a rich array of earth-mother goddesses, who were representative of the qualities of terror and beauty, regeneration and destruction; these deities were worshipped in cults concerned with the abundant powers of the earth, women, and fertility. Among the most prominent were Tlazolteotl, Xochiquetzal, and Coatlicue. Tlazolteotl was concerned with sexual powers and passions and the pardoning of sexual transgressions. Xochiquetzal was the goddess of love and sexual desire and was associated with flowers, feasting, and pleasure. A ferocious goddess, Coatlicue ("serpent skirt") represented the cosmic mountain that conceived all stellar beings and devoured all beings into her repulsive, lethal, and fascinating form. She is depicted in a huge statue now displayed at the National Museum of Anthropology in Mexico City. Her form is studded with sacrificial hearts, skulls, hands, ferocious claws, and a giant snake head. This image has been interpreted as a single, solid sculptural image of the layers and powers of the Mesoamerican cosmos.

Xipe Totec, a prominent deity, linked agricultural renewal with warfare; his gladiatorial sacrifice renewed vegetation and celebrated successes on the battlefield. Part of his ceremony, called the Feast of the Flaying of Men, including the flaying of the sacrificial victims and the ceremonial wearing of their skins by ritual specialists and their captors. Xipe Totec's insignia, including the pointed cap and rattle staff, was the war attire of the Mexica emperor.

Ceremony and Sacrifice

Sacrifice was another vital pattern of central Mexican religious practice, usually carried out for the purpose of nourishing or renewing the sun or other deities and forces in nature and society (or otherwise to appease them); it thus ensured the stability of the universe. One of the mythic models for mass human sacrifice was the story of the creation of the Fifth Age, in which the gods themselves were sacrificed in order to empower the sun. Tonatiuh, the personification of that sun (whose visage appears in the center of the Calendar Stone), depended on continued nourishment from human hearts.

Some of the large-scale sacrificial ceremonies re-created other sacred stories. For example, women and captured warriors were sacrificed in front of the shrine of Huitzilopochtli atop the Templo Mayor. Their bodies tumbled down the steps to rest at the bottom with the colossal stone figure of Coyolxauhqui, Huitzilopochtli's dismembered sister, symbolically reenacting the legendary slaughter of the four hundred siblings at Huitzilopochtli's birth.

The best setting in which to describe the significance of ritual sacrifice is the Aztec city of Tenochtitlán. Cosmology, pantheon, and ritual sacrifice were united and came alive in the exuberant and well-ordered ceremonies carried out in the more than eighty buildings situated in the sacred precinct of the capital and in the hundreds of ceremonial centers throughout the Aztec world. Guided by detailed ritual calendars, Aztec ceremonies varied from town to town but typically involved three stages: days of ritual preparation, death sacrifice, and nourishing the gods. The days of ritual preparation included fasting; offerings of food, flowers, and paper; use of incense and purification techniques; embowering; songs; and processions of deity-impersonators to various temples in ceremonial precincts.

Following these elaborate preparations, blood sacrifices were carried out by priestly orders specifically trained to dispatch the victims swiftly. The victims were usually captive warriors or purchased slaves. Although a variety of methods of ritual killing were used, including decapitation, burning, hurling from great heights, strangulation, and arrow sacrifice, the typical ritual involved the dramatic removal of the heart and its placement in a ceremonial vessel (cuauhxicalli) in order to nourish the gods. Amid the music of drums, conch-shell trumpets, rattles, and other musical instruments, which created an atmosphere of dramatic intensity, blood was smeared on the face of the deity's image and the head of the victim was placed on the great skull rack (tzompantli) that held thousands of such trophies.

All these ceremonies were carried out in relation to two ritual calendars: the 365-day calendar, or xiuhmopohualli, consisting of eighteen 20-day periods plus five intercalary days, and the 260-day calendar, or tonalpohualli, consisting of twenty 13-day periods. More than one-third of these ceremonies were dedicated to Tlaloc and the earth fertility goddesses. Besides ceremonies related to the two calendars, a third type of ceremony was associated with the many stages in the life cycle of the individual. In some cases, the entire community was involved in fasting and bloodletting rituals.

In the past ten years, important excavations carried out in the sites of Tlatelolco, Cacaxtla, and Xochicalco, as well as continuing work at the Templo Mayor, have uncovered important aspects of central Mexican religion that reflect considerable diversity and syncretism. For instance, periodic excavations at Tenochtitlán's sister city, Tlatelolco, show both continuity and change in ritual burials and architectural styles. While the former site had extraordinarily fine ritual objects buried in its floors, the burials at the monumental ceremonial center of the latter showed an abundance of buried human remains with ritual objects of mediocre quality. A number of children, some of whom appear to have been sacrificed, were buried with toys, dishes, and other household items. Another sign of architectural diversity appeared in a recent excavation of the Templo Calendario at Tlatelolco, which unearthed a rare mural painting that had been covered by the subsequent construction of a small circular structure. This mural depicts a scene, very similar to one found in the Codex Borbonicus, of the creator pair, Oxomoco and Cipactonal, in a ritual scene of creating the calendar and agriculture. Perhaps the most startling examples of pre-Hispanic syncretism have been uncovered in the

C

spectacular murals of Cacaxtla in Puebla and in the architectural assemblages of Xochicalco in Morelos. In the Cacaxtla images, we see lavishly costumed priests and warriors in ritual poses moving along the walls of various buildings. These figures and the accompanying symbols suggest that Cacaxtla was the site of impressive interactions and mixtures of Maya and central Mexican religious traditions. A similar pattern of integration appears in the marvelous hilltop ceremonial center of Xochicalco, where architectural forms, carved reliefs, and painted motifs combine Teotihuacán, Zapotec, Maya, and Gulf Coast elements. From these examples and many others, it is clear that important contacts, conflicts, and negotiations were taking place between various communities, cults, and the gods who influenced them.

FURTHER READINGS

Berrin, K., and E. Pasztory (eds.). 1993. *Teotihuacan: Art from the City of the Gods.* New York: Thames and Hudson.

Carrasco, D. 1990. *Religions of Mesoamerica: Cosmovision and Ceremonial Centers.* San Francisco: Harper and Row.

Leon Portilla, M. 1963. *Aztec Thought and Culture.* Norman: University of Oklahoma Press.

López Austin, A. 1988. *The Human Body and Ideology: Concepts of the Ancient Nahuas.* 2 vols. Salt Lake City: University of Utah Press.

———. 1993. *Myths of the Opossum: Pathways of Mesoamerican Mythology.* B. R. Ortiz de Montellano and T. Ortiz de Montellano (trans). Albuquerque: University of New Mexico Press.

López Luján, L. 1994. *The Offerings of the Templo Mayor of Tenochtitlan.* Niwot: University Press of Colorado.

Manzanilla, L., and L. López Luján. 1994–1995. *Historia antigua de México.* 3 vols. Mexico City: Inistituto Nacional de Antropología e Historia, Universidad Nacional Autónoma de México, y Porrúa.

Matos Moctezuma, E. 1995. *Life and Death in the Templo Mayor.* Niwot: University Press of Colorado.

Nicholson, H. B. 1971. Religion in Pre-Hispanic Central Mexico. In *Handbook of Middle American Indians,* vol. 10, *Archaeology of Northern Mesoamerica,* part 1, pp. 395–446. Austin: University of Texas Press.

Ortiz de Montellano, B. R. 1990. *Aztec Medicine, Health, and Nutrition.* New Brunswick: Rutgers University Press.

Pasztory, E. 1983. *Aztec Art.* New York: Abrams.

Townsend, R. 1979. *State and Cosmos in the Art of Tenochtitlan.* Studies in Pre-Columbian Art and Archaeology, 20. Washington, D.C.: Dumbarton Oaks.

Davíd Carrasco

SEE ALSO
Cosmology; Teotihuacán: Religion and Deities

Ceramics
Articles of fired clay served important functions in many aspects of prehistoric life throughout Mesoamerica. Pottery containers, including ceramic vessels for the storage, preparation, and serving of food and drink, were the most prevalent type of ceramic artifact. In addition, a broad range of non-container ceramic articles were employed for ritual, utilitarian, and decorative purposes.

Ritual and Ceremonial Articles
Figurines are one of the primary ceramic objects associated with ritual activities. Figurines first appeared in the Early Formative and continued in vogue until the Conquest and on into Colonial times. During the Formative, figurines were always hand modeled; most are solid, three-dimensional representations of people and activities

Fragment of cylindrical tripod vessel with relief design of blow-gun hunter, from Teotihuacán. Illustration found in Michael D. Coe, *Mexico: From the Olmecs to the Aztecs* (New York: Thames and Hudson, 1921), p. 114 (figure 28).

from daily life. But Formative craftsmen also modeled somewhat larger, hollow figurines; particularly famous are the baby-face Olmec figurines from the Gulf Coast and central Mexico.

The use of molds for figurine production appeared during the Classic; thereafter, figurines were generally mold made. Most common are the solid, so-called gingerbread man type, for which clay was pressed into a one-piece mold; many are standardized representations of deities. Less common are the jointed or "puppet" figurines, in which the solid body and limbs were molded separately but punched with holes for articulation. Hollow figurines, including rattles, were molded in several parts and the pieces assembled after drying.

A somewhat enigmatic category of figurines are the wheeled animals—small toylike figures mounted on wheels—which have a wide but not abundant distribution throughout Central Mexico and Mesoamerica. Found in both household debris and as grave goods, their purpose (whether for ceremony or amusement) is unknown.

Larger ceramic sculptures are rare in Mesoamerica, perhaps owing to the technical difficulties presented by the manufacture of figures of such size. However, two magnificent examples of monumental ceramic art are the life-sized (c. 190 cm) representations of Aztec eagle-warriors found guarding the entrance to the elite warriors' precinct, adjacent to the Templo Mayor in Teotihuacán.

Ceramic ear plugs from Central America. Courtesy University of Michigan Museum of Anthropology.

Musical instruments of fired clay also played a significant role in ceremonial and religious life. At the time of European contact, ceramic wind instruments included modeled whistles, flutes, ocarinas, and panpipes; many of these instruments have considerable time depth and were widely represented as early as the Middle and Late Formative. Percussion instruments included a small ceramic drum and clay rattles.

Pottery vessels associated with ritual contexts include censers (incensarios) used to burn incense and braziers (large urns for burning incense or holding ritual fires). The latter may have served a more utilitarian function as well, as a heater or small stove.

Utilitarian Articles

More utilitarian ceramic manufactures included blowgun projectiles, net and line sinkers, spindle whorls, stamps, and smoking pipes. Round clay pellets were carefully shaped for employment as blowgun missiles. We know from a scene carved on an Early Classic vase from Teotihuacán that this weapon was used in hunting birds as well as in warfare. Larger ceramic balls may have functioned as slingshot projectiles. In other procurement activities, small, rectangular, notched sherds served as weights for fishing and birding nets and as sinkers for fishlines.

Ceramic artifacts also played an important role in the production of textiles. Ceramic spindle whorls (malacates) were used as weights on the wooden spindles used in drop-spinning plant fibers into thread. Molded or modeled malacates, generally of hemispherical shape, were common only in Epiclassic and Postclassic times, although Formative and Classic examples are known. The

Ceramic spindle whorls (malacates) from Central America, Aztec period. Smaller whorls were used for spinning cotton; larger ones were for maguey. Courtesy University of Michigan Museum of Anthropology.

C

perforated sherd discs found in earlier contexts presumably served as spindle whorls for earlier peoples. By Aztec times, *malacates* were produced in abundance and in standardized weights and hole diameters appropriate to spinning two different fibers, maguey and cotton.

Ceramic stamps with carved or molded designs were used to stamp decorative motifs onto woven cloth. Flat-based, generally rectangular stamps are a standard part of assemblages from Epiclassic through Postclassic times. Although stamps dating back to the Middle Formative are known, these early examples may have been used in the application of body paint. Carved cylinder seals (generally dating to the Middle and Late Formative) probably served to decorate textiles.

Clay smoking pipes appear to have been a Toltec invention and were common throughout the Postclassic of Mexico along an arc extending from western Mexico through the Basin of Mexico to the Gulf Coast. The typical Toltec pipe has a small, conical bowl with a flaring rim and a long stem decorated with an undulating serpent. Clay smoking pipes predating the Postclassic period are rarely found in Mesoamerica, although tubular pipes are known from the Classic Maya.

Articles for Adornment

Finally, ceramic objects served for personal adornment. Both solid earplugs and hollow earspools were fashioned out of clay, as were a wide variety of beads and pendants, some so finely worked and polished as to appear like carved stone. Ceramic jewelry enjoyed a widespread and enduring popularity from Middle Formative times until European contact.

FURTHER READINGS

Noguera, E. 1965. *La cerámica arqueológica de Mesoamerica.* Mexico City: Instituto de Investigaciones Históricas, Universidad Nacional Autónoma de México.

Parsons, M. H. Spindle Whorls from the Teotihuacan Valley, Mexico. In *Miscellaneous Studies in Mexican Prehistory,* by Michael W. Spence, Jeffrey R. Parsons, and Mary H. Parsons, pp. 45–79. Anthropological Papers, 45. Ann Arbor: University of Michigan Museum of Anthropology, 1972.

Leah Minc

SEE ALSO

Figurines, Terracotta; Music, Dance, Theater, and Poetry; Pottery; Weaving and Textiles

Cerén (Western El Salvador)

This thriving southern Mesoamerican village was suddenly buried in about A.D. 590 by 5 meters of volcanic ash from a nearby vent. The extraordinary preservation of Cerén architecture, artifacts, activity areas, plants in gardens, and organic items allows a detailed understanding of village life 1,400 years ago. Cerén had been occupied only for a century or two, by people who moved back into the Zapotitán Valley and founded the village as a part of the natural and human recovery from the earlier Ilopango volcanic eruption. That earlier eruption, which occurred about A.D. 200, was a massive regional natural disaster. The site is in a tropical seasonal environment, with 1,700 ±300 mm of mean precipitation; its elevation is 450 meters above sea level.

With the volcanic eruption of c. 590, people fled the village with such haste that they abandoned their everyday artifacts and valuable items, leaving virtually full inventories in both houses and special-purpose buildings. A small earthquake that occurred immediately before the eruption gave warning, and the eruption probably was preceded by steam emissions that indicated the danger was north of the village. No bodies have been found in the village to date; they may be found when excavations continue to the south. The eruption began in earnest when the hot basaltic magma chamber came into contact with water of the Río Sucio, the large river that drains the Zapotitán Valley. The first component of the eruption was a huge scalding cloud of water vapor, volcanic ash, and gases that hurtled through the town at about 100 kilometers per hour. That was shortly followed by direct airfall of ash, with the larger lava bombs retaining temperatures over 575°C. These bombs penetrated the thatched roofs and set them on fire. Succeeding phases of the eruption alternated steam explosions and airfall deposits, eventually forming fourteen layers. Not only did the five meters of volcanic ash effectively block the site from later human disturbance; the ash also packed around many organic items such as crops and trees, preserving their forms as hollow spaces after the original items decomposed.

Even though research has only recently begun at Cerén, four zones of the ancient community have been uncovered. A civic zone occupies the center of the known site. Structure 3, a large, 5 × 8-meter, solid, earthen-walled building, was evidently used as a public building. The benches in the front room may have been symbols of authority; certainly a liquid was dispensed from the large

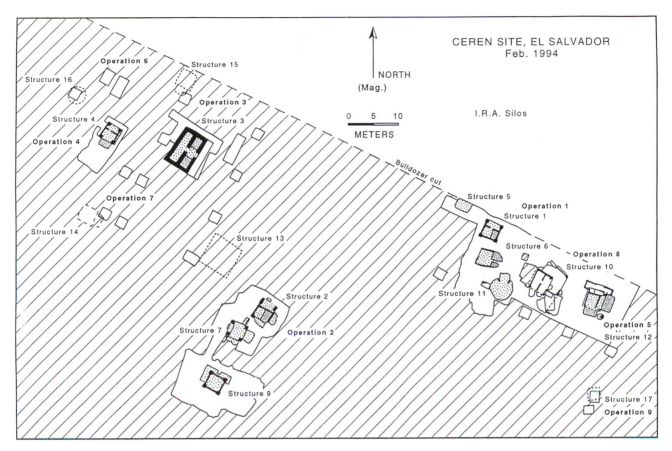

Map of the Cerén site. Blank area was destroyed by bulldozing in 1976, hatched area has yet to be excavated. The site extends an unknown distance to the south and west. Illustration courtesy of the author.

ceramic jar on one bench, ladled out with the polychrome hemispherical vessel found sitting on top of the wall above it. The building faces a hard-packed and well-maintained plaza. Structure 13, only partially excavated but clearly constructed like Structure 3, faces the same plaza from the south. It may have been a storehouse for civic artifacts. Structure 9, a few meters south of these buildings, is a large steam bath—probably public, because it could seat a dozen people inside and outside on its ample benches. It has solid earthen walls and a stone firebox in the center, and it is capped with an engineering marvel: an earthen dome. The building was protected from the elements by a thatched roof.

The second, residential, zone of the site is presently known in three areas. Virtually all of House 1 has been excavated, and much of two other houses has been excavated as of this writing. Each household constructed at least three functionally specialized buildings: a domicile, a storehouse, and a kitchen. The domicile, which was the principal building, was for sleeping, production of various household crafts, and food consumption. The usual construction procedure was to make a low but wide earthen mound to drain rainwater away from the earthen architecture. Then a formal square platform measuring about 4 × 4 meters was built on top, extending 0.5 to 1 meter above the surrounding terrain. That was dried and fired, creating a thin zone of hard, oxidized adobe as a hard floor. Then wattle-and-daub (bajareque) walls were built and tied tightly into the roof support beams. Grass and palm thatch was used for the roof. (Most of the thatched roofs were inhabited by at least one mouse.) Earthen columns were built in place to anchor the corners.

Households were surprisingly rich in material culture. Household 1 owned more than seventy ceramic vessels ranging from molded miniature pots to large scraped-slip storage vessels and fine, polychrome-painted, hemispherical food-serving vessels. They also had numerous

C

polychrome painted gourds, baskets, and other organic containers. Houses contained abundant chipped-stone and ground-stone implements for daily chores.

Associated with the houses is the third zone: agriculture. A variety of plants grew in kitchen gardens, including maize, medicinal plants, plants for fine fibers, and flowers. Farther from the household were *milpas* (fields) planted in maize, with three to five plants per locality, growing on top of low ridges. The eruption apparently occurred in August, so beans had not yet been interplanted that year. The maize stalks had been broken over to dry the ears in the field. Also found were tree crops, including nance, guayaba, cacao, and manioc. One garden was planted exclusively in maguey.

Structures 10 and 12 formed a religious complex at the eastern edge of the site. Structure 10 clearly belonged to a religious association; inside the two innermost rooms they stored their sacred artifacts, including a painted deer-skull headdress with the string used to attach it to a person's head, deer scapulas, and a large alligator-shaped vessel full of achiote seeds for making red paint. The outer room contained ceramic storage and cooking vessels along with considerable stored food, food-processing areas, and a zone for dispensing food to participants in rituals. Structure 12 has very complex architecture, with numerous isolated artifacts that appear to be offerings or payments for services. It may be where shamans performed.

Cerén research is overtly multi-disciplinary, with teams of archaeologists working with volcanologists, ethno-botanists, and geophysicists. Recent geophysical exploration has utilized ground-penetrating radar to map the Classic period buildings, plazas, drainages, and agricultural areas through the 4 to 6 meters of volcanic ash. The research is coordinated with architectural and objects conservation to give the fragile structures and artifacts a stable future. All work is done within a master plan that includes public access, an on-site museum, trained guides, and educational outreach programs.

FURTHER READINGS

Beaubien, H. 1993. From Codex to Calabash: Recovery of a Painted Organic Artifact from the Archaeological Site of Cerén, El Salvador. *Journal of the American Institute of Conservation* 32:153–164.

Sheets, P. (ed.). 1983. *Archaeology and Volcanism in Central America: The Zapotitán Valley of El Salvador.* Austin: University of Texas Press.

———. 1992. *The Cerén Site: A Prehistoric Village Buried by Volcanic Ash in Central America.* Fort Worth: Harcourt Brace Jovanovich.

Sheets, P., H. Beaubien, M. Beaudry, A. Gerstle, B. McKee, D. Miller, H. Spetzler, and D. Tucker. 1990. Household Archaeology at Cerén, El Salvador. *Ancient Mesoamerica* 1:81–90.

Payson Sheets

SEE ALSO
Zapotitán Region

Cerro de las Mesas (Veracruz, Mexico)

One of the largest centers in south central Veracruz during the period 600 B.C.–A.D. 900, this was possibly a regional capital from A.D. 300 to 600 or earlier. Situated in low-lying farmlands in an area known today as the Mixtequilla, the site's mounds surround an artificial lagoon, with a concentration of high conical mounds (up to 24 meters) at the northern end. Two ball courts and numerous carved stelae are part of the formal arrangement. Many stelae depict individuals who were probably rulers, accompanied by glyphs and long count dates in a system shared with La Mojarra and the Tuxtla Statuette; all are thought to display a Pre-Proto-Zoquean script. A lavish Terminal Formative burial was accompanied by a yoke, a carved turtle shell, and pottery. Large ceramic idols, jades, and cylinder tripod vessels were cached during the Classic period. Trace elements in prismatic blades indicate that obsidian was imported mainly from Zaragoza-Oyameles, Puebla, during the Classic period. Cotton thread production and textiles became prominent during the same period. Ceramics suggest change and continuity throughout the sequence until an interruption in the Postclassic period. Local elites drew on styles and practices at Teotihuacán, but Cerro de las Mesas was probably not dominated politically or economically.

FURTHER READINGS

Drucker, P. 1943. *Ceramic Stratigraphy at Cerro de las Mesas, Veracruz, Mexico.* Bureau of American Ethnology, Bulletin 141. Washington, D.C.

Stark, B. L. (ed.). 1991. *Settlement Archaeology of Cerro de las Mesas, Veracruz, Mexico.* Institute of Archaeology, University of California, Los Angeles, Monograph 34.

Stark, B. L., and L. A. Curet. 1994. The Development of Classic Period Mixtequilla in South-Central Veracruz, Mexico. *Ancient Mesoamerica* 5:267–287.

Stirling, M. 1941. Expedition Unearths Buried Master-pieces of Carved Jade. *National Geographic* 80:277–327.

———. 1943. *Stone Monuments of Southern Veracruz.* Bureau of American Ethnology, Bulletin 138.

Barbara L. Stark

SEE ALSO
Gulf Lowlands: South Central Region

Cerro de Moctehuma
See Chalchihuites Culture

Cerro de Trincheras (Sonora, Mexico)

The most visually impressive archaeological site of the Trincheras tradition in the Northern Arid Zone, Cerro de Trincheras is situated in the Río Magdalena drainage of northern Sonora. The site was occupied during the four-teenth and fifteenth centuries A.D. by a community of 1,000 to 2,000 individuals. They built more than 900 ter-races on a volcanic hill that covers about 100 hectares. These terraces ranged in height from a few decimeters to over three meters. They used the majority of these terraces as platforms for houses, but they grew crops such as agave on some, and they used others as platforms for ritual per-formances. The organization of the site is similar to hill-top sites such as La Quemada in Zacatecas, with a ceremonial and administrative center on the crest, elite residences directly below, and the mass of the population at still lower elevations. The architecture of Cerro de Trincheras is, however, less grand and formal than the Zacatecas sites. On the crest of the hill is a stone building with a spiral plan called El Caracol. At the base of the hill is a large rectangular structure (60 × 20 meters) called La Cancha. Craftspeople at the site obtained large quantities of shell from the Gulf of California and made it into jew-elry. Some of this shell was traded east to Casas Grandes in exchange for polychrome pottery. Randall McGuire and Elisa Villalpando directed the only excavations at the site in the spring seasons of 1995 and 1996.

FURTHER READINGS

Huntington, E. 1912. The Fluctuating Climate of North America—The Ruins of the Hohokam. In *Annual Report of the Board of Regents of the Smithsonian Institu-tion,* pp. 383–387. Washington, D.C.

———. 1914. *The Climatic Factor as Illustrated in Arid America.* Carnegie Institute of Washington Publication 192.

McGuire, R. H., and M. E. Villalpando. 1989. Prehistory and the Making of History in Sonora. In D. H. Thomas (ed.), *Columbian Consequences I: Archaeological and Historical Perspectives on the Spanish Borderlands West,* pp. 159–177. Washington, D.C.: Smithsonian Institu-tion Press.

Elisa Villalpando

SEE ALSO
Northwestern Frontier

Cerro el Chivo
See Acámbaro-Cerro el Chivo

Cerro Encantado (Jalisco, Mexico)

Situated in the semiarid Los Altos region of northeastern Jalisco, this site is on the edge and slope of a terrace above a small river. Excavations exposed buried masonry walls; one was stuccoed and brightly painted and may have sur-rounded a cemetery. Arroyo cuts exposed extensive terrac-ing probably used for habitation and other non-agricultural purposes. A pair of Zacatecas-style horned figurines *(cor-nudos)* was found with one of the inhumations. A tomblike feature contained numerous cremated individuals. A red-on-buff resist-decorated ceramic type, related to the Morales phase of Guanajuato (c. 300/200 B.C. to A.D. 200/400), was common. A highly polished buff ware with incised herringbone designs, probably representing another temporal component, also was present. Two uncorrected radiocarbon dates of 1800 ±80 B.P. were obtained. Bell, who tested the site in 1968 and 1970, suggested that the site and region were related to the shaft tomb tradition of West Mexico, as well as to Chupícuaro.

FURTHER READINGS

Bell, B. B. 1974. Excavations at El Cerro Encantado, Jalisco. In B. B. Bell (ed.), *The Archaeology of West Mexico,* pp. 147–167. Ajijic: Sociedad de Estudio Avanzada del Occidente de México.

Williams, G. 1974. External Influences and the Upper Rio Verde Drainage Basin at Los Altos, West Mexico. In N. Hammond (ed.), *Mesoamerican Archaeology,* pp. 21–50. Austin: University of Texas Press.

Michael Foster

SEE ALSO
Northwestern Frontier

C

Cerro Palenque (Cortés, Honduras)

The single largest site known from the Ulúa Valley of Honduras, Cerro Palenque probably began as a small monumental center in the Early Classic period and expanded to a peak in the Terminal Classic and initial Early Postclassic (c. A.D. 850–1050), when other sites in the region were being abandoned. Situated on a series of hilltops at the confluence of the Blanco, Ulúa, and Comayagua rivers, the site occupies a strategic location near fertile alluvial plains, with ready access to chert and quartzite cobbles, rhyolite for building stone, and lava flows for grinding stones.

In an area covering 3 square kilometers, 575 individual structures were mapped. The highest part of the site, a cluster of carved stone and stucco buildings, includes at least four residential clusters and a reservoir dating to the Classic period. Architectural sculpture in a style also known from Travesia was found here. The later part of the site, built on the lower hills, comprises 103 residential groups of small mounds around courtyards and a series of features forming a monumental architectural core. Terraces and ramps extending over 500 meters are linked by two paved walkways approximately 100 meters long to the 200-meter-long major plaza, which includes a ball court. During the site's period of maximum expansion, the inhabitants used local versions of Fine Orange pottery typical of the western Maya Lowlands, while obsidian was largely replaced by locally produced chert and quartzite tools.

FURTHER READINGS

Joyce, R. 1991. *Cerro Palenque: Power and Identity on the Maya Periphery.* Austin: University of Texas Press.

Stone, D. 1941. *Archaeology of the North Coast of Honduras.* Memoirs of the Peabody Museum of Archaeology and Ethnology, 9, part 1. Cambridge, Mass.: Harvard University.

Rosemary Joyce

SEE ALSO

Southeast Mesoamerica

Cerro Portezuelo (México, Mexico)

This large site in the eastern Basin of Mexico is notable for continuous occupation that encompassed both the Classic and Postclassic periods. The site, adjacent to rich agricultural land, displays an essentially linear settlement pattern, strung out along the northern flank of a knot of hills, the Sierra del Pino, which at the time of Contact divided the provinces of Acolhuacan and Chalco. Numerous mounds, both isolated and in clusters arranged around plazas, are scattered throughout the site; the largest group is in its eastern portion (San Antonio). First surface-collected in 1953/1954 by Paul Tolstoy, who named it "Cerro Portesuelo" from the peak just to the south, the site was excavated and mapped in 1954/1955 by George Brainerd; after his death in 1956, it was excavated briefly by H. B. Nicholson in 1957. It was also surface-collected and mapped by Jeffrey Parsons in 1967 during his Texcoco region survey.

A four-phase sequence has been worked out for the site, beginning some time in the Early Classic and continuing on through the Late Classic/Epiclassic, Early Postclassic (Toltec), and Late Postclassic (Aztec) periods. Nearly all of the ceramic and other artifact types of these phases correlate closely with those of coeval phases at Teotihuacán, Tula, Tenochtitlán, and other leading Central Mexican sites. Evidence from the Codex Xolotl indicates that the Postclassic site was probably known as Tlatzallan (Nahuatl, "gap between hills") and was entirely or largely abandoned owing to a military defeat (c. 1350?) by the neighboring Coatepec during the reign of Quinatzin of Tetzcoco.

FURTHER READINGS

Hicks, F., and H. B. Nicholson. 1964. The Transition from Classic to Postclassic at Cerro Portezuelo, Valley of Mexico. In *XXXV Congreso Internacional de Americanistas, México, Actas y Memorias,* vol. 5, part 1, pp. 493–506. Mexico City.

Nicholson, H. B. 1972. The Problem of the Historical Identity of the Cerro Portezuelo/San Antonio Archaeological Site: An Hypothesis. In *Teotihuacan: XI Mesa Redonda,* pp. 157–200. Mexico City: Sociedad Mexicana de Antropología.

Nicholson, H. B., and F. Hicks. 1961. A Brief Progress Report on the Excavations at Cerro Portezuelo, Valley of Mexico. *American Antiquity* 27:106–108.

Parsons, J. R. 1971. *Prehistoric Settlement Patterns in the Texcoco Region, Mexico.* Memoirs of the Museum of Anthropology, Ann Arbor: University of Michigan.

H. B. Nicholson

SEE ALSO

Basin of Mexico

Cerro Zapotecas (Puebla, Mexico)

Surface studies and excavations at this old volcanic crater and associated lava flow, 3.2 kilometers due west of the Cholula Pyramid, indicate that it was the site of a refugee settlement when the area around the Cholula Pyramid was abandoned in about A.D. 600. The refugees tried to maintain a semblance of their lowland society. They built two temple mounds with attached platforms, a ball court, and residential structures on platforms. They laid out farming plots on the broad main terrace and terraced the slope between the main terrace and the rim of the crater, irrigating the terraces with a system of water control that utilized small canals to distribute rainfall runoff. Judging from the great number of broken jars, the people appear to have had to store a lot of water for daily use, and they seem to have built a small dam and reservoir on the interior of the volcanic crater to catch and store runoff.

Two burned levels at residential and temple mounds seem to indicate that these people were not always successful in fending off their enemies during this period of apparent upheaval in the Valley of Puebla. This conflict may be related to strife between the two great powers of Teotihuacán in the Valley of Mexico to the west and El Tajín in the Veracruz coastal lowlands to the east—warfare that eventually led the Gulf Coast Olmeca-Xicallanca to establish a frontier outpost nearby at Cacaxtla in Tlaxcala about A.D. 650.

FURTHER READINGS

Mountjoy, J. B. 1987. The Collapse of the Classic at Cholula as Seen from Cerro Zapotecas. *Notas Mesoamericanas* 10:119–151.

Mountjoy, J. B., and D. Peterson. 1973. *Man and Land at Prehispanic Cholula.* Vanderbilt University Publications in Anthropology, 4. Nashville, Tenn.

Joseph B. Mountjoy

SEE ALSO

Puebla-Tlaxcala Region

Cerros (Corozal, Belize)

The ruins of Cerros (also known as The Bluff, Milagros, and Cerro Maya) are situated on Corozal Bay in northern Belize. The 5.5 hectares of public plazas and pyramidal acropolises presently jut out into the bay as the rough waters erode away the surrounding settlement zone coastline. There are indications that the water level has risen relative to the land here. Within the bay, concentrations of quarried rock mark the location of small platforms that once flanked the center farther north. At the same time, excavations of features within the center, and shoreline deposits under them, confirm that the center and the community were established on the ancient coast. South of the center, the settlement surrounds it in an arc defined by a 1200-meter-long artificial canal. Inside the canal, the 31 hectares contained eighty-one mounded features mapped by the original project. Within the canal perimeter, larger mounds and plazas, including two ball courts and an acropolis, formed a coherent civic plan oriented roughly to the cardinal directions, an arrangement also pervading the settlement zone, which was presumably otherwise comprised of dwellings. Outside the canal, settlement continued in lower density within the total 1.5 square kilometers mapped by the original project. The terrain of the core community had been significantly modified by the quarrying of stone and earth to build the center, which lowered the overall elevation and made the perimeter canal a necessary catchment to prevent seasonal rainwater from flooding the settlement.

Excavations in the center of Cerros documented that the community was founded as a nucleated village of fisherfolk and farmers at the beginning of the Late Formative period, around 300 B.C. There are three Late Formative ceramic phases for the site: Ixtabai (300–200 B.C.), C'oh (200–50 B.C.), and Tulix (50 B.C.–A.D. 150). Only the nucleated shoreline village is known to have been established in Ixtabai times. During C'oh times, the terrain around this core began to be settled and inhabitants built raised platforms in the dispersed settlement zone.

The Tulix phase witnessed the construction of the public buildings of the center and the completion of the settlement zone as a civic plan as well as a place of residence. During the late Tulix phase, Cerros was the seat of a kingdom of unknown size. The nearby smaller Formative center of Saltillo may have been a satellite secondary center during this period. Ceramic, lithic, and other artifactual data support the hypothesis that late Tulix phase Cerros functioned as a trading and transshipment center on a canoe network up the adjacent New River and along the Caribbean littoral of the peninsula.

Public buildings at Cerros were abruptly abandoned, in the context of termination rituals, at the end of Tulix times, before 200 A.D. An Early Classic ceramic phase, Hubul (200 A.D.), saw an brief attempt to rejuvenate the center with rituals on the summit of the largest pyramid,

C

Structure 4, in conjunction with some renewed settlement in the dispersed zone. However, this effort quickly collapsed, and Cerros remained virtually unoccupied until Terminal Classic times (Sihnal phase, about 850 A.D.), when a village of farmers and fisherfolk reused Formative mounded features for homes. In Middle to Late Postclassic times (Kanan phase, about 1300 A.D.), a small village population continued to inhabit the zone, and in Late Facet Kanan times the main pyramid was the site of elaborate offerings, including human sacrifice. In that late period, busy canoe traffic plied the New River, Corozal Bay, and Chetumal Bay; Cerros no doubt served, as it does today, as an important landmark.

The initial program of research at Cerros documented the existence of a major Late Formative center in a peripheral part of the southern Maya Lowlands. Because Cerros was abandoned at the end of the Formative, its public buildings, civic plan, and residential plan in this early phase of Maya civilization were accessible to extensive investigation. Analyses of material culture, flora and fauna, and environmental data generated detailed reconstructions of the adaptive dynamics of the Maya in a Caribbean coastal setting. Analyses of public architecture and residential features documented the strategies of construction, the modifications of the landscape, and the scale of labor efforts. The good preservation of architectural decoration and the presence of cached offerings allowed systematic analysis of material symbol systems pertaining to early Maya kingship. Historically, the original Cerros research was part of a broader effort in the 1960s and 1970s to investigate the origins of Maya central institutions and places. This effort has established that the Late Formative Lowland Maya civilization was elaborate, robust, and regional in scale, a distinctive phase of a mature society and not merely a prelude to Classic Maya civilization.

The original Cerros project contributed to methodology in Maya research through the definition of termination rituals as a class of context specified by a consistent range of associated artifacts and matrices. Although other Maya projects, most notably the Pennsylvania Tikal Project, had previously identified ritual deposits as terminal, the Cerros Project analysts proposed termination rituals as a formal class. Another methodological advance was the first functional analysis of Late Formative ceramics. Theoretically, the Cerros research contributed to the study of regional interactions between emergent complex communities in the Maya Lowlands as a conditioning factor in their development.

The second Cerros research project, directed by Debra Walker, is conserving and developing the ruins for public display while pursuing research prompted by the first project and more than a decade of work elsewhere in the Maya Lowlands. New discoveries include a third Late Formative period ball court; Cerros thus has the most such features known from a Lowland Maya site.

FURTHER READINGS

Lewenstein, S. M. 1987. *Stone Tool Use at Cerros: The Ethnoarchaeological and Use-Wear Evidence.* Austin: University of Texas Press.

Robertson, R. A., and D. A. Freidel (eds.). 1986. *Archaeology at Cerros, Belize, Central America: 1. An Interim Report.* Dallas: Southern Methodist University Press.

Scarborough, V. L., B. Mitchem, H. S. Carr, and D. A. Freidel. 1982. Two Late Preclassic Ball Courts at the Lowland Maya Center of Cerros, Northern Belize. *Journal of Field Archaeology* 9:21–34.

David A. Freidel

SEE ALSO

Maya Lowlands: South

Chac II

See Sayil and Chac

Chaco Canyon (New Mexico, United States)

From A.D. 950 to 1180, Chaco Canyon was the center of a regional system covering 75,000 square kilometers in what is now New Mexico, Arizona, and Colorado. The canyon contains ten "great houses," massive buildings with as many as eight hundred rooms. A variety of artifact types—cylinder vessels, shell, pseudo-cloisonné, and copper bells—as well as domesticated macaws, occur exclusively or predominantly in the great houses in the canyon. Most of the "great houses" contained at least one large kiva (circular semisubterranean ritual room), along with various special architectural features such as platform mounds and triwalled structures.

Smaller village sites also occur in the canyon, primarily along the wash's southern bank. Seven roads radiate out from the canyon. These roads may be several meters wide and up to 80 kilometers in length. They run in straight lines across mesas and washes and are built to maintain level surfaces. The settlements at the ends of these roads (and beyond) show a consistent pattern. They contain great house architecture and are built in the midst of small villages like those in the canyon. The canyon seemingly acted as a magnet for goods from within and beyond the system. Large quantities of painted ceramics entered the canyon from the outliers. The great houses used thousands of fir and pine beams that were carried in from the mountains at the ends of the road network. Turquoise came from the Cerrios mine near Santa Fe, and shell from the Gulf of California. The most exotic objects—copper bells, macaws, and cloisonné—originated in Mesoamerica.

FURTHER READINGS

Crown, P., and W. J. Judge. 1991. *Chaco and Hohokam: Prehistoric Regional Systems in the American Southwest.* Santa Fe: SAR Press.

Lekson, S. 1986. *Great Pueblo Architecture of Chaco Canyon.* Albuquerque: University of New Mexico Press.

Vivian, R. G. 1990. *The Chacoan Prehistory of the San Juan Basin.* Orlando: Academic Press.

Randall H. McGuire

SEE ALSO

Northern Arid Zone

Chahuite Escondido (Guanacaste, Costa Rica)

This site of the Greater Nicoya region is a large shell midden complex on the Santa Elena peninsula, occupied during the period A.D. 300–1520. In this dry tropical environment, multiple shell middens were loosely arranged around informal plazas. Artifacts include ceramics, lithics, mollusca, and archaeofauna. White-slipped ceramics from Pacific Nicaragua indicate interaction with other regions. Subsistence activities were hunting, fishing, harvesting marine mollusks, and plant gathering, with limited agriculture. Export of marine products to interior locations may have been an economic specialization.

FURTHER READINGS

Sweeney, J. W. 1976. Ceramic Analysis from Three Sites in Northwest Coastal Guanacaste. *Vínculos* 2:37–44.

Frederick W. Lange

SEE ALSO

Intermediate Area: Overview; Marías, Las; Nicoya, Greater, and Guanacaste Region; Vidor

C

Chalcatzingo (Morelos, Mexico)

Site in the Amatzinac Valley of eastern Morelos, noted for its Olmec-like Middle Formative period stone monuments. Chalcatzingo was first investigated in 1934 by Eulalia Guzmán, who recorded five carvings. Stratigraphic pits excavated there by Roman Piña Chán in 1953 provided some basic chronology. Extensive excavations in the 1970s, by a project codirected by David Grove, Jorge Angulo, and Raul Arana, sought to gather data on the Formative period village, its dwellings, public architecture, and general material culture in order to better understand the site's evolution and also its relationship with the Gulf Coast Olmec.

The archaeological zone lies on the northwestern side of the Cerro Chalcatzingo and Cerro Delgado, two granodiorite peaks dominating the valley's flat landscape. A small spring supplied water to the site's pre-Hispanic occupants, and the hill slopes offered good agricultural potential to the early corn farmers who settled there. The archaeological sequence for the Early and Middle Formative periods, when the site grew to its greatest prominence, has been subdivided into three phases: Amate (1500–1100 B.C.), Barranca (1100–700 B.C.), and Cantera (700–500 B.C.).

Potsherds from simple buff-colored bowls with red rims, dating to c. 1500 B.C., represent the earliest evidence of human occupation at Chalcatzingo and mark the beginning of the Amate phase. Most Amate phase levels were destroyed or deeply buried by later land modifications and cultural deposits, and so very little is known about that time period. Originally the settlement was a small farming hamlet built on the slopes below the peaks, but evidence suggests that it soon became the largest settlement in the valley. Excavations disclosed a unique aspect of the Amate phase village: stone-faced mound architecture, the only such public architecture known in highland central Mexico at this early date. By 1100 B.C. the site was apparently an important regional center with an active role in trade with nearby regions.

Early in the Barranca phase (1100–700 B.C.), the people of Chalcatzingo altered the hillslopes into a series of broad terraces. Evidence from this period is again scant, and only one house from this time period has been found. Data suggest that the site and its regional interactions continued to grow in importance, both reaching their peaks in the Cantera phase (700–500 B.C.). Remains of the Cantera phase settlement occur within the upper levels of the site, and the 1970s project retrieved good information on this period. Archaeological and stylistic

C

evidence indicate that the site's monuments were created and erected in the Cantera phase.

The upper (southern) end of the Formative settlement is marked by the talus slopes and cliffs of Cerro Chalcatzingo, and two groups of bas-relief carvings occur on the hill. The largest and most famous of the Chalcatzingo carvings, Monument 1 or "El Rey," depicts a personage sitting within a U-shaped niche that symbolizes a mountain cave. Rainclouds with falling raindrops are represented above the cave. El Rey is one of a linear arrangement of six bas-reliefs carved onto rock faces high on the hillside; all convey a rainfall theme. Six other carvings exist on boulders and slabs on the talus slopes at the base of the hill; these are primarily scenes of supernatural animals dominating humans.

The terraced hillside and Cantera phase settlement extends northward from the base of the two hills in a series of descending steps. The village's settlement pattern was dispersed, with apparently only one house structure situated on each terrace. The average floor area of these rectangular dwellings was more than 60 square meters. They were generally constructed with three adobe brick walls (the back and side walls) set on a wide stone foundation, and a front wall made of cane partially covered by mud plaster. All had thatched roofs. Subfloor burials were found in all houses excavated and were presumably of the house's deceased occupants.

The largest Cantera phase house excavated is separated from the others. Situated on the uppermost terrace, near the talus slopes of Cerro Chalcatzingo, it had thirty-eight subfloor burials, including the only house burials interred in stone-lined graves and associated with jade pieces. Evidence suggests that this was an elite household, probably of the community's leader. To the north of this elite residence is Chalcatzingo's largest public construction, a massive 70-meter-long earthen platform mound—the site's principal mound. Its final building stages are Cantera phase, but excavations indicate earlier Barranca and Amate phase components. No other Middle Formative mound of this size is known in the central highlands.

On several terraces beyond the principal mound (north, downhill) excavations uncovered Cantera phase rectangular platforms with stone exterior walls; each platform is about 15 to 20 meters in length and 1 to 1.5 meters tall. Carved monuments, including stelae, are associated with these platforms. Like Gulf Coast Olmec stelae, Chalcatzingo's depict individual personages, perhaps glorifying the village's past leaders. One stela commemorates a woman, the earliest such representation in Mesoamerican monumental art.

A terrace at the northern end of the site yielded a surprising discovery: a large Olmec-style tabletop altar, the only such altar ever found outside Gulf Coast Olmec centers. This monument, however, is constructed on large stone blocks, while altars at La Venta and San Lorenzo are monolithic. Furthermore, Chalcatzingo's altar sits within a large sunken rectangular patio, an architectural feature not known at Gulf Coast Olmec centers.

Chalcatzingo's stone monuments indicate the site's important interactions with Gulf Coast Olmec centers, while other data suggest that it was also interacting with sites in Guerrero, the Valley of Mexico, Puebla, and Oaxaca. It has been hypothesized that Chalcatzingo was a major "gateway city," a middleman in trade between the central highlands and Gulf Coast. However, the people of Chalcatzingo were not Olmec. Their material culture—the pottery, figurines, and other objects of daily and ritual use found in the archaeological excavations—was predominantly like that of other Formative period sites in central Mexico. Their language, probably related to the Zapotecan and Mixtecan languages, was also different from that of the Olmec.

About 500 B.C. Chalcatzingo declined in prominence and was abandoned. A few of the hillside terraces were apparently resettled during the Late Formative, and in the Late Classic a small village again developed there. The latter included a mound-plaza complex of modest size with a circular pyramid and adjacent ball court. Relatively simple painted rock art in shallow caves on Cerro Delgado apparently dates to this time. An Early Postclassic hamlet existed behind (i.e., northeast of) Cerro Delgado, and Late Postclassic mounds occur about a kilometer north of the site. During the Postclassic, a small shrine was built on the talus slopes of Cerro Chalcatzingo, adjacent to one of the Middle Formative monuments, perhaps venerating that ancient carving.

FURTHER READINGS

Arana, R. M. 1987. Classic and Postclassic Chalcatzingo. In D. C. Grove (ed.), *Ancient Chalcatzingo,* pp. 387–399. Austin: University of Texas Press.

Gay, C. T. E. 1972. *Chalcacingo.* Portland, Ore.: International Scholarly Book Services.

Grove, D. C. 1968. Chalcatzingo, Morelos, Mexico: A Re-appraisal of the Olmec Rock Carvings. *American Antiquity* 33:486–491.

———. 1984. *Chalcatzingo: Excavations on the Olmec Frontier.* London: Thames and Hudson.

———. (ed.). 1987. *Ancient Chalcatzingo.* Austin: University of Texas Press.

———. 1989. Chalcatzingo and Its Olmec Connection. In R. J. Sharer and D. C. Grove (eds.), *Regional Perspectives on the Olmec,* pp.122–147. Cambridge: Cambridge University Press.

Grove, D. C., and S. Gillespie. 1984. Chalcatzingo's Portrait Figurines and the Cult of the Ruler. *Archaeology* 37:27–33.

Guzmán, E. 1934. Los relieves de las rocas del Cerro de la Cantera, Jonacatepec, Morelos. *Anales del Museo Nacional de Arqueología, Historia, y Etnografía,* Epoca 5, 1(2):237–251.

Piña Chan, R. 1955. *Chalcatzingo, Morelos.* Informes, 4. Mexico City: INAH.

David C. Grove

SEE ALSO
Morelos Region

Chalcatzingo: Ritual Appropriation of the Sacred Landscape

By the early first millennium B.C., Olmec centers of power in southern Veracruz and Tabasco were extending outposts into other Mesoamerican regions. In the central highlands of Mexico, Olmec-related sites extend from southern Puebla and Morelos into the mountains of Guerrero. At Las Bocas, Chalcatzingo, Teopantecuanitlán, Juxtlahuaca, and Oxtotitlán, sculptors and artists familiar with the style of Olmec heartland capitals were commissioned to fashion ceremonial places in ritually interactive relationships with prominent mountains, caves, sources of water, and the east–west path of the sun. It was a central purpose of these works to affirm the legitimacy of rulers and to establish their religious participation in the annual cycle of fertility.

At Chalcatzingo a huge rock formation rises from the plain, aligned in an approximate north–south direction. By the foot of the cliffs, a burial tumulus and buildings associated with the elite overlook the residential district. Boulders sculpted with ritual scenes lie in the upper and intermediate zones. The viewer looks east toward the rock and its monuments, in the direction of the rising sun. The most imposing figures are carved in relief on a high rock face. A royal personage—perhaps an ancestor founder-

hero—is depicted in profile, enthroned within the abstracted mouth of a mask. Scrolls representing mist and clouds issue forth, and rainclouds appear above. Plants grow from the interstices of the mask. The mask represents a cave, an entrance into the "heart of the mountain," the watery underworld source of water and the earth's agricultural fertility. This theme is echoed by another stone cave-mask, almost certainly once the entrance to an inner temple chamber associated with the burial barrow below. This sculptural portal is now in the Munson Williams Proctor Institute, Museum of Art, Utica, New York. It is significant that Chalcatzingo's monuments are placed with a view toward the snow-capped volcano Popocatepetl and Mount Ixtaccihuatl beyond, where the great summer thunderclouds take form that irrigate a vast highland region. The sculptures appear to be early manifestations of a widespread Mesoamerican belief that ancestors within mountains were in communion with the earth's water-giving and regenerative forces. Propitiated by the living, they continued to play in afterlife an indispensable active role in bringing about the annual renewal. The mountain, the rock, the sculptures, and the burial barrow, as well as other historical monuments of rulership, embrace an immense landscape, participating in an ongoing colloquy between the living, the dead, and the natural environment and seasonal phenomena vital to the life of the community.

Richard F. Townsend

Chalcedony
See Silex

Chalchihuites Culture

Situated in the semiarid, rolling hill country of western Zacatecas and the foothills of central Durango on the Mesoamerican frontier, this cultural tradition is characterized by two distinct branches, Suchil and Guadiana. The Suchil branch of western Zacatecas represents the initial and more sophisticated development of the Chalchihuites tradition. J. C. Kelley believed that the Chalchihuites culture truncated the local Canutillo and subsequent Vesuvio phase developments in western Zacatecas around A.D. 750. The Canutillo phase represents the initial Mesoamerican development in western Zacatecas, featuring small villages with house platforms built around plazas. Ceramics include Canutillo Red-Filled Engraved and Gualterio Red-on-Cream. It is unclear whether the Canutillo phase represents a development

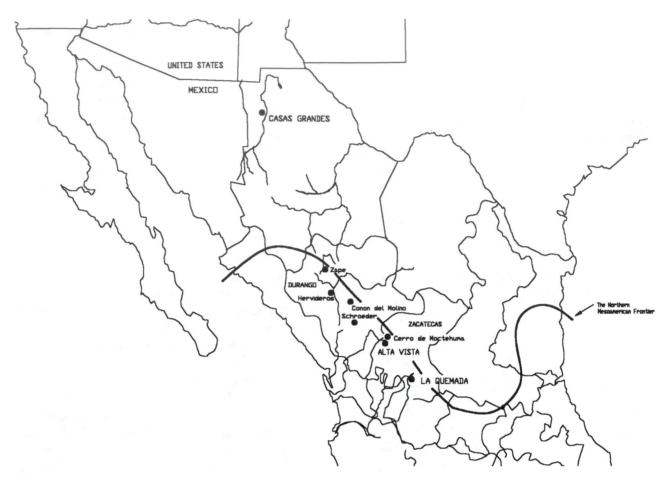

Extent of Chalchihuites culture area. Courtesy of Susan Toby Evans.

from local Loma San Gabriel populations or an occupation by Mesoamerican immigrants. The Vesuvio phase represents an elaboration of the Canutillo phase, with Vesuvio Red-Filled Engraved and Gualterio Exterior Red-on-Cream as dominant pottery types.

During the early Classic period, two major sites were constructed in the Chalchihuites core area: Alta Vista and Cerro de Moctehuma. Both had halls of columns and public buildings and spaces. Vista Paint Cloisonné and a negative pottery type indicate that both sites had ties to areas in West Mexico. By the mid-600s A.D. Cerro de Moctehuma was abandoned, giving way to the florescence of Alta Vista, beginning with the Alta Vista phase (c. A.D. 700–750). The site is on the Tropic of Cancer, and it has a ceremonial precinct that includes multiple plazas, a small pyramid with a crypt, and a unique observatory for equinox observations. As Alta Vista flourished, so did secondary centers and outlying villages. Ceramics

were dominated by well-made Suchil Red-on-Brown and Michilla Red-Filled Engraved, both decorated with geometric designs and life forms. Turquoise was common, as was the working of a soft white stone from local mines. The mining complex of the Chalchihuites culture was one of the most extensive in all of Mesoamerica.

By the mid-800s (Calichal and Retoño phases), Alta Vista declined, as did the Chalchihuites of western Zacatecas. By 1000 most of western Zacatecas was abandoned. After 1000, Chalchihuites developments occurred in the Guadiana branch in central Durango. The origins of the Durango branch are unclear; it could represent either a remnant population from Zacatecas or the adoption of the Chalchihuites tradition by local populations. Chalchihuites sites are found as far north as near the Durango-Chihuahua border. At many sites Chalchihuites components replace earlier Loma San Gabriel occupations. The earliest two Durango phases, Ayala and

Las Joyas (A.D. 875–1150), were clearly Chalchihuites. Moreover, there was an influx of pottery, copper, shell, and other items from the west coast. This probably represents the incorporation of the highland zone into the widespread and influential Aztatlan mercantile system, which linked northwestern with central Mexico. During the subsequent Río Tunal and Calera phases, this highland culture appears to represent a blending of the local Loma San Gabriel and Chalchihuites with Aztatlan traits and influence. By the mid-1400s the northwestern frontier collapsed, and remnant populations may have given rise to the Tepehuan and perhaps the Huichol.

FURTHER READINGS

Aveni, A. F., H. Hartung, and J. C. Kelley. 1981. Alta Vista (Chalchihuites), Astronomical Implications of a Mesoamerican Ceremonial Outpost at the Tropic of Cancer. *American Antiquity* 47:326–335.

Foster, M. S. 1985. The Loma San Gabriel Occupation of Zacatecas and Durango, Mexico. In M. S. Foster and P. C. Weigand (eds.), *The Archaeology of West and Northwest Mesoamerica*, pp. 327–351. Boulder: Westview Press.

Kelley, J. C. 1971. Archaeology of the Northern Frontier: Zacatecas and Durango. In R. Wanchope (ed.), *Handbook of Middle American Indians,* vol. 5, part 11, pp. 768–804. Austin: University of Texas Press.

———. 1985. The Chronology of the Chalchihuites Culture. In M. S. Foster and P. C. Weigand (eds.), *The Archaeology of West and Northwest Mesoamerica*, pp. 269–289. Boulder: Westview Press.

———. 1986. The Mobile Merchants of Molino. In F. J. Mathien and R. H. McGuire (eds.), *Ripples in the Chichimec Sea*, pp. 81–104. Carbondale and Edwardsville: Southern Illinois University Press.

———. 1991. The Known Archaeological Ballcourts of Durango and Zacatecas, Mexico. In V. L. Scarborough and D. R. Wilcox (eds.), *The Mesoamerican Ballgame*, pp. 87–100. Tucson: University of Arizona Press.

———. 1993. Zenith Passage: The View from Chalchihuites. In A. Wooley and J. Ravesloot (eds.), *Culture and Contact: Charles C. Di Peso's Gran Chichimeca*, pp. 227–250. Albuquerque: University of New Mexico Press.

Kelley, J. C., and E. A. Kelley. 1971. *An Introduction to the Ceramics of the Chalchihuites Culture of Zacatecas and Durango, Mexico. Part I: The Decorated Wares.* Mesoamerican Studies Series, 5. Carbondale: University Museum, Southern Illinois University.

Weigand, P. C. 1982. Mining and Mineral Trade in Prehispanic Zacatecas. *Anthropology* 6:87–134.

Michael Foster

SEE ALSO
Huistle, Cerro del

Chalchuapa (Santa Ana, El Salvador)

Comprising four architectural groups (El Trapiche, Casa Blanca, Pampe, and Tazumal) covering about three square kilometers, this site was occupied for around 2,700 years (c. 1200 B.C. to the Conquest), as documented by investigations by the University of Pennsylvania Museum. Initial Middle Formative (c. 900–650 B.C.) development was marked by a massive platform, about 20 meters high at El Trapiche, and Monument 12, a boulder with Olmec-style figures. A Late Formative (c. 200 B.C.–A.D. 200) peak saw large-scale constructions and carved stone monuments such as Monument 1, a Maya-style stela with a hieroglyphic text, representing a southern Maya tradition ancestral to Classic Maya sculpture and writing. Following a decline caused by the eruption of the Ilopango volcano (c. A.D. 200), a second peak during the Late Classic (c. 600–900) was centered on Tazumal and was probably linked to Copán.

FURTHER READINGS

Sharer, R. J. 1987. The Olmec and the Southeastern Periphery of Mesoamerica. In R. J. Sharer and D. C. Grove (eds.), *The Olmec and the Development of Mesoamerican Civilization*, pp. 247–271.

Sharer, R. J. (ed.). 1978. *The Prehistory of Chalchuapa, El Salvador.* 3 vols. University Museum Monograph 36. Philadelphia: University of Pennsylvania Press.

Robert J. Sharer

Chalco (México, Mexico)

The Aztec historian Chimalpahin reported that Chalco was an urban city-state in the early sixteenth century, and that it had been founded in the late 1100s A.D. and had led the Chalca political confederation until its conquest in 1456 by the Mexica-led Triple Alliance. Archaeological research confirms a florescence of occupation during the Postclassic, or Aztec, period. As identified by the regional surveys of Parsons and colleagues, Aztec period Chalco (c. A.D. 1150–1521) attained a maximum size of 2.5 square kilometers and a population of 12,500.

Excavations at Mound 65 by Hodge, and elsewhere in Chalco by Séjourné, disclosed ceramics from pre-Aztec cultural periods, including the Formative, Classic, Epi-classic, and Toltec (Coyotlatelco) periods. Regional surveys by Parsons and colleagues revealed that earlier occupation of Chalco was always less extensive than that of Aztec times. Excavations by O'Neill of a portion of Chalco situated on the shore of Lake Chalco traced Aztec ceramics to a depth of nearly 7 meters. Radiocarbon dates from Mound 65, obtained during Hodge's 1992 excavations, place the first appearance of Aztec ceramics (Aztec I Black-on-Orange and Chalco Polychrome) at c. 1200 (cal., Beta 57748 = A.D. 1010–1300). Chalco Polychrome was a distinctive style of pottery produced in the town; vessel forms included tripod dishes and bowls with multi-colored surface motifs. It was exported prior to Chalco's conquest by the Aztec Empire. Today the ancient city center of Aztec-period Chalco is buried beneath modern buildings and roads.

FURTHER READINGS

Hodge, Mary G. 1984. *Aztec City-States.* Memoirs of the Museum of Anthropology, University of Michigan, 18. Ann Arbor.

Parsons, J. R., E. Brumfiel, M. H. Parsons, and D. J. Wilson. 1982. *Prehispanic Settlement Patterns in the Southern Valley of Mexico: The Chalco-Xochimilco Region.* Memoirs of the Museum of Anthropology, University of Michigan, 14. Ann Arbor.

Schroeder, Susan. 1991. *Chimalpahin and the Kingdoms of Chalco.* Tucson: University of Arizona Press.

Séjourné, Laurette. 1983. *Arqueología y Historia del Valle de México de Xochimilco a Amecameca.* Mexico City: Siglo Veintiuno Editores.

Mary G. Hodge

SEE ALSO
Basin of Mexico

Chamá
See Alta Verapaz Region

Chametla
See Guasave and Related Sites

Chert
See Silex

Chetumal
See Santa Rita Corozal

Chiapa de Corzo (Chiapas, Mexico)

Chiapa de Corzo is situated in the center of the modern Mexican state of Chiapas and is the site from which the state derives its name. Bernal Diaz chronicled the initial conquest of the fierce Chiapanec warriors at Chiapa de Corzo in 1524 by the Spanish during their first incursion into the region. According to the chronicler, Chiapa de Corzo at this time had an estimated 4,000 inhabitants and "nicely laid out" streets and houses (Navarrete 1966:18). Chiapa de Corzo is on the left bank of the Río Grijalva in the modern town of the same name and near the modern capital of Tuxtla Gutierrez. The site occupies the most fertile riverbottom land along all of the Grijalva River at a juncture just before this river enters the impassable Sumidero Canyon. It was a favored site throughout all of prehistory and has been continuously occupied from 1400 B.C. until the present day. The Mangue-speaking Chiapanec peoples who inhabited the city at the Conquest are thought to have immigrated from the north and to have conquered the Zoque lands around Chiapa de Corzo during the Classic period, about A.D. 800. The Chiapanecs eventually conquered much of the central portion of the Middle Grijalva River Valley as well as subjugating nearby Zoque and Maya towns and making them tributaries. Contrary to some claims, the Chiapanecs were not conquered by the Aztecs.

The planned arrangement of large earthen mounds and plazas at Chiapa de Corzo was established about 700 B.C. (uncalibrated radiocarbon date), during the early part of the Middle Formative period. Chiapa de Corzo was one of many regional centers founded during the Middle Formative along the Grijalva River and Pacific Coast, the principal ones being Izapa, La Libertad, Mirador, and San Isidro. The local setting of Chiapa de Corzo was ideal for exploiting riverine resources, for taking advantage of the seasonally inundated river bottom lands, and for controlling river traffic and trade. The Grijalva was navigable from Chiapa upstream to near La Libertad, but rapids barred navigation downstream from Chiapa de Corzo until the river's exit from Sumidero Canyon near the site of San Isidro. The visible architecture at the site dates from the Late Formative period, in which dressed stone was used to face the mounds and platforms. A palace and temple complex dating to the Late Formative are visible in the center.

C

During the Middle Formative, Chiapa de Corzo was the principal paramount chiefdom in Chiapas. It may have evolved into a small kingdom or state at the very end of the Late Formative, at the time when the palace was constructed and the temple enlarged, owing principally to stimulus from the large polities of the Maya Lowlands. Considerable Maya influence is evident at the time that the community was reorganized around the palace and temple complex. However, Chiapa de Corzo does not appear to have adopted the stela-altar complex characteristic of the coeval Izapa culture or of their Maya neighbors. A few fragments of early stone monuments have been found, including Mesoamerica's oldest recorded long count date.

FURTHER READINGS

Lowe, G. W. 1977. The Mixe-Zoque as Competing Neighbors of the Early Lowland Maya. In R. E. W. Adams (ed.), *The Origins of Maya Civilization*, pp. 197–248. Albuquerque: University of New Mexico Press.

Lowe, G. W., and J. A. Mason. 1965. Archaeological Survey of the Chiapas Coast, Highlands, and Upper Grijalva Basin. In R. Wauchope and G. R. Willey (eds.), *Handbook of Middle American Indians*, vol. 2, pp. 195–236. Austin: University of Texas Press.

Navarrete, C. 1966. *The Chiapanec History and Culture.* Papers of the New World Archaeological Foundation, 21. Provo, Utah.

Gareth W. Lowe

SEE ALSO

Chiapas Interior Plateau

Chiapas Interior Plateau

Chiapas represents a paradox of Mesoamerican prehistory. Spatially, the region encompassed by this modern Mexican state occupied the center of Mesoamerica, being flanked on the north and east by Maya cultures of the lowlands and highlands and on the west by the cultures of Oaxaca and the Mexican Plateau (Zapotec, Mixtec, Toltec, and Aztec). Temporally and culturally, Chiapas was also central to the rise of Mesoamerican civilization during the Early and Middle Formative periods (c. 1800–500 B.C.). Nevertheless, the poorly known ancient cultures of Chiapas are presumed by many to have been peripheral to major developments in Mesoamerica. The opposite would be closer to the truth. Gareth Lowe argues that the

position of Chiapas at the spatial and cultural nexus of Mesoamerica prevented any grand civilizations from taking root there. Ancient peoples of Chiapas were conduits for cultural influences traveling through from either side or were casualties of conquest by more belligerent neighbors. In either case, Chiapas cultures were central to the interaction sphere and emerging world economic system that became Mesoamerica.

Two aspects of this claim are significant. Ancient cultural processes and events in Chiapas and those of adjacent regions cannot be understood apart from each other. The sensitivity of Chiapas communities to foreign influences provides an excellent measure of ancient power dynamics. The most hegemonic cultures of Mesoamerica left their marks on Chiapas societies. Consequently, beyond its own local prehistory, the archaeology of Chiapas also provides an important record of the waxing and waning of the political fortunes of Mesoamerica's most powerful civilizations.

A local saying proclaims that "everything in Chiapas is Mexico." This refers primarily to the varied ecological settings within this southernmost state of Mexico (ranging from arid to tropical and from montane to coastal), which constitute an ecological microcosm of Mexico; but the saying just as aptly captures the essence of Chiapas prehistory. Because of local tectonic geology and climate, the physiographic and ecological zones of the state form a series of bands, trending northwest to southeast, paralleling the shoreline of the Pacific Ocean and the upthrust Sierra Madre on the southern margin of the state. On the southern flank of this mountain chain lies the narrow Pacific coastal plain which, climatically, ranges from tropical conditions at its southeastern extremity (known as the Soconusco) to semiarid in its northwestern edge near the Isthmus of Tehuantepec. The southern mountain slopes enjoy wetter conditions than their northern counterparts.

The principal interior valley of the Grijalva River parallels the northwest-to-southeast trend of the Sierra Madre to the south, and a high plateau to the north. Thus, the Grijalva River Valley constitutes a central trench bracketed by a wide band of mountains to the north and a narrow band of higher mountains to the south. This central valley is known as the "Central Depression." North of the plateau or highlands, limestone hills slope down toward the Gulf of Mexico and the tropical lowlands. The majority of the ancient peoples of Chiapas occupied the semiarid Central Depression and the pine and oak forests of the northern highlands.

C

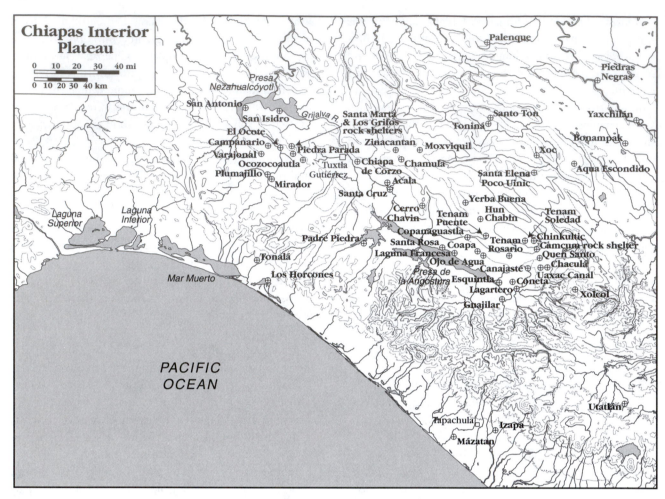

Chiapas Interior Plateau. Map design by Mapping Specialists Limited, Madison, Wisconsin.

Culturally, the interior of the state was sequentially occupied by ancestors of present-day Zoques, Mayas, and Chiapanecs. Chiapas derives its name from Chiapan (now known as Chiapa de Corzo), the principal city in the region and home of the warlike Chiapanecs encountered by the first Spanish invaders. The Chiapanecs, however, were relative latecomers to the region who had wrested the city from its Zoque former inhabitants sometime during the Middle or Late Classic period.

Today, the distribution of indigenous peoples cleaves the state down the middle: the western half is occupied by Zoque speakers, and the eastern half, including the central plateau and northern lowlands, by Mayan speakers. Archaeological evidence indicates that this situation dates

back to about 200 B.C. Prior to this time, the majority of the state was occupied by Zoque peoples, both in the interior valleys and along the Pacific coastal plain.

Given their rich history and extensive settlement, the Zoques' anonymity in Mesoamerican textbooks and museum presentations requires explanation. A simple one is readily at hand: the ancient Zoques are known archaeologically as "Olmecs." Prior to the advent and spread of "Olmec" culture about 1100 B.C., Chiapas was already occupied by Mixe-Zoquean speakers, ancestors to the later Mixes and Zoques.

Archaeological evidence indicates that Chiapas was occupied by Mixe-Zoquean peoples and their descendants for at least two thousand years before Maya peoples began to make inroads into the eastern sector of the region. Mayas immigrated from the tropical lowlands to the east and gradually pushed their Zoque neighbors out of the southern river valleys and the northern highlands. This process took several centuries to complete. Later, Chiapanec conquerors invaded the middle Grijalva River Valley, conquered Chiapa de Corzo and its environs, and enslaved the Zoques of this prime agricultural region. Aztecs tried to duplicate this feat in the fifteenth century. They conquered the Soconusco and annexed it to their empire, but they were unsuccessful in their attempts to subjugate the Chiapanecs or the Highland Mayas.

In their conquests the Spanish entered Chiapas territory from Tabasco in 1523. They first subdued Zoque cities in the northern lowlands, then Chiapanec domains in the interior of the state, and finally the Maya Highlands. A separate campaign plundered the Pacific slope as the initial step of Alvarado's conquest of Guatemala.

Historic records allude to earlier conquests of the Soconusco by the Quiché Maya and, much earlier, by unnamed peoples. Archaeological evidence also gives ample evidence of Toltec and Teotihuacán influence and contacts, but whether the artifact similarities resulted from conquest or merely strong cultural ties remains to be determined. The overall impression from a sweeping appraisal of Chiapas prehistory is of ethnic continuity in the face of multiple conquests. The major exception appears to be Maya-Zoque interactions; the early Mayas appear to have displaced or assimilated Formative Zoque communities of the upper Grijalva River Valley and the adjacent plateau to the north. The boundary between the two appears to have stabilized by about A.D. 200 and persists to this day.

The archaeological information available for the various regions and periods is uneven, but the general contours of Chiapas prehistory appear to parallel and be linked to those of its neighbors. The earliest known site in the Chiapas interior is the Santa Marta rock shelter. An ancient fluted projectile point was found in the lowest levels of a nearby alcove (Los Grifos) and indicates the presence of ancient hunters in the region about 11,000 B.C. Upper levels of the rock shelter also show evidence of Archaic period lifeways of hunting and foraging. The uppermost levels of occupation disclose a transition to settled village life, agriculture, and adoption of ceramics.

Other finds indicate that Archaic foraging peoples were in the northern highlands and living along the coastal estuary about 6000–2000 B.C. Evidence of early pottery from the Santa Marta and Camcum rock shelters indicates that the transition to a more settled lifestyle in the interior began about 1500 B.C., two centuries after large sedentary villages first appeared in the Soconusco.

The limited information for the earliest agriculturalists in the Central Depression indicates dispersal of small hamlets along the banks of the largest rivers. Similarities in pottery vessels and types of obsidian used for cutting tools indicate that the peoples of the interior were in significant contact with the coast-dwellers. The first large villages in the interior were at Plumajillo, Chiapa de Corzo, and Acala and date to about 1300 B.C. These sites show an early cultural tie to Pacific Coast groups and a later shift to early Olmec culture of the Coastal Lowlands to the north. Plumajillo was a special production site for iron ore, in the form of cubic "beads" that were exported to the Olmec capital of San Lorenzo in modern-day Veracruz. Chiapa de Corzo and Acala were situated at key locations along the Grijalva River; both communities constructed large terraces at this time rather than the large platforms arranged around plazas characteristic of the following period.

Perhaps the most dynamic centuries in Chiapas prehistory were from 900 to 500 B.C. During this period the region witnessed the rise of numerous large cities all along the Central Depression. These ceremonial centers were fairly regularly spaced, and all were based on a similar community plan copied from the Olmec capital of La Venta (Tabasco). The plan consisted of an axial arrangement of at least five platforms and two intervening courtyards, with the tallest pyramid in the north and a pyramid–long mound pair on the south. Goods found with elite burials from these same sites demonstrate the importance of long-distance trade in jade and other precious goods. Similarities among a range of artifacts and cultural practices indicate an integrated trade network that connected La Venta, at the northern terminus, to all the cities in central Chiapas and to Kaminaljuyú and perhaps Copán, on the southern terminus.

The network of centers along the Pacific Coast and in the Central Depression continued for several centuries, but by about 400 to 300 B.C. things started to fall apart, and many key cities were virtually abandoned. The demise of the Zoque network by 200 B.C. had at least two probable causes: the collapse of La Venta and/or the simultaneous rise of Maya cities (Nakbe and El Mirador) in the central Petén of Guatemala. The Late Formative period that ensued represented a restructuring of Chiapas peoples and an acculturation of foreign norms. Maya peoples began to settle the abandoned regions in the

C

upper Central Depression and the northern highlands. Those Zoque cities that did not collapse—Santa Rosa, Chiapa de Corzo, and Mirador—show a strong presence of Maya trade wares and architectural styles at this time. These changes probably relate to the rise and expansion of state societies in the Maya Lowlands. Chiapa de Corzo at this time became even more complex and powerful; a new palace and temple complex was constructed during the heyday of contact with the Lowland Maya. Interestingly, about 100 B.C. there appears to have been a local reaction to things Maya, and the Zoque inhabitants stopped using Maya-style crockery.

During the Classic period, the major Zoque cities of the middle and lower Central Depression were Chiapa de Corzo, Ocozocoautla, and Mirador; in the upper Central Depression, the principal Maya cities were Lagartero, Laguna Francesa, and Ojo de Agua. The largest Maya cities, however, were in the northern lowlands or along the Usumacinta River: Yaxchilán, Palenque, and Toniná. Teotihuacán influence in the region was spotty and appears to have been limited to the western portion of the Central Depression around Mirador. The more interior cities, such as Chiapa de Corzo, appear to have been little influenced, suggesting strong boundaries between Zoque polities at the time. Teotihuacán influence was pronounced, however, along the Pacific corridor at several strategic centers, principally Los Horcones (where Teotihuacán-style Tláloc sculptures have been recovered) and Izapa, and into Guatemala.

Late Classic occupation of the interior shows continuity in occupation, but the evidence is still too limited to reconstruct a detailed cultural history. Ethnohistoric legends claim that Chiapanecs invaded the region about this time, but to date there is no archaeological evidence of their conquest. This, in itself, suggests that these newcomers did not meddle with the basic infrastructure of Late Classic Zoque society. Of special interest, there appears to have been an emphasis on cave rituals and offerings in the Zoque area at this time.

Information from the Maya half of the Central Depression tells a different story: here the Late Classic period was the time of maximum population and activity, probably as a result of immigration from the lowlands to the north and east. Recent studies of language divergence indicate that Huastec Maya split from Chicomuseltec Maya about this time, suggesting an emigration of Chiapas Maya peoples from the Central Depression to northern Veracruz during the Classic period. Perhaps the Chiapanec entry into the adjacent portion of the central valley from the west coast and/or the westward push of Tzeltalan Maya groups on the east precipitated the Huastecs' departure. The first Pipil migrations to Central America date to this time, and these peoples would have passed through Chiapas along the Pacific coastal corridor. This period appears to be one of great movement of peoples within Mesoamerica.

A network of Maya statelets extended from the northern edge of the Sierra Madre, through the upper Central Depression, across the northern highlands, and down to the northern piedmont and northern lowlands. The principal state capitals in the interior were Lagartero, Tenam Rosario, Ojo de Agua, Tenam Soledad, Tenam Puente, Chinkultic, Yerba Buena, and Moxviquil. There seems to have been a special emphasis on ball courts and the ball game in local political rituals. This whole system fell apart several centuries later for reasons that remain obscure. One plausible proximate cause may have been a return to drier conditions, which would have made the semiarid lands of this subregion too marginal for rainfall agriculture.

Whatever the cause, the numerous Late Classic cities were abandoned and were succeeded by very few Postclassic centers. Enough is known of the Postclassic period, however, to demonstrate that the radical demographic decline is not a function of misidentification of archaeological remains. Rather, the break-up of the system appears to have been accompanied by increased hostilities and a marked decrease in interaction among different Maya groups. Much of the dialectal divergence for the western Maya (i.e., the splits in the Tzeltalan branch) dates to this period, suggesting a shift in interregional interaction as communities became more closed than before.

The Postclassic sites that are known in the upper Central Depression are remarkable for their extremely modest public buildings and nucleated settlement pattern. Most are also in defensive locations. The best-known site is Canajasté. The picture from elsewhere in the state is somewhat contradictory because Postclassic remains are rare, but ethnohistoric information exists. The few documentary sources portray the Late Postclassic as a time of extensive trade, especially by the Highland Maya of Zinacantan and the Chiapanecs of Chiapa de Corzo. Cotton and cotton cloth were the major Chiapan exports. The early colonial dictionaries portray small pre-Columbian kingdoms and elaborate hierarchies of rank, privilege, and responsibility, similar to coeval kingdoms in neighboring Guatemala and Oaxaca.

In their conquests, the Spanish left some pre-Columbian cities in place, especially Chiapa de Corzo, but for the most part they relocated the Indians into larger communities for the convenience of administrative control. In central Chiapas, a series of Catholic Indian towns and churches were established along the Camino Real, which followed the natural route of the Central Depression from the Isthmus of Tehuantepec on the west to Guatemala City on the east. Principal towns in central Chiapas were Chiapa de Corzo, Copanaguastla, Coapa, Coneta, and Esquintla. These colonial towns persisted for several centuries but were eventually abandoned because European diseases decimated the native populations. Indian communities that survived the Spanish Conquest, and continue to survive, were those in the rugged, marginal lands in the northern highlands. Prime lands for plow agriculture along the major rivers of the interior and along the Pacific coastal plain were quickly appropriated by Spanish overlords, and native populations were vanquished or assimilated—thereby following a grand tradition in Chiapas prehistory of conquest, assimilation, and acculturation.

FURTHER READINGS

Agrinier, P. 1970. *Mound 20, Mirador, Chiapas.* Papers of the New World Archaeological Foundation, 28. Provo, Utah.

Lowe, G. W., 1977. The Mixe-Zoque as Competing Neighbors of the Early Lowland Maya. In R. E. W. Adams (ed.), *The Origins of Maya Civilization,* pp. 197–248. Albuquerque: University of New Mexico Press.

———. 1978. Eastern Mesoamerica. In R. E. Taylor and C. W. Meighan (eds.), *Chronologies in New World Archaeology,* pp. 331–393. New York: Academic Press.

Lowe, G. W., and J. A. Mason. 1965. Archaeological Survey of the Chiapas Coast, Highlands, and Upper Grijalva Basin. In R. Wauchope (ed.), *Handbook of Middle American Indians,* vol. 2, pp. 195–236. Austin: University of Texas Press.

MacNeish, R. S., and F. A. Peterson. 1962. *The Santa Marta Rock Shelter, Ocozocoautla, Chiapas, Mexico.* Papers of the New World Archaeological Foundation, 10. Provo, Utah.

de Montmollin, O. 1995. Settlement and Politics in Three Classic Maya Polities. Monographs in World Archaeology, 24. Madison, Wisc.: Prehistory Press.

Ruz, M. H. 1985. *Copanaguastla en un espejo: Un pueblo Tzeltal en el Virreinato.* San Cristóbal de las Casas, Chiapas: Centro de Estudios Indígenas, Universidad Autónoma de Chiapas.

Santa María, D., and J. García-Bárcena. 1989. *Puntas de proyectil, cuchillos, y otras herramientas sencillas de Los Grifos.* Cuaderno 40. Mexico City: INAH.

John E. Clark

Chichén Itzá (Yucatán, Mexico)

The imposing Maya site of Chichén Itzá has been known to Europeans since Francisco Montejo II, first governor of the Yucatán Peninsula, briefly established his headquarters there in 1533, calling it Ciudad Real. At that time Chichén Itzá was still the goal of religious pilgrimage; it figured in contemporary Maya historical chronicles that related the ancient arrival of a new ruler and religious leader known as Kukulcan, or Feathered Serpent, who came from Mexico, home of feathered-serpent imagery. Kukulcan is said to have introduced at Chichén Itzá the distinctive architectural and sculptural traits that characterize the largest corpus of carved and painted images known in Mesoamerica; these reflect contact with Early Postclassic central Mexican Toltec culture. Maya chronicles also describe the earlier arrival of founding foreigners called the Itzá. Probably Maya from the south, the Itzá became guardians of the sacred well at Chichén Itzá, which means "mouth of the well of the Itzá" in Yucatec Mayan.

Among many debates over the history and archaeology of Chichén Itzá, questions persist about the span of occupation, the identity of of the "feathered serpent" people, and the identity of the Itzá, because there is little information available from scientific archaeology. Nevertheless, a

The Great Ball Court at Chichén Itzá. Courtesy Garland Publishing, Inc.

C

consensus on chronology is slowly emerging. A handful of sherds indicate that there was occupation in Late Formative times—as would be expected for a site with two large water sources—but strong evidence of settlement and the local use of ceramics are not encountered until the eighth century A.D., when stone structures were built in the southern main plaza. The eighth century also marks the beginning of ritual use of the Sacred Cenote, or Well of Sacrifice, as a repository of offerings. Maya hieroglyphic inscriptions with dates in the Maya calendar provide clear evidence of the presence of literate Maya at Chichén Itzá in the middle of the ninth century, when foreign architectural traits were also introduced in another part of the site. After this brief historically documented period, there followed two to three centuries (c. 900–1150) in which a relationship with the expansive militaristic Toltec culture of central Mexico is evident in the architecture, sculpture, and ceramics of the site. This was the time of Chichén Itzá's ascendancy, when the city ruled over most of the northern and western peninsula. A period of relative abandonment succeeded the collapse of the distant Toltec state, but by 1300, once the new capital of Mayapán had assumed the political role formerly held by Chichén Itzá, the latter continued to be a major religious pilgrimage center into the Colonial period. Chichén Itzá was thus important for about 800 years (A.D. 750–1550).

Chichén Itzá's local environment affords no surface water; a relatively thin layer of soil lies over bedrock, which is the porous karstic limestone that underlies the entire peninsula. The water table is reached only in caves, or in open sinkholes (cenotes) formed when the roofs of caves have collapsed. The site of Chichén Itzá extends well beyond the 5 kilometers mapped by the Carnegie Institution, and it includes several cenotes and caves; the largest two cenotes (the Sacred Cenote and Xtoloc Cenote) are 825 meters apart at the ceremonial center, while the biggest cave (Balankanche) is 4 kilometers to the southeast.

The site has more than thirty internal, raised, stone causeways (sacbes) that converge on the principal ceremonial terrace, situated in the northeastern part of the map. A north–south axis about 2.5 kilometers long joins three important southwestern groups with inscriptions (in the temples of the Four Lintels, Three Lintels, and One Lintel) to the great North Terrace with its focal Castillo Pyramid, and to the Sacred Cenote. These sight lines cross over the Nunnery (Monjas) Palace and the Observatory (Caracol) and extend just east of the Red House (Casa Colorada); all of these structures have inscriptions that

record ninth-century dates and refer to Kakupacal (Fire Shield), a ruler or a ruler's priestly title. Chichén Itzá was laid out with three different orientations that have both temporal and cultural significance. The earliest, about 10°–12° east of north, is evident in the Nunnery, the Red House, and the three temples with inscriptions to the southwest; this orientation is common in Puuc sites, from which Chichén Itzá's founders may have emigrated. The second, 16°–18° east of north, is an orientation associated with central Mexico and the Toltec; it is manifest in the High Priest's Grave (Osario), the Great Ball Court, the Skull Rack (Tzompantli), and the Eagles and Jaguars platform on the North Terrace. The third orientation, 21°–23° east of north, is found in the final platform of the Observatory, the Castillo Pyramid, and the Temple of the Warriors. Each of these geomantic alignments is associated with astronomical observations of particular religious importance in ancient Mesoamerica.

Most residents of Chichén Itzá lived in perishable structures made of poles, plaster, and thatch—an ephemeral population who were memorialized only in the great stone buildings they constructed for governance, for ritual, and for housing the ruling class. All stone sculpture and structures—buildings, platforms, plazas, and sacbes—were made of the local bedded limestone, which was quarried, worked, and then coated with lime plaster, as was true everywhere in the Maya Lowlands. It is the different styles and procedures of construction that provide clues to dating and cultural affiliation.

The southern part of Chichén Itzá has been called "Old Chichén" because the buildings there exhibit traits that resemble the architecture of the Puuc Maya region, where the style termed "Pure Florescent" developed in the eighth century. Many of these buildings are situated along the south–north axis noted earlier. Usually they have plain vertical lower façades made of roughly squared limestone blocks; the upper façades are decorated with complex horizontal moldings that frame stone mosaic designs and axial and corner long-nose Chac masks, all topped with similarly decorated roof combs. Inside, the buildings have stone corbel vaults and stone lintels, several carved with inscriptions. All known Maya inscriptions at Chichén Itzá were located south of the North Terrace. Except for one Initial Series Inscription, they register Calendar Round dates within baktun ten of the Maya long count, probably between A.D. 830 and 900. Most often carved on lintels, these may record the date of the lintel's dedication. One names a member of the Cocom lineage, while others register fire ritual and sacrifice performed by

Pyramid (El Castillo) at Chichén Itzá. Courtesy Garland Publishing, Inc.

individuals like Kakupacal (Fire Shield), with some indication of family relationships. Where more "Toltec" styles of architecture and sculpture are found south of the North Terrace, earlier constructions have been found beneath them—as at the High Priest's Grave, a radial pyramid that may be the prototype for the Castillo.

The southern and outlying parts of Chichén Itzá have been described as residential partly because of the presence of range-type buildings (sometimes called "palaces") that tend to be in the local Pure Florescent style and that are not found on the North Terrace where the ceremonial structures congregate (although small ceremonial structures are found in outlying groups).

The most specialized building south of the North Terrace is the Observatory or "Caracol," a round, concentrically vaulted structure set on rectangular platforms. The principal façade faces west, and different phases of construction indicate that this axial focus on the western sky was moved slightly over the years as this architectural astronomical instrument was calibrated to the setting of Venus, the Pleiades, the Sun, or the Moon, and other important celestial events. Because the latitude of Chichén Itzá (20° 41') is essentially the same as that of Tula (20° 05') in central Mexico, viewing of the night sky was also the same. The plan of the Observatory is a quartered circle, with doorways, viewing windows, and Chac masks that mark the eight cardinal and intercardinal directions.

The vast North Terrace is a raised, walled, irregularly shaped platform that measures 600 meters east to west and 500 meters north to south, at the widest points. Every structure on this northern platform has a special-

ized function, and every one, including underlying earlier constructions, displays traits characteristic of Chichén Itzá that have been called "Toltec" (usually meaning Central Mexican in origin). There are no Maya hieroglyphic inscriptions here. The earliest buildings are contemporary with some to the south, although they differ in design and function. Clearly, the nine-level stepped pyramidal structure found underlying the Castillo Pyramid predates it. The stepped pyramidal form of this early structure is associated at Chichén Itzá with the "foreign" style, and the upper façade of the simple vaulted two-room temple was decorated with stucco prowling jaguars and round shields, which are emblematic of Toltec style; there are, however, no feathered serpents on this structure. It may be contemporary with the early phases of the Nunnery and the Observatory.

It is difficult to date the Great Ball Court, which displays an abundance of painted relief sculpture, three-dimensional sculpture, and polychrome wall paintings in a variety of styles, all of which illustrate combined Maya and Toltec ritual and history. The Toltec personages and events are identified by their association with feathered serpents, also found on all the architecture of the North Terrace at Chichén Itzá. The Great Ball Court, built on the 17° east of north "Toltec" orientation, is two to three times larger than most ball courts (168 × 70 meters) and unusual in having high vertical walls that enclose the central playing field of the I-shaped court. The Lower Temple of the Jaguars, facing east into the Great Plaza at the base of the east range, is sequentially and stylistically early in the ball court's several phases of construction. This one-room building, with two carved square columns at the open east wall, depicts rows of deified Toltec warriors (dressed in central Mexican uniform, with round shields and spear-throwers [atlatls], and accompanied by rearing feathered serpents) at the top of its walls and vault, while other warriors, identified by their dress as local Maya and foreign, are portrayed as increasingly human as the five registers are read from the top to the bottom of the walls. At the highest, celestial level, the polychrome reliefs portray legendary forebears; ritual events, witnessed by the mortal Lords of Chichén Itzá and its realm, are performed at the lower levels.

Red-painted reliefs (stylistically related to the Lower Temple of the Jaguars) are found on the walls and vaults of the temples at the north and south ends of the Great Ball Court. The better-preserved North Temple also shows deified Toltec ancestors at the top, but here they preside over ritual events in the ruler's life, like accession

C

to power, bloodletting, decapitation, and funerary rites. The low, sloping playing benches of the Great Ball Court are edged with feathered serpents and have three long relief panels spaced along each side of the court. These show the outcome of the ball game, with different confronting teams of uniformed players who meet at the center of each panel, where the victorious team's captain decapitates his opponent at the central image of a skull. Above these, intertwined feathered serpents encircled two axially placed rings through which a rubber ball was supposed to pass, as part of the "game"—which was actually a ritual of profound religious significance. The ballplayer panels differ stylistically from those in the three lower ball court temples; they are probably part of a later construction phase, but not later than the reliefs, three-dimensional serpent columns, and painted walls of the Upper Temple of the Jaguars, which is on top of the south end of the ball court's east range, above the Lower Temple of the Jaguars. Unlike the other ball court temples with square carved columns, here the massive round bodies of twin descending feathered rattlesnakes, their open jaws on the floor and feathered rattles aloft, serve as columns at the open west side. These are early examples of this specialized "Toltec" architectural form at Chichén Itzá. The jambs at either side are carved with sixteen life-size figures dressed in the Toltec military uniform; they carry spear-throwers and darts and wear protective back shields and sleeves, butterfly-shaped pectorals, mosaic pill-box hats, and very little else—as was typical of these professional soldiers, who are identified by signs above their heads that may be written in a non-Mayan system. Although they wear the same uniform as the Toltec warriors in the other ball court temples, these men are carved in a different, elongated style more like the scores of column portraits at the architecturally analogous, but later, Temple of the Warriors, on the opposite east side of the Great Plaza. The Upper Temple of the Jaguars also has a carved wooden lintel that portrays two men, possibly deities; one with fiery sun attributes confronts the other who is in Toltec uniform and is protected by a feathered serpent. These facing figures also appear in painted murals inside the temple and on a carved stone table throne that was supported by richly dressed atlantid figures that probably symbolize tributary towns. Sometimes called Captain Sun Disc and Captain Feathered Serpent, these figures have been interpreted as both historical and mythological and identified with the Sun and the planet Venus. Brilliant murals depicting battles in foreign landscapes cover the walls of the inner room of this temple.

The Upper Temple of the Jaguars is an early example of a special type of temple of which four more are known on the North Terrace. All face west, with paired, descending, feathered-serpent columns at the entrance; they have squared columnar relief portraits, a vaulted painted inner room, and a table throne supported by atlantid figures. Three of these are the Temple of the Little Tables at the eastern extension of the North Terrace; the Temple of the Big Tables, just north of the Temple of the Warriors; and the Chac Mool Temple, which was excavated from underneath the Temple of the Warriors. Another characteristic element these temples share is the presence of a stone figure of a supine warrior, known as a "Chac Mool," which was probably used in a heart sacrifice ritual. The final, largest, and most elegant example of this architectural form is the Temple of the Warriors (covering the Chac Mool Temple), which multiplies the columnar portraits located within the temple and arrays them like an army in the colonnade below. The temple façade features stacks of Chac masks on the walls and corners, which alternate with images of Venus emerging from the open jaws of the feathered earth monster, thus using celestial imagery of the Maya storm god in conjunction and contrast with the introduced terrestrial symbolism of the Toltec militant Venus. The Temple of the Warriors exemplifies the later cosmopolitan architectural style at Chichén Itzá with carefully worked veneer stones covering lime concrete cores, a daring use of columns and vaults to enlarge interior spaces, and substructures that display a modified form of the central Mexican *talud* and *tablero*. Like its four earlier models, the Temple of the Warriors faces west at an azimuth of about 290° (20° north of west); this direction focused on the setting of the Pleiades and of the zenith Sun.

The Kukulcan (feathered serpent) Pyramid, the final phase of the Castillo, is the largest architectural expression of the combined cultures of ninth century Chichén Itzá. This pyramid pre-dates both the Temple of the Warriors and the four-stairway dance platforms in the Great Plaza; it probably symbolized the founding historic and religious role of Chichén Itzá. The Castillo, 55 meters on a side and 30 meters high, is built in a radial shape. Its four stairways have ninety-one steps each, which with the step of the temple platform on top total 365 steps—the days of the solar year. The overlapping panels on each side of the nine levels of the pyramid add up to fifty-two, the number of solar years in a Calendar Round cycle. The corner panels equal eighteen, the number of months in the solar year, and the quadripartite plan of the whole

130   **Chichén Itzá (Yucatán, Mexico)**

structure signifies the completion of a cycle. The orientation and design of the Castillo made the pyramid into a monumental sundial, which served to signal and celebrate solar events, of which the best-known example is the apparent descent of the temple's two feathered serpents down the balustrades of the northern stairway at sunset of the spring equinox. The architecture of the Castillo combines calendrically significant numbers to create a functioning three-dimensional model of a completed cycle. The pyramid's inaugural cycle was probably the completion of *baktun* 9 (10.0.0.0.0, A.D. 830), which commemorated the advent of *baktun* 10—a portentous new 400-year cycle in which a fusion of Mexican and Maya cultures were to be combined in a new state at Chichén Itzá.

Later constructions on the North Terrace elaborate the feathered-serpent themes of solar and militant Venus cycles: the radial Venus platform consecrates the combined completion of five Venus and eight solar cycles, every eight years. The smaller radial platform of the Eagles and Jaguars celebrates the role of the Eagle and Jaguar orders of warriors (which had solar connotations). Beside the Great Ball Court, the long north–south platform of the tau-shaped Skull Rack (Tzompantli) depicts three superimposed rows of skulls attached to an eastward-projecting platform with feathered serpents and burning skeletal warriors—perhaps signifying sacrificed captives, as was true of later Aztec skull racks. Like the substructure of the Temple of the Warriors, these three later platforms are constructed with projecting framed panels *(tableros)* above lower sloping façades *(taluds),* in a style reminiscent of central Mexico.

Another major construction in the later style is called the "Mercado" or "marketplace," although the actual marketplace would have been the large plaza in front of this specialized structure. The Mercado structure has an 80-meter-long open-columned and vaulted gallery that bounds the south side of the large eastern plaza, which is framed by colonnades. The inner wall of the long Mercado gallery was painted with huge coiling feathered serpents above a bench that ran the length of the wall, with a projecting thronelike bench at the center; this is carved with Venus signs, feathered serpents, and images of captives, while the contiguous door jambs depict warriors like those shown on columns and jambs in association with the five west-facing temples. The axial doorway, next to the throne, leads into a square enclosed gallery, 16 meters on a side, with an ambulatory and tall, thin columns surrounding a square sunken area. This enclosed

court recalls the interior courts, open to the sky with sunken areas for water, that were common in the apartment compounds of Teotihuacán several centuries earlier. The Mercado's architectural plan, with an outward-facing columned gallery attached to an enclosed patio with columns, is called a "gallery-patio"; it is characteristic of Chichén Itzá, and earlier and smaller variations on the plan are found in outlying groups, although its specialized function is unknown.

A *sacbe* leads 300 meters north from the North Terrace to the Sacred Cenote, a circular sinkhole, 60 meters in diameter and 36 meters deep, one-third filled with green water. One of two large cenotes at the center of Chichén Itzá, the Sacred Cenote appears to have been used exclusively for ceremonial purposes, while the more accessible Cenote Xtoloc, 825 meters south on an axis that incorporates the Castillo in between, served as the central source of water. The Sacred Cenote was still a goal of pilgrimage in the sixteenth century, when the Franciscan Bishop Diego de Landa observed that because of this well Chichén Itzá was as revered by the Maya as Jerusalem or Rome, and if there were gold in Yucatán, it would be found among the offerings in this cenote. The Sacred Cenote was also renowned as a recipient of human sacrifices in association with prophecies sought from it by the Maya. Landa's prediction intrigued antiquarians in the nineteenth century, and exploratory dredging between 1904 and 1911 proved he had been right: jade objects (most valuable to ancient Mesoamericans), as well as gold, copper, textiles, wood, ceramics, and copal incense, were found among the countless precious offerings made to the cenote, in addition to human remains that suggest children were sacrificed more often than adults. Most of these treasured objects had been broken or burned before they were proffered, but the fragments were well preserved in the anaerobic water at the bottom of the cenote, as were the more perishable materials. The dredged offerings indicate that the Sacred Cenote was used for this ceremonial purpose only after about A.D. 700.

Ceramics provide the clearest chronological evidence for use of the Sacred Cenote, as they do for occupation of the rest of Chichén Itzá. The earliest Classic period settlement is associated with a local variant of the ubiquitous slate wares found everywhere in Yucatán from about A.D. 700 to 1200. A new ceramic complex known as Sotuta, with Silho Fine Orange wares and plumbate vessels imported from outside the peninsula, was added to local wares between about 900 and the twelfth century. Late in the history of Chichén Itzá, when the capital had moved

C

to Mayapán, ceramics of the Hocaba and Tases complexes included specialized offertory tripod vessels and figurines that were found in the Sacred Cenote and near the surface at Chichén Itzá.

The large Sotuta phase population of Chichén Itzá, when it was a regional capital, surely exceeded 50,000 inhabitants. They subsisted on corn, beans, and the other Mesoamerican staples grown in *milpas,* supplemented by kitchen gardens and nut and fruit trees. Deer, turkey, other game, and salted fish added dietary protein. Salt may have been an important economic factor for Chichén Itzá if the capital controlled the vast salt beds along the north coast of the peninsula, as they did the northern island trading port of Isla Cerritos. Excavation of this island has confirmed the existence of the long-distance coastal trading routes long postulated on the basis of the imported ceramics, exotic cast gold from Lower Central America, and cast copper and turquoise from northern Mesoamerica that were offered to the Cenote of Sacrifice. The coastal traders, possibly Putún Chontal-speaking Maya who circumnavigated the Yucatán Peninsula in ocean-going canoes, may have been under the control of the powerful state of Chichén Itzá until the twelfth century. Later in Postclassic times, Yucatán supplied woven cotton and slaves as tribute to the Aztec, and the innumerable woven cotton offerings found in the Sacred Cenote suggest that growing and weaving cotton was an established industry.

As there are different styles of architecture and sculpture at Chichén Itzá, so there were different types of political organization during the 800 years of its occupation. In its first century Chichén Itzá was ruled by a few noble Maya families, who may have migrated from the Puuc region. The local Batab had the special distinction of managing a pilgrimage site with a sacred cenote and a celestial observatory, which implies the importance of religious specialists as well as the presence of an active market from the beginning at Chichén Itzá. The founding Maya probably counted among their ancestors emigrants from the ancient central Mexican city of Teotihuacán; such foreigners had married into southern Maya ruling families since the turn of the preceding *baktun* (9.0.0.0.0, about A.D. 430). This prized ancestry would have allowed the ruling Maya of Chichén Itzá to consider themselves "Toltec," or lineal carriers of the great tradition of Teotihuacán. After the fall of Teotihuacán, about A.D. 750, emigrants spread throughout Mesoamerica, founding new capitals that they called Tula (or Tollan), where they evoked, perpetuated, and elaborated the traditions of the ancient city of Teotihuacán—the original Tula, considered the source of civilization by its descendants. Chichén Itzá was one of these Tulas that received a direct infusion of central Mexican culture after A.D. 900, during the Sotuta ceramic phase, when Chichén Itzá dominated the northern and western parts of the peninsula, as symbolized by the unprecedented display of military power in the sculpture of the site. Although many captives are shown at Chichén Itzá, there are many more elite men portrayed on the columns, benches, and walls who are subordinate but probably still part of the government of the city. The long benches that flank table thrones may signify the participatory role of the many Maya chiefs who comprised the state of Chichén Itzá. After the twelfth century, evidence of long-distance trade and military might disappeared as the city lost all but its founding religious role, and Mayapán became capital of a much-reduced Maya polity that emulated Chichén Itzá.

FURTHER READINGS

Aveni, A. F. 1980. Astroarchaeology and the Place of Astronomy in Ancient American Architecture. In A. F. Aveni (ed.), *Skywatchers of Ancient Mexico,* pp. 218–318. Austin: University of Texas Press.

Coggins, C. C., and O. C. Shane III (eds.). 1984. *Cenote of Sacrifice: Maya Treasures from the Sacred Well at Chichen Itza.* Austin: University of Texas Press.

Kepecs, S., G. Feinman, and S. Boucher. 1994. Chichen Itza and Its Hinterland: A World Systems Perspective. *Ancient Mesoamerica* 5: 141–158.

Marquina, I. 1964. Arquitectura Prehispanica, pp. 831–902. Instituto Nacional de Antropología e Historia. Mexico.

Maudslay, A. P. 1889–1902. *Biologia Centrali-Americana: Archaeology* III:pls. III–LXVI. London: Dulau and Co.

Morris, J. C., J. Charlot, and A. A. Morris. 1931. The Temple of the Warriors at Chichen Itza, Yucatan, Mexico. Publication 406. Washington, D.C.: Carnegie Institution of Washington.

Ruppert, K. 1935. Caracol. Publication 454. Washington, D.C.: Carnegie Institution of Washington.

Ruppert, K. 1952. Chichen Itza: Architectural Notes and Plans. Publication 595. Washington, D.C.: Carnegie Institution of Washington.

Schele, L., and D. Freidel. 1990. *Forest of Kings,* pp. 346–347. New York: William Morrow.

Smith, R. E. 1971. The Pottery of Mayapan, Including Studies of Ceramic Material from Uxmal, Kabah, and

Chichen Itza. Papers of the Peabody Museum 66. Cambridge: Harvard University.

Tozzer, A. M. 1941. Landa's Relacion de las Cosas de Yucatan: A Translation. Papers of the Peabody Museum 18. Cambridge: Harvard University.

Tozzer, A. M. 1957. Chichen Itza and Its Cenote of Sacrifice: A Comparative Study of Contemporaneous Maya and Toltec. Memoirs of the Peabody Museum XI, XII. Cambridge: Harvard University.

Clemency Chase Coggins

SEE ALSO
Maya Lowlands: North

Chicomoztoc

See Quemada, La

Chiconautla (México, Mexico)

During the Late Postclassic period (A.D. 1150–1521), this urbanized center was a city-state capital *(altepetl)* with a resident lord *(tlatoani),* subject to Texcoco in the fifteenth century. Situated on the northeastern edge of aboriginal Lake Texcoco, Chiconautla was an important break-of-bulk point on one of the major trade routes between Tenochtitlán and the Gulf lowlands. Occupation has continued into the present, overlying most of the Aztec-era town. In the 1930s, excavations undertaken by Vaillant uncovered an extensive structure that Vaillant called the "Palace at Chiconautla." A survey of the site was conducted in the 1960s by the Teotihuacán Valley Project.

FURTHER READINGS

Sanders, W. T., J. R. Parsons, and R. Santley. 1979. *The Basin of Mexico: The Cultural Ecology of a Civilization.* New York: Academic Press.

Vaillant, G. C. 1966. *Aztecs of Mexico.* Revised by S. B. Vaillant. Baltimore: Penguin Books.

Susan Toby Evans

SEE ALSO
Basin of Mexico

Chihuahua, West Central

Before the 1990s northwestern Mexico received little attention from archaeologists, despite its obvious rele-

vance to prehistoric events north of the international border. Most research in Chihuahua has focused on remains of the Casas Grandes culture, particularly the complex legacy of C. C. Di Peso's Paquimé excavations (1958–1961). Archaeologists have practically bypassed the rest of Chihuahua. This is especially true of west central Chihuahua, essentially neglected between 1933, when E. B. Sayles surveyed there for Gila Pueblo, and 1989, when the Proyecto Arqueológico Chihuahua (PAC) initiated survey and excavation.

West central Chihuahua lies in basin and range country along the east flank of the Sierra Madre Occidental. The southern part of this area includes the Los Mexicanos, San Rafael, and Bustillos basins, all having interior drainages that create sizable intermittent lakes. Northward, the study area includes the Babícora Basin and two elongate grabens drained northward by the Santa María and Santa Clara rivers within the Municipio of Namiquipa. Study area elevations range between 1500 and 2700 meters, with most sites below 2200 meters. Larger sites are frequently situated along basin margins where floodwater farming remains precariously possible today.

Local plant associations include grasslands and Chihuahuan desert flora on basin floors below approximately 2200 meters elevation. Oak woodland occurs on basin margins and lower slopes, and pine forest on higher slopes. A recent study summarizes Holocene environmental conditions in the Babícora Basin as being semiarid during the past 3,000 years, following relatively arid conditions for the previous 3,000 years. Until recently, local fauna included rabbits, deer, coyotes, bears, and mountain lions. Shallow intermittent lakes and marshes of the Babícora Basin remain a major wintering area for migratory birds, including geese, ducks, and herons.

Hunter-gatherer sites occur throughout the study area but are most abundant on the northern side of the Laguna Bustillos Basin. Plainware sites are also more conspicuous in southern reaches of the study area, while pueblo sites with painted pottery are confined to the northern half.

Paleoindian and Early Archaic Periods

One isolated Clovis point base was found near Laguna Bustillos. Several sites in an active dunefield north of this lake contain probable late Paleoindian and early Archaic remains. These sites usually consist of small lithic scatters, or larger multi-component lithic scatters, with occasional later Archaic and ceramic period artifacts included.

C

Middle and Late Archaic Periods

Hunter-gatherer sites potentially from this interval are widespread but most abundant in the Bustillos Basin. On the basis of point typology, more than a dozen sites likely to pertain to this period exist north of Laguna Bustillos in the same dunefield as older sites. Archaic sites typically contain flaked tools and debitage from locally available stone, with exposed hearths that occasionally contain deer and rabbit bones. No related structures have been found.

Early Ceramic Period

Five sites along the north shore of Laguna Bustillos contain slab metates, tools flaked from locally available cobbles, and ceramic assemblages dominated by brownware. These sites evidently represent a pattern of small hamlets situated on arable land. At one site (Ch-125), PAC excavations exposed a circular pit-house that has been radiocarbon dated to sixteen centuries B.P. Small *jacal*-type structures at Ch-125—associated with brown and textured pottery, small projectile points of several forms, slab metates, 3/4-grooved axes, flour and flint corn, and two varieties of beans—date to c. 1,000 years B.P. Sites of this complex also exist on the west side of Bustillos Basin, and minimally another 50 kilometers farther west near Guerrero. These sites are broadly similar to Di Peso's (1974) descriptions of Viejo sites in the Casas Grandes Valley and may also extend much farther south. Smaller plainware sites, possibly from this time interval, also occur along the Santa María River.

Middle and Late Ceramic Period

This period corresponds with the emergence of Casas Grandes culture in northwestern Chihuahua. Sites in the Babícora Basin and the upper Santa María and Santa Clara valleys (usually referred to as "Babícora sites") fall within the Casas Grandes genre. Babícora room-blocks typically have puddled adobe walls, often with stone footings and, in more montane settings, stone architecture. At least one site includes small plazas. The largest Babícora site studied by PAC contains seventeen room-blocks. Small check dams and other water-control features also occur. Extensive survey in El Zurdo Valley shows a settlement pattern comprising one major village that was used for several centuries (Ch-159), several smaller satellite mound sites, and many special-use sites, such as field houses and lithic collection locales. Relationships between these valley sites and large Babícora mound sites in basin floors are unclear.

People from this time were dependent on agriculture, as is apparent from both macrobotanical remains and isotopic analysis of human bone from Ch-159. Analysis of Ch-159 fauna demonstrates that migratory fowl were part of the diet. Artifacts from Babícora sites include abundant locally made pottery, including Babícora polychrome, red-slipped, black-slipped, and brownware. There is little pottery from outside the region, although other Chihuahuan types in particular occur on Babícora sites. Radiocarbon assays from Ch-159 range from approximately A.D. 600 to 1400; these dates are consistent with the chronological revision of the Paquimé sequence developed by Dean and Ravesloot.

In spite of many similarities to the Casas Grandes culture (including general subsistence patterns, basic architectural style, general ceramic assemblages, macaw-raising, and turkey burials), Babícora sites are consistently different in important regards: no ball courts, platform mounds, or public cisterns have been observed; copper bells have never been reported; and little marine shell occurs. Babícora sites do not occur south of the Santa María watershed, where the Early Ceramic period pattern seems to persist.

Although our knowledge of west central Chihuahua is rudimentary, a basic understanding of adaptive patterns and regional dynamics is emerging. Important events in this zone include the appearance of sedentary farming, and, in northern portions of the study area, acceptance of many Casas Grandes traits, but evidently not full participation in Casas Grandes culture.

FURTHER READINGS

Dean, J., and J. C. Ravesloot. 1993. The Chronology of Cultural Interaction in the Gran Chichimeca. In A. I. Woosley and J. C. Ravesloot (eds.), *Culture and Contact: Charles Di Peso's Gran Chichimeca*, pp. 83–103. Albuquerque: University of New Mexico Press.

Di Peso, C. C. 1974. *Casas Grandes: A Fallen Trading Center of the Gran Chichimeca*. Vols. 1–3. Amerind Foundation Publications, 9. Flagstaff: Northland Press.

Di Peso, C. C., J. B. Rinaldo, and G. C. Fenner. 1974. *Casas Grandes: A Fallen Trading Center of the Gran Chichimeca*. Vols. 4–8. Amerind Foundation Publications, 9. Flagstaff: Northland Press.

Kelley, J. H., and M. E. Villalpando C. 1996. The View from the Mexican Northwest. In J. Reid and P. Fish (eds.), *Interpreting Southwestern Diversity: Underlying*

Principles and Overarching Patterns, pp. 69–77. Arizona State University Anthropological Research Papers no. 48. Tempe.

Ortega-Ramirez, J. R. Los Paleoambientes holocenicos de la Laguna de Babícora, Chihuahua, Mexico. *Geofísica International* 34:107–116.

Phillips, D. A., Jr. 1989. Prehistory of Chihuahua and Sonora, Mexico. *Journal of World Archaeology* 3:373–401.

Sayles, E. B. 1936. An Archaeological Survey of Chihuahua, Mexico. Medallion Papers, 22. Globe, Ariz.: Gila Pueblo.

Jane H. Kelley, Joe D. Stewart, A.C. MacWilliams, Loy C. Neff, David A. Phillips, and Karen R. Adams

SEE ALSO

Northern Arid Zone

Chingú

See Teotihuacán; Tula Region

Chipped Stone Tool Production and Products

Chipped stone tools and artifacts, because of their durability, are the most indelible evidence of human presence in Mesoamerica, where they are found in all time periods from Paleoindian to the twentieth century. Chipped stone can be used in culture-historical, processual, and symbolic studies because tools are sensitive to stylistic and functional changes, and because they retain critical technological and functional attributes that carry behavioral meaning. Furthermore, stone artifacts can carry powerful symbolic messages which may place them in contexts that convey social and religious meaning.

Chipped stone tools are manufactured from chert, chalcedony, or obsidian. Chert is microcrystalline rock that forms in sedimentary deposits such as limestone; the limestone regions in Mesoamerica, such as the northern Mexican deserts, central Mexico, the Yucatán Peninsula, the Petén, and Belize, contain cherts of various qualities and sizes. The best-documented and most extensively exploited source is the chert-bearing zone of northern Belize.

Chalcedony, also known as agate, is generally more translucent than chert and is often mistaken for it. The fibrous structure of chalcedony is sometimes intermingled with the microcrystalline chert in the same matrix, making visual identification even more difficult. Chalcedony may be formed under sedimentary or metamorphic conditions. It is found sporadically throughout Mesoamerica, but the best-known deposits are in northern Belize, the Petén, and southern Yucatán.

Obsidian, another highly valued resource for chipped stone tools, is a natural glass formed when lava is rapidly cooled. It is found in volcanic regions of central Mexico and highland Guatemala. In Mexico, the best-known obsidian sources are the Sierra de las Navajas and Otumba. Other important Mexican sources are Zinapécuro, Ucareo, and Pico de Orizaba and Zacualtipan. The major sources in Guatemala are El Chayal, Ixtepeque, and San Martín Jilotepeque (also known as Río Pixcaya).

Initially, elements of the chipped stone industry of the Clovis culture included the prismatic core-blade technologies of the Old World Upper Paleolithic from which it was derived. These earliest Old World-derived technologies quickly evolved into biface industries adapted to the diverse needs and resources of the New World. The high mobility of the earliest populations did not place severe restrictions on the Clovis-related technologies because they could move hundreds of miles to choice resource outcrops. Through time, however, as mobility became more restricted in Late Paleoindian to Historic periods, regional differences in quality and size of siliceous raw materials required new and different strategies of tool manufacture, resulting in more tool types and variable size ranges.

Variation in artifact form and style through time has been used for half a century to develop chronological sequences of stone tool types. Such cultural historical sequences spanning the last 10,000 years have been documented in the Tehuacán Valley, Tamaulipas, Coahuila, and Oaxaca.

The application of the linear reduction model to chipped stone studies has moved lithic analysis beyond its limited uses in cultural historical studies and has led to significant advances in the use of lithics to infer behavior. Because lithic reduction is a subtractive process, steps taken in reduction, as well as errors, are retained on the byproducts and fossilize the production steps. The lithic analyst can reconstruct the manufacturing trajectory and follow the decision-making process of the artisan through a complex system, beginning at the resource outcrop. In contrast to historical studies that emphasize finished or diagnostic tools, linear reduction studies focus on the entire history of lithic artifacts, tracing the steps of change in form and condition from the quarry to the place of

C

final discard. This analytical procedure examines quarry methods, blank preparation, steps in shaping and finishing, the finished products, chipping waste or debitage (which includes waste flakes, cores, and specimens broken or aborted in the course of production), tool use through use-wear analysis, breakage patterns, recycling, and final discard.

Stone was never replaced by metal as the material for tools used in daily maintenance activities or warfare in Mesoamerica. Chipped stone artifacts were used in some capacity in virtually every behavioral realm of Mesoamerican culture, from everyday life to the symbolic world, where stone was deified by the Maya. Chipped stone symbols, called "eccentrics," are artifacts of chert, chalcedony, or obsidian made in anthropomorphic, zoomorphic, or symbolic forms. They are found mainly in the southern Maya Lowlands, notably at Piedras Negras, Colhá, Altun Há, and Copán. Most of these non-utilitarian objects are fashioned bifacially, but some may have been made by simply chipping a sequence of notches along the edges of blades or flakes. They served as portable glyphic symbols placed in votive offerings and tombs; eccentrics are depicted in both Maya writing and iconography, often associated with bloodletting.

Changes in analytical approaches to chipped stone studies have required changes in field recovery methods. These new methods of recovery have replaced selective collecting of stone tools with quantitative sampling of all classes of lithic artifacts. The quantitative sampling strategies provide for detailed comparisons of lithic artifacts between households, mound groups or compounds, and sites; they offer a means to identify the presence and scope of craft specialists who were either making stone tools or using them in the craft activity.

Until about 3000 B.C., chipped stone sequences are dominated by biface tools—projectile points, uniface tools, and simple flake or expedient tools. Variability in style of projectile points from one area to another indicates traditional ways of meeting needs among Archaic groups. Variation in skill in achieving the style indicates household-based production. A lack of variation between regions and through time for the expedient core-flake tools may signify a stable adaptation to plant resources. In each case, the tool industries were the products of mobile hunting and gathering bands adapted to an arid landscape. Formal tools—those made to confirm to a formal design for hafting—consisted only of projectile points, triangular adze blades, and oval flakes for knife blades.

Stone technologies shifted from hunting and gathering to forest clearing and planting after 2500 B.C. throughout much of Mesoamerica. One of the best-documented regions for the transition to plant cultivation is the Tehuacán Valley in the Mexican Plateau. Here Richard A. MacNeish documented a gradual transition from hunting and gathering to agriculture and noted the evolution of chipped stone technology. Since then, work in Chiapas by John E. Clark, in Oaxaca by Kent Flannery, and in Belize by Thomas R. Hester and others has provided new evidence of how the process of change affected the chipped stone technologies.

Core-blade technology reemerges in both chert and obsidian industries by the Early Formative (or Preclassic). In northern Belize this process occurred in the Late Archaic–Early Formative transition, when massive chert macroblades were produced from large nodules and used for a variety of uniface and biface tools after 2500 B.C. Stone axes or celts and adzes replaced hunting assemblages in forested environments, and sharp-edged tools were used for wood working and plant processing. The stone axes were made by fixing a tear-shaped stone celt (an ungrooved axe-head) into a wooden handle, as shown by rare preserved examples such as the Puleston Axe from Belize. Most of the axe-heads were chipped into shape, if chert of sufficient size was available; some, however, were first chipped and then ground into shape. In regions that lack chert, such as the central Gulf Coast region of the Olmec, axe-blades were made of fine-grained igneous or quartzitic rocks. Sharp-edged or piercing tools were made of chert, chalcedony, or obsidian, depending on availability.

Prismatic blades of obsidian first appear about 1500 B.C., in the Early Formative, in northern and central Mesoamerica and on the Pacific Coast region of Chiapas. The object of a core-blade technique is the removal of one or more prismatic blades from a specially prepared core. A prismatic blade is a long, parallel-sided flake more than twice as long as wide that has been removed from such a core. Prismatic obsidian blades continued to be produced into the Colonial period.

Experiments by Don Crabtree and John Clark demonstrated that production of prismatic obsidian blades is a technology that requires special skill; furthermore, the blades were exchanged and distributed widely from the source of production. Such production and distribution indicate the beginning of cottage-level craft specialization in chipped stone technology around resource outcrops, a development that corresponds to growing complexity in the social and political systems of Early Formative Mesoamerica.

A survey of lithic studies in the Maya area, presented in *Maya Stone Tools: Selected Papers from the Second Maya Lithics Conference,* demonstrates the variability and complexities of stone technologies in correlation with the rise of complex society. For example, craft specialization is clearly evident in the chert workshops at Colhá (Belize). Here millions of stone tools were being made in chert workshops from Late Formative through Late Classic times. The chert workshops are marked by scores of massive debitage deposits, some measuring more than 100 cubic meters in volume. The chert workshops at Colhá produced largely utilitarian tools such as chipped stone biface celts, tranchet bit tools, elongated biface adzes, stemmed macroblades for hand-held staffs or thrusting spears, and large eccentrics. In the Terminal Classic, however, production shifted to core-blade technology and the production of stemmed blade points for atlatl spears. The vast numbers of stone tools were made in the Colhá workshops, which supplied the needs for consumers up to 100 kilometers distant in the densely occupied region north and west of the site. The workshops were spatially separate from residences, and one workshop may have accommodated several kin-related workers. The remarkable continuity in the lithic technology and strategies of reduction at Colhá arguably suggests a lineage-based tradition that endured through generations from the Late Formative Period through the Classic. This kind of organization, where access to lands and resources such as obsidian or chert was lineage-owned and lineage-governed, created situations for craft specialization to emerge and endure. Whether these specialists were independent or attached is unknown; most likely, they were attached to lineages whose powerful heads could commission the production of such items as stemmed macroblades or eccentrics for ritual consumption or as votive offerings or gifts to parallel or superordinate individuals.

The end of the Classic period brought about changes in chipped stone technologies. Craft specialists in Mexico and Guatemala continued to produce obsidian blades. Early and Middle Postclassic lithic craft specialization was redeveloped in northern Belize at Colhá. The principal items produced at Colhá were biface atlatl spear projectile points, biface knives, and small adze blades. Production ceased in these workshops when the bow and arrow were introduced in the late Postclassic throughout most of Mesoamerica; this event is marked by the presence of small, pressure-flaked, triangular side-notched arrow points, which quickly replaced the atlatl spear points.

FURTHER READINGS

Clark, J. E. 1988. The Artifacts of La Libertad, Chiapas, Mexico: An Economic Perspective. New World Archaeological Foundation Papers, 52. Provo, Utah: Brigham Young University.

———. 1989. Obsidian: The Primary Mesoamerican Sources. In M. Gaxiola G. and J. E. Clark (eds.), *La Obsidian en Mesoamerica,* pp. 299–319. Mexico City.

Darras, V. 1994. Las actividades de talla en los talleres de obsidiana del Conjuncto Zinaparo—Prieto, Michoacán. In E. Williams and R. Novella (eds.), *Arqueología del Occidente de Mexico: Nuevas Aportaciones,* pp. 139–158. Michoacán: El Colegio de Michoacán.

Dockall, J. E., and H. J. Shafer. 1993. Testing the Producer-Consumer Model for Santa Rita Corozal, Belize. *Latin American Antiquity* 4:158–179.

Flannery, K. V. (ed). 1986. *Guila Naquitz.* New York: Academic Press.

Healen, D. M. 1994. Talleres de obsidiana en Tula, Hidalgo. *Arqueología Mexicana* 2(7):35–37.

Hester, T. R. 1985. Maya Lithic Sequence in Northern Belize. In M. G. Plew et al. (eds.), *Stone Tool Analysis: Essays in Honor of Don E. Crabtree,* pp. 187–210. Albuquerque: University of New Mexico Press.

MacNeish, R. S., A. Nelken-Terner, and A. Garcia Cook. 1967. *The Prehistory of the Tehuacán Valley: The Non-Ceramic Artifacts.* Austin: University of Texas Press.

Shafer, H. J., and T. R. Hester. 1983. Ancient Maya Chert Workshops in Northern Belize, Central America. *American Antiquity* 48:519–543.

———, ———. 1986. Maya Stone-Tool Craft Specialization and Production at Colhá, Belize: Reply to Mallory. *American Antiquity* 51:158–166.

Sievert, A. K. 1992. *Maya Ceremonial Specialization: Lithic Tools from the Sacred Cenote at Chichén Itzá, Yucatán.* Monographs in New World Archaeology, 12. Madison, Wis.: Prehistory Press.

Harry J. Shafer and Thomas R. Hester

SEE ALSO

Lapidary Industry; Obsidian: Properties and Sources; Silex

C

Cacao glyph on a Codex-style vase. Late Classic period. Photograph © Michael D. Coe.

Chocolate and Cacao

The dried prepared seeds of the cacao tree *(Theobroma cacao)* were of supreme importance in Mesoamerica, both as the source of a highly prestigious drink, chocolate, and as a kind of money. The distribution of wild species of *Theobroma* suggests an origin in lowland South America, but the earliest evidence for the manufacture of chocolate—a complex process involving fermentation, drying, and roasting—comes from the Maya area. Historical linguistics also points to an origin for chocolate in lowland Mesoamerica: while the word *cacao* is Maya, it is a loan word from Mixe-Zoquean, the probable language family of the Olmec predecessors of the Classic Maya; thus, it may have been the Olmec who first domesticated the tree and elaborated the technique of processing raw cacao beans into chocolate.

By the Early Classic period, cacao and chocolate were in wide use among the lowland Maya: one part of the Primary Standard Sequence on Classic Maya pottery has been deciphered as "a drinking vessel for cacao" (i.e., chocolate) and a jar from a Río Azul tomb bearing the cacao glyph contained a residue chemically identified as chocolate. Among the late pre-Conquest Maya of both the highlands and lowlands, as among the contemporary Aztec, cacao was a universal currency, mainly used as small change in market transactions, but there are no archaeological data bearing on this function in earlier times. Cacao beans continued to be used as legal tender from Aztec times until the nineteenth century—so much so that they were often counterfeited.

At the time of the Conquest and during the Colonial period, the zones of intensive cacao production were the Chontalpa region of Tabasco, the Soconusco (where the most highly esteemed cacao originated), much of the Guatemalan Pacific Coast, Izalco in El Salvador, and the Naco region of Honduras (the Maya trading canoe intercepted by Columbus on his fourth voyage may have been carrying cacao from Naco). Less intensive production extended in favorable areas as far north as central Veracruz and as far south as Nicaragua and Costa Rica.

Chocolate is a mildly stimulating drink: among its estimated two hundred component substances are the two alkaloids theobromine and caffeine. It was widely used throughout Mesoamerica to seal marriage contracts and to be drunk during wedding banquets. Among the Aztec, it was taken hot, after pouring it from one vessel to another to raise foam, a delicacy that was eaten with a tortoise-shell spoon; however, only the elite class, merchants *(pochteca),* and warriors were permitted to drink chocolate, which was usually served at the end of a meal. Cacao had deep symbolic meaning to the Aztec: the pods were equated with the human heart, and the liquid chocolate with blood. The chocolate drink was flavored with honey, chiles, and spices, of which "ear-flower" *(Cymbopetalum pendiflorum)* was the most important.

Vast quantities of cacao were stored in huge bins in the royal palaces. The amount of chocolate reported to have been served annually in the palace of Nezahualpilli, king of Texcoco, was more than 11 million beans.

The origin of the word "chocolate" remains a puzzle, because it does not appear in the earliest Colonial period Nahuatl dictionaries or other primary sources (there, the correct Nahuatl word is *cacahuatl).* Some scholars believe "chocolate" to be a late sixteenth-century invention based on a Mayan term for the drink *(chocol ha,* "hot water"), with the Nahuatl word for "water" *(atl)* substituted for the Maya one, resulting in *chocolatl.*

FURTHER READINGS

Coe, M. D., and S. D. Coe. 1996. *The True History of Chocolate.* New York: Thames and Hudson.

Michael Coe

SEE ALSO
Food and Cuisine

Cholula (Puebla, Mexico)

Cholula has long been recognized as one of the most important cities of pre-Columbian Mesoamerica. It has been continuously occupied for more than three thousand years and has been a major religious center for much of that period. The Great Pyramid, Tlachihualtepetl, is the largest pre-Hispanic structure in the New World in terms of volume of construction material. As the Postclassic religious center for the cult of Quetzalcóatl, Cholula was influential over a vast domain: rulers from throughout central Mexico came there as pilgrims and for legitimation of their authority. Today Cholula remains the site of one of the major pilgrimages of Mexico, with as many as 350,000 visitors attending the annual festival centered on the church atop the Great Pyramid.

Yet despite more than a century of archaeological exploration, including several major projects, the culture history of Cholula is poorly understood. In fact, recent textbooks on Mesoamerican archaeology treat Cholula as a footnote in the great sweep of regional events, while noting that it remains one of the great enigmas of pre-Columbian history.

Physical Environment

Cholula is situated in the Puebla-Tlaxcala Valley of the central highlands of Mexico. It is surrounded by high mountains, including the snow-covered peaks Popocatepetl and Ixtacihuatl to the west, and Malinche to the north. Runoff during the summer rainy season and snowmelt throughout the year provide adequate water resources to permit irrigation agriculture in the fields surrounding Cholula. The confluence of several perennial streams with the Atoyac River creates a wetland to the north and east of the urban center that was even more extensive before modern pumping drastically lowered the water table.

The combination of rich alluvium and abundant water has resulted in excellent agricultural potential—during the colonial period Cholula was noted as the richest agricultural region of central Mexico. Maize is still the major crop in the surrounding area, and colonial accounts describe the excellence of Cholula maguey, chiles, and cochineal for dye. Flowers are still an important crop in irrigated fields adjacent to the archaeological zone and are sold in the marketplace for use in religious ceremonies. The natural *tepetate* subsoil of Cholula has a high clay content, and pottery and brick-making are important economic activities with a long history of production. Textiles have traditionally been another significant product, and although Cholula is too high to grow cotton, it was famous for the production of elaborately decorated capes.

A final environmental "resource" of Cholula is its geographical location at the intersection of trade routes connecting the Gulf Coast, Valley of Mexico, Tehuacán Valley, and Mixteca Baja through Izucar de Matamoros. Cholula was the center for the *pochteca* merchants, who traveled to distant corners of Mesoamerica to collect exotic merchandise that was then sold in the Cholula market, which was described as a center for the redistribution for "jewels, precious stones, and fine featherwork" (Durán 1971: 278).

Occupation History

The earliest positive evidence for settlement dates to the Early Formative period, and scattered discoveries have been made from subsequent periods. Perhaps because of the varied ecological niches provided by the wetlands, the earliest evidence for occupation has been found on the present campus of the University of the Americas, where Early Formative pottery was recently discovered during salvage excavations in advance of new construction. In the early 1970s, Mountjoy encountered waterlogged deposits dating to the late Middle Formative period near the ancient lakeshore. A mound group dating to the Late Formative period was discovered on an ancient island just north of the campus.

Extensive midden deposits from the Middle Formative period have been found in San Andrés Cholula. Ceramics are similar in style to those of Chalcatzingo and the Valley of Mexico, with the predominant decorated type having a thick kaolin slip with both incised and excised decoration, sometimes combined with red paint. One of the middens was associated with a cobble-filled platform about one meter in height.

The earliest construction evidence at the Cholula ceremonial center dates to the Late Formative period; Formative pottery was found inside the Edificio Rojo to the northeast of the Great Pyramid. Initial stages of the Great Pyramid itself probably date to the Terminal Formative period and show stylistic affinities to early Teotihuacán. Stage 1 of the Great Pyramid measured 120 meters on a side and reached a height of 17 meters. The top platform measured about 43 meters square and featured wall remains of a temple precinct.

Cholula was probably occupied continuously throughout the Formative period. Because of the buildup of later occupation it is impossible to estimate accurately the size and population of the site during these periods. On the basis of plotting the areas where Formative materials have been encountered, however, we can estimate that the site may have reached a maximum extent of 2 square kilometers, with a population of five to ten thousand.

C

Classic period Cholula is best known for the construction of the Great Pyramid. Close parallels between the material culture and architectural styles of Cholula and those of Teotihuacán have traditionally led to inferences of similar culture histories, but it is important to interpret Cholula's history in a new light. Numerous building phases at the Great Pyramid occurred during the Classic period, including at least two complete rebuilding episodes (stages 3 and 10). Stage 3 expanded the pyramid to 180 meters on a side, with a maximum height of 30 meters. The façades consisted of nine tiers completely made up of steps, in a unique architectural style that is distinctly non-Teotihuacanoid. Stage 10 was another complete expansion to about 350 meters on a side and 60 meters in height. The façades were in a *talud/tablero* style reminiscent of Teotihuacán. It should be noted, however, that the orientation of the Great Pyramid, and all of the Cholula urban grid, is at about 26° north of west, a clear deviation from the Teotihuacán orientation. This orientation is aligned with the setting sun at the summer solstice, and it may relate to worship of a solar deity related to the Mixtec 7 Flower, or Aztec Tonacatecuhtli.

Additional mounds dating to the Classic period have been found throughout the Cholula urban zone, including the Cerro Cocoyo, Edificio Rojo, San Miguelito, and probably even the Cerrito de Guadelupe. The central ceremonial precinct included the Great Pyramid, an extensive plaza to the west, and the Cerro Cocoyo as the westernmost pyramid of the plaza group. Classic period Cholula covered about 5 square kilometers, with an estimated population of fifteen to twenty thousand.

The material culture of Cholula also shows certain similarities to Teotihuacán, along with clear distinctions. The characteristic Classic period pottery is a burnished gray-brown ware with little decoration. Thin Orange pottery from southern Puebla (but closely associated with Teotihuacán culture) is relatively rare at Cholula. Some figurine types are closely related to standardized Teotihuacán styles, while others display more individuality. Virtually absent at Cholula are such Teotihuacán diagnostics as candelarios, composite braseros, or floreros.

Until recently, almost no information was available on Classic period domestic life. During the summer of 1993, a collaborative project involving the Puebla Regional Center and Brown University excavated an Early Classic house and associated tomb. The artifact assemblage resembled in many ways that of the Early Tlamimilolpa phase at Teotihuacán, but the elaborate stone-lined tomb beneath the house floor was distinctly different from Teotihuacán burial practices.

Archaeological evidence for a Classic period collapse at Cholula is nonexistent. The ceremonial center continued to be used into the Early Postclassic period, with an active building program including elaborately decorated carved and painted façades. It was at this time that final building programs expanded the Great Pyramid to its maximum extent, covering 16 hectares (400 meters on a side) and reaching a height of 66 meters. Ethnic change may have occurred, however, as suggested by an influx of Gulf Coast motifs and by the burial at the pyramid of an individual with Maya-style cranial deformation and inlaid teeth. Recent excavations on the northeast platform of the Great Pyramid, where Noguera discovered the Altar of the Carved Skulls, have uncovered a long sequence of elite residences spanning the Late Classic to Early Postclassic periods; these provide information on ethnic change as well as cultural continuity during this transitional period.

Cholula probably reached its maximum size and population during the Postclassic period, when it covered about 10 square kilometers and had a population of thirty to fifty thousand. Ethnic changes during this period, however, divide the historical sequence into two phases, designated the Tlachihualtepetl and Cholollan phases.

The Tlachihualtepetl phase (A.D. 700–1200) is named after the city of the Great Pyramid as it was recorded in the *Historia Tolteca-Chichimeca*. Cholula was the highland center for the Olmeca-Xicallanca group, with ethnic ties to the Gulf Coast and the Mixteca of Oaxaca. Numerous attributes from the final building phases of the pyramid demonstrate Gulf influences, including volute patterns at the Patio of the Altars, an extensive mosaic patio, the use of miniature pyramid-altars, and the painted style of the Bebedores mural. It was also during this phase that the origins of the Mixteca-Puebla stylistic tradition appeared, with the earliest examples again reflecting Gulf Coast influences. Polychrome pottery was already common by A.D. 1000, and many of the earliest motifs resemble Gulf Coast styles. Building façades at the Great Pyramid include mat and *greca* motifs that were later incorporated into the Mixtec codex style, but that had previously appeared in Maya and Gulf Coast architecture. One household compound (UA-1) from this period has been excavated, providing evidence for architectural style, mortuary and domestic ritual, and material culture.

At about A.D. 1200, ethnic Tolteca-Chichimeca conquered Cholula, causing the destruction of the Patio of the Altars and the movement of the ceremonial center (with the "new" Pyramid of Quetzalcoatl) to the present *zócalo* (main plaza) of Cholula. The architectural façade of the Great Pyramid may have been stripped to construct the center, which is probably beneath the modern town of San Pedro Cholula. During this period, identified as the Cholollan phase, Cholula became an ethnically divided city, a division still represented by that between San Andrés Cholula and San Pedro Cholula. Polychrome pottery from the Cholollan phase used distinctive design configurations but was a development out of earlier styles. The high quality *"laca"* pottery dates to this period; it includes codex-style glyphic elements relating to the Borgia group of codices. The Spanish conquistador Bernal Díaz del Castillo observed that the Aztec emperor Moctezuma possessed Cholula polychrome vessels for his personal use. Although Late Postclassic pottery is widely distributed on the surface, no architectural remains have been extensively investigated. One mass burial excavated from San Andrés Cholula contained a nobleman buried with about fifty sacrificed retainers, many of whom were associated with textile production implements. Another mass burial from the civic center may relate to victims of the Cholula massacre at the time of the Spanish conquest.

Ethnohistoric Sources

Much of the information relating to Postclassic Cholula is derived from ethnohistoric sources recorded soon after the Spanish conquest. These accounts include indigenous traditions, early observations of culture and religion, and more detailed sources such as notary transactions.

The Codex Borgia and related codices probably originated in the Puebla-Tlaxcala area, perhaps in Cholula itself, and vividly depict pre-Columbian religion and cosmology for the religious center. Among the important colonial sources, the *Historia Tolteca-Chichimeca* details the migration of the ethnic Tolteca-Chichimeca groups from Tollan to Cholula, where they defeated the Olmeca-Xicallanca around A.D. 1200, and ultimately to Cuauhtinchan. Alva Ixtlixochitl described an even earlier migration during which the Olmeca-Uixtotin conquered the *quinametin,* or giants, and then built the Great Pyramid for their god Ehécatl.

Early chroniclers include conquistadors such as Hernan Cortés and Bernal Díaz del Castillo, as well as priests such as Motolinía, Durán, and Sahagún. They described the rich agricultural resources of the area, the methods of house construction and costume, and particularly the reli-

gion and temple organization of the Cholultecas. According to these sources, the Pyramid of Quetzalcoatl was taller than the Great Temple of Tenochtitlán, and the city had more than four hundred additional temples. The abandoned Great Pyramid was discussed under the theme of mountain worship, and a shrine to a rain deity, Chiconauquiahuitl, was said to be situated on top of the mound.

The most detailed account is that of Gabriel de Rojas, the Spanish official who wrote the *Relación geográfica* in 1581. This invaluable document contains a wealth of ethnographic information on indigenous culture, economic production, urban organization, and religious practices. It also includes a plan of the town indicating barrio divisions and churches, an excellent complement to the Codex of Cholula, which depicts both the urban area and the regional kingdom.

Archaeological Investigations

Archaeological research at Cholula began in the late nineteenth century with such early explorers as Tylor, Charnay, and Bandelier. Intensive excavations at the Great Pyramid began in 1931 under the direction of Ignacio Marquina. Tunneling into the pyramid, researchers identified numerous stages of construction and details of the building façades. Excavations of stratigraphic pits around the pyramid allowed Eduardo Noguera to develop a preliminary ceramic sequence, and extensive investigations on the northeast platform of the pyramid exposed an elite compound with an elaborate altar burial dating to the Early Postclassic period.

In the mid-1960s the Proyecto Cholula, under the direction of Marquina, resumed investigations as a multidisciplinary program including archaeology, colonial architecture, ethnohistory, linguistics, physical anthropology, and ethnography. Archaeological investigations concentrated on the south and west sides of the pyramid, where associated platforms and plazas were exposed and reconstructed.

Beginning in 1968, archaeologists associated with the University of the Americas have conducted excavations away from the ceremonial center, primarily on the university campus in San Andrés Cholula. Sites from all phases of occupation are represented, and these studies are among the most completely analyzed and reported archaeological excavations from the site.

By far the most extensive archaeological program of recent years is that directed by Sergio Suárez Cruz and his

C

colleagues from the Puebla Regional Center of the Instituto Nacional de Antropología e Historia. Hundreds of salvage units have been excavated throughout the city, and numerous areas have received more extensive investigation. Specific sites have included a Late Postclassic mass burial; a Contact period house; and a platform, house, and extensive cache all dating to the Classic period.

Despite the wide range of archaeological and ethnohistoric evidence for the culture history of Cholula, many problems remain for investigation. Fundamental problems of site chronology and settlement size are still outstanding and must be addressed before more processual investigations can proceed. As one of the earliest major centers of the central highlands, Cholula has tremendous potential for the study of urbanization and state formation. Another important research question concerns the Classic/Postclassic transition: what was the relationship between the Classic period population and the newly arrived Olmeca-Xicallanca, including those settling at nearby Cacaxtla and Cerro Zapotecas? In the Late Postclassic period, documentary sources discuss the political interaction between Cholula and Tenochtitlán, yet Aztec ceramics are almost nonexistent at the site. As perhaps the longest continually occupied religious center in the New World, Cholula also holds research potential for understanding the role of religious ideology in promoting political and economic systems.

Unfortunately, modern Cholula is a rapidly developing suburb of the state capital of Puebla, and destruction of its archaeological resources is a serious problem. Management of the urban development and further archaeological research are urgently needed to rescue Cholula.

FURTHER READINGS

Bonfil Batalla, G. 1973. *Cholula: La ciudad sagrada en la era industrial.* Mexico City: Instituto de Investigaciones Historicas, Universidad Nacional Autónoma de México.

Díaz del Castillo, B. 1963 [1580]. *The Conquest of New Spain.* J. M. Cohen (trans.). Harmondsworth: Penguin.

Durán, D. 1971 [1576–1579]. *The Book of the Gods and Rites and the Ancient Calendar.* F. Horcasitas and D. Heyden (trans.). Norman: University of Oklahoma Press.

Marquina, I. (ed.). 1970. *Proyecto Cholula.* Serie Investigaciones, 19. Mexico City: Instituto Nacional de Antropología e Historia.

McCafferty, G. G. 1994. The Mixteca-Puebla Stylistic Tradition at Early Postclassic Cholula. In H. B. Nicholson and E. Quiñones Keber (eds.), *Mixteca-Puebla: Discoveries and Research in Mesoamerican Art and Archaeology,* pp. 53–78. Culver City, Calif.: Labyrinthos Press.

Mountjoy, J. 1987. The Collapse of the Classic at Cholula as Seen from Cerro Zapotecas. *Notas Mesoamericanas* 10:119–151.

Mountjoy, J., and D. A. Peterson. 1973. *Man and Land in Prehispanic Cholula.* Vanderbilt University Publications in Anthropology, 4. Nashville, Tenn.

Noguera, E. 1954. *La Cerámica Arqueológica de Cholula.* Mexico City: Editorial Guaranía.

Rojas, G. de. 1927 [1581]. Descripción de Cholula. *Revista Mexicana de Estudios Historicos* 1(6):158–170.

Simons, B. B. 1968. The Codex of Cholula: A Preliminary Study. *Tlalocan* 5(3):267–288.

Suárez C. S. 1985. *Un entierro del clásico superior en Cholula, Puebla.* Cuaderno de Trabajo 6, Centro Regional de Puebla. Mexico City: Instituto Nacional de Antropología e Historia.

———. 1989. *Ultimos descubrimientos de entierros postclásicos en Cholula, Puebla.* Cuaderno de Trabajo 7, Centro Regional de Puebla. Mexico City: Instituto Nacional de Antropología e Historia.

Geoffrey G. McCafferty

SEE ALSO
Puebla-Tlaxcala Region

Chupícuaro (Guanajuato, Mexico)

Situated in southeasternmost Guanajuato, this site is now covered by the waters of Solís Dam. Dating is still only approximate, but the range 600 B.C. to around the time of Christ is commonly accepted, largely because of comparative ceramic and figurine studies. Indeed, aside from these collections there is little else by which to characterize the postulated culture represented by the site. Small platforms and rock alignments have been found over the years, including one round structure at Cerro de la Crúz (which may or may not be coeval with the rectangular alignments). More recent studies are using a settlement pattern approach in the Chupícuaro region, though results are still quite preliminary.

Hundreds of burials have been located over the years. The greatest concentration (more than three hundred), found at Loma del Rayo, certainly qualifies as a cemetery. Burial positions varied, but offerings of beautiful polychrome and bichrome ceramics accompanied most of

C

them. Ollas and tecomates are common; figurines, zoomorphic vessels, pedestal supports, and high tripod vessels also occur. Hollow figurines are often polychrome (black and red over cream). Smaller, solid figurines, simpler than the hollow variety, are common, and often have distinctive "chokers" around their necks, along with elaborate headdresses. The site represents one facet of the Chupícuaro culture, whose influence is said to have extended from the Chalchuites area (Zacatecas) to Tlaxcala and large areas of western Mexico during the Middle and Late Formative.

FURTHER READINGS

Florance, C. A. 1985. Recent Work in the Chupícuaro Region. In M. Foster and P. Weigand (eds.), *Archaeology of West and Northwest Mesoamerica,* pp. 9–45. Denver: Westview Press.

Porter, M. N. 1956. Excavations at Chupícuaro, Guanajuato, Mexico. *Transactions of the American Philosophical Society* 46, part 5:515–637.

———. 1969. A Reappraisal of Chupícuaro. In J. D. Frierman (ed.), *The Natalie Wood Collection of Pre-Columbian Ceramics from Chupícuaro, Guanajuato, Mexico,* pp. 5–15. Los Angeles: University of California at Los Angeles and Los Angeles Museum and Laboratory of Ethnic Arts.

Schöndube, O. 1982. Epoca prehispánica: El horizonte formativo en el Occidente. In José María Muría (ed.), *Historia de Jalisco,* pp. 141–170. Guadalajara: Gobierno de Jalisco.

Phil C. Weigand

Cihuatán and Santa María (San Salvador, El Salvador)

Toltec-related, Nahua-speaking Pipils migrated from Mexico to Central America to found Cihuatán and a number of related centers in western and central El Salvador during the Early Postclassic period (A.D. 900–1200). They built the site on the west bank of the Acelhuate River, near its confluence with the Lempa, in a defensible location 50 meters above the floor of the basin. The primary regional center of the Paraíso Basin in north central El Salvador during this period, Cihuatán is at least 375 hectares in area. It consists of three major zones: a main ceremonial precinct, the West Ceremonial Center, which includes a large temple platform 18 meters in height, ten smaller monumental public buildings, two I-shaped ball courts, and an elite residential compound; an adjacent elite residential district combined with public buildings, known as the East Ceremonial Center; and non-elite residential zones dispersed on the slopes surrounding the two central sectors.

Santa María, situated 16 kilometers east-northeast of Cihuatán, is a closely related secondary regional center. Its material culture replicates that of Cihuatán: the settlement patterns, architecture, ceramics, chipped stone artifacts, and figurines of the two sites are essentially identical in form and content. Santa María extended over about 365 hectares.

Five of eight calibrated radiocarbon age determinations from the two sites range between A.D. 998 and 1150 with a calibrated mean of A.D. 1023. Stylistic dating of ceramics indicates a chronological alignment with the Early Postclassic Mazapan phase of central Mexico, conventionally dated to A.D. 950–1200, or with the Tollan phase at Tula, Hidalgo, dated to A.D. 1150–1200. Important horizon markers found at the two sites are Tohil Plumbate and Nicoya (Papagayo and related) Polychrome ceramics, which were widely traded throughout Mesoamerica.

Non-ceramic traits also link Cihuatán and Santa María with Toltec central Mexico. A partial list includes Mazapan-style figurines and wheeled figurines; technological and formal aspects of the chipped stone industry, especially bifacially thinned projectile points and arrow points made on segments of obsidian prismatic blades; and Mexican-derived architectural features such as *talud-tablero* construction, rubble-core columns, enclosed I-shaped ball courts, and drainage systems of fired clay tubes or stone-lined troughs. Some of these traits, such as the wheeled figurines and life-size ceramic effigies, suggest connections with the Gulf Coast as well as the central highlands of Mexico.

FURTHER READINGS

Bruhns, K. O. 1980. *Cihuatan: An Early Postclassic Town of El Salvador: The 1977–1978 Excavations.* University of Missouri Monographs in Anthropology, 5. Columbia, Mo.

Campbell, L. R. 1985. *The Pipil Language of El Salvador.* Berlin: Mouton.

Fowler, W. R. 1989. *The Evolution of Ancient Nahua Civilizations: The Pipil-Nicarao of Central America.* Norman: University of Oklahoma Press.

Fowler, W. R., and H. H. Earnest. 1985. Settlement Patterns and Prehistory of the Paraíso Basin of El Salvador. *Journal of Field Archaeology* 12:19–32.

C

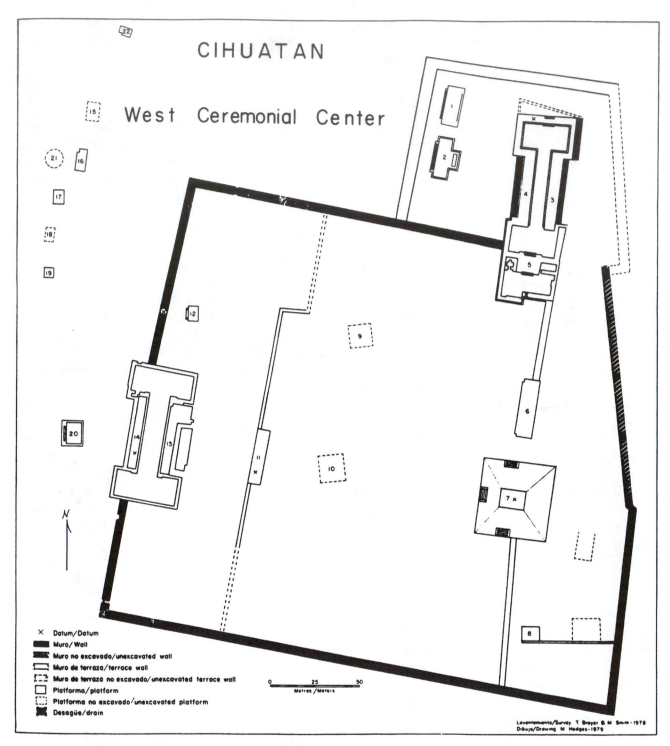

The west ceremonial center of Cihuatán. Courtesy of the author.

Kelley, J. H. 1988. *Cihuatán, El Salvador: A Study in Intrasite Variability.* Vanderbilt University Publications in Anthropology 35. Nashville.

William Fowler

SEE ALSO
Southeast Mesoamerica

Cihuatecpan (México, Mexico)

Occupied from the mid-Postclassic into the Early Colonial period (c. A.D. 1200–1600), Cihuatecpan exemplifies the dispersed rural village common to the piedmont zones of the central highlands during this period. Maguey *(agave)* farmers pioneered a settlement pattern of terraced house lots and garden plots, which permitted habitation and exploitation of land almost devoid of sources of potable water. Maguey sap *(aguamiel)* was maguey farmers' potable beverage and provided significant nutrition.

Maguey also provided fiber for textiles, which were produced by every Cihuatecpan household: spindle whorls were found everywhere, particularly in the probable *tecpan* (Nahuatl, "lord-place") or headman's house (Structure 6), a 25 × 25 meter building with suites of rooms around an interior courtyard. Another local industry, the production of unifacially and bifacially flaked tools of Otumba obsidian, is evidenced by an extensive obsidian debitage dump (Operation 8). Household devotions to Aztec deities are indicated by figurines representing Xochiquetzal, Quetzalcoatl, Ehecatl, and Tlaloc, among others. After the Spanish conquest, figurines show Spanish clothing and hairstyles. After a decline in population over the sixteenth century, Cihuatecpan was ordered abandoned in 1603.

FURTHER READINGS

Abrams, E. M. 1988. Investigation of an Obsidian Midden at Cihuatecpan, Mexico. In Evans 1988, pp. 235–238.

Evans, S. T. (ed.). 1988. *Excavations at Cihuatecpan, an Aztec Village in the Teotihuacán Valley.* Vanderbilt University Publications in Anthropology, 36. Nashville, Tenn.

Evans, S. T. 1990. The Productivity of Maguey Terrace Agriculture in Central Mexico during the Aztec Period. *Latin American Antiquity* 5:117–132.

Evans, S. T., and A. C. Freter. 1996. Hydration Analysis of Obsidian from Cihuatecpan, an Aztec Period Village in Mexico. *Ancient Mesoamerica* 7:267–280.

Susan Toby Evans

SEE ALSO
Basin of Mexico

Cinnabar and Hematite

Widely used by the ancient Maya in offerings, royal tombs, and probably ceremonies, no doubt because of its ritual importance derived from color-based association with blood, cinnabar (red mercuric sulphide) is often found smeared on or encasing carved jade objects, and it was frequently used to fill incised lines on shell, pottery, and other objects. Distributed throughout the Maya Lowlands by trade from Guatemalan and Honduran highland sources, it was related to and often associated with the apparently rare use in offerings of mercury—probably prized for its unusual physical properties and perhaps for its hallucinogenic effects.

Hematite (ferric oxide), also from highland sources, was extensively used as a pigment in pre-Columbian Mesoamerica. In the Maya area, laminae of the crystalline form were used in the manufacture of mosaics and headdress adornment, and in granular (specular) form crystalline hematite was incorporated in modeled and painted stucco architectural ornamentation and into red slip for decorating pottery vessels.

FURTHER READINGS

Barba P., L., and A. Herrera. 1986. San José Ixtapa: Un sitio arqueológico dedicado a la producción de mercurio. *Anales de Antropología* 23:87–104.

Pendergast, D. M. 1979, 1982. *Excavations at Altun Ha, Belize, 1964–1970.* 2 vols. Toronto: Royal Ontario Museum.

———. 1982. Ancient Maya Mercury. *Science* 217: 533–535.

Schele, L., and M. E. Miller. 1986. *The Blood of Kings.* Fort Worth: Kimbell Art Museum.

David M. Pendergast

SEE ALSO
Minerals, Ores, and Mining

Civic-Ceremonial Center

Traditionally defined as an urban zone of relatively small population ruled by a sacred monarch or the seat of a decentralized, unbureaucratized polity organized primarily according to religious principles. The term "civic-ceremonial center" as a type of settlement implies two things: a kind

C

of political organization, and a physical layout embedded in local beliefs of world order and sustained by the ritual performances of kings. Anthropologists have studied such centers comparatively and have arrived at several overlapping (and sometimes contradictory) understandings. Sjoberg describes such settlements as "preindustrial cities," an ideal type-city modeled on earlier work by Max Weber, who regarded strict definitions as useful bases for discussion. The preindustrial type encapsulates distinct ethnic groups and craft specialties, but its core consists of elite residences that preserve strategic access to subordinate groups within the city. Writing from an Asian perspective, Wheatley emphasizes the primacy of religion and the idiosyncratic, culturally determined features of "ethnocities" or "cosmic cities," which derive their internal arrangement from court ceremonial and cosmic structure replicated in urban design. In his "regal-ritual city," Fox achieves the most complete and flexible description of such urban settlements as cities in which state power tends to be "segmentary" (decentralized, with redundant centers of decision making), and the urban economy "dependent" (closely controlled by the court). This definition runs counter to conventional views of the city, in that population is relatively small, systems of communication and transportation underdeveloped, and political control largely religious in nature.

As applied to Mesoamerica, the concept of civic-ceremonial center displays similar characteristics, although with unique features taken from ethnographic analogies with small indigenous communities. The center contains a nucleus of civic and religious buildings. Its permanent population is generally small, but during festivals many people from dispersed agricultural populations congregate in the center. For this reason, scholars prefer "center" as a label, because, unlike "city," the term implies modest size and a smaller number of residents.

Aspects of the civic-ceremonial center exist in Mesoamerica. In their layout, all known urban zones show a pronounced concern with ceremonial processions and religious foci, principally temples of restricted access. Astronomical alignments partly dictate orientation and site layout. Broad avenues linking temple complexes occur in many cities, whether as links between new buildings or city sectors (larger Maya centers), or as part of massive, centralized city planning (Teotihuacán). Some formal roads even communicate between separate communities. Multi-room structures identified as royal palaces appear near central temples, suggesting the presence of state ritual orchestrated by rulers. Cities as diverse

as Palenque and Tenochtitlán mimic cosmological patterns and invoke metaphysically distant times and places. Thus, the Templo Mayor in Tenochtitlán represents both a national temple reflecting Aztec might and tributary extraction, and two sacred mountains recapitulating sacred verities. Hieroglyphs and ethnohistoric accounts suggest that rulers served as, among other things, sacred beings or pivotal intermediaries with the supernatural.

Nonetheless, the notion of civic-ceremonial center is deficient in other respects. An essential problem is the belief that similar physical features, such as buildings and overall layout, were created by similar social, economic, political, and religious systems. We now know this to be false. Current consensus holds that Mesoamerican cities possessed diverse economic functions and patterns of governance. Superficial resemblances, such as temples as sacred mountains, disguise profound differences. Tenochtitlán, once used to explain other Central Mexican cities, is now thought to be atypical in the region during its existence as an imperial capital. Maya cities such as Tikal and Dos Pilas share features—mortuary pyramids, ball courts, palaces, and central plazas—but their sizes and populations differed considerably. Events based on broadly held concepts occurred at these centers, but the scale of such activities varied quantitatively and qualitatively.

More debatable are two other features of the civic-ceremonial center and the related idea of regal-ritual cities: a small population surrounded by dispersed groups of agriculturalists who occasionally visited the center during pilgrimages, and dependent economies controlled by decentralized, nonbureaucratic governments. Recent research demonstrates that many centers contained relatively large permanent populations. Movement to and from outfields or remote villages probably took place during certain times of the agricultural year, but it involved uncertain, perhaps negligible numbers of people. Although patterns of nucleation shifted from area to area, population concentrations did not end abruptly at city margins; instead, urban building usually graded into low-intensity settlement. In contrast to earlier views, researchers even regard early centers, principally Olmec San Lorenzo and La Venta, as extensive, populous communities. As for politics and economy, larger cities doubtless had systems of governance based on an incipient bureaucracy (perhaps fused with the priesthood) and economies of varying, centralized control over the manufacture, distribution, and consumption of goods. Decentralized, nonbureaucratic polities would seem inherently unsuited to exercising close control over the economy. Available information indicates that "dependent" economies were not uniformly present in Mesoamerica (although the elites did control the production of some sumptuary goods), and, in some places, "segmentary" organization describes less a kind of polity than selected features of Mesoamerican kingdoms. The quadripartition of cities that characterizes the later phases of Teotihuacán and Tenochtitlán points to a level of centralized command not detectable in the layout of many other cities in Mesoamerica.

Like any other ideal type, the notion of civic-ceremonial center emphasizes and isolates features for further study. In this sense, it applies broadly to Mesoamerican cities; it fails, however, as a full description of actual settlements, especially in its problematic assumptions about ancient economies. With respect to the Maya, the specific elaboration of the concept of civic-ceremonial center rests on misleading analogies with modern ethnography. Nonetheless, the term has been productive, forcing scholars to reevaluate relations between cities and their hinterlands, leading to new, more refined estimates of urban populations and what they did to support themselves, and lending appropriate emphasis to the symbolic dimensions of Mesomerican cities.

FURTHER READINGS

Ball, J. W., and J. T. Taschek. 1991. Late Classic Lowland Maya Political Organization and Central-Place Analysis. *Ancient Mesoamerica* 2:149–165.

Becker, M. J. 1979. Priests, Peasants, and Ceremonial Centers: The Intellectual History of a Model. In N. Hammond and G. R. Willey (eds.), *Maya Archaeology and Ethnohistory*, pp. 3–20. Austin: University of Texas Press.

Fox, R. G. 1977. *Urban Anthropology*. Englewood Cliffs, N.J.: Prentice-Hall.

Marcus, J. 1983. On the Nature of the Mesoamerican City. In E. Z. Vogt and R. M. Leventhal (eds.), *Prehistoric Settlement Patterns: Essays in Honor of Gordon R. Willey*, pp. 195–242. Albuquerque and Cambridge: University of New Mexico Press and Peabody Museum of Harvard University.

Sanders, W. T., and D. L. Webster. 1988. The Mesoamerican Urban Tradition. *American Anthropologist* 90: 521–546.

Sjoberg, G. 1960. *The Preindustrial City: Past and Present*. New York: Free Press.

Wheatley, P. 1979. *City as Symbol*. London: University of London Press.

Stephen D. Houston

SEE ALSO
Architecture: Civic-Ceremonial

Classic Period

The term "Classic period" denotes a block of time when complex societies developed throughout Mesoamerica or increased dramatically in number, scale, and diversity compared to their Formative period antecedents. Most of these societies were integrated by the political form known as the "state," which based its power and authority on economic and social stratification backed by a state-supported administrative-military-judicial apparatus. Originally, archaeologists argued that the period represented the peak of civilization development in Mesoamerica; however, it is now apparent that later in the period, some regions declined in complexity while others developed full-blown empires based on the extraction of tribute from conquered polities.

Traditionally, it is assumed that the Classic period began around A.D. 200 and lasted until between 800 and 950, although it apparently started and ended earlier in some areas. Many Mesoamerican archaeologists divide the period into two phases: the Early Classic (A.D. 200–600) and the Late Classic (600–950). In recent years, however, the term "Middle Classic" has been introduced in the literature to describe the time period (c. 400–600) when objects made at the Central Mexican center of Teotihuacán, or imitations of materials produced there, were widely distributed in Mesoamerica. The term "Epiclassic" has been used to specify that block of time following the withdrawal of Teotihuacán influence.

In the Classic period no single political center dominated all of Mesoamerica. Rather, the region was split up into a large number of polities that varied greatly in scale, population, and complexity. The simplest systems during the Classic period existed in the Maya Lowlands. These polities were probably organized on a feudal basis, with political control involving a complex system of interrelationships among royal families. Maya polities were also comparatively small in size, covering areas of around 1,000 to 2,000 square kilometers. A few of these polities (e.g., Tikal, Calakmul, and possibly Copán, Sayil, and Palenque), however, probably dominated somewhat larger territories or had political influence on smaller ones situated around them. The largest centers contained populations in the range of twenty to thirty thousand people, but most probably had significantly smaller populations.

C

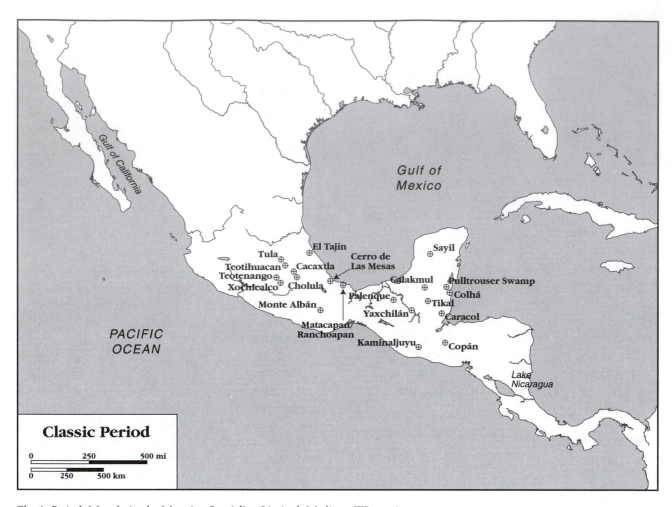

Classic Period. Map design by Mapping Specialists Limited, Madison, Wisconsin.

The polity centered at Monte Albán in the Valley of Oaxaca was probably organized on a more complex basis than those in the Maya Lowlands. In the Classic period Monte Albán was the center of a conquest state that dominated most of the southern highlands of Mexico. The site may have had a maximum population of thirty thousand. Monte Albán was a center of craft production, particularly of goods made from ceramic clays, shell, and various types of stone, which were distributed throughout the region. Several polities situated on the Gulf Coast may have been organized similarly. At Matacapan, for example, ceramic vessels were produced on a large scale, with distribution aimed at a clientele living throughout the Tuxtla Mountains and other parts of Mesoamerica. Great amounts of obsidian from the Zaragoza source in eastern

Puebla were also distributed up and down the Gulf Coast, although the center that controlled this exchange has yet to be determined.

The most complex system dating to the Classic period was centered at Teotihuacán, the largest Classic period site in Mesoamerica. It had a population of about 125,000 to 150,000 in Middle Classic times and probably directly dominated a substantial part of Central Mexico. A large proportion of its population were also craft specialists, manufacturing artifacts produced in obsidian, ground stone, ceramics, and possibly other media such as tropical feathers and semiprecious stones. In Middle Classic times Teotihuacán was also able to exert widespread influence throughout Mesoamerica, in contrast to other major Classic period centers. This influence has provided the basis for various models describing Teotihuacán's interaction with the rest of Mesoamerica. These models posit situations ranging from direct imperial dominance to economic and political influence, interaction, or hegemony.

All Classic period societies in Mesoamerica were agrarian civilizations. Farming was the major means of livelihood for most of their populations, including those at the largest centers, with craft and service specializations only weakly developed. In the Maya region, specialists rarely accounted for more than 10 to 15 percent of the population of the principal center. This underdevelopment in central-place economic functions was probably due to fact that most centers were not situated near localized resource deposits such as obsidian, salt, ceramic clay, and precious stone.

Classic period centers near special resources were in a different situation. Goods made from these media were distributed over larger areas, and the centers expectably supported greater numbers of specialists than elsewhere in Mesoamerica. At Teotihuacán, for example, about one-third of the population were craft specialists, and obsidian-working was the major industry, producing cores, blades, points, and other tools exchanged throughout Mesoamerica but probably largely restricted to central Mexico. Teotihuacán's obsidian production system was also internally differentiated, with some parts of the site producing only limited numbers of all kinds of tools, probably for distribution mainly within the city, and other, larger-scale workshops making only specific types of tools for exchange over much greater distances.

The ceramic production system at Matacapan was apparently organized very similarly, but large amounts of pottery were also produced in the countryside. At Colhá, a Maya site near the Rancho Creek chert source in Belize, hoes and large blade tools were produced by artisans in specialized workshops. A number of sites on the coast of northern Yucatán were involved in the production of salt in evaporation pans situated on the shore. The greater levels of specialization at these sites were probably due to a number of factors: their raw material deposits were localized, but goods made from them were in demand in neighboring areas; these goods could be readily transported over long distances in a cost-effective manner; and they were not consumed in great amounts per capita, making them affordable to clientele living far from the point of supply.

The question of how Classic period societies were organized politically has yet to be agreed on by archaeologists working in Mesoamerica. As mentioned above, the Maya region was probably organized on a feudal basis, with most of the area split into a number of polities controlling comparatively small areas, and with the major basis of political control and affiliation involving mainly regal-ritual functions based on dynastic ties. In addition, except for a few centers such as Tikal, Calakmul, Yaxchilán, Palenque, and Copán, political domination was generally short-lived; dominant centers frequently reconquered neighboring ones, and subordinate centers sometimes briefly controlled sites that previously had been dominant centers. The picture revealed by translations of documents on public sculptures largely confirms this reconstruction. Many monuments record information on territorial conquests, but few indicate that control was long-term, and none say that large amounts of resources were obtained from conquered territories.

The polity dominated by Teotihuacán may have been somewhat more centralized, but its structure has yet to be defined in detail. The Street of the Dead complex, now commonly acknowledged as the city's royal palace, is similar in size and general internal configuration to palaces described at later, Aztec period Tenochtitlán. Following this analogy, Teotihuacán's political system was also palace-centric, with the royal residence serving as the abode of the ruler, his immediate family, and their retainers and housing the state's top-level administrative apparatus. The Street of the Dead complex was also one of the largest buildings erected at Classic period Teotihuacán, indicating that the ruler invested considerable energy in state infrastructure. The city was the major center in Early and Middle Classic period Mesoamerica for at least seven centuries, in contrast to the pattern of short-term political dominance in the Maya region. Maya polities were probably also organized on a palace-centric basis, although the residence of the ruler and its outbuildings were generally much smaller in size than those at Teotihuacán, suggesting that the top-ranking authority in each wielded significantly less political and economic power.

These apparent differences in political and economic power were associated with variation in residential patterns. Residential settlement patterns in the Maya region—indeed, throughout most of tropical forest Mesoamerica—were generally quite dispersed. Most dependent communities were small in size, and many involved residences organized on the house lot plan: a unit consisting of a core of structures, an extramural work area kept clear of household debris during use, and family garbage dumps, all surrounded by a large garden where

C

special crops for household consumption were grown. Residence patterns at rural sites in highland Mexico were generally more nucleated. Here, residence was in dwelling units constructed next to one another or in compounds, with little intervening space used as gardens, and the basic unit of residence involved a comparatively small structural core bordered by exterior walls. In areas of sloping terrain, these buildings were constructed on terraces.

The Classic period was also a time of changing political relationships. During the Early Classic period, Teotihuacán, Monte Albán, and Tikal were politically the most important centers in central Mexico, in Oaxaca, and in the Maya Lowlands, respectively. The Middle Classic period is the time when Teotihuacán emerged as the most significant archaeological site in Mesoamerica. Although Teotihuacán probably never conquered all of the region, it was able to exert widespread influence throughout Mesoamerica. This influence had several aspects: the founding of enclaves at Kaminaljuyú, Matacapan, and other sites, either through military conquest or via the establishment of commercial colonies; the formalization of political and economic relationships at other major sites, such as Tikal, Monte Albán, and Cerro de las Mesas; and the exchange of goods produced at the city, particularly in obsidian, throughout a major part of Mesoamerica. Imitations of Teotihuacán goods were also made, generally in ceramics. Teotihuacán undoubtedly derived significant economic benefits from this control, which probably accounts for its larger size, its greater level of craft specialization, and its higher standard of living.

The Late Classic was a time of political restructuring on the South Gulf Coast, in Central Mexico, and in Oaxaca. In the Tuxtlas Mountains in southern Veracruz, Matacapan lost significant population and was replaced by Ranchoapan as the major center in the region. At this time El Tajín developed into the major center in central Veracruz, exercising control over a substantial part of the region. In Central Mexico, although Teotihuacán also lost significant population, it still retained its position as the major center in the Basin of Mexico. Other major sites like Cholula, Teotenango, Xochicalco, Tula, and Cacaxtla, however, had now emerged in other parts of central Mexico, indicating division of the region into a number of polities, all smaller in scale than the one that Teotihuacán had dominated. A similar pattern can be seen in the Valley of Oaxaca. Monte Albán's population declined in size until it was only one of a number of centers (e.g., Jalieza) that controlled different parts of the valley.

The Maya Lowlands also remained politically balkanized throughout the Late Classic, although centers varied greatly in size. Tikal retained its status as principal center early in the period, but it was replaced by Calakmul and possibly Caracol for a brief span of time, only to reassert dominance in the latter part of the Late Classic.

Population levels in Mesoamerica generally rose throughout the Classic period, but there was significant variability from region to region. In the Basin of Mexico population grew from around 125,000 persons in the late Terminal Formative to nearly twice that number in the Middle Classic, after which it largely stabilized until the beginning of the Aztec period. The rise of Teotihuacán as the preeminent state in Central Mexico in late Terminal Formative times was associated with the wholesale nucleation of population in the Basin at Teotihuacán; the city later operated as the center of recolonization for the region by the Middle Classic. The population during the succeeding Late Classic was very similar in size, although a large number of people moved from Teotihuacán to other centers in the region.

In the Valley of Oaxaca, the picture was much the same. Its population level grew during the period, and there were rearrangements in its distribution over the valley from Early to Late Classic times. During the Early Classic, population was distributed throughout the valley but concentrated at a few large centers, particularly Monte Albán and Jalieza. In the Late Classic, in contrast, there was a major nucleation at and around Monte Albán, although other parts of the valley still supported occupation. Finally, if Period IV is considered to be largely Epiclassic in date rather than Early Postclassic, the terminal part of the period was associated with the gravitation of population to a series of new centers as well as the first substantial occupation of the Tlacolula arm of the valley.

The population history of the Maya Lowlands is another case of growth throughout the period. The growth curve in many parts of the southern lowlands is exponential-like. Total population was very substantial by the Late Classic, amounting to densities of 100 to 200 persons per square kilometer in some rural areas. Figures of this magnitude make the Maya Lowlands one of the most densely settled regions of the world at the time. Population densities at centers, of course, were much higher than those in the countryside, but they were generally much less than at sites in highland Mexico such as Teotihuacán, Monte Albán, Tula, and Xochicalco. Another interesting characteristic of the Maya demographic profile is the crash that it experienced toward the end of the Late Classic. In several areas the level of decline approached 90 percent between A.D. 800 and 950, with even less occupation in the succeeding Postclassic period. Data from Copán suggest that the population fall there was much more protracted, but the pattern of decline was still much the same. Population levels in coastal areas were far less sharply affected: in some regions there were actually increases in population at the end of the Classic, while in others there were moderate decreases, combined with a redistribution of population.

These rises in population were associated with intensification of the agricultural landscape. In the Mexican highlands, intensification involved the adoption of various forms of hydraulic agriculture or dramatic increases in its scale. Water management in highland Mexico is indicated by archaeological evidence of irrigation canals, related features such as check, diversion, and impoundment dams, the drainage of marshes and other waterlogged areas, and changes in settlement patterns, with sites situated on or near major perennial streams. The most substantial amount of archaeological information on this subject, however, has come from the Maya Lowlands. In this area of more intensive agriculture, there was an increasing emphasis on modifying slope land environments, largely through constructing terraces to inhibit soil and nutrient loss, as well as by building raised fields in inundated areas. These raised fields were of two types. First, there were fields in comparatively flat humid areas that replicated the system later adopted by *chinampa* farmers in the Basin of Mexico. Second, in other areas—such as the one around Pulltrouser Swamp—raised field construction involved only the building of features around the edge of the *bajo* (swampy lowland). Raised fields, though an extremely labor-intensive operation, were capable of producing substantial surpluses. Unfortunately, little is known about the spatial extent of this mode of land use in the Maya Lowlands.

Perhaps the most spectacular archaeological event that occurred at the end of the Classic period was the Maya collapse. This phenomenon involved a wholesale system failure in landlocked parts of the Yucatán Peninsula; there, after A.D. 800–850, polities stopped erecting public buildings and monuments with datable inscriptions, and there was a great loss of regional population both at the major centers and in the countryside. The area did not recover demographically following the collapse, and apparently it has less population today than it did at the end of the Classic. Various theories have been offered to explain this collapse, including natural catastrophes, increased warfare, outside invasion, and a peasant revolt. The most convincing one involves a failure of the basic mode of food production, combined with a period of demographic instability stimulated by the increased impact of disease and malnutrition on population replacement capacity, and the inability of major centers to extract large amounts of basic goods as tribute from dependent polities.

Interestingly, other regions in Mesoamerica never went through a collapse comparable to that in the Maya Lowlands at the end of the Classic period. Although there were spatial rearrangements in populations following the decline of major Classic period centers in central Mexico, in Oaxaca, and in most other parts of highland Mexico, population numbers afterward persisted. In these areas, farming involved hydraulic agriculture from permanent water sources, complemented by irrigation using runoff during the rainy season. Irrigation systems with a floodwater component typically deposit new sediments on plots, renewing and maintaining soil fertility, depth, and structure with the application of only nominal amounts of human labor. Modes of food production based on floodwater farming should therefore be more long-lasting and more resilient than those relying mainly on rainfall. This explains why a comparable collapse never occurred throughout most of highland Mexico.

FURTHER READINGS

Ashmore, W. (ed.). 1981. *Lowland Maya Settlement Patterns.* Albuquerque: University of New Mexico Press.

Blanton, R. E. 1978. *Monte Albán: Settlement Patterns at the Ancient Zapotec Capital.* New York: Academic Press.

Culbert, T. P. (ed.). 1990. *Classic Maya Political History: Hieroglyphic and Archaeological Evidence.* New York: Cambridge University Press.

Culbert, T. P., and D. S. Rice (eds.). 1990. *Precolumbian Population History in the Maya Lowlands.* Albuquerque: University of New Mexico Press.

Diehl, R. A., and J. C. Berlo (eds.). 1989. *Mesoamerica after the Decline of Teotihuacán, A.D. 700–900.* Washington, D.C.: Dumbarton Oaks.

Flannery, K. V., and J. Marcus (eds.). 1983. *The Cloud People: Divergent Evolution of the Zapotec and Mixtec Civilizations.* New York: Academic Press.

Harrison, P. D., and B. L. Turner II (eds.). 1978. *Pre-Hispanic Maya Agriculture.* Albuquerque: University of New Mexico Press.

C

Millon, R. 1981. Teotihuacán: City, State, and Civilization. In J. A. Sabloff (ed.), *Supplement to the Handbook of Middle American Indians,* vol. 1, *Archaeology,* pp. 198–243. Austin: University of Texas Press.

Pasztory, E. (ed.). 1978. *Middle Classic Mesoamerica: A.D. 400–700.* New York: Columbia University Press.

Sanders, W. T., and D. L. Webster. 1988. The Mesoamerican Urban Tradition. *American Anthropologist* 90:521–546.

Sanders, W. T., J. R. Parsons, and R. S. Santley. 1979. *The Basin of Mexico: Ecological Processes in the Evolution of a Civilization.* New York: Academic Press.

Wilk, R. R., and W. Ashmore (eds.). 1988. *Household and Community in the Mesoamerican Past.* Albuquerque: University of New Mexico Press.

Robert S. Santley

SEE ALSO

Formative Period; Interregional Interactions; Monte Albán; Postclassic Period; Teotihuacán; Tikal

Clothing

Clothing requires broad, flat, flexible substances for its construction, and the size and shape of the fabrics available to a people dictate the nature of the garments they wear. In Mesoamerica, the costume repertory was one of unfitted apparel. The European concept of tailoring—the cutting and sewing together of pieces of cloth so as to follow the lines of the body—did not enter the New World until the sixteenth century, when the Spanish also introduced the Old World treadle loom, which could produce broad widths of material. In contrast, textiles produced on a Mesoamerican backstrap loom cannot exceed a weaver's working armspan, or about one meter. However, these relatively narrow pieces are woven with four completely finished edges, the selvages. As a result, in pre-Hispanic times a single piece of cloth could be draped on the body just as it came from the loom and thus serve as a loincloth or skirt; wider garments could be created simply by seaming together the selvages of two or more woven webs.

Unlike those of Egypt, far western China, or Peru and Chile, the climate and burial practices of Mesoamerica were such that almost no pre-Hispanic clothing has survived. As a result, costume repertories can be reconstructed only from garment depictions on wall murals, sculpture, ceramic vessels, figurines or—for the Late Postclassic (A.D. 1250–1521)—in pictorial codices or from eyewitness accounts by early Spanish chroniclers. Only a limited number of garment types appear in this archaeological and ethnohistorical record. Each ancient Mesoamerican culture displays its own distinctive subset of these forms, basic apparel that was further elaborated to serve as elite attire for rulers and deities. The following brief overview of Mesoamerican costume examines each of the basic clothing types, describing the variations of these garments in a chronological sequence of cultures from both the highland central plateau and the low-lying tropical regions.

Male Garments

For more than three thousand years, from the Middle Formative (1150–400 B.C.) to the Spanish Colonial era, the loincloth served as the basic male costume, worn in all successive Mesoamerican civilizations with the sole exception of west Mexico (see below). The loincloth of pre-Hispanic Mesoamerica was a continuous strip of material that covered the genitals, passing between the legs and tying at the waist; in most styles the ends of the loincloth hung down in front and back of the body.

In Mesoamerica, complex culture began to take shape in the Formative period (1500–100 B.C.). On Mexico's central plateau, the earliest small clay figurines wear only turbans and ribbons; clothing does not appear until the Middle Formative (1150–400 B.C.). At the Valley of Mexico site of Tlatilco, most of these early figures are female; the few extant males display some form of scanty loin covering.

Along the slow-moving rivers of the Gulf Coast, the Olmec peoples also first appeared during the Formative. Around 1150 B.C. this group began to sculpt permanent records of their gods and rulers. Among these were important personages who are sometimes depicted wearing a longer type of loincloth supported by a wide belt. These sturdy garments contrast with the skimpy genital coverings of the altar-supporting dwarfs, who wear a short, apron-like loincloth held in place by a narrow cord.

The outstanding site of the highland central plateau during its Classic period (A.D. 250–700) is Teotihuacán. The art of this great urban center is highly stylized, lacking dynastic indicators, portraits, or named individuals. Where humans do appear on the wall murals, they are depersonalized; they do not interact, and they are so richly bedecked with feathers that it is difficult fully to discern their clothing. Fortunately, small, simply dressed clay figurines abound at Teotihuacán; the males wear loincloths that provide short, apron-like coverings.

Returning to the lowland tropics, by this region's Classic period (A.D. 250–900) the numerous Maya city-states had reached an apogee of cultural refinement under the rule of dynastic kings. On carved stelae and polychrome ceramic pots, these rulers recorded the passage of time in connection with their portraits, parentage, and military victories. Their loincloths, often richly elaborated, appear to be made of a single long piece of cloth that passed between the legs, wrapped around the waist, and tied so that the long ends draped down in front and back of the body.

Following the eighth-century fall of Teotihuacán, the highland Toltecs—centered on their capital of Tula, Hidalgo—became the Early Postclassic (A.D. 900–1250) power on the central plateau. Around 900, the Maya site of Chichén Itzá in lowland Yucatán rose to prominence. Whether through voluntary alliance or through domination of one culture by the other, the Toltec and Maya developed new forms of architecture and sculpture that flourished at both centers. Whereas the old Maya order invested its power in the individual ruler and his cult, at Chichén and Tula it was the position and power of the warrior-king that held sway, rather than his lineage and portrait. The loincloths of the Maya males are the older form—the two long ends of the garment draping in front and back of the body—whereas the militant Toltec wear a new knotted style, discussed below, that subsequently became synonymous with one particular group of Aztecs: the Mexica of Tenochtitlán in the Valley of Mexico.

The most fully documented of all Mesoamerican cultures are those of the Late Postclassic (A.D. 1250–1521), particularly the Mexica. Their most typical loincloth was wrapped to encircle the waist so that both of the garment's ends could pass between the legs to the front of the body, loop over the waist-encircling "belt," and tie so as to create a large, distinctive knot whose short ends fell to above the knees. This "Aztec knot" often appears as a hieroglyph on tribute-list textiles, indicating the intended use of these cloths. The knot was apparently synonymous with virility, because the Nahuatl term for "loincloth," *maxtlatl,* was also used as a male given name.

The hipcloth, always worn in conjunction with the loincloth, was a square or rectangular textile that was folded and secured at the waist. It first appears in the archaeological record in the Olmec heartland, at Tres Zapotes. At Classic Period Teotihuacán, male figurines often wear hipcloths and loincloths of the same short length. The large hipcloths of the contemporary Maya are depicted in a variety of shapes: folded into triangular form

and tied at the waist so as to cover the buttocks, worn over the loincloth as a frontal apron, or bunched around the waist. The hipcloths of the Toltec-Lowland Maya sometimes were worn as frontal aprons, but more often in the triangular forms; the Mexica and Lowland Maya of the Late Postclassic are also depicted in triangular-shaped hipcloths.

From the Middle Formative to the time of Spanish contact, capes served as pre-Hispanic Mexico's premier status garments. These mantles consisted of a square or rectangle of cloth that tied around the neck and hung down to between waist and ankle. Clay figurines from Middle Formative Tlatilco wear waist-length capes, as do the lowland rulers who appear on Olmec sculptures. The Classic Period Maya are depicted in a variety of capes of varying lengths; the shorter versions seem more prominent. Feathered capes appear in the Early Postclassic archaeological record at both Tula and Chichén Itzá.

In the Late Postclassic, a short cape that covered only the chest appears. This is the *quemitl*—the so-called deity bib—that is often depicted in the pre-Hispanic Borgia Group ritual codices. Among the contemporary Mexica, an enveloping cloak—called *tilmatli* in Nahuatl—was the prestigious, status-denoting male garment; its fiber, decoration, and length were all reported by the Spanish friar Diego Durán to have been controlled by strict sumptuary laws. Supposedly, only the Mexica ruling class was allowed full-length, richly decorated cotton capes. However, modern research suggests that reports of such controlling regulations reflect a nostalgic colonial creed rather than a stringent pre-Hispanic reality.

The *xicolli,* a short, sleeveless jacket, has a diagnostic hem area that usually displays some form of elaboration, often a fringe. This garment was an important ritual costume in highland central Mexico from Middle Formative Tlatilco times through the Classic period at Teotihuacán and up to the Spanish colonial era. The *xicolli* appears on wall murals and ceramic vessels at Teotihuacán, worn by lavishly dressed males. These important personages—perhaps priests or deity impersonators—are shown in profile. Although they are heavily bedecked with ornate quetzal-feather headdresses and back ornaments, the diagnostic fringe of the *xicolli* is discernible. The combination of the fringe of these garments, their consistent knee length, and their use in a sacred context suggest that they were fore-runners of the sixteenth-century Mexica's ritual "godly jacket," whose Nahuatl name was *xicolli.*

The Classic period Maya also wore the *xicolli,* but as martial rather than religious attire. Clay figurines of warriors

	MIDDLE PRECLASSIC (1150–400 BC)		CLASSIC (AD 250–900)		EARLY POSTCLASSIC (AD 900–1250)		LATE POSTCLASSIC (AD 1250–1521)	
	TLATILCO	OLMEC	TEOTIHUACAN	LOWLAND MAYA	TOLTEC	LOWLAND MAYA	MEXICA	LOWLAND MAYA
LOIN CLOTH								
HIP CLOTH								
CAPE								
XICOLLI								
ARMOR								
KILT / SKIRT								
BODY SUIT								
BALLGAME ATTIRE								
ELITE HEADGEAR								

	MIDDLE PRECLASSIC (1150–400 BC)		CLASSIC (AD 250–900)		EARLY POSTCLASSIC (AD 900–1250)		LATE POSTCLASSIC (AD 1250–1521)	
	TLATILCO	OLMEC	TEOTIHUACAN	LOWLAND MAYA	TOLTEC	LOWLAND MAYA	MEXICA	LOWLAND MAYA
SKIRT								
HIPCLOTH								
CAPE								
WRAPAROUND DRESS								
HUIPIL								
QUECHQUEMITL								
ELITE HEADGEAR								

C

holding shields found on the island of Jaina, the Maya burial site off the Campeche coast, are sometimes attired in the sleeveless jacket. This garment is also worn by a Toltec warrior depicted on a metal disk found in the Cenote of Sacrifice at Chichén, as well as by a Maya valiant carved on a doorjamb at the early Postclassic Maya site of Cobá. On the latter example, the jacket's diagnostic hem area is not delineated by fringe but instead is depicted with a stepped scallop, a Maya fashion that continued into the Late Postclassic; Maya *xicolli* with scalloped hems are depicted in Codex Dresden as votive offerings. The Mexica *xicolli* was also ritual clothing, serving as special-purpose attire worn only by gods, priests, rulers, and constables.

Padded armor was worn in the form of a sleeveless, thickly padded tunic stuffed with raw cotton and encased by either reeds, animal hide, or quilted cloth. No doubt

An Olmec ball player, c. 1150 B.C., wearing a padded hip guard (Michael Coe and Richard Diehl, *In the Land of the Olmec: The Archaeology of San Lorenzo Tenochtitlan,* vol. 1. Austin: University of Texas Press, 1980, figure 466).

the armor was worn by warriors of all cultural groups and classes from the Classic period on, serving as Mesoamerica's basic martial attire. Indeed, the heavily quilted cotton armor was so effective that the Spanish conquistadors quickly adopted it.

Kilts and skirts were special-purpose garments reserved for deities, rulers, and priests. The earliest example of a male skirt is found on Middle Formative Tlatilco figurines, which probably portray shamans. The earliest kilt is worn by a personage who appears on a sculpture from the Olmec site of La Venta. Short kilts made of elongated jade beads strung in a diamond pattern are depicted being worn by Classic period Maya nobles; these garments are occasionally accompanied by matching diamond-patterned short capes. Early Postclassic Toltec–Lowland Maya priests appear in long, straight, decorated skirts. In the Late Postclassic, analogous long skirts appear in ritual screenfolds of the central Mexican Borgia Group; Mexica and Lowland Maya pictorials depict short kilts being worn in ritual contexts.

A garment type known as a "bodysuit" completely encased the trunk and limbs; it appears first at Tlatilco,

A god wearing a deity cape—the *quemitl,* bib of the gods— together with a long, decorated skirt (*Codex Fejervary-Mayer.* City of Liverpool Museums. Facsimile edition. Graz: Akademische Druck –u. Verlagsanstalt, 1971: 24).

A sixteenth-century drawing of a Tlaxcallan ball player wearing protective leather breeches at the Spanish court of Charles V (Christoph Weiditz, *Trachtenbuch: Historische Waffen und Kostume,* band II. Leipzig: Verlag von Walter de Gruyter & Co., 1927: Plates XIII and XIV).

worn by shamans. Subsequently, Teotihuacán males are depicted on murals dressed as jaguars and carrying shields and staffs. Similar bodysuits were worn by the Classic period Maya. The Mexica, too, had jaguar suits, but theirs were made of feathers, came in four colors, and served as but one of thirteen different martial styles; padded armor was worn under all of this feathered apparel.

Ball game attire includes a variety of special-purpose clothing—ranging from padded gloves to protective head and body garments—worn by those who took part in the deadly serious Mesoamerican games. From the Middle Formative period up to Spanish contact, the ball game was consistently played, and its participants of necessity donned a variety of protective clothing. Of special interest are the "jockey shorts" worn by the Middle Formative Olmec ruler, c. 1150 B.C., depicted on Monument 34 at the site of San Lorenzo, Veracruz. This same type of hip padding was still being worn at the time of Spanish contact, as is evident in Weiditz's sixteenth-century drawing of an animated Tlaxcalan ballplayer at the court of Charles V of Spain.

Throughout Mesoamerican history, members of the elite donned distinctive headgear that set them apart in their societies. Tlatilco shamans are depicted in impressive masks. Helmet-wearing Olmec rulers were commemorated with colossal heads. Teotihuacanos wore wide-frame headdresses bordered by exotic and expensive quetzal feathers. Classic period Maya rulers were adorned in magnificent, towering headdresses that sometimes included symbols representing their names; subsequent Toltec–Lowland Maya elite continued the use of sweeping quetzal-feather hair ornaments into the Late Postclassic. Mexica nobility regularly wore the *xiuhuitzolli,* the royal turquoise diadem.

Female Garments

The female costume repertory was far more limited than that of males. The basic garment—the female equivalent of the loincloth—was the wrap-around skirt, the indispensable, pan-Mesoamerican costume worn by all females

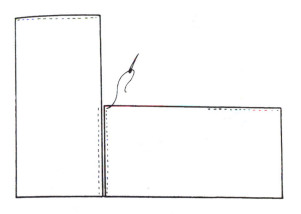

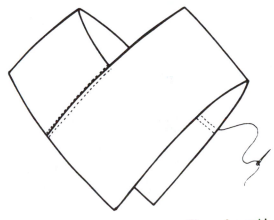

El quechquemitl.

The construction of the *quechquemitl* (Ruth Lechuga, *El traje indigena de Mexico.* Mexico: Panorama Editorial, S.A. 1982: 153).

from the Middle Formative period up through the Colonial era.

There were two principal upper-body garments. The *huipil*—a loose, sleeveless tunic composed of two or more joined webs of cloth that extend to between the knee and ankle—first appears among the Classic period Maya and was still in use at the time of Spanish contact. Following the Conquest, the *huipil* ceased to be worn in the area north of an imaginary line extending from Veracruz to Puebla to Guadalajara to the Pacific. In that northerly region, a different upper-body garment—the *quechquemitl*—has survived up to the present.

The *quechquemitl* is a unique costume composed of two rectangles of cloth joined in such a manner that when the garment's "points" are positioned front and back, a distinctive triangle is formed. This costume, uniquely rec-

A goddess wearing the ritual *quemitl* in one of the Borgia Group ritual screenfolds. (*Codex Laud* [M. S. Laud Misc. 678, Bodleian Library]: True-Color Facsimile of the Old Mexican Manuscript. Introduction by C. A. Burland. Graz: Akademische Druck –u. Verlagsanstalt, 1966: 15D).

ognizable in the archaeological/ethnohistorical record, appears to have been the attire of ancient fertility goddesses. It may have originated along the Gulf Coast, where the *quechquemitl* was—and still is—the region's quintessential female garment.

In addition to the more prevalent female clothing described above, Classic period female figurines at Teotihuacán sometimes wear capes over their *huipil*. Classic period Maya women are sometimes depicted on ceramic vessels wearing sarong-like, wrap-around dresses. During the Late Postclassic, goddesses in Central Mexican ritual codices sometimes wear the *quemitl*, or deity bib; Lowland Maya goddesses are sometimes depicted wearing short capes and hipcloths.

The earliest examples of elite female headgear are found on Middle Formative figurines from Tlatilco; one wears a distinctive conical hat. From Classic period Teotihuacán come depictions of goddesses wearing that site's distinctive wide-frame headdress bordered by exotic and expensive quetzal feathers, headgear often worn with a wide nose ornament. Equally impressive and lavish were the quetzal-feather headpieces worn by Classic period Maya noblewomen.

There is too little extant archaeological evidence to determine what type of headdresses were worn by the great ladies in the Early Postclassic Toltec or Lowland Maya societies; however, extant figurines and pictorial codices of the Late Postclassic Mexica offer depictions of the towering *amacalli* headdresses of corn goddesses, accouterments worn by priests and/or deity impersonators at certain great ceremonies. The Late Postclassic Lowland Maya continued the Classic tradition of using quetzal-feather headdresses to adorn their goddesses.

West Mexican Clothing: The Ecuadorian Connection

There are garment depictions in a West Mexican pictorial codex from the early colonial period that are inconsistent with what was being worn in the rest of Late Postclassic Mexico. Between 1539 and 1544, a Spanish missionary working with native informants and artists compiled the *Relación de Michoacan;* its scenes portray pre-Hispanic Tarascans in foreign attire. Whereas the Tarascan's Mesoamerican male neighbors all wore long, wrap-around loincloths and rectangular capes, Tarascan men are depicted in short breeches and tunic-like shirts, often checked. Mesoamerican females of the central plateau were modestly clad in long, wrap-around skirts and a *huipil* or *quechquemitl*, but Tarascan women—who lived at elevations of 2,100 to 2,700 meters, where it was often

A scene showing a Tarascan elite wedding group. The females of Michoacan wore short, tight, checked skirts and went virtually topless, despite living in elevations of more than 2,100 meters. Tarascan males wore tunics, often checked, and short breeches. (*Relacion de Michoacan* [*Lamina* XXXVII]).

C

cold—are depicted in short, tight, checked skirts, either worn with a tiny mini-mantle over one shoulder or completely topless. Although the style of the Tarascan garments was atypical for Mesoamerica, these costumes were also unfitted, as was all indigenous New World clothing.

These same types of Tarascan garments appear on figurines buried more than one thousand years earlier in West Mexican shaft tombs at Ixtlán del Rio, Nayarit. This clothing has analogs only in styles that were present in Ecuador from 1500 B.C. up to the time of Spanish contact. Clothing styles and textile design motifs represented on the ancient West Mexican mortuary figures indicate that these garment parallels existed in Nayarit as early as 400 B.C. Spanish colonial accounts and a variety of other data suggest that intermittent maritime contact persisted between Ecuador and West Mexico through the intervening period and into the sixteenth century.

FURTHER READINGS

Anawalt, P. R. 1976. The Xicolli: "Godly Jacket" of the Aztecs. *Archaeology* 29:258–265.

———. 1979. The Ramifications of Treadle Loom Introduction in 16th Century Mexico. In I. Emery and P. Fiske (eds.), *Looms and Loom Products,* pp. 170–187. Irene Emery Roundtable on Museum Textiles, 1977 Proceedings. Washington, D.C.: Textile Museum.

———. 1980. Costume and Control: Aztec Sumptuary Laws. *Archaeology* 33:33–43.

———. 1981. *Indian Clothing Before Cortés: Mesoamerican Costumes from the Codices.* Norman: University of Oklahoma Press.

———. 1982. Analysis of the Aztec Quechquemitl: An Exercise in Inference. In E. H. Boone (ed.), *The Art and Iconography of Late Post-Classic Central Mexico,* pp. 37–72. Washington, D.C.: Dumbarton Oaks.

———. 1984. Memory Clothing: Costumes Associated with Aztec Human Sacrifice. In E. H. Boone (ed.), *Ritual Human Sacrifice in Mesoamerica,* pp. 165–193. Washington, D.C.: Dumbarton Oaks.

———. 1985. The Ethnic History of the Toltecs as Reflected in Their Clothing. In *Gedenkschrift Gerdt Kutscher,* vol. 2, pp. 129–145. Indiana, 10. Berlin: Mann.

———. 1992. Ancient Cultural Exchanges between Ecuador, West Mexico, and the American Southwest: Clothing Similarities. *Latin American Antiquity* 3:114–129.

———. 1992. A Comparative Analysis of the Costumes and Accoutrements of the Codex Mendoza. In F. F. Berdan and P. R. Anawalt (eds.), *Codex Mendoza,* vol. 1, pp. 103–150. Berkeley: University of California Press.

Guzmán, E. 1959. Huipil y maxtlatl. In C. Cook de Leonard (ed.), *Esplendor del Mexico Antiguo,* pp. 957–982. Mexico City: Centro de Investigaciones Antropológicas.

Miller, M. E. 1986. *The Murals of Bonampak.* Princeton: Princeton University Press.

Taylor, D. 1991. Painted Ladies: Costumes for Women on Tepeu Ceramics. In *The Maya Vase Book: A Corpus of Rollout Photographs of Maya Vases,* vol. 3, pp. 513–525. New York: Kerr Associates.

Patricia Rieff Anawalt

SEE ALSO

Dyes and Colors for Cloth; Weaving and Textiles

Coapexco (México, Mexico)

One of the earliest village sites in the Basin of Mexico (c. 1150 B.C.), Coapexco is situated at the base of the volcano Ixtaccíhuatl, on the Amecameca Pass leading up from Morelos. The village is unusual for its size (c. 44 hectares), altitude (c. 2600 meters), brevity of occupation (c. 100

C

years), and setting (an environment where high rainfall favors maize farming despite cool temperatures). It was discovered by Parsons in 1972, and intensively collected and partially excavated by Tolstoy and Fish in 1973. Four dwellings were uncovered when the latter party cleared about 325 square meters. The population may have numbered about one thousand. Abundant obsidian blades from distant sources indicate contacts ranging from eastern Puebla to Michoacán, and possibly the presence of itinerant knappers and traders. It is one of the few village sites in the Basin in which ceramics and figurines are predominantly in the San Lorenzo Olmec tradition.

FURTHER READINGS

Boksenbaum, M. W., P. Tolstoy, G. Harbottle, J. Kimberlin, and M. Nievens. 1987. Obsidian Industries and Cultural Evolution in the Basin of Mexico Before 500 B.C. *Journal of Field Archaeology* 14:65–76.

Parsons, J. R. 1982. *Prehispanic Settlement Patterns in the Southern Valley of Mexico: The Chalco-Xochimilco Region.* Memoirs of the Museum of Anthropology, University of Michigan, 14. Ann Arbor.

Tolstoy, P. 1989. Coapexco and Tlatilco: Sites with Olmec Materials in the Basin of Mexico. In R. J. Sharer and D. C. Grove (eds.), *Regional Perspectives on the Olmec,* pp. 85–121. Cambridge: Cambridge University Press.

Tolstoy, P., and S. K. Fish. 1975. Surface and Subsurface Evidence for Community Size at Coapexco, Mexico. *Journal of Field Archaeology* 2:97–104.

Paul Tolstoy

SEE ALSO

Basin of Mexico; Formative Period

Cobá (Quintana Roo, Mexico)

The eastern half of the Yucatán Peninsula was dominated by one massive site during the Classic period and into the Postclassic: Cobá, in the state of Quintana Roo. Its strategic importance was perhaps related to its position: between the Caribbean and northern Yucatec trade networks, and linking the northern part of the peninsula to the Bay of Honduras and the southern lowlands. During the Classic horizon, many urban centers in this peninsula were placed 50 kilometers from the coast, with secondary centers and coastal outposts: Izamal with Temax and Dzilam Bravo; Cobá with Tancah; Edzná with Ah Kin Pech; Uxmal with Oxkintok and Celestún; Ichcansihó with Dzibilchaltún and Progreso.

In its origins, the city grew on the land between the two major lakes (Macanxoc and Cobá). Cobá's core covered 2 square kilometers and housed the three main architectural groups: the Cobá Group, a group of religious and civic constructions; the Nohoch Mul Group; and the Chumuc Mul Group, placed on a gigantic leveled platform. The suburbs (8 square kilometers) lodged the elite; the periphery (2 square kilometers) housed the terminal sites, where the zonal roads ended and probably where the main lineages dwelt.

Cobá reached a minimal extension of 70 square kilometers in the Terminal Classic period, thus being larger than Teotihuacán, but less compact. Its consolidation was achieved between A.D. 400 and 800, when the first cruciform *sacbe* causeway network was constructed, departing from the Cobá Group. It grew toward the east, and thus the Nohoch Mul, Chumuc Mul, and Macanxoc groups were constructed. From A.D. 800 to 1100, the second road network was built, emanating from the Nohoch Mul Group. These systems relate Cobá with the center of the Yucatán Peninsula through regional roads: the largest was 100 kilometers long and united Cobá with Yaxuná; the Cobá-Ixil road was 19 kilometers long; and the zonal roads led to satellite or terminal sites. Along these roads there are sites at regular intervals that mark day walks for transportation of goods.

The zonal *sacbes* are eight and give internal cohesion to Cobá. Each road reaches the major place of the construction group and ends in front of the major structure. Recently, scholars have suggested that causeways served political and economic functions by connecting political centers with outlying agricultural communities, and thus providing communication between rural production areas and exchange centers.

The terminal sites, at the ends of internal roads, have access plazas that may correspond to major lineages of the site. Some of the terminal sites are Kubulté, San Pedro, and Los Altares, to the north; Chan Mul and Mulucbacob, to the east; Lab Mul, Kucican, and Kitamná, to the south; and Chikín Cobá and Oxkindzonot, to the west. The main open spaces were areas to concentrate and redistribute goods and services, as well as congregational sites in front of the major temples: the Iglesia or the Nohoch Mul, enormous structures that rise over the 30-meter vegetational cover.

Many domestic compounds are situated near internal roads. These spaces bear strong resemblances to modern Maya *solares* (house lots): a low wall surrounds the space where kitchens, houses, storerooms, domestic animals, intensive cultivation sites in hollow trees *(caanché),* orchards, domestic altars (generally located to the east), and other components are found. Each household had circular and rectangular structures as functional areas. Some of the craft activities for self-consumption were carried out in the couryards.

Some *milpas* (cultivated fields) may have existed on the outskirts of the city, where maize, beans, squash, fruits, and so on were cultivated. The Maya at Cobá hunted deer, monkey, peccary, wild turkey, agouti, jaguar, and other animals of the tropical forest. They kept dogs, domestic turkeys, and honeybees. They also fished and collected marine mollusks and products from the forest.

There are traces of village society in Cobá during the Late Formative period. During the Early Classic period (A.D. 250–600) it developed into a chiefdom-level society, soon becoming an urban center. Its maximum development was achieved during the Late Classic period (A.D. 600–800). During the eighth century, Cobá may have had 20,000 stuctures that probably housed 55,000 inhabitants. It was the capital of a regional state, with a territory of 5,000 to 8,000 square kilometers.

Cobá has Petén characteristics, but it soon became the control site of the commercial route between the coast of Quintana Roo and the center of the Yucatán Peninsula. Robles and Andrews state that early Petén-related wares were replaced by the Cehpech ceramic tradition at Cobá, a tradition that may evoke commercial alliances with the Puuc cities during the Terminal Classic.

In the Postclassic horizon, Cobá was the largest polity encountered by the Itzá when they arrived in Yucatán; its western outpost was Cetelac, a site that resisted their penetration. The total absence of Silhó Fine Orange and Tohil Plumbate ceramic groups at Cobá and Yaxuná are considered good indicators of the inability of the Itzá to enter Cobá's domain.

Cobá declined as the Itzá circled its domain and cut off trade routes to the northwest and south. The terminal sites and causeways were abandoned around A.D. 1100.

FURTHER READINGS

Benavides, A. 1981. *Los caminos de Cobá y sus implicaciones sociales (Proyecto Cobá).* Mexico City: Instituto Nacional de Arqueología e Historia.

———. 1981. *Cobá: Una ciudad prehispánica de Quintana Roo.* Mexico City: Instituto Nacional de Arqueología e Historia.

Folan, W. J. 1979. La organización sociopolítica de los habitantes del área maya del norte a través del tiempo.
Boletín de la Escuela de Ciencias Antropológicas de la Universidad de Yucatán (Mérida) 34:34–45.

Folan, W. J., E. R. Kintz, and L. Fletcher. 1983. *Cobá: A Classic Maya Metropolis.* New York: Academic Press.

Freidel, D. A. 1981. The Political Economics of Residential Dispersion among the Lowland Maya. In W. Ashmore (ed.), *Lowland Maya Settlement Patterns,* pp. 371–382. Albuquerque: University of New Mexico Press.

Manzanilla, L. (ed.). 1986. *Cobá, Quintana Roo: Análisis de dos unidades habitacionales Mayas del horizonte Clásico.* Mexico City: Universidad Nacional Autónoma de México.

Manzanilla, L., and L. Barba. 1990. The Study of Activities in Classic Households: Two Case Studies from Cobá and Teotihuacán. *Ancient Mesoamerica* 1:41–49.

Marcus, J. 1983. On the Nature of the Mesoamerican City. In E. Z. Vogt and R. M. Leventhal (eds.), *Prehistoric Settlement Patterns: Essays in Honor of Gordon R. Willey,* pp. 195–242. Albuquerque: University of New Mexico Press.

Robles Castellanos, F., and A. P. Andrews. 1986. A Review and Synthesis of Recent Postclassic Archaeology in Northern Yucatan. In J. A. Sabloff and E. W. Andrews V. (eds.), *Late Lowland Maya Civilization: Classic to Postclassic,* pp. 53–98. Albuquerque: University of New Mexico Press.

Linda Manzanilla

SEE ALSO

Maya Lowlands: North

Coixtlahuaca (Oaxaca, Mexico)

This most northerly Postclassic Mixtec capital was renowned throughout the Mexican highlands as a major trading center until it was conquered by the Aztec Empire of the Triple Alliance in A.D. 1458. Although the city-state was composed of a mixed Chocho and Mixtec population, its kings claimed to be "Tolteca-Chichimeca" on the grounds that their ancestors had accompanied the Nahuas who migrated into the nearby Tehuacán Valley from Cholula sometime around the middle of the twelfth century. Ignacio Bernal excavated in and around what is believed to have been the principal Postclassic elite occupation site, defining a local ceramic sequence and locating a number of rich tombs. Several pictographic lienzos and maps, some of which remain in the possession of neighboring towns, portray a complex pre-Columbian history of community flux and fissioning, dual rulership, fac-

C

tional disputes, and marriage alliances throughout the Coixtlahuaca region between 1150 and 1520.

Linguistically and culturally closer to great Pueblan centers such as Cholula, Coixtlahuaca was a gateway for such centers to influence the rest of the Mixteca Alta. The city-state itself engaged the attention of the Mexica, who marched south from Tenochtitlán in 1458 with an army of 200,000 men to subdue the town after Mexica merchants were murdered there. Interaction with the Aztecs is evidenced by Aztec ceramics found by Bernal, who excavated there in the 1940s, also finding tombs with offerings like those of Monte Albán's Tomb 7.

FURTHER READINGS

Bernal, I. 1948. Exploraciones en Coixtlahuaca, Oaxaca. *Revista Mexicana de Estudios Antropológicos* 10:5–76.

Parmenter, R. 1982. *Four Lienzos of the Coixtlahuaca Valley.* Studies in Pre-Columbian Art and Archaeology, 26. Washington, D.C.: Dumbarton Oaks.

Pohl, J. 1994. *The Politics of Symbolism in the Mixtec Codices.* Vanderbilt University Publications in Anthropology, 46, Nashville, Tenn.

Susan Toby Evans and John M. D. Pohl

SEE ALSO

Mixtec History, Culture, and Religion; Tilantongo; Yanhuitlán

Colha (Orange Walk District, Belize)

This site is in northern Belize, at Milepost 47 along the Old Northern Highway, roughly 60 kilometers north of Belize City. It covers 7.5 square kilometers, with a small ceremonial center in the north central part of the site. The site sits atop exposures of high-quality chert (this is the northern end of the chert-bearing zone); on its east–northeast border is Cobweb Swamp; and Rancho Creek, a spring-fed stream, cuts through the middle of the site from southwest to northeast. Occupation began in Late Archaic or Preceramic times around 3000 B.C., with a major preceramic occupation on the margins of Cobweb Swamp around 1500 B.C. The initial Maya occupation was in the early Middle Formative, c. 900 B.C. A long sequence through Middle Postclassic times follows. Of paramount importance at the site was community-wide craft specialization in the mass production of chert tools (oval bifaces, adzes, stemmed blades, eccentrics, etc.) from Late Formative through Terminal Classic, for export to northern Belize and beyond. However, the site has also yielded significant data on the earliest farming cultures in the region,

on the complexity of Middle and Late Formative times (including bloodletting ritual and early writing), and on facets of the Terminal Classic and the Maya "collapse." In addition, there is compelling evidence of reoccupation of the site in Postclassic times by Maya from the Yucatán. During the Late Postclassic there were pilgrimages to the site, with incense burners smashed around one structure (Op. 2012) in the ceremonial center.

First recorded by Norman Hammond's Corozal Project in 1973, Colha has been systematically investigated by the authors, along with Jack D. Eaton, R. E. W. Adams, and G. Ligabue, during ten field seasons between 1979 and 1994.

FURTHER READINGS

Hester, T. R., and H. J. Shafer. 1994. The Ancient Maya Craft Community at Colha, Belize, and Its External Relationships. In G. M. Schwartz and S. E. Falconer (eds.), *Archaeological Views from the Countryside: Village Communities in Early Complex Societies,* pp. 48–63. Washington, D.C.: Smithsonian Institution Press.

Hester, T. R., H. J. Shafer, and J. D. Eaton (eds.). 1994. *Continuing Archeology at Colha, Belize.* Studies in Archeology, 16. Austin: Texas Archeological Research Laboratory, University of Texas.

King, E., and D. Potter. 1994. Small Sites in Prehistoric Maya Socioeconomic Organization. In G. M. Schwartz and S. E. Falconer (eds.), *Archaeological Views from the Countryside: Village Communities in Early Complex Societies,* pp. 64–90. Washington, D.C.: Smithsonian Institution Press.

Shafer, H. J., and T. R. Hester. 1983. Ancient Maya Chert Workshops in Northern Belize, Central America. *American Antiquity* 48:519–543.

———, ———. 1991. Lithic Craft Specialization and Product Distribution at the Maya Site of Colha, Belize. *World Archaeology* 17:79–97.

Thomas R. Hester and Harry J. Shafer

SEE ALSO

Maya Lowlands: South; Silex

Colonial Period

The invasion and conquest of Mesoamerica by Spaniards in the early sixteenth century brought about profound changes for indigenous Mesoamerican peoples. With the imposition of Spanish colonial rule, new political, eco-

Colonial Period. Map design by Mapping Specialists Limited, Madison, Wisconsin.

nomic, and religious institutions, technologies, plants and animals, and diseases were introduced, transforming Mesoamerican societies. Nevertheless, foreign ideas and materials were not always interpreted and implemented by native Mesoamericans in the ways that the Spaniards intended. Colonial Indian society in Mesoamerica developed in such a way that some pre-Columbian cultural traits were retained and others were modified, and many introduced Spanish traits were adopted but altered to meet local needs.

The Colonial period is defined as the period between 1521 and 1821 when Mesoamerica, as part of New Spain, was administered as a Spanish colony. The period began with the fall of the Aztec capital, Tenochtitlán, and the surrender of the last Aztec ruler, Cuauhtemoc, to Spanish forces led by Hernán Cortés and his Tlaxcalan Indian allies. In 1524 Pedro de Alvarado initiated the conquest of Central America with the defeat of the Quiché Maya under the leadership of Tecun in western Guatemala. The conquest of other Maya groups was a very protracted affair; the last independent Maya polity, the Itzá of the Petén region of Guatemala, did not fall to the Spaniards until 1697. The Colonial period ended in 1821 when creoles (Spaniards born in the New World) in Mexico declared independence from Spain following more than ten years of armed struggle. Central America also declared independence from Spain in 1821.

Initially, the most dramatic consequence of Spanish presence in Mesoamerica was the devastating population decline as introduced Old World diseases—smallpox, influenza, measles, typhus, yellow fever, and others—claimed the lives of millions of Indians. Disease proved to

C

be the Spaniards' most potent secret ally: epidemics struck many areas before the Spaniards themselves arrived. The magnitude of the demographic collapse varied from region to region, with most lowland regions experiencing higher mortality rates than highland regions. The native population of Mesoamerica was reduced by as much as 90 percent within the first one hundred years of colonial rule, declining from as many as 25 million people in 1520 to fewer than 2 million in the early 1600s.

Another demographic consequence of Spanish colonization was the biological mixing of European, African, and American Indian populations. By the end of the Colonial period dozens of *castas,* or biological castes, were recognized in Mesoamerica. Of particular importance was the emergence of a mestizo population—the result of Spanish and Indian unions. Today the population of Mexico is largely mestizo, but in pockets of southern Mexico, and in Guatemala, Indians still make up the majority of the population.

Many Spanish plants and animals and a wide range of other materials and technologies were introduced into Mesoamerica during the Colonial period and were readily accepted by the Indian population. Wheat, a Spanish staple, was never adopted—maize has always been preferred by Indians—but other plants such as onion, garlic, citrus fruits, banana, and mango were quickly integrated into native gardens and diets. Similarly, Indian families began to raise small domesticated animals such as chickens, goats, pigs, and sheep, and products from these animals were incorporated into Indian diets, and, in the case of sheep, Indian clothing. In some regions, cattle and horses also were adopted.

Metal tools and other implements quickly replaced stone tools. Spanish architectural features, many of which originated with the Romans or Moors, were introduced and influenced the construction of public and religious buildings. A common rural Spanish house type, a rectangular adobe structure with a red-tiled roof, became popular in some Indian towns.

Indian clothing was altered to incorporate introduced materials (e.g., silk thread, imported dyes) and certain stylistic elements (e.g., tailored shirts, jackets, and trousers; hats; shoes). But indigenous materials and designs also were retained, particularly in women's clothing, where the pre-Columbian *huipil* (blouse), wrapped skirt, and certain head coverings have remained popular to the present day. Weaving, too, combined pre-Columbian and European technology: Indian women continued to use the traditional back-strap loom, but introduced floor looms were adopted for some weaving tasks.

The introduction of certain Spanish technologies and practices had dire environmental consequences in Mesoamerica. Large herds of cattle overgrazed and destroyed Indian croplands. The use of the plow in tropical highlands caused serious soil erosion, a problem that has been exacerbated in modern times.

A number of Spanish economic and political institutions were imposed on Mesoamerican Indians to extract goods and services, ensure greater Spanish control over native communities, and try to make Indians behave more like Spaniards. The first such institution was the *encomienda,* in which the Spanish crown granted a deserving Spaniard—initially, a conquistador—rights to the goods (in the form of tribute) and labor of a specific native group, usually the residents of a particular town, in return for christianizing them.

When new regulations prevented *encomenderos* (the holders of *encomiendas*) from demanding labor from Indians, a new institution, *repartimiento,* was implemented. Under *repartimiento,* native communities were forced to provide labor for various public works projects, such as road-building and maintenance of public buildings, as well as for Spanish enterprises, such as mines and agriculture.

Under the Spanish tribute system, Indians were taxed either in goods or in money. Tribute payments went directly to the crown, or, if an Indian community was part of an *encomienda,* part of the payment went to the *encomendero.* In the mid-eighteenth century, the system was modified so that all tribute was paid in money. Many Mesoamerican Indians had been subjected to a tribute system in pre-Hispanic times, so the concept was not new. But it is generally agreed that Spanish tribute demands were more onerous in the Colonial period because tribute assessments for individual communities were seldom reduced to reflect declining populations.

The terms *congregación* and *reducción* refer to the institution that forced Indians to abandon isolated villages and hamlets and to resettle in larger, nucleated towns where it would be easier for Spanish officials and the clergy to "civilize" them. Colonial town locations, therefore, do not always correspond to their pre-Columbian counterparts. Moreover, these new *congregación* settlements were typically arranged in a prescribed fashion; streets were laid out on a grid plan, with public buildings and the church facing a public plaza in the middle of town.

Spanish authorities also regulated the internal governing of Indian communities, and the structure of town government was modeled after the Spanish system. A municipal council, the *cabildo,* oversaw all community affairs. Members of the *cabildo* were elected annually, and because Spanish officials had to approve the appointments, successful community leaders generally had to cooperate with colonial administrators. In some parts of Mesoamerica these policies provided social mobility to community members who were not part of the traditional hereditary elite. In other areas, however, the native nobility managed to circumvent official Spanish policies and effectively maintain control over their communities.

Intercommunity relationships were organized so that communities were grouped into *municipios* (townships) or *doctrinas* (parishes) in which one town served as the administrative center, the *cabecera,* and outlying towns were subject towns, or *sujetos* (sometimes annex towns, or *anexos*). In many regions this arrangement reflected a pre-Hispanic hierarchy among towns. Spanish officials—*corregidores* or *alcaldes mayores* (or sometimes governors), and their deputies—administered larger territorial units made up of several *municipios* or *doctrinas.* These administrators wielded considerable power, and their position enabled them to exploit native communities, forcing Indians either to buy goods from them at inflated prices *(repartimiento de mercancías)* or to sell goods at low prices.

The Spanish institution that had the greatest impact on native society in Mesoamerica was the Roman Catholic Church. Evangelization was, after all, a critical element of Spanish imperialist policy. It was not until 1492 that Christian forces in Spain, under King Ferdinand and Queen Isabella, had finally succeeded in defeating the last Moorish (North African Muslim) stronghold in Spain. After 700 years of Moorish occupation in Spain, the Christian reconquest, or Reconquista, was complete. In the wake of this success, religious fervor in Spain was strong, and for many, the evangelization of the New World was a logical continuation of the Reconquista, and a God-given opportunity to spread the faith.

The manner in which evangelization was to proceed became a hotly contested issue in Spain and among various Spanish factions in the colonies. At the center of this debate was Bartolomé de las Casas, a Dominican priest, who argued that Indians were intelligent, rational beings who could be persuaded to convert to Christianity without the threat of force. In fact, las Casas argued that the Spanish enterprise in the colonies was unjust and illegal, and his published accounts of Spanish brutality—some of which were exaggerated or even wrong—were widely read in Europe.

Spanish missionaries—Franciscans, Dominicans, and others—were charged by the Spanish crown with converting Indians to Christianity and teaching them to adopt a Christian lifestyle. The missionaries lived in Indian communities, learned native languages, and taught community members not only Christian doctrine but also how to read and write, how to utilize the Spanish legal system, and how to use Spanish tools and technology.

There is considerable debate regarding the actual conversion process and its relative success or failure. The entire process was fraught with misunderstanding and misinterpretation on the part of both missionaries and Indians. Mesoamerican Indians did, by and large, become nominal Christians. They were baptized, they faithfully attended religious services, they were devoted to the saints, and they participated enthusiastically in Catholic ritual. It is clear, however, that in the process of translating Catholic ideals and philosophy into native languages, many concepts were subtly altered to make them more meaningful to native peoples. Moreover, there is ample evidence to suggest that old beliefs and practices were never abandoned completely to be replaced with new ones. Instead, Mesoamerican Indians could at the same time be sincere and devoted Christians and retain pre-Columbian beliefs and practices, thus creating a new belief system that combined elements of old and new. Indians served in the church in certain capacities, as assistants to the priest *(fiscales),* as choirmasters *(maestros de coro),* and as sacristans, who oversaw church maintenance; however, they were not allowed to become priests or nuns.

The *cofradía* (a religious brotherhood or confraternity) was an important institution within the Roman Catholic Church that was eagerly adopted in Indian communities. *Cofradías* were voluntary organizations whose members venerated specific aspects of Catholic belief (e.g., the Virgin, the saints, and sacred activities like the Eucharist). They sponsored public rituals and celebrations to demonstrate their devotion. Perhaps more important, they served as community organizations that exercised a degree of autonomy from Spanish church authorities, and they were able to provide financial and psychological support for community members in times of need.

Another important church-related institution that was readily adopted among Mesoamerican Indians was *compadrazgo,* or co-parenthood. Begun as a custom of ritual kinship in which an adult sponsored a child at baptism or confirmation, this practice came to refer more to the social bond and mutual support between two adults, *comadres* (co-mothers) and *compadres* (co-fathers).

C

For Mesoamerican Indians, the arrival of Spaniards and the subsequent conquest and imposition of Spanish colonial rule had dramatic consequences, forever changing their way of life. In the first decades of the Colonial period, the native peoples of Mesoamerica experienced one of the most devastating demographic disasters known in human history. Moreover, a wide range of Spanish materials and institutions were introduced; some were readily adopted by Mesoamerican Indians, others were modified to meet local needs, and still others were forcibly imposed. The indigenous peoples of Mesoamerica played an active role in the creation of colonial Indian society; they were neither passive victims of Spanish domination nor did they cling rigidly to traditional ways. Instead, they made pragmatic decisions, incorporating pre-Columbian and Spanish-introduced beliefs and practices, creating a new, vibrant cultural system that has survived in many areas to the late twentieth century.

FURTHER READINGS

Chance, J. K. 1989. *Conquest of the Sierra: Spaniards and Indians in Colonial Oaxaca*. Norman: University of Oklahoma Press.

Cline, S. L. 1986. *Colonial Culhuacan, 1580–1600*. Albuquerque: University of New Mexico Press.

Farriss, N. M. 1984. *Maya Society under Colonial Rule: The Collective Enterprise of Survival*. Princeton: Princeton University Press.

Gerhard, P. 1993. *A Guide to the Historical Geography of New Spain*. Norman: University of Oklahoma Press.

———. 1993. *The Southeast Frontier of New Spain*. Norman: University of Oklahoma Press.

Gibson, Charles. 1964. *The Aztecs under Spanish Rule*. Stanford: Stanford University Press.

Haskett, R. 1991. *Indigenous Rulers: An Ethnohistory of Town Government in Colonial Cuernavaca*. Albuquerque: University of New Mexico Press.

Hill, R. M., and J. Monaghan. 1987. *Continuities in Highland Maya Social Organization: Ethnohistory in Sacapulas, Guatemala*. Philadelphia: University of Pennsylvania Press.

Jones, G. D. 1989. *Maya Resistance to Spanish Rule: Time and History on a Colonial Frontier*. Albuquerque: University of New Mexico Press.

Lovell, W. G., and C. H. Lutz. 1995. *Demography and Empire: A Guide to the Population History of Spanish Central America, 1500–1821*. Dellplain Latin American Studies, 33. Boulder: Westview Press.

Spores, R. 1984. *The Mixtecs in Ancient and Colonial Times*. Norman: University of Oklahoma Press.

Whitmore, T. M. 1992. *Disease and Death in Early Colonial Mexico: Simulating Amerindian Depopulation*. Dellplain Latin American Studies, 28. Boulder: Westview Press.

Janine Gasco

SEE ALSO
Postclassic Period

Comala (Colima, Mexico)

Never described or researched in detail, this site has monumental architecture of the Teuchitlán tradition style. Because no developmental sequence for this type of architecture exists locally, the site probably represents an intrusion from the Teuchitlán area of Jalisco into this section of Colima. Monumental circular buildings (the largest, c. 120 meters in diameter) display a formal concentric circular pattern. The largest circle has sixteen platforms around the patio; four are single platforms, and four more have two lateral platforms each. Kelly suggested that the fine polished red ceramic figurines and some of the latest shaft tombs dated to the Comala phase, which she placed in the centuries just before A.D. 500; this is supported by external ceramic associations. The phase (and site) clearly post-date the Ortices phase and pre-date Epiclassic developments such as those at Campana.

FURTHER READINGS

Kelly, I. T. 1980. *Ceramic Sequence in Colima: Capacha, an Early Phase*. Anthropological Papers of the University of Arizona, 37. Tucson.

Serna, C. R. 1991. Perspectivas de investigación a través del catálogo de sitios arqueológicos de Colima. *Barro Nuevo* 2.6:16–21. Colima: Centro Regional de Colima.

Phil C. Weigand

SEE ALSO
West Mexico

Comalcalco (Tabasco, Mexico)

The ruins of Comalcalco are situated on the broad coastal plain of Tabasco, about 3 kilometers northeast of the modern town of Comalcalco. The site covers nearly a square kilometer and consists of a central core area, where

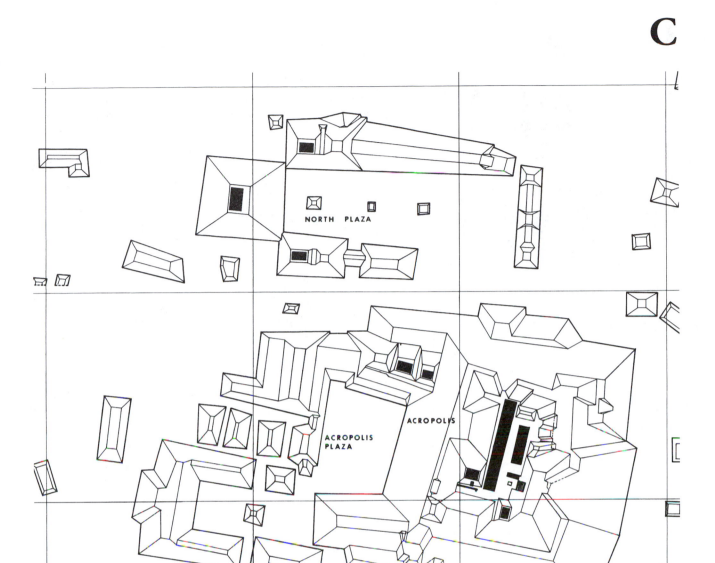

Site plan of Comalcalco, in Tabasco. Illustration courtesy of the author.

the largest and most important structures are found, surrounded by several "suburban" residential areas made up mostly of house mounds, interspersed with minor ceremonial structures. The central core area is dominated by the Great Acropolis, a huge pyramidal mound surmounted by the long Palace and several small pyramid temples. Just north of the Great Acropolis is the North Plaza, with a group of three recently excavated pyramid temples at its eastern end.

In contrast to all other parts of the lowland Maya area, where the omnipresent limestone base provided material for the construction of masonry buildings, the plain of Tabasco consists solely of clays, and the builders at Comalcalco were forced to find a substitute for the traditional

The south elevation (restored) of Temple VII and Comalcalco. Illustration courtesy of the author.

limestone. This ultimately led to the invention of fired clay bricks, which were cemented together with lime cement produced by burning oyster shells obtained from the nearby Gulf of Mexico.

During the Terminal Classic period, earthen substructures, faced with bricks, served to support superstructures in the form of vaulted brick masonry buildings. The largest brick buildings, such as the Palace and temples I–VII, were modeled after the temples and palace at Palenque, a major Maya site located some 165 kilometers to the southeast.

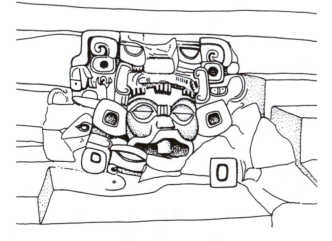

Stucco mask Kinich Ahau, Temple VII, Comalcalco. Illustration courtesy of the author.

Comalcalco is also noteworthy because of the numerous graffiti that were scratched into the surfaces of thousands of clay bricks prior to the time they were fired. What purpose these drawings may have served remains a mystery, since once the bricks were incorporated into the walls and vaults of buildings, the graffiti were lost to view forever, as far as those who made them were concerned.

FURTHER READINGS

Andrews, G. F. 1989. *Comalcalco, Tabasco, Mexico: Maya Art and Architecture.* Culver City, Calif.: Labyrinthos.
George Andrews

SEE ALSO

Gulf Lowlands: South; Maya Lowlands: South

Conchita, La (Veracruz, Mexico)

This small site near the northern Veracruz coast is notable for the presence of deep stratigraphic deposits containing terminal Pleistocene megafauna, Early to Late Archaic campsites, and Classic period agricultural terraces. Near the town of Gutierrez Zamora, La Conchita is situated by a former spring in the sandstone hills flanking the delta of the Tecolutla River. The basal stratum is a streambed bearing fossil remains of glyptodont, giant ground sloth, horse, and mastodon. On the overlying erosional surfaces are campsites for seasonal hunting that correlate with base camps at the nearby riverine site of Santa Luisa. The 7600 B.P. date from a hearth, with associated pebble chopper and flake tools, is currently the oldest confirmed presence of humans in eastern lowland Mexico. Near the present ground level is a series of catchment terraces illustrative of the intensive agricultural practices documented for the Classic period around Santa Luisa Paguas de Arroyo Grande, another site with extinct Pleistocene fauna and a very similar geologic context, which was found in 1994 five kilometers to the north. It contained bones of giant ground sloth, glyptodont, and horse, without evidence of contemporary or later human presence. Excavations were undertaken at La Conchita by Wilkerson in 1973–1974.

FURTHER READINGS

Wilkerson, S. J. K. 1975. Pre-Agricultural Village Life: The Late Preceramic Period in Veracruz. *Contributions of the University of California Archaeological Research Facility* 27:111–122.
———. 1980. Man's Eighty Centuries in Veracruz. *National Geographic Magazine* 158(2):202–231.

———. 1983. So Green and Like a Garden: Intensive Agriculture in Ancient Veracruz. In J. P. Duch (ed.), *Drained Field Agriculture in Central and South America,* pp. 55–90. BAR International Series, 189. Oxford.

———. 1987. Perspectivas sobre la prehistoria de Veracruz y la costa del Golfo de México. In *Origenes del hombre americano,* pp. 209–230. Mexico City: Secretaria de Educación Pública.

S. Jeffrey K. Wilkerson

SEE ALSO
Gulf Lowlands: North Central Region

Copán (Copán, Honduras)

Copán, one of the largest Classic Maya centers, was the capital of a polity covering several hundred square kilometers in the highlands of western Honduras between A.D. 400 and 820. The larger Copán region (see the following entry) occupies a southeastern frontier with non-Mesoamerican cultures, beyond which no Maya centers of comparable size are found. The site of Copán is especially notable for its rich, well-preserved corpus of sculpture and inscriptions, which provides detailed insights into ritual and dynastic history.

In 1576 Diego Garcia de Palacio, one of the first Europeans to visit Copán, was struck by the splendor of the ruins and recognized affinities with other ancient sites in northern Yucatán. Copán thus influenced early impressions of an extensive Maya culture area. The explorations of Stephens and Catherwood and their subsequent publications describing Copán's buildings and monuments drew popular and scholarly attention to the site in the mid-nineteenth century. Systematic archaeological research and reconstruction began in 1881 and continued more or less continuously until 1946, sponsored mainly by Harvard's Peabody Museum and the Carnegie Institution of Washington. Since 1975, renewed research by many institutions has focused on both the royal center of Copán and its larger sustaining region. Among other Classic Maya centers, only Tikal can boast a comparable history of intensive research.

Geographical and Environmental Setting

Copán's temples, palaces, and great plazas were built on an alluvial terrace of the Copán River, part of the larger Motagua drainage that ultimately discharges into the Gulf of Honduras. Although the river is not navigable, both the main valley and its tributaries provided access to other Maya regions to the west and north, and to the broad valleys of central Honduras to the east.

Five small pockets of alluvial soil are strung out along the floor of the Honduran segment of the valley, and the main site, known as the Main Group, lies in the largest and most fertile of these zones at an elevation of about 600 meters. The level bottomland is usually less than 2 kilometers wide, bordered by low foothills backed by steep mountain slopes that rise to elevations in excess of 1,300 meters. The population today, as in ancient times, is heavily concentrated on the valley floor or on the adjacent foothills.

Main Group

The Main Group, a huge concentration of beautiful masonry temples, palaces, ball courts, plazas, tombs, and carved stelae and altars, was the ritual/regal core of the polity, serving as the royal residence and political center of the Copán dynasty for more than four hundred years. Most of what is now visible was built during the reigns of the last four rulers, from about A.D. 695 to 800. The mature architectural pattern of the Main Group is quite compact compared to the scattered complexes found at some other major centers, such as Tikal. Today its buildings and plazas cover about 12 hectares, but the site was originally more extensive, probably once covering about 16 hectares, putting it solidly in the second rank of Classic centers in terms of size, though well behind such giants as Tikal and Calakmul. Major structures along the eastern edge were washed away by the Copán River until its diversion by Carnegie Institution archaeologists in the 1930s. The 40-meter-high vertical cut made by the river is the celebrated "Corte," a huge section exposing four centuries of cultural stratigraphy dating from c. A.D. 400–800.

Great Plaza

On the north is the Great Plaza, defined on three sides by monumental masonry stairways. Many of Copán's most imposing stelae and altars were set up in the huge open space defined by these stairways, which is capacious enough to have held the entire population of the polity at its height—at least 22,000 people. On the northwest corner of the Great Plaza is Group 1, possibly a royal palace. The excavated and restored Structure 223, on the northeast corner, was a dormitory for elite young men. A formal causeway probably led into the west side of the Great Plaza, with the entrance just to the west of the unusual

C

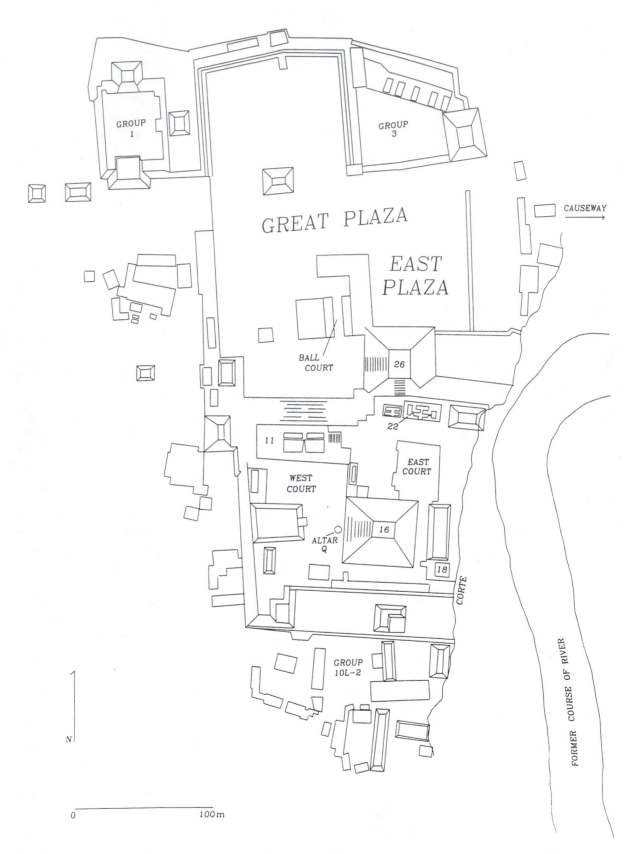

GROUP
1

GROUP
3

CAUSEWAY →

GREAT PLAZA

EAST
PLAZA

BALL
COURT

26

22

11

EAST
COURT

WEST
COURT

16

ALTAR
Q

18

CORTE

GROUP
10L-2

N

FORMER COURSE OF RIVER

0   100m

Plan of Copán Main Group showing principal structures. Courtesy Harcourt College Publishers.

four-stairway Structure 10L-4. A second, better-defined causeway extends to the west from the smaller East Plaza.

Plaza of the Hieroglyphic Stairway

Just to the south of the Great Plaza is the Plaza of the Hieroglyphic Stairway, named after the Temple of the Hieroglyphic Stairway (Structure 10L-26), which bounds it on the east. More than 2,200 glyphs on the risers of the stairs of this temple record the history of the Copán dynasty—the longest known Lowland Maya carved text. Statues of Copán rulers dressed as warriors were set into the center of the staircase, and other ancestral royal portraits appear to have decorated the now-fallen summit temple. Among the fallen façade sculptures recovered from this temple are glyphs that seem originally to have been part of an inscription in Maya, with a parallel text of Central Mexican derivation. Recent tunneling has revealed segments of at least six earlier construction stages. Also defining the plaza is the great Copán ball court, the second largest in the Maya Lowlands. It is one of the oldest monumental structures at Copán, begun by the second ruler and enlarged on several later occasions.

Acropolis

While the northern half of the Main Group is low and easily accessible, the whole southern section—the Acropolis—consists of a complex of buildings elevated as much as 30 meters above the level of the Great Plaza. Substantial buildings along the east side of the Acropolis have been washed away by the river. Surviving Acropolis architecture is arranged around two great open spaces, the East and West courts. On the northern side of the East Court is Structure 10L-22, a restored royal temple/residence famous for its sculptured entrance in the form of a giant cosmogram, its maize-god effigies, and the impressive *tun-witz* images, symbolizing stone mountains or hills, that adorn its corners. Next to it is a palace-like structure (Structure 10L-22a) with three doorways and large interior benches. The upper façade of this building is decorated with images of eight personages, each sitting on an individually distinctive glyph; these images alternate with those of conventionalized mats, symbols of authority in Maya culture. The excavators of Structure 10L-22a believe it to be a *popol nah*, a council or community house where powerful Copán lords met with the king. On the south side of the East Court is Structure 10L-18, one of the latest buildings at Copán. This temple covers a large vaulted tomb, looted long ago, which was prepared for

Hieroglyphic bench dating from A.D. 781, found in the elite-household Group 9N=8, Copán. Project photo by Jean-Pierre Courau.

Copán's last great king, whose image in military garb is carved on the door jambs of the superstructure.

Deep beneath the East Court is a succession of early buildings, beginning with what appear to be the modest fifth-century A.D. houses, shrines, and tombs of the dynastic founder and his associated family and nobles.

Two of the largest buildings at Copán dominate the West Court. The huge Structure 10L-11 along its northern edge actually fronts in two directions: on the north is an imposing stairway built of monumental stone blocks; the south side is the "Reviewing Stand," a series of terraces and inset niches redolent with metaphoric imagery of the Xibalba ball court and related themes of sacrifice. Although now largely ruined, the summit building of Structure 10L-11 was probably the largest and most imposing temple ever built at Copán. It also faced in two directions, with an enormous cosmogram on the north side; it had a massive interior bench on which were carved depictions of members of the royal dynasty.

On the east side of the West Court is Structure 10L-16, a huge temple pyramid whose stairway was embellished with carved images symbolizing death, war, and sacrifice. Altar Q, one of the most significant carved monuments in the Maya Lowlands, is set at the foot of the stairway. Commissioned by Yax Pac, Copán's last great king, the altar depicts sixteen successive rulers, each seated on his name glyph, with the first ruler, Yax K'uk Mo', shown symbolically passing a staff of royal authority

Excavated rural household remains at Copán Valley Site 11D-11-2. Project photo.

to Yax Pac himself. A cache of fifteen sacrificed jaguars was found beneath this altar.

Group 10L-2

Attached to the southern edge of the Acropolis is the recently excavated and restored Group 10L-2. Originally called "Los Cementerios" because Carnegie Institution archaeologists found rich tombs there, the group is actually an elite residential compound with impressive residences and other ancillary buildings oriented around several plazas (part of the eastern section has been washed away). Other compounds of similar scale and complexity are found elsewhere at Copán, but Group 10L-2 is distinctive in its formal attachment to the base of the Acropolis. Although there are traces of earlier occupation, the compound seems to have experienced its greatest growth between about A.D. 600 and 800. Inscriptions on its monuments and buildings associate Group 10L-2 with the royal dynasty. It probably served as the actual resi-

dence of the royal lineage during the last several reigns. Supporting this interpretation is the apparent deliberate destruction of major buildings around A.D. 850 and 900, followed by effective abandonment of the whole group, shortly after the dynastic collapse.

Urban Core

Around the Main Group, on the alluvial terraces to the northeast, west, and south, are zones of dense settlement. One thousand thirty-five masonry structures, ranging from small single mounds to buildings more than 40 meters in length, have been mapped in an area of about 0.6 hectares. The derived density of 1,449 structures per square kilometer is the heaviest concentration of architecture known at any Classic Maya center. Part of the urban core has been washed away by the river, and other sections along its northern edge have been buried by eroded sediments from the adjacent hills. Assuming that these sections had settlement densities equivalent to 25 to 75

Stela showing Copán's thirteenth ruler, Waxaklahun Ubah K'awil, set in the Great Plaza of the Main Group. Project photo by Jean-Pierre Courau.

Piece of mosaic sculpture fallen from the façade of STr. 66C, part of an elite residential group at Copán. Project photo by David Webster.

percent of those still intact, the urban core originally had about 1,300 to 1,827 structures in an area of about one square kilometer, and a population estimated in the range of 9,300 to 11,600 during the eighth century.

Two rather different residential enclaves have been formally identified within the urban core. To the west and southwest is the El Bosque enclave, which includes Copán's second ball court. Here much of the architecture clusters directly against the Main Group. To the east and northeast is the Las Sepulturas enclave, with impressive groups of mounds arranged along either side of a formal causeway extending from the East Court. Possibly these two different patterns reflect different settlement histories and relationships with the royal dynasty.

Extensive excavations as well as deep soundings have revealed the character and history of settlement, especially in the Las Sepulturas enclave. Essentially, the urban core was a huge residential zone dominated by the households of the Copán elite. Of forty-nine known groups of elite

scale and complexity in the valley as a whole, about twenty-eight are concentrated in the urban core within 850 meters of the Main Group. This pattern in part reflects early settlement on the floor of the most fertile and extensive alluvial pocket, as well as the apparently subsequent desire of elites to reside near the royal establishment. Elite groups are typically multi-plaza concentrations of well-built masonry structures, the most elaborate of which have façade sculpture as well as carved benches and altars. Associated inscriptions document the presence of sub-royal Maya lords of high social rank with impressive court titles. Apparently Copán's sub-royal elites had the prerogative of celebrating themselves with art and inscriptions to a degree unusual elsewhere. Several elite groups at Las Sepulturas have been fully restored.

Deep soundings revealed that parts of the urban core were occupied as early as 1100–900 B.C., but not until after about A.D. 700 did large buildings with masonry superstructures, sculpture, and inscriptions become com-

C

mon. Most of the architecture now visible was built in the eighth century, but some residential and construction activity continued at certain elite compounds for one to two centuries after the collapse of the royal dynasty.

Dynastic History

Although the Copán Valley was inhabited in Formative times, there was nothing particularly Maya, in the sense of Classic Maya elite culture, until the fifth century A.D. The abrupt appearance of distinctively Maya architecture, sculpture, iconography, and inscriptions may indicate an intrusion of elites from elsewhere in the Lowlands, but this suggestion, along with the linguistic affiliation of the original inhabitants, is much debated.

The wealth of inscribed and dated monuments and their association with architectural stratigraphy at the Main Group allow detailed reconstruction of Copán's subsequent dynastic history, as outlined in Table 1. Contributing heavily to the following summary is information from recent explorations of Structures 10L-26 and 10L-16, Group 10L-2, and the East Court. These efforts not only documented long construction sequences but also uncovered previously unknown inscribed monuments and several major tombs, some of which may be those of rulers. Uncertainties still exist concerning dynastic history, however, for two main reasons. First, the content of Copán's inscriptions emphasizes ritual and religion to an unusual degree, with less emphasis on a range of royal personages, their genealogies, their familial relationships, and important political/military events than is found at some other Classic sites. Second, prior to the reign of the thirteenth king, royal monuments were routinely destroyed or buried.

All subsequent kings reckoned their numerical order of succession from Ruler 1, the founder of the dynasty, who seems to have been on the throne by A.D. 426. Fragmentary Copán inscriptions, however, record dates before the fifth century—particularly one in the year A.D. 160—as well as earlier titled personages of obvious political importance. These individuals may have been members of an earlier, different dynasty at Copán or elsewhere. Although there are some early, low buildings in the Main Group that pre-date the fifth century as well, the tradition of monumental architecture seems to begin during the reign of the founder. Elite activity is apparent elsewhere, particularly at Group 9, an impressive site now destroyed or buried by the modern town of Copán Ruinas.

Little is known about the first eleven rulers. Their average reigns are comparatively short, collectively squeezed into an interval about the same length as that of the last five kings. One possible explanation for this compression of reign length is that succession may often have passed to siblings rather than offspring. Nevertheless, some of these early kings were patrons of architecture: they built many early structures on the Acropolis and beneath the later Structure 10L-26, and they also began the ball court and the Great Plaza. Ruler 12 had an extremely long reign of fifty-seven years and seems to have strongly consolidated the position of the royal dynasty, erecting in 652 a series of valley stelae that marks the demographic core of the polity. He also had relationships with rulers elsewhere, and he is known to have participated in rituals recorded on Altar L at Quirigua, the nearest large Classic Maya center, about 50 kilometers to the north. Little is known about his building projects, but the royal residence at Group 10L-2 seems to have begun its florescence around his time. During his reign the valley's population increased very rapidly; it continued to do so for 150 to 200 years.

The thirteenth ruler, who also had a long reign, was probably Copán's most powerful king and certainly one of its greatest builders. He was responsible for more stelae than any other ruler, and his images, dating between 711 and 736, dominate the Great Plaza, which he extensively enlarged and redesigned. He also commissioned structures on the Acropolis, most notably Structure 10L-22. Unfortunately, Ruler 13 was captured by Cuauc Sky of Quirigua in 738, and an "axe-event" ingloriously ended his life at that distant center.

Loss of face aside, the Copán polity suffered very little from this defeat, although the fourteenth ruler appears to have been a comparatively weak and short-lived king. He left no stelae, and only the *popol nah* building, where great lords came to confer with the king of a weakened dynasty, has been assigned to his reign. Consistent with this interpretation is the fact that many sub-royal elite groups in the urban core began to expand vigorously about this time. The final stage of the Hieroglyphic Stairway dates to the reign of the fifteenth ruler, and in part seems to represent an effort by 18 Rabbit's successors to reestablish royal prestige by glorifying their ancestors, especially as impressive military figures.

The sixteenth and last ruler had a problematical career. He raised no great self-glorifying stelae, but he did commission Altar Q and managed to complete impressive building projects such as Structure 10L-18 and the final stages of Structures 10L-11 and 10L-16. He was probably also responsible for the last great building phase at the royal residence at Group 10L-2. For all these projects he

TABLE 1.

Succession Order	Names, Titles, and Variants	Important Dates or Estimated Reigns (all A.D.)
Ruler 1 (founder)	**K'inich Yax K'uk Mo'** Mah K'ina Yax K'uk Mo' Blue Quetzal Macaw Sun-eyed Green Quetzal Macaw	Accession and death dates unknown; accession A.D. 426, death probably A.D. 435–437
Ruler 2	Unknown	Approximate date of reign mid-fifth century
Ruler 3	Mat Head	Approximate dates of reign 445–485
Ruler 4	Cu Ix	Approximate dates of reign 485–495
Ruler 5	Unknown	Short reign at end of fifth century
Ruler 6	Unknown	Short reign at end of fifth century
Ruler 7	Waterlily Jaguar	Approximate dates of reign first half of sixth century
Ruler 8	Unknown	Short reign in mid-sixth century
Ruler 9	Unknown	Short reign in mid-sixth century
Ruler 10	Moon Jaguar	Accession 553, death 578
Ruler 11	Butz' Chan	Birth 563, accession 578, death 628
Ruler 12	**Smoke Imix God K** Smoke Jaguar	Accession 628, death 695
Ruler 13	**18 Rabbit** XVIII-Jog Waxaklahun Ubah K'awil	Accession 685, death 738
Ruler 14	Smoke Monkey	Accession 738, death 749
Ruler 15	**Smoke Shell** Smoke Squirrel	Accession 749, death c. 763
Ruler 16	**Yax Pasah** Yax Pac, Madrugada, Yax Sun-at-Horizon New Dawn, First Dawn	Accession 763, death 820

was able to draft labor from a population of unprecedented size, estimated at 22,000 to 28,000 for the period from 750 to 800. Most of his construction efforts, however, seem to have been concentrated in the first half of his long reign. One possible indication of royal weakness is the extravagant growth of outlying elite residences after about 780, and the elaborate art and inscriptions many of them displayed.

The sixteenth ruler may have been something of an outsider, because his mother was a royal woman from Palenque and his father clearly was not the preceding king. He apparently took part in rituals at Quirigua late in his career in 810, and he was concerned with portraying himself as a warrior, although no enemy kings or centers are mentioned in his texts. Other poorly understood but very exalted royal personages are referred to in inscriptions from his reign, creating the impression of comparatively diffuse royal authority. The sixteenth ruler died in 820, bringing to an end Copán's four-hundred-year dynastic sequence, although some epigraphers believe that there were later ineffective claimants to the throne, such as the U Kit Tok' mentioned on the Main Group Altar L with an unfinished inscription dated 822.

Although the royal dynasty collapsed around 820 and the Main Group was effectively abandoned except for occasional and apparently intermittent ritual activity,

C

some urban core groups show signs of continued elite activity for another century or more. Population remained high for at least fifty years after the royal collapse, although beginning a long decline that lasted until 1200, by which time the Copán Valley was essentially depopulated.

FURTHER READINGS

Archaeology of Ancient Copán. 1992. Special section of *Ancient Mesoamerica* 3(1):61–197.

Baudez, C. F. (ed.) 1983. *Introducción a la arqueologia de Copán, Honduras.* 3 vols. Tegucigalpa: Instituto Hondureño de Antropología e Historia.

———. 1994. *Maya Sculpture of Copán.* Norman: University of Oklahoma Press.

Fash, B., W. Fash, S. Lane, R. Larios, L. Schele, J. Stomper, and D. Stuart. 1992. Investigations of a Classic Maya Council House at Copán, Honduras. *Journal of Field Archaeology* 19:419–442.

Fash, W. L. 1991. *Scribes, Warriors and Kings.* New York: Thames and Hudson.

Hohmann, H. 1995. *Die Architektur der Sepulturas-Region von Copán in Honduras.* Graz: Academic Publishers.

Hohmann, H., and A. Vogrin. 1982. *Die Architektur von Copán.* Graz: Academic Publishers.

Sanders, W. T. (ed.). 1986–1990. *Excavations en el area urbana de Copán.* 3 vols. Tegucigalpa: Instituto Hondureño de Antropología e Historia.

Schele, L., and D. Freidel. 1990. *A Forest of Kings.* New York: William Morrow.

Webster, D. L. 1988. Copán as a Classic Maya Center. In E. H. Boone and G. R. Willey (eds.), *The Southeast Classic Maya Zone,* pp. 5–30. Washington, D.C.: Dumbarton Oaks.

———. 1989. *The House of the Bacabs.* Studies in Pre-Columbian Art and Archaeology, 92. Washington, D.C.: Dumbarton Oaks.

Willey, G., R. M. Leventhal, A. A. Demarest, and W. L. Fash. 1994. *Ceramics and Artifacts from Excavations in the Copán Residential Zone.* Papers of the Peabody Museum of Archaeology and Ethnology, 80. Cambridge, Mass.: Harvard University.

David L. Webster

SEE ALSO
Maya: Motagua Region

Copán Region (Copán, Honduras)

Between A.D. 400 and 800 the Copán River Valley in western Honduras was the core of a regional Classic Maya polity extending over several hundred square kilometers. Because of the intensity and variety of archaeological projects carried out in many parts of the valley, we have an unusually clear picture of the growth and decline of the Copán polity. The following regional overview focuses on environment, chronological sequence, settlement, and agricultural history, and the relationships of these to the territorial extent and external relations of the polity.

Regional Environment

Unlike most parts of the Maya Lowlands to the west and north, the regional environment of Copán is strongly delimited and compartmentalized by natural hydrographic and physiographic features. Copán was accordingly much more isolated than most other Classic centers.

The core of the polity is a 30-kilometer-long section of the Copán River Valley, a tributary of the larger Motagua system that drains into the Gulf of Honduras. Though not navigable, the Copán River system nevertheless provides access to the Chamelecon Valley to the east, which in turn leads to the broad valley systems of west central Honduras. The major northern tributary, the Sesesmil, is the principal route to the lower Motagua Valley, and thus to the Classic center of Quirigua, which had political ties with Copán and was the nearest Classic Maya site of appreciable size.

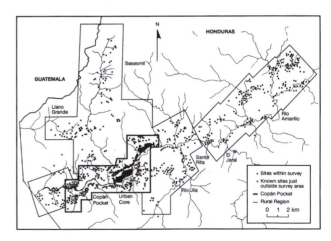

Map of the Copán Valley and archaeological survey zones, showing locations of all sites recorded by several survey projects. Drawing by AnnCorinne Freter. Courtesy Harcourt College Publishers.

The valley's prime agricultural resources are five wide pockets of alluvial soil along the valley floor. These pockets are generally less than one kilometer wide and together have maximally about 2,500 hectares of alluvium, over half of it in the Copán Main Group's pocket. Other small patches of alluvium are found in tributary valleys or intermontane basins. Upland forest soils tend to be heavily leached and, once cleared of vegetation, are very prone to erosion. Most of the modern population lives on or adjacent to the main pockets of alluvial soil, and the ancient population had a similar distribution.

Regional Cultural Sequence

The current reconstruction of the Copán regional cultural sequence derives from two main sources of evidence: ceramic stratigraphy and cross-dating, and a large sample of obsidian hydration dates. Ceramics of the Copán region relate more strongly to those of the highlands of Guatemala and El Salvador than to complexes of the Maya Lowlands proper. Since the 1940s, archaeologists have gradually refined a ceramic sequence for the valley. The latest published version of the Copán ceramic sequence is shown in the following table.

Pre-Acbi ceramics are comparatively rare and are largely confined to the Copán pocket. The Acbi phase itself begins with Maya intrusion into the Copán Valley and corresponds roughly to the reigns of the first eleven rulers and to the first major constructions at the Main Group. A distinctive painted pottery ware, Copador Polychrome, appears in the valley sometime after A.D. 500 and by 600–650 becomes widespread, initiating the beginning of the Late Classic/Epiclassic Coner phase. Coner ceramics are very abundant and are recovered from virtually all sites, and this is clearly the phase of maximum population growth and settlement expansion. An Epiclassic Ejar phase, partly overlapping with Coner, is defined on the basis of small amounts of imported wares, such as Tohil and San Juan Plumbate and Fine Orange, and by the apparent absence or low frequency of Copador Polychrome.

Until recently, the Coner phase was thought to end at 850–900 and to have no overlap with Ejar. In the latest version of the ceramic sequence such overlap occurs, and a generalized Epiclassic facet of the Coner phase has been extended to 950. In either case, the valley is postulated to be essentially depopulated by 850–950, following a very rapid decline from its Classic maximum at about 750–800.

This reconstructed ceramic sequence is supported by obsidian hydration dates (an unusually large sample of 2,263) derived from regional settlement excavations, except in one important respect: hydration dates indicate a much more gradual decline in population after the A.D. 750–800 peak, with occupation still detectable in the valley until approximately 1250. According to this reconstruction, post-800 populations continued to use a Coner or Coner-like ceramic assemblage, albeit with some changes in frequency and style, until at least the thirteenth century. Ejar ceramics do not represent a phase in their own right, but rather are imported vessels that are a sub-complex of an extended Epiclassic–Early Postclassic Coner assemblage. Recent AMS (Accelerator Mass Spectrometer) radiocarbon dates on burials from rural sites support the obsidian hydration chronology on this issue (one burial was made as late as the fourteenth century).

Regional Population and Agricultural History

Population reconstruction is based on a long program of settlement research, including survey and excavations, carried out in the Copán region by several projects. Variation among mapped sites was hypothesized by Harvard archaeologists in the 1970s to reflect a residential hierarchy based on wealth and status of the occupants. A typology of sites was developed. Type 1 and 2 sites were the simplest and most numerous. They consisted of comparatively small, low structures, single mounds, and simple mound groups of increasing size and quality. Type 3 and 4 sites had much larger and higher buildings, often with elaborate superstructures of finely cut stone, vaulted ceilings, and façade sculpture.

Period	Ceramic Complex	Dates
Epiclassic	Ejar complex	A.D. 800–1000 (overlaps with Coner)
Late Classic/Epiclassic	Coner complex	A.D. 600–950
Middle Classic	Acbi complex	A.D. 400–600
Early Classic	Bijac complex	A.D. 100–400
Late Formative	Chabij complex	300 B.C.–A.D. 100
Middle Formative	Uir complex (with Gordon funerary sub-complex)	800–300 B.C.
Early Formative	Rayo complex	1400–800 B.C.

C

All told, about 1,425 archaeological sites with more than 4,500 associated masonry buildings have been located over about 135 square kilometers of the valley. One distinctive feature of the settlement system is that almost all large elite residential groups are situated in the Copán pocket, and twenty-eight are in the urban core itself within 850 meters of the Main Group. Most of Copán's lords maintained their establishments right in the middle of the most productive resource zone, and also close enough to the royal establishment to be active in the affairs of the court.

A very large proportion of mapped sites, almost all of which had residential functions, have been test-pitted or extensively excavated; 17 percent of all excavated residential sites have associated obsidian hydration dates, which provide the primary basis for simulating the ancient population after A.D. 400.

Although a few hydration dates are as early as the ninth century B.C., we know comparatively little about the pre-Acbi population. Maize pollen shows up in one sediment core well before 2000 B.C. Ceramics from deep soundings in the Copán urban core and material from highland caves yield probable dates to 1400 B.C. Portions of a Middle Formative cemetery have been recovered from the urban core, where some individuals were buried with impressive jade artifacts. These early occupations probably were confined to the valley floor, especially that of the Copán pocket, and seem to have involved no more than a few hundred people. Unlike much of the rest of the Maya Lowlands, which experienced explosive Late Formative population growth, the Copán Valley seems to have been almost unpopulated during this period, although a large settlement is probably buried deep under sediments on the valley floor. By about A.D. 100–200 there are signs of architectural activity at the Main Group and also at Group 9 under the modern town, and inscriptions refer to dates and elite individuals about this time, but data for systematic population estimates are lacking.

For periods after A.D. 400 the data improve. Simulation indicates as few as 1,950 people in the valley as late as A.D. 550, but this is surely an underestimate; a more realistic guess is four to five thousand, most of whom practiced long-fallow maize agriculture on the deep soils of the Copán pocket. During the seventh century the population began to rise rapidly, peaking just short of 28,000 people between 750 and 800, and remaining at about this level for another century or so. Although 25 to 30 percent of the population may have lived in elite Type 3 and 4

groups during the eighth century, many of these people were of comparatively low rank. Copán's most privileged elites probably constituted less than 10 percent of the population.

Population growth was accompanied by increased cultivation of less fertile and more fragile upland soils after about A.D. 600, resulting in marked erosion of the Copán pocket uplands at least by 750–800, when overall population densities exceeded 100 people per square kilometer. By this time permanent cultivation was present in many parts of the valley, possibly supplemented by localized irrigation. Despite these high densities and intensive forms of cultivation, there are few signs of terracing, which would have helped to reduce erosion, and no indications of raised or drained fields like those found in Belize. The eighth century must have been a time of significant crisis for the regional subsistence economy, creating many managerial pressures for elites. By 750, production in the Copán pocket could supply less than 50 percent of the food requirements of the polity, yet most of its people still seem to have lived there, possibly as a result of elite decisions to keep the population heavily concentrated. This may also have been a time of increased stratification, as some elites established monopoly over the most risk-free and productive segments of an increasingly variegated agricultural landscape.

Up-valley alluvial pockets and foothills did not begin to fill in significantly until after 900, possibly as a partial consequence of the royal collapse. Still, at least half the population of the polity remained in the Copán pocket until 1050. By this time only a few thousand people remained in the whole valley, however, and elite activity was effectively finished, except for what appears to be a small enclave in the Río Amarillo pocket. A long overall decline began around 900, with the population dwindling away over the next three to four centuries.

Though not included in this simulation of the Copán region, the adjacent downstream segments of the valley, now in Guatemala, bear on the region's population history. Did the Copán core polity extend any significant distance into these lower reaches of the river? They have no large alluvial pockets comparable to those in Honduras, and rainfall becomes progressively lower and agriculture riskier farther down-valley. Preliminary surveys of the Guatemalan zones nearest the border failed to turn up evidence of a large Late Classic population, and in fact suggest that many sites there were abandoned at the end of Acbi times. Such abandonment correlates with the rapid rise of the Copán pocket population during the reign of the twelfth ruler, who may have encouraged people to settle around his royal establishment, leaving the lower reaches of the river comparatively unpopulated and effectively reducing the territorial size of the kingdom rather than expanding it.

The simulation from which this picture was derived was designed to produce maximal figures, and corollary simulations of agricultural carrying capacity suggest somewhat lower ones, with the peak at about 22,000. Nevertheless the overall pattern is clear—a single pulse of occupation, with rapid growth and decline. Evidence from fossil pollen in a long sediment core taken from an intermontane swamp in the Copán pocket independently supports this reconstruction of population history. Most of the valley apparently was extensively cleared of vegetation, including upland pine forest, by A.D. 900 (the earliest levels of the core), and regrowth of mixed-deciduous tropical species began only after about 1200.

The Copán Region in Interregional Exchange

Because of the long history and splendor of the Main Group and its location on main routes of communication between the Motagua Valley and central Honduras, many have long assumed that Copán must have been a main intermediary in regional exchange. Certainly exotic items flowed into Copán from the earliest times, as reflected by the Middle Formative jades recovered from the urban core. Jade, along with marine shell, stingray spines, and probably a host of other status items, appears to have been imported into Copán until the royal/elite collapse, but seemingly in small amounts. Pottery from the Maya Lowlands proper is surprisingly rare at Copán, especially in Late Classic contexts; ceramic imports from central Honduras are more abundant.

The one ubiquitous imported material found at virtually all Copán sites is obsidian, primarily from the Ixtepeque source about 90 kilometers distant in the highlands of western Guatemala. Ixtepeque was obviously outside Copán's direct control, so exchange is clearly indicated. Judging from its availability and amounts, obsidian, in the form of prismatic blades, was a cheap commodity consumed in small quantities by people of every status in the Copán Valley. Obsidian blades did not require high levels of labor or organization to import, produce, or distribute, and probably played only a small part in Copán's political economy. It thus seems improbable that, as some archaeologists suggest, Copán's rulers enriched themselves by controlling the flow of obsidian to other regions outside the valley.

One candidate for export is Copador Polychrome pottery, because the Copán Valley has long been seen as a center for production of this ware. It is at least as old in other parts of the southeastern Mesoamerican highlands, however, and it was clearly produced in more than one place. Copador is extremely rare at Quirigua and also in central Honduras and so seems an unlikely article of extensive trade. Other possible exports include tobacco and cacao.

Summary

Although culturally a Lowland Maya polity, Copán developed in a distinctive highland setting. In addition to its comparative isolation from comparable polities, it was situated on an ethnic/linguistic frontier and had exchange relations with both highland Maya and non-Maya societies. Claims that Copán was the capital of a much larger regional state are not strongly supported by our current knowledge of its epigraphy, its settlement system, or its population history. Copán appears to have had one great pulse of population growth, reached its maturity under its last five rulers after A.D. 600, then declined both politically and demographically after 820, partly owing to anthropogenic disruption of its fragile agricultural resources. By 1200 the Copán Valley was effectively abandoned, not to be heavily repopulated until the nineteenth century.

FURTHER READINGS

Abrams, E. M. 1994. *How the Maya Built Their World.* Austin: University of Texas Press.

Baudez, C. (ed.). 1983. *Introducción a la Arqueología de Copán, Honduras.* 3 vols. Tegucigalpa: Instituto Hondureño de Antropología e Historia.

Fash, W. L. 1991. *Scribes, Warriors and Kings.* New York: Thames and Hudson.

Freter, A. C. 1992. Chronological Research at Copán, Honduras: Methods and Implications. *Ancient Mesoamerica* 3:117–133.

Longyear, J. M. 1952. *Copan Ceramics: A Study of Southeastern Maya Pottery.* Carnegie Institution of Washington Publication 597. Washington, D.C.

Miller, M. E. 1988. The Meaning and Function of the Main Acropolis, Copán. In E. H. Boone and G. R. Willey (eds.), *The Southeast Classic Maya Zone,* pp. 149–194. Washington, D.C.: Dumbarton Oaks.

C

Morley, S. G. 1920. *The Inscriptions at Copán.* Carnegie Institution of Washington Publication 219. Washington, D.C.

Robicsek, F. 1972. *Copán: Home of the Mayan Gods.* New York: Museum of the American Indian.

Rue, D. 1987. Early Agriculture and Early Postclassic Maya Occupation at Copán, Honduras. *Nature* 326: 285–286.

Viel, R. 1993. Copán Valley. In J. S. Henderson and M. Beaudry-Corbett (eds.), *Pottery of Prehistoric Honduras,* pp. 12–19. Institute of Archaeology Monograph 35. Los Angeles: University of California, Los Angeles.

Webster, D., W. T. Sanders, and P. van Rossum. 1992. A Simulation of Copán Population History. *Ancient Mesoamerica* 3: 185–198.

David L. Webster

SEE ALSO

Maya: Motagua Region; Quirigua

Corralitos (Baja California, Mexico)

The site of Los Corralitos is on a mesa overlooking a canyon on the eastern side of the Sierra de San Francisco, Baja California Sur. The most notable features on the site are more than forty-five *corralitos,* "little corrals" or small, round, rock-walled structures. Such structures are common on the mesas of the Sierra de San Francisco, and the historically known Kiliwa Indians of Baja California used similar structures as the foundations for brush huts. An ancient lava flow created the mesa, and the desert vegetation on it is very dispersed. A rock tank, or *tinaja,* lies in the bottom of the canyon and would have been a year-round source of water for the inhabitants of the site. This *tinaja* was one of the very few permanent waterholes on the eastern side of the mountains and along the coast of the Gulf of California.

The material culture of the site included chipped stone, projectile points, manos, and metates. The styles of the projectile points indicate a long period of occupation from early Archaic times to the protohistoric period. The inhabitants of the site exploited its strategic location in the mountains to gather seeds, which they ground on the metates. They also traveled 12 kilometers to the sea to harvest sea mammals, fish, and shellfish, which they brought back to the site to consume. Investigations at the site have consisted of mapping, a systematic surface collection, and excavations in three of the *corralitos.*

Justin R. Hyland and María de la Luz Gutiérrez

SEE ALSO

Northern Arid Zone

Cosmetic Alterations of the Face and Body

At the time of Spanish contact, the people of Yucatán were still filing their teeth; piercing their noses, lips, and ears for the insertion of ornaments; painting and tattooing their faces and bodies; and intentionally shaping the heads and crossing the eyes of their children. Some scholars use pejorative terms such as cranial "deformation" (rather than "shaping") and dental "mutilation" (rather than "decoration") to refer to some of these practices.

The Indians told the Spaniards that such customs were "given to our ancestors by the gods," and head-shaping "gives us a noble air, and our heads are thus better adapted to carry loads." They stated that they did these and other body alterations for the "sake of elegance" and "beauty," while also attempting to make themselves look "ferocious and fierce" in order to frighten their enemies.

Archaeological evidence for the antiquity of these practices can be found in excavated artwork (vase and mural paintings, figurines, etc.) and body ornaments (ear spools, labrets, etc.). Our knowledge of soft-tissue alterations is confined to contemporary observations and surviving art and artifacts, but the recovered skeletons of the Indians themselves provide dramatic evidence of head-shaping and dental decoration.

Heads may be shaped unintentionally if the soft, thin bones of the immobilized infant's skull are pressed against the firm surface of a cradleboard or similar carrier for extended periods of time. It is also possible unintentionally to shape growing (and even mature) heads through the use of slings ("tump lines") for carrying loads on the back, or by balancing burdens on top of the head. The resulting accidental shapes may have encouraged ancient parents to seek further modifications through intentional use of boards and bindings.

Whatever the source of inspiration, groups in various parts of the New and Old Worlds have shaped their heads in distinctive fashion. Several shaping classifications have been used by scholars in the Americas. Imbelloni and Dembo's 1938 system appears to be the most accepted classification in Latin America. It consists of a "Tabular" category produced by fronto-occipital compression between thin boards and an "Orbicular" (or "Annular") category, involving circumferential compression using bands.

Each category of head-shaping is subdivided into "Erect" and "Oblique" varieties according to inclination of the occipital area on the Frankfort ("eye-ear") plane. In the Erect variety, pressure is confined to the upper portion of the occipital and adjacent portions of the parietalia (the lambdoid area), resulting in an essentially vertical orientation or occasionally an anterior inclination of the occipital bone. In the Oblique variety, the occipital is subjected to overall pressure to such an extent that it is flattened and tilted posteriorly. Additional variations occur, but seem to be due mainly to individual deviations in intensity and timing of the application of pressure, as well as differences in the bindings themselves.

According to Romero, the Tabular Erect style appears earliest (Early Formative, 1400–1000 B.C.) and Tabular Oblique is later (Late Formative, 500–200 B.C.), in the Valley of Mexico. Cuello, Belize, the earliest known Maya site, has yielded skulls with pronounced Tabular Oblique shaping as early as the Early Middle Formative (900–600 B.C.), whereas pronounced Tabular Erect shaping is later— Late Middle Formative, 600–400 B.C. The earliest Annular shaping is found in Oaxaca in the Middle Formative.

Mesoamericans also occasionally decorated their front upper (and sometimes lower) teeth by filing the incisal (biting) edges and/or drilling shallow holes in the labial (lip) surfaces of incisors, canines, and sometimes premolars, and installing inserts or incrustations of jadeite, iron pyrite (hematite), or turquoise. The now-oxidized dark, coffee-colored pyrite inserts probably resembled gold when freshly installed.

Any abrasive stone tool might have been used for filing teeth, but drilling holes for inserts probably required twirling (between hands or with a small bow) a tube of quartz, bird bone, or reed. Water and sand or a similar abrasive paste was probably needed. Once the hole was prepared, careful shaping of inserts and perhaps the use of a cement resembling Portland cement seems to have ensured retention. Some holes may actually have been filled with a ground pyrite paste.

Like head-shaping, dental decoration is found in both the Old World and the New. Types found in Mexico and Central America have been classified, and their distribution noted, by Romero. In addition to those listed by Romero, oversized, mushroom-shaped jadeite and pyrite inserts have been found in the upper teeth of an individual from Copán, and incised labial surface decorations have been found on lower teeth of an individual from Nohmul.

Romero's classification establishes types based on location and amount of incisal edge filing, alteration of the labial surface by filing grooves or drilling holes for inserts, and combinations of incisal and labial modifications. As of 1981, Romero had listed sixty-two types organized into seven categories. Filing may have begun in the Early Formative (1400–1000 B.C.) of the Valley of Mexico and may have continued into the Middle Formative (900– 600 B.C.), when inserts began to be used. The earliest known filing in the Maya area appears to be at Cuello in the Early Middle Formative (900–800 B.C.). In the New World, filing eventually extended from Argentina to Illinois in North America. Inlaying has been found as far south as Ecuador but only as far north as the Valley of Mexico.

Head-shaping and dental decoration sometimes occur together and were practiced by both males and females, but no significant correlation with social status (as judged by burial goods) has been found. However, Gill, working in Northwest Mexico, believes that a lack of cranial shaping may be associated with "somewhat lower social status," and dental decoration with puberty rites at about fifteen years of age in both sexes.

FURTHER READINGS

Comas, J. 1960. *Manual of Physical Anthropology.* Springfield: C. C. Thomas.

Gill, G. W. 1985. Cultural Implications of Artificially Modified Human Remains from Northwestern Mexico. In M. S. Foster and P. C. Weigand (eds.), *The Archaeology of West and Northwest Mesoamerica,* pp. 193–215. Boulder: Westview Press.

Romero, J. 1970. Dental Mutilation, Trephination, and Cranial Deformation. In T. D. Stewart (ed.), *Handbook of Middle American Indians,* vol. 9, *Physical Anthropology,* pp. 50–67. Austin: University of Texas Press.

Saul, F. P., and J. M. Saul, 1984. Osteopatología de los Mayas de las Tierras Bajas del Sur. In A. Lopez Austin and C. Viesca Trevino (eds.), *México Antiguo,* vol. 1, *Historia General de la Medicina en México,* pp. 313–321. Mexico City: Universidad Nacional Autónoma de México, Facultad de Medicina and Academia Nacional de Medicina.

———, ———. 1991. The Preclassic Population of Cuello. In N. Hammond (ed.), *Cuello: An Early Maya Community in Belize,* pp. 134–158. Cambridge: Cambridge University Press.

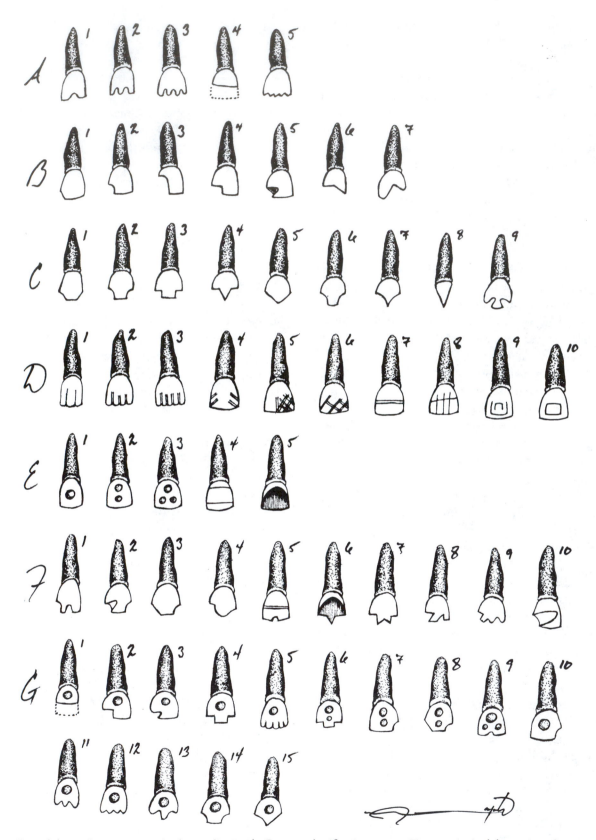

Dental decoration types organized according to the Romero classification system. Two new incised decorations from Nohmul are shown as D9 and D10. Illustration by Matthew J. Naujock.

C

————, ————. 1997. The Preclassic Skeletons from Cuello. In S. L. Whittington and D. M. Reed (eds.), *Bones of the Maya: Studies of Ancient Skeletons,* pp. 28–50. Washington, D.C.: Smithsonian Institution Press.

Schele, L., and M. E. Miller. 1986. *The Blood of Kings: Dynasty and Ritual in Maya Art.* Fort Worth: Kimbell Art Museum.

Stewart, T. D. 1975. Human Skeletal Remains from Dzibilchaltun, Yucatán, Mexico, with a Review of Cranial Deformation Types in the Maya Region. In *Archaeological Investigations on the Yucatán Peninsula,* pp. 199–226. Middle American Research Institute Publication 31. New Orleans.

Tozzer, A. M. (ed.). 1941. *Landa's Relación de las Cosas de Yucatán.* Papers of the Peabody Museum of Archaeology and Ethnology, 18. Cambridge, Mass.: Harvard University.

Frank P. Saul and Julie Mather Saul

SEE ALSO
Skeletal Analysis

Cosmology

All past societies had an explanation of how the world—the cosmos—operated. We call their perception of the world and its structure, layout, and origin "cosmology" or "worldview." Cosmology is often closely related to indigenous ritual and religious practices. It is also closely linked to ethnoscience, the study of how indigenous people classify all the elements of their world. How people group and divide elements of their world gives us clues about their beliefs and behavior.

Anthropologists are not just interested in how people explain the structure of their universe. Some scholars argue that the way people conceive of the universe—and all the things that dwell in it, such as animals and plants—directly affects how they exploit their environment for both subsistence and non-subsistence needs. Thus, knowing about a group's cosmology can enrich and complement our knowledge of other facets of their adaptation and lifeway.

Although every group within Mesoamerica had its own cosmology, some general principles and beliefs were widespread. One such concept was that the world was divided into three horizontal divisions: a multilayered upper world, a sacred earth, and a multilayered lower world. The composition of the upper and lower worlds varied from group to group. Even among the Aztecs, there are accounts of a nine-layered heaven and a thirteen-layered heaven; the number of layers in the lower world was most often given as nine.

Another widespread concept was the belief that from the center of the world extended four squares, or quadrants. Associated with each quadrant was a distinct color, bird, or tree. Just as groups differed in the number of levels they assigned to the heavens, they differed in their assignment of specific colors, trees, and birds to each of the four quadrants. For example, the Maya associated red with the east, white with the north, black with the west, and yellow with the south. The Tarascans also associated red with the east, but yellow with the north, white with the west, and black with the south. The Aztecs assigned yellow to the east, red to the north, blue-green to the west, and white to the south. The Aztecs assigned the following trees to the four directions: mesquite to the east, ceiba to the north, cypress to the west, and willow to the south. The birds associated by the Aztecs with the directions were the quetzal with the east, the eagle with the north, the hummingbird with the west, and the parrot with the south.

The Earth was conceived as a living creature by most Mesoamericans. Out of this creature's back grew plants. For the Maya, the Earth creature was a cayman they called *ain;* for the Aztec, it was one of two creatures—a supernatural being called *cipactli* that had attributes of a crocodile, or a crouching toad called *tlaltecuhtli.* Not only were living creatures thought of as the surface of the Earth, but they were also thought to be floating in a huge sea or ocean, which the Aztecs called *teoatl* ("divine water").

FURTHER READINGS
Flannery, K. V., and J. Marcus. 1993. Cognitive Archaeology. *Cambridge Archaeological Journal* 3:260–270.

Marcus, J., and K. V. Flannery. 1978. Ethnoscience of the Sixteenth-Century Valley Zapotec. In R. I. Ford (ed.), *The Nature and Status of Ethnobotany,* pp. 51–79. Anthropological Papers, 67. Ann Arbor: Museum of Anthropology.

Joyce Marcus

SEE ALSO
Caves; Central Mexican Religion; Maya Religion; Olmec Culture; Sacred Places and Natural Phenomena; Tarascan Culture and Religion; Underworld; Astronomy, Archaeoastronomy, and Astrology; Zapotec Culture and Religion

C

Cotton

Cotton (*Gossypium* spp.), a plant native to Asia and the Americas, has been domesticated independently in both world regions. The most important early species of Western Hemisphere cotton are *G. hirsutum,* the ancestor of modern American upland cotton, and *G. barbadense,* which forms the parental stock of silky Sea Island cotton as well as the Egyptian varieties. *Gossypium barbadense* was probably first domesticated in western South America; its use has been documented as early as 3500 B.C. in southwestern Ecuador and 2500 B.C. in coastal Peru. *Gossypium hirsutum,* the most commonly grown Mesoamerican cotton, probably derived from Central America and southern Mexico. Boll fragments are common in the Tehuacán Valley (central Mexico) by 3500 B.C., with two controversial fragments dated to two thousand years earlier. Cotton remains dating from 1000 B.C. to 400 B.C. have also been recovered in the Maya area, at Cuello, Belize. By at least 900–200 B.C. (and perhaps as early as 1500 B.C.) people in the Tehuacán Valley were weaving cotton cloth on looms.

Cotton is a lowland crop, growing in Mesoamerica along coastal plains and in inland valleys to an elevation of about 1,000 meters. The plant had many practical uses in pre-Columbian times: shoots, seeds, leaves, and flowers were applied as medicine for illnesses as varied as asthma and eye-twitching; cottonseed may have provided oil; and mature plants yielded excellent fibers for cloth production.

Cotton was cultivated primarily for its fibers, which ranged in color from white to tawny (*coyoichcatl* or "coyote-colored cotton," in Nahuatl). In Aztec times, and certainly earlier as well, cotton fibers were graded according to quality: the most highly valued were those produced on irrigated lands, followed by cotton grown in the "hot countries" (coastal lowlands), in the west, and in the northern deserts. The least valued was the tree cotton, or *pochotl,* from the Totonac lands near the Gulf Coast.

Maguey and yucca plants also yielded fibers; these were spun and woven into a relatively coarse cloth. Clothing of maguey or yucca fibers was generally designated "commoner" clothing, although some items were elaborately decorated and could have been worn proudly by a noble person. Cotton clothing, although produced by commoner and noble women alike, was reportedly restricted to noble wear.

The production of cotton cloth was women's work, and girls throughout Mesoamerica learned to spin and weave by their mid-teens. Cloth served many purposes: deity adornments and religious offerings; decorative hangings for palaces, temples, and marketplaces; household items such as tortilla covers; mummy bundle wrappings; gifts in marriage arrangements, rite-of-passage events, rulers' exchanges, and merchants' feasts; a form of money; and, of course, as clothing, plain or decorated. Cotton was also quilted into an effective body armor used widely by central Mexican warriors.

The use of cotton and cotton cloth in economic exchanges was pervasive in Late Postclassic Mesoamerica. By the time of the Spanish conquest, the Mexica of Tenochtitlán demanded an annual tribute of 16,000 loads of raw cotton from conquered lowland provinces (according to the *Matricula de Tributos;* 4,400 loads according to the Codex Mendoza). This included brown cotton from the Pacific coastal province of Cihuatlan. Tribute cotton may have been used in the imperial capital to manufacture cotton armor, or it may have been allocated to spinners and weavers for cloth production; particularly fine cloth was reportedly produced by women in temples. Beyond the tribute network, cotton moved through the many marketplaces from lowland production zones to highland spinners and weavers, carried by the producers themselves or by regional merchants.

In addition to raw cotton, Mexica tribute demands yielded 217,600 pieces of cotton clothing annually from all but two of their conquered provinces (according to the *Matricula de Tributos;* 128,000 according to the Codex Mendoza). These included cloaks (*tilmahtli*) of varying sizes, loincloths (*maxtlatl*), and women's tunics (*huipili*) and skirts (*cueitl*). Some of these items were plain, others ornately decorated. This clothing was either worn directly by the nobility who received the tribute, used in religious contexts, or presented as gifts in political exchanges.

Among the *tilmahtli* were 65,600 designated in the *Matricula de Tributos* as *quachtli,* or plain white cotton cloaks. These capes were used as a standard of value and means of exchange in the Aztec economy. Many goods (including slaves) were valued in terms of *quachtli;* these capes were applied as restitution for theft; they could be obtained on credit from merchants; and they were used to ransom slaves who had been ritually purified in preparation for sacrifice. Both *quachtli* and cacao beans served as means of economic exchange, and such cloaks of different grades were recorded in one source as equivalent to 100, 80, or 65 cacao beans; in another source, at 240 or 300 cacao beans.

Plain and decorated cloaks were traded widely in marketplaces throughout and beyond the Aztec domain. In

C

one documented exchange linking tribute, foreign trade, and marketplace exchange, the Mexica ruler Ahuitzotl (r. 1486–1502) gave sixteen hundred *quachtli* (probably obtained in tribute) to high-ranking professional merchants, who in turn took these cloaks to the bustling Tlatelolco marketplace and exchanged them for fancy capes to be transported to trading centers beyond the bounds of the empire. In addition to cotton and cotton cloth, multitudinous dyes, spun feathers and rabbit fur, spindle whorls, and surely other cloth producing tools and accouterments readily changed hands in the ubiquitous Mesoamerican marketplaces.

FURTHER READINGS

Berdan, F. F. 1987. Cotton in Aztec Mexico: Production, Distribution and Uses. *Mexican Studies/Estudios Mexicanos* 3:235–262.

Damp, J. E., and D. M. Pearsall. 1994. Early Cotton from Coastal Ecuador. *Economic Botany* 48:163–165.

Rodriguez Vallejo, J. 1982. *Ixcatl, el algodon mexicano.* Mexico City: Fondo de Cultura Económica.

Frances F. Berdan

SEE ALSO

Clothing; Exchange Media; Weaving and Textiles

Cotzumalhuapa Sites: Bilbao, El Baúl, and El Castillo (Escuintla, Guatemala)

The capital of an extensive Cotzumalhuapa (or Cotzumalguapa) state, and center of its unique art style was formed by three closely associated site groups: Bilbao, El Baúl, and El Castillo, all situated on the northern outskirts of modern Santa Lucía Cotzumalhuapa. Cotzumalhuapa is the generic name identifying an important but little-known Middle to Late Classic period culture on the Pacific piedmont of Guatemala; it is known mainly for the quantity of its unique Mexican-influenced sculptural art style (discussed in detail in the following entry). The site groups comprising its political core are situated at an altitude of 400 meters, approximately 50 kilometers inland from the Pacific Ocean. This region of the Pacific piedmont contains the majority of Cotzumalhuapa sites; the zone has some of the richest soils and most favorable agricultural climates in Mesoamerica. It was an important cacao-producing area, apparently from the earliest times.

The sites and associated sculptural art were discovered by nineteenth-century explorers, who from the beginning speculated on the origins of the non-Mayan characteristics of its art. Most pointed to migratory Nahua speakers, such as the Pipil or Toltec from central Mexico, as the originators of this distinctive art in the Late Classic to Postclassic periods. In the late 1800s, a major collection of more than thirty important sculptures, including magnificent ball court stelae, were transported to the Museum für Völkerkunde, Berlin, where they are currently housed.

Until recently, modern archaeological research by Thompson and Parsons was limited to excavations within the site centers of Bilbao and El Baúl and focused on the cultural history, the temporal placement of the art style, and its ethnic identity. Consequently, the research concentrated on major architecture associated with sculpture, although Parsons produced a preliminary but acceptable ceramic chronology. Parsons also believed that the style originated in the Middle Classic period and was closely linked to Teotihuacán influence from central Mexico. Others considered it to be an early manifestation of the widespread Mixteca-Puebla style of Postclassic Mesoamerica, while Braun in an art historical analysis favored eclectic sources with influences from many regions of Late Classic Mesoamerica, including lower Central America.

The rich agricultural zone was occupied from the Early Formative. Increasing populations combined with developing social political complexity evolved into a large Late to Terminal Formative center, as revealed by abundant ceramics, radiocarbon dates, the existence of a Late Formative period potbelly sculptural style, and Stela 1 at El Baúl (the Herrera Stela). Stela 1 is one of three Pacific Guatemalan monuments with early long count Terminal Formative calendrical dates; the other two are at Abaj Takalik in the western Guatemala piedmont. Stela 1 at El Baúl probably dates to A.D. 36 or 37 and suggests a temporary intrusive movement onto the piedmont region by adjacent Highland Maya groups, as in Abaj Takalik. The presence of Late Formative potbelly sculpture and Terminal Formative Stela 1 demonstrate the importance of the zone long before the Middle to Late Classic florescence of the Cotzumalhuapa culture manifested in its monuments and architecture.

Stratigraphic data coupled with radiocarbon and obsidian hydration dates suggest a sequential development of the main site groups. Bilbao was built earliest, followed by the El Castillo and El Baúl centers, although a continuous Middle to Late Classic occupation is present in widespread domestic areas around all three. The obsidian hydration data also strongly suggest occupation well into the Early Postclassic in virtually all areas of the central zone. These data are similar to recent published

C

results of the Copán, Honduras, project and call into question the validity of the so-called Terminal Classic population collapse in southern Mesoamerica.

Recent research has examined the Cotzumalhuapa cultural phenomenon from a regional perspective. These new data suggest that a well-developed hierarchical system was present, with the upper tiers sharing certain architectural traits apart from the presence of sculpture. District capitals are probably present at Palo Gordo, 45 kilometers west of Cotzumalhuapa, and at Los Cerritos Norte, 25 kilometers east; stylistic influences are present well into eastern Guatemala at Pasaco and La Nueva, and at Cara Sucia in nearby El Salvador. Political links were also present in the Antigua Basin of the adjacent Guatemala highlands. Monuments with Cotzumalhuapa stylistic elements are even found as far as Tonalá on the western coast of Chiapas, Mexico. The nature of political and economic relationships between Cotzumalhuapa and regional polities on the lower coast at Los Chatos–Manantial and the nearby Tiquisate region are also under study.

Socio-political and economic organization are currently being investigated on a regional basis. No population information is currently available, although controlled surveys give the impression of dense populations, particularly in and around the nuclear zone. Burial data are scarce in contrast to Early and Middle Classic sites such as Balberta and Los Chatos–Manantial on the lower coast. It is believed that Late Classic cemeteries with urn burials are found outside the political-ritual centers.

FURTHER READINGS

Bove, F. J., and L. Heller (eds.). 1989. *New Frontiers in the Archaeology of the Pacific Coast of Southern Mesoamerica.* Anthropological Research Papers, 39. Tempe: Arizona State University.

Bove, F. J., S. Medrano, B. Arroyo, and B. Lou (eds.). 1993. *The Balberta Project: The Terminal Formative– Early Classic Transition on the Pacific Coast of Guatemala.* University of Pittsburgh Memoirs in Latin American Archaeology, 6. Pittsburgh: University of Pittsburgh and Asociación Tikal.

Ford, J. B. 1968. A Stela at El Baúl, Guatemala. *Archaeology* 21:298–300.

Parsons, L. A. 1967–1969. *Bilbao, Guatemala: An Archaeological Study of the Pacific Coast Cotzumalhuapa Region.* 2 vols. Publications in Anthropology, 11–12. Milwaukee, Wis.: Milwaukee Public Museum.

———. 1986. *The Origins of Maya Art: Monumental Stone Sculpture of Kaminaljuyu, Guatemala, and the Southern Pacific Coast.* Studies in Pre-Columbian Art and Archaeology, 28. Washington, D.C.: Dumbarton Oaks.

Thompson, J. E. S. 1948. *An Archaeological Reconnaissance in the Cotzumalhuapa Region, Escuintla, Guatemala.* Carnegie Institution of Washington, Publication 574, Contribution 44. Washington, D.C.

Termer, F. 1973. *Palo Gordo: Ein Beitrag zur Archäologie des Pacifischen Guatemala.* Munich: Hamburgisches Museum für Völkerkunde.

Frederick J. Bové

SEE ALSO

Soconusco–South Pacific Coast and Piedmont Region

Cotzumalhuapa Style

A distinctive sculptural style and writing system were the hallmark of the Cotzumalhuapa culture, which developed on the Pacific coastal piedmont of Guatemala during the Late Classic period. Its main nucleus was at the sites of Bilbao, El Castillo, and El Baúl, which were actually part of a single settlement system encompassing at least 6 square kilometers. More than 140 sculptures in the Cotzumalhuapa style have been recorded from this area, which was probably the seat of a powerful state whose influence stretched over a 150-kilometer band along the piedmont and southern highlands. Cotzumalhuapa-style sculpture is found at the coastal sites of Palo Gordo, Aguná, Palo Verde, Pantaleón, Los Cerritos Norte, La Nueva–Pasaco, and many others. It is also present in the adjacent highlands, especially in the Antigua Valley of Guatemala.

The style was rendered mainly in volcanic basalt, in a variety of bas-relief and full-round formats, both in monumental scale and as portable pieces. A few examples in the form of jade artifacts are known. Architectural sculptures include pillars, carved pavement stones, and heads with horizontal tenons. Stelae and carved boulders show complex narrative scenes in which rulers and nobles interact with each other, with gods, and possibly with ancestors. They are also portrayed in three-dimensional statues. Individuals often have speech scrolls rendered as elaborate vines. Sculptures also display short inscriptions that probably convey dates and personal names in the Cotzumalhuapa writing system. The latter features combinations of numerals and figurative signs, of which twenty-seven have been catalogued. The structure and content of the system are yet undeciphered. Both the style and writing system were highly original but shared features with the roughly contemporaneous styles of Chichén Itzá, the Gulf Lowlands, and Central Mexico.

FURTHER READINGS

Bove, F. J., and L. Heller (eds.). 1989. *New Frontiers in the Archaeology of the Pacific Coast of Southern Mesoamerica.* Anthropological Research Papers, 39. Tempe: Arizona State University.

Chinchilla Mazariegos, O. 1996. *Settlement Patterns and Monumental Art at a Major Pre-Columbian Polity: Cotzumalguapa, Guatemala.* Dissertation, Vanderbilt University.

Habel, S. 1878. The Sculptures of Santa Lucía Cosumalwhapa in Guatemala. *Smithsonian Contributions to Knowledge* 23. (3):1–90. Washington, D.C.

Parsons, L. A. 1967–1969. *Bilbao, Guatemala: An Archaeological Study of the Pacific Coast Cotzumalhuapa Region.* 2 vols. Publications in Anthropology, 11–12. Milwaukee, Wis.: Milwaukee Public Museum.

Thompson, J. E. S. 1948. *An Archaeological Reconnaissance in the Cotzumalhuapa Region, Escuintla, Guatemala.* Carnegie Institution of Washington Publication 574, Contribution 44. Washington, D.C.

Oswaldo Chinchilla Mazariegos

SEE ALSO

Cotzumalhuapa Sites: Bilbao, El Baúl, and El Castillo; Soconusco–South Pacific Coast and Piedmont Region

Coxcatlan Viejo

See Tehuacán Region

Coyotera, La (Oaxaca, Mexico)

Formative period archaeological site near the present town of Dominguillo in the Cañada de Cuicatlán (Oaxaca), first occupied in the Perdido phase (600–200 B.C.). Excavations in 1977 and 1978 exposed more than 1,600 square meters of the 2.5-hectare Perdido phase settlement, situated on an alluvial terrace known as Llano Perdido. The village was organized into a series of (probably four) residential compounds, each measuring about 30–40 meters on a side and separated from the others by at least 25–35 meters. One of these compounds, Area A/B, was excavated completely. Arranged around three patios were eighteen structures, including residences, storehouses, ceremonial platforms, and a tomb. The associated artifacts reflect a diverse array of subsistence, craft, and ceremonial activities.

Around 200 B.C., the Cañada de Cuicatlán fell prey to the expansionist Zapotec state. At La Coyotera, the Perdido phase community on the Llano Perdido was burned and abandoned. A Lomas phase (200 B.C.–A.D. 200) settlement was established atop an adjacent piedmont ridge, Loma de la Coyotera. Major changes ensued in local economic, social, and politico-religious organization. Economic activities became more narrowly focused on agricultural production, which underwent intensification through canal irrigation. The basic unit of residence changed from the large multi-family compounds of Perdido times to a smaller, probably single-family form. The rich ceremonial life of the Perdido phase was supplanted by the fearsome presence of the Zapotec state, as shown by the skull rack excavated in front of the main Lomas phase mound.

FURTHER READINGS

Redmond, E. 1983. *A Fuego y Sangre: Early Zapotec Imperialism in the Cuicatlán Cañada.* Memoirs of the University of Michigan Museum of Anthropology, 16. Ann Arbor.

Spencer, C. 1982. *The Cuicatlán Cañada and Monte Albán: A Study of Primary State Formation.* New York: Academic Press.

Spencer, C., and E. Redmond. 1997. *Archaeology of the Cañada de Cuicatlán.* Anthropological Papers of the American Museum of Natural History, 80. New York.

Charles S. Spencer and Elsa M. Redmond

SEE ALSO

Monte Albán; Oaxaca and Tehuantepec Region

Coyotlatelco

The name "Coyotlatelco" has been used to refer to a pottery type, a ceramic complex, a ceramic tradition, an archaeological phase in the Basin of Mexico, and an ancient culture or people. The first archaeologist to use this term was Tozzer (1921), who named a red-on-brown pottery type "Coyotlatelco" (after a local place name); he excavated examples in strata above a Teotihuacán period residential compound at Santiago Ahuizotla near Azcapotzalco in the Basin of Mexico. Tozzer did not propose a specific dating for Coyotlatelco pottery, and its chronological position was not well established until Armillas (1950) formulated the Basin of Mexico cultural sequence

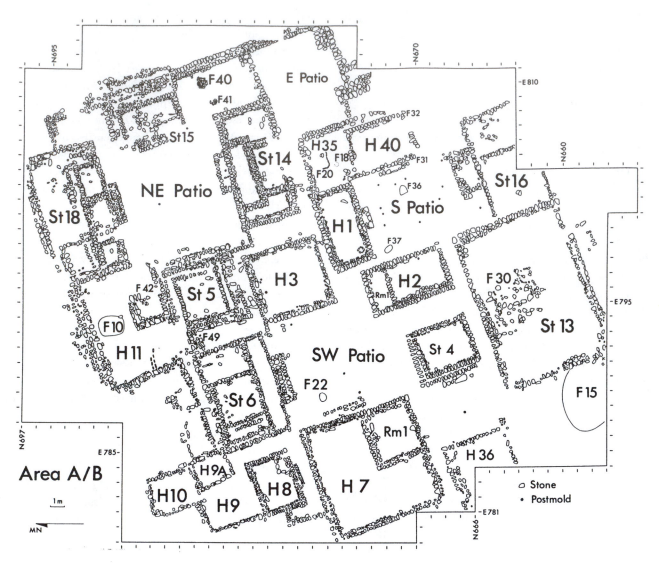

Plan of Area A/B, a Perdido phase residential compound at La Coyotera. Illustration courtesy of the authors.

for the Classic and Postclassic periods (Teotihuacán–Coyotlatelco–Mazapan–Aztec), which is still commonly accepted. The most detailed analysis of Coyotlatelco pottery is by Rattray (1966). Another key study is by Acosta (1945), who identified Coyotlatelco ceramics as being associated with the founding of the Toltec Tula sometime in the eighth or ninth century A.D.

Coyotlatelco ceramic complexes (the red-on-brown type and associated decorated and monochrome types) have a wide distribution throughout Central Mexico, and in many areas they coincide with the first occupations after the abandonment or collapse of Teotihuacan-related settlements. Coyotlatelco complexes are common in the Basin of Mexico, the Tula region, the Valley of Toluca, some sectors of the Puebla-Tlaxcala valleys, and areas of the southern Bajío covering parts of Querétaro, Guanajuato, and Michoacán. Until recently, the accepted chronology for this culture was c. A.D. 700–900, but recent radiocarbon dates from the Tula region and the Basin of Mexico suggest that some Coyotlatelco settlements were founded as early as A.D. 600–650 (Mastache 1996; Jeffrey Parsons and Mary Hodge, personal communications, 1995; Rattray 1996).

Archaeologists have presented two different models concerning the origins of the Coyotlatelco culture and its ceramics. Some investigators propose a largely local development within or near the Basin of Mexico after Teoti-huacán's collapse (Sanders, Parsons, and Santley 1979). Others postulate a northern origin for at least part of this culture because its ceramic and lithic complexes and its architecture are very similar to those of Early Classic (A.D. 300–600) cultures in the Bajío, Zacatecas, and some other areas of the northern Mesoamerican periphery (Braniff 1972, Mastache and Cobean 1989, Rattray 1996).

Early Coyotlatelco occupations in most of Central Mexico appear to coincide with a pattern of political fragmentation and lack of large pan-regional centers. Most early Coyotlatelco settlements do not seem to have possessed much political or social stratification, and they are not sufficiently large or complex to be considered cities or states. The ethnic composition of the Coyotlatelco people is poorly known, but ethnohistorical and archaeological studies suggest that some Coyotlatelco groups were Otomí, while others may have been Nahua.

Some late Coyotlatelco centers (after about A.D. 800) evolved a more complex socio-economic structure. Recent studies in the Tula region show that local Coyotlatelco people were the antecessors of the Toltecs, and many of the social and economic processes that eventually produced Tula's city and the Early Postclassic Toltec state began in the Coyotlatelco culture (Mastache and Cobean 1989, Mastache 1996).

FURTHER READINGS

Acosta, J. R. 1945. Las cuarta y quinta temporadas de exploraciones arqueológicas en Tula, Hidalgo, 1943–1944. *Revista Mexicana de Estudios Antropológicos* 7:23–64.

Armillas, P. 1950. Teotihuacan, Tula y los Toltecas. *Runa.* 3:37–70.

Braniff, B. 1972. Secuencias arqueológicas en Guanajuato y la Cuenca de México: Intento de correlación. In A. Ruz (ed.), *Teotihuacan: Onceava Mesa Redonda,* pp. 273–323. Mexico City: Sociedad Mexicana de Antropología.

Mastache Flores, A. G., and R. Cobean. 1989. The Coyotlatelco Culture and the Origins of the Toltec State. In R. A. Diehl and J. C. Berlo (eds.), *Mesoamerica after the Decline of Teotihuacán,* pp. 49–68. Washington, D.C.: Dumbarton Oaks.

Mastache Flores, A. G., R. H. Cobean, and D. M. Healan. Forthcoming. *Tula and Its Direct Interaction Area: A Regional Perspective of the Development of the Toltec State.* Niwot: University of Colorado Press.

Rattray, E. C. 1966. An Archaeological and Stylistic Study of Coyotlatelco Pottery. *Mesoamerican Notes* 7–8:87–211.

———. 1996. A Regional Perspective on the Epiclassic Period in Central Mexico. In A. G. Mastache et al. (eds.), *Arqueología Mesoamericana: Homenaje a William T. Sanders,* vol. 1, pp. 213–231. Mexico City: Instituto Nacional de Antropología e Historia.

Sanders, W. T., J. R. Parsons, and R. S. Santley. 1979. *The Basin of Mexico: Ecological Processes in the Evolution of a Civilization.* New York: Academic Press.

Tozzer, A. M. 1921. *Excavations of a Site at Santiago Ahuizotla, D.F., México.* Bureau of American Ethnology Bulletin 74. Washington, D.C.

Robert H. Cobean and Alba Guadalupe Mastache Flores

SEE ALSO
Basin of Mexico; Postclassic Period

Cozumel Island (Quintana Roo, Mexico)

An important Postclassic trading center and pilgrimage location, this island is situated about 16 kilometers off the eastern coast of the Yucatán Peninsula. The city flourished from A.D. 1250 to the early sixteenth century as a way station in the important seaborne trading route that circled the peninsula from Honduras to Campeche-Tabasco. The shrine of Ix Chel, the Maya goddess of the moon, childbirth, and weaving, was also on Cozumel, the easternmost point in the ancient Maya realm.

Cozumel Island is approximately 392 square kilometers in size. Its environment is characterized by dry forest and a thin soil cover. Most of the island lies near sea level, with a few rises that reach a maximum elevation of about 15 meters. Several lagoons, probably used as safe harbors for the large dugout canoes that plied the long-distance trading routes, exist on both the northern and southern ends of the island.

More than thirty archaeological sites have been found on Cozumel Island, evidence of occupation from Late Formative times into the historic period. These sites range from isolated shrines that line the eastern coast of the island and parts of the western coast (although modern construction has destroyed some of the latter) to larger inland sites. The coastal shrines may not only have had religious functions but may also have served as an early warning defense system for the inhabitants of the island's interior. At the time of European contact, the Spanish reported the lighting of what appeared to be warning fires

C

at coastal shrines as their ships first approached Cozumel Island. In addition, the island is covered by a system of dry-laid walls two to three courses in height. These walls appear to enclose agricultural fields and may represent property boundaries.

Some of the sites are linked by raised causeways. The largest site on the island, San Gervasio, is in the northern interior of the island and is linked by causeways to sites to the east and to the lagoons to the north. Parts of the causeways appear to cross seasonally flooded areas. The causeways may have been used to move trade goods from landing sites to interior storage areas, as well as to provide access for pilgrims and traders to key places such as San Gervasio. One of the causeways linking San Gervasio to the northern lagoons passed through an isolated shrine (with a circular foundation) and a freestanding arch near the settlement boundaries of the town.

San Gervasio probably was the political and economic center of the island and may also have been the location of Ix Chel's shrine. Four elite residential compounds, very similar in plan and architectural style to some found at the important Late Postclassic centers of Mayapan and Tulum, have been found at San Gervasio and may have been the homes of the ruling families of the island. Similar compounds are found at other sites, such as Buena Vista and La Expedición, but San Gervasio is the only site to have more than one of these residential units. All these sites, as well as several others, also have large rubble platforms, which may have served as warehouses. These platforms, from one to several meters in height, represented large labor investments and were significantly larger than the platforms that supported residential, public, or religious buildings. They may have been covered by perishable roofs and would have raised the stored goods above seasonal floods. They would have provided temporary shelter for traded materials that were off-loaded on Cozumel and subsequently shipped on to their final destinations. Goods may have been moved from coastal harbors to interior warehouses in order to protect them from potential raids.

The coastal shrine system, the widespread wall network, and the causeways linking sites and zones with different functions all lend weight to the inference that the island as a whole functioned as a trading center and that there was some kind of centralized authority, perhaps located at San Gervasio.

Cozumel Island was occupied from Late Formative times into the historic period. It was abandoned for parts of the seventeenth through mid-nineteenth centuries and was not fully reoccupied until after 1847. In recent years it has been the focus of major development and population buildup related to the growth of its tourist industry. Although the island was occupied for many centuries beginning before the start of the Common Era, it was not until the eighth century A.D. that it began its major florescence. Significant growth in population and construction characterized the centuries from the Terminal Classic period (A.D. 800–1000) until Spanish contact, with the Late Postclassic period (A.D. 1250–1519) witnessing the apogee of Cozumel's development.

Cozumel Island's growth was directly related to the expansion of the Chontal Maya (sometimes called the Putún) from their heartland in the Tabasco-Campeche lowlands near the end of the Classic period. The Chontal apparently were skilled merchants who emphasized waterborne movement of raw materials and finished goods. As many Classic Maya cities in the southern lowlands declined at the end of the eighth century A.D., the Chontal Maya expanded their influence along the western and eastern borders of that region, as well as in the northern lowlands at sites such as Chichén Itzá. Although waterborne trade along the coasts of Yucatán existed well before the Terminal Classic period, the Chontal Maya enhanced and expanded the earlier trading routes, emphasizing a variety of materials including obsidian and, inferentially, cacao, cotton, honey, and salt. In this new mercantile milieu at the close of the Classic period, the Chontal established an important base on Cozumel Island, which was strategically situated to serve as a way station in the circum-peninsular trade routes. The religious importance and sanctity of the shrine of Ix Chel, which featured a talking oracle, may well have complemented Cozumel's mercantile activities by ensuring the safety of pilgrims as they traveled through unfriendly areas en route to the island.

Much of Cozumel Island's visible remains date to the Late Postclassic period, and it is during this time that the island had its economic heyday; its population reached its maximum then, and its settlement its greatest extent. It also is the period when the Chontal Maya reached the pinnacle of their influence in southern Mesoamerica, and Cozumel was closely linked with the major political centers of the time, particularly Mayapan. After the fall of Mayapan in the mid-fifteenth century A.D., Cozumel continued to play a key role in the economic life of the greater Maya area. Hernán Cortés landed on the island in 1519; with the arrival of the Spanish and subsequent destruction of the long-distance trade routes, as well as the huge demographic loss resulting from the introduction of infectious diseases, the population of Cozumel Island rapidly declined. Its economic importance ceased, not to recover until the recent rise of the tourist industry.

John L. Stephens and Frederick Catherwood visited there in 1842, and numerous scholars, including William H. Holmes, Samuel K. Lothrop, Gregory Mason, Angel Fernandez, and Alberto Escalona Ramos, commented on the island's archaeological remains from the late nineteenth century to the mid-twentieth. In 1955, William T. Sanders examined the island through a brief survey and test excavations and was able to establish a ceramic chronology. The Harvard-Arizona archaeological project of 1972–1973, under the direction of Jeremy A. Sabloff and William L. Rathje, tackled the question of the nature of ancient Maya commercial systems and their development by undertaking a systematic survey of Cozumel Island's archaeological resources and mapping and excavating a number of sites. More recently, archaeologists from the Instituto Nacional de Antropología e Historia, such as Fernando Robles Castellanos and Thelma Noemi Sierra Sosa, have continued research on the island, with particular attention to the large site of San Gervasio.

FURTHER READINGS

Freidel, D. A., and J. A. Sabloff. 1984. *Cozumel: Late Maya Settlement Patterns.* Orlando: Academic Press.

Hamblin, N. L. 1984. *Animal Use by the Cozumel Maya.* Tucson: University of Arizona Press.

Robles Castellanos, F. (coord.). 1986. *Informe anual del Proyecto Arqueológico Cozumel: Temporada 1981.* Centro Regional de Yucatán, Instituto Nacional de Antropología e Historia, Cuadernos de Trabajo, 3.

Sabloff, J. A. 1977. Old Myths, New Myths: The Role of Sea Traders in the Development of Ancient Maya Civilization. In E. Benson (ed.), *The Sea in the Pre-Columbian World,* pp. 67–97. Washington, D.C.: Dumbarton Oaks.

Sabloff, J. A., and W. L. Rathje. 1975. The Rise of the Merchant Class among the Ancient Maya. *Scientific American* 233 (4):72–82.

———, ———. 1975. *A Study of Changing Pre-Columbian Commercial Systems: The 1972–1973 Seasons at Cozumel, Mexico, A Preliminary Report.* Peabody Museum of Archaeology and Ethnology Monographs, 3. Cambridge, Mass.: Harvard University.

Sabloff, J. A., W. L. Rathje, D. A. Freidel, J. G. Connor, and P. L. W. Sabloff. 1974. Trade and Power in Postclassic Yucatán: Initial Observations. In N. Hammond (ed.), *Mesoamerican Archaeology,* pp. 397–416. Austin: University of Texas Press.

Sierra Sosa, Thelma Noemi. 1994. *Contribución al estudio de los asentamientos de San Gervasio, Isla de Cozumel.* Seria Arqueología. Mexico City: Instituto Nacional de Antropología e Historia.

Jeremy A. Sabloff

SEE ALSO
Maya Lowlands: North

Crafts and Craft Specialization

Sixteenth-century Spanish documents describe the diversity of craft producers in late pre-Hispanic Central Mexico. Recorded observations, made primarily at the urban core (Tenochtitlán) of the late Aztec state, include vivid descriptions of feather workers, lapidaries, weavers, shell ornament producers, gold and silver workers, painters, and other craft specialists. For a second Central Mexican settlement, the important center of Texcoco, more than thirty kinds of occupational producers were distinguished in the written accounts, with each group of specialists relegated to its own *barrio* or residential district.

Many of the craft specialists described by Fray Bernardino de Sahagún and other early Spanish chroniclers manufactured highly valued goods that were reserved principally for the Aztec ruling families and other elite. Some makers of these finely crafted goods (like feathered attire, metal items, and lapidary ornaments) were directly employed in the palace of the Aztec ruler; other skilled specialists produced goods publicly for exchange at local markets or specifically for long-distance merchants. According to some sixteenth-century accounts, young Aztec women of the nobility were taught to weave in special seminaries annexed to temples. There is, however, little firm evidence for the large-scale mass production of craft goods in industrial workshops, a mode of production that was apparently more prevalent in other ancient states in both the Old (Rome) and New (Andean Inka) worlds. In fact, even though textiles served in Central Mexico as a valuable medium of exchange, many Aztec households spun their own cloth, and most of this fabric was produced in a residential context. In general, Aztec craft specialization was a domestic enterprise, with family members providing the labor force that undertook the manufacturing process from beginning to end.

In Aztec lore, the supernatural figure Quetzalcóatl, who was the patron of the earlier Toltecs (A.D.

C

900–1150), is credited with the invention of a range of luxury crafts. This historical association was so strong that master craftworkers in the sixteenth century were called *tolteca,* regardless of their specific ethnic origin. Archaeological evidence, however, indicates definitively that specialized craft production in stone, marine shell, pottery, and other materials did not originate with the Toltecs. For example, at sites like San José Mogote (Oaxaca), where a considerable number of houses have been excavated, specialization in shell ornament production and magnetite mirror manufacture is evidenced by Early Formative times. By the middle of that period (c. 1100 B.C.), the occupants of certain houses in the community produced shell objects and iron-ore mirrors in quantities much larger than were needed for immediate household consumption, while other households were not associated with these materials or their modification.

The production of shell and magnetite ornaments probably was not carried out full time at Early Formative period San José Mogote. The producers no doubt engaged in other economic pursuits, such as agriculture. Nonetheless, since the quantities of manufactured mirrors and ornaments exceeded household consumption needs, and production of these goods was enacted by skilled craftworkers who resided in only one *barrio* within the larger community, these non-farming activities constitute specialized craft production. The existence of stone-working and other craft specialists in Mesoamerica during the latter part of the Early Formative period is not really surprising when one considers the fabulous carved greenstone celts and other stylized artifacts that were made by Gulf Coast Olmecs and some of their trading partners at this time.

Although the specialized manufacture of certain craft goods has a long history in Mesoamerica, the nature of craftworking was not constant. Rather, the organization and character of craft production shifted along several important dimensions between Early Formative and later Aztec times and also exhibited significant variation across climatic and cultural regions. To examine these issues of temporal and spatial variation, scholars have had to supplement the interpretation of late pre-Hispanic documentary sources with the collection and analysis of archaeological findings. Certain pre-Hispanic crafts, like feather-working, are difficult, if not impossible, to recognize archaeologically; nevertheless, well-executed excavations can provide detailed information on the scale and intensity of other ancient crafts (such as pottery and shell ornament manu-

facture), as well as a perspective on the technologies that were employed in pre-Hispanic times.

Archaeologists use a broad range of factors to identify localities of craft manufacture. These criteria begin with the recognition that anomalous quantities of the crafted material are present. High densities of manufacturing debris, defective pieces, and the byproducts of the production process often are more instructive in this regard than the finished artifacts themselves, which could accumulate at a site for other reasons. At production locations, archaeologists often find tools and features associated with manufacture. For example, kilns or firing pits, molds for fabricating figurines, burnishing pebbles, and turning plates, or *moldes,* have all been recovered at Mesoamerican sites (e.g., Peñitas in Nayarit, Ejutla in Oaxaca) where specialized potters worked. Recently, careful study of micro-artifactual debris (the tiny, even microscopic, chippage and waste that is too small to have been swept away) has proved helpful in defining the specific work surfaces or production locations where craft activities were carried out.

Conceptually, the definition of several key attributes and aspects of economic specialization has also been important in recognizing change in the nature of ancient Mesoamerican craft production. For example, Early Formative period craft production seems largely to have been confined to relatively rare, status-related items (magnetite mirrors, shell ornaments, jade celts) that were sometimes exchanged over hundreds of kilometers. Alternatively, while some Aztec period (A.D. 1150–1520) craft specialists made similar kinds of elite-associated, precious goods, others manufactured basic utilitarian commodities, like ceramic vessels, which generally were consumed close to their place of manufacture. For the Early Formative, there is no indication of the great diversity of specialized economic activities that existed in Aztec period Texcoco or Tenochtitlán.

Another important temporal difference concerns the intensity of craft production—that is, the volume of goods produced and the proportion of work effort devoted to a given craft. In contrast to the specialists of the Early Formative period, many Aztec period craftworkers produced goods in considerable volume and probably were engaged in these activities full time. Nevertheless, the nature of Aztec craft specialization was neither monolithic nor restricted to urban centers. Recent archaeological findings from smaller centers (and even rural settlements) in the Basin of Mexico have shown that late pre-Hispanic craft specialists resided in these areas as well, although they generally may have worked at a lower intensity than their urban counterparts.

Like the production of status-related goods, utilitarian craft manufacture long pre-dates the Toltec period in Mesoamerica. In the Valley of Oaxaca, for example, specialized pottery production is evidenced during the latter half of the Formative period (c. 500–200 B.C.), roughly coincident with the foundation of a regional capital at Monte Albán. In the Maya region, specialized chert tool manufacture is documented at Colhá (Belize) at a roughly similar time during the Late to Terminal Formative period (B.C. 300–250 A.D.). In the Lowland Maya region as well, increasing economic specialization at Colhá corresponded with an episode of demographic expansion and increasing political complexity. For centuries, the occupants of Colhá continued to manufacture various kinds (both utilitarian and more elaborate) of chert objects for exchange, although the specific classes of tools changed through time.

Perhaps the clearest pre-Aztec period evidence for specialized production has been recorded at the Central Mexican urban center of Teotihuacán, where a range of goods, including diverse obsidian items, figurines, ceramic vessels, and shell and gemstone ornaments, were produced by specialists. The volume of production, particularly for obsidian blades, appears to have been great, and these artifacts were distributed across Mesoamerica. Much as in the Aztec period, most of this specialized production that has been firmly provenienced appears to have taken place within the site's apartment compounds (multi-family residential complexes) rather than in non-domestic workshops or factories.

The apparent disjuncture between intensity and scale in the craft production at Teotihuacán and Tenochtitlán would seem to represent a key difference between pre-Hispanic Mesoamerican economic specialization and that found elsewhere. Most general models of craft specialization presume that full-time, high-volume production necessarily occurs outside domestic contexts (in workshops and factories), an association that appears not to hold for much of ancient Mesoamerica. Even up to the present, full-time potters and other craftworkers in parts of Mexico often work in their house lots, a pattern that conforms to the pre-Hispanic findings. Nevertheless, neither the degree of effort (full-time versus part-time activity) nor the specific intensity of manufacture are easy factors to measure archaeologically or to compare across

global regions. At present, scholars cannot entirely reject the possibility that craft specialists in pre-Hispanic Mesoamerica generally produced at somewhat lower intensities than craftworkers in other ancient states. Certainly, Mesoamerican transportation technologies (human bearers or canoes) were more limited and generally less efficient, especially for land transport, than those of many other ancient societies where animal transport and wheeled vehicles were more readily available. The nature of pre-Hispanic Mesoamerican transportation may have placed upper limits on craft production intensity, especially for bulkier goods like pottery.

Archaeologists, with their broad temporal perspective, are often favorably situated to ask about origins or beginnings. Therefore, it is worth considering what conditions or factors may have triggered the advent of specialized production in Mesoamerica. Findings from across the region indicate that the specialized production of status-related goods preceded that for utilitarian items by several centuries (if not longer). Given this temporal disparity, it would seem unwarranted to expect that one factor or even a single set of conditions could explain the beginnings of all aspects of craft specialization.

During the Early Formative period, specialization focused on status-related goods that frequently were associated with personal ornamentation and societal ritual. These goods—like magnetite mirrors, shell ornaments, and jade celts—tended to be highly crafted, and they sometimes were made using non-local raw materials. Often the finished products were imbued with important symbols (such as those of the Olmec Horizon) and exchanged widely. Access to these goods was often limited by status, suggesting that these early specialists produced for (or in some ways were "attached" to) the emergent leaders or chiefs of this period. Although specific causal factors remain difficult to discern with precision, the advent of these early attached specialists appears related to the increasing consolidation of power and to the significance of interregional elite exchange networks (for goods and ideas) in that political process.

In highland Mexico, the specialized production of basic commodities like pottery also appears in conjunction with episodes of political development. In these transitions, however, the population nucleation, agricultural intensification, and reorganization of local exchange systems that frequently accompanied highland Mesoamerican state formation and urbanization seem more significant than long-distance networks. Again, it is not

C

easy to assign causal priority, because archaeologists do not yet know exactly what conditions prompted people to migrate into early urban centers like Teotihuacán and Monte Albán. Still, increasing urbanization had the effect of concentrating potential demand for basic commodities. This consolidation of consumption is important in Mesoamerica, where transportation possibilities were limited. At the same time, urban food demands may have spurred agricultural intensification in the immediate vicinity of those centers. If agrarian households indeed devoted more time and labor to farming, then this would have shifted them away from other production activities (like pottery manufacture), thereby opening up additional demand potential for utilitarian specialists.

In this regard, a comparison between the early urban highland Mesoamerican settlements of Teotihuacán and Monte Albán and roughly contemporaneous Maya Classic period (A.D. 300–900) centers is informative. Specialized manufacture of utilitarian goods is less evident, and was probably less intensive, in the Maya region, where population tended less to be concentrated in densely packed urban centers. At these lower urban densities, high-intensity commodity manufacture may have been somewhat more difficult to support and maintain, although it certainly existed. During the Maya Classic period, economic specialization was more directly associated with highly crafted status goods, such as polychrome ceramic vessels, shell ornaments, and carved stone monuments. This greater emphasis on highly crafted and status-associated goods may also reflect differences in rulership strategies and the principal modes for amassing and consolidating power. In comparison to their contemporaries in Central Mexico and the Oaxaca Highlands, the Maya placed greater emphasis on specific ruling individuals, the elaborate personal adornments of those lords, and their inter-elite gifting and exchange connections.

Soon after their arrival in Mexico, the Spanish chronicled the skill of the indigenous craft specialists, at times marveling at the beauty and diversity of the goods they made. The magnificent products of these artisans are exhibited in museums throughout the world. When we realize that the great majority of these pieces were crafted without metal tools or the true potter's wheel, using raw materials that frequently were transported by human bearers, the magnitude of these artistic and production achievements become even more impressive. Yet the admiration spurred by these craft goods should always inspire us to look beyond the objects themselves and lead

us to ask questions about the people, classes, and societies that were responsible. Although our knowledge of ancient Mesoamerican craft specialization—especially the ways that it was organized across time and space—has grown significantly over the past quarter century, there remains much more for future archaeologists, documentary analysts, art historians, and material scientists to discover and understand.

FURTHER READINGS

Brumfiel, E. M. 1987. Elite and Utilitarian Crafts in the Aztec State. In E. M. Brumfiel and T. K. Earle (eds.), *Specialization, Exchange, and Complex Societies,* pp. 102–118. Cambridge: Cambridge University Press.

Charlton, C. O., T. H. Charlton, and D. L. Nichols. 1993. Aztec Household-Based Craft Production: Archaeological Evidence from the City-State of Otumba, Mexico. In R. S. Santley and K. G. Hirth (eds.), *Prehispanic Domestic Units in Western Mesoamerica: Studies of Household, Compound, and Residence,* pp. 147–171. Boca Raton, Fla.: CRC Press.

Clark, J. E., and W. J. Parry. 1990. Craft Specialization and Cultural Complexity. *Research in Economic Anthropology* 12:289–346.

Costin, C. L. 1991. Craft Specialization: Issues in Defining, Documenting, and Explaining the Organization of Production. In M. B. Schiffer (ed.), *Archaeological Method and Theory,* vol. 3, pp. 1–56. Tucson: University of Arizona Press.

Feinman, G. M. 1986. The Emergence of Specialized Ceramic Production in Formative Oaxaca. *Research in Economic Anthropology,* Supplement 2:347–374.

Feinman, G. M., and L. M. Nicholas. 1993. Shell-Ornament Production in Ejutla: Implications for Highland-Coastal Interaction in Ancient Oaxaca. *Ancient Mesoamerica* 4:103–119.

Feinman, G. M., L. M. Nicholas, and W. D. Middleton. 1993. Craft Activities at the Prehispanic Ejutla Site, Oaxaca, Mexico. *Mexicon* 15:33–41.

Hodge, M. G., and M. E. Smith (eds.). 1994. *Economies and Polities in the Aztec Realm.* Albany: Institute for Mesoamerican Studies, University of Albany.

Marcus, J. 1989. Zapotec Chiefdoms and the Nature of Formative Religions. In R. J. Sharer and D. C. Grove (eds.), *Regional Perspectives on the Olmec,* pp. 148–197. Cambridge: Cambridge University Press.

McAnany, P. A. 1989. Economic Foundations of Prehis-

C

toric Maya Society: Paradigms and Concepts. *Research in Economic Anthropology,* Supplement 4:347–372.

Shafer, H. J., and T. R. Hester. 1991. Lithic Craft Specialization and Product Distribution at the Maya Site of Colhá, Belize. *World Archaeology* 23:79–97.

Stark, B. L. 1985. Archaeological Identification of Pottery Production Locations: Ethnoarchaeological and Archaeological Data in Mesoamerica. In B. A. Nelson (ed.), *Decoding Prehistoric Ceramics,* pp. 158–194. Carbondale: Southern Illinois University Press.

Gary M. Feinman

SEE ALSO
Lapidary Industry

Cuauhnahuac and Teopanzolco (Morelos, Mexico)

A Postclassic urban center in the Morelos region, Cuauhnahuac (modern Cuernavaca) was the capital of a large and powerful polity of the Tlahuica peoples. The city was first founded in the Middle Postclassic (A.D. 1140–1350) with the construction of a large temple pyramid at Teopanzolco—an excellent example of the Aztec twin-stair pyramid style later used in the Templo Mayor of Tenochtitlán. Associated with the Teopanzolco pyramid is a series of low ceremonial platforms, one of which contained the remains of a mass sacrificial burial (numerous severed heads, with pots and other goods).

During the Late Postclassic (A.D. 1350–1520), the city center was moved across a ravine with the construction of a new royal palace. Cuauhnahuac began a program of political expansion, conquering more than twenty Tlahuica city-states to become one of the most powerful states in Central Mexico. This expansion was halted with the conquest of Cuauhnahuac by the Mexica in 1438; the entire area was then incorporated into the Aztec Empire as the tributary province of Cuauhnahuac.

After the Spanish conquest, Cuauhnahuac was renamed "Cuernavaca," and Hernan Cortés built a large residence (the Palacio de Cortés) on top of the Aztec palace. The Cortés residence is now a museum of anthropology, with Aztec ruins visible in the courtyards. Apart from Teopanzolco, little of the Postclassic city remains intact today. Other excavated Postclassic sites in the Cuauhnahuac domain of western Morelos include Coatetelco, Coatlan, Cuexcomate, and Capilco.

FURTHER READINGS
Angulo Villaseñor, J. 1976. Teopanzolco y Cuauhnahuac, Morelos. In R. Piña Chan (ed.), *Los Señoríos y Estados Militaristas,* pp. 183–208. Mexico City: Instituto Nacional de Arqueología e Historia.

Smith, M. E. 1986. The Role of Social Stratification in the Aztec Empire: A View from the Provinces. *American Anthropologist* 88:70–91.

Michael E. Smith

SEE ALSO
Morelos Region

Cuajilotes
See Vega de la Peña and Cuajilotes

Cuayucatepec (Puebla, Mexico)

A Terminal Formative town site in the northern Tehuacán Valley, of the Early Palo Blanco phase (150 B.C.–A.D. 250), with two concentrations of public or ceremonial architecture. One is on the tip of a very steep-sided ridge looming nearly 100 meters above the level valley floor (at about 1,750 meters above sea level) and now consists of mounds defining several small plazas. The second is at the foot of the slope and is centered on a ball court. More than 30 hectares of residential occupation, ranging from sparse to quite dense, covered the ridgetop and spilled down the most gently sloping approach to it. Population was probably somewhat more than a thousand. Although there is no clear evidence of fortifications enclosing much of the occupied area at Cuayucatepec, the principal complex of public architecture on the tip of the ridge was separated from the rest of the settlement by a massive wall blocking the only easy access route along the ridge. Cuayucatepec was one of a half-dozen such towns in the valley in Early Palo Blanco times. All are of similar size and in similar hilltop locations; some have impressive fortifications. The valley at this time seems to have been divided into small independent polities that engaged at least sporadically in hostilities against one another.

FURTHER READINGS
Drennan, R. D. 1979. Excavations at Cuayucatepec (Ts281): A Preliminary Report. In R. D. Drennan (ed.), *Prehistoric Social, Political, and Economic Development in the Area of the Tehuacán Valley: Some Results*

C

of the Palo Blanco Project, Museum of Anthropology, University of Michigan, Technical Reports, 11. Ann Arbor.

Robert D. Drennan

SEE ALSO

Tehuacán Region

Cuello (Orange Walk, Belize)

Formative and Classic Maya site in northern Belize, covering an area of c. 1.6 square kilometers on the crest of the limestone ridge between the Río Hondo and New River. It includes a small ceremonial precinct of two plazas, each with a 9-meter-high pyramid and a series of long range buildings that lack masonry superstructures and date to the Classic period. Archaeological research there between 1975 and 1993, directed by Hammond, included extensive testing of mounds and intermound areas; findings indicated a population peak in the Early Classic estimated at more than three thousand. Most excavation has been carried out in Platform 34, a large (c. 80 meters square, 4 meters high) flat structure 300 meters south of the precinct. About 3,000 square meters of the superficial deposits of the Late Formative period and 300 square meters of the buried Middle Formative layers were dug as open areas, after initial test-pitting in 1975. This work exposed numerous Formative dwellings with low rubble walls, plaster surfacing, and perishable superstructures of which post molds and daub cladding remained. Multiple-screening, flotation, and other aids to data recovery were employed for the first time in the Maya area at Cuello.

Initial calibrated radiocarbon dates from the Cambridge and UCLA laboratories suggested occupation beginning in the late third millennium B.C., but further dates from La Jolla cast doubt on this; the problem was resolved by using human bone collagen from burials, dated by the Oxford AMS system, to link the radiocarbon dates with cultural materials (grave goods) and structural stratigraphy. The revised chronology begins with the Swasey phase (1200–900 B.C.), in which maize agriculture and ceramic technology were already established, followed by the Bladen phase (900–650 B.C.) when further ceramic developments included links to the Xe sphere of the Pasión basin and other lowland regions. Importation of obsidian and jade (including blue jades possibly of Olmec origin) began in Bladen; jade, together with locally worked marine shell jewelry, is found in child burials, suggesting asymmetrical wealth distribution and ascribed rank.

Bladen phase houses (construction periods II–IIIA) used apsidal-ended platforms clustered around a patio about 15 meters across, and were rebuilt and enlarged, with interim renewal of internal plaster floors, at frequent intervals. The overall size of the houses on the south side of the patio increased from 8 × 4 meters to 11.5 × 6 meters between 900 and 600 B.C.; similar though less dramatic enlargement took place on the north and west sides also, where after 600 B.C. rectangular buildings replaced those of apsidal plan during the Lopez Mamom phase (650–400 B.C.). The presence of mutilated burials in (and only in) the western buildings suggests a ritual focus that becomes visible in explicitly non-domestic architectural forms after 400 B.C. Other burials, in the floors of houses, are of both sexes and all ages, suggesting domestic sepulture; grave goods are modest.

Around 400 B.C. the patio group was ritually destroyed: superstructures were burned, substructure walls partly demolished, and the patio infilled with about a meter of limestone rubble. A mass burial in the rubble over the patio center included parts of thirty-two individuals, all (except possibly one) males of young to mature adult age; they may have been captives from another community. Several other burials, including some of decapitated individuals, took place during burial of the patio group by the construction of Platform 34 as a broad, raised open space with a small raised building (Structure 35) at the western end. Through the Cocos Chicanel phase (400 B.C.–A.D. 250), Platform 34 was resurfaced at intervals of about fifty years, with deposition of caches and the interment of another mass burial of twelve males around A.D. 100. The plain Stela 1 was also erected at this date, in front of the first stepped-pyramidal construction phase of Structure 35.

Buildings on the north side of the open area were subcircular in plan and were used as dwellings, with numerous subfloor burials in successive periods of enlargement and structural modification; the south-side buildings were largely destroyed by post-abandonment erosion, but those surviving suggest a similar residential function. The final Structure 35 was built in the Early Classic, c. A.D. 300–400; Platform 34 was then abandoned as a ceremonial focus, with a shift to the new ceremonial precinct of Cuello. Residence continued through the Late Classic, however, and in the Middle Postclassic, c. A.D. 1300, Structure 35 was refurbished and an effigy incensario installed (possibly in a temple) on its top.

The economy of the Formative community has been reconstructed from plant and animal remains recovered by screening and flotation. Maize was present in over 90 percent of samples from early Swasey times onwards, and root crops—including manioc and perhaps malanga (*Xanthosoma*)—were cultivated from Bladen or earlier. A wide range of forest tree crops was exploited. Animal protein came principally from hunting deer, from catching freshwater turtles, and from domesticated dogs, which were systematically killed at about ten months after the initial growth spurt. Dogs scavenged for food in the community and were not fed a special diet. Some freshwater fish were consumed, and in the Cocos Chicanel phase especially, large numbers of the edible snail *Pomacea flagellata,* collected at a perceived optimum size of c. 38 millimeters diameter. The proportion of maize in the diet was lower in the Formative than in the Classic period, and lower at Cuello than in areas farther west, perhaps because of a greater diversity of resources.

Resource procurement from beyond the immediate community included the importation of chert tools and/or raw chert from the Colhá workshop zone 26 kilometers to the southeast, and the utilization of local chalcedony. Sandstone mano and metate grinding stone fragments indicate contact with the Maya Mountains 150 kilometers to the south from early Bladen times onward, although most such domestic equipment was made from the harder varieties of northern Belize limestone. Marine shell from the Caribbean coast 50 kilometers to the northeast and animal bone from local species were worked into tools and ornaments. The earliest jades are of high quality and as yet unknown geological and cultural origin. Apart from decoration on pottery vessels and human figurine fragments, a complex art style does not emerge until after 500 B.C. Among the earliest pieces are a snarling mask made from a disc of human skull and a series of relief-carved bone tubes; several of the tubes bear the interwoven mat, or *pop,* design, which in Classic times denoted rulership, and others have more complex motifs.

Cuello is notable as the earliest Lowland Maya village community currently known (although both Colhá and K'axob in northern Belize have at least a Bladen phase occupation), and for the extensive excavations carried out there, which have documented early Middle Formative through Late Formative Maya material culture and architecture, economy, and ritual behavior. The 166 Formative burials form the largest sample from any Formative Maya site, and document demographic and health patterns over a period of 1,500 years. Numerous similar villages undoubtedly existed across the lowland zone, and these await discovery and exploration.

FURTHER READINGS

Gerhardt, J. C. 1988. *Preclassic Maya Architecture at Cuello, Belize.* British Archaeological Reports, International Series, 464. Oxford.

Hammond, N. (ed.). 1991 *Cuello: An Early Maya Community in Belize.* Cambridge: Cambridge University Press.

Robin, C. 1989. *Preclassic Maya Burials at Cuello, Belize.* British Archaeological Reports, International Series, 480. Oxford.

Norman Hammond

SEE ALSO

Maya Lowlands: South

Cuernavaca

See Cuauhnahuac and Teopanzolco

Cueva Blanca (Oaxaca, Mexico)

This cave, northwest of Mitla in the eastern Valley of Oaxaca, lies in a rocky canyon, almost obscured by thorn forest and scattered oak trees. Excavated by K. Flannery and F. Hole as part of a University of Michigan project, the cave yielded abundant remains from the period of hunting, gathering, and incipient agriculture that preceded village life and pottery-making in Mexico. The lowest level, dating to the Late Ice Age, contained the bones of animals no longer present in the Valley of Oaxaca. Later levels, such as C and D, were dated to 3300–2800 B.C. In Level D, men sat on one part of the cave floor making flint points for the atlatl or spear-thrower, while women sat on another part of the cave floor cutting and shredding agave leaves with flint flakes. Level C may be the remains of a camp made by a small, all-male deer-hunting group who later returned to a larger base camp on the valley floor.

FURTHER READINGS

Flannery K. V., and J. Marcus. 1983. *The Cloud People.* New York. Academic Press.

Marcus, J., and K. V. Flannery. 1996. *Zapotec Civilization.* London: Thames and Hudson.

Kent V. Flannery

SEE ALSO

Oaxaca and Tehuantepec Region

C

Cuicatlán Canyon (Oaxaca, Mexico)

The Cañada de Cuicatlán is a hot, low-lying canyon situated between the higher and cooler valleys of Oaxaca and Tehuacán. Archaeological fieldwork during 1977 and 1978 recovered evidence that the Cañada was conquered by the early Zapotec state toward the end of the Formative period. Just such a conquest had previously been hypothesized on the basis of certain inscriptions at Monte Albán in the Valley of Oaxaca.

A major disruption in settlement pattern occurred in the Cañada between the Perdido phase (600–200 B.C.) and the Lomas phase (200 B.C.–A.D. 200): all the Perdido phase sites were abandoned, and Lomas phase settlements were founded on nearby slopes and ridges. In the Quiotepec area at the Cañada's northern end, a small Perdido phase site was replaced by a 45-hectare complex of seven sites that sprawled across both sides of the natural pass into the Cañada from Tehuacán as well as occupying the strategic mountain peaks. Heavily fortified, the Quiotepec sites were undoubtedly a military frontier installation, designed to control movement through the northern frontier of the Cañada. The Quiotepec installation also marks the northern limit of Lomas phase pottery, some of which is very similar to the pottery of the contemporaneous Monte Albán Ic and II phases in the Valley of Oaxaca. At La Coyotera, a Perdido phase village (known as Llano Perdido) was burned to the ground, and settlement was shifted to an adjacent ridge, where major changes occurred in local economic, social, and politico-religious organization.

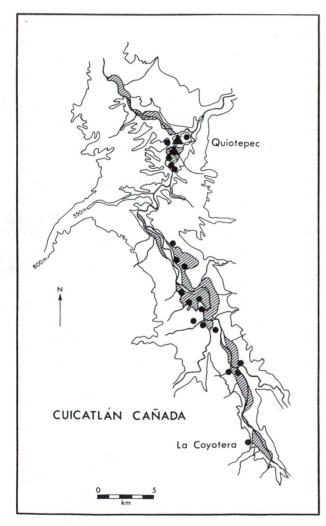

Cuicatlán Canyon Lomas phase regional settlement pattern map, 200 B.C.–A.D. 200. Sites smaller than 5 hectares are indicated by a bullet ●. Sites larger than 5 hectares are indicated by a triangle ▲.

FURTHER READINGS

Marcus, J. 1980. Zapotec Writing. *Scientific American* 242:50–64.

Redmond, E. 1983. *A fuego y sangre: Early Zapotec Imperialism in the Cuicatlán Cañada*. Memoirs of the University of Michigan Museum of Anthropology, 16. Ann Arbor.

Spencer, C. 1982. *The Cuicatlán Cañada and Monte Albán: A Study of Primary State Formation*. New York: Academic Press.

Spencer, C., and E. Redmond. 1997. *Archaeology of the Cañada de Cuicatlán*. Anthropological Papers of the American Museum of Natural History, 80. New York.

Charles S. Spencer and Elsa M. Redmond

SEE ALSO

Coyotera, La; Oaxaca and Tehuantepec Region; Tehuacán Region

Cuicuilco (D.F., Mexico)

During the Late Formative period (300–1 B.C.), Cuicuilco was the largest and most impressive site in the Basin of Mexico; its pyramid was the largest of its time, and its population was perhaps as great as twenty thousand. But in 50 B.C., Cuicuilco's fate was sealed by the eruption of the volcano Xitle, which covered the site with lava flows, some of them 10 meters deep. Cuicuilco's circular stepped pyramid, nearly 20 meters high and more than 110 meters across, was so well disguised by the lava flows that it was recognized as a built feature only in 1922, by Manuel Gamio and Byron Cummings. Excavation and consolidation of the pyramid were followed by other excavations at the site, recovering some settlement remains, but data recovery under these circumstances is extremely difficult.

The site was founded at about the same time as Coapexco, c. 1100 B.C., and it had one of the earliest irrigation systems in the Central Mexican highlands. Cuicuilco grew steadily throughout the Middle Formative period, with construction of the first version of the pyramid begun by 400 B.C. It dominated the Basin of Mexico until its demise, but toward the end of the Late Formative it was beginning to share power with the growing town of Teotihuacan in the northeastern basin.

Cuicuilco's stony entombment within the lava flow is the material relic of ten years of volcanic activity, and it is important to remember that for the survivors, the area directly affected by lava flow (c. 80 square kilometers) represented only a small part of the environmental horror of an exploding mountain right behind the town. Sharing the pan-Mesoamerican belief that the natural environment was infused with spiritual power, the Cuicuilcans must have been demoralized, and Teotihuacan's great growth spurt at this time almost certainly represented Cuicuilcan refugees, who then built the great monuments of Teotihuacan for that city's rulers.

Cuicuilco has been newsworthy recently because this important site is once again becoming engulfed, this time by Mexico City. Efforts to protect the site against encroaching development have resulted in a legal backlash by investors in a shopping mall and car park that have been built near the pyramid.

FURTHER READINGS

Cordova, C., A. L. Martin del Pozzo, and J. L. Camacho. 1994. Palaeolandforms and Volcanic Impact on the Environment of Prehistoric Cuicuilco, Southern Mexico City. *Journal of Archaeological Science* 21:585–596.

Heizer, R. F., and J. Bennyhoff. 1972. Archaeological Investigations at Cuicuilco, Mexico, 1957. *National Geographic Society Research Reports 1955–1960, Projects:* 93–104.

Muller, F. 1990. *La cerámica de Cuicuilco B: Un rescate arqueológico.* Mexico City: Instituto Nacional de Antropología e Historia.

Salazar Peralta, A. M. 1998. Cuicuilco: Public Protection of Mexican Cultural Patrimony in an Archaeological Zone. *Society for American Archaeology* 16(4):30–33.

Susan Toby Evans

SEE ALSO
Basin of Mexico; Formative Period; Teotihuacán

Culiacán

See Guasave and Related Sites; Northwestern Frontier

Cuyamel Caves (Colón, Honduras)

Situated in Cerro Cuyamel near the Aguan Valley in northeastern Honduras, three distinct ossuary caves (Matilde's, H-CN-14; Cuyamel, H-CN-15; Portillo, H-CN-16) had skeletal remains mixed with some stone artifacts (figures, vessels, T-shaped axes), and elaborate ceramic bottles and vases of types dating from the late Early Formative (c. 1200–900 B.C.) or Middle Formative (c. 900–400 B.C.) period. One vase displayed a variant of the Olmec "dragon" or "fire-serpent" motif, and a number of lobed bottles and effigy bottles. Comparison of the forms and decoration of these vessels with examples from Tlatilco in the Basin of Mexico has been used to suggest Honduran participation in widespread Mesoamerican networks during the Formative period, possibly related to cacao production in Honduras. Elsewhere in Formative period Honduras, caves were used for burials from the Copán Valley to Olancho, and Early to Middle Formative ceramics from Cuyamel Caves are similar to early material from Yarumela, Playa de los Muertos, and Gordon's Cave #3 at Copán. No associated occupation sites have been found near Cuyamel Caves.

FURTHER READINGS

Healy, P. F. 1974. The Cuyamel Caves: Preclassic Sites in Northeast Honduras. *American Antiquity* 39:433–437.

———. 1993. Northeastern Honduras. In J. S. Henderson and M. Beaudry-Corbett (eds.), *Pottery of Prehistoric Honduras,* pp. 194–213. Institute of Archaeology, University of California Los Angeles, Monograph 25. Los Angeles.

Joyce, R. 1992. Innovation, Communication and the Archaeological Record: A Reassessment of Middle Formative Honduras. *Journal of the Steward Anthropological Society* 20 (1–2):235–256.

Rosemary Joyce and James Brady

SEE ALSO
Southeast Mesoamerica

D

Dainzú (Oaxaca, Mexico)

Situated in the Tlacolula Valley, this town was founded in the Middle Formative period (during the Rosario phase, 600–400 B.C.) and was occupied until the Early Postclassic (beginning of Monte Albán V period, A.D. 1200). Its population may have been around five thousand in Monte Albán IIIa (A.D. 300–500).

Dainzú flourished during the Monte Albán II period, when it achieved a second-ranking position in the regional hierarchy of the Valley of Oaxaca. During period II, buildings A and B were constructed, and Dainzú shared a similar regional style of carved stone monuments, distinct from that of Monte Albán itself, with neighboring towns such as Abasolo, Macuilxóchitl, Teotitlán, and Tlacochahuaya. Dainzú's important carved stone reliefs depict ballplayers in motion, jaguar figures, and people. The best preserved are those from Building A. Tomb 7 shows a jaguar "lord of the night" carved on the façade. The ball court visible at the site belongs to a later period than the carvings.

Constructed over a hill slope facing west, the site's temples and administrative buildings were grouped around plazas, over a complex system of terraces. Thick layers of stucco covered and protected the walls and floors from water filtration. A well-designed underground drainage system was made using different techniques to protect the buildings from flooding and to collect the rainwater. There are at least six constructive phases, but these are not necessarily related to consecutive chronological phases. Dainzú has been only partially explored. Its residential zone extends to the modern town of Macuilxóchitl.

FURTHER READINGS

Bernal, I. 1968. The Ball Players of Dainzú. *Archaeology* 21:246–251.

———. 1974. *Bajorrelieves en el Museo de Arte Zapoteco de Mitla, Oaxaca.* Corpus Antiquitatum Americanensium, 7. Mexico City: Instituto Nacional de Antropología e Historia.

———. 1976. The Jaguar Façade Tomb at Dainzú. In J. V. S. Megan (ed.), *Essays on Archaeology presented to Stuart Piggott,* pp. 296–300. London.

———. 1981. The Dainzú Preclassic Figurines. In M. Coe et al. (eds.), *The Olmec and Their Neighbors: Essays in Memory of Matthew W. Stirling,* pp. 223–229. Washington, D.C.: Dumbarton Oaks.

Bernal, I., and A. Oliveros. 1988. *Exploraciones arqueológicas en Dainzú, Oaxaca.* Mexico City: Instituto Nacional de Antropología e Historia.

Bernal, I., and A. Seuffert. 1973. *Esculturas asociadas del Valle de Oaxaca.* Corpus Antiquitatum Americanensium, 6. Mexico City: Instituto Nacional de Antropología e Historia.

———, ———. 1979. *The Ball Players of Dainzú.* Graz: Academic Publishers.

Kowalewski, S. A., G. M. Feinman, L. Finsten, R. Blanton, and L. Nicholas (eds.). 1989. *Monte Albán's Hinterland, Part II: Prehispanic Settlement Patterns in Tlacolula, Etla, and Ocotlan, the Valley of Oaxaca, Mexico.* Memoirs of the Museum of Anthropology, University of Michigan, 23. 2 vols. Ann Arbor.

Marcus, J. 1983. Monte Albán II in the Macuilxochitl Area. In K. V. Flannery and J. Marcus (eds.), *The Cloud People: Divergent Evolution of the Zapotec and*

D

Mixtec Civilizations, pp. 113–115. New York: Academic Press.

Ernesto González Licón

SEE ALSO
Oaxaca and Tehuantepec Region

Dating Methods

Archaeologists bring a unique perspective to anthropology and culture history because they focus directly on changes in cultural processes through time. Time, therefore, is a central feature of archaeological research, with two major components: first, the development of regional sequences of time phases arranged in proper order, relative to one another; and second, the estimate of the age, in years, of materials and events, thus linking regional culture histories to calendars presently in use, such as the Gregorian (Christian, Western) calendar. Archaeologists determine the ages of phases, materials, and events through the use of dating methods including stratigraphy, seriation, radiocarbon dating, thermoluminescence, dendrochronology, obsidian hydration, archaeomagnetic dating, and interpretation of ancient calendars (see Table 1). These dating methods pertain either to determining an event or object's age relative to other things ("relative" dating methods) or to estimating its age in years ("chronometric" or "absolute" dating methods). Relative dating methods are not directly linked to a calendar and do not necessarily measure the number of years between events—only their relative positions in time. Chronometric ("time-measuring") methods produce calendar-year estimates. It should be noted that this distinction is blurred in the case of some methods, particularly those under active development, because they can sometimes operate in both capacities: they may serve as a chronometric method where enough is known about local conditions and the nature of the material under study to establish a chronometric estimate, and elsewhere they may help to establish relative chronology.

Archaeologists try to use as many dating methods as are available, routinely cross-checking one dating method against another in order to control empirically for the inherent limitations of each method while selectively capitalizing on their respective advantages. Successful applications depend on the recovery of datable remains, the presence of appropriate materials to analyze, and the general time period under study, as these factors pertain to the research issues.

Relative Dating Methods

These allow archaeologists to reconstruct the order or sequence of events at a site or in a region. Relative dating methods employed by Mesoamerican archaeologists include internal site stratigraphy, and artifact seriation—that is, putting artifacts into a series. Such methods do not indicate the amount of time elapsed between artifact use or discard and the present, nor do they produce a calendar-year estimate of their occurrence. For example, all over Mesoamerica, pottery sherds are found in archaeological sites. Based on their design, sherds in any region can be categorized as to pottery type, and such types will have an established association with one or more periods in a regional chronology that archaeologists have developed out of previous research. The calendar dates of these periods may be unknown, but to the archaeologist working in the region, finding pottery of a particular type will indicate that the remains may pertain to one or more specific periods whose place in the regional chronology is known. Such relative dating enables archaeologists to categorize sites and to make informed decisions about future research strategy. When cross-dated to known chronometric dates, relative dates may be interpreted as generalized calendar-year estimates. Relative dating methods have limits, though: they are not sufficiently time specific to answer many research questions; contexts of source materials may have been subject to mixing and disturbance by burrowing animals, tree roots, and later human occupants; and sequences may be difficult to extrapolate to other sites or regions.

Stratigraphy. The study of the strata, or layers, of an archaeological site provides a fairly clear record of the site's history. An archaeological site is established when people do something—sharpen a spear point, build a house—at a particular site, leaving some evidence of that activity. If cultural activity persists and increases, the site may become large and complex, encompassing many layers of cultural and natural deposits. Based on this depositional history, an archaeological cross-section can be drawn and interpreted in which a vertical soil profile is mapped, showing a plan view of the strata with their spatial and chronological relationships. Artifacts within each stratum can be ordered in time, and changes in artifact form and function through time analyzed. It is important to keep in mind, however, that the depositional sequence found in an archaeological site may have been subject to human, animal, or physical disturbances that could alter the relative positions of some strata.

In the 1970s Edward C. Harris produced a new technique, referred to as a "Harris Matrix," which schematically depicts stratigraphic relationships in archaeological sites. The Harris Matrix combines four laws of deposition (superposition, stratigraphical succession, original horizontality, and original continuity) into a schematic chart, allowing archaeologists to assess the various stratigraphic relationships within a site in greater detail than allowed by cross-section profiles or plan maps. The Harris Matrix has refined the use of stratigraphy as a means of relative dating, and it has allowed greater assessment of the potential disturbances that could negatively influence chronological reconstructions based on it. The application and further refinement of the Harris Matrix by N. Hammond, employing data from several Maya sites in Belize, has clearly demonstrated the utility of this approach to stratigraphic interpretation in Mesoamerica, where it should quickly become a standard technique.

Artifact Seriation. Seriation is a relative dating technique that orders artifact attributes into a relative time series based on frequency changes in either stylistic or functional attributes. This technique is based on the analogue of contemporary artifacts such as cars and clothing, which can be placed into approximate chronological order based on knowledge of their stylistic or functional attributes. When the relative frequencies of these particular attribute variants are diagrammed by time phase or archaeological stratum, their frequency is generally low to begin with, at the time the variant is introduced; the frequency becomes higher as popularity increases, and then declines and becomes low as popularity dies. The changing frequency pattern—thin on the oldest and youngest edges and fat in the middle—is known as a "double-lenticular" or "battleship-shaped" curve. Such frequency patterns may be linked to chronometric dates to determine the general time period spanned by each. Once an attribute sequence is established, it can be used as a reference during excavation to determine the approximate time period of the deposit, if combined with stratigraphic information. Nearly any artifact type can be employed for seriation studies, and many Mesoamerican artifact types have been seriated, including architecture, sculpture, figurines, ground stone, spindle whorls, and textiles, in addition to the more common traditional pottery and lithics.

Chronometric (or Absolute) Dating Methods

Chronometric dating methods produce an age estimate in years, with an associated error factor depending on the method and material under analysis. These methods are sometimes called "absolute" to contrast them with the "relative" methods, but most chronologists find this term inaccurate and misleading because it does not imply the error range around each age estimation. Many chronometric dating methods can be employed as relative methods when key data are unavailable, or when links to the calendar system cannot be determined.

Chronometric dating methods began with the development of dendrochronology (tree-ring dating; see below) in the 1920s. Their continued development and refinement profoundly influenced the field of archaeology because, in providing an age estimate in years, they allow archaeologists to compare sites and regions against the standard measurement of a calendar system. Chronometric dating methods are limited in that appropriate materials for analysis are not found at all sites, nor in contexts preferred for dating. A second limiting factor is expense, which often limits the number of dates that can be obtained. Chronometric dating methods include dendrochronology, radiocarbon, archaeomagnetic, thermoluminescent, and obsidian hydration dating, as well as interpretation of indigenous calendrical inscriptions.

Dendrochronology, or Tree-Ring Dating. Dendrochronology is the cross-dating of wood samples, based on comparison of patterns of variations of width in their annual growth rings. Some tree species, when exposed to annual environmental variation in rainfall, frost severity, and/or temperature, will grow slower or faster in a given year, so that over successive years a discernible sequence of tree-rings of distinctive widths occurs, which can be linked to a particular time period of growth. This regularity was recognized as having potential for archaeological dating by A. E. Douglass, who later developed dendrochronology as a means of dating archaeological features in the southwestern United States. The use of dendrochronology depends on the establishment of a master sequence of tree-ring patterns for a particular tree species within a region. Once established, the master sequence can be used by archaeologists to date additional wood samples through a comparison of the sequence of tree-rings in any wood sample with the established master chronology.

Dendrochronology is significantly more complex in application than in theory. If a wood sample lacks the tree's outermost ring of sapwood, then the date the tree was felled cannot be determined, and hence the date of the use of the wood may post-date the sample's sequence

TABLE 1. DATING METHODS EMPLOYED IN MESOAMERICA.

Dating Method	Type	Source Materials	Minimum Sample Size	Age Range	Limitations	Advantages
Stratigraphy	Relative	Soil and architecture layers	NA	All time periods	1) Physical or human disturbances 2) Missing or removed strata 3) Generalized time phasing only 4) Hard to extrapolate to other regions or sites	1) Can give feedback in the field 2) When combined with other methods yields great site-specific detail 3) Cost effective 4) Widely accepted
Artifact Seriation	Relative or chronometric	Ceramics—Pottery Figurines Spindle whorls Lithics—Obsidian Chart Flint Ground stone Architecture Sculpture Textiles	NA	All time periods	1) Generalized time phasing 2) Disturbance or mixed deposits make it difficult 3) Hard to extrapolate to other regions	1) Can give feedback in the field 2) When combined with other methods yields site specific detailed chronology 3) Cost effective 4) Widely accepted
Dendrochronology	Relative or chronometric—depending on gaps in the sequence	Wood	Depends on preservation	Depends on the master sequence reconstructed, so varies greatly from one region to another. Longest existing sequence is about 3,000 years	1) Lack of sap wood 2) Need to construct regional sequences 3) Limited to well-preserved, large wood samples 4) No sequence for Meso exists	1) Cost effective 2) Quick—once established 3) High level of accuracy 4) Widely accepted
Radiocarbon	Chronometric	Wood or charcoal Shell Bone Organic/soil mixed	25 grams 100 grams 300 grams 100–200 grams	Present to 50,000 years—can be pushed to 100,000 with large samples and specialized equipment	1) Sample sizes 2) Sample contamination 3) Cost—between $250 to $500 per date 4) Unknown variables of half-life determination and ^{14}C world distributions	1) Can be conducted on a wide range of materials 2) Acceptance of method 3) Relative accuracy
Archaeomagnetism	Chronometric	In situ burned clay features	5 to 7 1–2" squares of in situ material	Currently A.D. 1–1170 in Mesoamerica	1) Need to construct regional magnetic shift chronology 2) Limited source material 3) Need specialist to remove sample in the field 4) Occasional overlaps in master chronology so that more than one date is possible	1) Cost effective 2) High level of accuracy 3) Dates in situ features so no association problems

Dating Method	Type	Source Materials	Minimum Sample Size	Age Range	Limitations	Advantages
Thermo-luminescence	Chronometric or relative if lacking environmental controls	Fired clay or glass with ESR—unfired bone or shell	NA	Theoretically all time periods	1) Control over environmental variables requires extensive work to produce a regional TL rate 2) Different clay sources have different TL rates 3) Not widely accepted yet	1) Cost effective once established 2) Source materials are abundant at most sites 3) Has great potential if refined
Obsidian Hydration	Chronometric or relative under some environmental conditions	Obsidian artifacts	NA	500 to 250,000 years ago depending on the obsidian source and environmental conditions	1) Obsidian source must be determined 2) Regional or site-specific environmental conditions of EHT, PH, and RH must be determined 3) Deposit contents must be relatively uniform in environmental conditions 4) Not widely accepted	1) Cost effective 2) Can produce a large body of dates quickly if conditions are right 3) Source material common and abundant
Calendrical Inscriptions	Chronometric or relative	Inscriptions on wood, stone, plaster	NA	Long count A.D. 1–900 Short count A.D. 1200–1600	1) Determination of correlations 2) Limited number of inscriptions, generally in elite contexts 3) Problems of interpretation and association	1) Accepted 2) When present are accurate 3) When associated with written systems are invaluable in understanding chronology of political events

D

by an undetermined number of years. Because of this problem, most dendrochronology dates have an associated error range when employed for archaeological purposes, because uncertainties exist related to the wood artifact's preservation and condition.

Unfortunately, master chronologies of tree-rings can be developed only where environmental conditions produce noticeable fluctuations in tree-ring width, and where tree species with long lifespans exist in relative abundance. The southwestern United States and Europe are the two areas of the world where long master tree-ring chronologies have been established. In Mesoamerica, dendrochronology studies conducted in West Mexico in the 1960s by Scott and Wolfman produced encouraging results, and Jacoby has begun investigations in Guatemala into the use of tropical tree species for dendrochronology. Related work on frost-damaged tree-rings by LaMarche and Hischboeck offers a potential means of determining the date of major volcanic events in Mesoamerica with great accuracy. Much more research on dendrochronology, however, is needed to determine whether this dating method can be successfully or commonly employed in Mesoamerica.

Radiocarbon Dating. In 1960 the Nobel Prize for Chemistry was given to W. F. Libby for developing the use of a radioactive isotope of carbon for age determinations in many scientific disciplines, including geology, archaeology, and geophysics. Rarely has a single development in chemistry had such an impact on so many other scientific disciplines. Today the application of radiocarbon (^{14}C) dating to address issues of archaeological chronology remains one of the revolutionary advances in the field.

Radiocarbon dating measures residual amounts of carbon in long-dead organisms to determine the time elapsed since death. Compounds containing carbon are distributed and cycled through the environment on Earth. Living organisms naturally absorb carbon during their lives, in three isotopic forms: the isotopes ^{12}C and ^{13}C are stable, while ^{14}C is unstable or radioactive, decaying at a half-life rate of about 5735 ± 45 years. At death the organism's metabolic processes cease, and the amount of ^{14}C in its tissues starts to decay at the isotope's half-life rate. The radiocarbon age determination of a sample measures residual ^{14}C content and compares it to the natural levels of atmospheric ^{14}C.

Radiocarbon dating assumes that the half-life of ^{14}C has been correctly determined, that there is complete worldwide mixing of atmospheric ^{14}C, and that the atmospheric level of ^{14}C has remained stable through time and is accurately known. The practical limitations of ^{14}C dating (small archaeological sample sizes, sample contamination) have started to be addressed with the most recent introduction of accelerator mass spectrometer (AMS) dates, which can be run accurately on extremely small samples. Currently, the maximum range for this dating technique is between 40,000 and 50,000 years ago.

Archaeomagnetic Dating. The magnetic field surrounding the Earth shifts horizontally (the declination angle) and vertically (the dip angle) through time, altering the location of Earth's magnetic north. These shifts have been recorded in historic documents for more than two hundred years and their presence is well established. Iron particles, such as those occurring in clay soils, will naturally align to magnetic north—the operating principle behind the compass. When clay with iron particles is heated above a critical temperature, referred to as the "Curie point," the particles will reorient to magnetic north. When the clay is cooled, the iron particles retain that new orientation until reheated above the Curie point. Archaeological features such as hearths or baked clay floors can be dated by determining the declination and dip angles to which the iron particles last aligned and comparing them to a master magnetic north shift chart that maps the changes in magnetic north orientation through time for a specific region of the world.

Archaeomagnetic dating has become a very successful technique, but it has specific requirements. The master magnetic field shifts through time must be established for each region separately because they are a function of the location of the sample in respect to magnetic north. Thus, the master sequence for Japan is different from that for Mesoamerica because of their differing geographic orientations toward magnetic north. Furthermore, a fired clay sample must be in the original position in which it was heated; thus, only *in situ* fired clay features can be used as source material for archaeomagnetic dates. Fired clay vessels, figurines, and other clay artifacts, unless found in the position in which they were fired, cannot be employed because their alignment to magnetic north is no longer in context.

More than two hundred archaeomagnetic samples from Mesoamerica have been collected and measured by Daniel Wolfman since 1968. Based on these, a master curve for Mesoamerica from A.D. 1 to 1170 has been developed. In addition, a short section of the curve for the middle and early part of the Formative has been reconstructed. When additional key samples become available to bridge this gap in the current Mesoamerican archaeo-magnetic curve, a continuous curve from 900 B.C. to A.D. 1170 could quickly be established, producing an extremely powerful dating technique for Mesoamerican archaeologists.

Thermoluminescent Dating. Thermoluminescent (TL) dating is conduced by rapidly heating a sample of pottery, brick, tile, terracotta, or glass to between 400° and 500°C, depending on the material, and recording its weak but measurable emission of light. With a second heating of the same sample, the light emission is only thermal radiation. The difference in the amount of light measured between the two heatings is the thermoluminescent light from minerals in the pottery: the nuclear radiation emitted by radioactive impurities (potassium-40, thorium, and uranium) in the pottery and the soil it was buried in. Because these isotopes have extremely long half-lives (10^9 years or longer) this radiation is estimated as constant. Thus, the amount of TL observed is proportional to the amount of time that has elapsed since the pottery, or glass, was first fired. Heating the artifact for firing removes all previous TL, effectively resetting the sample at "zero." By measuring both the sensitivity of the sample for absorbing TL (through exposure to a calibrated radioisotope source) and the radioactive content of the sample and its surrounding soil matrix, it is possible to calculate an age of the artifact.

While simple in theory, practical complications of application are the necessity for site- and region-specific thermoluminescence rates, and the destruction of the sample in order to date it, making replication of the measurement difficult to obtain unless large samples are available. A new application of thermoluminescence is currently being developed for organic materials such as unburnt bone and shell artifacts. Electron spin resonance (ESR) gives a spectrum of the microwave power adsorbed by the samples as a strong magnetic field placed around the sample varies, thus measuring the trapped electrons in the sample. The advantages of ESR are that it does not destroy the sample and can be conducted on organic samples. However, it currently is much less accurate than TL, since its minimum detectable dose is significantly higher.

Attempts at TL dating in Mesoamerica began in the 1970s, but because of the many practical limitations of the technique, it has not yet been widely employed. It remains very promising, however, because pottery is one of the most common artifact types found in Mesoamerica, and a dependable technique that could quickly and cheaply date ceramic artifacts would be invaluable.

Obsidian Hydration Dating. Newly exposed surfaces of obsidian (a volcanic glass) adsorb water molecules, resulting in both a density increase and mechanical strain along the edges. This "hydration rim" or "rind" that forms on the exposed surfaces is visible in cross-section under a microscope's cross-polarized light source because it has different refractive properties than the nonhydrated obsidian interior. Considerable research has been devoted to understanding this chemical process and its application to archaeological materials because it can cost-effectively produce chronometric dates from obsidian artifacts, a source material present at most Mesoamerican sites.

Because obsidian hydration is a chemical process, physical environmental variables affect the rate at which it occurs. The factors that affect the rate of hydration in obsidian are divided into "primary" and "secondary" variables. Primary variables are those directly affecting the rate of the hydration process: the chemical composition or source of each obsidian artifact, the temperature conditions (effective hydration temperature or EHT) under which hydration occurred, and variations in site relative humidity (RH) and soil pH. Secondary hydration variables can also affect hydration rim width, and thus affect the age estimate, but they do not directly affect the rate of the hydration process itself. These variables include the spalling off of thick hydration rims as a result of mechanical strain, the exposure of an obsidian surface to burning, fire, or very high temperatures, the long-term weathering or erosion of a hydration rim after its formation, and artifact reutilization or modification. The successful application of hydration dating depends on a clear understanding of all these variables, along with extremely detailed information about soil chemistry and obsidian sourcing, which frequently is not available.

Obsidian hydration dating has many advantages: dates can be produced rapidly, at low cost, and consequently it has the potential to provide large bodies of chronological information. If a research project can afford to analyze five hundred obsidian hydration samples rather then five radiocarbon samples, at the same price, many more research questions can be addressed, using statistical approaches that are not applicable to smaller data sets.

Interpreting Indigenous Calendrical Inscriptions

Several pre-Hispanic Mesoamerican cultures developed their own means of calendrical notation, and this allows archaeologists to date features, artifacts, or architecture associated with inscribed dates. Calendrical systems based on rotating 52-year cycles, known as the short count

D

calendar, were in widespread use throughout Mesoamerica by the sixteenth century A.D. Such calendrical inscriptions have given archaeologists working in the Basin of Mexico and Oaxaca the data necessary to reconstruct master relative chronologies of sequences of events, which can be linked to events related to the period of European contact, recorded in both the short count and European Gregorian calendrical systems.

Classic Maya civilization operated under a different calendar system known as the long count, which had a fixed starting point about five thousand years ago and was commonly used between A.D. 1 and 900. However, the long count was no longer in use at the time of European contact, so no direct correlation with the Gregorian calendar system exists. Three correlations between the Maya long count and the Gregorian calendar system have been proposed: the Goodman-Martinez-Thompson (GMT), Spinden (about 260 years earlier than GMT), and Vaillant (260 years earlier than Spinden) correlations. These correlations were tested using radiocarbon dates from wooden lintels with associated long count inscriptions from the site of Tikal. The radiocarbon dates strongly supported the GMT long count correlation, which had fixed its starting point at 3113 B.C. The GMT correlation is the one accepted by most Mesoamerican scholars today, but debate over the correlation still arises and is likely to continue.

These calendrical systems have added greatly to Mesoamerican chronological reconstructions, and when associated with a true writing system, such as that of the Maya, they have allowed epigraphers and archaeologists to reconstruct dynastic sequences and their associated political events. Using these calendrical systems also has limitations: they can be misinterpreted when they lack direct association with text or behavioral context, they may intentionally misrepresent historical events, and they tend to be associated with only the elite segments of societies. Despite their limitations, the presence of these calendrical systems in Mesoamerica has added greatly to regional chronological reconstructions.

FURTHER READINGS

Aitken, M. J. 1985. *Thermoluminescence Dating*. London: Academic Press.

Baillie, M. G. L. 1982. *Tree-Ring Dating and Archaeology*. Chicago: University of Chicago Press.

Eighmy, J. L., and R. S. Sternberg (eds.). 1990. *Archaeomagnetic Dating*. Tucson: University of Arizona Press.

Friedman, I., and R. L. Smith. 1960. A New Method Using Obsidian Dating, Part I. *American Antiquity* 25:476–522.

Freter, A. C. 1993. Obsidian-Hydration Dating: Its Past, Present and Future Application in Mesoamerica. *Ancient Mesoamerica* 4:285–303.

Hammond, N. 1991. Matrices and Maya Archaeology. *Journal of Field Archaeology* 18:29–41.

Harris, E. C. 1989. *Principles of Archaeological Stratigraphy*. London: Academic Press.

Proskouriakoff, T. 1950. *A Study of Classic Maya Sculpture*. Carnegie Insitution of Washington Publication 593. Washington, D.C.

Taylor, R. E. 1987. *Radiocarbon Dating: An Archaeological Perspective*. London: Academic Press.

Ann Corinne Freter

SEE ALSO

Archaeology: Analytical Methods; Calendrics

Demographic Trends

The demographic characteristics of a human population and its dynamic trends are defined as the processes of fertility, mortality, and migration followed through time. Interest in demographic analyses in anthropology and archaeology has become prominent only since the 1960s, but the appearance of demographic anthropology and demographic archaeology was logical because of the mutual influence of demographic characteristics and culture. For archaeologists, demography is important in a number of ways. It is of theoretical interest because of its probable role in cultural development. It is crucial to the reconstruction of the past because both the characteristics of a population of a site or region and the trends of size and density through time are basic to the description of a past culture and to understanding culture history and culture change. The use of demographic methods to characterize demographic processes and to determine the vital rates of past populations from skeletal samples is called "paleodemography"; it is a distinct branch of demographic anthropology. Through paleodemography it is possible to investigate dynamic population processes that help to explain the florescence and decline of past cultures and to reconstruct their composition by age and sex. The study of demographic characteristics and trends has advanced archaeological methodology, theory, and practice in Mesoamerica.

Demography includes two major areas. The first is the population description or census: the actual enumeration of people at some point in time to determine a population's size, density, and actual composition by age, sex, and various other characteristics that may be measured in response to policy and research interests at a particular time. The second is vital statistics, the rates of mortality, fertility, marriage, and migration that affect census characteristics and explain changes in populations through time. Demographic archaeology does not have the kinds of sources and sample sizes available to demographers studying modern populations; instead, it depends on indirect indicators of population characteristics derived from small samples. Archaeologists study structures, artifacts, and other findings to determine population size, density, and census trends through time, while the human skeletons from archaeological excavations are studied by bioarchaeologists to determine population composition and some vital statistics. The research of both specialists is needed properly to characterize past demographic trends.

It is important to do this for two important theoretical reasons: first, to discover how demography has been involved in long-term cultural changes, such as the pattern in human history of increasing organizational complexity from small mobile societies to industrialized nation-states; and second, to understand the demographic characteristics typical of human populations in the past and how these affected the history and culture of a particular region or site. Ancient Mexico and Central America are important examples of regions with a clear trend toward increasingly complex cultures, and of places where demographic characteristics have affected cultural change and traits.

Demographic processes are often invoked as a prime cause of cultural change. The economist Ester Boserup argued that population increase is an independent factor fueling technological innovation for intensification of agriculture because the society feels pressure to provide ever more food. With more intensive subsistence techniques and more people, there are concomitant increases in the size of the economy and in socio-cultural complexity. This idea of population pressure as the prime mover in cultural evolution was attractive to many anthropologists and was used in several models to explain the rise of agriculture and the appearance of complex societies. For example, a recent model proposed by Johnson and Earle is dependent on population growth and pressure: as population increases, subsistence is intensified, which creates opportunities for economic control that ultimately leads

to inequality and social stratification—the complex societies of chiefdoms and states. Such a process can explain the transformation of societies from small groups of mobile foragers with a few hundred people completely dependent on wild resources, as in the Tehuacán Valley of the Archaic period, to complex agrarian states encompassing tens of thousands of people, such as Teotihuacán or Tikal, or even the millions controlled by the Aztec Empire.

In spite of their general utility in cultural evolution theory—because increasing population is a clear trend in the process wherever it occurs—population-pressure models have been strongly criticized. Several legitimate objections can be raised to such models. The most important is the difficulty of defining or quantifying population pressure. It is not caused merely by large population numbers or a high rate of population growth; rather, it is some function of density (people per unit of space) in relation to valuable resources. Proponents of population-pressure models have slightly varying definitions, but all incorporate some form of this function. Hassan has proposed that because human populations are well below the theoretical maximum that could be supported within their territories, given their subsistence technology, population must feel stress or pressure long before that theoretical threshold. Population pressure arises from the scarcity and limits of the resources utilized and valued by a culture; these limits vary according to ecological, cultural, and historical factors—hence the problems of definition. Pressure must be felt and reacted to by the people of a society for a population-pressure model to work, and no objective yardstick will be applicable to every situation. The experience of pressure will be pervasive in societies undergoing cultural change, but hard to measure. Proponents are comfortable with this vagueness, but critics never will be.

Population pressure as a prime cause of cultural evolution has also been criticized for the assumption that human populations tend to grow and do not regulate themselves; for depending on stress to lead to innovation and intensification, when it may in fact lead to conflict and disarray; and for oversimplifying the role of demography in culture change. All these criticisms have validity, but both proponents and critics often ignore two points about the rise of cultural complexity: it does not happen in all cases; and it is most evident in long regional archaeological sequences, not at individual sites. Those regions whose component cultures have become more complex and have encompassed larger populations over time are of particular theoretical interest.

D

As such a region, Mesoamerica has been central to this theoretical debate. Some researchers have found population to be a prime cause of cultural developments here, and others have found population growth and increasing density to be merely outcomes of other culture-change processes. Since increasing population size and density is a trend in this region, it seems logical that it was growing populations who were able to intensify economic activity, support more people, and integrate them into more complex social organizations; however, this debate will continually be tested in specific archaeological research.

The demographic trends that archaeologists often study are population size, density, migration, and growth or decline. Demographic estimation requires a determination both of the spatial extent of a past culture and of its settlement system through time. The number, size, and contemporaneity of settlements and their component residential units provide the basic data. Obviously, more complete settlement surveys and fine-grained chronological control provide better indicators of the size of a society at any point in time. A variety of techniques have been suggested for transforming the size of sites into numbers of inhabitants, using such data as site volume, amount of artifacts, roofed-over space, and food remains. A review of methods for determining population size in archaeology is given by Cook.

However, archaeologists must often use ethnographic analogies with living populations to determine realistic patterns for past populations. Some examples are the average number of inhabitants in various types of dwellings, or likely growth rates for populations practicing various types of agriculture. Archaeologists must take care to ensure the demographic characteristics they have postulated for the past are within the likely biological parameters of human populations as determined in the ethnographic present. Unbelievably high rates of population growth or excessively large family sizes reduce the credibility of estimates of past demographic trends.

One example of how archaeologists determine population size is provided by approaches to estimating Late Classic Maya population from various centers, as demonstrated in Culbert and Rice's compilation of case studies. Population can be calculated on the basis of survey samples of mounds, the platforms on which houses were built. Excavation is then used to determine the average number of nonresidential mounds, the presence of hidden or nonplatform residences, and the chronology of various house mounds to determine how many are likely to have been in use at one time. The archaeologist then must adjust the mound count by subtracting the percentage of nonresidential mounds and a percentage representing disused mounds, and adding a percentage for nonplatform residences, if present. This mound count is then multiplied by an average family size, usually determined from ethnohistorical or ethnographic sources; for the Maya, this is usually between four and six individuals per family. This gives an estimate of population for the sampled area. Differences are usually seen between rural areas and more nucleated settlement around centers, so the proportion of each type of settlement in a site should be determined. The resulting mound count is then multiplied by the whole site area to give a population estimate for a center during the Late Classic. From this, population density per square kilometer can also be calculated, especially to highlight the differences between center and rural areas.

Human skeletons recovered from archaeological excavations are another potential source of demographic information. They can provide data on vital events, such as fertility and mortality, and on population composition by age and sex. Before any demographic conclusions can be made about a past population, its skeletal sample needs to meet several criteria. First it should be a representative sample containing both sexes and all ages that were present among the living. This criterion is made difficult by past cultures' burial practices, by archaeological recovery techniques, and by the preservation environment of a site. A society may not have treated all its dead the same way, so variables of age, sex, or cause of death may mean that some individuals cannot be recovered archaeologically. Moreover, some archaeological techniques are not fine-grained enough to recover the small bones of babies and young children or incomplete, fragmentary remains of skeletons of any age. Archaeological excavation may not sample all areas of a cemetery or site equally, so there may be bias in the types of skeletons recovered. The soil may be chemically unsuited to the long-term preservation of skeletons, so that they are either absent or very fragmentary. All these problems will cause a skeletal sample to be biased and to underrepresent either the numbers of skeletons that were originally in a site or some age and sex component of the living population.

A second criterion is whether the skeletal sample can be treated as a valid biological population—a group of individuals who interact and interbreed. The shorter the period in which burials accumulated and the closer they are spatially clustered, the more likely it is that the sample is a valid population. Only such populations can provide accurate information on vital rates. In practice, however, paleodemographers often use skeletal populations accumulated over several hundred years and from several sites if there is clear evidence of cultural continuity over that time.

The demographic information depends on determining the age at death and sex of an individual skeleton as precisely as possible. Such information can be difficult to assess accurately because of poor preservation. Children under age fifteen usually cannot be sexed, and older adults are hard to age to within five or ten years because skeletal aging processes are so variable.

Even if a skeletal sample does meet the above criteria, it still represents only a representative distribution of the ages at which individuals died, and such a distribution has a complex relationship with the living population that produced it. It is affected by both mortality and fertility. Paleodemography depends on known characteristics of human populations to interpret a skeletal sample. For example, mortality rates—the proportion of individuals dying at age x out of all individuals age x—vary throughout the human lifespan: high at birth and infancy, often slowly declining through childhood to a low in early adolescence, and then rising slowly through the adult years until older ages, where it rises more steeply until the end of the lifespan. High-mortality populations tend to have more deaths during childhood and infancy, while low-mortality populations have more deaths during older adult ages. Fertility is measured only for females and is usually summed by the total fertility rate, the average number of children ever born to a woman during her reproductive years of age fifteen to fifty. High-fertility populations have more than six children per woman, while moderate fertility is from four to six children. The modern industrialized nations' pattern of low fertility and low mortality is a very recent historical development. For most of human history, moderate to high fertility has been coupled with moderate to high mortality in ways that are affected by cultural patterns, social organization, and ecological circumstances.

The main insight of paleodemography is that the proportion of individuals dying at any age in a skeletal sample is the result of both the mortality rate at that age and the number of living individuals in that cohort, which in turn is a result of the fertility of the population. Thus, it is difficult for paleodemography to determine fertility and mortality rates for the past. The easiest situation is that of a stationary population—one that is neither growing or declining—because then the actual proportion of deaths represents the mortality rates at various ages, and the reci-

procal of the mean age at death is the crude fertility rate, a measure of how many individuals are born per year per 100 persons in a population. Stationary populations are then easily compared as to their fertility rates and mortality rates at various ages, especially during infancy and childhood.

Most populations are not stationary, however, and there is reason to expect that for Mesoamerica growing and declining populations were the rule, as complex societies and civilizations flourished and disappeared. Paradoxically, relative fertility rates are easier to determine than mortality rates, because the former can be derived from the proportion of juvenile skeletons to adult ones. Thus, a proportion of over 50 percent juvenile skeletons in a sample is likely to indicate high fertility. Populations with validly determined smaller proportions of juveniles probably had moderate fertility rates. If fertility is high, children form an increasing proportion of the living population, and the absolute numbers of children dying will increase without any change in mortality rate; high-fertility populations thus have a majority of deaths during childhood. A trend through time of increasing numbers of juvenile burials would indicate that total fertility was increasing. The alternative explanation, increasing mortality rates during childhood, can be supported only if archaeologists can estimate the rate of population growth or decline for the society. If population growth is small or the population is declining, then a high proportion of juvenile deaths probably also indicates higher mortality during the vulnerable infant and childhood years.

Paleodemographic estimation techniques have been applied to the city of Teotihuacán (Mexico), and Storey's work on this subject can be consulted for further details on the problems and interpretations of skeletal samples for paleodemographic reconstruction. Unfortunately, paleodemographic techniques are only beginning to be applied to skeletal samples from Mesoamerica, so trends in fertility and mortality rates through time are poorly known. However, based on other anthropological populations, some predictions as to trends can be hazarded at this point.

In general, the evolution from foraging to incipient agriculture to intensive agriculture changes the fertility of a society from moderate to high and increases the mortality of juveniles. Fertility also tends to be high in societies that are growing quickly, whatever their mode of subsistence.

The initial Paleoindian colonization may have been characterized by high fertility and moderate mortality,

D

because there was ample territory in which to expand and there should have been ample resources to support the population. By Archaic times, however, there may have been more of a balance between fertility and mortality, as populations adapted to their various, more limited environments. With incipient agriculture, there would again have been more opportunity for populations to grow quickly, because more individuals could now be supported per unit of land. Thus, these societies may have had high fertility and moderate mortality, although preliminary results from Tlatilco, an early agricultural hamlet in the Basin of Mexico, indicate moderate fertility with moderate mortality. With the development of intensive agriculture and the rise of large, complex societies, mortality probably became high, and so populations had moderate to high fertility. As long as fertility was higher than mortality, the society grew; when mortality was higher, the society declined. The rise and fall of civilizations varied as their conditions of life affected the balance of fertility and mortality rates.

As a result of more than thirty years of settlement surveys, the Mesoamerican region overall can be characterized as showing increasing population size and ever larger settlements with increasing density through time. With the arrival of Europeans in the sixteenth century, the population of Mexico and Central America (and indeed the whole hemisphere) in general experienced a dramatic decline that continued for two hundred years. However, this overall trend during prehistoric times masks a great variety in local population history. For example, to use two prominent case studies, the Basin of Mexico and the Maya Lowlands have quite different population trends.

The Basin of Mexico in general had a pattern of increasing population growth, with only temporary declines, ranging from 0.1 percent per year to 0.7 percent per year from 1500 B.C. to Spanish contact at A.D. 1519. Thus, this is an area of fairly sustained long-term population growth that included several urban centers and an overall increase in population density from a few hundred people in the entire basin to about 200 people per square kilometer at Spanish contact.

In contrast, the Petén region of the Maya Lowlands had a period of sustained growth and a time of decline, followed by a period of approximately five hundred years (up to European contact) when there was little population in the area: the population density at 300 B.C. is estimated at 14.6 people per square kilometer, and at 4.1 per square kilometer in A.D. 1500. During the Classic period, from A.D. 300 to 800, this region witnessed a dramatic increase in population size and density associated with the Classic Maya civilization, in which the area probably supported two or three million people at its height. At the end of the Classic period, the civilization "collapsed" and the population virtually disappeared.

Demographic trends are an important adjunct to the study of the past. In Mesoamerica, they are important in studying cultural change and in the reconstruction of individual cultures and civilizations. The study of the dynamic processes of fertility and mortality is just beginning for the region but holds promise for understanding how demographic patterns and cultural practices were interrelated.

FURTHER READINGS

Boserup, E. 1965. *The Conditions of Agricultural Growth.* Chicago: Aldine.

Cook, S. F. 1973. *Prehistoric Demography.* Addison-Wesley Modules in Anthropology, 16. Reading, Mass.: Addison-Wesley.

Culbert, T. P., and D. S. Rice. 1990. *Precolumbian Population History in the Maya Lowlands.* Albuquerque: University of New Mexico.

Hassan, F. A. 1981. *Demographic Archaeology.* New York: Academic Press.

Johnson, A., and T. Earle. 1987. *The Evolution of Human Society: From Forager Group to Agrarian State.* Stanford: Stanford University Press.

Paine, R. R. (ed.). 1997. *Integrating Archaeological Demography: Multidisciplinary Approaches to Prehistoric Population.* Center for Archaeological Investigations, Occasional Paper 24. Carbondale: Southern Illinois University.

Sanders, W. T., J. R. Parsons, and R. S. Santley. 1979. *The Basin of Mexico: Ecological Processes in the Evolution of a Civilization.* New York: Academic Press.

Storey. R. 1992. *Life and Death in the Ancient City of Teotihuacan.* Tuscaloosa: University of Alabama Press.

Whitmore, T. M. 1992. *Disease and Death in Early Colonial Mexico: Simulating Amerindian Depopulation.* Dellplain Latin American Studies, 28. Boulder: Westview Press.

Rebecca Storey

SEE ALSO

Disease, Illness, and Curing; Settlement Patterns and Settlement Systems

Díaz del Castillo, Bernal (1496–1584)

One of the first Europeans to see the Aztec capital, Tenochtitlán, Bernal Díaz del Castillo recalled: "Gazing on such wonderful sights, we did not know what to say, or whether what appeared before us was real, for . . . on the land, there were great cities, and in the lake ever so many more . . . and in front of us stood the city of Mexico" (1984:192). As a soldier with Cortés, he took part in a profoundly important historical event—the Spanish conquest of the Aztec Empire. His extensive, vividly narrated account, *The True Story of the Conquest of New Spain,* is undoubtedly one of the most important Mesoamerican ethnohistoric documents, the best known and most complete eyewitness description of Mexico at the time of Contact.

Born in Spain, Díaz joined military expeditions to Cuba, Yucatán, and, in 1519, Tenochtitlán. In his later years he was determined to write the "true history" of the conquest, believing that soldiers like him had received little in return for the essential role they had played. Díaz took issue with the writings of other chroniclers, particularly Cortés's adulatory Spanish biographer, López de Gómara, whose polished account credited Cortés with the victory.

FURTHER READINGS

Cerwin, H. 1963. *Bernal Díaz: Historian of the Conquest.* Norman: University of Oklahoma Press.

Díaz del Castillo, B. 1963. *The Conquest of New Spain.* Baltimore: Penguin.

———. 1984 [1632]. *The Discovery and Conquest of Mexico 1517–1521.* A. P. Maudslay (trans.). New York: Farrar, Straus, and Giroux.

Mary Glowacki

Diet and Nutrition

Before the establishment of agrarian societies, foraging was the key food procurement strategy in Mesoamerica. In the Paleoindian period, until about 7000 B.C., small seminomadic bands lived in Mesoamerica. Their diet consisted of wild plants and wild game, including insects, eggs, snails, shellfish, rodents, reptiles, and amphibians, which they obtained by fishing, scavenging, and opportunistic killing. Archaeological remains of Paleoindians are rare, and so we have little direct evidence of their diets.

The Archaic period (c. 7000–2000 B.C.) is also poorly represented in terms of archaeological evidence. Subsistence adaptations were slowly changing as the climate altered from drier and cooler toward the modern pattern. Animal and plant distributions changed as well. Hunting became focused on smaller game as large animals such as the mammoth and horse became extinct. Although the subsistence pattern of foraging remained essentially the same, new food sources replaced old ones as the ecological structure shifted.

Many food plants important to Archaic peoples underwent initial morphological changes toward becoming domesticated crops during this period. In the final millennium of the Archaic, domesticated plants in western Mesoamerica included maize *(Zea mays),* beans, squashes, and chile peppers. Changes in stone tools indicate increasing reliance on plants. The predominant pattern was one of mobile bands making seasonal rounds of food resources. Remains of shell mounds in occupations along the Pacific Coast indicate the importance of estuary-lagoon resources in some regions. Marsh clams, fish, shrimp, turtles, iguanas, snakes, amphibians, birds, deer, and raccoons were eaten, along with plants. Thus, strategies for food procurement varied considerably with ecological circumstances during the Archaic.

The first known Formative (2000 B.C.–A.D. 250) peoples had a mixed farming and foraging economy. Local subsistence practices varied, with maize, beans, avocados, and other domesticated plants as part of the diet but not yet staples. Coastal populations depended on marine foods and plants, while inland sedentary communities relied on mixed farming and foraging or, in the highlands of Central Mexico, on seasonal rounds on a seminomadic basis.

By 1500 B.C., however, sedentary farming constituted a way of life in most of Mesoamerica, and maize was becoming the staple food. Our best archaeological information comes from the Classic period (A.D. 250–900) and later. Mesoamericans became reliant primarily on cultivated maize and secondarily on hunting, wild plant gathering, and fishing. Since they had few domesticated animals, they supplemented their protein requirements with dog *(Canis familiaris),* white-tailed deer *(Odocoileus virginianus)* and brocket deer *(Mazama americana),* collared peccary *(Tayassu tajacu nelsoni, T. t. yucatanensis,* and *T. t. nigrescens)* and white-lipped peccary *(Tayassu pecari* and *Dicotyles labiatus),* tapir *(Tapirus bairdi),* agouti *(Dasyprocta* spp.), rabbit *(Sylvilagus* spp.), and monkeys *(Alouatta villosa* and *Ateles geofroyi);* dwellers along lakes, rivers, and coasts added various fish and shellfish. Food plants of Neotropical origin include the grains amaranth *(Amaranthus hypochondriacus, A. cruentus);* stimulants

D

such as pulque (from *Agave salmiana*), monkey chocolate (*Theobroma angustifolium*), and cacao *(T. cacao)*; vegetable species of the family Curcurbitaceae (squashes and chayotes), such as *Cucurbita argyrosperma, C. moschata, C. pepo, C. ficifolia, Sechium edule*, and *S. tacaco;* tomato *(Lycopersicon esculentum)*; and tomatillo *(Physalis philadelphica)*. Legumes (beans) included *Phaseolus vulgaris, P. coccineus, P. polyanthus*, and *P. acutifolius*. Fruit trees included anona blanca (*Annona diversifolia*), custard apple (*A. reticulata*), soursop (*A. muricata*), white sapote (*Casimiroa edulis),* zapote or mamey (*Calocarpum sapota),* papaya (*Carica papaya),* avocado (*Persea americana),* and ramón (*Brosimum alicastrum).* Spices native to Mesoamerica include chile peppers (*Capsicum annuum* and *C. frutescens*) and vanilla *(Vanilla planifolia).*

Although they had access to a considerable variety of foods, maize was, in most of Mesoamerica, either the preferred food or the only one that was reliable and regularly available. Debate about the nutritional status of maize staple diets continues. Studies of modern peasant populations furnish evidence that maize-based diets, similar in composition to diets inferred for the ancient Mesoamericans, are deficient in niacin and riboflavin. Plant proteins are often deficient in some amino acids or have amino acid ratios inappropriate for human protein synthesis. The rate and level of protein synthesis is determined by the least abundant amino acid; an inadequate quantity of one amino acid is regarded as limiting because the remaining essential amino acids (i.e., those that the human body is incapable of building) will be metabolized at a level regulated by the amino acid present in the least amount. An imbalance can lead to protein synthesis stoppage and thus has detrimental health consequences.

Maize-based diets have increasingly been associated with physiological stress because maize is deficient in certain essential amino acids. The protein quality of maize is limited by a shortage of lysine and tryptophan, and an excess of leucine. The process in which maize kernels are soaked and then cooked with lime or wood ashes results in a lime-treated maize product the Aztecs called *nixtamal.* Lime liberates the vitamin niacin from an indigestible complex, which helps consumers avoid the deficiency disease pellagra. Nixtamalization aids in removal of the pericarp and the kernel becomes easier to grind. *Nixtamal* or alkaline-treated maize has an enhanced nutritional quality owing to the increased bioavailability of niacin and an improved amino acid balance, which increases protein quality.

The addition of legumes to a maize-based diet also improves protein quality. A 3:7 ratio of beans to maize provides the best protein complement by balancing the amino acid components. However, such a diet remains inadequate in quality for children because it is deficient in methionine and lysine and low in total protein content. Methionine is the limiting amino acid in diets containing a higher proportion of beans, while lysine is the limiting amino acid in diets having a greater proportion of maize. Nutrient quality improves with the addition of meat or green leafy vegetables.

Although early Mesoamerican diets may have been fundamentally adequate, caloric and animal protein intake may have been low. Observations from human skeletons reveal that iron deficiency anemia was a common affliction, particularly during Classic times. Iron deficiency anemia is often considered a product of diets high in maize and carbohydrates, but deficient in iron or copper. Individuals with poor-quality diets tend to suffer, in childhood, iron deficiency anemia brought on by infection or parasites. Iron is absorbed most efficiently from meat, and variably, although in general poorly, from plants. Some plant substances, such as phytates, can inhibit iron absorption, while ascorbic, citric, and lactic acids can promote iron bioavailability. Inferences from skeletal indicators of anemia, coupled with bone chemical studies, support a model of a maize-based diet poor in protein quality for many people of the Classic period. However, regional variability in resources led to regional variability in nutritional status.

FURTHER READINGS

Anderson, R. K., J. Calvo, G. Serrano, and G. C. Payne. 1946. A Study of the Nutritional Status and Food Habits of Otomí Indians in the Mezquital Valley of Mexico. *American Journal of Public Health and the Nation's Health* 36:883–903.

Callen, E. O. 1965. Food Habits of Some Pre-Columbian Mexican Indians. *Economic Botany* 19:335–343.

Cook, S. F., and W. Borah. 1979. Indian Food Production and Consumption in Central Mexico before and after the Conquest. In their *Essays in Population History: Mexico and California,* pp. 129–176. Berkeley: University of California Press.

Ebeling, W. 1986. *Handbook of Indian Foods and Fibers of Arid America.* Berkeley: University of California Press.

Etkin, N. L. (ed.). 1986. *Plants in Indigenous Medicine and Diet.* Bedford Hills: Redgrave.

Hassig, R. 1986. Famine and Scarcity in the Valley of Mexico. *Research in Economic Anthropology,* Supplement 2, pp. 303–317. Greenwich, Conn.: JAI Press.

Vargas, L. A., and L. E. Casillas. 1992. Diet and Food-ways in Mexico City. *Ecology of Food and Nutrition* 5:235–247.

Woot-Tsuen, W. L., and M. Flores. 1961. *Food Composition Table for Use in Latin America*. Bethesda, Md., and Guatemala City: Interdepartmental Committee on Nutrition for National Defense and Institute of Nutrition of Central America and Panama.

David M. Reed

SEE ALSO
Demographic Trends

Disease, Illness, and Curing

Pre-Columbian Mesoamerica was relatively free of disease in comparison with contemporaneous populations in the Old World. The original human migration across the Bering Strait, during the Ice Age, served as a "cold filter" because the long passage at low temperatures destroyed infectious disease pathogens and their insect vectors and prevented their transmission to the New World. In addition, the scarcity of domesticated animals in the New World diminished the number of possible zoonotic infections and parasites, which were a major source of disease in the Old World. Finally, dense urbanization in Mesoamerica occurred only a thousand years before the Spanish conquest; the large populations of three to five hundred thousand that are required to maintain "herd diseases" such as measles and smallpox in an endemic state had not existed for very long. The net result was that the inhabitants of Mesoamerica were spared the large variety of infectious and parasitic diseases that periodically devastated Europe, Asia, and Africa. This immunological innocence would have tragic consequences after the arrival of the Spanish.

Nutrition is an important factor in the ability of a population to resist disease. Although the shift to agriculture from hunting and gathering decreased the variety and quantity of food available, Mesoamericans had an adequate diet, high in fiber and low in fat. This diet, combined with a good amount of exercise, resulted in a low incidence of chronic diseases such as cancer and heart disease. The high birthrates and high infant mortality rates of Mesoamerican populations led to an overall short life expectancy—for the Aztecs, about thirty-seven years. This low life expectancy also decreased the significance of chronic diseases, which occur primarily in older people.

Public health and prevention are additional factors in

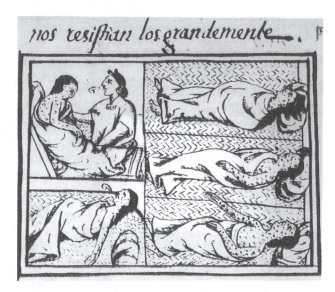

Smallpox was one of the major epidemics to strike Mesoamerica in the early sixteenth century. Illustration courtesy of the author.

determining the prevalence of disease. In this respect, Mesoamerica again compared favorably with contemporaneous Europe. The conquerors noted the frequency with which both Aztecs and Mayas bathed, in sharp contrast to prevailing European notions of hygiene; shampoos, deodorants, and dentifrices are mentioned frequently in Aztec herbals. Drainage systems were found in cities from the central highlands (Teotihuacán, Tula) to the Maya Lowlands. In Tenochtitlán, urine and excrement were collected and disposed of, and clean potable water was provided by an aqueduct.

Listed below are the diseases known to have been present before European contact:

Infectious diseases
    dysentery (bacterial and amoebic)
    viral influenza and pneumonia
    various viral fevers
    protozoan leishmaniasis
    bacterial pathogens such as *Streptococcus* and *Staphylococcus*
    non-venereal syphilis and pinta
    Salmonella and other food poisoning agents
    tuberculosis

Degenerative diseases
    various types of arthritis

Parasitic diseases
  roundworms, especially ascarids
  American trypanosomiasis, such as Chagas's disease

The diseases are not listed in order of prevalence; however, the humid tropical areas would enhance the survival and transmission of parasites, while the lacustrine people of the high central plateau would have had a greater incidence of gastrointestinal and respiratory ailments because of water pollution and dampness. Rheumatism was common, and arthritic lesions are almost universal in skeletons of individuals older than thirty-five. Dysentery and diarrhea were the major causes of death among children. Accidents, warfare, and respiratory infections were the major causes of death among adults.

There is controversy concerning several diseases. Some scholars claim that yellow fever existed among the tropical Maya but not among the inhabitants of the central highlands, like the Aztecs; the consensus, however, is that yellow fever was introduced from Africa after the conquest. Similarly, malaria seems to have been a late introduction into the New World, although there are intriguing hints of its possible pre-Columbian existence. The presence of syphilis is much more controversial and has not been definitely settled. The sudden appearance in Europe of a virulent venereal form of syphilis shortly after the discovery of the New World led to a claim that syphilis began in the New World; however, treponematosis (infection with spirochetes of the type that cause syphilis) is a single but extremely flexible disease that manifests itself in various ways. Yaws, pinta, non-venereal syphilis, and venereal syphilis are examples of forms it may take, depending on the environment and culture of the host. One of the most plausible interpretations is that a non-venereal treponemal infection was transformed into a venereal disease after its spread in Europe.

The arrival of the Spanish in Mesoamerica produced a demographic disaster for the natives. Estimates of the native population of Central Mexico in 1519, on the eve of the Conquest, range from six to twenty-five million, but eleven million is the most reasonable figure. By 1600, this population had decreased by 75 to 80 percent. Although forced labor and decreased nutrition were contributing factors, the primary cause of the population loss was the introduction of various forms of infectious disease. Diseases like measles, which had become endemic childhood diseases in Europe as children exposed to the pathogen developed lifetime immunity, had devastating

consequences for adults in immunologically naive populations. Table 1 lists the major epidemics in Mesoamerica after the arrival of the Spanish. The mortality in the first exposure of the natives to these diseases was in the range of 80 to 95 percent. The smallpox epidemic of 1520, which began through an infected African brought by Pánfilo de Narváez, had important political consequences. The epidemic struck while Cortés was besieging the Aztec capital of Tenochtitlán. The epidemic decimated the Aztec defenders, including the *tlatoani* (ruler), Cuitlahuac, who had succeeded Motecuhzoma II; it contributed greatly to the fall of Tenochtitlán. This epidemic spread to Guatemala and actually preceded the Spanish arrival there in 1523. Native medicine had no remedies for these infectious diseases, and treatments often made things worse. Measles, smallpox, and plague were considered to be "hot" diseases and were treated by bathing in cold water, which often led to pneumonia and even higher mortality.

A discussion of Mesoamerican medicine must begin with their religious thought and practices. Although beliefs varied and emphasis on one aspect or the other shifted, a basic unity of fundamental religious belief flourished in Mesoamerica, with roots in the distant past. There were local variations in worldview, just as there were epidemiological differences based on ecological variations. There is very little information about pre-

TABLE 1. MAJOR EPIDEMICS IN MESOAMERICA.

Years	Disease	Aztec Name
1520	smallpox	*hueyzahuatl*
1531–1532	measles	*tepitonzahuatl*
1545–1548	plague	*hueycocoliztli*
1550	mumps	*quechpotzahualiztli*
1562–1564	measles, whooping cough	*tepitonzahuatl, tlatlacistli*
1576–1581	plague, typhus	*hueycocoliztli, matlatzahuatl*
1590	whooping cough	*tlatlacistli*
1592–1593	measles, whooping cough	*tepitonzahuatl, tlatlacistli*
1595–1597	measles, mumps	*tepitonzahuatl, quechpotzahualiztli*

Columbian and early colonial medical practices for most Mesoamerican groups. The best and most abundant information deals with the Aztecs, so most of the following examples come from them. Nevertheless, the Aztecs are only the last chapter of a long cultural book and summarize a wide-ranging cultural tradition, both temporally and spatially. Because of this synthesis, it is possible to generalize from them to the rest of Mesoamerica.

Mesoamericans believed illnesses were caused by a wide variety of natural and supernatural causes; religion, magic, and morality were closely interwoven. Even if we separate causes of illness for heuristic purposes, pre-Columbians believed illness to be multicausal—the result of divine, magical, and natural forces. Diseases were believed to have both proximate and ultimate causes. *Yolpatzmiquiliztli,* an epileptic fit, was ultimately caused by the rain god, Tláloc, but the proximate cause could be either possession by one of the god's helpers or a rapid accumulation of phlegm in the chest.

The Aztecs believed that the structure and function of the human body paralleled and was linked to those of the universe. Consequently, astronomical events could affect the body; humans had the duty of preserving the existence of the universe by performing rituals such as human sacrifice. The three levels of their universe were homologous to the human body: *ilhuicatl* (sky) corresponded to the head and the animistic force *tonalli, tlalticpac* (earth) corresponded to the heart and the force *teyolia,* and the underworld corresponded to the liver and the force *ihiyotl.* A cosmic duality was another key organizing principle. The cosmos was divided into two great parts that created its organization and functions. These parts were paired, simultaneously opposed and complementary, and led to a number of relationships—hot/cold, father/mother, dry/wet, and fire/water. This classification scheme extended to diseases and their remedies.

The connection between the universe (including the supernatural) and the human body had consequences. The basic rules for maintaining health were equilibrium, moderation, and doing your duty (both to the deities and in the world). States of health and illness were related to equilibrium and disequilibrium, respectively. Social control was accomplished by holding the body hostage and punishing deviations with illness. A unique aspect of this balance was that this social control did not require the intervention of either human or supernatural beings: the properties and characteristics of animistic forces automatically produced illness in those who violated the rules. For

example, too much work and fatigue created disequilibrium and illness owing to the overheating of the *tonalli.*

Mesoamericans believed in the existence of several animistic forces ("souls") in humans, each with a specific function in the body's growth, development, physiology, and even fate after death. The pre-Columbian existence of this concept can be seen in documentary sources that show these forces leaving a corpse—for example, Codex Laud, 21D.

Tonalli (*wayjel* for the Tzotzil Maya) was the force that gave vitality and growth and, from the moment of birth, constituted a link to the gods and the universe. *Tonalli* was primarily located in the head. The word *tonalli* derives from the root *tona* (solar heat, irradiation, fate, astrological sign, soul). *Tonalli* was infused into a fetus before birth; it gave the baby particular propensities linked to the calendrical birth sign. For example, those born in the Aztec day 6 Dog or the Maya day *cauac* would be very susceptible to illness.

The amount of *tonalli* in a person determined his or her health and vitality. Besides the differences due to birth dates, men, old people, and nobles had more *tonalli* than women, young people, and commoners, respectively. *Tonalli* was a limited quantity, particularly among men. Engaging in sex prematurely or excessively diminished a man's *tonalli,* made him sick, and could even cause his death. On the other hand, *tonalli* could be increased by successful performance of official duties. *Tonalli* could leave the body either normally, in sleep or during intercourse, or abnormally, because of a frightful experience or through capture by a supernatural being. If a person's *tonalli* was not restored, the person would sicken and die. Loss of *tonalli* by fear is still widely found in present-day Mesoamerica as the folk syndrome *susto* ("fright"). Small children were particularly susceptible to soul loss because their open fontanelles allowed *tonalli* to escape, so special precautions were taken, such as not cutting the hair over the fontanelle. This illness corresponds to the modern *caida de mollera* ("fallen fontanelle"), although modern etiology is a purely mechanical sinking of the palate.

Teyolia ("that which gives life to the people," *ch'ulel* among the Tzotzil) was the animistic force that resided in the heart. *Teyolia* did not leave the body until death, and was the "soul" that went to the afterlife. It imparted vitality, knowledge, and intelligence to people because the heart was the center of thought, personality, and mental activity. *Teyolia* was also infused by the gods into the fetus before birth. The heart could be harmed by being crushed by phlegm or by immoral conduct. This connection can

D

be seen in the term used to describe the confession used to cure a type of sexual disease: *neyolmelahualiztli,* "the act of straightening out hearts."

Ihiyotl ("breath, respiration") was concentrated in the liver. It provided vigor, passion, and feelings such as anger or envy. Ordinarily, only shamans could release *ihiyotl;* however, sexual transgressions such as adultery or homosexuality would damage the liver, causing the sinner to release *ihiyotl.* Interestingly, this *ihiyotl* did not harm the sinner but functioned as a harmful miasma that produced a group of diseases called *tlazolmiquiliztli* ("filth death"): it affected children, who woke up screaming and sick; it produced incurable adult diseases, seizures in infants, or a consumptive weight loss. The close connection between physical illness and sexual transgression is shown in the word *cocoxqui,* which not only meant "sick" and "weak" but also "homosexual." A similar use of illness as method of social control was shown by the requirement among Maya healers that patients had to confess their sins before they could be treated.

Disease could be caused by deities, but because of the complementary/duality principle, gods could also cure disease. Some diseases were seen as divine punishment for human violations of taboos, for failure to observe ritual fasts or sexual abstinence, for sins, or for failure to perform one's duties. Plate 17b of the Maya Dresden Codex shows the lunar goddess Ix Chel bringing a sort of buzzard representing skin diseases to the world. The associated hieroglyph is *koch* ("sin, punishment"). Often the diseases produced were associated with characteristics of the particular god: Xipe-Totec ("Our Lord the Flayed One"), the god of spring and the renewal of the skin of the earth, produced diseases on the skin; rain gods like Tláloc or Itzamná produced diseases associated with water or cold.

The *mictecah,* human *teyolia* that had gone to Mictlan, the place of death, were messengers from the Aztec underworld. These messengers took the form of certain animals—owl, horned owl, weasel, spider, centipede, scorpion, and chafer—and were messengers of sickness and death. Maya names of diseases were often associated with animals, for example, "jaguar-macaw-seizure," "tarantula-eruption," "wasp-seizure," and "wind-of-the-purple-parrot." The exact etiological meaning of these terms is not clear because they were used in shamanic incantations that employed esoteric language.

The same deities that caused diseases also cured them. The cures for these diseases involved confession of sins, rituals, and efforts to propitiate the gods. People who had

TABLE 2. DISEASES ASSOCIATED WITH GODS.

Aztec

Xipe Totec	pimples, inflammation, eye diseases
Xochipilli	hemorrhoids
Tláloc	rheumatism, dropsy, leprosy, gout
Tezcatlipoca	epidemics
Chalchiuhtlicue	death by lightning
Atlatonan	leprosy, birth defects

Maya

Itzamná, Chacs	chills, asthma, respiratory ailments
Ix Chel	pustule diseases *(kak),* seizures, spasms *(tancaz)*
Chac-Mumul-Ain	ulcers
Ahav Xik ("Lord Hawk") and Patan ("Snare")	death on road, vomiting blood
Ahal Puh ("Pus Maker")	pus, inflammation
Ahal Zana ("Bile Maker")	jaundice

been afflicted with skin and eye diseases would make pledges to Xipe Totec that, if cured, they would participate in the ceremonies dedicated to him in the month of Tlacaxipehualiztli by wearing for several days the flayed skins of people sacrificed to Xipe. Hills and volcanoes were believed to be inhabited by and to incarnate water deities, members of the Tláloc complex. In the month of Tepeilhuitl, people who were afflicted by ailments attributed to these gods, or those who feared death by drowning, would perform a number of rituals. They would go to the hills and fashion anthropomorphic representations of the hills and volcanoes from amaranth dough. These images would be honored during four nights. On the fifth night, the images would be decapitated and the amaranth dough would be taken to the temple. Simultaneously, mock snakes made from gnarled tree branches covered with amaranth dough would be ritually "killed" and the dough would be distributed to the lame, the paralytic, and those suffering from pustules.

Certain gods were associated with particular medicines: Ixtlilton with "black water," used to cure children, and Tzapotlatenan with a salve called *axin* (made from an insect, *Coccus axin*). A group of goddesses (Toci, Tlazolteotl, and Ixcuina) were patrons of the health professions, particularly midwives.

Disease was also caused and cured by magic. Magic can be categorized as sympathetic magic (the magical effect is mirrored in reality) and contact magic (objects continue to produce effects at a distance or after a time). Magical disease causation and cure could also involve sorcerers and witches. Table 3 lists some categories of these practitioners. Sorcerers were predestined by their *tonalli,* and were born on days 1 Wind, and 1 Rain, which made these days propitious for casting spells. Apart from specific illnesses listed in Table 3, sorcerers (generically called "owl men") could produce illness by sending spells that would lodge in the body of the victim. Other sorcerers could cure the illnesses by sucking out the spells in the shape of small bones or pieces of obsidian.

Excellent examples of imitative magic are present in pregnancy taboos. Pregnant women were forbidden to eat tamales that had stuck to the pot lest the baby stick to the uterus; they should not chew gum lest their babies be born with swollen lips, unable to suckle; and they should not burn corncobs lest the baby be born pockmarked.

Magical diseases could be cured by a variety of mechanisms. The first step was to determine whether a particular illness was due to magic, divine intervention, or natural causes, and to obtain a prognosis. Divination procedures included casting corn kernels on the ground or into bowls of water, tying and untying knots, and counting the number of the diviner's handspans measured on the patient's forearm. Magical illnesses could be avoided by adhering to prohibitions such as those mentioned for pregnant women. Cures also involved the use of sympathetic and contact magic. People who had been frightened by lightning, which caused epilepsy, were anointed with sap from a tree struck by lightning. A number of plants, regardless of their chemical components, were clearly intended as agents of sympathetic magic: *yolloxochitl (Talauma mexicana),* a heart medicine, had heart-shaped flowers; *cocoztamal* ("yellow tamal"), which had a thick yellow root, was used as diuretic; and *tzotzoca xihuitl (Euphorbia helioscopa),* whose leaves were full of growths, was used as a treatment for warts.

Symbolic healing was a critical component in curing magical diseases. There was high regard in Mesoamerica for the power of language. Believers in magic believe that words, in themselves, have power. All types of cures (magical, supernatural, and natural) were accompanied by elaborate incantations using complex esoteric language *(nahuallatolli).* In fact, a number of magical or supernatural illnesses may have been cured by the placebo effect elicited by the procedures, incantations, and confidence in the healer. Even effective empirical cures could be enhanced by incantations referring to origin myths: bone fractures were treated by setting the bone, wrapping with a plaster made with *poztecpatli* ("fracture medicine"), and putting on a splint; the accompanying incantation referred to the myth in which Quetzalcóatl went to Mictlan to retrieve the bones, broken accidentally, which were used to create the first humans.

A number of conditions were considered to be natural in origin and were treated empirically. Treatment of bone injuries was possibly the most advanced aspect of Aztec surgery. Traction and countertraction were used to reduce fractures and sprains, and complications such as swelling around the break were treated. Intramedullar nails, not used in Western medicine until the twentieth century, were employed to consolidate bone callus. Snake and insect bites were treated by cutting the site, sucking out the poison, and rubbing ground-up tobacco on the wound. Plastic surgery was performed to repair harelips and lacerated lips by making clean cuts with an obsidian scalpel, suturing, and applying honey to promote healing and prevent infection.

Constant warfare provided much practice in treating wounds. The procedure was superior to contemporaneous European treatment and is still valid today. Wounds were washed with fresh urine, a sterile fluid, and bleeding was treated with the plant *matlaliztic (Commelina pallida).* The wound was dressed with concentrated agave sap

Table 3. Mesoamerican Sorcerers.

Aztec

teyolloquani	"produces insanity by eating hearts"
tecotzcuani	"he who eats people's calves"
tetlepanquetzqui	"he who prepares fire for people"
tlacatecolotl	"owl man"

Maya

ah pul a bick kik	"sorcerer caused blood in urine"
ah pul kazab	"sorcerer makes blood stop"
ah pul nach bach	"sorcerer produces pneumonia"
ajitz	"witch"

D

to which salt had been added. This type of dressing has been shown to kill bacteria commonly found in wounds and to heal effectively even septic and infected wounds in modern hospitals.

Two common natural etiologies involved diseases produced by phlegm or by the hot/cold dichotomy. Some diseases were considered to be "hot" or "cold," and remedies would involve the use of plants or materials with the opposite properties. Gout, a "cold" disease, was treated with either tobacco or *axin,* both of which were classified as "hot." Phlegm in the chest could produce a number of effects: fever (because it was hot), and madness or epilepsy (by damaging or crushing the heart). In both cases, the appropriate remedy would be to remove phlegm from the body with an emetic, a diaphoretic, a purgative, or a diuretic. Some 70 percent of all identifiable fever remedies used by the Aztecs could produce one of these effects. Table 4 lists a sample of medicinal plants used by the Aztecs. A study of a much larger sample showed that 85 percent would produce the effect desired according to Aztec etiology, and that 60 percent were effective to some degree by Western standards. Mesoamericans were acute observers of nature.

FURTHER READINGS

López Austin, A. 1988. *Human Body and Ideology.* B. R. Ortiz de Montellano and T. Ortiz de Montellano (trans.). 2 vols. Salt Lake City: University of Utah Press.

Orellana, S. 1987. *Indian Medicine in Highland Guatemala.* Albuquerque: University of New Mexico Press.

Ortiz de Montellano, B. 1990. *Aztec Medicine, Health, and Nutrition.* New Brunswick: Rutgers University Press.

Roys, R. L. 1976 [1931]. *The Ethno-botany of the Maya.* Philadelphia: Institute for the Study of Human Issues.

Bernard R. Ortiz de Montellano

SEE ALSO

Demographic Trends; Diet and Nutrition; Divination; Sweat Baths

Divination

Inquiry about obscure past, present, or future events through attention to omens and other signs sent by a supernormal power, god, or spirit was an essential element of Mesoamerican religious life. The Aztecs believed that a primordial couple, Oxomoco and Cipactonal, invented the 260-day divinatory almanac; the Quiché (K'iché) Maya primordial couple, Xpiyacoc and Xmucane, were thought to have performed divinatory sortilege at the time of human creation.

In Mesoamerican society there was no division between individuals who practiced priestly functions within religious cults, and individuals who practiced div-

TABLE 4. AZTEC MEDICINAL PLANTS.

Botanical Name	Aztec Name	English Name	Uses
Agave sp.	*metl*	agave	wounds
Annona cherimolia	*quauhtzapotl*	custard apple	diarrhea
Commelina pallida	*matlaliztic*	African day hemostat flower	wounds
Datura stramonium	*tlapatl*	jimson weed	fever, pain
Guaiacum sanctum	*matlaquauitl*	holy wood	fever
Ipomoea purga	*cacamatic*	jalap	purgative, phlegm
Montanoa tomentosa	*cihuapatli*	tree daisy	oxytocic
Psidium guajava	*xalxocotl*	guava	dysentery
Sambucus mexicana	*xumetl*	Mexican elder	laxative, diuretic
Schoenocaulon coulterii	*zozoyatic*	sabadilla	nosebleed
Tagetes lucida	*yauhtli*	"African" marigold	fever, diuretic
Teloxys ambroisiodes	*epazotl*	epazote	anthelminthic

ination and healing. Ehécatl-Quetzalcóatl, the Aztec personification of wind, and Tetoinnan-Toci, an Aztec earth goddess, were simultaneously important deities in the official religion and patrons of diviners. Priestesses of the goddess Toci were skilled physicians and herbalists who acted as midwives during childbirth and as priests and diviners during naming and dedication ceremonies. They consulted various almanacs within painted codices, or *tonalamatl* (*tonalli*, "day, sun, destiny"; *amatl*, "paper, book"), in order to discover prognostications related to the birthdate. The painted images in the text told them what ceremonies or ritual actions should be performed to encourage good luck or to ward off harmful influences.

These painted manuscripts, which from their earliest beginnings were used primarily to record divinatory information, can be traced back to the advent of pictorial writing (around 800 B.C.) on the stone commemorative monuments of Olmec civilization, and to fragments of codices found in early Classic Maya tombs. All intact screenfolds date to the Postclassic and early Colonial periods; in the Borgia, Borbonicus, Cospi, Vaticanus B, and other Aztec and Mixtec manuscripts, time is the most important factor, and almanacs within these books explain the divinatory associations of various units of time.

The Nahuatl term for diviners is *nahualli*, which also denotes the animal or object into which shamans could transform themselves. Divination was the prime function of healers and seers, and some individuals specialized in it. There were a number of divinatory techniques besides decoding the auguries in the *tonalamatl:* interpreting dreams and omens, tying and untying knots, scattering maize seeds on a white cotton mantle (or on the pages of an open *tonalamatl*) and observing the resultant patterns, water scrying, and looking into obsidian mirrors. Diviners also used their own and their clients' bodies for prognostications; they received messages through muscle twitching and the pulsing of blood. In Central Mexico, divination was performed by handspans: the diviner measured the left arm of the patient with the outstretched span of her right hand.

Another important type of divination consisted of inducing hallucinatory states by fasting and ingesting psychotropic plants. Although direct information concerning the use of visionary and trance-inducing agents is post-Columbian, there are earlier indications that oracular manifestations were sought during the period of altered consciousness and that divine replies to questions were announced by diviners. At the time of the Conquest, peyote, morning-glory seeds, tobacco, at least two species of *Datura*, and *Psilocybe* mushrooms were the most widely used divinatory hallucinogens.

FURTHER READINGS

Codex Vaticanus B. 1972. *Codex Vaticanus B (3773)*. In F. Anders (ed.), *Biblioteca Apostólica Vaticana*. Graz: Academic Publishers.

Ruiz de Alarcon, H. 1984 [1629]. *Treatise on the Heathen Superstitions That Today Live among the Indians Native to This New Spain, 1629*. J. R. Andrews and Ross Hassig (ed. and trans.). Norman: University of Oklahoma Press.

Sahagún, B. de. 1950–1982. *General History of the Things of New Spain (Florentine Codex)*. A. Anderson and C. Dibble (ed. and trans.). 13 vols. Santa Fe: School of American Research and University of Utah.

Seler, E. 1963. *Comentarios al Códice Borgia*. Mexico City: Fondo de Cultura Económica.

Tedlock, B. 1982. *Time and the Highland Maya*. Albuquerque: University of New Mexico Press.

Tedlock, D. 1985. *Popol Vuh*. New York: Simon and Schuster.

Barbara Tedlock

SEE ALSO

Cosmology; Disease, Illness, and Curing; Intoxicants and Intoxication

Dog

All domestic dogs of the New World, according to Schwartz (1997), are ultimately derived from the North American gray wolf. Their original domestication is credited to the Indians of North America (Canada and the United States), since remains of domestic dog go back at least 10,000 years in that region. Some zooarchaeologists, however, believe that North American dogs descend from animals brought by humans from the Old World, perhaps hybridized with American wolves.

There is currently no evidence for domestic dogs in Mesoamerica prior to 2000 B.C. Their remains have been found in caves in the Tehuacán Valley (Puebla) dating to approximately 1900–1400 B.C. Dogs were used as food by peoples of the Formative period, especially from 1150 to 150 B.C., when human populations were growing rapidly and a new meat source was needed. At one site in the Valley of Oaxaca there is evidence for a large communal feast at which more than 100 pounds of dog meat were consumed (dated at 850–700 B.C.).

D

Dogs of at least two or three different sizes (perhaps representing different varieties selected and bred by people) were present at Formative villages in the Basin of Mexico, Tehuacán, Oaxaca, and Chiapas. The smallest of these dogs sometimes show congenitally absent premolar teeth, suggesting that the genetic changes that ultimately led to the development of the breed known as *xoloitzcuintli* were under way by 500 B.C. The *xoloitzcuintli* was a small, hairless, voiceless dog, easily fattened, which was raised for food by the Aztecs at the time of the Spanish conquest. It is depicted in the ceramic sculptures of Colima in West Mexico and is believed to be ancestral to the modern breed of dog known as the Mexican Hairless. Many geneticists believe that the hairlessness, voicelessness, and tooth loss of these dogs are genetically linked, and it seems possible that human selection leading to this breed can be traced back to the Formative period.

FURTHER READINGS

Schwartz, M. 1997. *A History of Dogs in the Early Americas.* New Haven: Yale University Press.

Kent V. Flannery

Don Martín (Chiapas, Mexico)

Situated on the bank of the Grijalva River in the Chapatengo-Chajel region, this site was explored during salvage operations at the Angostura Dam and is now under water. On the basis of ceramic dates, the site was occupied during the Middle to Terminal Formative period (Chiapa de Corzo phases II, IV, V, VI, and VII, c. 1000 B.C. to A.D. 200), contemporaneous with sites such as Cuicuilco, Tlapacoya, Kaminaljuyú, Monte Albán, Tlalancaneca, Santa Rosas, and Santa Cruz. The site consisted of five earth mounds, the highest being 3.5 meters high and 25 meters across. It is near a series of foundations made of river-rolled stones. In the barranca cuts made by the river one can see trunco-conical (bell-shaped) pits about 1.6 meters deep and 2.5 meters in diameter, filled with Postclassic period trash.

Archaeological investigations focused on the exploration of these trash deposits, which revealed such material culture remains as all the vessel forms of San Jacinto Black ware, which is found in the Grijalva Valley and the Guatemala Highlands. Vegetable food remains included beans, maize, *Canavalia, Manihot,* amaranth, chile peppers, and other plants. Animal remains included white-tailed deer, rabbits, field mice, reptiles such as iguana, and amphibians such as toads. These materials indicate that this community had a developing agricultural system and obtained most of its animal protein from game. Other material remains are of construction materials, among them conical adobes, and artifacts related to stoneworking and the manufacture of personal adornments in shell and green stone. These indicate that they possessed established trade routes and specialized technology of artifact manufacture, based on local material such as river-rolled cobbles.

FURTHER READINGS

Martínez Muriel, A. 1991. La utilización de la flora y fauna durante el Formativo Tardío, en el centro de Chiapas. In *Trace* 15: 25–30. Mexico City: CEMCA.

Alejandro Martínez Muriel

Dos Pilas (Petén, Guatemala)

Dos Pilas is an important archaeological site of the Maya civilization located in the Petexbatún region of the Petén rainforest. Recent archaeological and epigraphic researches there have shown that Dos Pilas was the capital of a Classic Maya state that was remarkable for its late and rapid trajectory of florescence, expansion, and violent collapse.

The major occupation at the site began in the seventh century when outcast members of the royal family of the great city of Tikal arrived at Dos Pilas and rapidly constructed the site center. From this new base, the first rulers concentrated their political and military efforts on defeating their relatives and rivals at Tikal. In the late seventh century, Dos Pilas defeated and sacrificed the king of Tikal, enhancing the prestige of this newly created Maya polity. During the next century, the Dos Pilas state expanded across the Petexbatún region through marriage, alliance, and warfare. Even some large ancient centers such as Seibal were subjugated by Dos Pilas. By A.D. 740 this kingdom controlled much of the Pasión River valley, one of the major trade routes of the Maya world. During this period of expansionism the Dos Pilas center acquired great wealth and prestige, as reflected in its tombs, cave deposits, and numerous stone monuments. The site's many sculpted stelae and its four hieroglyphic stairways present military themes in text and imagery.

The fall of Dos Pilas was as rapid and dramatic as its rise. In A.D. 761, previously subordinate Petexbatún centers defeated the ruler of Dos Pilas. Archaeological remains corresponding to this date show that the site was besieged and destroyed. After the fall of Dos Pilas, the Petexbatún kingdom fragmented into intensively warring smaller polities. This final violent period of Petexbatún history ended by A.D. 830 with the virtual abandonment of most of the region.

FURTHER READINGS

Demarest, A. 1993. The Violent Saga of a Maya Kingdom. *National Geographic* 183:94–111.

Houston, S. D., and P. Mathews. 1985. *The Dynastic Sequence of Dos Pilas, Guatemala.* Monograph 1. San Francisco: Pre-Columbian Art Research Institute.

Arthur Demarest

SEE ALSO

Petexbatun Region

Durán, Diego (c. 1537–1588)

Born in Seville, Spain, Durán was brought by his parents to New Spain (Mexico) while still a child. He grew up in Texcoco, an Aztec city that was a center of intellectual refinement in both the Postclassic and Colonial periods. All this influenced Durán, who later claimed that the Nahuatl language spoken there was the most polished of all Aztec varieties. His knowledge of Nahuatl proved invaluable to understanding people of all stations in his adopted country. After moving to Mexico City, the boy probably studied in monastery schools before entering the Dominican Order in 1556.

Like other friars in sixteenth-century Mexico, Durán was commissioned by his order to produce a study of the religion and customs of local people as a guide for their conversion to Christianity. Therefore, he undertook extensive field work in Central Mexico, talking to informants of all ages and social classes, and studying native manuscripts (now lost), including an official history of the Aztecs in Nahuatl, now known as the *Crónica X*. The results of this research are the *Book of the Gods and Rites* (1574–1576), *The Ancient Calendar* (1579), and the *History of the Indies of New Spain* (finished 1581). Other late sixteenth-century friars, such as the fellow Dominican Agustín Dávila Padilla and the Jesuits Juan de Tovar and Joseph de Acosta, drew heavily on Durán's works. Durán's writings, however, languished in the National Library of Madrid until they were discov-

ered there by the Mexican scholar José Fernando Ramírez in the 1850s.

Durán was one of the great ethnographers of his time, and his writings are also invaluable to archaeologists. His descriptions of ceremonies and other customs, both majestic and humble, are a guide to the identification of material remains. For example, he noted that slaves buried with a distinguished master to serve in the otherworld were dressed in finery belonging to the master. The archaeological remains of the richly dressed slave could well be misinterpreted as those of the master, in the absence of documentation of this practice. Durán's works are a trove of information on pre-Conquest and Early Colonial history, providing many unique descriptions of the Aztec world.

FURTHER READINGS

Durán, D. 1964 [1581]. *The Aztecs: The History of the Indies of New Spain.* Doris Heyden and Fernando Horcasitas (trans. and ed.). New York: Orion.

———. 1971 [1579]. *Book of the Gods and Rites* and *The Ancient Calendar.* Fernando Horcasitas and Doris Heyden (trans. and ed.). Norman: University of Oklahoma Press.

———. 1994 [1574–1581]. *The History of the Indies of New Spain.* Doris Heyden (trans. and ed.). Norman: University of Oklahoma Press.

Doris Heyden

SEE ALSO

Ethnohistorical Sources and Methods; Texcoco

Dyes and Colors for Cloth

Archaeological material evidence for Mesoamerican cloth and dyes remains scarce, despite the eloquent testimony of sixteenth-century chroniclers regarding the stunning polychromatic range of textile colors, the records of gifts sent to the king of Spain, and the illustrations in the Matrícula de Tributos and Codex Mendoza of dyed and colored cloth. Fifty-seven sites in Mexico and Guatemala have yielded textile fragments of significance, but color appears in only a handful, and only a few of these have undergone sophisticated analysis (spectrophotometric analysis, microqualitative chemical analysis, and optic mineralogy). There are also serious deficiencies in dating because many specimens were found in sites that had

D

undergone looting and thus lost the information obtainable from association with related materials in context.

Outstanding examples of dyed or colored textiles come from the following sites (in chronological order): Coxcatlán Cave in the Tehuacán Valley (Palo Blanco Phase, Classic period, A.D. 700) with brown, red, and black stripes; Sierra Madre Cave in southwestern Chihuahua (Rio Fuerte Basket Maker period) with pigmented stripes of orange, green-black, and blue-black; Ejutla Cave in Oaxaca (Postclassic) with traces of blue; Romero Cave (Sierra Madre of Tamaulipas, c. A.D. 1450) with blue and white; La Candelaria Cave in Coahuila (c. A.D. 1500)

with red painted pigment; Chilapa Cave in Guerrero (c. A.D. 1500) with red painted pigment; Chiptic Cave in Chiapas (c. A.D. 1500) with three fragments (top, red, Maya blue, black, turquoise painted pigments; middle, *Purpura pansa* violet; and lower, light brown batik); and finally, La Garrafa Cave in Chiapas (c. A.D. 1500) with dyed indigo, and Maya blue, smoke and carbon black, red and yellow ochre, dark and light green, and dark and light brown painted pigments.

Various techniques were used to apply color and dyes to fibers processed from cotton, agave, rabbit hair, yucca, and native hemp *(Apocynum).* One method was to paint the surface of the finished cloth with pigments derived mostly from inorganic minerals, combined with some organic sources, along with a medium to make them adhere, similar to stucco. A second technique was to dye or paint the surface of the cloth. A third consisted of resist-dyes such as batik (wax or resin resist), ikat (bound and dyed threads), and plangi (tie-dye). A fourth was to pre-dye yarns in water baths, either hot or cold, with the aid of mordants and color enhancers, and to incorporate them into weaving as stripes or as supplementary threads for patterns.

Sixteenth-century references by chroniclers are invaluable sources on the use of dyestuffs (dyes) and mordants. Dyes were derived from vegetation, animals, and inorganics/minerals. Vegetable dyes are the most numerous, derived from plants, flowers, fruits, roots, wood, bark, and lichens. Animal dyes include the cochineal insect *(Dactylopius coccus),* and the marine shellfish *Purpura pansa.* Inorganic/mineral dyes include ferrous oxide, ochre, carbon, and Maya blue (combined with organic indigo). Mordants (alum, iron sulphate, copper sulfate, sodium carbonate) were added to dyebaths to modify colors and expand hues.

TABLE 1. OUTSTANDING EXAMPLES OF MESOAMERICAN DYED AND COLORED TEXTILES.

Site	Date	Description
Coxcatlán Cave, Tehuacán Valley	Palo Blanco phase, Classic, A.D. 700	brown, red, and black stripes
Sierra Madre Cave, SW Chihuaha	Rio Fuerte Basket Maker period	pigmented stripes: orange, green-black, blue-black
Ejutla Cave, Oaxaca	Postclassic	traces of blue
Romero Cave, Sierra Madre of Tamaulipas	c. A.D. 1450	blue and white
La Candelaria Cave, Coahuila	c. A.D. 1500	red painted pigment
Chilapa Cave, Guerrero	c. A.D. 1500	red painted pigment
Chiptic Cave, Chiapas	c. A.D. 1500	three fragments: top, red Maya blue, black, turquoise painted pigments; middle, *Purpura pansa* violet; lower, light brown batik
La Garrafa Cave, Chiapas	c. A.D. 1500	dyed indigo; Maya blue, smoke and carbon black, red and yellow ochre, dark and light green, dark and light brown painted pigments

FURTHER READINGS

Dahlgren de Jordan, B. 1963. *La Grana Cochinilla.* Nueva Biblioteca Mexicana de Obras Históricas, 1. Mexico City: José Porrua y Hijos.

Donkin, R. A. 1977. Spanish Red: An Ethnogeographical Study of Cochineal and the Opuntia Cactus. *Transactions of the American Philosophical Society* 67, part 5.

Hernandez, F. 1959–1960. *Obras completas: Historia natural en la Nueva España.* 3 vols. Mexico City: Universidad Nacional Autónoma de México.

Kasha, M. 1948. Chemical Notes on the Coloring Matter. In L. O'Neile (ed.), *Textiles of Pre-Columbian Chihuahua,* pp. 151–161. Contributions to American

TABLE 2. ETHNOHISTORICAL REFERENCES TO COLORS.

Vegetable Dyes	Raw Materials (Common Names)	Botanical/Mineral Identification	Geographic Distribution	Evidence
Red	Nocheztli, grana cochinilla, cochineal	*Dactylopius coccus*	Tribute to Aztec Empire by Mixteca Alta (High-lands) and Oaxaca Valley Semiarid ecosystem	Matricula de Tributos, 11 talegas annually Sahagun
Fine red	Tezoatl with alum and tlaliatl	*A shrub's leaves (?) with fetid mineral mud*	Tropic sub-humid ecosystem	Sahagun
Blackish-red	Uitzquauitl	*Haematoxylon Brasiletto, or Caesalpinia echinata*	Tropic humid ecosystem	Sahagun
Orange	Madder (or alizarin) with inorganic mordent	*Rubia tinctorium mor-danted with hydrous ferric oxide or aluminum hydroxide*	Tropic sub-humid ecosystem	Sierra Madre cave
Vermillion	Chiotl (or annatto) with axin	*Bixa orellana with coccus axin*	Tropic sub-humid ecosystem	Sahagun
Fine yellow	Xochipalli	*Cosmos sulphureus (?)*	Tropic sub-humid ecosystem	Hernandez
Light yellow	Zacatlaxcalli, barba de leon	*Cuscuta americana or Cuscuta tinctoria*	Tropic sub-humid ecosystem	Sahagun Hernandez
Dark green	Ixpalli: zacatlaxcalli with texotli and tzacutli (orchid bulb)	*Cuscuta spp. with blue mineral earth (?) and Epidendrum pastoris*	Tropic sub-humid ecosystem	Sahagun
Fine light green	Texotli with more yellow	*Blue mineral earth (?) with more Cuscuta spp.*	Tropic sub-humid ecosystem	Sahagun
Blue	Mohurtl, sacatinta, muicle, hierba purpurea	*Justicia spicigera*	Tropic sub-humid ecosystem	Hernandez
Fine blue	Matlali, matlalitztic	*Commelina coelestis (?)*	(?)	Hernandez Sahagun
Dark blue	Xiuhquilitl, anil, indigo, Xiuhquilitipitzahoac	*Indigofera suffruticosa Indigofera tenuifolio*	Tropic humid ecosystem	Sahagun Romero, Ejutla, and La Garrafa caves
Light blue	Texotli or xoxouic matlalli	*A blue mineral earth (?)*	(?)	Sahagun
Purple	Nocheztli with tlalxocotl and tzacutli (orchid bulb)	*Dactylopius coccus with alum and Epidendrum pastoris*	Semiarid ecosystem	Sahagun
Purple	Cuauhayohuachtli, Piñon de Indias, sangregado	*Jatropha spp.*	Tropic sub-humid ecosystem	Hernandez
Blackish-purple	Palo de tinte, Palo de Campeche, logwood	*Haematoxylon campechamim*	Tropic humid ecosystem, Yucatán Peninsula	Sahagun
Violet-purple	Marine shellfish dye	*Purpura pansa Purpura patula pansa*	Pacific Coast Atlantic, Caribbean coast	Chiptic Cave, middle fragment
Black	Tlilliocotl, humo de ocote, or smoked pinewood	*Pinus spp.*	Broad	Sahagun
Black	Capulin	*Ardisia escallonoides and Eugenia capuli*	Temperate sub-humid ecosystem	Sahagun

D

TABLE 2. ETHNOHISTORICAL REFERENCES TO COLORS. (*continued*)

Vegetable Dyes	Raw Materials (Common Names)	Botanical/Mineral Identification	Geographic Distribution	Evidence
Inorganic pigments used to paint on textiles or threads				
Red-orange	Tlauitl, almagre rojo, hematite, or red ochre	*Ferrous oxide*	Broad	Sierra Madre, Chilapa, Chiptic, La Candelaria, and La Garrafa caves
Red	Cinabrio, Cinnabar	*Native red mercuric sulfide*	(?)	
Yellow-ochre	Tecozahuitl, almagre amarillo, ochre, or lemonite	*Hydrous ferric oxide, or iron ore*	Tribute to Aztec Empire by nahuas, matlames, and tuxtecos. Broad.	Matricula de Tributos, 20 gourds full every 80 days
Light brown (Leonado)	Tecoxtli with tzacutli (orchid bulb)	*Brown mineral with epidendrum pastoris*	Tropic sub-humid ecosystem	Chiptic Cave: batik on lower fragment
Blues and greens	Malaquite and Azurite	*Copper carbonates*	(?)	
White	Tizatlalli (chalk)	*Limestone*	(?)	
White	Chimaltizatl (gypsum)	*Hydrous calcium sulfate*	(?)	
Compound vegetable and inorganic pigment				
Maya blue	Xiuhquilitl (indigo) with attapulgita (a kind of clay)	*Indigofera spp. with mineral clay (?)*	Humid tropic ecosystem, Maya culture	La Garrafa, Chiptic caves
Black	Palli, Tlaliatl	*A fetid mineral mud (?)*	Temperate sub-humid ecosystem	Sahagun
Mordants				
	Tlalxocotl, alum	*Potassium aluminum sulfate*	Desert areas near sulphur springs	Sahagun
	Tlatliac, "aceche," caparrosa, color enhancer	*Iron sulfate*		Sahagun
	Alcaparrosa, color enhancer	*Copper sulfate*		Sahagun
	Sal de estaño, tin	*Tin*	Broad	Sahagun
	Cal, lime	*Lime*	Broad	Sahagun
	Tequesquite	*Sodium carbonate or sodium chloride*	Broad	Sahagun
	Tzacutli, orchid bulb	*Epidendrum pastoris*	Tropic sub-humid ecosystem	
	Salitre	*Potassium nitrate*	Broad	Sahagun

Anthropology and History, 45; Carnegie Institution of Washington, Publication 574. Washington, D.C.

Sahagún, B. de. 1950–1969. *Codex Florentino: General History of the Things of New Spain.* A. J. O. Anderson and C. E. Dibble (ed. and trans.). Books 1–14. Santa Fe: University of Utah and School of American Research.

Marta Turok Wallace

SEE ALSO
Painting; Weaving and Textiles

Dzibilchaltún (Yucatán, Mexico)

The location of Dzibilchaltún appears to be a compromise between agricultural potential and proximity to coastal resources. Salt from brackish lagoons behind the Gulf beaches has always been a valuable commodity, but Dzibilchaltún lies 22 kilometers from the salt-producing area, on the nearest fertile terrain. Any sizable, self-sufficient community had to be situated inland, beyond the mangrove swamps and expanses of bare limestone bedrock that border the north coast of Yucatán. Although soil at Dzibilchaltún is seldom more than a few centimeters deep and precipitation is light, farmers there can support a considerable population.

The largest cenote (water-filled sinkhole) in the vicinity marks the center of the ruins, indicating that the presence of an unlimited supply of potable water was also a strong attraction. The cenote was once the focus of a religious cult, judging by materials retrieved by divers. These findings, together with arrangement of the settlement around the water source, underscore the material value of cenotes in a landscape where rainfall quickly filters underground through fissures and cracks in the limestone.

This strategic site enjoyed a long occupation, from Formative times through the Spanish conquest, as Andrews IV and Brainerd have detailed. While excavators found some Formative sherds under later architecture near the central cenote and at other many places over the entire site, they encountered concentrations of Formative materials at large platforms located about 2 kilometers west of the central cenote. The Dzibilchaltún project included excavations at the Formative Mirador and Komchen groups, but these places are far from the center of the site and should be considered separate settlements.

Most of the architecture at the site and the general configuration of the settlement represent Late Classic phases, but several Postclassic buildings are present at the center. Occupants of the site modified and reused various structures and erected various shrines during the century preceding the Spanish conquest. A sixteenth-century chapel situated near the cenote served a Colonial period population.

The Main Plaza, an open area east of the cenote that is surrounded by monumental ruins, was the center of the site during Late and Terminal Classic times. Ruben Maldonado's 1993–1994 investigations showed that Late Classic builders enlarged the plaza, demolishing the existing structures and covering them with buildings having a uniform orientation. These later buildings, especially Structure 44, contrast with dwellings found at the site. Structure 44 forms the south side of the plaza. It is 120 meters long; a row of thirty-five doorways fills the front façade of the superstructure. Instead of small rooms with single doors leading to the exterior, the building contained three huge halls. Structure 44 was probably a communal building that was not primarily built or controlled by a single kin group.

The layout of Dzibilchaltún is exceptionally clear and complete. The nucleus of the site is a concentration of ruins around the cenote and Main Plaza, covering about 50 hectares. Three masonry causeways *(sacbes)* connect the Main Plaza to architectural complexes beyond the nucleus. One causeway ends about 600 meters due east of the Main Plaza at the Temple of the Seven Dolls group; the other two terminate at smaller plazas, one about 1,400 meters west, and one 900 meters south of the Main Plaza. Altogether, the center of the site can be considered a single interconnected aggregate of architecture that measures 1.5 kilometers north to south and 2.5 kilometers east to west. The density of ruins within 500 meters of the causeways—a T-shaped area of 4 square kilometers—diminishes with distance from the center. Beyond this causeway zone and farther from the center of the site, isolated compounds of elite dwellings and groups of less costly houses formed the outskirts of the community.

The dwellings used by the inhabitants of Dzibilchaltún range from single-room structures with thatched roofs to multi-room palaces with vaulted roofs. Particularly abundant are wall foundations for single-room houses with a round-ended ground plan, analogous to the thatch-covered cottage used in rural Yucatán today. Although such remains are rare at other sites, paintings and sculpture at Uxmal, Labna, and Chichén Itzá show that this type of structure was the common pre-Columbian house. The presence of metates near vaulted buildings, and the presence of domestic pottery, show

D

that most of these structures also functioned as houses. Multi-room buildings with thatched roofs, easily distinguished by the absence of the cut-stone debris that results from the collapse of vaulted roofs, are a third category of dwelling. The variation in the energy cost of different dwelling types suggests a strongly stratified society.

Dzibilchaltún is an excellent place to study the Early period architectural style; the remains of 150 Early period vaulted structures, including various standing buildings, exist at the site. If the average vaulted room is about 5 meters long, these buildings represent a total of more than 500 rooms. The walls of Early period buildings are made with crudely dressed blocks, and vaults consist of corbeled slabs. Façade decoration is achieved with molded stucco. Andrews IV observed structural problems resulting from excessively wide vaults and big doorways with wooden lintels at the Early period buildings of the Temple of the Seven Dolls group. The builders of these faulty buildings either abandoned the structures, covering them with new construction, or progressively braced and reinforced them by sealing doorways and adding walls. Structures 38-sub and 44-sub, near the cenote, are smaller and more stable buildings. The Standing Temple, west of the Main Plaza, includes stone lintels and other evolved features of Early period vault construction.

Although scholars often associate Pure Florescent concrete-veneer architecture with Puuc sites such as Uxmal, surveyors found seventy-three Pure Florescent vaulted buildings representing more than 300 rooms at Dzibilchaltún. The squared and dressed blocks used in veneer walls are a popular contemporary construction material, so recent inhabitants of the area have quarried these sites. No Florescent architecture remains intact at the site, but the Structure 38 complex illustrates the superposition of concrete-veneer Pure Florescent masonry over Early period buildings.

The Main Plaza contains various stelae, but most of these were plain or badly eroded. Excavators found two stelae embedded with carved surfaces exposed in the lower retaining walls of Structure 36, a pyramidal building in the northeast corner of the Main Plaza. One set of Maya leaders probably broke up these sculpted monuments and displayed them as political propaganda to commemorate their victory over another group.

FURTHER READINGS

Andrews, E.W., IV, and E. W. Andrews V. 1980. *Excavations at Dzibilchaltun, Yucatan, Mexico.* Middle American Research Institute Publication 48. New Orleans.

Andrews E. W., V. 1981. Dzibilchaltún. In J. A. Sabloff (ed.), *Supplement to the Handbook of Middle American Indians,* vol. 5, part 1, pp. 13–341. Austin: University of Texas Press.

Coggins, C. 1983. *The Stucco Decoration and Architectural Assemblage of Structure 1-sub, Dzibilchaltún, Yucatán, Mexico.* Middle American Research Institute Publication 49. New Orleans.

Folan, W. J. 1970. The Open Chapel of Dzibilchaltún. In Middle American Research Institute Publication 26, pp. 181–199. New Orleans.

Kurjack, E. B. 1974. *Prehistoric Lowland Maya Community and Social Organization: A Case Study at Dzibilchaltún, Yucatán, Mexico.* Middle American Research Institute Publication 38. New Orleans.

Stuart, G. E., J. C. Scheffler, E. B. Kurjack, and J. W. Cottier. 1979. *Map of the Ruins of Dzibilchaltún, Yucatán, Mexico.* Middle American Research Institute Publication 47. New Orleans.

Edward B. Kurjack

SEE ALSO
Maya Lowlands: North

E

Economic Organization

Economic organization has been defined as the answer "to such questions as what is to be produced, who is to share in the production process, how the resulting goods are to be consumed, where power and discretion in industrial matters are to lie and how fully and to what . . . ends the human and material resources of society are to be employed" (Hamilton 1937: 438). This discussion of ancient Mesoamerican economic organization uses these overarching questions as a guide, making concessions for gaps in present knowledge.

Indigenous peoples of Mesoamerica survived and flourished for more than a hundred centuries before the arrival of the Spanish. Native Americans first arrived in the region as foragers and, in certain places, they eventually built great cities and civilizations. Pre-Hispanic Mesoamericans lived in environments as diverse as highland valleys, tropical forests, scrubby plains, and steep mountain zones. At the time of Spanish conquest, they spoke a diversity of languages and were composed of an array of different ethnic and cultural populations. Despite these axes of variation, the absence of a single or uniform economic organization, and the variation of patterns of production, exchange, and consumption across time and geographic space, a few broad generalities and parameters characterize the ancient Mesoamerican economy.

This essay establishes these parameters, then describes three key components of economic organization: production, both agricultural and craft; exchange, or distribution; and consumption, or access. These components are discussed as they pertain to the definitional questions outlined above. For each economic dimension, discussion relies most heavily on the case of the Aztecs of Central Mexico, because only from them can we draw on native texts, Colonial period documents, and recent archaeology. In spite of this emphasis, however, I do not propose that the Aztecs were typical of all of pre-Hispanic Mesoamerica. Consequently, whenever data pertinent to the economic behavior of other Mesoamerican peoples are available, this discussion stresses variation in these behaviors across time and space.

General Parameters

Ancient Mesoamerican economic organizations were integrally related to the region's subsistence, transportation, and tool technologies. The earliest inhabitants depended exclusively on wild plant and animal resources. These peoples were largely mobile and lived at relatively sparse population densities. Sometime between 5000 and 3500 B.C., key agricultural food crops, such as maize, were domesticated and then rapidly disseminated across the cultural region. Yet it was not until sometime after 2000 B.C. that much of Mesoamerica's population began to reside in relatively sedentary villages. During the last three millennia before Spanish conquest (c. 1500 B.C.– A.D. 1519), most of them relied heavily on some combination of the indigenous domesticates: maize, beans, squash, and amaranth. A wide range of other domesticated and wild foods, which varied according to local environmental conditions, always supplemented these crops. Significantly, few animals (hairless dog, turkey, and honeybee) were domesticated in Mesoamerica. The comparative dearth of domesticated fauna not only had implications for diet and household economies but also placed

E

constraints on long-distance, land-based transport, since no Mesoamerican domesticated species could serve as a beast of burden.

In late pre-Hispanic times, long-distance Aztec traders traversed considerable distances by foot. They generally were accompanied by human porters, who carried loads weighing over 20 kilograms on their backs. The heavier the load carried, the shorter the trip a porter could make in a day. Although wheels are present on a few late pre-Hispanic Mesoamerican toys, wheeled vehicles were never employed for transportation. Because of the friction of distance (with all land-based transport by foot), light-weight, high-value goods tended to be exchanged much farther than heavy items of lesser value (such as maize).

Archaeological findings reveal that such goods as marine shell, gemstones, and obsidian were exchanged over great distances throughout the pre-Hispanic period in Mesoamerica. In later times, we know from documents that such perishable items as cloth, feathers, cacao, and animal skins were moved across mountains. Likewise, at the time of Spanish conquest, it is said that the Aztec ruler in Tenochtitlán ate fresh fish from the Gulf Coast, a distance that would take 16 to 20 hours to run.

In the lake system of the Basin of Mexico, water-borne canoes carried heavy loads in a more energetically efficient manner. Canoes also traversed the rivers and coastlines. One of the first glimpses of Mesoamerican peoples reported by Europeans was of the large ocean-going canoes used by Yucatecan traders, who voyaged to ports in Central America.

The first metal items in Mesoamerica do not date until A.D. 650–700. Yet even after the advent of metallurgy, Mesoamerican peoples used metals as adornments and valuables for exchange rather than for utilitarian tools. Their ancient civilizations were founded on a stone tool technology and continued to rely on it until Spanish conquest.

Despite their significant intellectual and organizational achievements, the civilizations of pre-Hispanic Mesoamerica can be considered low-energy societies in which human labor was the basic building block of economic activity and political power. In this world, which lacked beasts of burden, animal-driven plows, utilitarian metal tools, and wheeled vehicles, there were few effective sources of energy beyond human muscle power.

Agricultural Production
Agrarian production was the economic basis of most Mesoamerican societies, although craft production and exchange also were important to varying degrees. In general, the primary factors of production and sources of wealth and power were land and labor. In Aztec Central Mexico, which provides the most ample record, power and a life of comfort were derived not so much from the direct ownership of land as from control over labor. Despite occasional exceptions, the main means of production (land and labor) were distributed through the political system and not through the market. Land was assigned by the Aztec ruler to a subservient noble or state institution, and was inherited thereafter. Most agriculture was organized locally, but some was administered more centrally by the state. While land and labor were generally distributed (although not necessarily managed) by the state sector, the market served principally for the distribution of basic commodities and certain elite goods.

In the Basin of Mexico during the Aztec period, some agricultural households were nearly self-sufficient. These peasant families engaged in generalized rain-fed or small-scale irrigation farming in which they grew basic food staples (e.g., maize, beans) supplemented by xerophytic plants such as maguey. Maguey is not only an important source of food and alcohol, but also of fiber that can be used to produce everything from rope to clothes. Other Aztec households followed more specialized strategies, taking advantage of irrigation and/or market opportunities to produce maize more intensively. In the wetland *chinampa* zones at the edge of Lake Texcoco, labor-intensive regimes, along with multiple cropping, permitted maize returns per unit of land that were several times higher than under other conditions. These farmers probably exchanged surplus maize for the xerophytic crops that they still required for basic household use. In marginal upland and drier parts of the Basin of Mexico, Aztec period farmers grew maguey and nopal, the products of which were marketed in exchange for other household necessities.

Less is known about the organization of agricultural production in other pre-Hispanic Mesoamerican contexts, although there are many reasons to suspect that it did not strictly mirror Aztec organization. In the Lowland Maya region, settlements—even cities—often were more dispersed (less nucleated) in layout than the Aztec centers, so that gardens may have been interspersed with household clusters to a greater degree. Population densities and the sheer size of the Aztec capital, Tenochtitlán, were rarely matched elsewhere in this region. Beyond the Aztecs, we have little knowledge about the role of Mesoamerican market systems.

We do know that the pre-Hispanic peoples of Mesoamerica developed technologies and management practices that allowed them to crop a diverse range of ecological settings, giving rise to a multiplicity of agricultural landscapes. Cultivation strategies ranged from swidden (slash and burn) to multi-cropped, hydrologically transformed wetlands (such as the Aztec *chinampas*). However, long before the Aztecs, during the last millennium B.C., the drainage of swamps created and maintained fertile wetland zones in the Maya region. Thus, pre-Hispanic Maya farmers in Belize and the Petén probably employed more labor-intensive farming strategies than were practiced by farmers in the same regions during the early part of the twentieth century. In the lowlands, these wetland fields could be used to grow high-value crops such as cocoa and cotton, as well as more basic food sources.

In upland regions, Mesoamerican farmers often constructed agricultural terraces to catch soil runoff and to create flattened fields that were more amenable to farming. Various practices, including dam construction, wells dug down to high water table (pot irrigation), and canal irrigation also frequently were employed to direct precious water to fields. Many of these practices were first used shortly after the advent of sedentary communities. Truly monumental irrigation systems—the kinds that would require centralized management—were relatively rare in pre-Hispanic Mesoamerica. In general, many of the more labor-intensive Mesoamerican agricultural systems can be considered a kind of "landesque capital." That is, their initial construction required a fair amount of household or community labor, but with regular, though generally small, labor inputs, they could be readily maintained, sustaining only minor degradation. Nevertheless, when population displacement or political disruption caused these agrarian features to be abandoned or inadequately maintained, major environmental consequences (such as episodes of heavy erosion) often resulted.

Craft Production and the Division of Labor

Aztec society was composed of market sellers, long-distance merchants, craft workers, wood collectors, priests, nobles, and a variety of other specialists, as well as farmers. Nevertheless, the majority of (but not all) commoner households engaged in at least some agriculture. In many Aztec households, women spun maguey and/or cotton into cloth; some of this was for household use, but some was sold in the market. Cotton mantles served as a unit of currency in the regional market system. The extent to which Aztec households engaged in textile production varied according to agricultural, market, and political forces (and so temporally and spatially). Although the Aztec ideological ideal was that women should be involved in weaving and cooking, specific women participated in those activities to varying degrees.

In addition to weaving, the documents describe an array of craft specialists in Aztec society, including potters, metallurgists, stone-workers, basket-weavers, feather ornament producers, wood-carvers, reed mat makers, and many others. Some of these craft workers produced directly for the ruler in the palace, while others manufactured goods for the market or long-distance merchants. At present, we have little firm archaeological or documentary evidence for the large-scale mass manufacture of craft goods in industrial workshops, a mode of manufacture that apparently was more prevalent in other ancient states in both the Old (Rome) and New (Andean Inka) worlds. In general, Aztec craft production was a domestic enterprise, with family members providing the labor force for the manufacturing process from start to finish.

Specialized production for exchange (rather than for immediate use) has a long history in pre-Hispanic Mesoamerica, extending back to the Early Formative period (c. 1100 B.C.). Some of the earliest indications of craft production are evidenced in ornamental or status-related materials such as marine shell and magnetite. The specialized manufacture of more utilitarian items, such as basic ceramics, appeared during the later half of the Formative period (c. 500–200 B.C.). While the importance of specific crafts varied over space and time, these activities generally took place in domestic contexts.

For the Classic Maya (c. A.D. 250–900), like the Aztecs, textual sources suggest that certain artisans, such as the makers of polychrome vases and the carvers of stone monuments, produced their goods directly for the elite. Yet archaeologists strongly suspect that other Maya craft workers were more independent of direct political control. Ancient Mesoamerican craft production was not confined to centers of political power or urban contexts but also occurred in smaller communities and more rural settings. This pattern has been particularly well documented in the Lowland Maya region for pottery and chipped stone tool manufacture, which often was dispersed in smaller village communities. Such non-urban production does not appear to have been centrally controlled or administered. At present, it is not known whether such goods were moved partly through market exchange networks or entirely by non-commercialized, kin-based transactions.

E

Exchange

Three distinct but interlocking circuits accounted for the complex exchange and distribution systems that characterized the late Aztec economy. Two of these networks were largely commercial in focus. The first involved long-distance professional merchants called *pochteca* or *oztomeca*. Through these exchanges, exotic raw materials were transported to markets and craft producers in the Basin of Mexico, while finished elite goods were traded outside the region. The second commercial circuit was the Basin of Mexico market system, a regional institution that moved a wide range of materials, including local utilitarian products and commodities as well as exotic items that entered the basin through long-distance exchange. The third circuit was tribute, which brought products and labor from inside and outside the Basin to the region's political elite. The tribute system channeled goods and labor from producers through their local lords to the central elite of the Aztec Triple Alliance (Tenochtitlán, Texcoco, and Tlacopan), as well as more direct flows from landless tenants to landholding lords and the state. Tribute demands were the consequence of Triple Alliance military domination.

The interlocking linkages among these distributional circuits have been amply demonstrated. Tribute included taxes paid by craft specialists and merchants, in addition to special fees collected on market transactions. Triple Alliance rulers derived an important segment of their economic support by manipulating aspects of commercial exchange. Raw materials derived through trade from outside the basin were distributed in the market system, thereby affecting exchange values. At the same time, the flow of costly goods through the tribute system was inadequate to meet the needs of elite consumption, requiring the acquisition of these valuable finished products through market vendors.

In the late pre-Hispanic period, the three circuits of Aztec exchange interconnected a large segment of Mesoamerica. While long-distance exchange was important at least from the advent of sedentary village life here (c. 2000–1500 B.C.), the extent and the mechanisms of pre-Aztec period exchange are less well understood. At some of the earliest Mesoamerican villages, archaeologists have recovered items of obsidian, marine shell, jade, and magnetite that were procured from hundreds of kilometers away. By 1100 B.C., shared symbols and iconographic motifs depicted on highly crafted items indicate that ideas as well as finished goods were being transmitted over considerable distances. This interregional interaction was centered on emergent chiefs or elites, who shared greater access to specific classes of goods and information through down-the-line networks covering considerable distances. The total volume of local and extraregional exchanges, however, was still much lower than in late pre-Hispanic times.

In the highlands of Mesoamerica during the last centuries B.C., the emergence of cities and towns, along with increasing population densities, entailed critical shifts in the volume and nature of exchange relations. No longer could the inhabitants of larger communities grow enough food to feed themselves from the lands immediately surrounding their sites. In regions such as the Valley of Oaxaca and the Basin of Mexico, neighboring villages had to supply grain to provision the occupants of the early cities of Monte Albán and Teotihuacán, respectively. At this time, we see increasing evidence for the specialized production of such utilitarian goods as pottery. In many regions, the local circulation of basic goods (e.g., food and pottery) increased. The extent to which these transactions occurred through tribute, market, or kin-based reciprocal exchanges is a matter for further debate and investigation.

Studies of obsidian and other goods exchanged over long distances also indicate that the volume of interregional trade increased during the Classic and Postclassic periods. For example, Central Mexican obsidian has been found at Early Classic Maya centers, while highly valued marine shell was recovered with some frequency at Teotihuacán. The relative role of long-distance exchange, particularly the export of obsidian for Teotihuacán's economy, remains a key question in Mesoamerican research.

Access to precious and exotic goods appears to have been a particularly important key to Classic Maya economic organization. In burials and numerous graphic depictions, Classic Maya lords are lavishly adorned with exotic and highly crafted items. Movement of these precious goods probably followed riverine routes in the Classic period, with the peoples of the Gulf Coast serving as key intermediaries between the highlands and the Petén lowlands. Water-borne commerce was certainly an ancient practice among the Maya, extending back to the Late Formative; by the Postclassic period, however, they employed seagoing vessels that could carry much heavier loads. Such a Maya vessel had the now famous encounter with Columbus off the northern coast of Honduras on his fourth voyage. This canoe, described as being as long as a galley and two and a half meters wide, had a crew of about two dozen men plus the captain and a number of women and children. The vessel carried a cargo of cacao, metal products (e.g., bells and ornamental axes), pottery, cotton clothing, and wooden swords with inset blades of obsidian.

The expanded Postclassic period sea trade around the coast of Yucatán is characteristic of the increased volume of long-distance exchange that occurred across much of Mesoamerica following the decline of Teotihuacán, Monte Albán, and most major Classic Maya centers (c. A.D. 650–950). Although the volume of exchange probably always was less than for much of the contemporaneous Old World, the kinds of goods that were traded, exemplified by those in the canoe, were significant for warfare, status ascription, exchange (currency), rituals of social reproduction, and hence the region's basic political economy.

Consumption

In Aztec society, exotic and highly crafted goods were used and consumed for many reasons: to award military success, attract clients, mark social status, gift allies, pay tribute debts, and commemorate ritual events. Sixteenth-century texts chronicle Aztec nobility who ate more richly and dressed more finely than commoners. While the former tended to wear garments of exotic cotton, the later dressed in coarser fabrics of local maguey. These textual accounts of differences in consumption and access are not at all surprising for a stratified, hierarchical, urban society.

Socially defined differences in access to specific goods, labor, and/or information were typical of most ancient Mesoamerican societies (although to greatly varying degrees) for more than 2,500 years before the arrival of the Spanish. Excavations of houses and burials have revealed that patterns of consumption and access were not egalitarian as early as the Early Formative period and that burial treatment at death also reflected degrees of status differentiation. In certain cases these distinctions were rather stark; recall the impressive funerary temples that were erected above the tombs of certain Classic period Maya lords, who were then interred with jade funerary masks, shell adornments, polychrome vessels, and other grave wealth. Likewise, at the Classic Maya center of Copán (Honduras), a comparison of urban and rural household architectural complexes revealed that urban structures were more architecturally elaborate, with more costly building features. These urban groups were associated with higher percentages of decorated pottery, finer burial goods, and greater amounts of exotic items, and were perhaps occupied for longer durations. Many of

these same axes of variation were found within the sample of rural households around Copán, reflecting the fact that access distinctions involved more than a simple urban-rural dichotomy.

In certain other studies of domestic contexts, however, the differences in consumption practices between elite and commoner populations have been found to be relatively minor. For example, in Postclassic Morelos, excavations in two rural villages (Cuexcomate and Capilco) indicate that architectural (and not artifactual) distinctions exclusively segregate elite from commoner segments. A number of ceramic varieties were recovered somewhat more frequently, but certainly not exclusively, in elite contexts; however, other likely sumptuary items (jade beads, obsidian lip plugs, and shell pendants) were found regularly in non-elite contexts. In pre-Hispanic Mesoamerica, the social significance and consumption of portable wealth and exotic goods was apparently variable through time and across space. Furthermore, in certain situations actual practice probably varied markedly from the social codes regarding noble/commoner status and access that have been preserved in Spanish documents from the Contact Era.

A Look Back and Ahead

Over the past half-century we have learned a tremendous amount about the economic organization of the peoples of ancient Mesoamerica. Intensive wetland agriculture was a critical aspect of many lowland and lakeshore production systems. Most of these areas were once thought to have been dependent on more extensive swidden farming systems alone. Specialized craft production has been shown to date to the Formative period, indicating that relatively few ancient Mesoamerican households were completely self-sufficient. While the intensity of craft production at times may have been great, such producers almost always worked in domestic rather than workshop-factory contexts.

Mesoamerican exchange and distribution systems clearly were diverse and complex. We now suspect that Aztec exchange spheres cannot serve as a full or an adequate model for central Mexican Teotihuacán. For example, redistributional exchange between social and ethnic segments may have had a larger role in the latter city. Consequently, blanket extrapolations from the Aztecs to the Maya or other regions probably are even less appropriate. The extent of geographic and temporal diversity certainly was not recognized five decades ago. As archaeological findings modify and expand earlier known textual

E

accounts, even Aztec economic organization itself is now envisioned as much more internally variable, with greater interconnections among the market, tribute system, entrepreneurial long-distance trade, and political power than suggested in earlier accounts. Recent archaeological work also indicates that Aztec patterns of consumption were more heterogeneous than depicted in the sixteenth-century texts, which draw a more finite division between commoners and elite.

Although our understanding of ancient Mesoamerican economic organization has advanced considerably in the past fifty years, there is still much that we do not know, or that we could comprehend better. When and why did market systems emerge, and how broadly distributed were they? What percentage of craft specialists also participated in agriculture, or were they full-time artisans? How much gardening and farming took place within the limits of Mesoamerican cities? How prevalent were large-scale grain storage facilities in the region? How much control did ancient Mesoamerican rulers exert over production and exchange, and how did this vary over space and time? Can we understand why exotic and highly crafted adornments seem to have had such a key role for the Classic Maya? How important was obsidian production and export to the Teotihuacán economy? These and other questions provide an intellectual "road map" for the next generations of archaeologists. Answering them will require multi-generational commitments of field work and analysis. The results will be important both for understanding diversity and change in ancient Mesoamerican populations and for providing a basis to judge how these native societies differed from or were similar to archaic chiefdoms and states in other global regions.

FURTHER READINGS

Berdan, F. F., R. E. Blanton, E. Boone, M. Hodge, M. E. Smith, and E. Umberger. 1996. *Aztec Imperial Strategies.* Washington, D.C.: Dumbarton Oaks.

Blanton, R. E., G. M. Feinman, S. A. Kowalewski, and P. N. Peregrine. 1996. A Dual-Processual Theory for the Evolution of Mesoamerican Civilization. *Current Anthropology* 37:1–14.

Blanton, R. E., S. A. Kowalewski, G. M. Feinman, and L. M. Finsten. 1993. *Ancient Mesoamerica: A Comparison of Change in Three Regions.* 2nd ed. Cambridge: Cambridge University Press.

Brumfiel, E. M. 1991. Weaving and Cooking: Women's Production in Aztec Mexico. In J. M. Gero and M. W. Conkey (eds.), *Engendering Archaeology: Women and Prehistory,* pp. 224–251. Oxford: Basil Blackwell.

Brumfiel, E. M., and T. K. Earle. (eds.). 1987. *Specialization, Exchange, and Complex Societies.* Cambridge: Cambridge University Press.

Hamilton, W. H. 1937. Organization, Economic. In E. R. A. Seligman (ed.), *Encyclopaedia of the Social Sciences,* pp. 484–490. New York: Macmillan.

Hicks, F. 1986. Prehispanic Background of Colonial Political and Economic Organization in Central Mexico. In R. Spores (ed.), *Supplement to the Handbook of Middle American Indians,* vol. 4, *Ethnohistory,* pp. 35–54. Austin: University of Texas Press.

Hirth, K. G. (ed.). 1984. *Trade and Exchange in Early Mesoamerica.* Albuquerque: University of New Mexico Press.

Hodge, M. G., and M. E. Smith (eds.). 1994. *Economies and Polities in the Aztec Realm.* Albany: Institute for Mesoamerican Studies, State University of New York at Albany.

Isaac, B. L. (ed.). 1986. *Research in Economic Anthropology,* Supplement 2, *Economic Aspects of Prehispanic Highland Mexico.* Greenwich: JAI Press.

Manzanilla, L. 1992. The Economic Organization of the Teotihuacan Priesthood: Hypotheses and Considerations. In J. C. Berlo (ed.), *Art, Ideology, and the City of Teotihuacan,* pp. 321–338. Washington, D.C.: Dumbarton Oaks.

McAnany, P. A., and B. L. Isaac (eds.) 1989. *Research in Economic Anthropology,* Supplement 4, *Prehistoric Maya Economies.* Greenwich: JAI Press.

Gary M. Feinman

SEE ALSO

Exchange Media

Edzna (Yucatán, Mexico)

Edzna (Spanish, Edzná) lies in a shallow basin within the Yucatecan thorn forest region. Annual precipitation of between 1,000 and 1,300 millimeters occurs in a six-month period, leaving a long dry season. Thirty-one kilometers of canals and twenty-seven reservoirs were carved into the clay soil, draining lands that may have allowed the practice of intensive agriculture. The canals were laid out like the spokes of a wheel radiating from a huge Late Formative platform on which rests a Late Classic pyramidal building called Cinco Pisos. The hydraulic system brought water to several areas and allowed storage of water for more than 700 house mounds and public build-

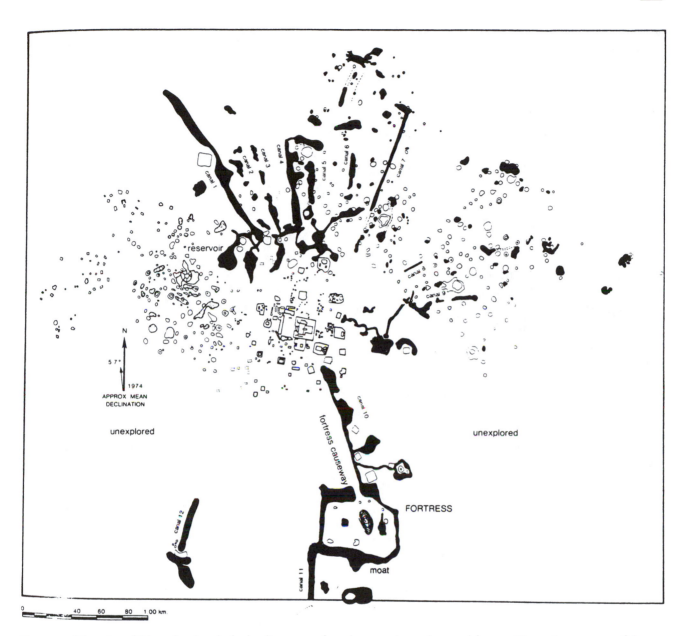

Site map of the ruins of Edzna showing the hydraulic system of canals, reservoirs, and moated fortress. Illustration courtesy of the author after Matheny et al., 1983.

ings. The canals were mapped by color infrared aerial photography during the wet season and by ground survey. More than 2 million cubic meters of soil were excavated in creating the hydraulic system, requiring an estimated 4 million man-days of labor to complete it; this suggests a powerful polity far beyond that of a chiefdom. A fortress-like complex, connected by canal to the ceremonial area, is surrounded by water-filled moats. One hundred fifty excavations demonstrated that most of the hydraulic sys-

tem was constructed by about 150 B.C. and that there was diminished use of it by Late Classic times.

FURTHER READINGS

Matheny, R. T., D. L. Gurr, D. W. Forsyth, and F. R. Hauck. 1980–1983. *Investigations at Edzná, Campeche, Mexico.* New World Archaeological Foundation Papers, 46.

Ray T. Matheny

E

SEE ALSO
Maya Lowlands: North

Emblem Glyphs

The honorific titles in Maya inscriptions that link a ruler to a specific kingdom are known as "emblem glyphs." Each is based on the term *k'ul ahaw*, "divine lord," which accompanies a varying hieroglyphic element that stands for the ancient name of a place or political unit. Thus, each ruler of Tikal was called *K'ul Mutul Ahaw*, or "Divine Lord of Mutul"; the kings of Palenque were called *K'ul Bakal Ahaw*, or "Divine Lord of Bakal," and so forth. Emblem glyphs are but one of several elaborations on the *ahaw* title; others are *cli 'ok ahaw*, "young lord, prince," and *ix-ahaw*, "noblewoman, queen." Typically these appear after a personal name. The emblems of approximately thirty sites are now known, apparently labeling the greater political unit over which that site had domain.

Although the decipherment of the emblem glyph title is recent, they were first recognized by Heinrich Berlin in 1958. His realization that at least some Maya glyphs are tied to particular places set the stage for the hypothesis that Maya texts relate royal history, advanced by Tatiana Proskouriakoff and Berlin in the years that followed. Emblem glyphs have since been used to study the nature of Classic Maya geopolitics, beginning with the pioneering work by Joyce Marcus in the 1970s, and continuing most recently with the "superstates" model advanced by Simon Martin and Nikolai Grube. Martin and Grube suggest that Calakmul and Tikal were the two most powerful kingdoms in the Maya Lowlands and that the *k'ul ahaw* of each competed for the allegiance of many smaller centers in the southern Maya Lowlands. The study of place names in Maya inscriptions has also become more refined since Berlin's work, with the identification of specific locations within kingdoms.

FURTHER READINGS

Berlin, H. 1958. El glifo émblema en las inscripciones mayas. *Journal de Ia Société des Américanistes*, n.s. 47:11–12.

Marcus, J. 1976. *Emblem and State in the Classic Maya Lowlands*. Washington, D.C.: Dumbarton Oaks.

Mathews, P. 1991. Classic Maya Emblem Glyphs. In T. P. Culbert (ed.), *Classic Maya Political History: Hieroglyphic and Archaeological Evidence*, pp. 19–29. Cambridge: Cambridge University Press.

Stuart, D., and S. Houston. 1994. *Classic Maya Place Names*. Washington, D.C.: Dumbarton Oaks.

David Stuart

SEE ALSO
Maya Culture and History

Epiclassic

See Classic Period; Postclassic Period

Ethnicity

Ethnicity is a complicated and sometimes controversial topic in Mesoamerican studies. Ethnic groups are categories of ascription and identification employed by social actors, especially categories concerning origins and background (here following Barth 1969). The cultural features that the actors use to define ethnic categories may be rather arbitrary and are subject to change over time. Ethnic boundaries may differ from cultural boundaries, and a population sharing basically the same culture may be ethnically divided.

Ethnicity is also a highly situational phenomenon that applies to various levels of socio-cultural integration. For example, one's barrio (neighborhood), community, region, or language group may all serve as ethnic reference points, depending on the context of social interaction. Finally, it is axiomatic that ethnicity is not equally important in all societies or all social contexts. It flourishes especially in competitive settings marked by sharp differences in language, political power, and access to economic resources, including labor. These differences became important in ancient Mesoamerica as complex social organization developed. Mesoamerican chiefdoms, states, and empires subsumed previously separate communities into new organizational forms and brought different groups into new contexts of ethnic interaction. They also participated in long-distance exchange and diplomacy that crossed ethnic boundaries.

Ethnographically, the expression of ethnicity in modern Mesoamerica varies markedly from region to region, and even from town to town within the same region. One study in the Morelos Highlands of Nahuatl-speaking Central Mexico concluded that Indian identity in the community was largely forced on the inhabitants by mestizo outsiders (people of mixed racial heritage with a predominantly Hispanic culture). At the other end of the spectrum is the Isthmus of Tehuantepec city of Juchitán

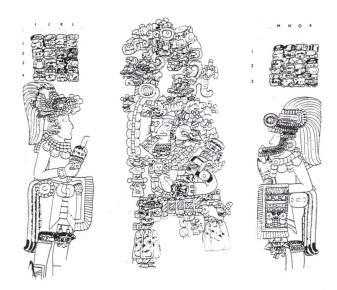

Illustration of the front and lateral faces of Stela 31 at Tikal, Guatemala. Early Classic Maya. Courtesy of the University Museum, University of Pennsylvania.

(Oaxaca), where Zapotec language and ethnicity are badges of honor and constitute the foundation of an important political movement. Some other towns in the region share Juchitán's militancy, yet still others—notably the city of Tehuantepec—reject it and are oriented more toward the national mestizo mainstream.

In general, indigenous ethnicity today receives its greatest expression in highland regions that are linguistically diverse and characterized by microenvironmental differences. The Maya Highlands of Chiapas and western Guatemala are especially noted for their rigid distinction between ladinos (people of Hispanic descent) and Indians. The Maya themselves are not a unified group and are divided in their ethnic loyalties along the lines of language and community membership.

In the Maya Highlands, the most basic unit of ethnic identification is the *municipio* (roughly equivalent to a U.S. township), as Tax was the first to recognize. *Municipios* are recognized political units in contemporary Mexico and Guatemala, but they have deep cultural roots, and their boundaries frequently follow those of pre-Hispanic communities or city-states.

Common language is often viewed as ethnically distinct, and wherever an indigenous language is spoken, it will be an important factor in ethnic identity. These linguistic groups usually include more than one *municipio*, although within a group a number of recognized municipal dialects often exist. Linguistic affiliation is somewhat less important in determining ethnicity than is identification with the local community (*municipio*), and it would be a mistake automatically to equate linguistic and ethnic boundaries in an unambiguous fashion. Ethnic identity is relative, and situational factors must also be taken into account. Among the Sierra Zapotec of Oaxaca, for example, de la Fuente found a gradient of identification and classification, starting with the *pueblo* or *municipio*, progressing to the linguistic group (speakers of the Cajonos, Nexitzo, or Bixanos Zapotec languages), and at the most general level including speakers of all Zapotec languages. The particular ethnic units and symbols relevant to a given social encounter are context dependent.

Many symbols or "badges" of ethnicity have been reported by ethnographers. Dress is highly expressive of ethnic difference: type of cloth or weave, colors used, design, men's hat styles, women's hairstyles, footwear, jewelry, and so on. Artisan specialization may also be a mark of ethnic identity, because some groups specialize in particular crafts (pottery, weaving, etc.) or produce special market commodities such as flowers or salt. Thus, Chiapas Highlanders might categorize the male residents of the town of Zinacantan as follows: "Zinacantecos wear big, flat hats with coloured ribbons, white shorts, pink scarfs, and sandals with tall leggings. They are salt traders and live in the municipality of Zinacantan" (Siverts 1969:103).

Worship of particular gods, spirits, or saints is also frequently relevant to the expression of ethnicity. The phenomenon of patron saints or deities for named communities (and even barrios within them) did not originate with the Spanish but was in many places an old Mesoamerican concept. Local variants of the belief system are part of whole "bundles" of traits that denote ethnic distinctiveness; in Guatemala today, for instance, a sign of indigenous identity is active participation in *costumbre*— the community-based, civil-religious hierarchy and its associated ritual. These are just some of the most common ethnic symbols recognized today in Mesoamerica.

Native ethnohistorical sources use the same traits mentioned above to express ethnic affiliation. For example, Nahuas writing near the time of the Spanish conquest occasionally describe ethnic groups in terms of language or city-state origin, or mention articles of clothing or occupational or behavioral traits that were used to distinguish people in terms of origin (Sahagún 1950–1969, book 10:165–197). However, while many such indicators of ethnicity have great time depth, their specific manifestations (dialects recognized, particular items of clothing,

E

etc.) are highly variable and often unpredictable. No list of indicators can be exhaustive, because the relevant traits are constantly changing.

Obviously, there can be no simple projection of modern patterns of ethnicity into the Mesoamerican past, nor can Colonial ethnohistorical sources be used uncritically to predict pre-Hispanic patterns. Spanish-Indian contacts introduced a new dimension of ethnic relations, including new biological traits as an aspect of ethnicity. Colonial administration may have strengthened the importance of the community through restrictions on access to land. However, native accounts from the time of early Spanish contact identify city or town origins as a prominent feature of ethnic identity, and the settlement pattern in many parts of Mesoamerica in the Late Postclassic period exhibited multiple, often independent cities or towns. Although ethnohistorical sources suggest that language, clothing, and community of origin were among the most important dimensions of ethnicity in pre-Conquest times, the information is complicated by a large number of migrations and unstable political alliances of various sizes. Shifting ethnic identities and relations were especially characteristic of the Postclassic period, and in this period, as in others, there was considerable overlap between ethnic and class differences. In ancient Mesoamerica it was not uncommon for ruling elites to distinguish themselves from commoners by a number of "ethnic" traits mentioned above, such as dialect, vocabulary, religious ritual, and dress.

Ethnic identities may be detectable archaeologically, because ethnicity structures interactions within and among societies, and ethnic groups may use arbitrary symbols of identity. However, the ethnic pattern will seldom be unambiguous, and its detection must rely on the consistent contrast between juxtaposed behavioral patterns not easily ascribed to class, rank, or occupation. Occasionally, recovery of associated burials and skeletal analysis may reveal variant biological populations or practices.

Despite the problems with studying ethnicity archaeologically, certain bodies of evidence provide a means of substantiating its importance as a basis for structuring social relations. Often, ethnohistoric patterns are an important starting point. For example, clothing depicted in native codices follows broad patterns in regional dress that are likely to have been utilized to ascribe social identities and structure interactions, according to Anawalt. Another example is that of the Otomí. Xaltocan, a Post-

classic Otomí-dominated town in the Basin of Mexico, yielded archaeological evidence that was interpreted using ethnohistoric descriptions: a concentration of a particular kind of lip plug at Xaltocan matched descriptions of its use by the Otomí, and it may have been one signal about ethnic identity, according to Brumfiel's research. Ceramic figurines may be another such symbol, applicable to earlier periods.

For earlier periods, and for contexts lacking written documentation of ethnic traits, representational sculpture occasionally shows figures with contrastive clothing and other attributes that may reflect ethnic identities. Two possible examples date to the Classic period. Stela 31 at Tikal shows a Maya ruler in typical regalia flanked by two attendants garbed in Teotihuacán style. Possibly they were local Maya who affected Teotihuacán dress, but probably ethnic Teotihuacanos are shown. At Monte Albán in the Valley of Oaxaca, the Lápida de Bazán carving and stelae at the corners of the South Platform show individuals in Teotihuacán-style clothing; this suggests that in foreign situations, Teotihuacanos (perhaps ambassadors or other important personages) were recognizable and designated in part through costume, especially a particular tassel headdress.

Archaeological patterning in artifacts, buildings, and social or religious ritual also can reveal possible ethnic groups. Ethnic residential areas, or "barrios," at the city of Teotihuacán in the Valley of Mexico are an example. Tlailotlacan, the "Oaxaca barrio," displays an enduring pattern of pottery forms and finishes different from those that predominated at Teotihuacán. Although locally made, this pottery is typical of styles in the Valley of Oaxaca. In addition, tomb construction and aspects of burial ritual, including funerary urns, resemble patterns in Oaxaca, not Teotihuacán. Some other artifacts, as well as the "apartment compound" style of dwelling, are typical of Teotihuacán, suggesting that the inhabitants adopted some Teotihuacán practices but persistently maintained styles and ritual in family life that distinguished them from other urban dwellers. Although osteological burial analyses could provide a basis for identification of a non-local biological population, insufficient data are available in the case of this barrio.

Another possible ethnic barrio at Teotihuacán may have been inhabited by people from the Gulf Coast, as round buildings and importation of Gulf Coast and Maya ceramics in considerable quantities distinguish the occupants of what is called the "Merchants' barrio." Persistent juxtaposition of a constellation of non-local traits for which a distant zone of origin can be suggested creates a case for these ethnic barrios.

Ethnic enclaves of Teotihuacanos at distant locations are suggested by styles of temple architecture (*talud* and *tablero*) and artifacts (e.g., two-holed *candeleros*) at Kaminaljuyú in the Guatemala Highlands and at Matacapan in the Tuxtla Mountains. Certain areas at Kaminaljuyú may have been inhabited by Teotihuacanos in an otherwise Maya settlement, and Matacapan may have been an enclave of Teotihuacán affinity among southern Gulf Coast groups.

Ethnohistoric language patterns provide a different basis for inferring earlier ethnic identities. In the case of ancient Oaxaca, many researchers view Monte Albán as the capital of an ancient Zapotec state and use modern and historic Zapotec cultural practices as a basis for archaeological interpretations. On a large scale, Zapotec language and cultural practices are one basis of ethnic identity today and may have served similarly in the past, but at other, smaller scales, community affiliations may have been more important.

Pockets of Nahua speakers in locations distant from the main concentration of this language in the Central Mexican Highlands and northwestern Mexico provide another linguistic case of possible contrastive ethnic identity. Groups called Pipil and Nicarao were Nahua speakers as far south as El Salvador and Nicaragua. The timing of arrival and the cultural and social characteristics of these groups is a matter of debate, as is their exact geographic origin. Excavations have revealed some instances of Central American settlements, such as Cihuatán in El Salvador, in which artifact styles diverge from local patterns and seem to be intrusive, substantiating the linguistic evidence for groups that may have been recognized as ethnically distinct.

Generally, however, it is risky to assume that contrastive cultural patterns necessarily operated as markers of ethnic identity, because the situation may have been subdivided in more complex ways by the ancient inhabitants. Ethnic markers in pre-Columbian Mesoamerica may have been traits that do not preserve archaeologically, or symbols that we cannot interpret accurately. Moreover, stylistic patterns were often an active basis for manipulation and presentation of identities. One result is that the spread or adoption of foreign styles or cultural traits may be accomplished by local people who imitate practices elsewhere.

FURTHER READINGS

Anawalt, P. 1981. *Indian Clothing before Cortés: Mesoamerican Costumes from the Codices.* Norman: University of Oklahoma Press.

Auger, R., et al. (eds.). 1987. *Ethnicity and Culture.* Calgary: Archaeological Association, Department of Archaeology, University of Calgary.

Barth, F. 1969. Introduction. In F. Barth (ed.), *Ethnic Groups and Boundaries,* pp. 9–38. Boston: Little, Brown.

Brumfiel, E. 1994. Ethnic Groups and Political Development in Ancient Mexico. In E. Brumfiel and J. Fox (eds.), *Factional Competition and Political Development in the New World,* pp. 89–102. Cambridge: Cambridge University Press.

Emberling, G. 1997. Ethnicity in Complex Societies: Archaeological Perspectives. *Journal of Archaeological Research* 5:295–344.

Fowler, W., Jr. 1989. *The Cultural Evolution of Ancient Nahua Civilizations: The Pipil-Nicarao of Central America.* Norman: University of Oklahoma Press.

de la Fuente, J. 1965. *Relaciones Interétnicas.* Mexico City: Instituto Nacional Indigenista.

Sahagún, B. 1950–69. *Florentine Codex: General History of the Things of New Spain.* A. Anderson and C. Dibble (trans.). 13 vols. Salt Lake City: School of American Research and University of Utah.

Santley, R., C. Yarborough, and B. Hall. 1987. Enclaves, Ethnicity, and the Archaeological Record at Matacapan. In R. Auger et al. (eds.), *Ethnicity and Culture,* pp. 85–100. Calgary: Archaeological Association, Department of Archaeology, University of Calgary.

Siverts, H. 1969. Ethnic Stability and Boundary Dynamics in Southern Mexico. In F. Barth (ed.), *Ethnic Groups and Boundaries,* pp. 101–116. Boston: Little, Brown.

Spence, M. 1992. Tlailotlacan: A Zapotec Enclave in Teotihuacán. In J. Berlo (ed.), *Art, Ideology, and the City of Teotihuacán,* pp. 59–88. Washington, D.C.: Dumbarton Oaks.

Tax, S. 1937. The Municipios of the Midwestern Highlands of Guatemala. *American Anthropologist* 39:423–444.

John K. Chance and Barbara L. Stark

SEE ALSO

Languages at the Time of Contact

E

Ethnohistorical Sources and Methods

Ethnohistory, in contrast to archaeology, relies on written and/or illustrated texts as its primary source of data. The ethnohistoric study of pre-Hispanic Mesoamerica depends heavily on the written words and art of Spaniards and Indians; most of the texts, noteworthy in number and quality, were produced during the early post-Conquest era. These sources allow scholars to write detailed histories of individual pre-Columbian cultural groups, syntheses of micro- and macrogeographic and cultural regions, and intensive analyses of political, economic, social, and religious aspects of social life. They also show that indigenous ways of life survived longer into the Colonial period than nineteenth-century and early twentieth-century scholars—such as Lewis Henry Morgan, William Prescott, and Hubert Bancroft—understood.

Anthropologists often define ethnohistory as the application of anthropological theory and methods to written documents, whereas historians generally view it as the study of peoples for whom written documents are sparse and for whom anthropological data are applied for historians' goals. Anthropologists, archaeologists, and historians began to use the term "ethnohistory" in the 1940s to describe their researches combining documentary, oral, and sometimes archaeological data on the aboriginal peoples of North America. By the 1950s, ethnohistoric interest developed in regard to Mesoamerica and South America.

The roots of Latin American ethnohistory, especially Mesoamerican ethnohistory, lie less in archaeology and more in the strong, persistent interest in the massive amounts of documentation that emerged out of the Spanish conquest and colonial aftermath. Although aboriginal peoples worldwide fall under the purview of ethnohistory, most such scholarship concentrates on the New World.

Ethnohistorians of Mesoamerica have focused on the geographic area spanning present-day Mexico, Guatemala, and Belize, with the United States "borderland" areas (formerly part of New Spain and later of Mexico) and Central America receiving less attention. Anthropological specialists, for the most part, investigate the pre-Columbian peoples of Mesoamerica, especially those of the fourteenth and fifteenth centuries—the Late Postclassic period—and historical specialists concentrate on the Colonial period histories of these peoples. This article treats ethnohistorical sources dealing with pre-Columbian groups, even though most of these sources were written during the Colonial era, and concentrates on the primary regions of population of Mesoamerica as already defined.

Printed materials, both textual and pictorial, constitute the primary source for pre-Columbian ethnohistory. Scholars recognize the codex (Spanish, *códice*), a native-tradition pictorial and/or written manuscript, as the most authentic representation of aboriginal historical, cultural, and artistic expression. Codices took a variety of forms in the pre-Hispanic era; screenfold books (manuscripts "folded, accordian-pleat fashion, like a screen," Glass 1975:8) are the most common type. They depict a variety of kinds of information, especially ritual and calendrical themes (for example, the Codex Dresden), group and dynastic histories (e.g., the Codex Boturini or the *Tira de la Peregrinación,* as it is also commonly known), and economic and cartographic records (e.g., the Codex Mendoza or the *Historia Tolteca-Chichimeca*). Codices use both pictures and a limited pictographic or hieroglyphic writing system to convey information. Of the hundreds still extant, the vast majority were produced in the post-Conquest era; some are copies or slightly edited versions of earlier, pre-Hispanic records.

Textual, printed materials form the bulk of sources used by scholars of pre-Columbian ethnohistory. The most common include eyewitness accounts of conquerors (Cortés's letters to Emperor Charles V are only the best known of a substantial genre); historical and ethnographic accounts by both Spanish civil bureaucrats (for example, Alonso Zorita) and religious personnel (the Sahaguntine corpus is the supreme representative of this subgenre) and Indian and mestizo writers (such as Chimalpahin or Gaspar Antonio Chi); administrative reports and records (for example, the *Relaciones geográficas*); and grammars and dictionaries. While most texts were written in Spanish, many examples of native-language texts exist. The majority of the latter are in Nahuatl, but texts in Otomí, Mixtec, Quiche, Cakchiquel, Chontal, and Yucatec may also be found. Indigenous and Spanish writers often had strikingly different views of events as well as contrasting ways of expressing ideas and recounting histories.

The very number and richness of both the pictorial and textual sources indicates that there are significant problems of interpretation. The meanings of pictorials (whether visual images or, more commonly, the signs used in indigenous writing systems) are not alway immediately apparent and are subject to varying explanations. Textual sources, while seemingly easier to interpret, also pose challenges, most of which fall under the category of "reliability." Scholars must always be aware that written texts vary in quality, and even the richest pose interpretive

TABLE 1. CODICES (C = CODEX).

Title/Author C[omposition], P[ublication] date (Modern Ref.[a])	Type of Document	Region or Town
C. Aubin; C: after 1576 (1963)	calendrical	Mexico City
C. Borbonicus; C: pre-Conquest or early sixteenth century (1979)	calendrical	Mexico City
C. Magliabecchiano; C: before c. 1566 (1970)	calendrical, historical, ethnographic	Valley of Mexico
C. Ríos (also known as C. Vaticanus A); C: c. 1566–1589 (1979)	calendrical	Valley of Mexico
C. Telleriano Remensis; C: c. 1562–1563 (1964)	calendrical	Valley of Mexico
C. Borgia; C: pre-Conquest (1993)	calendrical	western Oaxaca[b]
C. Cospi; C: pre-Conquest (1968)	calendrical	western Oaxaca[b]
C. Féjéváry-Mayer; C: pre-Conquest (1971)	calendrical	western Oaxaca[b]
C. Laud; C: pre-Conquest (1966)	calendrical	western Oaxaca[b]
C. Porfirio Díaz; C: sixteenth or seventeenth century (1892)	calendrical, historical	northern Oaxaca
C. Vaticanus B; C: pre-Conquest (1972)	calendrical	western Oaxaca
C. Vienna (aka Codex Vindobonensis Mexicanus I); C: pre-Conquest (1963)	calendrical, historical	western Oaxaca (Mixtec)
C. Dresden; C: pre-Conquest (1975)	calendrical	southeastern Mexico
C. Madrid (aka Codex Tro-Cortesianus); C: pre-Conquest (1967)	calendrical	southeastern Mexico
C. Paris; C: pre-Conquest (1994)	calendrical	southeastern Mexico
C. Boturini (aka *Tira de la Peregrinación*); C: sixteenth century (1944)	historical	Mexico City
C. Xolotl; C: sixteenth century (1951)	historical	Texcoco region
Lienzo de Tlaxcala; C: c. 1550 (1979)	historical	Tlaxcala
C. Becker; C: pre-Conquest (1961)	historical	western Oaxaca
C. Bodley; C: c. 1521 (1960)	historical	western Oaxaca
C. Colombino; C: pre-Conquest (1966)	historical	western Oaxaca
C. Nuttall; C: pre-Conquest (1987)	historical	western Oaxaca
C. Selden; C: pre-Conquest (1964)	historical	western Oaxaca
C. Fernández Leal; C: sixteenth century (1942)	historical	northern Oaxaca

[a]The accompanying bibliography cites a significant modern reference for each work. In rare cases (for especially important works), English translations are also cited. For fuller lists of citations, see the bibliographic essays in volumes 12 through 15 of the *Handbook of Middle American Indians*.

[b]Because of disagreement over the identification of the location of these codices, I follow the "western Oaxaca" designation of Glass (1975). Also see Sisson (1983) and Nicholson and Quiñones Keber (1994).

E

TABLE 2. NATIVE-LANGUAGE PROSE SOURCES.

Title/Author; C[omposition], P[ublication] date (Modern Reference)	Type of Document	Region or Town
Anales de Cuauhtitlan; C: c. 1570 (1885)	historical	central Mexico
Cantares mexicanos; C: sixteenth century (Bierhorst 1985)	poems and songs	central Mexico
Anales de Tlatelolco; C: seventeenth century (1950)	historical	Mexico City
Historia de los Mexicanos, Cristobal Castillo; C: 1600 (1991)	historical	central Mexico
Diario, Chimalpahin Quauhtlehuanitzin; C: c. 1615 (1963–1965)	historical	Mexico City
Relaciones, Chimalpahin Quauhtlehuanitzin; C: c. 1600–1631 (1965)	historical	central Mexico
Crónica mexicana, Tezozomoc, Fernando Alvarado; C: late sixteenth or early seventeenth century (1980)	historical	central Mexico
Crónica mexicayotl[a]; C: early seventeenth century (1949)	historical	Mexico City
Estas son las leyes; C: 1543 (1941)	legal	central Mexico
Historia de los mexicanos por sus pinturas; C: c. 1535 (1988)	historical	central Mexico
Historia Tolteca-Chichimeca; C: c. 1550 (1976)	historical	Cuauhtinchan, Puebla
Relaciones, by Fernando de Alva Ixtlilxochitl; C: c. 1600–1640 (1975–1977)	historical	Texcoco
Historia Chichimeca, by Fernando de Alva Ixtlilxochitl; C: c. 1600–1640 (1975–1977)	historical	central Mexico
Leyenda de los Soles; C: c. 1558 (1993)	religious	central Mexico
Relación de Texcoco, by Juan Bautista Pomar; C: 1582 (1975)	historical	Texcoco
Relación sobre las costumbres, by Gaspar Antonio Chi; C: 1582 (1941)	historical	Yucatan
Books of the Chilam Balam; C: eighteenth and nineteenth centuries[b] (Barrera Vásquez and Rendón 1948)	religious	Yucatan
Anales de los Cakchiqueles; C: c. 1605 (1967)	historical	Solola, Guatemala
Popol Vuh; C: c. 1544–1558 (Edmonson 1971)	historical	Santa Cruz del Quiche, Guatemala

[a]Although this work has been attributed to Fernando Alvarado Tezozomoc, Chimalpahin may well be its main author.
[b]Many of these works were written in the eighteenth and nineteenth centuries, but they include earlier materials.

issues. Because early chroniclers often copied from each other, giving little or no credit, the ethnohistorian must make judgments about the independence of such sources. The quality of information must also be judged by asking of every source who was its author, as well as when, where, and why its author wrote it.

The researcher may encounter two particular problems. First, the cyclical ordering and patterning of historical events that was part of Mesoamerican worldviews and his-torical consciousness makes reliable identification and ordering of actual events problematic. Second, regionally varying calendars and year counts make conversion of dates to the Gregorian calendar difficult. Nevertheless, while the quality of both Spanish-language and native-language pic-torial and textual sources varies and their meanings are not always as literally transparent as earlier scholars believed, the Mesoamerican corpus remains unique for its size and the variety and richness of the sources.

E

TABLE 3. CONQUERORS' ACCOUNTS.

Title/Author; C[omposition], P[ublication] date (Modern Reference)	Type of Document	Region/ Town
Brief Account of the Conquest *(Relación breve de la conquista),* by Francisco Aguilar; C: after 1559 (1977)	conquest history	Mexico City
Account of Some Things of New Spain *(Relación de algunas cosas de la Nueva España),* by an Anonymous Conqueror; C: 1556 (1941)	conquest history	Mexico City
Letters *(Cartas de relación),* by Hernan Cortés, C: 1519–1526 (1960, 1986)	conquest history	Mexico City
True History of the Conquest *(Historia verdadera de la conquista),* by Bernal Díaz del Castillo; C: c. 1568 (1944)	conquest history	Mexico City
Account *(Relación)* by Pedro Alvarado; C: 1525 (1954)	conquest history	Guatemala

TABLE 4. OFFICIAL CHRONICLES AND GENERAL HISTORIES.

Title/Author; C[omposition], P[ublication] date (Modern Reference)	Type of Document	Region or Town
Historia general de los hechos de los castellanos, by Antonio de Herrera y Tordesillas; C: 1601–1615 (1991)	official chronicle and history	Spanish America
Geografía y descripción universal, by Juan López de Velasco; C: 1574 (1971)	official chronicle and history	Spanish America
De novo orbe decades, by Peter Martyr (Pietro Martire d' Anghiera); C: 1530 (1989)	official chronicle and history	Spanish America
Opus epistolarum, by Peter Martyr (Pietro Martire d' Anghiera); C: 1530 (1953–57)	official chronicle and history	Spanish America
Historia general y natural, by Gonzalo Fernández Oviedo y Valdés; C: 1535 (1959)	official chronicle and history	Spanish America
Política indiana, by Juan de Solórzano Pereira; C: 1648 (1972)	legal compilation	Spanish America
Relaciones geográficas; C: 1579–1585[a] (Acuña 1982–1986)	answers to a standard questionnaire, many with maps	Central Mexico, Oaxaca, Yucatan
Historia natural, by José de Acosta; C: 1590 (1940)	general history	Spanish America
Brevísima relación, by Bartolomé de las Casas; C: 1552 (1945)	general history	Spanish America
Apologética historia, by Bartolomé de las Casas; P: 1909 (1967)	general history	Spanish America
Historia de las Indias, by Bartolomé de las Casas; P: 1875–76 (1957–58)	general history	Caribbean
Historia de las Indias y la conquista de México, by Francisco López de Gómara; C: 1552 (1943)	general history and conquest narrative	Central Mexico

[a]Other such *relaciones* were produced later but are of less ethnohistorical significance.

E

TABLE 5. CIVIL AND RELIGIOUS CHRONICLERS.

Title/Author; C[omposition], P[ublication] date (Modern Reference)	Type of Document	Region/ Town
History of the Indians of New Spain (*Historia de la Indias de Nueva España*), by Diego Durán; C: c. 1570s–1581 (1964, 1967, 1971ª, 1971)	political history, religious description	Central Mexico
Economic and Social Life of New Spain (*La vida económica y social de Nueva España*), perhaps by Gonzalo Gómez de Cervantes; C: 1599 (1979)	descriptive chronicle	Central Mexico
Indian Eccesiastical History (*Historia eclesiástica indiana*), by Jerónimo de Mendieta; C: 1571–1596 (1945)	religious description, history of evangelization	Central Mexico
History of the Indians of New Spain (*Historia de los indios de la Nueva España*), by Toribio de Motolinía; C: 1536–1541 (1969)	political, religious, and social history	Central Mexico
Memoriales, by Toribio de Motolinía; P: 1903 (1971)	political and religious history	Central Mexico
History of Tlaxcala (*Historia de Tlaxcala*), by Diego Muñoz Camargo; C: 1576–1595 (1979)	historical chronicle	Central Mexico/Tlaxcala
Treatise on superstitions and customs (*Tratado de las supersticiones y costumbres*), by Hernando Ruíz de Alarcón; P: 1629 (1988)	religious history and description	Central Mexico/ Atenango del Río
Florentine Codex, by Bernardino de Sahagúnª; written by 1569 (1950–1982)	descriptive chronicle	Central Mexico
Historia general, by Bernardino de Sahagúnª; written after 1569 (1956)	descriptive chronicle	Central Mexico
Monarquia indiana, by Juan de Torquemada; P: 1615 (1969)	descriptive and religious chronicle	Central Mexico
Tovar Manuscript, by Juan de Tovar; written by 1579 (1972)	historical chronicle	Central Mexico
Tovar Calendar; C: c. 1585	calendrical description	Central Mexico
Brief and Summary Account (*Breve y sumaria relación*), by Alonso de Zorita; C: c. 1570s	descriptive chronicle	Central Mexico
History of New Spain (*Historia de la Nueva España*), by Alonso de Zorita; P: 1909	descriptive chronicle	Central Mexico
Descripción de la provincia, by Diego de Muñoz; C: c. 1583	descriptive and religious chronicle	Michoacan
Relación de Michoacan, by Jerónimo Alcalá; C: c. 1539–1541	historical chronicle	Michoacan
Palestra historial, by Francisco del Burgoa; 1670	religious history	Oaxaca
Geográfica descripción, by Francisco del Burgoa; 1674	religious history	Oaxaca
Account of the Things of Yucatán (*Relación de las cosas de Yucatán*), by Diego de Landa; 1688	historical chronicle	Yucatan
Historia de Yucatán, by Diego López de Cogolludo; 1688	historical chronicle	Yucatan
Informe contra idolarum cultores, by Pedro Sánchez de Aguilar; 1639	religious history	Yucatan
Historia general de las Indias Occidentales, Antonio de Remesal; 1639	conquest and religious history	Guatemala
Relación historico-descriptivas, by Martín Alfonso Tovilla; C: 1635	historical chronicle	Guatemala
Crónica de la Provincia del Santisimo Nombre de Jesús de Guatemala, by Francisco Vásquez; c. 1600	religious history	Guatemala

ªNote that this work was based on substantial collaboration with native informants and artists who shaped its strong linguistic and pictorial contents.

Pre-Columbian ethnohistory relies on textual, documentary analysis as its primary method. This historical methodology is supplemented by several distinctly anthropological methods. Ethnohistorians often rely on space–time relationships to organize and interpret their data. Among the concepts used are diffusion (the wavelike spread of ideas or technologies from a center), cultural evolution (the development of societies through patterned, predictable stages), and the "direct historical approach" in which archaeologically known sites and regions are tied to recognized sequences of historical and ethnographic data so that lengthy histories of sites and regions can be developed. Ethnohistorians therefore employ methods that allow the creation of detailed cultural analyses of one point in time (synchronic analysis) or of extended developmental sequences (diachronic analysis). They may also rely on oral traditions or linguistic data, especially kinship terminologies, to draw inferences about cultural development and group interrelationships.

Mesoamerican ethnohistorians have used these sources and methods to produce three kinds of historical analyses. One kind focuses on long-range developmental sequences of cultures or regions. Another kind consists of historical ethnography—that is, the intensive reconstruction and description of a cultural group within a fairly narrow timespan. The third kind of ethnohistorical analysis is theoretical, using data and theory to analyze patterns of political economy, cultural belief and practice, and social organization. Topics such as trade, warfare, urbanization, religious belief and practice, and kinship and family structure draw significant attention. Anthropologists have recently shown interest in analyzing archival sources in addition to the chronicles and codices they have previously emphasized. They also have turned toward analyzing colonial Indian societies, their relationships with Europeans, the changing ecological, economic, political, and ideological contexts shaping them, and the emergent interethnic relationships in which they were enmeshed. Because of the use of both native-language and Spanish-language archival texts, such work explores not only indigenous cultures and histories but also indigenous perspectives, emphasizing colonial Indians as actors within and commentators on their changing societies.

Tables 1–5 list significant ethnohistorical sources for Mesoamerican prehistory, categorized by genre of document. Modern published editions of many of these are cited in the bibliography that follows.

FURTHER READINGS
Primary Sources

Acosta, J. 1940. *Historia natural y moral de las Indias.* Mexico City: Fondo de Cultura Económica.

Acuña, R. 1982–1986. *Relaciones geográficas del siglo XVI.* 10 vols. Mexico City: Universidad Nacional Autónoma de México.

Aguilar, F. 1977. *Relación breve de la conquista de la Nueva España.* Mexico City: Universidad Nacional Autónoma de México.

Alvarado, P. 1954. *Relación hecha por Pedro de Alvarado a Hernando Cortés, en que se refieren las guerras y batallas, para pacificar las provincias del antiguo reino de Goathemala.* Mexico City: José Porrua e Hijos.

Annals of Cuauhtitlán (Codex Chimalpopoca). 1885. *Anales de Cuauhtitlán: Noticias históricas de México y sus contornos.* Mexico City: I. Escalante.

Annals of the Cakchiqueles. 1967. *Anales de los Cakchiqueles.* Havana: Casa de las Americas.

Annals of Tlatelolco. 1950. *Anales de Tlatelolco.* Número uno. Mexico City: Vargas Rea.

Anonymous Conqueror. 1941. *Relación de algunas cosas de la Nueva España y de la gran ciudad de Temistitán México.* Mexico City: Editorial América.

Barrera Vásquez, A., and S. Rendón. 1948. *El libro de los libros de Chilam Balam.* Mexico City and Buenos Aires: Fondo de Cultura Económica.

Bierhorst, J. 1985. *Cantares mexicanos: Songs of the Aztecs.* Stanford: Stanford University Press.

Burgoa, F. 1934a. *Palestra historial de virtudes, y exemplares apostólicos.* Mexico City: Talleres Gráficos de la Nación.

Burgoa, F. 1934b. *Geográfica descripción de la parte septentrional.* Mexico City: Talleres Gráficos de la Nación.

Castillo, C. 1991. *Historia de la venida de los mexicanos y otros pueblos; e, Historia de la conquista.* Mexico City: Instituto Nacional de Antropología e Historia, Proyecto Templo Mayor; GV Editores; Asociación de Amigos del Templo Mayor.

Chi, G. 1941. *Relación sobre las costumbres de los indios.* In A. Tozzer (ed.), *Landa's relación de las cosas de Yucatán: A Translation.* Papers of the Peabody Museum of American Archaeology and Ethnology, 18. Cambridge, Mass.: Harvard University.

Chimalpahin Quauhtlehuanitzin, D. 1965. *Relaciones originales de Chalco Amaquemecan.* Mexico City: Fondo de Cultura Económica.

Chimalpahin Quauhtlehuanitzin, D. 1997. *Codex Chimalpahin: Society and Politics in Mexico, Tenochtitlan,*

E

Tlatelolco, Texcoco, Culhuacan, and Other Nahua Altepetl in Central Mexico. A. Anderson and S. Schroeder (ed. and trans.). 2 vols. Norman: University of Oklahoma Press.

Chronicle Mexicayotl. 1949. *Crónica mexicayotl.* Attributed to F. Tezozomoc. Mexico City: Universidad Nacional Autónoma de México.

Codex Aubin. 1963. *Historia de la nación mexicana: Reproducción a todo color del Códice de 1576 (Aubin).* Madrid: Ediciones José Porrua Turanzas.

Codex Becker. 1961. *Codices Becker I/II.* Graz: Akademische Druck- und Verlagsanstalt.

Codex Bodley. 1960. *Codex Bodley 2858.* Mexico City: Sociedad Mexicana de Antropología.

Codex Borbonicus. 1979. *Códice Borobonico: Manuscrito mexicano de la Biblioteca del Palais Bourbon.* Mexico City: Siglo Veintiuno.

Codex Borgia. 1993. *The Codex Borgia: A Full-Color Restoration of the Ancient Mexican Manuscript.* New York: Dover.

Codex Boturini. 1944. *Tira de la peregrinación mexica.* Mexico City: Anticuaria.

Codex Colombino. 1966. *Códice Colombino.* Mexico City: Sociedad Mexicana de Antropología.

Codex Cospi. 1968. *Codex Cospi: Calendario messicano 4093 Biblioteca universitaria Bologna.* Graz: Akademische Druck- und Verlagsanstalt.

Codex Dresden. 1975. *Codex Dresdensis: Sachsische Landesbibliothek Dresden.* Graz: Akademische Druck- und Verlagsanstalt.

Codex Féjérváry-Mayer. 1971. *Codex Féjérváry-Mayer.* Graz: Akademische Druck- und Verlagsanstalt.

Codex Fernández Leal. 1942. Codex Fernández Leal. *Pacific Art Review* 2:39–59.

Codex Laud. 1966. *Codex Laud.* Graz: Akademische Druck- und Verlagsanstalt.

Codex Madrid. 1967. *Codex Tro-Cortesianus (Codex Madrid).* Graz: Akademische Druck- und Verlagsanstalt.

Codex Magliabecchiano. 1970. *Codex Magliabecchiano.* Graz: Akademische Druck- und Verlagsanstalt.

Codex Nuttall. 1987. *Codex Zouche-Nuttall.* Graz: Akademische Druck- und Verlagsanstalt.

Codex Paris. 1994. *The Paris Codex: Handbook for a Maya Priest.* Austin: University of Texas Press.

Codex Porfirio Díaz. 1892. *Códice Porfirio Díaz. Homenaje a Crístobal Colón: Antigüedades mexicanas.* Mexico City: Oficina Tipográfica de la Secretaria de Fomento.

Codex Ríos. 1979. *Codex Vaticanus 3738.* Graz: Akademische Druck- und Verlagsanstalt.

Codex Selden. 1964. *Codex Selden 3135 (A.2).* Mexico City: Sociedad Mexicana de Antropología.

Codex Telleriano-Remensis. 1995. *Codex Telleriano-Remensis: Ritual, Divination, and History in a Pictorial Manuscript.* Eloise Quiñones Keber (ed.). Austin: University of Texas Press.

Codex Vaticanus B. 1972. *Codex Vaticanus 3773.* Graz: Akademische Druck- und Verlagsanstalt.

Codex Vienna. 1963. *Codex Vindobonensis Mexicanus I.* Graz: Akademische Druck- und Verlagsanstalt.

Codex Xolotl. 1951. *Códice Xolotl.* Mexico City: Publicaciones del Instituto de Historia.

Cortés, H. 1960. *Cartas de relación.* Mexico City: Editorial Porrua.

Cortés, H. 1986. *Letters from Mexico.* A. Pagden (trans. and ed.). New Haven: Yale University Press.

Díaz del Castillo, B. 1944. *Historia verdadera de la conquista de la Nueva España.* Mexico City: Editorial Porrua.

———. 1963. *The Conquest of New Spain.* J. M. Cohen (trans.). Baltimore: Penguin.

Durán, D. 1967. *Historia de las Indias de Nueva España e islas de la tierra firme.* 2 vols. Mexico City: Editorial Porrua.

———. 1971. *Book of the Gods and Rites and the Ancient Calendar.* F. Horcasitas and D. Heyden (trans.). Norman: University of Oklahoma Press.

———. 1994. *The History of the Indies of New Spain.* D. Heyden (trans. and ed.). Norman: University of Oklahoma Press.

Estas son las leyes. 1941. *Estas son las leyes que tenjan los Indios de la Nueva España.* In J. García Icazbalceta (ed.), *Nueva collección de documentos para la historia de México,* vol. 3, pp. 280–286. Mexico City: Editorial Chávez Hayhoe.

Gómez de Cervantes, G. 1944. *La vida económica y social de Nueva España, al finalizar el siglo XVI.* Mexico City: Antigua Librería Robredo, de J. Porrua e Hijos.

Herrera y Tordesillas, A. 1991. *Historia general de los hechos de los castellanos en las Islas y tierra firme de mar oceano, o decadas.* 4 vols. Madrid: Universidad Complutense de Madrid.

History of the Mexicans from Their Pictures. 1988. *Historia de los mexicanos por sus pinturas.* Paris: Association Oxomoco y Cipactomal.

History of the Tolteca-Chichimeca. 1976. *Historia de la Tolteca-Chichimeca.* P. Kirchoff, L. Odena Guemes, and L. Reyes García (eds.). Mexico City: Instituto Nacional de Antropología e Historia.

Ixtlilxochitl, F. de Alva. 1975–1977. *Obras historicas: incluyen el texto completo de las llamadas. Relaciones e Historia de la nación Chichimeca.* 2 vols. Mexico City: Universidad Nacional Autónoma de México.

Landa, D. 1941. *Landa's Relación de las cosas de Yucatán: A Translation.* A. Tozzer (trans.). Papers of the Peabody Museum of American Archaeology and Ethnology, 18. Cambridge, Mass.: Harvard University.

———. 1985. *Relación de las cosas de Yucatán.* Madrid: Historia 16.

las Casas, B. de. 1945. *Brevisima relación de la destrucción de las Indias.* Mexico City: SEP.

———. 1951. *Historia de las Indias.* 3 vols. Mexico City: Fondo de Cultura Económica.

———. 1967. *Apologética historia sumária.* 2 vols. Mexico City: Universidad Nacional Autónoma de México.

Legend of the Suns. 1993. *La leyenda de los soles.* Mexico City: Fondo de Cultura Económica.

Lienzo of Tlaxcala. 1979. *Lienzo de Tlaxcala.* Mexico City: Editorial Cosmos.

López de Cogolludo, D. 1957. *Historia de Yucatán.* Mexico City: Editorial Academia Literaría.

López de Gómara, F. 1943. *Historia de la conquista de México.* 2 vols. Mexico City: Editorial Pedro Robredo.

———. 1964. *Cortés: The Life of the Conqueror by His Secretary.* L. Simpson (trans. and ed.). Berkeley and Los Angeles: University of California Press.

López de Velasco, J. 1971. *Geografía y descripción universal de las Indias.* Madrid: Atlas.

Martire, P. (Peter Martyr). 1953–1957. *Epistolario.* 4 vols. Madrid: Imprenta Góngora.

———. 1989. *Decadas del Nuevo Mundo.* Madrid: Ediciones Polifemo.

Mendieta, J. 1945. *Historia eclesiastica indiana.* Mexico City: Editorial Salvador Chavez Hayhoe.

Motolinía, T. 1969. *Historia de los indios de la Nueva España.* Mexico City: Porrua.

———. 1971. *Memoriales; o, Libro de las cosas de la Nueva España y de los naturales de ella.* Mexico City: Universidad Nacional Autónoma de México.

Muñoz, D. 1951. *Descripción de la provincia de San Pedro y San Pablo de Michoacán, en las Indias de la Nueva España.* Guadalajara: Junta Auxiliar Jalisciense de la Sociedad Mexicana de Geografía y Estadística.

———. 1979. *Historia de Tlaxcala.* Mexico City: Editorial Innovación.

Oviedo y Valdés, G. 1959. *Historia general y natural de las Indias.* 5 vols. Madrid: Ediciones Atlas.

Pomar, J. 1975. *Relación de Tezcoco.* Mexico City: Biblioteca Enciclopedia del Estado de México.

Popol Vuh. 1971. *The Book of Counsel: The Popol Vuh of the Quiche Maya of Guatemala.* M. S. Edmonson (ed.). New Orleans: Middle American Research Institute, Tulane University.

Relation of Michoacán. 1988. *La relación de Michoacán.* Mexico City: Secretaría de Educación Pública.

Remesal, A. 1988. *Historia general de las Indias Occidentales, y particular de la gobernación de Chiapa y Guatemala.* Mexico City: Editorial Porrua.

Ruiz de Alarcón, H. 1984. *Treatise on the Heathen Superstitions That Today Live among the Indians Native to This New Spain, 1629.* J. Andrews and R. Hassig (trans. and ed.). Norman: University of Oklahoma Press.

———. 1988. *Tratado de las supersticiones y costumbres gentilicas que hoy viven entre los indios naturales desta Nueva España.* Mexico City: SEP.

Sahagún, B. 1950–1982. *Florentine Codex: General History of the Things of New Spain.* A. Anderson and C. Dibble (trans. and ed.). 14 vols., 13 parts. Salt Lake City: University of Utah and School of American Research.

———. 1956. *Historia general de las cosas de Nueva España.* Mexico City: Editorial Porrua.

Sánchez de Aguilar, P. 1937. *Informe contra idolarum cultores del obispado de Yucatán.* Mérida: E. G. Triay e Hijos.

Solórzano Pereira, J. 1972. *Política indiana.* 5 vols. Madrid: Ediciones Atlas.

Tezozomoc, F. 1980. *Crónica mexicana.* Mexico City: Editorial Porrua.

Torquemada, J. 1975–1983. *Monarquía indiana. De los veinte y un libros rituales y monarquía indiana, con el orígen y guerras de los indios occidentales.* 7 vols. Mexico City: Universidad Nacional Autónoma de México.

Tovar, J. 1951. *The Tovar Calendar.* New Haven: The Academy.

———. 1972. *Tovar Ms. Manuscrit Tovar: Origenes et croyances des Indiens du Mexique.* Graz: Akademische Druck- und Verlagsanstalt.

Tovilla, M. 1960. *Relaciones historico-descriptivas de la Verapaz, el Manche y Lacandón en Guatemala.* Guatemala: Editorial Universitaria.

Vásquez, F. 1938–1944. *Crónica de la provincia del Santísimo Nombre de Jesús de Guatemala.* 4 vols. Guatemala: Sociedad de Geografía e Historia.

Zorita, A. 1909. *Historia de la Nueva España.* Madrid: Librería General de V. Suarez.

E

———. 1942. *Breve y sumaria relación de los señores de la Nueva España*. Mexico City: Universidad Nacional Autónoma de México.

Secondary Sources

Berdan, F. 1982. *The Aztecs of Central Mexico: An Imperial Society*. New York: Holt, Rinehart and Winston.

Burkhart, L. 1989. *The Slippery Earth: Nahua–Christian Moral Dialogue in Sixteenth-Century Mexico*. Tucson: University of Arizona Press.

Carrasco, P. 1971. Social Organization of Ancient Mexico. In G. Ekholm and I. Bernal (eds.), *Handbook of Middle American Indians: Archaeology of Northern Mesoamerica*, vol. 10, part 1, pp. 349–75. Austin: University of Texas Press.

Glass, J. 1975. A Survey of Native Middle American Pictorial Manuscripts. In H. Cline (ed.), *Handbook of Middle American Indians: Guide to Ethnohistorical Sources*, vol. 14, pp. 3–80. Austin: University of Texas Press.

Hill, R. 1992. *Colonial Cakchiquels: Highland Maya Adaptation to Spanish Rule, 1600–1700*. Fort Worth: Harcourt Brace Jovanovich.

Kellogg, S. 1995. *Law and the Transformation of Aztec Culture, 1500–1700*. Norman: University of Oklahoma Press.

Nicholson, H. 1975. Middle American Ethnohistory: An Overview. In H. Cline (ed.), *Handbook of Middle American Indians: Guide to Ethnohistorical Sources*, vol. 15, pp. 487–505. Austin: University of Texas Press.

Restall, M. 1997. *The Maya World: Yucatec Culture and Society, 1550–1850*. Stanford: Stanford University Press.

Spores, R. 1980. New World Ethnohistory and Archaeology, 1970–1980. *Annual Review of Anthropology*, 9:575–603.

Sturtevant, W. 1966. Anthropology, History, and Ethnohistory. *Ethnohistory* 13:1–51.

Susan Kellogg

SEE ALSO
Colonial Period

Etlatongo (Oaxaca, Mexico)

This site lies in the Nochixtlán Valley of the Mixteca Alta. It was initially defined through the Vanderbilt survey (from 1966 to 1971) as two separate sites: a Formative site between two rivers, and a Classic and Postclassic site on a low hill to the north. Further research revealed that these two sites represent components of a larger site, with a Postclassic occupation covering 208.2 hectares.

Radiocarbon dates document the precocious settlement of this fertile land during the Early Formative period. Etlatongo shares an early settlement date with Yucuita, 10 kilometers to the north, but unlike that large village it had limited occupation during the Early Cruz (1500–1150 B.C.) phase. There was a sudden and substantial population increase in the Middle Cruz (1150–850 B.C.), with settlement debris concentrated throughout the portion of the site lying between the rivers, an area of 26.2 hectares. Etlatongo's obsidian, some ceramics, and figurines were obtained from distant sources, indicating the settlement's participation in an interregional exchange network during the Middle Cruz, including interaction with contemporaneous Zapotecs in the Valley of Oaxaca, Gulf Coast Olmecs, and groups from the Valley of Mexico.

Public architecture, first detectable in the Middle Cruz phase, expanded in the Early Classic period, as did site size. Massive modification of the landscape occurred with the construction of a large platform adjoining the Yanhuitlán River. Population expanded and shifted during the Classic period, with most of the occupation and public architecture—including a ball court—concentrated on the low hill. The Postclassic occupation blankets all explored portions of the site for more than 2 kilometers north to south.

FURTHER READINGS

Plunket, P. 1990. Patrones de asentamiento en el Valle de Nochixtlán y su aportación a la evolución cultural en la Mixteca Alta. In M. Winter (ed.), *Lecturas históricas del estado de Oaxaca*, vol. 1, *Epoca prehispánica*, pp. 349–378. Mexico City: Instituto Nacional de Antropología e Historia.

Spores, R. 1972. *An Archaeological Survey of the Nochixtlán Valley, Oaxaca*. Vanderbilt University Publications in Anthropology, 1. Nashville.

Winter, M. 1989. El Preclásico en Oaxaca. In M. Carmona Macias (ed.), *El Preclásico o Formativo*, pp. 461–479. Mexico City: Instituto Nacional de Antropología e Historia.

Zárate Morán, R. 1987. *Excavaciones de un Sitio Preclásico en San Mateo Etlatongo, Nochixtlán, Oaxaca, Mexico*. BAR International Series, 322. Oxford.

Jeffrey P. Blomster

Etzatlán (Jalisco, Mexico)

Much of the 650-hectare area of this Postclassic site is covered by modern Etzatlán. Excavations have explored the Huistla sector, where most materials date to the Santa Cruz de Barcenas phase (A.D. 900–1250). At the Santa Clara sector, a radiocarbon date belongs to the Etzatlán phase (A.D. 1250–1520), its most prosperous period, when it was the capital of a small state that controlled most of the area west of Tlala to Ahuacatlán in Nayarit. It was strong enough to resist Tarascan conquest efforts during the fifty-year period prior to the arrival of the Spanish. It was visited by the Spanish on a number of occasions between 1525 and 1542, when it was definitively conquered, but Contact era sources disagree about the size, social complexity, and nature of the settlement.

Systematic investigations indicate a large and complex ancient settlement, divided into barrios, with an estimated population of ten thousand. Habitation compounds, averaging three per hectare, were usually comprised of four platforms around a common patio. Some of the superstructures were stone and faced with veneer slabs, which were occasionally carved. Freestanding stelae marked the tributary ceremonial patio at Atitlán. A structure similar to that shown in the Codex Quinatzin exists at Ocomo, another tributary settlement. This structure, the Oconahua Palace, is 120 meters square, with a large interior plazuela. Ceremonial structures at Etzatlán itself have been destroyed.

The defining local ware is the Huistla polychrome tripod molcajete. Materials from trade include ceramics from all over western Mesoamerica, especially the coastal regions of Nayarit; turquoise from New Mexico is also found in this area. The major exports were copper and silver objects, blue-green stones, quartz crystals, and high-quality prismatic obsidian blades. Etzatlán controlled the La Joya obsidian mines.

FURTHER READINGS

Glassow, M. A. 1967. The Ceramics of Huistla, a West Mexican Site in the Municipality of Etzatlan, Jalisco. *American Antiquity* 32:64–83.

Weigand, P. C. 1974. The Ahualulco Site and the Shaft Tomb Complex of the Etzatlán Area. In B. Bell (ed.), *The Archaeology of West Mexico*. Ajijic, Jalisco: West Mexican Society for Advanced Study.

———. 1993. *Evolución de una civilización prehispanica: Arqueología de Jalisco, Nayarit, y Zacatecas*. Zamora, Michoacan: 120–131. Colegio de Michoacan.

Weigand, P. C., and A. García de Weigand. 1994. Mineria prehispanica de Jalisco. *Estudios Jaliscienses* 17:5–21.

Phil C. Weigand

SEE ALSO

West Mexico

Exchange Media

Exchange media are goods and services used in economic transactions. In pre-Hispanic Mesoamerica, exchange media were employed in three types of transactions: gift exchange, in which exchanges of goods and services establish and reaffirm social relations among the exchanging parties; barter exchange, in which the comparative values of exchanged commodities are determined by the bartering parties; and market exchange, in which the comparative values of exchanged commodities reflect the prevailing prices of a market. Many different goods and services were employed in exchange transactions; addressing their variety is a complex topic because we find both change over time and regional variation. In addition, goods used in one category of exchange transaction might not have been suitable for use in others—for example, in cases where sumptuary regulations restricted certain goods from market transactions.

From the Early Horizon until the end of the pre-Hispanic sequence, many exchange transactions in Mesoamerica, especially those taking place over long distances, involved exotic goods whose value was due to their distant origin or their production by means of special skills or high levels of labor. However, it is also likely that basic commodities increased in frequency in exchange transactions over time. The most important goods involved in Early Horizon exchanges included fine pottery and lapidary items (especially jade) invested with serpent and jaguar symbolism, magnetite mirrors, and marine shells. By contrast, in Teotihuacán's expansive economic sphere during the Classic period, although exotics such as jade and serpentine were exchanged, obsidian (a good in ordinary household use) figured most importantly.

We have abundant data on exchange media for the latest pre-Hispanic period, based in part on early Spanish accounts. Among the Aztecs, many goods were utilized in exchange transactions, and several functioned in a manner similar to money in modern economies. I refer to these as "money-like goods," rather than as true money, because they retained both exchange functions and use

E

functions; for example, cacao beans served as currency but also were readily processed into an elite food item, chocolate. With these goods, exchange values of a wide range of other goods and services (including land and labor) could be calculated as equivalencies in the money-like goods. In Aztec society, the most important money-like goods were cotton cloaks (*mantas* in Spanish, *quachtli* in Nahuatl), cacao beans, and quills filled with gold dust, along with other items of lesser importance like copper beads, copper axes, and jade beads. In the Lowland Maya area, similar money-like goods included cacao beans, copper bells, marine shells, and jade beads.

FURTHER READINGS

Berdan, F. F. 1982. *The Aztecs of Central Mexico: An Imperial Society.* New York: Holt, Rinehart and Winston.

Blanton, R. E., and G. M. Feinman. 1984. The Mesoamerican World System. *American Anthropologist* 86: 673–682.

Durand-Forest, J. 1971. Cambios económicos y moneda entre los Aztecas. *Estudios de Cultura Nahuatl* 9:105–124.

Flannery, K. V., and J. Marcus. 1994. *Early Formative Pottery of the Valley of Oaxaca, Mexico.* Museum of Anthropology, University of Michigan, Memoirs, 27. Ann Arbor.

Landa, D. 1941. *Relación de las Cosas de Yucatan.* A. M. Tozzer (ed.). Papers of the Peabody Museum of American Archaeology and Ethnology, 18. Cambridge, Mass.: Harvard University.

Pires-Ferreira, J. W. 1976. Shell and Iron-Ore Mirror Exchange in Formative Mesoamerica, with Comments on Other Commodities. In K. V. Flannery (ed.), *The Early Mesoamerican Village,* pp. 311–328. New York: Academic Press.

Santley, R. S., J. M. Kerley, and R. Kneebone. 1986. Obsidian Working, Long-Distance Exchange, and the Politico-Economic Organization of Early States in Central Mexico. In *Research in Economic Anthropology,* Supplement 2, pp. 101–132. Greenwich, Conn.: JAI Press.

Richard E. Blanton

SEE ALSO

Economic Organization

Fábrica San José (Oaxaca, Mexico)

This Middle Formative village site in the piedmont zone of the Valley of Oaxaca was first occupied during the Early Guadalupe phase (c. 850–700 B.C.) by about three nuclear families of maize farmers living in wattle-and-daub houses. During the Late Guadalupe phase (700–550 B.C.), population grew to eleven households, and in the Rosario phase (550–450 B.C.) it increased slightly. Burials and artifactual evidence indicated ascribed (inherited) status differences among villagers, as well as part-time craft specializations, including the manufacture of luxury ornamental goods, and salt production from salt springs adjacent to the site. A part-time specialization in subsistence activities beyond maize farming is suggested by higher than usual incidence of remains of avocado and deer at this village. The apparent absence of public-scale architecture suggests dependence on the nearby center of San José Mogote for ritual activities. Fábrica San José is one of several village sites in Oaxaca whose excavation has documented patterns of Formative life; others include San José Mogote, Huitzo, Tierras Largas, and Santo Domingo Tomaltepec. The Middle Formative occupation of Fábrica San José has been the focus of research, and later occupations there (Terminal Formative, Classic, and Postclassic) have not been explored.

FURTHER READINGS

Drennan, R. D. 1976. *Fábrica San José and Middle Formative Society in the Valley of Oaxaca.* Memoirs of the Museum of Anthropology, University of Michigan, 8. Ann Arbor.

Robert D. Drennan

SEE ALSO
Oaxaca and Tehuantepec Region; San José Mogote

Family and Household

As habitation sites have become a strong focus of investigation for Mesoamerican archaeologists, so have family and household, respectively the social structural and behavioral features represented by residential remains—the house and its accompaniment of artifacts, burials, and surrounding space. Family and household in ancient Mesoamerica are further illuminated by ethnographic, epigraphic, ethnohistoric, and linguistic information.

"Household" and "family" are not synonymous: the household is an activity group defined by behavioral functions of production, distribution, reproduction, enculturation, and coresidence. Families are defined by kin relations, and, as Murdock states, a kinship system is not a social group and does not correspond to an organized aggregation of individuals. However, families often occupy houses and comprise households, facilitating archaeological inferences.

Residential architecture has been a primary source for analyses of ancient family organization, but a more appropriate object of research for the household is the house lot. Santley and Hirth define three types of Mesoamerican residential units: the house lot, composed of a structural core, clear area, intermediate area, and garden; the house compound, a bounded unit encompassing structures surrounding a patio; and the dwelling unit, which shares exterior or boundary walls with another unit in a nucleated settlement.

For complex societies in Mesoamerica, archaeological

F

data and ethnohistoric documents are biased in favor of elites, both because elite facilities attract more scholarly and public interest, and because elite architecture has greater visibility and permanence, and ancient writings record genealogical data for the elite only. In the contact period, Spanish chroniclers recruited elite informants.

Cultural Evolution of Family and Household

A very generalized model of the evolution of the family in Mesoamerica would begin with small groups of mobile foragers, perhaps independent nuclear families (parents and their dependent children) who joined their relatives to live in larger "macroband" groups at some times of the year. With the adoption of sedentary village agriculture, people resided in nuclear and extended family dwellings. As craft specialization became more important, and the exchange of goods and services an integral part of life, households functioned as economically interdependent units of production and consumption. We assume that suprafamilial kin groups, such as lineages, existed prior to the Classic period; their existence is well documented for the Classic Maya and for Postclassic populations as well. Complex societies encompassed a variety of families and households; most continued the nuclear and extended family, joint household patterns of village farmer-artisans, while elite establishments were polygynous and had servants and even artisans and other specialists attached to the household.

Paleoindian and Archaic Periods (to c. 2500 B.C.)

Little habitation evidence has been recovered from these periods, but cave sites (e.g., those in the Tehuacán Valley) provide information on subsistence practices. Probably the early inhabitants of Mesoamerica were mobile foragers who erected temporary shelters as they made their seasonal rounds of resource exploitation. Based on ethnographic analogy with contemporary foragers, small social groups oriented around nuclear families may have predominated, seasonally fluctuating between microbands and macrobands.

Formative Period (2500 B.C.–A.D. 300)

Small single houses, the dwellings for nuclear families, seem to have predominated during the Early Formative, based on architectural and burial information for the Early and Middle Formative phases of the Valley of Oaxaca. House sizes were fairly consistent, suggesting egalitarian organization, a pattern that is reflected in similar burial treatment of adults. During the Middle Formative,

house clusters become apparent in the archaeological record, suggesting the coalescence of nuclear families into extended family compounds. The quintessential courtyard arrangement of structures so common throughout Mesoamerica arose after this time.

A similar development occurred in other locations throughout Mesoamerica. At Late Formative Loma Torremote (Basin of Mexico), the house compound was the basic residential unit. A number of compounds were clustered together, with vacant areas between clusters. These two patterns of residential distribution are indicative of two types of organization: one at the level of the family (nuclear or extended), and the other representing some simple type of corporate organization.

We know little about residential patterns in Olmec culture, one of the first complex societies to arise in Mesoamerica. Olmec society was hierarchical, but the nature and degree of its complexity are debatable. Extremely dense vegetation has masked hundreds of smaller sites. Presumably, settlement in villages may have been organized around larger kin groupings.

In the Maya Lowlands, sites such as Cuello evidence thriving village life, while at El Mirador and Cerros public architecture complemented the developing hierarchy of housing. Numerous Maya sites, such as Tikal, were settled during the Formative; however, repeated use of building sites, for commoners and elite alike, has made excavations of such remains difficult.

Classic Period (A.D. 300–900)

The Classic period saw the zenith of state-level societies in three main areas of Mesoamerica: the Valley of Oaxaca (Monte Albán), the Basin of Mexico (Teotihuacán), and the Maya Lowlands (Classic Maya). Extensive excavations at Copán and its region show that people of all statuses most often arranged their houses in courtyard groupings, suggestive of large household configurations, a pattern found in both urban and rural contexts. Similar patterns are found at dozens of other Maya sites, such as Tikal, Barton Ramie, and Cobá. Oval or rectangular perishable structures were most commonly built on stone platforms. Evidence for average family size is based on ethnographic modeling. Common population figures are given as 5.6 people per residence, or 4 to 5 people per room. Preindustrial family size would have been much smaller than today because of high infant mortality rates. A common assumption is that house size or number of structures correlates with number of occupants. However, variations in house size and structure number may also be due to functional differences, status variation, or the developmental cycle. Residences comprised of a single structure were still an option, as is well documented by Tourtellot at Seibal, and some of these single residences may have served as houses for newlyweds.

The position of a household head within a courtyard group can be identified archaeologically in several ways. It is likely that the household head's residence was larger, had a longer history of occupation, was the focus of more activities, and had greater wealth and better courtyard position than other structures in the courtyard. The wealthiest families may have practiced polygyny, as determined through architectural patterns, recurring activity kits, and the adult male-to-female burial ratio.

The issue of descent has not been fully resolved for the ancient Maya, although there is a tendency among many researchers to accept a patrilineally based society; some, however, see epigraphic evidence for the importance of matrilines, along with patrilines. Strict rules of postmarital residence cannot be determined for the Classic Maya, but the level of household affluence was probably an important factor in determining residence locale. In an agrarian society, households that have access to more and better farmlands tend to have larger family groups. Wilk has found in both ethnographic and ethnohistoric sources the widespread practice of bride service, in which the newlywed couple resides for a time with the wife's family, after which time the couple may either permanently remain in the uxorilocal situation, or switch to patrilocality or neolocality. Inter-site royal marriages have been documented for several Maya sites; these alliances served to bind together elites both politically and socially.

Survey and excavation at Teotihuacán have revealed that many inhabitants of the city lived in apartment-like dwellings. These dwelling units were comprised of a number of rooms or structures built side by side, enclosing one or more courtyards. Compound residents were a cognatic kin group, a corporate entity responsible for craft production, group ritual, and external ties. Within the compound, each apartment suite was occupied by an individual family, the unit of reproduction and consumption, and practitioners of household ritual. There is no epigraphic evidence from Teotihuacán providing genealogical information relating to royal marriages or conquests, as exists for the Classic Maya.

Postclassic Period (A.D. 900–1521)

There are rich ethnohistoric sources for the Aztecs, and they complement archaeological research in reconstruct-ing the household and family. The Aztecs organized groups of related families into a larger corporate residential grouping called the *calpulli,* localized within a neighborhood or village or ward of a city. Individual houses, featuring rooms around courtyards, were the residences of extended families with several family heads, the most senior of whom served as household head, representing the household to the *calpulli* headman (or, very occasionally, headwoman). The headman, who organized tributes, kept records, and settled disputes, lived in a house large enough for meetings of household heads as well as for the residential and artisanal functions of his polygynous family. At the Aztec village of Cihuatecpan (Basin of Mexico), the residence presumed to be the headman's *tecpan* (Nahuatl, "lord-place") was three times larger than the next largest house. Excavations in Postclassic villages and towns in Morelos show a similar pattern of variation in architecture of houses and organization of households.

In Tenochtitlán, the Aztec capital, were eighty-seven large *calpulli*s. Among a *calpulli*'s corporate functions were religious worship, land ownership, tax-paying, and education. The *telpochcalli,* or "house of young men," instructed boys on proper behavior and thought, prepared them to be soldiers, and organized them for community service. Likewise, girls were probably socialized into appropriate roles by *calpulli* members. Outside the *calpulli,* the *calmecac* was a priestly training school, mostly for the elite. If the *calpulli* was large enough, endogamy was practiced; otherwise, members sought spouses outside of their own group.

Polygyny was practiced by any man who could afford it, because many wives indicated a prosperous man, both as a sign of the wealth necessary to support wives and children, and as a function of greatly expanded capacity of the household to produce textiles. All Aztec women spun thread and wove cloth, and these products were mainstays of the Aztec economy. An Aztec polygynous household had one principal wife, whose children were the legitimate principal heirs, with other wives ranked according to the status of their own lineages and other more ambiguous factors, such as connubial affection. Arranged political marriages ensured ties throughout the empire, with higher-ranking lords arranging for their daughters to be principal wives for their lower-ranking allies.

Reconstruction of the Postclassic Maya family and household organization is accomplished through ethnohistoric documents that cite three royal/noble groups—the Cocoms, the Xius, and the Chels—to whom ancestral lineage was very important. The descent group, as

F

recorded by Landa in the sixteenth century, was non-localized, exogamous, and patrilineal; further, the non-localized patriclan for the Maya is supported by kinship terminology, as Sharer notes. Lineage lines cross-cut social statuses incorporating both nobles and commoners, leading to increased social solidarity. Matrilines were also present, and children inherited the father's patronymic and the mother's first name.

Multiple-family houses were numerous, as documented by archaeological surveys of the region, and each extended family compound had a head. Marriages occurred by the age of twenty years and were sometimes arranged by a matchmaker employed by the parents of the prospective spouses. Many couples followed the custom of bride service, living with the bride's family and contributing to the economic prosperity of that household, after which patrilocal or neolocal residence was assumed. Among commoners, monogamy was the rule, with frequent separations and informal marriages to other individuals. Polygyny was the prerogative of the upper class, with a man taking a principal wife of the same social rank and other wives of lower rank. All offspring bore the patronymic of the father, and it is certain that offspring of the principal wife inherited the status of the father, but the children of lower-ranking wives did not necessarily do so.

Information about daily life was also recorded by Landa, who provides details of house construction and layout. "The way they built their houses was to cover them with straw which they have of very good quality and in great abundance, or with palm leaves, which is very well fitted for this, and they have very steep slopes, so that the rain water may not penetrate. And then they build a wall in the middle dividing the house lengthwise, leaving several doors in the wall into the half which they call the back of the house, where they have their beds; and the other half they whitened very nicely with lime" (quoted in Tozzer 1941: 85). House walls were constructed of stone, wattle and daub, or poles.

Summary

Throughout the development of settled life in Mesoamerica, we see a standard pattern in which common people lived as small nuclear families (average size probably between 4 and 6 people) among their relatives in extended family households. These households inhabited sets of rooms around a common patio. As societal complexity emerged, a major effect of growing differentials in wealth was to permit some individuals to support larger households in larger residences. With the emergence of the state at Monte Albán, Teotihuacán, and other Classic period centers, the ruler signaled the power of office and individual by amassing a large household with many wives, children, and servants and housing them in palaces.

FURTHER READINGS

Calnek, E. 1992. The Ethnographic Context of the Third Part of the Codex Mendoza. In *The Codex Mendoza,* vol. 1, *Interpretation,* pp. 81–91. Berkeley: University of California Press.

Carrasco, P. 1984. Royal Marriages in Ancient Mexico. In H. Harvey and H. Prem (eds.), *Explorations in Ethnohistory,* pp. 41–81. Albuquerque: University of New Mexico Press.

Evans, S. T. 1991. Architecture and Authority in an Aztec Village: Form and Function of the Tecpan. In H. R. Harvey (ed.), *Land and Politics in the Valley of Mexico,* pp. 63–92. Albuquerque: University of New Mexico Press.

Flannery, K. V. (ed.). 1976. *The Early Mesoamerican Village.* New York: Academic Press.

Gonlin, N. 1994. Rural Household Diversity in Late Classic Copán, Honduras. In G. M. Schwartz and S. E. Falconer (eds.), *Archaeological Views from the Countryside: Village Communities in Early Complex Societies,* pp. 177–197. Washington, D.C.: Smithsonian Institution Press.

Haviland, W. A. 1968. Ancient Lowland Maya Social Organization. *Tulane University, Middle American Research Institute, Publications* 26(5):93–118.

MacEachern, S., D. J. W. Archer, and R. D. Garvin (eds.). 1989. *Households and Communities: Proceedings of the 21st Chacmool Conference.* Calgary: University of Calgary Archaeological Association.

Murdock, G. P. 1966. *Social Structure.* New York: Macmillan.

Nutini, H. G., P. Carrasco, and J. Taggart (eds.). 1976. *Essays on Mexican Kinship.* Pittsburgh: University of Pittsburgh Press.

Santley, R. S., and K. G. Hirth (eds.). 1993. *Prehispanic Domestic Units in Western Mesoamerica.* Boca Raton: CRC Press.

Schele, L., and P. Mathews. 1991. Royal Visits and Other Intersite Relationships among the Classic Maya. In T. P. Culbert (ed.), *Classic Maya Political History: Hieroglyphical and Archaeological Evidence,* pp. 226–252. Cambridge: Cambridge University Press.

Sharer, R. J. 1993. The Social Organization of the Late Classic Maya: Problems of Definition and Approaches. In J. A. Sabloff and J. S. Henderson (eds.), *Lowland Maya Civilization in the Eighth Century A.D.,* pp. 91–109. Washington, D.C.: Dumbarton Oaks.

Smith, M. E., et al. 1989. Architectural Patterns at Three Aztec-Period Sites in Morelos, Mexico. *Journal of Field Archaeology* 16:185–203.

Tourtellot, G. 1988. *Excavations at Seibal, Department of Petén, Guatemala: Peripheral Survey and Excavation, Settlement and Community Patterns.* Peabody Museum, Memoir 16. Cambridge, Mass.: Harvard University.

Tozzer, A. M. 1941. *Landa's Relación de las Cosas de Yucatán.* Papers of the Peabody Museum of American Archaeology and Ethnology, 18. Cambridge, Mass.: Harvard University.

Wilk, R. R., and W. Ashmore (eds.). 1988. *Household and Community in the Mesoamerican Past.* Albuquerque: University of New Mexico Press.

Nancy Gonlin and Susan Toby Evans

SEE ALSO
Gender Roles

Famine

Severe food shortages that lead to chronic malnutrition and increased mortality have social as well as ecological causes. Most famines are predominantly social, caused by factors under the immediate control of the society in question, including government policies, transportation inadequacies, and hoarding. Enough food is available to sustain the population, but social practices or political decisions prevent its distribution. Examples of social famines abound in the modern world, but ecological famines were more significant in ancient Mesoamerica, including those caused by floods, insect infestations, droughts, and frosts. Such ecological reversals are usually spatially limited, and their impact depends on the society's ability to import food from beyond the area affected. Mesoamerican transportation constraints made this difficult or impossible; and although food storage ameliorates temporary shortages, sustained ecological reversals ultimately exhaust these stores and lead to famine.

During a major famine in central Mexico in 1454, many died and many more migrated to the unaffected Gulf Coast region of Totonicapan; parents sold their children into slavery so they would be fed. This famine was followed by massive agricultural intensification and the construction of extensive hydraulic works in the Basin of Mexico, and greater political expansion and the creation of a vastly larger tribute network, although establishing causality is difficult, even in the historical record. However, mass migrations and the resultant cessation of building activities, the disproportionate deaths of young and old and the usual drop in fertility, and even food stress reflected in the osteological record should, in principle, be detectable archaeologically.

FURTHER READINGS

Hassig, R. 1981. The Famine of One Rabbit: Ecological Causes and Social Consequences of a Pre-Columbian Calamity. *Journal of Anthropological Research* 37:171–181.

———. 1986. Famine and Scarcity in the Valley of Mexico. In *Research in Economic Anthropology,* Supplement 2, pp. 303–317. Greenwich, Conn.: JAI Press.

Ross Hassig

SEE ALSO
Diet and Nutrition

Fauna

Middle America, from the northern Mexican border to the Isthmus of Panama, is one of the richest biotic zones in the world. Its tremendous diversity of animal species, both invertebrate and vertebrate, results from the combined effects of high rates of endemic speciation in the heterogeneous environments of the region and from a complex evolutionary history that has included periodic admixture of northern and southern faunal populations. The classification of the Mexican and Central American fauna as either Nearctic (North American) or Neotropical (predominantly South American) has been the subject of considerable debate. As a whole, the group is best considered a transitional population dominated by Neotropical families and genera. The fauna of the Mexican plateau is, however, predominantly Nearctic. The transitional zone between the two regions includes the mountains and associated lowlands of southern Mexico.

Many species in this highly diverse group had both socio-economic and symbolic importance for the early residents of Middle America. Despite regional faunal variability and mixed Nearctic and Neotropical animal populations, the ancient significance of some species appears to have been pan-regional. Many are part of what appears to have been a chronologically stable core of symbolism and

F

mythology shared throughout the Mesoamerican culture area. While it is beyond the scope of this discussion to provide a complete zoogeographic analysis of the Middle American fauna, this essay will combine modern faunal distributions, ethnography, ethnohistory, iconography, and zooarchaeology to present a biogeographical account of many of the biologically and culturally important species.

Mammalia

Middle American marsupials are represented by several species of opossum, two of which (the common and Virginia opossums) are exploited today as game animals. The meat is considered inferior, but medicinal use of the animal's tail has a long tradition in parts of Mesoamerica.

The primarily Nearctic insectivores of Middle America include two families, the Talpidae (moles) and Soricidae (shrews). Talpids are generally restricted to northern North America, although a few species enter Mexico, while soricians are more uniformly distributed. Only one insectivore genus extends to South America.

Edentates (sloths, anteaters, and armadillos), with a single exception, are restricted to the humid tropics, and their greatest diversity is found in the southern regions. While sloths occur only to eastern Honduras, anteaters range north to southeastern Mexico, and an armadillo enters the United States. Most edentates are considered unpalatable, but the burrowing armadillo, in ancient times symbolizing fertility and the underworld, is as enthusiastically hunted today as it was in the past.

The most diverse mammalian faunas in Mexico and Central America are rodents and bats. Nine bat families are reported for the area, and more than 240 species are estimated to occur in the Neotropical region alone. The most diverse are the leaf-nosed bats, with five subfamilies including the common fruit bats and vampires. These groups and the funnel-eared bats are southern in origin; the many vespertilionid and free-tailed bats, although distributed throughout, are predominantly northern. The characteristic leaf-nose of the Phyllostomidae is prominent in most pre-Columbian bat representations, and the vampire bat with its peculiar blood diet was an important inhabitant of the ancient underworld. Although bats were primarily associated with death, sacrifice, and blood, the role of some species as pollinators of night-blooming flowers may be one reason bats were also strongly associated with fertility and agriculture.

New World primates, common motifs in ancient Mesoamerican art, were often depicted as artists, musi-cians, and dancers. Essentially southern in distribution, the primates are represented by two families (monkeys and tamarins) and eleven species in the tropical lowlands. Only three monkey species (the howler monkeys and one spider monkey) extend into Mexico, while the tamarin, the night and squirrel monkeys, and the Colombian black spider monkey range only to southern Costa Rica. The capuchin today ranges north to Honduras. Monkeys, a preferred food for many modern groups, are rare in archaeological deposits.

Carnivores are represented by five Middle American families. Canids occur throughout, although the family affinities are Nearctic. Red fox, coyote, and wolf are at their southern limits in northern Mexico, but the domestic dog is found wherever there are human populations. Gray foxes reach South America, and the southern bush dog ranges to Panama. Dogs, the oldest domesticates, were pets, hunters, and sacrificial victims throughout Middle America and were primary food sources for many pre-Columbian peoples. In many areas dogs or dog depictions were buried with the deceased to act as companions along the difficult path to the underworld.

Bears, restricted to the highlands of Mexico, are represented by a single genus. Almost extinct in this area today, they may be the basis for the legendary Nahuatl monster *cuetlachtli,* a participant in the Mexican "gladiator sacrifice."

Procyonids are represented by both northern and southern elements. The northern raccoons and ringtails extend from Mexico to Panama, overlapping with the southern olingos, kinkajous, and coatis, many of which range into the southern United States. Frequent agricultural pests, all were symbolic of human gluttons and thieves.

Three of the mustelid subfamilies—the badgers, skunks, and river otters—are northern in origin, although various species occur through the lowland tropics. Both tayra and grison are southern species that extend north to the Mexican lowlands. Predatory mustelids are often associated with bad luck and witchcraft in modern Central America, and the tradition is deeply rooted. The seventh lord of Tenochtitlán was named after the river otter, *ahuizotl,* reputed to drown greedy fishers and innocent victims alike at the command of the rain god Tláloc. For the ancient Maya, the malevolent weasel symbolized oppression, and, not surprisingly, a skunk in the house was considered extremely bad luck.

Seven Middle American cats are distributed through three genera. The Nearctic lynx barely enters Mexico, and the oncilla occurs only from Costa Rica south. The remaining felids range throughout the region and, except for the highly adaptable mountain lion, are restricted to the humid rainforests. The largest cat, the jaguar, is an exclusively nocturnal predator and has long been associated with sorcery and the supernatural underworld throughout Mesoamerica. Priests and rulers alike appropriated the jaguar symbol as validation of their divine royalty. Although the jaguar is the most common cat in ancient artworks, sculpted and painted depictions of the randomly spotted pelt of the ocelot may represent the lesser elite orders of Maya royalty.

The perissodactyls and artiodactyls are northern immigrants, although tapirs, the only living American perissodactyls, are now restricted to tropical America. The tapir is the largest indigenous and extant Central American mammal, and its semiaquatic, nocturnal nature and prodigious appetite explain its association with the underworld and fertility for the ancient Maya.

Modern indigenous artiodactyls are represented by four Middle American families, and three species are entirely restricted to the Nearctic areas of Mexico—the pronghorn antelope, bison, and mountain sheep. While both peccaries are found throughout, only one cervid (white-tailed deer) is ubiquitous. The mule deer occurs no farther south than northern Mexico, while the brocket deer are southern in distribution, extending to southern Mexico (red brocket) and Panama (brown brocket). Artiodactyls are and were favorite sources of meat, bone, and hides, and both peccaries and deer had rich symbolic associations for pre-Columbian peoples. One of the most widespread species and most valuable resources in the area, the white-tailed deer is the primary fertility symbol in Mexico and Central America. It plays a central role in creation myths and is commonly associated with the sky and sun. Although neither the peccary nor the white-tailed deer was truly domesticated, they may have been husbanded in various places. Archaeological and soil analyses suggest that animals were penned for accessibility, while dietary studies document corn-feeding in some regions.

Rodents are the most abundant mammals of Middle America and are represented by fifteen families in three groups. Although rodent diversity increases southward, most of the families are of Nearctic origin, and many are restricted to arid environments. The squirrels are most numerous in the northern and highland locations. Although four geomyid genera occur in the region, only one extends to the tropical biomes. One of the Nearctic heteromyid genera, however, is restricted to that domain.

One beaver barely reaches northern Mexico. The originally Nearctic rats and mice are the most abundant and widely distributed rodents in Middle America. In contrast to the Nearctic groups, the caviomorphs are southern in origin. Only one porcupine genus occurs north of the Rio Grande; two others are found from Mexico southward, and a third extends south from Panama. The capybara ranges north from South America into Panama, while the agoutis and pacas are distributed throughout the tropical lowlands. Many of these larger rodents were, and still are, important food sources throughout their ranges. This is particularly true of the pacas and agoutis, whose rich, fatty meat was a favorite dish, but the pocket gopher was also enjoyed where it was abundant.

Throughout their ranges, the hares and rabbits are second only to deer as favorite food and fur animals, and archaeological evidence supports a long history for this preference. All three Middle American leporid genera have Nearctic affinities. The geographic distribution of the volcano rabbit is restricted, and the hares extend only as far south as the Isthmus of Tehuantepec. Rabbits occur throughout, but most are found in the arid highlands, and there is only one rabbit common in the humid tropical forest. The appetites and reproductive ability of the leporids easily explain their ancient association with fertility and vegetation, but like the deer, they were also sky elements, in this case associated with the moon—the mythical residence of the rabbit.

Several aquatic mammals are resident on Middle American coasts, and one, the West Indian manatee, ranges into brackish and freshwater habitats all along the Atlantic. An important source of meat, fat, hides, and bone for most ancient coastal residents, this animal is represented in such large numbers at some coastal sites that inland trade of manatee meat has been suggested. Fur and harbor seals are common off the coasts of both Baja California and the Mexican mainland, while the West Indian seal occurs south to Honduras. Various whales, porpoises, and dolphins frequent both oceans and were also incorporated into ancient diets.

Birds

The permanent and overwintering avian fauna of Mexico and Central America includes approximately two thousand species in more than one hundred families. Except for the albatrosses, which are limited to the Pacific Ocean, most of the pelagic and littoral birds occur on both Atlantic and Pacific coasts. Many of the land-based species are similarly cosmopolitan in distribution. Most

F

of the avian families have their greatest representation in the tropical southern lowlands, but some species (such as loons, flamingos, and cranes) are predominantly Nearctic. The ducks, geese, and swans, though occurring throughout the entire area, have a much higher diversity in the north. Most of the perching birds are Neotropical in origin. Some families are specifically southern and do not extend north of Costa Rica (e.g., potoos); the majority, however, are more generally pantropical, ranging into the lowlands of Central Mexico (the enormous, monkey-eating harpy eagle, most of the cracids, the parrots and macaws, and many of the toucans and woodpeckers). Hummingbirds and swifts are best represented in the tropics, as are kingfishers and motmots. Several groups, including the New World quails and jays, exhibit their highest diversity in the transitional Mexican zone.

The most important food species are galliformes, including the currassows, chachalacas, guans, pheasants, grouse, quails, and turkeys. All are considered excellent eating today, and many have symbolic associations that reach into prehistory. The guans symbolized the dawn in much of Mesoamerica, although it was the chachalaca that was likened by the Spanish to the crowing rooster, and the quails that were sacrificed in dedication to the sun each morning by Aztec priests. The currassow, resident of the dense tropical forests of Middle America, symbolized fertility, water, and agriculture, as did both turkey species. The natural ranges of the bronze and ocellated turkeys do not overlap: the ocellated turkey occurs on the Yucatán Peninsula and extends through the Mexican lowlands to Guatemala; the bronze or common turkey, the most famous New World domesticate, was exported from its natural range in the pine-oak uplands of northern Mexico in pre-Columbian times. Although the ocellated turkey is not well adapted to true domestication, ethnohistoric sources suggest that many galliformes were captured and penned, and that chicks of various species were raised from eggs stolen from natural nests. Also hunted for meat in the past and today are the ground-dwelling tinamous, ducks and their relatives, and the herons, cranes, and rails, as well as the larger pigeon and dove species.

Acting as messengers between earth and the heavens, many birds assumed particular symbolic importance. The diurnal birds of prey were often associated with the sun, while night hunters such as the owls, and the carrion-feeding vultures, were animals of the dark underworld and harbingers of bad luck. The tiny, aggressive, brilliant hummingbird symbolized fertility, sacrifice, and rejuve-

nation. Many Central American birds were most valued for the colorful feathers used to decorate everything from clothing to warriors' shields. The most important of these were the quetzals, whose intensely green feathers adorned the god Quetzalcóatl and were considered more valuable than jade. White egret feathers were worn by Tláloc, and the feathers of the roseate spoonbill mimicked the dawn colors. Deities, lords, and warriors decorated their attire with the blue and purple feathers of the cotinga, multi-hued parrot and macaw feathers, and the metallic feathers of the hummingbird and Mexican trogon.

Herpetofauna

The herpetological fauna of Mexico and Central America includes over one thousand species, many of which were both economically and ceremonially important to past inhabitants; all were strongly symbolic of fertility, rain, and water. Most of the almost five hundred amphibian species belong in ten frog and toad families. Only four salamander families and one caecilian (legless lizard) occur in the area. Also diverse, the reptilian fauna includes about twenty-three families in three orders. More than seven hundred reptilian species occur in Mexico; close to four hundred have been reported in the Neotropical region. Amphibian diversity is greatest at the two geographical extremes of the region because of the extension of nine Nearctic genera into Mexico and eight South American genera into Panama. Reptiles, particularly the lizards and snakes, are most diverse north of the Isthmus of Tehuantepec.

Historic references suggest that many amphibian species were a part of ancient diets. Frogs were eaten in tamales and stews, and tadpoles were considered a special delicacy by the Aztecs. Toads, unpalatable eating, were associated with shamanistic ritual, and the poisons secreted by the marine toad may have been a ritual hallucinogen. The prized Mexican amphibian was a larval mole salamander common in the highlands of Mexico and so enjoyed as a culinary delicacy by the Aztec and Spanish alike that it was hunted almost to extinction in the eighteenth century.

Snakes, crocodilians, and turtles all played pivotal roles in ancient Mesoamerican myth and legend. The inclusion of saurians and turtles in creation mythology is almost ubiquitous in Mesoamerica, and the image of the crocodilian earth-monster is one that can be traced from modern legend to the earliest Olmec art. Two crocodilians—one southern (spectacled caiman) and one northern (American crocodile)—extend throughout the drainages of Middle America, while a third (Morelet's crocodile) is restricted to southern Mexico, Belize, and Guatemala. At least seven species of marine turtle occur along the coasts of Mexico and Central America. Threatened today by overhunting, they were valued in the past for their meat, eggs, and carapace. Many of the Middle American freshwater turtles, most belonging to the kinosternid family, were also valued for both meat and shell. While mud, musk, and river turtle remains are common in most midden deposits, the river turtle was often the preferred elite fare. Limited to aquatic systems, very few of the turtle species are ubiquitous in distribution.

More than 95 percent of the Mexican and Central American reptiles are lizards and snakes. Although most saurian families are represented by a few species throughout, the majority are generally (for example, iguanas and skinks) or strictly (the poisonous beaded lizards) northern in distribution. The spiny lizards, including the iguanas and ctenosaurs prized for food throughout the area both today and in the past, are the most common lizards in Middle America.

Contrary to popular legend, the great diversity of snake species in Middle America is not indicative of high numbers of individual snakes. Nevertheless, the snake was, and still is today, one of the most powerful panregional animal symbols. Associated with water and fertility, as are all of the herpetofauna, the snake is also strongly associated with blood, the second life-giving fluid. The combined serpent/avian motif, which merges the rattlesnake with the quetzal to become the feathered serpent Quetzalcóatl or Kukulcan, is found throughout the regions and time periods of Mesoamerica. Modern snakes are represented by eight families containing close to five hundred species. Approximately seventy-five of these species are dangerously venomous to humans, including the coral snakes and pitvipers (moccasins, copperhead, lanceheads, bushmasters, and rattlesnakes, among others). Other important non-venomous species include the single python restricted to the Pacific Coast, and the boas, only one species of which is common throughout the lowlands from Mexico south.

Fishes

The freshwater Nearctic and Neotropical fish populations of Mexico and Central America are more sharply defined than those of other vertebrate classes. Between the Atlantic coastal plain north of the Tropic of Cancer and the Rio Papaloapan, the fish fauna shifts from approximately seventy-five percent Nearctic to predominantly Neotropical. Some three hundred primary (obligatory freshwater) and secondary (salt-tolerant) freshwater species in thirty-six families occur in Mexico north of this transitional zone. Over half of the species are included in four cypriniform families (the tetras and billums, minnows, suckers, and freshwater catfishes) and three cyprinodontoid families (the flagfishes and allies, the Mexican live-bearers, and the mollies and alligator fishes). The nearly five hundred known Neotropical freshwater fishes include both primary and secondary species, as well as approximately fifty-seven marine derivatives that have become permanent freshwater residents. Included in this group are sharks and sawfishes, known to occur well inland in lakes Nicaragua and Izabal, and several marine catfish, tarpons, jacks, snooks, marine mojarras, and snappers. The Neotropical species are dominated by cyprinodontoids and cichlids, as well as the secondary and marine derivative species. Most of the primary fishes (all cypriniformes) are restricted to Panama and parts of Costa Rica, and only three northern groups (two suckers and one freshwater catfish) penetrate the southern region. Between Costa Rica and the Isthmus of Tehauntepec the fish fauna is extremely depauperate. Many of these freshwater fishes are and were regionally important dietary elements, the most common being the freshwater cichlids, snooks, mullets, and catfish.

The Middle American marine ichthyofauna is remarkably diverse. The marine fish population for Mexico alone includes some 375 continental marine fish species (those found primarily in brackish waters, coastal lagoons, and estuaries) and more than 1,300 strictly oceanic species. Marine fishes include both Nearctic and Neotropical species, as well as some of Indopacific and eastern Atlantic origin, and diversity in both Atlantic and Pacific oceans is equally high. The richest zones are also those most accessible to ancient and modern fishers—the shallow inland estuaries and lagoons and the nearshore coral reefs. Marine fish remains are found at all coastal sites, indicating a long history of use of this valuable resource. Common dietary species included marine snappers, jacks, groupers, parrotfish, and the estuarine saltwater catfish, mullets, marine mojarras, snooks, and tarpon. The use of shark teeth and stingray spines as votive offerings throughout Mesoamerica, and the recovery of marine fish bones from both ceremonial and subsistence deposits at many inland sites, suggest that marine fish were also valuable trading commodities.

F

TABLE 1. TAXONOMY OF IMPORTANT MEXICAN AND CENTRAL AMERICAN FAUNA.

Taxonomic Name	English (Spanish) [Nahuatl] {Maya}
Phylum Mollusca: Marine Species	
Class Bivalvia	clams, oysters
Pteriidae	pearl oysters
Spondylidae	spondylus
Class Gastropoda	snails (caracoles)
Trochidae	pearly top shells
Strombidae	strombs
Strombus gigas	Queen conch (caracol marino) [tecciztli] {huub}
Cassididae	helmet shells
Thaididae	
Purpura patula pansa	Wide-mouthed rock shell
Melongenidae	crown conch
Olividae	olive shell
Xancidae/Turbinellidae	chank shell
Marginellidae	marginella
Conidae	cone shell
Class Scaphopoda	
Dentaliidae	
Dentalium spp.	tusk shell
Phylum Mollusca: Freshwater Species	
Class Bivalvia	
Sphaeriidae	
Unionidae	freshwater clams
Amblemidae	
Mutelidae	
Class Gastropoda	
Pilidae	
Hydrobiidae	
Pleuroceridae	
Ampullariidae	
Pomacea spp.	apple snails
Thiaridae	
Pachychilus spp.	{jute}
Phylum Arthropoda: Arthropods	
Arachnida	arachnids
Scorpionida	scorpion (alacran) [colotl] {sina'an}
Araneida	spider (araña) [tocatl] {toy}
Crustacea: Malacostracea	shrimps, crabs, lobsters, crayfish
Insecta	insects

Taxonomic Name	English (Spanish) [Nahuatl] {Maya}
Odonata	dragonflies
Orthoptera: Acrididae	grasshoppers (saltamontes) [chapolin] {saak}
Hemiptera: Corixidae	water boatmen [axayacatl/ahuauhtli]
Homoptera: Dactylopiidae	
Dacylopius coccus	cochineal scale insect (cochinilla) [nocheztli]
Lepidoptera: Papilionoidea	butterflies (mariposas) [papalotl] {(ah) pepen}
Lepidoptera: Hesperiidae	skippers
Agathymus spp.	maguey worms (gusanos de maguey) [meocuillin]
Lepidoptera: Cossidae	carpenter moths [chilocuillin]
Hymenoptera: Apidae	bees (abejas) [xicotli/pipiolin] {kab}
Hymenoptera: Formicidae	ants (hormigas) [azcatl] {sinik}
Coleoptera: Elateridae/Lampyridae	click beetles/firefly beetles [icpitl] {kokay}
Phylum Chordata: Pisces (Primary Freshwater Species)	
Osteichthyes	bony fishes (pez) [michin] {kay}
Characidae	tetras and billums
Cyprinidae	minnows
Catostomidae	suckers
Ictaluridae	freshwater catfishes
Cyprinodontidae	flagfishes and allies
Goodeidae	mexican live-bearers
Poeciliidae	mollies, alligator fish, and allies
Cichlidae	cichlids (mojarras)
Centropomidae	snooks
Atherinidae	silversides
Muglidae	mullets
Phylum Chordata: Pisces (Marine Species)	
Chondrichthyes	
Carcharhinidae	sharks
Pristidae	sawfishes

Taxonomic Name	English (Spanish) [Nahuatl] {Maya}
Dasyatidae/Myliobatidae	stingrays and eagle rays
Osteichthyes	
Ariidae	saltwater catfish
Elopidae	tarpon
Carangidae	jacks
Centropomidae	marine snooks
Gerreidae	marine mojarras
Labridae	hogfishes
Lutjanidae	snappers
Serranidae	groupers
Scaridae	parrotfishes and chubs
Phylum Chordata: Amphibia–amphibians	
Gymnophiona	caecilians
Caudata	salamanders
Ambystoma mexicanus	mole salamander (ajolote) [axolotl]
Anura: Ranidae	frogs (rana) [tamazolin] {bab}
Anura: Bufonidae	toads (sapo) [cueyatl] {uo/wo}
Bufo marinus	marine toad
Phylum Chordata: Reptilia–reptiles	
Crocodilia	crocodilians (lagarto) [cipactli] {ain}
Caiman crocodilus	Spectacled caiman (caiman)
Crocodylus americanus	American crocodile (Lagarto)
Crocodylus moreleti	Morelet's crocodile (Lagarto)
Testudinia	turtles (tortuga) [ayotI] {ak}
Cheloniidae	loggerhead, green, hawksbill, and allied turtles
Dermochelyidae	leatherback turtles
Kinosternidae	mud and musk turtles
Dermatemydidae	river turtles
Dermatemys mawii	Central American river turtle (tortuga blanca)
Squamata	
Sauria: Scincidae	skinks
Sauria: Iguanidae	spiny lizards/iguanas (lagartija) [cuetzpalin] {mach}
Sauria: Helodermatidae	beaded lizard
Serpentes: Elapidae	
Microrus spp.	coral snakes (coralillo) [tlapapalcoatl] {chak k~an}
Serpentes: Viperidae	
Bothrops spp.	lanceheads (barba amarilla/terciopelo) [nauhyacacoatl]
Serpentes: Pythonidae	pythons
Serpentes: Boidae	boas
Phylum Chordata: Aves–birds	
Tinamiformes: Tinamidae	tinamous
Gaviiformes: Gaviidae	loons
Podiciformes: Podicipedidae	grebes
Procellariiformes: Diomedeidae	albatrosses
Pelecaniformes	pelicans, cormorants, anhingas, frigatebirds
Ciconiiformes: Ardeidae	herons
Casmerodius albus	Great egret (garza blanca) [aztlatl] {sak bok}
Ciconiiformes: Threskiornithidae	ibises and spoonbills roseate spoonbill
Ajaja ajaja	(pico de cuchara) [tlauhquechol] {chak kaanal ok chi'ch'il ha'}
Phoenicopteriformes: Phoenicopteridae	flamingos
Anseriformes: Anatidae	ducks, geese, swans (patos) [canauhtli] {chi'ich'ilha'}
Falconiformes	birds of prey
Falconiformes: Cathartidae	American vultures
Sarcoramphus papa	King vulture (zopilote rey) [cozcacuauhtli] {kuch}
Cathartes aura	Turkey vulture (zopilote) [tzopilotl] {ch'om}
Falconiformes: Accipitridae	hawks, eagles (aguila) [cuauhtli] {kunk'uk}

F

TABLE 1. TAXONOMY OF IMPORTANT MEXICAN AND CENTRAL AMERICAN FAUNA. (*continued*)

Taxonomic Name	English (Spanish) [Nahuatl] {Maya}	Taxonomic Name	English (Spanish) [Nahuatl] {Maya}
Harpia harpyja	Harpy eagle	*Pharomachrus mocinno*	Resplendent quetzal [quetzaltototl] {(ah) k'uk'um}
Aquila chrysaetos	Golden eagle		
Galliformes: Cracidae		*Trogon mexicanus*	Mexican trogon
Penelope purpurascens	Crested guan (pava de monte) [cox-coxtli] {koox}	Coraciiformes: Alcedinidae	kingfishers
		Coraciiformes: Momotidae	motmots
Crax rubra	Currassow (hoco faisán) [tepetototl] {k'anbul}	Piciformes: Ramphastidae	toucans
		Piciformes: Picidae	woodpeckers (carpintero) [chiquimolli] {(ah) kolomte}
Ortalis spp.	chachalacas (chachalaca) [chachalaca] {bech}		
		Passeriformes	perching birds
Galliformes: Phasianidae	quails and allies (codorniz) [zolin] {bech}	Passeriformes: Cotingidae	cotingas
		Cotinga amabilis	Lovely cotinga (azulejo real) [xiuhtototl] {yaaxun}
Galliformes: Meleagrididae	turkeys (pavo) [huexolotl/totolin] {ulum}		
		Passeriformes: Corvidae	jays, crows, and allies
Meleagris ocellata	Ocellated turkey		
Meleagris gallopavo	Bronze/Common turkey	Class Mammalia–mammals	
		Marsupialia	marsupials
Gruiformes: Gruidae	cranes	Didelphidae	opossums (tlacuache/zorro) [tlacuatzin] {och}
Gruiformes: Rallidae	rails, coots, gallinules		
		Didelphis marsupialis	Common opossum
Columbiformes: Columbidae	pigeons, doves (palomas, tórtolas) [cocotl] {tuuch?}	*Didelphis virginianus*	Virginia opossum
		Insectivora	insectivores
Psittaciformes: Psittacidae	parrots, macaws and allies	Talpidae	talpids
		Soricidae	soricians
Ara spp.	macaws (guacamayo) [alo] {kato/mo'}	Xenarthra	edentates
		Myrmecophagidae	anteaters
Amazona spp.	parrots (papagayo) [toznene] {ix k'an}	Bradypodidae	three-toed sloths
		Megalonychidae	two-toed sloths
Strigiformes	owls (buho/tecolote) [tecolotl] {cui}	Dasypodidae	armadillos (armadillo) [ayotochtli] {huech}
Strigiformes: Tytonidae	barn owls (lechuza) [chicuatli] {puhuy}		
		Dasypus novemcinctus	Nine-banded armadillo
Strigiformes: Strigidae	typical owls (buho) [tecolotl] {(ah) iikim}	Chiroptera	bats (murcielago) [quimichpatlan] {sot's}
Caprimulgiformes: Nyctibiidae	potoos		
Apodiformes: Apodidae	swifts	Phyllostomidae	leaf-nosed bats
Apodiformes: Trochilidae	hummingbirds (colibri) [huitzitzilin] {ts'unu'un}	Phyllostomidae: Stenodermatinae	Neotropical fruit bats
		Phyllostomidae: Desmodontinae	vampire bats {ukum tsek}
Trogoniformes: Trogonidae	trogons	Natalidae	funnel-eared bats

Taxonomic Name	English (Spanish) [Nahuatl] {Maya}
Vespertinionidae	vespertilionid bats
Molossidae	free-tailed bats
Primata	primates
Callitrichidae	tamarins (tamarin/titi)
Cebidae	monkeys
Aotus spp.	night monkeys
Saimiri oerstedii	Central American squirrel monkey (mono ardilla)
Cebus capuchinus	white-throated capuchin monkey
Alouatta spp.	howler monkeys (saraguato) {batz/ba'ats'}
Ateles spp.	spider monkeys (mono araña) [ozomatli] {chuen/ma'ax}
Carnivora	carnivores
Canidae	canids
Canis familiaris	dog (perro) [itzcuintli (xoloitzcuintli/techichi)] {pek'}
Canis latrans	coyote (coyote) [coyotl] {ch'umak}
Canis lupus	wolf (lobo)
Vulpes macrotis	red fox (zorra roja)
Urocyon cinereoargenteus	gray fox (zorra gris)
Speothos venaticus	southern bush dog (perro de monte)
Ursidae	bears (oso) [cuetlachtli]
Procyonidae	procyonids
Procyon spp.	raccoons (osito lavador) [mapachtli] {k'ulu'}
Nasua spp.	coatimundis (coati/pizote) [pitzotl] {chi'ik/tziz}
Bassaricyon gabbii	Olingo
Potos flavus	kinkajou (oso mielero/mico de noche) {ak'ab' ma'ax}
Bassariscus spp.	cacomistles (cacomixtle/mico de noche)

Taxonomic Name	English (Spanish) [Nahuatl] {Maya}
Mustelidae: Melinae	badgers (tejon/tlalcoyote)
Mustelidae: Mephitinae	skunks (zorrillos) [epatl] {pay}
Mustelidae: Lutrinae	river otters (nutria) [ahuitzotl] {pek'i ha/ts'ula'ilha'}
Mustelidae: Mustelinae	weasels
Mustela frenata	long-tailed weasel (comadreja) [cuzamatl] {sabin}
Galictis vittata	grison (grison) {zabin}
Eira barbara	tayra (cabeza de viejo/tolomuco) {sacol}
Felidae	cats
Felis pardalis	ocelot (ocelote/tigrillo)
Felis wiedii	margay (gato tigre/tigrillo) {chulul}
Felis tigrina	oncilla (tigrillo)
Felis yagouaroundi	jaguarundi (yaguarundi) {ekmuch}
Felis concolor	mountain-lion (puma/leon) [miztli] {koh}
Panthera onca	jaguar (jaguar/tigre) [ocelotl] {balam}
Lynx rufus	lynx (lince/gato montes)
Pinnipedia	pinnipeds
Otariidae	sea lions
Phocidae	seals
Cetacea	cetaceans
Physeteridae	sperm whales
Balaenopteridae	fin-backed whales
Delphinidae	porpoises and dolphins
Perissodactyla	perissodacyls
Tapiridae	tapir (tapir/danta) [tlacaxolotl] {tzimin}
Artiodactyla	artiodactyls
Tayassuidae	peccaries (jabali/coche de monte) [coyametl] {kitam/ac}
Cervidae	deer

F

Taxonomic Name	English (Spanish) [Nahuatl] {Maya}	Taxonomic Name	English (Spanish) [Nahuatl] {Maya}
Odocoileus hemionus	mule deer (bura/venado mula)	Geomyidae	pocket gophers (tuza) [tozan] {ba}
Odocoileus virginianus	white-tailed deer (venado cola blanca) [mazatl] {keh}	Heteromyidae	pocket mice
		Castoridae	beavers (castor/ nutria)
Mazama americana	red brocket deer (temazate) [temazate] {chan yuc}	Rodentia: Myomorpha	rats and mice (ratones) [quimichin] {ch'o}
Mazama gouazoubira	gray or brown brocket deer (venado plomo)	Rodentia: Caviomorpha Erethizontidae	caviomorphs porcupines (puerco espin) [huitztlacuatzin] {ki'ix och}
Antilocapridae	antelopes		
Antilocapra americana	pronghorn antelope (berrendo)	Hydrochaeridae	capybaras (capibara)
Bovidae	bovids	Agoutidae	agoutis (paca/tepezcuintl)
Bison bison	bison (bisonte)		
Ovis canadensis	mountain sheep (carnero salvaje/ borrego cimarron)	Dasyprodidae	pacas (aguti) [cuauhtozan] {tsub}
Sirenia		Lagomorpha	lagomorphs
Trichechus manatus	West Indian manatee (manati) {baclam}	Leporidae	leporids
		Romerolagus diazi	volcano rabbit (zacatuche)
Rodentia: Sciuromorpha	sciuromorphs	*Lepus* spp.	hares (liebres)
Sciuridae	squirrels (ardilla) [techalotl] {kuuk}	*Sylvilagus* spp.	rabbits (conejos) [tochtli] {tu'ul/tan kah}

Invertebrates

The invertebrates are an enormously diverse faunal group, encompassing many phyla, classes, and families. While the ancient Middle Americans used or recognized many of these, the Mollusca and Arthropoda were the most significant dietary, economic, and ritual invertebrates.

Separation of freshwater aquatic systems and low molluskan motility result in a highly diverse Middle American freshwater molluskan fauna. The Sphaeriidae, Unionidae, Amblemidae, and Mutelidae dominate the bivalves, while the principal gastropod families include the Pilidae, Hydrobiidae, Pleuroceridae, and Thiaridae. Freshwater gastropods, particularly the apple snails, *jutes,* and various riverine and lacustrine unionid bivalves, are still an important local source both of nutrition, and of utilitarian and ceremonial artifacts.

Marine mollusks, one of the most diverse faunal groups in Middle America, appear in coastal archaeologi-

cal deposits at all time periods and are also common at most inland sites. A comprehensive analysis of the mollusks of the Yucatán coasts lists almost 780 shallow-water species alone. Faunas from the two coasts are related, both being derived from an early Caribbean population, and tropical species predominate. The influence of Nearctic species is strong north of Baja California, and along the northern Atlantic coast, but southward sub-provincial differences are small. Symbolizing death and rebirth, and artistically represented in association with various deities, marine shells were also valuable trade commodities throughout Mesoamerica. An impressive diversity of marine invertebrates, including many bivalve and gastropod species, was included in ceremonial deposits at both inland and coastal sites. The most highly valued ceremonial mollusks at most Maya sites were the colorful spiny spondylus. Olive, cone, and marginella shell tinklers were common decorations on clothing and textiles. Other artifacts were often fashioned from the colorful conch, stromb, and helmet shells, and the thick pearl oyster shells. Other molluscs of direct commercial importance were the dye-producing wide-mouthed rock shells common off the coast of Mexico, and the tusk shells, which occur only in small quantities in Middle American deposits but which were used as currency in many parts of North America.

Thousands of arthropod species occur in Mexico and Central America, including scorpions, spiders, crustaceans, and insects. The majority are distributed among the diverse insect families. Throughout Mesoamerica spiders were associated with weaving and witchcraft. In Aztec iconography butterflies represent beauty and joy, but also symbolize flames and fire. Many arthropod species were important in both diet and economy. Freshwater shrimps, crayfish, and crabs formed a large part of any ancient Mesoamerican diet, as did dragonflies, grasshoppers, crickets, bugs, and ants. True delicacies for the ancient Aztecs were the water boatmen bugs and their eggs, eaten even by the Spanish on meatless days. Larval skipper moths are still famous as the maguey-eating "tequila worms." While these edible larvae were roasted or fried, larval carpenter moths collected from the same maguey plants were used as a spice.

Two economically important insect species were domesticated and their products were traded throughout Mesoamerica. The brilliant red coloring agent produced from the cochineal insect, used as both dye and ink, was one of the most valuable Mesoamerican commodities. The second domesticated Middle American insect was the indigenous honeybee. There are almost 160 bee genera in Mexico and Central America, and several species were exploited to produce different varieties of the wax and honey so important in tribute and trade, medicine, and religious ceremonies.

FURTHER READINGS

Aguilera, C. 1985. *Flora y Fauna Mexicana: Mitología y Tradiciones.* Editorial Everest Mexicana.

Bussing, W. A. 1985. Patterns of Distribution of the Central American Ichthyofauna. In F. G. Stehli and S. D. Webb (eds.), *The Great American Biotic Interchange,* pp. 453–473. New York: Plenum Press.

Campbell, J. A., and W. W. Lamar. 1989. *The Venomous Reptiles of Latin America.* Ithaca: Cornell University Press.

Davis, L. I. 1972. *A Field Guide to the Birds of Mexico and Central America.* Austin: University of Texas Press.

Emmons, L. H. 1990. *Neotropical Rainforest Mammals: A Field Guide.* Chicago: University of Chicago Press.

Hurlbert, S. H., and A. Villalobos-Figueroa (eds.). 1982. *Aquatic Biota of Mexico, Central America and the West Indies.* San Diego: Department of Biology, San Diego State University.

Keen, A. M. 1958, 1975. *Sea Shells of Tropical West America: Marine Mollusks from Lower California to Colombia.* Stanford: Stanford University Press.

Lange, F. W. 1971. Marine Resources: A Viable Subsistence Alternative for the Prehistoric Lowland Maya. *American Anthropologist* 73:619–639.

Leopold, A. S. 1959. *Wildlife of Mexico: The Game Birds and Mammals.* Berkeley: University of California Press.

Miller, R. R. 1966. Geographical Distribution of Central American Freshwater Fishes. *Copeia* 4:773–785.

Morris, P. A. 1975. *A Field Guide to Shells of the Atlantic and Gulf Coasts and the West Indies.* Boston: Houghton Mifflin.

Ramamoorthy, T. P., R. Bye, A. Lot, and I. Fa (eds.). 1993. *Biological Diversity of Mexico: Origins and Distribution.* New York: Oxford University Press.

Savage, J. M. 1966. The Origins and History of the Central American Herpetofauna. *Copeia* 4:719–765.

Stuart, L. C. 1964. Fauna of Middle America. In R. C. West (ed.), *Handbook of Middle American Indians,* vol. 1, *Natural Environment and Early Cultures,* pp. 316–362. Austin: University of Texas Press.

Kitty Emery

SEE ALSO
Flora; Geography and Climate

Feathered Serpent

In Mesoamerica, the iconographic union of different animal species into one powerful god or spirit symbolized an imaginative combination of magical qualities. The very ambiguity of visual forms spoke of supernatural power. One of the most mythologically and iconographically important of such fantastic creatures was the Feathered Serpent, called Quetzalcóatl in Nahuatl, the language of the Aztecs. The term is made up of two words: *quetzal,* the magnificently plumed quetzal bird, and *coatl,* meaning "snake." For Mesoamerican peoples, quetzal feathers were a sign of elite status and power, while serpents dramatically swallowed their prey whole and regularly shed their slick, shiny skins. Amongst the Olmec, Teotihuacanos,

F

Maya, and Aztec, precious quetzal plumes and snake imagery adorned the ritual costumes and paraphernalia of rulers, warriors, and gods. Both animals thus possessed strong associations with magical powers and ideas of supernatural shamanic transformation.

Feathered Serpent imagery pervades the iconography of many Mesoamerican civilizations, beginning with the Olmec. It finds its greatest architectural expression in the monumental Temple of Quetzalcóatl at Teotihuacán. Here an ornate façade shows snarling serpent heads emerging from petaled collars on a design alternating with images of Tláloc or the War Serpent. The rippling body of the snake is flanked with seashells, linking the sinuous figures with water, fertility, and possibly also blood sacrifice.

In later, Postclassic times, Quetzalcóatl appears in human form, wearing a conical headdress and symbolic manifestations of the sea in jewelry made of cut conch shells. For the Aztec in particular, Quetzalcóatl was a wind god who announced the coming of rain.

Quetzalcóatl's imagery in these later times is complex, and he was seen also as a culture hero who played a central role in the creation of the world. During the sixteenth century, the king of the Toltec capital of Tula took the name Ce Acatl Topiltzin Quetzalcóatl and was associated with a cult of the celestial feature we know as the planet Venus, as the patron of war and sacrifice. In mythology, Quetzalcóatl was cast out of Tula by his archrival Tezcatlipoca; he then journeyed to the Yucatán, where he became known as Kukulkan, which means "Feathered Serpent" in the Maya language. Throughout Mesoamerica, the powerful mix of bird and serpent imagery made the Feathered Serpent a patron of rulers and priests, whose far-seeing powers and divine qualities were embodied in the strange iconography of this distinctive creature.

FURTHER READINGS

Miller, M. E., and K. Taube. 1993. *The Gods and Symbols of Ancient Mexico and the Maya*. Thames and Hudson, London.

Sahagún, B. de. 1950–1978. *Florentine Codex: General History of the Things of New Spain*. A. J. O. Anderson and C. E. Dibble (eds.). Santa Fe and Salt Lake City: School of American Research and University of Utah.

Nicholas J. Saunders

Figurines, Terracotta

Figurines—small images made of baked clay, representing humans and, less frequently, animal forms—were used throughout Mesoamerica from the beginning of settled village life into the Colonial period. With few exceptions, figurines are associated with households, recovered archaeologically in refuse middens or mixed up in the fill of residential debris. They are almost always broken and eroded. Figurines seem to be part of household ritual paraphernalia, because they are only occasionally recovered as burial goods or offertory caches. Whistles, flutes, and ocarinas occur in similar contexts and may provide a clue to the nature of household ritual. The items are easily portable; the largest rarely exceed 20 cm in height.

Whistles in the Formative period feature canines, felines, birds, and monkeys, represented consistently in all geographical regions; less numerous and more climate specific are the peccary, coatimundi, and various water-related zoomorphs. Beginning in the Classic period, the human form predominates on whistles, but the animal theme continues.

The earliest figurines were made by the hand-modeling technique, which was replaced with the use of the mold in the Early Classic period, a technological innovation that is significant as a chronological marker. In the Central Highlands, molded figurines continued to be small and solid, whereas to the southeast in the Gulf Coast and Maya areas, and to some extent in Oaxaca, they were replaced by hollow whistles.

Mesoamerican figurines are divided into four geographical regions: Mexican Central Highlands, West Mexico, Gulf Lowlands and Oaxaca, and the Maya area. Figurines are similar throughout Mesoamerica in the Formative period and develop distinctive regional differences in the Classic period. Figurines have been neglected in the literature, particularly evident in the lack of sufficient illustrations; only Noguera's 1975 publication covers the entire Mesoamerican corpus, and even this compendium has serious gaps.

Formative Period

Terracotta figurines were first produced as part of the pottery-making tradition that developed with settled village life (approximately 1500 B.C.). The tradition of figurine manufacture and use seems to appear full blown, but there must have been a period of experimentation that has been lost from the archaeological record. Two examples, dated to c. 2300 B.C., are reported from Zohapilco/Tlapacoya, a lacustrine site in Central Mexico (Fig. A;

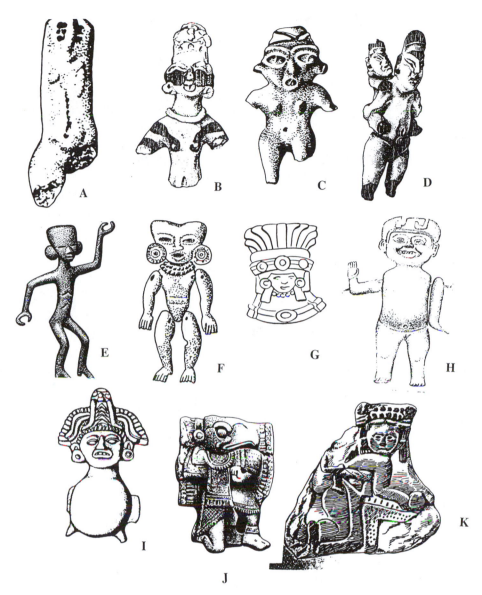

A. Zohapilco (Niederberger 1976: Lam. XVC. Height 5.4 cm) Clay cylinder in human form, with facial features and body parts suggested rather than carefully delineated. Associated RC date 2300 110 B.C.; **B. El Arbolillo** (Vaillant, George. *Excavations at El Arbolillo*. New York: Anthropological Papers of the American Museum of Natural History 35(2), 1935: Fig. 16-4. Height 9.6 cm) Type C head and torso, showing body paint; **C. Zohapilco** (Niederberger 1976: Lam. LXXVII-9. Height 5.5 cm) Vaillant's Type K, exaggeratedly large eyes; **D. Gualupita** (Vaillant, Suzannah B., and George C. Vaillant, *Excavations at Gualupita*. New York: Anthropological Papers of the American Museum of Natural History 35(1), 1934: Fig. 1. Height 10.3 cm) Vaillant's Type D; mother carrying child; **E. Teotihuacán** (Covarrubias, Miguel. *Indian Art of Mexico and Central America*. New York: Alfred A. Knopf, 1957: Fig. 54, center right. Height: approximately 10 cm) Classic period standing "dancer" figure; heads are usually molded, the torso and limbs made by hand modeling; **F. Teotihuacán** (von Winning 1991: Fig. 8. Height approximately 12 cm) Classic period articulated figure with heart-shaped head; **G. Teotihuacán** (Sejourne 1966: Fig. 109. Height: approximately 5 cm) Classic period seated figure wearing cape and feather panache headdress; **H. El Zapotal, Veracruz** (von Winning 1991: Fig. 20. Height 37 cm) Late Classic period hollow figure, articulated arms. The form evolved from smaller, Preclassic versions with whistle in the back of the head; **I. Monte Albán** (Martínez López and Winter 1994: Fig. 49e; Height: approximately 20 cm) Classic period whistle; human head wears animal headdress; **J. Jonuta, Tabasco** (Alvarez and Casasola, *Las Figurillas de Jonuta, Tabasco*. Mexico: Universidad Nacional Autonoma de Mexico, 1985. Lam. 16 Height approximately 15 cm) Late Classic period figurine-whistle; kneeling human figure wears bird headdress; **K. Lubaantun, Belize** (Joyce, Thomas A. "The Pottery Whistle-Figurines of Lubaantun." *The Journal of the Royal Anthropological Institute of Great Britain and Ireland,* vol. 63: xv–xxv, 1933: Plate VI-8. Height approximately 15 cm) Late Classic figure-whistle; profile female grinds on metate; carries infant on her back.

Niederberger 1976:213), and from Puerto Marques on the Pacific coast of Guerrero.

All Mesoamerican Formative period figurines are marked by similarity rather than difference. Hand-modeling allows for an enormous variety of detail, and indeed, no Formative period figurine exactly resembles any other. Coils of clay were joined to make the torso, limbs, and head. Details of facial features, headgear, and jewelry were added by incising, appliqué strips, and punctate. Postures are standing (less frequently, sitting), with legs separated and arms extended or placed against the chest. Heads, headgear, jewelry, and clothing (although scanty) are shown in detail, whereas fingers and toes are poorly defined. The process allows for a three-dimensional view of figurines, many times whimsical in demeanor and pose. Occasionally genital features are indicated, especially female breasts and protruding abdomens to indicate pregnancy. The theme of a female carrying a baby begins in the Early Formative and continues into Late Classic times. Body decoration such as painting and facial scarification is indicated (Figs. B, C, D).

Within these general parameters, there are regional and temporal variations that have served as diagnostic traits. In the 1930s George Vaillant excavated the Basin of Mexico village sites Zacatenco, Ticomán and El Arbolillo, and Gualupita (in Morelos) to establish a chronological sequence and develop a classification system; this works relatively well for Central Highlands material but, with rare exceptions, is not more generally applicable, and it became meaningless as more excavations were carried out in regions far from Central Mexico. Large, generalized "types" may be recognized, but the hand-modeling technique allows for a wide range of variation in detail. Important collections of Early Formative figurines have been made at Tehuacán Valley sites, at Chalcatzingo (Morelos), San José Mogote (Oaxaca), and Uaxactún (southern Maya Lowlands). Some of the differences may represent specific physical types: for example, the Olmec "baby face" (slightly bulbous head, turned-down mouth, slanted eyes) is consistently found on small, solid figurines from all sites with Olmec components.

Late Formative, Classic, and Postclassic Periods

Mexican Central Highlands. With the rise of Teotihuacán, figurines underwent a radical change. Clothing became important: female figures are shown wearing the traditional overblouse *(quechquemitl)* and skirt, and males wear loincloths and capes. The hand-modeling process continued, but the emphasis was on clothing that covered the body. By the time the Classic period was fully under way, the process of using molds became widespread. Figurines lost their vital spontaneity and assumed a rigid conformity, a trend that continued to the Conquest.

The figurine tradition is particularly visible at Teotihuacán because of its large population. Molded figurines are divided into four major groups based on morphological traits: (1) the stick figure, termed "dancer," may have been covered by garments made of perishable material (Fig. E); (2) the figurine with articulated limbs, usually with an enigmatic heart-shaped head (Fig. F), frequently wearing a close-fitting cap or sidelocks; (3) the seated individual covered by cape from neck to toes (Fig. G), with a seemingly endless variety of headdresses, some laden with diverse ornaments, including feathers, or shaped as animal heads; and (4) males dressed in protective clothing that suggests ballplayer costume, with carefully delineated heads seeming to depict individuals. Animals make up approximately 10 percent of the figurine corpus, with canines, felines, birds, and monkeys predominating. The musical flute was decorated by a monkey head.

The figurine tradition seems to lose its vitality in the Highlands outside Teotihuacán; either the Teotihuacán craft-workers had dominated their neighbors, or people were not producing many figurines, or else the archaeological record is simply incomplete. Late Classic sites such as Cholula show new but uninformative figurines. Xochicalco and Cacaxtla either did not use figurines or they have not been reported.

Toltec (c. A.D. 1100) figurines mark a significant change in clothing. Females wear long skirts, but no upper-body clothing. The texture of the fabric is shown in detail by either careful molding or paint. Whistles are not known from the Toltec corpus. The figurines are large and two-dimensional. Late Postclassic (A.D. 1250) Aztec figurines are either hollow rattles, or flat with perforations for suspension. Central Highland traits continue into Aztec times, greatly diminishing in themes and variations from the Classic period.

West Mexico. The West is famous for its abstract, fanciful large tomb figures, few of which have been recovered in controlled excavations. Nonetheless, some small, solid figurines have been recovered, again in refuse deposits. Late Formative figurines from Chupícuaro are highly stylized and laden with appliqué, and are thought to mark a cultural link with the Central Highlands, sharing traits such as diagonally placed eyes and heavy appliqué.

Thin, slant-eyed Chupícuaro figurines probably were used in domestic contexts, as well as occasionally serving as grave goods. Hand-modeling continued in West Mexico until the early Postclassic, when Toltec-style figurines appeared.

Gulf Coast and Oaxaca. The Gulf Coast region, like West Mexico, lacks much archaeological information on domestic architecture and content. The area had a prodigious ceramic industry, particularly in its exquisite sculptures, some of which are life-sized. Figurines that dominated the Classic period assemblage are problematic as to context. Archaeologists working on the Gulf Coast have focused on the larger, more elaborate sculptures, and many of these lack field reports. Whistles, flutes, and ocarinas are abundant in human and animal forms. The "smiling" figures from Remojadas and other sites (Fig. H) evolved from Late Formative solid figurines, and have been recovered in burials as well as trash deposits.

Figurines typical of Monte Albán have been recovered from sites all over the Valley of Oaxaca. The female figurines are flat and slablike, whereas many male figurines are whistles (Fig. I). Females wear traditional garb, and males are noted for elaborate headdresses, some of which depict the open maw of an animal. Figurines are virtually unknown for the Postclassic Mixtec.

Maya Area. The Maya shared in the hand-modeled tradition in the Formative period. Figurine manufacture diminished in the Early Classic period, only to be revived in the Late Classic with a rich tradition of elegant, detailed figurines in the tradition (or style) known as "Jaina" after the island type site off the western coast of the Yucatán Peninsula. The distinction between figurines used in burials and as purely household ritual items becomes blurred because Jaina was a burial ground and figurines have come from controlled excavations. "Jaina" figurines are far more numerous from excavations at inland Maya sites, such as Altar de Sacrificios and Seibal. A workshop has been identified at Jonuta (Tabasco) which probably supplied many areas with figurines (Fig. J). Figurines connect the Maya area to the Gulf Coast in the Late Classic period. "Nopiloa-Mayoid" and other figurines with articulated limbs have been recovered both at Jaina and along the central Gulf Coast.

Maya figurines are rich in ethnographic details of dress, daily activity, and probably social status. Ballplayers have been identified, as well as males carrying staffs, shields, and other accouterments. Women are shown holding children, weaving, and grinding corn (Fig. K). Since all these figurines are whistles or some sort of musical instrument, they may have played a part in the celebration of village life by recording actual portraits of individuals and their statuses within the community.

Summary

Figurines offer insights on the people who made and used them as no other artifact category can do. Mesoamericans in the Formative period lived in small and apparently egalitarian villages. They made small images of themselves and their animals, with which they performed household rituals, probably involving music, dance, songs, and chants. Individualistic art forms are fully developed in the Formative, with abstraction carried to extremes that seem highly sophisticated to the modern eye.

When social differentiation became widespread and cities such as Teotihuacán developed, figurines may have served to demonstrate some sort of social affiliation within the community. The symbols and motifs on Teotihuacán's figurines reflect similar themes in their ceremonial art, such as incensarios, and are even found in Zapotec funerary ceramic sculpture. Mesoamerican figurines provide important information about daily life, and they communicate a humanity that is not found in other Mesoamerican media of self-expression.

FURTHER READINGS

Diehl, R. A., and M. D. Mandeville. 1987. Tula, and Wheeled Animal Effigies in Mesoamerica. *Antiquity* 61:239–246.

Grove, D. C. 1984. *Chalcatzingo: Excavations on the Olmec Frontier.* London: Thames and Hudson.

MacNeish, R. S., F. A. Peterson, and K. V. Flannery. 1970. *The Prehistory of the Tehuacan Valley,* vol. 3, *Ceramics.* Austin: University of Texas Press.

Marcus, J., and K. V. Flannery. 1996. *Zapotec Civilization: How Urban Society Evolved in Mexico's Oaxaca Valley.* London: Thames and Hudson.

Niederberger, C. 1976. *Zohapilco: Cinco milenios de ocupación humana en un sitio lacustre de la cuenca de México.* Colección Científica, 30. Mexico City: Instituto Nacional de Antropología e Historia.

Noguera, E. 1954. *La cerámica arqueológica de Cholula.* Mexico City: Editorial Guarania.

———. 1975. *La cerámica arqueológica de Mesoamérica.* 2nd ed. Mexico City: Instituto de Investigaciones Antropológicas, Universidad Nacional Autónoma de México.

Porter Weaver, M. 1969. A Reappraisal of Chupícuaro. In J. D. Frierman (ed.), *The Natalie Wood Collection of*

F

Pre-Columbian Ceramics from Chupícuaro, Guanajuato, Mexico, at UCLA, pp. 5–15. Los Angeles: Museum and Laboratories of Ethnic Arts and Technology, University of California, Los Angeles.

Rands, R. L., and B. C. Rands. 1965. Pottery Figurines of the Maya Lowlands. In G. R. Wiley (ed.), *Handbook of Middle American Indians,* vol. 2, pp. 535–560. Austin: University of Texas Press.

Ricketson, O. G., and E. B. Ricketson. 1937. *Uaxactun, Guatemala: Group E—1926–1931.* Washington, D.C.: Carnegie Institution of Washington.

Séjourné, L. 1966. *El lenguaje de las formas en Teotihuacan.* Mexico City: Siglo XXI.

Vaillant, G. 1941. *The Aztecs of Mexico: Origin, Rise and Fall of the Aztec Nation.* Garden City: Doubleday, Doran.

von Winning, H. 1991. Articulated Figurines from Teotihuacan and Central Veracruz—A Reanalysis. In T. Stocker (ed.), *The New World Figurine Project,* vol. 1, pp. 63–83. Provo, Utah: Research Press.

Sue Scott

SEE ALSO
Ceramics

Filobobos

See Vega de la Peña and Cuajilotes

Flora

See Agave; Agriculture and Domestication; Diet and Nutrition; Food and Cuisine; Maize

Flowers

Biologically, flowers are sexual reproductive organs of highly evolved vascular seed plants. Flowers are also the most striking feature of plant life, which in various Mesoamerican cultures has been considered to be of sacred origin. In an Aztec creation myth, flowers arose from the skin of the earth goddess Cipactli. In another myth, flowers came from the love goddess Xochiquetzal's genital flesh, bitten off by a bat made from Quetzalcóatl's semen.

At different times and places in Mesoamerica, flowers represented the sun, the maternal matrix, fertility, creation, the place of emergence, and the place of rest. The association of flowers with the life-giving sun is exempli-

Offering based upon maguey crown (Span. *Agave*) and draped with garlands of white, pink, and yellow flowers of *Plumeria rubra* (or *P. rubra acutifolia*) and used as offerings at the Water Petition Ceremony in Guerrero (May 1, 1990).

fied in the Mayan glyph *k'in,* which represents the sun as well as the day of Mayan sun god and resembles the stylized four-part flower motif of other Mesoamerican cultures. Blossoms were sustenance for the elite classes of Mesoamerican societies. Warriors killed in battle were said to have been transformed into birds and butterflies, feeding on flowers in the luxuriant garden paradise of Tlalocan, as depicted in a mural at Tepantitla, Teotihuacán.

Some gods arose from the union of flowers. The red-flowered and white-flowered forms of *nikte'* (Plumeria) were a kind of ancestral couple for the Lacandon Maya; their son was Nohoch-chac-yum, head of the Lacandon pantheon. Other deities are associated with the physiological effects of flowering plants; Tohil, the Maya god of justice and revenge, is linked with *tohk'u (Datura),* the neurotoxic alkaloids of which induce delirium and even insanity.

Flowers epitomize relationships in both biological and cultural contexts. In the natural world, they mark phenological changes through time and seasons; morphogenic change in terms of organized organ formation and development, evolutionarily expressing the advanced, derived condition of plant reproduction on earth; and ecological relationships with pollinators. The use of flowers in every culture reflects a society's view of nature and assists in establishing, maintaining, and ending relationships—with dead and living, with divinities and humans.

The flowering of certain plants marked seasonal activities. Among the Maya of Yucatán, *ch'oy* (*Cochlospermum*) indicated the time to fell trees in the dry forest to create agricultural fields. The ornamental *azcalxochitl* (*Sprekelia*) signaled to the highland Aztec farmers that the rainy season would soon start.

Flower offerings by Aztec nobles and merchants to their deities and guests consisted of blooming stalks of aroids and *Helianthus,* as well as bouquets and crowns of various flowers of attractive color, form, and fragrance. *Polianthes* (tuberose), with its penetrating perfume, was one of the flowers used by the Aztecs to mask the odors of sacrifices; today in Mexico it is valued as a pleasantly fragrant cut flower for use in weddings, house blessings, funerals, churches, and shrines. *Plumeria* is also much used today and has deep pre-Hispanic roots in Mesoamerica; its flowers adorn altars and offerings, and it is tucked into women's coiffures to attract suitors—probably an extension of the pre-Hispanic Maya *K'ay Nikte'* ceremony. Various color forms of this flower were identified with the erotic ritual dedicated to Macuilxochitl, Aztec goddess of music and dance and a solar deity associate of Xochipilli, which was introduced to the Maya of Yucatán during the Toltec occupation.

Aromatic flowers in Aztec neck charms, along with other plant, animal, and mineral products, maintained a protective relationship between the public officials wearing them and the natural and supernatural environments. To protect important travelers as well as to alleviate fatigue, the nobility used many fragrant local summer blossoms, as well as exotic flowers such as *Plumeria, Magnolia, Philodendron, Cymbopetalum,* and *Bourreria.* The use of flowers was restricted to elites; commoners were permitted only aromatic herbs to treat similar conditions.

Flowers and their representations have been used for utilitarian and esthetic purposes—decorative, edible, and medicinal—and as signifiers of events and message carriers. Flower representations especially involved vocal descriptions and expressions in words (imagery) and visual comprehension through images. Flower representations (phytomorphs) vary from stylized and abstract glyphs and ideographs to detailed, realistic depictions. Artistic manifestations can be found in clothing, ceramics, painting and writing, sculpture, and architecture.

Early post-Contact documents with texts and illustrations derived directly or indirectly from native informants attest to the prominence of flowers in Mesoamerican cultures. Hernández's *Natural History of New Spain* describes twenty-six ornamental flowers. In other Nahuatl culture sources, flowers are also well represented. The Florentine Codex lists forty-eight species of plants with esthetic purposes, of which thirty-six are flowers; of eighty-one ceremonial plants, thirty-three are flowers. These blossoms, along with tubes of tobacco (*Nicotiana tabacum),* were essential elements of the dances of the nobility.

The semantic range of the root *xoch* ("flower") in Nahua culture was broad. *Xochitl* is a metaphoric name for one of the many inebriating mushrooms (e.g., *Psilocybe aztecorum*); *temixoch* is a flowery dream, while *xochinanáncatl* is a divinatory plant or "flower" mushroom. The fermented fruits of *Vanilla* were considered flowers and were included in the aromatic pouches that protected rulers; they also provided a favorite flavoring in cacao-based drinks of royalty. Flowers were strongly linked with elegant communication: *In xochitl, in cuicatl* ("flower and song," or "poetry") was considered the only proper manner in which to communicate with the life-giving forces, to aid a saddened heart, and to speak the truth. Within this concept, flowers were considered to be the only memory that humans left on this earth. Nahuatl poetry was absorbed with flowers in general, but it rarely names any plants specifically, which is unusual, given the detailed plant taxonomy of the Aztecs.

The military-economic-religious domination of the Aztec Triple Alliance was also characterized by *xochiyaoyotl,* the "flowery wars." These staged, non-conquest conflicts between the Aztecs and their enemies were arranged to provide military training and to obtain enemy prisoners for religious offerings in Tenochtitlán. During the sacrificial procedures, the enemy rulers secretly observed the ceremonies while concealed from the spectators by a wall of flowers.

A common representation of the generic flower among Mesoamerican cultures is the stylized four-part flower, although variants may have three, five, or seven components. The top view usually presents four petals, while the

F

side perspective reveals three of the four petals (one complete petal, two half petals; it is assumed that the balance is on the unseen half). The flower symbolizes the perfect Mesoamerican universe with its fourfold division of time and space, as well as the four-part universe of the creation stories. Quadripartite motifs are seen in such works as the pecked quartered circles on floors of buildings in Teotihuacán and the quartered universe of the pre-Conquest Fejerváry-Mayer Codex from the Cholula region of Oaxaca. Such floral imagery may have inspired a sense of harmony and order among the people. More detailed flowers of *Nymphaea* (waterlily), associated with Tláloc (Aztec god of rain) and Chaak (Mayan water deity), have been found on murals at Teotihuacán and Palenque and in the Maya Dresden Codex.

Some flower depictions are realistic, such as the body decorations on Xochipilli, Prince of Flowers. This masked figure manifests a state of ecstasy with his trancelike pose. Decorations on his body include flowers of such hallucinogenic plants such as *Rivea, Heimia,* and *Nicotiana.* He is depicted seated on a base decorated with metamorphosing butterflies that are feeding on "flowery" mushrooms. The clothes of the aristocratic class, such as the capes of rulers and noblemen, were embellished with a wide array of floral designs based on *Philodendron, Magnolia, tlapaltecuxuchio* ("colored lord's flower," unidentified), *Dahlia, Plumeria,* and *Euphorbia.*

Restriction of flower use to elites probably changed rapidly after European intrusion. Even though the Florentine Codex and Bernal Díaz's *History of the Conquest of Mexico* provide vivid and detailed descriptions of the central markets of early post-Conquest Mexico and their contents, the only flower noted for sale was that of *Cucurbita* (squash). After the Spanish conquest, Francisco Hernández recorded in *Natural History of New Spain* (written 1571–1576) the abundant trade in *Cymbopetalum* as a flavoring for the cacao beverage *cacáoatl;* this probably reflected the collapse of class restrictions on the employment of this blossom as well as a reorientation of market demands.

The general public also appreciated flowers but had access only to wild, seasonal blossoms for offerings, such as that of *tlaxochimaco* to Huitzilopochtli (often represented as a flowering-feeding hummingbird) during the ninth month of the year. The royalty controlled plants that had more visible and fragrant blossoms and that were available all year. These plants were cultivated in diverse, elegant gardens, the pleasure retreats where the noble class liked to relax. These royal gardens were spectacular,

according to the first notices of the Spaniards who encountered them at Anáhuac, Iztapalapa, Chapultepec, and Tetzcotcingo in the Valley of Mexico as well as in warmer regions of the Aztec Empire, as at Huaxtepec. These gardens concentrated exotic flora from various ecosystems of Mesoamerica and permitted the acclimation of the plants for subsequent transplanting in different ecological zones. Many of the garden flowers specified in the early post-Conquest documents are trees that originated in distant lands of the Aztec Empire.

Often a local gardener migrated with and tended the relocated plants; the cultivation of special flowering plants required specialists to ensure survival and florescence. Among the Aztecs flower horticulture was a distinguished occupation, and the horticulturist, or *quilchiuhqui,* was an honored professional differentiated from the farmer *(tlalchiuhqui).* A good horticulturist was considered to be a careful and diligent individual, familiar with books and with signs of the days, months, and years. Caring for cut flowers also required specialized knowledge of how to construct the floral garlands, necklaces, bouquets, and wreaths used in ceremonial offerings.

Continued introduction of new flowering species from around the Aztec Empire, attention to genetic variants among garden plants, and subsequent selection for more attractive plants resulted in the domestication of horticultural varieties. Illustrations in pre- and post-Contact sources present blossoms with numerous floral parts in multiples of four, suggesting horticultural forms with "doubled" flowers. The domesticated forms have more petals than their wild ancestors (resulting from transformation of other floral parts) and thus deliver greater visual impact and more fragrance; examples are the ball-headed marigolds and dahlias depicted on the necklace of Xipe-Tótec (goddess of vegetation and of regeneration of the earth) and in the illustrations in book 11 of the Florentine Codex.

The Mesoamerican flower heritage has been passed down to the present, a continuity perceived through the etymology of Nahuatl words based on *xochitl* ("flower") and the Mayan words *nik* and *lol* ("small" and "large" flowers, respectively). Such contemporary Nahuatl toponyms as Xochicalco ("place of the house of flower"), Xochimilco ("among cultivated flowers"), Xochipala ("soaked flower"), Xochipilan ("among cut flowers"), and Xochitepec ("flower-covered hill") place human activities and geographical features in context with flowers since pre-Hispanic times.

The flowers of the Mesoamerican royalty of the past are part of present-day rituals of Mexican society. In cen-

TABLE 1. FLOWERS IMPORTANT IN MESOAMERICAN CULTURES.

Taxonomic Name	English (Spanish) [Nahuatl] {Maya}
Araceae family	arum [chimalxochitl]
Bourreria huanita	(juanita) [yzquixochitl]
Cochlospermum vitifolium	yellowsilk shellseed {ch'oy}
Cosmos diversifolius	cosmos
Cucurbita spp.	squash blossom (calabaza) [ayotli] {k'uum}
Cymbopetalum penduliflorum	ear-flower [xochinacaztli]
Dahlia coccinea	dahlia [acocoxochitl]
Datura inoxia	angel's trumpet {tohk'u}
Euphorbia pulcherrima	poinsettia [cuetlaxochitl]
Heimia salicifolia	[sinicuichi]
Helianthus	sunflower
Magnolia dealbata	magnolia [eloxochitl]
Nicotiana tabacum	tobacco [y[i]etl] {k'uts}
Nymphaea	waterlily [atzatzamolli] {na'ab, lolha}
Philodendron spp.	philodendron [huacalxochitl]
Plumeria rubra	frangipane (flor de mayo) [cacaloxochitl] {nikte' ch'om}
Polianthes tuberosa	tuberose (nardo) [omixochitl]
Rivea corymbosa	morning glory [ololiuhqui] {xtabentun}
Sprekelia formosissima	Aztec lily [azcalxochitl]
Tagetes erecta	marigold (flor de muerto) [zempoalxochitl] {xkanlol}
Tagetes lucida	sweet marigold (pericón) [yauhtli]
Vanilla planifolia	vanilla [tlilxochitl] {siisbik}
unidentified	colored lord's flower [tlapaltecuxuchio]

tral Mexico, crosses of wild-collected, blooming stems of *Tagetes* (marigold) are placed over doors and windows as well as on the corners of cultivated fields in order to prevent the entrance of evil spirits on September 28, St. Michael's Day—an association demonstrating the syncretism of the Archangel Michael and Tláloc (with whom *yauhtli* was originally associated), as well as the acculturation of floral elements on a local scale in the states of Morelos and México. On a wider scale, *Tagetes* is used ceremonially throughout Mexico during the feast of the Day of the Dead (October 31–November 2). The spectacular and fragrant orange-yellow doubled heads of marigold adorn cemeteries and home altars where images and personal effects of the recently deceased are displayed, and the petals are spread along the path connecting these two ceremonial sites in order to aid the departed soul's return to the human community.

Since pre-Hispanic times, flowers have been an essential element of all aspects of life in Mesoamerica. Vestiges of their utilitarian, esthetic, and symbolic benefits are shared by all contemporary socio-economic classes of Mexico and Central America, as well as by people around the world.

FURTHER READINGS

Bye, R. A., and E. Linares. 1990. Mexican Market Plants of 16th Century, 1: Plants Recorded in *Historia Natural de Nueva España*. *Journal of Ethnobiology* 10:151–168.

Cruz, Martin de la. 1991 [1552]. *Libellus de medicinalibus indorum herbis, segun traducción latina de Juan Badiano*. Mexico City: Fondo de Cultúra Económica, Instituto Mexicano del Seguro Social.

Emboden, W. A. 1983. The Ethnobotany of the Dresden Codex with Especial Reference to the Narcotic *Nymphaea ampla*. *Botanical Museum Leaflets* (Harvard University) 29:87–132.

Hernández, Francisco. 1959. *Historia de las plantas de Nueva España*. In *Historia natural de Nueva España Volumenes I y II*, in his *Obras Completas*, vols. 2–3. Mexico City: Universidad Nacional Autónoma de México.

Heyden, D. 1985. *Mitología y simbolismo de la flora en el México prehispánico*. Mexico City: Universidad Nacional Autónoma de México.

Hicks, F. 1979. "Flowery Wars" in Aztec History. *American Ethnologist* 6:87–92.

F

Leon-Portilla, M. 1963. *Aztec Thought and Culture: A Study of the Ancient Nahuatl Mind.* Norman: University of Oklahoma Press.

Linares, E. 1994. Los jardines botánicos de México, su historia, situación actual y retos futuros. *Revista Chapingo, Serie Horticultura* 2:29–42.

Lot, A., and M. G. Miranda-Arce. 1983. Nota sobre las interpretaciones botánicas de plantas acuaticas representadas en codices mexicanos. In J. F. Peterson (ed.), *Flora and Fauna Imagery in Precolumbian Cultures: Iconography and Function,* pp. 85–92. B.A.R. International Series, 171. Oxford.

Ortiz de Montellano, B. R. 1990. *Aztec Medicine, Health and Nutrition.* New Brunswick: Rutgers University Press.

Sahagún, B. de. 1950–1982. *Florentine Codex, General History of the Things of New Spain.* C. E. Dibble and A. J. O. Anderson (trans. and ed.). Salt Lake City and Santa Fe: University of Utah Press and School of American Research.

Wasson, R. G. 1980. *The Wondrous Mushroom: Mycolatry in Mesoamerica.* New York: McGraw-Hill.

Robert Bye and Edelmira Linares

SEE ALSO
Gardens; Intoxicants and Intoxication

Fonseca, Gulf of (El Salvador, Honduras, Nicaragua)

The Gulf of Fonseca region demonstrates the difficulties in carrying out research in a naturally defined area that is subdivided among three modern political republics, with a historical and ongoing pattern of border and other conflicts. Around the Gulf of Fonseca, research has been limited to preliminary excavations: on the Honduran side by Baudez; on the El Salvadoran side, unpublished preliminary research at the Asanyamba site; and in Nicaragua, preliminary excavations by Montealgre Osorio near Chinandega. The known cultural sequence is limited to three phases defined by Baudez, covering the period from A.D. 300 to 950. Ceramics include Usulutan Negative, Ulua-Yojoa polychromes, and Choluteca polychrome, as well as local variations of the Greater Nicoya types Papagayo polychrome and Vallejo polychrome. Small artificial mounts suggest minimal site hierarchies. There are no mortuary, lithic, or subsistence data available.

FURTHER READINGS

Baudez, C. 1973. Les camps de Saliniers de la côte méridionale du Honduras: Données archéologiques et documents historiques. In *L'Homme, hier et aujourd'hui.* Paris: Editorial Lujas.

———. 1976. Llanura costera del Golfo de Fonseca, Honduras. *Vinculos* (National Museum of Costa Rica, San José) 2:15–23.

Healy, P. 1984. The Archaeology of Honduras. In F. W. Lange and D. Stone (eds.), *The Archaeology of Lower Central America,* pp. 113–161. Albuquerque: University of New Mexico Press.

Frederick W. Lange

SEE ALSO
Southeast Mesoamerica

Food and Cuisine

Cuisine is the culturally defined manner in which food is prepared and combined for presentation and consumption. There are as many cuisines as there are cultures in the world, and there were probably many in ancient Mesoamerica. Unhappily, most of these have been lost or severely altered since the Conquest. With the exception of a few tidbits on chocolate and maize-drink preparation among the Maya, there is little or no information on the cuisines of the Classic and Formative (Preclassic) periods. The richest data on food preparation concern the Aztec, thanks to the unparalleled efforts of the sixteenth-century Franciscan Bernardino de Sahagún.

Contemporary and nineteenth-century ethnographic data have some relevance, but they must be used with caution, since acculturative forces have played their role in diet and cookery as well as in other aspects of post-Conquest Mesoamerican life. Apart from the plants and animals used as food, one vital difference between the Spanish cuisine and those of the entire native New World is the pervasive use of oils and fats (especially lard) in the former, not only in frying but as additions to foods during their preparation. In contrast, Native Americans eschewed such substances: their recipes relied not on frying, but on roasting, boiling, steaming in pits, and the like. The tamale bought in a modern Oaxaca food stall may look pre-Columbian, but its heavy lard content reveals its hybrid nature.

How much diversity was there in pre-Conquest Mesoamerica? We know that the basic foodstuffs, apart from genetic diversity within some species, were largely the same everywhere. It is taken for granted by most scholars that three plant foods constituted an ever-present "triad" in the Mesoamerican diet: maize (consumed as tortillas, tamales, and gruels), beans, and squash. Yet an analysis of ethnohistoric documents shows that chile peppers were far more omnipresent than squash, and that when squashes were heavily used, as among the Yucatec Maya, their seeds were valued more than their flesh. Our early sources tell us very little about the native cuisines of civilizations other than the Aztec and the Maya, but we can see some interesting differences between these two. In Central Mexico, the basic way that maize is consumed has always been the flat, thin tortilla made from nixtamalized (lime-softened) maize dough and toasted on a griddle; but among the Maya, such a tortilla is by no means universal, being replaced in some areas by a variety of much thicker maize cakes. The Maya also place as much emphasis on maize gruels, such as *atolli* and *posolli*, as on solid foods. We have mentioned the considerable use by the Maya of ground squash seeds. Finally, the Yucatec Maya *pib* or pit oven, while probably not unique to them, has produced a specialized cuisine still famed throughout Mexico.

In addition to their general indifference to native cuisine, the documentary sources on Mesoamerica have one other defect: for the most part, they are more concerned with formal banquets than with the everyday fare of ordinary people. The most famous description of Aztec food habits is the account of Motecuhzoma's banquet by Bernal Díaz del Castillo. Even Sahagún's fine ethnography concentrates on the banquets given by the *pochteca,* the long-distance merchants. On the other hand, through such accounts we learn much of eating etiquette: for example, that among the Aztec, dishes containing sauces *(molli)* were held on the palm of the right hand, and rolled up tortillas in the left, and that one dipped the tortilla into the sauce; and that among the elite, the chocolate drink and smoking tubes generally were passed at the conclusion of a meal.

Aztec Ingredients

Maize was the Aztec staple food, and the focus of a large part of Aztec religion, but other grains play an important role in the imperial tribute lists and in Sahagún's *General History.* The second most important tribute seed was the common bean, for which Sahagún describes twelve varieties. Beans could be stewed or parched, or added to maize in a dish like North American succotash. The third tribute seed was *chian (Salvia hispanica),* which was apparently made into a gruel, although today it is the basis of a refreshing drink.

The Aztec word *huauhtli* could denote species of both *Amaranthus* and *Chenopodium.* Its ground seeds had an immense ritual significance: the dough was fashioned into the images of gods—especially Huitzilopochtli—and eaten by worshippers in a kind of communion. In modern Mexico, a variety of grain amaranth is popped and made into a candy sweetened with sugar syrup; whether *alegría,* as it is called, has pre-Conquest roots is unknown. Although sugar did not arrive in Mexico until after 1521, there were native sweeteners such as honey and syrups made from maguey sap or maize cane.

Squash seeds were the fourth most common item among the tribute seeds. While Sahagún describes, without much enthusiasm, the cooking of the flesh of squash in an *olla* (stew), it is clear that the Aztecs preferred the seeds and ate them parched as well as added to recipes (e.g., ground squash-seed tamales).

There were many varieties of chile, varying in size, color, and degree of hotness. So important was this plant to the native diet and cuisine that "fasting" basically meant going without chile and salt. Certainly the Aztec *macehualli,* or commoner, could and did exist on a daily fare of tortillas, beans, and chile peppers. But this would have been a monotonous diet, and many other plant and animal foods were available in the Valley of Mexico and surrounding areas to add to it. There were tomatoes, pot herbs like the greens of *Amaranthus* and *Chenopodium,* cactus pads and fruits, root crops such as the chayote *(Sechium edule)* and jícama *(Pachyrrhizus erosus),* and many kinds of fruit. The multiple uses of the maguey plant are legendary; apart from the fiber produced from its leaves, pulque (Nahua, *octli*) was fermented from its sap, and its leaves were made edible by cooking them in a pit oven.

The domesticated animals that entered the Aztec cuisine were the turkey, the Muscovy duck, and the dog. The last may have been the principal source of animal protein in the Aztec diet, and dogs were raised by the tens of thousands by professional breeders; dog meat was highly regarded by the natives and, after the Conquest, by the Spaniards (who salted it down for consumption on ocean voyages). Huge amounts of turkeys were sold in the markets and brought into Tenochtitlán as tribute. All sorts of wild game were offered in the markets of the island capital, especially waterfowl from the lake (which could be fattened in cages), and even snakes. Besides waterfowl, the lake filling the Valley of Mexico produced a wealth of

F

edible foods, including algae or pond scum (*Spirulina geitleri),* which was eaten as sun-dried cakes, and lake shrimp, small fish, and the axolotl (a larval salamander).

The question of the extent and importance of Aztec cannibalism has been hotly debated for centuries. Most scholars now agree that it never was practiced on a massive scale, since the consumption of human flesh was surrounded by restrictions and taboos. Only selected war captives were so treated, their flesh being consumed in small quantities by the captor—apparently no more than about 15 grams (half an ounce, or about a tablespoon) being allowed per person. In the recipe given by Sahagún, the meat was placed on cooked maize and the dish was to be eaten without chile or salt (emphasizing its purely religious nature).

Aztec Cooks and Menus

As far as we know, cooking was exclusively women's work; it was part of the education of every Aztec girl and was learned at home from her mother. The most important items of kitchen equipment were the maize-grinding stones, the *mano* and *metlatl (metate),* used for grinding nixtamalized maize kernels into dough for tamales and tortillas; the *molcaxitl (molcajete),* a stone or clay three-legged bowl with roughened interior, for grinding ingredients into sauces with a pestle; the *comalli,* a clay griddle; and the three hearthstones for supporting the *comalli.* In addition, there were necked jars (Spanish, *olla),* and neckless jars (Nahua, *tecomatl)* for stewing, boiling, and steaming.

Although we have no detailed recipes, Sahagún gives the ingredients and sometimes the names of a great many dishes. For the upper ranks of society, there were many kinds of tortillas, as well as tamales (such as tamales layered with maize dough and beans, and rolled into a spiral). For these lords there were roast game-birds like quail, and even whole fowl wrapped in maize dough and cooked. Elite food, especially that served in banquets, included a variety of stews and sauce dishes or casseroles. *Chilmolli* was a basic chile-and-tomato sauce that varied according to the variety of chile; it could be used with both meat and fish dishes. Chile with or without tomatoes was ubiquitous. Other ingredients used in luxury recipes were ground squash seeds and the hog plum (*Spondias* spp.).

The "street foods" sold in the marketplace were of a bewildering variety; Sahagún lists about fifty kinds of tamales alone, including such items as tamales made from turkey meat, rabbit, fish, pocket gophers, frogs, fruit,

turkey eggs, maize flowers, honey, and even bees. All kinds of tortillas were for sale, and a plethora of sauces, including the still-famous avocado-based *ahuacamolli* (guacamole). There was not only street food in quantity, but street drink as well. *Atolli* was a gruel made from maize dough (nixtamalized or not), and was a thoroughly nourishing food as well as a refreshing drink; it could be flavored in a number of ways, and/or mixed with beans and other ingredients. For travelers on the road, there was *pinolli,* ground toasted maize to which water could be added as an instant meal; marching rations for the Aztec armies included this, as well as toasted tortillas and dried maize dough (for mixing with water). In fact, it was the task of the market cooks to produce such rations when needed.

Although *atolli, pinolli,* and the like were drinks available to all, there were considerable restrictions about the use of *octli* (pulque) and chocolate. *Octli,* the fermented juice of the maguey plant, was surrounded with taboos, and drunkenness was severely punished (except in the case of old people); consuming three cups of the drink was all right, but a fourth was thought to inebriate. The Aztecs were distinctly ambivalent about chocolate. Its use was confined to the elite, to the *pochteca* merchants, and to the warriors. Although it was highly esteemed—especially the froth on top of the bowl in which it was drunk—the native philosophy classed it as a luxury product that could sap the will of a tough warrior nation. As a part of the Aztec cuisine, it appeared only as the finale to a feast, and it was almost never taken in solid form. Chocolate seems never to have been incorporated as an ingredient in dishes prior to the Conquest; its appearance in the famous *mole poblano* is a Colonial innovation.

Maya Food Sources

Food (especially tamales) and drink appear in palace scenes painted or carved on Classic Maya pictorial vases, and references to chocolate and the sacred maize gruel appear in the hieroglyphic texts, but very little information on Classic Maya cuisine can be gleaned from such sources. Epigraphic research has shown that chocolate was stored in cylindrical vases, that gruel was drunk from hemispherical cups, and that flat-bottomed plates and dishes held maize tamales. The beautiful Panel 3 from Piedras Negras shows a chocolate-drinking scene attendant on a diplomatic banquet given in A.D. 761 by the king of that city. But most of the Classic texts are silent on the subject of elite food habits, and they have nothing at all to say about the everyday fare of commoners.

Unfortunately, the ethnohistoric sources on the late pre-Conquest Maya are disappointingly scanty when compared with Sahagún on the Aztecs; they certainly fail to give us the wealth of named dishes that are available for the Aztec. The best source is Diego de Landa, but even he presents only a fragmentary picture of Maya cuisine. Further details must be sought in early Colonial dictionaries, in other historic sources, and in ethnographies of contemporary Maya groups like the Lacandón.

Maya Ingredients

Maize was, and is, the Maya "staff of life," and it was even more central to Maya religion and mythology than it was to the Aztec. As a staple, it was consumed in tamales, in various Maya forms of the tortilla, and in gruels. In both highlands and lowlands, beans, chiles, and squash seeds were vital elements in the diet, but the Petén–Yucatán Peninsula provided many tropical fruits, pot herbs, and condiments that were absent from the frost-prone higher elevations (cacao being the most important of these). Prominent among Maya produce were root crops, three of which are mentioned in the riddles asked in the *Book of Chilam Balam* of Chumayel: sweet manioc; *macal (Xanthosoma nigrum)*, a species of aroid that could be used for its edible leaves and shoots as well as its tuber; and *jícama (Pachyrhizus erosus)*. Sweet potatoes *(Ipomaea batatas)* must be considered fourth in this tetrarchy of Maya root crops.

Yucatán was famous for its abundance of turkeys and deer; both the domestic and wild (ocellated) turkey were eaten. Other lowland food animals included peccaries, spider monkey, howler monkey, armadillo, turtles, two species of iguana, crocodile, and turtles. Marine and freshwater fish played prominent roles in the lowland cuisine, sometimes being salted and sun-dried or smoked for storage and export; we are told that even manatee and tapir meat was so treated.

Maya Solid Staple Foods

The Aztec *comalli* (comal), a flat clay griddle, was apparently absent in much of the Maya area during the late pre-Conquest era, and presumably so were the thin, flat tortillas made on it. The flat cakes of nixtamalized maize that were consumed by the Maya were often much thicker than the Aztec variety, and could as well have been cooked in the ashes as on a comal. Once the nixtamal was ground on the *metate,* the Maya cook (probably always a woman, as among the Aztec) had many choices. Seasonings could be applied to the dough or mixed into it. Maya cooks mixed chiles with their maize dough, as well as ground toasted squash seeds, honey, and achiote *(Bixa orellana)*. Especially common, and often used for ceremonies, were bread doughs that incorporated beans, a kind of food used today in *chaachak* rites in Yucatán. The beans, usually the small black variety favored by the Maya, could be added cooked whole, cooked and then ground to a paste, or used partially ripe and whole, like shell beans. In the last case, the dough could be used only to form tamales, because they had to be cooked for a long time (otherwise, the beans would have remained uncooked).

The choice of tamale fillings was endless. The same bean preparations that were mixed with the dough could be used to fill it, as could ground toasted squash seeds, meat, fish, and fowl stews; flowers such as squash flowers; and all the many greens used by the Maya, especially *chaya (Jatropha aconitifolia)*. Landa mentions special breads for offerings made with egg yolks, deer hearts, or quail. Tamales were wrapped in leaves and usually steamed in a jar with a tight opening, but they could also be cooked on a comal (where that was in use), or in or under the coals.

Solid foods made of bread were often cooked in the *pib* or earth oven. In the *chaachak* rite, a special bread is constructed from many layers of dough with ground toasted squash seeds or bean paste between the layers, and baked in a *pib* under the supervision of the *hmen* (shaman).

Maya Liquid Foods

Two kinds of *atolli* or maize gruel are attested both in old Yucatec dictionaries and in Classic ceramic texts: *saka'*, made from ground maize kernels and water, and sometimes mixed with cacao, and *ul*, made from young maize. To these one must add *keyem,* a nutritious gruel based on sourdough mixed with water. So important were these gruels to the Maya diet that Landa tells us they made up two of the three meals of the day—in fact, most of the average Maya intake of maize may have been in liquid form.

Cacao had the same prestigious significance as it did among the Aztec; while the Aztecs took their chocolate drink cold or at room temperature, the evidence suggests that the Maya preferred theirs hot. Although we have little data on whether it was subject to the same sumptuary laws as it was in the Aztec state, chocolate seems to have been ubiquitous in Maya betrothal and wedding ceremonies. Several Late Classic Maya vases depict marriage go-betweens in royal courts; they bear in their hands

F

nosegays of "ear-flowers" (*Cymbopetalum penduliflorum*), a prized chocolate flavoring throughout Mesoamerica.

As an intoxicating drink, in place of the Aztec maguey-based *octli*, the lowland Maya had a strong, honey-based mead called *balché,* named from the tree the bark of which was used as a flavoring. The contemporary Lacandón produce this in wooden dugout canoes, probably a pre-Conquest practice. There seem to have been no restrictions placed on the consumption of *balché*—in fact, drunkenness was a universal feature of both banqueting and the most sacred rituals. Although it is true that *octli* (Maya, *chih*) is not mentioned in the ethnohistoric sources, several Late Classic vases marked with its hieroglyph show that it was stored in necked jars during banquets and apparently imbibed to the point of intoxication.

FURTHER READINGS

Bayless, R., and D. G. Bayless. 1987. *Authentic Mexican: Regional Cooking from the Heart of Mexico.* New York: William Morrow.

Coe, S. D. 1994. *America's First Cuisines.* Austin: University of Texas Press.

Sophie Coe and Michael Coe

SEE ALSO
Diet and Nutrition

Formative Period (c. 1600 B.C.–A.D. 250)

For descriptive and analytical convenience, archaeologists divide the long history of Mesoamerica into epochs designated as the Formative (also called the Preclassic), Classic, and Postclassic periods. Each of these is subdivided into more specific components (e.g., Early, Middle, Late, and Terminal Formative). These temporal designators provide a general framework that facilitates interregional comparisons of cultural developments within Mesoamerica.

When first proposed, these periods were purposely developmental as well as chronological, and referred to levels of civilizational complexity, which were thought to correspond generally to evolutionary time. The pivotal point of reference was the "classic" manifestation of greatest artistic achievement, in a manner analogous to "Classical" civilizations of the Old World. As originally conceived, the Classic period in Mesoamerica represented the climax of Lowland Maya civilization with its carved stone monuments, calendrical inscriptions, and impressive stone temples. The Classic was anticipated by a long period of nascent development (Preclassic or Formative) and was followed by an epoch of denouement (Postclassic).

The principal difficulty in using this developmental sequence as a chronological scheme is that it overgeneralizes the histories of three cultures (Maya, Zapotec, and Teotihuacán) to all of Mesoamerica. Not all Mesoamerican cultures developed at this pace. To avoid characterizing societies inappropriately, several investigators have proposed more neutral chronological terms representative only of time periods. Thus, for the Basin of Mexico, some scholars have adopted a scheme of sequential "horizons" and numbered "intermediate" periods. The period represented by the Formative (1600 B.C. to A.D. 250; all dates in radiocarbon years) is designated in the Basin of Mexico scheme as the Initial Ceramic period, Early Horizon, and First Intermediate period. This scheme is not as neutral as it first appears, and the terminology has not really caught on. Most investigators still prefer the old terminology but use it strictly to refer to periods of time rather than to relative development, as once intended. With improved dating techniques, Mesoamericanists hope eventually to describe time in terms of the Western calendar rather than by arbitrary phases and periods.

As its name implies, the Formative period was originally thought to be the epoch in which the basic characteristics of Classic civilizations began to form and develop. As such, it represented a major transitional period from a hunting-and-gathering, seminomadic way of life (characteristic of the preceding Archaic period) to the development of true civilization during the Classic period. The major innovation of the Formative was the shift to sedentism and village life based on horticulture and full-time agriculture. Concomitant changes were thought to include the first theocratic village societies, fertility cults, economic specialization, long-distance exchange, ancestor worship, and social stratification.

The first two millennia of Mesoamerican history (beginning c. 1600 B.C.) were a time of successive, dynamic transformations in economic, social, and political institutions. The beginning date marks the first adoption of ceramic technology and sedentary village life in the region. It is doubtful, however, that 1600 B.C. represents the critical shift in subsistence techniques; these changes began well before the first Formative villages were established. The arbitrary terminal date of A.D. 250 for the Formative approximates the beginning of the Mayan emphasis on long count dates and calendrical monuments. Most of Mesoamerica was probably under the

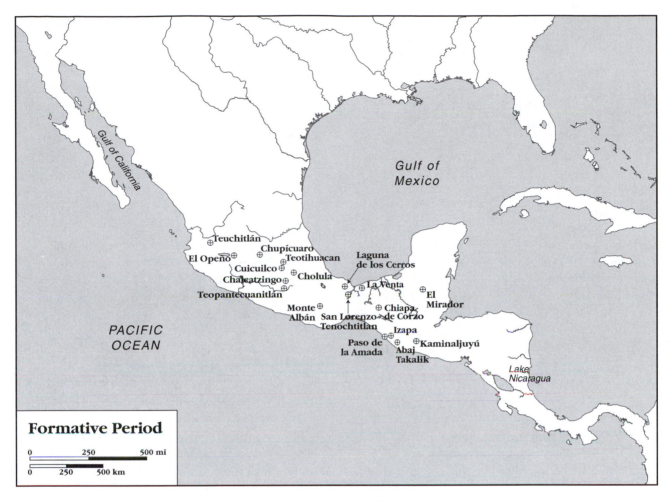

Formative Period. Map design by Mapping Specialists Limited, Madison, Wisconsin.

dominion of regional state societies by this time; these arose during the Late and Terminal Formative periods, beginning about 200 B.C. It would probably be inaccurate to characterize all Formative cultures prior to this time as pre-state societies, because the early Olmecs of 1100 B.C. may have comprised three or more city-states. Nonetheless, the Formative was clearly the period in which the institutional and material bases for state organizations were established in almost all regions of Mesoamerica. One significant developmental difference with the Classic period does remain: true empires in Mesoamerica first arose during the Classic.

The Formative period witnessed the creation of Mesoamerica as a cultural area and its near-maximal extension. The developmental process characteristic of the Formative was the spread of the Mesoamerican pattern or way of life. This was a historic process with clear spatial consequences. In contrast, the Classic period represents, in essence, a slight elaboration of basic Mesoamerican institutions, but not a notable spatial extension, nor a significant alteration of content. The Mesoamerican pattern consisted of seven major elements: (1) sedentary village and town life; (2) reliance on basic cultigens such as beans, avocados, chiles, and maize; (3) employment of intensive

F

farming and water control techniques; (4) expansion of public economies based on surplus production of foodstuffs and specialized production of luxury goods and other commodities for long-distance exchange; (5) establishment of complex social and political systems, including social stratification, divine kingship, ceremonial centers, and commemorative art; (6) promotion of a particular view of a quadripartite, multi-layered cosmos, creation myths, a pantheon of deities, notions of spirit essences and animism of nature, and the human journey of life and death; and (7) the influence of these and other concepts on social mores and behavioral norms.

Two processes of critical importance are suggested by this brief summary of the Formative period: the origins of the various traits that became part of the Mesoamerican pattern, and the spread of these traits to other regions. The current understanding of Formative developments in Mesoamerica is still too limited to address either process convincingly, but extant data suggest that the genesis and spread of traits, innovations, and beliefs were temporally and spatially irregular, with no one regional culture being responsible for all critical developments.

As viewed from any single vantage point, the development of Mesoamerica during the Formative presents a checkered history, with various regional cultures taking turns at preeminence. Any generalization of pan-Mesoamerican processes, therefore, will always be controversial from any regional point of view. Only rarely during the Formative did all Mesoamerica undergo parallel, coeval development. There is good evidence for at least four significant processes or episodes. Unfortunately, these no longer correspond very well to the chronological subdivisions of the Formative as once intended, because more recent archaeological research has shifted the dating of these changes. They can be considered as (1) the beginnings of village life, (2) the emergence of Olmec civilization, (3) a period of more regional developments and the emergence of a network of paramount chiefdoms, and (4) the emergence of regional states. For convenience, each of these periods is here discussed from the perspective of five regions of Mesoamerica—the Mexican Highlands, the Valley of Oaxaca, the Gulf Coast Lowlands, coastal Chiapas and Guatemala, and the Maya Lowlands.

Beginnings of Village Life

The transition from seminomadic hunting and gathering to settled village life and the adoption of ceramic technology took place throughout the Early Formative period, beginning about 1600 to 1400 B.C. among cultures of the coastal lowlands of northern Veracruz, the Gulf Coast Lowlands, coastal Chiapas and Guatemala, the highlands of West Mexico, and the valleys of Oaxaca, Puebla, Morelos, and México. Toward the end of the Early Formative period (c. 1000 B.C.), small agricultural villages were also established in the highlands of Chiapas, Guatemala, and El Salvador, and in the Maya Lowlands. The best information for the early village period comes from coastal Chiapas and Guatemala (known as the Soconusco) and from the Valley of Oaxaca. Comparison of these data demonstrate significant differences between developments in the Mexican Highlands and the Maya Lowlands, with more extensive settlements found in the tropical lowlands.

The highland cultures appear to have been committed to maize agriculture, small villages, and dispersed settlement. Early pottery was simple and utilitarian. Abundant evidence exists for interaction among many of the early village societies; obsidian, iron-ore mirrors, jade and greenstone, colorful feathers, marine shells, and probably cacao and other perishables were exchanged. Judging from similarities in decorated pottery vessels and clay figurines, the highland societies comprised one major interaction zone, and the lowland societies another.

By conventional standards of archaeological measurement, the tropical lowland societies were socially more complex than those of the highlands. In the Soconusco, villages were larger and more closely clustered than in the highlands, and there is good evidence for the development of ranked societies by about 1400 B.C. Agriculture was significant (and probably included root crops as well as maize), but the overall economy remained mixed, with significant continuing reliance on wild resources, especially fish, turtles, and deer. Ceramic inventories include a variety of fancy forms that may have been used for ritual serving and feasting. Special lapidary items include carved jade, greenstone, and mica. Evidence from the Soconusco is suggestive of the development of simple chiefdom societies and the presence of shaman-chiefs during the first part of the Early Formative. Corroborating evidence is seen in elaborate residences, ball courts, settlement patterns, representations in figurines, some burials, and differential distribution of imported and specially crafted goods.

The Early Olmecs

Developments during the Early Formative can be usefully divided into two categories: those that preceded the early

Olmecs and those that followed. Olmec civilization arose by 1150 B.C. in the Gulf Lowlands, with its most spectacular manifestation being the capital of San Lorenzo Tenochtitlán (Veracruz). This center, notable for its evidence of massive earth-moving activity and erection of multi-ton basalt sculptures, was large enough to have been a true city of more than 10,000 inhabitants. It was also the center of a unique art style of "supernatural" creatures such as "were-jaguars" and "fire-serpents," which spread quickly across Mesoamerica about 1100 to 1000 B.C. The roots of this Olmec development undoubtedly lie in the antecedent lowland village societies. The spread of Olmec stylized iconography and other artifacts across early Mesoamerica was probably a continuation of the very interactive processes that brought Olmec civilization into existence in the first place.

The distribution of San Lorenzo–style objects is quite spotty across Mesoamerica and seems to have concentrated in the regions with the largest populations. Ceramic vessels with early Olmec motifs and Olmec clay figurines and cylinder seals have been found in the Valley of Mexico, Guerrero, Oaxaca, Puebla, Tehuacán, northern Veracruz, Chiapas, coastal Guatemala, Honduras, and El Salvador. Their presence in these distant regions signals continuing contact among most Early Formative societies, as well as the dominance of the Olmecs in the ideological sphere, and perhaps others. The Olmecs were clearly the principal players in Mesoamerica at the end of the Early Formative period. Most scholars readily concede that the polity centered at San Lorenzo was a complex chiefdom, if not Mesoamerica's first state. Contemporaneous societies were much smaller and more simply organized and may have formed alliances with the Olmecs as a first, but necessary, step toward increased socio-political complexity. The Olmecs of the Gulf Coast undoubtedly benefited from these arrangements in a number of ways, principally in access to foreign material and social resources.

The Olmecs appear to have had an indelible effect on the rest of early Mesoamerica, although the nature and means of their influence remain hotly contested issues. Many of the societies that were in early contact with the Olmecs demonstrated rapid development to complex chiefdoms shortly thereafter, but the particular impact of the interregional contact has not been determined. Exchange, marriage alliances, and conquest may all have been important in the spread of the Mesoamerican way of life during the Early Formative.

Regional Development of Complex Chiefdoms

The cessation of San Lorenzo as a regional center and of its elite as cultural brokers in Mesoamerica at about 900 B.C. signals the end of the Early Formative and the beginning of the Middle Formative (900–400 B.C.). Significant developments continued to occur in the Gulf Lowlands among the Olmecs, especially at the centers of La Venta and Laguna de los Cerros, but the influence of these communities on the rest of Mesoamerica is less apparent.

In the Basin of Mexico during the Middle, Late, and Terminal Formative, no pan-Mesoamerican horizon style is apparent, and regional developments appear to have been the norm; for this reason, Sanders et al. characterize this as the First Intermediate period. Complex chiefdoms centered on impressive pyramid sites arose all over Mesoamerica during the Middle and Late Formative. Perhaps the most significant Middle Formative development was the spread of the Mesoamerican pattern to the Maya Lowlands.

This episode of regionalization consisted of two significant, related processes. As mentioned, the first pulse of chiefdom development across Mesoamerica was linked to the initial spread of San Lorenzo–style artifacts and influence and appears to have been stimulated by the early Olmecs. This led to a patchy development of widely spaced, small clusters of chiefdoms in the Soconusco, Veracruz, and possibly Oaxaca, Morelos, Puebla-Tlaxcala, and the Valley of Mexico. This was followed by what was essentially an infilling process, with population growth within the original polities and its spread to adjacent regions. In this regard, the developments in the Maya Lowlands appear unprecedented. The regional developments there during the Middle and Late Formative seem to have kept pace or surpassed those of other regions with documented earlier occupations. One plausible explanation is that archaeologists have yet to find the earliest large communities of the Maya Lowlands from which the Middle Formative Maya chiefdoms sprang. The general archaeological situation of early deposits deeply buried under later cities in the Maya Lowlands makes this a likely possibility.

Obvious innovations of the period of regional chiefdom development include large towns or cities with planned plaza arrangements comprised of tall pyramids and special buildings, including ball courts; high-status pyramid burials with significant amounts of jade jewelry and other burial goods; the beginning of a "stela cult" and other expressions of bas-relief narrative sculpture; and shifts in luxury goods and exchange patterns.

F

Much of the population expansion and demographic infilling may have become possible with the development of more productive varieties of maize; because of steady enlargement of cob sizes through time, maize achieved a sufficient degree of energetic efficiency (compared to human labor investment) by the Middle Formative that it constituted a viable surplus-producing crop for most environmental situations with adequate rainfall or irrigation water. Most of the large chiefdoms were situated in the center of prime agricultural land, in the most productive valleys and along major rivers and coastal plains.

The political and social dynamic of the Middle Formative can be appreciated only by comparing the details of specific regions. Complex chiefdoms came and went throughout the period, with various centers gaining prominence in rapid succession. Most polities probably had a radius no greater than one day's walk from the center. This situation of rival chiefdoms of relatively equal power changed toward the end of the Late Formative with the simultaneous formation of regional states in many areas of Mesoamerica. The particular dynamic leading to these changes remains unknown, but the close timing among all of them indicates some mechanism of interregional interaction.

Emergence of Regional States

Whether or not scholars can agree to designate the large, regional polities that emerged at the end of the Late Formative as "states" is less significant than the fact that a major change in social and political organization occurred at this time. Near the end of the Late Formative, the various chiefdoms in the Valley of Oaxaca appear to have been consolidated under the domination of one center at Monte Albán. Evidence from the Maya Lowlands suggests the presence of several large regional polities, quite possibly states, best known from El Mirador in the central Petén. Other likely candidates for states are the Terminal Formative polities at Chiapa de Corzo and Izapa in Chiapas, and Kaminaljuyú in the Valley of Guatemala. Developments in the Basin of Mexico and surrounding valleys are more difficult to interpret because the major Middle and Late Formative center at Cuicuilco is covered by lava; the relationship of this major community to the development of Teotihuacán remains to be determined. In any event, a major state emerged in the Basin of Mexico toward the end of the Terminal Formative, perhaps somewhat later than those in Oaxaca, Chiapas, and the Maya region. The situation at Cholula in the Puebla Valley is also unclear; it may eventually prove to have been coeval in development with Oaxaca.

Each of these large regional polities was characterized by its own individual style in a range of material media, especially architecture, sculpture, pottery, and figurines. Writing and complex calendars were clearly in place at this time but may have been developed in the earlier period. The processes that led to the consolidation of clusters of chiefdoms into single-state societies remain to be determined. The only region for which adequate data are currently available for documenting the formation of regional states from a network of complex chiefdoms is the Valley of Oaxaca. In Oaxaca, the capital hilltop center at Monte Albán appears to have been constructed as a planned, defensible city in which to establish a confederation government formed by the alliance of leaders of the various chiefdoms in the three conjoining valleys. The factors that prompted this alliance remain unknown. Evidence at Monte Albán indicates that an early activity of the state was the conquest of neighboring chiefdoms and their incorporation into the state, at least in a tributary capacity. Clear evidence of state organization for the other areas mentioned is more circumstantial and consists of settlement patterns, site hierarchies, and the distribution of specific stylistic similarities (ceramic wares, architectural and sculptural styles, burial programs). These data indicate the emergence at the end of the Late Formative and Terminal Formative of very large polities—in the Maya case, larger than those that followed in the Classic period.

FURTHER READINGS

Clark, J. E. 1997. The Arts of Government in Early Mesoamerica. *Annual Review of Anthropology* 26:211–234.

Coe, M. D. 1981. San Lorenzo Tenochtitlán. In J. A. Sabloff (ed.), *Handbook of Middle American Indians, Supplement 1: Archaeology,* pp. 117–146. Austin: University of Texas Press.

Cyphers, A. 1996. Reconstructing Olmec Life at San Lorenzo. In E. P. Benson and B. de la Fuente (eds.), *Olmec Art of Ancient Mexico,* pp. 61–71. Washington, D.C.: National Gallery of Art.

Grove, D. C. 1997. Olmec Archaeology: A Half-century of Research and Its Accomplishments. *Journal of World Prehistory* 11:51–101.

Lowe, G. W. 1978. Eastern Mesoamerica. In R. E. Taylor and C. W. Meighan (eds.), *Chronologies in New World Archaeology,* pp. 331–393. New York: Academic Press.

Marcus, J., and K. V. Flannery. 1996. *Zapotec Civilization: How Urban Society Evolved in Mexico's Oaxaca Valley.* London: Thames and Hudson.

McCafferty, G. G. 1996. The Ceramics and Chronology of Cholula, Mexico. *Ancient Mesoamerica* 7:299–331.

Niederberger, C. 1996. The Basin of Mexico: A Multimillenial Development toward Cultural Complexity. In E. P. Benson and B. de la Fuente (eds.), *Olmec Art of Ancient Mexico,* pp. 95–103. Washington, D.C.: National Gallery of Art.

Oliveros, J. A. 1989. Las tumbas mas antiguas de Michoacán. In *Historia General de Michoacan,* vol. 1, pp. 123–134. Michoacan: Instituto Michoacano de Cultura.

Sanders, W. T., J. R. Parsons, and R. S. Santley. 1979. *The Basin of Mexico: Ecological Processes in the Evolution of a Civilization.* New York: Academic Press.

Sharer, R. J. 1994. *The Ancient Maya.* 5th edn. Stanford: Stanford University Press.

Stark, B. L. 1981. The Rise of Sedentary Life. In J. A. Sabloff (ed.), *Handbook of Middle American Indians, Supplement 1: Archaeology,* pp. 345–372. Austin: University of Texas Press.

Winter, M. 1989. *Oaxaca: The Archaeological Record.* Mexico City: Minutiae Mexicana.

John E. Clark

SEE ALSO

Archaic Period; Classic Period; Interregional Interactions

Fortifications

Fortifications and defensible arrangements of architecture were commonplace in pre-Hispanic Mesoamerica. The specific nature of a fortified place depended on the social and economic resources of the particular culture, as well as on available materials, topography, and characteristic patterns of combat. Motivations for the construction of fortifications included protecting a central (usually elite) place, creating a safe refuge, defending territory and resources, and providing a logistical and symbolic support base. Much Mesoamerican warfare, however, was carried out in landscapes where fortifications were absent or poorly developed, as in the Postclassic Basin of Mexico.

Mesoamerican warfare was technologically and logistically unsophisticated—for example, there were no effective siege weapons, artillery, or efficient transport—so even minor and simple artificial barriers were serviceable as fortifications. For example, Cortés encountered small communities defended by wooden palisades and screens of thorny plants in the Maya Lowlands in the early sixteenth century. Such barriers required minimal skill and labor to erect and were possibly used as early as Preclassic times. They are, however, very difficult to detect archaeologically, thus complicating reconstructions of chronological trends in the use of fortifications. The evidence we have nevertheless suggests an accelerating use of fortifications through time.

Few examples of Formative period fortifications are known. Around 500 to 300 B.C. the large Formative urban center of Monte Albán was established in a naturally defensible, strategic location—a high, steep hill commanding the central Valley of Oaxaca. Both the ceremonial/elite core and much of the surrounding residential architecture were protected not only by the rugged topography, but also by a system of supplementary walls later built on the flanks of the hill. Smaller fortified centers appeared elsewhere in the Valley of Oaxaca by Late Formative times.

Near the end of the Formative period, one of Mesoamerica's largest fortifications was built at Becan, a Maya center in southern Campeche, Mexico. Becan's defenses consisted of a ditch and earthwork system, probably supplemented by timber palisades. Inside were major temples and palaces, and the defenses probably also provided refuge for the outlying population during attacks.

In the Classic period fortifications were common in some parts of Mesoamerica. To increase its dominance as a regional highland state, Monte Albán established military outposts on its frontiers, such as Cañada de Cuicatlán; by A.D. 500 roughly 64 percent of the estimated population of the Valley of Oaxaca lived at thirty-eight fortified or defensible sites. Little is known about Classic period defensive architecture in other parts of highland Mesoamerica. Teotihuacán, the dominant urban center of the time, had no formal fortifications, but its very scale probably discouraged attackers. In the Maya Lowlands, impressive Early Classic earthworks were built at Tikal, Guatemala, to protect both the site core and more than 100 square kilometers of Tikal's hinterland. Becan's earthworks continued to function throughout the Classic period, and other large Maya centers such as Calakmul have what appear to be defensive walls.

Fortifications become more common during the Terminal Classic and Postclassic periods. After the decline of Teotihuacán many new highland centers, such as

F

Cacaxtla, Teotenango, and Xochicalco, were situated on defensible hilltops. In some cases, as at Xochicalco, systems of terraces and defensible causeways further strengthened the topographic position. After A.D. 780, the collapse of many Maya polities in the central and southern Lowlands was accompanied by warfare and the construction of fortifications in some regions. Core architecture at Dos Pilas was hurriedly fortified by a ramshackle wall, and Dos Pilas refugees fortified a stronghold at Aguateca, protected by natural chasms and stone and timber palisades. About the same time the nearby Punta de Chimino center, situated on a peninsula in Lake Petexbatun, was cut off from the mainland by a massive earthwork and parapet system.

After A.D. 750, many northern Maya centers—including Uxmal, Chacchob, Dzonot Ake, Cuca, Chinchucmil, and Ek Balam—were wholly or partly enclosed by wall systems, sometimes as integral parts of the site plan and sometimes as later defensive precautions. Murals at the great northern capital of Chichén Itzá show warriors attacking walled towns. One of the most extensive stone walls surrounded Mayapán, a northern Maya urban center that functioned as a regional capital until about A.D. 1450. Tulum, a walled commercial maritime center on the eastern coast of Yucatán, was probably still inhabited when the first Spaniards arrived, and older walled sites, such as Ixpaatun and Xelha, exist elsewhere on this coast.

Our best evidence for fortifications and how they were used dates to the Late Postclassic and Contact periods, for which we have oral and written accounts of both native Mesoamericans and the Spanish. During the 1520s, Spanish armies in the highlands of Guatemala encountered native capitals, such as Iximché, situated on defensible promontories and further defended by walls and ditches. In Central Mexico the main temple complexes of cities often served as the defensive structures of last resort, and the conquest of a Mesoamerican polity was sometimes symbolically expressed by the picture of a burning, destroyed temple.

As their empire expanded, Aztec armies often encountered enemies entrenched in strong fortifications, as at the Zapotec hilltop center of Guiengola. The Aztecs themselves established systems of fortifications along frontiers where they faced especially formidable enemies. During the long Aztec-Tarascan war, both empires established chains of fortified sites from the Lerma River to the Balsas River that maintained visual communication with each other or were no more than about a day's march apart. Other extensive fortified zones are described for the boundary between Cempoala and Tlaxcala.

The principal proprietors of the Aztec Empire, the Mexica-Tenochca, established their capital of Tenochtitlán on a defensible group of islands in Lake Texcoco, Basin of Mexico. Though not formally fortified, access (except by watercraft) was along causeways that could easily be cut. Even with boats and artillery, the Spanish and their Indian allies found it hard to subdue the Mexica forces defending the capital during the final stages of the conquest in 1521. Almost two centuries later, in 1697, the Spanish conquered Noj Petén, the capital of the Itzá Maya, which was built for defensive reasons on a hilly island in Lake Petén Itzá, northern Guatemala. This conquest of the last independent Mesoamerican polity brought to an end the long tradition of native fortifications.

FURTHER READINGS

Armillas, P. 1951. Mesoamerican Fortifications. *Antiquity* 25(8): 77–86.

Elam, J. 1989. Defensible and Fortified Sites. In S. Kowaleski et al. (eds.), *Monte Albán's Hinterland, Part II*, pp. 385–407. Memoirs of the Museum of Anthropology, 23. Ann Arbor: University of Michigan.

Hassig, R. 1992. *War and Society in Ancient Mesoamerica.* Berkeley: University of California Press.

Inomata, T. 1997. The Last Day of a Fortified Classic Maya Center: Archaeological Investigations at Aguateca, Guatemala. *Ancient Mesoamerica* 8:337–351.

Palerm, A. 1956. Notas sobre las construcciones militares y la guerra en mesoamerica. *Ciencias Sociales* 7(39): 189–202.

Puleston, D., and D. Callender. 1967. Defensive Earthworks at Tikal. *Expedition* 9(3):48–48.

Webster, D. 1976. Lowland Maya Fortifications. *Proceedings of the American Philosophical Society* 120(5):361–371.

Jay Silverstein and David L. Webster

SEE ALSO
Weaponry

G

Gamboa, Hector (1934–1993)

As head of the National Museum of Costa Rica's Department of Anthropology and History through the 1970s, with interpersonal skills worthy of a diplomat, Hector Gamboa Paniagua fostered the development of modern archaeology in Costa Rica by bringing out the cooperative best in both young, developing Costa Rican archaeologists and the foreign archaeologists who came to conduct research there in the mid-1970s. He visited more archaeological sites in more remote corners of Costa Rica than perhaps anyone else, and was always available for consultation and pushing for excellence. Later, as head of technical services at the museum, he oversaw the development and deployment of the greatly successful, and innovatively scientific, international exhibition "Between Continents/ Between Seas: Precolumbian Art of Costa Rica" from 1981 to 1984.

Frederick W. Lange

Games and Gambling

In pre-Columbian Mexican cultures, the practice of gambling on games of chance and skill was a popular activity. Soustelle goes so far as to say that the Aztecs were probably addicted to gambling. The prevalence of gambling may indicate that it served an adaptive function in Aztec society, because it fostered the personal qualities of confidence and risk-taking necessary for individuals to flourish as military men and entrepreneurs.

The game of chance on which players bet was called *patolli* by the Aztecs. It was a dice game played on a crossed grid of fifty-two squares drawn on a large mat or on the floor. Two persons could play against each other, or

four individuals might compete by forming two-person teams (see illustration). When two individuals played as a team, one was designated the dice-thrower and the other as the scorekeeper. Each side had six little pebbles that served as markers; one set was colored blue, the other red. The game drew its name from the large, flat beans, called *patoles,* that were used as dice. Each *patole* was marked on one side with points that represented numbers, and when four were cast together they indicated how many squares a player was permitted to move his pebble. The goal of the competition was for an individual, or a team,

Game of patolli, as illustrated in the *Florentine Codex,* Book 8, illustration 63. Feathers and precious stones are being wagered, and the individual on the right is speaking. As indicated by speech scrolls (redrawn from the *Florentine Codex*).

G

to be the first to get all six pebbles completely through the course of squares along the arms of the cross.

According to Fray Diego Duran, *patolli* players "were given to the vice of gambling. Some of the items wagered in the game were jewels, precious stones, and a gambler's own home and his wife's personal jewelry. When a gambler had lost everything, he might even go so far as to stake himself at a set price and, if he lost, the gambler would then become his victor's slave" (1971:301).

Like most forms of entertainment in ancient Mexico, *patolli* appears to have had a hidden meaning. Soustelle claims that the fifty-two squares on the mat represented the number of years that were present in the combined divinatory and solar cycles; at the end of this time span a final cataclysmic event might occur that would destroy all life in the universe. A *patolli* victory, therefore, symbolized the continuation of life, whereas a defeat represented the anticipated end of the world. Another hidden meaning of *patolli* has been proposed by Kendall, who believes that the Aztec dice game may have been used as an instrument of divination in which the fifty-two squares were perceived as fifty-two days, or one-fifth of the 260-day divinatory calendar. The result of the game would forecast a happy or an unhappy situation during the next fifty-two days for the winner and the loser, respectively.

Whereas *patolli* was a game played by all classes in Aztec society, *tlachtli,* the Aztec game of skill, was mainly for the enjoyment of the aristocracy. It was a ball game in which players, using only their knees and their hips, were expected to hit a hard rubber ball up to one foot in diameter through a four-foot stone ring attached vertically to a stone wall. According to the Franciscan friar Bernardino de Sahagún, who arrived in Mexico shortly after the Conquest, there was widespread gambling among the players concerning the outcome of the game. It was not unusual for the athletes to wager extremely valuable items such as gold, golden necklaces, fine turquoise, precious capes, and armbands of quetzal feathers. Like *patolli,* the game of *tlachtli* was thought to have religious significance. Soustelle claims that the athletes were duplicating what was taking place in the heavens, where the sacred sky was a ball court and the ball was a heavenly body, such as a star or a planet, which was being passed back and forth by divine entities.

The Aztec games of *patolli* and *tlachtli* each had antecedents in pre-Columbian Mesoamerica. In the case of *patolli,* Smith and Wiley discovered two game boards, similar to the type the Aztecs used, at the Maya ceremonial center of Seibal. Each of these game boards was carved into the base of a stela; the first is dated at A.D. 849, while the second bears a date equivalent to A.D. 771. Game boards of the same type have been found in Mexico at the Maya sites of Uxmal and Palenque. At Uxmal, a game board painted black was discovered inside the remains of Temple II of the Pyramid of the Magicians. At Palenque, a game board was scratched into the plaster floor of the Temple of the Inscriptions.

In Mexico's Central Highlands, additional game boards have been unearthed. At Teotihuacán, several game board designs attributed to the seventh century A.D. have been discovered engraved on floors or patios. At Tula, six gaming grids were found incised in plaster pavement; it is estimated that these designs were carved during the mid-twelfth century or earlier.

The ball game was another focus of gambling. As in Aztec Mexico, Maya athletes wagered heavily on the game, some of them losing all their worldly possessions as a result. Furthermore, it is claimed that as an additional incentive to play well, a competitor getting the ball through the ring had the right to demand the jewels and the clothing of the spectators.

FURTHER READINGS

Acosta, J. 1961. La doceava temporada de exploraciones en Tula, Hidalgo. *Anales del Instituto Nacional de Antropología e Historia* 13:29–58.

Barry, H., III, and J. Roberts. 1972. Infant Socialization and Games of Chance. *Ethnology* 11:296–308.

Duran, D. 1971. *Book of the Gods and Rites and the Ancient Calendar.* F. Horcasitas and D. Heyden (trans.). Norman: University of Oklahoma Press.

Kendall, T. 1980. *Patolli: A Game of Ancient Mexico.* Boston: Boston Museum of Fine Arts Publication.

Ruz Lhuillier, A. 1952. Exploraciones en Palenque: 1950. *Anales del Instituto Nacional de Antropología e Historia* 5:25–46.

———. 1956. *Uxmal: Official Guide of the Instituto Nacional de Antropología e Historia.* F. and M. Camara Barbachano (trans.). Mexico City: Instituto Nacional de Antropología e Historia.

Sahagun, B. de. 1954. *Kings and Lords, Book 8 of the Florentine Codex: General History of the Things of New Spain.* C. E. Dibble and A. J. 0. Anderson. Santa Fe and Salt Lake City: School of American Research and University of Utah Press.

Sejourne, L. 1959. *Un Palacio en la Ciudad de los Dioses, Teotihuacán.* Mexico City: Instituto Nacional de Antropología e Historia.

Smith, A. L. 1977. Patolli at the Ruins of Seibal, Petén, Guatemala. In N. Hammond (ed.), *Social Process in Maya Prehistory: Studies in Honor of Sir Eric Thompson,* pp. 349–365. New York: Academic Press.

Soustelle, J. 1964. *Daily Life of the Aztecs.* Harmondsworth: Pelican.

Wasserman, M. 1983. Transcending Ethnocentrism in Sport Research: The Case of Aztec Player Gambling. *Anthropos* 78:874–878.

Martin Wasserman

SEE ALSO

Ball Game; Divination

Gamio, Manuel (1883–1960)

Gamio, one of Mexico's most important archaeologists and a pioneer in applying broad anthropological principles to the study of ancient cultures, received his doctorate in 1924 from Columbia University, where he studied with Franz Boas. From 1908 to 1925 he served as General Inspector of Archaeological Monuments in Mexico, and also as director of the International School of American Archaeology and Ethnology. During that time he explored such sites as Chalchihuites, Azcapotzalco, Chichén Itzá, Teotihuacán, Copilco, Chalco, the Templo Mayor of Tenochtitlán, and Naucalpan.

One of his main contributions was *La población del Valle de Teotihuacán,* an interdisciplinary study of the Teotihuacán Valley, in which he emphasized archaeology as part of anthropology. He not only coordinated archaeological explorations at Teotihuacán (such as the Temple-Pyramid of the Feathered Serpent) but also supervised the study of the geological, geomorphological, faunal, floral, and biophysical dimensions of the region, the architecture and crafts of the Teotihuacanos, the economic and religious life of the Colonial period, and the conditions of the inhabitants of the Teotihuacán Valley in the twentieth century.

FURTHER READINGS

Gamio, M. 1922. *La Población del Valle de Teotihuacán.* Clásicos de la Antropología Mexicana, 8. 5 vols. Mexico City: Instituto Nacional Indigenista.

———. 1972. *Arqueología e indigenismo.* Mexico City: Secretaría de Educación Pública (SepSetentas 24).

Various authors. 1956. *Estudios antropológicos publicados en homenaje al doctor Manuel Gamio.* Mexico City:

Universidad Nacional Autónoma de México, Dirección General de Publicaciones, y Sociedad Mexicana de Antropología.

Linda Manzanilla

Gardens

In addition to the house lot gardens (called *calmil* and *milpa* in the Aztec language) that provided food for farming families throughout ancient Mesoamerica from the Formative period on, formal and informal pleasure gardens were numerous and noteworthy for their beauty during the Late Postclassic, and may have had Classic (or earlier) antecedents. Most documentary information concerns Aztec horticulture and landscape architecture. Lords of Tenochtitlán and Texcoco developed gardens as part of their main palace complexes, as special-purpose pleasure parks (zoos and aviaries, for example), as monumental royal retreats (Chapultepec and Texcotzingo), and as horticultural nurseries (Huaxtepec, Acatetelco). Groves of *ahuehuetl* trees (*Taxodium* spp., a relative of the cypress and redwood, and the national tree of Mexico) were established in royal parks, and plants were treasured for their flowers, fragrance, and foliage.

Evidence for gardens elsewhere in Mesoamerica is sparse. Some murals at Teotihuacán may depict gardens. But given the widespread evidence and great time depth of veneration of plants, traditions of landscape modification, and site planning, we may assume that gardens were an integral part of many Mesoamerican sites. Mesoamerican gardeners pioneered many propagation and cultivation techniques, and their botanical gardens may have influenced the early European botanic gardens which were established in the mid to late sixteenth century.

FURTHER READINGS

Evans, S. T. Forthcoming. Aztec Royal Pleasure Parks: Conspicuous Consumption and Elite Status Rivalry. *Garden History.*

Heyden, D. 1979. Flores, creencias y el control social. *Actes du XLIIe Congrès International des Américanistes* 5(6):85–97.

Killion, T. W. (ed.). 1992. *Gardens of Prehistory: The Archaeology of Settlement Agriculture in Greater Mesoamerica.* Tuscaloosa: University of Alabama Press.

Musset, A. 1986. Les jardins préhispaniques. *Trace* 10:59–73.

Nuttall, Z. 1925. The Gardens of Ancient Mexico. In *Annual Report of the Board of Regents of the Smithsonian*

G

Institution, 1923, pp. 453–464. Washington, D.C.:
Government Printing Office.

Peterson, J. F. 1993. *The Paradise Garden Murals of Malinalco: Utopia and Empire in Sixteenth-Century Mexico.*
Austin: University of Texas Press.

Susan Toby Evans

SEE ALSO

Agriculture and Domestication; Flowers; Huaxtepec; Texcotzingo

Gender Roles

Gender was one of the most important organizing principles in Mesoamerican society. Male and female gender
identities were recognized from birth, and a child's education was devoted to preparing him or her for gender-
specific roles in adulthood. Costume and hairstyles clearly
indicated gender distinctions. Daily activities such as
hunting, cooking, warfare, child care, and textile production were defining characteristics of the gender-based
division of labor.

In part because of this superficially unambiguous
structure, gender has often been ignored in anthropological reconstructions of the pre-Columbian world. Normative presentations of Mesoamerican society focus on
predominantly male activities such as dynastic politics,
warfare, exchange, and sacrifice; the role of women has
often been minimized and dealt with stereotypically.
Recently, however, scholars have pointed out the inherent
androcentrism in these characterizations, based on both
biases of Colonial period chroniclers and on research
interests of modern investigators. Critical rereadings of
the ethnohistorical documents and an engendered
approach to the archaeological record provide an opportunity to revise interpretations of gender relations in
Mesoamerica.

Ethnohistoric sources represent eye-witness accounts
of Contact period indigenous culture. Spanish *conquistadores* and priests recorded a wide array of cultural information, yet their eurocentric preconceptions often
blinded them to the activities of women. For example,
Sahagún recorded that women did not sell things in the
marketplace, but the accompanying illustrations (painted
by indigenous artists) clearly depict women selling food
goods. Spanish chroniclers often used elite males as informants and then further filtered the information through
their own gender prejudices. Consequently, the accounts
of female gender roles are fragmented, and they can be
characterized more as prescriptions for proper behavior
than as descriptions of actual practice.

Information on alternative or ambiguous gender identities is even more problematic. Descriptions of hermaph-
rodites and other "deviant" groups appear in the
Florentine Codex, and passing reference is made to
"sodomites" throughout the chronicles, but always in a
condemnatory sense lacking specific details. Dwarfs and
hunchbacks were considered to be sexually ambivalent in
much the same way as children, and were favored by the
nobility as servants and as sacrificial "messengers" to the
gods. Spanish priests also paid considerable attention to
the *ahuianime* (pleasure women), who were interpreted as
harlots but without recognition of their possible affiliation with the Mother Goddess cult.

In contrast to the Colonial accounts, pre-Hispanic
texts are free from Western biases, but they were often created as propaganda designed to legitimize the ruling lineage, and thus they preserve elite bias. Males predominate
in most contexts, as rulers, priests, supernaturals, and
warriors. Women appear in these roles to a lesser degree,
suggesting that, at least structurally, there was complementarity in female status.

Archaeology provides a window into an expanded
panorama of pre-Columbian lifeways, including domestic
activities, household ritual, mortuary systems, and public
and domestic art. These data present a more democratic
perspective on both male and female activities. The challenge faced by a gendered archaeology, however, is to
overcome the androcentrism inherent in Western scholarship in order to produce a nonprejudicial reconstruction
of the Mesoamerican past.

Previous studies of Mesoamerican gender relations
tend to fall into two distinctive theoretical positions:
those that emphasize gender hierarchy, and those that recognize a complementarity in male and female identities.
The argument that males enjoyed a dominant position
over women within a gender hierarchy is supported by
ethnohistoric accounts from Aztec Central Mexico. Evidence is cited that women were excluded from public ritual, politics, trade, and militarism—all arenas in which
males were able to enhance their status. This social structure was not universal, however, and the subordination of
women is viewed as a consequence of the emergence of
the Aztec state.

Gender complementarity implies that males and
females were part of a structural duality that permeated
Mesoamerican ideology. Susan Kellogg identifies a "structural equivalence" in gender that is found in kinship,

inheritance, and religion. For example, women who gave birth were hailed as warriors who took a captive in battle, while a woman who died in childbirth joined the warriors killed in battle in accompanying the sun on its daily journey through the sky.

Both systems of gender relations probably existed simultaneously and were adopted situationally, depending on specific cultural context. Because of the wealth of ethnohistoric information on the Aztec, it is deceptively easy to generalize from this exceptional case to other Mesoamerican cultures. As critical evaluation of the ethnohistoric sources continues to question gender stereotypes, and as archaeological research focuses on gender practice in diverse cultural contexts, Mesoamerican gender relations will become increasingly complex and informative.

Ethnohistory of Gender

Several Colonial sources address indigenous gender relations, with the most comprehensive discussion appearing in Sahagún's *Florentine Codex*. Other valuable sources are the Codex Mendoza and the accounts of Durán, Motolinía, and Zorita for the Aztec, and Landa for the Maya. Pre-Columbian sources that offer provocative insights in passing include the Mixtec, Borgia Group, and Maya codices. Finally, Colonial period legal documents provide important information on gender relations in practice.

For the Aztec, gender identities were assigned at birth. The umbilical cord of a boy was buried on a battlefield, while that of a girl was buried near the household hearth. At the bathing ceremony a baby boy was presented with the symbols of male identity: shield, bow and arrow, and loincloth; a baby girl received spinning and weaving tools and female costume. Children learned practical skills and performed household tasks under the supervision of their parents respective of gender identity; girls learned to spin, weave, and cook, while boys learned to fish and hunt.

After adolescence boys entered schools to prepare further for adulthood: the *calmecac* school trained nobles for the priesthood, while the *telpochcalli* school provided military training for young men who also performed public works projects. Young women generally stayed in the household until marriage, though there is some evidence for temple schools where they performed religious services and produced elaborate textiles for ceremonial functions.

Mature men and women were described in relation to their occupations, with distinctions made between good and bad practitioners. Thus, a good middle-aged woman was a skilled weaver and cook, chaste and hard working; a bad woman was foolish and lazy, prone to wearing gaudy dress and prostitution. Similarly, a mature man was a resolute worker, stout hearted and wise; but a bad man was irresponsible, lazy, "a lump of flesh with two eyes." Noblewomen were respected as efficient adminstrators, and women were explicitly mentioned as officials overseeing the marketplace. Additional female occupations that did not fit the domestic stereotype included merchants, midwives/healers, and priestesses.

Insight into the political acumen of noblewomen is found in the accounts of Malinche, or Doña Marina, the translator and consort of Cortés. Malinche was the daughter and heir of a chief from the southern Gulf Coast, and so was undoubtedly educated in the art of statecraft. To alter the line of succession, however, she was given to a neighboring polity, probably as an adolescent, and eventually was given to the Spanish *conquistadores*. She was bilingual in Mayan and Nahuatl, and her language skills were essential to the Spanish conquest; also obvious is Malinche's key role as a negotiator, manipulating both Spaniards and Aztecs. Malinche was the principal spokesperson of the Conquest, as demonstrated in Colonial illustrations in the Lienzo de Tlaxcala, to the extent that Cortés himself was referred to as "Malinche." Following the fall of Tenochtitlán, she took the name Marina and married a Spaniard gentleman, but her son Martín Cortés inherited titles and estates from his father, and later led a brief uprising against the Spanish crown.

Other examples of powerful noblewomen are found in Aztec, Mixtec, and Maya dynastic histories. Aztec lords married women from Culhuacan in order to legitimize their dynasty through Toltec bloodlines, and queens had the authority to rule in their own right. Aztec kings were referred to as both father and mother of the people, in reference to the complementary roles that constituted the fundamental social unit. The Mixtec practiced cognatic descent; Codex Becker II, for example, records matrilineal descent for ten generations of a ruling dynasty. Codex Nuttall records the creation of the Xipe dynasty at Zaachila, uniting ethnic Zapotecs and Mixtecs, but the preceding genealogy that legitimized the new dynasty was that of the wife, Lady 4 Rabbit. Similarly, it was the semi-mythological matriline that the Palenque ruler Pacal used to assert his political claims. At Yaxchilan, the autosacrifice of Lady Xoc produced the ancestral link to solidify the dynastic rule of her husband.

Mesoamerican religious pantheons featured both male and female supernaturals. Male deities such as Huitzilopochtli, Quetzalcóatl, and Tláloc were predominant in Aztec society, where they were affiliated with major

G

temples, ceremonies, and state religion. Female deities of the Mother Goddess complex (e.g., Toci, Tlazolteotl, Xochiquetzal, Cihuacóatl) were probably more important at the household level, where they were associated with fertility, reproduction, and domestic craft. The goddess 9 Grass was among the most prominent deities for the Mixtec, where she paralleled Cihuacóatl as a skeletal earth mother as well as supporting an important politico-religious oracle. The Maya goddess Ix Chel, associated with weaving and fertility, was worshipped at an important pilgrimage shrine on the island of Cozumel.

Ethnohistoric accounts describe the training and activities of male priests during rituals. Complementary female practices, however, are rarely noted, though this is probably due to androcentric bias on the part of the Spanish chroniclers. Brown, for example, contrasts the minimal role of women in written accounts of religious ritual with their prominence in depictions of the same ceremonies. Women associated with the priesthood were often referred to as *ahuianime* ("pleasure girls"), and their duties apparently included temple prostitution. Adolescent girls entered temple schools, where they learned the hymns and dances of the different festivals and produced elaborate textiles for religious costumes and tribute.

Colonial period texts provide a wealth of information on gender relations. Yet as noted, discrepancies between texts and their accompanying images highlight biases that underlie these sources. Pre-Columbian codices and hieroglyphic texts offer indigenous perspectives on gender that avoid some, but not all, of these biases. Archaeological data provide an alternative with which to evaluate the ethnohistorical accounts, challenging male and elite biases while exploring contexts for which no textual references exist.

Archaeology of Gender

Archaeological interest in gender relations is a relatively recent theoretical development, but in the past decade it has become a prominent research goal in Mesoamerican archaeology. Gender has been the focus of analyses of mortuary remains, household production, and both public and domestic art (i.e., figurines). Archaeological evidence offers a contrast to the "top-down" perspective of ethnohistorical accounts, reflecting cultural practice rather than elite opinion about social structure.

Based on ethnohistoric models of Aztec society (and supported by additional evidence from other pre-Columbian cultures), spinning, weaving, and food preparation were tasks associated with women, while hunting,

agriculture, certain crafts, and especially warfare were associated with male identity. Archaeological correlates of these activities can therefore be used to study gender relations for different groups at different times, while critically assessing the degree to which these gender stereotypes were practiced.

From Postclassic Cholula, for example, artifact classes from domestic contexts were considered as correlates of a variety of overlapping cultural identities, including gender, occupation, status, ethnicity, and religion. A large number of ceramic spindle whorls, as well as a kitchen tool kit for food preparation (manos and metates, comales, ollas, etc.), provided evidence for women's activities in the household compound. Projectile points, clay balls, celts, and polishing stones were among the artifact classes associated with male production.

Evidence for women's production has also been studied in the Valley of Mexico, where spindle whorls and utilitarian vessels are contrasted diachronically between Early Postclassic and Late Postclassic assemblages to identify changes in female production relating to the rise of the Aztec state. Textile production has also been studied for the Maya. At Cholula, spindle whorls have been interpreted in relation to spinning technology and the fiber materials used in textile production, while the iconography of the decorated whorls is related to female gender ideology.

Spinning and weaving tools found in Tomb 7 at Monte Albán have been used to reinterpret the context of one of the most elaborate burials of the pre-Columbian world. Carved bone weaving battens, picks, combs, and ceramic spindle whorls associated with the principal individual of the tomb provide a basis for identifying it as female. The published data on the skeletal remains is less definitive but also supports the identification of the principal individual as female. The ritual nature of Tomb 7, together with the iconography of the elaborate grave goods, indicates that this may have been an oracular shrine dedicated to the Mother Goddess complex.

Figurines are another artifact class that has been used for evaluating pre-Columbian gender relations. Olmec-style figurines from domestic contexts at Formative Chalcatzingo depict stages of the female life cycle: puberty, pregnancy, and childbirth. Celebrations of female rites of passage may have been important social events for the creation of group identity. The figurines may indicate a policy of elite intermarriage between Olmec women and Chalcatzingo males. Figurines from

Central America were also used to negotiate gender status, but in different ways, depending on the relative degree of social stratification of the particular culture. In lower Central America, male and female roles were represented as distinct but complementary; in later, more complex Maya society, gender distinctions are represented through the acts and products of female labor—weaving and cooking—in contrast to male activities in warfare and public ritual. Figurines from the Gulf Coast present a different diachronic shift, from a majority of figurines representing males in the Early Classic to figurines of women in elaborate costume in the Middle and Late Classic. The relative prestige of women, and particularly the value of female production, became the subject of material discourse as female status was negotiated through this medium. Finally, in Aztec society female figurines were used in domestic rituals of fertility and curing, both activities under the control of women.

Several studies have contrasted the representation of women in public versus minor art. Yet it was not until 1961 that female figures were identified on Maya stelae, and the preeminent deity of Teotihuacán has only recently been identified as the Great Goddess rather than a male rain deity. Women in Maya monumental art are typically depicted as important ancestors to legitimize dynastic succession. In other scenes, particularly from Yaxchilan, noblewomen practice autosacrificial rites to induce visions that are again linked to dynastic politics. Women are often depicted in finely woven clothing, carrying bowls with food or ritual objects, in reference to the products of female labor.

The polychrome murals of Cacaxtla depict women dressed in elaborate costumes as captives in a battle between distinct ethnic groups. The two women (or, more likely, the same woman depicted twice) wear the headdress of the defeated Quetzal army, including possible military insignia, and are paired with the captain of the victorious Jaguar army, Lord 3 Deer Antler. It is likely that this mural commemorates the capture of the founding queen of the Jaguar/Quetzal dynasty, with the woman shown in her finery in contrast to the other Quetzal warriors, who are stripped to signify the humiliation of defeat.

Female supernaturals appear in Aztec monumental art, including skeletal goddesses such as Coatlicue and the dismembered moon goddess Coyolxauhqui. Mortal women are shown giving birth, seated in council, or as warriors. On the Tizoc Stone, an Aztec lord is depicted repeatedly in the act of conquering rival war chiefs from neighboring polities; in two cases the defeated rulers are women, who carry battens in substitution for the weapons of their male counterparts.

Conclusion

In summary, evidence for pre-Columbian gender is available from several different sources, but with distinct advantages and disadvantages. Ethnohistoric sources provide vivid details of male and female roles in Aztec society based on the accounts of elite male informants, filtered through the eurocentric gender bias of the Spanish chroniclers. Archaeology can produce a broader view of gender for a range of cultural contexts, with the added advantage of a diachronic perspective that allows interpretation of gender as one of several interrelated social identities.

But archaeological insights are most productive when integrated with ethnohistoric and ethnographic analogies where contrasts between ethnohistorically derived models and archaeological evidence expose the dynamics of gender practice. For example, at Postclassic Cholula, males are buried with spindle whorls and spinning bowls. Is this evidence for a breakdown in the gender stereotype, or is this a class distinction in which servants/slaves were less closely governed by a gender-based division of labor? Were women depicted as warriors in Mixtec and Aztec accounts simply mythological anomalies, or did women actually participate in the military?

Another potential for an archaeology of gender is the identification of resistance to an ideology of male dominance. Spindle whorls decorated with shield motifs and weaving battens used in ritual sacrifice became substitutes for male weapons, perhaps in an attempt to subvert male authority and express a female gender ideology of complementarity.

Despite the wealth of information in the encyclopedic ethnohistoric accounts, gender relations in pre-Columbian Mesoamerica were not unambiguous. Rather, they were dynamic processes that varied through time and space, and they were continuously negotiated in social practice. As such, gender has become a rich field of investigation with significant implications for anthropological understanding of the past and the present.

FURTHER READINGS

Brumfiel, E. 1991. Weaving and Cooking: Women's Production in Aztec Mexico. In J. M. Gero and M. W. Conkey (eds.), *Engendering Archaeology: Women and Prehistory,* pp. 224–251. Oxford: Basil Blackwell.

G

Guillen, A. C. 1993. Women, Rituals, and Social Dynamics at Ancient Chalcatzingo. *Latin American Antiquity* 4:209–224.

Joyce, R. A. 1993. Women's Work: Images of Production and Reproduction in Pre-Hispanic Southern Central America. *Current Anthropology* 34:255–274.

Kellogg, S. 1988. Cognatic Kinship and Religion: Women in Aztec Society. In J. K. Josserand and K. Dakin (eds.), *Smoke and Mist: Mesoamerican Studies in Memory of Thelma D. Sullivan,* pp. 666–681. BAR International Series, 402. Oxford.

McCafferty, S. D., and G. G. McCafferty. 1994. Engendering Tomb 7 at Monte Albán, Oaxaca: Respinning an Old Yarn. *Current Anthropology* 35:143–166.

Miller, V. E. (ed.). 1988. *The Role of Gender in Pre-Columbian Art and Architecture.* Lanham, Md.: University Press of America.

Motolinía, Toribio de Benavente. 1951 [1540]. *History of the Indians of New Spain.* F. B. Steck (trans.). Washington, D.C.: Academy of American Franciscan History.

Proskouriakoff, T. 1961. Portraits of Women in Maya Art. In S. K. Lothrop et al. (eds.), *Essays in Pre-Columbian Art and Archaeology,* pp. 81–99. Cambridge, Mass.: Harvard University Press.

Rodriguez-Shadow Valdés, M. J. 1988. *La mujer Azteca.* Toluca: Universidad Autónoma del Estado de México.

Sahagún, B. de. 1950–1982 [1547–1585]. *Florentine Codex: General History of the Things of New Spain.* C. E. Dibble and A. J. D. Anderson (trans. and ed.). Santa Fe and Salt Lake City: School of American Research and University of Utah Press.

Sullivan, T. 1982. Tlazolteotl–Ixcuina: The Great Spinner and Weaver. In E. H. Boone (ed.), *The Art and Iconography of Late Post-Classic Central Mexico,* pp. 7–36. Washington, D.C.: Dumbarton Oaks.

Zorita, A. de. 1994 [c. 1570] *Life and Labor in Ancient Mexico: The Brief and Summary Elation of the Lords of New Spain.* B. Keel (trans.). Norman: University of Oklahoma Press.

Geoffrey G. McCafferty

SEE ALSO

Family and Household

Geography and Climate

In response to a request to sketch the complex physical patterns of Middle America, Cortés abandoned pen and ink altogether, crumpled up a sheet of paper, and laid it

TABLE 1.

Physiographic Regions	Significant Mineral Resources
I. Sierra Madre Occidental	basalt, copper, gold, silver
II. Mexican Pacific Lowland	basalt, copper, gold, salt, shell, silver
III. Baja California Peninsula	asphalt, copper, gold, pearls, salt, shell, silver
IV. Sierra Madre Oriental	basalt, limestone
V. Gulf Lowland	asphalt, basalt, gold, salt, shell
VI. Mexican Plateau	
VIa. Mesa Central	basalt, cinnabar, copper, gold, hot springs, ice, obsidian, salt, silver, turquoise
VIb. Mesa del Norte	basalt, cinnabar, copper, flint, gold, hematite, jadeite, salt, silver, turquoise
VII. Balsas Depression	basalt, copper, gold, jade, jadeite, limestone, serpentine, silver, turquoise
VIII. Mexican Southern Highland	basalt, gold, limestone, salt, shell, silver, turquoise
IX. Isthmus of Tehuantepec	gold, limestone, salt, shell
X. Yucatan Peninsula	chert, flint, limestone, salt, shell
XI. Central American Highland	basalt, gold, hot springs, jade, jadeite, limestone, obsidian, serpentine, silver
XII. Central American Pacific Lowland	salt, shell
XIII. Central American Caribbean Lowland	salt, shell

on the table. Pithy and evocative, this anecdote emphasizes the dramatic elevational differences that characterize the region's physical geography and underpin an unmatched environmental diversity. Squeezed among the margins of six lithospheric plates, the ancient rocks have folded and faulted into a rugged topography, while volcanism has mantled the surface with younger rocks and built the highest peaks—with Volcán Pico de Orizaba's glacial cap gleaming within sight of the Gulf Coast's mangrove swamps. While the eruptions and earthquakes associated with such energetic tectonism produce relatively brief and localized catastrophes, the more enduring lithological and structural patterns have endowed some general order on the landscape.

Thirteen physiographic regions (see map) thus define the environments of ancient Middle American cultures—a suite of landforms, drainage patterns, soils, mineral resources (see Table 1), and climates characterizing each region. As a preliminary overview, three extensive highlands dominate Middle America. In the north, the Sierra Madre Occidental (Region I) and Sierra Madre Oriental (Region IV) flank the Mexican Plateau (Region VI). The Mexican Southern Highland (Region VIII) occupies the center. The Central American Highland (Region XI) extends from southern Mexico to the Isthmus of Panama. Lowlands bound and divide those highlands. The Mexican Pacific Lowland (Region II) abuts the Sierra Madre Occidental, separated from the Baja California Peninsula (Region III) by the Gulf of California. The Gulf Lowland (Region V) separates all three highlands from the Gulf of Mexico, grading into the Yucatan Peninsula (X) at the foot of the Central American Highland, itself fringed by narrower, discontinuous lowlands: the Central American Pacific Lowland (XII) and the Central American Caribbean Lowland (XIII). The Balsas Depression (Region VII) and Isthmus of Tehuantepec (Region IX) flank the Mexican Southern Highland.

The Sierra Madre Occidental (I) rose during Tertiary time, 65 million–2 million years ago (mya); the Farallon

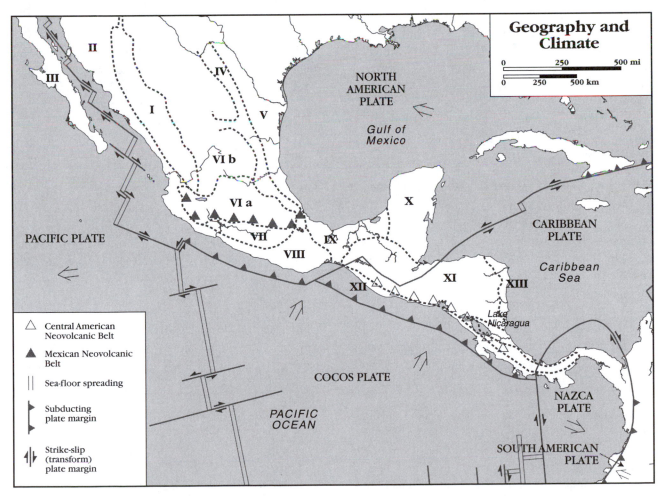

The physiographic regions of Mexico. Map design by Mapping Specialists Limited, Madison, Wisconsin, after original provided by Andrew Sluyter.

G

Plate, an extinct sector of the Cocos Plate, subducted beneath the North American Plate, melting and welling upward into a western backbone of volcanic peaks built of rhyolite and andesite. Continued tectonism during the Pleistocene (2–0.01 mya) further uplifted the range and faulted its eastern versant (slope) into parallel (northwest–southeast) ridges and valleys, where streams carved out a labyrinth of lava-capped mesas that grade into those of the Mesa del Norte. In contrast, the streams plummeting down the western escarpment to the Pacific Lowland have cut deep canyons (e.g., Barranca del Cobre). From a relatively modest northern terminus, the range gains elevation toward the south (e.g., Cerro de la Mohinora, 3,250 meters)—in total, a massive barrier with daunting heights, a few slightly less daunting passes cut headward by the major streams (Río Yaqui, Río Fuerte) of the Pacific drainage, and isolated pockets of valley bottom scattered along the eastern fringe and the drainage axes.

The Mexican Pacific Lowland (II) consists of ranges of granite that predate the Tertiary, eroded nearly to sea level, the nubs largely buried beneath sediments deposited by streams descending from the Sierra. It tenuously perches on the edge of the San Andreas Rift, which was inundated during the Tertiary by the Gulf of California as subduction consumed the Farallon Plate and the Pacific and North American plates came into contact and ground past each other. To the south, where the lowland clings to the Sierra along the open Pacific, longshore currents have extended sand spits to enclose lagoons. To the north, the rock has faulted into parallel (north–south) basins and ranges that grade from a continuous foothill margin along the Sierra to isolated ranges along the coast, in places forming the headlands of bays (Bahía Kino) but largely buried by alluvium and by dune fields (Desierto Altar) of sand blown southwest from the Colorado River Delta. The alluvial soils of the floodplains and coastal deltas (Río Mayo) punctuate an otherwise forbidding landscape of ancient, rounded hills smothered under detritus eroded from the younger Sierra. The north even lacks the deltas; its streams (Río Sonora) disappear into the coarse sediments and evaporate in the arid heat before reaching the coast.

Two granite ranges bracket the Baja California Peninsula (III) between elevational highs in the north (Sierra San Pedro Mártir, 3,100 meters) and south (Sierra de la Victoria, 2,100 meters). Erosion since before Tertiary times has rounded the summits and carved broad headwater basins with deep soils. As the San Andreas Rift

opened, the block comprising the peninsula uplifted and tilted westward, and the sedimentary rocks lying between the two ranges presented a jagged fault scarp (Sierra de la Giganta, 1,500 meters) to the east. Subsequent volcanism mantled the sedimentary rocks, and the intermittent streams draining westward have carved narrow valleys between mesas capped with lava and tuff, with springs bubbling from the volcanic rocks. Continued uplift has restricted lowland to isolated pockets along the west coast, where the sand dunes of small deserts (Desierto Vizcaíno) merge into the barrier islands and spits that enclose bays (Bahía Magdalena).

The Sierra Madre Oriental (IV) counterposes the western orogenic belt with an eastern backbone of marine limestones and shales deposited during Jurassic and Cretaceous times (213–65 mya). During the latest Cretaceous and early Tertiary, as the Farallon and North American plates pressed together, the sedimentary rocks compressed and folded into a series of parallel valleys and ridges: some stretch for hundreds of kilometers, and all increase in elevation westward to a crest at 2,000–3,000 meters. Faulting and limited volcanism complicates the folded structure and occasionally interrupts the regular crest with higher peaks (Cerro Peña Nevada, 3,540 meters). Karst features, the result of limestone solution, occur throughout the Sierra and flanking foothills: streams plunge into sinkholes (resumideros), flow for kilometers through caverns, and reemerge as springs (ojos de agua); sinkholes coalesce to form flat-bottomed valleys filled with alluvium. The larger streams (Río Pánuco–Moctezuma) draining the Sierra and the Mexican Plateau have cut deep canyons and passes through the echelon of ridges, in places interconnecting the well-watered stretches of fertile soils in the intervening valleys and facilitating passage between high plateau and coastal lowland.

Along the Gulf Lowland (V), streams draining the highlands deposited piedmonts of detritus—now conglomerates, sandstones, and shales—in fans and deltas along the Tertiary coastline, entrenching meanders and cutting terraces as sea levels fell during the Pleistocene glaciations; the canyons are thus separated by eastward-sloping plains and, where capped with volcanics, by mesas. The piedmont's hilly fringe grades into a coastal plain which, although bisected by the Neovolcanic Belt (Sierra de Chiconquiaco, 2,850 meters) at Punta Delgada, stretches the length of the Gulf of Mexico. Streams with drainage basins dominated by the limestone of the Sierra Madre Oriental did not deposit major fans of detritus, and so there is a more abrupt transition from folded foothills to coastal plain. Low ranges divide the lowland into a series of broad basins filled with fertile alluvium by the large, perennial streams (Río Pánuco, Río Papaloapan, Río Grijalva). While some of the low ranges represent the dissected sandstones and shales of the Tertiary deltas, others formed as isolated volcanism uplifted and faulted the thick marine rocks (Sierra de Tamaulipas, 1,250 meters). In the north, volcanic necks (Bernal de Horcasitas, 1,100 meters) thrust up isolated needles of basalt to signal extinct and highly eroded volcanoes. In the south, the Sierra de los Tuxtlas (1,700 meters) harbors small lakes (Lake Catemaco, 340 meters) and valleys of well-watered and fertile basaltic soils. Except at the Mexican Neovolcanic Belt, where the Gulf nearly laps the foothills, the streams meander across a broad coastal plain and are flanked by cordons of levees, backswamps, abandoned channels, oxbow lakes, and salt-intruded uplands that stand above the copious annual floods. Along the littoral, mangroves root in the muds of extensive delta-estuary systems and fringe lagoons protected by reefs, barrier islands, spits, and dune fields—some of them active and low, and some dating to Pleistocene times and having crest elevations over 100 meters.

The Mexican Plateau (VI)—a crustal block of Cretaceous and older marine sedimentary rocks, uplifted during the Tertiary formation of the paired Sierra Madres—crouches atop those two mountainous backbones; the Mesa Central (VIa) in the south grades into the Mesa del Norte (VIb). The Tertiary volcanics of the western range and the Cretaceous, folded sedimentary rocks of the eastern range converge on the Mesa Central. This is a landscape born of the volcanism which, as the Cocos Plate subducted beneath the North American Plate, began to intrude and cloak the plateau's older limestones and shales in late Tertiary times, a process that has continued to the present; it is manifest in high andesite peaks (La Malinche, 4,461 meters), swarms of low cinder cones (Paricutín, 2,500 meters), and flows of basalt, welded ash, and mud-rafted boulders. This Mexican Neovolcanic Belt—anchored by Volcán de Colima (4,240 meters) in the west and Pico de Orizaba (5,610 meters) in the east, where volcanics almost completely bury the folded marine sedimentary rocks of the southern Sierra Madre Oriental—cuts across the breadth of the continent, uplifting the Mesa Central to over 2,000 meters, bounding its verge with a dramatic suite of peaks, and bridging the southern termini of the two Sierra Madres. Those peaks, the high-

est scarred with cirques and draped with moraines dating to Pleistocene glaciations, enclose a series of basins (Toluca, 2,600 meters; Puebla, 2,100 meters). Most of them were periodically closed by lava flows during the Pleistocene, inhibiting exterior drainage and forming large, shallow lakes rich in aquatic resources and fringed by plains of fertile alluvium. The lakes left flat basin floors after eventual drainage, infilling, or desiccation. Four streams drain the Mesa Central: the Balsas and Santiago-Lerma Rivers to the Pacific, and the Papaloapan and Pánuco-Moctezuma Rivers to the Gulf.

The Basin of Mexico remained closed until it was drained in the Colonial period through a tunnel to the Pánuco-Moctezuma system. Its floor is underlain by hundreds of meters of sediment and covered by a series of shallow, interconnected lakes (Lake Texcoco, 2,250 meter). Deposits dating to the terminal Pleistocene and early Holocene (Upper Becerra Formation) contain remains of Paleoindians (e.g., the Tepexpan Woman) and extinct mammals such as mammoths. Between the fertile soils of the lacustrine plain—derived from erosion of basalt and andesite—and the enclosing peaks (Iztaccíhuatl, 5,300 meters; Popocatépetl, 5,465 meters), alluvial fans of volcanic detritus dating to the Pleistocene form a piedmont apron. Topsoil erosion in some piedmont sectors has exposed the underlying duricrusts (tepetate), indurated but friable soils cemented by chemical precipitation. More recent basalt flows cover other piedmont sectors, such as the Pedregal de San Angel that flowed from Volcán Xitle.

As the Mexican Plateau gradually drops in elevation northward from the Mexican Neovolcanic Belt, ultimately to less than 1,000 meters, a series of lower basins (El Bajío, 1,800 meters)—occupied by lakes (Lake Chapala, 1,500 meters) and drained by the Santiago-Lerma River—marks the transition to the Mesa del Norte. Squeezed between the Sierra Madres, with marine rocks predominating to the east and volcanics to the west, fault blocks form a series of parallel (north–south to northwest–southeast) ridges and valleys (bolsones), flanked by fans and aprons of coarse sediments (bajadas) and floored by expanses (playas) of fine sediments (barriales) ephemerally occupied by shallow lakes that precipitate salts on evaporation (Bolson de Mapimí, 1,100 meters). Except for the Conchos River draining northward into the Rio Grande (Río Bravo del Norte), drainage is interior and intermittent, and ultimately evaporates from the playa lakes. Elevations increase from east to west; the western ranges comprise the foothills of the Sierra Madre Occidental, a

G

labyrinth of sediment-filled basins walled by lava-capped mesas.

Draining the peaks and basins of the Mexican Neovolcanic Belt, streams (Río Atoyac, Río Cutzamala) plunge into the Balsas Depression (VII), fragmenting the southern escarpment of the Mexican Plateau. The highly dissected terrain in the western ranges (Sierra de Mil Cumbres) gives way to a series of broad, gently sloping valleys (Atlixco) in the east, which are filled with more recent volcanic ash, mudflow, and alluvial deposits—highly fertile soils. The valleys are well watered and facilitate passage to the south. Outcrops of Cretaceous limestones introduce karst features such as caverns, sinkholes, and springs. The depths of the depression—floored with Cretaceous granite, limestone, and even older metamorphosed rocks that dropped in relation to the uplift of the Mexican Plateau—comprise a crazy-quilt of low hills and tiny swatches of alluvium, only a few of any appreciable size (Ciudad Altamirano, 300 meters).

To the south of the Balsas Depression rises the Mexican Southern Highland (VIII). On the west, the ranges of the Sierra Madre del Sur plunge into the Pacific and have a lithology similar to the Balsas Depression, in places mantled by Tertiary lavas. Only a few pockets of coastal plain front the Pacific, formed by the deltas of major streams (Río Balsas) and including lagoons guarded by barrier islands. In the interior, similar rocks comprise the Mesa del Sur, a dissected plateau of knife-edged ridges and steep, narrow valleys, carved into a labyrinth by the headwaters of the Balsas drainage. Only a few remnants of the ancient plateau surface and a few fault-block valleys relieve the sea of ridges with extensive flats; the Valley of Oaxaca (1,600 meters), watered by the headwaters of the Río Atoyac, comprises the largest expanse of alluvium. The Sierra Madre de Oaxaca—parallel (northwest–southeast) folds of marine sedimentary rocks, similar to the Sierra Madre Oriental—bounds the eastern flank of the Mesa del Sur. Volcanic peaks (Cerro Zempoaltepec, 3,390 meters) provide the highest elevations.

The Isthmus of Tehuantepec (IX), associated with the strike-slip fault where the Cocos and North American plates have ground past each other, provides a lowland pass between the Gulf Coast Lowland and the Pacific littoral, separating the similar lithologies of the Mexican Southern Highland and the Central American Highland. Meandering streams descend toward the coasts from a divide in the Sierra Atravesada (Cordón la Cordillera, 750 meters), crossing alluvial plains sprinkled with low hills

that grade into the lagoons and barrier islands of the Pacific littoral and Gulf Lowland. Tertiary and Pleistocene tectonism raised the carbonate rocks of the Yucatán Peninsula (X) above sea level, with a gentle tilt toward the northwest, thus forming the only extensive lowland in Middle America. The northern and western coasts have gradually resubmerged with Holocene (0.01–0 mya) sea-level rise, merging into the shoals and reefs of the Campeche Banks. Lagoons and mangrove swamps fringe the shorelines, with numerous saltpans (Celustún) along the low-lying northern and western coasts, and with cliffs (Tulum) fronting reef-enclosed lagoons along the higher eastern coast. The pitted plain of limestone, marl, and gypsum in the north is unrelieved by surface drainage; the soils are thin and stony, with settlements clustering around the numerous cenotes (sinkholes accessing underground streams) and aguadas (clay-lined, shallow sinks collecting runoff). The plain abuts a scarp (northwest–southeast) that formed as the northern sector dropped relative to uplift. The Puuc Hills (350 meters) anchor the western terminus of the scarp, with elevations decreasing toward the southeast. South of the scarp, the higher, and thus longer exposed, limestones form a rolling surface (100–300 meters) underneath the expanse of the Petén forest. High precipitation leaches the already nutrient-poor soils, and the water table lies farther below the surface than north of the scarp. Nonetheless, the soils are older, deeper, and more fertile; the karst topography is more mature, cloaked by soil, and subdued; and surface streams augment subterranean channels and caverns. In the southwest, the karst grades into the alluvial plain of the Gulf Lowland. To the east, faulted valleys and low ridges parallel the coast, controlling the drainage pattern of the moderately sized surface streams (Río Hondo, New River) and forming bays (Bahía de Chetumal) and islands (Cozumel) upon reaching sea level. Stretches of alluvium, swampy *bajos* (clay-bottomed, coalesced sinkholes), and lakes (Lake Sacnab, 200 meters) occupy the fault valleys. The Maya Mountains (Victoria Peak, 1,122 meters)—a highly dissected block of granite and metamorphosed sedimentary rocks—comprise the only extensive highland, isolated from the Central American Highland to the south.

The Central American Highland (XI) rises from the Yucatán Peninsula and the Isthmus of Tehuantepec, continuing largely uninterrupted southeastward to the Isthmus of Panama. To generalize an immensely complex and still poorly understood region, the deep Montagua Valley forms the suture between the North American and

Caribbean plates, marking an impact that formed a cordon of folded ranges during latest Cretaceous times and bounded the Yucatán Peninsula on the south. Along the Pacific, the Central American Neovolcanic Belt became active during Tertiary times, as the Cocos Plate subducted beneath the Caribbean Plate; volcanism, continuing to the present, has capped a jumble of older granites, volcanics, and sedimentary rocks, building a chain of high peaks (Tajamulco, 4,210 meters). Basins (Quetzaltenango-Totonicpan, 2,400 meters) enclosed by those peaks harbor lakes (Atitlan, 1,560 meters; Ilopango, 450 meters) surrounded by fertile soils developed on ash, similar to the landforms of the Mexican Neovolcanic Belt. The Pacific versant slopes precipitously toward the coastal plain, frayed by deep canyons. In the north, the eastern drainage descends more gradually, with streams (Río Grijalva–Grande de Chiapas) flanked by broad terraces and intervening fault-block mountains capped by karsted limestone, with fertile soils on substrates of alluvium and on volcanic ash blown from the south. Southeastward, limestones become less frequent, but the general pattern continues of high volcanoes along the Pacific and lower, faulted ranges and basins toward the Caribbean. Elevations generally decrease from highs in Guatemala to a low at the Isthmus of Panama. One fault-block depression, occupied by large lakes (Lake Nicaragua, 35 meters), interrupts the highland: the Nicaraguan Graben. Where the Central American Highland peters out at the Isthmus of Panama, spurs of sedimentary and volcanic rocks rise to form the northern terminus of the Andes.

From the Isthmus of Tehuantepec, the Central American Pacific Lowland (XII) widens (the Soconusco) before pinching out on meeting the Nicaraguan Graben at the Gulf of Fonseca. Detritus from the neovolcanic chain forms an apron of gently sloping alluvial fans (Boca Costa) grading into a coastal plain; fertile soils form on substrates of weathered ash and detritus eroded from the volcanic slopes. Sand spits and barrier islands enclose lagoons. Southeastward from the Gulf of Fonseca, mountains front the Pacific more closely except where fault blocks form lowland peninsulas.

The Miskito Coast comprises the only extensive Central American Caribbean Lowland (XIII). Tertiary marine sediments extend a sloping plain between highland and coast, with streams cutting shallow valleys separated by laterite-capped mesas. Large deltas extend into shallow lagoons enclosed by reefs, atolls, and barrier islands. From Mosquitia eastward to the Maya Mountains, only small deltas intervene between mountain spurs that abut the sea. Southward, the large delta of the San Juan River, draining the Nicaraguan Graben, presses out into the sea, rife with estuaries, lagoons, and swamps; longshore currents carry its sediments to build a coastal plain to the southeast. Eastward, the reefs continue, but only small deltas punctuate the mountainous shore.

Climate

Extending from 8° to 33° north latitude, Central America and Mexico bridge the transition from tropical to temperate climates. This, together with climate change over the course of the Quaternary (2–0 mya), further increased the diversity of the environments of ancient Middle American cultures. Central America and southern Mexico enjoy a tropical climate (more than 1,600 mm precipitation per annum) all year round, while central and northern Mexico are under the influence of subtropical climates (250–1,000 mm precipitation per annum). Mid-latitude weather systems prevail in the north of Mexico, but in winter they may also penetrate deep into the tropics. Altitude conspicuously affects the temperature distribution from hot lands at sea level to cold lands upward of 3,000 meters. The local diversity of climates is further controlled by the mountain ranges, which help to accentuate land-sea breezes along the coastlines and to produce rain shadow effects on the leeward side of the mountains and over the Mexican Plateau (250–500 mm precipitation per annum). During the winter dry season, the subtropical westerly jet dominates the upper tropospheric circulation, and the North Pacific and North Atlantic anticyclones, which are closest to the equator in this season, influence the surface circulation. The trade winds affect only Central America and southeastern Mexico, while the mid-latitude westerlies influence mainly northern and central Mexico, meaning that less precipitation falls in the latter two regions. The occurrence of a cold cyclonic vortex over northwestern Mexico (the Sonora Track) may account for most of the rain in this area and for the occasional snowfall on the Sierra Madre Occidental.

During strong meridional flow conditions over northwestern Canada, cold air masses may enter the Mexican Plateau, the Gulf of Mexico, and even as far south as Central America. These cold surges, or *nortes,* are associated with light rains, low temperatures, and frosts. The El Niño/Southern Oscillation (ENSO) warm events (cold ENSO events are known as La Niña) also have an impact on the winter circulation by enhancing strong meridional

G

flow over northwestern Canada and a strong subtropical westerly jet that extends across Mexico and the Gulf of Mexico. Consequently, El Niño (warm ENSO) events have been documented as producing colder, wetter weather over northeastern Mexico during winter, with La Niña (cold ENSO) events having the opposite effect. El Niño events also seem to be associated with dry conditions in some parts of Central America.

During summer, the subtropical westerly jet disappears and the North Atlantic and North Pacific highs and the equatorial trough of low pressure shift northward. Easterly flow aloft along the Bermuda-Azores anticyclone brings moist air over Mexico and Central America and the main rainy season develops. Convective clouds, orographic lifting, and abundant rains are produced over the windward slopes of the mountain ranges. In general, the rainy season lasts from May through November, with a maximum in July on the Mexican Plateau, in July and August in northwestern Mexico (when the Mexican monsoon occurs), and in September in coastal regions. The exceptions include the northwestern part of the Baja California Peninsula, which experiences winter rains (Mediterranean climate); the coastal plains of the southern Gulf of Mexico (tropical wet-dry, with 1,500–2,000 mm precipitation per annum); and Central America, which has rainfall throughout the year. The northeasterly trades, tropical storms, and hurricanes account for the September rainfall maximum in Central Mexico as well as the coastal regions of the Gulf of Mexico and the Caribbean. The northeastern coasts of Central America, which face the Caribbean Sea, are usually wetter (tropical rainy, more than 2,000 mm per annum) than the southward ones, which are on Pacific Ocean, leeward side of the mountains (tropical wet-dry, 800–1600 mm per annum). The equatorial southwesterlies, associated with the northward location of the Intertropical Convergence Zone (ITCZ), account for the September-October precipitation on the Pacific coast of Central America, while tropical storms and cyclones are responsible for the maximum on the Pacific coast of Mexico. However, between June and September there is a relatively dry period, called Canícula in Mexico and Veranillo in Central America. Drought conditions along the Gulf of Mexico and the Caribbean coasts are established during summer when the upper tropospheric circulation is dominated by a trough (cyclonic flow) over the Caribbean and a ridge over the Mexican Plateau. Therefore, large-scale ascending motion over the sea decreases or changes to subsidence, dampening precipitation processes. Recent studies also indicate that reduced seasonal upper tropospheric anticyclonic flow over the western Atlantic should be associated with weak hurricane activity. Moreover, low hurricane activity in the Atlantic basin seems to be associated with the occurrence of a moderate to strong El Niño event. Accordingly, several studies document that during ENSO warm events summer rainfall decreases in some regions of Mexico and Central America.

Several studies based on pollen and lake-level records show that climates in Mexico and Central America have changed over the past 20,000 years. Despite much uncertainty, the most consistent inferences indicate that before 14,000 years ago, climates in general were colder and drier than present. Subsequently, wetter periods (but still colder than present) seem to correspond with glacial advances and changes in the position of the polar front. Several studies generally agree that in relative terms, the Formative period was humid, the Classic dry, and the Postclassic humid.

FURTHER READINGS

Craig, A. K., and R. C. West (eds.). *Geoscience and Man*, vol. 33, *In Quest of Mineral Wealth: Aboriginal and Colonial Mining and Metallurgy in Spanish America*. Baton Rouge: Geoscience Publications, Department of Geography and Anthropology, Louisiana State University.

Dengo, G., and J. E. Case (eds.). 1990. *The Geology of North America*, vol. H, *The Caribbean Region*. Boulder: Geological Society of America.

Markgraf, V. 1989. Palaeoclimates in Central and South America since 18,000 BP Based on Pollen and Lake-Level Records. *Quaternary Science Reviews* 8:1–24.

Morán Zenteno, D. J. 1994. The Geology of the Mexican Republic. American Association of Petroleum Geologists Studies in Geology, 39. Revision and translation of J. L. Wilson and L. Sanchez-Barreda. 1984. *Geología de la República Mexicana* Mexico City: Secretaria de Programación y Presupuesto.

Mosiño, P., and E. García. 1974. The Climate of Mexico. In R. A. Bryson and F. H. Hare (eds.), *World Survey of Climatology*, vol. 11, *Climates of North America*, pp. 345–390. Amsterdam: Elsevier.

Salvador, A. (ed.). 1991. *The Geology of North America*, vol. J, *The Gulf of Mexico Basin*. Boulder: Geological Society of America.

Siemens, A. H. 1978. Karst and the Pre-Hispanic Maya in the Southern Lowlands. In P. D. Harrison and B. L. Turner II (eds.), *Pre-Hispanic Maya Agriculture*, pp.

117–143. Albuquerque: University of New Mexico Press.

Tamayo, J. L. 1980. *Geografía Moderna de México.* Mexico City: Editorial Trillas.

Thom, B. G. 1967. Mangrove Ecology and Deltaic Geomorphology: Tabasco, Mexico. *Journal of Ecology* 55:301–343.

West, R. C. (ed.). 1964. *Handbook of Middle American Indians,* vol. 1, *Natural Environment and Early Cultures.* Austin: University of Texas Press.

Weyl, R. 1980. *Geology of Central America.* D. and I. Jordan (ed. and trans.). Berlin: Gebrüder Borntraeger.

Williams, B. J., and C. A. Ortíz-Solorio. 1981. Middle American Folk Soil Taxonomy. *Annals of the Association of American Geographers* 71:335–358.

Andrew Sluyter and Maria Tereza Cavazos Perez

SEE ALSO

Fauna; Flora; Hydrology; Minerals, Ores, and Mining

Gheo-Shih (Oaxaca, Mexico)

Gheo-Shih (Zapotec, "River of the Gourd Trees") is a 1.5-hectare open-air site of the hunting, gathering, and incipient cultivation era in highland Mexico. It lies along the right bank of the Río Mitla in the eastern Valley of Oaxaca and was excavated by Frank Hole as part of a University of Michigan expedition. The most interesting feature of Gheo-Shih is a cleared area 20 meters long and 7 meters wide, swept clean of artifacts and lined with boulders. It resembles a dance ground or ritual area like those used by the Indians of the Great Basin of the western United States. There were also oval concentrations of stone tools and fire-cracked rocks, which may indicate ephemeral shelters or huts of some kind. Scattered among them were areas for tool manufacturing, including some where flat river pebbles had been drilled as pendants. Gheo-Shih, which probably dates somewhere in the period 5000–3000 B.C., provides a glimpse of the kind of open-air encampment that could be the ancestor of the earliest Mesoamerican villages.

FURTHER READINGS

Flannery K. V., and J. Marcus. 1983. *The Cloud People.* New York: Academic Press.

Kent V. Flannery

SEE ALSO

Oaxaca and Tehuantepec Region

Gibson, Charles (1920–1985)

Perspectives, methods, and scholarly standards of the American ethnohistorian Charles Gibson shaped subsequent research on Indian and colonial societies of Latin America. Gibson (Ph.D., History, Yale University, 1950) welded primary documents from Mexican and Spanish archives into his monumental book, *The Aztecs Under Spanish Rule,* an account of the Valley of Mexico's indigenous peoples in the Colonial period. Its topics include society; town political organization, taxation, and finances; Spanish colonial *encomiendas;* religious institutions; labor; land and agriculture; production and exchange; and the city of Mexico during the years 1519–1810. One of Gibson's major contributions to community studies is *Tlaxcala in the Sixteenth Century.* His investigations of colonial institutions provided new insights into pre-Columbian practices; these studies include "Llamamiento General, Repartamiento, and the Empire of Acolhuacan" and "The Structure of the Aztec Empire." Gibson's "Survey of Prose Manuscripts in the Native Historical Tradition" and, with John Glass, "Census of Middle American Prose Manuscripts in the Native Historical Tradition" are important bibliographic tools for students and scholars of all levels of expertise.

FURTHER READINGS

Chevalier, F. 1986. Charles Gibson (1920–1985). *Hispanic American Historical Review* 66:349–351.

Gibson, C. 1960. The Aztec Aristocracy in Colonial Mexico. *Comparative Studies in Society and History* 2:169–196.

———. 1964. *The Aztecs under Spanish Rule: A History of the Indians of the Valley of Mexico, 1519–1810.* Stanford: Stanford University Press.

———. 1967. *Tlaxcala in the Sixteenth Century.* Stanford: Stanford University Press.

———. 1971. Structure of the Aztec Empire. In R. Wauchope (ed.), *Handbook of Middle American Indians,* vol. 5, part 10, pp. 376–394. Austin: University of Texas Press.

Mary G. Hodge

SEE ALSO

Ethnohistorical Sources and Methods

Grillo, El (Jalisco, Mexico)

Situated in the Atemajac Valley on the northern outskirts of Guadalajara, this site's surface remains and salvage excavations indicate occupation during the Tabachines, El Grillo, and Atemajac phases. The primary occupation and architecture is El Grillo phase, which Galván places at c. A.D. 300–600, and Beekman at A.D. 550–800. The site was cleared and excavated in 1959 by Corona Nuñez (at about the same time as his work at Ixtépete), with subsequent minor salvage excavations. Test pits and trenches were excavated in 1972 by Bell, Winnie, and Gussinyer, but the collections were never analyzed. Looting and construction damage have been extensive, and the beltway around Guadalajara cuts through the northern part of the site.

Because the site is surrounded by modern construction, minor structures have been eradicated, and only the monumental core of the settlement remains. There are seven major structures, six of them grouped around a large plaza and covering an area of fourteen hectares. Three of these structures form a U-shaped complex atop a common structure; highway construction exposed a talud-tablero façade on the platform. Another 80-meter-long "palace" structure was described by Corona Nuñez as having the Tarascan yácata form, but its current state no longer allows a determination. Stone architecture is present at El Grillo, but much has been destroyed or carried away. More distinctive is the extensive use of adobe, including the practice of first forming a compartmentalized core around which the building was constructed.

The site is critical for any interpretation of the nature of the El Grillo phase. Galván points to the talud-tablero and compartmentalized core construction as indicators of a Middle Classic Teotihuacán influence, while Beekman emphasizes the U-shaped complex form and its connections to the Epiclassic and Guanajuato.

FURTHER READINGS

Beekman, C. S. 1996. El complejo El Grillo del centro de Jalisco: una revision de su cronologia y significado. In E. Williams and P. C. Weigand (eds.), *Las Cuencas del Occidente de Mexico, epoca prehispanica*, pp. 247–291. Zamora: Colegio de Michoacan.

Luís Javier Galván Villegas and Christopher S. Beekman

SEE ALSO
Atemajac Region; West Mexico

Ground Stone Tools

Tools made of stone shaped through a process of pecking and grinding occur commonly throughout Mesoamerica. Pecking with a hard stone roughs out the general shape of the tool; grinding then produces the desired shape and smoothness. Some ground stone tools, such as *manos* and *metates,* come to have polished surfaces, but this polish is the result of use, not an intentional result of the manufacturing process. Researchers usually classify artifacts with intentional polish in the polished-stone category. Ground stone tools were made from wide range of raw materials; the most common are andesite, basalt, chert, fossil coral, granite, gneiss, limestone, quartzite, rhyolite, sandstone, and schist.

A *metate* is a stone basin used for grinding maize (Fig. a,b,c). A *mano* is an oblong stone held in the hand, or both hands, that is pulled and pushed across the grinding surface of the *metate* (Fig. h,i,j). *Metates* occur in many shapes and sizes and can be legged or legless. Legless *metates* are the most common and occur in two basic subforms, trough and rimmed. Trough *metates* have a trough-shaped grinding surface that is open at one or both ends (Fig. b). Rimmed *metates* have a rim that surrounds the grinding surface (Fig. a). This rim becomes more pronounced as the grinding surface wears down. The backs and sides of both forms show varying degrees of shaping; some were carefully shaped and smoothed, while others are rough and irregular. Central Mexico has a higher frequency of *metates* with carefully flattened backs. Some researchers refer to these legless *metates,* either trough or rimmed, as "turtle-backed" *metates* because of their rounded backs; many were made from boulders. Most *metates* are large enough for use with a two-handed *mano* (Fig. h,i), although some clearly were for use with a smaller one-handed implement (Fig. j).

Legged *metates,* usually made from volcanic stone, frequently show extensive work on the underside and legs (Fig. c). In cross-section, the legs or feet can be round, square, ovoid, rectangular, or triangular. Three-legged *metates* are more common than four-legged ones. A typical tripod *metate* has a leg at both corners of one end and a single leg centered at the opposing end. This third leg is usually larger and taller than the other two, giving the grinding surface a downward slope. Legged *metates* were most popular in the Postclassic period but were present in Classic times as well. In some areas, such as the Valley of Mexico, they occasionally occur in Late Formative contexts.

Miniature *metates* are relatively uncommon but occur throughout Mesoamerica. Some have a grinding surface that is only 10.0 cm by 10.0 cm—clearly too small for domestic maize grinding. Their function might have been to grind special herbs, pigments, or maize for ritual purposes. More than 350 miniature metates were found in Balankanche Cave near Chichén Itzá in the northern Maya Lowlands as part of a rain god shrine. Nine miniature *manos* and *metates* were found in a cache at Kaminaljuyú.

Manos also occur in a wide variety of shapes and sizes (Fig. h,i,j). In cross-section, *mano* forms include circular, square, rectangular, oval, triangular, and plano-convex. In outline, forms include oval, square, rectangular, round, elongated, and overhang or "dogbone." Many *manos* are long enough for use with both hands—similar to those still in use today. Others were clearly used one-handed. Many of the latter show evidence of breakage and may originally have been two-handed. Overhang *manos* are wider than their associated *metates,* and thus, as the working surface of the *mano* is worn down, the unworn ends appear bulbous (Fig. i). Because of their shape, overhang *manos* are sometimes called "dogbone" *manos.* Like *metates, manos* frequently show evidence of pecking on their surfaces after these surfaces had been smoothed by use; this pecking served to resharpen the *mano* or *metate* to increase its abrasive action. Some raw materials, such as vesicular volcanic stones or fossil coral, were self-sharpening owing to natural pit exposure as the piece was worn down.

Archaeologists find *manos* and *metates* in domestic contexts along with other subsistence-related refuse. At many sites they also occur in the construction fill of monumental architecture in higher frequencies than expected; perhaps they were left as votive offerings by the laborers who constructed the mounds. High frequencies of *manos* and *metates,* both full sized and miniature, have been recovered within caves in the Maya Lowlands. Additionally, several tripod *metates* and their *manos* were recovered within tombs at Kaminaljuyú. The presence of *manos* and *metates* within monumental architecture, tombs, and caves suggests that they carried a special meaning beyond their subsistence function. In the *Popul Vuh* creation story of the Highland Maya, the Lords of Underworld ground the bones of the Hero Twins on a *metate* and threw them into a river; the Hero Twins later emerged as fish-men. Perhaps the prehistoric Maya perceived the *mano* and *metate* as instruments of transformation that played a role in the life-death-rebirth continuum.

Mullers, used in conjunction with milling stones, are similar to *manos* and *metates,* except that mullers are used with a rotary motion as opposed to the back-and-forth motion of a *mano* in a *metate.* It is often difficult to determine, by form alone, the difference between a muller and a *mano* or a milling stone and a *metate.* Researchers may use a microscope to determine the direction of grinding. Mullers and milling stones generally occur in earlier contexts when wild foods still made up a significant portion of the diet. After the development or introduction of domesticated maize, *manos* and *metates* dominate as the principal ground stone tools used to process food.

Pestles are elongated stones with an end flattened by pounding or rotary action, either intentionally or through use (Fig. e). Pestles, used in conjunction with mortars, are stone artifacts that have a concave surface that shows evidence of pecking or rotary grinding (Fig. f,g). Mortars and pestles are assumed to have been used to process nuts, seeds, berries, and other vegetable substances. The archaeological excavation of stratified deposits in the Tehuacán Valley showed a chronological sequence of pestle forms. From earliest to latest these are long, conical, and cylindrical; cuboid; bell-shaped and flatiron; truncated cone; and thumbtack. Mortars showed less variability, with three basic forms: tecomate (Fig. f), flat-bottomed (Fig. g), and hemispherical (Fig. d).

Bark beaters are specialized ground stone tools used in the production of cloth paper (Fig. n). They occur throughout Mesoamerica, except in the northernmost regions. They are generally made from dense stone. The characteristic feature of all bark beaters is a series of parallel incised grooves. There are two basic bark beater forms. The first is rectangular in outline and fist sized, with two flattened or slightly convex faces. The incised face or faces have a series of ten to twenty parallel grooves that are approximately 0.2 cm wide and generally 0.5 to 1.0 cm apart. A U-shaped groove encircles the sides and ends to facilitate hafting to a wooden handle. The less common club-shaped bark beater did not need a handle. One end has the parallel grooves and the other is plain, serving as the handle. In this form, the grooved end is square or round in cross-section and the handle is round. The Mesoamerican technology and process of making paper closely resembles that of Southeast Asia, and some researchers have suggested that this may be a trait that was transmitted to Mesoamerica by sea. Found in both highland and lowland contexts, bark beaters (and, by implication, paper) appear at the end of the Formative period and continue through the Postclassic.

Grooved stones or girdled stones vary considerably in size and shape, indicating several functions for this class of artifacts. They are found throughout Mesoamerica. Their characteristic feature is an encircling, or partially encircling, groove. Use wear, such as battering marks and pitting,

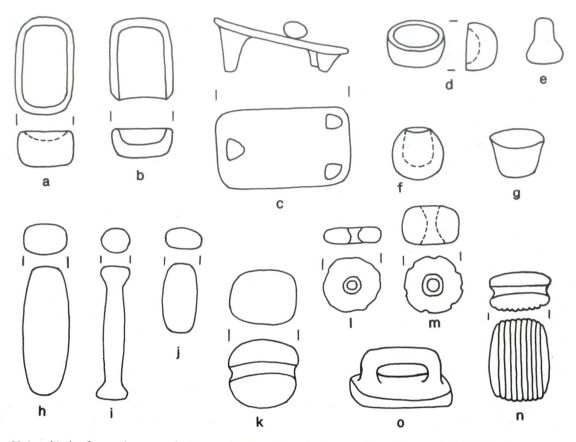

Various kinds of ground stone tools. See text for discussion of each type. Illustration courtesy of the author.

suggests that some functioned as mauls (Fig. k). The groove facilitated hafting to a wooden handle. Larger specimens possibly functioned as net weights or canoe anchors; small specimens possibly served as toggles for clothing.

Donut stones are stone spheroids or disks with centrally positioned, biconically drilled holes. There are two basic forms: one is round or nearly so (Fig. m), and the other is flattened or disk shaped (Fig. l). A variety of simple patterns adorns some oval and round specimens, but elaborately decorated specimens are rare. Most round or oval specimens are approximately 10.0 to 15.0 cm in diameter. The disk-shaped specimens are typically in this diameter range, but 3.0 to 5.0 cm thick. The biconically drilled hole in both forms is typically 3.0 cm in diameter at its narrowest point. The material used to make these stones varies: some specimens are of soft stone such as limestone, whereas others are of dense volcanic or metamorphic rock. The function of these stones is not clear, and it is quite possible that the two forms functioned differently. Suggested functions include digging-stick weights, net weights, mace heads, field markers (used with a pole), and flywheels.

Ground stone spindle whorls are stone versions of the more common ceramic spindle whorls, which functioned as counterweights on a spindle to spin thread. They are made from a variety of materials and are generally 3.0 to 5.0 cm in diameter and 2.0 to 3.0 cm thick, with a central hole approximately 1.0 cm in diameter. Most are disk shaped, although some resemble the common dome shaped ceramic forms that are flat on one side and dome shaped on the other. An encircling groove decorates some specimens.

Abraders are fist sized or smaller stones, usually made from highly abrasive materials such as pumice or sandstone. Pumice does not occur naturally in the lowlands but floats down from highland sources. Abraders occur in a variety of forms: flat abrading surfaces characterize some, whereas others are rounded or egg shaped. The variability of form suggests multiple uses for this artifact class—possibly as multipurpose or general-purpose abrading tools. Abraders of various forms occur from Formative times to the present throughout Mesoamerica.

Polishing stones were used to rub or polish other objects or materials. They vary considerably in size and shape. The smallest are stream pebbles with a flattened surface or surfaces. Some possess specially prepared flattened surfaces, and on others the flattening resulted from use. Pebble polishers are identical to the "pot burnishers" used by present-day Mesoamerican potters to polish the surfaces of ceramic vessels. Larger fist-sized specimens apparently functioned as plaster spreaders and polishers, since many have traces of plaster still adhering to them. Some of the more carefully shaped specimens have well-shaped tenons that may have served as grips; others have loop-shaped handles (Fig. o). Others closely resemble one-handed corn-grinding *manos,* except that they have a flatter working surface. Evidence from some sites suggests the recycling of broken *manos* as plaster smoothers or polishers. Some specimens classified as plaster polishers or smoothers may actually have functioned as pestles.

Whetstones, as a category of ground stone tools, are quite variable and include all stones that show evidence of being used to sharpen other objects. Most are made from an abrasive material such as sandstone. Whetstones vary considerably in overall form, but almost all show a flat face with either grooves or a depressed area resulting from another object being rubbed on it. Whetstones were probably used to sharpen pointed tools of wood and bone that would then be used for purposes such as piercing, sewing, and weaving.

FURTHER READINGS

Garber, J. F. 1989. *Archaeology at Cerros, Belize, Central America.* Vol. 2, *The Artifacts.* Dallas: Southern Methodist University.

Kidder, A. V., J. D. Jennings, and E. M. Shook. 1946. *Excavations at Kaminaljuyú, Guatemala.* Carnegie Institution of Washington, Publication 561. Washington, D.C.

MacNeish, R. S. 1967. *The Prehistory of the Tehuacán Valley: Nonceramic Artifacts.* D. S. Byers (ed.). Austin: University of Texas Press.

Sheets, P. D. 1978. Artifacts. In R. J. Sharer (ed.), *The Prehistory of Chalchuapa, El Salvador,* vol. 2, pp. 1–131. University Monographs, University Museum. Philadelphia: University of Pennsylvania.

Willey, G. R., and P. H. Auerbach. 1965. Artifacts. In G. R. Willey et al., *Prehistoric Maya Settlements in the Belize Valley,* pp. 391–522. Peabody Museum, Archaeological and Ethnological Papers, 54. Cambridge, Mass.: Harvard University.

James F. Garber

G

Gualjoquito (Santa Bárbara, Honduras)

Occupying 8 hectares of the Río Ulúa's eastern bank in west central Honduras, Gualjoquito's forty-eight buildings represent the compact civic center of a non-Maya community; its sustaining populace gathered into four distinct residence clusters spatially separate from Gualjoquito itself. Although radiocarbon analyses and ceramic cross-dating indicate that local settlement spanned the Late Formative through Colonial periods, Gualjoquito supported only occasional squatters after the Late Classic. A Late Formative settlement there was destroyed and replaced by an Early Classic civic center.

Classic period growth and prosperity correlate most closely with florescence at Maya Copán, in probably the fifth and late seventh or early eighth centuries A.D. Although Gualjoquito's construction employs cobbles rather than masonry, structures in this non-Maya site resemble Copán's in use of space. In its final, eighth-century form and some fifth-century details, Gualjoquito's plan mimics Copán's core, especially in placing the main public plaza to the north, the ruler's enclosed residence to the south, and a ball court in between. Architectural and artifactual styles, especially in ceramics, join with developmental specifics to imply strong if fluctuating connections to outside authorities, especially Copán. Together, these data imply that local authority derived from control of a strategic crossroads linking the Ulúa and Jicatuyo rivers and an overland pass eastward to Lake Yojoa. When communication intensified between societies at the crossroads termini, Gualjoquito thrived. When such interaction declined, authority in this part of the Ulúa Valley shifted 13 kilometers south, to the agriculturally richer Tencoa Valley.

FURTHER READINGS

Ashmore, W. 1987. Cobble Crossroads: Gualjoquito Architecture and External Elite Ties. In E. J. Robinson (ed.), *Interaction on the Southeast Mesoamerican Frontier: Prehistoric and Historic Honduras and El Salvador,* pp. 28–48. BAR International Series, 327. Oxford.

Ashmore, W., E. M. Schortman, P. A. Urban, J. C. Benyo, J. M. Weeks, and S. M. Smith. 1987. Ancient Society in Santa Bárbara, Honduras. *National Geographic Research* 3:232–254.

Schortman, E. M., and P. A. Urban. 1995. Late Classic Society in the Río Ulúa Drainage, Honduras. *Journal of Field Archaeology* 22:439–457.

Schortman, E., P. Urban, W. Ashmore, and J. Benyo. 1986. Interregional Interaction in the SE Maya

G

Periphery: The Santa Bárbara Archaeological Project 1983–1984 Seasons. *Journal of Field Archaeology* 13:259–272.

Wendy Ashmore

Gualupita (Morelos, Mexico)

In this brickyard on the northern outskirts of Cuernavaca, Suzannah and George Vaillant in 1934 excavated four trenches in areas not destroyed by brickyard activities. Digging in 50-cm levels and without screening, they uncovered twelve burials and defined three major occupation periods. The distinctive pottery vessels and figurines associated with four Gualupita I burials represent the first important discovery of Early Formative period (c. 1100–900 B.C.) artifacts in Central Mexico; however, that temporal position was not recognized for several more decades. Gualupita I burial goods are virtually identical to those found at Tlatilco in the Valley of Mexico. Gualupita II ceramics are a regional variation of Late Formative (c. 400–200 B.C.) Valley of Mexico pottery, and Gualupita III is typical of the Morelos Late Postclassic period (c. 1350–1521 A.D.).

FURTHER READINGS

Vaillant, G. C., and S. Vaillant. 1934. Excavations at Gualupita. American Museum of Natural History, Anthropological Papers 35, no. 1. New York.

David C. Grove

SEE ALSO

Morelos Region

Gualupita Las Dalias (Puebla, Mexico)

Fortified town occupied during the Late to Terminal Formative period, situated in the eastern central part of the modern state of Puebla. It was occupied by groups bearing West Mexican culture. The settlement lies between two deep *barrancas,* one of which zigzags at the beginning of its course, forming two spaces that provide separate quarters of the community. At the site there remain seventeen structures on raised platforms; two of these were built at the edge of the eastern *barranca* in strategic positions, and one more was found at the convergence of the *barrancas,* where it could control access to and egress from the site.

FURTHER READINGS

García Cook, A., and F. Rodríguez. 1975. Excavaciones arqueológicas en "Gualupita Las Dalias, Puebla." *Comunicaciones* 12, F.A.I.C., Puebla, Mexico.

Angel García Cook

SEE ALSO

Puebla-Tlaxcala Region

Guasave and Related Sites (Sinaloa, Mexico)

Guasave and related sites pertain to the Huatabampo and Aztatlán cultures in northern Sinaloa and date from between A.D. 700 and perhaps A.D. 1400. Ekholm excavated a burial mound at Guasave and recovered a variety of ceramic, shell, metal, and stone artifacts. Both urn and extended burials were recovered. Ceramics include elaborate polychromes, incised and engraved types, polished Red-on-Buff, red, and plain wares, and grooved wares in the form of bowls, tripods, and jars. Also found were spindle whorls, smoking pipes, masks, clay plaques, figurines, whistles, beads, earplugs, and a cylinder stamp. Paint cloissoné occurred on gourd fragments. Stone bowls, a pipe, *manos, metates,* pestles, and axes were recovered, along with shell and copper artifacts; turquoise found was suggested to be from a Cerrillos, New Mexico, source.

The elaborate nature of the Guasave burial mound assemblage demonstrates that the Aztatlán phenomenon was more complex than initially envisioned. Ekholm recognized forty-four traits common to Guasave and Central Mexico, including depictions of the gods Xochipilli and Nanautzin. Mixteca-Puebla influence was so strong that Ekholm suggested that a migration of people must have occurred.

Isabel Kelly excavated at several localities near Chametla. The Chametla sequence dates from A.D. 250–1250, and its latter three phases are Aztatlán related. Chametla Aztatlán ceramics are characterized by Red-Rim Decorated, Black-on-Buff, and several polychromes. The El Taste-Mazatlán ceramic assemblage was dominated by a Red-Bordered type, polychromes, a highly polished buffware, and a textured type. Other Aztatlán-related materials include smoking pipes, large incised spindle whorls, and slab figurines.

Culiacán excavations by Kelly revealed a cultural sequence extending from A.D. 900 to 1530; its first three phases are Aztatlán related. Artifacts included Aztatlán-related ceramics, ceramic cylindrical stamps, figurines,

Guasave and related sites in western Mexico. Map courtesy of the author.

rattles, smoking pipes, and incised spindle whorls, horn and bone tools, shell jewelry, copper artifacts, *manos, metates,* and axes, and projectile points.

Other excavations in the highlands of Durango prompted a revision and better temporal definition of West Coast sequences. Excavations at Peñitas showed many stylistic similarities between Peñitas and Central Mexico, especially Cholula. Peñitas was occupied between c. A.D. 400 and 1300; ceramic types recovered had strong affinities to Amapa and Chametla. Culiacán- and Aztatlán-related materials were also present.

The 1959 Amapa excavations, the most extensive at any site on the West Coast, established a chronology for the site that parallels Chametla's. Occupation from A.D. 250 to 1550 is indicated by ceramic cross-dating; occupation from 250 B.C. to A.D. 1400 is suggested by obsidian hydration measurements. The middle phases appear Aztatlán related, and there are many specific resemblances between Amapa ceramics and Aztatlán-related materials from Chametla, Guasave, and Culiacán.

Numerous copper artifacts were also recovered. Amapa's graveyard and numerous mound groups with associated plazas were tested, and a fairly elaborate ball court was excavated. Two varying chronologies have been presented for Amapa.

North of Amapa, along the Nayarit and Sinaloa border, lies the Marismas Nacionales, a vast estuary-lagoon system where a multi-year research effort involved testing a number of sites, generally dating from A.D. 250–1400, and recovering materials from both burial and shell midden contexts. Most of the ceramics were typologically similar to those of Chametla or Amapa. Subsistence data indicate an intensive exploitation of the estuary and nearby marine environments. Radiocarbon determinations suggest a date of c. 1750 B.C. for Cerro El Calón, which consists of a heap of articulated bivalve shells nearly 30 meters high in the form of a truncated temple mound.

Other artifacts from the Marismas sites included smoking pipes, spindle whorls, and Mazapan figurine fragments. Pieces of copper were recovered, along with

G

ceramic whistles, balls, beads, pendants, obsidian blades and projectile points, *manos,* and *metates.* Some 250 human burials were excavated from earthen mounds, and the skeletons exhibited various forms of skull deformation and tooth mutilation. The several burial types included urn burials like those of Chametla and Guasave.

Recent excavations at Mochicahui, northern Sinaloa, produced ceramics with Guasave and Aztatlán polychromes. Ceramic cross-dating suggests dates for the materials of between A.D. 900 and 1350.

From the Guasave excavations, Ekholm also defined the Huatabampo complex, a tradition now dated between A.D. 700 and 1000. Vessel forms include unique composite shapes, and some figurines exhibit affinities with Chametla.

Clearly the Aztatlán phenomenon, defined by its four- to six-color polychromes, copper, and sometimes silver and gold, is an important element of the prehistory of the West Coast. However, there exists a great deal of ambiguity about its nature: Is it a culture, time horizon, complex, tradition, or ceramic style? Most recently, its late manifestation is viewed as part of a mercantile system linking West and Northwest Mexico with Central Mexico. Although ill defined, it was a dynamic, fairly long-lived, and widespread phenomenon that tied the cultures of West and Northwest Mexico together.

FURTHER READINGS

Alvarez Palma, A. M. 1990. Huatabampo. *Noroeste de Mexico* 9:9–93.

Bordaz, J. 1964. Pre-Columbian Ceramic Kilns at Penitas, a Post-Classic Site in Coastal Nayarit, Mexico. Dissertation, Columbia University.

Ekholm, G. F. 1942. *Excavations at Guasave, Sinaloa, Mexico.* Anthropological Papers of the American Museum of Natural History, vol. 38, part 2. New York.

Kelley, J. C. 1986. The Mobile Merchants of Molino. In F. J. Mathien and R. H. McGuire (eds.), *Ripples in the Chichimec Sea,* pp. 81–104. Carbondale and Edwardsville: Southern Illinois University Press.

Kelly, I. T. 1938. Excavation at Chametla, Sinaloa. *Ibero-Americana* 14:1–110.

———. 1945. Excavations at Culiacan, Sinaloa. *Ibero-Americana* 25.

Meighan, C. W. (ed.). 1976. *The Archaeology of Amapa, Nayarit.* Monumenta Archaeologica, 2. Los Angeles: Institute of Archaeology, University of California, Los Angeles.

Sauer, C., and D. Brand. 1932. *Aztatlán: Prehistoric Mexican Frontier on the Pacific Coast.* Ibero-Americana, 1. Berkeley: University of California Press.

Scott, S. D. 1985. Core Versus Marginal Mesoamerica: A Coastal West Mexican Perspective. In M. Foster and P. Weigand (eds.), *Archaeology of West and Northwest Mesoamerica,* pp. 181–191. Boulder: Westview Press.

Michael Foster

SEE ALSO

Aztatlan Complex; Northwestern Frontier; West Mexico

Guatemala Highlands Region
Environment

The highlands of Guatemala, loosely defined as an area above 800 meters elevation, is characterized by several climatic and environmental zones. The southern highlands of Guatemala, part of the rugged Sierra Madre volcanic range, parallel the Pacific coastal plain and are bordered on the south by active volcanoes. North of these volcanic peaks is an older igneous complex with extensive valleys covered with volcanic ash. Surface erosion has dissected these deposits to form deep gullies, or *barrancas.* The fertile volcanic soils of the valleys and basins within this area have supported large human populations for thousands of years; the largest valleys are those of Guatemala and Quezaltenango.

North of the continental rift marked by the Motagua Valley are the metamorphic northern highlands with elevations reaching 3,000 meters. To the west are three successive ranges: the Sierra de los Cuchumatanes of northwestern Guatemala, the Sierra de Chuacús in central Guatemala, and the Sierra de las Minas extending eastward to the Caribbean.

In the Alta Verapaz region the metamorphic mountains yield to limestone formations with karst topography. Much of the northern highlands are poor for agriculture. Farther north, good soils, rainfall, and cool temperatures make the basins of the Alta Verapaz a prime area for present-day coffee cultivation. Stretching in a great arc along the western and southern flank of the lowlands, the foothills of the cordillera mark the transition to a region of steep slopes and broken terrain.

The cool interior region, called *Los Altos,* consists of fertile valleys and pine/oak-covered plateaus enclosed by rugged mountain chains. To the north and south are cypress-covered subtropical foothills *(tierra templada).* Most of the region has been deforested, although stands

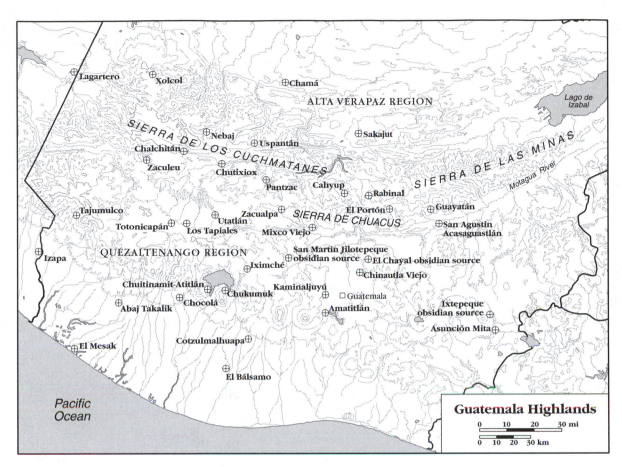

Guatemala Highlands. Map design by Mapping Specialists Limited, Madison, Wisconsin.

of oak, laurel, sweetgum, dogwood, and pine are still found in remote areas and at higher elevations. The original flora of the highlands appears to have been a mixed evergreen and deciduous forest. The area is largely drained by tributaries of the Río Usumacinta, which flow into the southern lowlands and to the Gulf of Campeche. The main tributary of the Río Usumacinta, the Río Chixoy, drains most of the central portion of the northern highlands. The eastern slope of the highlands is emptied by the Motagua and Polochic drainage, which flows to the lowlands of the Caribbean coast.

The alternation of wet and dry seasons dominates weather patterns and the farming cycle throughout the area. The rainy season extends from May through October or November. During the dry season, beginning in November or December, there is little or no rain, and farmers turn to clearing new fields. By April the vegetation is dry.

The climate of the southern highlands is temperate with mean annual temperatures between 15° and 25° C. Above the 3,000-meter level much cooler temperatures

prevail, with frequent frosts and occasional snow accumulations. Annual rainfall totals average 2,000 to 3,000 mm annually in most areas. Rainfall is much less in areas sheltered from the prevailing easterly trade winds, such as the interior of the Río Motagua valley.

The climate of the northern highlands ranges from annual means below 15° C in the *tierra fria* of the Altos Cuchumatanes to the tropical *tierra caliente* typical of the lowlands. Most of the populated valleys are in *tierra templada* environments. Rainfall generally follows the same pattern as in the southern highlands, but the length of the wet season tends to increase toward the north. On the northern fringes of the highlands, in Alta Verapaz and Chiapas, rainfall totals average over 3,000 mm per year.

Settlement History and Cultural Processes

Highland Guatemala has a long record of human settlement, extending from Lithic through Late Postclassic or Protohistoric times. The archaeological record reflects a pattern of cultural development consistent with the broad evolutionary features outlined for the region as a whole.

Guatemala Highlands Region   307

G

There has been little systematic archaeological research in the Guatemala Highlands because of the physical isolation and inaccessibility of many parts of the region, and the greater potential for investigation offered by other areas of Mesoamerica. Nonetheless, several significant archaeological programs have been conducted in the Guatemala Highlands. The most important are excavations at Kaminaljuyú by the Carnegie Institution of Washington and by Pennsylvania State University. Other programs include the French Archaeological Mission at Mixco Viejo and the Río Chixoy valley, the Spanish Archaeological Mission in the Totonicapán and Quezaltenango region, the State University of New York at Albany Quiché Project, the United Fruit Company excavations at Zaculeu, and the University Museum University of Pennsylvania Verapaz Archaeological Project in the northern highlands.

The Lithic stage (ending c. 6000 B.C.) began with the initial human entry into the Guatemala Highlands, possibly as early as 15,000 B.C., and lasted roughly until 6000 B.C. This period was characterized by small nomadic hunting and gathering groups who relied on seasonal growth cycles of food plants and availability of food animals as the first step toward the establishment of permanent villages and the domestication of certain food plants and animal species.

Lithic occupations are indicated by a Clovis-like obsidian point found near San Rafael, west of Guatemala City, and by an andesite flake complex from Los Tapiales near Totonicapán, probably occupied around 9000 B.C. by hunters using fluted points.

The Archaic stage (c. 6000–2000 B.C.) was marked by the development of settled communities along the Pacific coast and the domestication of such food plants as maize, beans, squash, avocado, chile peppers, pumpkin, and tomato, which led to the establishment of permanent village life. Distinctive obsidian tools at the El Chayal obsidian source probably represent Archaic hunting groups in the highlands. Recent research in the Quiché Basin of the southern highlands has identified numerous preceramic sites, marked by basalt implements, dating to a span from about 11,000 to 1200 B.C.

Highland Guatemala underwent a profound cultural transformation during the Preclassic or Formative (c. 2000 B.C.–A.D. 250) period. The inhabitants developed sophisticated religious and economic institutions, hereditary leadership, and chiefdoms as a basic cultural pattern.

The origins of village life in the central and eastern highlands is evident by 1500 B.C., when a more stratified society emerged from the simple, spatially confined village style of life. This change was paralleled by an intensification of the agricultural subsistence base and rapid population growth. By the Middle Formative, probable Olmec enclaves were established along the Pacific coastal plain, corresponding to the innovation of monumental sculpture and architecture and other evidence of the origins of complex social, political, and economic systems. Kaminaljuyú and other communities grew to great size. The Late Formative was marked by Izapan-style sculptured stone monuments, often with hieroglyphic texts and dates, as well as the probable development of dynastic rule. Izapan art styles and symbols formed a major component of the emerging Maya tradition. Many southern sites peaked in size and population during the Late Formative/Protoclassic.

The Classic period (c. A.D. 250–900) saw the emergence of civilization with an increasingly complex political organization, the state, with powerful sanctions to support political authority. Although the zenith of the Classic period in the Maya area is closely associated architecturally and artistically with the great lowland settlements, a number of Classic settlements also developed in the Guatemala Highlands. The most important of these was the settlement of Kaminaljuyú. During the Early Classic there was a Teotihuacán "colony" at Kaminaljuyú with economic and political ties to the lowlands. There evolved a highly organized and sophisticated society, the theocratic orientation of which is indicated by temple mounds located around ceremonial plazas to form acropolis-like complexes.

Classic period settlements in the highlands were situated on open valley floors or hillslopes in close proximity to water resources. They were essentially undefended but strongly nucleated ceremonial centers. Large populations were supported in the vicinity of these centers by an intensive agricultural base that utilized as farm land areas peripheral to the ceremonial complex, in which terracing and irrigation played a major role. Direct Teotihuacán influence in southern Mesoamerica diminished by A.D. 600 with the local development of a poorly understood period of regionalization. The florescence of Classic Maya civilization evidently did not include central and eastern highland societies. Communities in these areas did not produce the monumental architecture, sculpture, and hieroglyphic inscriptions associated with lowland Classic centers. The nature of the relationship between the Maya Highlands and Lowlands during the Classic period remains to be resolved.

The Postclassic period (c. A.D. 900–1500) was marked by the development of some of the most complex and powerful states in the New World prior to European colonization. The settlement pattern during the Early Postclassic period (c. A.D. 900–1250) indicates a shift from open valley sites to defensive centers constructed on hilltops or promontories surrounded by ravines. The tendency toward locational change was precipitated by internal conflict and endemic warfare, possibly resulting from population pressure. According to Robert Carmack, the most significant event of the Postclassic period in highland Guatemala was the arrival around A.D. 1250 of mexicanized Putún Maya warrior groups from the Gulf Coast lowlands who established themselves in Yucatán from their capital at Chichén Itzá. The sites of Chalchitán near the headwaters of the Río Chixoy and Chuitinamit-Atitlán on the south shore of Lake Atitlán exhibit architectural parallels with Chichén Itzá.

The Late Postclassic period (c. A.D. 1250–1525) has been well investigated. Numerous documents in indigenous languages agree on the importance of a series of highland Maya groups and their major centers, many of which are described with considerable detail in the documents. Identified are many powerful regional capitals and secondary centers, most of which were built in defensive positions. Warfare was endemic throughout the region, and several groups, notably the Quiché and Cakchiquel, extended their influence into the Pacific coastal plain to gain control over cacao and other resources.

The major highland centers included Mixco Viejo and Chinautla Viejo (Pokomam), Chuitinamit-Atitlán (Tzutujil), Utatlán (Quiché), Zaculeu (Mam), and Iximché (Cakchiquel). Major excavations have been undertaken at Zaculeu, Mixco Viejo, Iximché, and Utatlán, as well as at secondary centers such as Zacualpa and Chisalin.

In the closing centuries of the pre-Hispanic period a number of highland groups competed for political hegemony in the Guatemala Highlands. At the western border of the highlands were the Kanjobal, Jacalteca, and Chuj, whose role in regional culture history is obscure. The Mam, Ixil, and Aguacateca languages diverged by 1500 B.C. and apparently changed least from Proto-Maya of all the Mayan languages. The Mam dominated much of the western highlands from their capital at Zaculeu until, just before the Conquest, they came under heavy pressure from the Quiché. Quiché, Cakchiquel, and Tzutujil diverged in the central highlands as separate languages about A.D. 1000, and by the early sixteenth century these groups had developed into antagonistic independent states. The arrival of the Spaniards interrupted the Quiché rise to dominance. To the east were the Kekchí and Uspanteca in the north and the Pokom in the east. In the foothills along the southeastern lowlands were the Cholan Chortí. Pokom speakers lived to the east and south along the frontier of the Maya area. Beyond the Pokom were non-Mesoamerican groups such as the Lenca, Jicaque, and Xinca.

The ethnohistorical information available for the Postclassic period of highland Guatemala is especially rich with indigenous texts, including the *Popol Vuh, Annals of the Cakchiquels,* and *Título Totonicapán.* These documents outline the conquest of highland areas by outsiders who claimed descent from Tollan (possibly Chichén Itzá). The *Popol Vuh* relates how the Quiché traveled to their former homeland to gain authority and symbols of their legitimate right to rule in the highlands. The southern Maya area was affected by the same expansion of mexicanized Maya groups that dominated the Yucatán Peninsula throughout the Postclassic.

Until further archaeological and ethnohistorical investigations are conducted, an understanding of the protohistoric experience of the region and its peoples must be tentatively derived from an extrapolation of the work of Robert Carmack in the Quiché area. It should be noted that some scholars disagree with what they view as Carmack's "literal interpretation" of the documentary sources and argue that, contrary to the ethnohistorical account of Toltec invasion from the north, the archaeological record of the Quiché Basin shows strong continuity from Classic to Postclassic times.

Important Resources

Archaeological research in the Maya Lowlands has disclosed a variety of resources that originated in the highlands. Jade has been identified from the Manzanel-Acasaguastlán-Guaytan area of eastern Guatemala. The ancient Maya quarried obsidian (volcanic glass) at several locations, including El Chayal and San Martín Jilotepeque on the upper flanks of the Motagua Valley, and Ixtepeque, about 85 kilometers to the southeast. Localized resources such as hallucinogenic mushrooms are known to grow in the southern part of the Quiché Valley, and salt beds are found along the middle Río Chixoy at Sacapulas and near Salinas de los Nueve Cerros. Polished celts of diorite and grinding stones of basalt and other igneous stone common throughout the lowlands probably originated in the volcanic areas of the highlands. Volcanic ash and mica for temper and clay for pottery-

G

making have a wide distribution. Hematite and cinnabar, used in the manufacture of red paint and pottery, are rare in the lowlands but common in the highlands. Iron pyrite used in the manufacture of mosaic mirrors, and copper and some gold for ornaments and utensils, are found in the highlands. The prized feathers of the quetzal bird were obtained in the cloud forests of the Cuchumatanes Mountains in Huehuetenango and the Sierra de las Minas of Alta Verapaz.

Summary

The chronology of the Guatemala Highlands, with characteristic ceramics, is outlined below. Table 1 gives approximate dating for the two major sequences.

Late Postclassic: Establishment of regional conquest states based on hilltop settlements; Chinautla Polychrome and White-on-Red pottery

Early Postclassic: Arrival of mexicanized warrior-groups who extend influence throughout region; commerce in glazed effigy pottery, Tohil Plumbate; Tile Ware pottery

Late Classic: Teotihuacán influence diminishes as groups move into highlands from the Gulf Coast of Mexico; valley sites are abandoned for slope and hilltop locations; Red-on-Cream, Tiquisate, and San Juan Plumbate pottery

Early Classic: Mexicanization of Kaminaljuyú reflects beginnings of western Mesoamerican influence from Kaminaljuyú into lowlands; Thin Orange and Fine Polished Black pottery

Late Formative: Izapa-style sculptured stone monuments and artifacts with long count dates appear along the Pacific slope of Guatemala; Usulutan pottery

Middle Formative: Olmec style influences from Chiapas and Pacific coastal Mexico into highlands; beginning of monumental architecture and sculpture; Streaky Gray-brown pottery

Early Formative: Early sedentism along the Pacific coast

Archaic: Development of settled communities along the Pacific and Caribbean coasts; plant and animal domestication leads to establishment of permanent village life

Lithic: Small hunting and gathering bands preceded the establishment of permanent villages and the domestication of food plants and animals

TABLE 1. REGIONAL CHRONOLOGY.

Southern Highlands: Kaminaljuyú Sequence

Chinautla	c. A.D. 1200–1500	Late Postclassic
Ayampuc	c. A.D. 1000–1200	Early Postclassic
Pamplona	c. A.D. 800–1000	Late Late Classic
Amatle 2	c. A.D. 600–800	Early Late Classic
Amatle 1/ Esperanza	c. A.D. 400–600	Middle Classic
Aurora	c. A.D. 200–400	Early Classic
Arenal	c. A.D. 0–200	Late Terminal Formative
Verbena	c. 0 B.C.–A.D. 200	Early Terminal Formative
Providencia	c. 500–200 B.C.	Late Formative
Las Charcas	c. 1000–500 B.C.	Middle Formative
Arevalo	c. 2500–1000 B.C.	Early Formative

Northern Highlands: Verapaz Sequence

Chican	c. A.D. 1250–1540	Late Postclassic
Samac	c. A.D. 1000–1250	Early Postclassic
Coban 2	c. A.D. 550–1000	Late Classic
Coban 1	c. A.D. 300–550	Early Classic
Quej	c. A.D. 0–300	Terminal Formative
Uc	c. 200–0 B.C.	Late Formative
Tol	c. 500–200 B.C.	Middle/Late Formative transition
Max	c. 800–500 B.C.	Middle Formative
Xox	c. 1200–800 B.C.	Early Formative

FURTHER READINGS

Arnauld, M.-C. 1986. *Archéologie de l'Habitat en Alta Verapaz (Guatemala)*. Mexico City: Centre d'Études Mexicaines et Centraméricaines.

Brown, K. L. 1980. A Brief Report on Paleoindian-Archaic Occupation in the Quiché Basin. *American Antiquity* 45:313–324.

Carmack, R. M. 1973. *Quichean Civilization: The Ethnohistoric, Ethnographic, and Archaeological Sources*. Berkeley: University of California Press.

———. 1981. *The Quiché Mayas of Utatlan: The Evolution of a Highland Guatemala Kingdom.* Norman: University of Oklahoma Press.

Fox, J. W. 1978. *Quiché Conquest: Centralism and Regionalism in Highland Guatemalan State Development.* Albuquerque: University of New Mexico Press.

———. 1987. *Maya Postclassic State Formation: Segmentary Lineage Migration in Advancing Frontiers.* Cambridge: Cambridge University Press.

Sanders, W. T., and J. W. Michels. 1977. *Teotihuacán and Kaminaljuyú: A Study in Prehistoric Culture Contact.* University Park: Pennsylvania State University Press.

Sharer, R. J., and D. W. Sedat. 1987. *Archaeological Investigations in the Northern Maya Highlands, Guatemala: Interaction and Development of Maya Civilization.* University Museum, University of Pennsylvania, Monograph 59. Philadelphia.

Smith, A. Ledyard. 1955. *Archaeological Reconnaissance in Central Guatemala.* Carnegie Institution of Washington, Publication 608. Washington, D.C.

Wallace, D.T., and R. M. Carmack (eds.). 1977. *Archaeology and Ethnohistory of the Central Quiché.* Institute for Mesoamerican Studies, State University of New York, Publication 1. Albany.

Wauchope, R. 1975. *Zacualpa, El Quiché, Guatemala: An Ancient Provincial Center of the Highland Maya.* Middle American Research Institute, Tulane University, Publication 39. New Orleans.

Weeks, J. M. 1983. *Chisalin: A Late Postclassic Maya Settlement in Highland Guatemala.* British Archaeological Reports, International Series, 169. Oxford.

Woodbury, R. B., and A. S. Trik. 1953. *The Ruins of Zaculeu, Guatemala.* 2 vols. New York: United Fruit Company.

John M. Weeks

SEE ALSO

Chiapas Interior Plateau; Maya Lowlands: South

Guayabo de Turrialba (Cartago, Costa Rica)

This site's principal occupation occurred between A.D. 700 and 1300, but ceramic evidence suggests initial occupation as early as 1000 B.C. Extending over a broad, irregular ridge for about 747 hectares, Guayabo's central portion covers about 32 hectares. More than fifty major architectural features have been detected, including forty-four mounds (mostly circular), two plazas, a large paved ceremonial walkway (*calzada*), and a walled rectangular enclosure. Among these are numerous smaller *calzadas*, bridges, and paved ramps. A palisade may have surrounded the site.

Most of the mounds once supported perishable houses made of logs, cane, and thatch. Mounds were constructed of superimposed circular levels consisting of low retaining walls of river cobbles filled with compacted earth. Mound 1 (4.5 meters high, c. 28 meters across) and two rectangular mounds form an impressive entrance to the site. An adjacent plaza measures c. 900 square meters. The site's hydraulic system consists of three aqueducts, four dams, a reservoir, bridges, and three vertical drainage pits.

Petroglyphs at Guayabo are carved in low relief on irregular boulders; some represent semirealistic human or animal figures, most commonly felines and saurians (lizards or crocodiles). Turrialba Bichrome pottery was found in abundance at Guayabo and appears to have been a local ware.

FURTHER READINGS

Fonseca Zamora, O. M. 1981. Guayabo de Turrialba and Its Significance. In *Between Continents/Between Seas: Precolumbian Art of Costa Rica.* New York: Harry N. Abrams.

Fonseca Zamora, O. M., and V. Acuña C. 1986. Los petroglifos de Guayabo de Turrialba y su contexto. In F. W. Lange and L. Norr (eds.), *Prehistoric Settlement Patterns in Costa Rica* (*Journal of the Steward Anthropological Society* 14.1–2), pp. 237–254.

Hurtado de Mendoza, L., and A. C. Arias. 1986. Cerámica y patrones de asentamiento en la región de Guayabo de Turrialba. In F. W. Lange and L. Norr (eds.), *Prehistoric Settlement Patterns in Costa Rica* (*Journal of the Steward Anthropological Society* 14.1–2), pp. 281–322.

John Hoopes

SEE ALSO

Intermediate Area: Overview

Guerrero Region

The Mexican state of Guerrero is a recent geopolitical unit, created in 1843. There is no correlation between the modern territory and its pre-Hispanic counterpart. On all frontiers of the modern state, there are linguistic affinities with bordering states: for example, Tarascan in the Tierra

G

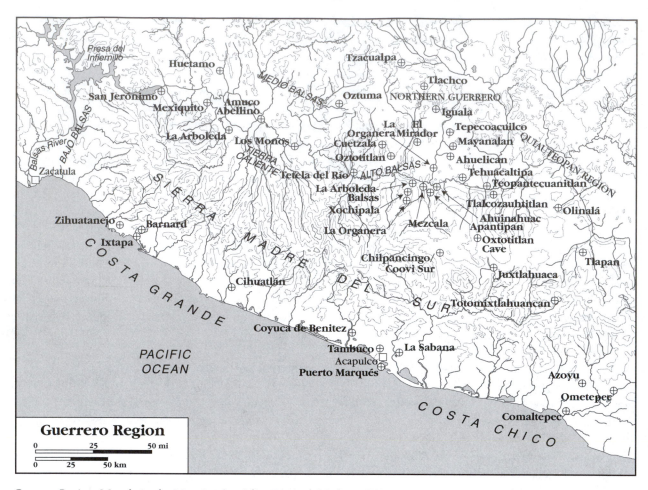

Guerrero Region. Map design by Mapping Specialists Limited, Madison, Wisconsin.

Caliente's western border with Michoacan, Matlazinca at the northern limits of Guerrero, Mixtec at the southeastern limits of Guerrero and the state of Oaxaca. Despite this arbitrariness, pre-Hispanic Guerrero can be defined as one of the regions pertaining to the Mesoamerican sphere or culture area, on both developmental and historical grounds.

Indeed, from an evolutionary standpoint, pre-Hispanic Guerrero shares the defining cultural characteristics of Mesoamerica: village life based on the production of maize, squash, and beans, with its correlated lithic and ceramic technology; active participation in complex interaction networks, implying goods, persons, and ideas, at the regional and interregional levels—networks that served as the integrating mechanism for the regions defining Mesoamerica; socio-political complexity, as expressed by architectural and artifactual diversity, and hierarchy, at least at some point in its history; and, finally, expression of a shared thought system. Guerrero did not develop all these characteristics to the extent that they were developed in

the Basin of Mexico or the Maya Lowlands, for example, but, whether owing to internal development and/or to integration in more complex socio-political units, it shares these with Mesoamerica.

For at least the last 5,000 years, Guerrero was occupied by various human groups who can be individually identified by their cultural practices. Archaeologically, this implies the development of generally distinct architectural and artifactual styles; ethnohistorically, it implies distinct linguistic groups. Several authors have proposed archaeological subdivisions for pre-Columbian Guerrero, based on artifactual characteristics and distributions. I propose the archaeological regions and subregions shown in Table 1. Given our uneven knowledge of pre-Hispanic Guerrero at this juncture, and the fact that the spatial limits of the cultural subregions have fluctuated through time, this classification is tentative and primarily geographical.

Throughout the pre-Hispanic history of Guerrero, these subregions remained in close contact with one

TABLE 1. ARCHAEOLOGICAL REGIONS AND SUBREGIONS OF GUERRERO, MEXICO.

Number of Region	Name of Region	Subregions	Geographical Location
1	*Northern Guerrero*	a) Taxco b) Teloloapan c) Iguala d) Tlaxmalac e) Tepecoacuilco	An area covering the northern part of Guerrero. Mountains and valleys of the upper portions of the Cocula, Tepecoacuilco, and Amacuzac Rivers.
2	*Alto Balsas or Mezcala*	a) Mezcala-Balsas b) Amacuzac c) Xochipala d) Cocula	Along the Alto Balsas River bordering Mayanalan to the north, Xochipala to the south, and Tlalcozoutitlan and Balsas to the east and west respectively.
3	*Medio Balsas or Mezcala*	a) Amuco b) Arcelia c) Huétamo	Along the Media Balsas River, bordering to Huétamo to the north, Placeres del Oro to the south, Balsas to the east and the confluence of the Temazcaltepec and the Balsas Rivers to the west.
4	*Bajo Balsas*	a) Infiernillo	Lower portion and estuary of the Balsas River. Southwestern border of Guerrero with Michoacan.
5	*Sierra Madre del Sur*	a) Western SMS b) Eastern SMS: La Montaña	Chain of mountain south of the Balsas River drainage system and north of the Pacific coast.
6	*Pacific Coast*	a) Costa Grande b) Costa Chica	a) From Zacatula to Acapulco. b) From Acapulco to the Oaxaca border.

Regions 1 and 2 correspond more or less to the Taxco-Zumpango region of the 1948 Mesa Redonda El Occidente de México and to Covarrubias's Mezcala region (1948). Actually, Lister subdivides the region into three subregions: a) Teloloapan, b) Tepecoacuilco, and c) Mezcala. In Postclassic times, one finds a certain homogeneity in material culture over the area, but in earlier times, it is not the case.

another, but at no point is there any sign of economic or political centralization of the kind seen in the neighboring Basin of Mexico, Michoacan, or Oaxaca areas. Although there is no evidence for the internal development of state-level organization in any one of these subregions, at sites like Teopantecuanitlán (Middle Formative period) or La Organera–Xochipala (Classic period), site hierarchies involving urban agglomerations in the Late Formative and Classic Periods show distinct signs of complex sociopolitical developments. Parts of Guerrero were nevertheless involved in state-level formation, at least in Postclassic times; ethnohistorical evidence conclusively shows the penetration into this region of the Mexica Aztecs and of the Tarascans.

Pre-Hispanic Guerrero had constant contacts with neighboring and even distant regions. The presence of remains related to the great stylistic traditions of Meso-america—Olmec, Teotihuacán, Toltec, Aztec, and Tarascan—points to active participation of the local cultures in the Mesoamerican sphere of economic, social, and ideological interactions. Guerrero is also known to have produced and exported raw materials, finished goods, and skills: the Mezcala art style, copper, cacao, varnished goods, conch shell, and perhaps jade, to name a few. The value of the Mezcala lapidary tradition on the modern art market in pre-Hispanic antiquities and the very well organized tradition of looting and faking are partly responsible for its renown. The sad consequence of this is that, until quite recently, Guerrero had produced evidence of activities and art styles that could not be related to specific cultural contexts or societies, because so many "Guerrero" materials had no archaeological context. This situation is slowly changing; it is now possible to present and discuss, in a more structured framework, the characteristics and

G

great moments of Guerrero's pre-Hispanic history, to understand its internal development, and to show the dynamics of its relations with the rest of Mesoamerica.

Our knowledge of pre-Hispanic Guerrero results from the past 100 years of investigations—archaeological, ethnographic, and ethnohistorical. Some parts of the state have received much more systematic attention than others, which remain *terra incognita* from an archaeological point of view. Thus, it is difficult to present an adequate overview of its pre-Hispanic history, and one must focus on the better-known areas and sites.

Environment

Guerrero, in southwestern Mexico, is dominated by mountains. Even at the Pacific coast, the mountains leave barely enough space for a narrow stretch of renowned beaches, such as Acapulco and Zihuatanejo. From north to south, Guerrero encompasses the following physiographic features: the Neovolcanic Axis, the Río Balsas Depression, the Sierra Madre del Sur, and the Pacific coast.

The southern flank of the Neovolcanic Axis dominates northern Guerrero; it is of recent geologic age and volcanism is still active, with large expanses of lava covering mountaintops and slopes. More ancient geologic formations show up at the surface of eroded places: metamorphic rocks of the Paleozoic, limestone from the Cretaceous, and clastic rocks of the Tertiary era. Through these young mountains, with altitudes ranging between 1,000 and 2,000 meters, rivers have carved deep gorges as they drain into the Río Balsas. Agriculture is practiced wherever possible, on mountain slopes and in the infrequent narrow valleys and terraces. Minerals and rocks have been and are exploited with more success; Taxco and Iguala's marketplaces are locally and internationally renowned for the production of gold, silver, and many other mineral products.

The Río Balsas is one of the most important rivers in Mexico. With its sources in the Neovolcanic Axis and in the Sierra Madre del Sur, this hydrographic system drains a basin of 105,900 square kilometers. It runs across a geosyncline oriented east to west, thus creating a deep depression between the Neovolcanic Axis and the Sierra Madre del Sur. The river crosses strikingly varied regions and, apart from rare exceptions like the Middle Balsas River Basin, very few flat alluvial surfaces. At a mean altitude of 500 meters, the Río Balsas receives generally less than 800 mm of rain yearly, concentrated during the rainy season (June–October); thus, its tributaries are seasonal and torrential. Semiarid vegetation includes grasses, cacti and shrubs, and a few epiphytic trees. Here again, land for cultivation is a luxury; corn is grown on the narrow river terraces and slopes of the adjacent mountains. Nahuatl speakers have been known to live in the Alto and Medio Balsas since the twelfth century A.D.

The Sierra Madre del Sur is part of a mountain range, with a west–east orientation, which originates in southern Mexico and extends toward the Greater Antilles through northern Central America. It constitutes the oldest geological formation and the most complex physiographic region of Mesoamerica. Its basement is formed of metamorphic rocks and, in a few instances, Tertiary lava covering the metamorphic rocks. The mean altitude varies between 1,000 and 2,000 meters, with a landscape of abrupt slopes and tapered ridges. The vegetation cover evidences a slightly less arid climate as one moves south: below 2,000 meters, one finds juniper, copal, and palms together with cacti and shrubs. Once more, the topographic and climatic conditions leave little space for agriculture, which is mostly practiced on mountain slopes. The remaining forest resources are exploited, as are metals (gold) and rocks (quartz, serpentine). Nahuatl, Tlapanec, and Mixtec groups are settled in the *La Montaña* eastern portion of the Sierra Madre del Sur.

At the end of our north-south journey across Guerrero, we find a narrow coastal plain between the Sierra Madre del Sur and the Pacific Ocean (Region 6). In this subtropical semiarid environment, the alluvial soils on the coastal plain are very fertile, despite a very short growing season and constant threat of drought. Today the main crops are copra and coconut from two species of palm, and coffee, which has replaced the cacao grown there in pre-Hispanic times. Other resources include marine and mangrove products. Today, maritime activities as well as the tourism industry are highly developed, and Acapulco and Zihuatanejo have been known as harbors since the sixteenth century.

In terms of the resources available, the various regions provide mountain forest products (wood), rocks and minerals (gold and copper; serpentine and other metamorphic rocks, quartz and other semiprecious stones like amethyst and possibly jade; salt) and river and sea products (fish, mollusks, and shellfish; conch and other shell). Ecological conditions do not favor agriculture; the scarcity of agricultural land is and probably has always been a constant source of conflict among populations of Guerrero. Still, the hot, dry climate allowed the culture of cotton and cacao in pre-Hispanic times, making the region an important source of tribute for the Aztec Empire.

The environment also shaped human patterns of mobility and sedentism. Guerrero's mountainous configuration created a situation of isolation, while the internal dendritic network of the Balsas drainage system provided a central northeast–southwest circulation axis, with north–south circulation provided by the drainages of Balsas affluents.

Settlement History and Cultural Processes
Early Occupation

Guerrero was once thought to be a good candidate for very early traces of incipient agriculture, but in spite of early evidence—for example, the Puerto Marqués shell midden (c. 3000 B.C.) and the occurrence there of Pox pottery, among the oldest in Mesoamerica—the first well-documented signs of human settlement show up in Guerrero around 1500 B.C. (Table 2).

Depending on the chronology in use, this time corresponds to either the Early to Middle Formative, the Initial Ceramic Period, or the Olmec Horizon. Most regions of Guerrero were occupied by groups practicing agriculture, living in hamlets or villages, and using pottery. At this early stage, Guerrero's ceramic traditions show marked cultural individualism and the influence of contacts with other regions. For example, although the inhabitants of the Tierra Caliente produced ceramics stylistically distinct from those of the Mezcala region or of the Costa Grande, all three areas shared common stylistic elements characteristic of a representational system found throughout Mesoamerica—the Olmec art style.

For nearly a millenium, the Olmec art style was found in all of Guerrero's cultural regions except the Lower Balsas. The style is expressed in Guerrero by many shapes and forms, both stationary (monumental architecture, sculptures, stelae, and mural paintings) and portable (pottery, figurines, and other ornaments). In most of Guerrero's regions, however, Olmec art represents only a minority of all cultural artifacts, and thus may be considered intrusive into a local tradition.

Guerrero played a precocious role in Olmec culture. Chronologically, Olmec-style objects appear very early in some regions of Guerrero—in fact, earlier than in the lowlands of Veracruz-Tabasco, regarded as the source of the Olmec representational system. Two Olmec-style figurines found in a residential zone at the Amuco Abelino site in Guerrero's Tierra Caliente have radiocarbon dates ranging between 1530 B.C. ± 230 and 1220 B.C. ± 110.

The site of Teopantecuanitlán, in the Mezcala region, was saved from looters in the early 1980s by the archaeologist Guadalupe Martínez Donjuán. With the help of Christine Niederberger and Rosa Reyna Robles, Martínez Donjuán uncovered traces of a complex civic-religious center, marked by the presence of Olmec style, associated with residential zones, and an elaborate system of irrigation canals. According to Martínez Donjuán, Teopantecuanitlán was first occupied during the Early Formative (1423 B.C. ± 112–1,393 B.C. ± 126) and was continually occupied up to the Spanish conquest. The Olmec art style is represented both during the first two construction stages of the ceremonial center, which date to between 1400 and 800 B.C., and to contemporary occupation in the residential zone.

From a social standpoint, the discovery of Teopantecuanitlán has revealed indisputable social complexity in which the Olmec art style played an important role; it is the only such complex site in Olmec Horizon Guerrero. Before Teopantecuanitlan was uncovered, Guerrero's Olmec Horizon sites were known to display only egalitarian social organization. Villages such as Amuco Abelino in the Tierra Caliente region and Ahuelican in the Mezcala-Balsas region, shell mounds in the Costa Grande, workshops in La Arboleda in Tierra Caliente, and a few other sites along the Río Balsas in the Mezcala region all suggested non-hierarchical social organization. The cultural contexts of other sites, such as the caves of Oxtotitlan and Juxtlahuaca with their elaborate mural paintings, and the burial complexes of Xochipala and Coovi Sur, remain to be investigated. In the future they may provide evidence of emergent social complexity and differentiation.

The presence of an Olmec system of representation in pre-Hispanic Guerrero can be seen as both a part and a consequence of the exchange system that characterized Mesoamerica during the Middle Formative (1200–800 B.C.). The various regions of Guerrero would have supplied this exchange network system with jade and other hard stones, either as raw material or as small objects from the developing lapidary tradition of the Mezcala region. Cotton, cacao, and other similarly valued products grown in the hot lands of Guerrero are other possible exchange items, together with shells and related maritime products from the Pacific coast. Finally, obsidian, widely used in the production of tools in a country that never used metal for that purpose, could have traveled from Michoacan through Guerrero, via the Río Balsas, toward Oaxaca and Veracruz-Tabasco, where it has been found. These economic patterns and the distribution of Olmec-style artifacts in

TABLE 2. CHRONOLOGICAL SEQUENCES IN PRE-HISPANIC GUERRERO.

Time	North Guerrero	Mezcala-Balsas	Alto Balsas Teopan-Tecuanitlan	Xochipala	Medio Balsas	Bajo Balsas	Costa Grande	Chronological Periods
1520								
1400		3 Arroyos		Tinaco		El Poche		Late
1300								Postclassic
1200			Amacuzac-					
1100			Balsas					Early
1000		Ixpan Moto		*Magueyitos		El Remanse		Postclassic
900								
800						O		
700				Tepenacaxtla		J		
600						O		Classic
500						De	Yax/*Xlop	
400				Gogongoro		Agua	Acapulco 2	
300			El Caserio					
200				Xaltipan		IN		
100						F		Proto
0		*Trinchera			Guacamole 2	I	Fal/Etna	Classic
−100				Campanario		ER		
−200						N		
−300		*Ahuinahuac				I		Late
−400				Chichitlantepec		L		Preclassic
−500					Guacamole 1	LO	*Et/Slup	
−600			*3				Acapulco 1	
−700								Middle
−800		Ahuelican	*2	*Tejas			Rin	Preclassic
−900	Tecolotla				Sesame 3			
−1000			(Lomerios)					
−1100	Atopula				*Sesame 2		Tom	Early
−1200	Cacahuananche							Preclassic
−1300			*1		*Sesame 1			
−1400								
−1800							Uala	
−2300							*Pox	Initial Ceramic

Sources of data: North Guerrero (Henderson 1979); Mezcala Balsas (Paradis 1992, 1995; Paradis & Bélanger 1986); Teopantecuanit-lan (Martínez Donjuán 1986; Niederberger 1986); Xochipala (Schmidt Shoenberg 1986); Medio Balsas (Paradis 1978, 1981); Bajo Balsas (Cabrera Castro 1986); Costa Grande (Ekholm 1948; Brush E. 1968; Brush C. F. 1969).
*phases established on the basis of uncorrected radiocarbon dates

pre-Hispanic Guerrero indicate two communication routes: the Río Balsas and its tributary, the Amacuzac, and the Pacific coast.

The exchange and presence of Olmec-style artifacts in Guerrero undoubtedly represented not only the effects of Olmec ideological hegemony but carried social implications as well. From a political standpoint, the incipient cultural regions of Mesoamerica developed relations of power among themselves. According to Flannery's model, Veracruz-Tabasco, which some researchers maintain to be the origin of the Olmec art style, was a precursor to the establishment of social complexity in Mesoamerica. This anteriority gave Veracruz-Tabasco an edge and, for a time at least, gave it the balance of power in its relations with the other Mesoamerican regions. These relations seem to have been strongest with regions or sites that also showed incipient social complexity, and here Olmec symbolism is the most pronounced: San José Mogote in the Valley of Oaxaca, Tlatilco in the Basin of Mexico, Chalcatzingo in Morelos, and Teopantecuanitlán in Guerrero.

In sum, sedentary occupation of Guerrero started as early as 1400 B.C. with agricultural hamlets and villages, settled by cultural groups of unknown ethnic affiliation who developed their own local ceramic tradition and culture, in most of Guerrero's regions. Teopantecuanitlán, an elaborate civic-religious center situated at the eastern border of the Mezcala region, may have been the head of a chiefdom and shows strong affiliations with the pan-Mesoamerican symbolic network, reflected by the integration of the Olmec art style into its own artistic production. Its location at the crossing of east–west and north–south routes of communication, and its access to resources like conch shell and possibly jade and cacao, may have been motives for its participation in the Mesoamerican interaction sphere of that time.

Villages and Urban Agglomerations at the Beginning of the Common Era

The Olmec Horizon was followed by a period of regional revival throughout Mesoamerica (500 B.C.–A.D. 200). The Basin of Mexico, Valley of Oaxaca, and Maya Lowlands were all developing new ways of meeting the needs of growing populations. Contacts based on the exchange of goods, ideas, and people continued, but rather than constituting a pan-Mesoamerican network, this process was now taking place at an intra- and interregional level. This period of regional florescence led to varying forms of social complexity that would achieve full expression in the Classic period. Some regions, like the Basin of Mexico

and the Valley of Oaxaca, developed highly centralized urban states; in others, like the Maya Lowlands, there emerged confederations of regional states united by a sophisticated ideology.

During this period, Guerrero's cultural regions expanded local patterns established earlier. On the other hand, its inclusion and participation in the Classic period Mesoamerican interaction sphere is evidenced by the sporadic presence of Teotihuacán and other Classic stylistic markers in Guerrero, and by the presence of Mezcala-style objects and other products in highland Mexico.

This pattern is present in the various archaeological subregions of Guerrero; the Mezcala region is by far the best-documented example. The Mezcala region flourished, and investigations in the Mezcala-Balsas subregion show it at the peak of its internal development. The settlements grew in number, diversity, and complexity as population increased, extending habitation and developing agricultural practices and craft production. Urban agglomerations such as Ahuinahuac, Apantipan, and Tehuacaltipa appeared—densely settled sites with elaborate architectural features such as temple mounds, ball courts, and residential complexes. The alluvial terraces around these urban complexes were densely occupied by villages, hamlets, and workshops. The workshops were producing the small polished stone objects characteristic of the well-known Mezcala art style, as documented in their large concentrations of lithic artifacts, completing all the technological steps in the production of Mezcala polished objects, except for the finished products: raw material, chipped and ground pre-forms, and waste flakes. The workshops are situated on alluvial terraces along the Río Balsas and are bordered by deep gullies that provided the water, hard cobbles and pebbles, sand and gravel necessary to the producers of Mezcala objects (Table 4).

The Mezcala art style is expressed in small polished-stone objects from Guerrero. Covarrubias first identified this style, in which the most common representations are those of human and animal masks and figurines, ornaments such as beads, necklaces, and earspools, and miniature replicas of temples. An analysis of Guerrero's lapidary tradition reveals a long history and a great deal of stylistic variation that shows both local tradition (Mezcala style proper) and foreign influences. This tradition probably started in the Olmec Horizon (c. 1200 B.C.) and bloomed during the Late Formative and Classic periods. Mezcala-style objects continue to appear, probably as heirlooms, throughout the history of Mesoamerica. Mezcala objects were found during the excavation of the Mexica Templo

G

TABLE 3. OLMEC-STYLE REPRESENTATIONS FROM GUERRERO, MEXICO.

Localization	Cultural Subregion	Nature of Findings	Cultural Context	Dates	References
Amuco Abelino	Medio Balsas (3)	1 ceramic masquette 1 ceramic figurine	Residential	1530 B.C. ± 230 1220 B.C. ± 110	Paradis 1974, 1978, 1981, 1990
La Arboleda	Medio Balsas (3)	1 jadeite masquette	Workshop	(100–800 B.C.)	Paradis 1974, 1978, 1981, 1990
Amuco Village	Medio Balsas (3)	1 stela	Probably Residential	(800–500 B.C.)?	Grove & Paradis 1971; Paradis 1974, 1978, 1981, 1990
Atopula	Tepecoacuilco (1)	Pottery and figurines	Midden	(1000–800 B.C.)	Henderson 1979
Teopantecuanitlán	Mezcala (2)	Monumental architecture, sculptures and figurines	Ceremonial Precinct and residential units	1423 B.C. ± 112 1393 B.C. ± 126 844 B.C. ± 58 822 B.C. ± 117 790 B.C. ± 42 623 B.C. ± 69 610 B.C. ± 12	Martínez Donjuán 1986; Niederberger 1986
Coovi Sur	Chilpancingo (2)	Olmec style pottery and false vault	Mortuary	(1000–800 B.C.)	Martínez Donjuán & Reyna Robles 1989
Puerto Marqués	Costa Grande (6a)	"Baby face" figurines	Shell midden	(1000–800 B.C.)	Brush 1969
Zanja	Costa Grande (6a)	"Baby face" figurines	à vérifier	(1000–800 B.C.)	Brush 1968

ABSENCE OF CULTURAL CONTEXT

Localization	Cultural Subregion	Nature of Findings	Cultural Context	Dates	References
Oxtotitlan	SMS (5b)	Mural painting	Rockshelter	No context	Grove 1968, 1969, 1970
Juxtlahuaca	SMS (5b)	Mural painting	Cave	No context	Grove 1968, 1969, 1970
Ahuelican	Mezcala (2)	Serpentine plaque Middle Preclassic ceramics	Unknown; surface	(1000–800 B.C.)	Paradis et al. 1983, Paradis 1990
Mezcala, Xalitla, etc.	Mezcala (2)	Jadeite and serpentine ornaments	Unknown	No context	Covarrubias 1948, 1957
Zumpango del Río	Mezcala (2)	Jadeite and serpentine ornaments	Unknown	No context	Covarrubias 1948, 1957
Xochipala	Mezcala (2)	Jadeite ornaments pottery and figurines	Unknown	No context	
Cañon de la Mano	Mezcala (2)	Wooden mask	Unknown	No context	
Tlacotepec	Mezcala (2)	Small stone yokes	Unknown	No context	
	Medio Balsas (3)	Jadeite ornaments	Unknown	No context	Armillas 1948:75
	Costa Grande (6A)	Jadeite ornaments and "La Venta" figurines	Unknown	No context	Armillas 1948:75; Covarrubias 1948:86
	Costa Chica (6B)	Jadeite ornaments	Unknown	No context	Piña Chan 1960:74

TABLE 4. MEZCALA OBJECTS IN ARCHAEOLOGICAL CONTEXT.

Sites	Type	Context	Date	References
Guerrero				
Ahuinahuac	Mezcala 2	Residential	Late Preclassic: 500–100 B.C. (radiocarbon dates)	Paradis et al. 1991; Paradis 1991
Cuetlajuchitlan	Mezcala 2	Residential	Late Preclassic	Manzanilla & Talavera 1993 and pers. com.
El Mirador	Mezcala 2	Residential	Late Classic	Cabrera 1986
La Organera–Mezcala	Mezcala 2	Offering in ball court	Late Classic to Early Postclassic	Rodríguez 1986
La Organera–Xochipala	Mezcala 2	Residential	Late Classic to Early Postclassic	Reyna Robles (pers. com.)
Teopantecuanitlán	Mezcala 2	Surface	? Late Preclassic or Late Postclassic	Martínez Donjuán 1986
Outside Guerrero				
Teotihuacán	Teotihuacán	Residential	Classic	De la Borbolla 1964
Tenochtitlán	Mezcala 1, 2, 3;	Offerings in residential Teotihuacán; indefinite	Late Postclassic context and in Templo Mayor	Batres 1902; Angulo 1966; Contreras 1979; González & Vera 1986; González 1987
Xochicalco Valley	Olmeca; Teotihuacán; Anthropo- morphic figurine	Mortuary	Early and Late Classic Tlahuica Postclassic	Noguera 1961; Saenz 1961, 1963 Litvak King in González 1987

Mayor in Tenochtitlán. Replicas of Mezcala-style objects are still being produced and sold today.

Until 1989, no Mezcala-style object had been found in archaeological contexts in Guerrero, which precluded the possibility of dating or interpreting them in cultural terms. However, at Ahuinahuac seven objects in this style were found under the floors of residential complexes and were radiocarbon dated to between 500 and 200 B.C. Since then more Mezcala-style objects have been found in context in Guerrero, all in the Mezcala region (Ahuinahuac, Cuetlajuchitlan, El Mirador, La Organera–Mezcala, and La Organera–Xochipala). These are related to the second variant of Covarrubias's classification, spanning the period between the Middle to Late Formative (c. 700 B.C.) and the end of the Classic (A.D. 900).

Thus, the Mezcala region was at the peak of its cultural development during the first centuries of the common era.

As in other parts of Mesoamerica, it underwent a process of demographic growth that led to increasing social complexity and urbanization, as exemplified by sites such as La Arboleda–Balsas, Apantipan, Ahuinahuac, and Tehuacaltipa, scattered along the Río Balsas. The area of Xochipala to the south and that of Mayanalan to the north show similar patterns. The Mezcala art style is the trademark of this successful region, which participated in the larger Mesoamerican sphere dominated by Teotihuacán.

Archaeological data show similarities between Teotihuacán and three cultural regions of Guerrero, suggesting that Teotihuacán's influence took different forms in these three regions. In the Medio Balsas and Costa Grande regions, Teotihuacán contact seems to have been intrusive and generally late, whereas in the Mezcala region it was important and reciprocal, and affected not only the technological but also the ideological domains of culture.

G

What were the reasons for interaction between Teotihuacán and Guerrero? The Middle Balsas River region maintained contact with some regions; the presence of a few objects of Olmec and Teotihuacán origin can be interpreted as the product of the travels of the Middle Balsas people, as their means of adjusting to their region's relative geographical and cultural marginality, and of ensuring the circulation of goods, people, and ideas in and out of the region. More powerful regions had no economic incentives to invest in this area, and they did so only when the Postclassic period Aztec and Tarascan empires clashed as they expanded against each other, and the Middle Balsas became a strategic buffer zone. As a consequence, the region showed an important economic and social development. Nothing of the sort can be inferred from the archaeological record in the Classic period; Teotihuacán was in contact with the Middle Balsas region but did not control it.

In the Costa Grande, Teotihuacán's influence was quantitavely and qualitatively more important than in the Middle Balsas. In Tambuco and Coyuca de Benitez, a local ceramic tradition was maintained but was strongly affected by Teotihuacán. Teotihuacán may have been interested in ocean products (fish and mollusks, conch shell, shark, stingray) or in hot-region products such as cacao. Costa Grande's history and socio-cultural characteristics are not sufficiently known to evaluate its relationship with Teotihuacán. On the basis of its more recent history (no Mexica influence, no copper), I infer that it remained generally isolated, and thus Teotihuacán's influence was probably unidirectional and certainly late.

In the Mezcala area, the situation is altogether different. Teotihuacán's influence is pervasive in the regional culture, seen in a few examples of ceramic attributes (annular bases) and figurines, Teotihuacán-style stone objects, stelae, and architectural traits such as *talud* and *tablero* (slope and panel) walls. But there is also evidence for the presence of Mezcala-style objects and of Granular ware in Teotihuacán, the latter certainly proceeding from the Mezcala region. A case has to be made for the possible association of Mezcala craftsmen with a ceramic tradition that would include the Granular ware. If so, these craftsmen could have produced their art in Guerrero and also in Teotihuacán, creating masks in pure Teotihuacán style, as M. D. Coe suggested.

Accounting for the presence of Granular ware in Teotihuacán as the products of a resident population of Mezcala artisans would mean that relationships between Teotihuacán and the Mezcala region were bidirectional and reciprocal. Teotihuacán may have dominated the Mezcala region, however: it employed its artists, probably imported raw material through tribute or commerce, and thus exerted economic control.

Guerrero in the Postclassic

In Guerrero, the last pre-Columbian period dates from the end of the Classic period (A.D. 900) through the arrival of the Mexica Aztecs in the area (c. 1450), and up to the Spanish conquest. It was marked by transformations related to the incursion of new linguistic groups and, most important, to the fifteenth-century conquest of the area by the Aztec and Tarascan states.

Ethnohistorical documents disclose that around A.D. 1250, the first Nahua group, the Coixca, settled in northern Guerrero and the Mezcala region; the Mexica, also linguistically Nahuatl, probably colonized it two centuries later. Around 1370, between the Coixca migration and the Mexica invasion, the Tierra Caliente region of western Guerrero was conquered by its powerful neighbor, the Tarascan state. The Middle Río Balsas came to divide the newcomers and the resident local population, the Cuitlatecos. Meanwhile, the Mexica of Tenochtitlán initiated a policy of expansion that brought them to Guerrero. Under the reign of Itzcoatl (1427–1440), the Mexica conquered northern Guerrero, then inhabited by Chontales to the west and Coixca to the east. Iguala, Tepecoacuilco, Cuetzala, and Tzacualpa are among the towns mentioned in the list of Mexica conquests. The next Mexica ruler, Motecuhzoma Ilhuicamina, put down insurrections in northern Guerrero and conquered the remaining Tlahuica, Coixca, and Chontal groups of Morelos and northern Guerrero. Towns were conquered in the tributary provinces of Tlachco, Tlalcozauhtitlán, Tepecoacuilco, and Quiauhteopan. Mexica expansion continued southward during Tizoc's reign with the conquest of Tetela del Río and Tlapan, and under Ahuizotl with the conquest of Zacatula on the Costa Grande. However, northern Guerrero continued to rebel against Mexica rule up to the Spanish conquest.

The Mexica territorial conquest of Guerrero had economic and political motives. Guerrero promised much in terms of raw materials and finished products. The Aztec tribute lists of the six conquered Guerrero provinces—Tlachco, Tepecoacuilco, Tlalcozauhtitlán, Quiauteopan, Tlapan, and Cihuatlan—are impressive, featuring subsistence goods such as beans and corn; luxury items like cotton and cacao; and regional specialties like honey, copal, gold, and copper ornaments, varnished gourds, and necklaces made of green stone. Many of these articles, including the green stone objects (probably jadeite or serpentine) and the varnished gourd bowls, came from the province of Tepecoacuilco and therefore from the Mezcala region. Conquest was not only economically motivated; there was a political stimulus as well. The Mexica state needed to defend its southwestern border from the threatening advances of the Tarascan state. Indeed, this was perhaps the prime catalyst for the conquest of many territories in Guerrero, particularly in the northwestern portion of the state.

This cycle of conquest, rebellion, and reconquest had dramatic consequences for Guerrero's inhabitants. In the final eighty years before the Spanish conquest, its cultural regions, politically autonomous up to the mid-sixteenth century, were colonized and came to form part of a centralized state system. Moreover, Mexica tribute policy compelled the intensification of production and a reorganization of economic activities at the internal as well as "national" level.

FURTHER READINGS

Covarrubias, M. 1946. El arte "olmeca" o de La Venta. *Cuadernos Americanos* 28:153–179.

———. 1948. Tipología de la industría de piedra tallada y pulida de la cuenca del Río Mezcala. In *El Occidente de México*, pp. 86–90. Mexico City: Sociedad Mexicana de Antropología.

———. 1956. *Mezcala, Ancient Mexican Sculpture.* New York: A. Emmerich Gallery.

Hendrich, P. R. 1946. *Por tierras ignotas: Viajes y observaciones en la región del Río Balsas.* 2 vols. Mexico City: Editorial Cultura.

Lister, R. H. 1971. Archaeological Synthesis of Guerrero. In G. E. Ekholm and I. Bernal (eds.), *Handbook of Middle American Indians,* vol. 11, pp. 619–631. Austin: University of Texas Press.

Litvak King, J. 1971. Cihuatlán y Tepecoacuilco. In *Provincias tributarias de México en el siglo XVI.* Instituto de Investigaciones Históricas, Serie Antropológica, 12. Mexico: Instituto Nacional de Antropología e Historia.

Martínez Donjuán, G. 1986. Teopantecuanitlán. In *Arqueología y Etnohistoria del Estado de Guerrero,* pp. 55–80. Mexico City: Instituto Nacional de Antropología e Historia and Gobierno del Estado de Guerrero.

Niederberger Betton, C. 1986. Excavación de un área de habitación doméstica en la capital "olmeca" de Tlacozotitlan: Reporte Preliminar. In *Arqueología y Etnohistoria del Estado de Guerrero,* pp. 83–103. Mexico City: Instituto Nacional de Antropología e Historia and Gobierno del Estado de Guerrero.

Paradis, L. I. 1990. Revisión del fenomeno olmeca. *Arqueología* 3:33–40.

———. 1991. El Estilo Mezcala en contexto en Guerrero, México. *Arqueología* 5:59–68.

———. 1995. The Prehispanic History of the Mezcala Region. In Jonathan Amith (ed.), *The Amate Tradition: Innovation and Dissent in Mexican Art,* pp. 113–128. Mexico City: Mexican Fine Arts Center Museum and Grupo Editorial Casa de las Imagenes.

Schmidt Schoenberg, P., and J. Litvak King. 1986. Problemas y perspectivas de la arqueología. In *Arqueología y Etnohistoria del Estado de Guerrero,* pp. 27–51. Mexico City: Instituto Nacional de Antropología e Historia and Gobierno del Estado de Guerrero.

Louise I. Paradis

SEE ALSO
Aztec Culture and History; Mezcala Lapidary Style; Settlement Patterns and Settlement Systems; Teopantecuanitlán; Xochipala Style

Guiengola (Oaxaca, Mexico)

This Zapotec site on the Isthmus of Tehuantepec was possibly part of a series of fortified sites that guarded Late Postclassic trade routes between the Soconusco and the Valley of Oaxaca. Guiengola carries the name of the 1,070-meter limestone mountain on which it sits, a strategic position at the eastern end of the Sierra Madre del Sur, overlooking the western bank of the Tehuantepec River and giving the fortress command of passages through the river valley and over the fertile coastal plain between the mountains and the Pacific Ocean.

Guiengola has been dated through ceramics and ethnohistoric sources. The ceramics belong to the Postclassic Ulam phase (A.D. 900), with the greatest proportion being Reu Silty pottery (A.D. 1300) of the Late Postclassic. Ethnohistoric sources confirm that the Zapotec were driven into the Isthmus during the fourteenth century. During the early sixteenth century, Cocijoeza, the Zapotec ruler, was besieged at Guiengola for seven months by the Aztecs. The conflict ended with a marital alliance that ensured Aztec trade through the region.

G

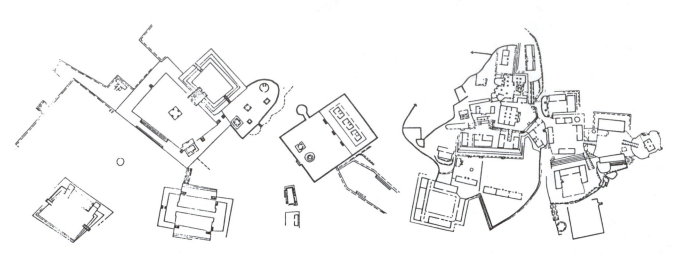

THE SITE CENTER   GALAHUI LA' YU' YU' DU'
GUIENGOLA, OAXACA

D. Peterson, S. Stebbins, S. Rasnick, R. Russell, H. Ball, C. Olson

INSTITUTO de ESTUDIOS OAXAQUEÑOS

Guiengola, a Late Postclassic fortified hilltop site. On the right, the palace complex. Illustration courtesy of the author.

The site comprises a central group—which lies in a saddle formation between two summits of the mountain—three residential groups, and an extensive system of walls. Two pyramids and a ball court define the central group as the ritual and administrative center. The walls around the site consisted of at least two tiers, averaging three meters in height, with an estimated total length of more than forty kilometers.

FURTHER READINGS

Burgoa, F. 1934 [1647]. *Geográfica Descripción*. Vol. 2. Mexico City: Publicaciones del Archivo General de la Nación.

Covarrubias, M. 1947. *Mexico South*. New York: Alfred Knopf.

Peterson, D. A., and T. B. Mac Dougall. 1974. *Guiengola: A Fortified Site in the Isthmus of Tehuantepec*. Vanderbilt University Publications in Anthropology, 10. Nashville, Tenn.

Wallrath, M. 1967. Excavations in the Tehuantepec Region, Mexico. *Transactions of the American Philosophical Society* 57(2).

Jay Silverstein

SEE ALSO

Oaxaca and Tehuantepec Region

Guila Naquitz (Oaxaca, Mexico)

This small cave in the mountains bordering the eastern Valley of Oaxaca is set in oak woodland and thorn forest at an elevation of 1,926 meters. Between 8000 and 6500 B.C. the cave was occupied on at least six occasions, according to the results of University of Michigan research directed by K. V. Flannery. This was a period of seminomadic hunting and gathering; the occupants of the cave (probably families of four to six people) hunted deer, rabbits, and mud turtles and collected a variety of local wild plants. Plant materials, preserved by desiccation within the cave, included acorns, pinyon nuts, cactus fruits, agaves, mesquite pods, hackberries, West Indian cherries, wild onions, and other species. Also present were the remains of gourds, squashes, and small black runner beans, some wild and others possibly in the early stages of domestication. Guila Naquitz seems to document a period of "incipient cultivation," or significant use of the wild ancestors of beans and squashes. However, it was apparently abandoned too early to document the domestication of maize, which took place later.

FURTHER READINGS

Flannery, K. V. (ed.). 1986. *Guila Naquitz: Archaic Foraging and Early Agriculture in Oaxaca, Mexico.* New York: Academic Press.

Kent V. Flannery

SEE ALSO

Oaxaca and Tehuantepec Region

Guinéa, La (Guanacaste, Costa Rica)

Situated in the Greater Nicoya region, on the Tempisque River in a dry tropical habitat, this site had habitation and cemetery features and was occupied during A.D. 300–1520. Funerary remains were primary interments with associated ceramics, mortuary patterns similar to those of La Ceiba. Artifacts included White-slipped ceramics from Pacific Nicaragua.

FURTHER READINGS

Baudez, C. F. 1967. *Rechèrches archéologiques dans la Vallée du Tempisque, Guanacaste, Costa Rica. Travaux et Memoires de l'Institut des Hautes Études de l'Amérique Latine,* 18. Paris: Institut des Hautes Études de l'Amérique Latine.

Frederick W. Lange

SEE ALSO

Ceiba, La; Nicoya, Greater, and Guanacaste Region

Gulf Lowlands

The cultural subareas of the Mexican Gulf Lowlands covered an immense region that stretched for nearly 1,000 kilometers along the Gulf of Mexico from the northeastern periphery of Mesoamerica to the Yucatán Peninsula. The western limits were well above the humid lowlands, in certain periods reaching elevations as high as 2,400 meters or more in the Sierra Madre Oriental, or even to the dry eastern margins of the central Mexican plateau. Within this topographically and ecologically diverse zone lie the western portions of the modern state of Tabasco, all of Veracruz, the southern half of Tamaulipas, parts of northern Puebla, and the lower eastern reaches of Hidalgo, Querétaro, San Luis Potosí, and Oaxaca. Flowing eastward across the often hilly coastal plain are some of the largest rivers in Mexico, including the Pánuco-Tamesi, Tuxpan, Tecolutla, Papaloapan, and Coatzalcoalcos. Lesser mountain ranges such as the Sierra de Tamaulipas, Sierra de Otontepec, Sierra de Chinconquijaco, and the Tuxtlas verge on the sea, grouping the intervening river drainages into rich natural regions that also reflected cultural subareas at different points in time.

By the Early Formative period there were two Gulf Lowlands subareas, Northern and Southern. During the Middle Formative, the former split into the North and the North Central. By the Late Formative, four subareas, including the South and South Central, were in existence. Situated strategically between the southeastern lowlands and the central Mexican plateau, the Gulf Lowlands were not only a passageway for long-distance contact but also a major and highly dynamic regional manifestation of Mesoamerican civilization that frequently spilled over into adjoining zones.

Each subarea has its own culture history and also shares a long chronology of interaction; each is noted for distinctive archaeological manifestations. The Southern Lowlands region was, in large part, the focus of the initial lowland Olmec florescence with its characteristic massive stone sculpture during the Early and Middle Formative periods. The South Central Lowlands region generated a huge volume of expressive ceramic figurines and monumental clay statuary associated with localized cults during the Classic period. The North Central Lowlands was the core region for the metropolitan cities of El Pital and El Tajín, where Classic Veracruz culture and art attained their apogee. The North Lowlands region was the Postclassic home of the bellicose, artistically staid, and mostly Huastec-culture societies of the labile Mesoamerican frontier.

The entire Gulf Lowlands region was intensely populated when the Spanish conquest began here in 1519 but declined almost immediately because of epidemics of European diseases. There followed catastrophic depopulation and generalized site abandonment, as well as an accelerated reversion to rainforests and wooded savannas, the predominant environmental contexts for the first archaeological discoveries in the late eighteenth century.

FURTHER READINGS

Wilkerson, S. J. K. 1974. Sub-Culture Areas of Eastern Mesoamerica. In *Primera Mesa Redonda de Palenque,* part 2, pp. 89–102. Pebble Beach, Calif.: Robert Louis Stevenson School.

G

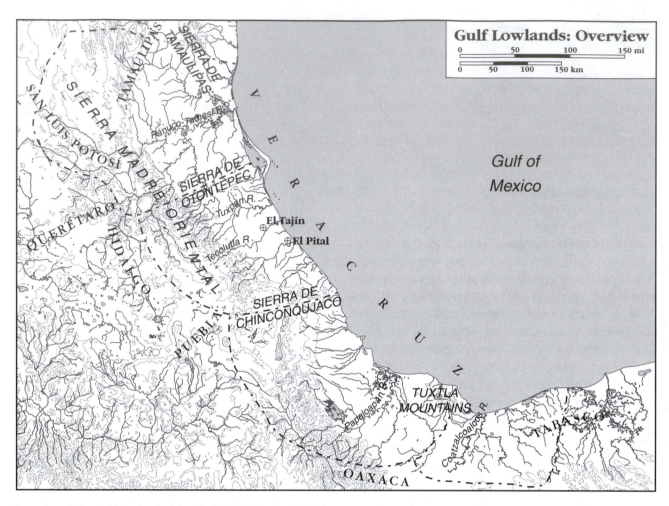

Overview of the Gulf Lowlands. Map design by Mapping Specialists Limited, Madison, Wisconsin.

———. 1988. Cultural Time and Space in Ancient Veracruz. In M. M. Goldstein (ed.), *Ceremonial Sculpture of Ancient Veracruz,* pp. 6–17. New York: Hillwood Art Gallery–Long Island University.

———. 1997. Die Geschichte der archäologischen Forschung an der Golfcuste. In *Prakolumbische Kulturen am Golf von Mexiko,* pp. 15–18. Zurich: Museum Rietberg.

S. Jeffrey K. Wilkerson

SEE ALSO

Gulf Lowlands: North Region, North Central Region, South Central Region, and South Region

Gulf Lowlands: North Central Region

One of four principal cultural subareas of the Mesoamerican Gulf Lowlands, the North Central area is archaeologically highly significant for its terminal Pleistocene fauna finds and its long cultural sequence beginning in the Early Archaic period, and as a focus of major urban centers from the Late Formative period through the Postclassic. Here Classic Veracruz culture, art, and architecture reached their apogee, and here some of the largest Gulf Coast cities were situated. Defined by both cultural and environmental parameters, the area was largely within the modern state of Veracruz but included adjoining portions of the states of Puebla and Hidalgo. The lowland portion was comprised primarily of the Tuxpan, Cazones, Tecolutia, and Nautla river drainages, while the higher elevations were limited by the Sierra Madre Oriental on the west, and by lesser mountain spurs known as the Sierra de Otontepec on the north and the Sierra de Chiconquiaco on the south. With rich alluvial soils and high rainfall on a compressed, hilly coastal plain traversed by navigable rivers, the area had diverse resources in abundance to sustain ancient populations. Gulf Coast archaeology began here with the eighteenth-century discovery of El Tajín.

While occasional chance finds of megafauna are known from Mexico's eastern lowlands, in the North Central Gulf Lowlands remains from the terminal Pleistocene period have come from both explorations and salvage contexts. Concentrated in the low hills of the Tecolutla catchment near the sea, sites such as La Conchita and Paguas de Arroyo Grande have bones or teeth of mastodon, giant ground sloth, glyptodont, and horse. Although not positively correlated with humans, both the geological and archaeological contexts strongly suggest that eventually, reliable human-megafauna associations are likely to be encountered here.

Archaic occupations are also known from the coastal zone, particularly in the Tecolutla River delta, which formed as sea level rise lessened about 8000 B.P. Early Archaic (c. 7000–4000 B.C.) campsites and some stone artifacts were encountered at La Conchita, but much of the data, especially for the Late Archaic, comes from Santa Luisa. This chronologically pivotal site has provided the major part of a nearly continuous 8,000-year culture sequence that has widespread applications throughout the area; this is the primary basis for dating period references in this overview. Beginning with island base camps that evolved into Late Archaic (c. 4,000–2400 B.C.) villages subsisting on the abundant riverine-estuarine resources, principally shellfish, there is evidence for an ample Archaic population and even long-distance obsidian commerce. The nonagricultural subsistence base demonstrates a very successful preceramic Mesoamerican pattern for coastal sedentarism. During the Archaic, the North Central and North Gulf Lowlands regions were very probably a single northern Gulf macrounit.

Early Formative (c. 2400–1000 B.C.) island villages of large size—containing the region's first ceramics in the form of jars (*tecomates* and *ollas*)—are found at Santa Luisa. The artifact corpus suggests that agriculture, initially a minor factor in subsistence, accelerated in significance only during the last centuries of the second millennium B.C. Maize-grinding tools increased as obsidian chips, probably used for grating manioc and preparing shellfish, gradually decreased in number. Stone vessels, some finely made, persisted, while ceramics, particularly grater bowls for chile and beans, became abundant. Cotton was grown and woven for garments. House construction with clay-and-pole walls, as well as carefully fired clay floors and hearths, became common. The first low temple platforms may have been built at this time. The artifacts of the end of the period are, for the most part, decidedly not Olmec, although there are local imita-

tions and some direct imports. Though receptive to influence from the more dynamic Southern Gulf throughout the later Early Formative, this region was apparently a frontier with limited Initial Olmec penetration. The concentrated abundance of local food resources and the proximity to the Olmec, however, made it more populous and culturally vigorous than the upper reaches of the Northern Gulf.

The Middle Formative (c. 1000–300 B.C.) was an extremely active time in which the North Central area appears to have separated from the far more conservative North Gulf. At Santa Luisa, again the principal site known from the period, there were large perishable structures, massive hearths, thick burnt-clay floors, composite-silhouette ceramics, inverted rims with double-line break motifs, and a larger population concentrated on riverbanks or islands. Some similar data come from surface survey in the Nautla River delta around El Pital. During this time grater bowls decreased in importance, and maize-grinding instruments became quite common as obsidian chips rapidly declined in number. Long-distance trade diversified further. Green obsidian prismatic blades from the Pachuca highlands and Olmec portable art were traded among the elite. Examples of Olmec jade or fine stone figurines are known from Necaxa, Tuzapan, and Zaragosa near El Pital. The nearest confirmed Olmec site is El Viejón, perhaps a control station for commerce, at the extreme southern edge of the area.

Following a prolonged span of precipitation, extensive flooding, and silt deposition throughout the area, probably reflecting a very intensive El Niño climatic event, extensive deposits of the Late Formative period (c. 300–1 B.C.) are found at several riverine locations. Santa Luisa remains the best understood, but data also come from El Pital, Tabuco, and Las Higueras, all of which share similar blackware and domestic ceramics. There was a considerable increase in population; in fact, there may have been an important coastal migration from the north of early Nahua speakers. Spacious deltaic and riverbank zones were occupied by sprawling towns, suggesting an ever more intensive agricultural use of the rich terrace soils. Raised fields and canal systems may have begun at this time at both El Pital and Santa Luisa.

By at least the last century of the Formative, the first huge, probably multiethnic, city of the area came into being at El Pital. Massive earthen buildings with burnt-clay coatings, street grids, ball courts, port zones, expansive plazas, satellite centers, canal systems, and gateway communities mark the beginning of intensive urbanism in the

G

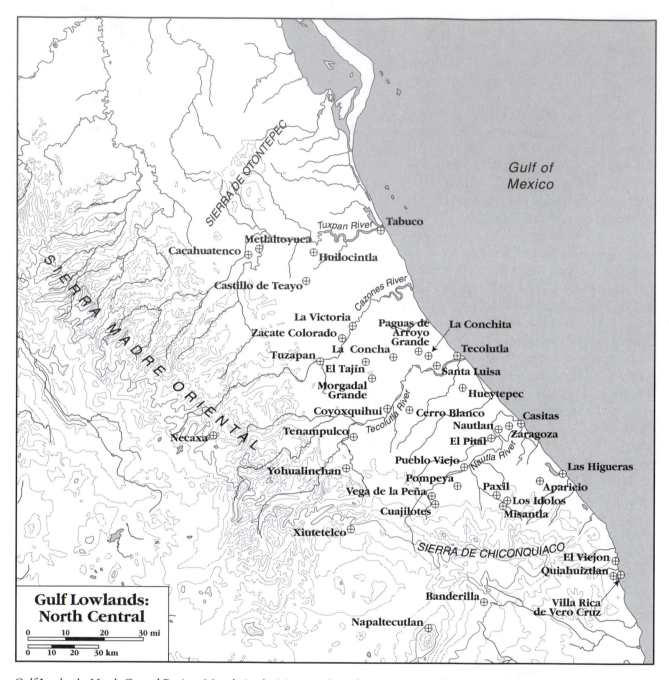

Gulf Lowlands: North Central Region. Map design by Mapping Specialists Limited, Madison, Wisconsin.

North Central region. Probably a very successful city-state with ample hegemony, El Pital represented a major population and social centralization on a scale that—at its probable peak in the Protoclassic (c. A.D. 1–300)—surpassed even much later cities in the area. Its geographic placement was excellent for commerce with the highlands in general and with cities such as Cantona and Teotihuacán in particular. This was the first metropolitan center of incipient Classic Veracruz culture in the North Central Gulf Lowlands. The growth of the city and environs was such that some sites in the adjoining coastal regions, such as Las Higueras, were largely deserted by the end of the Late Formative, their populations probably absorbed by the great urban center and its expanding, labor-intensive civic and agricultural works. This regional process may also account for the generally sparse settlements of this date in the interior, particularly in locations away from large waterways.

The Protoclassic may have begun earlier at El Pital than in the rest of the region. At Santa Luisa, probably at this point a major subordinate center of El Pital, there was a sizable occupation. In the interior, riverbank settlements were present at Zacate Colorado and La Victoria (Kilometer 47) on the Cazones, and probably in small settlements like Morgadal Grande and El Tajín on the edges of the Tlahuanapa plain in the Tecolutla catchment. About El Pital itself there was an expanding population, much temple construction—at times utilizing thin stucco coating on sanctuaries—and continued canal-building. The city's sphere of control may have extended well up and down the coastal zones, and perhaps even beyond the borders of the North Central Gulf region. In these regions there was expanding emphasis on hydraulic systems for agriculture.

At the beginning of the Early Classic period (c. A.D. 300) El Pital was still the principal city of the area. Other significant population centers included Santa Luisa with its ample canal systems, riverbank La Victoria, Los Idolos by a major source of incense, Morgadal Grande at the convergence of intravalley access routes, and, of gradually emerging importance, El Tajín. Preliminary evidence suggests that El Pital suffered a rapid, overwhelming eclipse during the latter portion of the Early Classic, possibly triggered or hastened by a climatic alteration (perhaps another El Niño event having an impact on intensive agricultural production). El Pital and its satellite communities were all but abandoned. Concomitantly, there was a pervasive expansion southward of mostly defensively placed sites with the architecture, art, and artifacts associated primarily with El Tajín. Centers such as Pueblo Viejo, Paxil, Pompeya, Vega de la Peña, and Aparicio, all in the immediate hinterland of El Pital, strongly suggest the deliberate and forceful isolation of the formerly preeminent city. To the west, astride a key trade route to the highlands, the growing regional projection of El Tajín was manifest in the gateway center of Yohualinchan.

El Tajín expanded its influence rapidly and clearly came to dominate the area during the Late Classic (c. A.D. 600–900) and Epiclassic (c. A.D. 900–1100) periods. Distinguished by its unique flying-cornice-over-niche architectural profile, elaborate structural use of cement, abundant stone sculpture, and an extraordinary emphasis on the ball game cult, this metropolitan center of mature Classic Veracruz culture was situated inland, away from the older coastal population centers. Although it appears to have derived many of its initial ceramics and ball game obsession from earlier El Pital, it evolved its own distinctive characteristics.

Occupying most of a steep-sided valley well back from major waterways, El Tajín was the largest city of its time, although smaller in both extent and urban population than El Pital at its zenith. Buildings were clustered on the valley floor and on immense terraces that served both elite and defensive purposes. Large satellite communities, such as Morgadal Grande and Lagunilla, formed part of the urban periphery of El Tajín. Canal systems at delta sites such as Santa Luisa, around El Pital, and near Las Higueras functioned at this time, almost certainly under the direct domination of El Tajín.

Bellicose in orientation, the city apparently controlled or strongly influenced practically all of the North Central region, as well as adjacent regions. Sites such as Napaltecutlan and Xiutetelco in the eastern highlands, Banderilla and Coatepec in the upper reaches of the South Central Gulf Lowlands area, and Cerro Cebadilla and Cuatlamayan in the distant North Gulf area all manifest architectural influence from El Tajín. Throughout this immense territory, but especially in the core zone of ascendancy, ritual ball game sculptures known as yokes, *hachas,* and *palmas* attest to the strength of the El Tajín cult focus. Ceramics associated with the city have a similar, though more restricted, distribution. Mural techniques, themes, or iconography of the metropolitan center also appear at coastal Santa Luisa and Las Higueras.

From the very end of the Classic, and extending through the local Epiclassic, there was a considerable intensification of construction at El Tajín. This last florescence greatly altered the urban surface through prodigious earth movement. Earlier middens were utilized as fill and many older structures covered. Sculptural depictions indicate that warfare and conquest were important activities, and the deliberate destruction of sculpture and buildings suggests that the city's demise was violent. From a regional perspective, both the zenith and rapid decline of the metropolitan center and its hitherto influential culture came in this brief period.

The tumultuous migration of aggressive groups down the coast from the North Gulf region may have been responsible for despoiling the city and causing the southward flight of populations affiliated with El Tajín. Significant regions for intensive agriculture, such as at Santa Luisa and the former El Pital hinterland of the Nautla delta, were greatly depopulated and replaced by hamlets

G

or scattered homesites. Centers on the southern periphery of the North Central region, such as Cuajilotes and, perhaps, Aparicio and Paxil, may have briefly increased in importance before suffering the same disruption. Fortified mountaintop sites of small size, such as Cerro Blanco and Coyoxquihui, appear in the region just south of El Tajín. The architectural and artistic attributes of Classic Veracruz culture, as well as the portable sculptures of the ball game cult, cease throughout the region. The events that led to the destruction of El Tajín and its associated culture were apparently sudden and extremely pervasive.

The Early Postclassic period (c. A.D. 1100–1300) has had limited research in general, but particularly in the key northern reaches of the region. Beginning with an explosive movement of peoples originating in the vast North Gulf region, apparently triggered by a prolonged drought typical of severe El Niño events in those latitudes, large numbers of Huastecs and intermingled groups debouched into the area.

Internecine warfare, labile alliances, and political balkanization appear to characterize the time. It is unlikely that any one center dominated the entire area, except perhaps ephemerally. None rivaled earlier El Tajín in size, grandeur, or regional influence. Populous fortified hilltop or mesa cities, such as Iluilocintla, Metlaltoyuca, and Cacahuatenco, emerged in the Tuxpan catchment. Southward, in the former El Tajín heartland, the intrusive population may have been less numerous and more dispersed. Artifacts reflect the strong influence of the North Gulf: fine paste, almost temperless ceramics became common. Stone slab effigy stelae and "old men with staff" sculptures were utilized at least as far south as La Concha. In many respects, the area became a part of the greater Huasteca.

During the Late Postclassic (c. A.D. 1300–1520), Metlaltoyuca and Cacahuantenco continued as important centers, and Tabuco, just back from the mouth of the Tuxpan River, undertook the conquest of portions of the Cazones and Tecolutla valleys. Farther south, fortified Tuzapan and Tenampulco had important populations and controlled small kingdoms. Although still lacking stratigraphic exploration, Castillo de Teayo, previously assumed to be the principal post–El Tajín site, appears increasingly to be primarily situated in the terminal Postclassic. Abundant Huastec and Aztec-like sculptures are found there, as well as a large temple in a format common in the central Mexican highlands. This center in the Cazones catchment is likely associated, in its latter occupation, with a predominately Nahua-speaking enclave.

Two important processes influenced the last century of the Late Postclassic period in the area: the intensive reutilization of the riverine, deltaic, and unfortified locations depopulated earlier, and the Aztec (Triple Alliance) conquest. The first is manifest in the reestablishment and rapid growth of riverbank towns such as Tabuco, Santa Luisa, and Nautlan, as well as the partial reoccupation of previously significant locations such as El Pital and El Tajín. There was major structure refurnishing at a satellite of the former, and some sculpture and building summit reuse at the latter. Coastal communities such as Casitas and Tecolutla were also revived. Much of the earlier raised field and canal systems were revived and worked, mostly for cacao and cotton. The gradual increase in polity size may have facilitated this phenomenon. The second process, known historically from abundant documentation, is archaeologically manifest by the "Mar del Norte" garrison placed at Vega de la Peña. The suppression of local warfare under Aztec rule, and the regional organization necessary for massive tribute payments, may have accelerated the reactivation of the field systems.

The aftermath of the Spanish conquest of the region in the early sixteenth century, initiated from Villa Rica de Vera Cruz near Quiahuistlan, is represented by extensive cemeteries at sites such as Santa Luisa. These are almost certainly the result of the catastrophic epidemics of European diseases, a major factor in the rapid abandonment of practically all lowland population centers. By the end of the first century of the Colonial period, none of the major Postclassic coastal sites remained occupied, and even those at higher elevations were greatly reduced. Although Spanish-owned fishing stations and *estancias* (ranches) were established in this demographic void, none have been excavated or formally surveyed. With minimal land use, the entire area rapidly reverted to rainforest, which remained largely intact until oil exploration brought roads and deforestation in the mid-twentieth century.

Archaeological interest in the area was stimulated by the 1785 publication of a Spanish official's drawing of the Pyramid of the Niches at El Tajín. Throughout the nineteenth century there were further descriptions of the building (e.g., by Marquez, Humboldt, and Fage) and depictions (e.g., by Nebel and Velasco). Other sites, such as Tuzapan, Paxil, Idolos, and possibly El Pital, were eventually recorded (e.g., by Nebel and Strebel). In 1891, a government expedition under the direction of the historian Paso y Troncoso undertook inspection and measurements at El Tajín. There followed visits to El Tajín, Castillo de Teayo, Yohualinchan, and Tuzapan by photographers (Maler, Jimenez), archaeologists (Fewkes, Palados), and art historians (Seler, E. Spinden). In 1935, formal government work began with the clearing and topographic operations at El Tajín by Garcia Vega.

Beginning in 1938 with the first direct regional field study (Misantla) on the Gulf Coast, Garcia Payon began four decades of research. His pioneering work included regional data collection, mapping, survey, explorations, reconstruction, and museum formation. His principal efforts were at Paxil, El Tajín, Castillo de Teayo, Xiutetelco, Yohualinchan, and a complex of sites around Zempoala in the adjacent margin of the South Central Gulf region. Within his research program at El Tajín, stratigraphic studies were undertaken by DuSolier in 1938 and Krotzer in 1970. In coordination with Garcia Payon at El Tajín, and in order to place the city in a regional chronology, Wilkerson in 1968 began a decade of stratigraphic explorations at Santa Luisa.

Other research in the area included testing at Tabuco, and survey at Cacahuatenco, Metlaltoyuca, and Tuzapan by Ekholm in 1947. Medellin Zenil in 1950 inspected Vega de la Peña; in an effort to derive comparative data for his Remojadas finds, as well as to establish state-wide collections for Veracruz, he probed a number of sites in 1952, including Hueytepec, Zacate Colorado, and La Victoria. In 1951 he commenced explorations at El Viejón, and beginning in 1969 he directed the mural salvage and testing at Las Higueras. Kampen published drawings of the El Tajín sculptural corpus in 1972. Wilkerson explored the Pleistocene and Archaic deposits at La Conchita in 1973–1974, examined the aftermath of the El Tajín collapse at Cerro Blanco in 1973–1976, and initiated the survey of a pipeline that traversed the area in 1978. Instituto Nacional de Antropología e Historia began reconstruction at Coyoxquihui in 1981. By 1984 reconstruction resumed at El Tajín with joint state government–INAH projects that continued intermittently until 1992. Following an inspection by Wilkerson in 1990–1991, a reconstruction effort was undertaken by INAH at Cuajilotes and Vega de la Peña in 1993–1994. Reconnaissance, mapping, and stratigraphic probing was initiated at El Pital in 1993 by Wilkerson. In 1996 Pascual began a Universidad Nacional Autónoma de México reconnaissance project at Morgadal Grande.

Two centuries of archaeological research have brought much knowledge of site locations and considerable structural reconstruction, but only a preliminary delineation of culture history. Nevertheless, there is ample evidence to suggest that the eight millennia or more of human presence in the North Central Gulf Area are critical to understanding the course of civilization in eastern lowland Mesoamerica.

FURTHER READINGS

Garcia Payon, J. 1947. Exploraciones arqueológicas en el Totonacapan Meridional (Region de Misantla). *Anales del Instituto Nacional de Antropología e Historia* 11:73–111.

———. 1965. *Bibliografia arqueológica de Veracruz.* Cuadernos del Instituto de Antropologia. Xalapa: Universidad Veracruzana.

———. 1971. Archaeology of Central Veracruz. In *Handbook of Middle American Indians,* vol. 11, pp. 505–542. Austin: University of Texas Press.

Wilkerson, S. J. K. 1975. Pre-agricultural Village Life: The Preceramic Period in Veracruz. *Contributions of the University of California Archaeological Reseach Facility* 27:111–122.

———. 1980. Man's Eighty Centuries in Veracruz. *National Geographic* 158(2):202–231.

———. 1983. So Green and Like a Garden: Intensive Agriculture in Ancient Veracruz. In J. P. Darch (ed.), *Drained Field Agriculture in Central and South America,* pp. 55–90. BAR International Series, 189. Oxford.

———. 1994. The Garden City of El Pital: The Genesis of Classic Civilization in Eastern Mesoamerica. *National Geographic Research & Exploration* 10:56–71.

———. 1994. Nahua Presence on the Mesoamerican Gulf Coast. In E. Quinones-Keber (ed.), *Chipping Away on Earth,* pp. 177–186. Culver City, Calif.: Labyrinthos Press.

S. Jeffrey K. Wilkerson

SEE ALSO
Gulf Lowlands

Gulf Lowlands: North Region

Forming the northeastern frontier of Mesoamerica, this is the largest and, archaeologically, the least-known cultural subarea of the Gulf Lowlands. Its geographic core is the great Pánuco-Tamesí basin, the fourth-largest river system in Mexico, draining large portions of the modern states of Veracruz, Tamaulipas, San Luis Potosí, Querétaro, and Hidalgo. Resource-rich and with a long cultural chronology, but remote from the dynamic core regions of Mesoamerica, it initially evolved slowly. Throughout its

G

history the area bore the impact of intrusive migrations. Eventually influences from neighboring regions, particularly the North Central Gulf Lowlands, brought it more into the Mesoamerican mainstream. By the final centuries of the pre-Columbian era it was both very populous and vigorous, with labile, bellicose polities. Noted for its unique sandstone slab sculpture, round buildings, distinctive Black-on-White pottery, and enormous quantities of small clay figurines, this huge area has had remarkably little attention from archaeologists. Hundreds of sites are recorded, but only a few have been surveyed or have undergone reconstruction efforts, and still fewer have been excavated for chronological purposes. The culture history of the area is complex and interwoven with that of adjoining regions.

Maya-speaking Huastecs, the area's most numerous pre-Hispanic inhabitants, reached the upper Gulf Lowlands from the south during the first half of the Formative period. There they prospered and later expanded into neighboring zones. Although traditionally considered the Huastec heartland, the area also had enclaves of other important groups, some of great time depth, including Nahua, Otomi, Pame, and Chichimec. The limits of the culture area fluctuated as the Mesoamerican borderland waxed and waned, or as outward movements led to overlapping into adjacent regions. At its greatest extent, the northern and most unstable border was the Sierra de Tamaulipas and the southern limit was in the Sierra de Otontepec, while the fluid western margins surged well inland past the outliers of the Sierra Madre Oriental. Ringed by mountains, humid and sometimes swampy lowland savannas predominate toward the center, with dry hills in the south, and plains in the north and west. To the southeast lies the Laguna de Tamiahua, a huge, island-studded coastal lagoon.

The temporal parameters for the ancient exploitation of this immense area are still largely imprecise. Although an initial regional sequence for the lower Pánuco has been established, and site chronologies have been developed in the far west and extreme north, as well as regional syntheses derived from surveys in the east, north, northwest, and western margins, the culture chronology for the lowland zone as a whole remains in many instances vague or disjunctive. In most regions accuracy is greatest for more recent phases. With some probable dating variation, most of the basic Mesoamerican period classification is applicable to the area. However, the Proto-Classic and Epiclassic, present in the adjoining North Central Gulf Low-

lands, seemingly do not occur here, except perhaps in highly localized districts influenced by this southern neighbor.

In part, the lack of a generally reliable area-wide chronological framework has led to oversimplified generalizations and blanket interpretations of cultural conservatism. A genuine contributing factor to evolutionary time lag, primarily in early time levels, was the distance from the Mesoamerican core regions and the dynamic processes that propelled their more rapid cultural evolution. The North Gulf Lowlands region was never immune to events elsewhere but was often simply isolated from centers of Mesoamerican innovation. At certain points in time, nevertheless, it was the focus of expansive ritualism; moreover, it was the first Gulf Lowlands region to be modified by innovations wrought by new groups migrating from beyond the Mesoamerican frontiers.

Although a Paleoindian presence is known from the dry caves and shelters of the Sierra de Tamaulipas, at and beyond the area's borders, there is currently no known evidence for this period in the North Gulf Lowlands. Archaic period (c. 7000–2400 B.C.) occupations are still unconfirmed but are likely to have been similar to those known from the North Central Gulf Lowlands, where shellfish were exploited from sometimes densely settled delta and riverbank locations. One possible preceramic, or aceramic, site that may be from the end of this period is on the Laguna la Tortuga, in the swampy area between the Pánuco and Tamesí rivers. Apart from the fact there has been little archaeological emphasis on detecting such time levels anywhere in the Gulf Lowlands, the massive alluvium caps of the Holocene in the lower river valleys have left most early surfaces deeply submerged and largely inaccessible except by chance finds.

Primarily riverbank sites are known from the Formative period (c. 2400 B.C.–A.D. 300). Although it is not yet clear how densely populated the greater lowlands were during most of this long timespan, there were at least ample villages by its midpoint in regions of plentiful riverine and estuarine resources. At Pánuco, two phases (Pavón and Ponce) have been defined at the termination (c. 1400–900 B.C.) of the Early Formative. Ceramics include abundant grater bowls and whitewares, which predominate to such an extent, and are sufficiently distinct from the corpus of neighboring areas, to suggest a major regional focus of ceramic development. Maize-grinding implements occur in moderate numbers, but obsidian and flint chips that may well have been used in root grating or shellfish preparation are relatively numer-

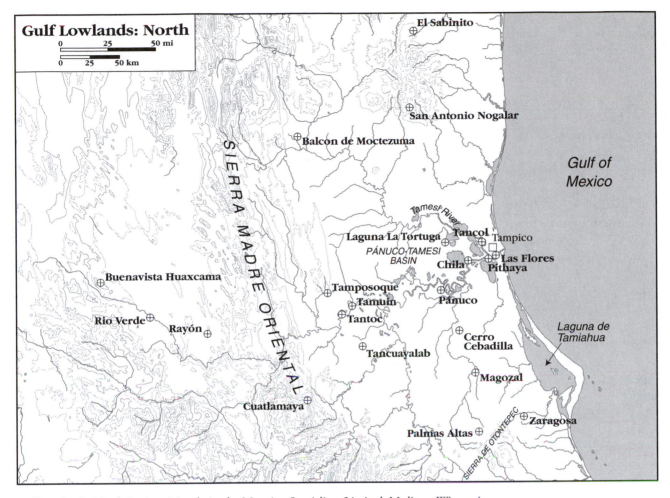

Gulf Lowlands: North Region. Map design by Mapping Specialists, Limited, Madison, Wisconsin.

ous. Agricultural activities may have coexisted with successful older lifestyles for a long time in the northern lowlands of the Gulf Coast. Based on limited evidence, Olmec influence from the south is weak until the Middle Formative (c. 900–300 B.C.), and even then is apparently not pervasive. These circumstances may reflect a generally sparse receptive population or, more likely, an inadequate archaeological corpus.

Villages grew larger during the Middle Formative, initially stretching for at least 1.5 kilometers along the river at Pánuco (Aguilar phase), and perhaps as much as 2.5 kilometers by the end of the period (Chila phase). Domestic structures included apsidal shapes, with wattle-and-daub walls and thatched roofs. These may have first appeared about the end of the previous period, but they can be confirmed at these later time levels. Ritual struc-

tures were mostly of modest height, as at Chila, where there are conical mounds of earth with burnt-clay floors, but without apparent plaza groupings. Shellfish remains progressively declined in midden deposits. White (surface wash) grater bowls and stone chips continued to be abundant, and maize-grinding implements were only slightly more numerous than earlier, suggesting continuity and gradual change from the diet of the terminal Early Formative. In the latter portion of the period at Pánuco, white-wares, now sometimes with true slips, remained popular, as were composite-silhouette forms. Although it is probable that earlier evidence of cotton-weaving will be found, the first known sherd spindle whorls and fabric impressions on pottery occur in these levels. In some regions there may be discontinuities between this and the following period.

G

The Late Formative (c. 300 B.C.–A.D. 300) was a time of rapid change, migrations from the north, and general population increase. Towns expanded farther, as at Pánuco and Laguna de la Tortuga. Locations for the exploitation of shellfish, as at Pithaya, were still occupied. Cities—such as Tantoc, with the largest earthen buildings in the North Gulf Lowlands—may have come into being by the latter portion of this period or the beginning of the next. Some of the bigger population centers may have been multiethnic polities. Both round and rectangular structures occurred, as well as plazas, and some structures may have had stone slab facings. Fired earthen floors continue in both domestic and ritual structures. Artifacts reflect considerable cultural diversity.

While ceramics at Pánuco appear initially to be transitional from the preceding period, those downstream at Tancol are quite distinct and regionally intrusive. Blackwares are abundant. At Pánuco some ceramics had fresco exterior, or incised interior, decoration, and most were polished. Bowls with insloping sides and inverted lips were popular, and both ladles and whistles began to appear in significant numbers. The Tancol complex contains coarse paste ceramics with black-slipped, unpolished exteriors. Hemispherical bowls with flattened rims were common, as were *molcajetes*. Decoration was mostly by incision and grooving, occurring on the exterior, rim, or interior. Red paint was sometimes used on decorated exteriors. The geographical extent of the Tancol culture has never been determined.

The Classic period (c. A.D. 300–900) is represented at numerous sites situated throughout the area. Riverbank and lagoon settlements such as Pánuco and Pithaya continued to be important, but a great diversity of locations conducive to agriculture were occupied throughout the lowlands. During the early centuries of the period, settlement expanded well into the neighboring uplands along trade routes or canyons with agriculturally exploitable microenvironments, particularly in the mountain border zone to the north. At such locations, sprawling sites (San Antonio Nogalar, El Sabinito, Balcón de Moctezuma) had abundant round domestic and small ritual structures, as well as an occasional ball court. By the end of the period, the western margins were also amply settled (Río Verde, Rayón) and there were even notable sites more than 250 kilometers inland at over 1,200 meters elevation (Buenavista). With the possible exception of Tantoc on the fringe of the central Pánuco lowland basin, this appears to have been a time of mostly small and medium-sized polities. In many instances, ball game ritualism and architecture were significantly influenced by concepts emanating from the North Central Gulf Lowlands and its dynamic urban centers, especially El Pital and later, in the middle and latter years of the period, El Tajín. Classic Veracruz architectural elements, such as the cornices diagnostic of ritual constructions, have been found at diverse locations, including Cerro Cebadilla and Cuatlamayan; they are also depicted in miniature on shell work from Pánuco. Stone yokes, although never so abundant as on the central Gulf Coast, have been found dispersed throughout the west central and southern portions of the area. Sculptural depictions with Classic Veracruz–style scrolls are also known from Tantoc, which may also have had its apogee at this time.

Ceramics reflect some outside influence, primarily in forms—such as cylindrical tripod vessels of the Early Classic—but once more largely suggest the elaboration of regional norms. Red and black wares, and especially open bowl forms, at times with exterior incised designs, were common throughout the period. Some vessel shapes (incurved bowls, jars) and decoration (exterior incision motifs, indented ridges) of the Late Classic are likely to imitate similar ceramics from the North Central Gulf (El Tajín). Clay figurines, mostly solid but with many mold-made by the Late Classic, are ubiquitous and highly diverse, many of them apparently representing both male and female ballplayers. Wheeled clay zoomorphic figures, probably used ritually rather than as toys, first appear at this time. Shell carving was a true specialty of the area and is manifest in a wide assortment of pectorals, gorgets, and ear ornaments. These vary greatly in quality from very rustic to highly detailed narrative scenes; the best are clearly among the highest-quality Mesoamerican shell work. Both rectangular and round structures are known from this period, some with asphalt coatings and many with stone facings. The North Gulf Lowlands has the greatest number of known round temples and structures in Mesoamerica. By the end of the period in some lowland regions (Tamuín, Tamposoque), large platforms, which in turn supported temples, palaces, and tombs, were in use. Stone sculptures of standing figures in sub-human scale, for which the North Gulf Lowlands region is noted, may have been initiated about this time, but most are likely to date to the following period. Many sites that flourished toward the end of the Classic (Tamuín, Buenavista, Pánuco) appear to have had continuous occupation into the next period.

G

The first centuries of the Postclassic period (c. A.D. 900–1520) were a time of florescence, followed by sudden dispersal and then partial resettlement. At sites such as Tamuín, Pánuco, Tancol, and Las Flores there were ample populations. Nevertheless, with extensive evidence of warfare, any large polities are likely to have been ephemeral. The use of cement-over-veneer masonry was now common on ritual structures, both rectangular and round. In some instances, as at Tamuín, there were monochrome or bichrome murals of processions, deity impersonators, and reticulate designs. Carved shell ornaments were extremely abundant and widely dispersed; many depict rulership, conquest, or ball game rites that may have been derived from the North Central Gulf Lowlands.

Copper, in the form of solid cast bells as well as thin beaten sheets modified for pendants, earplugs, and masks, first appeared at this time. Fine-paste redwares, often with black paint designs, were produced in great numbers. Incurved plates and small, decorated ollas were prevalent. The ceramic corpus also includes older shapes revived from the Terminal Formative, such as tetrapod supports, bowls with inverted rims, and some composite-silhouette profiles. Decoration and iconography, as well as trade wares, often indicate influence from the central Gulf Coast at the initiation of the period. Pipes appear in significant numbers and probably represent the spread of a significant tobacco cult. Although found throughout the lowlands, these objects appear to have been particularly popular in the western margins of the area, around Río Verde and Rayón, where they may have still greater time depth.

Many of the larger sculptures known from the area date to this period. Most are anthropomorphic, 25 to 75 percent life size, and carved from sandstone flags. The majority appear to have been utilized in a freestanding mode on or about low ritual structures. A number have insertion points in their chests or hands for stones, staffs, and other ritual accouterments. Depicted primarily are tattooed rulers (at Tamuín and Tancuayalab), warrior-rulers (at Cerro Cebadilla and Zarogosa), and women (at Mogazal and Palmas Altas). The female depictions are thought to be indicative of a widespread lowland adoration of Tlazolteotl-Ixcuina, a popular goddess associated with a host of lunar, warfare, and fertility attributes. The cult, widespread in the Postclassic, may have reached its apogee here in northeastern Mesoamerica. Small sculptures of old men with staffs are also found throughout the area and in adjoining regions. The quality of depiction of the area's sculptural corpus is highly variable, the best being fully comparable to any other Mesoamerican sculpture of the time.

After approximately two centuries there appears to have been a massive disruption of settlement. Probably occasioned by climatic alteration in the form of widespread and prolonged drought, it led to the abandonment of many sites. There was extensive migration both within and beyond the borders of the area. Among the neighboring regions feeling the impact of this phenomenon and subsequent movements were the higher elevations to the west, the coast of Tamaulipas, and the North Central Gulf Lowlands. In the northern portions of the last there are many sites of this period with sculpture and architecture that are largely indistinguishable from that of the North Gulf Lowlands region. This general southward dispersal is likely to have been a contributing factor in the destruction of important earlier cities such as El Tajín. Some Gulf Coast ritualism, particularly elite forms of the ball game cult and, perhaps, certain tobacco rites, may have traveled beyond the Mesoamerican frontiers at about this time.

Following the twelfth-century dispersal, warfare remained important, but population apparently increased in many previously abandoned or affected lowland zones, as along the Pánuco River. Even frontier sites in the Sierra de Tamaulipas (e.g., San Antonio Nogalar) were reoccupied. Peoples from the North Gulf Lowlands, probably primarily Huastecs, are likely to have traveled or migrated widely at this time. Most sites were small or medium sized, although a few, such as Cerro Cebidilla, were large. Shell and bone ornaments were common, as were small stone death bundle masks in some regions. Extremely popular throughout the area were fine-paste Black-on-White vessels, one of the most distinctive ceramic complexes in Mesoamerica. Examples have been found as far north as the Rio Grande valley and as far south as central Veracruz. Incurved plates with central designs were most abundant; anthropomorphic and zoomorphic effigy vessels, some spouted, were also prevalent. During the final half-century of the period Aztec tribute conquests began, but these were not consolidated before the European arrival in 1519.

The Spanish conquest of the North Gulf Lowlands met prolonged and fierce resistance from the Huastecs. There followed large-scale, European-induced epidemics of catastrophic proportions, which depopulated most of the lowlands by the end of the sixteenth century. Much of the area reverted to rainforest or wooded savanna,

G

particularly in the south and around the Pánuco River. Resettlement was slow, accelerating only toward the end of the eighteenth century and during the nineteenth century, when ancient sculptures and buildings began to be reported by travelers. By the beginning of the twentieth century, oil exploration resulted in an expanding road network, deforestation, and still more archaeological finds, some competently reported by oil geologists (Staub, Adrian, Muir) and dedicated enthusiasts (Meade). Formal explorations did not begin until the excavations of DuSolier and Ekholm in the early 1940s. Recent INAH reconstruction projects have been undertaken in the 1990s at Tantoc and Tamuín, as well as El Sabinito in the Sierra de Tamaulipas. There has been no exploration of early Spanish settlements. In general, given the vast geographic extent and the considerable number of sites, extremely little systematic research has been undertaken in the North Gulf Lowlands, leaving one of Mesoamerica's most complex and distinctive areas still a major archaeological frontier.

FURTHER READINGS

Du Solier, W., A. D. Krieger, and J. B. Griffin. 1947. The Archaeological Zone of Buena Vista, Huaxcama, San Luis Potosí, Mexico. *American Antiquity* 13:15–32.

Ekholm, G. F. 1944. Excavations at Tampico and Pánuco in the Huasteca, Mexico, *American Musuem of Natural History Anthropological Papers* 38:319–512.

MacNeish, R. S. 1958. Preliminary Archaeological Investigations in the Sierra de Tamaulipas, Mexico. *Transactions of the American Philosophical Society* 48:1–209.

Meade, J. 1957. Las Ruinas de la Huasteca Potosina. *Letras Potosinas* (San Luis Potosí) 15 (125–126).

Merino Carrion, B. L., A. G. Cook, and L. A. Castaneda Zerecero. 1989. Proyecto definición del Formativo en la cuenca baja del Río Pánuco. *Boletin, Consejo de Arqueologia, Instituto Nacional de Antropología e Historia,* pp. 82–85.

Michelet, D. 1996. *Río Verde, San Luis Potosí.* Mexico City: Instituto de Cultura San Luis Potosí and Centre Français d'Études Mexicaines et Centraméricaines.

Sanders, W. 1978. *The Lowland Huasteca, Archaeological Survey and Excavation, 1957 Field Season.* University of Missouri Monographs in Anthropology, 4. Columbia: Museum of Anthropology.

Stresser-Pean, G. 1964. Première campagne de fouilles à Tamtok, près de Tamuín, Huasteca. *International Congress of Americanists,* 1962, Acta 1:387–394.

———. 1977. *San Antonio Nogalar.* Études Mesoaméricaines, 3. Mexico City: Mission Archéologique et Etnologique Française au Mexique.

Wilkerson, S. J. K. 1980. Huastec Presence and Cultural Chronology in North-Central Veracruz, Mexico. *Actes du XLII Congres Internationale des Américanistes* 9-B: 31–47.

———. 1994. Nahua Presence on the Mesoamerican Gulf Coast. In E. Quinones-Keber (ed.), *Chipping Away on Earth,* pp. 177–186. Culver City, Calif.: Labyrinthos Press.

———. 1996. The Huasteca. In B. Tenanbaum (ed.), *Encyclopedia of Latin American History and Culture,* vol. 3, p. 215. New York: Charles Scribner's Sons.

S. Jeffrey K. Wilkerson

SEE ALSO

Gulf Lowlands; Gulf Lowlands: North Central Region

Gulf Lowlands: South Central Region

The Veracruz South Central Gulf plain is delimited topographically by the Sierra de Chiconquiaco to the northwest, the Tuxtla Mountains to the southeast, and the Sierra Madre Oriental to the west. Elevations vary dramatically as a consequence of mountains framing the plain. Rainfall varies markedly because of rain shadow effects and the higher rainfall on mountain slopes, ranging from an average of 2,500–3,000 mm annually in piedmont or montane locations down to 1,000 mm in part of the central coastal plain, sometimes referred to as the "semiarid zone." The force of northerly winter storms is partly absorbed by exceptionally high dune ridges fronting the Gulf of Mexico, which protect inner waterways and lagoons.

The Papaloapan River and its tributaries (such as the San Juan, Tesechoacan, and Blanco) form a particularly large drainage system in the south of the region, with extensive estuarine lagoons and mangrove swamps near the Gulf. The Papaloapan drainage includes the western Tuxtlas. The Cotaxtla, Jamapa, Antigua, and Actopan rivers serve smaller drainages that transect the coastal plain to the northwest. Isla de Sacrificios and smaller nearby coral islands off the Bay of Veracruz were part of the landscape. Native inhabitants used them for ritual purposes such as temples and burials; they may also have served as lookouts for coastal canoe movements.

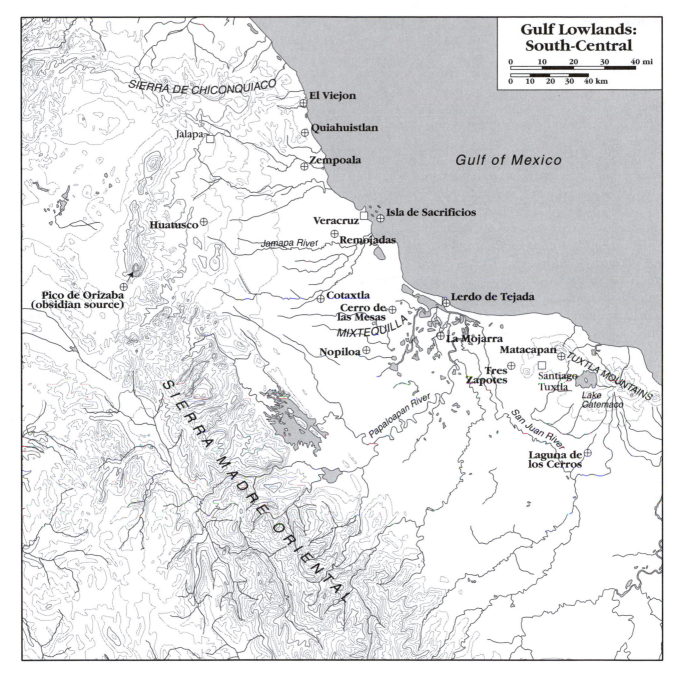

Gulf Lowlands: South Central Region. Map design by Mapping Specialists Limited, Madison, Wisconsin.

Summer rains are relatively reliable for rainfall farming throughout the region, but multi-cropping depends on a few locales with a potential for three farming techniques: canal irrigation, practiced in the pre-Hispanic period mainly around the archaeological site of Zempoala; raised fields, documented mainly at Neveria and Mandinga and at some spots in the lower Papaloapan basin; and well or "pot" irrigation, in which people pump or dip water from a high water table, as practiced today in the Ignacio de la Llave area. Terraces were constructed on some of the

G

mountain slopes. Winter storms crossing the Gulf are unreliable in the South Central Gulf area for rains to sustain winter crops, in contrast to their role in multi-cropping in the South Gulf region. The relatively dry winter months in the South Central region were significant, however, for pre-Hispanic and historic cotton farming, which involved multi-cropping with winter cotton and summer foods.

Mineral and stone resources in south central Veracruz are restricted to montane and piedmont areas, with the exception of low-grade salt, which according to early documents was produced in the lower Papaloapan drainage. The nearest obsidian sources are Pico de Orizaba, Veracruz, nearby Guadalupe Victoria in the Sierra Madres, and Zaragoza-Oyameles in the Puebla-Tlaxcala area. Volcanic stone in the Tuxtlas was selected for many Olmec monuments as well as for *manos* and *metates*. Volcanic stones from the Sierra Madres, however, were probably the common materials for monuments and grinding tools for most of south central Veracruz.

Organic products were the chief natural riches of the region, mainly through agricultural production. A broad range of Mesoamerican staple crops, tropical fruits, and fiber plants were grown reliably with rainfall farming, and riverine locations benefited from annual flooding that renewed soils. By the Classic period, cotton fiber was spun using fired ceramic spindle whorls, and elaborate textiles were depicted on figurines; however, poor preservation means that no ancient textiles have been recovered archaeologically. Late Postclassic tribute to the Aztec Triple Alliance emphasized finished textiles, many of them elaborately decorated, as well as raw cotton. Additionally, brightly colored feathers were an important local product and export item. The rivers and estuaries of the region provided opportunities for fishing and shellfish gathering, and land animals could be hunted—for example, deer for meat or jaguars for pelts.

Reliable annual agriculture meant that the South Central Gulf sustained continued human settlement and land use. We have little information about endemic tropical diseases prior to European settlement, and the region seems to have been well populated before epidemic diseases spread in the wake of European contact and conquest.

Archaeological work in the South Central Gulf has lagged in comparison with better-known parts of Mesoamerica. Instead, much attention has been directed toward the Olmecs in the South Gulf area and to El Tajín in the North Central Gulf region. Chronologies are poorly anchored by chronometric dates, and consistent procedures are not characteristic among investigators in their definitions of artifact types and phases. For some sites, such as Tres Zapotes, multiple-phase schemes have been proposed. In Table 1, only selected phases from accessible publications are shown. There are insufficient well-published stratigraphic excavations to provide a backbone of evidence to understand social variability and change. Perhaps the lack of stone for masonry construction at most centers has led to under-appreciation of this region, since many of the spectacular local achievements have been discovered through salvage or excavation. At most centers, rammed earth construction was used for major building platforms, and the buildings on top were made from perishable materials; Postclassic Zempoala is one exception, with masonry architecture. Archaeological zones open to the public include the Late Classic site of Zapotal, the Postclassic sites of Zempoala and Quiahuistlan, and the historic site of Antigua and the fortifications of San Juan de Ulúa. A state museum of anthropology in Jalapa and an archaeological museum at Santiago Tuxtla are among the institutions that offer archaeological information for visitors.

Some pre-Hispanic periods in particular are poorly known, especially the Paleoindian and Archaic, but also the Early and Middle Formative. By Late and Terminal Formative times, excavations at Cerro de las Mesas, Chalahuite-Trapiche, Remojadas, and La Mojarra begin to flesh out the archaeological record. The Classic and Postclassic periods likewise can be addressed with a variety of evidence. As in many other parts of Mesoamerica in recent decades, there have been several salvage projects, but pending publication, these projects remain out of reach for a wider audience.

No Paleoindian remains have been reported, but this does not mean there was no human presence at that time. Alluviation, erosion, and lush vegetation make it especially difficult to locate small, ephemeral sites. For the Archaic period, we have hints about human activities. Aceramic levels with lithics at Colonia Ejidal were associated with a Late Archaic radiocarbon date. At El Viejón, Archaic lithics were mentioned from surface observation, but no details are known. A lake core pollen sequence and radiocarbon dates from the Tuxtla Mountains indicate agricultural disturbance near the close of the Late Archaic period.

Early ceramic occupations prior to the Olmec era have not yet been found in south central Veracruz. There are possible traces of Early Formative people on the basis of ceramics, but little can be said about the South Central

TABLE 1. SOUTH CENTRAL GULF LOWLANDS.

Dates and Processes/Events	Chronology: Phases	Sites, Artifacts
Spanish conquest	**Colonial**	Antigua; Veracruz; Villa Rica
Aztec Triple Alliance conquest	**PC: L.** Cerro de las Mesas Upper II	Cempoala; Cotaxtla; Quauhtochco; Quiahuistlan
Change toward highland-related styles in most of area	**PC: M.** Cerro de las Mesas Upper I	El Sauce
Events of period not yet well defined	**PC: E.** Soncautla Complex	
Flourishing local tradition of elaborate ceramics, both vessels and figurines; increase in Maya-related styles	**CL: L.** Limon; Matacapan F; Tres Zapotes IV	Nopiloa; Patarata 52; Tres Zapotes; Zapotal
Teotihuacán influence, enclave	**CL: M.** Matacapan D, E	Cerro de las Mesas; Matacapan
Local figurines and pottery diversify; cotton becomes important; obsidian blades widespread	**CL: E.** Camaron; Upper Remojadas; Matacapan C; Tres Zapotes III	Cerro de las Mesas; Patarata 52; Remojadas; Tres Zapotes
La Mojarra and Tuxtlas script; stela C at Tres Zapotes; long count dates	**PrCl: T.** Tres Zapotes II	Cerro de las Mesas; Mojarra; Remojadas; Tres Zapotes; Tuxtla Statuette
Regional style in pottery and figurines	**PrCl: L.** Lower Remojadas; Matacapan B; Pozas	Bezuapan; Cerro de las Mesas; Chalahuite; Remojadas; Tres Zapotes
Little involvement in Olmec iconography	**PrCl: M.** Matacapan A; Lower Tres Zapotes	Joya; Tres Zapotes; Viejon
Little occupational evidence	**PrCl: E.**	Joya
Little occupational evidence	**Arch.**	Colonia Ejidal
No finds yet	**PaleoInd.**	

Legend: **PrCL:** Formative; **CL:** Classic; **PC:** Postclassic; **E:** Early; **M:** Middle; **L:** Late; **T:** Terminal.

Gulf area during this period. During the Middle Formative period, ceramic evidence shows occupation at scattered sites, but most of the region seems to have been scarcely involved in the Olmec style in either monumental or portable form. One exception is El Viejón, Actopan, where a low-relief of a standing figure was carved on a block of stone, and some testing yielded a blackware vessel with a stylistic variant of the frontal earth monster visage. This site, like Los Ídolos, Misantla, in the North Central Gulf area, is near the Sierra de Chiconquiaco, well removed from the Olmec heartland. In this respect, these two sites are more comparable to scattered instances of Olmec-style sculpture along the Pacific coast of Chiapas and Guatemala. One possible reason that the South Central Gulf region was not as active as the South Gulf area in the development of chiefly centers and Olmec symbols is that the former's population may have been smaller and less concentrated. Multi-crop rainfall farming is more favorable in the South Gulf area and may have contributed to the attraction of that region.

In the Late and Terminal Formative periods, the growth of centers and the elaboration of new styles in monument carving, calendrics, and writing show that the lower Papaloapan Basin was a key region politically. External sculptural stylistic relationships are mainly with the Pacific coast of Chiapas and Guatemala, showing that the "trans-Isthmian lowlands" continued to maintain long-distance interactions after the Olmec era. The best-known centers in the South Central Gulf region are Tres Zapotes on the eastern side of the lower Papaloapan Basin and Cerro de las Mesas to the west, but other locations, such as Lerdo de Tejada, have produced carved monuments dated stylistically to epi-Olmec times and may have been important settlement or political nodes. La

G

Mojarra yielded a stela with an elaborately garbed leader and lengthy inscription dating to the Terminal Formative period. Testing at the associated mounds revealed mainly Classic occupation, however, giving the stela an anomalous context. The script on the La Mojarra stela, like that on the small Tuxtla statuette, is interpreted as reflecting a pre-Proto-Zoquean language. The long count dates on these carvings anchor this script in the Terminal Formative period and thus suggest the possible language group of Late and Terminal Formative peoples in the lower Papaloapan Basin. Iconographic and ceramic continuities from earlier Olmec times and those leading into the Classic period raise the possibility that this same language group was present in the region for a long time. If so, some portion of the South Central Gulf area that previously was attributed to Totonac speakers may instead have been occupied by Mixe-Zoquean speakers. Totonac speakers were present at Spanish contact to the northwest—for example, at Zempoala.

Pottery and figurines, artifacts in wider circulation or of broader access than inscribed monuments, indicate a degree of regionalization in stylistic traits by the Late and Terminal Formative periods; for example, Lower Remojadas–style figurines are characteristic in the South Central Gulf area except in the Tuxtlas; so, too, is the "minute incision style" on bowls. Regionalization is part of a wider trend in Mesoamerica and may be tied to proliferation of hierarchical polities, greater competition among them, and population growth.

A lavish central burial in a low mound at Cerro de las Mesas contained an extended adult accompanied by a stone yoke and elaborate pottery vessels in Late or Terminal Formative styles. Stone yokes are linked symbolically to ball game heavy belts. This burial is one of the specific indications of marked hierarchical social differentiation, in addition to the figural representations on stelae.

The precise details of settlement hierarchy remain obscure for these two periods, in part because there is also considerable Classic period occupation and construction at centers such as Cerro de las Mesas and Tres Zapotes. Near Cerro de las Mesas there was at least one small village dating to the Late Formative period, represented by a cluster of domestic mounds, and residential occupation seems limited to the Cerro de las Mesas environs, only spreading eastward in the Mixtequilla (the area surrounding Cerro de las Mesas) with the Classic period. In the lower Cotaxtla drainage, where a pattern of growth and dispersion of settlements into different ecological zones can be detected in the Late and Terminal Formative periods, there are differentials in the visibility of earlier occupations that hinder understanding of settlement processes. In the Tuxtlas, survey of the Catemaco River area shows that hierarchical settlement differentiation was slow to develop during the Formative period, compared with the riverine Olmec area in the South Gulf region; in the Tuxtlas, periodic volcanic eruptions led to occasional relocation and disruptions of population.

In several respects the Classic period shows cultural and social developments that build on Late and Terminal Formative patterns, but considerable reorganization occurred in the economy. Classic period economies show a thoroughgoing shift to prismatic blades from flake or flake-and-blade assemblages. Apparently blades were mainly from the Zaragoza-Oyameles source. This contrasts with greater diversity in obsidian sources during the Formative period and greater variability in whether blade technology was employed; for example, some locales show considerable use of a flake technology until the Late Formative period. Cotton spinning is well documented for the Papaloapan Basin and Tuxtlas on the basis of ceramic spindle whorls from the Classic period, including the Early Classic. Whether this was more generally the case in the South Central Gulf region remains to be determined. Classic figurines frequently depict elaborate clothing, which suggests that cloth became important in social displays. Additionally, there is evidence of specialized pottery production in the Classic period, but we cannot judge to what degree this contrasts with the Formative period until we have more systematic investigations for earlier times. Cotton production and specialized pottery manufacture are signs of a more complex and diversified economy in the Classic period for the South Central Gulf area. Since obsidian blades from the highlands were widely distributed, Gulf Lowlands inhabitants were tied to reliable exchange processes with the neighboring highlands, perhaps exporting complementary lowland products such as textiles or feathers.

Classic period settlement in the lower Cotaxtla basin shows a settlement hierarchy with indications of three sizes of centers and a likely division of the area into several settlement systems. Ball courts are common at all types of centers. The Classic period also witnessed striking growth in occupation remains and monumental architectural investment in the Cerro de las Mesas area. Numerous carved monuments from Cerro de las Mesas, mainly Early Classic stylistically, include two stelae with long count dates that fall within the Early Classic period. Monumental construction in the Cerro de las Mesas area is not associated with nucleated settlement; rather, residential occupation was dispersed in the countryside in a fashion analogous to the Maya Lowlands.

The Classic period role of Tres Zapotes remains ill defined, but farther eastward in the Tuxtla Mountains, Matacapan became an important center, dominating the Catemaco drainage. Matacapan has architectural (*talud* and *tablero* temple platforms) and artifactual (candeleros, cylinder tripods) ties to Teotihuacan. Matacapan has been interpreted as partly an ethnic enclave of Teotihuacanos, perhaps relocated to the site for entrepreneurial or state economic reasons. It also had a specialized ceramic industry that contrasts with the otherwise scattered, less concentrated evidence of Classic period pottery production from the lower Papaloapan basin at Patarata 52, La Mojarra, and in the Cerro de las Mesas environs. We lack direct evidence of ceramic production from the rest of the South Central Gulf region during the Classic period, but this is probably a result of the kinds of archaeological investigations conducted.

In contrast to Matacapan, there is little evidence for close connections with Teotihuacan in the case of Cerro de las Mesas, where elites were aware of and emulated some stylistic features of Teotihuacan but maintained a strongly local cultural tradition. Instead, elite emulation appears likely as an important process that led to selective Teotihuacan-style traits. The lively and quite diverse Classic figurine tradition in the South Central Gulf area is a good index of the elaboration of local cultural practices that are quite distinct and independent from Teotihuacan in the Classic period. Perhaps most widely recognized are the "laughing-face" figurines, which typically show a grimacing or laughing expression and a posture with upraised arms and hands. The symbolism of these figurines remains unclear, although drug-induced states or ritual sacrifice have been suggested. Also distinctive of at least part of the South Central Gulf area is the Patarata scroll style, executed primarily on bowls and figurines. It contrasts spatially and stylistically with the interlace scroll style from the North Central Gulf region, apparent in carved stone ball game paraphernalia—yokes, *hachas,* and *palmas*—as well as on later bas-reliefs at El Tajín.

After the fall of Teotihuacan as a major power, Matacapan declined somewhat in size but continued to function as a ceramic production center. Major constructions and offerings continued in the Cerro de las Mesas area—for example, at El Zapotal, where an unfired, near life-sized, painted clay effigy of the underworld death god, seated in his temple, was buried accompanied by elaborate offerings and human burials with valuable funerary items. It is difficult to point to any major disruptions in the South Central Gulf area following the demise of Teotihuacan, but there were changes of a more subtle nature that remain to be investigated. Some exchange patterns and possibly political relations shifted. For example, this is the period when Tuxtlas Polychrome became either closely imitated or, more likely, imported to the Cerro de las Mesas area. Tuxtlas Polychrome and some figurine and vessel styles share a few traits with materials from the Maya Lowlands, perhaps indicating new political alignments.

The Classic period traditions of the South Central Gulf region do not show continuity into the Postclassic period, or at least with the Middle Postclassic period. On the basis of systematic data from the lower Cotaxtla Basin and the Cerro de las Mesas area, this portion of the region underwent dramatic settlement reorganization by Middle Postclassic times, and possibly earlier. Earlier centers were abandoned, and new centers display distinct organizational plans. The Early Postclassic period remains poorly known, but the Middle Postclassic displays new ceramic patterns of central highland affinity, including *guinda* pottery, *comales* (griddles), a local Black-on-Orange pottery, *fondo sellado,* and Cholula-like polychromes, as well as local polychromes. Still other polychromes are more common to the northwest, such as Tres Picos or Isla de Sacrificios Polychromes. These latter two polychromes appear only rarely in the Cotaxtla and Blanco drainages, suggesting economic and political divisions among Gulf Lowlands groups. These general pottery configurations continue into the Late Postclassic period, when Aztec III Black-on-Orange pottery and Texcoco Molded censers are occasionally imported, but more commonly just closely imitated, in the Cotaxtla and Blanco drainages.

To the northwest at Zempoala, related changes occurred that led to ceramics similar to those in the highlands. In contrast, in the western Tuxtlas these highland-related ceramic patterns do not appear. The Postclassic remains poorly defined in the Tuxtlas on the basis of archaeology, but early historic documents indicate a large population and many settlements. The dramatic switch to mainly highland-related pottery styles in much of the South Central Gulf region raises many interpretive issues. Some archaeologists interpret the change as deriving from the intrusion of new ethnic groups from the highlands into the coastal plain. Or did the Classic patterns undergo a decline and collapse prior to highland intrusion, leaving

G

something of a vacuum? Or did local populations continue, with the adoption of new foreign styles?

Ethnohistory recounts late processes affecting the South Central Gulf region. The Aztec Triple Alliance attacked and incorporated several provinces and extracted tribute. Aztec personnel were reportedly stationed at Zempoala and Cotaxtla, for example. Later, this region was one of the early foci of Spanish colonial settlement, with successive relocations of Cortes's coastal headquarters from near Quiahuistlan to Antigua, and finally to Veracruz City. Spanish rule brought a series of economic changes to the region, with cattle ranching, sugar cane cultivation, and shipping as new activities. Native population dropped drastically as a result of new diseases and Spanish policies, and today native language populations are found only in the Tuxtla Mountains or in the Sierra Madres.

FURTHER READINGS

Coe, M. D. 1965. Archaeological Synthesis of Southern Veracruz and Tabasco. In G. R. Willey (ed.), *Handbook of Middle American Indians,* vol. 3, *Archaeology of Southern Mesoamerica,* Part 2, pp. 679–715. Austin: University of Texas Press.

Curet, L. A., B. L. Stark, and S. Vásquez Z. 1994. Postclassic Change in South-Central Veracruz, Mexico. *Ancient Mesoamerica* 5:13–32.

Ethnic Arts Council of Los Angeles. 1971. *Ancient Art of Veracruz.* Los Angeles.

Justeson, J. S., and T. Kaufman. 1993. A Decipherment of Epi-Olmec Hieroglyphic Writing. *Science* 259:1703–1711.

Medellín Zenil, A. 1960. *Cerámicas del Totonacapan: Exploraciones Arqueológicas en el centro de Veracruz.* Jalapa: Instituto de Antropología, Universidad Veracruzana.

Pool, C. A., and R. S. Santley. 1992. Middle Classic Pottery Economics in the Tuxtla Mountains, Southern Veracruz, Mexico. In G. J. Bey III, and C. A. Pool (eds.), *Ceramic Production and Distribution: An Integrated Approach,* pp. 205–234. Niwot, Colo.: Westview Press.

Santley, R. S., and P. J. Arnold III. 1996. Prehispanic Settlement Patterns in the Tuxtla Mountains, Southern Veracruz, Mexico. *Journal of Field Archaeology* 23: 225–259.

Stark, B. L. 1989. *Patarata Pottery: Classic Period Ceramics of the South-Central Gulf Coast, Veracruz, Mexico.* Anthropological Papers of the University of Arizona, 51. Tucson: University of Arizona Press.

Stark, B. L., and P. A. Arnold III (eds.). 1997. *Olmec to Aztec: Settlement Pattern Research in the Ancient Gulf.* Tucson: University of Arizona Press.

Stark, B. L., L. Heller, M. D. Glascock, J. M. Elam, and H. Neff. 1992. Obsidian Artifact Source Analysis for the Mixtequilla Region, South-Central Veracruz, Mexico. *Latin American Antiquity* 3:221–239.

Stark, B. L., L. Heller, and M. A. Ohnersorgen. 1998. People with Cloth: Mesoamerican Economic Change from the Perspective of Cotton in South-Central Veracruz. *Latin American Antiquity* 9:1–30.

Barbara L. Stark

Gulf Lowlands: South Region

The South Gulf Coast region has the dual distinction of being widely acknowledged as the central hearth of early Mesoamerican civilization and, ironically, as being virtually unknown archaeologically. This region includes the lower courses of the Coatzacoalcos and Uxpanapa River drainages of southernmost Veracruz and westernmost Tabasco. A lowland, swampy, tropical zone of lagoons, estuaries, oxbows, and sluggish meandering rivers, this region is bordered on the north and west by the volcanic Tuxtla Mountains, on the east by the swampy Chontalpa region, and on the south by the foothills of northern Chiapas and Tehuantepec. The earliest and largest cities of Mesoamerica are found in this region. Perhaps because of the current lack of information, these cities appear archaeologically almost out of nowhere, with no clear cultural or historic antecedents, and disappear nearly as suddenly.

The South Gulf Coast region boasts four of the most important Formative sites in Mesoamerica—San Lorenzo, El Manatí, Las Limas, and La Venta—but it is otherwise almost unknown archaeologically. The spectacular Maya site of Comalcalco is on the eastern margin of the region and represents the westernmost extension of Maya speakers into the Gulf Lowlands. Thus, the eastern boundary of the South Gulf Coast represents a cultural and linguistic boundary between Maya and non-Maya peoples. Many of the daily practices and tools for living in this environment, however, would have been essentially the same among all the different cultural groups.

Archaeology in the South Gulf Coast has focused on Formative Olmec developments (c. 1300–400 B.C.) to the near exclusion of all other time periods and groups. Evidence of later occupations overlies some Olmec sites, but little is known of these more recent peoples other than what can be determined from surface remains and maps.

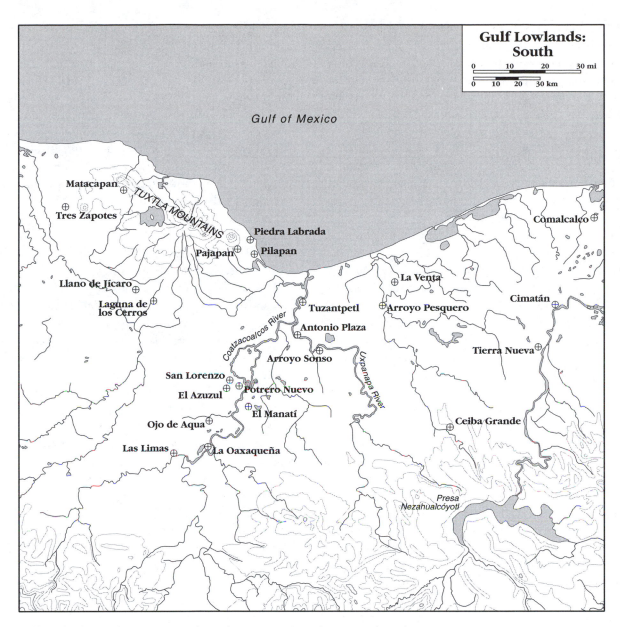

Gulf Lowlands: South Region. Map design by Mapping Specialists Limited, Madison, Wisconsin.

Apparently they were more numerous than the early Olmecs and tended to live in more nucleated cities. The city plan from the Late Classic/Postclassic occupation at Las Limas, for example, shows modest civic architecture and numerous tight arrangements of courtyard groups of four low-mound structures arranged in a rectangular pattern around a central courtyard. The general demographic pattern for the region shows two strong periods of occupation that date respectively to the Formative (1500–400 B.C.) and the Late Classic/Postclassic periods (A.D. 1000–1300). In between, the Late Formative and Early Classic was a period of minimal population.

Overall, the region appears to be characterized archaeologically by dramatic shifts of population and settlement locations. This may be due in large part to local environmental circumstances, such as shifting river courses, and/or to geological events, such as volcanic eruptions in the Tuxtla Mountains just to the northwest. Interregional politics may also have played a critical role. Summaries of the archaeological research in the South Gulf Coast region of necessity focus on the Olmecs and Formative period developments. It is worth noting that most models of Olmec civilization and ethnicity presume cultural continuity in the region despite the ragged pattern of site

G

settlement and abandonment. Currently, the most credible model identifies the Olmec as Mixe-Zoquean speakers and as related to the adjacent peoples of the Chiapas coast and interior. At the moment, however, this claim remains an unsubstantiated presumption, because sustained continuities in settlement and/or artifact traditions in the South Gulf Lowlands region have not been demonstrated. To the contrary, there is a bewildering variety of artifact types in all media, and these are interpreted as shifting cultural styles adopted by a stationary group, but they can just as easily be seen to signal population movements of different cultural groups.

At the time of the Spanish conquest, the South Gulf Coast region was occupied by at least four different ethnic groups: Mixe and Zoque (both also called "Popolucas"), Nahua, and Chontal Mayan speakers. Especially intriguing is the discontinuous distribution of these peoples; different ethnic groups were juxtaposed in a jumbled mosaic of isolated groups. The main body of the Chontal Maya inhabited the Chontalpa region on the eastern border of the region, with some enclaves within the region itself. The very complexity of the pattern suggests frequent movements of peoples and of intrusions by foreigners, such as the late-arriving Nahua-speakers from the Mexican plateau.

Because of environmental constraints, all groups shared a basic lifestyle oriented to the large rivers and lagoons abundant in this tropical region. Many of the communities specialized in trade. The famous port of trade, Xicalango, frequented by Aztec traders (*pochteca*) was situated just to the east of the South Gulf Coast region (in modern-day Campeche), and the region of the famous Putún traders was just to the south and east of this city. Cities observed by Spanish conquerors were thin ribbons of settlement, some over a league (c. 5 kilometers) in length, that paralleled major rivers. The peoples in this region and the adjacent Chontalpa region of Tabasco were middlemen traders who mediated between the highland traders of the Chiapas interior, just upstream, and the circum-peninsular traders to the east. These were very much canoe cultures, with a focus on trade, water transport, and fishing; it seems probable that earlier peoples in this region had a similar emphasis. All the major Olmec cities of this region were built on what were principal rivers at the times of their occupation.

The Olmec story of the Gulf Coast Lowlands is usually told in two acts that focus on the sequentially important capital centers of San Lorenzo and La Venta. San Lorenzo came to power by 1300 B.C. (calibrated time) and col-lapsed by 900 B.C. It continued to be occupied for several centuries, but the number of inhabitants does not appear to have been significant. For its part, La Venta came into power by at least 850 B.C. and persisted until 400 B.C. It is not known why either city arose when and where it did, nor why each collapsed, but shifting river courses may have been involved in the decreased importance of both. San Lorenzo was occupied by sedentary agriculturalists several centuries before it became a major center. The earliest pottery there shows strong connections to that used by peoples of the Soconusco. Recent finds at the ceremonial site of El Manatí have substantiated that the ceramic-using peoples were in the South Gulf Coast region by at least 1650 B.C. and that they were already concerned with rituals connected to freshwater springs.

The data for pre-Olmec occupations in the South Gulf Lowlands are still too sparse to make strong claims for their indigenous roots in the region, and this remains a major topic for investigation. There is little doubt, however, that the bulk of subsequent developments were locally inspired. By 1000 B.C. San Lorenzo had become Mesoamerica's first city, and, at 690 hectares in extent, one of its largest ever. The center of the city consisted of massive terraces that required thousands of person-hours to construct. Also evident and prominent for the first time were massive, three-dimensional stone sculptures depicting humans, presumably kings, as well as animals and supernatural beings. The hallmark of early Olmec sculpture is the colossal basalt heads weighing up to ten tons or more, which depict obese, helmeted individuals—probably portraits of chiefs or kings depicted as warriors or ballplayers. There is abundant evidence of elite culture and differential privilege at San Lorenzo, especially in differences in residential architecture and in the consumption of special goods imported from outside regions.

One of the persistent questions for the early Olmec is whether or not they were a true state. San Lorenzo was clearly more elaborate and complex than contemporaneous centers in the same region, such as Las Limas (or Tres Zapotes, or Laguna de los Cerros in the Tuxtlas region to the west), but did the elites at San Lorenzo hold sway over those at smaller centers? Extant evidence is insufficient to decide the matter convincingly. However, the evidence for a single large political system, with its center at San Lorenzo, is more convincing than the alternative of numerous, competing, contemporaneous centers. If one considers relative site sizes and the presence or absence of large stone monuments, a clear four- or five-tiered settlement pattern becomes evident for the early Olmec. Early colossal heads are found only at San Lorenzo, thrones and smaller statuary are found at San Lorenzo and several smaller centers in its immediate orbit, and smaller sites lack sculpture altogether. In terms of site size, San Lorenzo during its apogee (c. 1100–950 B.C.) was nearly 700 hectares in extent; Las Limas was probably between 50 and 70 hectares; La Oaxaqueña and Ojo de Agua, subsidiaries to Las Limas, would have been third- and fourth-level settlements, respectively. When combined with evidence of influence in foreign regions, such as the Soconusco, the data suggest a state-level society at San Lorenzo.

The principal data in support of a network of competing Olmec chiefdoms come from La Venta and Tres Zapotes. Monumental sculpture at these sites is stylistically and thematically similar to that at San Lorenzo, especially the colossal heads. These data are problematic, however, because they are at odds with the ceramic and figurine data from these same sites. This is most clearly evident at La Venta, where evidence of occupation contemporaneous to San Lorenzo has yet to be found. The early-style sculptures at these sites require a different explanation; I suspect that they were reused. This interpretation is controversial, but it explains some major disjunctions between the two cities.

Rather than being an antagonist to San Lorenzo, La Venta was its successor. A novel innovation at La Venta was the incorporation of tall pyramids into the city center. Large, elevated basal platforms for special buildings, presumably temples and elite residences, were organized along a north–south alignment. Special offerings and sculptures were arranged along the same axial line. La Venta became the model for most early Middle Formative cities (c. 750–600 B.C.), especially those in the Chiapas interior, with which La Venta was linked by trade. Jade artifacts (polished celts and figurines) appear abundantly in La Venta offerings and elite burials.

Another innovation at La Venta was a shift from sculpture in the round to low-relief sculptures that depict multiple individuals on the same monument. Thematically, much of the art of La Venta appears to have been dedicated to rulers who dressed as gods, or to the gods themselves. Some monuments of gods were incorporated into the façade of the main pyramid in an arrangement that anticipated later Maya developments of stucco façades on temples. The influence of La Venta throughout greater Mesoamerica surpassed that of San Lorenzo. Low-relief monuments in the La Venta style show up as far north as Guerrero and as far south as El Salvador. These carvings have been variously interpreted as traders, priests, or kings, but the dress of the elite males depicted favors the last interpretation.

In sum, a good case can be made that La Venta was a state-level society with widespread influence. It is not clear why this city was abandoned about 400 B.C., but this date signals the end of Olmec culture as normally conceived. After the fall of La Venta, the whole South Gulf Coast region remained nearly uninhabited for over six centuries. Beginning about the Middle Classic period, a process of repopulation and infilling began that culminated in the early Postclassic settlement. Lowland Maya groups encroached on the region from the east, Zoques entered from the south, and Mixes and Popolucas came from the south and west. Toward the end of its prehistory, Nahua groups immigrated from the far north, probably representing two different waves of settlement related to Toltec and Aztec trade and expansion. Their interest was commerce, an emphasis that continued well into the Colonial period.

FURTHER READINGS

Cobean, R. H., 1996. La Oaxaqueña, Veracruz: Un centro Olmeca menor en su contexto regional. In A. G. Mastache et al. (eds.), *Arqueología Mesoamericana: Homenaje a William T. Sanders,* vol. 2, pp. 37–61. Mexico City: Instituto Nacional de Antropología e Historia and Arqueología Mexicana.

Coe, M. D., and R. A. Diehl. 1980. *In the Land of the Olmec.* Austin: University of Texas Press.

Cyphers, A. C. 1996. Reconstructing Olmec Life at San Lorenzo. In E. Benson and B. de la Fuente (eds.), *Olmec Art of Ancient Mexico,* pp. 61–71. Washington, D.C.: Dumbarton Oaks.

Drucker, P., Heizer, R. F., and Squier, R. J. 1959. Excavations at La Venta, Tabasco, 1955. Bureau of American Ethnography Bulletin 170. Washington, D.C.: Smithsonian Institution.

Gómez Rueda, Hernando. 1996. Las Limas, Veracruz, y otros asentamientos prehispánicos de la región Olmeca. Collección Científica, no. 324. Mexico City: Instituto Nacional de Antropología e Historia.

González, R. 1996. La Venta: An Olmec Capital. In E. Benson and B. de la Fuente (eds.), *Olmec Art of Ancient Mexico,* pp. 73–82. Washington, D.C.: Dumbarton Oaks.

Lee, T. A., Jr. 1978. The Historical Routes of Tabasco and Northern Chiapas and Their Relationship to Early

G

Cultural Developments in Central Chiapas. In T. A. Lee, Jr., and C. Navarrete (eds.), *Mesoamerican Communication Routes and Cultural Contacts,* pp. 49–66. Papers of the New World Archaeological Foundation, 40. Provo, Utah.

Rodríguez, M. d. C., and P. Ortíz Ceballos. 1997. Olmec Ritual and Sacred Geography at Manatí. In B. L. Stark and P. J. Arnold III (eds.), *Olmec to Aztec: Settlement Patterns in the Ancient Gulf Lowlands,* pp. 68–95. Tucson: University of Arizona Press.

Ruz, M. H. 1994. *Un rostro encubierto: Los Indios del Tabasco colonial.* Mexico City: Instituto Nacional Indigenista.

Symonds, S. C., and R. Lunagómez. 1997. Settlement System and Population Development at San Lorenzo. In B. L. Stark and P. J. Arnold III (eds.), *Olmec to Aztec: Settlement Patterns in the Ancient Gulf Lowlands,* pp. 144–173. Tucson: University of Arizona Press.

Tejedo, I. F., M. Gaxiola, J. L. Camacho, and E. Ramírez. 1988. *Zonas arqueológicas: Tabasco.* Mexico City: Instituto Nacional de Antropología e Historia and Gobierno del Estado de Tabasco.

John E. Clark

H

Herramientas (Puntarenas, Costa Rica)

This single-component late Sapoa period and Ometepe period site on Chira Island in the Gulf of Nicoya was occupied from A.D. 1200 to 1520. In this dry tropical environment, the subsistence base was mixed: marine resources, some agriculture, and gathering and collecting. A local economic specialization was salt production.

Material culture remains included ceramics, lithics, mollusks, and archaeofauna. Mortuary remains consisted of poorly preserved primary interments with some associated grave goods, including a gold eagle pendant. Obsidian flakes were probably from the Guinope source in Honduras. Herramientas is contemporaneous with late Sapoa and Ometepe period components at Las Marías and Chahuite Escondido, and on the Bay of Culebra.

FURTHER READINGS

Creamer, W. 1983. *Production and Exchange on Two Islands in the Gulf of Nicoya, Costa Rica, A.D. 1200–1550.* Ph.D. dissertation, Tulane University.

Frederick W. Lange

SEE ALSO

Nicoya, Greater, and Guanacaste Region

Higueras, Las (Veracruz, Mexico)

Noted for its murals, this small coastal center in north central Veracruz was occupied intensively in the Late Formative (c. 300–1 B.C.) and Late Classic (c. A.D. 600–900) periods. Situated beneath a modern fishing and farming village of the same name, the site consists of a series of low mounds and half a dozen principal structures, the present heights of which range from 6 to 13 meters; these are placed on a natural levee between the seasonally low-volume Colipa River and a lagoon. Beginning in 1971, Las Higueras received archaeological attention as a result of the looting of painted stucco fragments from a temple sanctuary. Over the next few years, the supporting structure was cleared, partially consolidated, and provisionally roofed, and the multilayered murals were removed by a team from the Instituto de Antropología in Jalapa under the direction of Alfonso Medellín Zenil. More than twenty mural fragments are on display in Jalapa's Museo de Antropología.

By at least the Early Classic (c. A.D. 300–600), and possibly by the Protoclassic (c. A.D. 1–300), Las Higueras almost certainly was dominated by El Pital, 32 kilometers distant. It was probably one of several modest centers in an intensively cultivated area of canal systems located on estuary and lagoon margins. During the Late Classic, it would have been in the political orbit of Aparicio, a fortified El Tajín–related center about 9 kilometers away.

The murals appear to date to this period and to the Epiclassic (c. A.D. 900–1100), corresponding to the last florescence of El Tajín culture. Many of the depictions stylistically and thematically resemble the Building of the Columns at El Tajín, while a few are earlier. Most are processional scenes with musicians, warriors, deity impersonators, and rulers. These are probably elite rites associated with the ruler's affirmation and ascension. There are ball game and maguey beer *(pulque)* cult references, and one dynamic narrative scene portrays beheading in a ball game.

Most of the murals are on the exterior walls of the very narrow temple sanctuary and the upper surfaces of a

H

plain, stepped pyramidal platform devoid of niches. Several artists were involved, and the murals were probably frequently refurbished, with numerous overlays of stucco and the painting of new images. Although many figures were initially elaborated from black cartoons, reds tend to predominate, and Maya blue, yellow, and green pigments are also present. The beige-white stucco surface often serves as the background, but red and occasionally yellow or blue were also used.

Although the Las Higueras murals are simpler in theme and coarser in line and depiction than the known examples from metropolitan El Tajín, they show this art form's strength in a provincial setting, suggesting the potential for further mural discoveries at other small sites in the humid lowlands of Veracruz.

FURTHER READINGS

Medillín Zenil, A. 1979. El Clásico Tardio en el Centro de Veracruz. *Cuadernos Antropológicos* 2:205–213. Jalapa: Instituto de Antropología, Universidad Veracruzana.

Sanchez Bonilla, J. 1992. Similaritudes entre las pinturas de las Higueras y las obras plásticas del Tajín. In J. K. Brueggeman et al. (eds.), *Tajín,* pp. 133–159. Mexico City: El Equilibrista.

Wilkerson, S. J. K. 1983. So Green and Like a Garden: Intensive Agriculture in Ancient Veracruz. In J. P. Darch (ed.), *Drained Field Agriculiure in Central and South America,* pp. 55–90. BAR International Series, 189. Oxford.

———. 1994. The Garden City of El Pital. *National Geographic Research and Exploration* 10:56–71.

S. Jeffrey K. Wilkerson

SEE ALSO
Gulf Lowlands: North Central Region

Hochob (Campeche, Mexico)

Situated about 8 kilometers southwest of the modern village of Dzibalchen, these ruins stand on a low hill that has been artificially leveled and terraced on top; they comprise a small group of structures arranged around a series of interconnecting courts and plazas. The buildings that can be seen presently were excavated and consolidated in 1982. They were built during the Late Classic period and show virtually all the diagnostic features of the Chenes architectural style.

Structure 2, a three-room, range-type building that occupies the north side of the main plaza, is the site's best-known building. It consists of a central room flanked on both sides by slightly projecting one-room wings. Above the central room are the remains of a high roof comb, which once carried stucco sculptures of human figures. The doorway of the central room is surrounded by a gigantic zoomorphic mask, while the upper wall zones of the two wings were filled with large partial masks, with long-nosed masks at the corners. Teobert Maler, who was the first person to report on the site, called Structure 2 "the richest and most beautiful example of a stucco façade that exists in Yucatán at this time." Both wings have fallen considerably since Maler's time, but the central portion is still well preserved; notably missing, however, are the two large stucco heads that graced the roofs of the thatched huts at the top of the piers adjacent to the central mask.

Structure 1, occupying the east side of the Main Plaza, also carried a large zoomorphic mask around its central doorway (a later addition). Structures 5 and 6 form a three-part complex on the south side of the plaza, with pyramid temples at both ends of a six-room range structure. The two temples at the ends supported high, slotted roof combs, and numerous projecting stones can be seen in or on their medial and cornice moldings; these stones probably supported stucco sculptures, long since fallen.

FURTHER READINGS

Robina, R. de. 1956. *Estudio preliminar de las ruinas de Hochob, Municipio de Hopelchén, Campeche.* Mexico City: Atenea.

George Andrews

SEE ALSO
Maya Lowlands: North

Holmul (Petén, Guatemala)

This large Maya center is situated at the eastern edge of the central Petén region, between the centers of Nakum and Yaloch and near the modern Guatemala-Belize border. Although the site has not yet been completely mapped, Holmul's main architectural groups were the first Maya buildings to be excavated stratigraphically—by Raymond E. Merwin on a 1910–1911 Peabody Museum expedition. Merwin's excavations provided the strati-

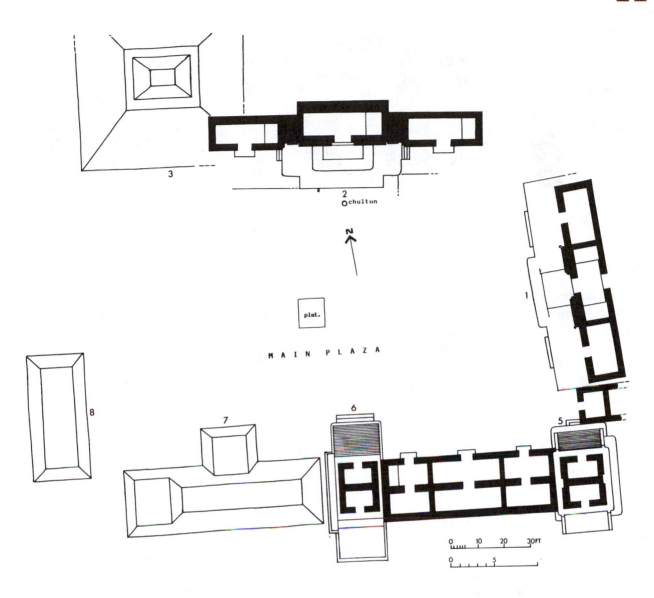

Site plan of Hochob, Campeche, Mexico. Illustration courtesy of the author.

graphic basis for the first chronological sequence of Maya ceramics, published by George C. Vaillant in 1932. The Holmul I through V ceramic sequence spans the Proto-classic (A.D. 150–250) through the Late Classic (A.D. 600–900) period. The Holmul I ceramics include early examples of polychrome painted decoration and mammi-form tetrapod vessel forms, comprising the controversial "Q complex" or "Protoclassic" assemblage. Subsequently, in Holmul V times, the site was one of the loci of produc-tion of a distinctive regional style of polychrome painted vessels that appeared in many Late Classic elite burials of

the eastern Maya Lowlands. The satellite center of Cival has an early stela, probably Cycle (Baktun) 8 in date, thus dating to the period before c. A.D. 430.

FURTHER READINGS

Merwin, R. E., and G. C. Vaillant. 1932. *The Ruins of Holmul, Guatemala*. Memoirs of the Peabody Museum of Archaeology and Ethnology, 3.2. Cambridge, Mass.: Harvard University.

Reents-Budet, R. L. 1991. The "Holmul Dancer" Theme in Maya Art. In V. M. Fields (ed.), *Sixth Palenque*

H

Hochob, Structure 2, south elevation. Illustration courtesy of the author.

Round Table, 1986, pp. 217–22. Norman: University of Oklahoma Press.

———. 1994. Painting Styles, Workshop Locations and Pottery Production. In D. Reents-Budet (ed.), *Painting the Maya Universe: Royal Ceramics of the Classic Period,* pp. 164–234. Durham: Duke University Press.

Francisco Estrada Belli

SEE ALSO
Maya Lowlands: South

Huacas, Las (Guanacaste, Costa Rica)

This cemetery site in the Greater Nicoya region produced the first evidence of the association of carved stone ceremonial stools ("metates") and jadeite/greenstone pendants from the late Tempisque and early Bagaces periods (300 B.C.–A.D. 500). In some tombs, ceramics were also associated with human skeletal remains. Jadeite and greenstone are not locally available, but the source is unknown. Las Huacas is contemporaneous with Nosara Valley and other sites on the Pacific coast of the Nicoya Peninsula.

FURTHER READINGS

Fonseca Z., O., and J. B. Richardson. 1978. South American and Mayan Cultural Contacts at the Las Huacas Site, Costa Rica. *Annals of the Carnegie Museum of Natural History* 47(13):299–317.

Fonseca Z., O., and R. Scaglion. 1978. Stylistic Analysis of Stone Pendants from Las Huacas Burial Ground, Northwestern Costa Rica. *Annals of the Carnegie Museum of Natural History* 47(12):281–298.

Hartman, C. V. 1907. Archaeological Researches on the Pacific Coast of Costa Rica. *Memoirs of the Carnegie Museum of Natural History* 3(1).

Frederick W. Lange

SEE ALSO
Nicoya, Greater, and Guanacaste Region

Huandacareo (Michoacán, Mexico)

This site in the Lake Cuitzeo Basin, a natural corridor that links Central and West Mexico, was occupied during the Late Postclassic period (A.D. 1300–1530), when this area was dominated by the Tarascans. Huandacareo has a sunken plaza on its highest point, surrounded by walkways, and a building of the *yácata* type (which combines rectangular and round shapes, and is typical of the Tarascans), as well as the only known pre-Hispanic temple in Michoacán.

In the Courtyard of the Tombs were found six burial chambers, each of which contained a primary burial and a variety of offerings: bowls and jars of brown polished clay; obsidian tools from Zinapécuaro; several prismatic blades of green obsidian from Cerro de las Navajas (Pachuca, Hidalgo); metates (querns); cinnabar; shell beads; cut and perforated conch shells; anthropomorphic figurines made of shell; and bone spatulas.

Huandacareo is one of the few sites where metal objects have been found in archaeological context and professionally excavated and studied: 115 of these objects have been identified as ornaments (bells, rings, pendants, pins, beads), and seventeen as tools or weapons (tweezers, points for "scepters," awls, needles, an axe). All the metal objects seem to have been associated with the elite and to have been of a ritual or sumptuary nature. Copper is the predominant raw material, but bronze and silver are also present.

FURTHER READINGS

Macías Goytia, A. 1990. *Huandacareo: Lugar de juicios, tribunal.* Mexico City: Instituto Nacional de Antropología e Historia.

————. 1994. Análisis de los materiales prehispánicos tarascos de Huandacareo, Michoacán. In E. Williams (ed.), *Contribuciones a la arqueología y etnohistoria del Occidente de México,* pp. 157–188. Zamora: Colegio de Michoacán.

Eduardo Williams

SEE ALSO

Michoacán Region

Huatusco (Veracruz, Mexico)

Archaeological Huatusco, across the Río Atoyac from the modern town of Santiago Huatusco, is a fortress site with a distinctively Aztec style pyramid—one of only a few remaining with parts of the shrine intact. The site is also noted for the highest density of Aztec and Aztecoid ceramic wares anywhere in the empire. Medellín, who explored it archaeologically, identified it as the Aztec provincial capital Quauhtochco pictured in the Codex Mendoza, but this has been questioned. The rival candidate, the town of San Antonio Huatusco, is closer to Quauhtochco's tributaries, as pictured in the codex. Other scholars, following Medellín, maintain that the archaeological site was the Aztec capital and that its inhabitants moved to Santiago Huatusco after the Spanish conquest. If this is the case, Huatusco/Quauhtochco's proximity to Cuetlaxtlan, the site that was once capital of the neighboring province, may reveal an Aztec pattern of clustered fortresses, also seen in the Oztoma area of Guerrero.

Situated on a meseta in the semiarid plain of southern Veracruz, Huatusco is surrounded by steep embankments and walls and has remains of terraces, enclosed rooms, a possible *tecpan* or palace, and a large platform with a standing room in the vicinity of the pyramid. Also striking is the high percentage, relative to other wares, of Aztec III Black on Orange, local imitations of Black on Orange, and Aztec-style long-handled incensarios, as well as other Mexican relic types collected by Medellín.

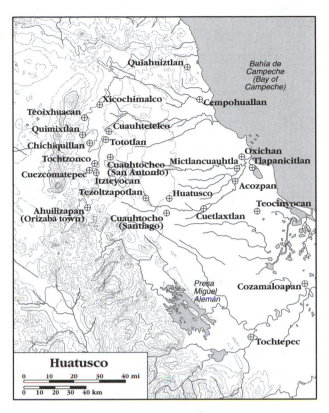

Huatusco. Map design by Mapping Specialists Limited, Madison, Wisconsin.

FURTHER READINGS

Berdan, F., R. Blanton, E. Boone, M. Hodge, M. Smith, and E. Umberger. 1996. *Aztec Imperial Strategies.* Washington, D.C.: Dumbarton Oaks.

Medellín Zenil, A. 1952. *Exploraciones en Quauhtochco.* Jalapa: Gobierno de Veracruz and Instituto Nacional de Antropología e Historia.

Smith, M. 1990. Long-distance Trade under the Aztec Empire: The Archaeological Evidence. *Ancient Mesoamerica* 1:153–169.

Emily Umberger

SEE ALSO

Gulf Lowlands: North Central Region

Huaxtepec (Morelos, Mexico)

At Huaxtepec, a sixteenth-century town in the hills of Morelos, Cortés and his company came upon one of the world's most beautiful gardens—as Bernal Díaz describes them, "the best that I have ever seen in all my life, and so said . . . our Cortés" (Díaz del Castillo 1956 [1560]:375). The gardens, established in the 1460s by Motecuhzoma I,

H

were the private property of the Aztec emperors, whose capital, Tenochtitlán, was 100 kilometers distant and nearly 1,000 meters higher in elevation. Huaxtepec was a perfect spot for an imperial pleasure garden; the region had springs, good arable land, and a warm, subhumid climate. Aztec landscaping and gardening procedures are described by Durán, who notes that tribute received by the rulers included rare plants and gardeners to tend them. Rulers had privileged access to medicinal plants, and Huaxtepec was a botanical garden as well as a paradise of bloom and foliage.

Huaxtepec, an Aztec regional capital in the Late Postclassic, had a long history of occupation, beginning in the Middle Formative period (1100–650 B.C.) and continuing through the Classic period, with settlement by local groups and by Teotihuacanos. In the Postclassic, the town's population was Tlahuica and Mexica. In addition to its agricultural resources, the region had lime and flint beds.

FURTHER READINGS

Díaz del Castillo, B. 1956 [1560]. *The Discovery and Conquest of Mexico*. A. P. Maudslay (trans.) New York: Farrar, Straus, and Cudahy.

Durán, Diego. 1994 [1581]. *The History of the Indies of New Spain*. Doris Heyden (trans. and ed.). Norman: University of Oklahoma Press.

Maldonado Jiménez, D. 1990. *Cuauhnáhuac y Huaxtepec (Tlalhuicas y Xochimilcas en el Morelos Prehispánico)*. Cuernavaca: UNAM Centro Regional de Investigaciones Multidisciplinarias.

Octavio Rocha Herrera and Susan Toby Evans

SEE ALSO

Gardens; Morelos Region

Huexotla (México, Mexico)

Huexotla is an Early and Late Aztec (i.e., Middle and Late Postclassic) site in the eastern Basin of Mexico. It consists of two segments. A nucleated urban core of about 300 hectares lies at the western end of the site, where the gently sloping lower piedmont meets the flat lakeshore plain. The northern edge of the urban core is obscured by the modern town of Huexotla. The modern town contains the remains of a large, walled complex that was partially excavated and reconstructed by L. Batres in the early 1900s; this was probably the palace of Huexotla's ruler. South of the modern town, thirteen substantial structures

and moderate concentrations of surface artifacts define the extent of the nucleated urban core. The second sector, an area of dispersed occupation, extends up the piedmont slope east of the urban core for a distance of 10 kilometers. Scattered concentrations of artifacts mark the residences of rural households.

Potsherds, obsidian tools and waste flakes, grinding stones, maguey-fiber scrapers, ceramic spindle whorls, figurines, stamps, and blowgun pellets are common in both sectors of the site. Black-on-Orange and Black-on-Red pottery are the most common decorated wares. These decorated ceramics are much more frequent in the urban core than in the zone of dispersed occupation. Black-on-Orange II, III, and IV ceramics are common in the urban core, suggesting an Early and Late Aztec through Early Colonial occupation (c. A.D. 1150–1560), but the area of dispersed occupation contains Black-on-Orange III and IV ceramics almost exclusively, suggesting a Late Aztec and Early Colonial occupation (c. A.D. 1430–1560).

Intensive, systematic surface collection revealed few indications of full-time craft specialists in either the urban core or the area of dispersed occupation. The extraction of maguey sap and fiber is visible archaeologically in the form of plano-convex obsidian scrapers and trapezoidal felsite maguey-fiber scrapers. Huexotla is frequently mentioned in native histories from the Basin of Mexico. Prior to 1408, it was an important autonomous city-state; with the formation of the Triple Alliance in 1430, however, it became dominated by the nearby city of Texcoco.

FURTHER READINGS

Batres, L. 1904. *Mis exploraciones en Huexotla, Texcoco y Monumento del Gavilan*. Mexico City: J. I. Guerro.

Brumfiel, E. M. 1980. Specialization, Market Exchange and the Aztec State: A View from Huexotla. *Current Anthropology* 21:459–478.

———. 1983. Consumption and Politics at Aztec Huexotla. *American Anthropologist* 89:676–686.

García García, M. T. 1987. *Huexotla: Un sitio del Acolhuacan*. Colección Científica, 165. Mexico City: Instituto Nacional de Antropología e Historia.

Parsons, J. R. 1971. *Prehistoric Settlement Patterns in the Texcoco Region, Mexico*. Memoirs of the Museum of Anthropology, 3. Ann Arbor: University of Michigan.

Elizabeth M. Brumfiel

SEE ALSO

Basin of Mexico; Postclassic Period

Huistle, Cerro del (Jalisco, Mexico)

This mesa-top site lies in the upland valley of the Río Huejuquilla, above the deep Río Chapalagana Canyon, which drains this portion of the south central Sierra Madre Occidental. Perched about 60 meters above the valley floor, Cerro del Huistle maintained an easily defended position. This 1.4-hectare site exhibits evidence of extensive masonry and adobe architecture in the form of rectangular patios or plazas, structure platforms, carved stone column bases, and small bedrock cisterns that may have been used to collect rain and runoff. Cerro del Huistle had three continuous phases of occupation spanning the period A.D. 1–900; these are marked by distinct building episodes and changing burial patterns.

Cerro del Huistle has been associated with the Chalchihuites culture, primarily because of its ceramic affinities; in general, it shares many other traits with sites on the north central frontier of Mesoamerica, including Alta Vista, La Quemada, and El Teúl. Archaeological excavations have revealed skull racks, enigmatic sculptures that have been compared with the Postclassic reclining Chac Mool statues found at Mesoamerican sites such as Tula, and metal objects (including copper bells). Other ceramics found at Cerro del Huistle include Chinesco wares, spindle whorls, and ceramic figurines suggestive of West Mexican/coastal traditions; resist wares that resemble types found in the Bolaños Valley and areas farther to the southeast; and pseudo-cloisonné, which appears throughout the north central frontier. Abundant Pacific Coast shell, particularly from burials, also points toward interaction between highland societies and coastal groups. The site was the focus of six seasons of excavation (1978–1987) undertaken by the Belgian Archaeological Mission in connection with the Sierra del Nayar Project.

FURTHER READINGS

Fauconnier, F. 1992. Projet: Sierra del Nayar, Résultats des travaux menés par la mission archéologique belge au Mexique. *Mexicon* 14(2):24–30.

Hers, M. A. 1989. *Los Toltecas en tierras Chichimecas.* Mexico City: Instituto de Investigaciones Estéticas, UNAM.

Hosler, D. 1994. *The Sounds and Colors of Power: The Sacred Metallurgical Technology of Ancient West Mexico.* Cambridge, Mass.: MIT Press.

Kelley, J. C. 1971. Archaeology of the Northern Frontier: Zacatecas and Durango. In G. F. Eckholm and I. Bernal (eds.), *Handbook of Middle American Indians,* vol. 11, *Archaeology of Northern Mesoamerica, Part Two,* pp. 768–801. Austin: University of Texas Press.

López Luján, L. 1989. *Nómadas y sedentarios. El pasado prehispánico de Zacatecas.* Colección Regiones de México. Mexico City: Instituto Nacional de Antropología e Historia.

J. Andrew Darling

SEE ALSO

Northwestern Frontier

Huitzilapa (Jalisco, Mexico)

This ceremonial center in central Jalisco was occupied during the Early Classic period (c. A.D. 1–300). Excavation at this site in 1993 discovered the most important shaft tomb found to date in unlooted condition in West Mexico. The site presents a series of architectural units, including plazas, mounds, ball courts, terraces, cross-shaped residential units, and circular complexes; the last pertain to the Teuchitlan tradition.

The two-chambered shaft tomb, 7.6 meters in depth, contained six individuals—three in each chamber—buried with rich offerings. Osteological analysis of the individuals has revealed that they may have been related, so this tomb may have been a crypt for a group of relatives or members of a specific lineage. A male individual approximately forty-five years of age is by far the most important person interred in this tomb, judging by the quality and quantity of the offerings associated with the skeleton. He was elaborately adorned with jade and shell bracelets, noserings, earrings, greenstone beads, carved jade pendants, and a cloth sewn with thousands of shell beads. Conch shells ornamented with painted stucco were placed on his loins and at his sides, along with atlatl hooks. Two female skeletons were found associated with artifacts that pertain to the feminine sphere of life: pottery spindle whorls and metates (grinding slabs) made of volcanic stone. The tomb offerings also include pottery figures that represent ballplayers, as well as clay vessels, decorated with geometric and zoomorphic designs, which still contained food remains.

Huitzilapa was one of many sites that flourished in the Jalisco-Colima-Nayarit area during the Classic period. Most of them are characterized by shaft tombs and circular architecture, traits that have been used to define the Teuchitlan tradition of West Mexico.

H

FURTHER READINGS

Ramos de la Vega, J., and L. Lopez Mestas. 1998. Excavating the Tomb at Huitzilapa. In *Ancient West Mexico: Art and Archaeology of the Unknown Past*. Chicago: Art Institute of Chicago.

Eduardo Williams

SEE ALSO

Shaft Tombs; West Mexico

Huitzo (Oaxaca, Mexico)

The Formative period archaeological site now called Barrio del Rosario Huitzo is near the upper Atoyac River in the northwestern Valley of Oaxaca. Excavated in 1967 by a University of Michigan expedition, it is most notable for having a superimposed series of public buildings of the Guadalupe phase (850–700 B.C.) and Rosario phase (700–500 B.C.). The best-preserved of these, Structure 3, consists of a wattle-and-daub temple on an adobe platform 1.3 meters high and 11.5 meters long, equipped with a three-step stairway 7.6 meters wide. A domestic refuse midden not far away yielded the carbonized remains of maize, beans, squash, chile peppers, avocados, prickly pear and organ cactus seeds, acorns, hackberry pits, and seeds of acacia, all dated to the Guadalupe phase.

FURTHER READINGS

Flannery, K. V., and J. Marcus. 1983. *The Cloud People*. New York: Academic Press.

Marcus, J., and K. V. Flannery. 1996. *Zapotec Civilization*. London: Thames and Hudson.

Kent V. Flannery and Joyce Marcus

SEE ALSO

Oaxaca and Tehuantepec Region

Hydrology

Early complex societies needed and emphasized a variety of primary and processed resources, ranging from pottery to obsidian to bronze, in order to maximize the use of their environment; but it was the immediacy of food production and the availability of water that underlay basic survival. Synonymous with life itself, water was perhaps the most precious of natural resources for Mesoamerican cultures. Hydrology (water management) is a society's interruption and redirection of the natural movement or collection of water.

Water Management Techniques

Although climate and geomorphology strongly influenced the techniques used by Mesoamerican societies, most of their environments were at least partially transformed into agricultural settings through various technological adaptations and labor investments in water management. Generally speaking, water systems were adapted to either of two basic environments: arid, semiarid, and temperate settings associated with both rugged and low relief, or humid surrounds occupying gentle topographic contours. The Mesoamerican Highlands, defined by the extent of the Sierra Madre and much of northern and western Mexico, represent the elevated, dry to semiarid terrain that is best modified by canalization. The wet and frequently swampy Gulf Lowlands and the greater Yucatán Peninsula reflect a different manipulation of the landscape that emphasizes flood recessional techniques and swamp-margin reclamation projects.

Highland Mesoamerica

Doolittle's analysis of canal irrigation techniques for much of highland Mexico shows that the earliest evidence for deliberate diversion of watercourses occurred by about 1000 B.C. The reasons why these water diversion systems were built remain unclear: possibly they were built to drain water away from habitation areas, or perhaps the need for simple floodwater control, within the context of a dry farming adaptation, inspired people to build brush and rock weirs that slowed and spread water over an otherwise parched soil.

The earliest known Mesoamerican water system is one believed to be associated with the Olmec site of Teopantecuanitlan in northern Guerrero. It consists of a stone "gravity dam"—one that resists perpendicular flow because of its mass—and a slabrock-lined canal segment issuing from it. Dated to 1200 B.C., this feature is at present somewhat temporally isolated in its precocious sophistication, and further information is needed. The next earliest example of canalization dates from 700 B.C. and is situated at Santa Clara Coatitlan in the northern section of present-day Mexico City. Excavated by Nichols, this canal system is a less well constructed water management system than the Guerrero example; lacking a dam, it was probably designed to channelize less predictable gully runoff into agricultural plots.

The Purron Dam, a gravity dam in the Tehuacan Valley, was examined by Woodbury and Neely during their pioneer studies of water systems. At the time of the Santa Clara canal (700 B.C.) the dam was a diminutive feature, but by the Early Classic period (A.D. 100–300) it had been incrementally enlarged to a maximum plan of 100 × by 400 meters, reaching a maximal height of 18 meters. One of the most impressive hydraulic works in highland Mexico, the Purron Dam was constructed in an area relatively peripheral to centralizing developments elsewhere. In fact, it appears to have fallen into disrepair by A.D. 200–300, a period of accelerated growth in the nearby Basin of Mexico. In addition to the major storage dam, the Purron reservoir contained a substantial cofferdam, probably constructed to entrap sediment before it could enter the main body of the reservoir as well as to allow the diversion of water during periods of reservoir dredging or dam maintenance. The precise function of the feature remains enigmatic because evidence for canalization issuing from the dam is ill defined.

Perhaps the best understood of the early storage reservoirs associated with a canal system is in the Xoxocotlan Piedmont, immediately below Monte Albán, Oaxaca. Doolittle states that the dam, 10 meters high and 80 meters long, "was V-shaped in plan with the apex pointing upstream" (1990:30); it was thus an "arch dam," its strength dependent on curvature rather than weight. Additionally, the dam had a floodgate that directed water into the 2-kilometer-long main canal, a portion of which was carved into bedrock. The entire system dates to the Late Formative period (between 550 and 150 B.C.) and was designed to irrigate as much as 50 hectares of field plots.

Near Mitla, Oaxaca, the well-reported but controversial spring-fed irrigation system at Hierve el Agua left an intricately latticed network of canals "fossilized" in travertine and covering an artificially terraced area of 50 hectares. The system is dated to c. 300 B.C., coeval with the nearby reservoir-driven irrigation system at Xoxocotlan. Some have argued that salt production was the primary aim of the Hierve el Agua system, but this seems less convincing today. Kirkby and others speculate that water was hand-lifted from small circular pits (*pocitos*) dug into the course of diminutive branch canals flanking the outer margins of the terraced plots. These depressions would pond water and permit the hand-watering of plants—a form of "pot irrigation," more commonly associated with shallow wells and an elevated aquifer closer to the valley bottom.

By the close of the Formative period and throughout the subsequent Classic, the highlands continued to develop canal technology. Two developments—poorly known at an earlier date—appear to be well defined: raised fields and aqueducts. Drained-field swamp-margin agriculture began much earlier in the humid lowlands of Mesoamerica, but as early as 500 B.C., and more assuredly by 200 B.C., lacustrine soils were deliberately drained and low-gradient canal systems maintained.

Amalucan in the Puebla Valley provides the oldest evidence for valley-bottom agriculture in the highlands. Although ample precipitation allows one crop, this reservoir-fed system could facilitate another harvest during the dry season over an area of 70 hectares. Lake-margin field systems are suggested as early as the Late Formative in the Basin of Mexico, with well-documented pre-Aztec *chinampa* systems in the northwestern portion of the lakes region. Other extensive Classic period lake-basin, *chinampa*-style drained-field systems have recently been documented in Jalisco.

The earliest evidence of an aqueduct comes from the course of the Xiquila Canal south of Tehuacan. Here, a portion of the canal—dated by settlement association to A.D. 400–700—was forced over and across a natural tributary, perhaps by means of perishable hollowed log segments suspended from a wooden trestle. No doubt aqueducts of this type were widespread at this time, but few can be reconstructed. It is not until the Aztec period (A.D. 1150–1519) that well-documented sources reveal the complexity and sophistication of aqueduct construction in the Basin of Mexico. From the celebrated springhead at Chapultepec Hill, water was carried across the western embayment of the large central lake of Texcoco to the island city of Tenochtitlan in an elaborate aqueduct. This was first constructed of packed clay, supported by man-made islands and linked by hollowed logs; later, it was secured by the stone buttressing of the underlying support islands and the use of lime-masonry construction for the aqueduct segments themselves.

Woodbury and Neely indicate the presence of a *qanat* (*galería*) system in the Tehuacan Valley, but most research suggests a Spanish origin for these "tunnel wells." Dependent on a deep aquifer at the elevated margins of the valley, these systems were excavated laterally, extending from the source to the hamlet or field surfaces to be watered. More than 230 kilometers of subterranean tunnels are reported.

At the Olmec site of Chalcatzingo, and later at Postclassic Maravilla near Teotihuacan, rather ephemeral dikes were constructed to divert natural channel movements. The most formidable dikes—also used as causeways—were constructed during the Late Aztec period to accommodate unstable lake levels and elevated salinity

H

rates. One dike separated the embayment surrounding the island of Tenochtitlan from the rest of Lake Texcoco, and permitted the sweet water from the surrounding foothill springs to dilute the otherwise saline concentration of this portion of the lake. Additionally, the sluice gates of the dike were used to control water levels within the dammed area and to facilitate *chinampa* cultivation by moderating fluctuations in stream discharge into the lake.

In the arid northern portions of Mexico, less is known about canalization. *Trincheras,* or rock water-spreaders, on low terraces and in the floodplains of arroyos are reported to have been in use by A.D. 1000. Nevertheless, the area of Casas Grandes, Chihuahua, suggests more complicated water management systems by c. A.D. 1100. In addition to a canal system that issued from a spring source 6 kilometers away, the ancient site of Casas Grandes had two centrally located reservoirs with a large water retention basin and a stone-lined settling tank. A "walk-in well" was also featured at the site, defined by a stepped entranceway descending 12 vertical meters from the surface before reaching water.

Doolittle has shown that, contrary to general belief, irrigation systems in the U.S. Southwest were far superior to contemporaneous ones in Mexico. In the Hohokam area of present-day Arizona, more than 500 kilometers of major canal bed have been identified. This and the complex water systems at neighboring Casas Grandes are matched only by Late Aztec period developments in the Basin of Mexico in terms of investment in highland water management. Palerm states that the river at Cuauhtitlan was dammed, diverted, and finally redirected into a newly widened channel 2 kilometers long, nearly 3 meters wide, and about 3 meters deep. Nevertheless, even this enterprise pales in comparison to the canalization efforts of the Hohokam. Howard has recently demonstrated that the Hohokam systems were "explosive," or rapid, investments in labor and resources, rather than slow, incremental developments. These systems were probably implemented as grand schemes, planned and organized by an authority above the level of the immediate community.

Humid Lowlands

Water management in the lowlands of Mesoamerica functioned differently than in the highlands. Many of the techniques identified on the lake margins of the highlands were probably pioneered in the vast, internally drained, seasonal swamps *(bajos)* of the central Yucatán Peninsula. Although canalization as defined in the highlands was never as developed here, reservoirs and tank systems, in concert with drainage channels and raised fields, were greater in both scale and complexity in the humid lowlands than in the semiarid highlands.

The earliest dates for shallow ditches draining the margins of swamps—a cropping technique useful in areas with a high water table—are around 1000 B.C. in northern Belize. Water development accelerates during the Late Formative in the southern Maya Lowlands, culminating in intensive wetland reclamation at Cerros (Belize), at Edzná (Campeche), and probably at the huge, *bajo*-flanked center of El Mirador (Petén, Guatemala). At Cerros, a 1.2-kilometer-long drainage canal, 6 meters wide and 2 meters deep, enclosed the site core, an area of 37 hectares. The main canal acted as a drainage device for the paved and plastered surfaces of the core area during the rainy season, and it stored water for agricultural use through the four-month-long dry season. Further, raised fields were excavated and identified with buttress stones positioned to prevent slumpage into adjacent basin canals; during the dry season, water presumably was dispatched from the basin canals by pot or splash irrigation techniques. A causeway segment or dike separated the diminutive agricultural zone within the core area at Cerros from a potable water source associated with residential occupation; the employment of dikes as causeways and water-purity dividers is attested nearly a millennium and a half earlier in the humid lowlands than in the Basin of Mexico.

Edzná reveals a massive program of landscape modification within a shallow valley on the northwestern Yucatán Peninsula. More than 20 kilometers of canals are reported, with numerous associated reservoirs. The total storage capacity of the canal basins is 2 million cubic meters. Edzná, Cerros, and perhaps El Mirador are characterized as dependent on "concave" microwatersheds, or the movement of water from little-altered upland settings into well-managed low-lying zones associated with the core architecture of the community.

During the Classic period in the Maya Lowlands, sites like Tikal, La Milpa, and Kinal can be shown to represent a deliberately sculpted landscape in which runoff across the surface of a "convex" micro-watershed permitted far greater control over the resource than did the earlier lowland systems. The hillocks on which these sites rest—away from permanent springs or streams—were heavily paved with plastered surfaces canted toward elevated reservoirs. The most elevated central precinct catchment at Tikal covered an area of 62 hectares; because seepage loss was limited by the impervious plaza pavements and plastered monumental architecture, it could collect more than 900,000 cubic meters of water (based on 1,500 mm of rainfall annually). The runoff from this and adjacent catchment areas easily filled the associated reservoirs during the eight-month wet season. Eventually, each catchment area terminated in the *bajo*-margin reservoirs or natural *aguadas* (shallow, bowl-shaped sinks), ultimately leading into the flanking *bajos.*

The tiered character of the reservoir system at Tikal allowed the controlled downhill release of water during the dry season. Causeways connected many portions of the site. As at Cerros perhaps 500 years earlier, these same features functioned to retain water and to define the outer margins of the reservoirs. The causeways are believed to have acted as dams.

The largest and most elevated reservoirs were associated with the central precinct, occupying the gentle slopes of the hillock. Collectively, the six central precinct reservoirs contained 100,000 to 250,000 cubic meters of water. Some domestic structures were associated with smaller tanks, but all were near one of several drainage channels issuing from the central precinct reservoirs. After passing through the community, water was caught and held for agricultural purposes in *bajo*-margin reservoirs. Although partially fouled by domestic use, such "gray" water could be cycled into raised or ditched fields at the margins of the community, allowing nearly continuous cropping year round.

During the Postclassic period in the Maya Lowlands, principal occupation occurred on the northern Yucatán Peninsula. Although *chultuns*—large subterranean chambers with constricted orifices—were used for food and beverage storage earlier to the south, they were most commonly used as cisterns in the arid northern Maya Lowlands. Roof surfaces and paved, dish-shaped household catchments directed water into sometimes cavernous *chultuns,* supplying potable water to smaller, more autonomous groups than did the Tikal water system with its centralizing influence. Because of the karstic topography, natural limestone sinks *(cenotes)* dropping to an exposed water table were also important water sources. Large caverns were sometimes formed because of the deep subterranean water channels and the natural formation of solution cavities that contacted these underground streams. People often carved the soft limestone to accommodate foot access, resulting in "walk-in" wells.

Although the amount and kind of agriculture practiced in the extensive *bajos* remains unclear, drained fields and associated channels are well documented in northern Belize along the perennial rivers there. Pulltrouser Swamp and Albion Island on the Rio Hondo/Rio Azul system reveal well-documented wetland reclamation projects during both the Formative and Classic periods. Siemens and Puleston were the first to identify raised fields and associated channels in the lowlands near the early Postclassic site of Acalan in southern Campeche.

Siemens and colleagues have reported wetland reclamation via shallow canals flanking planting platforms near Veracruz, Mexico. This research suggests that channelizing efforts occurred by A.D. 500, and perhaps earlier, within the floodplain and backwater margins of the San Juan River Basin.

Water management in ancient Mesoamerica could be expedient or sophisticated, local and autonomous, or state managed and complex. These systems reflect the processes by which the landscape was transformed and open a window onto Mesoamerica's human ecology and economy.

FURTHER READINGS

Armillas, P. 1971 Gardens on Swamps. *Science* 174:653–661.

Doolittle, W. E. 1990. *Canal Irrigation in Prehistoric Mexico.* Austin: University of Texas Press.

Fowler, M. L. 1987. Early Water Management at Amalucan, State of Puebla, Mexico. *National Geographic Research* 3:52–68.

Kirkby, A. 1973. The Use of Land and Water Resources in the Past and Present, Valley of Oaxaca, Mexico. Memoirs of the Museum of Anthropology, 5. Ann Arbor: University of Michigan.

Nichols, D. L. 1982. A Middle Formative Irrigation System near Santa Clara Coatitlan in the Basin of Mexico. *American Antiquity* 47:133–144.

O'Brien, M. J., R. D. Mason, D. E. Lewarch, and J. A. Neely. 1982. *A Late Formative Irrigation Settlement below Monte Albán.* Austin: University of Texas Press.

Scarborough, V. L., and B. L. Isaac (eds.). 1993. *Economic Aspects of Water Management in the Prehispanic New World.* Supplement 7 of *Research in Economic Anthropology.* Greenwich: JAI Press.

Siemens, A. H., R. J. Hebda, M. Navarrete Hernandez, D. R. Piperno, J. K. Stein, and M. G. Zola Baez. 1988. Evidence for a Cultivar and a Chronology from

H

Patterned Wetlands in Central Veracruz, Mexico. *Science* 242:105–107.

Siemens, A. H., and D. E. Puleston. 1972. Ridged Fields and Associated Features in Southern Campeche. *American Antiquity* 37:228–239.

Wolf, E. R., and A. Palerm. 1955. Irrigation in the Old Acolhua Domain, Mexico. *Southwestern Journal of Anthropology* 11:265–281.

Woodbury, R. B., and J. A. Neely. 1972. Water Control Systems of the Tehuacan Valley. In R. S. MacNeish and F. Johnson (eds.), *Chronology and Irrigation, The Prehistory of the Tehuacan Valley,* vol. 4, pp. 81–153. Austin: University of Texas Press.

Vernon Scarborough

SEE ALSO

Agriculture and Domestication

I

Ihuatzio (Michoacán, Mexico)

This sprawling site (c. 50 hectares) is one of the biggest and most architecturally complex in Michoacán. Together with Tzintzuntzan and Pátzcuaro, Ihuatzio formed a core area in the Lake Pátzcuaro Basin, where the political and economic powers of the Tarascan state were centered. Ihuatzio had two periods of occupation: A.D. 900–1200, which may correspond to occupation by Nahuatl-speaking groups, and A.D. 1200–1530, pertaining to the epoch of Tarascan rule.

Ihuatzio is one of the most complex sites in western Mexico, although it has been little explored. There are structures with rectangular, rectangular-circular, and circular layouts, as well as monumental walls and causeways. The Tarascan archaeological complex is fully represented at this site: there are metal (primarily copper and bronze) objects such as bells, tweezers (worn as ornaments by high priests and members of the nobility), adzes, and needles; ceramic vessels decorated with "negative" or resist paint, including jars with handle and spout; clay pipes; obsidian ear and lip plugs; and shell ornaments. Large-scale stone sculptures were found at Ihuatzio, in the shape of a throne-like coyote ("Ihuatzio" means "place of coyotes") and a *Chac Mool,* in a style reminiscent of other areas of Mesoamerica, mainly to the east.

Subsistence was based on agriculture (maize, beans, squash, chile peppers, etc.), exploiting the rich lands around the lake basin. Fishing, hunting (waterfowl, deer, rodents, reptiles), and gathering wild plants complemented the diet.

FURTHER READINGS

Acosta, J. 1937. Exploraciones arqueológicas realizadas en el estado de Michoacán durante los años de 1937 y 1938. *Revista Mexicana de Estudios Antropológicos* 3:85–99.

Caso, A. 1929. Informe preliminar de las exploraciones realizadas en Michoacán. *Anales del Museo Nacional de Arqueología, Historia y Etnografía* 4(6):446–452.

Pollard, H. P. 1993. *Taríacuri's Legacy: The Prehispanic Tarascan State.* Norman: University of Oklahoma Press.

Eduardo Williams

SEE ALSO

Michoacán Region

Innocentes, Los (Guanacaste, Costa Rica)

The first cemetery complex from Greater Nicoya to be found with cremations, this site dates from A.D. 200–800. Cremated remains were found in globular, open-mouthed vessels, some with pendants of jadeite from an unknown source outside the Greater Nicoya subarea.

Frederick W. Lange

SEE ALSO

Nicoya, Greater, and Guanacaste Region

Intermediate Area: Overview

The cultural-geographical region known as the Intermediate Area has been included, entirely or in part, in a number

I

of different spatial and culture area schemes, among them Mesoamerica, Central America, lower Central America, and Middle America. Archaeologists have employed these various units in attempts at a cultural characterization of the geographical space between the areas occupied by the "high civilizations" of Mesoamerica and the South American Andes. Fonseca defines the Intermediate Area as conforming rather precisely to what he calls the area of "Chibchan tradition," a spatial zone defined by parameters of linguistic distribution; Fonseca notes that his model also appears to be supported by genetic data.

While the genetic data generally coincide with the linguistic distribution, there are significant gaps in the genetic database (especially in Atlantic Nicaragua and Honduras). The problem remains of correlating the rich and variable archaeological record with the broad outlines of linguistic and genetic knowledge. Relatively little evidence exists to aid understanding of the time depth or spatial integrity of the area, and although Fonseca's model may direct us toward productive cultural-processual inquiries, it remains to be tested. It also remains to be shown that these prehistoric Central Americans and northern South Americans inhabited an area that can also be characterized by Porter's (1993:3) description of Mesoamerica as a "unique civilization that grew up . . . beginning with the time it was first settled until the arrival of the Europeans in the sixteenth century."

The perceived unity of Mesoamerica is increasingly developing cracks, and I suspect that a careful evaluation of the data for the Intermediate Area, or area of Chibchan tradition, will further weaken the case for areal unity. Paradoxically, however, the lower level of socio-political complexity achieved in the Intermediate Area may have resulted in a unity, in the sense of a kind of amorphous homogeneity. Whatever the outcome, the evaluation should be instructive in refining our view of the ancient history of this geographical-cultural region of the Western Hemisphere.

The Area, whether called "Intermediate" or "Chibchan," must still be considered a largely artificial construct with indistinct boundaries that conform to neither natural nor modern political boundaries. Nonetheless, this area is worthy of our attention and interest for a number of reasons. It reflects both apparent linguistic and genetic unity and stability with time depth. It contains evidence of both the fluted and fish-tail traditions of Paleoindian projectile points. Although it incorporates the southern margins of what we call "Mesoamerica" and reflects faint influences of Maya, Olmec, and Central Mexican cultures, it nonetheless overwhelmingly demonstrates autochthonous cultural development. The region encapsulates the middle steps in the northern dispersal of gold-working techniques and artifacts from South America to Mesoamerica, and it has some of the earliest ceramics and evidence of settled village life in the Western Hemisphere, as well as excellent examples of jade, ceramic, and gold-working technologies and traditions. Finally, it presents a dynamic alternative to the architecturally dominant "bigger is better" models of New World civilization characteristic of Mesoamerica and the Andes. Given these important features, it is reasonable to expect ongoing assessment of the utility of this cultural-temporal-spatial unit.

Historically, the tendency has been to interpret the cultural development of various sectors of this area, and of the whole area, in terms of influences from adjacent areas of Mesoamerica or South America rather than in terms of local developments. Major debates have ranged over the source, direction, and nature of external influences. Modern research did not begin until the 1960s, and then only in a dispersed and spotty fashion. Unfortunately, many who initiated early investigations here were subsequently lured to the more visually exciting architecture of Mesoamerica and South America, and to the supposedly greater theoretical challenges of more complex societies. When preliminary investigations were not followed up with more detailed work, preliminary results gradually became imbued with the ring of truth through repetition, most often by uncritical readers rather than by the original researchers. This is particularly true with regard to cultural artifacts and traits that were identified as reflecting elite behavior, external influence, and even cultural/political dominance from external sources (Maya, Olmec, Teotihuacán, Aztec, and others).

There are extensive data for a long cultural sequence only in western Panama, where evidence dates human occupation to before 8000 B.C. The earlier parts of these sequences deal with more general hemisphere-wide developmental patterns; the integrity of the sequences provides strong support for an interpretation that the major forces for cultural evolution were in situ rather than borrowed, diffused, or imposed. In addition to Lange, John Hoopes, Payson Sheets, and Oscar Fonseca have been strong proponents of a *sui generis* developmental model. The entire cultural sequence is summarized below, in general for the period prior to 2000 B.C. and more specifically after that.

Overview of Intermediate Area. Map design by Mapping Specialists Limited, Madison, Wisconsin.

Environment

The Intermediate Area is characterized by a wide diversity of climates, from seasonally dry (northern Pacific Costa Rica, southern Pacific Nicaragua, and the Santa Elena Peninsula of Ecuador) to the highest levels of precipitation in the New World (the Atlantic watersheds of Costa Rica and Panama). The area is composed of what is commonly classified as either wet or dry tropical (Aw, Afw, Amw, and Anw climates) in the Köppen classification.

Meandering and seasonally raging rivers drain the Atlantic watershed, while there are few such rivers on the Pacific coast. On the Caribbean coast, most rivers drain into an open coastline, while the principal rivers on the Pacific generally drain into bays such as the Gulf of Fonseca (El Salvador, Honduras, and Nicaragua), the gulfs of Nicoya and Osa in Costa Rica, the bays of Parita and Panama in Panama, and the Gulf of Guayaquil in Ecuador. Principal exceptions are the bays of Chiriqui (Panama) and Uraba (Colombia), and the Gulf of Venezuela (Venezuela) on the Caribbean/Atlantic side.

The principal elevations in the area are the volcanic chain of central Nicaragua, the Central Valley and

I

volcanic cordillera of Costa Rica, and the northern extension of the Andean chain in Ecuador, Colombia, and Venezuela. The large interior basins that seem to have promoted the concentration of larger populations and the emergence of more complex societies in Mesoamerica are absent from the area.

In Nicaragua, Costa Rica, Panama, and north coastal South America, the prehistoric inhabitants enjoyed bicoastal opportunities. Nowhere is one coast more than a week's walk from the other (assuming that the weather was relatively good and that any of the numerous natural passes was utilized). The limited research that has focused on Caribbean-Pacific contacts has produced preliminary evidence of long-term, regular contacts, although the precise mechanisms and patterns of these remain to be elucidated.

In Costa Rica, the sharing of forms and iconography of jade pendants among the Pacific coast, the central cordillera, and the Atlantic coast suggests some shared ideology that spanned these three ecologically distinct areas. Grieder has noted that, throughout the area, polychrome ceramics are generally limited to the Pacific coast, and modeled and incised/engraved/brushed/punctated ceramics are much more common on the Caribbean/Atlantic coast.

Settlement History and Cultural Processes

Regional cultural patterns characteristic of the Intermediate Area can be identified as early as 1500 B.C. and continued until Spanish contact. Prior to this, peoples in the area participated in the more generalized Northwest South American Littoral tradition. Based on linguistic data, Fonseca claims a starting point of 4000 B.C. for the area of Chibchan tradition, but there are few archaeological data available to test the suggested time depth.

Richard G. Cooke and Anthony J. Ranere have documented the longest currently available sequence of evolution from simple hunters, gatherers, and collectors to ranked societies. In contrast to Mesoamerica and the Andes, there are no strongly developed temporal "horizons" that serve to integrate the area at particular moments in time. There were broad common trends and ongoing contacts and communication, but the most salient feature is a long tradition of subareal, subregional developmental independence—what John Hoopes has called "associated but distinct" cultures. Not all parts of the area have deep developmental sequences; it is not clear whether this reflects differing research objectives or different patterns of early settlement and adaptation.

For interpretation of cultural evolution and process, the rate and pattern of cultural development is as important as the length of the sequence. Payson Sheets notes that the rates of development in the Intermediate Area were much slower than those in Mesoamerica and the Andes. In the Intermediate Area, significant changes occurred over spans of 300 to 400 years or more. This suggests much greater stability and a more peaceful existence for these peoples than were known by their more "civilized" neighbors. An assessment of the cultural development of the Intermediate Area begins with an overview of settlement and subsistence data, the basic building blocks on which further developments in the area depended.

Period I (?–6000 B.C.). The earliest data from the northern part of the Intermediate Area are from the Turrialba site in Atlantic Costa Rica and from Lake Alajuela (Lake Madden) in western Panama. In both locations, projectile points related to both the northern fluted point and the southern fish-tail traditions have been recovered from surface collections and excavations. Isolated finds in the Lake Arenal area of Costa Rica, and a fluted "Clovis-like" projectile point reportedly surface-collected in Guanacaste province of Costa Rica, suggest that this pattern was widespread in northern Costa Rica, although poorly known at present. The site of La Mula–West on the shore of Parita Bay has yielded only fluted fragments, as well as engraving, boring, and scraping tools also thought to be part of the Paleoindian tool kit. Four rock shelters tested during the Proyecto Santa María in the Parita Bay region yielded radiocarbon dates between 6600 and 5000 B.C.

To the south, the El Inga projectile point complex from highland Ecuador, dated to approximately 7000 B.C., also shows a combination of fish-tail form and fluting treatment. The presence of leaf-shaped point complexes in northern South America, such as the El Jobo complex from Venezuela, also dates to this time. This complex may represent independent development, but it may also be related to the leaf-shaped point tradition of North America. Widely scattered individual finds of presumably early stemmed, fluted, fish-tail, or leaf-shaped lithic industries suggest that Paleoindian peoples occupied both highland and lowland areas—and that we still have much to learn about the earliest periods of human occupation.

Although no artifacts or sites are directly associated, core samples from Lake Yeguada sediments indicate human presence and ecological changes from clearing and burning by 9000 B.C. Based on similarities in stone tool assemblages and burial modes, Karen Stothert has proposed a Preceramic "interaction sphere" extending from northern Peru and the Vegas culture of the Santa Elena Peninsula of Ecuador to the Cerro Mangote shell mound on Parita Bay, Panama.

Finally, despite claims made in the 1970s by Jorge Espinoza, the El Bosque site in northern Pacific Nicaragua is now recognized as a redeposited paleontological site rather than an archaeological one.

Period II (6000–4000 B.C.). Data from this period are extremely limited, except for the Proyecto Santa María area in Panama. At about this time, the coastlines stabilized after a prolonged period of glacial melting; this favored the formation of mangrove swamps and other niches exploitable by ever-expanding human populations. The footprints at the Acahualinca site in the Managua metropolitan area in Nicaragua and the Río Antiguo surface finds in northwestern Costa Rica are both thought to date to this period. To date, the former site lacks artifacts in association with the footprints (although its chronological position is well fixed by geological cross-dating); the latter consists entirely of surface finds, with the chronological placement suggested by geomorphological interpretation and weathering rate analysis of the patina on the lithic artifacts.

Near Parita Bay, Proyecto Santa María investigators recorded a twentyfold increase in the number of sites during this period; temporary sites and permanent hamlets are recorded, and rock shelters were occupied year round. Maize pollen and phytoliths are found in cave deposits, and lake sediment data indicate that deforestation of primary forests continued as human occupation intensified. The unexplained contrast between relatively dense population in this area and the apparent absence of coeval populations on the Pacific coasts of Nicaragua and Costa Rica farther north is one of the great mysteries of Central American archaeology.

Period III (4000–1000 B.C.). There is very little evidence of sites from the early part of this period, but by its end there is evidence of the use of ceramics and settled village life throughout the Intermediate Area. As Hoopes has pointed out, though there are general similarities among ceramic complexes, the overriding impression is one of local development from a common technological base, rather than technological and stylistic diffusion from a central source or a single direction. In northeastern Honduras, the Cuyamel phase dates to about 1400 B.C.; in Nicaragua, the Dinarte phase on Ometepe Island in

Lake Nicaragua had the first documented ceramics from the northern part of the area and dates to the middle of the period, c. 2000 B.C. The Dinarte phase is important not only because it is relatively early and comparable to other regional ceramic complexes of the same approximate date, but also because it demonstrates—albeit indirectly—a rafting or sailing technology well developed by that time.

The Tronadora site in the Lake Arenal area of the Cordillera of Guanacaste is also from this period (pre-2000 B.C.). The Chaparron and La Montana sites on the Atlantic watershed of Costa Rica come at the very end, or transition to the following Period IV. Published dates range from 1515 to 280 B.C., clustering around 500 B.C.; Hoopes believes that they may date closer to 800 B.C., a time period that may include the Loma B phase at the Vidor site on the Bay of Culebra.

The earliest ceramics in the area (the Monagrillo style) are from this period, and use of ceramics expanded over the region beginning in approximately 2500 B.C. in Chiriqui, Panama, to approximately 1000 B.C. in eastern Panama. Hoopes's careful review of the existing collections led him to conclude that there was a pattern of multiple origins and stylistic regionalism that negated the possibility of the spread of ceramic technology from a single source. In Caribbean Colombia, ceramics and habitational shell middens occur for the first time.

The development of a reliable subsistence base is a key variable in the accumulation of wealth, the emergence of elite personages or groups, and the evolution of hierarchical rankings of communities. The area had no single crop, such as maize, that was the staple for the entire area. Much of the area had access to coastal environments, and marine resources were certainly important; all investigators working in the area have reported mixed subsistence economies from all time periods, and Norr's trace element analyses of human skeletal remains from a broad range of time periods from coastal Panama and coastal and highland Costa Rica also support this view of a diversified prehistoric subsistence pattern.

Multiple food resources limited the ability of individuals and communities to regulate subsistence, or to manipulate subsistence-related activities such as accumulation and redistribution. There is no evidence that cultigens and ceramics were introduced simultaneously as part of any broad-scale "Formative" expansion from either Mesoamerica or South America. This lends independent support to the inference drawn from the ceramic data, as outlined above.

I

Using the site of La Mula as an example, Cooke and Ranere draw a correlation between food specialization (maize) and the emergence of site hierarchies around 1000 B.C. in western Panama. However, they emphasize that the hierarchical relationships were based on advantageous locations and kinship-based redistribution systems, rather than on the emergence of centralized political-economic control. This model seems to be widely applicable throughout the area at this time, and subsequently. Few comparable sites have been excavated, and understanding the nutritional and social role of the various dietary patterns for which we already have evidence will require additional bone collagen analysis from a wide variety of skeletal populations from the entire area, and from a wide range of time periods.

We can touch on almost all the important sites in discussing these early periods, but the next period sees a virtual explosion of sites and population, and our discussion will become much more generalized.

Period IV (1000 B.C.–A.D. 500). Various authors in the volume *Wealth and Hierarchy in the Intermediate Area* (Lange 1992) suggest that the earliest evidence for wealth and hierarchy, and ranking and ritual, comes from around 1000 B.C. In central Honduras, the sites of Los Naranjos at Lake Yojoa and Yarumela in the Comayagua Valley were under construction with corporate labor and specialized architecture. Although such sites are peripheral to our focal area, they serve to emphasize the sharp differences between groups in western Honduras and those to the south and to the east. Sites from this period are also present in the other principal subdivisions of the Intermediate Area: the Atlantic watershed of Central America, Greater Nicoya, the Central Valley of Costa Rica, Greater Chiriqui, and northern South America. Polychrome ceramics first appear by the beginning of the period.

Around 500 B.C., jade and other greenstone artifacts came into widespread use. In northern and central Costa Rica, a specialized funerary complex developed, including various combinations of zoned bichrome ceramics, ceremonial stools or thrones, jade pendants, and mace-heads. According to Bruhns, most of the stone sculpture from San Agustín and other northern South American sites dates to this period.

Maize is first evident in Panama in the Chiriqui Highlands. In comparison with the situation in the Parita Bay area of Panama, this crop seems to have arrived late, at least in archaeologically detectable quantities, in the central highlands and the northwestern Pacific coast of Costa

Rica, and in southwestern Nicaragua. By the end of this period, there is evidence of continuous human occupation (permanent villages and extensive cemeteries that may reflect clans, lineages, or other social units) in settings previously occupied by less permanent communities, as well as in many places that appear to have been previously uninhabited. Jade artifacts and ceramics of various styles (zoned engraved, Usulutan) evidence interregional and intergroup contacts, although the specific mechanisms are still poorly understood; it is important to note that in the case of Usulutan, researchers are documenting the distribution of a decorative technique, and not of the finished ceramics themselves. In general, ceramic studies indicate that, through the end of this period, ceramic production was fundamentally locally controlled and directed.

Period V (A.D. 500–1000). The A.D. 500 time line is a major marker of change in many regions of the Intermediate area. The types of change that are most easily identifiable archaeologically are shifts in settlement patterns and the introduction of new types or styles of artifacts. In eastern Honduras, status goods are present after this time; in the southern sector of Greater Nicoya, there is a rapid buildup in coastal habitation; and in Atlantic Costa Rica, striking changes took place in settlements and larger, concentrated villages are evident. In central Panama, the Boruca Valley, and the Arenal region of the volcanic highlands of northern Costa Rica, population shifts appear to have been less significant.

In central and Atlantic Costa Rica, Michael Snarskis interprets changes in house forms and sizes as evidence of the emergence of elites and the development of a warrior-chieftain hierarchy. Large sites such as Guayabo de Turrialba and Las Mercedes were constructed of large river cobbles and stone slabs and are visually and dimensionally quite different from earlier, smaller sites in that region and from more homogeneous site forms in other regions. Because distinctions among site forms and sizes proliferated during this period, it can be generalized that the larger sites are in the wetter central valleys and highlands, and in the Atlantic watersheds, while greater homogeneity was maintained on the drier Pacific slopes. In the Diquis area, Robert Drolet noted a major settlement shift around A.D. 700. As in Period IV, sites representative of Period V are found in all major subdivisions of the Intermediate Area.

Most of the stone sculpture from lower Central America appears to date from this and the following period.

This was also the time of the principal dispersal of gold metallurgical technology throughout the northern tier of the Intermediate area.

Period VI (A.D. 1000–1520). At the time of the Spanish invasion, travelers described chiefdoms in Panama and Colombia (the Sinu and the Tairona) with larger populations and more complex societies than those in Costa Rica, Nicaragua, and eastern Honduras. Regional ceramic patterns became more distinct during Period VI, and gold metallurgy was widespread.

This historical overview shows that the broad diversity of this area provided its prehistoric populations with long-term cultural stability, in contrast to the cyclical upheaval and competition that were characteristic of the centers of both highland and lowland Mesoamerican peoples, as well as of Andean societies.

Material and Ideological Resources

The following data summary demonstrates the limitations of the artificial boundaries of the Intermediate area as it is currently drawn, as well as some limitations of the more culturally defined Chibchan area linguistic boundaries advocated by Fonseca. I note important resources that either are present in the area, or are outside the area but were obtained and utilized by its residents. Most data suggest that the usual manner of acquisition and transfer was the point-to-point process.

The accumulation of wealth, the emergence of ranked societies, and the evolution of economic/political (regional and extraregional) hierarchies have traditionally been identified as the consequences of mature, settled village life. Although such an evolutionary sequence is appropriate to the Andes and to the Valley of Mexico and the Maya Lowlands, the process was truncated at a lower level—the chiefdom—in some parts of the Intermediate area, and at the tribal level in others.

Jade. The manufacture and use of jade artifacts (primarily pendants and beads) was limited mostly to northwestern, central, and Atlantic coastal Costa Rica from approximately 300 B.C. to A.D. 700. In this context, the term "jade" includes all lithic materials—jadeite, quartz, serpentine, and others—used in the manufacture of earplugs, pendants, and beads. The closest presently known source of jadeite is outside the Intermediate area, in the Motagua Valley of Guatemala. In addition, there exists a group of artifacts that are geologically and chemically jadeite but are unrelated to Motagua or any other known source, posing a tantalizing challenge to geological and archaeological researchers. The geographical distribution of jade artifacts in northern Costa Rica crosses major ecological and archaeological culture boundaries and strongly suggests sharing of specialized knowledge among the elite members of societies in different regions. In contrast to the Maya area, where jade objects and manufacturing debris are found in both domestic and ceremonial contexts, in Central America such objects have, to date, been found only in association with interments or ceremonial settings.

There has been extensive speculation regarding Olmec and Maya influence on the Costa Rican jade-carving tradition, but it is best to view the three archaeological cultures as having distinct carving traditions. Cruder greenstone (but non-jadeite) artifacts are known from Honduras, and to a limited extent from northern South America, but these too are from entirely separate carving traditions. Jade artifacts have been found in limited quantities in Nicaraguan sites near the Costa Rica border, and recent finds in the area of El Ostional have expanded the known distribution of the Tempisque period (300 B.C.–A.D. 300) complex—Zoned Bichrome ceramics, maceheads, jade, and carved *metates*—into the Nicaraguan sector of the Bay of Salinas.

Obsidian. Obsidian from sources in Guatemala (Pixcaya and Ixtepeque) and Honduras (Guinope) is found at sites beyond the northern limits of the Intermediate area, but from there it was traded south into Nicaragua and northern Costa Rica. From central Costa Rica southward, obsidian is very rare and usually absent. There is also a strong contrast between Pacific coastal sites in Nicaragua and Costa Rica, which more frequently have obsidian, and those sites in the central and Atlantic areas that tended to make more use of locally available raw materials. Where it does appear, obsidian is most frequent after A.D. 800.

Gold. The principal cultural occurrences of gold in the Intermediate area are in the Chontales region of Nicaragua, the Diquis region of Costa Rica, western Panama, and Colombia. The gold-working tradition is part of a northward-moving process during the pre-Columbian era, as gold metallurgy techniques moved from Colombia to the western coast of Mexico. Symbols for gold are found on ceramics in the Greater Chiriqui and Greater Nicoya areas, where both symbolism and actual artifacts usually postdate A.D. 800, although both the temporal range and the geographical distribution are occasionally and superficially distorted by isolated

I

finds. Gold symbols are also seen on some stone statuary from Nicaragua, Panama, and the San Agustín area of Colombia.

Copper. Relatively few copper artifacts, all of them bells or earspools, have been found. They are all thought to have been made in Honduras or Mexico, and then imported.

Clay Resources. In this volcanically active area, erosional deposits of clays of variable quality are widely distributed, and most populations would have had access to ceramic-quality clays in their immediate vicinity. In northwestern Costa Rica and Pacific Nicaragua, the most carefully studied region for ceramic typology, a combination of stylistic and chemical studies have divided the region into nine divisions of ceramic production, closely mirroring major volcanic, erosional, and river drainage patterns.

Perishables. Although samples of woods, fibers, drug plants, feathers, and skins are seldom recovered from archaeological contexts, depictions and symbolism on ceramics and stone statuary and in jade and gold figures indicate that they were important components of the cultural assemblage. In the Intermediate Area, differences between the wealthy and the non-wealthy were neither so pronounced nor so obvious as in the central Mexican and Maya areas or in the Andean zone, and therefore these distinctions are more difficult to identify archaeologically.

Interaction with Other Regions

Although the Intermediate Area and Central America have been considered transitional areas, corridors, and/or the recipients of strong cultural influences from external sources (more from the north than from the south), the direct archaeological evidence of such incursions or passages is relatively limited and usually indirect. The degrees of Olmec influence on the jade-carving tradition, Mesoamerican influence on the ceramic tradition, and Mesoamerican influence in the subsistence system—especially in the northern part of the area—are vigorously debated.

There seems to be little doubt that the inspiration for gold-working technology and many forms and symbols were derived from northern South America, and after A.D. 800 some obsidian arrived from Guatemalan and Honduran sources. However, the Usulutan technique in evidence from A.D. 200–500, and the Mexican symbolism on ceramics after A.D. 800, both suggest more indirect and probably filtered influences. One interesting

category is the Early Classic Maya belt celts, which have been recovered more frequently in Costa Rica than in the Maya area proper, and which are absent from the intermediate terrain of Honduras and Nicaragua.

Data Gaps and Interpretative Blanks

There seems to be general agreement that a different model of cultural development and the evolution of social complexity is needed for the Intermediate Area. The more traditional, idealized models developed for the civilizations of highland and lowland Mesoamerica and the Andes may be of little applicability except as contrasts to Intermediate Area patterns. How do we go about developing new models for these overlapping areas?

We need to focus our attention on filling in the missing space-time gaps in clearly defined, ecologically bounded basins, plains, and valleys. We have begun to make some progress in this aspect of Central American research, after a lapse (with a few exceptions) for the past twenty years. The most ambitious project under way is the systematic archaeological inventory of Nicaragua developed in cooperation between the government of Sweden and the Organization of American States. This recent sense of urgency to fill in some existing space-time gaps has been stimulated by an unprecedented surge of site-destructive economic development in the area, combined with a sense of how many areas about which we still know nothing.

FURTHER READINGS

Barrantes, R., P. E. Smouse, H. Mohrenweiser, H. Gershowitz, J. Azofeifa, T. Arias, and J. V. Neel. 1990. Microevolution in Lower Central America: Genetic Characterization of the Chibcha Speaking Groups of Costa Rica and Panama, and a Consensus Taxonomy Based on Genetic and Linguistic Affinity. *Journal of Human Genetics* 46:63–84.

Bishop, R. L., F. W. Lange, and P. Lange. 1988. Ceramic Paste Compositional Patterns in Greater Nicoya Pottery. In F. W. Lange (ed.), *Costa Rican Art and Archaeology: Essays in Honor of Frederick R. Mayer,* pp. 11–44. Boulder: Johnson Books.

Bonilla V. L., M. Calvo M., J. V. Guerrero M., S. Salgado G., and F. W. Lange (eds.). 1990. *Tipos ceramicos y variedades de la Gran Nicoya. Vinculos* 13 (1-2):1–327. San José, Costa Rica: Imprenta Varitec.

Constenla U. A., 1991. Las lenguas del Area Intermedia: Introducción a su estudio areal. San José: Editorial de la Universidad de Costa Rica.

Cooke, R., and A. J. Ranere. 1992. The Origins of Wealth and Hierarchy in the Central Region of Panama (12,000–2,000 BP), with Observations on Its Relevance to the History and Phylogeny of Chibchan-Speaking Polities in Panama and Elsewhere. In Lange 1992, pp. 243–316.

Fonseca Z., O., 1994. El concepto de area de tradicíon chibchoïde y su pertinencia para entender Gran Nicoya. In R. Vazquez L. (ed.), *Taller sobre el futuro de las investigaciones arqueológicas y etnohistóricas en Gran Nicoya* (*Vinculos* 18/19), pp. 209–277. San José: Museo Nacional de Costa Rica.

Grieder, T. 1993. A Global View of Central America. In M. M. Graham (ed.), *Reinterpreting Prehistory of Central America,* pp. 39–50. Niwot: University Press of Colorado.

Haberland, W. 1959. A Pre-appraisal of Chiriquian Pottery Types. In *Actas, 33rd International Congress of Americanists,* vol. 2, pp. 339–346.

Hirth, K. G., and S. G. Hirth. 1993. Ancient Currency: The Style and Use of Jade and Marble Carvings in Central Honduras. In Lange 1993, pp. 173–190.

Hoopes, J. W. 1992. Early Formative Cultures in the Intermediate Area: A Background to the Emergence of Social Complexity. In Lange 1992, pp. 43–83.

Lange, F. W. (ed.). 1992. *Wealth and Hierarchy in the Intermediate Area.* Washington, D.C.: Dumbarton Oaks.

————— (ed.). 1993. *Precolumbian Jade: New Cultural and Geological Interpretations.* Salt Lake City: University of Utah Press.

Lange, F. W., and S. Abel-Vidor (eds.). 1980. *Investigaciones arqueológicas en la zona de Bahía Culebra, Costa Rica (1973–1979). Vinculos,* San José: Museo Nacional de Costa Rica.

Lange, F. W., and L. Norr (eds.). 1986. *Archaeological Settlement Patterns in Costa Rica. Journal of the Steward Anthropological Society* 14(1–2). Urbana-Champaign: University of Illinois.

Lange, F. W., P. D. Sheets, A. Martinez, and S. Abel-Vidor. 1992. *The Archaeology of Pacific Nicaragua.* Albuquerque: University of New Mexico Press.

Lange, F. W., and D. Z. Stone (eds.). 1984. *The Archaeology of Lower Central America.* Albuquerque: University of New Mexico Press.

Linares, O., and A. J. Ranere. 1980. *Adaptive Radiations in Prehistoric Panama.* Peabody Museum Monographs, 5. Cambridge, Mass.: Harvard University.

Rouse, I. 1962. The Intermediate Area, Amazonia, and the Caribbean Area. In R. J. Braidwood and G. R. Willey (eds.), *Courses Toward Urban Life.* Viking Fund Publications in Anthropology, 32. New York: Wenner-Gren Foundation for Anthropological Research.

Sheets, P. D. 1992. The Pervasive Pejorative in Intermediate Area Studies. In Lange 1992, pp. 15–41.

————— . 1994. Taller sobre el futuro de las investigaciones arqueológicas y etnohistóricas en Gran Nicoya. *Vinculos* 18/19:209–227. San José: Museo Nacional de Costa Rica.

Weaver, M. P. 1993. *The Aztecs, Maya, and Their Predecessors.* 3d ed. San Diego: Academic Press.

Willey, G. R. 1971. *An Introduction to American Archaeology.* Vol. 2, *South America.* Englewood Cliffs, N.J.: Prentice-Hall.

Frederick W. Lange

Interregional Interactions

Mesoamerica's original designation as a culture area was predicated on the widespread distribution of a set of distinctive behavior patterns, or traits, among its constituent societies. These features range from elements of technology and subsistence—for example, cultivation of maize, beans, and squash with a distinctive digging stick, the *coa*—to more abstract principles of time reckoning (the 260-day calendar), conceptions of the supernatural (deities such as the Rain God and the Feathered Serpent), and sacred practices such as autosacrificial bloodletting. It was assumed, in keeping with U.S. anthropological theory of the early to mid-twentieth century, that the integrity of this eclectic group of traits was not due to functional interrelations among its components but resulted from a shared history of diffusion and migration linking Mesoamerican societies. These processes, often combined in retrospective considerations of anthropological theory, are points on a continuum of cultural dislocation and population movement.

The term "diffusion" generally refers to the passage of ideas ("stimulus diffusion") and/or goods among societies, accompanied by the movement of at most a few individuals who serve as the means of dissemination. Diffusion has traditionally been offered as the explanation for the appearance of a few new behavior patterns or locally unprecedented items in archaeological components.

The term "migration" denotes the permanent transfer of a sizable number of people from one territory to another, along with much of their cultural baggage (both

I

goods and ideas). An immigrant group may range in constitution from a subset of the original population (e.g., warrior males) to an entire social unit including both sexes, all ages, and all occupations. Intentional migrations span a continuum from hostile and acquisitive, as in wars of conquest, to peaceful movements in search of employment, protection, or arable land. Population movement has usually been invoked to account for such dramatic changes in the archaeological record as the sudden appearance of a number of new behavior patterns and their material manifestations ("trait complexes"). Despite these differences, both migration and diffusion have been treated as mechanisms of trait dispersal that contributed to Mesoamerica's cultural integrity.

Little attention was initially devoted to establishing the operational and behavioral effects of these interaction processes. Diffusion and migration, as employed in early to mid-twentieth century Mesoamerican archaeology, generally presupposed a unilinear sequence of development leading to increasing cultural elaboration and political complexity. Unlike the rigidly circumscribed evolutionary trajectories of nineteenth-century anthropology, this view did not generalize sequences of change within culture areas to all human societies nor propose them to be the products of inevitable biological shifts underlying expansion of mental capacity. Instead, the enduring cultural uniformity of Mesoamerica and its development through time were seen to result from the actions of a sequence of core societies which, for largely undetermined reasons, took the lead in formulating innovations that spread, by diffusion and migration, outward to the margins of the culture area.

It has long been recognized that some commonalities underlying the Mesoamerican culture pattern resulted from a shared history predating culture cores. Mesoamerica, like all of the New World, was occupied as a result of migrations originating in northeastern Asia, though the number and dates of these peregrinations are still debated. Once established in Mesoamerica, these dispersed populations remained in contact, exchanging goods, ideas, and—after 8,000 to 5,000 B.C.—crops over wide areas. Most traits used to define Mesoamerica, however, are related to the development of complex, hierarchically organized socio-political forms whose appearance is traditionally identified with innovating cores.

The Olmecs of the Mexican Gulf Coast (1500–500 B.C.) were the first of these inventive central societies. An early and enduring interpretation of the Olmecs' significance in Mesoamerican culture history posits that Gulf Coast elites precociously developed concepts of political

hierarchy and religion that underlay all later Mesoamerican developments (the so-called Mother Culture hypothesis). Diffusion of these principles and a set of related material traits, especially ceramic and sculptural styles, extended throughout Mesoamerica, imparting to all subsequent phases a unity born of a shared history of intersocietal contact.

Teotihuacan, in the northeastern corner of the Basin of Mexico, played a similar role later (200 B.C.–A.D. 650). Architectural, ceramic, and sculptural styles abundantly represented at Teotihuacan are found to varying degrees over wide portions of Mesoamerica and even, in attenuated forms, beyond its borders (diagnostic traits include *talud/tablero*-style architecture and slab-footed tripod ceramic cylinders). Teotihuacan, like the Olmec heartland before it, seems to have been politically advanced; its rulers fashioned a polity of unprecedented scale and centralized power. This preeminence gave Teotihuacan's rulers a telling edge in interregional competition, leading to the rapid and widespread distribution of innovations derived from the central Mexican core.

Coexisting with Teotihuacan were cores whose influences were more spatially circumscribed: Monte Albán in the Oaxacan highlands, and large Maya centers such as Tikal in the southern lowlands. Diffusion of innovations originating at these foci defined subsidiary culture areas that are distinguished by enduring variations on general Mesoamerican stylistic, ideological, and organizational themes. Teotihuacan was still seen as the largest political center of the time, exercising the most extensive and pervasive influence.

Core status was retained by central Mexican polities until the Spanish conquest, focused first on the northern Toltec center of Tula and later on the Aztec capital, Tenochtitlan. Each was a center of political and military innovations, an advantage that facilitated extensive dispersal of concepts and material items associated with these cores.

Diffusion up through A.D. 650 was generally envisioned as a peaceful process conducted by such agents as merchants and religious proselytizers. There was little doubt, however, that the spread of innovations associated with the Toltec and Aztec states was accomplished in large part through military action and migrations of varying scale.

Migration in Mesoamerica, as in much of the world, has been called on to account for that residual class of dramatic behavioral and material changes that resisted explanation by diffusion. Population movement did not play a central role in twentieth-century anthropological thought and, to this day, there is little evidence of a coherent body of concepts that can be referred to as "migration theory." This does not mean that the significance of population movements in Mesoamerican prehistory has been denied: quite the opposite. Migration's enduring appeal in Mesoamerica owes much to the following lines of evidence: detailed statements appearing in native documents concerning prominent figures within, and the itineraries of, ancient population movements; linguistic evidence of migrations, based primarily on genetic relations among languages, their historically known distributions, and timing of language divergences obtained using such techniques as glottochronology; the sudden appearance in some areas of new populations recognized primarily by their renditions on monuments, murals, and/or ceramic figurines; and traditional archaeological markers of population movement, especially the rapid introduction of a large number of locally unprecedented material styles. Of particular importance in the last case are aspects of nonportable media, such as architecture and monuments, whose appearance cannot easily be explained by intersocietal goods exchange. Where two or more of these lines of evidence converge, Mesoamerican archaeologists continue to invoke migration. This process is, however, largely confined to the late prehistoric intervals described in native accounts.

The Gulf Coast lowlands play an important role in most discussions of Mesoamerican migrations. This area is usually seen as a frontier between two Mesoamerican subareas: the Central Highlands and the Maya Lowlands. Gulf Coast populations, therefore, fashioned a culture composed of elements derived from both zones. The resulting mix is generally acknowledged to have imbued its creators with "hybrid vigor," or at least with cultural and political flexibility, that gave them advantages in contests with neighboring cores when the latter were undergoing episodes of political decentralization. Given the importance attributed to this lowland zone in Epiclassic (A.D. 700–900) and Early Postclassic (A.D. 900–1250) culture history, it might better be seen as an innovating center than as a periphery. It was from this cultural crucible that the Nonoalcas, a poorly understood, culturally complex group, are supposed to have migrated to the Central Highlands. Their joining at Tula with immigrants from Mesoamerica's northern margins, the ethnically and linguistically protean Chichimecs, is reported in ethnohistoric accounts to have been a crucial event in the creation of the Toltec state (A.D. 900–1100).

Most Gulf Coast migrations, however, involved relatively small, well-organized groups of elite merchants and/or warriors who, by dint of superior military technology and organization, established hegemony over autochthonous populations. Olmeca-Xicalanca movement into the highlands following Teotihuacan's decline (A.D. 700–900) is one postulated example of Gulf Coast incursions. Evidence of this migration takes the form of "international" painting and architectural styles that combine Lowland Maya and Central Mexican elements. Physically distinct Central Mexican and Lowland Maya individuals also appear in murals at highland Olmeca-Xicalanca centers such as Cacaxtla.

The sudden, widespread introduction of Central Mexican stylistic and behavioral innovations—beginning by c. A.D. 800 at such northern and southwestern Lowland Maya centers as Seibal, Altar de Sacrificios, Becan, and Chichén Itzá—has been attributed to successive waves of Chontal-Putun warrior-traders. These "mexicanized" Maya, some of whom may appear on monuments at Seibal and murals at Chichén Itzá, were carriers of a syncretic culture whose origins are traced to the Gulf Coast.

Similarly, establishment of late prehistoric (after A.D. 1250) Quiché, Cakchiquel, and Tzutujil conquest states over much of the Maya Highlands has been traced to mobile warrior bands whose ultimate source was the Gulf Coast. Even more far-reaching spatially are the postulated migrations of Nahua-speaking Pipil and Nicarao populations. They apparently set out on a long, complex trek that originated in the Central Mexican highlands sometime between A.D. 650 and 850, passed through the Gulf Coast, and proceeded down the Pacific littoral of Guatemala into El Salvador, Honduras, and ultimately western Nicaragua. These groups may have been preceded into eastern El Salvador by another people of Gulf Coast origin whose distinctive material culture, most notably stone sculpture associated with the ball game, appeared at Quelepa during the seventh century A.D.

Archaeological diagnostics of Gulf Coast population movements include the following: the *talud/tablero* architectural style; the appearance of central Mexican deities, particularly Quetzalcoatl, Tlaloc, and Xipe Totec; the sacrifice of war captives; I-shaped ball courts; skull racks *(tzompantlis);* sculpted themes of fertility and sacrifice associated with the ball game; an increased emphasis on conquest warfare; colonnaded and round structures; fine-paste ceramics and Tohil Plumbate, especially for migrations predating A.D. 1250; green obsidian, presumably from the Central Mexican Pachuca source; *Chac Mool*

I

(reclining figure) sculptures; wheeled figurines; and foreign portraits on monuments and in figurines. These elements do not comprise a functionally coherent complex that must be present in its entirety before Gulf Coast migrations are accepted. Instead, these traits are an eclectic assortment of styles and objects from diverse sources and are presumed to have arrived in the areas outlined earlier as a result of Gulf Coast intermediaries. In addition to dispersing traits, Gulf Coast immigrants are credited with establishing high-volume, competitive commodity trading and conquest states whose persistent efforts to acquire new lands bred endemic warfare. Epiclassic and Postclassic peregrinations, therefore, are the agents by which the mercantilist and militaristic spirit of late Mesoamerican prehistory was disseminated. Migration, in these models, powerfully supplements diffusion, forging a new unity in Mesoamerican cultural patterns.

The development and spread of the Aztec Empire and its extensive influence within Mesoamerica are also commonly explained by recourse to migration. Following indigenous accounts of their own history, the Aztecs are depicted as late arrivals in the Valley of Mexico, imbued with the militaristic skills and spirit often attributed to the Chichimecs. Like Tula's founding and expansion, Aztec success is credited to their synthesis of northern frontier toughness with the established Mesoamerican cultural patterns they adopted from preexisting Central Mexican societies.

Subsequent dispersal of innovations from this latest of pre-Hispanic cores in the Valley of Mexico was due to a combination of military expansion and extensive trading operations involving specialized merchants such as the *pochteca*. Both processes entailed limited core-periphery migration as trading colonies and garrisons were established at various points within and on the fringes of the empire. Once again, a late pre-Columbian theme is reiterated: creation of an innovating core from the synthesis of diverse populations, at least some of whom are recent immigrants, and dispersal of traits by means of aggressive mercantile and military action.

The migration that brought independent pre-Columbian developments to an end, the Spanish conquest in the sixteenth century, was also a product of powerful commercial interests backed by strong military forces. In a sense, this intrusion of warrior bands from the Iberian Peninsula propelled Mesoamerica into a wider interaction sphere that would eventually see the spread of goods, ideas, and diseases throughout the world.

Anthropologists and archaeologists from at least the 1940s onward realized that there were severe problems with the concepts of diffusion and migration. It was felt, for example, that both terms were used too loosely. Research on migration in the 1950s and 1960s focused on specifying canons of evidence by which population movements could be reconstructed. Comparable work on diffusion attempted to standardize terms used in describing this process and to categorize its diversity with reference to such variables as the nature and numbers of contact agents and the behavioral impact of interactions on donor and recipient societies. Even more worrisome was the increasing awareness that calling on diffusion and migration did not explain observed patterns. They were, at best, names given to interaction processes that, by themselves, did not entail a clear theory of causation. Scholars need to develop an explicit body of concepts dealing with the behavioral consequences of, and factors affecting, intersocietal transfers of goods, ideas, and people. Initial steps taken in this important direction during the 1940s and 1950s, especially by Bennett and Willey, were not immediately pursued.

The waning of interest in diffusion and migration was due in large part to the growing popularity of cultural ecological theory in archaeology. This perspective emphasized relations among demographic, economic, technological, and physical environmental variables to explain cultural patterns and change processes. Traits became components of cultural systems whose forms and histories were now accounted for by the functions they served in adapting populations to their physical environments. Causes of cultural stability and transformation were to be found in relations among factors *internal* to specific societies and their ecological settings. Exogenous processes such as intersocietal contacts were not systematically incorporated in these new models. Diffusion, in fact, was repeatedly cited as a cause of superficial differences among cultures—variation that obscured essential functional and developmental regularities.

This debate was part of a broader argument over the scientific status of anthropology and archaeology. Cultural ecologists and their materialist successors were committed to a generalizing, scientific approach that sought to identify and explain cross-cultural regularities in human behavior. Diffusion and migration were seen as unscientific, linked with unpredictable historical forces that concealed behavioral commonalities.

Archaeological interpretations, however, still employ migration and diffusion to account for the appearance of those cultural features that have no obvious adaptive significance, most notably material styles. As in the past, diffusion is invoked to explain the advent of a few isolated stylistic innovations; migration is employed where such changes are more extensive. Inference of population movement is particularly attractive when supported by data from ethnohistory, linguistics, and/or the appearance of new physical types (the cases cited above continue to be explained, in part at least, by migration). Even leading proponents of materialist perspectives, therefore, still find a place for migration and diffusion in their interpretations. These processes, however, are not explicitly integrated within materialist theories but instead are used to account for a residual class of phenomena that defy other interpretations.

Even the most extreme hypothesized scenarios of migration and diffusion—transoceanic contacts between Mesoamerica and the Old World before the sixteenth century—still enjoy some currency, though more in the popular than in the scholarly literature. The appeal of such unconventional contacts can be traced to the dramatic image of heroic sea voyages and an unfortunate tendency in Euro-American thought to see Old World societies as primary sources of significant cultural innovations. Most claims of long-distance migration are based on incomplete New World sequences that create the false impression of sudden innovation without local precedent. Many also rely on superficial formal resemblances in art and architecture among historically unrelated cultures. Thus, Mesoamerican and Egyptian pyramids were equated, despite their differing functions, and the long, curling noses on *Chac* masks decorating northern Yucatecan buildings became elephant trunks indicative of Hindu contacts. As understanding of Mesoamerican cultures and occupation sequences increases, there is a general consensus that these and other formal similarities are merely fortuitous, and that Mesoamerican prehistory is an indigenous process that owes little to transoceanic input.

Diffusion and migration have imparted a subtle and pervasive legacy to Mesoamerican investigations that goes far beyond their ad hoc use in specific cases. Perhaps the most enduring consequence of this research tradition is the tendency to view changes in Mesoamerica according to a unilinear model in which a series of precocious cores stimulated changes in surrounding peripheries. The Olmecs, for example, may no longer be the Mother Culture of diffusion studies, but they are still generally seen as catalysts for cultural and political developments through-

out Mesoamerica. A widely accepted formulation posits that Olmec elites provided early models for complex social organization and the use of religion in legitimizing political hierarchies, concepts whose adaptive and strategic values were recognized by emergent rulers outside the Gulf Coast lowlands. Contact, in this view, sped up endogenous processes and imparted a general commonality to Mesoamerican prehistory. A comparable case could be made for many models of Teotihuacan's role in ancient Mesoamerica, and the persistent significance of migration in explanations of Epiclassic and Postclassic developments has already been noted. Though the above remarks do not do justice to the complex models employed by some investigators in recent years, they highlight the continuing attraction that innovating cores hold for Mesoamerican researchers.

The central issue in interregional interaction studies is not whether diffusion and migration ever occurred, or whether interaction or adaptive processes are more significant for interpreting human behavior. A wide array of intersocietal contacts have characterized Mesoamerican prehistory, and explanations of cultural form and change that ignore endogenous or exogenous factors grossly oversimplify causal relations in which both sets of variables are significant. The major problem is that a coherent body of archaeological theory specifying the behavioral significance of intersocietal interaction has not yet been articulated. Concepts such as diffusion and migration, therefore, have been employed as vague, ad hoc interpretive principles in the past, and they continue to be imperfectly and often covertly incorporated within explanatory schemes in which they have no systematic role.

This unsatisfactory situation has begun to change over the past three decades as archaeologists, inspired by work in related disciplines, have come to realize that societies cannot be studied meaningfully in isolation from the interaction networks in which they were originally embedded. All social systems depend to some extent on inputs of energy, ideas, and/or goods from beyond their boundaries to sustain and reproduce themselves each generation. Change, in many cases, also requires external stimuli, whether in the form of an influx of people, novel concepts, or new technologies. This is especially true for hierarchically organized societies whose complex political forms are partially sustained by external resources and alliances under paramount control. The challenge has been to integrate a more sophisticated appreciation of interaction processes than that found in the older diffusion/migration school with insights provided by

I

materialist perspectives on human-environment relations. It is only in this way that diffusion and migration can be shorn of their particularistic and disruptive connotations and made the subject of investigations designed to identify regularities in their behavioral effects.

Various perspectives have been advanced to accomplish this objective. Trade studies initially set out to establish contacts among societies by charting the flow of goods. Researchers pursuing this avenue enjoy great success in developing chemical and mineralogical tests by which sources of such items as obsidian, ceramics, and jade can be identified and exchange routes inferred. This marks a significant advance over earlier diffusion studies in which intersocietal contacts were more assumed than proved. As interesting and important as trade investigations are, they have not given rise to a consistent theory concerning the behavioral significance of intersocietal interaction. More recently, archaeologists inspired by Immanuel Wallerstein's world systems theory have begun to address the latter topic. Though varying in detail, world systems formulations tend to conceive of intersocietal transactions as occurring within a matrix of unequal economic and political relations in which powerful cores systematically exploit smaller, less centralized peripheral societies. Peripheries suffer underdevelopment as resources needed to sustain local economic growth and political complexity are siphoned off to support these processes in the core states. Such relations have clear behavioral implications for both cores and peripheries, strongly affecting economic, political, technological, and sometimes ideological patterns throughout the interaction network. The late prehistoric Aztec state has been viewed by several authors as the political and economic center of an extensive world system, as have Teotihuacan and Monte Albán. Putative peripheries of these foci as distant as the U.S. Southwest have also been examined from a world systems perspective.

Such efforts have sparked a debate over the applicability of world systems theory to prehistoric situations. These discussions focus largely on the suitability of many basic world systems assumptions to the study of non-modern economies. Wallerstein's scheme was developed to account for the spread of capitalism from Europe over the last 400 to 500 years. Application of this framework to pre-Hispanic Mesoamerica, therefore, requires reformulation of concepts and variables central to the original model. In particular, the political and economic value of "preciosity" exchanges, including transfers of status-defining goods such as jade, is stressed in opposition to

Wallerstein's disavowal of their importance in linking cores and peripheries. The possible incorporation of multiple cores within interaction networks has also been considered, running counter to both traditional world systems theory and the unilinear legacy of diffusion and migration. Questions have also been raised concerning the degree of underdevelopment suffered by peripheries. This last issue has to do with the extent to which a single pre-Hispanic core ever successfully monopolized political, economic, and/or military resources, thereby gaining a significant advantage in dictating the terms of intersocietal exchange. In the absence of such monopolies, core-periphery relations are likely to be much more ambiguous than they are in the modern world, and the behavioral significance of intersocietal ties more fluid and complex.

Finally, attention has turned to how external contacts and the goods acquired through them figured in local struggles to secure and enhance power. Much of this literature concerns the ways in which would-be social leaders maneuver to control exclusively extraregional transactions, thereby becoming the sole purveyors of valued exotic goods within their immediate societies. Such monopolies may have served as bases for local preeminence. To date, there has been far too little interest in the nature and behavioral impact of transactions involving non-elites in different societies.

Migration, that most enduring of concepts, has not been much affected by these developments. Core-periphery formulations, like earlier diffusion models, presume a matrix of spatially localized, immobile populations linked by a wide range of interaction processes. Goods and ideas, but not people, move through the network. Migration, now as in the past, is used to account for those "anomalous" cases where the above assumption is not met. There is no reason why migration should continue to exist as an intellectual loophole to be used only to explain unpredictable historical events. Because we cannot deny that migration has occurred in Mesoamerica, as the examples noted above indicate, we must face the challenge of systematically incorporating this process into our models, searching for regularities in its causes and behavioral consequences.

A growing literature has begun to coalesce around these issues, covering all periods of Mesoamerican prehistory but with most attention devoted to those intervals characterized by complex socio-political systems. The situation is very fluid, with a coherent interaction perspective yet to emerge. At the very least, we have moved away from sterile diffusion/migration vs. ecological and history vs. science debates to an appreciation of the complex interplay among local and extralocal factors in all cultural processes.

FURTHER READINGS

Blanton, R., and G. Feinman. 1984. The Mesoamerican World System. *American Anthropologist* 86:673–682.

Carmack, R. 1981. *The Quiche Mayas of Utatlan: The Evolution of a Highland Maya Kingdom.* Norman: University of Oklahoma Press.

Fowler, W. 1989. *The Cultural Evolution of Ancient Nahua Civilizations: The Pipil-Nicarao of Central America.* Norman: University of Oklahoma Press.

Fox, J. 1987. *Maya Postclassic State Formation: Segmentary Lineage Formation in Advancing Frontier.* Cambridge: Cambridge University Press.

Hirth, K. 1978. Interregional Trade and the Formation of Prehispanic Gateway Communities. *American Antiquity* 43:34–45.

McVicker, D. 1985. The "Mayanized" Mexicans. *American Antiquity* 50:82–101.

Miller, A. (ed.). 1983. *Highland–Lowland Interaction in Mesoamerica: Interdisciplinary Approaches.* Washington, D.C.: Dumbarton Oaks.

Sabloff, J., and C. C. Lamberg-Karlovsky (eds.). 1975. *Ancient Civilization and Trade.* Albuquerque: University of New Mexico Press.

Sanders, W., and J. Michels (eds.). 1977. *Teotihuacan and Kaminaljuyu: A Study in Prehistoric Culture Contact.* University Park: Pennsylvania State University Press.

Schortman, E., and P. Urban (eds.). 1992. *Resources, Power, and Interregional Interaction.* New York: Plenum Press.

Sharer, R., and D. Grove (eds.). 1989. *Regional Perspectives on the Olmec.* Cambridge: Cambridge University Press.

Whitecotton, J., and R. Pailes. 1986. New World Precolumbian World Systems. In F. Mathien and R. McGuire (eds.), *Ripples in the Chichimec Sea*, pp. 183–204. Carbondale: Southern Illinios University Press.

Edward Schortman and Patricia Urban

SEE ALSO

Economic Organization; Ethnicity; Settlement Patterns and Settlement Systems

Intoxicants and Intoxication

"Mexico represents without a doubt the world's richest area in diversity and use of hallucinogens in aboriginal societies—a phenomenon difficult to understand in view of the comparatively modest number of species comprising the flora of that country. Without any question, the Peyote cactus is the most important sacred hallucinogen, although other cactus species are still used in northern Mexico as minor hallucinogens for special magico-religious purposes." So wrote Schultes and Hofmann (1979:27). Schultes, former director of Harvard's Botanical Museum, is the leading authority on the "hallucinogenic" flora of the New World; Hofmann, the Swiss research chemist who discovered lysergic acid diethylamide (LSD), has isolated and/or synthesized many of the alkaloids in the most important species employed by Mexican Indians.

Fermentation

Mexican Indians also practiced ritual intoxication with alcohol made from fermented fruits, maize, honey, and sap (distillation was unknown anywhere in the Americas prior to the Spanish invasion). Although there are differences between the contexts, purposes, and effects of the two kinds of inebriation, and the plant hallucinogens are vastly more potent than fermented beverages, there is also some overlap. Both were intended to facilitate communication with the spirit world, and the consumption of both was usually limited to ceremonial and ritual contexts.

A mildly intoxicating ceremonial maize drink the *Raramuri (Tarahumara)* and other groups call *tesgüino* (probably from Nahuatl *tecuin*, "to inflame") was and still is made by fermenting the ground kernels. To the south, the Maya made and still make their ceremonial drink *balché* from fermented honey and an extract of the bark of the *balché* tree *(Lonchocarpus longistylus);* occasional reinforcement with an extract of morning glory seeds has been reported. Not well known is an intoxicating cacao beverage made not from the beans, as has long been thought, but by fermenting the gelatinous pulp surrounding the beans inside the pod of the cacao tree (*Theobroma* spp.). This may explain the frequent representation of cacao pods on Maya pottery vessels.

The most important and most widely used ceremonial drink was *pulque,* called *octli* in Nahuatl. It is made by extracting and fermenting the sweet sap of several species of *Agave,* or *maguey* (the word is related to the name of the Aztec *pulque* goddess, Mayahuel). In Aztec art, some of the most elaborate sculptures are vessels used for the

I

pulque rituals. However, *pulque* is much older than the Aztecs, who were late-comers to Central Mexico. The most interesting early evidence is the fragmentary painting called "Los Bebedores" ("The Drinkers"), dated to c. A.D. 300–300 and discovered during tunneling into the great pyramid at Cholula. The painting consists of four panels: the two on the south side are 9.70 and 5.20 meters long, and the two on the north side, 9.80 and 7.4 meters long. It depicts a ceremonial *pulque* orgy, perhaps historical or perhaps mythological, with numerous participants, some with the heads of birds or wearing bird masks. The later Aztecs had strict rules governing who was permitted to drink *pulque,* and under what circumstances, with severe penalties for violations, suggesting that drinking to excess and addiction were already a problem. That the Aztecs might have been aware of the danger of exposing the developing fetus to alcohol is suggested by the rule that except on certain ritual occasions, the only women permitted to drink were those past child-bearing age.

Plant Hallucinogens

Among the most important of the many plants Mexican Indians discovered and used for ecstatic-visionary purposes are *Lophophora williamsii,* the *peyotl* of the Aztecs and *hikuli* of the modern Huichols; the "sacred mushrooms" that the Aztecs venerated as *teonanácatl* ("divine food" or "flesh of the gods"), most of which belong to the genus *Psilocybe* or closely related genera (family Strophareaceae); *Datura inoxia* (*toloátzin,* hispanicized as *toloache*) and other species of this solanaceous genus (principal alkaloids: scopolamine, hyoscyamine, and atropine); and their close relatives, *Solandra brevicalyx* and *S. guerrerensis* (Nahuatl, *tecomaxóchitl, hueipatl;* Huichol, *kiéri*). Tobacco also belongs in the solanaceae, and several species were employed as ecstatic-divinatory intoxicants; they are also the only psychotropic plants that are addictive in the clinical sense. The most important tobacco species is *Nicotiana rustica,* the *piciétl* of the Aztecs. With several times the nicotine content of commercial brands, *N. rustica* is still widely employed as a ritual intoxicant in South American shamanism. There is evidence for a comparable role in Mexico and Central America, especially among the Maya.

Of special significance, widely used in ecstatic divination, were the seeds of two morning glories: the white-flowered *Turbina* (formerly *Rivea*) *corymbosa,* and the blue- or violet-flowered *Ipomoea violacea* (family Convolvulaceae). In Nahuatl, the round, brown seeds of the former were called *ololiuqui,* and the vine itself *coatlxoxouhqui* ("green snake plant"). It is this species that is depicted in the "Tlalocan" mural at Tepantitla, Teotihuacan, as a great flowering vine towering above a female deity, probably the Great Goddess of this early city-state, who is dispensing life-giving water and agricultural bounty. The seeds of the second species were known to the Aztecs as *tlitliltzin,* from *tlilli,* "black," with a reverential prefix. All these plants, and some others of more limited distribution, were thought to be invested with divine powers; notwithstanding strenuous efforts at suppression by the colonial authorities, they continued to be highly esteemed and used in the old ways by shamans, diviners, and curers. Some also served—and still serve—a double purpose: as ecstatic intoxicants and, depending on dosage and method of application, as therapeutic agents (e.g., peyote as an antibiotic, *Datura* as an analgesic, and *Nicotiana rustica* as a poultice and fumigant).

Intoxicating Snuff. The Europeans' initial encounter with non-alcoholic ritual intoxication as a phenomenon of indigenous religion and ritual dates to Columbus's first landfall. On his second voyage in 1496, the admiral commissioned Fray Ramón Pané to report on the ceremonies and "antiquities" of the Arawakan-speaking Taino. Pané described rites in which the natives of Hispaniola inhaled an intoxicating powder called *kohobba,* "so strong that those who take it lose consciousness," believing themselves to be in contact with the spirit world. When *kohobba* was employed in healing, he wrote, the "sorcerers"—i.e., shamans—customarily took it along with their patients so that both might learn the nature, cause, and most effective cure of the affliction. The Spanish thought *kohobba* was tobacco; it is now identified as the pulverized seeds of *Anadenanthera peregrina* (formerly *Piptadenia peregrina*), a leguminous tree native to the South American tropical lowlands and related to acacias and mimosas. Snuff prepared from the seeds is used today among Venezuelan Indians of the Orinoco Basin, where it is best known as *yopo.* A sister species native to the Andean highlands, *A. colubrina,* is the source of the sacred *wilka* seeds of Quechua-speaking Indians. Nevertheless, along with *A. peregrina* and *Virola,* tobacco remains a major source of intoxicating snuffs in South America.

Curiously, there is no mention in the colonial literature of intoxicating snuff among Mexican Indians. Yet we now know from the archaeological and iconographic evidence—including numerous ceramic effigy snuffers or nose pipes, probable snuff tablets, and even some figurines (from shaft tomb burials in Colima) holding snuffing pipes to their noses, with eyes closed and ecstatic expressions—that the practice was not limited to the Caribbean and Central and South America but was also common in Mexico as far back as the Olmecs. Almost any psychotropic species could have been dried and pounded into snuff, but *N. rustica* tobacco is considered a good candidate.

Intoxicating Enemas. Rectal administration of *pulque* by means of enemas was reported for the Huastecs by Sahagún, whose *Florentine Codex* also illustrates therapeutic use of the enema in Central Mexico. The *Tratado* of 1629 by Ruiz de Alarcón describes medicinal/divinatory use by Aztec physicians of enemas of peyote, *ololiuhqui* (morning glory seeds) and *atlinan* (lit., "its mother [is] water," *Datura ceratocaula,* an aquatic species), accompanied by magical incantations (Ruiz de Alarcón 1984 [1629]:183, 200, 203, 293, 299–300). But it is only in recent years that the ritual and/or medicinal use of enemas has been identified in Classic Maya art. Scenes on polychrome vases depict both self-application and the insertion of enema syringes into their clients by female shamans or priestesses. On other figure-painted or carved vessels, Maya gods and priests are shown with enema syringes in their hands or stuck in their sashes. If the Maya clysters were intoxicating, *balché,* liquefied tobacco, or morning glory infusions are among the prime candidates. Self-administration of enemas also occurs in Maya figurines from the island of Jaina, Campeche, and in whistle figurines and murals found in Veracruz.

Chemistry of Plant Hallucinogens. To the Spanish, two of the worst offenders, next to *peyotl,* were the sacred mushrooms and the seeds of morning glories. Morning glory seeds had a purely descriptive Nahuatl name, giving no hint either of their impressive psychoactive potency or of the awe in which they and their visionary effects were held by Aztec priests. After the priesthood and their temples had been destroyed, this veneration was maintained by village shamans who preserved, if not the old gods and great ceremonies, many of the magico-religious beliefs and practices of the pre-Christian past. Thus, a century after the fall of the Aztecs, Nahuatl-speakers in Guerrero not only continued to venerate *ololiuqui* but also personified it as a male deity, whom the friars could only assume to be the devil himself. Indeed, the clergy generally attributed the strange powers of these plants not to their chemistry but to deceptions of the devil. In 1960, Hofmann finally identified the compounds responsible for the effects of *ololiuqui* as *d*-lysergic acid amide (ergine) and *d*-isolysergic acid amides, indole alkaloids closely related to lysergic acid diethylamide, or LSD. This was the first time that LSD-like ergot alkaloids—the active principles of the primitive ergot fungus, *Claviceps purpurea* (an Old World infestation of grasses, principally rye)—had been discovered in one of the higher plants.

The identification of the active principles of the *teonanacatl* mushrooms also fell to Hofmann, who not only identified the agents responsible for the extraordinary effects of these mushrooms but also was able to reproduce them synthetically. The psychoactive compounds in the mushrooms turned out to be, like those in the morning glories, indole-tryptamine derivatives, which he named psilocybine and psilocine after the genus to which most of the divinatory fungi of ancient and contemporary Mexico belong.

Peyote *(Lophophora williamsii)* is a small, round, gray-green cactus crowned by tufts of silky hair (one translation of *peyotl* is "furry thing"); it is native to the north central high Mexican desert and the lower Rio Grande Valley. It was widely traded over much of pre-Hispanic Mexico; today its use as a shamanistic-ecstatic intoxicant is largely confined to one group, the Huichols of the Sierra Madre Occidental, who have preserved much of their pre-Christian religion. They go on annual 500-kilometer pilgrimages to hunt the sacred cactus, which they identify with deer, in the desert in the state of San Luis Potosí. North of the border, it was adopted toward the end of the nineteenth century as a sacrament in the syncretistic rituals of the pan-Indian Native American Church.

Peyote has a very long archaeological record. Its earliest known occurrence, in a Desert Culture rock shelter in the Amistad Basin on the Texas-Mexican border, has been radiocarbon dated to c. 5000 B.C. In these sites, peyote occurs in association with ceremonial caches of the red, bean-shaped toxic seeds of a flowering shrub, *Sophora secundiflora,* which, with ^{14}C dates as far back as 8440 B.C., holds the world record for antiquity among plant hallucinogens. Ceremonial caches of the seeds occur in all occupational levels of Desert Culture sites north and south of the Mexican border; the oldest were found in association with the remains of extinct bison and Folsom and Plainview-type projectile points, with ^{14}C dates between 8440 and 8120 B.C. Notwithstanding its high toxicity (its principal constituent, cytisine, can, in overdoses, cause death from respiratory failure), the use of *Sophora* in initiation rites of ecstatic shamanistic medicine

I

societies on the southern Great Plains persisted until the last quarter of the nineteenth century.

Peyote also has the longest record of ethnographic, ethnobotanical, and pharmacological investigation. Popularly, it is identified with its best-known and strongest alkaloid, misnamed mescaline, but Schultes was right to call peyote a "veritable factory of alkaloids." More than fifty have been detected since a German chemist, Arthur Heffter, isolated four pure alkaloids from the cactus in 1895–1896. He named one of these *mezcalin* (now rendered as "mescaline"), thereby initiating the unfortunate linguistic confusion, continuing to this day, between peyote ("mescal buttons") and *mescal,* a distilled liquor made, like *pulque,* from the *maguey* plant. Seven years before Heffter's work, the German toxicologist Louis Lewin had reported his isolation of an alkaloid from peyote, which he named *Anhalonin* (peyote's first scientific name was *Anhalonium lewinii*). This may, in fact, have been a mixture of several alkaloids that included mescaline, but it was nevertheless a historic moment in the history of phytochemistry: the first time that any compound with effects on the mind had been recognized in one of the Cactaceae.

Animal Sources

Claims to the contrary notwithstanding, the extreme toxicity of toxin from the giant toad *Bufo marinus* rules out its use for ecstatic-visionary purposes. Some of the twenty-six compounds in the secretions of *Bufo marinus* are benign, being allied to dopamine, epinephrine, and norepenephrine, and bufotenine is also found in some South American snuffs; but others are so toxic that ingestion by any method would cause cardiac failure long before the user could have an ecstatic experience. This is not the case with another amphibian, however: the Sonoran desert toad, *Bufo alvarius.* The principal psychoactive compound in its skin secretions, toxic when taken orally but powerfully psychoactive when dried and smoked, is 5-methoxy-N,N-dimethyltryptamine (5–Me-O-DMT), which also accounts for much of the psychoactivity of the *Anadenanthera* and *Virola* snuffs of the South American Indians. However, there is no archaeological or ethnographic evidence for such use of *Bufo alvarius.*

Plant Hallucinogens and Brain Chemistry

The discoveries by ethnobotanists and phytochemists among the culturally important psychoactive flora of Mexico and Central and South America were accompanied by the realization that the major botanical hallucinogens are structurally related to biologically active compounds occurring naturally in the brain, where they play a role in the biochemistry of mental functions. Thus, psilocybine and the LSD-related alkaloids in morning glory seeds are similar in chemical structure to the brain hormone serotonine (5-hydroxy-tryptamine). Mescaline has the same basic chemical structure as norepinephrine (noradrenaline). All these brain hormones belong to the category of physiological agents that play a role in the chemical transmission of impulses between nerve cells (neurons), and hence are known as "neurotransmitters."

Shamanism and the Quest for Ecstatic Vision

The question remains why the Indians of Mexico and other Native Americans seem to have been so much more interested in the intoxicating properties of plants than any other peoples in the world. The anthropologist Weston La Barre provided an answer that has yet to be contradicted. The base religion of American Indians, he wrote, from Pleistocene hunter-gatherers to the Aztecs, and down to the present day, was shamanism. Shamanism is deeply rooted in the individual ecstatic-visionary experience, for which Siberian shamans and their colleagues across Eurasia employed the fly agaric, *Amanita muscaria,* and perhaps other botanical intoxicants. This was the religion the Pleistocene big-game hunters carried with them out of northeastern Asia across the Bering Strait. They and their descendants were thus culturally programmed, so to speak, to explore their new environments for natural agents that might, in the manner of the fly agaric, aid them in attaining the desired mental states.

FURTHER READINGS

Furst, P. T. 1974. Archaeological Evidence for Snuffing in Prehispanic Mexico. *Botanical Museum Leaflets* (Harvard University) 23(10):368–.

———. 1976. *Hallucinogens and Culture.* San Francisco: Chandler and Sharp.

Furst, P. T., and M. D. Coe. 1977. Ritual Enemas. *Natural History* 86:88–91.

Guerrero Guerrero, R. 1980. *El Pulque: Religión, Cultura, Folklore.* Mexico City: Instituto Nacional de Antropología e Historia.

La Barre, W. 1970. Old and New World Narcotics: A Statistical Question and an Ethnological Reply. *Economic Botany* 24:368–373.

Ott, J. 1993. *Pharmacotheon: Entheogenic Drugs, Their Plant Sources and History.* Kennewick, Wash.: Natural Products Co.

Ruiz de Alarcón, H. 1984 [1629]. *Treatise on the Heathen Superstitions that Today Live among the Indians Native to This New Spain, 1629*. J. R. Andrews and R. Hassig (trans. and ed.). Norman: University of Oklahoma Press.

Schultes, R. E. 1941. *A Contribution to Our Knowledge of Rivea corymbosa, the Narcotic Ololiuhqui of the Aztecs*. Cambridge, Mass.: Botanical Museum of Harvard University.

Schultes, R. E., and A. Hofmann. 1979. *Plants of the Gods: Origins of Hallucinogenic Use*. Springfield, Ill.: Charles C. Thomas.

Wasson, R. G. 1980. *The Wondrous Mushroom: Mycolatry in Mesoamerica*. New York: McGraw-Hill.

Wilbert, J. 1987. *Tobacco and Shamanism in South America*. New Haven: Yale University Press.

Peter T. Furst

Isla [del] Caño (Puntarenas, Costa Rica)

Isla Caño, off the coast of the Osa Peninsula, has habitation and cemetery features scattered across the island, which has a wet tropical environment. There have been no controlled excavations; surface-collected artifacts from the area include ceramics, lithics, sculptural stone, and stone spheres. Mortuary remains include skeletons and grave goods. The span of occupation is 300 B.C. to A.D. 1520. Interaction with other regions is evidenced by ceramics from Greater Nicoya and from the adjacent Greater Chiriqui zone.

FURTHER READINGS

Finch, W. O., and K. Honetschlager. 1986. Preliminary Archaeological Research, Isla del Caño. *Journal of the Steward Anthropological Society* 14 (1982–1983): 189–206.

Frederick W. Lange

Isla de Sacrificios (Veracruz, Mexico)

This small coral island (c. 4 hectares) is situated at the entrance to the port of Veracruz on the Gulf Coast of Mexico. Its name was bestowed by the members of the Juan de Grijalva expedition of 1518, who on arrival found victims of heart sacrifice on two large altars. A Postclassic (A.D. 900–1521) ceremonial and funerary site, it is known principally for giving its name to a distinctive Fine Orange ceramic type with white designs, typical of central Veracruz.

Summary excavations at the turn of the century, then again in the 1950s and 1990s, indicated the existence of structures of stuccoed stone of Early and Late Postclassic date, dedicated to the cult of the Feathered Serpent, Quetzalcóatl. Numerous primary and secondary burials were found, with food and ceramic offerings, principally Fine Orange ceramics (Isla de Sacrificios, Tres Picos, Plumbate) and Mixteca-Puebla wares (Cholulteca Laca, Black-and-White-on-Red). Mutilations are frequent in the skeletons (beheading, cut hands).

Isla de Sacrificios represents the southernmost outpost of a particular Postclassic cultural subarea of central Veracruz that is traditionally identified as Totonac; its meridional limit was the Antigua River, 25 kilometers farther north. The island must have had great importance as a sanctuary and as a strategic military and commercial point, like the island of Jaina (Campeche) and the cays along the coast of the Yucatán Peninsula; however, investigations to date have been too scarce and random to offer any broad interpretation. Past lootings, modern construction, and erosion have obliterated a major part of the data, adversely affecting any future research.

FURTHER READINGS

Birch, S. 1884. Report upon the Antiquities Discovered by Captain Nepean. *Archaeologia* 30:139–143. London: Society of Antiquaries of London.

Díaz del Castillo, Bernal. 1956 [1560]. *The Discovery and Conquest of Mexico*. Genaro García (ed.), A. P. Maudslay (trans.). New York: Farrar, Straus, and Cudahy.

Du Solier, W. 1938. *Isla de Sacrificios (entierros)*. Mexico City: Revista de Educación.

———. 1943. A Reconnaissance on Isla de Sacrificios, Veracruz, Mexico. *Carnegie Institution of Washington, Notes on Middle American Archaeology and Ethnology* 1(14):63–80.

Medellín Zenil, A. 1955. *Exploraciones en la Isla de Sacrificios*. Jalapa: Gobierno del Estado de Veracruz.

Nuttall, Z. 1910. The Island of Sacrificios. *American Anthropologist* 12:257–295.

Annick Daneels

SEE ALSO

Gulf Lowlands: South Central Region

Isla Muerto

See Isla Zapatera

I

Isla Solentiname (Río San Juan, Nicaragua)

Isla Solentiname and the Archipelago de Solentiname, in a wet tropical environment at the mouth of the San Juan River drainage in the southeastern corner of Lake Nicaragua, had a strategic location for contacts with Atlantic Costa Rica and Honduras and with Pacific Greater Nicoya. It was occupied from A.D. 500 to 1300. Its material culture remains include ceramics, stone sculpture, and petroglyphs. Interments were accompanied by ceramics and elaborately carved stone stools *("metates")*. Non-scientifically recovered stone and ceramic artifacts suggest regular contacts with eastern and southern Honduras, the central highlands and Atlantic watershed of Costa Rica, and the Pacific coast of northwestern Costa Rica and western Nicaragua.

FURTHER READINGS

Sini, S. 1994. *La collezione archeologica di Solentiname (Nicaragua).* Milan: Asociación de Cooperación Rural en Africa y América Latina.

Frederick W. Lange

SEE ALSO

Isla Zapatera; Nicoya, Greater, and Guanacaste Region

Isla Zapatera (Granada, Nicaragua)

Isla Zapatera and neighboring Isla Muerto had the largest known concentrations of stone statuary and petroglyphs in Nicaragua, as well as habitational and architectural remains. Occupied from A.D. 500 to 1350, the islands have been only partially mapped, locating features such as retaining walls, terraces, and artificial mounds. Artifacts include ceramics, petroglyphs, and stone sculpture. Stone sculptural styles on the islands are related to those on Isla Ometepe in the department of Chontales, and to those of Nacascolo on the Bay of Culebra, Costa Rica; they are also related to petroglyph traditions throughout the rest of lower Central America. Polychrome ceramics from the Greater Nicoya white-slipped ceramic tradition are also present. The different petroglyph and sculptural styles are thought to represent social subdivisions of the islands, and it is generally assumed that the large petroglyph platform on Isla Muerto was of ceremonial significance.

FURTHER READINGS

Arellano, J.E. 1979–1980. La colección "Squier-Zapatera": Estudio de estatuaria prehispánica (primera parte). *Boletín Nicaraguense de Bibliografía y Documentación* 32–33:1–149; 34:1–48.

Matillo Vila, J. (Hno. Hildeberto Maria). 1968. *El Muerto, Isla Santuario: Estudio de su arte rupestre.* Managua: Imprenta Nacional.

Frederick W. Lange

SEE ALSO

Intermediate Area: Overview

Itzan (Petén, Guatemala)

This medium-sized Maya center is situated 6 kilometers north of the lower Río de la Pasión; it was occupied from the early Middle Formative period through the Terminal Classic. Itzan evidently remained independent from the powerful Petexbatun polity (30 kilometers distant), which ruled the upper Pasión Basin during the eighth century A.D. The linear site layout extends over 3 square kilometers along an escarpment crest and centers on a site core. This dense concentration of monumental architecture is built atop a hillock that was broadened and flattened in the construction of massive terraces and platforms. The core consists of one large acropolis and three major plazas bordered by pyramidal mounds. In this zone, the Classic period Maya erected sculpted and inscribed stone monuments, thirty-six of which have been recovered.

Excavations in the site area outside the core revealed simple, minimally platformed residential structures that had no mounded remains and thus had been undetectable in surface survey. The evidence of these otherwise "invisible" structures confirmed, for the Maya Lowlands, that such modest architectural remains are houses.

FURTHER READINGS

Tourtellot, G., N. Hammond, and R. Rose. 1978. *A Brief Reconnaissance of Itzan.* Memoirs of the Peabody Museum, 14.3. Cambridge, Mass.: Harvard University.

Kevin J. Johnston

SEE ALSO

Maya Lowlands: South

Ixcuintepec

See Peñoles Region

Iximché (Chimaltenango, Guatemala)

One of the major political centers of Guatemala at the time of the Spanish conquest was Iximché, the capital of the Cakchiquel kingdom, whose hegemony extended over much of Guatemala's central highlands. The site is surrounded by deep ravines, with the only direct access route blocked by a dry moat and wall. According to the sixteenth-century *Annals of the Cakchiquels,* written by descendants of a ruling family, the Cakchiquel lords established themselves at Iximché around A.D. 1470–1480, after breaking off from the Quiché of Utatlan. From there they expanded their domains over neighboring Cakchiquel and Pocomam peoples, in the midst of constant feuding with their former allies and other rival kingdoms—the Tzutuhil of Atitlan and the Pipil of Izquintepec.

The site center includes two major compounds with similar architectural layouts, but they are distinctly separated from each other. Each has a large plaza with two temple pyramids, an I-shaped ball court, a council house, and a palace with its own temple and patio. Such dual partition is consistent with Cakchiquel rulership as described in colonial documents. The buildings are finely dressed with cut stone and stucco. Excavations by Guillemin uncovered portions of murals whose style is related to the Borgia Group codices, as well as rich burials provided with gold paraphernalia. No information is available on the site's history before the Late Postclassic, nor has there been any research on commoner residential patterns. Part of the site was burned by the Spaniards in 1526.

FURTHER READINGS

Guillemin, G. F. 1965. *Iximché, capital del antiguo reino Cakchiquel.* Guatemala City: Instituto de Antropología e Historia de Guatemala.

———. 1967. The Ancient Cakchiquel Capital of Iximché. *Expedition* 9:22–35.

———. 1977. Urbanism and Hierarchy at Iximché. In N. Hammond (ed.), *Social Process in Maya Prehistory: Studies in Honour of Sir Eric Thompson,* pp. 227–264. New York: Academic Press.

Recinos, A., and D. Goetz (eds.). 1953. *The Annals of the Cakchiquels: Title of the Lords of Totonicapán.* Norman: University of Oklahoma Press.

Oswaldo Chinchilla Mazariegos

SEE ALSO

Guatemala Highlands Region

Ixtapa (Jalisco, Mexico)

This 60-hectare site is located in the southern half of the Banderas Valley on the southern side of a remnant channel of the Mascota River, about 10 kilometers northeast of Puerto Vallarta. Archaeological data, including six radiocarbon dates and associated cultural materials from eleven excavations, indicate that the site was occupied from at least 300 B.C. into the Spanish contact period, until about 1600.

Ceremonial mounds date from at least 770 A.D. and later, but the development of the site as a major ceremonial and administrative center for the Banderas Valley was accomplished about A.D. 1165 by colonists of the Aztatlan archaeological culture. The site features that were probably built by these people include three pyramidal temple mounds of earth and river cobbles, about 75 meters on a side and up to 8 meters high; five or more smaller ceremonial mounds, including one with eight rustic stone stelae; two large platforms, one of which had a ball court on top; an area of elite multi-room residential structures; and a cemetery for burial of the deceased elite.

Aztatlan presence at the site is also evidenced by pottery decorated with an encircling band of red painted or incised geometric designs, and mold-made figurines of the Mazapan style. There is also a local industry of prismatic blades of obsidian imported from the area of the Tequila volcano, west of Guadalajara.

The Aztatlan occupation at Ixtapa appears to have been relatively short-lived, and its termination appears to have involved conflict, as evidenced by the destruction of the ceremonial structure and some associated stelae atop the stela mound. Thereafter, the site continued to be occupied up into Spanish contact times by local people who were using pottery decorated with motifs derived from or inspired by the Aztatlan culture, and who were still conducting ceremonies on the Aztatlan mounds as well as on smaller mounds they constructed themselves.

FURTHER READINGS

Mountjoy, J. B. 1993. El pasado prehispánico del municipio de Puerto Vallarta. In J. Olveda (ed.), *Una aproximación a Puerto Vallarta,* pp. 23–40. Puerto Vallarta: Colegio de Jalisco.

Joseph B. Mountjoy

Ixtépete, El (Jalisco, Mexico)

Situated in the Atemajac Valley on the western outskirts of Guadalajara, next to a small stream that has eroded

I

away some small sections, El Ixtépete is the site of one of the few archaeological parks in western Mexico. The earliest archaeological excavations were carried out in the late 1950s by José Corona Nuñez, who began the longstanding tradition of referring to the site as Teotihuacan-influenced. He also reconstructed the main rectangular platform mound and its *talud/tablero* façade. In the 1960s, Saenz repaired some of the older reconstruction work and recovered further information. Marcia Castro-Leal, Luis Galván, and Lorenzo Ochoa did further excavation and reconstruction in the early 1970s, and later minor rescue operations recovered a rich box tomb in one of the mounds. More recently, an earlier house and an empty shaft tomb were excavated by Daria Deraga and Rodolfo Fernández. Little of this has been published, and there has been no synthetic report.

The central core of the site is fenced, but the thirty identified mounds continue into the surrounding properties and cover around 6 hectares. The primary structure is a rectangular platform more than 6 meters high, with a *talud-tablero* façade; it was built up over five construction episodes. Except for the single shaft tomb and a small Tabachines phase occupation, the vast majority of the ceramics and architecture from Ixtépete are all El Grillo phase (A.D. 550–850). Weigand has speculated that the later platform modifications may belong to the Postclassic, but no ceramic evidence supports this, and no chronometric dates are available for the site.

FURTHER READINGS

Castro-Leal, M., and L. Ochoa. 1975. El Ixtépete como un ejemplo de desarrollo cultural en el Occidente de México. *Anales del Instituto Nacional de Antropología e Historia* 7(5):121–154.

Saenz, C. 1966. Exploraciones en el Ixtépete. *Boletín del Instituto Nacional de Antropología e Historia* 23:14–18.

Schöndube Baumbach, O., and L. J. Galván Villegas. 1978. Salvage Archaeology at El Grillo-Tabachines, Zapopan, Jalisco, Mexico. In C. L. Riley and B. C. Hedrick (eds.), *Across the Chichimec Sea: Papers in Honor of J. Charles Kelley*, pp. 144–164. Carbondale: Southern Illinois University Press.

Weigand, P. C. 1993. The Political Organization of the Trans-Tarascan Zone of Western Mesoamerica on the Eve of the Spanish Conquest. In A. I. Woosley and J. C. Ravesloot (eds.), *Culture and Contact: Charles C. Di Peso's Gran Chichimeca*, pp. 191–217. Dragoon: Amerind Foundation.

Christopher S. Beekman

SEE ALSO
West Mexico

Ixtlan del Río (Nayarit, Mexico)

A town, and by extension an archaeological zone, in the highlands of Nayarit near the west coast of Mexico. It came to scientific attention with the 1946 surface survey by E. W. Gifford, who also published a looted collection of ceramic human figurines recovered from deep shaft tombs. Gifford did no excavations, but he defined a sequence based on comparison of his surface sherds with types defined by Isabel Kelly, Gordon Ekholm, and others. He recognized a Late period, equating it with Late Culiacán (Protohistoric); a Middle Period, equated with Aztatlan and Aztec 2, and probably Early Postclassic; and an Early period, equated with Early Chametla (early centuries A.D.). Gifford recognized the large, hollow human figurines from shaft tombs as early and suggested that they were contemporaneous with late Teotihuacan. They are now considered to be slightly older, toward the beginning of the Christian era; but considering the absence of either excavation evidence or radiocarbon dates at the time, Gifford's interpretations were remarkably correct.

The large human figurines have attracted much attention because of their esthetic and museum value. They are also quite useful for ethnographic reconstruction because of the clothing, ornaments, and activities portrayed. Furst has offered numerous interpretations based on analogy with contemporary Huichol shamanism.

Excavations carried out at Ixtlan by José Corona Nuñez in 1948 were oriented toward reconstruction of the site so that it could be visited by tourists. A particular focus was the circular structure named the Temple of Quetzalcoatl, possibly because Central Mexican temples to Quetzalcoatl's wind god avatar, Ehecatl, are circular, and at the time of excavation this was the only circular structure known in West Mexico. Subsequent research elsewhere has revealed the circular complexes of the Teuchitlan tradition, the basic public architecture for a large portion of West Mexico during the Formative and Classic periods. Excavations and mapping in the 1960s by Eduardo Contreras and José Luis Lorenzo, also geared toward reconstruction, revealed a series of columned range structures and determined that the site dates primarily to the late part of Gifford's sequence; however, the systematic linkage of ceramic and architectural phases has been weak. More recent research by Gabriela Zepeda has focused on the establishment of a corrected architectural and ceramic baseline.

FURTHER READINGS

Gifford, E. W. 1950. Surface Archaeology of Ixtlan del Rio, Nayarit. *University of California Publications in American Archaeology and Ethnography*, 43(2): 183–302.

Kan, M., C. W. Meighan, and H. B. Nicholson. 1970, 1989. *Sculpture of Ancient West Mexico.* Albuquerque: Los Angeles County Museum of Art and University of New Mexico Press.

Schöndube Baumbach, O., and L. J. Galván Villegas. 1978. Salvage Archaeology at El Grillo–Tabachines, Zapopan, Jalisco, Mexico. In C. L. Riley and B. C. Hedrick (eds.), *Across the Chichimec Sea: Papers in Honor of J. Charles Kelley,* pp. 144–164. Carbondale: Southern Illinois University Press.

Weigand, P. C. 1976. Circular Ceremonial Structure Complexes in the Highlands of Western Mexico. In R. B. Pickering (ed.), *Archaeological Frontiers: Papers on New World High Cultures in Honor of J. Charles Kelley,* pp. 18–227. Carbondale: Southern Illinois University.

Zepeda García M., G. 1994. *Ixtlan. Ciudad del Viento.* Mexico City: Instituto Nacional de Antropología and Grupo ICA.

Clement Meighan and Christopher S. Beekman

SEE ALSO

West Mexico

Izamal (Yucatán, Mexico)

The ruins of Izamal ("Dew of Heaven" in Maya) are in the town of the same name, located about 56 km (35 mi) southeast of Merida, the modern capital of Yucatán. Early Spanish observers in the mid-sixteenth century were astonished at the size and grandeur of the large pyramids that make up the site core. Fray Diego de Landa, later notorious for his destruction of Maya books, oversaw the leveling of one of these great buildings on which a Franciscan convent and church were built in 1553. Another pyramid, named Kinich K'akmo, is still relatively intact and is possibly the largest structure ever built in the northern Maya Lowlands. It consists of a massive basal platform with multiple terraces and a second, smaller pyramidal structure on its summit. Very little archaeological work has been done at Izamal. Its largest buildings appear to be Early Classic in date, but according to ethno-

historic accounts the town remained an important commercial center, especially for the salt trade, until the mid-fifteenth century; it also attracted many pilgrims because of its associations with Kinich Ahau, the sun god.

FURTHER READINGS

Garza, S. T., and Kurjack, E. B. 1980. *Atlas arqueológico del estado de Yucatán.* Mexico, D. F.: Instituto Nacional de Antropología e Historia.

Kelly, J. 1982. *The Complete Visitor's Guide to Mesoamerican Ruins.* Norman: University of Oklahoma Press.

David L. Webster

SEE ALSO

Maya Lowlands: North

Izapa (Chiapas, Mexico)

Izapa, the largest Late Formative site in coastal Chiapas, is best known for its large corpus of narrative-style carved stone monuments. The site was occupied continuously for 3,000 years, beginning by 1500 B.C., but the bulk of the pyramidal mounds and all of the sculpture date to the Late Formative period (400–100 B.C.). The site extends over 2.3 kilometers north to south; it consists of eight major mound groups, each with a plaza, large earthen pyramids, and several stelae-altar pairs. Izapa was a regional capital during the Late Formative and Early Classic periods.

Izapa is situated about 240 meters above sea level in the piedmont zone of the southern Soconusco region, in an area of evergreen tropical forest ideal for growing cacao. It is thought that cacao and other tropical products, such as bird plumes and jaguar pelts, were the major exports of this capital during its heyday. The political control of the Izapa polity probably never extended beyond the south coast of Chiapas, Mexico, and parts of adjacent Guatemala. The narrative art style characteristic of its bas-relief stelae, however, was popular throughout eastern Mesoamerica. This Late Formative art style has come to be known as "Izapan" and is a horizon marker that fits chronologically between the earlier Olmec and later Classic Maya styles. It is unlikely, however, that the style originated at Izapa, even though it is best represented there.

FURTHER READINGS

Ekholm, S. M. 1969. *Mound 30a and the Early Preclassic Ceramic Sequence of Izapa, Chiapas, Mexico.* Papers of the New World Archaeological Foundation, 25. Provo, Utah.

Lowe, G. W., T. A. Lee, Jr., and E. Martínez Espinosa. 1982. *Izapa: An Introduction to the Ruins and Monuments.* Papers of the New World Archaeological Foundation, 31. Provo, Utah.

John E. Clark

SEE ALSO

Izapa Style; Soconusco–South Pacific Coast and Piedmont Region

Izapa Style

Artworks in the Izapa style consist primarily of the upright stone stelae and associated frog-shaped altars carved in low relief from the site of Izapa, near Tapachula, Chiapas (Mexico), within the environmentally rich Soconusco region. The style is highly narrative, distinctive, and specialized, depicting widespread Mesoamerican themes—such as diving figures—in the unique context of coastal estuary-swamp-slough forms and suggesting a cult focused on supernatural beings related to this ecosystem. The subjects of the carvings emphasize estuary fauna and flora, such as crocodiles, fish, marsh birds, jaguars, sapodilla, and other fruit-bearing trees. These are shown in scenes involving humans engaged in dramatic action such as wrestling, diving, or beheading someone, surrounded by dripping, running, or falling water.

The stelae do not bear dates, but they have been assigned to the Late Formative and Protoclassic based on stylistic comparison with other carved monuments from the region and beyond. Even though the site of Izapa was occupied more or less continuously from c. 1500 B.C. through the Postclassic period, the carving style is remarkably consistent. Smith's comparisons of Izapa subjects, the context in which subjects are shown, and carving techniques with those of Formative carved monuments that bear dates suggest that most or all of the stelae were erected over a relatively short timespan (200 B.C.–A.D. 1) and are contemporary with the building activity that greatly enlarged the earlier Middle Formative site.

FURTHER READINGS

Coe, M. D. 1962. *Mexico.* New York: Frederick A. Praeger.

Norman, V. G. 1973, 1976. *Izapa Sculpture.* Part I, *Album;* Part 2, *Text.* New World Archaeological Foundation Papers, 30. Provo, Utah.

Parsons, L. A. 1986. *The Origins of Maya Art: Monumental Stone Sculpture of Kaminaljuyu, Guatemala, and the Southern Pacific Coast.* Dumbarton Oaks Studies in Pre-Columbian Art and Archaeology, 28. Washington, D.C.

Quirarte, J. 1973. *Izapa Style Art: A Study of Its Form and Meaning.* Dumbarton Oaks Studies in Pre-Columbian Art and Archaeology, 10. Washington, D.C.

———. 1976. The Relationship of Izapan-Style Art to Olmec and Maya Art: A Review. In H. B. Nicholson (ed.), *Origins of Religious Art and Iconography in Preclassic Mesoamerica,* pp. 73–86. UCLA Latin American Studies Series, 3. Los Angeles: University of California Press.

Smith, V. G. 1984. *Izapa Relief Carving: Form, Content, Rules for Design, and Role in Mesoamerican Art History and Archaeology.* Dumbarton Oaks Studies in Pre-Columbian Art and Archaeology, 27. Washington, D.C.

Virginia G. Smith

SEE ALSO

Izapa; Soconusco–South Pacific Coast and Piedmont Region

J

Jade

Among the items highly prized by the pre-Columbian people of Mexico and Central America were objects carved in hard, lustrous jade. During the conquest of Mexico, precious stones of *chalchihuites* (jade) were offered as gifts to the king of Spain; each stone was held to be equal in worth to two loads of gold. From the time of the early explorers, and continuing today, the fascination with New World jade has fed speculation about the location of the prehistoric sources of the stone and about the cultural significance of the carved imagery.

The term "jade" has been used to refer to a variety of different minerals and greenstones, including albite, quartz, hornblende, and glucophane, among others. Most commonly, however, "jade" denotes nephrite, an amphibole, or jadeite, a pyroxene. Nephrite, used in Asian jade carving, is a compact, interfelted crystalline aggregate of minerals in the tremolite-actinolite series; it is not known to occur in the artifacts of Mexico and Central America.

Jadeite, $NaAlSi_2O_6$, is a sodium aluminum silicate member of the pyroxene family of minerals. When very pure, it consists of essentially colorless needles and is difficult to carve. Impurities in the structure and intergrowths of the needles give jadeite an extremely "tough" quality that takes a high luster. Minor substitution in the crystal structure of the Si by Al occurs, as well as limited replacement of the Al by $Fe+_3$; the latter gives rise to jadeite's iron-rich, greenish-black isomorph, chlormelanite. The valence state of the iron and the amount of chromium oxide present in the mineral contribute to the well-known green color of jade.

Mineral jadeite forms under complex geological conditions that are not well understood. It is rarely found alone but rather occurs as a component of jadeitites—rocks in which impure jadeite is a constituent. Jadeitites were formed from ultramafic parent rock in highly limiting conditions of extreme pressure and low-temperature metamorphism; a slight lowering of the pressure would favor the development of albite over jadeite. Jadeitites evolve from hydrothermal solutions where both crystallo-chemical effects and stability in solutions influence the chemical composition of the mineral. They are then subject to mixing and additional geological processes prior to their arrival at the Earth's surface.

Archaeological regions of jade-working can be identified for the Olmec of Mexico, the Maya Lowlands, central Honduras, and northern Costa Rica. Other regions—the Valley of Mexico, the Valley of Oaxaca, and highland Guatemala—were mainly recipient consumers of already finished products. There are, in addition, occasional looted jade artifacts that are attributed to areas in the Mexican state of Guerrero.

Four distinct jade-carving traditions are definable, the earliest of which is that of the Olmec of the tropical Mexican Gulf Coast, approximately 1000 to 400 B.C. Although jades have been recovered from caches in buildings and from beneath plaza floors at such Olmec sites as La Venta and San Lorenzo, hundreds of nonprovenienced jades, carved in a style that shares Olmec stylistic elements, are abundant in museum collections; many of these nonprovenienced pieces are reported to be from areas outside the Olmec heartland.

South and east of the Olmec Gulf Coast is the region that was occupied by the ancient Maya. Jaditic and albitic rocks were used extensively in Maya society from the Formative period through Postclassic (1100 B.C.–1200

J

A.D.). Among the earliest recovered jades are undecorated beads from Cuello (Belize) burials that date between 1100 B.C. and 400 B.C. The Maya expressed a preference for jade that was bright emerald-green. Based on the jadeitite compositional evidence for Belizean samples presented by Bishop and colleagues, there appears to have been continuous mining of at least one jadeite source for that material from the Formative period through the arrival of the Spanish.

Jade artifacts functioned as items of personal adornment and as dedicatory offerings associated with commemoration of the construction of public architecture and with the ritual termination of public building. Excavations by Garber, however, demonstrate that jade artifacts also occurred in domestic contexts. The artifacts depict people, some of whom may have wielded religious and secular power over broad areas, and their personal accouterments (earspools, necklaces, etc.). A general discussion of the significance of jade in Maya society is found in Hammond et al. (1977).

At the southern periphery of the Maya, in northern Honduras, the frequency of emerald-green jade artifacts gives way to a greater prevalence of a duller green albitic jade. More than three thousand jades have been excavated from the region of the El Cajón Dam. Chemical data from sampled pieces indicate that the raw material was acquired from sources along the Motagua River, 185 kilometers to the east. Within central Honduras, jade assemblages evidence a carving tradition that existed between A.D. 200 and 500. This tradition is believed to represent strong local cultural norms and practices that were influenced by the Maya to the north through sporadic trading contacts. Most of the central Honduran jades appear to have been placed in caches associated with architectural dedications, rather than buried as mortuary offerings.

The majority of the carved forms—including beads, bead-pendants with zoomorphic images of monkey heads, variously shaped pendants, hunchback pendants, pectorals, and earspools—have no close correlates outside the region. They are carved in a style that emphasizes "pebble carving," in which the carving conforms to the shape of the largely unaltered stone. Central Honduras appears to have witnessed attenuation in the importance of Maya jade-carving styles as well as a change in the type of material that was carved. A few heirloom objects, including Olmecoid material, have also been found, but these pieces stand out in contrast among the products of the local carving tradition.

Jade is infrequent in El Salvador and virtually unknown in Nicaragua; only two pieces of jade have been reported from the southern border of the latter. In northern Costa Rica, however, a strong jade tradition flourished between 300 B.C. and A.D. 700. Jade occurs in mortuary contexts from a period that is marked by the introduction of polychrome ceramic techniques and possible Maya influences. Jade disappears from the archaeological record in Costa Rica during a time that may coincide with major political changes that were occurring in the Maya Lowlands.

In contrast to the patterns of raw-material exploitation in the Maya area, the prehistoric inhabitants of Costa Rica carved a much broader range of greenstone materials; apparently, any of a range of greenstones was socially acceptable. An important distinction between the various greenstones and true jadeite relates to the latter's physical properties. On the Mohs' scale of hardness, jadeite is 6.5 to 7, compared to frequently associated pyroxenes and amphiboles with hardness between 5.0 and 6.5. This use of a greater range of softer materials can be interpreted as evidence for a lessening of societal investment in the carving. Nevertheless, the finest carving appears to have been executed in stones that were predominately jadeite or albite. The Costa Rican jaditic specimens, while ranging widely in color, tend toward a "bluish to sea green" hue (Easby 1968:15). They are also distinct from the Maya jadeitites in their virtual absence of mica.

Axe god pendants, representing human, avian, and mythical figures, were produced through the alteration of naturally occurring cobbles that were cut into halves or smaller segments. The tendency to segment raw material is also seen in the reduction of the Maya belt plaques that reached Costa Rica, where they were often cut, fragmenting or obliterating the original image or text. Prehistoric Costa Rican artisans also used the "string-saw" technique (sawing between a set of drilled holes) and developed the technical ability to cut thin "sheets" of jade that were used to make serpentine spirals and other delicate figures.

Sources of Jadeitites

The location of prehistoric jade sources is a matter of speculation, exploration, and analysis. Jadeitites are found near ancient tectonic suture zones in only six locations worldwide. One area of occurrence is along the tectonically active continental margin of the Motagua River in Guatemala. Here jadeite constitutes a primary constituent that is accompanied by other major mineral components, such as albite, muscovite, paragonite, and sphene. The rarity of occurrence, with but a single known source in all of Mexico and Central America, might reasonably suggest that all of the jaditic material used by the Olmec, Maya, and Costa Rican carvers was derived from a single source. This view, however, is called into question both by chemical analysis of jadeitites and by the archaeological distribution of the artifacts.

One proponent of the "single source" hypothesis is the mineralogist George Harlow. He approaches the question of source from a geological perspective that draws heavily on plate tectonic theory, observational data derived from the examination of petrographic thin sections, and chemical analyses using an electron microprobe. His model of jadeite occurrence is based on experimental findings that produce synthetic jadeite, and on interpretation of jadeite formation processes and linkage to tectonic conditions and mineralogical associations (e.g., serpentinite). The occurrences of the known jadeite sources and associated serpentinites are observed to be correlated with faults that tend to be large and active and to show horizontal movement, and that occur in relatively young geologic environments. Thus, Harlow postulates a "generic" relationship among plate tectonics, jadeitite formation, and the way the area of formation appears on the surface. He reasons that the conditions under which jadeite forms are so demanding that the Motagua Valley is the only area of Mesoamerica or Central America where the conditions that he sets forth are met.

Mineralogical heterogeneity within the Motagua source materials or within the jaditic artifacts reflects the diverse suite of rock that can make up the jadeitites. Jadeitites, as found in Guatemala, contain sodium pyroxenes, including jadeite, most frequently occurring with other minerals as major constituents, such as albite, mica (muscovite-paragonite), and sphene. Color variation in the artifacts can also be accommodated by Harlow's model: the emerald-green jade could result from the mixing of chromium containing chromite into jadeite, while the darker hues of jade could be a function of varying amounts of chromium omphacite. Even the blue-green Olmec or Costa Rican artifacts could be accommodated within the potential range of mineralogical or chemical mixing.

The "multiple source" hypothesis is based on chemical data derived predominantly through the use of Instrumental Neutron Activation Analysis (INAA). In the early 1970s, Hammond explored the compositional variation of jadeite and related minerals from the Sierra de Las Minas area on the northern side of the upper Motagua River. Hammond's project provided basic data on the

compositional variation of jadeite and associated minerals found in the Motagua Valley and provided the stimulus for a more extensive compositional approach to the investigation of jade procurement and distribution. Bishop and his colleagues greatly increased the sampling of the jadeitites from the Motagua River region and carried out INAA characterization of several hundred Maya and Costa Rican jade artifacts. Within the chemical data there are observable patterns of relative homogeneity in the form of "clusters" of data points that are more similar to one another than they are to other clusters. When supplemented by structural analysis of the artifacts, the chemical patterns are found to covary with mineralogical assemblages or regularities in X-ray peak shifts.

Among the jaditic rocks of the Motagua Valley a fundamental chemical distinction can be observed that corresponds to "light" green or "dark" green-black specimens. Similar compositional profiles are found among the analyzed Maya region artifacts, including those recovered from the nearby Classic Maya center of San Agustín Acasaguastlan and, farther away, from the Sacred Cenote of Chichén Itzá in Yucatán. The light green jadeitites of the Motagua are characterized as consisting of major abundances of jadeite and albite with minor occurrences of paragonite and analcite. In contrast, the dark green analyzed jadeitites are comprised of jadeite with omphacite and variable amounts of analcite.

Chemically and mineralogically distinct from the Motagua Valley's jadeite-bearing rocks are data derived from the analysis of visually distinctive emerald-green Maya artifacts (see table). Composed of jadeite, trace amounts of omphacite, and relatively low abundances of albite, muscovite, and analcite, these specimens possess much higher chromium values than the Motagua source and matching artifact analyses.

The analyzed Costa Rican samples also reveal compositionally distinct divisions into light and dark groups. These chemically defined groups are statistically separable from those of the Maya region and can be observed to differ mineralogically in having low occurrences of the micas, paragonite, and muscovite.

Research findings from neutron activation and structural analyses have been interpreted to suggest the following conclusions. (1) The jadeite-containing rocks of the Motagua River Valley were exploited by the Maya, with analytically matching specimens having been recovered from nearby Maya sites as well as from such distant regions as Chichén Itzá in northern Yucatán. (2) A compositional group consisting of emerald-green specimens

EXAMPLES OF OXIDE CONCENTRATION MEANS AND STANDARD DEVIATIONS (PERCENT) OF REPRESENTATIVE MAYA AND COSTA RICAN JADEITITE GROUPS.

	Motagua Light	Motagua Dark	Chichén Green	Maya Green	Costa Rican Light	Costa Rican Dark
n =	24	28	34	49	37	12
Na_2O%	12.8 (11)	8.09 (25)	11.5 (18)	11.5 (12)	12.7 (9)	8.74 (24)
Fe_2O_3%	.959 (301)	2.40 (34)	0.698 (43)	1.26 (12)	1.29 (36)	6.06 (30)
Sc_2O_3	1.02 (120)	4.55 (38)	1.28 (107)	3.77 (37)	3.47 (55)	25.3 (46)
Eu_2O_3	27.8 (100)	80.8 (78)	29.6 (88)	0.148 (25)	0.193 (98)	1.04 (107)
Lu_2O_3	24.0 (60)	65.9 (43)	21.7 (66)	97.1 (31)	44.9 (201)	0.644 (190)
Yb_2O_3	0.119 (55)	0.314 (60)	0.117 (76)	0.567 (26)	0.255 (173)	4.28 (179)
HfO_2	1.30 (54)	1.11 (89)	0.829 (207)	0.317 (34)	2.60 (53)	4.57 (99)
Cr_2O_3	18.7 (411)	513. (120)	393. (312)	1530. (80)	6.74 (111)	60.5 (301)
CoO	3.85 (64)	17.3 (39)	4.30 (50)	7.06 (22)	3.76 (38)	18.1 (33)

(Bishop et al. 1993, Table 3). Data derived by instrumental neutron activation and reported as parts per million, except for Na and Fe, which are given as percent.

cannot be shown to match the analyzed specimens of the Motagua source area. (3) The emerald-green artifacts reveal a similar compositional pattern that lasts almost three thousand years in the Maya area. (4) Greenstones that were albite, as well as those that were jadeite, were preferred by the Maya for carving. (5) With a few notable exceptions, analyzed Costa Rican jadeite artifacts are compositionally distinct from those of the north.

The reported recovery of reworked Maya jade belt-pendants in Costa Rica (few are known from scientific excavation) can be taken to indicate some form of contact between the Maya region and lower Central America. The INAA data have shown a few of the analyzed specimens from the Belizean sites of Cuello and Cerros to be chemically indistinguishable from the members of one of the Costa Rican compositional groups, indicating that jade flowed in both directions. When we consider only the emerald green jadeitites, long-distance exploitation of a common resource area is suggested. The problem is that the emerald-green jadeitites do not chemically match the known source area. Still, given the reality of only a single known source and the inherent limitations of our sampling for analysis, Harlow's single source hypothesis may be correct.

Should the Motagua Valley be the only source of carved jadeitites, they could have been transported down the Motagua River. Goods could have moved northeast along the river to the Gulf of Honduras, around the coast of Nicaragua, and into Costa Rica from the Atlantic side. Subsequently, they could have been dispersed to northern Pacific Costa Rican sites. Jade could have taken a Pacific route from Guatemala to the Gulf of Nicoya. This route, however, is unlikely because seaborne travel was subject to severe navigational hazards. As an alternative to seaborne trade, jade could have moved overland; but this, too, is unlikely, given the different jade-carving traditions, the differing use of jadeitites and other greenstones, and the absence of jade artifacts in Nicaragua.

If contact between regions did occur—and it seems likely that some contact did occur—we do not know the extent of contact, its frequency and duration, or its influence. Certainly, to the extent that additional sources of jadeitites are yet to be found, the importance of long-distance trade and its meaning become even more complex. At present, in spite of the field and laboratory investigations that have taken place, the source of Mexican and Mesoamerican jade remains a matter for speculation and future exploration.

FURTHER READINGS

Bishop, R. L., and F. W. Lange. 1993. Sources of Maya and Central American Jadeitites: Data Bases and Interpretations. In F. W. Lange (ed.), *Precolumbian Jade: New Geological and Cultural Interpretations,* pp. 125–130. Salt Lake City: University of Utah Press.

Bishop, R. L., E. V. Sayre, and J. Mishara. 1993. Compositional and Structural Characterization of Maya and Costa Rican Jadeitites. In F. W. Lange (ed.), *Precolumbian Jade: New Geological and Cultural Interpretations,* pp. 30–60. Salt Lake City: University of Utah Press.

Bishop, R. L., E. V. Sayre, and L. van Zelst. 1985. Characterization of Mesoamerican Jade. In P. A. England and L. van Zelst (eds.), *Application of Science in Examination of Works of Art,* pp. 151–156. Boston: Research Laboratory, Museum of Fine Arts.

Easby, E. K. 1968. *Pre-Columbian Jade from Costa Rica.* New York: André Emmerich.

Foshag, W. F. 1957. Mineralogical Studies on Guatemalan Jade. *Smithsonian Miscellaneous Collections,* 145.5. Washington, D.C.: Smithsonian Institution.

Garber, J. F. 1986. The Artifacts. In R. A. Robertson and D. A. Freidel (eds.), *Archaeology at Cerros Belize, Central America,* vol. I, *An Interim Report,* pp. 117–126. Dallas: Southern Methodist University Press.

Hammond, N., A. Aspinall, S. Feather, J. Hazelden, T. Gazard, and S. Agrell. 1977. Maya Jade: Source Location and Analysis. In T. K. Earle and J. E. Ericson (eds.), *Exchange Systems in Prehistory,* pp. 35–68. New York: Academic Press.

Harlow, G. E. 1993. Middle American Jade: Geologic and Petrologic Perspectives on Variability and Source. In F. W. Lange (ed.), *Precolumbian Jade: New Geological and Cultural Interpretations,* pp. 9–29. Salt Lake City: University of Utah Press.

Lange, F. W., and R. L. Bishop. 1988. Abstraction and Jade Exchange in Precolumbian Southern Mesoamerica and Lower Central America. In F. W. Lange (ed.), *Costa Rican Art and Archaeology: Essays in Honor of Frederick R. Mayer,* pp. 65–88. Boulder: University of Colorado Press.

Sharer, R. J. 1984. Lower Central America as Seen from Mesoamerica. In F. W. Lange and D. Z. Stone (eds.), *The Archaeology of Lower Central America,* pp. 63–84. Albuquerque: University of New Mexico Press.

Ronald L. Bishop

SEE ALSO

Minerals, Ores, and Mining

J

Jaguars

The jaguar (*Panthera onca*) is the largest American cat, and for three thousand years it was one of Mesoamerica's most important symbolic animals. Its dramatic image haunts the iconography of every major pre-Columbian civilization, from Olmec to Aztec. A deadly nocturnal predator, the jaguar sees in the dark through mirrored eyes and hunts all manner of prey on land, in trees, and in water. Its feline stealth, strength, and razor-sharp claws make it the epitome of hunting success. It was probably this impressive combination of talents that inspired the jaguar's all-powerful supernatural form as "Master of Animals" and spiritual ally of transforming shamans and priests.

As a cunning, beautiful, but deadly killer, the jaguar evoked powerful emotions in many Mesoamerican civilizations, and it came to embody key social and religious concepts. Throughout Mesoamerica it was associated with shamans, hunters, warriors, blood sacrifice, royal status, and fertility. Jaguar imagery in painting, sculpture, clothing, and ritual paraphernalia associated elites with the divine power of the animal's supernatural form.

The jaguar symbol appears first in Olmec iconography, in carved stone sculptures adorning sites such as San Lorenzo and La Venta. Strange half-human, half-feline creatures may represent were-jaguars, the supernatural offspring of Olmec rulers and mythical jaguar beings. The creature's associations with rulership and warfare are evident also among the Classic Maya, where the jaguar's brilliant pelt served as emblematic clothing for kings and covered royal thrones, which were often carved in the animal's form.

Linguistic evidence supports this association. The Maya term *balam* refers to the jaguar, to rulers, and to their shared qualities of strength, ferocity, and valor. In the Bonampak murals, jaguar apparel is a prominent feature of war regalia, and the animals' remains have been found in elite burials. In Postclassic times, "spreading the jaguar skin" was a sign for war, and the "jaguar mat" was the seat of authority in a Maya council. Even today, powerful Maya men have a jaguar spirit-familiar.

Among the Aztec, the jaguar held a similarly important place in iconography and symbolism. In the *Florentine Codex,* the jaguar is called *ocelotl,* the bravest and fiercest of animals, whose proud disposition made it the ruler of the animal world. Like the Maya, the Aztec jaguar imagery associated with warfare, and terms that include the animal's name, are metaphors for valiant soldiers, including the elite Jaguar-Warrior society, who were privileged to wear costumes with jaguar designs. The animal's supernatural associations are also apparent in mystical

J

beliefs: jaguar skins and claws were used by Aztec sorcerers in their magical rites. Aztec rulers had an especially close relationship with the jaguar, wearing capes and sandals of jaguar skin into battle, and holding court seated on jaguar-skin thrones. The patron deity of Aztec royalty was the all-powerful Tezcatlipoca, who could appear transformed as a huge jaguar known as Tepeyollotli. Today, the jaguar retains a hold on the Mesoamerican imagination, appearing as brightly colored masks and costumed dancers in springtime festivals to petition for rain.

FURTHER READINGS

Furst, P. T. 1968. The Olmec Were Jaguar Motif in the Light of Ethnographic Reality. In E. P. Benson (ed.), *Conference on the Olmec,* pp. 143–175. Washington, D.C.: Dumbarton Oaks.

Saunders, N. J. 1990. Tezcatlipoca: Jaguar Metaphors and the Aztec Mirror of Nature. In R. G. Willis (ed.), *Signifying Animals: Human Meaning in the Natural World,* pp. 159–177. New York and London: Routledge.

———. 1994. Predators of Culture: Jaguar Symbolism and Mesoamerican Elites. *World Archaeology* 26: 104–117.

Nicholas J. Saunders

SEE ALSO
Fauna

Jaina (Campeche, Mexico)

This island off the western coast of the Yucatán peninsula served ritual and particularly funerary functions during the Late Classic period (A.D. 600–900). The site is most famous for the figurines found there as grave goods. These small figurines, otherwise uncommon for Classic Maya culture, depict upper-class Maya men and women in many occupations, attitudes, and costumes (some removable), thus providing an important corpus of information about social relations, roles, and status, and how these were related to age and sex. Figurines also depict individuals engaged in activities pertaining to economic specialization, ritual, and military activities. The figurines are famous for the delicacy of their modeling and polychrome painted details.

FURTHER READINGS

Aveleyra Arroyo de Anda, L., and G. F. Ekholm. 1966. Clay Sculpture from Jaina. *Natural History* 75:40–46.

Corson, C. 1976. *Maya Anthropomorphic Figurines from Jaina Island, Campeche.* Ballena Press Studies in Mesoamerican Art, Archaeology, and Ethnohistory, 1. Ramona, Calif.

Piña Chan, R. 1968. *Jaina, la casa en el agua.* Mexico City: Instituto Nacional de Antropología e Historia.

Schele, L. 1997. *Hidden Faces of the Maya.* Impetus Comunicación. Poway, Calif.: Alti Publishers.

Susan Toby Evans

SEE ALSO
Figurines, Terracotta; Maya Lowlands: North

Jalieza (Oaxaca, Mexico)

Extending over more than 8 square kilometers of hilltops and piedmont, Jalieza is the largest known archaeological site in the Valley of Oaxaca. It consists of 2,149 pre-Hispanic residential terraces, 91 mounds, and large expanses of unterraced but inhabited area. Jalieza's occupational history is known from surface survey, surface collection, and mapping of 249 terraces. The site's three large components overlap very little with one another spatially, and there are a number of much smaller components as well. Among the latter are two very small Late/Terminal Formative occupations.

In the Early Classic period, Jalieza was one of two secondary centers in the Valley of Oaxaca. Second in size only to Monte Albán at this time, its population is estimated to have been more than 12,000. Jalieza's Early Postclassic occupation, estimated at about 16,000, is the largest known for this period in the state of Oaxaca. Its most significant Late Postclassic component, believed to date to the earlier part of this very long phase, had an estimated population of 6,600 inhabitants.

The more intensively studied Early Classic and Early Postclassic settlements have revealed evidence of widespread manufacture of local chipped stone expediency tools, production of a variety of ceramic wares, at least one obsidian workshop, and some textile production. Obsidian was obtained from a range of sources in the Central Plateau region, although material from Zaragosa in Puebla is predominant.

FURTHER READINGS

Finsten, L. 1995. "Jalieza, Oaxaca: Activity Specialization at a Hilltop Center." Nashville: Vanderbilt University Publications in Anthropology, Number 47.

Laura Finsten

SEE ALSO
Oaxaca and Tehuantepec Region

K

Kabah (Yucatán, Mexico)

The archaeological zone of Kabah, meaning "strong hands," is situated at the southern end of a 20-kilometer-long intersite Maya causeway that links it with two other large Puuc sites, Nohpat and Uxmal. It is classified as a rank two center by the *Atlas arqueológico,* but recent work by Carrasco and his colleagues suggests that the total mass of architectural construction may be greater at Kabah than at the rank one center of Uxmal, prompting researchers to reassess its role in the regional settlement hierarchy. Kabah was first settled during the Middle Formative period (600–300 B.C.) in the dry-forest, water-poor hill region of northern Yucatán. Its economy was based on agriculture. Kabah grew into one of the key politico-economic centers of the region in Terminal Classic times (A.D. 800–1000).

The site covers about 5 square kilometers, with monumental Puuc-style architecture found at the site core of 1 square kilometer. These buildings were of rough limestone concrete masonry covered with fine veneer stone façades. Like most sites in the Puuc region, however, Kabah seems to have been abandoned shortly after A.D. 1000. Several building groups have been partially restored, including the freestanding arch over the intersite causeway entering the site, the Red Hands building with interior red-hands murals, and the *Codz Pop* or Palace of the Masks. Recent work by Ramon Carrasco at the *Codz Pop* included the restoration of the east façade and the rediscovery of two sculpted door jambs with hieroglyphic inscriptions dating to A.D. 987. The remains of six monumental sculpted figures found here are believed to represent the kings *(kin ich ahua)* of Kabah.

FURTHER READINGS

Andrews, G. 1975. *Maya Cities: Placemaking and Urbanization.* Norman: University of Oklahoma Press.

Carrasco V., R. 1992. El Rey de Kabah (The King of Kabah). *Mexicon* 14:66–67.

Dunning, N. P. 1992. *Lords of the Hills: Ancient Maya Settlement of the Puuc Region, Yucatán, Mexico.* Madison, Wis.: Prehistory Press.

Garza Terrazona de Gonzales, S., and E. B. Kurjack. 1980. *Atlas arqueológico del Estado de Yucatán.* 2 vols. Mexico City: Instituto Nacional de Antropología e Historia.

Pollock, H. E. D. 1980. *The Puuc: An Architectural Survey of the Hill Country of Yucatán and Northern Campeche, Mexico.* Peabody Museum of Archaeology and Ethnology Memoirs, 19. Cambridge, Mass.: Harvard University.

Michael Smyth

SEE ALSO
Maya Lowlands: North

Kaminaljuyu (Guatemala, Guatemala)

This large, important archaeological site in the Valley of Guatemala is concentrated particularly in what are now the southwestern sections of modern Guatemala City. It originally consisted of about two hundred mounds distributed throughout an area of approximately 5 square kilometers. Most of these were remains of platforms that supported perishable structures, organized around patios or plazas or in linear arrangements along what were probably wide avenues. Since 1940, the majority of the

K

mounds have been destroyed by the constant growth and spread of Guatemala City.

Kaminaljuyu (in Spanish, Kaminaljuyú) was occupied continuously from the Middle Formative period (possibly even earlier) to the end of Late Classic times (roughly, from 1000 B.C. to A.D. 900). In Kaminaljuyu's chronological sequence, the Formative is divided into seven phases: Arevalo, 1200–1000? B.C.; Las Charcas, 1000–750 B.C.; Majadas, 750–700 B.C.; Providencia, 700–400 B.C.; Verbena, 400–300 B.C.; Arenal, 300 B.C.–A.D. 100; and Santa Clara, A.D. 100–200. The Early Classic is divided into the Aurora phase, A.D. 200–400, and the Esperanza phase, A.D. 400–550, and the Late Classic into the Amatle phase, A.D. 550–800, and the Pamplona phase, A.D. 800–900. Kaminaljuyu was abandoned in the Postclassic period, but elsewhere in the Valley of Guatemala the occupation during this time can be divided into the Ayampuc phase, A.D. 900–1200, and the Chinautla phase, A.D. 1200–1524.

Very little is known about the Arevalo phase. It was identified by ceramic types that were mixed in the fill of platform mounds constructed in Las Charcas times. The Arevalo ceramics are of excellent quality and, up to the present time, seem to have no antecedents in the valley, nor any close relationship to those of Las Charcas. By contrast, the Las Charcas phase is represented by a number of formal platforms (such as Mounds C-III-9 and C-III-10) that supported wattle-and-daub structures; the Valley of Guatemala lacks stone that could be employed for construction. The presence of administrative complexes and their association with fine ceramics and imported items indicate that the society was already hierarchically organized under some central control. The economy was apparently based on maize agriculture supplemented by other foods. The numerous trash pits contained tools of wood, obsidian, and other stones; indications of obsidian workshops; local and imported ceramics of good quality; and remains of baskets, ropes, mats, and textiles. Censers and fired clay figurines indicate the existence of standardized religion and ceremonial practices.

The Majadas phase, its definition based on a cache buried within Mound C-III-6, represents a brief period of transition between the Las Charcas and Providencia phases. Some Olmec or Olmecoid influence is reflected in the jade objects in the cache, but otherwise the changes are steady and gradual from one phase to next. Population continued to grow in size and complexity. The Providen-

cia phase is recognized on the basis of certain changes in ceramic styles and types, although the total cultural inventory continued basically the same. One of the important structures dated to the Providencia phase is Mound D-III-10.

One innovation—possibly a response to the increasing number of people dependent on the Kaminaljuyu economic network—was an enormous agricultural project to intensify food production. A system of canals was dug to drain water from a lake in the southwestern section of the valley for the purpose of irrigating an extensive zone of cultivated raised beds. This must have considerably augmented the local food supply by allowing year-round production and harvesting of vegetables and fruits. These endeavors would have required a well-organized administration to direct the labor force required to maintain the system, to manage the distribution of goods within the society, and to effect exchange with distant regions. Trade involved importing obsidian and jade from the Motagua Valley to the east, and ceramics and other goods from the northwestern highlands; salt, cacao, fruits, and other items were brought in from the southern coast of Guatemala and western El Salvador. Kaminaljuyu undoubtedly played a central role in the redistribution of these goods to other regions.

The Verbena phase witnessed the disruption of trade ties and communication between Kaminaljuyu and the northwestern highlands of Guatemala. The largest structure at Kaminaljuyu, Mound E-III-3, dates to this phase. It contained the tombs of two successive, high elite personages (perhaps a father and son), who may have resided there while governing the center. From Verbena times until the end of the Late Formative, relations between Kaminaljuyu and the northwestern highlands seem to have remained hostile, whereas economic and cultural interaction steadily increased among the Valley of Guatemala, the southern coast, El Salvador, and the lower Motagua Valley. Evidence of this interaction is revealed in the distribution of traded items, shared ceramic styles (including the use of Usulutan decoration), and the "potbelly" sculptural motif, which was probably associated with a body of religious belief.

The climax of Formative cultural development at Kaminaljuyu occurred in the Arenal phase. Most of the constructions date to this phase, when the population reached its maximum density. The canal system was enlarged and improved with more sophisticated hydraulic engineering to further increase agricultural production. A great amount of sculptural activity is associated with the phase, including monuments with early Maya hieroglyphic texts, such as Monument 10, which, although yet undeciphered, probably commemorates an important event. The employment of early Maya hieroglyphic writing suggests that the Formative occupants were probably Maya speakers. In addition, the presence of potbelly sculptures indicates affinities with peoples of the southern coast of Guatemala and western El Salvador. However, the corpus of sculptures also includes purely local styles and innovations.

The Formative period terminates at Kaminaljuyu with the Santa Clara phase, a period of marked decline, collapse of centralized authority, and at least partial abandonment of the site. Ecological factors may have been involved as the lake dried up and the canal system could no longer function. Political problems are implied by the fact that no constructions have been found that date to this phase. Figurines and sculptured monuments ceased to be produced, and ceramics deteriorated markedly in quality and variety of types manufactured. The Formative traditions finally disappeared at the end of the period.

The Early Classic Aurora phase is the product of an intrusive population that apparently took over Kaminaljuyu, either by blocking trade routes and other indirect means or by outright force, causing the exodus of the former occupants. The ceramics they brought in have no local antecedents; instead, they exhibit affinities with those of the northwestern highlands of Guatemala. The intruders seem to have established themselves first at the site of Solano, southwest of Kaminaljuyu, before entering and taking over the Valley of Guatemala. In addition to the abrupt change in ceramic types, the cultural inventory suggests that the new population was associated with an ideology noticeably different from the Formative one; this is reflected in the style of censers and in the lack of sculptures and figurines. Mound D-III-13 is one of the few structures associated with the Aurora phase.

During the Esperanza phase, the new population began to spread farther throughout the site. The tombs of the elite rulers in mounds A and B indicate apparent connections with the great site of Teotihuacan in Mexico, with which they traded and which they emulated in architectural and ceramic styles. This connection persisted for about a century but ceased at the end the of the Early Classic period, although the population remained at the site until the end of the Late Classic.

The Amatle and Pamplona phases at Kaminaljuyu exhibit some decentralization and development of local culture. A great deal of building activity dates to the Late Classic period, including the construction of eleven ball courts. The number of structures and amount of cultural debris scattered over the entire surface of the site indicates that the population reached a density as least as great as that of the Late Formative Arenal phase. However, in terms of the quality and amount of elite ceramics and other goods, as well as the level of sophistication in art and engineering accomplishments, Kaminaljuyu lagged far behind the heights attained in the Petén lowlands.

Kaminaljuyu was abandoned at the end of the Late Classic period; the circumstances of this are not yet understood. The fact that Postclassic ceramics of the central Guatemalan highlands appear to have evolved from Classic types at Kaminaljuyu suggests that the population remained in the region and may have been ancestors of one of the present-day Quiché/Cakchiquel-related ethnic groups.

The earliest scientific investigations at Kaminaljuyu were carried out by Manuel Gamio in 1925, followed by C. A. Villacorta and his son J. Antonio Villacorta in 1927. More extensive research and excavations were conducted between 1935 and 1953 under the sponsorshop of the Carnegie Institution of Washington, directed by Kidder and Shook. In the 1970s, a large project of investigation was undertaken by the Pennsylvania State University, directed by Sanders and Michels. Since then the Instituto de Antropología e Historia has actively engaged in several salvage operations, maintaining and preserving one sector as a national park.

FURTHER READINGS

Kidder, A. V., J. D. Jennings, and E. M. Shook. 1946. *Excavations at Kaminaljuyu, Guatemala.* Washington, D.C.: Carnegie Institution of Washington, Publication 561.

Michels, J. W. 1979. *The Kaminaljuyú Chiefdom.* University Park: Pennsylvania State University Press.

———. (ed.). 1979. *Settlement Pattern Excavations at Kaminaljuyú, Guatemala.* University Park: Pennsylvania State University Press.

Popenoe de Hatch, M. 1997. *Kaminaljuyú/San Jorge: Evidencia arqueológica de la actividad económica en el Valle de Guatemala, 300 a.C. a 300 d.C.* Guatemala City: Fundación para la Cultura y el Desarrollo.

Shook, E. M., and A. V. Kidder. 1953. Mound E-III-3, Kaminaljuyú, Guatemala. *Carnegie Institution of*

Washington, Contributions to American Anthropology and History 53:33–127.

Sanders, W. T., and J. Michels (eds.). 1977. *Teotihuacan and Kaminaljuyú: A Study in Prehistoric Culture Contact.* University Park: Pennsylvania State University Press.

Wetherington, R. K. 1978. *The Ceramics of Kaminaljuyú, Guatemala.* University Park: Pennsylvania State University Press.

Marion Popenoe de Hatch

SEE ALSO

Maya Lowlands: South

L

Labna (Yucatán, Mexico)

The archaeological zone of Labna, meaning "stone house," is one of several major ruins along the modern "Puuc Route" highway. It is situated in a small, semiarid valley of dry forest vegetation surrounded by steep "haystack" hills. Labna has been classified by the *Atlas arqueológico* as a rank three settlement, with about 3 square kilometers of architectural settlement remains dating to the Terminal Classic period (A.D. 800–1000), although initial agricultural settlement probably occurred sometime during the late Formative (300 B.C.–A.D. 300). Building complexes of the Main Group had core and veneer masonry, stone vaulted roofs, and elaborate decorative façades. The Palace complex, a plaza and multi-room, two-story range structure, is connected to two southern complexes by a north–south causeway; it includes the Mirador, a temple-pyramid bearing a high roof comb that was adorned with a seated figure, ball game players, and a row of skulls, as well as a courtyard group highlighting a famous freestanding arch. The Peabody Museum's explorations of the Labna *chultuns* (bell-shaped underground water storage cisterns) and mapping of the site by Edward Thompson in 1888–1891 represented the first scientific work at the site. In the 1970s, three Main Group buildings were partially restored by archaeologists of the Central Regional de Yucatán. In recent work on settlement pattern and building consolidation, Tomás Gallerta Negrón and colleagues have excavated and restored the causeway, consolidated the Palace, and mapped a large portion of the site.

FURTHER READINGS

Andrews, G. 1975. *Maya Cities: Placemaking and Urbanization.* Norman: University of Oklahoma Press.

Dunning, N. P. 1992. *Lords of the Hills: Ancient Maya Settlement of the Puuc Region, Yucatán, Mexico.* Madison, Wis.: Prehistory Press.

Garza Terrazona de Gonzales, S., and E. B. Kurjack B. 1980. *Atlas arqueológico del Estado de Yucatán.* 2 vols. Mexico City: Instituto Nacional de Antropología e Historia.

Kurjack, E. B., S. Garza T., and J. Lucas. 1979. Archaeological Settlement Patterns and Modern Geography in the Puuc Hills Region of Yucatán. In L. Mills (ed.), *The Puuc: New Perspectives,* pp. 36–45, Scholarly Studies in the Liberal Arts, 1. Pella, Iowa: Central College.

Pollock, H. E. D. 1980. *The Puuc: An Architectural Survey of the Hill Country of Yucatán and Northern Campeche, Mexico.* Peabody Museum of Archaeology and Ethnology Memoirs, 19. Cambridge, Mass.: Harvard University.

Michael Smyth

SEE ALSO

Maya Lowlands: North

Lacandón Maya

A century ago, the Lacandón Maya were scattered throughout the lowland jungles of Petén, Guatemala, and Chiapas, southeastern México. Today only a few hundred Lacandones—recognized by their white tunics, long hair, and distinctive dialect of Yucatec Maya—live in small, dispersed settlements in Chiapas. The Lacandón

L

are egalitarian agriculturalists and hunters whose few pole-and-thatch houses are built among their fields in forest clearings. The typical settlement consists of a house, a kitchen, storage huts, and a "god house" containing incense burners, serving vessels, and ritual items. Their foods include maize, beans, squash, roots, fruits, peccaries, deer, and birds. The Lacandón trade tobacco, honey, meat, and arrows to nearby peoples for salt, metal tools, grinding stones, cloth, sweets, and other household sundries.

Ethnohistoric sources mention larger Lacandón populations and villages—some having defensive perimeters of thorny plants. Documents also provide clues to Lacandón ethnogenesis: they are descended from Maya Lowlands peoples and refugees escaping Spanish colonization from adjacent areas, especially from Yucatán and the highlands. Additionally, there once were political leaders, warriors, diverse kin organizations, and religious specialists; the Lacandón have been transformed through intruding outsiders. Lacandón archaeological sites contain diagnostic brown and black hemispherical bowls, made of hard-fired clay with coarse sand temper, modeled incensarios, small chert blades and arrowheads, remnant fruit trees, and exotics (metal pots, knives, painted ceramics, bottles, etc.).

FURTHER READINGS

Bruce, R. D., and V. Perera. 1982. *The Last Lords of Palenque: The Lacandón Mayas of the Mexican Rain Forest.* Berkeley: University of California Press.

McGee, R. J. 1990. *Life, Ritual, and Religion Among the Lacandón Maya.* Belmont, Calif.: Wadsworth.

Palka, J. W. 1998. Lacandón Maya Culture Change and Survival in the Lowland Frontier of the Expanding Guatemalan and Mexican Republics. In J. G. Cusick (ed.), *Studies in Culture Contact: Interaction, Culture Change, and Archaeology,* pp. 457–475. Carbondale: Center for Archaeological Investigations, Southern Illinois University.

Tozzer, A. M. 1907. *A Comparative Study of the Mayas and Lacandones.* London: Macmillan.

Joel W. Palka

SEE ALSO

Maya Lowlands: North

Lagartero and Environs (Chiapas, Mexico)

Lagartero is a major Classic Maya center situated in the Upper Grijalva River Basin, in Mexico near its border with Guatemala, and just a few kilometers north of the Pan-American Highway. It is accessible to tourists and is the most frequently visited site in the region. The local environmental setting is spectacular. Lagartero lies at the foot of the Cuchumatan Mountains at an elevation of 600 meters, in a marshy area of calcareous springs, streams, sinkholes, and azure lakes. The central portion of this capital center is on Limonal Island; other plaza groups and residential zones spread out over other islands and peninsulas, a total area of 8.6 square kilometers. The Limonal Group with its eleven plazas, 170 mounds (the tallest, 18 meters), and a formal ball court (with a playing alley of 28 × 13 meters) has been the focus of archaeological investigations and architectural restorations. The discovery by Susanna Ekholm of a ceremonial dump in the main plaza revealed thousands of broken polychrome vessels and mold-made figurines in a local style, now known as the Lagartero style.

Lagartero was probably the capital center of a small state during the Classic period, with more than a dozen other states or kingdoms existing to the west in the same region. Limited evidence suggests that Lagartero was occupied in Protoclassic and Early Classic times. Several large fragments of stelae in the Protoclassic style have been recovered from the site.

FURTHER READINGS

Ekholm, S. 1979. The Lagartero Figurines. In N. Hammond and G. R. Willey (eds.), *Maya Archaeology and Ethnohistory,* pp. 172–186. Austin: University of Texas Press.

Montmollin, O. de. 1995. *Settlement and Politics in Three Classic Maya Polities.* Monographs in World Archaeology, 24. Madison, Wis.: Prehistory Press.

Sonia Rivero Torres

SEE ALSO

Chiapas Interior Plateau; Soconusco–South Pacific Coast and Piedmont Region

Laguna de los Cerros (Veracruz, Mexico)

This major Formative and Classic period site in southern Veracruz lies south of the Tuxtla Mountains in an area of upland plains, distant from any river. The site has nearly 100 mound structures, including a 20-meter-tall main mound at the north end of a 170-meter-long plaza. Brief excavations there in 1960 by Medellín Zenil suggest that the major mound constructions and configurations date from the Classic period. However, that research also recorded more than two dozen Olmec monuments, a quantity indicating that a millennium earlier the site had been a major Olmec center. The dating of the latter status remains speculative, for although Early Formative period potsherds were recovered in some excavation units, the stone monuments are stylistically of the Middle Formative period. Those monuments were apparently produced at a nearby basalt quarry and Olmec monument workshop, Llano del Jícaro, which was investigated by Medellín Zenil in 1960 and by Gillespie in 1991.

FURTHER READINGS

Bove, F. J. 1978. Laguna de los Cerros: An Olmec Central Place. *Journal of New World Archaeology* 2(3):1–56.

Gillespie, S. D. 1994. Llano del Jícaro: An Olmec Monument Workshop. *Ancient Mesoamerica* 5:223–242.

Medellín Zenil, A. 1960. Monolitos ineditos olmecas. *La Palabra y el Hombre* (Jalapa) 16:75–97.

———. 1971. *Monolitos Olmecas y Otras en el Museo de la Universidad de Veracruz.* Corpus Antiquitatum Americanensium, 5. Mexico City.

David C. Grove

SEE ALSO

Gulf Lowlands: South Region

Laguna Moyua (Matagalpa, Nicaragua)

This area in central Nicaragua has sites on two intermittent islands and the surrounding lakeshore, which is alternately dry and inundated. One of the islands has a complex of low stone mounds with one larger, central, stone mound. Occupation dates from approximately A.D. 500 to 1520. The cultural assemblage reflects both Greater Nicoya ceramics from the south and southern Honduras ceramics from the north.

FURTHER READINGS

Finlayson, K. 1996. Prospección y excavación preliminar en la zona de la Laguna Moyua. In F. W. Lange (ed.), *Abundante Cooperación Vecinal: La Segunda Temporada del Proyecto "Arqueologia de la Zona Metropolitana de Managua,"* pp. 133–152. Managua: Alcaldia of Managua, Managua.

Frederick W. Lange

SEE ALSO

Intermediate Area: Overview

Laguna Zope (Oaxaca, Mexico)

By several orders of magnitude the largest Formative period settlement on the Pacific Isthmus of Tehuantepec, Laguna Zope was also the longest lived. Radiocarbon dates place its occupation from about 1500 B.C. to A.D. 300. The singular growth and importance of the site may be attributable in part to its role in the procurement and export of locally available ornamental seashell, the possession of which symbolized high status in ancient Mesoamerica. Laguna Zope's importance in the network of exchange between lowland and highland regions would have been further enhanced by its location at the hub of routes linking Formative period centers of cultural development along the central and southern Gulf Coast, the Valley of Oaxaca, the Southern Highlands, and the Soconusco.

Early ceramic affiliations suggest close cultural ties with regions along the southern Pacific Coast and piedmont, but beginning around 800 B.C. Maya influences can be discerned. Around 200 B.C., a shift of ceramic affiliation to a greyware tradition resembling that of the developing Monte Albán civilization in the Valley of Oaxaca indicates a new set of relationships. By 500 B.C., Laguna Zope had grown in size to more than 90 hectares and an estimated 1,000 inhabitants. Three earthen mounds, the tallest over nine meters high, were constructed as the residential and perhaps administrative locus for rulers of what had probably evolved into a chiefdom society. Seashell collection and ornament-making for export to places such as Monte Albán, along with the importation of obsidian from distant highland sources, indicate the ongoing prominence of Laguna Zope in interregional exchange, and its role for almost two millennia as the principal settlement for the entire southern Isthmian region.

FURTHER READINGS

Delgado, A. 1965. *Archaeological Reconnaissance in the Region of Tehuantepec, Oaxaca, Mexico.* Papers of the New World Archaeological Foundation, 18. Provo, Utah.

Zeitlin, R. N. 1982. Toward a More Comprehensive Model of Interregional Commodity Distribution: Political Variables and Prehistoric Obsidian Procurement in Mesoamerica. *American Antiquity* 47:260–275.

———. 1990. The Isthmus and the Valley of Oaxaca: Questions about Zapotec Imperialism in Formative Period Mesoamerica. *American Antiquity* 55:250–261.

L

———. 1993. Pacific Coastal Laguna Zope: A Regional Center in the Terminal Formative Hinterlands of Monte Albán. *Ancient Mesoamerica* 4:85–101.

Robert N. Zeitlin

SEE ALSO
Oaxaca and Tehuantepec Region

Lamanai (Orange Walk, Belize)

This important northern Belize lakeside Maya center was excavated by the Royal Ontario Museum during 1974–1986. It is the first known southern Maya Lowlands site with continuous occupation from c. 1500 B.C. to A.D. 1650/1700, defined by ¹⁴C dates, architectural stratigraphy, and ethnohistoric documentation. There are extensive Postclassic (c. A.D. 1100–1544) and Colonial (1544–1650+) remains, including European imports in the latter period. An agriculturally based economy, with a small raised-field area, was supplemented by lacustrine resources. The central precinct features plaza groups with temples to 33 meters in height, arranged in a lakeside strip. Unusual royal tombs (c. A.D. 450–500) have cloth-covered wooden hoopwork enclosures. Carved monuments include a stela depicting the seventh-century ruler Smoking Shell. Imported metal artifacts from Oaxacan, West Mexican, and other sources were found in deposits of the twelfth and thirteenth centuries; the sixteenth century saw the local development of metal-working. There are close, probably bidirectional ceramic and other links with the northern Yucatán Peninsula during the Postclassic, and close Middle Postclassic (c. A.D. 1200–1300) ceramic ties to the small island site of Marco Gonzalez (Ambergris Caye, Belize).

FURTHER READINGS

Pendergast, D. M. 1986. Stability through Change: Lamanai, Belize, from the Ninth to the Seventeenth Century. In J. A. Sabloff and E. W. Andrews V (eds.), *Late Lowland Maya Civilization: Classic to Postclassic*, pp. 223–249. Albuquerque: University of New Mexico Press.

———. 1990. Up from the Dust: The Central Lowlands Postclassic as Seen from Lamanai and Marco Gonzalez, Belize. In F. S. Clancy and P. D. Harrison (eds.), *Vision and Revision in Maya Studies*, pp. 169–177. Albuquerque: University of New Mexico Press.

———. 1991. The Southern Maya Lowlands Contact Experience: The View from Lamanai, Belize. In D. H. Thomas (ed.), *Columbian Consequences*, vol. 3, pp. 336–354. Washington, D.C.: Smithsonian Institution Press.

David M. Pendergast

SEE ALSO
Maya Lowlands: South

Lambityeco (Oaxaca, Mexico)

Situated in the Valley of Oaxaca, about 26 kilometers from Oaxaca City, Lambityeco is considered by some to be the type site for the period Monte Albán IV, which followed the collapse of Monte Albán at the end of the period Monte Albán IIIB. Other scholars, however, see no evidence for separating periods IIIB and IV, lumping them into a single phase known as Xco (A.D. 600–800), during which Lambityeco would have been contemporaneous with Monte Albán. An intensive surface survey revealed that Lambityeco was first inhabited in the Rosario phase (700 B.C.) but reached its maximum size during the Xco phase, when 168 of the 213 mounds showed evidence of occupation, and the area of habitation covered nearly 64 hectares, with a population estimated at 4,000. Excavations have uncovered the remains of elite houses with associated tombs and sweat baths dated by five radiocarbon analyses to between A.D. 640 and 755. Tomb 6, the most elaborate, had its façade decorated with two life-size portrait heads of a named male and female. Above Tomb 6 was an altar with friezes depicting named male and female couples. The named couples probably were buried in the tomb and constitute a genealogy over several generations. Another elite house contained a room with two 1-meter plaster busts of Cocigo, Zapotec deity of lightning and rain. Tomb 11, in another elite house, contained murals with named personages and carved bones.

FURTHER READINGS

Lind, M. 1994. Monte Albán y el Valle de Oaxaca durante la fase Xco. In M. Winter (ed.), *Monte Albán: Estudios Recientes,* pp. 99–111. Proyecto Especial Monte Alban, Contribución 2.

Lind, M., and J. Urcid. 1983. The Lords of Lambityeco and Their Nearest Neighbors. *Notas Americanas* 9:78–111.

———,———. 1990. La zona arqueológica de Lambityeco. In M. Winter (ed.), *Lecturas históricas del estado de Oaxaca: Época prehispánica,* vol. 1, pp.

287–307. Mexico City: Instituto Nacional de Antropología e Historia and Gobierno del Estado de Oaxaca.

Paddock, J. 1983. Lambityeco. In K. Flannery and J. Marcus (eds.), *The Cloud People*, pp. 197–204. New York: Academic Press.

Michael Lind

SEE ALSO
Oaxaca and Tehuantepec Region

Landa, Diego de (1524–1579)

Diego de Landa, third bishop of Yucatán, was born in Cifuentes. He went to Yucatán in 1549. Until 1563 he lived in Izamal, Conkal, and Mérida; he then left for a decade in Spain. He returned to Yucatán in 1573, and held the bishopric until his death in Mérida in 1579. Landa's life among the northern Maya during the earliest days of the Spanish presence in Yucatán produced the two deeds for which he is best known: burning Mayan hieroglyphic books in Yucatán, and writing the famed *Relación de las cosas de Yucatán*. The former Landa believed necessary as a strategy against native idolatry; the latter serves as our best single source on Lowland Maya culture as it was in the decades immediately following the Conquest. The fate of the original manuscript of the *Relación*, written in Spain around 1566, remains unknown. It exists only as a copy, rendered in several hands, in the Academy of History in Madrid, Spain, where it was brought to light by the French cleric Etienne Charles Brasseur de Bourbourg in 1863. Various editions of the *Relación* have come into print since Brasseur's French version of the following year; the most useful in English are those of Tozzer and Pagden.

FURTHER READINGS
Landa, D. 1978 [1566]. *Yucatán before and after the Conquest.* New York: Dover.

Pagden, A. R. (trans. and ed.). 1975. *The Maya: Diego de Landa's Account of the Affairs of Yucatán.* Chicago: J. Philip O'Hara.

Tozzer, A. M. (trans. and ed.). 1941. *Landa's Relación de las Cosas de Yucatán: A Translation.* Papers of the Peabody Museum of Archaelogy and Ethnology, 18. Cambridge, Mass.: Harvard University.

George Stuart

SEE ALSO
Ethnohistorical Sources and Methods

Languages at the Time of Contact

The Native American language families of Mexico and Central America include the following, from north to south: Uto-Aztecan, Totonac-Tepehua, Otomangean, Tarascan, Cuitlatec, Tequistlatec-Jicaque, Huave, Mixe-Zoque, Mayan, Xinca, Lenca, Chibchan, and Misumalpan. Uto-Aztecan extends north into the Great Basin of the United States. Chibchan extends well into South America. At time of European contact, the distribution of these language families was approximately that shown in Map 1. When we compare this with Map 2, the modern-day distribution, two major differences meet the eye: the incursion of Spanish as a dominant language, replacing native languages in some areas and circumscribing others; and the arrival of Arawakan on the eastern coast of Belize and Guatemala and on the northern shore of Honduras. Spanish is now spoken as a second language, or as a first language in replacive bilingual situations, throughout most if not all of the area shown as the homeland of indigenous languages. English and English Creole are also spoken in Belize and along the northern and eastern coasts of Honduras and Nicaragua in those areas shown as Arawakan and Misumalpan.

Immigration to Mexico and Central America

There were people scattered throughout this region by 10,000 B.C. These people lived in small groups, probably family units, of hunter-gatherers. It is impossible to say with certainty what languages they spoke, except by projecting backward in a least-moves theory. Proto-languages for each family can be reconstructed, and the resulting vocabulary provides some clues of cultural inventory, but the time depth of such reconstructions does not exceed 6000 B.C. No lexicon indicative of point of origin can be projected back to the hunter-gatherer period. Evidence for initial homelands comes from archaeology and ethnohistorical accounts, and from applying optimization theory to glottochronological projections.

Uto-Aztecan

Starting from the north, the Uto-Aztecan group diffused south from the Great Basin. They inhabited the upper Sonoran area of what is now New Mexico and Arizona and the lower Sonoran area in Mexico, reaching the Central Mexican highlands, where they lived among Otomangean and Tarascan speakers. Northern outliers differentiated, giving rise to ancestral forms of Ute and Hopi. Within Mexico, the proto-language moved toward ancestral Nahuatl. There was variation within this group,

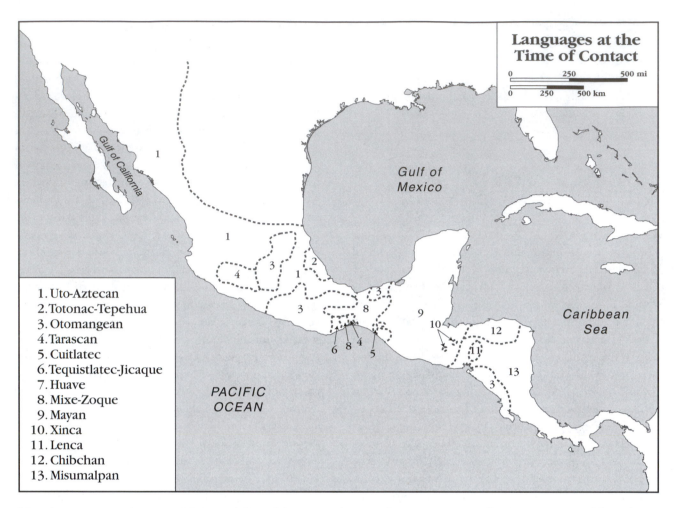

Languages at the Time of Contact

| 0 | 250 | 500 mi |
| 0 | 250 | 500 km |

1. Uto-Aztecan
2. Totonac-Tepehua
3. Otomangean
4. Tarascan
5. Cuitlatec
6. Tequistlatec-Jicaque
7. Huave
8. Mixe-Zoque
9. Mayan
10. Xinca
11. Lenca
12. Chibchan
13. Misumalpan

Major language groups in ancient Mexico and Central America at the time of European contact. Illustration courtesy of the author.

both linguistically and culturally. Successive waves of Nahuatl speakers overran the Valley of Mexico, moving south from the arid north, but vigorous pockets of other language groups persisted within their newly won territories. Three main dialects of the Nahuatl language developed. The undifferentiated language group is referred to as "Nahua." Its three principal divisions are identified by a shibbolethic consonant distinction. The group that was in power at Tenochtitlan at the time of contact, popularly referred to as "Aztecs," used [tl] for this phoneme, and their language is known as "Nahuatl." The Nahuatl (/tl/ speakers) occupied the Central Mexican region at contact. To their west were related speakers who simplified /tl/, the voiceless dental lateral affricate, to voiceless lateral, /l/;

this group is called "Nahual." Around these groups, to the north, east, and south, were another group of speakers who had simplified /tl/ to /t/, the voiceless dental stop; this group is known as "Nahuat."

One group of Nahuat speakers, the Pipil, migrated south to El Salvador. Interpretations of the ethnohistoric record differ as to the date of this migration. Campbell suggests that they came originally from the area around Cholula and Puebla in Mexico. They first moved south to southern Veracruz, then were displaced to the Soconusco. They were driven out of the Soconusco by the Olmec and moved on southward, leaving colonies in Guatemala, El Salvador, and Nicaragua, and even a few isolated communities in Costa Rica and Panama. The move south from the Soconusco is dated at c. A.D. 800 on the basis of early Colonial texts that refer to the last migration having occurred seven or eight ages of an old man earlier. The "age of an old man" is taken to be 104 years, or two 52-year cycles.

There were a few known intervening pockets of Nahuat and/or Nahuatl speakers in Guatemala and southern Mexico. While the Nahaut speakers may represent communities of Pipiles who settled out on the trek south, or support colonies for the *pochteca* (the Aztec merchants), the Nahuatl are almost certainly post-Contact settlers—soldiers who accompanied the Spanish south and were rewarded with land for their help.

Totonac-Tepehua

This familial trunk was situated in Central Mexico, in the area around the Valley of Mexico, the site of Teotihuacan, and in the states of Veracruz, Puebla, and Hidalgo. Subsequent Nahua invasions isolated some communities and displaced others. At the time of contact, Totonac peoples considered themselves traditional enemies of the Aztec and aided Cortés in his military campaigns.

Otomangean

The Otomangean family is much dispersed. The northernmost group is Pamean; below them lies the Otomian group, followed by Popolocan, Subtiaba-Tlapanec, Amuzgo, Mixtecan, Chatino-Zapotec, Chinantecan, and Chiapanec-Mangue. These languages are spoken as far south as Nicaragua and Costa Rica. Glottochronological calculations project the initial breakup and differentiation of this group to 4500 B.C. The Otomangean homeland is a matter of some debate; the reconstructed flora and fauna for the place of origin are compatible with either the Valley of Tehuacan or the Tamaulipas area.

Tarascan

At the time of Contact, the Tarascans were established in the Mexican states of Guanajuato, Querétaro, Guerrero, Colima, Jalisco, México, and Michoacán. The language is also known as Michoacano or Purépecha. Their oral traditions hold that they were relative newcomers to the area when the Spanish arrived. Some scholars, such as Swadesh and Greenberg, detect South American linguistic relationships, possibly linking Tarascan to a posited Macro-Kechua-Chibchan. Some ceramics and copper items found in archaeological sites of Michoacán share stylistic traits with northern South American finds. However,

most linguists treat Tarascan as an isolate, with its homeland and macro-affiliation undetermined. Since Contact the Tarascan community has shrunk, the bulk now lying within the state of Michoacán. Migrations of the past century, in response to economic pressures, have placed small groups of Tarascan speakers in the states of Aguascalientes and Baja California Norte.

Cuitlatec

This language is now extinct, but at the time of Contact it was spoken in the state of Guerrero. The sketchy information collected on Cuitlatec suggests no close family ties, so it is treated as an isolate. This may be the group referred to in Colonial documents as the Chontal of Guerrero. Note that several unrelated languages were designated "Chontal"; some retain this label today. Etymologically, *chontal* means "foreigner, stranger," from the root of the Nahuatl word *chontalli*. The Cuitlatecs were engulfed by Nahua migrations but retained some of their lands and community structures. The extinction of the language resulted from post-Contact assimilation.

Tequistlatec-Jicaque

At the time of Contact, these languages were separated by groups of Maya, Xinca, and Lenca. Often, such spatial distribution of a language, peripheral to insurgent groups, is indicative of a former continuous and contiguous occupation, with later incursions by the intervening groups. This model is hard to adjust to the Tequistlatec-Jicaque case, however, because the reconstructed proto-lexicon includes names of cultigens, which suggests relatively late differentiation; moreover, the Xinca and Lenca groups seem to have been in situ for an indefinite but long period. Whatever their original homeland, by time of Contact the Tequistlatec and the Jicaque were two separate groups. The Jicaque are also known as Tol. Tol communities within Honduras have increasingly become monolingual in Spanish since the nineteenth century.

Huave

The Huave homeland was to the north of the Mixe-Zoque groups, but Zapotec expansion from as early as 1200 B.C. began to put pressure on their communities and eventually confined them to the Pacific Coast. In colonial times, they were spread from Oaxaca through El Mar Muerto de Chiapas and Tonalá. Today, only the Oaxacan communities survive. The Huave speakers have also been referred to as Mareños and Huapis.

L

Mixe-Zoque

Mixe-Zoquean groups probably moved into Mesoamerica from the north. However, they were in approximately their current position—the region of the Olmec cultural florescence—by the time of agricultural beginnings in the area, c. 1200 B.C. They have remained in place while other groups moved into and through the area. This physical coincidence and lack of evidence of other groups' presence in the area at the critical period has led to the hypothesis that the Olmec were Mixe-Zoque speakers. Proto-Mixe-Zoque would have been a unified language group, consistent with its use by a single speech community, at the time of the emergence of the Olmec tradition in sculpture, architecture, and ceramics, c. 1150 B.C. Campbell and Kaufman argue for Proto-Mixe-Zoque as the language of the Olmec on the basis of core Mesoamerican cultural and agricultural vocabulary that diffused from the Olmec sphere into other language and culture areas of the region. Basic concepts in Mesoamerican religion, the Calendar Round, vigesimal counting, and deities were passed on to neighboring groups; basic cultigens, such as corn, beans, and squash, along with elements of their associated agricultural round, were named in Proto-Mixe-Zoque, and thence spread throughout Mesoamerica. Groups as diverse as the Maya, Totonac, Lenca, and Paya borrowed from this "Olmec" collection of terms. From their position straddling the Mesoamerican heartland, the Mixe-Zoque did not wander; at the time of European contact, Mixe-Zoque communities stretched across the isthmus from the Bay of Campeche, interspersed with Zapotec groups. On the Gulf Coast, they were intermingled with Nahuat speakers.

Mayan

There are two main hypotheses concerning the location of the Maya homeland: the northwestern Cuchumatanes Mountains of Guatemala, or the northern highlands of El Salvador. The latter hypothesis holds that the Maya were forced out of their original holdings by a volcanic eruption. They then moved out northward, primarily by way of the Gulf Coast. New dates for settlements in the lowlands, especially Belize, show fairly dense habitation before the relevant volcanism in El Salvador. The northwestern Cuchumatanes hypothesis offers no driving engine for the out-migration, but it suggests a least-moves model for positioning groups in their approximate modern locations. In this model, the contemporary Q'anjob'alan area is the homeland. Little archaeological

excavation has been done in this area. Surface collections and test pits reveal late Classic and Postclassic ceramics and structures, though Classic and even earlier structures probably underlie these throughout the zone. We lack confirming archaeological data for a "mother" Mayan community in the high Cuchumatanes in the year 4000 B.C., when the family would have been a single unit just beginning to diversify.

The first group to emigrate were the Huastec. They reached the Gulf Coast of Mexico and headed north, later to be cut off from the rest of the Mayan family by successive migrations of Otomangean, Totonac-Tepehua, and Uto-Aztecan groups. The next out-migrations were by Yucatecan and Cholan peoples, who moved from the highlands to the lowlands of the Yucatán Peninsula, the Petén, Belize, El Salvador, and Honduras. Subsequent migrations distributed the remaining Mayan groups throughout the Guatemala and Chiapas highlands. In Guatemala, they incorporated or displaced the Xinca; in southern Mexico, they overran Otomangean and Zoquean areas. These invasions of Zoquean areas brought new loan words, but they well post-date the early loan period when the basic agricultural vocabulary and ritual calendrical terms were diffused into the Mayan family. At the time of Contact, the Maya formed a bloc from the Isthmus of Tehuantepec east to the Gulf and the sea, and south as far as northern El Salvador and Honduras, with isolated pockets of Xinca and Pipil (Nahuat) speakers encysted along their southern border.

Xinca

Speakers of this language group seem to have settled early in southern Guatemala and in El Salvador, and they may at one time have occupied highland and lowland areas from the southern Pacific coast of Guatemala through to the northern coast of Honduras. There is some evidence of reconstructible vocabulary shared with Lenca, suggesting a much earlier proto-community that bridged, or was central to, this area. By Contact times, Xinca and Lenca communities had long been separate and distinct, cut off from one another by Mayan immigrations.

Lenca

At Contact, Lenca was found in Honduras and in eastern El Salvador. Lenca speakers, along with Xinca, settled in this area early in Mesoamerican prehistory. Lenca territory was isolated from Xinca lands by Mayan incursions. Later, pockets of Nahuat-Pipil speakers moved into the western fringes of Lenca territory. By Contact times, the Lenca communities had contracted to northern and central Honduras. Subsequent immigrations of Caribs and Miskitos cut the Lenca off from the coast. Today the remaining isolated communities are rapidly becoming monolingual in Spanish.

Chibchan

Most Chibchan languages are in South America. Paya, the Chibchan language found in Honduras, seems to have moved north along with a cluster of language groups who settled out in Nicaragua and Costa Rica: the Rama, Guaturo, Bribri, Cabecar, Boruca, Tiribí, Guaymí-Movere, Bocotá, Dorasque, and Kuna. The Paya, however, have loan words that are reconstructible to Proto-Mixe-Zoque; these, if borrowed at the time of the existence of that community, would place Paya in Mesoamerica from around 1200 B.C. It is possible that these words were borrowed later, from the Maya or from other Olmec heirs. In this case, contact presumably dates to the apogee of the Maya expansion southward, 1000–200 B.C. At the time of Spanish contact, Chibchan languages alternated in pockets with Misumalpan throughout southern Central America.

Misumalpan

Misumalapan languages today are fairly isolated within Nicaragua. Their internal lexical diversity suggests a time depth for separation of about 3,700 years. They may have been in place since 1700 B.C. Misumalpan communities were later separated by Chibchan immigrations. Matagalpa, the northernmost outlier, once extended into Honduras and El Salvador. At Contact, there were still Matagalpan communities bordering Pipil settlements. Cacaopera, which is in the northwestern part of Misumalpan territory, also reached El Salvador, where it survived until the early twentieth century. The Sumo occupied the eastern interior of northern Nicaragua and parts of Costa Rica. Misumalpan peoples of the northern and eastern coastal areas, especially the Miskito, had heavy post-Contact interaction with pirates and displaced African populations.

Conclusion

Central America, especially the northern area of culturally denominated Mesoamerica, was densely populated at the time of Contact, though generally less so than would have been the case in the tenth century A.D. The highland areas saw uninterrupted habitation, interspersed with both economic and administrative centers. The eastern lowlands of the Gulf Coast through northern Honduras were organized in contiguous spheres of economic and political influence. The Pacific coast, though fairly densely populated in Mexico, was less developed from Guatemala south. Some areas had organized redistribution and ceremonial centers, which interacted with highland areas; others seem to have been only seasonally exploited. Commercial, and sometimes marital, ties tightly interwove Mesoamerica. There is evidence for both overland and sea-going (coast-hugging) trade from Maya and Aztec centers south to the Chibchan and Misumalpan areas. The Aztec *pochteca* also may have traveled north into what is now the U.S. Southwest.

The Spaniards found an intricate pattern of political and economic alliances and counteralliances, which they exploited, when possible, in their stepwise military campaigns throughout the zone. The highly organized states of Mesoamerica were generally able to retain some of their social, and even political, structure after Contact. Areas of densest indigenous populations on the modern map generally reflect this pre- and post-colonial autochthonous organization. Areas in which social organization was simpler, based on small family units with nomadic or semi-sedentary horticultural bases, withstood the onslaught of europeanization much less successfully.

FURTHER READINGS

Campbell, L. 1985. *The Pipil Language of El Salvador.* New York: Mouton.

Campbell, L., and T. Kaufman. 1976. A Linguistic Look at the Olmecs. *American Antiquity* 41:80–89.

Greenberg, J. 1987. *Language in the Americas.* Stanford: Stanford University Press.

Ligorred, F. 1992. *Lenguas indígenas de México y Centroamérica (de los jeroglíficos al siglo XXI).* Madrid: Mapfre.

Suárez, J. A. 1983. *The Mesoamerican Indian Languages.* Cambridge: Cambridge University Press.

Swadesh, M. 1959. *Mapas de clasificación lingüística de México y las Américas.* Cuadernos del Instituto de Historia, Serie Antropológica, 8. Mexico City: Universidad Nacional Autónoma de México.

Judith M. Maxwell

SEE ALSO

Ethnohistorical Sources and Methods; Interregional Interactions

L

Lapidary Industry

Mesoamerica has a rich tradition of lapidary production going back at least to the Early Formative period. Lapidary items were produced from a broad range of raw materials; some of them were exotic, such as jadeite and marine shell, often obtained from distant sources. The lapidary industry produced a distinct inventory of both prestige and utilitarian artifacts. These were used for personal ornament and jewelry, ritual display, ritual offerings including caches and burials, political gifts, and social prestation (gift, offering). Many lapidary products represented "social currency," made out of expensive exotic materials such as marine shell, turquoise, jadeite, and other greenstones, worn as insignia of high status and social position, and used as offerings and burial furniture. However, many other lapidary artifacts were produced from less valuable materials such as slate and fuchsite. The relative value of these artifacts can be determined by the frequency with which we find their materials and the contexts in which they are found. For example, at Classic period Teotihuacan, in the lower-class apartment compound Tlajinga 33, identical lapidary items were made from a number of different media: jadeite/greenstone and marine shell were the rarest, while slate was the most common.

Lapidary production techniques are well documented for the historic Aztec by Sahagún in the *Florentine Codex*. He describes the use of the string saw and hollow reed and bone drill for working the material. A series of grit slurries of increasing fineness facilitated grinding; the final polishing was done with a cane burnisher. These techniques seem to have been in use in the Classic period as well, but at shell workshops from the Oaxaca area, chert microdrills seem to have been used for perforation. No such tools have been reported for lapidary workshops from the Classic period workshops at Teotihuacan or those of the Classic Maya.

Within ancient Mesoamerica, lapidary production and use operated within distinct social and economic contexts. During the Formative period and in many Classic contexts, particularly among the Classic Maya, lapidary production was conducted by elites for elite use. At Copán (Honduras), one elite residential compound with a population of about 250 people had a number of lapidary workshops in one patio. Three of these workshops contained in situ evidence of media such as marine shell, schist, and greenstone. In addition, tools such as sharpening stones and a stone working surface were found in situ on benches and floors of these rooms. Debris from lapidary production was found in the sheet middens directly in front of these rooms. All three rooms are typical high-status elite domiciles with interior benches characteristic of other residences, and one even has a vaulted stone roof, indicating an expensive building and high social status of its occupants. This implies that lapidary production was associated with domestic activities in elite contexts, and that elites were producing lapidary items in their own residences as part of their everyday domestic activities. The lack of differentiation of space or location for lapidary manufacturing, and the direct in situ evidence in the form of unfinished and worked lapidary items and tools, indicate that lapidary activity took place on the benches that also served as sleeping places. The two adjacent lapidary workshops were very different, lacking benches and having restricted access to their interiors. Under one was a subfloor burial chamber that contained five elite burials with lapidary raw materials, including greenstone and shell; the skeletons exhibited cranial deformation characteristic of Maya elites. The direct association and spatial link of the burial features with lapidary production implies that the ancestors in the tomb, as members of the supernatural realm, in some way sanctified or ritually charged these artifacts during their production because they would ultimately have a sacred function.

The highest expression of high-status sumptuary lapidary production occurred among the Late Postclassic period Aztec. The most spectacular collection of lapidary items was found as offerings in the Templo Mayor pyramid complex of Tenochtitlan. Not only were lapidary items produced locally out of exotic precious material, such as jadeite and *Spondylus* shell, but many of the offerings were tribute or gift items made by lapidary artisans in outlying provinces of the Aztec Empire. Thus, we see another level of elite sumptuary lapidary activity: as production for meeting tribute requirements of the Aztec emperor.

FURTHER READINGS

Boone, E. H. (ed.). 1983. *The Aztec Templo Mayor.* Washington, D.C.: Dumbarton Oaks.

Sahagún, B. de. 1959. *Florentine Codex, Book 9—The Merchants.* C. E. Dibble and A. J. O. Anderson (trans. and ed.). Monographs of the School of American Research and the Museum of Mexico, 14, part 10. Santa Fe: School of American Research.

Turner, M. H. 1992. Style in Lapidary Technology: Identifying the Teotihuacan Lapidary Industry. In J. C. Berlo (ed.), *Art, Ideology, and City of Teotihuacan*, pp. 89–112. Washington, D.C.: Dumbarton Oaks.

Widmer, R. J. 1991. Lapidary Craft Specialization at Teotihuacan: Implications for Community Structure at 33:S3W1 and Economic Organization in the City. *Ancient Mesoamerica* 2:131–147.

Randolph Widmer

SEE ALSO
Jade

Leadership and Rulership

Leaders existed in Mesoamerica's earliest villages, but it is difficult to say much about them because they are usually only known from their graves (1500–1200 B.C.). Based on modern studies of various "tribal societies," we might suggest that these early Mesoamerican leaders emerged because of their personal qualities, such as charisma, honesty, speaking ability, hunting prowess, or military skills. While a son might inherit some of his father's personal qualities, there was no mechanism that guaranteed that a son would follow his father in the post of community leader. Instead, each man in turn had to achieve his own prestige and respect. The post of community leader was not inherited.

By 1200–1000 B.C., some Mesoamerican infant burials display artificially deformed skulls and special grave offerings (jade beads and pendants, magnetite mirrors, and pottery vessels incised with the depiction of the supernatural being Lightning). From such data one could infer that these infants were born into high-ranking lineages, because they were far too young to have achieved anything.

With the emergence of chiefdoms in Mesoamerica, depictions of leaders began. In some chiefdoms, colossal heads or other kinds of monumental stone sculpture were carved (e.g., on Mexico's Gulf Lowlands at sites such as San Lorenzo Tenochtitlan and La Venta). In other chiefdoms, depictions of hundreds of slain captives proved their chief's proclaimed powers (e.g., in the Valley of Oaxaca, at San José Mogote, and at Monte Albán). By 600–500 B.C., chiefly societies such as the Zapotec in the Valley of Oaxaca provided the names of elite captives taken in raids; in doing so they developed the first hieroglyphic writing known from Mesoamerica.

Although chiefs in Mesoamerica used their labor forces to create monumental stone heads, sculptural galleries of slain captives, and defensive structures, Mesoamerican kings used their workers to construct elaborate palaces, roads and causeways, and a series of distinct, standardized government buildings that probably witnessed activities performed by different kinds of specialized personnel. Both chiefs and kings linked themselves to the supernatural, to deceased ancestors, and to military feats, but it is clear that kings during the Classic period (A.D. 250–900) had more institutionalized powers. Kings were able to commission monuments that commemorated events in their personal lives—their births, marriages, inaugurations, and deaths. Mesoamerican rulers could, and did, commission stone monuments (with scenes and associated hieroglyphic texts) to put themselves in the best possible light. Such monuments were erected by rulers in their efforts to legitimize themselves and to ward off competition from other claimants to the throne.

In Mesoamerica, the depiction of a person seated on a woven mat or on a jaguar pelt symbolized occupying a seat of authority. For example, among the Aztec, rulers are shown seated on woven-reed, high-backed seats or thrones. The Nahuatl expression *in petlatl, in icpalli* ("the mat, the seat/throne") was used as a metaphor for "rulership." The Aztec ruler was referred to as "he who is on top of the mats," and their expression for "to govern" meant "on top of the mats." Similarly, among the Maya, the ruler was said to be seated on *(cumaan)* the jaguar-mat *(ix pop ti balam)* when he was inaugurated and held office. Other metaphors for the Aztec ruler were *iyollo altepetl,* "the heart of the city"; *tlazotli,* "precious one"; and *in ahuehuetl, in pochotla,* "bald cypress tree, silk cotton tree," comparing the ruler to two huge trees that could create enough shade to protect all his people.

FURTHER READINGS
Marcus, J. 1992. *Mesoamerican Writing Systems.* Princeton: Princeton University Press.
Sullivan, T. D. Tlatoani and Tlatocayotl in the Sahagún Manuscripts. *Estudios de Cultura Nahuatl* 14 (1980): 225–238.

Joyce Marcus

SEE ALSO
Names and Titles

León Viejo (León, Nicaragua)

This was the first Spanish capital of Nicaragua, settled in 1524 by Francisco Hernandez de Cordoba on the northwestern shore of Lake Managua in the shadow of Volcán Momotombo. The Spaniards chose the location in part because of the native population, living in surrounding villages, who could provide labor to build the capital.

L

Although no known Spanish plan or maps exist of León Viejo, archaeological work demonstrates that it was a small but typical early Spanish colonial town laid out on a grid system. Spanish buildings, both public and private, were of thick double-sided brick walls with mud fill. Along the main north–south avenue there are at least two churches and numerous public administrative buildings. The town served as the administrative center of all Spanish activities (taxation, slave records, import/export, *encomiendas*) in Nicaragua until it was abandoned by the Spanish in 1610, most likely because of volcanic activity. At that point León (Nuevo) was established farther to the northeast.

Deborah Erdman-Cornavaca

SEE ALSO
Intermediate Area: Overview

Libertad, La (Chiapas, Mexico)

La Libertad, the largest Middle and Late Formative regional center in the upper Grijalva River Basin, was founded about 750 B.C. and persisted until about 300 B.C. The site lies at the edge of the Cuchumatanes Mountains, only 100 meters from the Mexican border with Guatemala, and occupies a relatively flat peninsula between four rivers, just a kilometer south of the Lagartero lakes. La Libertad was one of a chain of paramount chiefdom centers that were rather evenly spaced along the Grijalva River from La Libertad downstream to Chiapa de Corzo. La Libertad was the southernmost center on the river and appears to have been founded to control trade coming from highland Guatemala into the Chiapas region and then down into the Gulf Coast lowlands. La Libertad's massive architecture covers about 45 hectares and dates to 700 B.C. Like most Chiapas Middle Formative centers, it has an early "C-group" arrangement, here formed by three principal earthen mounds faced with puddled adobe. An elongated cruciform mound more than 100 meters long is flanked on its short axial line by twin pyramids measuring about 20 meters high and 50 meters square at their bases. Elite burials found in the principal pyramids indicate a close relationship to the center of Chiapa de Corzo.

FURTHER READINGS
Clark, J. E. 1988. *The Lithic Artifacts of La Libertad, Chiapas, Mexico.* Papers of the New World Archaeological Foundation, 52. Provo, Utah.

John E. Clark

SEE ALSO
Chiapas Interior Plateau

Lightning and Thunder

Lightning was perhaps the most powerful supernatural being and force for many ancient groups of Mesoamerica. The Maya called it *chac*. The Zapotec called the lightning bolt *cociyo*, while thunder was called *xoo cociyo*, "the motion, or earthquake, of lightning."

Why did lightning achieve this prominent position? One answer is that it was one of the most dramatic sights the ancient populations saw. Another is that lightning seemed to have the power to pierce clouds and send rain to earth, where humans could use it and manipulate it through hydrology.

Many sixteenth-century documents supply information on the kinds of offerings made to lightning, either in gratitude or to petition it to split the clouds to release rain. Offerings include one's own blood (autosacrifice), as well as sacrificed quail, turkey, dog, human infants, and captives.

FURTHER READINGS
Marcus, J. 1978. Archaeology and Religion: A Comparison of the Zapotec and Maya. *World Archaeology* 10:172–191.

———. 1983. Zapotec Religion. In K. V. Flannery and J. Marcus (eds.), *The Cloud People*, pp. 345–351. New York: Academic Press.

Joyce Marcus

SEE ALSO
Blood and Bloodletting

Lime and Limestone

These widespread minerals had many uses in ancient Mesoamerica. Limestone was a primary material for stone masonry in elite architecture. Lime wash and lime plaster (stucco) were used on buildings and artifacts to protect surfaces and prime them for painting—on walls and floors in elite and commoner structures, stelae, ceramic figures, and paper for writing. Nutritionally, the addition of limestone to the soaking water of dried maize (a process called "nixtamalization") provided calcium in a diet otherwise deficient in it.

Limestone, a sedimentary rock of high solubility and workability, dominates the surface geology of the Yucatán

Peninsula and the eastern portion of northern Mexico, and is distributed throughout the highlands of southern Mexico, central Guatemala, and western Honduras. Limestone was easily quarried in large blocks (sometimes these were columnar blocks to be carved as stelae), either by prying the stone loose with a hardwood bar from a hillside quarry or by cutting the blocks directly from a subsurface quarry. These blocks were then transported to building sites by human porters.

Limestone blocks were manufactured into masonry quite easily with chert tools, because freshly quarried limestone is relatively soft, only assuming considerable strength and durability after exposure to the elements. The use of limestone masonry correlates well with its natural distribution and relative ease of access; thus, it was used in elite architecture more widely in the Maya region than in other parts of Mesoamerica, such as the Gulf Lowlands.

Lime plaster was produced from limestone (calcium carbonate) by calcining (burning) the stone in pit ovens, open-air kilns, and walled kilns. The burning process releases carbon dioxide from the calcium carbonate, but subsequent absorption of oxygen and water turn the burned limestone back into calcium carbonate. The addition of an aggregate (often *sascab,* or naturally decomposed limestone) completes the process of manufacturing lime plaster. In effect, the process reshapes quarried limestone into smooth layers of limestone contoured to the form of the building. Lime plaster was produced by part-time lime plaster makers who, at other times of the year, were farmer-artisans. A thin plaster wash, a combination of crushed limestone (or *sascab*) and water, coated the surfaces of vernacular architecture, but preservation of lime wash is poorer than that of lime plaster. Under normal archaeological conditions, chunks of lime plaster are recoverable, preserved in part by the collapsed stones fallen from the elite structure on which the lime plaster was set.

The clearing of trees for fuelwood in plaster manufacture contributed to some degree to the deforestation that periodically undermined the economy of ancient societies; however, its role in deforestation was secondary to that of tree-clearing for agricultural and domestic needs.

FURTHER READINGS

Abrams, E. M. 1994. *How the Maya Built Their World: Energetics and Ancient Architecture.* Austin: University of Texas Press.

———. 1996. The Evolution of Plaster Production and the Growth of the Copan Maya State. In A. Guadalupe M. et al. (eds.), *Arqueología mesoamericana: Homenaje a William T. Sanders,* vol. 2, pp. 193–208. Mexico City: Instituto Nacional de Antropología e Historia.

Abrams, E., and A. Freter. 1996. A Late Classic Lime-Plaster Kiln from the Maya Centre of Copan, Honduras. *Antiquity* 70:422–428.

Littmann, E. 1962. Ancient Mesoamerican Mortars, Plasters, and Stuccos: Floor Constructions at Uaxactun. *American Antiquity* 28:100–103.

West, R. 1964. Surface Configuration and Associated Geology of Middle America. In R. Wauchope (ed.), *Handbook of Middle American Indians,* vol. 1, pp. 33–83. Austin: University of Texas Press.

Elliot M. Abrams

SEE ALSO

Minerals, Ores, and Mining

Llano de Jícaro
See Laguna de los Cerros

Llano Perdido
See Coyotera, La

Loma San Gabriel
See Northwestern Frontier

Loma Torremote (México, Mexico)

This large Formative period village is situated in the Cuautitlán region of the Basin of Mexico. Although the site was occupied throughout the period, its most substantial occupation dates to the early part of the Late Formative (650–550 B.C.). Occupation at Loma Torremote was highly nucleated, with most of its population living in small residential units adjacent to one another.

Several levels of settlement are represented at Loma Torremote. The most fundamental is the house compound: a residential unit consisting of one or more wattle-and-daub earthen-floored structures, a series of extramural activity areas, bell-shaped pits, and in some cases a small garden, all enclosed by an adobe wall. Individual compounds group into clusters of four to six of these residential units, which are separated from one

L

another by vacant areas free of domestic occupation. Compound clusters in turn may be grouped into neighborhoods.

Different compounds within each cluster were hierarchically organized and economically differentiated. Each cluster contains a residence that was significantly larger in size and occupied by a household of higher status. This compound also performed a number of specialized functions, including obsidian blade production, centralized storage, and ritual. The presence of domestic refuse in most compounds indicates that each was occupied by a household of some sort, probably a nuclear or an extended family. Clusters were probably occupied by domestic groups, which were incipiently stratified above one another based on the patron-client relationship. Whether stratification was also present on the neighborhood level is unknown.

FURTHER READINGS

Sanders, W. T., J. R. Parsons, and R. S. Santley. 1979. *The Basin of Mexico: Ecological Processes in the Evolution of a Civilization.* New York: Academic Press.

Santley, R. S. 1993. Late Formative Society at Loma Torremote: A Consideration of the Redistribution versus the Great Provider Models as a Basis for the Emergence of Complexity in the Basin of Mexico. In R. S. Santley and K. G. Hirth (eds.), *Prehispanic Domestic Units in Western Mesoamerica: Studies of the Household, Compound, and Residence,* pp. 67–86. Boca Raton, Fla.: CRC Press.

Robert S. Santley

SEE ALSO

Basin of Mexico; Formative Period

Los Angeles (Rivas, Nicaragua)

Occupation at this Greater Nicoya site spans the period from 2000 B.C. to A.D. 1520. Its most important features include Nicaragua's earliest known ceramics (from the site's earliest phase, Dinarte, 2000–500 B.C.) and, from the Gato phase (A.D. 1000–1200), the largest human skeletal collection yet excavated in Nicaragua. Los Angeles is an open site, with various levels separated by layers of volcanic tephra. Subsistence was mixed: fishing, collecting, and some cultivation. Artifacts include ceramics, lithics, bone implements, and portable stone sculpture. Some of the fifty-nine skeletons exhibit cranial deforma-

tion and dental mutilation. Grave goods were limited, but "extra" mandibles were placed with one of the burials.

FURTHER READINGS

Fleischhacker, H. 1972. Praekolumbische skelettfunde von der Ometepe-Insel im Nicaragua-See. *Verhandlungen des XXXVIII Internationalen Amerikanistenkongresses* 4:401–414. Munich: Klaus Renner.

Haberland, Wolfgang. 1992. The Culture History of Ometepe Island. In F. W. Lange et al. (eds.), *The Archaeology of Pacific Nicaragua,* pp. 63–117. Albuquerque: University of New Mexico Press.

Frederick W. Lange

SEE ALSO

Intermediate Area: Overview

Lothrop, Samuel K. (1892–1965)

In Gordon R. Willey's words, Samuel K. Lothrop was "a gentleman, a scholar, and an absolutely first-rate archaeologist" (1988:216). His pre-World War II legacy in Central American archaeology is unparalleled, partially because, almost from the beginning, he forged a bond between archaeology and pre-Columbian art history. In Central America, he began with the still frequently cited *Pottery of Costa Rica and Nicaragua* (1926). He went on to Cocle and other famous sites in Panama, and also worked in El Salvador. Although he never held a formal teaching position, he left a direct imprint on a whole generation of archaeologists with his wide-ranging interests, and an indirect but still strong imprint on succeeding generations.

FURTHER READINGS

Lothrop, S. K. 1924. *Tulum: An Archaeological Study of the East Coast of Yucatán.* Carnegie Institution of Washington, Publication 335. Washington, D.C.

———. 1952. *Metals from the Cenote of Sacrifice, Chichén Itzá, Yucatán.* Memoirs of the Peabody Museum of Archaeology and Ethnology, 4.2. Cambridge, Mass.: Harvard University.

——— (ed.). 1961. *Essays in Pre-Columbian Art and Archaeology.* Cambridge, Mass.: Harvard University Press.

Willey, Gordon R. 1988. *Portraits in American Archaeology.* Albuquerque: University of New Mexico Press.

Frederick W. Lange

Lubaantún (Toledo, Belize)

This major Maya ceremonial center was occupied for only a short period of time, between A.D. 700 and 850, in the Late Classic period. Its occupation was perhaps the result of a single migration episode into the Río Grande basin by groups that may have originated at Pusilhá (although Early Classic occupation is known at Uxbenká, a few miles west of Lubaantún).

The site lies in the low foothills that rise from the coastal plain to the Maya Mountains, at a natural crossroads along the foothills and upriver, with access to mineral resources such as quartz, building stone, and chert from the upper hills, to staple crops from the lower foothills, and to marine resources from the coast. Several areas around Lubaantún were ideal for the cultivation of cacao.

The ceremonial complex was built in five successive phases over a period of 120 to 150 years. Arranged around the complex's sixteen plazas are religious, administrative, and residential buildings in a pattern of progressively secluded enclosures from the north toward the south end of the ridge. The most peripheral and most secluded spaces are plazas II and III at the southern tip of the ridge, where residential buildings and a ball court are situated. It thus appears that the ball game was played in an area secluded from the rest of the site and accessible only through the religious core, under the exclusive supervision of the elite who lived within the ceremonial complex, until a second court was built late in the site's history. Imported artifacts demonstrate the site's long-distance trade links with the central Petén, the Guatemala highlands, and northern Yucatán.

FURTHER READINGS

Hammond, N. 1975. *Lubaantún: A Classic Maya Realm.* Peabody Museum of Archaeology and Ethnology, Monograph 2. Cambridge, Mass.: Harvard University.

Francisco Estrada Belli

SEE ALSO

Maya Lowlands: South

M

Machomoncobe (Sonora, Mexico)

A coastal site of the Huatabampo Culture, occupied c. 17 B.C.–A.D. 1004, near the modern city of Huatabampo in southern Sonora, on the coastal plain about seven kilometers from the Gulf of California. The subsistence base at the site included a mixture of agricultural plants (maize and beans), wild terrestrial foods, and marine resources. The site's occupants built *jacals* (houses of perishable materials) along the river. They made a redware pottery, ceramic beads, and female ceramic figurines with "tattooed" faces.

People at Machomoncobe specialized in the exploitation and working of marine shell and produced large quantities of shell jewelry, including pendants, bracelets, and beads. The site was a node supplying shell to a coastal trade network that linked western Mexico with the southwestern United States. Excavators in 1979 encountered a secondary inhumation, a dog burial, and several presumed offerings of ceramics, turquoise, and shell ornaments. These offerings resemble those found at Chametla and Amapa. Prismatic green obsidian blades found in some of the offerings probably originated from Jalisco, and the turquoise most likely came from New Mexico. There is evidence at the site for social ranking, as well as craft specialization, particularly in shell-working. Catastrophic flooding probably caused the abandonment of the area, and the population appears to have shifted south to the area of Gusave in Sinaloa.

FURTHER READINGS

Alvarez, A. M. 1982. Archaeological Investigations at Huatabampo. In P. H. Beckett (ed.), *Mogollon Archaeology*, pp. 239–250. Ramona, Calif.: Acoma Books.

———. 1990. Huatabampo: Consideraciones sobre una comunidad agricola prehispánica en el Sur de Sonora. *Noroeste de México* 9:9–93.

Ana María Alvarez P.

SEE ALSO

Northern Arid Zone

Maize

Maize (*Zea mays* L.) is a member of the Gramineae (grass) family and belongs to the tribe Maydeae. It was domesticated in Mexico, probably between 7,000 and 5,000 years ago, and spread to Central, South and North America over the ensuing millennia. By the time Native American and European cultures came into contact, maize provided a significant portion of the subsistence base of most sedentary New World populations, supplemented by locally available traditional crops. The diversification of maize into numerous land races is a testimony to its successful expansion into diverse human ecosystems, ranging from lowland tropics to temperate highland zones.

The origin of maize has been the subject of controversy for more than a century. Many aspects of the current views concerning its development were established during the 1930s. Two main positions developed concerning the origin of maize. The first, attributed to P. C. Mangelsdorf, postulated that domesticated maize was derived by selection from an extinct wild pod popcorn, with small, hard kernels enclosed in glumes. The second, and generally accepted, position holds that maize evolved from teosinte (*Zea mexicana*), its nearest wild relative. Recent research has been directed toward determining how this process

M

occurred and what races or species of teosinte were involved. In contrast, Mangelsdorf considered teosinte to be a product of the hybridization of wild maize with *Tripsacum,* a wild grass of the Andropogoneae tribe.

Several species and races of teosinte are distributed in Mexico and Guatemala. Both annual and perennial forms occur, and their morphological characteristics are susceptible to variation depending on growth conditions, making their identification difficult. Although earlier investigators observed morphological similarities between maize and the Chalco race of teosinte (*Z. mexicana* subsp. *mexicana*), recent molecular evidence supports the position that the annual teosinte, *Z. mays* subsp. *parviglumis,* is most similar to the domestic plant. The modern distribution of this species is concentrated in a limited area of the Balsas River drainage that includes northern Guerrero, eastern Michoacán, and western México. Introgression between these species as a cause of their similarity is rejected because hybrids rarely occur, owing to the fact that the wild species does not generally grow near cornfields. The close morphological similarity between Chalco teosinte and maize, on the other hand, is now considered to be the result of the convergence of vegetative characters as a consequence of adaptation to the same ecological conditions in certain areas. Molecular evidence suggests that they are not in fact as similar as they may appear, nor do they undergo constant gene exchange despite their common occurrence in the same habitat in some areas. The limited degree of introgression of Chalco teosinte into maize that is evident, however, may have played a role in helping the domesticate to adapt to higher elevations.

In spite of considerable evidence to the contrary, Mangelsdorf maintained his position that domesticated maize evolved from an extinct wild form. He did, however, modify his view about the role of teosinte and later suggested that *Z. diploperennis* (a perennial teosinte distributed in the Balsas region) hybridized with maize to produce the earliest domesticated form.

The development of the characteristic maize ear has also been the subject of ongoing research, and again two principal positions have developed, both of which assume that teosinte is the ancestor of maize. Galinat holds that the maize ear developed directly from the teosinte ear; whereas Iltis argues that the central spike of the teosinte tassel positioned at the tip of a lateral branch transformed into the maize ear by means of a process called "sexual transmutation." Such sexual reversals may be induced by environmental effects, such as light intensity and duration or temperature decrease.

Efforts to classify races of maize and to develop models of phylogenetic relationships, based largely on morphological characters of the ears, received much attention during the 1950s and 1960s. The most influential classification postulated phylogenetic relationships based essentially on external ear characteristics such as size; row number; and kernel shape, size, and color, most of which were affected by cultural selection based on the preferences of human populations.

Racial diversification of maize took place in different ecological zones in Mexico, and later throughout North and South America. Genetic variation in maize has been shown to be closely correlated with ecological factors related to altitude, such as length of the growing season and temperature and moisture regimes that limit gene flow between races adapted to different conditions. Recent efforts to classify Mexican maize consider biochemical evidence, and the results contrast sharply with earlier schemes. Mexican maize is generally classified into three broad groups: the so-called Pyramidal races, adapted to higher elevation zones, largely in Central Mexico; the northern and northwestern races; and low-elevation dent and flour races found in southern and western Mexico.

Races of maize from Guatemala form two distinct groups based on their adaptation to highland or lowland ecological zones. The race known as Nal-Tel has been recognized in both contexts, in Mexico as well as Guatemala. Mangelsdorf suggested that this race may originally have had a prehistoric distribution so broad as to cover most of Mexico. However, recent evidence indicates that the highland and lowland types reported in Guatemala are in fact separate races, the populations of which developed similar ear morphology as a result of convergent evolution. Biochemical evidence suggests that the highland Guatemalan Nal-Tels share some similarity with Mexican highland races of maize.

The preservation of archaeological maize specimens varies greatly, and it is often difficult to recognize characters that permit racial identification. This is particularly true in the case of fragmentary, charred remains. In Mexico, archaeological remains of maize were extremely well preserved in dry caves in two of the regions excavated by R. S. MacNeish—Tamaulipas and the Tehuacan Valley (Puebla). Mangelsdorf's position concerning the origin of maize had a strong impact on the identification and classification of Mesoamerican archaeological specimens. Some of the specimens of early maize recovered from caves in the Tehuacan region were identified by him as "wild" maize, whereas others were judged to reflect the sequence of evolution under domestication. Dates from charcoal associated with the archaeological deposits provided the basis for a chronological framework within which maize domestication was believed to have taken place, in relation to socio-cultural development and subsistence changes manifest in the transition of mobile hunter-gatherers into semisedentary and later fully sedentary agricultural village communities.

Archaeological evidence for teosinte is currently insufficient to contribute additional information to the study of the origin of maize. Macrobotanical archaeological remains of teosinte have been reported only from Valenzuelas's Cave in the Ocampo region of southwestern Tamaulipas, in a San José phase context at Fábrica San José in the Valley of Oaxaca (c. 1150–850 B.C.), and from Tlapacoya in the southern Basin of Mexico (c. 5000 B.C.). Mangelsdorf interpreted the absence of archaeological remains of teosinte as evidence that it had developed following the advent of domesticated maize; however, more probable explanations include poor preservation and the relative absence in the archaeological record of preceramic sites that correspond to the period during which maize developed.

Based on established chronology, maize in Mesoamerica appears to be earliest in the Tehuacan region between 5000 and 2500 B.C. (Coxcatlan phase) and, possibly, in the Basin of Mexico. It is present in somewhat later contexts in the Valley of Oaxaca (3295 B.C.). Expansion to the north is evident from its appearance in south central Tamaulipas (3000–2200 B.C.) and southwestern Tamaulipas (2200–1800 B.C.). To the south, the earliest maize reported to date on the Gulf Coast at La Venta corresponds to about 2250–1750 B.C., and on the southwestern Pacific Coast to around 1550–1400 B.C. MacNeish and Peterson cite maize pollen from Santa Marta Cave in Chiapas dated to around 2500 B.C., although no macrobotanical specimens were recovered.

In the lowland Maya region, macrobotanical remains of maize were recovered from Cuello in northern Belize, dated by the Accelerator Mass Spectrometry (AMS) technique to 920–770 B.C.; these specimens had originally been reported as dating to 2500–2400 B.C. Maize pollen in the Yojoa region of Honduras is interpreted to indicate possible slash and burn agriculture after approximately 2500 B.C. Maize pollen and phytoliths are reported from Panama corresponding to contexts dated to 3000–2500 B.C., although macrobotanical remains do not appear until around 15 B.C.

Other early maize specimens have been reexamined in light of the recent theoretical perspectives referred to above, using more effective measurement techniques that consider additional morphological characteristics of the cobs, as well as direct AMS dating of the specimens. The new dates indicate that the specimens originally associated with the Coxcatlan and Abejas phases in the Tehuacan region (c. 5000–2300 B.C.) are more recent by approximately 1,500–2,000 years. Also, careful analysis of the cobs revealed that the so-called wild maize was in fact fully domesticated. Recent AMS dating of cobs from the Ocampo region in the Sierra Madre mountains of Tamaulipas suggests that maize appeared in this area around 2500 B.C. Similar results have recently been obtained from direct AMS dating of archaeological specimens of beans and squash from these and other areas in Mesoamerica.

The recovery of archaeological remains of maize, particularly macrobotanical specimens from well-defined contexts that can now be dated directly, is a fundamental part of excavation. More reliably dated archaeological plant remains will permit a better understanding of how maize developed, diversified, and spread throughout the Americas and how it came to be incorporated into established subsistence patterns.

FURTHER READINGS

Beadle, G. W. 1977. The Origin of *Zea mays*. In C. Reed (ed.), *Origins of Agriculture*, pp. 615–635. The Hague: Mouton.

Benz, B. F., and H. H. Iltis. 1990. Studies in Archaeological Maize, I: The Wild Maize from San Marcos Cave Reexamined. *American Antiquity* 55:500–511.

———, ———. 1992. Evolution of Female Sexuality in the Maize Ear (*Zea mays* L. subsp. *mays*–Gramineae). *Economic Botany* 46:212–222.

Doebley, J. 1990. Molecular Evidence and the Evolution of Maize. *Economic Botany* 44(3S):6–27.

Galinat, W. C. 1971. The Origin of Maize. *Annual Review of Genetics* 5:447–478.

Long, A., B. F. Benz, D. J. Donahue, A. J. T. Jull, and L. J. Toolin. 1989. First Direct AMS Dates on Early Maize from Tehuacan, Mexico. *Radiocarbon* 31:1035–1040.

Mangelsdorf, P. C. 1974. *Corn: Its Origin, Evolution and Improvement.* Cambridge, Mass.: Belknap Press, Harvard University.

———. 1986. The Origin of Corn. *Scientific American* 254:80–86.

M

Mangelsdorf, P. C., R. S. MacNeish, and W. C. Galinat. 1967a. Prehistoric Maize, Teosinte and Tripsacum from Tamaulipas, Mexico. *Botanical Museum Leaflets* 22:33–63. Cambridge, Mass.: Harvard University.

———, ———, ———. 1967b. Prehistoric Wild and Cultivated "Maize." In D. S. Byers (ed.), *The Prehistory of the Tehuacan Valley,* vol. 1, *Environment and Subsistence,* pp. 178–200. Austin: University of Texas Press.

Wellhausen, E. J., L. M. Roberts, and E. Hernández X., with P. C. Mangelsdorf. 1952. *Races of Maize in Mexico.* Cambridge, Mass.: Bussey Institution of Harvard University.

Wilkes, H. G. 1972. Maize and Its Wild Relatives. *Science* 177:1071–1077.

Emily McClung Heumann de Tapia

SEE ALSO

Agave; Agriculture and Domestication; Diet and Nutrition; Food and Cuisine; Maize

Malinalco (México, Mexico)

The Malinalco rock-cut temple forms part of a Mexica Aztec ritual and administrative center begun at the Matlazinca town of Malinalco around A.D. 1495–1501. The buildings overlook a mountain valley 75 kilometers southwest of Mexico City. The entrance to the rock-cut temple is framed by the relief sculpture of a frontal serpentlike visage, whose forked tongue forms the threshold. The image is a hieroglyphic sign for *oztotl* ("cave"). Within the circular chamber, feline and eagle pelts are carved three-dimensionally on a semicircular stone bench

Interior view of the Malinalco rock-cut temple. Illustration courtesy of Richard F. Townsend.

and the floor below. A small, circular orifice in the floor functioned as a sacrificial receptacle.

In Mesoamerica, caves were places of ritual communion with the Earth's interior. The Malinalco cave-temple was a place of transition between levels of the universe, functioning as a place of remembrance and communion among the living, the ancestors, and the sources of the earth's fertility. Specific functions are also indicated by the eagle and feline seats, which are emblems of ranked Aztec military officers in the provincial government at Malinalco. Such structure is also expressed in the imperial government capitol at Tenochtitlan. The circular receptacle for blood offerings was used by the rulers in rites of taking office. On the highest level, such offerings were made at the Yopico earth temple in Tenochtitlan by the supreme Aztec ruler as the final act of kingship rites. In this respect, the Malinalco rock-cut temple is a variant of Yopico. Such rites also signify appropriation, and the Malinalco temple thus symbolically affirmed imperial possession of the land. Excavations were carried out in the 1930s by Federico Garcia Payón.

FURTHER READINGS

Townsend, R. F. 1982. Malinalco and the Lords of Tenochtitlan. In E. H. Boone (ed.), *The Art and Iconography of Late Post-Classic Central Mexico,* pp. 111–140. Washington, D.C.: Dumbarton Oaks.

Richard F. Townsend

SEE ALSO

Aztec Culture and History; Militarism and Conflict; Tenochtitlán: Ceremonial Center; Tenochtitlán: Imperial Ritual Landscape; Tenochtitlán: Palaces; Tenochtitlán-Tlatelolco

Manatí, El (Veracruz, Mexico)

Between about 1600 and 1200 B.C., the freshwater spring at El Manatí was the site of rituals and offerings. The wetness of the site has resulted in exceptional preservation of a variety of materials, including wooden sculptures, rubber balls, and remains of burials of infants, as well as finely worked stone celts and stone sculptures. The site's excavators, Ponciano Ortiz and María del Carmen Rodríguez, believe that the springs were a focal point of religious activity for Early Formative communities in the area.

Susan Toby Evans

SEE ALSO

Gulf Lowlands: South Region

Maps and Place-Names

Maps—graphic records of space—were made throughout Mesoamerica, probably from the time of the earliest complex societies. Most surviving examples, however, date to the fifteenth and sixteenth centuries; these and other written works employ pictorial images, logographs, and abstract signs. The most common type of pre-Hispanic map, as far as we can reconstruct it, was the community map sometimes called a *lienzo* (Spanish, *canvas*), after its medium. Community maps were not planimetric reductions of landscape but rather depicted relative arrangements of logographic place-names and landscape features. Typically, a community map showed the city-state's boundaries, using logographic place-names. These were constructed along the lines of rebus writing. In addition, a historical narrative was often written within the frame of boundaries. This history centered on the migrations of community founders, the battles fought, and the alliances struck in order to cement rights to the territory shown. The Codex Xolotl (c. A.D. 1540) is perhaps the earliest of such community maps known from the Basin of Mexico; the Mapas de Cuauhtinchan 1, 2, and 3 are notable sixteenth-century community maps made near Cholula. Mixtec examples emphasize genealogy, specifically that of each community's ruling family, as seen on the Lienzo of Zacatepec I (A.D. 1540–1560) and the Relación Geográfica map of Teozacoalco (A.D. 1580).

A number of pre-Hispanic-style maps survive from the Aztec heartland, the Basin of Mexico, showing us that complex states like that of the Aztec used a wide variety of maps at all levels of society. Individuals had carefully measured property maps of house lots and gardens. In these, units of measurement include the *quahuitl* (about 2.5 meters) and the *cemmatl* (ranging from 2.5 to 1.77 meters). Community leaders within urban neighborhoods used maps like the Maguey Plan, which depicts a part of Aztec Tenochtitlan, to apportion lands and collect tribute. Towns held cadastral records that included individual maps of each family's plot. Imperial military commanders commissioned maps from Aztec military spies showing layouts of foreign cities to help them in planning battles of conquest.

Mesoamericans also mapped their cosmos, as we see in the Central Mexican Codex Fejervary-Mayer fol. 1 and the Maya Codex Madrid, pages 75–76. The latter is one of the few examples of native-style Maya maps known; post-Conquest Maya maps show the heavy influence of European forms and convention, and other Maya records of territory take the form of alphabetically written records, not pictorial maps.

While the Spanish conquest inexorably changed Mesoamerican culture, native communities continued to make traditional maps to document boundaries and community history; often these maps were accepted as land titles in adjudications overseen by Spaniards. In these late examples, place-names are often written in alphabetic script. Post-Conquest community maps are known from Nahuatl-speaking and Mixtec-speaking communities, as well as from the Otomí, Zapotec, Totonac, Huastec, Chinantec, Cuicatec, and Mazatec.

One notable group of land titles that draw on the tradition of community maps is known as the Techialoyan Documents. Once dismissed as fakes, the Techialoyans were created in the early eighteenth century and were purposefully antiquated to appear to be sixteenth-century land titles. Although community maps have little legal standing today, they are still held by many traditional towns and villages. Often redrawn and reinterpreted, these maps are the present flowering of pre-Conquest traditions.

FURTHER READINGS

Boone, E. H. 1992. Glorious Imperium: Understanding Land and Community in Moctezuma's Mexico. In D. Carrasco and E. Matos Montezuma (eds.), *Moctezuma's Mexico: Visions of the Aztec World*, pp. 159–173. Niwot: University Press of Colorado.

Calnek, E. 1973. The Localization of the 16th-century Map Called the Maguey Plan. *American Antiquity* 38:190–195.

Mundy, B. 1996. *The Mapping of New Spain: Indigenous Cartography and the Maps of the Relaciones Geográficas*. Chicago: University of Chicago Press.

———. 1998. Mesoamerican Cartography. In D. Woodward and G. M. Lewis (eds.), *The History of Cartography*, vol. 2.3, pp. 183–256. Chicago: University of Chicago Press.

Robertson, Donald. 1994. *Mexican Manuscript Painting of the Early Colonial Period: The Metropolitan Schools*. Norman: University of Oklahoma Press.

Smith, M. E. 1973. *Picture Writing from Ancient Southern Mexico: Mixtec Place Signs and Maps*. Norman: University of Oklahoma Press.

Williams, Barbara J. 1984. Mexican Pictoral Cadastral Registers: An Analysis of the Códice de Santa María Asunción and the Codex Vergara. In H. R. Harvey and H. J. Prem (eds.), *Explorations in Ethnohistory: Indians*

M

of Central Mexico in the Sixteenth Century, pp. 103–125. Albuquerque: University of New Mexico Press.

Barbara E. Mundy

Marías, Las (Guanacaste, Costa Rica)

This Greater Nicoya site is on the Bay of Salinas, in a dry, tropical environment on the border between Pacific Nicaragua and Costa Rica. It has an extensive shell midden complex, as well as the most extensive excavation of Ometepe period (A.D. 1350–1520) materials from Greater Nicoya. The span of occupation is c. A.D. 300–1520. The subsistence base was fishing, hunting, collecting marine mollusks, plant gathering, and collecting, with limited agriculture. Economic specializations may have included salt collecting and exporting marine products to interior locations. The architecture and site layout consist of multiple shell middens loosely arranged around informal plazas. Artifacts include ceramics (including White-slipped wares from Pacific Nicaragua), lithics, shell, and archaeofauna; there are some skeletal remains with associated grave goods. Exotic obsidian from southern Honduras (flakes) and Guatemala (mostly blades) indicates contact with these areas. Similar and contemporaneous sites include Chahuite Escondido on the Santa Peninsula, and Vidor on the Bay of Culebra.

FURTHER READINGS

Lange, F. W. 1971. Culture History of the Sapoa River Valley, Costa Rica. *Occasional Papers in Anthropology*, 4. Logan Museum of Anthropology, Beloit College, Wisconsin. Ann Arbor: University Microfilms.

———. 1996. The Bay of Salinas: Cultural Crossroads of Greater Nicoya. In F. W. Lange (ed.), *Paths to Central American Prehistory*, pp. 119–143. Niwot: University of Colorado Press.

Frederick W. Lange

SEE ALSO

Nicoya, Greater, and Guanacaste Region

Market Systems

A flourishing market system was strikingly evident to Spanish eyewitnesses at the Aztec imperial capital, Tenochtitlan, in A.D. 1519. Hernán Cortés wrote, "This city has many squares where trading is done and markets are held continuously. There is also one square twice as big as that of Salamanca [Spain], with arcades all around, where more than sixty thousand people come each day to buy and sell, and where every kind of merchandise produced in these lands is found" (1986:103). A market system links a number of marketplaces into a network or hierarchy. Exchange of goods through market systems is a central characteristic of Mesoamerica's civilizations.

To understand the source of the colorful market system observed in Contact period Mesoamerica, archaeologists have investigated the origins of market systems. One cause cited for the existence of market systems in Mesoamerica is this continent's pronounced ecosystem diversity, which creates differences in the resources and raw materials available to communities. In fact, a market system characterized by village specialization still operates in modern Oaxaca, where each village produces and markets locally made products such as grinding stones (*metates*), blankets, rope, or pottery.

It is believed that market systems in Mesoamerica appeared when agricultural villages began to trade their surplus of raw materials, crafts, or produce for goods originating elsewhere. Early Mesoamerican market systems thus integrated regions characterized by varied resources. An additional contributor to the growth of market systems in ancient Mesoamerica was the emergence of urban centers whose elites demanded or sponsored specialized craft or agricultural production.

Economic anthropologists agree that for market systems to exist, the markets must be regular or predictable. Market systems prosper when distances to markets are manageable, when goods are reasonably priced and of adequate quantity, when the region is politically integrated so that buyers and sellers may move safely to and from the market, and often when professional as well as part-time traders participate. In hierarchically organized market systems, the largest (with the most patrons and traders) and most frequently held markets offer the greatest variety of goods, while smaller, less frequently held markets (sometimes called "periodic markets") offer lesser variety and quantity of products. Communities too small and isolated may be linked to a market system by visits from itinerant traders. The scheduling of markets in prehistoric and nonindustrial societies often parallels other cultural institutions, such as religious festivals or political events. Markets are social gatherings where participants share information, gossip, and meet friends.

Archaeological identification of marketplaces in Mesoamerica is difficult because markets would have been held in plazas that also served other purposes, and goods would have been removed at the close of the market day. Thus, to identify these market systems archaeologists have traced the manufacture and distribution of products, particularly ceramics, that are stylistically distinctive, that are in common use as prestige objects during feasts and other celebrations, and that tend to be preserved over long periods so that archaeologists can collect and study them.

Cycles of market system development have been recognized in several areas of ancient Mesoamerica. The first market system in the Oaxaca Valley emerged about 500 B.C., according to the regional survey reports. At this time, production refuse (failed ceramics, called "kiln wasters") found in some but not all villages and the spatial concentration of ceramic varieties show that ceramics were produced by specialist potters in a few villages. This contrasts with the earlier practice of pottery-making in each village and/or household. The ceramic-producing communities' spacing over the landscape, combined with evidence of distribution of ceramics from the production sites, suggests that a regional market system orchestrated exchange.

In the Basin of Mexico, the Postclassic market system changed from a regionally decentralized pattern to a hierarchical and centralized one, based on changes in the distribution of ceramics. Variations in clay composition and decorative styles show that during the early Aztec period (A.D. 1150–1350), a number of territorially discrete market systems distributed serving dishes: within each market system certain stylistically distinct vessels, made by local potters, circulated. Early Aztec market systems corresponded to political confederations composed of small communities clustered geographically around head towns that hosted the major markets. Trade was most active among communities within each confederation's boundaries. Changes in these exchange patterns followed political centralization under the Aztec Empire (A.D. 1430–1521); serving dishes produced by each confederation were then distributed more widely, beyond the confederation borders, indicating that a wider hierarchy of markets had taken over the distribution of goods. Further evidence of the emergence of this wider market system is the ceramics' increased stylistic similarity. Late Aztec imperial period ceramics look so much alike that chemical testing is often required to distinguish the products of different workshops. The communities at the pinnacle of this hierarchy, with the largest markets, were the Aztec imperial political centers of Tenochtitlan and Texcoco. While pro-duction remained local, esthetic choices were conditioned by the leading political centers.

The Aztec market hierarchy operated through a series of periodic markets: market days were held at different intervals, depending on the size and centrality of the community. Some markets operated daily, while others met only every five, nine, thirteen, or twenty days. In periodic market systems, varied market days concentrate scarce goods at known times and places. Mobile traders can then move their goods from one market to another and from higher-level markets to lower-level ones. In Aztec society, the market system was more than an economic institution, however; according to Fray Diego Durán, market days coincided with communities' religious celebrations, and each marketplace had its own shrine and deity. Durán reports that people from surrounding communities unfailingly traveled to attend markets in major towns because market days were important social events.

Aztec markets in the Basin of Mexico were part of an exchange system that linked much of Mesoamerica. Specialized zones of activity differentiated Aztec traders. Local traders dealt primarily in utilitarian goods and local products. In contrast, long-distance traders called *pochteca* traveled to the far reaches of the Aztec Empire and acquired rare and valuable goods such as tropical feathers, cacao beans, and cloth, to be carried back to the Basin of Mexico by professional porters. *Pochteca* resided in twelve Aztec cities and probably brought their goods to their home cities' markets. Of six *pochteca* groups that traded outside the imperial borders, the foremost was that of Tenochtitlan-Tlatelolco. The *pochteca* of Tenochtitlan-Tlatelolco acquired from foreign territories not only goods for their own trade but also goods and information for the Aztec imperial rulers.

The Aztec Empire's need for trade to acquire goods used as wealth and to reward political allies is evident from imperial economic policies. In some cases, the Aztec capital created or moved markets to ensure access to goods. For example, the city of Tepeaca was situated on an important trade route. After it was conquered, Tepeaca was charged with sponsoring a regional market that Tenochca (Aztec) merchants could attend. Within the Basin of Mexico, giving and taking away cities' rights to specialized markets—where exchange of particular goods such as edible dogs, birds, or slaves occurred—was a tool for political control of dependent cities. The importance of markets to imperial rulers and to those of provincial city-states is clear from documents that enumerate rulers' incomes from market taxes.

M

Regional market systems characterized much of Mesoamerica during the Postclassic period (A.D. 900–1521). In Oaxaca, a network of markets based on village specialization continued to integrate the valley. In the Maya region, archaeological evidence from obsidian and pottery as well as from documentary accounts reveals that a network of markets emerged during the Postclassic. Maya marketplaces coincided with the towns where important elite families resided, some of whom were traders. Other exchanges in the Yucatec market system occurred at the sources of particular products. In the West Mexican Tarascan state, sixteenth-century chronicles report, several equally ranked trading centers were established at politically important communities, forming a "heterarchical" rather than hierarchical market system.

Throughout Mesoamerica—in the Maya area, in Zapotec Oaxaca, in the Tarascan state, and in the Basin of Mexico (all studied intensively by archaeological survey and excavation)—it is clear that market systems emerged more than once during Mesoamerica's prehistory. An aspect of the ancient Mesoamerican economy to be explored by further research is the suppression or control of market exchange under some conditions, particularly during the Classic period, which was characterized by centralized urban systems and polities, in contrast to the Formative and Postclassic periods, characterized by strong, relatively independent market systems.

FURTHER READINGS

Anderson, A. J. O., Frances Berdan, and James Lockhart (eds.). 1976. *Beyond the Codices.* Berkeley: University of California Press.

Berdan, F. F. 1989. Trade and Markets in Precapitalist States. In S. Plattner (ed.), *Economic Anthropology*, pp. 78–107. Stanford: Stanford University Press.

Carrasco, P. 1982. The Political Economy of the Aztec and Inca States. In G. A. Collier et al. (eds.), *The Inca and Aztec States 1400–1800*, pp. 23–40. New York: Academic Press.

Cortés, H. 1986 [1519–1525]. *Letters from Mexico.* A. Pagden (transl. and ed.) New Haven: Yale University Press.

Diskin, M. 1976. The Structure of a Peasant Market System in Oaxaca. In S. Cook and M. Diskin (eds.), *Markets in Oaxaca*, pp. 49–65. Austin: University of Texas Press.

Hassig, R. 1982. Periodic Markets in Precolumbian Mexico. *American Antiquity* 47:346–355.

Hirth, K. G. 1998. The Distributional Approach: A New Way to Identify Marketplace Exchange in the Archaeological Record. *Current Anthropology* 39:451–476.

Hodge, M. G. 1992. The Geographical Structure of Aztec Imperial Period Market Systems. *National Geographic Research and Exploration* 4:428–445.

Plattner, S. 1989. Markets and Marketplaces. In S. Plattner (ed.), *Economic Anthropology*, pp. 171–208. Stanford: Stanford University Press.

Pollard, H. P. 1993. *Taríacuri's Legacy: The Prehispanic Tarascan State.* Norman: University of Oklahoma Press.

Sanders, W. T., J. R. Parsons, and R. Santley. 1979. *The Basin of Mexico: The Cultural Ecology of a Civilization.* New York: Academic Press.

Smith, C. A. 1976. Introduction: The Regional Approach to Economic Systems. In C. A. Smith (ed.), *Regional Analysis,* Vol. 1, *Economic Systems,* pp. 1–63. New York: Academic Press.

Mary G. Hodge

SEE ALSO

Economic Organization; Exchange Media; Transport

Matacapan and the Tuxtla Region (Veracruz, Mexico)

Matacapan is a large urban center situated in the Tuxtla Mountains of southern Veracruz. The site has a long history of occupation beginning as early as the Early Formative, but its most substantial occupation dates to the Middle Classic period, a time when objects produced in Teotihuacan style were widely distributed in Mesoamerica. Occupation is also evident at the site from the Early and Late Classic periods; however, the frequency of these finds is nominal compared with that from the Middle Classic.

The central part of the site is dominated by a large complex of public buildings and other mounded architecture, covering approximately 2.5 square kilometers. This complex contains seventy-one mounds, many of them arranged around small plazas that in turn are situated around a large, central plaza. Two types of buildings are present: multi-stage temple mounds and low, rectangular platform mounds that presumably housed the community's top-ranking elite and their retainers. Many of these platforms are quite substantial in size, suggesting the presence of large multi-family residential groups. The excava-

M

tion of one platform structure (Mound 61) indicates that it consisted of a complex of rooms arranged around patios and separated by intervening corridors.

Distributed around this central core is a large area of suburban occupation covering at least 20 square kilometers. The settlement pattern in this area is dispersed, with groups of residential mounds separated by areas of relatively little occupation. Many of these platforms are also quite large, again suggesting the presence of large residential groups. In general, the pattern is one of decreasing density of occupation with greater distance from the site center. Through time, the picture is somewhat different. In the late Early Classic (A.D. 300–450), Matacapan was a small, compact community centered on the Teotihuacan *barrio* (neighborhood). The Middle Classic period (A.D. 450–650), in contrast, was a time of explosive growth, with the main occupation zone expanding to cover more than 20 square kilometers. At 463 hectares, the early Late Classic center (A.D. 650–800) was smaller in size, but it was more densely nucleated. Matacapan also dominated a large rural hinterland during the Middle Classic. Survey of a 400-square-kilometer area around the site indicates a well-developed settlement hierarchy, with two large centers set up at Ranchoapan and Teotepec and smaller ones founded at other sites, as well as a history of settlement that was very similar to the occupation sequence at Matacapan.

Matacapan has long been recognized as a site containing objects produced in Teotihuacan style. This assemblage involves of a variety of different types of artifacts (figurines, incense burners, *candeleros,* cylindrical tripod vases, *floreros, braseros,* etc.), as well as a series of formal architectural characteristics (*talud-tablero* platforms and large multi-room residences). Most of the artifacts produced in Teotihuacan style were locally manufactured imitations, not materials imported from Central Mexico. The presence of this assemblage indicates that the inhabitants of Matacapan were greatly concerned with Teotihuacan-style domestic and community-wide ritual, which suggests that the site supported a Teotihuacan enclave. Teotihuacan-style domestic artifacts occur throughout Matacapan, and they also are present at rural sites, indicating that elements of enclave behavior penetrated well into the countryside.

Artifacts produced in Teotihuacan style occur at Matacapan during the late Early Classic, the first phase of occupation at the site during the Classic period. This occupation was also associated with an abrupt shift in set-

tlement pattern from the region to the southwest of Matacapan to the area around the site, implying that Matacapan may have been physically founded by Teotihuacan or by persons with close connections to the Central Mexican center. The frequency of Teotihuacan-style materials peaks in the early Middle Classic and then falls off. Interestingly, the assemblage is still present at Matacapan in the early Late Classic, a time when population levels at the site and throughout the region were declining. The rapid growth in occupation at Matacapan and in its hinterland indicates major immigration in Middle Classic times. Much of this population probably came from regions adjacent to the Tuxtlas (e.g., the Coatzacoalcos River drainage), but some of it may have derived from Teotihuacan. The drop in population and Teotihuacan influence at Matacapan, as well as throughout the region, in the Late Classic implicates an emigration process working in the other direction.

The polity that Matacapan dominated also supported a large-scale, internally differentiated ceramic industry. Some of the pottery produced by this industry was undoubtedly destined for local consumption, but some was probably intended for distribution throughout a broad area that included not only the Tuxtlas but also other regions. The scale of this ceramic production system largely paralleled the history of occupation and Teotihuacan influence at Matacapan, implying that contacts with the Central Mexican center were somehow involved in the establishment and maintenance of the industry.

Most ceramic production in "downtown" Matacapan was small scale and not internally differentiated. Thus far, fifteen ceramic production areas have been identified within the urban zone. Production in all areas took place in domestic contexts, and most potteries manufactured the complete suite of wares used throughout the region. Each of these areas probably represents a household industry, with pottery production supplying part of the domestic group's income and farming or other activities providing the remainder. Small-scale ceramics production also took place at rural sites around Matacapan.

Ceramic production in suburban contexts at Matacapan was larger in scale. These production areas vary greatly in size and internal configuration, suggesting major differences in the organization of production. Twenty-five of these production areas were small in scale. Seven areas in suburban Matacapan were much larger in size and contained more substantial quantities of refuse. Of these, six qualify as workshop industries or nucleated

M

industries. Ceramic production here was always oriented to a few wares, indicating a much higher level of product specialization. Pottery-making at two rural sites, El Salado and La Lomita, may have been of comparable scale.

The most intensive production took place at Comoapan, a small suburb of Matacapan. The ceramic production area here covered 8 hectares, with groups of kilns and waster dumps most concentrated in the eastern half of the site. Production at Comoapan was also highly specialized, involving the manufacture of only a few wares. Interpretations of the organization of production at Comoapan vary: some posit that it functioned as a nucleated industry, maintained by different groups of workshops, while others believe it operated as a single, large-scale industry such as a manufactory.

Recent work in the Tuxtla Mountains indicates a series of interrelationships among the sequence of occupation at Matacapan, the pattern of Teotihuacan influence, the scale and degree of differentiation in specialized ceramic production at the site, and the history and character of occupation throughout in the region. It appears that Matacapan was initially founded as a Teotihuacan enclave sometime in the late Early Classic. In the Middle Classic period it grew dramatically in size; at this time there was also explosive growth in its craft ceramic craft industry, influence from Teotihuacan, and population throughout the region. The Late Classic period, in contrast, was a time of population loss, reduction in influence from Teotihuacan, and decreases in the scale and complexity of its pottery production industry. It is likely that Teotihuacan was a major player behind these developments, although other agents cannot be discounted at present.

FURTHER READINGS

Arnold, P. J., C. A. Pool, R. R. Kneebone, and R. S. Santley. 1993. Intensive Ceramic Production and Classic-Period Political Economy in the Sierra de los Tuxtlas, Veracruz, Mexico. *Ancient Mesoamerica* 4:175–191.

Santley, R. S. 1989. Obsidian Working, Long-Distance Exchange, and the Teotihuacan Presence on the South Gulf Coast. In R. A. Diehl and J. C. Berlo (eds.), *Mesoamerica after the Decline of Teotihuacan A.D. 700–900,* pp. 131–151. Washington, D.C.: Dumbarton Oaks.

Santley, R. S. 1994. The Economy of Ancient Matacapan. *Ancient Mesoamerica* 5:243–266.

Santley, R. S., P. J. Arnold III, and C. A. Pool. 1989. The Ceramics Production System at Matacapan, Veracruz, Mexico. *Journal of Field Archaeology* 16:107–132.

Santley, R. S., C. Yarborough, and B. A. Hall. 1987. Enclaves, Ethnicity, and the Archaeological Record at Matacapan. In R. Auger et al. (eds.), *Ethnicity and Culture,* pp. 85–100. Calgary: Archaeological Association, University of Calgary.

Robert S. Santley

SEE ALSO
Gulf Lowlands: South Central Region; Gulf Lowlands: South Region

Matanchén (Nayarit, Mexico)

A non-ceramic Archaic period shell midden covering more than 3,600 square meters and exceeding 3 meters in depth, situated at the base of Ceboruco Hill on the Pacific coast, 3 kilometers southeast of San Blas. Investigation focused on extensive profiles exposed by quarrying for road construction material. Three uncalibrated and uncorrected radiocarbon dates were obtained on shell samples: 1810 ±80 B.C., 2000 ±100 B.C., and 2100 ±100 B.C.

The shellfish were probably harvested using nets in Matanchén Bay immediately to the southeast. Three stone net weights were found among the shells. The shellfish include many large conchs and great quantities of bivalve mollusks. These were probably boiled or baked in the upslope area of the site. The conch shells were bashed open to more easily extract the meat; this was probably a secondary function of some net weights. Rare obsidian flakes may have been used to cut meat out of the bivalves.

The alkalinity of shell middens serves to preserve bone, yet only ten bones were recovered, representing fish, sea turtle, and pelican. This is surprising given the biological diversity of the local microenvironments.

FURTHER READINGS

Mountjoy, J. B., R. E. Taylor, and L. Feldman. 1972. Matanchén Complex: New Radiocarbon Dates on Early Coastal Adaptation in West Mexico. *Science* 175: 1242–1243.

Joseph B. Mountjoy

SEE ALSO
West Mexico

Mathematics

The Aztecs and the Maya had a well-developed system of arithmetic, suggesting that such knowledge was pan-

Mesoamerican. In both areas, the number system was vigesimal (base 20) rather than decimal (base 10) like our own. In addition, Texcocan Aztecs, at least, used positional or place-value notation. They also employed two systems to record numbers. One system, used in tribute records, consisted of a dot or circle for one, employed to create the numbers 1–19 through the process of repetition; a flag for 20, repeated to form multiples up to 399; a glyph for a feather or tied bundle for 400 (20^2); and a glyph for a bag of copal incense to represent 8,000 (20^3). Each symbol denoted a cardinal place in the numeral system. These symbols could be subdivided by drawing a quarter of a flag for 5 or three-quarters for 15. One advantage of this notation is its high visual impact, useful for denoting quantities of commodities paid in tribute.

The other system consisted of a positional line-and-dot notation (analogous to the Maya bar and dot). Although written evidence for this is scarce, its existence is demonstrated by two census-cadastral codices from the town of Tepetlaoztoc, near Texcoco in the Valley of Mexico: Codex Vergara and Codice de Santa María Asunción. Each codex consists of three sections, or registers. The first register of each contains a census of households. The second register depicts individual fields with their dimensions and their soil types glyphically written, as well as the name glyph of the one who owned or worked the field. In the third register, the same fields are depicted in stylized fashion as rectangles, some with a flag in the upper right protuberance. The numbers in the flag record units of 20, which are indicated by 1 to 19 lines, and groups of 5 are bundled together with a line at the top. Fields may also contain a dot, which has a value of 20 and appears only in the third register. When there is no entry in the third register, the protuberance is left blank; a *cintli* glyph is drawn toward the top of the rectangle and signifies zero in the third register. The number in the third register is multiplied by 20, then added to the second register, and the sum never exceeds 399.

Measures

The 2.5-meter *quahuitl* was a standard lineal measure used in determining external boundaries of agricultural fields in the area of Acolhuacan of the Valley of Mexico. There appear to have been several other measures widely used in ancient Mexico, such as the *betan* (91 cm) and *azab* (4.55 cm).

Geometry

Opinion is divided as to whether ancient Mexicans had a system of geometry. Evidence from archaeological sites—regular use of the right angle and its precise construction, the recurrent use of other angles, symmetry in site layout, use of the square, circumscribing circles in wall murals, and so on—points to the regular employment of geometric concepts by builders and artists, indicating that there was a developed system of geometry, which may well date to early Olmec times. Horst Hartung has hypothesized a relationship between the development of geometry for community or architectural planning, and geomancy and/or well-developed mathematics. Furthermore, he believes that the Maya conception of the four world directions strongly implies the notion of a right angle. He also points to the use of isosceles triangles and the regular use of 30° angles. The zero symbol used in Maya numerical notation implies the existence of geometry.

FURTHER READINGS

Calderon, H. M. 1966. *La ciencia matematica de los Mayas.* Mexico City: Editorial Orion.

Harvey, H. R., and B. J. Williams. 1980. Aztec Arithmetic: Positional Notation and Area Calculation. *Science* 210:499–505.

Williams, B. J., and H. R. Harvey. 1977. *The* Códice de Santa María Asunción: *Facsimile and Commentary; Households and Lands in Sixteenth-Century Tepetlaoztoc.* Salt Lake City: University of Utah Press.

Herbert Harvey

SEE ALSO

Maps and Place-Names

Maudslay, Alfred Percival (1850–1931)

Born in London, Maudslay obtained a bachelor's degree in natural science from Cambridge and spent nearly five years in the colonial service, holding posts in Trinidad, Samoa, Tonga, and Fiji. In Fiji, Maudslay became a collector of ethnographic material; this collection, with several others, became the nucleus of the University Museum of Archaeology and Ethnology at Cambridge University. Maudslay's interest then shifted to archaeology, and in 1880 he embarked for Guatemala in order to see the ruins of Copán and Quirigua. So great was his new enthusiasm that before returning home he had also visited the distant ruins of Tikal.

At Quirigua Maudslay pulled moss from apparently shapeless stones, revealing hieroglyphs and bas-relief

M

carvings. He immediately grasped that recording these inscriptions was an urgent and important task, worthy of his time, money, and skills as an experienced photographer. As this work progressed, he saw that, in addition to photographs, plaster casts were needed. In six expeditions he recorded sculpture and inscriptions at Quirigua, Copán, Tikal, Yaxchilan, Palenque, and Chichén Itzá and mapped the sites. Casts made from his molds were displayed at the South Kensington Museum, and graphic depictions were published in the section entitled *Archaeology* (1889–1902) in *Biologia Centrali-Americana.* To this day, these volumes are an essential reference work. Pieces of sculpture brought back by Maudslay from Copán and Yaxchilan were exhibited at the British Museum.

In 1912 Maudslay was elected president of the Royal Anthropological Institute; in the same year he received an honorary D.Sc. degree from Oxford University; an honorary Sc.D. was conferred on him by Cambridge University in 1925.

FURTHER READINGS

Maudslay, A. P. 1883. Explorations in Guatemala and Examination of the Newly Discovered Ruins of Quirigua, Tikal, and the Usumacinta. *Proceedings, Royal Geographical Society,* 5:185–204.

———. 1889–1902. *Archaeology: Biologia Centrali-Americana.* 5 vols. London: Porter and Dulau.

Ian Graham

Maya: Motagua Region

The Motagua Maya area has long been known for its two major Lowland Maya centers, Copán and Quirigua, and their Classic period (A.D. 200–900) demographic and political florescence. Recent archaeological and epigraphic investigations are establishing the broader context for these impressive developments, focusing on events leading up to and following the Classic, and the range of contacts enjoyed by Copánec and Quirigua residents with neighboring societies over a long prehistoric span. We are now better able to appreciate the complex network of varied societies that comprised the Motagua Maya zone.

The Region

The Motagua Maya region is an environmentally diverse zone encompassing the middle and lower drainages of the Motagua River. The Motagua rises in the Guatemala highlands, and its 350-kilometer-course passes through a number of different environmental zones, from high, cool mountains at its headwaters, through the arid middle stretch, to the hot, moist lowlands of its lower valley and the Caribbean coast. The Motagua Maya region encompasses the river's lower 200 kilometers. Most tributaries of the middle and lower Motagua are relatively short, making rapid descents from the bordering hills. The principal exception is the Copán Valley river system.

Three zones of the Motagua Maya region have been subject to persistent archaeological scrutiny: the Copán Valley; the middle Motagua Valley, especially near the town of San Agustín Acasaguastlán; and the lower Motagua Valley, where most work has focused on the site of Quirigua. There is significant variation among these zones in resources that would have been attractive to prehistoric settlers. Least welcoming of the triad for agricultural populations—because of its low rainfall, high evaporation, and generally shallow, infertile soils—is the middle Motagua Valley. Arable land here is largely restricted to small, discontinuous segments of alluvium on low terraces formed along the Motagua and its principal tributaries. Partially compensating for these relatively bleak prospects is the wealth of mineral resources, especially jade, found in large exposures such as the Mazanal quarries in the southern flanks of the Sierra de las Minas. Jade was highly valued for the manufacture of status markers, such as jewelry, throughout southern Mesoamerica from the Formative through Postclassic, and those controlling its extraction almost certainly benefited from their strategic position. The middle Motagua also provides easy, direct passage to the extensive El Chayal obsidian flows, lying about 55 kilometers to the southwest in the upper Motagua drainage. This volcanic material, valued for the manufacture of utilitarian and esoteric implements, could have been acquired easily by middle Motagua inhabitants.

The Motagua creates a broad, very fertile floodplain as it meanders sluggishly through its lower valley. Lower Motagua populations could have produced considerable agricultural surplus from this zone's well-watered, rich soils. Mineral resources are, however, lacking in the Motagua's lower reaches. Natural communication corridors converge in the lower Motagua Valley, and local populations may have occupied a strategic position on several exchange networks linking various portions of southeastern Mesoamerica. The Motagua itself links the Caribbean coast with the highlands to the southwest, while passes breach the bordering hills, leading southeast toward Copán and the Chamelecon drainage of Honduras and northwest to Lake Izabal and the Petén.

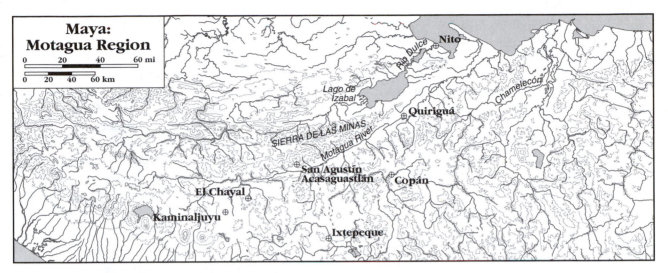

Maya: Motagua Region. Map design by Mapping Specialists Limited, Madison, Wisconsin.

The Copán Valley, watered by the river of the same name, is intermediate in resources between the aforementioned zones. Deep, fertile alluvial soils comprise the valley bottoms, but these are limited in extent and bordered by relatively steep slopes that are vulnerable to erosion when cleared. Easily worked stone is readily accessible in the valley and was extensively used in the fabrication of the structures and monuments for which Copán is famous. Other mineral resources are not known for the zone, though valley residents apparently enjoyed easy access to obsidian from the large Ixtepeque flows about 65 kilometers to the southwest. The Copán Valley's position near the divide between the Chamelecon and Motagua watersheds may have given its residents a privileged position in interregional exchanges. These diverse environments have variable potential for sustaining prehistoric socio-political growth and the demographic expansion that accompanied it.

Previous research in the Motagua Maya region tended to focus on the Lowland Maya centers of Copán and Quirigua, and their architectural cores have benefited from over a century of study. The great size and imposing construction of these sites encouraged archaeological scrutiny, as did their eccentric locations on the far southeastern margin of the Lowland Maya culture zone. Initial work, from the late nineteenth to the mid-twentieth century, concentrated on recording the numerous sculpted monuments recovered at these centers, with limited excavation. These investigations were an outgrowth of prevailing concerns with iconography, hieroglyphic decipherment, chronology, and elite culture. Systematic programs of regional survey and excavation conducted over the past two decades within and outside Copán and Quirigua reflect a growing concern with the sequence of events leading up to the imposing architectural florescences and the environmental and socio-political contexts in which those apogees were achieved. The nature of the societies that coexisted and interacted with the scions of Copán and Quirigua has remained, until recently, largely unknown. Pioneering surveys here, some beginning by the late nineteenth century, were followed by a long hiatus in archaeological interest. Limited reconnaissance and excavation were conducted along the middle stretches of the Motagua River near the town of San Agustín Acasaguastlán by Carnegie Institution staff in 1935 and 1940, while the lower Motagua Valley between Quirigua and the Caribbean coast enjoyed even less attention up through the 1960s. It has only been since the late 1970s that systematic investigations combining survey and excavation have been initiated in both zones. Even so, limited portions of the middle and lower Motagua Valley have been surveyed, and excavations are still restricted to a few locales. Many other areas, especially the mountainous terrain bordering the Motagua and its principal tributaries, remain unknown archaeologically.

We are confronted, therefore, with a research mosaic in which two major centers and their environs are well

M

documented, two other areas are just entering the first research stages, and many other zones are archaeological ciphers. This uneven history of investigation frustrates efforts at regional synthesis. Consequently, what follows must be treated as hypotheses subject to evaluation as our knowledge of this culturally complex area increases.

Events predating the Classic are most clearly attested in the Copán Valley, where intensive research over many years has reconstructed one of the longest occupation spans in southern Mesoamerica. Early Formative occupation here was apparently initiated by egalitarian, agricultural populations dispersed in small settlements across the valley alluvium.

Population gradually increased during the subsequent Middle Formative, though settlements remained small and scattered over fertile low-lying areas. Evidence of emergent ranking now takes the form of differential burial treatment, noted in a cemetery unearthed below a large Late Classic floodplain site. Most of the more than thirty-two interments found in the fill of two adjacent Middle Formative platforms were not associated with burial goods. Burial VIII-27, however, was outfitted with large quantities of items, including stone beads, engravers, jade effigy teeth, and four ceramic vessels, one of which was decorated with motifs apparently derived from the contemporary Olmec tradition. This individual's youth implies that his status was inherited. These interments contrast with the contemporary use of caves for burial, as recorded by Gordon at the beginning of this century on the valley margins. Such natural shelters apparently served as ossuaries; in them, partially cremated human remains were found associated with ceramic offerings, a pattern replicated in the coeval Cuyamel Caves on the lower Aguan River, approximately 350 kilometers to the northeast. Early and Middle Formative Copán ceramics fit comfortably with what is known concerning contemporary southeastern Mesoamerican pottery traditions, but they differ from those found in the neighboring Maya Lowlands.

Population and evidence for socio-political complexity decline dramatically in the Copán Valley during the subsequent Late Formative. Sites dating to this interval are fewer, and there is no clear evidence of social differentiation. We may be witnessing less a demographic drop than increasing nucleation, with evidence pertaining to the period largely buried beneath the Copán acropolis, where low, cobble-faced platforms dating to A.D. 100–400 have been identified through deep tunneling. Still, no monumental constructions (platforms of 1.5 meters or higher) have been dated to this span. Copán may therefore be

something of a developmental anomaly. While polities in the Maya Lowlands and other portions of southeastern Mesoamerica experienced population growth and political centralization, Copán seems to have been in decline.

The first signs of occupation in the middle and lower Motagua Valley date to this span; the available information, however, is insufficient to describe the nature of these early societies. Residents of all three zones participated in exchange networks linking them with people to the east and south. Usulutan wares—fine-paste, well-fired, orange-slipped ceramics decorated with negative-painted linear and blobby designs—are prevalent in Late Formative Honduran and Highland Maya assemblages and have been recovered from the Copán, lower, and middle Motagua valleys. These vessels are especially common at Copán, where they assume a wide array of forms. Stone pedestal sculptures, probably dating to the Late Formative, have also been recovered from Copán and Quirigua and provide another link to the Maya Highlands. Late Formative Motagua Maya material patterns are distinct from those reported from the coeval Maya Lowlands, suggesting that ties in this direction were weak.

Gradual but significant growth of the Copán and Quirigua polities occurred during the Early Classic. A ceremonial and administrative center developed on the northern margin of the later Quirigua site core from A.D. 400 to 500, focused on architectural groups 3C-7 and 3C-8. References to a ruling dynasty appear for the first time. Monument 26, probably erected in Group 3C-7, dates to A.D. 493 and depicts an early ruler; its hieroglyphic text also mentions two preceding monarchs. There are no known competitors for political preeminence within the contemporary lower Motagua Valley, and it appears that the residents of groups 3C-7 and 3C-8 were well on their way to concentrating power in their own hands. The degree of population growth contemporary with these political shifts remains unknown owing to difficulties in locating nonmonumental sites buried under the deep Motagua alluvium. This burst of dynasty-building apparently came to an abrupt end between A.D. 500 and 650, when Early Classic constructions were buried by Motagua flood deposits. It is unknown whether these inundations curtailed continued political growth or were symptoms of other environmental problems that undermined centralized power.

Copán rebounded vigorously from its apparent Late Formative decline, beginning a process of demographic growth and political centralization that would continue throughout the Classic. Sustained population increase marked the Early Classic, with most of the expansion concentrated on the fertile alluvium in the environs of the Copán site core. There may have been some initial competition for regional preeminence among the leaders of three political foci: the site core, Cerro de las Mesas in the foothills, and a center now buried by the town of Copán. Residents of the first settlement, however, soon established their local preeminence, possibly under the leadership of Yax Kuk' Mo', who ruled from A.D. 426 to 435. The dynasty founded by Yax Kuk' Mo', celebrated on numerous hieroglyphic texts, was to last until the early ninth century. Copán's emergent elites may have been aided in this struggle by their privileged access to fertile alluvial soils that could be used to attract and support large numbers of clients. Leaders of competing centers, surrounded by less productive terrain, would have been at a decided disadvantage in this contest. The victory of the site core rulers is reflected here in the accelerated pace of monumental construction in the early fifth century. Comparable labor control is not evident elsewhere in the valley, strongly suggesting that Copán's lords had attained the rank of regional paramounts by A.D. 400.

The Quirigua and Copán ceramic assemblages, marked by the persistence of Usulutan-decorated wares, continue to have close ties with Honduran and Highland Maya pottery traditions. A few serving vessels at both centers exhibit formal and decorative modes reminiscent of Lowland Maya Tzakol containers, especially in the use of polychrome decorations and basal flanges on bowls. Monumental architecture at Quirigua and Copán also reflects strong ties to the contemporary Maya Lowlands, especially the prevalence of faced stone masonry and, at Copán, polychrome-painted stucco decorations, including hieroglyphs, on substructure façades. Large earthen platforms, however, were also raised at both sites, pointing to Highland Maya inspiration. Carved stone stelae bearing hieroglyphic texts, found at Quirigua and Copán, derive from Lowland Maya models. This and other evidence suggest that the newly ascendent Quirigua and Copán rulers maintained close ties with established centers of power in the Maya Lowlands, Highlands, and western Honduras, expressing these linkages in various media. It remains to be established whether this means that scions of ruling houses hailed from distant centers or that they were autochthonous elites who adopted foreign identities and their material trappings.

The status of Early Classic occupation within the middle Motagua Valley is uncertain. This area may have been temporarily abandoned at this time, the exodus hastened by volcanism affecting the zone during the second to third centuries. If this was the case, reoccupation of the middle Motagua began around A.D. 450, pioneered by peoples bearing a material culture with strong Highland Maya influences. This reconstruction coincided with the ties maintained between Early Classic Quirigua and the major highland center of Kaminaljuyú. The Motagua Valley was probably the channel linking these two zones, with middle Motagua residents serving as intermediaries.

The Late Classic was a period of maximum political and demographic growth in all three of the areas considered here. Quirigua recovered from its earlier political troubles, while Yax Kuk' Mo''s successors at Copán enjoyed continued success in accruing power and attracting clients. Population expanded dramatically throughout the Late Classic near both centers. Most growth in the Copán Valley was concentrated in the site core's environs, though significant occupation of the surrounding foothills is attested. Demographic increase is also noted on the Motagua floodplain near Quirigua. Late Classic growth rates undoubtedly responded in part to political pressures, especially the desire of powerful elites to secure ever-larger labor pools. Such strains would have encouraged both larger families and immigration. Evidence of political centralization, reflected in the size and pace of monumental construction at regional capitals, is strong in both the Copán and lower Motagua Valleys. The Copán and Quirigua cores were scenes of unprecedented building activity. Quirigua's newly founded acropolis and Great Plaza, replacing Groups 3C-7 and 3C-8 as architectural foci, were enlarged many times during the seventh through early ninth centuries.

Rulers of both capitals also oversaw bursts of stela erection, peaking in the eighth century. Butz Chan and Smoke Imix God K, the eleventh and twelfth Copán monarchs respectively, figure prominently in these texts. They consolidated control over the Copán Valley and extended the polity's sway, by military or other means, to distant realms. Newly renascent Quirigua may have been one of their prizes; Quirigua's Altar 12 (L) contains a reference to Smoke Imix God K, strongly suggesting that Quirigua was subordinate to its southern neighbor by A.D. 672. Each capital also dominated a settlement hierarchy composed of at least three levels and including subsidiary elite centers through which the realms were administered.

Quirigua and Copán elite power was, however, limited by both internal and external factors. Copán's continued expansion under its thirteenth ruler, 18 Rabbit, was at

M

least partially curtailed by the secession of Quirigua from Copánec hegemony in A.D. 737. At this time 18 Rabbit was defeated, captured, and ultimately sacrificed by Quirigua's best-known ruler, Cauac Sky, who then began a program of unprecedented monumental construction and stela erection at Quirigua. The audaciousness of some of Cauac Sky's post-victory monuments, including examples that surpass in height and elaborate carving those known from the Classic Lowland Maya heartland, hint at the great pride this monarch took in his newly won independence. Nevertheless, the spatial extent of the Quirigua domain was restricted by the post-A.D. 700 development of at least five large, complexly organized polities within the lower Motagua Valley whose borders may have reached to within 25 kilometers of Quirigua. Capitals of these political units—Las Animas, Quebrada Grande, Las Quebradas, Playitas, and Choco—dominated a three-tier site hierarchy. Each contains from one to four monumental court groups, with as many as 295 total constructions.

After 18 Rabbit's fall, his successors may have been forced to share power with lesser elites. This concession is physically represented by the construction of a council house, or *popol nah,* at the center of elite power, the acropolis. Magnates from throughout the realm apparently gathered here to confer with the reigning paramount on matters of state. Such conferences imply that monarchs no longer ruled absolutely but had to build support among the nobility for any large-scale enterprise. Hieroglyphic inscriptions from the reign of Copán's last major monarch, Yax Pak, also suggest that he was forced to concede paramount elite prerogatives, including monument raising, to lesser notables in order to retain their loyalty. There is no comparable evidence for the dispersion of power at Quirigua.

Politics was a dynamic, contested field in which actors within and outside polities competed for dominance. Through time the balance shifted, and by A.D. 800–850 forces were set in motion that weakened centralized rule.

Population growth and political centralization within the middle Motagua drainage focused on the 3-kilometer-long Lato River, a Motagua tributary, near the town of San Agustín Acasaguastlán. At least four large sites with more than a hundred platforms each are found in this zone, and roughly a thousand constructions have been reported along the Lato. Late Classic occupation thins out considerably east and west of this location. The four largest settlements dominate a four-tier site hierarchy, though it is uncertain whether each "capital" was the focus of a distinct polity or all four were integrated within a single realm, possibly part of the same extensive site.

Middle Motagua centers are best known for the evidence of both jade- and obsidian-working that they yield. Jade workshops, drawing on plentiful nearby sources for raw materials, are widespread throughout the San Agustín Acasaguastlán zone, though the largest production areas are concentrated at the biggest sites, such as Guayatan on the west bank of the Lato. Manufacture of obsidian tools, probably using cores imported from such nearby flows as El Chayal, was also a major enterprise engaged in by middle Motagua residents. The large scale of jade and obsidian working at sites such as Guayatan suggests that the zone was a center of production for export. No comparable evidence of craft specialization is forthcoming from the lower Motagua and Copán valleys.

Material remains from all three areas indicate that the ruling elites were embedded in far-reaching interregional networks. Copán and Quirigua paramounts were clearly linked to lowland Maya rulers by shared traditions of architecture, monumental site organization, and stela carving. They diverged from their northern neighbors in ceramics; Quirigua almost entirely lacks the tradition of polychrome decoration so common in the Lowland Maya zone. Quirigua's Late Classic pottery, in fact, most closely resembles that of its lower Motagua neighbors to the northeast, where polychrome decoration is also rare. Copán, on the other hand, was a production center of the distinctive Copador ware, cream-slipped vessels decorated with hematite red and black figurative and geometric designs. Copador ware diverges markedly in motifs and composition from contemporary Lowland Maya polychromes and seems to have been used in place of the latter at Copán. These distinctive vessels were exported in varying quantities to peoples living in western Honduras and El Salvador. Whatever the significance of these ceramic distributions may be, they suggest that identities and affiliations expressed through monumental architecture and sculpture differed from those manifest in pottery.

The monumental centers sharing the lower Motagua Valley with Quirigua appear to have been part of an entirely different cultural tradition. Each is dominated by at least one complex quadrangle composed of adjoining closed courts surrounded by monumental platforms faced not with cut masonry, but with unworked river cobbles and schist slabs set in long, narrow terraces. Very few pieces of sculpture are reported from these sites; the few freestanding monuments consist of plain stelae, pecked stone spheres, and large natural boulders and slabs. This tradition extends into areas linked to the northern lower

Motagua Valley by natural communication corridors, including the massive settlements of Techin and Tres Cerros in highland valleys on the Honduras/Guatemala border and newly discovered centers on the southeastern shore of Lake Izabal. The above distribution suggests that the lower Motagua polities northeast of Quirigua were part of a late-developing interaction network whose residents were excluded from, or consciously strove to avoid identification with, the system symbolized by the adoption of Lowland Maya material forms. Quirigua, sharing numerous ceramic similarities with these centers, may have been a nexus connecting this system with the Lowland Maya exchange network.

Middle Motagua elites also participated in a cosmopolitan mixture of interaction reflected in their material culture. The most distinctive of Lowland Maya architectural traits, the corbel vault, was employed here in the construction of elaborate crypts. Many of these tombs have benches and red-painted walls; they were used for protracted periods before being buried beneath stone-faced platforms. Ball courts are reported at several of the larger middle Motagua settlements, but carved monuments are absent—only a few plain stelae having been found at Guayatan. Middle Motagua ceramics continue to have their strongest affinities with the Maya Highlands, though some modes link this area with the adjacent lowlands and Quirigua. Middle Motagua jade was distributed over large portions of Central America, including the Maya Lowlands, from the Formative onward, reinforcing impressions of the area's extensive and enduring connections.

Available evidence indicates that each zone underwent demographic and socio-political decline beginning by the eighth century. Monuments recording dynastic rule at Copán ceased to be raised early in the ninth century. This fact and the persistence of small-scale elite centers in the Copán Valley and its immediate environs throughout the Terminal Classic imply that the diffusion of power begun after 18 Rabbit's demise accelerated in the ninth through twelfth centuries. Processes of political decentralization coincided with gradual demographic decline, both possibly spurred by massive sheet erosion caused by overfarming of the valley slopes. The Copán polity had apparently overshot its environmental limits, creating a subsistence crises that led in turn to malnutrition, disease, and out-migration. By A.D. 1250, the formerly prosperous Copán Valley was abandoned.

Quirigua underwent a comparable decline over the same span. The center's last named ruler, Jade Sky, took office in A.D. 800 and probably commissioned that site's latest monumental text, an architectonic inscription on Structure 1B-1. Clear evidence of centralized dynastic rule is absent after this date, though Quirigua remained a center of occupation and, possibly, political leadership into the early Terminal Classic. Its residents made several additions to the acropolis. They were also involved in transactions linking them with societies on the Pacific and Yucatecan coasts through which distinctive ceramics, such as Plumbate ware, and sculptural styles, including a *Chac Mool,* were introduced to the center. Despite these contacts with vital foci of late prehistoric trade, Quirigua continued to decline and was finally abandoned in the thirteenth century. The lower Motagua centers northeast of Quirigua had ceased to function somewhat earlier, possibly at the end of the Late Classic. Population and power apparently migrated northeast within the lower Motagua Valley throughout the Postclassic. The archaeologically unknown site of Nito, situated somewhere on the Caribbean coast near the Río Dulce, was thriving as a major center in the coastal trade by the time of the Spanish conquest.

Middle Motagua centers apparently continued as capitals of complexly organized polities through the Terminal Classic; Plumbate ceramics and some copper artifacts appear as late offerings in Guayatan tombs. Nevertheless, there is little evidence of Early Postclassic occupation in the area, suggesting a rapid shift in interrelated demographic and political processes. Population grew in or returned to the middle Motagua during the final pre-Columbian centuries, and early Spanish accounts record the existence of several towns within the zone, possibly the capitals of small polities. There is no evidence that ecological disasters like of those of Copán hastened the demise of hierarchically organized lower and middle Motagua societies in the Late and Terminal Classic. Their fall remains something of a mystery, though shifts in exchange networks during the Postclassic, especially the growing importance of coastal routes, may have undercut the ability of inland elites to attract and hold clients with promises of access to exotic goods.

The declines noted above conform with broader trends toward political decentralization and dwindling populations that are recorded at about the same time throughout southern Mesoamerica. The general simultaneity of these events hints at their interconnectedness, as though the fall of a ruling house in one polity undermined the ability of other leaders to remain in power. There is, however, much work to be accomplished before we can specify the processes involved and their relations to local environmental variables.

M

FURTHER READINGS

Ashmore, W. 1984. Quirigua Archaeology and History Revisited. *Journal of Field Archaeology* 11:365–386.

Baudez, C. (ed.). 1983. *Introducción a la arqueología e historia de Copán, Honduras.* 3 vols. Tegucigalpa: Secretaria del Estado en el Despacho de Cultura y Turismo.

Boone, E. H., and G. Willey (eds.). 1988. *The Southeast Classic Maya Zone.* Washington, D.C.: Dumbarton Oaks.

Fash, W. 1991. *Scribes, Warriors, and Kings: The City of Copán and the Ancient Maya.* New York: Thames and Hudson.

Houston, S., and W. Fowler, Jr. (comps.). 1992. Special Section: The Archaeology of Ancient Copán. *Ancient Mesoamerica* 3:61–197.

Schortman, E., and S. Nakamura. 1991. A Crisis of Identity: Late Classic Competition and Interaction on the Southeast Maya Periphery. *Latin American Antiquity* 2:311–336.

Sharer, R. 1990. *Quirigua: A Classic Maya Center and Its Sculpture.* Durham: Carolina Academic Press.

Smith, A. L., and A. V. Kidder. 1943. Explorations in the Motagua Valley, Guatemala. *Contributions to American Anthropology and History* 8:109–184.

Urban, P., and E. Schortman (eds.). 1986. *The Southeast Maya Periphery.* Austin: University of Texas Press.

Walters, G. 1980. *The San Agustín Acasaguastlán Archaeological Project, 1979 Field Season.* Museum Brief 25. Columbia: University of Missouri, Museum of Anthropology.

Webster, D. (ed.) 1989. *The House of the Bacabs.* Studies in Pre-Columbian Art and Archaeology, 29. Washington, D.C.: Dumbarton Oaks.

Webster, D., and A. C. Freter. 1990. The Demography of Late Classic Copán. In T. P. Culbert and D. S. Rice (eds.), *Precolumbian Population History in the Maya Lowlands,* pp. 37–62. Albuquerque: University of New Mexico Press.

Edward Schortman and Patricia Urban

SEE ALSO
Copán; Quirigua

Maya Culture and History

The term "Maya" refers to the cultural patterns characteristic of speakers of Mayan, a family of thirty closely related languages and dialects that are widely spoken in southern and eastern Mesoamerica ("Mayan" is usually used when referring to language). On a more general level, "Maya" refers to the ethnic identity of speakers of Mayan languages, and to their long traditions of cultural development. Because Mayan languages have a highly contiguous spatial distribution in southern Mesoamerica (with the exception of an isolated enclave of Huastec speakers along the northeastern coast), the word "Maya" also has a geographical meaning. Mayan speakers today occupy the southeastern highlands of Mexico (especially the modern state of Chiapas), all of the adjacent highlands of Guatemala farther to the southeast, and some highland valleys in western Honduras and El Salvador. The northern lowlands of Guatemala, sparsely populated only a few decades ago and now being rapidly colonized by migrants from many places, before A.D. 900 were the heartland of Classic Maya civilization, which also extended throughout the territory of modern Belize. Finally, Mayan speakers are firmly established throughout the low-lying northern parts of the Yucatán Peninsula, comprising the modern Mexican states of Yucatán, Campeche, and Quintana Roo.

Within this vast Maya homeland, which covers about 324,000 square kilometers, anthropologists and archaeologists distinguish between Highland and Lowland Maya regions, each with its own distinctive cultural traditions. The Highland Maya live at elevations above 800 meters in the southern mountains; the much more extensive lowlands, about 250,000 square kilometers in area, lie to the north at lower elevations. There was considerable cultural variety within these subareas as well. For example, the culture history of the Maya of the northern Yucatán Peninsula was rather different from that of the lowland areas to the south.

Linguists offer various reconstructions of the origins and geographical spread of Mayan languages, but several patterns are clear. First, these languages are quite different from those of most neighboring regions. Second, the major Mayan language groups resemble one another closely, exhibiting about the same amount of variation as is found among the European Romance languages. Finally, the region of most linguistic complexity is the highlands of Chiapas and Guatemala. The first pattern strongly suggests that the Mayan family of languages is old and well established. (According to some linguists, it belongs to a more inclusive linguistic subgroup called "Amerind," whose languages are the oldest and most widespread in the New World.) The similarity of Mayan languages argues for a common origin in fairly recent times, a high degree of interaction, or both. Although reconstructions of linguistic origins are difficult and controversial, most Mayanists believe that the southern highlands were the original home of the ancient Proto-Mayan language, and that separation of its main branches took place between about 2000 B.C. and A.D. 100, as populations migrated into the northern lowlands or otherwise diverged from one another. Knowledge of the Mayan languages spoken in Colonial times and still spoken today immeasurably aids in the decipherment of ancient texts.

Mayan speakers were the first Mesoamericans to be encountered by Europeans in the early sixteenth century. Contrary to a widely held popular belief in a general and dramatic Maya cultural and demographic collapse, numerous complex Maya political systems and dense populations existed throughout northern Yucatán and the Mexican-Guatemalan highlands at that time. European conquerors and colonists were impressed by the cultural sophistication of the Maya and by the many abandoned buildings and monuments that had apparently been built by their ancestors. Not the least impressive of Maya accomplishments was writing, primarily recorded in screen-fold books called codices. Unfortunately, the Spanish regarded such books as idolatrous and made a concerted effort to destroy them in the second half of the sixteenth century. Only four pre-Contact books are known today, but many other inscriptions are found carved or painted on stone, pottery, and other durable materials. These inscriptions, recorded in the most sophisticated of indigenous Mesoamerican writing systems, are—along with archaeology and ethnographic observations—our principal means of reconstructing the ancient Maya past.

Largely because of the sophistication of their art, writing, and architecture, the Maya, especially the Lowland Maya, have been intensively investigated by archaeologists, epigraphers, art historians, geographers, ethnographers, and scholars of many other disciplines for well over a century. As a result, we have detailed reconstructions of the world of the ancient Maya, and particularly of the Classic Maya (A.D. 250–900). Although such reconstructions were traditionally focused heavily on great Classic centers such as Tikal, Palenque, and Copán, since the 1960s settlement surveys have added much information about whole regions and polities. Beginning about the same time, and especially since 1980, ever-accelerating breakthroughs in deciphering Maya texts have contributed new understandings of kings, nobles, politics, ritual, and war. No other pre-Columbian people so clearly speak to us through their own records.

Environment

All of the Maya homeland lies well within the tropics, but nonetheless the region as a whole exhibits considerable environmental variety owing to differences in elevation, topography, soils, and prevailing weather patterns. This is even true in the Maya Lowlands, entirely at elevations below 800 meters. These low-lying hot lands receive most of their precipitation, ranging from 4,000 mm (157 inches) in the southwest to less than 500 mm (20 inches) in extreme northwestern Yucatán, from about May through January. Crops are grown primarily during this rainy season. The intervening dry season severely dries up vegetation in many places, but "dry" is a relative term, and some regions get rainfall and remain quite green during all months of the year. Most rainfall derives from summer storms moving in from the eastern seas.

Paradoxically, there is little available surface water in much of the Maya Lowlands. The Yucatán Peninsula is basically a huge, recently emerged platform of limestone that absorbs water, which finds its way to the sea through underground drainage channels. Permanent water sources are found in *bajos,* or swamps, and in the north in cenotes—places where the surface limestone strata have collapsed, exposing underground water. A localized system of large lakes has formed in limestone faults in the northeastern Petén region of Guatemala. Rivers are scarce, except along the western frontier, in Belize, and along the Honduran-Guatemalan border, and none of them provides a major avenue of transportation and trade comparable to the great rivers associated with Old World civilizations.

Although the Maya Lowlands seem deceptively flat on a map, the central and southern portions have considerable topographic relief, ranging from the hilly country of the Petén to the karst-formed solution valleys and steep escarpments of the southwest. Fertile, well-drained soils develop on the upland limestone parent material, but they are generally shallow and prone to nutrient loss and erosion if cleared of vegetation. Lower-lying *bajo* soils are more stable, but less fertile and often waterlogged. A small but rugged range of older igneous and metamorphic rock, the Maya Mountains, lies in central and southern Belize.

In the absence of human disturbance, dense tropical vegetation would cover the Maya Lowlands, although only remnants of the original forest cover exist today. High, multiple-canopy tropical forest blankets the Petén and fingers the east side of the peninsula. Some of the

M

heaviest undisturbed tropical forests are found along the drainage of the Usumacinta River in the southwest. Lower, semideciduous forest occurs farther north, grading into the scrubby, thorny vegetation of northwestern Yucatán. Specialized plant communities form locally in *bajos* and other microenvironments. Many of the tree species are of considerable economic importance to human populations.

The great forests support a rich tropical fauna. Large mammals include two kinds of deer, peccaries, tapir, jaguars, and several species of monkeys. Fish are abundant in rivers and along the coasts, and there are many tropical birds, including the wild turkey.

On the south rise the Maya Highlands, a complex region of very young and geologically active mountains. A line of towering volcanic peaks, the tallest 4,410 meters (14,332 feet) high, runs east–west along the southern highland margin from Mexico to El Salvador. Eruptions periodically blanket much of the highlands with rich volcanic ash and, together with earthquakes, may dam deep valleys so that extensive lakes form. Although the eruptions are destructive in the short run, this volcanic material weathers into deep, mineral-rich soils which, watered by abundant highland rains, produce bumper crops of New World cultigens. Another volcanic product is obsidian, a volcanic glass long prized by pre-Columbian peoples for cutting tools and extensively exported to lowland regions.

Highland climates are temperate, with temperatures ranging from 15° to 25° C (59°–77° F), and frost is never a problem for farmers. Most areas get from 200 to 3,000 mm of rainfall annually. Although now heavily altered, upland forests originally consisted of mixed evergreen and deciduous forests, dominated at high elevations by pines. These forests also supported a rich variety of animals, the most famous of which is the now threatened quetzal bird, whose tail feathers were traded throughout Mesoamerica for use on elite costumes.

Sandwiched between this high southern volcanic belt and the Maya Lowlands is a zone of lower, older, less geologically active mountains consisting of metamorphic rocks and complexly folded limestones. Great rivers such as the Usumacinta and Grijalva drain these highlands, whose foothills and valleys were ancient sources of jade and serpentine.

Finally there is the Pacific coastal piedmont, a narrow strip of fertile soils brought down from the uplands to the north by many small rivers. This hot, low-lying region is now largely cleared of its natural cover of tropical forests and coastal mangrove swamps. In ancient times it was famous as one of the richest cacao-producing zones of Mesoamerica, and it still is a rich source of fish, shrimp, and other aquatic resources.

Chronology and Culture History

Several slightly different chronological schemes have been applied to the general Maya cultural tradition. Most archaeologists conventionally use one that is divided into time periods roughly as follows.

Because Maya long count dates could be translated into European calendrical equivalents by the beginning of the twentieth century, this chronology is anchored by the Classic period, when most such dates occur. Surviving Maya books with dates in other calendars provide the framework for later periods, but before about A.D. 250 the tradition is essentially prehistoric. For these early times, chronology is determined by local ceramic sequences, stylistic comparison, stratigraphy, and chronometric techniques such as radiocarbon and obsidian hydration dating.

Early Hunter-Gatherers

The Maya Highlands and Lowlands must have been occupied well before 13,500 years ago, because they form a funnel-like corridor leading to South America, where human settlements have been dated to this time. The first inhabitants were ancient hunter-gatherers. A few controversial traces of these people, dating to perhaps as early as 9000 B.C., have been recovered by archaeologists in the Lowlands, but we know little of their ways of life, nor do we know that they were Maya speakers. In the Maya Highlands, the situation is much the same. Finds of ancient fluted points resembling those used more widely in North America show that people were certainly present in the mountain valleys of Guatemala by about 11,000 years ago.

Late Postclassic	A.D. 1250–1500
Early Postclassic	A.D. 1000–1250
Terminal Classic	A.D. 800–1000
Late Classic	A.D. 600–800
Early Classic	A.D. 250–600
Protoclassic	A.D. 100–250
Late Formative	400 B.C.–A.D. 100
Middle Formative	1000–400 B.C.
Early Formative	2500–1000 B.C.
Archaic	before 2500 B.C.

The First Farmers

More controversial and significant is the issue of the first appearance of settled farming populations. Staple Meso-american cultigens such as maize and beans were first domesticated not in the Maya region but rather in the temperate or subtropical highlands of Mexico to the north and west. These cultigens spread widely throughout Mesoamerica after about 3000 B.C. by diffusion, by the movement of populations, or in both ways. The earliest known remains of the houses, tools (including pottery), and weapons used by Lowland Maya farmers date to about 900 B.C. Environmental studies, particularly fossil pollen from lowland sediment cores, suggest that forest clearance for farming began much earlier, around 2500–2000 B.C. Fossil maize pollen itself has been recovered from levels dating to before 1700 B.C. in the Copán Valley in western Honduras. Such evidence suggests that small communities of farmers—possibly Mayan speakers—were probably widespread in the Early Formative, but that human population numbers were very small. A mixed economy of hunting-gathering and farming seems likely for this period. Agriculture was clearly important, how-ever, probably in the form of upland, long-fallow slash-and-burn cultivation. Some Mayanists believe that early farmers also cultivated the margins of low-lying wetlands, where drained field systems increased production and provided protection against drought.

Middle Formative

By Middle Formative times, there is no doubt that a vig-orous farming culture was present in the Maya Lowlands, especially in riverine locales. Sites of this period yield the earliest Lowland ceramics (classified as the Xe and Swasey complexes), dated to about 900–700 B.C. These early vil-lagers were probably Mayan speakers. The slightly later spread of distinctive Mamom ceramics and the increasing number of sites after about 700 B.C. reflect a rising popu-lation, perhaps stimulated by increasingly productive forms of maize. Excavated communities have yielded remains of burials and the foundations of pole-and-thatch houses, and perhaps community buildings, as well as tools and weapons. Apparently the farming village was the basic unit of political and social life during the first part of the Middle Formative. Some people were buried with more grave goods than others, but this is to be expected even in egalitarian social contexts. These little communi-ties were not isolated, however; obsidian, jade, serpentine, feathers, and other exotic goods were widely exchanged.

Ceramic vessels from as far afield as Copán show influ-ences from the Olmec region of the Gulf Coast, where impressive Middle Formative polities, centered on capi-tals such as San Lorenzo and La Venta, were thriving under powerful rulers.

Signs of political hierarchy and complexity, perhaps stimulated by such contacts, appear at Nakbe in northern Guatemala between 600–400 B.C. People at this center built structures as tall as 10 to 14 meters, beginning a tra-dition of monumental architecture that was to characterize the Maya Lowlands thereafter. About the same time, and possibly also as a result of Olmec contacts, even bigger structures were erected at Chalchuapa in El Salvador. Boulder sculptures there, and along the Pacific coast of Guatemala and Mexico, show Olmec-like and other sophisticated symbolic motifs. Large centers such as Kam-inaljuyú began to emerge elsewhere in the Maya High-lands. At other highland centers, elaborate burials, large structures, stone stelae, and what may be early glyphs and numerals all appeared by about 400 B.C.

Late Formative

The Late Formative period brought spectacular changes. Distinctive Chicanel pottery characterizes Lowland sites of this time, which are much more numerous and widespread than those of the Middle Formative, reflecting a vast in-crease in population. Even more significant than popula-tion growth and the elaboration of agricultural economies, however, is the rapid appearance of many of those cultural markers formerly thought to be innovations of the Classic period. Most conspicuous are massive ceremonial build-ings and palaces at centers such as El Mirador, Nakbe, and Cerros in the central Lowlands, and the emergence of complex communities such as Komchen in northern Yucatán. Building designs and techniques prefigure those of the later Classic period, as do façade decorations, which include early versions of religious and royal symbols later integral to Classic society. Late Formative remains are buried beneath later Classic constructions, as at Tikal, where huge Formative platforms were erected. Other signs of emerging social and political complexity in the Maya Lowlands include increased trade, rich burials, human sac-rifice (probably associated with war), stone monuments, and, most significant, evidence for the use of early hiero-glyphs and perhaps calendrical inscriptions. The Lowland Maya almost certainly borrowed some of these innova-tions from their Highland cousins, as well as from Mixe-Zoquean speakers on their southwest frontier, who seem

M

to have developed the distinctive long count calendar. Other influences, particularly in sculpture, came from the Izapan culture of the Pacific coast of Chiapas. Large carved-stone monuments depicting humans in elaborate costumes, accompanied by glyphs and dates (as yet unreadable), also appear early in Late Formative contexts in highland Guatemala and El Salvador, and also along the Pacific coastal zone of Guatemala. Late Formative centers such as Kaminaljuyú in the Valley of Guatemala also have large mounds with spectacular interior burial chambers and impressive carved stelae.

Wherever these innovations originated (and it is clear that some, such as writing, came from outside the Maya homeland), several themes of the Late Formative stand out, apart from population growth. First, there were complex exchanges of ideas as well as things over broad regions. Second, ranking and possibly stratification emerged, as did the central political institution of the Maya—kingship. We also begin to see the earliest cycles of regional political growth and abandonment that are common in later Maya culture history. Finally, by A.D. 100 many of the technical innovations, symbols, and ideologies fundamental to the elite Classic Maya Great Tradition were firmly in place.

Among the major Late Formative centers that peaked during the Late Formative and then were wholly or largely abandoned during the Protoclassic were El Mirador, Nakbe, and Cerros. There may have been localized problems with overpopulation around these sites even this early, but the eruption of the Ilopango volcano in western El Salvador devastated much of the southeastern highlands, and it may have caused severe population disruptions as well. Shifting political fortunes caused conflict in the form of large-scale warfare, best reflected by the impressive fortifications of Becan, built at the end of the Formative or perhaps during the Protoclassic period. Many centers thrived, however, and the stage was set for the spectacular recovery and florescence of Classic Maya culture.

Classic Maya

The beginning of the Classic period is conventionally signaled by the presence of large, non-portable stone monuments inscribed with dates in the long count calendar. The earliest known such inscription appears from A.D. 292 at Tikal, where a ruling dynasty was probably founded about a century earlier. Thereafter royal lines proliferated, particularly in the fifth century, at centers as distant as Copán. Traditions of elite culture in the form of architecture, art, iconography, and writing also spread widely,

especially in northern Guatemala, and became increasingly standardized. Emblem glyphs were used as parts of royal titles, and the term *ahaw,* signifying "lord," is also conspicuous in carved or painted texts, many of which come from royal or elite tombs. Although inscriptions allow historical insights into Early Classic Lowland Maya society, texts of this time are rare and difficult to read. Nevertheless, texts, along with the art associated with them, make it clear that kingship was well established and that rulers were preoccupied with celebrating their distinguished descent and their participation in ritual and war. Where inscribed monuments are abundant and well preserved, as at Copán and Tikal, sequences of as many as fifteen successive Early Classic rulers can be identified, and it seems that the latter center, along with others such as Calakmul, emerged as important regional powers.

During the Early Classic there are clear indications of trade, with attendant political and cultural influences from the great metropolis of Teotihuacan in the Basin of Mexico. Contacts with highland Mexico occurred either directly, or indirectly through Teotihuacan enclaves such as Kaminaljuyú in highland Guatemala. Maya rulers adopted Teotihuacan military imagery, and according to some interpretations, the first large-scale territorial war took place during the late fourth century, when Tikal conquered the neighboring center of Uaxactun.

Roughly between A.D. 530 and 590, people at some previously dynamic centers, most conspicuously Tikal, stopped erecting dated monuments, building large structures, and interring royal burials. This curious cessation of elite activity is called the "Classic hiatus." Although it was once thought to be a pan-Maya phenomenon, we now know that while particular events, such as major military conflicts, may have seriously disrupted the affected centers, many others remained vigorous during this period. Nevertheless, the hiatus provides one convenient means of distinguishing the Early Classic from the Late Classic period.

In many respects, the period between A.D. 600 and 800 marks the mature phase of Classic Maya civilization, and certainly it is the best documented historically and the most visible archaeologically. There were more major centers with local dynasties of kings than ever before— about forty had their own distinctive emblem glyphs. The general elite Maya Great Tradition, archaeologically reflected in shared conventions of art, long count dates, inscriptions, and architecture, achieved its broadest distribution—so much so that archaeologists once spoke of the Late Classic as the "period of uniformity." This label is not strictly appropriate, however, because we now know that there were many regional variants even of elite Maya culture, as reflected by local styles of art and architecture and details of hieroglyphic expression. Moreover, many impressive centers in the central and northern Maya Lowlands never used basic elements of the southern Great Tradition, such as long count dates or hieroglyphic writing, at least in ways detectable by archaeologists.

The basic political unit was the regal-ritual center of the hereditary ruler and its supporting hinterland, which together typically encompassed a territory on the scale of hundreds of square kilometers, or even a few thousand. Great plazas, palaces, ball courts, and temples for the worship of nature deities and royal ancestors attested to the splendor of the ruler's court. Scribes and sculptors, some of royal descent, recorded important events in the lives of kings. Lesser nobles had their own elaborate establishments, and kings and nobles alike were supported by common people, mostly farmers, who lived in outlying zones and comprised the vast bulk of the population.

The largest polities of this kind had populations in excess of 100,000, but most were much smaller. Kings and other nobles formed reciprocal marriage alliances and visited one another for important ceremonies. Coexisting with this veneer of shared elite kinship and culture, however, were protracted wars involving not only local dynasties but also networks of military allies. Warfare and alliance situationally created larger polities in which lesser or dependent rulers were dominated by paramount kings of centers such as Tikal, Calakmul, Caracol, and Dos Pilas. Mayanists debate the scale and character of these expanded polities. Some characterize them as "superstates," while others envision less stable and cohesive coalitions based on mutual interest and shifting alliances. No single center, however, was able to conquer all the others and create an enduring Late Classic polity that united a significant portion of the Maya Lowlands.

Populations peaked during the eighth century, with densities in many regions exceeding 100 people per square kilometer. Most archaeologists believe that upland agriculture provided the bulk of the food supply, and that fields had to be cropped very frequently or perhaps permanently. Intensive cultivation based on agricultural terracing and drained fields has been detected, but remains of such features are spotty, and archaeologists debate their productivity and chronological placement. Although the Late Classic was in many respects a cultural high point for Maya civilization, it clearly was also a time of increasing economic stress, conflict, and political fragility.

Cessation of dated monuments and royal building projects signals troubles at many centers in the late eighth century, and over the next 150 years of the Terminal Classic, dynasty after dynasty failed. Some kings continued to erect long count inscriptions until quite late—at Tikal until A.D. 889, and at Tonina until A.D. 909 (the latest certain date recorded in this calendrical style). Some centers were abruptly abandoned when kings lost their power; elsewhere, there was a more gradual decline as lesser nobles and some of the supporting population persisted for a time. Internecine warfare, internal factionalism, and environmental degradation are all implicated in this "collapse" of Maya civilization, but it certainly was not a universal process. Some centers, particularly in Belize, remained vigorous, and large construction projects continued. Nevertheless, there seems to have been a widespread rejection of the old Classic traditions of kingship in the central and southern Lowlands.

The archaeology and culture history of the northern Maya is much less well known, but it seems clear that many northern centers were unaffected by the crisis in the south. Sites heavily occupied in the Late Classic, such as Dzibilchaltun, continued to thrive until about A.D. 1000. Cobá, in northeastern Yucatán, also prospered. There was a spectacular florescence of Maya culture during the Terminal Classic in the Puuc hill country of northwestern Yucatán, where thousands of farmers supported elites at impressive centers such as Uxmal, Kabah, Labna, and Sayil. Other centers exhibiting distinctive Puuc architecture and ceramic styles were founded on the flat plains farther to the north.

Postclassic Maya

Beginning in the mid-ninth century, the great northern center of Chichén Itzá, which exhibits a mixture of Maya and Mexican architectural and sculptural styles, began its rise to power. Successful wars with the Puuc centers and with Cobá and its allies made Chichén Itzá the preeminent capital of the Early Postclassic, when it dominated much or all of northern Yucatán. Despite its fame, the chronology of Chichén Itzá is still debated. According to native documents, Chichén Itzá was overthrown early in the thirteenth century, to be replaced by a Late Postclassic confederated government focused on the less impressive walled city of Mayapan. Recent research suggests that the heyday of Chichén Itzá was considerably earlier, between about A.D. 800 and 950. Mayapan, the center of a later political confederation, succumbed to factional strife about A.D. 1450. Just half a century after

M

the fall of Mayapan, Spanish explorers first encountered the northern Maya and left eyewitness accounts of what they saw.

There were sixteen loosely defined polities in northern Yucatán in the early sixteenth century, with a combined population of perhaps 600,000 to 1 million. Towns were numerous, their central precincts dominated by temples with images of gods, the palaces of nobles, and the houses of rich families. Everywhere the town, ruled by a local lord, or *batab,* and surrounded by its supporting hinterland, was the basic political unit. Distinguished families such as the Xiu, Cocom, and Itzá dominated the political landscape. Strong rulers with the title *halach uinic* ruled large numbers of lesser *batabob* (plural) in some provinces. Elsewhere, polities consisted of alliances of related *batabob,* or fragile coalitions of unrelated rulers. A class of nobles who retained the old Classic title *ahaw* was supported by common farmers who owned and cultivated land communally. Commerce was controlled by nobles, who traded cotton, cacao, honey, slaves, and other commodities by land and sea. Warfare was common, waged for territory, slaves, strategic advantage, and to avenge insults. Writing and calendrics still flourished in the hands of native scribes and priests.

Strong kingdoms also flourished in the Maya Highlands of Guatemala in the early sixteenth century. By far the most important were the Quiché kingdom centered on Utatlan and the Cakchiquel kingdom with its capital at Iximché. Elites in both kingdoms claimed foreign "Toltec" origins and dominated local populations of highland farmers. Unfortunately, no pre-Columbian native books survive from the Highlands, but colonial documents describe the histories of these groups, and one such book, the *Popol Vuh,* also preserves ancient Maya accounts of the origin of the world and of humans, as well as dynastic accounts of the Quiché.

Spanish armies and their highland Indian allies quickly conquered the Quiché and the Cakchiquel by in the mid-1520s. The northern Maya in Yucatán resisted much more effectively, repelling many Spanish attacks until their final subjugation in the 1540s. More isolated Maya groups remained independent in the interior of the peninsula for much longer. In the old Petén heartland of Classic Maya culture, the forest kingdom of the Itzá held out until 1697. By the end of the seventeenth century, however, all Maya regions were under at least indirect Spanish control, although there were rebellions and uprisings throughout the Colonial and Republican periods. The most successful was the Caste War of the 1840s, which sparked a tradition of resistance to Spanish and Mexican authorities that remained strong in Quintana Roo until well into the twentieth century.

Today about 4 million Mayan speakers still inhabit southern and eastern Mesoamerica, especially the southern highlands and northern Yucatán. Many are farmers who live in small, rural communities where pre-Spanish cultural practices and beliefs still survive, albeit often in altered forms. In the New World, only the central and southern Andes have a comparable contemporary concentration of native peoples who preserve many of their cultural traditions. The living Maya have been heavily studied by ethnographers, in part because their life yields insights concerning their pre-Spanish ancestors.

FURTHER READINGS

Ashmore, W. (ed.). 1981. *Lowland Maya Settlement Patterns.* Albuquerque: University of New Mexico Press.

Culbert, T. P. (ed.). 1991. *Classic Maya Political History.* New York: Cambridge University Press.

Culbert, T. P., and D. S. Rice (eds.). 1990. *Precolumbian Population History in the Maya Lowlands.* Albuquerque: University of New Mexico Press.

Fox, J. 1978. *Quiché Conquest.* Albuquerque: University of New Mexico Press.

Harrison, P., and B. L. Turner. 1978. *Pre-Hispanic Maya Agriculture.* Albuquerque: University of New Mexico Press.

Houston, S. 1989. *Maya Glyphs.* Berkeley: University of California Press.

Jones, G. 1998. *The Conquest of the Last Maya Kingdom.* Stanford: Stanford University Press.

Sabloff, J., and J. Henderson (eds.). 1993. *Lowland Maya Civilization in the Eighth Century A.D.* Washington, D.C.: Dumbarton Oaks.

Schele, L., and M. Miller. 1986. *The Blood of Kings.* Fort Worth: Kimbell Art Museum.

Sharer, R. 1994. *The Ancient Maya.* Stanford: Stanford University Press.

Roys, Ralph. 1943. *The Indian Background of Colonial Yucatan.* Carnegie Institution of Washington Publication 528. Washington, D.C.

Thompson, J. E. S. 1954. *The Rise and Fall of Maya Civilization.* Norman: University of Oklahoma Press.

David L. Webster

SEE ALSO

Chiapas Interior Plateau; Guatemala Highlands Region; Maya Lowlands: North; Maya Lowlands: South; Maya Religion

Maya Deities

To the ancient Maya, deities were not simply abstract, remote beings from the time of creation; they actively influenced all aspects of everyday life, including health and prosperity. Thus, the gods were frequently invoked for such matters as curing, good harvests, or the success of business ventures. However, despite their importance in daily life, the gods of the ancient Maya are known far less than those of the Postclassic Aztec. Whereas many detailed Colonial accounts exist for Aztec gods and mythology, there are relatively few comparable sources pertaining to the sixteenth-century Maya. Although such early sources as the *Relación* of Fray Diego de Landa and the Quichean *Popol Vuh* contain invaluable information regarding Maya gods and religion, much of our current understanding of Maya deities comes not from the Colonial period but from pre-Hispanic Maya writing and art.

Among the first scholars to approach systematically the varied attributes and meanings of the ancient Maya gods was Paul Schellhas. In a work published in English in 1904, Schellhas analyzed the many deities appearing in the three known pre-Hispanic Maya screen-fold books—the Dresden, Paris, and Madrid codices. In addition to describing and interpreting the meaning of the various gods appearing in these books, Schellhas identified many of their accompanying name glyphs. Rather than labeling these beings with Maya names then poorly known, Schellhas designated each god with a character of the Roman alphabet, beginning with the letter *A*. Although the ancient Maya names for many of these gods can now be uttered, the Schellhas system of deity terminology is still widely used.

In his study of Maya gods, Schellhas was restricted to the Postclassic period (A.D. 900–1521), during which the extant pre-Hispanic codices were painted; however, the writing and art of the preceding Classic period (A.D. 250–900) are filled with descriptions and representations of Maya divinities. Although the Classic gods appear on stelae, altars, and other stone monuments, they are especially well represented on fine ceramic vases used for feasting and the drinking of cacao. In these vessel scenes the gods often appear in narrative mythical events with accompanying hieroglyphic texts. In these texts, the deities at times even speak in the first or second person, much as if actual conversation was being recorded. In addition to containing many deities not appearing in the Postclassic codices, the Classic period material has virtually all the major gods who appear in the Schellhas god list. In addi-

tion, a number of these gods, such as the rain and lightning deity Chac, or God B, can be traced still further back to the Late Preclassic period and the beginnings of Maya civilization (100 B.C.–A.D. 100). For the ancient Maya gods, the general pattern appears to be one of gradual development and continuity rather than sudden episodes of innovation and change.

Our increasing understanding of the phonetic nature of Maya hieroglyphic writing now makes it possible to decipher the names and attributes of many gods. For example, the skeletal death deity, God A, is glyphically named Cimi, meaning "death." In one Madrid Codex passage, however, he is also called Cisin, a Yucatec Mayan word meaning "flatulent one." The god of rain and lightning, Chac (God B) had a number of epithets, including Chac Xib Chac and Yaxha Chac—terms probably referring to particular aspects of this being. The name for God D, the old, wizened creator god, was Itzamna, and in ancient texts he is described as an *ah dzib,* or scribe, and an *idzat,* meaning "learned person." Another old being, God N, was named Pauahtun; he appears to be the quadripartite world-bearer who supports the heavens. Although many have considered the goddess Ix Chel a young and comely woman, the name "Chel" is actually reserved for the old and powerful Goddess O, who appears to have been named Chac Chel.

Among the stranger deities in the Schellhas god list is God C. In hieroglyphic texts, he appears to be the personification of a particular sign read as *ku* or *ch'u,* a word signifying sacredness in Mayan languages. Rather than representing a particular being, this deity seems to be a more generalized personification of divinity or sacredness. Thus, in ancient Maya texts the face of God C can introduce the names of particular gods.

Although the ancient texts are an excellent means to identify particular gods, these beings can also be recognized readily by their physical features, costume, and accouterments. Maya gods tend to be anthropomorphic, but many possess specific faunal attributes: thus, the long-nosed being known as God K or Kauil has a serpent nose, belly scutes, and a burning serpent foot. A number of deities possess jaguar characteristics, including the Sun God (God G), the aged merchant God L, and the old goddess Chac Chel, who often appears with spotted jaguar ears and paws. Facial features are especially telling forms of identification. Although some of these facial traits may appear fairly obvious, such as a fleshless skull for the Death God, others are more subtle. Thus, both the Sun God and Itzamna possess the same large eye and "Roman-nose"

M

profile; however, the sun god is represented as mature man at his peak of strength, while Itzamná typically appears with a snaggle-toothed or chapfallen mouth to indicate his advanced years. In terms of costume, headdresses are especially important sources of identification. Itzamná tends to have a central flower-like diadem on his brow, perhaps referring to a divinatory mirror; God L typically wears a broad-brimmed hat topped by an owl. The deities often appear with specific accouterments that not only help identify particular gods but also provide clues to their significance. Thus, along with his broad hat, God L also commonly occurs with a walking stick and merchant's bundle, identifying him as a god of commerce. Chac typically wields an axe, the preeminent lightning symbol in ancient Mesoamerica.

Aside from the distinguishing traits of particular deities, there are other characteristics widely shared among the various gods. One common trait is "god markings," rounded cartouches that commonly appear on the limbs and torsos of divine beings. Although they have been often interpreted as circular mirrors, they are actually oval and probably represent stone celts. In the earlier art of Izapa and other Late Preclassic sites, figures often appear with celts bound to their limbs.

Aside from the old Pauahtun world-bearer, other Maya gods can be quadripartite, including Chac, Kauil, and the Maize God. The quadripartite aspect of these beings surely reflects their orientation to the four world directions or quarters. It is noteworthy that the quadripartite deities tend to correspond to powers of agricultural fertility, and they may relate to the widespread Maya concept of the four-sided world as a maize field.

A third trait common among Maya gods is their tendency toward hybridization—that is, the intentional merging of distinct gods. Although this may be at first sight a source of confusion, such conflation indicates important overlaps in meaning between deities. For example, the frequent merging of Chac and Kauil probably corresponds to their shared role as lightning gods; indeed, the serpent-footed Kauil is a personification of the lightning axe wielded by Chac.

In view of the importance of agriculture among the ancient Maya, it is not surprising that many of their deities personify forces of agricultural fertility. It has been noted that both Chac and Kauil are identified with lightning and rain. Rather than being considered as purely destructive, lightning was seen as a fertilizing force, and in both ancient and contemporary Maya mythology it is lightning that first releases maize from the enclosing underworld. It is now apparent the Maize God was a central being in Classic Maya creation mythology, and he is one of the more common gods appearing on Classic vessel scenes. Whereas the Postclassic form of the Maize God, God E, appears with a foliated head, the Classic period being commonly displays an elongated cranium topped with a tuft of hair; both versions have the same underlying meaning—the head of the Maize God is an ear of corn. In other words, harvesting is an act of decapitation. The Maize God tends to wear copious amounts of jade and quetzal plumes, precious items that not only allude to verdant corn but also mark this being as the ultimate source of prosperity and wealth.

One of the most exciting recent developments in the study of ancient Maya gods is the reconstruction of ancient Maya mythology. It is now increasingly apparent that many of the myths and deities appearing in the creation episode of the early colonial Quiché *Popol Vuh* were present among the Classic Maya. Research by Michael Coe and others has revealed that the hero twins, Hunahpu and Xbalanque, commonly appear on Classic Maya vases in scenes that correspond to episodes in the *Popol Vuh*. One such episode, the defeat of the monster bird Vucub Caquix, can be traced even further back, to Stelae 2 and 25 of Late Preclassic Izapa. It is now evident that the father of the *Popol Vuh* hero twins, Hun Hunahpu, is the richly dressed Maize God commonly depicted on Classic vessels. In the ceramic scenes, the Hero Twins often assist the Maize God, who rises out of a turtle shell symbolizing the green, rounded earth. In a number of these scenes, Chac splits the carapace open with his lightning weapons. The early Colonial *Popol Vuh* does not elaborate on the resurrection of Hun Hunahpu out of the underworld, but this seems to have been a central theme of Classic Maya creation mythology. In a similar line, certain mythological episodes appearing in Classic art are absent from the Quichean *Popol Vuh*. One such myth concerns a trickster rabbit who steals the hat and regalia of old God L, an episode known from a number of Classic vessel scenes. But although such episodes cannot readily be linked to the *Popol Vuh* or to contemporary Maya mythology, these myths are probably not forever lost. The richness and complexity of Classic Maya epigraphy and iconography promise to provide vital clues for reconstructing Classic Maya belief. Moreover, although it is unlikely that additional pre-Hispanic codices will soon come to light, we are dealing with an open system for the Classic period, with vast amounts of art and writing still awaiting discovery and study. Thus, although our current understanding of ancient Maya gods is relatively limited, this will surely change in years to come.

FURTHER READINGS

Hellmuth, N. 1987. *Monster und Menschen in der Maya-Kunst.* Graz: Akademische Druck-u. Verlagsanstalt.

Houston, S., and D. Stuart. 1995. Of Gods, Glyphs, and Kings: Divinity and Rulership Among the Classic Maya. *Antiquity* 70:289–312.

Schellhas, P. 1904. *Representations of Deities of the Maya Manuscripts.* Papers of the Peabody Museum, 4. 1. Cambridge, Mass.: Harvard University.

Taube, K. 1992. *The Major Gods of Ancient Yucatan.* Studies in Pre-Columbian Art and Archaeology, 32. Washington, D.C.: Dumbarton Oaks.

Karl Taube

SEE ALSO

Maya Culture and History; Maya Religion

Maya Lowlands: North

This artificially defined region extends south from the Yucatán Peninsula's northern coast to an arbitrary east–west line running between the Caribbean coast of Belize and the Campeche Gulf Coast, comprising an area of about 120,000 square kilometers, including the present-day Mexican states of Yucatán, Campeche, and Quintana Roo, together with the northernmost tip of Belize. It is characterized by a north-to-south environmental gradient. The far north's coastal salt flats and mangrove estuaries grade into dry scrub vegetation, thorn forest, deciduous forest, and finally dense tropical forest in the far south. Annual rainfall grades from less than 500 mm in the far northwest to over 2,000 mm in the south. The north's red laterite soils, only a few centimeters deep, grade to black-brown rendzina soils over a meter deep in the south. The terrain of the northern plains—a low, flat, limestone shelf relieved only by the low range, the Puuc Hills, which only rarely exceed 100 meters—slopes rapidly upward to the rolling limestone hills and ridges of the south.

Surface water is scarce. A few shallow lakes fluctuate in size and depth with the annual seasonal rains. Laguna Bacalar, 56 kilometers long by 10 kilometers wide, is the only really large body of water in the region. A few shallow rivers drain the immediate inland areas of the south central eastern and western coasts. The only other available surface water is provided by seasonal ponds *(bajos)* in the south and by cenotes in the north. Cenotes (from Yucatec Mayan *dz'onot*) are natural sinkholes formed where the limestone shelf has collapsed to expose the peninsula's subterranean water table; their depths vary from 5 to 40 meters.

The peninsula itself is a sloping limestone shelf, still slowly emerging from the sea. Geological resources include an overall abundance of limestone and marl, pockets of chert, and extensive coastal deposits of solar-evaporated sea salt. A wealth of tropical botanical products and fauna—all now depleted or extinct—were also available; their use is attested by archaeological data and early Colonial documents. Archaeologically, the area is a mosaic of architectural styles and pottery traditions.

Early Occupation and Settlement

Late Paleoindian or Archaic occupation is known from the Loltun Cave system, but this is regarded as an isolated occupational episode. Continuous human settlement in the region began in the Middle Formative period (c. 1000–400 B.C.). Sometime after 700 B.C., slash-and-burn farmers moved into the southern forests, a long, slow process extending over 200 years. Middle Formative pioneers moved into the north by two routes. The first involved a comparatively rapid expansion from the southern Petén up a westerly route to the northwestern corner, dating to between 700 and 600 B.C.; it included occupation at Dzibilchaltun and Komchen (Yucatán), Dzibilnocac (Campeche), and sites along the western edge of the Puuc Hills. The second, more easterly route out of the northeastern Petén and northern Belize into the central and northeastern peninsula started perhaps a century later; people moved slowly northward and outward along an ever-widening front, not reaching many localities until the late sixth century B.C. (Becan) or even later. The initial settlement of far northern Quintana Roo and the northeastern coast of the peninsula may have occurred in the late fifth century B.C. or later. The Cobá area, for example, was not occupied until after 400 B.C.

The hamlets and villages of these pioneer farmers comprised the first permanent settlements in the northern Maya Lowlands. Dzibilchaltun in the sixth century B.C. was a small agricultural hamlet, containing houses with plaster floors and packed earth walls, and the earliest known example of a Maya sweat bath. Even in the Middle Formative period, long-distance exchange was important. Obsidian from the Guatemalan highlands and status-related exotics such as jadeite and hematite were already obtainable.

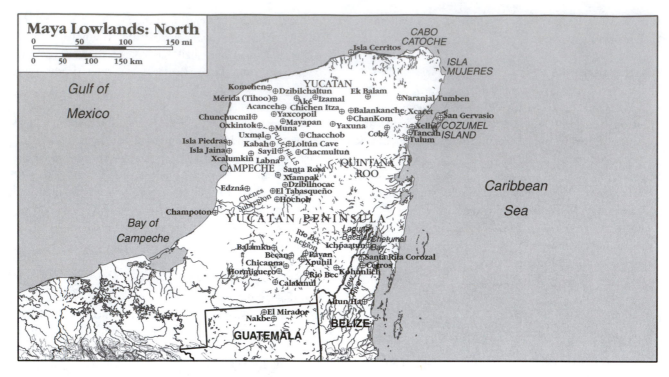

Maya Lowlands: North. Map design by Mapping Specialists Limited, Madison, Wisconsin.

Throughout the area, Middle Formative pottery shows clear derivation from and relationships to the Mamom ceramic sphere of the southern Maya Lowlands, although local variations in vessel forms, surface finishes, and decorative treatments suggest the isolation and independent development commensurate with low population density and slash-and-burn mobility of these pioneering village agriculturalists. In the north during the Middle Formative period, no public architecture, monumental art, or formal centers have been identified that are comparable to southern Lowlands centers such as Nakbe and Mirador.

Late Formative Period (c. 400 B.C.–A.D. 250)

Throughout the northern Lowlands, this period witnessed the earliest evidence of complex socio-political organization, with large-scale platform architecture, monumental art, formal public centers, massive hydraulic works, and artifactual indications of social ranking. Komchen on the northwestern coastal plain is the most thoroughly investigated center. By its height at A.D. 150, Komchen consisted of 900 to 1,000 structures spread over 2 square kilometers. At the center of its concentric arrangement were five monumental platforms, three of which exceeded 8 meters in height. The earliest known

sacbe (raised causeway; Yucatec, "white road") linked two of these. Komchen's development and florescence may have been based on control of the northern coast's salt fields, warfare linked with population pressure, or participation in maritime commerce. Artifactual and ceramic data link Komchen into a coastal maritime network extending around the peninsula and including another important Late Formative center, Cerros (Belize).

Situated on the southern edge of Chetumal Bay near the mouth of the New River, Cerros was established as a small village of farmers, fishers, and traders toward the end of the Middle Formative. By the first century B.C., Cerros had grown into a monumental center, its civil and religious authority in the hands of an elite ruler and expressed through complex architectonic and artifactual symbolism. Four principal pyramidal platforms—the largest around 22 meters high—were enclosed, along with two ball courts and numerous other structures, by a moatlike canal that served dual defensive and irrigation purposes. One platform was adorned with giant stucco masks of the Underworld Jaguar Sun deity and Venus as Morning and Evening Star. The analysis and interpretation of these masks have become a model for similar studies throughout the Maya Lowlands. The Late Formative emergence of "kingship" and its intimate linkage with divinity, postulated for Cerros, is alluded to in a larger-than-life bas-relief of a Maya king in full regalia carved into the rock face above one of several entrances to the Loltun Cave system.

Other large Late Formative architectural centers were at Ake, Yaxuna, Edzna, and Becan. At Yaxuna, a cut-stone masonry platform of this date measures more than 60 by 128 meters and over 18 meters high. Edzna is most impressive for an extensive waterworks system of canals, ponds, ditches, and causeways that combined water storage and irrigation facilities with a central precinct defensive works. More than 22 kilometers of waterways drained 220 square kilometers into a reservoir and irrigation system capable of holding some 220 million cubic meters of water and irrigating more than 450 hectares of land. The entire system appears to have been constructed during the Late Formative.

At Becan, an imposing dry moat—nearly 2 kilometers long, 5.5 meters deep, and 16 meters wide—was complemented by an inner earthworks rampart 5 meters high, enclosing the core of the Late Formative center. At least one pyramidal platform over 14 meters high dates from this period, and extensive Formative construction at the site makes it likely that others existed.

The Becan moat has been dated to the late second or early third century A.D., the same interval during which Edzna, Komchen, and Cerros have been documented as going into rapid decline and failing; data suggest a general demographic decline and societal collapse, perhaps because of endemic local warfare, the inherent instability of early state and ranked (chiefdom-type) societies, or a major shift of communication and trade routes from the circumpeninsular coastal margins to transpeninsular inland routes. Although some centers failed (Komchen, Cerros, Edzna) and some populations declined, others did not (Santa Rita Corozal, Kohunlich, Becan), and some cases (Dzibilchaltun, Cobá) present an even more complex archaeological picture.

Early Classic Period (Early Period I; A.D. 250–600)

This period remains poorly understood for the northern Lowlands. The extent of population decline is questionable; data from Dzibilchaltun and Cobá in particular suggest a persistence of "Late Formative" ceramics and other temporal indicators well into the fifth century. Major Early Classic architectural centers with impressive monumental platform architecture include Ake, Izamal, Acanceh, Yaxuna, Chac II, Edzna, Balamku, Kohunlich, and Calakmul.

Richly furnished high-status burials have been recovered at Dzibilchaltun, Yaxuna, Oxkintok, and Calakmul, and at Becan there was an unbroken, thriving occupational presence within the Terminal Formative defensive system. Monumental architectonic façade decorations consisting of enormous modeled and polychrome-painted stucco depictions of the Sun God and Venus are known from Kohunlich, Balamku, Edzna, and Izamal. As always in the northern Lowlands, hieroglyphic inscriptions are rare; the earliest known occur at Calakmul (A.D. 431) in the western Puuc Hills.

There are few but strong indications of contact with central highland Mexico. In addition to green obsidian blades, dart points (Becan), and even eccentrics (Altun Há), these include a stela fragment from Yaxuna bearing a "Mexican" warrior carved in profile, a set of wall frescoes in pure Teotihuacan style and colors at Xelha, and a cached structural offering from Becan consisting of a hollow Teotihuacan-style terracotta statuette and ten solid figurines of Teotihuacan gods and warriors. All these are believed to date to between the middle fifth century and late sixth. Interaction between the northern Lowland Maya and Teotihuacan probably was based on trade of highland obsidian, lowland salt, and lowland forest products.

The Late and Terminal Classic Period Continuum (Early Period II and Pure Florescent Periods; A.D. 600–750 and 750–950)

Northern Maya Lowlands chronology employs a simple division at approximately A.D. 550–600 between Early and Late Classic. During this and the subsequent Terminal Classic (or Pure Florescent, A.D. 750–950), several distinctive regional architectural and ceramic traditions emerged and flourished, and kaleidoscopic cultural zonation became pronounced. Concurrent social, political, and economic zonation was also more evident than in earlier times, and this became the focus of archaeological, ethnohistoric, and epigraphic research during the 1970s and 1980s. It is most effective to review this era in the Northern Lowlands by subregion.

Central Yucatán Region, Río Bec Subregion. The Río Bec subregion extends across adjacent central eastern Campeche and central western Quintana Roo; it is environmentally transitional between the high rain forest of the southern Lowlands and the dry thorn forest of the northwestern peninsula. Its topography consists of rolling hills and ridges interspersed with low-lying *bajos*. The zone is defined by the presence of the Río Bec architectural style

M

(named for its type site), which is characterized by block masonry range buildings ("palaces") that are frequently equipped with twin or triple decorative towers constructed to appear to be temple-topped pyramids with outset frontal stairs. In reality, these towers were ornamental: the stairs are nonfunctional low-relief sculptures, and the temples either dummies or single-chamber lookouts. Many of the towers are solid; others contain narrow, twisting stairways leading to small chambers within the imitation temple buildings on top. The façades of many Río Bec range buildings were also adorned with central doorways sculpted as gaping monster-mouths flanked by wall panels of profile sky-serpent and *witz* (mountain) monsters. Most decoration involved thickly applied and deeply modeled polychrome-painted stucco over rough-cut stone armatures. Elaborately embellished openwork roof combs are another common feature throughout the zone.

Río Bec centers generally are much smaller and less compact than those of the southern Lowlands. Important recorded sites include Río Bec (actually a cluster of fourteen separate sites), Hormiguero, Xpuhil, Payan, Chicanna, and Becan. Many smaller plaza group or "manor house" sites are scattered throughout the zone. Their abundance and architectural richness probably reflect the region's high agricultural productivity, evidenced by the 10,000 square kilometers of hillside terraces, walled garden plots, drained fields, and other agricultural features recorded in the area. The largest and most complex site, and probably the primary center for the region, was Becan, with ditch-and-earthworks fortification. The zonal ceramic tradition is related closely to the monochrome red, brown, black, and polychrome glosswares of the south and shares many features and some actual pottery with them. No distinctive local "palace school" of pottery production has been identified for the Río Bec region.

Central Yucatán Region, Chenes Subregion. Farther north and west, straddling the dry thorn-forested border region of northeastern Campeche and southwestern Yucatán, the Chenes subregion is defined by the presence of an architectural style that is plainly related to Río Bec but that lacks imitation temple-pyramid towers and has much greater elaboration of ornately modeled stucco façade decoration. The Chenes zone was probably a separate small regional state or cluster of small states. Style and region are named for the numerous natural sinkholes (*chenes*) that provide water throughout the zone. Among the most important recorded Chenes sites are Hochob, Santa Rosa Xtampak, Dzibilnocac, and El Tabasqueño.

The ceramic tradition of the region is quite distinct from Río Bec's and combines southern-like monochrome and polychrome "glosswares" with the low-polish, soapy-luster "slateware" tradition common to northern Campeche, Yucatán, and Quintana Roo. The zone was home to a well-known palace school of ceramic art featuring bright red and black supernatural *muan* birds painted on the interiors of orange-slipped tripod dishes.

Both Río Bec and Chenes architectural styles have been dated to the early seventh into ninth centuries. Centers and smaller sites probably continued to be occupied, and recent data from the Río Bec zone suggests ongoing activities and occupation at Chicanna as late as the early twelfth century. Beyond that time, there is scant evidence of occupation until well into the Colonial era.

Although not associated with widespread, distinctive architectural styles as are the Río Bec and Chenes sites, several other sites probably represented small, independent Late to Terminal Classic regional states, notably Edzna in the Campeche coastal zone, Oxkintok at the southwest tip of the Puuc Hills, Yaxcopoil in central east Yucatán, Dzibilchaltun on the northwestern coastal plain, Izamal on the north central coastal plain, Xcalumkin in northernmost Campeche, Yaxuna in central Yucatán, and Ek Balam in northeastern Yucatán. They vary in architecture, ceramics, art, and the use of hieroglyphic inscriptions, but all express a similar underlying theme, and their distinctiveness is best understood as reflecting political or social organizational segmentation rather than cultural differentiation. The Late Postclassic period (A.D. 1450–1550) has come to be known as an era of small independent states, but such a description would be equally appropriate for the Late and Terminal Classic periods.

In the far northeast of the peninsula, spread out among five small lakes, lies the enormous site of Cobá (Yucatec, "ruffled waters"). One of the largest dispersed centers in all the Lowlands, at its eighth- and ninth-century height Coba sprawled across more than 30 square kilometers, not including numerous satellite communities. Characterized by a distinctly Petén-like architectural style and construction tradition, the central core includes two tenoned-ring ball courts, a number of temple-pyramids more than 24 meters high, and thirty-two stelae, twenty-three of which were sculpted with narrative images and glyphic texts. Inscriptions on Stela 1 (A.D. 682) hint at links to Naranjo and Dos Pilas in the south. Cobá's most notable feature is its urban plan, which comprised a complex multi-plaza core linked via a branching system of sixteen elevated trunk causeways (*sacbeob*) to a series of variably distanced outlying groups and other centers. The causeways range from 50 cm to 2.5 meters above ground, average about 4.5 meters wide, and range in length from less than 1 kilometer to 100 kilometers. The longest causeway, built around A.D. 800, linked Cobá to the central Yucatán center of Yaxuna. To the east, Xelha and Tancah on the Quintana Roo coast probably served Cobá as port facilities.

The Late through Terminal Classic ceramics of Cobá comprise one of two major divisions of the slateware tradition common to the northern peninsula (Eastern Cehpech sphere). Glossy polychrome tradewares and giftwares from the south suggest interactions with the Chenes, Río Bec, and northern Belize coastal regions. There is general comparability between the Eastern and Western (Puuc) Cehpech spheres, but enough differences exist in surface finish characters, vessel shape inventories, and decorative emphases to intimate the cultural separateness of the Cobá and Puuc regions and to suggest a complementary independence in the social and economic realms, if not the political as well.

The emergence of Chichén Itzá as a major power in the early ninth century is believed to have been accompanied by a violent confrontation between the "Itzá" and the Cobá state. Yaxuna was situated on what may have been an important boundary between the existing Cobá and Puuc regional polities, and the site was apparently the scene of combat between the "Itzá" and Coba Maya. After A.D. 900 Cobá's center languished, and it may even have been abandoned by the eleventh century, but it was revitalized and its principal structures refurbished during the Late Postclassic period. Several new East Coast–style (or Tulum-style) temples were built, with wall frescoes in the hybrid Maya-Mixteca-Puebla style of the Late Postclassic period. The precise time of this resurgence has yet to be established satisfactorily.

Puuc

Puuc architectural style and the archaeological culture region named for it take their name from the low range of hills (puuc) that zigzags through the heart of their distribution. Puuc style has its roots in central western and northern Campeche, where Early Puuc architecture has been dated to between A.D. 700 and 800 at Edzna, Oxkintok, and Xcalumkin. Late or Classic Puuc architecture, seen in its fullest grandeur at such sites as Uxmal, Labna, Sayil, and Kabah, is dated to between A.D. 800 and 950. Classic Puuc architecture is regarded by many authorities as the finest of all the ancient Mesoamerican architectural

traditions. It combines true concrete-core and veneer-facing masonry with intricate geometric and symbolic stone mosaic façades. These façades combine tens of thousands of standardized precut and sculpted stone elements into intricate, repetitive geometric designs and masks. In-the-round statues of rulers, warriors, gods, animals, and appropriate paraphernalia were tenoned into the concrete core-backed façades. Low-relief doorjambs and lintels of similar subjects often completed the work. The availability of hard, fine-grain limestones in a range of warm earth colors added to the beauty of the final product.

Hieroglyphic texts are rare in the zone, as throughout the north, but they occur at Uxmal, Kabah, Labna, Oxkintok, and Xcalumkin. Among the little information garnered from them to date is the name of the last and perhaps greatest Uxmal ruler, Lord Chac, who commissioned construction of the city's finest building, the Palace of the Governor, shortly after A.D. 900. Lord Chac is also named in texts at Kabah and Chichén Itzá. Other renowned gems of Classic Puuc architecture include the Nunnery Quadrangle palace complex and Pyramid of the Magician in Uxmal; the Great Palace at Sayil; the Palace and Portal Arch at Labna; and the Palace of the Masks, or Codz Poop, at Kabah.

Uxmal, Kabah, Sayil, Labna, Chacmultun, and other Puuc centers probably formed nuclei of culturally related small polities, with Uxmal perhaps enjoying some preeminence at the regional level, a role in which it may have succeeded Oxkintok, Nohpat, and Kabah. The economic underpinnings of Puuc society remain poorly understood; control over northern coastal salt extraction and trade, more generalized mercantilism, and intensive agricultural production and surplus marketing all have been proposed in recent years. The zone was among the most densely occupied on the northern peninsula and is characterized by the deepest and most fertile soils to be found in the far north. Still, it is a region of very low rainfall, and specialized large-capacity, plaster-sealed water storage cisterns, or chultunes, were cut into the limestone bedrock or incorporated into platforms at almost all sites examined. Despite the shared name, the northern Lowland chultunes differ both morphologically and functionally from those of the central peninsula and southern Lowlands.

Fortifications suggest the pervading social and political tenor of the Terminal Classic or Pure Florescent period in the north. Uxmal itself was a walled center, and as Puuc influences spread northward after A.D. 800, fortification systems also appeared at existing and new centers. On the

M

northern plains, Chacchob, Muna, Chunchucmil, Ake, and Cuca are known for defensive walls dating to this period. Puuc influence ultimately spread as far as northeastern Yucatán state, where it is reflected in the Uxmal-like architecture of Culuba. The actual history of the era is still poorly understood, but from shortly after A.D. 900 on, there are site failures and abandonments. While economic competition and warfare plainly were involved, the overall underlying reasons for the site abandonments of the tenth through twelfth centuries remain matters of ongoing investigation and debate.

The ceramic tradition associated with Puuc architecture is the Western Cehpech sphere, a slateware-dominated assemblage given scant color only by Puuc Redware and low frequencies of the dull, burnished orange and white fine-paste pottery produced along the Tabasco-Campeche Gulf coast. Even rarer are occasional polychrome glossware vessels from the southern peninsula or northern coastal Belize.

Western Cehpech ceramics provide a valuable tracer for the direction and timing of Puuc interactions and movements, and they have been used to evaluate relationships between the core centers of the Puuc Hills zone, the Cobá regional state, and Chichén Itzá. Thin-slate ware and Puuc Redware, possibly representing the "palace school" tradition of Uxmal and its peers, have been especially important in this regard. One other palace school tradition—the so-called Chochola style of deeply and intricately carved polished blackware, brownware, and slateware bowls depicting rulers, gods, and mythological scenes and bearing hieroglyphic texts—appears to have been produced at either Xcalumkin or Oxkintok.

Linked by ceramics to the Puuc, Chenes, and Edzna zones are two offshore cemetery islands, Isla Jaina and Isla Piedras. Neither island possesses ruins of any importance, two small plaza groups and a ball court on Jaina constituting the principal local site; however, the islands hold hundreds upon hundreds of graves, each one accompanied by slateware or glossware pottery furnishings and one to three beautifully modeled or mold-cast and modeled ceramic figurines. Jaina-style figurines, naturalistic and exquisitely detailed, are generally regarded as the finest figurine art produced throughout the ancient Americas. In the form of solid statuettes, hollow figurine-whistles, and rattles, they depict men and women, rulers, warriors, weavers, gods, and mythological couples. All the figurines seem to have been produced specifically as burial accompaniments. The identity of the burial population remains undetermined, but consensus favors

elites from the neighboring Edzna, Chenes, and Puuc regions.

Terminal Classic–Early Postclassic Continuum (Pure and Modified Florescent Periods; A.D. 750–950 and 950–1250)

Chichén Itzá is without question the best-known site in the northern Lowlands. Its architecture, art, inscriptions, pottery, and other artifactual remains have been studied, drawn, photographed, and written about for decades, but it is a center whose actual history remains murky and controversial; only in recent years has it started to become clear. Situated on the north central coastal plain of Yucatán, some 125 kilometers east of present-day Mérida (ancient Tihoo, a major Late Classic/Early period II through Conquest era center renowned in the early Colonial period for its now-vanished Terminal Classic Puuc-style architecture), and 90 kilometers inland from the coast, the ruins of Chichén Itzá's architectural core are known to spread over at least 5 square kilometers.

Two sharply distinct architectural styles are represented among the center's principal structures, and much of the controversy about the site concerns two issues: whether these styles were contemporaneous or sequential, and the ethnic affiliation of their respective builders. The two styles are divided spatially to a large degree into separate southern and northern clusters at the site's core.

The southern cluster is characterized by a local expression of the Puuc style that more closely resembles Early than Classic Puuc in construction technology but is nonetheless believed to date to the ninth century and later; it is generally assigned to the Terminal Classic or Pure Florescent period. Its builders have been identified variously as Yucatec Maya, Itzá-Maya, and Putun-Chontal Maya. Well-known examples of Chichén Itzá Puuc architecture include the *Monjas* palace complex, the Akabdzib, the Casa Colorada, and the Caracol observatory. A series of hieroglyphic inscriptions associated with several southern zone structures ranges from A.D. 840 to 889, clustering after 866. The texts differ in structure and content from southern Lowland Maya examples in recording dedications and ritual activities carried out by groups of elites rather than documenting the dynastic histories and achievements of individuals. Rulership at Chichén Itzá may have been shared among a group, council, or confederation of "brothers" rather than being held by a single king or lord. This form of governance is described in later Maya chronicles as *mul tepal,* or "joint rule." One major figure, Kakupacal, is named repeatedly in the inscriptions and may be the same individual described in Colonial era sources as a valiant leader of the Itzá-Maya.

Chichén Itzá's northern cluster of buildings is dramatically different, with "Toltec" or "Maya-Toltec" style architecture. Some scholars believe these structures to be fully contemporaneous in construction and use with the Puuc-style buildings of the southern group; most, however, have placed the northern group in the subsequent Early Postclassic or Modified Florescent period (A.D. 950–1250). Its builders or patrons have been identified variously as Toltecs, Itzá-Maya, and mexicanized Maya. Colonial era sources also associate Chichén Itzá's founding or refounding with the arrival in Yucatán of Kukulcan (Feathered Serpent), the Maya manifestation of the semi-mythological, semi-historical Mexican god-king, Topiltzin Quetzalcoatl.

The principal monuments of the northern zone—the Temple of the Warriors, Thousand Columns Group, Castillo or Temple of Kukulcan, Temple of the Jaguars, Great Ball Court, Tzompantli (Skull Rack), Mercado, and two "dance platforms"—either are closely analogous to others at Tula (Hidalgo), in highland Central Mexico, or are decorated with reliefs, paintings, and sculptures pronouncedly Toltec in content and style. The nature, raison d'être, actual players involved, and even the direction of the interaction documented continue to be debated. That a multiplicity of "foreign" (Central Mexican) cultural features were represented at Chichén Itzá with intensity is one of few certain facts.

Apart from its Toltec-flavored art and architecture, Chichén Itzá is widely known for its seven ball courts, more than any other site in Mesoamerica, and for the life-size and larger-than-life sculptures of semi-reclining, supine human captives, the so-called *Chac Mools.* These may have played a role in periodic New Fire ceremonies. The single most famous feature of Chichén Itzá, however, is its Cenote of Sacrifice and associated "cenote cult." Actual ritual use of Cenote Chen Ku for sacrificial offerings has been established to have involved two discrete episodes. The first was a single massive ceremony of dedication or termination that occurred sometime during or toward the end of the city's florescence, during which the bulk of its famous treasure of gold, jadeite, wood, shell, and bone artifacts were cast into it. The second episode was a prolonged period postdating A.D. 1200, involving intermittent offerings of pottery dishes, copal incense, and an occasional jadeite ornament. When the hundred or so people—male adults, children, and a few women—whose remains have been recovered from the cenote's depths were thrown in has not been determined.

Chichén Itzá's ceramic assemblage, the Sotuta complex, is in many respects nothing more than another strongly regionalized variant of the widespread northern slateware and redware traditions. Real distinction lies in the favored exotic fine ware, Silho or "X" Fine Orange, probably a product of the northern Campeche coastal zone. Also imported was Plumbate ware from the western highlands of Guatemala, but this popular Mesoamerican tradeware of the tenth through twelfth century was equally common at Uxmal and far more abundant at sites along the southern transpeninsular trade route such as Becan and Chicanna, so it ought not to be regarded as a Chichén Itzá diagnostic.

Evidence of "Toltec" presence is scarce elsewhere in the northern Lowlands, but it exists in the form of elaborate ceremonial deposits of hourglass-shaped Tlaloc-effigy incense burners from underground cave shrines at Balankanche, east of Chichén Itzá, and from Xelha, on the Quintana Roo coast. Ninety kilometers north of Chichén Itzá, an offshore island, Isla Cerritos, served the inland center as a port facility; its role is apparent in the presence of such highland Mexican imports as turquoise and obsidian from several sources known to have been exploited or controlled by the Tula Toltec.

Exactly when Chichén Itzá failed remains uncertain. Traditional chronologies based on Colonial era native histories and a meager body of archaeological data place the event sometime in the mid-twelfth to early thirteenth century. Following its collapse, Chichén Itzá and especially the Cenote of Sacrifice remained a focus of periodic pilgrimages and offerings through the Postclassic and Colonial eras and into the late twentieth century.

Late Postclassic Period (Decadent; A.D. 1250–1550)

Archaeology and early Colonial literary accounts combine to document the history of Mayapan, established as a small local center in the late eleventh century. It emerged in the mid-thirteenth as the successor to Chichén Itzá as the preeminent power on the northern plains following the latter's fall. Tradition assigns the Itzá-Maya and Cocom lineage to rulership at this center and also records their engagement of "Mexican" mercenaries from Tabasco to back up their authority. The city survived on a tribute-based economy, with the ruling families of other small northern polities housed as virtual hostages within its walls. A bloody rebellion by these rulers and their followers in the mid-1400s resulted in the slaughter of the

M

Cocom family and the destruction of Mayapan. Archaeology confirms the fact and dating of the center's violent end. As a city, Mayapan was a ramshackle affair of structurally and esthetically inferior architecture, manifesting obvious efforts to replicate that of Chichén Itzá. The principal temple-pyramid of Mayapan, El Castillo, mimics its Chichén Itzá namesake on a smaller, less grand scale. Several other structures are scaled-down copies of Chichén Itzá originals. There are no ball courts, no sweat baths, and no use of the elsewhere ubiquitous corbel arch. The ceremonial and administrative core of about 120 buildings was demarcated by a low stonewall, and an outer defensive wall enclosed the entire settlement of about 12,000 people, densely packed into 4 square kilometers. This genuinely urban character of Mayapan's demography and use of space is one of the site's most interesting features.

Late Postclassic ceramics in general emphasized unslipped plainwares and redwares of highly variable technological and esthetic quality. The most outstanding feature of the period is the elaborately molded, modeled, appliquéd, and brightly postfiring-painted effigy censers in the forms of gods and mythological beings. These were used in formal public ceremonies and in private household ancestor rites; they occur commonly in Late Postclassic ritual contexts from Santa Rita Corozal on Chetumal Bay and Champoton on the Campeche Gulf to Mayapan, Chichén Itzá, Dzibilchaltun, and numerous other northern peninsula sites.

Mayapan economy has traditionally been emphasized as tribute based, but evidence from throughout eastern Mesoamerica suggests that at least as important was the city's intense involvement in the circumpeninsular maritime trade that flourished from the thirteenth century until the Conquest.

No single center dominated the final pre-Conquest century in the northern Lowlands. Instead, a mosaic of sixteen variably sized independent polities shared the peninsula, their governing systems differing in structure and membership. A single lineage generally governed each of these from a sometimes fortified capital center. Mercantile activities provided the economic underpinnings for a new order of families, centers, and states that outlasted Mayapan and continued a well-established way of life. Of several centers known to have been active during this era but likely to have been contemporaries of Mayapan as well, Santa Rita Corozal, Ichpaatun, Tancah, Tulum, San Gervasio (Isla Cozumel), and Champoton are best known archaeologically.

Tulum is representative of these mercantile Postclassic centers. Situated on a cliff overlooking the Caribbean, the town is fortified on its three inland sides by a wall 3 to 5 meters high, with parapets and towers. Within the 6.5 hectares enclosed by the wall, the planned layout includes not only administrative and ceremonial buildings but also residences, a marketplace, a permanent freshwater source, and canoe-landing facilities. No evidence has been found of associated settlement outside the wall. Tulum's late fifteenth-century mural art, like that of Tancah, Xelha, and Santa Rita Corozal, was executed in the "international" Maya-Mixteca-Puebla style popular throughout southern Mesoamerica during the century before the Conquest. It was of Tulum that Juan Diaz, chaplain of the Grijalva expedition, wrote in 1518, "Towards sunset we saw from afar off a town or village so large that the city of Seville could not appear greater or better; and in it was seen a very great tower."

FURTHER READINGS

Andrews, E. W., IV, and E. W. Andrews V. 1980. *Excavations at Dzibilchaltun, Yucatan, Mexico.* Middle American Research Institute, Tulane University, Publication 48. New Orleans.

Andrews, E. W., V. 1990. Early Ceramic History of the Lowland Maya. In F. S. Clancy and P. D. Harrison (eds.), *Vision and Revision in Maya Studies,* pp. 1–19. Albuquerque: University of New Mexico Press.

Ball, J. W. 1977. *The Archaeological Ceramics of Becan, Campeche, Mexico.* Middle American Research Institute, Tulane University, Publication 43. New Orleans.

Brainerd, G. W. 1958. *The Archaeological Ceramics of Yucatan.* Berkeley and Los Angeles: University of California Press.

Dunning, N. P., and J. K. Kowalski. 1994. Lords of the Hills: Classic Maya Settlement Patterns and Political Iconography in the Puuc Region, Mexico. *Ancient Mesoamerica* 5:63–95.

Eaton, J. D., and J. W. Ball. 1978. *Studies in the Archaeology of Coastal Yucatan and Campeche.* Middle American Research Institute, Tulane University, Publication 46. New Orleans.

Gendrop, P. 1983. *Los Estilos Río Bec, Chenes, y Puuc en la arquitectura Maya.* Mexico City: Universidad Nacional Autónoma de Mexico.

Kurjack, E. B. 1974. *Prehistoric Lowland Maya Community and Social Organization: A Case Study at Dzibilchaltun, Yucatan, Mexico.* Middle American Research

Institute, Tulane University, Publication 38. New Orleans.

Miller, A. G. 1982. *On the Edge of the Sea: Mural Painting at Tancah-Tulum, Quintana Roo.* Washington, D.C.: Dumbarton Oaks.

Pollock, H. E. D., R. L. Roys, T. Proskouriakoff, and A. L. Smith. 1962. *Mayapan, Yucatan, Mexico.* Carnegie Institution of Washington, Publication 619. Washington, D.C.

Prem, H. J. (ed.) 1994. *Hidden among the Hills: Maya Archaeology of the Northwest Yucatan Peninsula.* Moecmsuehl, Germany: Anton Saurwein.

Sabloff, J. A., and G. Tourtellot (eds.). 1991. *The Ancient Maya City of Sayil: The Mapping of a Puuc Region Center.* Middle American Research Institute, Tulane University, Publication 60. New Orleans.

Joseph W. Ball

SEE ALSO

Chichén Itzá; Maya Culture and History; Mayapan

Maya Lowlands: South

This cultural area of Maya affiliation extends across the southern Yucatán Peninsula, bounded on the east by the Caribbean, on the west by the Gulf of Mexico and Isthmus of Tehuantepec, and to the north and south, approximately, by latitudes 18° and 16°. The southern Maya Lowlands represent one of the focal points of Mesoamerican civilization: a region of large if variable population, rich craft tradition, cities of considerable size, and a literate elite who commissioned public sculptures for the glorification of self, ancestors, and gods. The Lowlands also witnessed dramatic changes in settlement and society during the course of their occupation, including the demographic convulsion known as the "Maya collapse." These changes, along with the increasing pace of hieroglyphic decipherment, have fascinated popular audiences and scholars and have led to an unusual intensity of research over the past century. Today, the Lowlands lie within the Mexican states of Chiapas, Tabasco, Campeche, and Quintana Roo, the Guatemalan departments of Petén and Alta Verapaz, and the country of Belize.

Environment

The southern Maya Lowlands cross-cut several environmental zones. The region contains a great diversity of underlying geology, including an ancient massif of meta-morphic stone, now eroded into the peaks and valleys of the Maya Mountains. The remainder of the area consists largely of Mesozoic and Cenozoic limestones folded tectonically, faulted into blocks, and dissolved by karstic processes. Caves, many with evidence of intensive ritual use by Maya, result from subterranean flow and dissolution of limestone. Several important drainage systems, their courses determined in part by faults, pass through the region. They range from the docile Pasión River to the fast-moving and nearly impassable Usumacinta River and its more benign tributaries. Most of these sweep eventually into the Gulf of Mexico, winding through flat alluvial plains. Coastal plains also characterize the eastern portion of the Lowlands. Beyond lies a barrier reef used by Maya traders and fishermen. Over the Lowlands, surface elevation seldom exceeds 200 meters. The most notable exceptions are the Maya Mountains (Victoria Peak, 1,120 meters) and the broken terrain to either side of the Usumacinta River (500+ meters). The elevation of the Sierra Lacandón, in the Mexican state of Chiapas, is particularly high and grades into colder, volcanic highlands.

In contrast to popular views of torrid, dense rain forest, climate and vegetation vary greatly in the southern Lowlands. Temperature, for example, changes with elevation. Most of the Lowlands lies in a zone known to Spanish speakers as the *tierra caliente,* or "hot land," up to about 800 meters, with the remainder in the *tierra templada,* or "temperate land." Prevailing winds come from the east, bringing seasonal rains of varying duration and accumulation. The heaviest rains arrive in May or June and last, with some breaks, until December and beyond. At this time rivers can be swollen, and flooding occurs in low, swampy areas of poor drainage, known as *bajos.* Parts of the Lowlands, particularly the far south and west, seldom have "dry" months, and mean annual rainfall can surpass 3,400 mm. To the north, annual rainfall diminishes by at least 1,000 mm.

The vegetation depends on a number of factors, especially soils, drainage, amount of rainfall. Not surprisingly, some evergreen rain forests exist, with many distinct canopies and, typically, "plank" root buttresses to compensate for thin soil. *Palo de tinta,* or logwood (*Haematoxylum* sp.), often predominates in low-lying areas. Other plants, including the iron-hard *chicozapote* (*Achras* sp.), the related mahogany (*Switenia macrophylla*) and cedro (*Cedrela mexicana),* and vaulting ceiba trees (*Ceiba* sp.), whose seed fiber supplies stuffing, abound in better-drained forest, at least until cut by modern settlers and

M

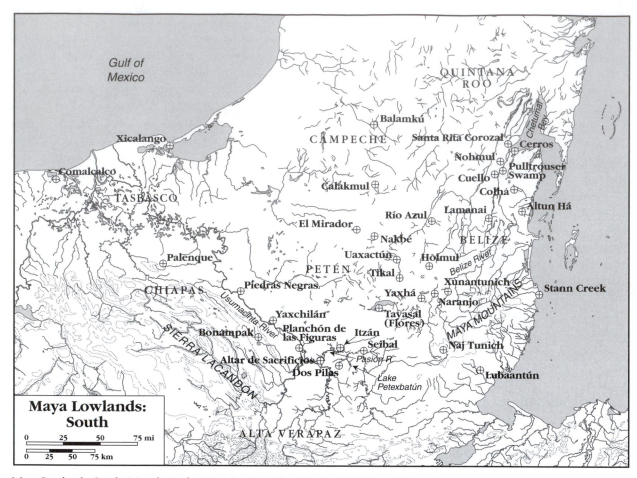

Maya Lowlands: South. Map design by Mapping Specialists Limited, Madison, Wisconsin.

loggers. The ramon tree *(Brosimium alicastrum)*, with its brightly colored fruits around hard kernels, occurs commonly on well-drained soils, leading some researchers to argue for its intentional planting by the Maya, a view not widely shared among scholars. Gums and other binding mastics may have come from the rubber *(Castilla elastica)* and gumbo limbo *(Bursera simaruba)* trees. Local residents continue to use the huano palm *(Sabal mayarum)* for thatching. Yet these are only the most prominent flora. There is a great abundance of palms, vines, bromeliads, and other species, nurtured by forests with some of the highest indices of biodiversity in the world. Rich but understudied flora exist in the mangrove swamps of the Belizean coast, although relatively few Maya lived near such locations.

A striking feature of the Petén and adjacent areas of Belize is an unusual zone of vegetation. A compact clay soil and pattern of interior drainage formed a savanna just south of a string of lakes in the central Petén. Scattered signs of occupation show fitful use by the Maya, who probably hunted there. Just to the east of the Maya Mountains are stands of pine trees, known in Belize as "pine ridge," that flourish on the sandy, leached soils of the area. Generally the Maya preferred to settle near soils with a limestone substrate or on well-drained levee or alluvial soils. Tragically, the removal of forest cover led in some areas to considerable soil erosion, at least until agriculturalists adopted slope-management techniques, depending on the degree of slope and underlying bedding planes of stone. Recent, apparently unstoppable settlement in the area begins anew this cycle of environmental degradation.

In terms of diversity and biomass, most of the fauna in the southern Maya Lowlands consists of insects, of which the most visible examples are stingless bees, mosquitoes, butterflies, wasps, and especially ants, including the prodigiously hard-working leafcutter. The Maya occasionally depicted such insects in their art, but of far greater interest to them were reptiles, amphibians, fish, birds, and terrestrial animals. Among the more prominent of these are an irritable and highly dangerous snake, the fer-de-lance *(Bothrops asper)*, the tasty iguana *(Ctenosaura similis)*, and various species of toad and frog, whose mating calls crescendo during the rainy season. Fish used for consumption include the catfish (Fam. Siluriformes) and mojarra (Fam. Gerreidae). The scarlet macaw *(Ara macao)*, a spectacular seed-eater of the high canopy, occurs in Classic Maya art, apparently depicted as a pet, as does the quetzal bird *(Pharomachrus mocinno)*. The Maya doubtless imported this trogon from cloud forests to the south (the quetzal's natural range lies between 1,500 and 2,500 meters, well above elevations in the southern Lowlands). Small hovering nectarivores, the hummingbirds (Fam. Trochilidae), intrigued the Maya enough to appear in iconographic scenes. Domesticated birds, such as the turkey *(Meleagris* sp.), seldom occur in Maya art. The paca *(Agouti paca)* provided (and still provides) delicious, fatty meat, as did the peccary (Fam. Tayassuidae), the brocket deer *(Mazama* sp.), and the white-tailed deer *(Odocoileus virginianus)*. Various kinds of feline, including the now-scarce jaguar *(Felis onca)*, exist throughout the southern Lowlands, although in low-intensity distribution. At least two primates—the howler monkey *(Alouatta palliata)* and the spider monkey *(Ateles geoffroyi)*, and possibly the Capuchin monkey in ancient times—live in the jungle canopy. All are threatened by forest clearance, road penetration, and uncontrolled hunting.

These flora and fauna bear the imprint of human activity. The turkey was domesticated, and deer and peccary probably were herded loosely or even kept in corrals. Trees of economic value, such as the avocado *(Persea americana)* and mamey *(Calocarpum mammosum)*, may be found near communities abandoned by Lacandón Maya, who occupied the western Petén until the early years of the twentieth century and still live, partly acculturated and in much reduced numbers, in Chiapas, Mexico. Species of plant were domesticated, including beans *(Phaseolus* sp.), squashes *(Cucurbita* sp.), a small-fruited chile *(Capsicum annuum)*, cacao *(Theobroma* sp.), and particularly maize *(Zea mays)*, which relies on human intervention for its propagation and whose cob size increased throughout the early years of Maya occupation in the southern Lowlands. Even before their modern destruction, the forests, grasslands, and riverine and lakeside habitats of the southern Lowlands, as well as the creatures and plants that inhabit them, can hardly be regarded as pristine or untouched by humans. Cutting, burning, and landscape modification have introduced large changes to the region since agriculturalists arrived several millennia ago.

Settlement History and Cultural Processes

Human occupation and societal development in the southern Lowlands can be divided into several phases, each characterized by a distinctive constellation of economy, settlement, and social and political organization. These phases are: (1) hunting and gathering, with dispersed, probably mobile settlement (the Archaic); (2) early agriculturalists, congregated into isolated homesteads and, increasingly, villages (Early to Middle Formative); (3) larger communities with public architecture, some of it monumental in scale (Middle Formative); (4) urban centers with massive architecture and terraforming (Late Formative); (5) urban centers with literate elites organized dynastically (Classic); and (6) smaller communities settled in riverine and lakeside settings (Postclassic). Of these, Phase 1 and possibly Phase 2 are not certainly "Maya" in any linguistic or ethnic sense. The broad distribution of a particular group of Mayan languages in the Yucatán Peninsula suggests a relatively late introduction of Mayan to the region from its linguistic homeland in the Guatemalan highlands. Regrettably, neither the unreliable estimates of glottochronology—a method for determining the time when languages diverged—nor studies of material culture, such as ceramics, are likely to resolve the question of linguistic or ethnic affiliation for this early period. Moreover, culture has its own dynamic and cannot easily be divided into discrete phases for the convenience of scholars. Hunting and gathering doubtless continued throughout the sequence, just as every phase (except Phase 1) possessed isolated homesteads. A study of ceramic, stone-working, or architectural technology, or a categorization of agricultural systems or trade routes, might result in different conceptions of chronological shifts and continuities. Archaeologists have adopted conventional labels for these periods, but settlement and other cultural developments do not always coincide with these. Another point to keep in mind is that archaeological accounts of the southern Maya Lowlands inevitably reflect what researchers have found and the sites they have investigated. Patterns and perceptions can, and will, change with further work, as ideas are refined or rejected. (For a summary of chronology, see the table.)

Phase 1 (the Archaic) embraces a long, preceramic period that remains very poorly understood. Finds in Belize of stone tools, often in uncertain stratigraphic position, suggest the existence of such a phase, possibly extending back to the beginning of the Holocene, when glacial recession prompted massive changes in sea level, climate, and environment; this phase lasted until the

M

CHRONOLOGY, CULTURAL PROCESSES, AND SALIENT ARTIFACTS.

Phase 1: Archaic (c. 9000–2500 B.C.)	Hunting and gathering	Inga, Madden Lake–like points
Phase 2: Early to Middle Formative (2500–600 B.C.)	First maize agriculture, isolated farmsteads and hamlets	Swasey, Xe, Eb ceramics
Phase 3: Middle to Late Formative (600–400 B.C.)	First monumental architecture, villages	Mamom ceramics
Phase 4: Late Formative (400 B.C.–A.D. 250)	First cities, complex iconography, triadic architecture, road systems, first writing, systems of water capture, organized trade, migrations?	Chicanel ceramics
Phase 5: Classic (A.D. 250–900)	Widespread literacy, dynastic rulership, alliance and antagonism, hegemonic polities, palaces, mortuary pyramids, peak population in most sites, intensification of agriculture	Tzakol and Tepeu ceramics
Phase 6: Postclassic (A.D. 900–1600)	Riverine and lakeside settlement, towns, strong connections with northern Yucatán, refugee zone	New Town and Dos Lagos ceramics

fourth millennium B.C. Speculations about the nature of these peoples or their adaptation to variable environments cannot be verified on present evidence, other than to point to analogous, better-documented groups elsewhere. In the future, this phase will need to be subdivided through study of more secure archaeological contexts.

Phase 2 (Early to Middle Formative, or Preclassic) is almost as obscure. Cores from lakes in the central Petén reveal the existence of maize pollen at about 2500 B.C., in calibrated radiocarbon dates. This accords with evidence from Honduras, southeast of the southern Lowlands, where similar disturbances linked with maize pollen occur about 500 years earlier. This phase is also a time of transition, in that some of the earliest ceramics appear at this time, with marked signs of regional styles, a situation making comparisons of pottery difficult and controversial. (Usually, archaeologists believe the appearance of ceramics indicates a considerable break with the past, but this shift has been overstressed: many other aspects of local culture continue unbroken.)

Most researchers place the advent of ceramics at between 1200 and 1000 B.C., depending on the region. One center of ceramic production lies in the Pasión River drainage and is linked by some researchers to non-Mayan peoples. Slightly earlier sherds, of the enigmatic Swasey complex, are documented in Cuello (Belize). Ceramics of this period are simple in form, although they probably result from an even longer, as yet unattested sequence of technological development. Cuello also offers the earliest known architectural evidence from the southern Lowlands: low, platformed courtyard groups, probably domestic and residential in function, with perishable buildings and evidence of replastering and refurbishment. The archaeological sample is too limited to speak meaningfully of the nature of society during this period; presumably, however, it resembled early village cultures elsewhere in Mesoamerica. Figurines satisfied some need, perhaps a religious one, but very little imagery at this time anticipates later Maya symbolism.

Phase 2 extends to approximately 600 B.C., after which increased ceremonialism, expressed through bulky, massive structures and ritual caches, comes into play. At this time, Phase 3 (Middle to Late Formative, c. 600–400 B.C.), archaeological evidence becomes far richer than for earlier periods. New varieties of pottery, with enough material to reconstruct a full set of adventurous forms and surface treatments, appear archaeologically: the most attractive pieces of this "Mamom" pottery display resist decoration, so called because undulating streaks (probably coated with some waxy material) "resisted" the application of another coat of paint, leaving visible the underlying surface. Settlement expanded into more remote, less riverine areas of the southern Lowlands. Most communities were small villages, but recent investigations at Nakbe (Petén, Guatemala), and much more modest architecture from Altar de Sacrificios (Petén, Guatemala), reveal the beginnings of a complex society in which vast labor, centrally organized, was dedicated to the construction of immense platforms and terraces, some close to 20 meters high.

Phase 4 (Late Formative, 400 B.C. to c. A.D. 250) represents the crystallization of southern Lowlands civilization. The Maya elite announced unambiguously its arrival on the scene. Iconography, an elaborate set of visual symbols recording broadly shared meanings, appears for the first time in the region. Its form and content are recognizably Maya, emphasizing a selection of deities, including the Sun God and a creature known as the Principal Bird Deity, who later is associated with royal accession and is one of the main Maya deities. Monumental building reached great height and size. The "triadic" complex—three temples resting symmetrically on immense basal pyramids—figures at sites such as Calakmul, Lamanai, Mirador, and Nakbe. At Mirador, these constructions may reach a height of nearly 70 meters above the jungle floor. Gigantic masks, sometimes recognizable as deities, flank the stairways leading up these pyramids. Population experienced one of its peaks at this time. Settlement extended into new areas, apparently with grave results agriculturally, as unprecedented quantities of soil washed into lakes and rivers. Formal road systems—we presume that trails and paths existed before—radiated out from the Petén city of Mirador. A red pottery known as Sierra Red achieved an unusual degree of uniformity and spread throughout much of the southern Lowlands.

All signs point to unprecedented levels of population, an elaborate iconography that presages later imagery, and architectural forms replicated at different sites. Such features reflect similar religious or processional customs, well-developed trade routes involving specialized traders, and widely shared pottery styles. Whatever created these patterns resulted in part from heightened interaction, but also from a potent combination of religious and political power, leading some researchers to discern the origins of divine kingship at this time. Royal tombs and massive constructions indicate the presence of profound social inequality, doubtless with roots in the preceding phase and perhaps beyond. Toward the end of Phase 4, scribes began to record hieroglyphic texts. Although opaque to modern researchers, these hieroglyphs seem to be remarkably sophisticated, despite the lack of clear antecedents. Overall, the archaeological and textual record continues to be uncertain and shadowy: probably divine kingship came into existence, but the nature of society eludes understanding.

Temptations to interpret this pinnacle of Maya civilization in terms of later periods are misleading—as mistaken as seeing the Classic period through a Postclassic lens. Continuities existed, but changes too, as the southern Lowlands headed into another demographic decline. Scholars label the last years of this phase the "Protoclassic," a time with a new set of ceramics. One interpretation explains these ceramics as the result of actual migration from the southeast; another prefers to see them in terms of local development, adopted for social or political reasons.

Phase 5 (the Classic period, A.D. 250–900) is the best-understood period in the southern Lowlands: a time of literacy, intellectual and religious achievement, peak population, and urbanism. Both earlier and later periods contain some features of the Classic, including stepped or corbelled masonry vaults, polychrome ceramics, and hieroglyphic writing, but they possess neither its abundance of historical documents nor the sheer intensity of archaeological study devoted to it. Most major projects in the southern Lowlands concentrate on the Classic period, although simultaneously uncovering earlier and later remains.

The initial years of the Classic, the Early Classic (A.D. 250–550), represent a distinct subperiod with clear architectural continuities from the Formative. The Early Classic also anticipated the dynastic emphases of the Late Classic, although in different form: ancestor worship played a large role, and the names of kings occur clearly, if without the elaborate parentage statements of later times. The key site in the southern Lowlands was Tikal. Glyphic records attest to the great age of its dynasty, apparently without breaks in succession, and its architecture is vast in size and complexity. Links existed with close sites such as Uaxactun and, evidently, distant ones such as Teotihuacan, a contemporary metropolis in highland Mexico. Yet it would be mistaken to see Tikal as the one Maya center of importance at this time, as archaeologists tend to do because of intensive excavations at the site. Many other Early Classic settlements dot the central and eastern Petén. When told, their stories will supplement Tikal's to produce a fuller account of the Early Classic.

M

A final feature of the Early Classic continues to mystify scholars. In many areas, Early Classic ceramics are almost as scarce as those of the Middle Formative and Postclassic periods, suggesting a dramatic reduction in population at this time, or at least a heavy clustering of people in a few cities. The factors leading to the famous Terminal Classic "collapse," some social, some ecological, may have resembled those affecting the Early Classic. Whatever the population, early dates and counts of succession from dynastic founders show that most major dynasties began toward the middle of this period, the major exceptions being those of the central and northern parts of the southern Lowlands.

After a brief period with fewer texts (a time known as the "hiatus") came the Late Classic period. This was the most literate period, with by far the greatest number of dynastic texts and, for the first and last time in the southern Lowlands, the heightened possibility of reconstructing the overall political composition of the landscape. Historical events, particularly patterns of alliance and antagonism, help to explain archaeological remains to an extent inconceivable before this period. Recent research points to a complex political mosaic. Several old, large centers, especially Tikal and Calakmul, an understudied but crucial site on the northern edge of the southern Lowlands, exercised great influence over kingdoms in the area. Locked in sustained hostility, these centers maneuvered against one another by seeking allies and battling enemies, until a key event in which Tikal seized the ruler of Calakmul. Scholars disagree, however, about the nature of their hegemonic control over the southern Lowlands. Where some see tight control over smaller kingdoms by Tikal and Calakmul, other perceive mutually beneficial voluntary alliances.

Because of recent decipherments, elite behavior of the Late Classic has come into relatively clear focus. The maximal rank was that of "holy lord"—no imperial titles are yet known from Tikal or Calakmul—with the extension of "lordly" rank to only a few people, probably close relatives of the ruler. Rulers sponsored dances, often with sacred regalia, dedicated monuments and buildings with special fire ceremonies, and waged warfare that may have been singularly vicious. Some centers were probably burnt, their sculptures toppled, and members of the royal family taken captive, either for sacrifice or for service as long-term hostages at foreign courts. Royal visits and mingling of dynastic bloodlines through marriage consolidated alliances and probably operated as a mechanism for the exchange of valuable objects and foodstuffs. An increasing elaboration of nonroyal titles and patronage of monuments dedicated to subroyal elites hint at a new dynamic of power. Elites laid greater claim to royal prerogatives, suggesting a situation of decentralization and political fragmentation.

Population estimates, derived from detailed mapping of extensive settlement, underscore the unique demographic profile of the Late Classic period. It ranks among the most populous of all preindustrial societies on the globe, with close to 100,000 people around Tikal and densities of rural settlement that exceed 190 people per square kilometer. A pervasive problem for research is the agricultural basis of these populations. Slash-and-burn agriculture, the cutting and burning of regrowth or pristine forest for impermanent food production, seems unlikely to have provided the necessary food. Techniques of soil capture—soil loss constitutes a major problem with heavy use of tropical soils—and intensification, principally by raised- or drained-field agriculture, are now well documented archaeologically, although local conditions of slope gradient and shifts in water level determine the distribution of such methods for maintaining and increasing yields. In the southern Lowlands, the greatest concentration of these techniques exists in parts of Belize, adjacent parts of Petén, Guatemala, and terrain to the west of Calakmul, in Campeche, Mexico, with a few terracing systems in the Pasión drainage. The limited area given over to these techniques raises serious problems for Maya archaeology. Did the Late Classic Maya trade in food? (From the Formative to the Postclassic, the Maya benefited from ample trade networks both through and around the Yucatan Peninsula.) Was a combination of intensive and extensive agriculture sufficient to feed the burgeoning population? Did enough forest remain to supplement the diet with other foods? Scholars also recognize that a difference exists between living and living well. Late Classic skeletons show widespread evidence of pronounced dietary deficiencies, except for the robust, protein-laden bones of the elite.

The Maya collapse remains as perplexing as the demographic decline of the Early Classic period. Some researchers downplay its scope and extent, but this view is not justified in the southern Lowlands, where populations diminished from urban densities to scattered, mostly riverine settlement. Current perspectives explain the collapse in terms of political fragmentation, migration to other parts of the Yucatán Peninsula, and serious environmental decline. Doubtless a combination of factors resulted in this demographic crisis, with varying effects in different portions of the southern Lowlands. A group of sites near Lake Petexbatún, Petén, reveals late, hurried defensive constructions around site cores, suggesting different kinds of warfare involving populations with changed patterns of interaction. But there is also a paradox here: the period of the collapse, known conventionally as the Terminal Classic period, represented a period of pan-Yucatecan contact, with extensive trade in certain fine goods (some marked with royal names). Greater mobility, expressed in goods but probably involving people as well, contributed as much to population decline in the southern Lowlands as did starvation and warfare.

The final phase, Phase 6 (the Postclassic, A.D. 900–1600), coincides with the denouement of southern Lowlands civilization. Current fashion sees it as a time of vitality and broad interaction, but the fact remains: in the central southern Lowlands, although less so in Belize, populations dropped dramatically, constructions diminished in size, and literacy shifted, we presume, to perishable records, since inscribed monuments disappear. Settlement clustered largely in riverine, coastal, and lakeside areas, where residual populations of Maya, all Yucatecan speakers, remain today. Similarities in ceramics and architecture underscore deep relations with sites to the north. Eventually these connections became even more important as the southern Lowlands developed in response to Spanish incursions and onerous tributary demands. The Lowlands thrived as places of refuge and even accommodated the occasional *visita* church, a chapel for intermittent visits by Spanish clerics.

The end of the Maya tradition in the southern Lowlands has been neither clear-cut nor conclusive. Refugees from the Caste War, a Maya rebellion in Yucatan, settled the area anew in the mid-nineteenth century, probably following well-established routes of escape. Other Maya, culturally and perhaps linguistically related to the Lacandón of Chiapas, Mexico, continued to live in the Petén well into the twentieth century. To the dismay of Spanish authorities, English-speaking populations—the descendants of slaves, logwood cutters, and pirates—occupied the Belizean coast, making inroads into the Belize River Valley. The result was a novel variant of Maya culture and an enrichment of the cultural and linguistic texture of that country. At this writing, only a few dozen speakers of Itzá Maya remain in the central southern Lowlands, and a few thousand of another Yucatecan language, Mopan, live in the southern portion of this region. But other Maya, the Kekchi from the south, are moving steadily into the zone, fleeing political persecution in their homelands and seeking new opportunities in the lowland forests. The Maya, residents of the region for more than three thousand years, will leave their imprint on the southern Lowlands for many years to come.

FURTHER READINGS

Andrews, E. W. 1990. The Early Ceramic History of the Lowland Maya. In F. S. Clancy and P. D. Harrison (eds.), *Vision and Revision in Maya Studies,* pp. 1–19. Albuquerque: University of New Mexico Press.

Chase, A. F., and P. M. Rice (eds.). 1985. *The Lowland Maya Postclassic.* Austin: University of Texas Press.

Culbert, T. P., and D. S. Rice (eds.). 1990. *Precolumbian Population History in the Maya Lowlands.* Albuquerque: University of New Mexico Press.

Dunning, N. P., and T. Beach. 1994. Soil Erosion, Slope Management, and Ancient Terracing in the Maya Lowlands. *Latin American Antiquity* 5:51–69.

Hammond, N. (ed.). 1991. *Cuello: An Early Maya Community in Belize.* Cambridge: Cambridge University Press.

Hansen, R. D. (ed.) 1993. *Investigaciones arqueológicas en Nakbé, Petén: El resumen de la temporada de campo de 1993.* Report submitted to the Instituto de Antropología e Historia, Guatemala.

Houston, S. D. 1993. *Hieroglyphs and History at Dos Pilas.* Austin: University of Texas Press.

Jones, G. D. 1989. *Maya Resistance to Spanish Rule: Time and History on a Colonial Frontier.* Albuquerque: University of New Mexico Press.

Mathews, P. 1985. Maya Early Classic Monuments and Inscriptions. In G. R. Willey and P. L. Mathews (eds.), *A Consideration of the Early Classic Period in Maya Lowlands,* pp. 5–54. Institute for Mesoamerican Studies, Publication 10. Albany: State University of New York at Albany.

Rue, D. J. 1985. Archaic Middle American Agriculture and Settlement: Recent Pollen Data from Honduras. *Journal of Field Archaeology* 16:177–184.

Scarborough, V. L., and G. G. Gallopin. 1991. A Water Storage Adaptation in the Maya Lowlands. *Science* 252:658–662.

Sharer, R. J. 1994. *The Ancient Maya.* 5th edn. Stanford: Stanford University Press.

Stuart, D., and S. D. Houston. 1989. Maya Writing. *Scientific American* 262:82–89.

Stephen D. Houston

SEE ALSO

Maya Culture and History; Maya Lowlands: North; Tikal

M

Maya Religion

Maya religious beliefs and practices were shared widely with other Mesoamerican cultures, but at the same time they were expressed in uniquely Maya ways. Our most direct evidence about religion comes from ethnohistoric sources and ethnographic descriptions. For all periods before the early sixteenth century, we must rely instead on native oral traditions and written texts, art, and the archaeological record. Religious beliefs and institutions varied somewhat according to geographical region, ethnic group, and polity; and while it is clear that certain basic themes and images are very ancient, there were episodes of major transformation in the past.

Animism and Shamanism

Among the most ancient, fundamental, and tenacious beliefs of the Maya (and of Mesoamericans in general) is the notion that things we may regard as inanimate are actually endowed with spiritual energy, and in some cases with sentience. Active spiritual forces emanate from these things and affect important aspects of human life. It is of utmost importance that these forces be in proper balance, lest disorder or chaos result. Since the earliest times Maya shamans have divined the causes of disorder, sometimes while in trances induced by exertion, privation, or hallucinogenic drugs. Through rituals, shamans intervene magically in the supernatural world to restore order, benefiting both individuals and the larger community. Shamans are often associated with soul-like companion animals or "co-essences," particularly jaguars, and are sometimes believed to be "shape-shifters" who can actually transform themselves into animals. Maya shamans are still active today in northern Yucatán and the highlands of Guatemala and southern Mexico. Most are valued members of their communities, but some are regarded with fear and anxiety, because evil shamans or sorcerers can be dangerous and antisocial.

An important element in Maya shamanism and religion more generally is that of prophecy, perhaps best reflected in the various Books of Chilam Balam. These books, written as traditional Maya narratives shortly after the Spanish conquest, make prophetic predictions based in part on earlier cycles of historical events. Prophecies were essential to native resistance to Spanish rule, and in the mid-nineteenth century prophetic oracles figured prominently in Maya rebellions against the Mexican government.

Closely related to prophecy is the concept of omens. Shamans and other religious practitioners are alert to any unusual events in the natural world that may be portents—harbingers of familiar events such as birth or death, or calamitous ones such as world destruction.

Divine Kingship

Many anthropologists believe that the institution of Maya kingship, which appeared at least as early as the first century A.D., was strongly rooted in earlier shamanistic traditions. By the Classic period (A.D. 300–900), Maya kings certainly professed to be ritual guarantors of cosmic order and of the prosperity and well-being of their subjects. Whether kings were considered divine during their lifetimes is debatable, but they were definitely charged with unusual supernatural potency that enabled them to function as privileged intermediaries with the ancestors and gods. Classic period art and texts, such as those on the sarcophagus of Pakal at Palenque, depict rulers being transformed into divine beings or sacred ancestors at the moment of death. Such depictions are related to larger themes of death and resurrection associated with the cycles of the seasons, of vegetation, and particularly of maize, a plant fundamental to the Maya economy and of great symbolic significance. Classic Maya kings projected images of themselves as great "domesticators" who held at bay the disorder of nature, ensured the fertility of the land, and presided over cycles of death and rebirth. At the end of the Classic period, conceptions of divine kingship probably were radically transformed, partly because kings were no longer effective in controlling natural or social disorder.

Presumably there were many other kinds of lesser religious practitioners who assisted rulers and presided over rituals. Classic inscriptions include titles of people who were wise and learned, and who understood the sacred books, calendars, and rituals, but so far no specific glyph for the actual office of priest has been found, nor is there evidence of a complex institution of priesthood comparable to that of the Aztecs.

Souls and Ancestors

A belief shared by ancient and modern Maya is that humans have souls or spiritual co-essences (sometimes called *uay*) associated with their physical bodies. Misfortune such as illness is caused if a soul part becomes unhealthy or is inappropriately separated from the body, both being forms of spiritual imbalance. Shamans divine the causes of misfortune and either prescribe remedies or actively intervene as spiritual practitioners to restore well-being. Souls of certain prominent individuals, especially

Classic Maya kings, became ancestral spirits associated with mountains, caves, or other natural features. Many of the large pyramid-temples that dominate Classic Maya centers are now known to be mortuary monuments, dedicated not so much to dead rulers as to their still vital spirits. Ancestors had to be conjured up and propitiated at appropriate times because they retained power over the affairs of the living community. Ancestor veneration on the household and community level was, along with shamanism, probably one of the earliest shared themes of Maya religion. Later, the dynastic ancestors of living Classic period kings became important objects of veneration by members of the polity as a whole.

Sacrifices and Offerings

Like all other Mesoamerican peoples, the Maya made (and still make) sacrificial offerings to ancestors and deities, both as signs of respect and to nourish or influence them. Sacrifices were extraordinarily varied and involved a wide range of materials, depending on the particular sacrificial context and method. In some cases, precious offerings of jade, pottery, and metal were thrown into cenotes or placed in caves, because both of these geological features were conceived to be portals to other worlds where the gods and ancestors resided. Offerings were also placed in tombs or sealed into building elements as architectural caches. Individual Maya pierced their tongues, earlobes, genitals, or other body parts and offered the resulting blood to the ancestors or gods. Sometimes the blood was caught on paper and then burned so that the smoke carried the offering—one form of the widespread use of incense in ceremonies. Kings, their close relatives, and other high-ranking people were especially important participants in this form of auto-sacrifice.

Animals (notably jaguars) were sacrificed, but the most precious offering was a human victim. Human sacrifice was noted by the first Spanish explorers of Yucatán, and texts, art, and archaeological remains indicate that it was practiced at least as early as Formative times. The capture, torture, and eventual sacrifice of high-ranking warriors seized on the battlefield, and particularly of enemy rulers, was an essential element of Classic Maya religion, although it was carried out on a much smaller scale than were similar rituals among the Aztecs.

Deities

In addition to impersonal animistic spiritual forces and ancestors, the Maya recognized certain anthropomorphic, personified deities who had their own distinct characters, histories, jurisdictions, ritual associations, and graphic forms. Many of these gods are portrayed in the four surviving pre-Columbian screenfold books, or codices, and some have great time depth, as evidenced by art and inscriptions. Many individual gods were ranked in comparative importance. Colonial sources indicate that at the head of the pantheon was a deity called Itzamna; his prominence appears to be an ancient concept. Although the entire pantheon was collectively recognized and worshipped by the Maya, certain deities were especially identified with particular centers or dynasties during Classic times. Gods could manifest themselves in or be represented by images, and Classic rulers were personal custodians or "owners" of bundles that contained sacred objects—perhaps effigies of patron gods, or the bones of deceased ancestors. Some bundles are depicted wearing god masks. The capture of such bundles was an important aim of Maya warfare. Rulers or other individuals could wear god costumes, and the Maya apparently believed that the deity manifested itself in the impersonator.

Gods were extremely powerful, but by no means omnipotent, omniscient, or universally admired by humans. Death gods in particular could be ruthless and cruel, and they inspired fear and dread. They could be tricked, injured, and even killed, and many Maya myths, especially those involving the Hero Twins of the *Popol Vuh*, recount how humans outwit and defeat the gods of the underworld.

Scholars today usually give the Maya deities letter designations. Individual deities presided over particular aspects of nature or human experience. For example, God A was the skeletal god of death; God B was the Postclassic form of the much older Chac, the god of rain and lightning; God C personified the concept of sacredness; God D was an aged creator god, God G, the sun god, and God E, the maize god. Deities were associated not only with particular centers or dynasties but also with categories of people or institutions; thus, God K was closely identified with kings and the institution of rulership, and God L was a patron of merchants. Various gods presided over specific activities, such as writing and time-keeping, and gods are frequently represented as diviners.

Deities were worshipped in major temples and also had important shrines where they were venerated and provided with offerings. In the sixteenth century, for example, many pilgrims journeyed to Isla Mujeres and Cozumel, the sites of important shrines to Ixchel, a goddess of childbirth, fertility, and pregnancy. The great

M

sacred cenote at Chichén Itzá was another destination, and presumably pilgrimage is an ancient pattern, though difficult to perceive archaeologically.

Death and the Afterlife

Information on how the Maya regarded the afterlife is sketchy and contradictory. Death and regeneration were likened by Maya to the cycle of the growth of maize, and some individuals were reincarnated as divine ancestors. The Postclassic Maya, as shown by the *Popol Vuh,* seem to have believed that the dead undertook a harrowing journey through the underworld (called Xibalba, or "place of fright," by the Quiché Maya), where they experienced many ordeals at the hands of the gods of death. At least some people outwitted these gods and were reborn. It was partly to provision the soul on its journey that the Maya placed offerings in the graves of rich and poor alike. Presumably these are very ancient concepts.

Cosmogony

Judging from the best-known Maya book, the *Popol Vuh,* the pre-Columbian Maya, like other Mesoamerican peoples, believed in multiple cycles of creation. One section of the *Popol Vuh* relates how the gods tried on three occasions to create a viable world inhabited by plants, animals, and humans, but failed each time. On their fourth attempt, a primordial ancestral couple ultimately succeeded in creating humans from maize. These new people were able properly to worship and make sacrifices to the gods to whom they owed their existence. Although this myth is specifically associated with the highland Quiché Maya, variants of it may have been common in pre-Spanish times throughout the larger Maya culture area. The Classic Maya long count calendar begins on August 11, 3114 B.C., a date that might have been identified with the creation of the present world.

Cosmology

The Maya generally conceived of a tripartite world composed of the main elements of heaven, earth, and underworld. Heaven and underworld were each subdivided into multiple layers. The underworld was identified both with the gods of death and with the primordial sea. The central element, the surface of the earth, was thought of in a variety of ways: as a rectangular house or maize field, as a great crocodile, or as the back of a great turtle. A central axis, sometimes represented as a great ceiba tree, united heaven, earth, and underworld. Sky-bearer gods called *pauahtuns* supported the four corners of the world;

they correspond to the four cardinal directions, each associated with a specific color: red with east, black with west, white with north, and yellow with south. Green was the color of the fifth "direction," or center.

Natural Cycles, Astronomy, and Calendars

From the earliest times the Maya observed and measured various natural cycles, particularly those related to the astronomical movements of the Sun, Moon, Venus, and other celestial bodies. They were particularly interested in commensuration, or the permutations of independent cycles of different lengths. On the basis of individual or combined cycles they devised a variety of calendars; the most important are the 365-day *haab,* or solar calendar; the 260-day *tzolkin,* a ritual calendar possibly based on the human gestation period; and the 52-year Calendar Round, created by meshing the *haab* and *tzolkin.* The long count is a linear count of days (or more properly, an immensely long cycle) that began in 3114 B.C. Important dates or period endings in all these calendars were used by the Classic Maya to commemorate significant events in the lives of gods, kings, and other important people, such as births, deaths, wars, succession to office, and sacrifices or other rituals. Some activities appear to have been timed to correlate with specific cycles; for example, some war events are associated with the cycle of the planet Venus.

Esoteric knowledge concerning all these cycles, and the complex symbolism that accompanied them, was internalized by accomplished scribes or wise men and preserved in books, now called "codices," that often were essentially astronomical almanacs. Information about calendars and other cycles was used in part for prophetic and divinatory purposes.

FURTHER READINGS

Carrasco, D. 1990. *Religions of Mesoamerica.* New York: Harper and Row.

Edmonson, M. 1982. *The Ancient Future of the Itza: The Chilam Balam of Tizimin.* Austin: University of Texas Press.

Houston, S., and D. Stuart. 1996. Of Gods, Glyphs, and Kings: Divinity and Rulership among the Classic Maya. *Antiquity* 70:289–312.

Landa, D. 1941. *Landa's Relación de las Cosas de Yucatán.* A. Tozzer (ed.). Papers of the Peabody Museum, 18. Cambridge, Mass: Harvard University.

Miller, M., and K. Taube. 1993. *The Gods and Symbols of Ancient Mexico and the Maya.* London: Thames and Hudson.

Roys, R. 1943. *The Indian Background of Colonial Yucatan.* Carnegie Institution of Washington Publication 548. Washington, D.C.

Schellhas, P. 1904. *Representations of Deities in the Maya Manuscripts.* Papers of the Peabody Museum, 4.1. Cambridge, Mass.: Harvard University.

Schmidt, P., M. Garza, and E. Nalda (eds.). 1998. *Maya.* New York: Rizzoli.

Taube, K. 1992. *The Major Gods of Yucatan.* Studies in Pre-Columbian Art and Archaeology, 32, Washington, D.C.: Dumbarton Oaks.

Tedlock, D. (trans.). 1986. *Popol Vuh.* New York: Simon and Schuster.

Thompson, J. E. S. 1970. *Maya History and Religion.* Norman: University of Oklahoma Press.

David L. Webster

SEE ALSO

Central Mexican Religion; Maya Culture and History; Maya Deities

Mayapan (Yucatán, Mexico)

The last major pre-Columbian political capital of Yucatán, Mayapan (Spanish Mayapán) was founded c. A.D. 1200–1250, following the fall of Chichén Itzá. It held sway over a group of provinces in northwestern Yucatán until it collapsed around 1450 as a result of the stress of internecine warfare between competing ruling groups.

The city was surrounded by a wall enclosing more than 4,000 structures in an area of 4.2 square kilometers. Of these, more than 3,500 are believed to have been domestic (residences and associated outbuildings), housing an estimated 12,000 people, with an urban population density of 2,850 people per square kilometers. At the center of the city was a civic-ceremonial complex of pyramids, temples, palaces, and related buildings, the seat of a confederated government (*multepal*) made up of the ruling families of northwestern Yucatán. Archaeological mapping and excavation by the Carnegie Institution of Washington was conducted from 1949 to 1955.

FURTHER READINGS

Andrews, A. P. 1993. Late Postclassic Maya Lowland Archaeology. *Journal of World Prehistory* 7:35–69.

Pollock, H. E. D., R. L. Roys, T. Proskouriakoff, and A. L. Smith. 1962. *Mayapán, Yucatán, Mexico.* Carnegie Institution of Washington, Publication 619. Washington, D.C.

Proskouriakoff, T. 1955. The Death of a Civilization. *Scientific American* 192(5):82–88.

Sabloff, J. A., and E. W. Andrews V (eds.). 1986. *Late Lowland Maya Civilization.* Albuquerque: University of New Mexico Press.

Smith, R. E. 1971. *The Pottery of Mayapan.* 2 vols. Papers of the Peabody Museum, 66. Cambridge, Mass.: Harvard University.

Anthony P. Andrews

SEE ALSO

Maya Lowlands: North

Mazatan Region

This region lies in the heart of the Soconusco, a zone of rich tropical forests, inland swamps, rivers, and estuaries flanking the Pacific coast of Chiapas in southeastern Mexico. It has long been recognized as important for understanding the origins and evolution of early village life in Mesoamerica and is unique in its abundance and excellent preservation of a wide range of settlement features and artifacts in a tropical lowland setting.

Although there was a continuous pre-Hispanic occupation of the Mazatan region from Early Formative times through to the Spanish conquest and beyond, by the Middle Formative period the focus of cultural development shifted to neighboring regions within the Soconusco. This article, therefore, concentrates on the Early Formative period from approximately 1600 to 800 B.C., a period spanning several archaeological phases that, grouped together, are called the Mokaya Tradition.

The Mazatan region is a strip of Pacific coastal plain that extends 30 kilometers inland from the sandy ocean beaches to the steeply rising piedmont slopes of the Sierra Madre mountain range. It is bounded on the northwest by the huge Cantileña Swamp (also called Hueyate) and extends 15 kilometers southeast to the Coatan River. Meandering waterways cross-cut the coastal plain and empty into a series of lagoons, estuaries, and swamps that interconnect along the length of the Soconusco shoreline. These fresh and brackish water habitats abound with aquatic resources: fish, amphibians, reptiles, mammals, waterfowl, and plants.

Little evidence of Archaic period occupation exists in the Mazatan region, in contrast to the neighboring Chantuto region, where Voorhies has excavated several late Archaic sites. Permanent settlement of the Mazatan region began during the Early Formative period, in the

M

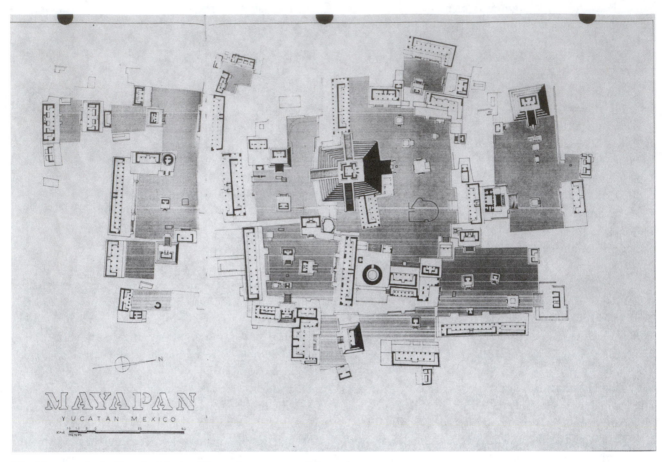

The Mayapan site in Yucatán, Mexico. Illustration courtesy of the author.

Barra phase (c. 1550–1400 B.C.). Fifteen Barra phase sites have been found, but only a handful of them have been test excavated, including Altamira, San Carlos, and Paso de la Amada. Remnants of house floors, hearths, postholes, and middens—which contain pottery remarkable for its elegance and sophistication—show that the Mokaya people were among the earliest sedentary villagers in Mesoamerica.

The Locona phase (1400–1250 B.C.) is much better known, with more than thirty sites recorded and several of these excavated. Both the number and size of sites increased, eventually producing a two- or possibly three-tier settlement hierarchy. At the top of the hierarchy were large sites such as Aquiles Serdan, Chilo, San Carlos, La Calentura, and Paso de la Amada, ranging in size from 20 to 75 hectares. Surrounding these centers were dozens of smaller hamlets only 1 to 5 hectares in size. Excavations have provided evidence suggesting the emergence of simple chiefdoms, with a number of traits that presage developments in later, more complex Mesoamerican societies such as the Olmec. At the largest sites, high-status Mokaya villagers lived in dwellings on raised platforms more than twice the size of common residences. Excavations at Paso de la Amada in 1995 discovered Mesoamerica's earliest ball court, built between 1400 and 1300 B.C.

Mokaya villagers cultivated maize, beans, and avocados, but they were also prodigious fishers and hunters. Remains of fresh and brackish water fish, turtles, and snakes, as well as terrestrial mammals such as deer, peccary, dogs, and other species, confirm that these animals made up a significant portion of the diet. Isotopic analysis of stable carbon and nitrogen in the skeletal remains of these Mokaya villagers shows that maize probably did not comprise a very large part of the diet until after about 900 B.C.

By about 1250–1100 B.C., the Ocos phase, Mokaya villagers were coming increasingly in contact with neighboring regions. Imported obsidian continued to come from far-away sources in highland Guatemala, including San Martín Jilotepeque and El Chayal. Other items—such as jade for manufacturing beads, pendants, and bloodletters—may have come from more local sources. Ocos phase ceramics are similar in many respects to contemporary ceramics in the Gulf Coast region, Oaxaca, central Chiapas, and neighboring Guatemala. It is not yet possible to determine the full range of goods that moved in and out of the Mazatan region during the Formative period, but by the Postclassic period many perishable items, such as skins, feathers, chocolate, and tropical fruits, made their way into the neighboring highlands.

By the Cherla phase (1100–1000 B.C.), a wide range of new ceramic styles and figurine types, not part of the previous Mokaya tradition, were introduced into the Soconusco. These new styles of pottery and figurines show marked similarities to those found in many other parts of Mesoamerica, particularly the Gulf Coast region. Increasing interactions between the Mokaya and their neighbors in adjacent regions—the Grijalva River valley, highland Guatemala, the Gulf Coast, and Oaxaca—may have lessened the autonomy of Mazatan's villages. Some large village sites like Paso de la Amada show their first major disruptions: buildings were abandoned and new ones were built in different locations; pottery and figurine styles were replaced with new ones from abroad; and the sources and quantities of imported goods, such as obsidian, declined. One possible explanation for these changes is that the impact of the Gulf Coast Olmec, centered on San Lorenzo Tenochtitlan, was starting to be felt in relatively far-flung regions like the Soconusco. We still do not know the exact nature of the interactions between these distant regions, but we know that they involved importation and emulation of foreign styles and symbols that disrupted the six-century-long Mokaya Tradition and brought the region into view along the Olmec horizon.

Subsequent phases led to increasing contact and interaction with neighboring regions. The Mazatan region lost its early primacy by the Cuadros phase (1000–900 B.C.) and never recovered. Other regions within the Soconusco developed into political centers that may have drawn population away from villages in the Mazatan region. For example, during the Conchas phase (850–600 B.C.), the neighboring site of La Blanca in Guatemala grew into a huge center at the time when many of the Mazatan region's villages were abandoned. By Late Formative times, new sites were settled in the Mazatan region and other important centers grew up in the Soconusco. Perhaps the most famous is the site of Izapa, about 50 kilometers northeast of Mazatan. During much of the Classic and Postclassic periods, the Mazatan region may have remained a province of larger centers such as Izapa. Whatever its political status in later times, it never again enjoyed the leading role it played during the Early Formative Mokaya Tradition.

FURTHER READINGS

Blake, M., B. S. Chisholm, J. E. Clark, B. Voorhies, and M. W. Love. 1992. Early Farming, Fishing and Hunting along the Pacific Coast of Mexico and Guatemala. *Current Anthropology* 33:83–94.

Blake, M., J. E. Clark, B. Voorhies, G. Michaels, M. W. Love, M. E. Pye, A. A. Demarest, and B. Arroyo. 1995. Radiocarbon Chronology for the Late Archaic and Formative Periods on the Pacific Coast of Southeastern Mesoamerica. *Ancient Mesoamerica* 6:161–183.

Clark, J. E., and M. Blake. 1994. The Power of Prestige: Competitive Generosity and the Emergence of Rank Societies in Lowland Mesoamerica. In E. M. Brunfiel and J. W. Fox (eds.), *Factional Competition and Political Development in the New World*, pp. 17–30. Cambridge: Cambridge University Press.

Clark, J. E., and D. Gosser. 1995. Reinventing Mesoamerica's First Pottery. In W. K. Barnett and J. W. Hoopes (eds.), *The Emergence of Pottery*, pp. 209–221. Washington, D.C.: Smithsonian Institution Press.

Hill, W. D., M. Blake, and J. E. Clark. 1998. Ball Court Design Dates Back 3,400 Years. *Nature* 392:878–879.

Lesure, R. G. 1997. Early Formative Platforms at Paso de la Amada, Chiapas, Mexico. *Latin American Antiquity* 8:217–236.

Love, M. W. 1993. Ceramic Chronology and Chronometric Dating: Stratigraphy and Seriation at La Blanca, Guatemala. *Ancient Mesoamerica* 4:17–29.

Lowe, G. W., T. A. Lee, Jr., and E. Martinez E. 1982. *Izapa: An Introduction to the Ruins and Monuments*. Papers of the New World Archaeological Foundation, 31. Provo, Utah: Brigham Young University.

Voorhies, B. (ed.). 1989. *Ancient Trade and Tribute: Economies of the Soconusco Region of Mesoamerica*. Salt Lake City: University of Utah Press.

Michael Blake

SEE ALSO
Soconusco–South Pacific Coast and Piedmont Region

M

Mendez (Guanacaste, Costa Rica)

Situated within the Río Naranjo–Bijagua Valley, just on the side of the dry Pacific watershed in the transition to the wet tropical Atlantic coastal environment, in the gap between the Miravalles and Tenorio volcanoes, Mendez is the only site in this region with extensive excavation of mortuary architectural features. These are accretional large burial mounds of river boulders with tombs underneath; there are associated petroglyphs on boulders in the surrounding fields. The interments are poorly preserved and have very limited grave goods. The primary span of occupation was A.D. 300–800, contemporary with Bagaces period (A.D. 300–800) sites in the Cañas-Liberia project area on the east side of the Tempisque River, and with the late Arenal and early Silencio phases in the adjacent Arenal area.

FURTHER READINGS

Guerrero M., J. V., F. S. del Vecchio, and A. Herrera V. 1988. Zona Arqueologica Cañas-Liberia: Planteamiento de un problema de investigación. *Vinculos* 14:67–76.

Guerrero M., J. V., and F. S. del Vecchio. 1997. *Los pueblos antiguos de la Zona Cañas-Liberia.* San José: Museo Nacional de Costa Rica and SENARA.

Hoopes, J. W. 1984. A Preliminary Ceramic Sequence for the Cuenca de Arenal, Cordillera de Tilaran region, Costa Rica. *Vinculos* 10:129–148.

Norr, L. 1986. Archaeological Site Survey and Burial Mound Excavations in the Río Naranjo-Bijagua Valley. *Journal of the Steward Anthropological Society* 14 (1982–1983):135-156.

Frederick W. Lange

Mesak, El (Retalhuleu, Guatemala)

This Early to Middle Formative site (2000–700 B.C.) on the western Pacific coast of Guatemala has shell middens, extensive village deposits, and small early temple mounds, providing an excellent archaeological record of the earliest village societies and their local evolution into chiefdoms. El Mesak lies around and within mangrove swamps and estuaries of the Río Jesús. The earliest occupations are of the Locona period (c. 1500–1200 B.C.), as defined in Chiapas, although sherds and artifacts of the even earlier Barra phase have been found. The midden deposits at the site include more than fifty wide but low mounds of Early Formative date. These were all tested or excavated between 1985 and 1990 by the Vanderbilt University El Mesak Archaeological Project. Some mounds had more than thirty sequential living floors, revealing the gradual growth of villages and social complexity here.

The earlier levels showed a heavy reliance on shellfish, fish, and collecting, although grinding stones and year-round sedentism indicate that agriculture was present. Later midden levels and cleared occupation floors show mixed adaptation. Massive quantities of sherds and broken vessels of crude, poorly fired standardized bowls have been cited by Pye and Demarest as evidence of salt production and coastal-to-inland exchange systems in the Early Formative period.

The upper levels of mounds at El Mesak are Middle Formative house floors (c. 900–700 B.C.). Domestic middens associated with these include so-called Olmec-style diagnostics, including fragments of hollow Olmec-style figurines and Olmec motifs carved on local ceramics, among them "flame-eyebrows" and "were-jaguars." This evidence and the presence of a few a jade objects suggest the local evolution of chiefdoms.

FURTHER READINGS

Demarest, A. A. 1989. The Olmec and the Rise of Civilization in Eastern Mesoamerica. In R. Sharer and D. Grove (eds.), *Regional Perspectives on the Olmec,* pp. 303–344. London: Cambridge University Press.

Pye, M. E., and A. A. Demarest. 1991. The Evolution of Complex Societies in Southeastern Mesoamerica: New Evidence from El Mesak, Guatemala. In W. R. Fowler, Jr. (ed.), *The Formation of Complex Society in Southeastern Mesoamerica,* pp. 77–100. London: CRC Press.

Arthur Demarest

SEE ALSO

Soconusco–South Pacific Coast and Piedmont Region

Mesoamerica Septentrional (Northern Mesoamerica)

See Bajío Region; Northern Arid Zone; Northwestern Frontier

Metal: Tools, Techniques, and Products

Metallurgy developed in western Mexico between A.D. 600–800 in a region archaeologists designate as the West Mexican metal-working zone. Although elements of Mesoamerican metallurgy were introduced from the earlier metallurgies of Colombia (casting) and Peru and Ecuador (cold-working), West Mexican metalworkers incorporated those elements and transformed them in keeping with

West Mexican social realities and the range of native metals and ore minerals available to them. Mesoamerican metallurgy, which was largely extinguished at the time of the Spanish invasion, was one of the most varied and technically imaginative metallurgies of the preindustrial world.

The first evidence for metal-working in Mexico comes from archaeological sites on the Pacific coast: along the Balsas River, at Tomatlan (Jalisco), and at Amapa (Nayarit). Metal was unknown elsewhere in Mesoamerica at this time. It is not surprising that metallurgy developed in the west, since Michoacán, Jalisco, and Nayarit are rich in deposits of copper, silver, and other ore minerals. The social infrastructure necessary to master the intricacies of this complex technology also existed in this region, where village-based agricultural peoples had been flourishing for hundreds of years.

Between A.D. 600–800 and about 1200 (Period 1 in terms of this technology), West Mexican metalworkers worked primarily with copper, which occurs as native copper and also in copper ore minerals. Native copper is easy to manage: it can be heated and cast, or a lump of the native metal can be hammered to the desired shape. The common Mexican copper ore minerals—malachite, cuprite, and chalcopyrite—present a more complex technical problem. Ores are composed of one or more metallic minerals in a rocky matrix. The metal must be won from the ore through a process known as "smelting." Smelting requires designing a furnace or crucible to contain ore and fuel (wood charcoal, for example). To smelt malachite, sufficient heat and reducing gases must build to allow the oxygen in the ore to combine with carbon monoxide produced from incomplete burning of the wood, yielding copper metal.

Archaeological and laboratory evidence (studies of artifact chemical composition and microstructure) show that Period 1 West Mexican artisans occasionally used native copper, but they made most objects from metal smelted from its ore. Period 1 smiths also shaped metal using several quite different approaches. One was to cast the metal using the lost wax method. Metalworkers cast hundreds of bells in this way, in a range of sizes and shapes. This complex technique requires constructing a model of the bell in wax, surrounding it with clay and charcoal, melting out the wax, and then casting the liquid metal into the hollow mold. The other approach was to shape metal by hammering it from a cast blank. Tools fashioned by cold-working include needles, tweezers, awls, and axes, as well as rings worn as earrings or hair ornaments and certain other ornamental objects.

Our data indicate that the technique of lost wax casting and some of the bell designs had been introduced to West Mexico from Colombia around A.D. 600–700. Colombian metal-workers cast thousands of intricate ritual objects in one- and two-piece molds and also by using the lost wax method. The earliest of these date to about 200 B.C. Some of these items are bells, and the designs of some Colombian types are identical to the earliest West Mexican examples. Prototypes for the West Mexican cold-worked tools and ornaments, such as tweezers, rings, and needles, also appear in South America, but in Ecuador and northern Peru, where they date to before A.D. 500. These are identical to their later West Mexican counterparts in fabrication methods and design.

All evidence suggests that these elements of South American metallurgy were introduced to West Mexico from Ecuador and Colombia via maritime trade. South American artifacts too were undoubtedly brought to West Mexico, but South American mariners primarily introduced technical know-how rather than large numbers of artifacts.

The striking characteristic of Period 1 metallurgy lies in the cultural interest in bells and their sounds. In fact, bells comprise the vast majority of all metal objects made during this period. Copper is an adequate though not ideal material for tools because the hardness of the blade or working tip of the implement can be increased by hammering; however, Mesoamerican smiths only occasionally used metal for this purpose. They focused instead on using metal for its sonority and its resonance. We know from ethnographic and sixteenth-century ethnohistoric data that bell sounds were considered sacred and creative. They protected their wearer from malevolent influences; they replicated the sounds of thunder and rain, and the rattle of the rattlesnake; and they promoted human and agricultural fertility.

After A.D. 1200 (Period 2), West Mexican smiths greatly expanded the range of ore minerals they exploited. They began to mine and smelt cassiterite, the oxide ore of tin, to produce copper-tin bronze. They also made objects from alloys of copper-arsenic bronze and of copper and silver. Laboratory and compositional analyses of many hundreds of artifacts shows that the two bronzes, copper-arsenic and copper-tin, became nearly standard materials during this period. Copper-tin and copper-arsenic artifacts have been recovered from Atoyac (Jalisco), Milpillas, Urichu, and Tintzunzan (Michoacán), from the Balsas region, and from coastal Guerrero. They also have been found outside the metal-working zone, at Cuexcomate in

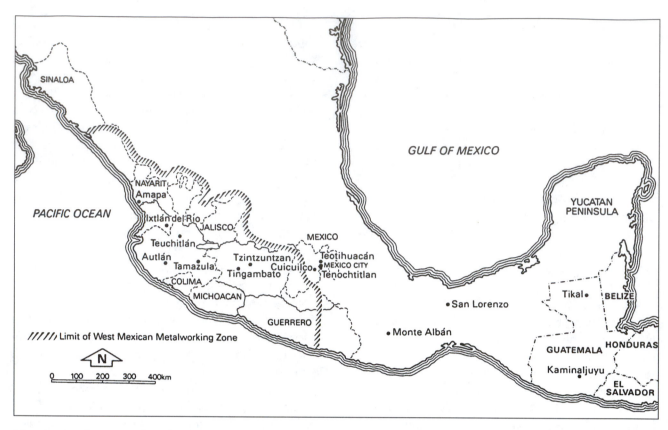

Map showing the extent of metalworking in western Mexico. Illustration courtesy of the author.

Morelos, at Paredon, in Chiapas, in Belize, and at Platanito and other sites in the Huastec region. Our research shows that the latter bronze objects were made in the west from Jalisco or Michoacán metal and exported to other Mesoamerican areas.

The widespread use of copper-tin bronze is especially intriguing because cassiterite is uncommon in Mesoamerica and very rare in West Mexico. Cassiterite deposits, which are small and scattered, appear in a region known as the Zacatecas Tin Province, situated along the eastern slope of the Sierra Madre Occidental. Making the tin bronze alloy requires smelting the tin metal to produce metallic tin, smelting copper ore such as malachite to produce the metallic copper, and then melting the two together. Another approach is to co-smelt cassiterite ores with copper or copper ores. In either case, metalworkers in Michoacán and Jalisco, the heart of the metalworking zone, had to acquire either tin ore or metallic tin from distant sources. To produce copper-arsenic bronze, smiths apparently used arsenopyrite, which is the most common ore of arsenic in Mexico and is abundant in West Mexico.

We do not completely understand how metalworkers produced the copper-arsenic alloys, but the co-smelting of copper ores with arsenopyrite or its weathered products is a likely possibility.

What is even more interesting is the way Mexican smiths used bronze. Metalworkers used both bronzes—copper-arsenic and copper-tin—to refine and streamline the designs of artifacts they had previously made in copper, taking advantage of the increased fluidity, strength, and hardenability of these alloys. They continued casting bells, producing them in far greater numbers than any other artifact class. But Period 2 bells were cast finer, thinner, and larger and were designed with intricate, raised, wirelike designs. Metalworkers also elaborated the design of tweezers. Bronze tweezers possess complex three-dimensional curvature and are thinner, larger, and wider than their copper counterparts. The increased strength of these bronze alloys made such design changes possible. The properties of bronze also allowed artisans to optimize tool design and performance, making thinner, harder, and finer cutting tools and longer, more durable needles.

The most remarkable feature of Period 2 metallurgy is metalsmiths' use of bronze to alter a metal's color. Some bells contain tin in concentrations as high as 22 percent, and others contain arsenic in concentrations as high as 23 percent. When arsenic appears in such high concentrations, the metal looks silvery; when tin concentrations increase in copper, the metal looks increasingly golden. Metalworkers systematically added tin and arsenic in concentrations far higher than necessary simply to realize certain designs; they also were interested in changing the color of the metal to resemble gold or silver. Apart from bells, metalworkers also used high-tin alloys to fashion large golden-colored tweezers and rings. The tweezers, which were hammered to shape, usually contain tin in concentrations to about 10 percent. The large, golden-colored, beautifully crafted tweezers became symbols of political and sacred power and were worn by elites and nobility. Metalworkers consciously controlled the amount of tin or arsenic in copper in elite and sacred items—in bells, rings, and tweezers—by adding these elements in much higher concentrations than necessary to achieve the particular design.

Mesoamerican peoples believed that gold and silver metals were divine substances, according to linguistic and other evidence. Gold was associated with the sun in both Purépecha, spoken by the Tarascan people in Michoacán, and in Nahuatl, common throughout the Aztec Empire. For example, in Nahuatl the word for "gold," *cuztic teocuital*, literally means "yellow divine excretions" and is taken to mean excretions of the solar deity, Tonatiuh, whose name comes from the verbal root *tona*, "to shimmer, to shine, to give off rays"; thus, gold shines, shimmers, and gives off rays or heat like the sun or Tonatiuh. The Nahuatl term for "silver," *iztac teocuitlatl*, means "white divine excretions," which may mean excretions of the moon.

But if these metalworkers' interest lay in achieving the divine golden and silvery metallic colors, why did they not use gold and silver metal to do so? Gold, metallic silver, and silver ore minerals are abundant in West Mexico. The answer lies in the design of these particular artifacts. Gold and silver metals lack the strength, solidification characteristics, and toughness required for these designs: it is technically impossible, for example, to cast extremely thin-walled bells from pure gold or pure silver, or to use the pure metal to craft large, thin shell-shaped tweezers. Their ingenious technical solution to this problem was to use bronze—copper-tin for gold and copper-arsenic for silver—with the alloying element, tin or arsenic, present in sufficiently high concentrations to produce metals of the desired colors.

The most fascinating characteristic of West Mexican metallurgy is that these people were intensely interested in metal for its sound and for the golden and silvery colors they achieved by using bronze. This path of technological development is remarkable, given their technical expertise and the broad range of raw materials available to them. They certainly could have developed a technology of bronze tools and weapons, and they occasionally did use bronze for these purposes. However, the social context in which this metallurgy developed may have militated against this. By A.D. 700, Mesoamerican peoples already had been managing technologies in stone, bone, clay fiber, and other materials for centuries to solve subsistence problems and to meet the needs of social life. The critical issue for elites and religious functionaries in these societies was symbolic power, and they communicated such power through metal objects: visually through golden and silvery divine metal colors in tweezers, bells, and other items, and aurally through the sacred and powerful sounds of bells.

FURTHER READINGS

Hosler, D. 1988a. Ancient West Mexican Metallurgy: Andean Origins and West Mexican Transformations. *American Anthropologist* 90:832–855.

———. 1988b. West Mexican Metallurgy: A Technological Chronology. *Journal of Field Archaeology* 15:191–217.

———. 1994. *The Sounds and Colors of Power: The Sacred Metallurgical Technology of Ancient West Mexico.* Cambridge Mass.: MIT Press.

Hosler, D., and A. Macfarlane. 1996. Copper Sources, Metal Production and Metals Trade in Late Postclassic Mesoamerica. *Science* 273:1819–1824.

Hosler, D., and G. Stresser-Pean. 1992. The Huastec Region: A Second Locus for the Production of Bronze Alloys in Ancient Mesoamerica. *Science* 257:1215–1220.

Lothrop, S. K. 1952. *Metals from the Cenote of Sacrifice, Chichén Itzá Yucatán.* Memoirs of the Peabody Museum, vol. 10, no. 2. Cambridge, Mass.: Harvard University.

Pendergast, D. 1962. Metal Artifacts in Prehispanic Mesoamerica. *American Antiquity* 27:520–545.

Dorothy Hosler

SEE ALSO

Minerals, Ores, and Mining

M

Mezcala Lapidary Style

A pre-Columbian art style and lapidary tradition first identified by Miguel Covarrubias in the 1940s, the Mezcala Lapidary style is characterized by small, geometrically shaped stone objects in the form of standing and kneeling figures, miniature temples, beads, masks, earspools, and animals. These small objects are usually composed symmetrically and skillfully executed in an opposition of volumes and planes. Such objects were produced in the north central area of Guerrero. Mezcala-style objects were first recovered archaeologically from excavations at Ahuináhuac, Guerrero, and were dated securely to between 500 and 200 B.C. Recent archaeological evidence suggests that the style originated before 500 B.C., reaching its height the late Formative and Classic periods. In the Postclassic period, Mezcala-style objects were highly prized as heirlooms, and several were deposited in the dedication offerings associated with the Templo Mayor in Tenochtitlan.

FURTHER READINGS

Gay, C., and F. Pratt. 1992. *Mezcala: Ancient Stone Sculptures from Guerrero.* Geneva: Balsas.

Paradis, L. I. 1995. Archaeology, History and Ethnography: The Precolumbian History of the Mezcala Region. In *The Amate Tradition: Innovation and Dissent in Mexican Art*, pp. 113–128. Chicago and Mexico City: Mexican Fine Arts Center Museum.

F. Kent Reilly III

SEE ALSO

Guerrero Region

Michoacán Region

When the first Europeans moved west in 1522 after their conquest of the Aztecs, the modern state of Michoacán and adjacent parts of Guanajuato, Jalisco, and Guerrero were under the control of the Tarascan Empire. Despite early archaeological interest in the region, which allowed Eduardo Noguera to produce the first regional synthesis of the prehistory of the Tarascan zone in 1948, modern research has been sporadic and uneven. Nevertheless, the region includes one of the core zones for the emergence of states and empires in the New World, and it contains primary evidence for the testing of major theories of cultural dynamics. It also produced a distinctive cultural tradition that persists to the present in modern Tarascan, or "Purépecha," culture.

Tarascan Zone

The Tarascan domain spanned the lands between two of Mexico's greatest rivers, the Lerma-Santiago to the north and the Balsas to the south. The Tarascans controlled four major geographic regions and an enormous variety of resources. The Tarascan Central Plateau is a high volcanic region that constitutes the western extension of the central Mexican Mesa Central. It is dominated by Cenozoic volcanic mountains and small lake basins above 2000 meters. Human occupation of this region has been focused on the lake basins, such as Pátzcuaro, and the marshes, such as Zacapu. The absence of large surface streams and rivers has led to a dispersal of settlements adjacent to springs in the remainder of the region. Nevertheless, the central plateau offers abundant forest resources and opportunity for temperate agriculture, with few recorded droughts.

The semitropical rims of the Central Plateau contain volcanic mountains and plains that decrease in elevation from 2,000 meters to 1,200 meters, to the north and south of the plateau. The northern rim includes the Lerma River Basin, Lake Chapala, Lake Cuitzeo, and Lake Yuríria. In the northeast and northwest are thermal springs, obsidian flows (Zinapécuaro-Ucareo in the northeast and Zináparo in the northwest), and, in the northeast, small deposits of silver and gold. The southern rim, often referred to as the "southern escarpment," is characterized by fertile black soils *(vertisols)*, which have attracted human settlement, and mountain soils *(andesols)*, which support pine-oak forests. A large variety of subtropical domesticated plants, including fruits, vegetables and cotton, can be grown here.

South of the escarpment lie the two remaining regions, the Balsas Depression and the southern Sierra Madre, which are often treated as one. Directly south of the Central Plateau is the Balsas Depression, including the middle and lower Balsas Basin and the tributary Tepalcatepec Basin, both below 500 meters. The complex geomorphology offers a number of resources of particular value to human occupation, including marble deposits in the southwest Tepalcatepec Basin and copper, gold, silver, iron pyrites, and lead deposits in the eastern and central Balsas Basin.

The final major region of the Tarascan domain is the southern Sierra Madre, largely situated southwest of the Tepalcatepec Basin. It is composed of volcanic mountains and small intermontane valleys, mixed with metamorphic and sedimentary deposits. Mineral deposits of copper, gold, and silver are found in the southeastern portion of this region near Huetamo and in the southwestern portion near Coalcomán. Human settlement has always been dispersed and primarily focused on the mineral resources.

Lithic Period

The earliest occupation of Michoacán was by small groups of hunter-gatherers during the Paleo-Indian or Lithic period (before 2500 B.C.). The evidence for these earliest inhabitants is limited to fluted projectile points and other stone implements found in association with Pleistocene mammoth and bison. While the best documentation comes from the Lake Chapala Basin, it is reasonable to suggest that similar occupations were taking place along other late Pleistocene lakes, such as Sayula in the west and Cuitzeo, Zacapu, and possibly Pátzcuaro in the center and east.

Archaic Period

The Archaic period is virtually unknown in Michoacán. During the Zacapu Project, preceramic deposits dating to 2500–2200 B.C. were found in Los Portales Cave. The associated artifacts included waste flakes of basalt and obsidian, one projectile point, and one *mano*. The obsidian is believed to have come from the Zináparo and Prieto flows, about 10 kilometers from the site.

Formative Period

By the Early Formative, populations were settled in agriculturally based villages, known from El Opeño in the west and the Balsas Basin in the south. From the remains of these earliest known ceramic-producing societies, it is clear that the region was occupied by many localized cultures, each with its distinct history and patterns of interaction with adjacent zones and with its neighboring communities. This diversity remained characteristic of Michoacán until the emergence of the Tarascan state.

El Opeño culture, one the best-documented Formative cultures, is known from eleven excavated shaft tombs dating from 1500–800 B.C. Five were excavated in 1938, four in 1970, and two in 1991. The burial cult revealed by these tombs, including ceramic vessels, figurines, and the shafts themselves, suggests cultural interaction along the Santiago-Lerma river system with cultures to the west in Jalisco and Nayarit, as well as linkages to the east. Of the large number of exotic raw materials, the jadelike greenstone is believed to have come from the Motagua Valley (Honduras), indicating probable long-distance exchanges between Central America and the Pacific coast from Nayarit to Guerrero, and exchanges between the West Mexican coast and highlands. Farther south, in the middle and lower Balsas Basin, El Infiernillo small village sites containing ceramics suggest ties to the Capacha culture of Colima and the Pacific coast from Nayarit to Guerrero. From the Tarascan highlands we have as evidence only pollen cores from the Lake Pátzcuaro Basin, which reveal domesticated maize pollen from approximately 1500 B.C. These botanical data suggest that human settlement was far more widespread in the Early and Middle Formative than the current archaeological evidence reveals.

By the late Formative there were at least three regional cultures in Michoacán: the Chupícuaro culture of the northern and central zones, the Chumbícuaro culture of the Tepalcatepec Basin in the southwest, and the Balsas/Mezcala culture (El Infiernillo and La Villita phases) of the central Balsas to the south. Each zone was characterized by small village societies, and each has been identified primarily by variation in burial-associated ceramics. The best-known is the Chupícuaro culture, found along the middle Lerma drainage in southern Guanajuato, the Lake Cuitzeo Basin, and, with localized variants, near Morelia (Santa María) and in the Zacapu and Pátzcuaro basins. Chupícuaro communities appear to have been adapted primarily to lacustrine ecosystems, building their villages either on islands within marshes or along lakeshores or rivers (e.g., Chupícuaro, Acámbaro, Zacapu-Loma Alta, Lake Pátzcuaro, and the many Lake Cuitzeo sites along the southern shore of the lake).

Classic Period

During the Early Classic period, local changes in ceramic style and more elaborate public architecture are found at the site of Santa María, near Morelia and Chehuayo in the Cuitzeo Basin. In the related but locally distinct culture in the Zacapu Basin, the Loma Alta occupation includes some Thin Orange sherds and sunken patio architecture similar to contemporary sites in Guanajuato. This evidence, along with more widely known variations in burial artifacts, suggests that by the first centuries A.D. social ranking may have existed at the larger settlements. Nevertheless, the location of settlements on the floors of lake basins, and the general absence of settlements in defensible positions, indicates minimal local aggression and/or movements of peoples. Chupícuaro or stylistically similar artifacts are found along the upper Lerma in the Toluca Basin, and farther east into the Basin of Mexico and Tlaxcala, so there was significant, if indirect, social interaction between northern Michoacán and Central

M

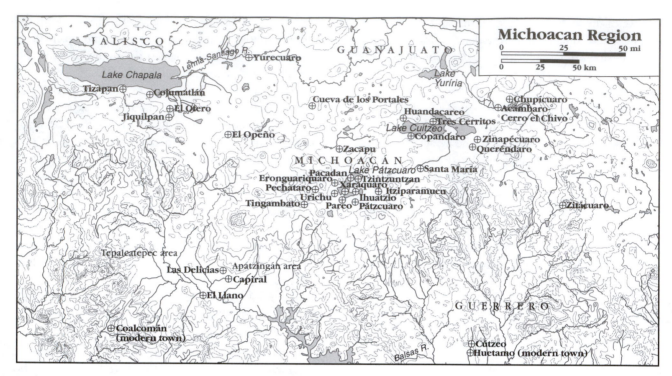

Michoacán Region. Map design by Mapping Specialists Limited, Madison, Wisconsin.

Mexico at this time. The Chumbícuaro culture is known primarily from the plain of Apatzingán and is dated from 100 B.C. to A.D. 100. The Balsas/Mezcala culture existed along the central Balsas. While regionally distinct, each appears to be related to adjacent zones to the south and west.

A major cultural transformation took place between A.D. 400 and 900. After centuries of autonomous village societies, distinguishable by stylistic variation in artifacts and local economic adaptations, a new form of settlement—the ceremonial center—appeared in Michoacán. The ceremonial centers known from this period are widely dispersed in central Michoacán: El Otero, near Jiquilpan; Tres Cerritos, near Cuitzeo, with possible minor centers at Queréndaro and/or Zinapécuaro (Lake Cuitzeo Basin); and Tingambato, near the Pátzcuaro Basin. They were separated by lands occupied by populations that were essentially continuing regional traditions, although in interaction with these new centers. In the Zacapu Basin, this was a time of rapid population growth, as evidenced by the doubling of the number of sites in the

Jarácuaro phase (from thirteen to twenty-two) and another doubling in the Lupe phase (from twenty-two to forty-two in the early part, A.D. 600–700, and forty-three in the latter part, A.D. 700–850). By the end of the late Classic (La Joya phase, A.D. 850–900) there were fifty-eight sites. Moreover, settlements by this time are also located away from the lakeshore, especially in the zone between Zacapu and the Lerma River, and include pyramids, plazas, and ball courts.

The major centers themselves contain architectural forms and artifacts indicating direct contact with the Teotihuacan culture of the Basin of Mexico. At El Otero this includes a ball court, plazas, pyramids, stucco painting, and large group tombs, one of which held forty-two individuals along with jade, rock crystal, pyrites, and turquoise. At Tres Cerritos, a site that continued to be occupied until Spanish contact, there are three large mounds and two sunken plazas. The earliest architecture at this site includes *talud-tablero* facing one of the mounds and at least two large tombs, one of which contained more than thirty individuals, 120 vessels, marine shell, jade, turquoise, rock crystal, and an alabaster Teotihuacan-style mask.

At Tingambato there is a series of plazas, altars, a central pyramid, a ball court, and a large tomb that contained the remains of at least thirty-two people. Among the artifacts were a cloisonné decorated vessel, marine shell, and mosaic disks inlaid with pyrites, jadeite, jade, and turquoise. For the first time, there was evidence of dental mutilation; six of the Tingambato male burials exhibited A-2, A-4, and B-4 patterns. The *talud-tablero* architecture on the pyramid and plazas reveals links to Central Mexico, although all but a few ceramics are local. Based on the ball court architecture, Eric Taladoire suggests a date of A.D. 800–900 for Tingambato.

Outside these centers, from the Lerma River and Lake Cuitzeo Basin to the middle Balsas, a few sites in each zone contain Thin Orange pottery, cloisonné decoration, mosaic disks, Teotihuacan-like figurines, and occasional *talud-tablero* architecture. In all cases the number of such artifacts is low, often a handful, and represents only a small proportion of the material goods associated with central Mexican Classic period culture. Thus, for example, while dental mutilation appears for the first time at Tingambato, it represents only a limited sample of the types of such mutilation found at this time, and it includes practices known elsewhere since the Middle Formative; dental incrustation (Romero's types E and G) is never found in Michoacán.

The meaning of these new centers and Teotihuacan-style artifacts is unclear. Owing to the salvage nature of most research, none of the deposits at the larger centers has been dated more precisely than to A.D. 400–900. This means that these, and the more dispersed artifacts, may date to the Middle Classic and may reflect populations interacting with the extensive Teotihuacan economic network; or they may date to the Epiclassic (A.D. 700–900) and may reflect small groups of elite, priests, and/or artisans who migrated out of the Basin of Mexico following the collapse of Teotihuacan, bringing some aspects of their heritage with them. A third possibility remains: that the archaeological evidence reflects a complex mixture of both processes, with the added impact of the independent emergence of complex societies in Jalisco during the Classic period. There are strong adherents of all alternatives, although the current evidence suggests Teotihuacan interaction along the Balsas during the Middle Classic, while significant Central Mexican interaction with central and northern Michoacán occurred after A.D. 600. Thus, Thin Orange pottery, a Teotihuacan mask, and "al fresco" decoration on a few sherds in the Zacapu Basin are not to be associated with major changes in settlement patterns or ceramic styles during the Loma Alta and Jarácuaro phases (A.D. 0–600). When major changes are seen in settlement patterns and ceramics during the Lupe and La Joya phases (A.D. 600–900), they are associated with populations moving from lakeshore sites and occupying the zone between Zacapu and the Lerma River. This pattern raises the possibility that Central Mexican traits introduced at this time may have entered Michoacán via Classic period populations in southern Guanajuato in the north, rather than directly from the east.

The effect of these contacts was to increase the ongoing process of social differentiation and to stimulate the emergence of territorially discrete and competing polities. It is unclear what they, or more precisely their elites, were competing over, but it may have included access to inter- and intra-regional trade to both the east and west. The high proportion of Zinapécuaro-Ucareo obsidian utilized at Tula (Hidalgo) from A.D. 800 to 1000 suggests that by A.D. 800 portions of northeastern Michoacán were interacting more directly with Central Mexico. Such long-distance exchange may have stimulated the increased production at the Zináparo obsidian mines, which can be documented by A.D. 700.

Postclassic Period

By A.D. 900 the effects of these changes resulted in major shifts in settlement patterns. In the Cuitzeo and Zacapu basins, the best-known areas for this time period, but also along the Lerma and Balsas rivers, there are indications of population nucleation at defensible locations. In many zones this is the beginning of a pattern that grows until the emergence of the Tarascan state. Along with these settlement changes came the widespread adoption of Red-on-Cream ceramics, which are integrated with local ceramic traditions. Such shifts in style are known from a wide region of north and central Michoacán, including Zinapécuaro, Cuitzeo, Tiristarán, Morelia, Teremendo, Zacapu, Lake Pátzcuaro, Carapan, Zamora, and Tangamendapio. In the Pátzcuaro Basin at the site of Urichu, we can document the appearance by A.D. 400–500 of polychrome pottery with negative decoration that bears strong similarity to earlier ceramics of southern Guanajuato (Morales phase) and later Tarascan polychromes.

The appearance of metallurgy in Michoacán after A.D. 900 (possibly earlier in Nayarit and Jalisco, and in the lower Balsas Basin) suggests that cultural exchange and/or population movements linked Michoacán directly

M

to societies to the north and west. Again, the Santiago-Lerma river drainage and Balsas-Tepalcatepec rivers appear to have been the primary routes of change. Dorothy Hosler suggests that metallurgy was introduced by merchants plying the coastal canoe trade from southern Ecuador up the West Mexican coast. Hosler's suggestion is based on technical analyses of the metal objects themselves. Oliveros has noted that at the time of Spanish contact, canoe traders along that coast would put in at the port of Zacatula, at the mouth of the Balsas River, for as long as six months before their return voyage was possible. During the early Postclassic, the metal objects, known almost exclusively from burials, were made of copper and copper-silver by means of cold hammering, annealing, and lost wax casting in styles and types of objects known earlier from coastal Ecuador.

By the Middle to Late Postclassic (A.D. 1200), societies throughout the region had little direct interaction with Central Mexico but were instead participating in regional cultures, sharing traits and beliefs that later were characteristic of the Tarascans. Some of these traits appear to have diffused from farther west in Mexico, particularly along the Santiago-Lerma river system; others were products of local cultural change. Specific traditions appearing or dominating assemblages now include complex metallurgy, ceramic pipes, polychrome pottery with negative decoration, large-scale rubble-filled mounds clustered into plazas and located on hillslopes or *malpaís,* and petroglyphs later associated with the Tarascan sun-hunting deity Curicaueri. Sites occupied at this time were later endowed with sacred significance.

Hosler notes that a number of metallurgical techniques and styles were introduced at this time into West Mexico. The source of these innovations appears to be trade from south coastal Peru to coastal Ecuador, and then from Ecuador to West Mexico. Among the new features were loop-eye needles, axe money (of sheet metal), and wirework bells, which, in addition to previously made forms, were worked hot. New alloys were produced during the late Postclassic, including copper-arsenic, copper-tin, and copper-arsenic-tin.

The current archaeological evidence suggests that during the Early to Middle Postclassic local elites competed for communities, marking their relative success with polychrome pottery, metal goods, and patron deities. The absence of strong regional authority in the face of what appear to have been increasing populations led to the formation of highly nucleated populations in some areas.

The best-documented example is Zacapu (known as El Palacio in the literature), with an estimated occupation of the *malpaís* of eleven square kilometers and 20,000 or more people, while the lake-marsh below was abandoned.

According to the *Relación de Michoacán,* the legendary history of the Tarascan state written down in 1541, during the late Postclassic there were a series of migrations of peoples into central Michoacán. These included groups referred to as Chichimec and Nahua, and the ancestors of the Tarascan royal dynasty, known as Uacúsecha (Eagles). They are said to have been hunters and gatherers, especially deer-hunters, who migrated from the north and settled in discrete communities within and adjacent to the Lake Pátzcuaro Basin, joining the existing Tarascan-speaking population. Current evidence indicates either that the numbers of migrants were very small or that they had assimilated local cultural traditions before actually entering central Michoacán. Although there are clear ties between some late Postclassic traits and the Lerma River Basin, there is no evidence of movement of Chichimecs, in the sense of hunter-gatherer Uto-Aztecan speakers from north of the Mesoamerican frontier. To what extent this origin legend is myth or history will probably always be uncertain; but while the Postclassic period in the Basin of Mexico saw the spread of the Nahuatl language associated with population movements from the north, Tarascan remained the language of the Michoacán Central Plateau.

Nevertheless, even if the migrants' numbers were relatively small, in the context of the late Postclassic their effects may have been great. There were several different language/ethnic groups in the Pátzcuaro Basin by A.D. 1200, but their size must have varied greatly. For example, the Nahuatl speakers of Xaráquaro (Jarácuaro) claim in the *Relación de Michoacán* that "we are many more than they for there are not many Chichimecs," referring to the Uacúsecha of Pátzcuaro. The subsequent competition between their elites for access to basic resources is given as the cause for a succession of wars in which political and economic power was concentrated in the Uacúsecha elite. According to official Tarascan history, the warrior-leader Taríacuri united the several independent polities of the Pátzcuaro Basin into a unified state during the first half of the fourteenth century. Following his death, his son and nephews extended the state beyond the Pátzcuaro Basin and began the political and economic changes that saw the emergence of a new Mesoamerican civilization. Current archaeological research in the Pátzcuaro Basin at the Postclassic site of Urichu is targeted on these centuries of transformation in order to understand the process by which the Protohistoric (A.D. 1450–1530) kingdom came into being.

Protohistoric Period

Archaeological research in Michoacán has been limited and sporadic, and much of what has been done relates to the Tarascan state. The greatest amount of research has been carried out at the Tarascan capital, primarily under the auspices of the Mexican Instituto Nacional de Antropología e Historia (INAH). In 1930, when modern archaeological research began, Alfonso Caso and Eduardo Noguera placed test pit excavations in two of the ethnohistorically known Tarascan centers—Tzintzuntzan and Ihuatzio—in an effort to provide collections for the National Museum. Caso returned in 1937 and 1938 to begin mapping and excavations on the Great Platform at Tzintzuntzan; in 1940, 1942–1944, and 1946, these were continued under Daniel Rubín de la Borbolla, along with reconstruction of several pyramid bases; in 1956, under Orellana, limited excavations were continued; in 1962, 1964, and 1968, Román Piña Chan continued this work on the Great Platform at Tzintzuntzan. The tenth season of work by the INAH at the ceremonial core of Tzintzuntzan was carried out by Ruben Cabrera Castro in 1978–1979, and Efraín Cárdenas has just completed restoration and test excavations on INAH projects in the official archaeological zones of Tzintzuntzan and Ihuatzio (1992–1994). In 1970 Helen Perlstein Pollard conducted an intensive surface survey of the urban extent of Tzintzuntzan.

On the regional level, the Protohistoric political system of the Lake Pátzcuaro Basin included ninety-one settlements occupied during the apex of the Tarascan state, identified in a study by Gorenstein and Pollard (1976–1980). In the eastern half of the basin, eighty-three sites, of which more than thirty were tentatively assigned to the Protohistoric, were recorded in 1981–1982 as part of the Proyecto Arqueológico Gasoducto (Tramo Yuríria-Uruapan), under the direction of Carlos Silva Rhoads. In the western half of the lake basin, sixty sites, forty-four of which were assigned to the Protohistoric, were identified by surface survey in 1983.

Similar surveys in the Zirahuén and Cuitzeo lake basins have documented an abundance of Tarascan-associated sites, although the speed and incompleteness of these salvage surveys have limited the data obtained. The far more detailed surveys in the Balsas River Basin undertaken

before the construction of dams in the zones of Infiernillo (1963) and La Villita-Palos Altos (1967–1968) provide archaeological documentation of Tarascan presence in this important southern zone of the empire. Current research in the Sayula Basin of southern Jalisco, under the auspices of the Laboratory of Anthropology of the University of Guadalajara, the French Foundation for Scientific Development, and the Regional Center of Jalisco (INAH), has documented Tarascan occupation of this important salt- and metal-rich region. Though none of these projects focused on Tarascan archaeology, they all have provided archaeological evidence of the nature of the expansion of the empire.

Outside the Lake Pátzcuaro Basin, the period of Tarascan domination has been the focus of two studies. The first, carried out from 1971 to 1974 under the direction of Shirley Gorenstein, was a study of the Tarascan-Aztec military frontier. Several of the Tarascan fortified sites were located and surveyed, with major excavations focused on Cerro del Chivo, Acámbaro. The second study entailed excavations and mapping at the Tarascan center of Zacapu, a regional survey of the Zacapu Basin, and study of the obsidian quarries in the region of Zináparo, carried out by the Centre d'Études Mexicaines et Centraméricaines (CEMCA) under the direction of Dominique Michelet, from 1983 to 1987.

In addition to the research within the Pátzcuaro Basin, the regional surveys, and targeted study of Tarascan archaeology, many other archaeological projects carried out within the territory once held by the Tarascan State have provided some information. These have been summarized by Chadwick for the period through 1970, and many have appeared as salvage reports, rarely published, for the period since 1970. The Cuitzeo Basin project, under the direction of Macías Goytia, has included excavations at Huandacareo, an administrative center founded after Tarascan conquest of the basin, and at Tres Cerritos (Cuitzeo), an earlier center that continued in use under the Tarascans. Technical analyses of Tarascan artifacts from museum collections provide information about raw materials, technology, style, and economic interaction. Finally, paleoecological studies in the Pátzcuaro and Zacapu basins have determined resource distribution and human impact under the Tarascan state.

Despite all this archaeological research, the only chronology for the late Postclassic/Protohistoric periods comes from sixteenth-century ethnohistoric and historic documents, especially the *Relación de Michoacán*. From

M

these documents it has been possible to map the geographical expansion of the empire, to analyze the imperial political economy, to detail the social structure and incorporation of subject peoples, and even to describe Tarascan religious and political ideology.

Michoacán Prehistory and Mesoamerica

In the prehistory of western Mesoamerica, Michoacán occupies a key position between Central Mexico and the highland lakes of Jalisco to the west. Since the turn of the twentieth century, the monumental architecture of the Tarascan monumental platforms (*yácatas*) and the epic legends of the *Relación de Michoacán* have been incorporated into the understanding of Mesoamerica's past. At least two versions of this past have dominated the interpretation of regional prehistory. The first version describes a powerful, centralized Tarascan Empire that emerged from culturally homogeneous societies as a small-scale replica of the same evolutionary sequence as occurred in the Basin of Mexico, albeit "delayed" in its unfolding. This focus on Tarascan evolution as an example of secondary state development carries with it two implicit notions: that only the Tarascan period is worthy of study, and that the regional prehistory is redundant to an understanding of Mesoamerica as a whole.

A second version of the past sees the Tarascan state as a barbarian, quasi-Mesoamerican polity that emerged following the conquest of culturally isolated Chupícuaro-like villages by Chichimecs, who then ruled by "copying" their Aztec relatives. In this version, Michoacán prehistory is not merely marginal to Mesoamerica, it is only partially Mesoamerican.

This a priori marginalizing of the region has impeded research without reflecting the culture-historic dynamics revealed by the available evidence. The assumption that the ethnic, linguistic, political, and economic patterns of the Protohistoric period reflect a "culmination" or apex of cultural evolution in the region misinterprets the reality of patterns of interaction within the long prehistory of Mesoamerica. However, until there are more regionally focused, long-term archaeological projects in the state that are able to produce chronometrically dated cultural sequences, the questions raised in 1948 will continue to go unanswered, and Michoacán will continue to be devalued in the construction of Mexico's past.

FURTHER READINGS

Florance, C. A. 1985. Recent Work in the Chupícuaro Region. In M. S. Foster and P. C. Weigand (eds.), *The Archaeology of West and Northwest Mesoamerica*, pp. 9–45. Boulder: Westview Press.

Hutchinson, G. E., R. Patrick, and E. Deevey. 1956. Sediments of Lake Pátzcuaro, Michoacán, Mexico. *Bulletin of the Geological Society of America* 67:1491–1504.

Michelet, D. (coord.). 1992. *El Proyecto Michoacán 1983–1987: Medio ambiente e introducción a los trabajos arqueológicos*. Collection Études Mésoaméricains, 11–12; Cuadernos de Estudios Michoacános 4. Mexico City: Centre d'Études Mexicaines et Centraméricaines.

Miranda, F. (ed.). 1980 [1541]. *La Relación de Michoacán: Versión Paleográfica, Separación de Textos, Ordenación Coloquil, Estudio Preliminar y Notas*. Morelia: Estudios Michoacanos V. Fimax.

Piña Chan, R. 1977. *Bitacora: Cento Regional de México-Michoacán*. Mexico City: SEP and Instituto Nacional de Antropología e Historia.

———. 1982. *Exploraciones arqueológicas en Tingambato, Michoacán*. Mexico City: Instituto Nacional de Antropología e Historia.

Pollard, H. P. 1980. Central Places and Cities: A Consideration of the Protohistoric Tarascan State. *American Antiquity* 45:677–696.

———. 1982. Ecological Variation and Economic Exchange in the Tarascan State. *American Ethnologist* 9:250–268.

Pollard, H. P., and S. Gorenstein. 1980. Agrarian Potential, Population and the Tarascan State. *Science* 209: 274–277.

Pollard, H. P., and T. Vogel. 1994. Late Postclassic Imperial Expansion and Economic Exchange within the Tarascan Domain. In M. Hodge and M. Smith (eds.), *Economies and Polities in the Aztec Realm*, pp. 447–470. Albany: Institute for Mesoamerican Studies.

Porter, M. N. 1956. Excavations at Chupícuaro, Guanajuato, Mexico. *Transactions of the American Philosophical Society*, no. 46, pt. 5.

Street-Perrott, F. A., R. A. Perrott, and D. D. Harkness. 1989. Anthropogenic Soil Erosion around Lake Patzcuaro, Michoacán, Mexico, during the Preclassic and Late Postclassic–Hispanic Periods. *American Antiquity* 54:759–765.

Helen Perlstein Pollard

SEE ALSO

Tarascan Culture and Religion; Tzintzuntzan

Militarism and Conflict

Evidence of systematic armed conflict in Mesoamerica begins in the Formative period, with the Olmecs, and extends through the Spanish conquest. This was not simple savagery or a military ethos run amuck; rather, warfare appears to have been an essential element in the development and expansion of complex societies in Mesoamerica.

Perhaps the best approach to exploring militarism in Mesoamerica is to begin with the best-described and best-understood case, the Aztecs, before delving into earlier, more poorly known examples. For the Aztecs, attacks on other armies involved an orderly sequence of weapons use and tactics. Signaled by the commander's drum or trumpet, the assault typically started at dawn, thereby making best use of daylight, since battles ceased at night. Fighting began with a deadly projectile barrage of arrows and slingstones from about 60 meters, while the soldiers closed. As they advanced, the soldiers cast short spears, or darts, with their spearthrowers *(atlatls)*, which had a much shorter range than bows and slings but had greater striking force at close range; thus, they could penetrate cotton armor and disrupt the opposing formation. The two sides closed as quickly as possible, since only when they met did the barrage lift, and *atlatls* were dropped in favor of the greater effectiveness and protection of a sword or thrusting spear and shield.

The most experienced soldiers led the attack: first the knightly orders, followed by the veteran soldiers leading organized units, and novice warriors last. Archers and slingers were unarmored and remained out of hand-to-hand combat; they fired at isolated targets, harassed enemy reinforcements, covered withdrawals, and prevented encirclement by the enemy.

Aztec movements into and out of battle were orderly to maintain a solid front, but once the army closed with the enemy, combat was inevitably an individual affair, although small skirmishing units remained cohesive. Units could not be kept together through voiced commands in the din of battle, so the soldiers followed the standards of their leaders—feather banners visible above the fray—to see where their comrades were going. If the standard-bearer was killed, the banner fell; its followers were effectively blinded and withdrew.

The battle was heaviest at the front, the only place where hand-to-hand weapons could be brought to bear, and the Aztecs typically sought to broaden the front to exploit their usual numerical advantage. If the Aztecs penetrated the opposing line, either through the center or around the ends, they would pour through and envelop the enemy troops, cutting them off from reinforcements

and resupply. Though standard, this tactic did not preclude the use of ambushes. Ambushes were favored at locations such as narrow mountain passes where the advantage lay with the attacker. The most spectacular ambushes, however, involved feigned retreat during battle. If executed convincingly, the enemy troops pressed their advantage and followed the retreating Aztecs until they were drawn into a compromised position. Then, hidden troops attacked from the sides and behind while those fleeing turned and attacked as well.

Given the usual Aztec advantage in numbers and experience, some enemies chose to wait behind city fortifications rather than fight in the open. Extensive urban fortifications were uncommon at this time, but a few cities were encircled by walls, especially smaller towns on hilltops. More common was the small stronghold adjacent to the city, where the advantage of height and a difficult ascent added to defensive walls and battlements. These typically did not protect the town itself, but they could serve as refuges for dependents and political leaders while the city's tributary status was negotiated.

The Aztecs faced five options when they encountered fortifications: breach them, scale them, besiege the city, gain entry by deceit, or withdraw. Breaching the fortifications was difficult, time-consuming, and uncommon in Aztec warfare. Scaling walls with ladders was a quicker alternative but was also relatively uncommon, probably because the attackers typically needed a three-to-one advantage over the defenders to succeed. Laying siege to the town was feasible within the Valley of Mexico, where the besiegers could be resupplied by canoe, but elsewhere the logistical difficulties of supporting a lengthy siege at a significant distance were enormous, given the transportation available. Most often, trickery, deceit, or traitors opened the way into fortified cities. Otherwise, withdrawal was the best option.

Although fortified defenses could obviously be effective, they were scarce because the various Aztec tactics were often successful. Moreover, dispersing defenders along the walls of a fully encircled city could dilute and weaken the defenders' forces. Most important, even if walls protected the city itself, its dependent towns, fields, and stores beyond the walls were still vulnerable, and their loss meant the defeat of the town in any case. Thus, only meeting and vanquishing an attacker before he could lay waste to the region would guarantee the city's safety.

The Aztecs' primary objective, however, was to acquire tributaries, not to destroy them. Even in fiercely contested battles, cities were not generally destroyed, although

M

temples might be burned. Beyond the symbolic defeat of the local gods, the temples were usually the most heavily fortified sites within the city, and their destruction signaled loss of their associated armories and the defeat of the strongest resistance. Only if resistance continued thereafter might an entire town be razed.

One thing that set the Aztecs apart was their ability to project force at a distance, which meant mustering troops, gathering supplies, and coordinating mass movements. Simply moving large numbers of men posed enormous problems because there were no wheeled vehicles or draft animals in Mesoamerica. Aztec armies (each being 8,000 men, or a *xiquipilli*) began their marches on separate days, for practical rather than ritual reasons. Like preindustrial armies elsewhere, the Aztec army moved slowly, probably averaging roughly 2.5 kilometers per hour, or 20 kilometers per day. The Aztecs did not build roads for military purposes; instead, they relied on local roads, which meant the army could march in no more than double files. This stretched out a *xiquipilli* over a distance of 12.5 kilometers, which meant the last men both started and stopped their march five hours after the first. Thus, separating each *xiquipilli* by a day was the only way a unit could complete its march by nightfall, although this practice greatly increased the time needed to assemble the entire army at the point of attack. Consequently, Aztec armies frequently used several alternative routes simultaneously to shortened the overall march time.

Speed was crucial because of the enormous logistical constraints in Mesoamerican warfare. Accompanying porters (*tlamemes*) carried more than 20 kilograms of food each and, at one porter for every two warriors, the normal daily per capita consumption rate of about 1 kilogram meant that the army carried food for only eight days, giving it a combat radius of 60 kilometers—three days going, one day fighting, one day recuperating, and three days returning.

These constraints affected all Mesoamerican armies, but the Aztecs adapted their tributary system to extend their range, demanding supplies en route. Messengers were sent along the designated route two days before the march to alert all tributary towns so they could gather foodstuffs from their surrounding dependencies (campaigns were conducted from December to April, during the dry season after the harvest when large numbers of men were available). Nevertheless, the great cost of supplying armies in the field limited the Aztecs' ability to march at will or to besiege towns for significant periods, and it profoundly affected the nature of conquest.

The Aztecs could march to a city-state and fight. Victory meant the subjugation of the city and all its dependencies, but the same was not true of confederacies and empires. Because they controlled large hinterlands, these large polities could march to their borders to meet the Aztecs. Even if the Aztecs won, a victory meant the conquest of that place only: confederated and imperial armies could withdraw into their interiors, where the Aztecs, lacking tributaries for logistical support, could not follow. Thus, defeat meant subjugation for a city-state, but not for a confederacy or empire. Mesoamerican logistical limitations offered large polities a protection their armies could not, and their total defeat was a long-term project achieved only gradually by chipping away at the edges. The Aztecs were unable to deliver a single, decisive blow to the heart of an empire.

Conquered cities were not structurally integrated into the Aztec Empire. Instead, the Aztecs left local rulers in place and merely exacted tribute. Conquered rulers complied because they perceived the Aztecs as powerful and able to force compliance, and this self-policing greatly reduced the Aztecs' political, administrative, and military costs. However, should that perception of power be undermined, tributary obedience was not ensured. The Aztecs' concern with maintaining their tribute empire affected their large polities: even if they could conquer powerful opponents, they might be left so weakened by the struggle that their control elsewhere might be challenged. The costs of such a "victory" were too high for an empire that had to balance many strategic interests. To deal with larger polities, the Aztecs fought "Flower Wars" (*xochiyaoyotl*) instead.

Unlike traditional wars of conquest, Flower Wars were reported in early accounts to have been fought for military training, to take captives for sacrifice to the gods, and to display individual military skill. This is all true, but Flower Wars were also part of a larger military strategy for dealing with major powers.

As conventionally viewed, Flower Wars were ritual battles fought for the purpose of taking sacrificial captives. However, this ritualistic combat was merely the first part of a longer, strategic conflict. Flower Wars began as demonstrations of individual military prowess with relatively few combatants. An impressive display could lead to the enemy's capitulation without further conflict, but if the opponent remained unintimidated, Flower Wars escalated in ferocity over a period of years, even decades, until they resembled wars of conquest. Thus, what began as low-cost exercises in military intimidation escalated until they became wars of attrition that the numerically superior Aztecs were unlikely to lose.

Flower Wars required considerably longer to defeat an enemy than wars of conquest, but they allowed the Aztecs to pin down strong opponents, to reduce their offensive threat, and gradually to encircle them, cutting off allies and external support. Then, after slowly chipping away at the enemy territory, the Aztecs would ultimately crush their enemies, all at a relatively low cost in men and materiel and without endangering their expansion or control elsewhere.

Although the Aztecs conducted expeditions into the north against non-state groups, these were not successful. They could defeat such groups in battle, but without fixed assets or a centralized political hierarchy, they were unable to control them after conquest. Accordingly, with few exceptions they aimed their campaigns at states and empires.

At the service of the state, Aztec militarism added tributaries and created expanded trading areas. War also enjoyed broad support in the society because military success offered even commoners additional wealth and a significant avenue of social mobility. However, the same was not true of all societies in Mesoamerica, and simply projecting Aztec capabilities and practices onto other groups or into earlier times is inaccurate. Weapons, population size, logistical capabilities, and social organization all differed, and so must the role of their militaries, though we see these earlier societies less clearly than the Aztecs.

Many written accounts exist for the Aztecs but for earlier periods records of military practices are few and incomplete, and most of our knowledge derives from archaeology, which offers the best evidence for population (and hence logistics and imperial structure), site locations, and fortifications. Such practices as Flower Wars, or their equivalents, may not be detectable at all in the absence of written records, but works of art provide information on many aspects of warfare that would otherwise remain unknown, including battle tactics, weaponry, and other combat practices from which broader patterns can be inferred. Such self-depictions are not without problems, however, since they may reflect what their patrons wished to portray rather than what actually happened. For instance, figures such as the Aztec king Tizoc or many of the Maya rulers left monuments attesting to their own military greatness which other evidence suggests are not accurate; and the Aztec broadsword was widely used, yet it is totally absent from pre-Columbian depictions. Thus, indigenous depictions, though important cultural evidence, are not always historically accurate. Moreover, pre-Columbian art is largely elite and urban, so while these data are problematic, they nevertheless record matters that are otherwise inaccessible.

Warfare among the earliest Mesoamerican hunter-gatherers was probably limited to occasional raids, but by 1500 B.C., as agriculture led to permanent settlements, raids gave way to more serious conflicts. Once assets became fixed, they could be seized, destroyed, or defended: with flight no longer an acceptable alternative, conflicts escalated.

The Olmecs offer the first evidence of military professionalization, based on the existence of arms used exclusively for military purposes. Yet their conflicts appear to be intimately tied to the rise of kings and were only incidentally related to external threats; there is little evidence of military conflict and no concern for security obvious in their settlements. Nevertheless, the Olmecs were the first society in Mesoamerica to project force significantly beyond their homeland, overcoming the inertia of timing, distance, and logistics. They used their military to protect their trade, but small numbers and vast distances prevented them from compelling it.

Following the Olmec decline around 400 B.C., low populations, difficulties in long-distance travel, and a rough military parity kept conflicts local. This was, however, a period of increasing military professionalism among local elites, and specialized arms now dominated warfare, reflecting the general Late Formative shift away from guerrilla warriors relying on stealth and weapons that could be used from concealment and toward soldiers formally trained in military skills. One response was the development of fortifications.

Fortifications compensate for small populations by substituting labor for soldiers. Using labor when available—for instance, after the agricultural season—magnifies the fortified center's military effectiveness because a successful assault normally requires three attackers for each defender. However, while small fortified sites can deter minor or random threats such as raids, they cannot effectively dominate a sizable hinterland.

There were numerous defensively fortified sites at this time, but Monte Albán, the largest of its day, employed its fortifications not just defensively but offensively as well, serving as the powerful nucleus of a small, expansionary state that united the Valley of Oaxaca and beyond. Expansive control from fortified centers did not prove to be the pattern for empires in Mesoamerica, however. Its

M

first large empire was centered at Teotihuacan, and it fielded the first army composed of complementary arms units, indicating formal military training, a chain of command, and centralized control of arms.

Like the Aztecs, Teotihuacan's military underwrote a trade empire, though a more extensive one based on colonial entrepôts beyond its area of relatively direct control, which extended out perhaps 140 kilometers from the capital. Even with the largest army in Mesoamerica, many cities, such as Monte Albán, remained independent, but Teotihuacan influence linked areas producing goods of interest by trade corridors. Only late in Teotihuacan's history did its military play a significant internal role, maintaining order as the empire contracted.

Warfare was widespread among the Classic Maya but was primarily raiding rather than wars of conquest. Geared more toward maintaining boundaries between the various areas of dominance of city-states than toward conquest, these clashes appear to have been used internally primarily to buttress the claims of kings to rule. Moreover, the eclectic nature of Maya arms indicates a lack of state control and a concomitant lack of a chain of command, which suggests a significantly less organized and capable military that could conduct raids but not large-scale offensive actions. In any event, despite numerous monuments boasting of conquests, no large political systems arose in the Maya Lowlands.

Following Teotihuacan's demise, Mesoamerica fragmented into numerous semiautonomous areas, and a new series of fortified hilltop centers arose, including Xochicalco, Cacaxtla, and Teotenango. Apparently trade cities with economic ties throughout Mesoamerica, these centers maintained prominent militaries, which were essential during this unstable period. Although the centers could defend themselves and even dominate their surrounding areas, they were ultimately unsuccessful—witness the demise of Xochicalco—and they could not be maintained as new Mexican powers emerged.

The Toltec capital of Tollan was the center of the next extensive, military-supported trade network, which was based on merchant enclaves and settlements throughout the region. Smaller than Teotihuacan, Tollan could not control a comparable area, but its military helped to secure trade. A similar pattern was transplanted to Chichén Itzá, which dominated northern Yucatán for 300 years before the region reverted to warring city-states. Central Mexico again broke into competing city-states and mini-empires with the abandonment of Tollan after years of political unrest tied to the deteriorating ecology of the area. Then,

250 years later, Central Mexico was again integrated, this time by the Aztec Empire.

During the previous 2,500 years, the dominant organizational form in Mesoamerica was the city-state, punctuated by the periodic success of a city that expanded to create an empire before it ultimately collapsed, reverting to a series of city-states. Militarism accompanied the rise of all these polities; it was tied to the emergence of new leaders, as evidenced by glorifying monuments, but primarily it reflected and supported the exercise of new and unprecedented internal powers. Occasionally, polities arose in which the exercise of military power went well beyond internal political purposes to underwrite the expansion into empire and to protect trade networks and colonies.

It is difficult to identify tributary empires archaeologically—though there is no reason to think they did not exist—but imperial trade links are amply attested, and trade was a major motive behind imperial expansion. Yet only those polities able to field large armies could secure expansive trade links, and army size depends not only on total size but also on how many of the people participate, and this varied by internal social organization.

All states have classes, and those in Mesoamerica had hereditary nobles occupying the upper rungs of society and benefiting accordingly. How rigidly class barriers were maintained varied. Some societies had insurmountable class barriers while others were permeable, even into the ranks of the nobility. All the major Mesoamerican empires had societies that permitted some social mobility, which is suggested by analogy with the Aztecs and evidenced by the significant influx of people, including ethnically different groups. Outsiders were attracted because they were permitted to succeed in this new setting in a way they could not in their places of origin. In the Mesoamerican empires, this mobility was achieved primarily through military success, which led to a greater distribution of rewards throughout society and encouraged broader-based participation in warfare.

Societies that permitted social mobility through military success could raise large, well-trained, highly motivated armies to support extensive military adventures, giving those societies enormous imperial potential. By contrast, societies that limited military participation to the nobility produced small armies that simply lacked the size and capability to support imperial expansion. These small forces were useful for defense, police, and internal political support, but their foreign military adventures were restricted largely to raids that helped to maintain boundaries between city-state hinterlands and to support the political legitimacy of the rulers. They were wholly inadequate in the face of large empires, except when distance or other intervening variables limited any confrontation. Moreover, with wealth and power concentrated in the hands of the elite, societies that permitted little mobility offered few incentives for broad-based participation in war and sacrificed greater military potential in favor of preserving the noble-dominated social hierarchy.

These different social arrangements produced distinctly different outcomes. Societies offering avenues of advancement were able to mobilize a much greater proportion of their populace for military service—as much as ten times larger. The more closed a society was to social mobility, the less likely it was to arm and train commoners in elite warfare, the smaller the army it could muster, and the more limited the area it could dominate. In short, the large Mesoamerican empires were all open to social advancement and capable of mobilizing large numbers of well-trained and motivated soldiers.

Although supernatural sanctions supported all state societies in Mesoamerica, these were probably greater in societies without significant mobility than in those where it was possible. To whatever extent social and political legitimacy was tied to divine right, societies permitting social advancement could count on the added support generated by a somewhat more equitable distribution of benefits and the potential for social mobility, especially when the economy was expanding. Lacking these, societies without social mobility probably relied more heavily on the twin supports of supernatural sanction and limiting access to arms and training. So while taking captives for rituals supporting the state was common throughout Mesoamerica, it is interesting that the less socially mobile societies elevated their rulers by depicting captives naked, bound, and underfoot, whereas more mobile societies did not so depict them, but simply emphasized the fact of conquest.

Societies that did not offer social mobility generally lacked the military size and capacity to control large, competing cities and polities. Societies offering social advancement could integrate large areas, but they typically ruled indirectly over a loosely integrated empire, but one that cost little to maintain, freeing imperial resources for further conquest.

Technology played a role in military success, but innovations were not automatically adopted and employed. Rather, new technology was adopted as it benefited the existing society, notably the elites. Otherwise it was ignored, even when it offered overall enhanced military capability, if it could threaten existing social relations—that is, if it might undermine elite control. Sometimes innovations in weaponry gave one polity an advantage over others, but which weapons were adopted was largely determined by the nature of a society. As empires grew, they relied increasingly on specialized training of both nobles and commoners. Moreover, greater size and superior training encouraged the use of organized combat units, if not formations, and complementary, reinforcing weapons systems. These advantages were simply unattainable by smaller polities. The degree of training also fostered the use of specialized weapons rather than tools turned to martial use.

Specialized weapons requiring formal training were adopted by both socially mobile and immobile societies, but if using the weapons required little training or adapted existing utilitarian skills, it was less likely to be adopted by societies lacking mobility because it promised to place more power in the hands of commoners. That same weapon in a society that allows social advancement, however, is not destabilizing, and in fact increases the power of the empire. At least in Mesoamerica, the major weapons innovations arose in or were quickly adopted by socially open societies, giving them an additional advantage. However, not all weapons rendered societies socially porous: some increased the differences embodied in stratification. An innovation requiring additional training would increase class distance in societies without mobility, though not necessarily in those that permitted it. Expensive objects like cotton armor favored the elite, but neither greater cost nor specialized training had this effect where arms and armor were controlled by the state, as was typical of mobile societies, rather than by individuals, as in societies that lacked significant opportunities for social advancement.

In sum, warfare and violence pervaded Mesoamerican prehistory. Tied to the rise of kings and the expansion of states and empires, warfare was an integral part of the expansion of control, both internal and external. However, the way this was carried out, and the way it was expressed in cultural remains, differed according to both the scale of the societies involved and their internal organization.

FURTHER READINGS

Davies, N. 1978. The Military Organization of the Aztec Empire. In T. A. Lee and C. Navarrete (eds.),

M

Mesoamerican Communication Routes and Cultural Contacts, pp. 223–230. Papers of the New World Archaeological Foundation, 40. Provo, Utah.

Hassig, R. 1988. *Aztec Warfare: Imperial Expansion and Political Control.* Norman: University of Oklahoma Press.

———. 1992. *War and Society in Ancient Mesoamerica.* Berkeley: University of California Press.

Hicks, F. 1979. "Flowery War" in Aztec History. *American Ethnologist* 6:87–92.

Hirth, K. G. 1989. Militarism and Social Organization at Xochicalco, Morelos. In R. A. Diehl and J. C. Berlo (eds.), *Mesoamerica After the Decline of Teotihuacan A.D. 700–900,* pp. 69–81. Washington, D.C.: Dumbarton Oaks.

Isaac, B. L. 1983. Aztec Warfare. *Ethnology* 22:121–131.

Marcus, J. 1983. Aztec Military Campaigns against the Zapotecs: The Documentary Evidence. In K. Flannery and J. Marcus (eds.), *The Cloud People,* pp. 314–318. New York: Academic Press.

Ross Hassig

SEE ALSO

Transport; Warfare; Weaponry

Milpa, La (Orange Walk District, Belize)

This large Late Classic Maya site in northwestern Belize covers an estimated 78 square kilometers on the elevated scarp between the Río Azul and the Río Bravo. Research from 1992 directed by N. Hammond and G. Tourtellot shows that it was founded in Late Formative (Preclassic) times, with a modest prosperity in the Early Classic that included dedication of at least five stelae and the construction of some public buildings, as well as a royal tomb of the fifth century. Almost abandoned in the sixth and seventh centuries, La Milpa flourished dramatically in the period after A.D. 700 through 830: almost 70 percent of the ceramics found in the central precinct and 85 percent of those from the settlement date to this phase. The period of decline, observable also at neighboring centers including Río Azul, may be connected with long-term, large-scale conflict between Calakmul and Tikal, which both lie about 100 kilometers from La Milpa.

The center occupies a ridgetop at 190 meters elevation, with two main groups of buildings linked by a north–south *sacbe* (causeway). The Great Plaza to the north is flanked by four major pyramids and other structures and contains two ball courts as well as sixteen of the site's nineteen stelae; some of these are fragmentary and were relocated in Postclassic times, however. Only one, Stela 7, has a legible Initial Series date of 9.17.10.0.0. (A.D. 780). The southern sector includes several large plazas enclosed by long range structures, and an elevated acropolis, apparently the palace of La Milpa's Late Classic rulers. Several painted thrones have been found in the acropolis and in adjacent large courtyard groups. The southernmost court of the acropolis, and other buildings, including a major pyramid, were left unfinished when La Milpa was abandoned: the scarcity of Terminal Classic markers such as Fine Orange pottery suggests that this occurred around A.D. 830.

Extensive surveys, including transects up to 6 kilometers long and randomly placed blocks, document a heavily engineered landscape with terracing, stony banks and berms, interpreted as attempts to raise agricultural production and minimize soil erosion after deforestation. A peak population of 46,000 within a 5-kilometer radius has been estimated.

FURTHER READINGS

Hammond, N. 1991. The Discovery of La Milpa. *Mexicon* 13:46–51.

Hammond, N., G. Tourtellot, S. Donaghey, and A. Clarke. 1996. Survey and Excavation at La Milpa, Belize, 1996. *Mexicon* 18:86–91.

———, ———, ———, ———. 1998. No Slow Dusk: Maya Urban Development and Decline at La Milpa, Belize. *Antiquity* 72:831–837.

Tourtellot, G., A. Clarke, and N. Hammond. 1993. Mapping La Milpa: A Maya City in Northwestern Belize. *Antiquity* 67:96–108.

Norman Hammond

Minerals, Ores, and Mining

Utilization of mineral resources was of supreme importance in ancient Mesoamerica. From the highland Aztec to the lowland Maya and from the earliest hunters and gatherers to the last civilizations of the contact era, the native societies of Mesoamerica thrived mainly on the basis of stone technology, with limited use of metals. Minerals were required for virtually every activity. They were used in making weapons, obtaining and processing food, and building; they provided pastes for ceramics, precious gems for jewelry, supernatural substances for ritual, medicinal resources for healing, and media for the sculpture and painting that have made Mesoamerica famous.

A tremendous variety of mineral materials was employed. Obsidian, which can hold an edge more than a thousand times sharper than surgical steel, was utilized for cutting tools such as knives. Basalt and granite were used for grinding stones. Hematite and manganese oxide provided bases for pigments. Magnetite was ground into mirrors, and jadeite was carved into portable sculpture and ornaments.

Processing ranged from informal household production to massive, highly organized manufacturing operations. The vast majority of processing was conducted at the household level to meet daily needs, and recent findings suggest that many of the larger deposits of manufacturing waste may have resulted from household processing sustained over many years. Household production remained prominent even in very complex economies.

Mineral materials and finished products were traded over great distances, especially when they were particularly useful or highly prized. Blades made from obsidian that came from Central Mexico have been found in Belize, some 1,200 kilometers away in a straight line, and even farther along the trails and waterways traveled by ancient merchants. Nevertheless, the greatest share of mineral exchange was fairly local; people tended to employ readily available materials to fulfill their everyday requirements.

As is generally the case in areas where complex societies have developed, minerals were obtained by three primary means: opportunistic gathering, open-pit quarrying, and subterranean mining. The most common method was clearly the least intensive—opportunistic gathering, the simple collecting of surface materials. Open-pit quarrying, the extraction of materials from broad, superficial excavations, was also fairly widespread. Subterranean mining or tunneling after underground deposits was the least frequent and most intensive mode of acquisition.

The earliest form of mineral procurement employed in prehistoric Mesoamerica was opportunistic gathering. While no actual remains of the practice have been documented—the act of collecting rarely leaves identifiable traces—this technique must have been utilized from the start. The oldest artifacts from Mesoamerica, fluted dart tips of Paleoindian vintage (11,000 to 10,000 years ago), were fashioned of chert, obsidian, and basalt, but the responsible groups were presumably too few and too small to have sustained or required much intensive exploitation.

Open-pit quarrying undoubtedly intensified as social complexity increased during the Archaic period (7000–2000 B.C.). Settled communities needed more materials and were better able to support intensive extraction. Most of these initial quarries, however, have been destroyed or obscured by subsequent exploitation. Later quarries were often devoted to the extraction of materials for construction, as in the case of the massive reservoirs at Classic Maya ruins (A.D. 250–900), many of which originated as borrow pits. Quarries were also used to obtain scarce commodities, such as jadeite in the middle Motagua Valley of Guatemala. Typically such quarries were small, although some attained considerable size over the centuries. The obsidian pits at Cruz del Milagro (Pachuca), Mexico, reach 10 meters in depth, with spoil heaps exceeding 10 meters in height, and the operation extends over hundreds of hectares.

Formal mining probably commenced during the Formative period (2000–100 B.C.), when complex societies began to emerge. Large populations generated the demand and support for truly intensive exploitation. The great cinnabar mine atop Calentura Mountain near Soyatal in Mexico's Sierra de Queretaro contains Olmecoid ceramics that date back as far as the Middle Formative (900–300 B.C.). The Olmec and their associates are renowned for their ritual and elite use of cinnabar and its derivative, liquid mercury. Mining would appear, then, to have been initiated at Calentura in the wake of the first major complex development in Mesoamerica. It evidently peaked in conjunction with the end of the Teotihuacan ascendancy (A.D. 500–800) and lasted into the Postclassic (A.D. 900–1500), with connections to Veracruz and West Mexico. Calentura may have been the oldest and longest operating mine in pre-Columbian Mesoamerica.

The most extensive of the known mines in pre-Hispanic Mesoamerica are undoubtedly those of Chalchihuites (Zacatecas), also in Mexico. These mines were exploited mainly during the Middle Classic apogee of Teotihuacan (A.D. 400–600), at a time of pronounced Central Mexican influence in the region. They were named after *chalchihuitl*, the blue-green gemstone of the Aztec. The prime target material was probably blue-green chrysocolla, but other materials may also have been sought, including hematite, flint, and rhyolite. Dozens of mines occur in several clusters, some extending for kilometers through semiconsolidated alluvial gravels and forming mazes of interconnecting tunnels and arching chambers. There were occasional ventilation holes and colossal support pillars, but the mines were (and are still) dangerous. The remains of one ancient miner were found crushed beneath debris from a collapse. Phil Weigand has

M

described the harsh conditions the miners faced: "The combination of smoke from the pine torches, high temperatures, lack of circulation of air, and the dust from the blows of the hammers, in addition to the constant threat of collapse, must have made the work in the mines a horrible nightmare."

Unfortunately, the hazards of pre-Hispanic mining were probably not unique to Chalchihuites, nor did they end with the Spanish conquest. While the Spaniards abandoned the old mines in search of others for precious metals, they built on the pre-Contact mining tradition and established a harsh mining regime that remains infamous to this day. The mines of Mesoamerica enriched the royal coffers of Spain and its colony, and the native people of Mesoamerica continued to brave the hellish life of the artificial underworld.

FURTHER READINGS

Barba L., and A. Herrera. 1986. San José Ixtapa: Un sitio arqueológico dedicado a la producción de mercurio. *Anales de Antropología* 23:87–104.

Pendergast, D. M. 1982. Ancient Maya Mercury. *Science* 217:533–535.

Weigand, P. C., and G. Gwynne (eds.). 1982. *Mining and Mining Techniques in Ancient Mesoamerica. Anthropology* 6 (1-2), special issue.

Peter S. Dunham

SEE ALSO

Jade; Metal: Tools, Techniques, and Products; Obsidian: Properties and Sources; Obsidian: Tools, Techniques, and Products; Geography and Climate; Salt

Mirador (Chiapas, Mexico)

Mirador was the major regional center of the western interior valley of Chiapas. The site lies on the northern edge of the Sierra Madre near the headwaters of the La Venta River, overlooking the semiarid Cintalapa Valley. This large ceremonial center of thirty-two large earthen mounds covers 1.5 square kilometers and is similar in layout to contemporaneous Middle and Late Formative centers of Chiapas along the Grijalva River and the Pacific coast, most notably Chiapa de Corzo. Like these other paramount chiefdom capitals, Mirador has a C-group architectural arrangement of a long mound flanked by a pyramid at its short axis.

The Mirador site was first occupied about 1400 B.C., but the large pyramids and plazas at the site were not built

until the Middle Formative period, about 700 B.C. During early Olmec times (c. 1100 B.C.), the region around Mirador was the locus of a specialized community of artisans who fabricated small iron-ore cubes (ilmenite) which they exported by the tens of thousands to the Olmec community at San Lorenzo. In the Late Formative and Classic period, the region was known for its fine ceramic wares and human figurines, which were exported to neighboring regions. Trade goods from Teotihuacan are also known at Mirador for the Classic period. The site was probably occupied by Zoque speakers throughout its history.

FURTHER READINGS

Agrinier, P. 1970. *Mound 20, Mirador, Chiapas.* Papers of the New World Archaeological Foundation, 28. Provo, Utah.

Lowe, G. W. 1977. The Mixe-Zoque as Competing Neighbors of the Early Lowland Maya. In R. E. W. Adams (ed.), *The Origins of Maya Civilization,* pp. 197–248. Albuquerque: University of New Mexico Press.

Gareth W. Lowe and John E. Clark

SEE ALSO

Chiapas Interior Plateau; Formative Period

Mirador, El (Petén, Guatemala)

This Late Formative Lowland Maya city displays the greatest concentration of public architecture known throughout Maya history. All of the complexes of buildings and plazas thus far investigated show a massive construction period from the second century B.C. to about A.D. 100; the site was abandoned about fifty years later. Two great structures, over 50 meters high, can be seen from the air 125 kilometers away and appear as natural hills. These two structures, the Tigre Pyramid to the west and the Danta Pyramid to the east, oppose each other in a cosmological orientation to honor the rising and setting sun, consistent with a theme observed at other sites. Between these giants, the ceremonial center dominates the Central Acropolis, about 335 meters long. The center axis of the Central Acropolis focuses on a huge plaza that terminates at the north with the Cascabel Complex of three principal buildings. This triadic architectural pattern exists at all the large complexes of buildings and probably relates to the Maya cosmological concept of deities.

The Tigre Temple, attached to the Tigre Pyramid plaza, exhibits enclosed rooms, in contrast to the solid-fill rock and earthen structures at the site. Facing north, a stairway is flanked by two giant modeled stucco god masks painted in colors. The symbolism incorporated in the masks presages the later Classic period hieroglyphic writing system, suggesting that a ruler or dynasty was sanctioned by the gods to rule and build this magnificent city. Coercion of the population to build these extraordinary public buildings, plazas, walls, water collection system, and connecting causeways to nearby sites is thought to have been under the organization of a primitive city-state. The public constructions are so vast that it seems reasonable to assume that its ruling dynasty held political power for a considerable time.

El Mirador lies about 7 kilometers south of the Mexican border, almost in the center of the base of the Yucatán land mass. It is situated in a strategic position to have controlled overland trade networks from the heart of the Petén forest to the Yucatán Peninsula in the north, and routes to the southern highlands of Guatemala. These distant connections apparently were significant in maintaining the political and ritual importance of El Mirador. Volcanic ash has been found in the clay of Late Formative monochrome pottery, and the art style found on stelae at the site strongly suggests an important ritual tie with the Guatemalan highland site of Kaminaljuyú.

That the site was revered in later times is manifest in the use of its principal buildings by Early Classic peoples. The upper platform of the Tigre Pyramid and the main building of the Central Acropolis both have large Early Classic deposits of ritually broken ceramics and lithics that are restricted to the center line of the structures. No significant Early Classic occupation of the site has been found; however, during the Late to Terminal Classic period squatters built their houses on the lower platform of the great Danta Pyramid, apparently flaunting its ritual sacredness. The Late to Terminal Classic occupation of the site was of little significance in the Petén, where political power had shifted to the south at sites like Tikal.

FURTHER READINGS

Demarest, A. A. (ed.). 1984. Proyecto El Mirador de la Harvard University 1982–1993. *Mesoamérica* 5(7): 1–160.

Matheny, R. T. 1986. Investigations at El Mirador, Petén, Guatemala. *National Geographic Research* 2(3): 332–353.

Ray T. Matheny

SEE ALSO

Maya Lowlands: South

Mirrors

Fashioned from various types of stone, mirrors had a major role in ancient Mesoamerican ritual and symbolism. The types of stone and forms of manufacture varied considerably according to period and culture. Among the Formative Olmec, mirrors were typically fashioned from single pieces of grey metallic iron ores, including hematite, ilmenite, and magnetite. Marvelously polished, these mirrors have concave reflective surfaces that invert as well as reverse an original image. Concave mirror pectorals are commonly represented on Olmec figures, many of them ballplayers. In Classic Mesoamerica, including the societies of Teotihuacan, the Zapotec, and the Maya, mirrors usually were made of carefully fitted iron pyrite mosaic glued to a slate or sandstone backing. Typically circular in form, these golden mosaic mirrors were often worn by warriors against the small of the back. Pyrite mosaic back mirrors continued among the Early Postclassic Toltec, although usually made with a broad band of turquoise mosaic surrounding the central mirror surface. Pyrite mirrors were also used by the Late Postclassic Aztec, but they also had highly polished obsidian mirrors. The Central Mexican deity known as Tezcatlipoca, or Smoking Mirror, is essentially a personification of the obsidian divinatory mirror. In the sixteenth-century *Relación Geográfica* of Texcoco by Juan Bautista de Pomar, the image of Tezcatlipoca is described as a mirror enclosed in a sacred bundle.

Although stone mirrors could also be used for cosmetic purposes, they were primarily tools of prophecy and divination. Through divinatory scrying, mirrors served as conduits of communication with the supernatural world. In fact, as is true among the modern Huichol of western Mexico, mirrors were often considered to be much like caves or passageways for the gods and ancestors. Frequently, mirrors represented the middle place, or *axis mundi,* a symbolic means of gaining access to the heavens and underworld. Thus, in Classic and Postclassic Mesoamerican art, circular mirrors appear on the abdomens of figures as the earth navel (Nahuatl, *tlalxicco*). As well as being identified with caves and the middle place, mirrors had a wide range of other meanings in Mesoamerica, including reflective pools of water, fiery hearths, flowers, eyes, the circular Earth, and the Sun.

FURTHER READINGS

Carlson, J. 1981. Olmec Concave Iron-Ore Mirrors: The Aesthetics of a Lithic Technology and the Lord of the Mirror. In E. P. Benson (ed.), *The Olmec and Their*

M

Neighbors: Essays in Memory of Matthew W. Stirling, pp. 117–47. Washington, D.C.: Dumbarton Oaks.

Taube, K. 1992. The Iconography of Mirrors at Teotihuacan. In J. C. Berlo (ed.), *Art, Ideology, and the City of Teotihuacan*, pp. 169–204. Washington, D.C.: Dumbarton Oaks.

Karl Taube

SEE ALSO
Divination

Mitla (Oaxaca, Mexico)

Its magnificent buildings rank Mitla as one of the most important archaeological sites in Mexico. The site's Zapotec name is Lyobaa; the name "Mitla" is from the Nahuatl word *mictlan,* meaning "place of the dead," apparently in recognition of a bloody battle there around A.D. 1494 between Aztecs and Zapotecs. Unlike almost all other monumental sites in Mexico, which were abandoned long before the arrival of the Spaniards, Mitla was an active community at the time of the Conquest. The town's name became San Pablo Mitla in honor of the patron saint the Spaniards imposed on the local population. San Pablo Mitla lies at the base of the Sierra Mixe about 40 kilometers east of the city of Oaxaca. Traditionally, Mitla served as a major trade center for the Sierra, but today it depends heavily on tourism and craft production associated with the archaeological site.

The Mitla area experienced early human settlement in the Tlacolula Valley, but Mitla itself was of minor consequence until the Postclassic, when the decline of Monte Albán's hegemony fostered the emergence of small citystates governed by military chieftains. In addition to local conflict, the Aztecs arrived in the Oaxaca Valley and sought to establish control over their trade route to Chiapas and Guatemala by subjugating the Zapotec communities. In turn, the Zapotecs, who could not defeat the Aztecs by themselves, sought alliances with the Mixtecs. Ultimately these circumstances affected Mitla, stimulating the development of fortifications, quarries, tombs, and other construction. Mitla gradually grew in importance; beyond its political and military significance, it was (and continues to be) a commercial and religious center holding sway over communities in the eastern end of the Tlacolula Valley and nearby settlements in the Sierra Mixe. Coincident with the construction of much monumental architecture in the thirteenth and fourteenth centuries, groups of Mixtecs began to enter the Oaxaca Valley

from the mountains to the northwest. Perhaps dislodged by the Aztecs, Mixtecs settled in the area of Cuilapan and Xoxocotlan. Archaeological data show the Mixtecs entered into contact and exchange with Zapotecs, and subsequently Mixtec influence began to appear in sites such as Mitla and Yagul.

Mitla's core consists of five monumental groups scattered, but not aligned, along a north–south axis amid residential and commercial buildings, arranged within a rectangle of approximately 460 by 276 meters. All but one of the groups are on gently sloping ground to the north of the river; the South Group, the oldest, is largely lost among houses on the south bank of the river. Each of the five groups consists of structures or platforms surrounding a plaza or patio. Each of the two oldest groups, the South Group and the Adobe Group, consists of four mounds or platforms, the largest being the easternmost. The platforms are made of stone, rubble, or adobe blocks (which had a stone facing, now often missing). Some are of substantial volume; the largest platform in the Adobe Group (so named because of its construction material) is nearly 46 meters long and 11 meters high.

One of the most impressive features of the Mitla site is its stonework. Great volumes have been laid up in long, low, unmortared courses in the hope of withstanding earthquakes that rock the region, one of the most seismically active in the Western Hemisphere. Builders spanned doorways, passageways, and other open spaces with massive stone lintels. The largest of these weigh more than twelve tons and were transported to the site over irregular terrain from quarries several kilometers away. Some of the quarries still contain blocks in an unfinished state or damaged during preparation. While most blocks and lintels have a smooth finish, some are incised with precise, repetitive designs. Many of these same designs appear as friezes of thousands of small pieces of stone in the façade of the Hall of the Columns, where intricate mosaic patterns have been built up and locked in place by lintels without the use of mortar. The contrast between these pieces, often weighing just a few ounces, and the heavy lintels is visually and architecturally striking, and it attests to both a well-developed esthetic sense and sophistication in construction techniques among Mitla's builders.

Unlike the South and Adobe groups, with their simple arrangement of platforms around a small central plaza, the somewhat later Arroyo, Columns, and North Groups consist of multiple units of rooms and patios. In the Columns Group, with one notable exception, the rooms face open, apparently public plazas, while in the Arroyo and North Group rooms are at ground level around smaller patios. The design suggests a concern for privacy or controlling access. The exception noted above in the Columns Group consists of indirect access to a patio and rooms heavily decorated with elaborate friezes. This patio can be reached only by passing through the Hall of the Columns, so named because of the six monolithic columns which once helped to support the roof. In turn, the Hall of the Columns opens to a large plaza via a steep staircase. The conjunction of elements—plaza, staircase, Hall of the Columns, and elaborate chambers—suggests that this building served some public or ceremonial purpose. Like the North Group, the Hall of the Columns retains a few vestiges of painted plaster, and it appears that the elaborate frieze work was painted red, with the smooth lintels covered by designs or codices.

Immediately to the south of the Hall of the Columns and its plaza lies a second plaza bounded on three sides by platforms supporting the remains of other buildings. Under the north and east platforms, tombs from the Postclassic period have been discovered. Both are heavily decorated with fretwork, cruciform in shape, and are reached via underground entrances from the plaza.

While archaeologists and explorers have probed Mitla's monumental architecture since the nineteenth century, much less is known about its household and daily life. Unfortunately, much of early Mitla lies beneath the contemporary community, making systematic study difficult. Population estimates for the late pre-Conquest population range as high as 10,000, but such figures are quite tentative. Mitla's role as a gateway to the Sierra and its favorable location on trade routes to the Oaxaca coast, the central valleys, the Isthmus of Tehuantepec, and more distant destinations facilitated contacts with peoples and cultures elsewhere. In addition to acting as a conduit for the exchange of styles, taste, and ideas, Mitla's participation in Postclassic trade relationships had the practical benefits of supporting a relatively large population and channeling wealth into the community, perhaps thereby partially underwriting the construction of its monumental architecture.

FURTHER READINGS

Paddock, J. 1966. *Ancient Oaxaca.* Stanford: Stanford University Press.

Parsons, E. C. 1936. *Mitla: Town of Souls.* Chicago: University of Chicago Press.

Robles García, N. M. 1992. *Mitla: 1992 Guia de la Zona Arqueológica.* Mexico City: Instituto Nacionalde Antropología e Historia.

———. 1995. *Las Canteras de Mitla, Oaxaca: Tecnologia para la arquitectura monumental.* Vanderbilt University Publications in Anthropology, 47. Nashville, Tenn.

Robles García, N. M., R. Gonzalez Medina, V. Jimenez Munoz, and A. J. Moreira Quiros. 1989. *Mitla, Libro Guia.* Mexico City: Tule.

Robles García, N. M., and A. J. Moreira Quiros. 1990. *Proyecto Mitla: Restauración de la zona arqueológica en su contexto urbano.* Colección Cientifica, 193. Mexico City: Instituto Nacional de Antropología e Historia.

Winter, M. 1992. *Oaxaca, the Archaeological Record.* Mexico City: Editorial Minutiae Mexicana.

Nelly M. Robles García

SEE ALSO

Oaxaca and Tehuantepec Region

Mixco Viejo (Chimaltenango, Guatemala)

One of the largest and best preserved Late Postclassic sites in highland Guatemala, Mixco Viejo (elevation 900 meters) is situated on a naturally fortified hilltop overlooking the gorges of the upper Motagua River. Major buildings are distributed in several plaza groups along patterns largely dictated by the narrow plateau, whose flanks were extensively reinforced with stone terraces. All major groups contain plazas, temple pyramids, and elongated buildings. Major structures were dressed with thin stone slabs and sometimes covered with stucco. One of the large plaza groups has twin temples, and two have I-shaped ball courts. One horizontally tenoned sculpture was found in ball court B-1. Dwelling platforms that cluster on the limited space around major building complexes, studied by Fauvet-Berthelot, are typically rectangular and delimited by stone banquettes. A population of 1,500 to 2,000 inhabitants has been estimated on the basis on 250 probable houses in the immediate site center. Excavations in an adjacent dwelling area by Ichon and Grignon revealed commoner cemeteries, where sixty-two burials were excavated. The majority were placed in circular pits in seated position, accompanied by modest lithic and ceramic furnishings, contrasting with urn burials found in the major groups.

According to seventeenth-century chronicler Fuentes y Guzmán, Mixco Viejo was a stronghold of the Pocomam Maya and fell to the Spaniards after a prolonged battle. An alternative explanation, espoused by Carmack, interprets the site as a center of the Chajomá, a Cakchiquel people who occupied the territory in colonial and modern times.

M

FURTHER READINGS

Carmack, R. 1979. *Historia Social de los Quichés*. Guatemala City: Seminario de Integración Social Guatemalteca.

Fauvet-Berthelot, M. F. 1986. *Ethnohistoire de la Maison Maya (Guatemala 1250–1525)*. Mexico City: Centre d'Études Mexicaines et Centraméricaines.

Ichon, A., and R. Grignon. 1984. Pratiques funéraires et stratification sociale dans les hautes terres Mayas: les cimetières protohistoriques de la campana a Mixco Viejo, Guatemala. *Journal de la Société des Américanistes de Paris* 70:89–126.

Lehmann, H. 1968. *Mixco Viejo: Guia de las ruinas de la plaza fuerte Pocomam*. Guatemala City: Tipografia Nacional.

Oswaldo Chinchilla Mazariegos

SEE ALSO

Guatemala Highlands Region

Mixtec History, Culture, and Religion

The term "Mixtec" is often used in vague and contradictory ways. It can refer to a language, an ethnic group, an endogamous elite, a geographical area, and an art style, none of which coincides, point for point, with any of the others. In ancient times there were speakers of the Mixtec language living in regions far outside the Mixteca; there were also large groups of non-Mixtec speakers (such as the Trique, Amuzgo, Chatino, Chocho, and Cuicatec) who were native to that region, and who may even have made up the majority of the population of some "Mixtec" kingdoms. Similarly, the Mixtec writing style, one of the four major scripts in use in Postclassic Mesoamerica, appears to have inspired non-Mixtec scribes outside the Mixteca region. Nor are ethnonyms—local geographical and social categorizations—any more straightforward. In the sixteenth century, the name Ñusavi, or "People of the Rain," was used for the inhabitants of single kingdoms, for the people who spoke Mixtec, for the inhabitants of the Mixteca Alta, and even for the peoples of the eastern half of Oaxaca. Because the term "Mixtec" embraces such heterogeneous things, one might conclude that it is a term of little analytic value. It is perhaps best to see it as reflecting the nature of most ancient Mesoamerican civilizations, where cultural, social, ethnic, historical and ecological variables combined in complex ways to produce recognizably distinct but always overlapping traditions.

We can trace the origins of Mixtec civilization to at least 1000 B.C., when people living in the Mixteca Alta—a region in the high western mountains of the present-day Mexican state of Oaxaca—began to isolate themselves from other Otomanguean groups, and their language took on recognizably "Mixtec" characteristics. Subsequently, these people followed the major river courses out of their core mountain area south and west into the coastal region of Oaxaca, now called the Mixteca de la Costa, and north and west into the semiarid zone along the borders of the states of Oaxaca, Puebla, and Guerrero, called the Mixteca Baja. By the time the Spanish arrived in 1522, Mixtec-speaking kings and queens ruled over much of the western Valley of Oaxaca as well. They had incorporated most of the Chocho, Chatino, Nahuatl, Amuzgo, and Trique-speaking regions of Oaxaca into their kingdoms, and there is evidence that they controlled groups of Tlapanec speakers in Guerrero, as well as Popoloca and Mazatec speakers in Veracruz and Puebla.

Although we have long recognized the Mixteca as the home of a unique and influential civilization, relatively little anthropological or historical research has been carried out in the region. Archaeologists have thoroughly surveyed the neighboring Valley of Oaxaca, but most of the Mixteca is archaeologically unknown. Important ethnohistorical documents on Maya and Aztec societies are available in reasonably priced critical editions, but similar works for the Mixteca remain rare or in manuscript form. And although contemporary Mixtec speakers make up the fourth-largest indigenous group in Mexico, our basic ethnographic knowledge of the region is embarrassingly incomplete.

The natural environment in which an ancient civilization develops is important for understanding its economic, political, and social dynamics, and the Mixteca is no exception. The indigenous terms for subareas of the Mixteca highlight the importance of environmental variation to the ancient Mixtec. The Mixteca de la Costa, for example, was called "land of corn," perhaps because the warm climate and ample rainfall allow for the production of large corn surpluses. We traditionally divide the Mixteca into three broad geographical zones: the Mixteca Alta, a mountainous region in eastern Oaxaca; the Mixteca Baja, a dry region northwest of the Alta; and the Mixteca de la Costa, a low-lying, humid strip of land alongside the Pacific Ocean. These subdivisions, however, obscure the great diversity that exists in the area, where changes in altitude and rainfall patterns create many distinct microclimates, often within a small area. In some

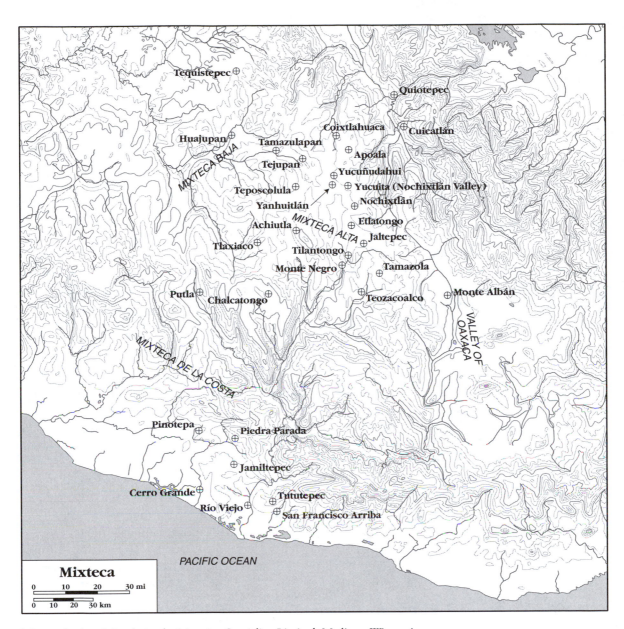

Mixteca Region. Map design by Mapping Specialists Limited, Madison, Wisconsin.

areas one may begin walking in high pine forests, where potatoes, *maguey,* and other cold-weather crops are grown, and within an hour or two descend to a tropical valley full of banana groves and mango trees. The proximity of different ecological floors encourages their vertical integration, something that was an important factor in settlement patterns, ritual exchanges, and the political dynamics of ancient Mixtec societies.

Chronology

Little is known of the preagricultural settlement in the Mixteca. In the Nochixtlán Valley, a half-dozen small farming villages dating to approximately 1350 B.C. were found in the course of research by Spores; in the adjacent Tamazulapan Valley, similar sites were discovered in Byland's survey. These settlements were established along rivers and streams and near good farmland. Residents used a smoothed, thin-walled, buff-colored pottery, and they produced stone tools from locally available chert and basalt.

Between 750 and 200 B.C. the number of settlements expanded greatly in the Nochixtlán and Tamazulapan valleys, and villages appeared in the once largely uninhabited lower Río Verde Valley in the Mixteca de la Costa. More-

M

over, ceramic styles and a local figurine complex show clear affinities with broader Formative stylistic traditions, indicating contact with other areas in Mesoamerica. Although the settlements remained small, unusual structures have been excavated, such as a large earthen platform at Etlatongo. Clear evidence of socio-political stratification dates from after 200 B.C., the Early Classic period. In the Nochixtlán Valley, Yucuita became the core settlement, expanding from a small cluster of houses covering 100 to 150 square meters in the early Formative to a large urban center with internally differentiated structures covering 1.5 square kilometers. For about 500 years, Yucuita occupied a position at the apex of a regional settlement hierarchy consisting of at least thirty smaller sites. Exotic goods are also found in abundance, indicating extensive contacts with areas far beyond the Mixteca.

The Classic period in the Mixteca, from A.D. 300 to 800, was a time of unprecedented growth and development. More than a hundred sites dating to this period have been located in the Nochixtlán Valley alone, three of which—Yucuñudahui, Cerro Jazmín, and Etlatongo—cover more than two square kilometers. Similarly, Río Viejo in the Río Verde Valley developed an urban center with settlement spread over three square kilometers. These sites were characterized by clearly demarcated civic-ceremonial centers with large plazas, ball courts, and large temple mounds. Residential areas show a complex stratification of the population, and richly decorated tombs with painted murals have been found.

Because many large Classic settlements are associated with caves, springs, distinctive stone outcroppings, and unusually shaped mountains, they may have been built on ancient sacred sites. As populations increased, so did the use of techniques to intensify agricultural production. These included extensive irrigation works developed in favorable areas, vertical integration of different microclimes, and one of the most unusual agricultural technologies in the world: the *lama-bordo* technique of controlled erosion, which is designed to bring moist fertile soil off steep mountainsides onto terraced agricultural plots.

Postclassic Mixtec Kingdoms

The best-understood period of pre-Conquest Mixtec history is the Postclassic, from the collapse of the Classic period urban centers (c. 800 A.D.) to the Spanish conquest of the region in the 1520s. Archaeologists have excavated a number of Postclassic sites, and the Mixtec people themselves produced a comparatively extensive corpus of manuscripts documenting their genealogies, religion, and mythology. In addition, beginning in the sixteenth century Spanish colonialists and some native Mixtecs began to produce accounts of ancient Mixtec society in European script.

It is the remarkable art and writing style patronized by the rulers of its Postclassic kingdoms that has done most to bring the Mixteca to the world's attention. Mixtec artists produced delicate jewelry, like the pieces found in the famous Tomb 7 at Monte Albán, as well as intricately carved bones, polychrome pottery, and illuminated manuscripts. The artistic style associated with the Mixteca has been classified as a variant of the Mixteca-Puebla or "International" style, with other variants found throughout Postclassic Mesoamerica. Postclassic Mixtecs appear to have been less concerned with monumental architecture, focusing their efforts instead on fine, precise, geometric, and vividly colored work.

We know that the Postclassic was the period of small kingdoms, or *yuhuitayu* (*cacicazgo* in Spanish), whose rulers were linked by a network of kinship and marriage ties. The typical Mixtec kingdom consisted of a single major site and its immediate surroundings. If a kingdom was ruled by kings and queens of a particularly prestigious line, and if they were astute military leaders and able to form strategic alliances, a single kingdom might dominate other, lesser kingdoms, and form a major kingdom.

Major kingdoms at the time of the Spanish conquest included Coixtlahuaca, Yanhuitlán, Teposcolula, Tilantongo, Achiutla, Tlaxiaco, Teozacualco, Chalcatongo, Tequistepec, Tecomaxtlahuaca, and Tututepec on the coast. Several of these were, in turn, subordinate to the Central Mexican Triple Alliance. In most cases, subject kingdoms were free to rule themselves, being required only to provide regular tribute payments and occasional military support in war. They may even have made strategic alliances with other centers independent of the dominant kingdom. The exception was the region dominated by the large coastal kingdom of Tututepec, whose rulers seem to have appointed officials in subject kingdoms.

The ruling stratum was divided into two groups: those having royal lineage (*iya tnuhu* or, as the Spanish called them, the *caciques*), and the *tay toho*, a hereditary nobility (*principales* in Spanish). The elite held power and authority in most kingdoms, with the nobility playing advisory and administrative roles. Mythology portrayed the elite as having a different origin from other people; they spoke a special language, known as the Iya vocabulary, which was reputed to be the speech of the first rulers of the Mixteca, who were born from trees around the sacred site of Apoala; the Iya vocabulary is in fact a series of elaborate metaphors, whose meaning was not apparent to the uninitiated. At least some tribute to the elite was considered sacrificial offerings rather than a tax. Sixteenth-century Dominican lexicographers translated the Mixtec word for "royalty," *iya*, as "saint" and "divine." All these facts suggest that the ancient Mixtec elite were considered godlike beings.

The great mass of people in the Mixteca in Postclassic times were, of course, not members of the elite, and early colonial sources refer to them as "local people" (*tay nuu*) and "rural people" (*tay yucu*). Although we tend to think of the nonelite in broad terms, in many Mixtec kingdoms this sector of society appears to have contained important internal divisions. Thus, there were people we might call "commoners," organized into communities or barrios, like the Central Mexican "Big House," with both corporate and individual rights to lands and other resources. There were groups of landless tenant farmers, who worked the royal patrimony. Their lord would sometimes move them from one area to another, if the lord also changed residence upon marriage or succession to a throne. Finally, there were slaves, who were people captured in battle, born to slaves, purchased, or received in tribute.

Our knowledge of nonelite social patterns, the ways in which they were linked to elites, and the political role they played in the dynamics of Mixtec kingdoms is only sketchy. In part this is due to the nature of the Mixtec documents that survived the Conquest, which deal either with religious themes or with elite genealogy and history. But it is also due to the lack of archaeological research in nonelite contexts. We do know that the nonelite sector was ethnically diverse. The kingdom of Tututepec on the coast, for example, contained large number of Chatino, Nahuatl, Zapotec, and perhaps Amuzgo speakers, and non-Mixtec speakers may have made up the majority of the population. The same may have been true of the Mixtec kingdoms in the Valley of Oaxaca, in Guerrero, and in the Mixteca Baja, where Chocho, Cuicatec, Ixcatec, and Nahua people lived in proximity to one another, often in different barrios of the same settlement.

"Mixtec" speakers were themselves a diverse group. The principal languages of the Otomanguean family, Mixtec and Zapotec, have fragmented into a continuum of many dialects (or languages) that tend to be mutually unintelligible beyond about a day's journey on foot. Modern linguistic studies show that there are least twenty-nine dialects that fall below the level of 70 percent mutual intelligibility, which is considered the minimum necessary for effective communication. Linguists agree that Mixtec, like Zapotec, is really a group of related languages, although the presence of dialect continua prevents the drawing of absolute language boundaries.

Some suggest that this linguistic diversity is somehow an artifact of Spanish colonial rule, but the documented cases of sixteenth-century interpolity and interregional communication almost all involve the elite, who were often polyglot, speaking the lingua franca of Nahuatl, or merchants, who spent much of their time traveling from one place to another and would have become familiar with systematic variations between the speech of one Mixtec area and another (a situation that holds true today). Thus, Antonio de los Reyes wrote that he based his 1593 grammar on the Mixtec of Teposcolula, since the elite and merchants of all regions could understand it. He went on to say that the common people would only be able to pick out a few words here and there. This suggests that Mixtec linguistic diversity also characterized the Postclassic period, although the number of distinct Mixtec dialects was probably not as high as it is today.

Each of the social strata enumerated above—kings and queens, nobles, commoners, tenants, slaves—was largely endogamous. It is true that the elite practiced polygyny, and their second or third wives might be commoners; however, only the children of the principal wife inherited titles and property. The first wife had to be from the aristocracy, since caste endogamy was required to inherit or retain a royal title. Consequently, the ancient Mixtec elite and nobility were very concerned with genealogy, and cousin marriage was frequent among royalty. The Mixteca are also one of the few societies in the world where true brother-sister marriage occurred.

Mixtec kingdoms, then, should be seen as made up of many different ecological, social, and cultural units, with rulers and ruled being, in many cases, ethnically and linguistically distinct (the old Mixtec term for noble, *toho*, means "foreigner" in many places today). Thus, it is no great surprise that throughout history, Mixtec kingdoms appear to have been relatively easily broken up and reconfigured, with pieces divided and added. Although this process of segmentation was in part a consequence of elite

M

inheritance rules and alliance strategies, which tended to divide titles and privileges among several heirs in each generation, it was greatly facilitated by the social, ethnic, and linguistic divisions that existed in the Mixteca, which defined ready-made segmentary units.

The Spanish conquest of the Mixteca, from 1522 to 1524, brought wrenching changes to the area. The colonial regime curbed the power of Mixtec kings and encouraged the breakup of the great kingdoms by granting local segmentary units administrative autonomy. Dominican friars destroyed religious shrines and persecuted people who continued to practice the old religion. Added to this, the new diseases the Spanish brought with them ravaged the population, sometimes wiping out entire settlements. Prior to the Spanish conquest, the population of the Mixteca was over 500,000 (earlier estimates of a pre-Conquest population of 700,000 for the Mixteca, based on projections from colonial sources, are being revised downward). The plagues of the sixteenth century reduced the population by almost 90 percent. The demographic collapse, coupled with difficult terrain, the region's lack of mineral resources, and isolation from major trade routes increasingly marginalized the Mixteca, and few Spaniards chose to live there.

Despite the calamities of the sixteenth century, members of the Mixtec elite came to occupy leading roles in the new colonial regime. In some places, descendants of the hereditary nobility, still called by the term *iya*, or "holy lord," continued to hold lands and occupy prominent places into the twentieth century. The indigenous population of the region, after reaching a nadir in the early seventeenth century, began to increase again. In the nineteenth and twentieth centuries outsiders began to move into the Mixteca in increasing numbers, and commercial agriculture expanded. At the same time, the region became a center for several armed political movements, and Mixtec-speaking peoples actively participated in the Mexican struggle for independence, as well as the Wars of the Reform and the Mexican Revolution of 1910–1920.

A lack of economic opportunity has caused many to migrate from this area, and there are now substantial colonies of Mixtec speakers in the Isthmus of Tehuantepec, Oaxaca City, Mexico City, Baja California, and various places in the United States. Today there are about 400,000 speakers of Mixtec in the region, occupying the same territory once ruled by their ancient kings and queens, and Mixtec culture remains a living presence. Although most contemporary speakers of Mixtec are what anthropologists call "peasants," there is a growing Mixtec middle class made up of teachers, government workers, technicians, politicians, health officials, scholars, and other professionals.

Research among modern inhabitants of the Mixteca has shed considerable light on the region's pre-Hispanic history. Many of the incidents recorded in the pre-Conquest codices and post-Conquest *lienzos* remain part of contemporary oral tradition, and folkloric research has helped to elucidate the content of these manuscripts. Moreover, since these manuscripts were not simply reference works but were part of a tradition of recitational literacy, studies of contemporary Mixtec verbal art have helped us to illuminate the way the poetics of oral performance inform these texts. Oral history and toponymic research have also been used to identify archaeological sites and ancient boundaries, and studies of contemporary social and ritual practices have helped in understanding ancient rituals and institutions.

FURTHER READINGS

Byland, B., and J. Pohl. 1994. *In the Realm of Eight Deer.* Norman: University of Oklahoma Press.

Dahlgren de Jordón, B. 1954. *La Mixteca: Su cultura e historia prehispánica.* Mexico City: Cultura Mexicana.

Flannery, K., and J. Marcus (eds.). 1983. *The Cloud People.* New York: Academic Press.

Furst, J. L. 1978. *Codex Vindobonensis Mexicanus I: A Commentary.* Albany: Institute for Mesoamerican Studies, State University of New York.

Monaghan, J. 1995. *The Covenant with Earth and Rain: Exchange, Sacrifice and Revelation in Mixtec Sociality.* Norman: University of Oklahoma Press.

Pohl, J. 1994. *The Politics of Symbolism in the Mixtec Codices.* Vanderbilt University Publications in Anthropology, no. 46. Nashville, Tenn.

Romero Frizzi, M. 1990. Economía y vida de los españoles en la Mixteca Alta: 1519–1720. Mexico City: Instituto Nacional de Antropología e Historia.

Smith, M. E. 1973. *Picture Writing of Ancient Southern Mexico.* Norman: University of Oklahoma Press.

Spores, R. 1967. *The Mixtec Kings and Their People.* Norman: University of Oklahoma Press.

———. 1984. *The Mixtec in Ancient and Colonial Times.* Norman: University of Oklahoma Press.

John Monaghan

SEE ALSO

Coixtlahuaca; Languages at the Time of Contact

Mixteca-Puebla Style

This distinctive painting style has been found at many Postclassic sites in the "Mixteca-Puebla" region (northwestern Oaxaca and southern Puebla) of Central Mexico; it dates from the twelfth or thirteenth century A.D., after the fall of the Toltec state. It employs vivid colors in a standardized, precise, and geometric delineation of images. Common symbols include animals, plants, sky elements, ritual objects, and deities. "Imaginative exaggeration of prominent features, strong black outlines, and bright, flat colors, resulted in images of striking boldness and visual impact" (Nicholson and Quinones 1994:vii). Works painted in the Mixteca-Puebla style are a major source of information on Postclassic religion and iconography.

The Mixteca-Puebla style occurs in a variety of media. Two groups of codices, or pictorial manuscripts, provide the most elaborate examples of the style. The Codex Borgia and related pictorial manuscripts (the "Borgia group") are ritual almanacs from the Mixteca-Puebla area (probably Cholula) that were used by priests for divination. The Mixtec codices (e.g., the Codex Nuttall) are historical annals from northwestern Oaxaca that recount the genealogies and exploits of the Mixtec kings. Mural paintings in the style have been found at several sites in the Mixteca-Puebla area, including Tehuacan Viejo and Tizatlan.

The most abundant objects bearing the Mixteca-Puebla style are the many polychrome ceramic vessels from the same area. The best-known examples are the Cholula polychromes, from Cholula (often suggested to have been the central focal point of the style); similar polychromes from southern Puebla and Tlaxcala; Mixtec polychrome ceramics from the Mixteca Alta area; and Chalco polychromes, an extension of the style into the Valley of Mexico. Most of the manuscripts, murals, and ceramics pertain to both the Middle and Late Postclassic periods, A.D. 1200–1520, and as chronological research continues, our ability to date the origin and evolution of the style should improve.

During the Late Postclassic period (A.D. 1350–1520), murals and manuscripts painted in the Mixteca-Puebla style were used throughout Mesoamerica, including areas outside Central Mexico. These works have been grouped together as the "International style" to distinguish them from the objects of the Mixteca-Puebla area proper. One variant of this style is found in Aztec historical codices from the Valley of Mexico and several provincial cities in the Aztec Empire, including Xilotepec, Tlappa, and Tochpan. The economic and political dynamics of Aztec imperialism may account for the spread of this manuscript style from the Aztec capital, Tenochtitlan, to distant parts of the empire. Another variant of the International style consists of complex polychrome murals from a broad area of central and southern Mesoamerica, including Mitla, Cempoala, Tulum, Santa Rita, and Iximche. The latter three sites lie in Maya-speaking areas far beyond the limits of the Aztec Empire. The style probably spread to these areas through busy Late Postclassic networks of commerce and elite interaction not involving the Aztecs.

Painted ceramics with standardized motifs similar to those of the Mixteca-Puebla style are found in widely scattered coastal areas of Mesoamerica. Originally, scholars proposed diffusionist models to account for the presence of these objects so far from their presumed Central Mexican hearth. Later research, however, has shown that most examples of this coastal style date to the Epiclassic and Early Postclassic periods (A.D. 750–1200), long before the emergence of the Mixteca-Puebla style in Central Mexico. This earlier style has been called the "Postclassic Religious style" by Smith and Heath-Smith. It does not occur in Central Mexico, whose cultures at that time were cut off from major coastal trade networks. The distribution of this style supports the hypothesis that coastal areas were critical in the control of trade and communication in peripheral Mesoamerica following the fall of Teotihuacan. The Mixteca-Puebla style thus evolved out of the Postclassic Religious style.

The three styles discussed above are related as follows. The Postclassic Religious style evolved in coastal Mesoamerica during a period of active sea trade that was not controlled by a large empire (c. A.D. 750–1200). Local elites probably used these standardized religious symbols to express their links with distant cultures. After A.D. 1200, the people of the Mixteca-Puebla area selected some of the earlier symbols and developed them into the more elaborate Mixteca-Puebla style. This style was applied to a wider range of media and became very popular in Central Mexico. In Late Postclassic times (after A.D. 1350), the International style, a broader version of the Mixteca-Puebla style, was carried to distant corners of Mesoamerica. Although the Aztecs may have been responsible for part of this process, much of it occurred through commercial and cultural networks largely independent of the Aztec Empire.

FURTHER READINGS

Berdan, F. F., R. E. Blanton, E. H. Boone, M. G. Hodge, M. E. Smith, and E. Umberger. *Aztec Imperial Strategies.* Washington, D.C.: Dumbarton Oaks.

M

Mixteca-Puebla image. Illustration courtesy of the author.

Diaz, G., A. Rodgers, and B. E. Byland (eds.). 1993. *The Codex Borgia: A Full-Color Restoration of the Ancient Mexican Manuscript.* New York: Dover.

Nicholson, H. B., and E. Quiñones Keber (eds.). 1994. *Mixteca-Puebla: Discoveries and Research in Mesoamerican Art and Archaeology.* Culver City, Calif.: Labyrinthos.

Nuttall, Z., and A. G. Miller (eds.). 1975. *The Codex Nuttall: A Picture Manuscript from Ancient Mexico.* New York: Dover.

Robertson, D. 1970. The Tulum Murals: The International Style of the Late Post-Classic. In *Verhandlungen der XXXVIII Internationalen Amerikanisten-Kongres, Stuttgart-Munchen, 1968,* pp. 77–88. Munich: Klaus Renner.

Smith, M. E., and C. M. Heath-Smith. 1980. Waves of Influence in Postclassic Mesoamerica? A Critique of the Mixteca-Puebla Concept. *Anthropology* 4:15–50.

Michael E. Smith

SEE ALSO

Mixtec History, Culture, and Religion

Mixtequilla

See Cerro de las Mesas; Gulf Lowlands: South Central Region

Mojarra, La (Veracruz, Mexico)

The archaeological site of this name, occupied from the Late Formative period until at least the early Postclassic (c. 300 B.C.–A.D. 1000), has been little studied; it consists of small earthen mounds and modest plazas covering an area of about one square kilometer on a bend of the Acula River. Of far greater significance than the mounds is Stela 1, accidentally discovered in the water adjacent to the riverbank.

Stela 1, an irregular trapezoidal stone slab, measures 2.34 by 1.42 meters. It depicts an elaborately costumed standing male accompanied by a very long hieroglyphic text recorded in a nearly unknown script variously called Epi-Olmec, Intermediate, and Tuxtla script. Two dates included in the text can be read as 21 May A.D. 143 and 13 July A.D. 156 in the Maya long count, making the stela one of Mesoamerica's oldest known texts; it is also one of the longest. Publication of the monument and its text in

1988 sparked ongoing disputes about the authenticity of the stela and the correct decipherment of the text. Although most scholars accept the stela as genuine, a few claim that the text is a modern forgery added to an authentic pre-Hispanic monument.

Decipherment is inextricably tied to the language spoken by the scribes who carved the text. The linguists John Justeson and Terrence Kaufman believe the inscription is in Pre-Proto-Zoquean, an ancestral form of the Mixe, Zoque, and Populuca languages still spoken today in the region; other epigraphers consider it an early form of Mayan, and still others pursue nonlinguistic decipherments. Justeson and Kaufman have proposed the only tentative reading of the inscription so far, suggesting that the text proclaims the accession to power and subsequent deeds of the man depicted on the stela. Neither the authenticity of the writing system nor its correct decipherment can be ascertained until additional, similar monuments and texts become available for study.

FURTHER READINGS

Diehl, R., A. Vargas González, and S. Vásquez Zárate. 1997. Proyecto arqueológico La Mojarra. In S. Ladrón de Guevara and S. Vásquez Zárate (eds.), *Memoria del Coloquio Arqueología del centro y sur de Veracruz,* pp. 197–209. Jalapa: Universidad Veracuzana.

Richard A. Diehl

SEE ALSO
Gulf Lowlands: South Central Region

Monagrillo (Herrera, Panama)

Situated near the mouth of the Parita River on Parita Bay in Panama, this is one of the earliest sites of ceramic-using peoples in Central America. Its material culture remains include crude pottery, pebble choppers, simple grinding stones, and stone bowls, along with remains of estuarine fauna dating to the fourth millennium B.C. Monagrillo is currently interpreted as a seasonal camp for the procurement of aquatic resources, used by people who moved between the coast and inland regions. It was occupied between 3500 and 1500 B.C. (calibrated radiocarbon dates) and was characterized by an increase and decline in permanence of occupation.

The site's occupants consumed mostly small fish, shellfish, and crustaceans. They also processed palm nuts and other plant foods with edge-ground cobbles. This may have been a location for salting and drying small fish caught in fine nets. Monagrillo is the type site for the Monagrillo Ceramic Complex, now known from several locations, including Aguadulce Shelter and Cueva de los Ladrones farther inland. The complex is simple in technology and style. Although the initial dates for Monagrillo vessels remain unclear, these most likely appeared between 3800 and 3000 B.C. The degree of sedentism at Monagrillo and the question of whether its occupants were horticulturalists are topics of current investigation.

FURTHER READINGS

Cooke, R. 1995. Monagrillo, Panama's First Pottery. In W. K. Barnett and J. W. Hoopes (eds.), *The Emergence of Pottery: Technology and Innovation in Ancient Societies,* pp. 169–184. Washington, D.C.: Smithsonian Institution Press.

Willey, G. R., and C. R. McGimsey III. 1954. *The Monagrillo Culture of Panama.* Papers of the Peabody Museum, 49. 2. Cambridge, Mass.: Harvard University.

John Hoopes

SEE ALSO
Intermediate Area: Overview

Monte Albán

Monte Albán is one of the most important and most thoroughly studied archaeological sites in Mesoamerica. Its massive array of pyramid platforms, plazas, carved stone monuments, residential terraces, roads, defensive walls, and many other features, which so impresses the modern visitor to the site, represents the remains of the political and cultural center of the Zapotec state during the period from its origin in 500 B.C. to A.D. 700. Through studying this ancient center and its impact on surrounding regions, we gain insight into the factors that brought about the evolution of one of the earliest complex political systems in the New World.

Monte Albán is located in the semiarid Valley of Oaxaca, a region of roughly 2,000 square kilometers in the modern Mexican state of Oaxaca. By comparison with the rugged terrain of the surrounding Southern Highlands region, the site's valley setting is characterized by comparatively flat terrain suitable in many areas for intensive irrigation agriculture. The Valley of Oaxaca's climate is mild owing to its elevation, about 1,400 meters above sea level, and this factor too contributes to the region's

M

potential for agricultural development. Monte Albán is situated on and around the summits and slopes of a cluster of hills, the highest of which reaches 400 meters above the valley floor. The Main Plaza, situated along the highest ridgeline of the major hill, was the city's, and the region's, major civic-ceremonial concourse.

City Origins and Growth in Period I

Monte Albán was founded suddenly at the end of the Middle Formative period, around 500 B.C., during what Caso, Bernal, and Acosta call Monte Albán Period I (ceramic periods predating Monte Albán's Period I have been discovered in other sites of the region by Flannery and his colleagues). The community was established in a previously unoccupied area. Its site is well above the surrounding valley floor but central to the Valley of Oaxaca's three main archaeological subregions, each of which occupied one of the three arms of the Y-shaped valley. Each subregion was occupied by a politically autonomous chiefdom dating to the ceramic phase preceding Period I, the Rosario phase (600–500 B.C.). Siting the new capital in a central but previously unused location probably reflected a strategy aimed at the creation of a new polity that could transcend the territorial limits of the prior chiefdoms, integrating them into a new political system of larger scale and greater hierarchical complexity. Thus, Monte Albán can be called a "disembedded capital," given the fact of its location in a political neutral zone, away from existing centers and in the interstices of prior political territories.

Period I remains at Monte Albán are largely obscured by those of later occupational periods, but enough information is available for us to draw several conclusions about the early settlement. During the initial phase of Period I (Early I, 500–350 B.C.), the center's population grew to approximately five thousand, quickly surpassing long-established communities in the valley's other regions and making Monte Albán by far the most populous community in the valley. The Main Plaza area was not yet architecturally enclosed, as it came to be in later periods, but several public buildings built there—one a probable temple—indicate that it was already a center of public activity. One of the new Main Plaza buildings, a gallery of carved stone monuments called *Danzantes,* dates to this and the subsequent ceramic phase (Late I, 350–200 B.C.). These near-life-size monuments, numbering more than 300 at Monte Albán but not constructed elsewhere in the region during Period I, depict slain individuals who were probably war captives. We may infer from the monumen-

tal scale of this building's display that warfare was an important factor prompting the development of a new political order and the establishment of the new capital. Three distinct clusters of Early I ceramics found along the edges of the Main Plaza area and one cluster at a greater remove from the Main Plaza suggest the presence of discrete neighborhoods (barrios) in the early city. This pattern of neighborhood organization was maintained in later periods, although in more complex form; fifteen barrios can be recognized by the Late Classic phase. During the Late I phase, Monte Albán's population continued to grow rapidly, reaching a maximum estimated at roughly sixteen thousand.

Evidence from the valley-wide settlement pattern survey provides us with an incomplete but tantalizing picture of changes that occurred in many aspects of society during the Early I and Late I phases. Although the exact sequence of events cannot be reconstructed with great accuracy, it is reasonable to conclude from the information we have that the development of a new, larger-scale political system, manifested by the construction of Monte Albán, brought in its wake fundamental social, cultural, and demographic changes throughout the region. Many existing communities increased in population size, and many new communities were founded, particularly in the area encircling the city at about 20 kilometers in radius, the area of its most direct influence. Piedmont irrigation systems were constructed within this same area, representing one dimension of an overall increase in production intensity. Many households abandoned the traditional wattle-and-daub construction in favor of the more substantial mud-brick, perhaps reflecting an increased standard of living for large sectors of the population. The region's economy exhibited more specialized production, and, evidently, although this is difficult to study archaeologically, an increase in market exchange. There is evidence of the first use of the griddle *(comal),* indicating the beginnings of the technique of preparing corn in the form of tortillas.

Regional Reorganization in Period II

During the lengthy Monte Albán Period II (200 B.C.–A.D. 300), the center's influence appears to have diminished somewhat within its local domain, though it maintained its role as regional political capital. Although Monte Albán was still the region's most populous community, changes in political and economic structure during this time resulted in a decline in its population from the preceding Period I, to an estimated 14,500. Ceramic and architectural evidence from other major valley sites is consistent in suggesting some increase in the autonomy of local centers of government, to Monte Albán's detriment, although there was not a total breakdown in regional integration. During this troubled time (or at the very end of the Late I phase), a massive defensive wall was built around Monte Albán's difficult-to-defend northern and western slopes, extending over a distance of more than two kilometers. It was also during Period II that the city's rulers extended their political reach far outside the Valley of Oaxaca—as far as 100 kilometers into the mountainous region of the Cañada de Cuicatlan. This imperial strategy may have been necessary, given the city's apparent inability to control resources and loyalties within its home region. Within the city, an active construction program leveled the Main Plaza and added new buildings to it, including a new military gallery.

Growth and Decline During Period III

The Early Classic period (A.D. 300–500, locally referred to as Phase IIIA) was a period of substantial population growth and political change at Monte Albán and in the Valley of Oaxaca. Monte Albán grew substantially to an estimated 16,500, and the valley's population in some regions (particularly its southern arm) reached densities higher than in any subsequent period up to the present day. Extensive construction in the Main Plaza area included the South Platform (the massive structure defining the southern edge of the Main Plaza) and the addition of other buildings and walls whose positioning made the plaza a more isolated, formal, and architecturally impressive space.

In addition to the population growth and architectural elaboration that took place within the city, several other lines of evidence point to Monte Albán's growing regional dominance during Phase IIIA. By this time, carved stone monuments in the Monte Albán style were erected throughout the valley, and, in the Main Plaza, stelae publicly depict rulers ascending to positions of power, declaring military victories, and greeting diplomatic visitors from Teotihuacan. The regional survey data indicate the development of a more centralized Phase IIIA social system, in which we can detect an increase in the degree of state involvement in production and the flow of commodities between specialized sectors of an integrated region-wide economy.

The episode of population growth that is so clearly evident during Phase IIIA was reversed in the subsequent phase. By the Late Classic period (locally known as the IIIB ceramic phase, A.D. 500–700), the massive development of the valley's southern region had collapsed. The IIIB regional system centered on Monte Albán was considerably reduced in scale and was focused within the city's immediate local hinterland. In the capital, however, growth continued, and the city attained its maximum pre-Hispanic population size of nearly twenty-five thousand.

The Main Plaza was the site of additional construction, and it was at this time that it took the final form that is still visible today. New construction reflected a continuing policy of making the Main Plaza architecturally formalized, isolated, and awe inspiring. As a result, by Phase IIIB it had been developed into a space so visually impressive that even modern visitors are strongly affected by it. The architectural strategy aimed at the creation of a space that is both monumental and spatially coherent. The plaza is bounded by uninterrupted lines of pyramid platforms along its eastern and western edges, while two massive platform mounds define the northern and southern edges. The staircase of the South Platform, about twelve meters in elevation, faces a central spine of buildings that connect it visually to the staircase of the North Platform, which it faces. The North Platform, accessible from the Main Plaza by a massive staircase, contained the living and working areas of Monte Albán's rulers.

Outside the Main Plaza, the city grew to its largest pre-Hispanic population size. By this time, more than two thousand terraces had been constructed on the sloping terrain to create spaces for residential and public buildings. Major and minor roads, still detectable on the surface today, directed traffic through the various barrios of the city, but they only weakly connected the isolated, forbidding Main Plaza to the main traffic flows. The city's residential barrios are recognizable by their characteristic form: a cluster of residential terraces surrounding a complex of pyramid platforms and adjacent open spaces, some of which may have been neighborhood market plazas. The pyramids always include one or two buildings that were probably elite residences, and one or more associated temples. To some degree, craft specialization has been found to occur by barrio, although in this period, as in previous periods, Monte Albán was never a major center of basic commodity production of any type; however, evidence for elite goods production, such as shell-working, is found in higher frequency in the city than in other valley centers.

Changing Urban Patterns of the Postclassic Period

By the end of Phase IIIB construction had ceased in the Main Plaza area, and its buildings were allowed to fall into

M

disrepair. During the subsequent Early Postclassic period, or Period IV, Monte Albán was still occupied but was much reduced in population size; it had a more scattered settlement pattern and was no longer the region's major political center. An increase in interregional warfare is indicated by the construction of new defensive walls within the city.

By the Late Postclassic, locally called Period V, Monte Albán was again the region's major city, at least in demographic terms, with a population of roughly fourteen thousand. But the city's regional role during Period V cannot be compared to what it had been during the Classic period or earlier. The Main Plaza remained deserted, and the city (known then in the Mixtec language as Sa'a Yucu) was dispersed over a broad area along the lower slopes of the complex of hills, well beyond the limits of the old city. No complex of buildings comparable to the Main Plaza was ever built again, and the palaces of the Zapotec rulers of Period V were situated elsewhere, in Zaachila, a small center to the south of Sa'a Yucu.

Monte Albán has attracted the attention of several generations of archaeological researchers because it was the political, cultural, and urban focal point of one of the earliest and most influential Mesoamerican polities. Earlier in the twentieth century, major research projects were conducted by Mexican archaeologists Alfonso Caso, Ignacio Bernal, and Jorge R. Acosta, who mapped and excavated in and around the vicinity of the Main Plaza. These researchers established the main features of the site's ceramic sequence, excavated tombs and described their artifacts, and offered interpretations of the large corpus of carved stone monuments found in and around the Main Plaza. More recently, Joyce Marcus carried forward the study of written texts and other carved stone monuments, and Richard Blanton completed a surface survey of the site, documenting the city's history of population growth and its urban layout. A systematic settlement pattern survey of the entire Valley of Oaxaca by Blanton, Stephen Kowalewski, Gary Feinman, Laura Finsten, and Linda Nicholas allows us to interpret many aspects of Monte Albán's changing role in a densely populated regional political and economic system.

FURTHER READINGS

Blanton, R. E. 1978. *Monte Albán: Settlement Patterns at the Ancient Zapotec Capital.* New York: Academic Press.

Blanton, R. E., S. A. Kowalewski, G. M. Feinman, and J. Appel. 1982. *Monte Albán's Hinterland, Part I: Prehispanic Settlement Patterns of the Central and Southern Parts of the Valley of Oaxaca, Mexico.* Museum of Anthropology, University of Michigan, Memoirs, 15, Ann Arbor.

Blanton, R. E., S. A. Kowalewski, G. M. Feinman, and L. Finsten. 1993. *Ancient Mesoamerica: A Comparison of Change in Three Regions.* 2nd edn. Cambridge: Cambridge University Press.

Caso, A. 1965. Zapotec Writing and Calendar. In G. R. Willey (ed.), *Handbook of Middle American Indians,* vol. 3, *Archaeology of Southern Mesoamerica,* part 2, pp. 931–47. Austin: University of Texas Press.

———. 1969. *El Tesoro de Monte Albán.* Memorias del Instituto Nacional de Antropología e Historia, 3. Mexico City.

Caso, A., and I. Bernal. 1952. *Urnas de Oaxaca.* Mexico: Memorias del Instituto Nacional de Antropología e Historia, 2. Mexico City.

Caso, A., I. Bernal, and J. R. Acosta. 1967. *La Cerámica de Monte Albán.* Memorias del Instituto Nacional de Antropología e Historia, 13. Mexico City.

Kowalewski, S. A., G. M. Feinman, L. Finsten, R. E. Blanton, and L. Nicholas. 1989. *Monte Albán's Hinterland, Part II: Prehispanic Settlement Patterns in Tlacolula, Etla, and Ocotlán, the Valley of Oaxaca, Mexico.* Museum of Anthropology, University of Michigan, Memoirs, 23. Ann Arbor.

Marcus, J. 1992. *Mesoamerican Writing Systems: Propaganda, Myth, and History in Four Ancient Civilizations.* Princeton: Princeton University Press.

Richard E. Blanton

SEE ALSO

Oaxaca and Tehuantepec Region

Monte Negro (Oaxaca, Mexico)

This archaeological site lies near Tilantongo in the Mixtec-speaking highlands of Oaxaca. Alfonso Caso discovered the site in 1936, and along with Jorge R. Acosta and Alberto Ruz Lhuillier, he conducted excavations there from 1937 to 1940.

Monte Negro's physical setting is similar to that of Monte Albán, the better-known Zapotec city in the Valley of Oaxaca. Both sites are set on defensible 400-meter mountaintops that have been modified to create ceremonial centers and numerous residential terraces. But unlike Monte Albán, whose occupation spanned nearly two millennia, Monte Negro was occupied for only a few hundred years.

Its peak was between 300 and 100 B.C., and during that period Monte Negro's pottery shows strong stylistic affinity to that of Period Ic and earliest Period II of Monte Albán. During this period the Zapotec of Monte Albán were expanding militarily and incorporating many regions into an emerging state. It is not clear whether Monte Negro represents an outpost of Zapotec expansion or a mountain that was fortified to resist such expansion. Hints that the former may be the case can be found at Monte Negro in the form of braziers depicting an anthropomorphized Cociyo, the Zapotec version of the god Lightning. Monte Negro lies only 50 kilometers north of Huitzo, one of the northernmost sites in the Valley of Oaxaca.

After A.D. 200, the Zapotec seem to have abandoned their efforts to expand into what is today Mixtec-speaking territory. As the territorial borders of the Zapotec state shrank, Monte Negro and other sites on the northern frontier were abandoned. Unlike Monte Albán, Monte Negro has no overburden of later structures and thus provides important examples of elite residences and public buildings from 300 to 100 B.C.

FURTHER READINGS

Acosta, J. R., and J. Romero. 1992. *Exploraciones en Monte Negro, Oaxaca: 1937–38, 1938–39, y 1939–40.*

Flannery, K. V. 1983. Monte Negro: A Reinterpretation. In K. V. Flannery and J. Marcus (eds.), *The Cloud People*, pp. 99–102. New York: Academic Press.

Marcus, J., and K. V. Flannery. 1996. *Zapotec Civilization*. London: Thames and Hudson.

Joyce Marcus

SEE ALSO

Formative Period; Mixtec History, Culture, and Religion; Oaxaca and Tehuantepec Region

Morelos Region

The Morelos region, corresponding to the present-day Mexican state of Morelos, was a key part of Central Mexico throughout the pre-Columbian epoch. Favorable environmental conditions coupled with a central location in the Mexican highlands led to the growth of complex and dynamic cultures that interacted heavily with groups in the Basin of Mexico and other areas. Archaeological and ethnohistorical research in Morelos has contributed greatly to the understanding of many key developments in the Mesoamerican past.

Morelos lies just south of the Basin of Mexico, across the Ajusco Mountains. Most of the state is below 1,500 meters in elevation and thus has a subtropical climate. Rainfall averages between 800 and 1100 mm annually, and mean annual temperatures are between 20 and 24° C; winter frosts are virtually unknown below the northern Ajusco slopes. This favorable climate permitted cultivation of warm-country crops, such as cotton and various fruits, that could not grow in the adjacent Basin of Mexico. Archaeological and ethnohistoric research on the Postclassic period reveals that cotton textiles and bark paper were important exports from Morelos; production of these items probably began far earlier, although direct evidence is scanty.

The extent and productivity of agriculture in Morelos are limited by its topography and soils. Much of the state is mountainous, with thin and rocky soils. Today only 27 percent of the state's 4,900 square kilometers is sufficiently level to support rainfall agriculture. The alluvial soils along the rivers are deep and rich, however, and much of this land (about 500 square kilometers) is irrigated today. Pre-Hispanic populations were concentrated in the river valleys of Morelos, and ethnohistoric sources describe Late Postclassic irrigation systems along the Cuernavaca, Yautepec, and Amatzinac rivers.

Early Cultures

Little is known of cultures in Morelos during the Paleoindian and Archaic periods. Mammoth remains have been uncovered in several areas, but without associated human artifacts. Preceramic sites are probably deeply buried, and none have been investigated by archaeologists.

Formative Period

The earliest evidence for human occupation in Morelos dates to the Early Formative period. Sedentary farming villages supported by maize agriculture were first established in alluvial valley settings. Communities do not appear to have exceeded one or two hundred persons, with leadership authority restricted to kinship and social interaction within community boundaries. Evidence for village-level ceremonialism is found in the construction of a small burial mound at San Pablo and a civic-ceremonial platform at Chalcatzingo; both sites were excavated by Grove. Sites throughout Morelos shared similar mortuary customs, with individuals often buried with distinctive red-on-brown bottles and stirrup spout vessels in the Rio Cuautla style. These practices link Morelos with the Basin of Mexico, where elaborate burial offerings at the site of Tlatilco parallel Rio Cuautla mortuary traditions in form, meaning, and social complexity.

M

The Middle Formative period was marked by population growth and increasing socio-political complexity, particularly in eastern and central Morelos. In a few areas, ranked societies or chiefdoms developed with internal socio-economic differentiation, integrated regional site hierarchies, and special civic-ceremonial places. Chalcatzingo in the Amatzinac Valley of eastern Morelos emerged as one of the most important and influential civic-ceremonial centers in Central Mexico during this period, with a population of five hundred to one thousand. Its inhabitants participated in interregional networks of economic exchange and stylistic interaction with the Olmec area of the Gulf Coast, the Valley of Oaxaca, Guerrero, and the Valley of Puebla. The presence of large-scale civic-ceremonial architecture at Chalcatzingo, together with limited craft activity and the use of a special cemetery area for members of the elite, indicates the kind of socially diverse and economically differentiated resident population characteristic of chiefdoms. Chalcatzingo functioned as the dominant regional center in Morelos until around 500 B.C. The preservation of many "Olmec-style" rock carvings at Chalcatzingo make this one of the most impressive Formative sites in Central Mexico. Other Middle Formative sites include Iglesia Vieja.

The Late and Terminal Formative periods witnessed processes of regional differentiation and continuing population growth throughout Morelos. Three-tier site hierarchies and political integration at the regional level signaled the appearance of rank societies or chiefdoms in nearly all parts of the state. Interregional trade was more limited in scope than in Middle Formative times, with most interaction occurring with the Basin of Mexico and adjacent regions of Central Mexico. Regional variation is found in ceramic assemblages at this time. Sites in western Morelos had relatively strong contacts with Guerrero, while sites in some parts of eastern Morelos show greater similarities with the Valley of Puebla. Large regional centers during this period include Amacuitlapilco in the Amatzinac Valley, Pantitlan in the Yautepec Valley, and Coatlan del Rio; Gualupita in present-day Cuernavaca was a small Late Formative site.

Classic and Epiclassic Periods

The Classic period witnessed a demographic peak in most parts of Morelos. This was a time of marked socio-political change. Chiefdoms and other groups in eastern and central Morelos were incorporated into the expanding Teotihuacan empire. Changes associated with increased interaction with Teotihuacan include shifts in regional population location, strong participation in trade networks centered on the Basin of Mexico, and the adoption of political, economic, and ideological norms from Teotihuacan as the basis for local elite power and authority. These traits are evident at the eastern Morelos sites of Las Pilas and San Ignacio, and at Classic period sites in the Yautepec Valley excavated by Montiel. Las Pilas is noteworthy for its rich Classic period burials, which had hundreds of ceramic vessels and other objects, and for a small civic-ceremonial plaza with an extensive system of underground drains.

Cultural and economic affiliations with Teotihuacan were far weaker in western Morelos. Regional settlement was transformed from a pattern dominated by nucleated village communities to one of many small, dispersed hamlets dominated by a single large community at the site of Miahuatlan. Sites in the Río Chalma survey area show less evidence of direct interaction with Teotihuacan in terms of either imported tradewares or the emulation of locally manufactured ceramics. Although western Morelos clearly was incorporated into Teotihuacan's broader economic sphere, the strength of its political involvement was weaker or less direct than in eastern Morelos.

During the Epiclassic period, regional populations dropped, Teotihuacan's influence came to an end, warfare became prominent, and Xochicalco emerged as a major supraregional religious and political center. Xochicalco is the largest and most impressive archaeological site in Morelos today, with many research projects investigating the monumental buildings of the site's central core as well as residential areas and obsidian workshops on the terraced hillslopes around the central zone.

At its height in the ninth century, Xochicalco had a population of ten to fifteen thousand. In addition to its domination of political relations in western and central Morelos, Xochicalco had clear commercial and ceremonial importance throughout northern Mesoamerica. Imported artifacts and iconographic styles provide evidence for long-distance contact as far away as the Gulf Coast, the Valley of Oaxaca, Michoacán, the Pacific Coast, and perhaps the Maya region.

The art and architecture of Xochicalco reflect changing social and political conditions and the emergence of a new militarism throughout Central Mexico. An extensive system of fortifications was constructed at the site. Major monuments such as the Pyramid of the Plumed Serpents and three carved stelae record the names of conquered towns paying tribute to Xochicalco during this period. Iconography at Xochicalco also suggests the development of knight or warrior societies as a basis for elite power, upward social mobility, and imperial expansion. Many other Epiclassic cities in Morelos were also built in fortified hilltop locations, including Cerro Jumil near Xochicalco and Cerro Tenayo in Yautepec. Xochicalco met an abrupt end in the tenth century A.D., when most of the city was burned and destroyed, but the causes and context of this destruction are not yet understood.

Postclassic Period

The Early Postclassic period in Morelos, after the fall of Xochicalco, was a time of ruralization and isolation. Relatively few Early Postclassic sites have been located in regional surveys, and no site of this period has yet been excavated. Surface collections at these sites reveal ceramic similarities with cultures of the Basin of Mexico and Guerrero.

The Middle Postclassic period was a time of population growth and political development. Immigrant Nahuatl-speaking populations from the semimythical Aztec homeland of Aztlan founded new towns and established city-states throughout Morelos. The Aztlan groups who settled Morelos were the Tlahuica and Xochimilca. Their arrival was signaled by increases in the numbers and sizes of sites discovered in regional surveys, and by the start of the Tlahuica Polychrome pottery tradition in most parts of Morelos; these ceramics are painted with red and black simple geometric designs on a white background.

The peoples of Morelos in the Middle and Late Postclassic periods can be termed "Aztecs" on the basis of their extensive linguistic, cultural, and social similarities with the Aztecs of the Basin of Mexico. One such similarity is the twin-stair temple-pyramid, popular in both areas during Middle Postclassic times (this style was later adopted by the Mexica for the Templo Mayor of Tenochtitlan). The Middle Postclassic site of Teopanzolco, in Cuernavaca (Cuahnahuac), contains a particularly well preserved example. In a low platform across the plaza from this structure, archaeologists excavated a sacrificial burial consisting of numerous severed crania placed in a stone chamber with ceramic vessels and other offerings. Teopanzolco probably served as the center of the city of Cuauhnahuac during Middle Postclassic times. Another Middle Postclassic temple is at the Tepozteco site on cliffs high above the town of Tepoztlan. This single-stairway structure contains carved reliefs depicting Aztec pulque gods and rituals. A number of Middle Postclassic domestic contexts have been excavated at Xochicalco, Capilco (near Xochicalco), Yautepec, and Tetla (near Chalcatzingo).

The Late Postclassic period in Morelos witnessed a continuation of demographic and social trends begun in the previous period. Populations expanded greatly, and agriculture was intensified as terraces covered available slopes and canal irrigation was initiated or expanded in the river valleys. Powerful polities arose at Cuauhnahuac, Yautepec, Huaxtepec, and several other cities whose armies conquered neighboring city-states. These Morelos polities were in turn conquered and incorporated into the Aztec Empire under the Mexica kings Itzcoatl and Motecuhzoma I. The Cuauhnahuac domain of western Morelos became the Aztec tributary province of Cuauhnahuac, while Yautepec, Huaxtepec, and other polities were organized into the Huaxtepec tributary province.

The Teopanzolco site was abandoned in Late Postclassic times, and the city center of Cuauhnahuac was moved to the location now covered by downtown Cuernavaca. Excavations inside the sixteenth-century Palacio de Cortés (the residence of the conqueror Hernando Cortés) uncovered the remains of the royal palace of Cuauhnahuac. In Cuernavaca's main plaza were Late Postclassic deposits from the Cuauhnahuac urban core. In the Cuauhnahuac hinterland in western Morelos, the city center of Coatetelco has been excavated and reconstructed, including a ball court, temple-pyramid, and other civic buildings arranged around a public plaza. The nearby city-state center of Coatlan Viejo and the urban center of Cuentepec and other sites in the Buenavista Lomas north of Xochicalco have also been studied.

At the village site of Capilco and at the town site of Cuexcomate, Late Postclassic houses were excavated. Like their Middle Postclassic antecedents, Late Postclassic households were very active economically. Cotton textile production was carried out at all houses, and many households also manufactured paper from the bark of the wild fig tree (*Amate* sp.). Imported goods were abundant at these houses, including ceramics and obsidian from throughout Central Mexico and copper-bronze tools from the Tarascan empire. Residents of Cuexcomate farmed agricultural terraces.

The most extensively excavated Postclassic urban center in Morelos is Yautepec. Excavations of the Yautepec palace, a large platform (more than 6,000 square meters), have revealed one of the only surviving Aztec royal palaces in Central Mexico. Smith conducted an intensive survey of the 2-square-kilometer Aztec city of Yautepec and excavated seven houses as well as other domestic deposits. Small-scale excavations have been conducted at a number of additional Late Postclassic sites in central and eastern

M

Morelos, including Tepoztlan, Huaxtepec, Olintepec, Coacalco, and Itzamatitlan.

Morelos is rich in sixteenth-century ethnohistoric documentation, including such typical sources as *Relaciones Geográficas* and numerous lawsuits and *encomienda* documents. Particularly noteworthy are census reports from five Morelos communities that are among the most important Nahuatl-language documents from anywhere in Central Mexico. Compiled within three decades of the Spanish conquest, these reports provide unusually rich information on kinship and household organization, demography, land tenure, tribute obligations, and territorial organization on the level of the *calpolli* and the *altepetl*. The documents are from the towns of Huitzillan, Molotla (part of Yautepec), Panchimalco, Quauhchichinollan, and Tepoztlan. There is close agreement between the content of these reports and the results of excavations and surveys at Late Postclassic sites.

In comparison with the Basin of Mexico, lower levels of modern development have helped to preserve sites in many archaeological resources in Morelos, permitting research that has illuminated a variety of pre-Hispanic processes that characterized not just Morelos but the entire area of Central Mexico. In general, cultural developments in Morelos paralleled those in the adjacent Basin of Mexico. The Formative period was a time of growing populations and increasing social complexity. The Chalcatzingo chiefdom in eastern Morelos was one of the dominant cultures of Middle Formative Central Mexico. The Classic period witnessed a demographic peak and the establishment of varying levels of economic and political interaction with Teotihuacan. In the Epiclassic period, Xochicalco emerged as a large city and polity whose influence was felt throughout northern Mesoamerica. After a period of demographic and social decline in Early Postclassic times, the Middle and Late Postclassic periods saw major processes of population growth and increasing socio-political complexity. In the decades prior to the Spanish conquest, the peoples of Morelos were incorporated into the expanding Aztec Empire.

FURTHER READINGS

Cline, S. L. (ed. and trans.). 1993. *The Book of Tributes: Early Sixteenth-Century Nahuatl Censuses from Morelos.* Los Angeles: U.C.L.A. Latin American Center.

González Crespo, N., S. Garza Tarazona, H. de Vega Nova, P. Mayer Guala, and G. Canto Aguilar. 1995. Archaeological Investigations at Xochicalco, Morelos: 1984 and 1986. *Ancient Mesoamerica* 6:223–236.

Grove, D. C. (ed.). 1974. *San Pablo, Nexpa, and the Early Formative Archaeology of Morelos, Mexico.* Vanderbilt University Publications in Anthropology, 12. Nashville, Tenn.

———— (ed.). 1987. *Ancient Chalcatzingo.* Austin: University of Texas Press.

Hirth, K. G. 1980. *Eastern Morelos and Teotihuacan: A Settlement Survey.* Vanderbilt University Publications in Anthropology, 25. Nashville. Tenn.

————. 1984. Xochicalco: Urban Growth and State Formation in Central Mexico. *Science* 225:579-586.

Hirth, K. G., and J. Angulo Villaseñor. 1981. Early State Expansion in Central Mexico: Teotihuacan in Morelos. *Journal of Field Archaeology* 8:135-150.

Maldonado Jiménez, D. 1990. *Cuauhnahuac and Huaxtepec: Tlalhuicas y Xochimilcas en el Morelos Prehispánico.* Cuernavaca: Centro Regional de Investigaciones Multidisciplinarias, Universidad Nacional Autónoma de México.

Smith, M. E. 1992. *Archaeological Research at Aztec-Period Rural Sites in Morelos, Mexico.* Vol. 1, *Excavations and Architecture.* University of Pittsburgh Monographs in Latin American Archaeology, 4. Pittsburgh.

————. 1994. Economies and Polities in Aztec-Period Morelos: Ethnohistoric Overview. In M. G. Hodge and M. E. Smith (eds.), *Economies and Polities in the Aztec Realm,* pp. 313–348. Albany: Institute for Mesoamerican Studies.

————. 1996. *The Aztecs.* Oxford: Blackwell.

Michael E. Smith and Kenneth G. Hirth

SEE ALSO

Chalcatzingo; Gualupita; Xochicalco; Yautépec

Morett (Colima, Mexico)

This multi-component habitation site lies on low hills near the mouth of the Cihuatlan River on the Jalisco-Colima border. Morett was a small farming village of wattle-and-daub houses. There are no constructed mounds and no ritual areas, although the site is contemporaneous with the shaft tomb complex of Western Mexico. It was extensively occupied in the Late Formative period (300 B.C. to A.D. 100), with later occupation extending to about A.D. 750. Subsistence activities included farming, harvesting shellfish, and hunting, primarily for deer.

The population in the Formative was no more than a few hundred, judging from the site area. Features of the Formative occupation include extended burials with small, solid figurines and small pottery vessels. Dogs were present, and one dog burial was found. The early pottery types include blackware, plain and engraved buffware (most common), purple-on-red pottery, and an early polychrome (red and white).

Morett was a key site in developing a chronology for Western Mexico, based on 115 obsidian hydration dates and 16 radiocarbon dates determined for various cultural contexts in its unusually deep deposits (some up to 3 meters deep). The site was excavated in three seasons (1960–1962) by teams from the University of California, Los Angeles. At the time of excavation, this was the most northerly site on the west coast with "typical" Late Formative occupation; recent work by Mountjoy has extended the range well north into Jalisco.

FURTHER READINGS

Meighan, C. W. 1972. *Archaeology of the Morett Site, Colima.* University of California Publications in Anthropology, 7. Berkeley and Los Angeles.

Meighan, C. W., L. Foote, and P. V. Aiello. 1968. Obsidian Dating in West Mexican Archaeology. *Science* 160:1069–1075.

Clement Meighan

SEE ALSO

West Mexico

Morley, Sylvanus Griswold (1883–1948)

Born in Chester, Pennsylvania, Morley graduated as a civil engineer from Pennsylvania Military Academy. At Harvard he came under the influence of Alfred Tozzer; he received a bachelor's degree in 1907 and a master's degree in 1908. After visits to Chichén Itzá and Copán, Morley was appointed to the School of American Research, in Santa Fe, to conduct glyphic research. There he wrote an introduction to Maya writing and stimulated research into the glyphic "Supplementary Series" by publishing a compilation of them. In 1912, the Carnegie Institution of Washington funded his proposal for work at Chichén Itzá. However, political unrest ruled out work there, so Morley made an expedition to Petén, Guatemala, finding the first Baktun 8 stela at a site he named Uaxactun. His monograph on Copán was the first to discuss all the inscriptions from a single site; it prompted Harvard to confer an honorary doctorate on him.

In 1923, Morley secured a contract to work at Chichén Itzá, and soon after, another to excavate Uaxac-

tun. Both projects flourished, latterly under the direction of Alfred Kidder, leaving Morley to concentrate on a multi-volume survey of inscriptions (1937–1938). His popular book on the Maya, both ancient and modern, was written in lively and lucid style, though flawed by adherence to his outmoded concept of Old and New Empires (1946); in revised editions, it has remained in print for fifty years.

FURTHER READINGS

Morley, S. G. 1913. Archaeological Research at the Ruins of Chichén Itzá, Yucatán. In W. H. Rivers et al., *Report upon the Present Condition and Future Needs of the Science of Anthropology,* pp. 61–91. Carnegie Institution of Washington, Publication 200. Washington, D.C.

———. 1915. *An Introduction to the Study of Maya Hieroglyphs.* Smithsonian Institution Bureau of American Ethnology, Bulletin 57. Washington, D.C.

———. 1920. *The Inscriptions at Copán.* Carnegie Institution of Washington, Publication 219. Washington, D.C.

Thompson, J. Eric S. 1949. Sylvanus Griswold Morley, 1883–1948. *American Anthropologist,* n.s. 51:293–297.

Ian Graham

Mural Painting

The ruins that we see today are earth colored, but in ancient times, Mesoamerican cities large and small were brilliantly colored in simple, vivid tones that covered most building façades, while richly painted narrative scenes were found in interior spaces such as patios, porticos, niches, hallways, rooms, and alcoves. The natural environment provided the model for the greens of the valleys and woods, the blues of the mountains, the placid lakes and raging rivers. White and blue tonalities evoked the firmament.

Colors were compounded of various organic and inorganic materials, achieving coloristic effects that are difficult to equal even today, with chemical colors. Mural paintings were one element of this world of color, visually perceived in the cities and their buildings, in the statues that ornamented them and objects offered in the markets, on the documents that preserved sacred wisdom, and in costume and cosmetics.

Our knowledge of Mesoamerican mural paintings is relatively recent. Until a century ago, the only known references to murals were to those of Teotihuacan (Valley of Mexico), Mitla (Oaxaca), and Maya sites of the Yucatán Peninsula. Since then there have been numerous discoveries showing the variety of pictorial styles. Olmec-style wall

M

paintings were discovered in Guerrero—at Oxtotitlán, Juxtlahuaca, and Cacahuiziqui—and disclosed a previously unknown Olmec influence in that area. Wall paintings from the Maya sites of Río Azul (Guatemala) and Bonampak (Chiapas) extended our knowledge of Classic Maya culture; Cacaxtla (Tlaxcala) murals showed the warlike presence of peoples from the nearby Central Highlands, and those from the Aztec capital, Tenochtitlan-Tlatelolco (Mexico City), revealed change and continuity in Mesoamerica's mural tradition.

Techniques

In general, Mesoamerican murals feature flat areas of color, but the mural traditions of several regions, particularly the Lowlands and tropics (such as Veracruz and the Maya lowlands) produce the illusion of superposition of dimensions and of volume by varying pigment saturation. Most figures in murals are outlined, providing the images with visual structure that is enlivened by varying the width of the line. The other generally shared element is the absence of perspective, with increasing distance indicated by diminished size and relative spacing (for example, the portico of the "Diosas Verdes," Tetitla compound, Teotihuacan); not a few murals, however, succeed in giving the impression of depth and the sensation of distance. There is an exceptional example of intentional foreshortening in the reclining image of Room 2 at Bonampak.

The essential mural technique in Mesoamerica was affixing colored media to the surface of a building. Stucco plaster invariably served to support the application of pigments that were oxidized in diverse proportions. These pigments were of mineral origin, with the exception of the blues and greens, which have organic components. In this way the artists created a type of tempera, bound by gummy plant fluids such as the sap of the nopal cactus, and a fresco that was applied over still-damp plaster.

Themes and Styles

Themes of the murals varied according to the function of the architectural spaces that supported them: funerary motifs in the tombs found in Oaxaca, symbolic repeated figures in interior murals in the apartment complexes of Teotihuacan, and heroic narratives in the buildings of the Maya region. Narrative murals exist in the Gulf Lowlands at Las Higueras, and murals depicting mythic and real history of the Basin of Mexico after the fall of Teotihuacan can be seen at Cacaxtla.

The abundant murals of the Classic period (A.D. 300–900) had as their iconographic antecedent the presumably Olmec-influenced cave paintings of Guerrero, perhaps contemporaneous with the apogee of the Gulf Lowlands centers, 1000–600 B.C. True mural painting—the application of colors to stuccoed walls prepared to receive polychromes—is first known at Teotihuacan (A.D. 300–600), at such sumptuous buildings as Tetitla, Zacuala, Atetelco, La Ventilla, Tepantitla, and many others that have been partially reconstructed, as well as those that have remained permanently hidden. In Teotihuacan one appreciates the sensitive use of the distinctive exterior walls of the buildings, with two-dimensional scenes depicted on the sloping *talud* walls as well as in the vertical *tablero* walls, always delimited by an enclosing line. The precise repetition of the lines suggests the use of a stencil to outline the figures. In Teotihuacan there are several recurring themes, always expressed in an abstract mode with an essential concept: agriculture, war, or mythology, components of a cosmology that seems to exclude individuals as historic characters. One can identify representations of deities and sacred principals, as well as various animals that combine references to natural features and fantasy, like plumed serpents or were-jaguars. These, as sacred mediators, are distinguished by their accouterments and their attributes, but not by individual characteristics. Among all the buildings embellished with murals, Tetitla stands out as a kind of painting museum for Teotihuacan: it has 120 painted walls in all styles of Teotihuacan painting.

While Teotihuacan maintained its hegemony over the Central Highlands, other cities continued to develop. Cholula, situated in the Puebla-Tlaxcala region, was built in a strategic spot on a route that linked the Basin of Mexico with the Gulf Lowlands and with the Oaxaca region. Cholula's Great Pyramid and its first construction phases feature polychrome figures facing front, with their bodies in profile. Another mural at this site, dating from c. A.D. 200–350, is known as "The Drinkers" and features one hundred anthropomorphic figures painted in diverse colors. Garbed in loincloths, turbans, earrings, and other adornments, they are grouped in pairs, standing or squatting. Some raise vessels and others drink the liquid. It has been suggested that this represents a libation, the pulque (agave beer) ritual, or the celebration of harvest. There are also floral forms, lozenge shapes with volutes and braids. The scenes originally occupied a surface 56 meters long. Its iconographic content makes this mural unique in the known pictorial art of Mexico.

Another style and function are evident in the painted tombs of Oaxaca, principally at Monte Albán and Suchiquitongo (Huijazoo). They include stylistic elements familiar from other Mesoamerican paintings, particularly those of Teotihuacan, but they are more narrative, and their scenic quality is reinforced by the presence of glyphs of names and toponyms. Depersonalized human and animal figures are generally depicted in profile, but ornaments and features of clothing are shown frontally. In tombs 112, 103, 104, 105, and 123 at Monte Albán, as in that of Suchilquitongo, rigid postures mark deities in scenes of religious ritual; this is not realistic portrayal, but a reality founded in religious ceremonial and beliefs. Oaxacan tomb murals show corteges that accompany the deceased, as well as cosmological elements—celestial skybands with stellar eyes, and processions of deities that set the dead on the road to the afterworld.

The tomb at Suchilquitongo (Huijazoo), near Monte Albán, is magnificent, with two large rooms. Its very well preserved mural paintings cover an area of 40 square meters, with a representation of a funeral involving sixty people: priests with great capes, priestesses with *huipils* and bags of incense, warriors, nobles, old chiefs in mourning. It is an exceptional example of Oaxaca tomb painting.

Maya mural painting is outstanding, distinguished by its naturalism and historic and cosmological content. The oldest known murals have been found in funerary contexts, such as Tomb 1 at Río Azul (Guatemala). On its red-painted walls is the date A.D. 417; figures of deities, serpents, and aquatic symbols allude to the underworld. At Uaxactun (Guatemala), a mural found in Structure BXIII has historic scenes expressed in a mode common in Maya mural painting: groups of personages on foot and in profile, perhaps nobles, accompanied by hieroglyphic inscriptions arrayed over horizontal registers.

Late Classic period (A.D. 600–900) murals share this thematic tradition. The ancient Maya were famous for expressing cosmological and political concepts and activities of the powerful elite, depicted on interior and exterior walls, lintels, jambs, and cornices. In the scenes, the rulers narrate their participation in war, the taking of captives, rituals of autosacrifice and sacrifice, and their relation to and communication with their ancestors and with gods, themes that stress their power and dynastic legitimacy. This is the content of the scenes that cover the interiors of the three rooms of Structure 1 of Bonampak (Chiapas). These paintings, dated to A.D. 792, show events in the life of the ruler Chan Muan II. Other Maya sites, Mulchic and Chacmultun (Yucatán), have murals with scenes of war and processions of personified deities.

A regional characteristic of the Río Bec, Chenes, and Puuc zones of the Yucatán Peninsula is the decoration of the capstones of vaults. Most of the scenes painted on central stones of vault covers in Maya buildings depict gods, particularly God K, connecting the ruling lineage to supernatural power.

In the late Classic (A.D. 600–900 or later), artists painted the battle scenes on the interior walls of the Temple of the Jaguars at Chichén Itzá. In these we recognize certain compositional features similar to those of the Central Highlands of Mexico but foreign to the Classic Maya pictorial tradition. Murals from the Postclassic period (A.D. 900–1521) exist in sites of the eastern coast of the Yucatán Peninsula. There are representations of Maya deities, but the importance of individuals, so characteristic of Classic Maya murals, declines. Predominant iconographic themes are agriculture, and the cosmos and its three levels—heaven, earth, and underworld. It has been said that stylistic characteristics of Tulum and Santa Rita Corozal are related to the Mixteca-Puebla style, present in this epoch in the Central Highlands of Mexico.

Along the Gulf Lowlands we find important cities with mural paintings that covered much of the structures. The murals of Las Higueras were painted around A.D. 800–900. In Structure 1 there were nineteen superimposed levels of painting. The mural fragments (now in the Jalapa Museum) depict birds and serpents; processions of personages with lances, standards, and long trains; and other individuals who play musical instruments, personifying dancers or ballplayers.

The murals at El Tajín recall the paintings of Structure 1. In this case there appear human faces, at times covered by masks and ornamented with a bunch of plumes, as well as symbolic elements within cruciform designs and the famous intertwined motifs. The zoomorphic figures are highly ornamented, having diverse quadrupedal forms, clawed feet, and jaws with canine teeth.

In the 1970s, the site of Cacaxtla was discovered in the Puebla-Tlaxcala region. The first versions of the "Battle" mural and the paintings of the Jaguar-Man, Bird Man, and Dancer date from c. A.D. 650. In 1984, new paintings were discovered in the Red Temple and the Temple of Venus. Ethnohistoric sources attribute the painted images to the Olmeca-Xicalanga, the ethnic group of that region. In the murals one recognizes elements that form part of the iconography of older cultures—Teotihuacan, Xochicalco, and Monte Albán—along with similarities to the pictorial tradition of the Classic Maya. These elements indicate that Cacaxtla was a multicultural community.

M

The theme of war is characteristic of this period, and in the "Battle Mural" the principal element is the human figure, depicted in naturalistic proportions and positions.

The polychrome decorating the architecture of Xochicalco (Morelos) remains only in symbolic elements like borders and blue lines that may refer to water, a sacred liquid. Other Late Postclassic (twelfth through fifteenth centuries) paintings of the Central Highlands have been found in Tizatlan and Ocotelulco, two cities that formed part of the four-city Tlaxcalan capital (the *"cuatro señorios"*).

The Mixteca-Puebla style, expressed in the style of the Borgia Group codices, is quite distinctive. The images depict deities, sacrifice, and the underworld through the use of skulls, hearts, stingray spines, knives, and aquatic symbols. In the northern Gulf Lowlands, in Huasteca, mural paintings on a building frieze at Tamuín show local characteristics in the facial features and headdresses of human figures, but they also display elements of Mixteca-Puebla style in the adornments and objects the figures carry, and in the appearance of certain gods.

In the Northwest periphery region, home of the Chalchihuites culture and the site of Alta Vista, mural painting is evidenced by red and blue pigments over mud plaster. Other mural fragments have been found in Postclassic cities of the Central Highlands of Mexico. The mural of Tenayuca now removed from its original place, depicts crossed bones and human skulls. The mural of Malinalco, attributed to the Matlatzinca ethnic group, shows warriors, shields, and lances.

Mexica or Aztec mural art is known from magnificent examples dating to the fourteenth and fifteenth centuries, uncovered in excavations of the Templo Mayor of Tenochtitlan, 1978–1982. They emphasize the Aztec concept of duality. On top of the Templo Mayor were two shrines, one dedicated to the Mexica patron god, Huitzilopochtli, and the other to the water and agriculture god, Tlaloc. The exterior of Tlaloc's shrine was painted with concentric circles, horizontal red-and-blue bands, and vertical black-and-white bands, symbols that allude to the deity. On the interior of this wall were the remains of a mural—the feet of a figure on a stream of water. Within the complex of structures that surround the Templo Mayor are various altars and shrines. The Red Temple, on the south side of the Templo Mayor, retains traces of red, white, and black paint depicting paper strips, and over the molding there are circles of red-painted stone. The exterior walls were decorated with designs bearing Teotihuacan features, like the "weeping eye" motif and elements shaped like cross sections of conch shell. Similar art survives from Tlatelolco (Mexico City).

FURTHER READINGS

Boone, E. H. 1985. The Color of Mesoamerican Architecture and Sculpture. In E. H. Boone (ed.), *Painted Architecture and Polychrome Monumental Sculpture in Mesoamerica*, pp. 173–186. Dumbarton Oaks, Washington D. C.

de la Fuente, B. (coord.). 1996. *La pintura mural prehispánica en México: Teotihuacán, México*. Vol. 1, *Cátalogo*; vol. 2, *Estudios*. Mexico City: Instituto de Investigaciones Estéticas, Universidad Nacional Autónoma de México.

Fahmel Beyer, B. 1995. La pintura mural zapoteca. *Arqueología Mexicana* 16:36–41.

Gendrop, P. 1971. Murales prehispánicos. *Artes de México*, no. 144.

Miller, A. G. 1973. *The Mural Painting of Teotihuacan*. Washington, D.C.: Dumbarton Oaks.

———. 1982. *On the Edge of the Sea: Mural Painting at Tancah-Tulum, Quintana Roo, Mexico*. Washington, D.C.: Dumbarton Oaks.

———. 1995. *The Painted Tombs of Oaxaca: Living with the Dead*. Cambridge: Cambridge University Press.

Pascual Soto, A. 1995. Los pintores de El Tajín. *Arqueología Mexicana* 16:42–47.

Solís, F. 1995. Pintura mural en el Altiplano central. *Arqueología Mexicana* 16:30–35.

Staines Cicero, L. 1995. Los murales mayas del Postclásico. *Arqueología Mexicana* 16:42–47.

Tejeda, A. 1955. *Ancient Maya Paintings of Bonampak, Mexico*. Carnegie Institution of Washington, Supplementary Publication 46. Washington, D.C.

Villagra Caleti, A. 1971. Mural Painting in Central Mexico. In G. F. Ekholm and I. Bernal (eds.), *Handbook of Middle American Indians*, vol. 10, *Archaeology of Northern Mesoamerica*, pp. 135–156. Austin: University of Texas Press.

Beatriz de la Fuente and Leticia Staines Cicero

SEE ALSO
Cacaxtla; Caves of Guerrero; Painting; Teotihuacán

Museums, Archives, and Libraries

There are substantial collections of pre-Columbian artifacts in many museums. More than sixty museums spread throughout the United States feature ceramics, sculpture, carvings, jewelry, stone tools, and other artifacts of various pre-Columbian cultures, as well as ethnographic materials from Mexico and Central America. The states of New York, Massachusetts, and California, and the District of Columbia have numerous museums with such holdings, and some of the largest collections are in these locations. The accompanying table gives details of museums and their holdings.

The Museo Nacional de Antropología, Mexico City, has the most extensive collection of pre-Columbian and ethnographic materials from Mexico and is probably the premier institution of this kind in the world. The artifacts date from the earliest discoveries to the Aztec period, while ethnographic materials cover the Cora-Huichol, Tarascans, Otomí, Puebla peoples, Oaxacans, Gulf Coast cultures, Maya, and northwestern Mexicans.

In Mexico, each state has a regional museum (museo regional) featuring artifacts from the pre-Columbian cultures of that state as well as colonial and historical artifacts. In addition, at many of the archaeological sites throughout Mexico and Central America, small museums on the site or nearby display excavated sculptures, carvings, and artifacts. Each Central American country has a large museum in its capital city, with centralized holdings representative of the cultures within that country.

The process of collecting museum-quality pre-Columbian artifacts in the United States changed radically in the 1970s, when international legislation went into effect that established each nation's right to protect its cultural patrimony by forbidding the export of archaeological materials. In consequence, American museums do not accept, even as gifts, objects that have entered the United States since 1971 without proper documentation from their country of origin. For this reason, many collections have remained relatively stable over the past few decades, and many artifacts have remained in their countries of origin rather than being exported to the United States or to European countries. Thus, the value of existing museum collections is stronger than ever, because they provide an important and irreplaceable research resource. Many collections are available for detailed study and professional analysis. Museum work will always be an integral part of archaeology and may become even more important in the future as research opportunities for excavation decline owing to destruction of sites and reduction of funding for research.

FURTHER READINGS

Kelly, J. 1982. *The Complete Visitor's Guide to Mesoamerican Ruins.* Norman: University of Oklahoma Press.

The Official Museum Directory. 1992. 23rd edn. New Providence, N.J.: R. R. Bowker.

The World of Learning. 1994. 44th edn. London: Europa Publications Limited.

Nancy Gonlin

MUSEUMS WITH COLLECTIONS OF PRE-COLUMBIAN ARTIFACTS FROM MESOAMERICA AND CENTRAL AMERICA.

UNITED STATES

State, *City*	*Museum*	*Holdings*
Alabama		
Birmingham	Birmingham Museum of Art 2000 8th Avenue, N. Birmingham, AL 35203 205-254-2566	Pre-Columbian art.
Arizona		
Dragoon	Amerind Foundation, Inc. Dragoon Road Dragoon, AZ 85609 602-586-3666	Archaeological collections from Mesoamerica and South America; ethnological material from Mexico.
Tucson	Arizona State Museum University of Arizona Tucson, AZ 85609 602-586-3666	Devoted to the study of U.S. Southwest archaeology and living Indians of the region; includes northwestern Mexican ethnographic items; photographic items of U.S. Southwest and Sonoran vertebrate zooarchaeological specimens.

M

UNITED STATES
State, *City* | *Museum* | *Holdings*

California

State, City	Museum	Holdings
Fresno	Fresno Art Museum 2233 N. First Street Fresno, CA 93703-9955 209-441-4221	Pre-Columbian, Mexican works and art.
Fullerton	Art Gallery California State University 800 N. State College Boulevard Visual Arts Center Fullerton, CA 92634-3262 714-773-3262	Pre-Columbian artifacts.
Los Angeles	Fowler Museum of Cultural History University of California Los Angeles, CA 90024 310-825-4361	South American art, archaeology, and material culture.
Los Angeles	Los Angeles County Museum of Art 5905 Wilshire Boulevard Los Angeles, CA 90036 213-857-6111	Textiles and costumes from the Americas.
Los Angeles	Los Angeles County Museum of Natural History 213-744-3382	New World ethnology and archaeology.
Los Angeles	Southwest Museum 213-221-2164	North, Central, and South American historic and contemporary materials; Spanish Colonial and Mexican provincial artifacts and decorative arts; manuscript collections.
San Diego	San Diego Museum of Man 1350 El Prado, Balboa Park San Diego, CA 92101 619-239-2001	Ethnological and archaeological collections pertaining to peoples of the western Americas.
San Francisco	Fine Arts Museums of San Francisco M. H. de Young Memorial Museum 415-863-3330	Significant holdings in ancient art.
San Francisco	Mexican Museum 415-441-0445	Mexican and Mexican American fine arts; pre-Hispanic colonial, folk, Mexican, and Mexican American.
Santa Ana	Bowers Museum of Cultural Art 714-567-3695	Pre-Columbian ceramics; nineteenth- and twentieth-century South American Indian and African ethnic arts.
Santa Barbara	University Art Museum University of California 805-893-2951	Pre-Columbian art.

MUSEUMS WITH COLLECTIONS OF PRE-COLUMBIAN ARTIFACTS. (*continued*)

UNITED STATES *State, City*	*Museum*	*Holdings*
Colorado		
Denver	Denver Art Museum 303-640-2295	Pre-Columbian and Spanish colonial art.
Denver	Denver Museum of Natural History 303-370-6388	Archaeology.
Connecticut		
New Haven	Peabody Museum of Natural History Yale University 203-432-3770	Aztec sculpture of 5 Suns; major collection of figurines from Allbers; ceramics from Costa Rica and Panama.
District of Columbia		
Washington	Art Museum of the Americas Organization of American States 202-458-6016	Latin American twentieth-century art.
Washington	Dimock Gallery George Washington University 202-994-1525	
Washington	Dumbarton Oaks 202-399-6400	Pre-Columbian artifacts, paintings, sculpture, decorative art (Olmec, Teotihuacan, Maya, Aztec, Peru).
Washington	Explorers Hall National Geographic Society 202-857-7588	Indian artifacts.
Washington	Smithsonian Institution National Anthropology Archives 1000 Jefferson Drive SW Washington, DC 20560 202-357-2700	Anthropology, archaeology.
Washington	Smithsonian Institution National Museum of the American Indian 1000 Jefferson Drive SW Washington, D.C. 20560	
Washington	Textile Museum 2320 S Street NW Washington, DC 20008 202-667-0441	Textiles of Peru, Guatemala, Mexico, and Panama.
Florida		
Coral Gables	Lowe Art Museum University of Miami 305-284-3536	Samuel K. Lothrop collection of Guatemalan textiles; pre-Columbian art.
Gainesville	Florida Museum of Natural History University of Florida 904-392-1721	Caribbean area.
Miami	Art Museum Florida International University	Pre-Columbian artifacts; contemporary Hispanic art.
Miami	Museum of Science 305-854-4247	Anthropology, archaeology.

M

MUSEUMS WITH COLLECTIONS OF PRE-COLUMBIAN ARTIFACTS. (*continued*)

UNITED STATES

State, City	Museum	Holdings
Georgia		
Atlanta	High Museum of Art 404-892-3600	Pre-Columbian artifacts.
Indiana		
Notre Dame	Snite Museum of Art University of Notre Dame 219-239-5466	Pre-Columbian sculptures, textiles, ceramics.
Illinois		
Chicago	Art Institute of Chicago 312-443-3600	Pre-Columbian art.
Chicago	Field Museum of Natural History 312-922-9410	Anthropology, archaeology.
Dekalb	Anthropology Museum Northern Illinois University 815-753-0230	Ethnographic materials from Mexico and South America.
Kentucky		
Lexington	University of Kentucky Art Museum 606-257-5716	Pre-Columbian arts.
Louisiana		
New Orleans	New Orleans Museum of Art 504-488-2631	Pre-Columbian sculpture collection from Central and South America; Native American art.
Maine		
Orono	Hudson Museum 207-589-1901	Ethnology collection from South America; archaeological material from Central and South America.
Maryland		
Baltimore	Baltimore Museum of Art 410-396-4930	Pre-Columbian art.
Massachusetts		
Andover	Robert S. Peabody Museum of Archaeology Phillips Academy 508-749-4490	Archaeology of Mexico.
Boston	Museum of Fine Arts 617-267-9300	Pre-Columbian art; Peruvian art.
Cambridge	Harvard University Art Museums 617-495-9400	Fine arts collection covering prehistoric to modern Eastern and Western art; serves as lab for training museum professionals, art historians, and conservators.
Cambridge	Peabody Museum of Archaeology and Ethnology Harvard University 617-495-2248	North and South America.

MUSEUMS WITH COLLECTIONS OF PRE-COLUMBIAN ARTIFACTS. (*continued*)

UNITED STATES

State, City	Museum	Holdings
Massachusetts (*continued*)		
Salem	Peabody Museum of Salem Essex Institute 508-745-1876	Pre-Columbian artifacts.
Worcester	Worcester Art Museum 508-799-4406	Pre-Columbian pottery, sculpture, and gold.
Michigan		
Ann Arbor	University of Michigan Museum of Anthropology 313-764-0485	Archaeology and ethnology.
Detroit	Detroit Institute of Arts 313-833-7900	New World cultures art.
Missouri		
St. Louis	Saint Louis Art Museum 314-721-0072	Pre-Columbian arts, artifacts.
New Jersey		
Princeton	Art Museum Princeton University 609-258-3788	Pre-Columbian art.
New Mexico		
Albuquerque	Albuquerque Museum 505-243-7255	Artifacts from Middle Rio Grande Valley, 1500–present.
Albuquerque	University Art Museum University of New Mexico 505-277-4001	Spanish colonial art.
Santa Fe	Museum of New Mexico	Indian arts and culture.
Santa Fe	Wheelwright Museum of the American Indian 505-982-4636	Artifacts, archives, sound recordings, photos, documenting Native American culture (both historic and contemporary).
New York		
Brooklyn	Brooklyn Museum 718-638-5000	Pre-Columbian collection; Native American art; Peruvian textiles; pre-Columbian gold; Costa Rican sculpture.
Hempstead	Fine Arts Museum of Long Island 516-481-5700	Pre-Columbian art.
New York	American Museum of Natural History 212-769-5375	
New York	Metropolitan Museum of Art 212-879-5500	Pre-Columbian cultures; painting, sculpture, architecture, drawings, manuscript collections, decorative art.

M

UNITED STATES

State, City	Museum	Holdings
New York (*continued*)		
New York	National Museum of the American Indian Smithsonian Institution 212-283-2420	American Indian archaeology and ethnology from Central, South America, and Caribbean; artifacts, textiles, anthropology, sculpture, decorative arts.
Utica	Munson Williams Proctor Institute Museum of Art 315-797-1100	Pre-Columbian art.
North Carolina		
Durham	Duke University Museum of Art 919-684-5135	Pre-Columbian pottery and textiles.
Ohio		
Cleveland	Cleveland Museum of Art 216-421-7340	Art from cultures worldwide.
Dayton	Dayton Art Institute 513-223-5277	Pre-Columbian artifacts.
Oklahoma		
Tulsa	Thomas Gilcrease Institute of American History 918-582-3122	American Indian artifacts from Arctic to Mexico.
Pennsylvania		
Philadelphia	University Museum of Archaeology and Anthropology 215-898-4000	North, Middle (Mayan), and South American archaeological and ethnographic materials.
Pittsburgh	Carnegie Museum of Natural History 412-665-2600	Extensive collection of Costa Rica artifacts; other pre-Columbian artifacts.
University Park	Matson Museum of Anthropology Pennsylvania State University 814-865-3853	Pre-Columbian artifacts.
Rhode Island		
Providence	Roger Williams Park Museum of Natural History 401-785-9450	Native American, archaeology.
Texas		
Austin	Texas Memorial Museum University of Texas 512-471-1604	Civic and natural history of Latin America, including archaeology and anthropology.
Dallas	Dallas Museum of Art 214-922-1200	Pre-Columbian art.
Houston	Museum of Fine Arts 713-639-7300	Pre-Columbian art and archaeology.

UNITED STATES **State,** *City*	*Museum*	*Holdings*
Virginia		
Norfolk	Chrysler Museum 804-622-1211	Pre-Columbian art.
Richmond	Virginia Museum of Fine Arts 804-367-0844	Pre-Columbian art.
Washington Seattle	Seattle Art Museum 206-625-8900	Pre-Columbian art.

COUNTRY **Dept.,** *City*	*Museum*	*Holdings*
BELIZE		
Belize City	Bliss Institute	Monuments from Caracol.
COSTA RICA **San José**		
San José	Museos Banco Central	Pre-Columbian gold and coins.
San José	Museo Nacional de Costa Rica	Pre-Columbian art.
EL SALVADOR **La Libertad**		
San Andrés	Museo San Andrés	On-site museum.
San Salvador San Salvador	Museo Nacional David J. Gutzmán	Pre-Columbian archaeology of El Salvador, colonial period, and local costumes and artifacts of inhabitants.
Santa Ana Tazumal	Museo Tazumal	On-site museum.
GUATEMALA **Guatemala**		
Guatemala City	Museo Nacional de Arqueología y Etnología de Guatemala	Artifacts, sculptures, stelae from pre-Columbian sites in Guatemala; large model of Tikal; ethnology.
Guatemala City	Museo *Popol Vuh*	
Guatemala City	Museo Nacional de Artes e Industrias Populares	Collections of metal, ceramic, textile and wooden objects of native peoples; costumes.
Petén Tikal	Museo Sylvanus G. Morley	Stelae, altars, pottery, other artifacts from Tikal.
Quiché Chichicastenango	Museo Regional de Chichicastenango	Artifacts from Maya-Quiché and Pacific Coast of Guatemala.
Huehuetenango Zaculeu	Museo Zaculeu	On-site museum.

M

COUNTRY *Dept.*, City	*Museum*	*Holdings*
HONDURAS		
Comayagua		
Comayagua	Museo Arqueológico de Comayagua	Archaeological and colonial collections.
Copán		
Copán	Museo Regional de Arqueología Maya	Artifacts from site of Copán and nearby sites.
Francisco Morazán		
Tegucigalpa	Museo Nacional	Artifacts from Honduras; site model of Copán; ethnological collection.
MEXICO		
Campeche		
Campeche City	Museo Regional de Campeche	Artifacts, drawings, photographs, sculpture.
Chiapas		
Palenque	Museo Palenque	On-site museum; artifacts, sculpture.
Toniná	Museo Toniná	On-site museum; sculpture.
San Cristóbal de las Casas	Museo Na Bolom	Artifacts from Moxviquil site and other sites in Chiapas; photographs, maps; ethnological collection.
Tuxtla Gutiérrez	Museo Regional de Antropología e Historia	Archaeology, colonial, anthropological collections.
México, D.F.		
Mexico City	Museo de las Culturas	Archaeology and ethnology from all over the world.
Mexico City	Museo Etnográfico de Esculturas de Cera	Wax sculptures of indigenous dancers, idols, figures from temples.
Mexico City	Museo Nacional de Antropología	Finest extensive collection from all pre-Columbian cultures of Mexico; ethnological collection.
Mexico City	Museo Nacional de Artes e Industrias Populares del Instituto Nacional Indigenista	Popular Mexican art from all periods; conservation and encouragement of traditional handicrafts.
Mexico City	Museo Nacional de Historia	History of Mexico from the Conquest to 1917.
Hidalgo		
Actopán	Museo Regional de Actopán	Collections relating to Otomí Indians.
Tula	Museo Tula	On-site museum; sculpture and artifacts.
Jalisco		
Jalisco	Museo del Estado de Jalisco	Anthropology, archaeology, historical research; folk art and costumes.
Guadalajara	Museo Regional de Guadalajara	Pre-Columbian and Colonial art and paintings.
Nayarit	Museo Regional de Nayarit	Regional and Mexican archaeology and history.

MUSEUMS WITH COLLECTIONS OF PRE-COLUMBIAN ARTIFACTS. (*continued*)

COUNTRY *Dept.,* City	*Museum*	*Holdings*
MEXICO (*continued*)		
México		
Santa Cecelia	Museo Santa Cecelia	On-site museum; artifacts, sculpture, models of Aztec temples.
Teotihuacan	Museo Teotihuacán	On-site museum; artifacts, interpretation of prehistory; site model.
Michoacan		
Morelia	Museo Regional Michoacano	Archaeology, ethnography.
Patzcuaro	Museo Regional de Artes Populares	Ancient and modern exhibits relating to Tarascan Indians; native art.
Tzintzuntzan	Museo Etnográfico y Arqueológico	Ethnography and archaeology relating to Tzintzuntzan and Tarascans.
Morelos		
Cuernavaca	Museo Cuernavaca	Artifacts from Paleoindian to Postclassic periods, and from Colonial to modern.
Tepotzlán	Museo Tepotzlán	Artifacts from Mexico, with emphasis on Mayan antiquities.
Nuevo León		
Monterrey	Museo Regional de Nuevo León	Regional and Mexican history; archaeology and painting.
Oaxaca		
Huamelulpan	Museo Huamelulpan	Local artifacts.
Oaxaca City	Museo Regional de Oaxaca	Artifacts from Oaxacan sites; ethnological collection; artifacts from Tomb 7, Monte Albán.
Oaxaca City	Museo Rufino Tamayo	Art collection from Olmec to Aztec.
Mitla	Museo Mitla	Artifacts from Oaxaca, particularly the Valley of Oaxaca.
Monte Albán	Museo Monte Albán	Ceramics from the site.
Puebla		
Cholula	Museo Cholula	On-site museum; artifacts and reconstruction drawings and model.
Puebla	Museo Amparo	
Puebla	Museo Regional del Estado de Puebla	Notable historical collections.
Querétaro		
Querétaro	Museo Regional de Querétaro	Local history and art.
Quintana Roo		
Cozumel	Museo San Miguel de Cozumel	Artifacts, carvings, photographs.
Tabasco		
Villahermosa	Museo La Venta	Sculpture from La Venta, including colossal heads.
Villahermosa	Centro de Investigaciones de las Culturas Olmecas y Mayas	Olmec and Maya artifacts.
Villahermosa	Museo Regional de Tabasco	Artifacts from numerous Mexican cultures.

MUSEUMS WITH COLLECTIONS OF PRE-COLUMBIAN ARTIFACTS. (*continued*)

COUNTRY **Dept.,** *City*	*Museum*	*Holdings*
MEXICO (*continued*) **Veracruz**		
Jalapa	Museo de Antropología Universidad Veracruzana	Regional Gulf Coast collection of Olmec, Totonac, and Huastec.
Santiago Tuxtla	Museo Tuxteco	Sculpture, artifacts from Gulf Coast.
El Tajín	Museo El Tajín	On-site museum; sculpture and artifacts.
Tampico Alto	Museo Tampico Alto	Huestec sculpture from Postclassic; ceramics.
Tres Zapotes	Museo Tres Zapotes	Monuments from Tres Zapotes site.
Zempoala	Museo Zempoala	On-site museum; artifacts.
Yucatán		
Dzibilchaltún	Museo Dzibilchaltún	On-site museum; artifacts and excavation photographs.
Mérida	Museo Regional de Antropología	Olmec, Mayan artifacts; precious stones, ceramics, jade, copper, gold.
NICARAGUA **Managua**		
Managua	Museo Nacional de Nicaragua	Archaeology, ceramics.
PANAMA **Panamá**		
Panamá	Museo del Hombre Panameño	Archaeology and ethnography.

Music, Dance, Theater, and Poetry

Performing arts were essential to rituals, feasts, and secular festivities in ancient Mesoamerica. Documentary sources frequently mention the importance of these arts but seldom describe them precisely, and they are not as well studied and documented as are architecture, painting, or ceramics. Recent research, inspired by the growing interest in saving the traditions of these arts, has focused on the many archaeological objects related to them and on descriptive terms in Colonial dictionaries and writings. Some musical instruments are illustrated in sculptures, murals, painted vessels, and surviving pre-Hispanic books or codices, and others have been found in excavated sites.

The cultures of Mesoamerica had few different types of musical instruments, and those were mainly percussion and wind instruments (see table, p. 507). With these they obtained a large variety of tones and tunes, from the low, sad tone of the shell trumpet that announced night ceremonies to the delicate sound of the five-tone flute accompanying the performance of palace dancers.

Three basic types of percussion instruments created sounds of rattling, rasping, and beating. The best-known rattle consisted, in its basic form, of a gourd serving as a resonator for its own dried seeds. Its handle was usually made of wood. Such rattles were spherical or ovoid, of various sizes; some were engraved, painted, or ornamented with feathers. Many artistic representations show anthropomorphic and zoomorphic figures holding one or two rattles. In the murals of Room 1 at Bonampak (Chiapas), five persons are depicted, each holding two big rattles crowned by yellow feathers, which indicate motion and rhythm: while some feather clusters are shown very open, others are closed as in the instant of the pause.

Another rattling percussion instrument was the bell. Small bells were made of clay, copper, or gold; tinklers, which produce noise by striking each other, were common shells or little stones. Bells were used on necklaces, bracelets, or anklets to complement another instrument played by the wearer. Tinklers, such as seeds, shells or stones, were placed in hollowed sticks to produce a sound

Drawing of the musicians in the murals of Bonampak, Chiapas, Mexico. Illustration courtesy of Sophia Pincemin.

similar to the sound of a rattle if shaken, and to the sound of rain or poured water if moved slowly. These instruments are well represented in Mesoamerican art, and copper bells have been retrieved from numerous excavations.

The rasp is the only rasping instrument. Its sound was created by rubbing a stick or bone over a notched stick or bone, often a long bone such as a human femur.

Beaten instruments form the largest class of percussion instruments, and the drum is by far the most important. Drums were vertical or horizontal, made of wood or ceramic. The *pax* or *zacatan* of the Mayas, known as the *huehuetl* by the Aztecs, is a high vertical drum made of hollowed tree trunk covered by an animal skin; it is played by beating on the skin with fingers and hands. The form is generally cylindrical, with a triangular opening at the base; the size ranges from miniature drums to a height of 1.5 meters. Drummers could either stand or sit. This drum could be totally or partially covered with incised decoration, as in Aztec examples, painted with various motifs, or adorned with moldings as shown in a Bonampak example.

Other hand-beaten drums were made of ceramic and could have a single or double bulbous body, sometimes placed on a tall pedestal. Another type of drum was played with sticks: it, too, was fashioned from a tree trunk. These instruments have a split in the front forming a U or H shape and were used horizontally. The Maya called this drum *tunkul,* and the Aztecs, *teponaxtli.* Writers of the sixteenth century mention that it had a heavy, sad sound. These drums could be ornamented and engraved. The Maya and Aztec also drummed on tortoise shells, beaten with the hands or with wooden sticks or deer antlers.

Wind instruments, their sound generated by vibrating air, are the second major category. Bishop Landa mentions wood and gourd trumpets, conch-shell trumpets, clay flutes, reed pipes, and whistles. Representations of wooden trumpets show they were very long and may have produced a wide range of notes. Conch *(Strombus gigas)* was the main source of shell trumpets, which produced low tones. Reed pipes and flutes made of bone or clay could be simple or double—there are a few examples of

Music, Dance, Theater, and Poetry 505

M

multiple flutes—and had from one to five finger holes. The pipes were very plain, but flutes could be exuberantly ornamented. Whistles and ocarinas made of clay present a wide range of zoomorphic, phytomorphic, and anthropomorphic forms; they are found throughout the area in various archaeological contexts.

The instruments were honored as if they were gods, and people offered incense and other offerings to them. Today in the highlands of Chiapas, this tradition survives: "San Sebastiancito" is a drum of the *tunkul* type that is dressed and honored as the representation of San Sebastian during the celebration of his feast at Zinacantan.

A single musician could play one or more instruments, generally two: drum and rattle or flute are the best-known combinations, but tinklers could be added, or a musician may hold two rattles. There were, however, specialists for each instrument. Specific names for musicians include drum players, Aztec *quaquacuiltzin,* Maya *ah pax,* Zapotec *penihuijillaxeni,* Tarascan *ataparba; tlamacazque,* who played trumpet shell and flute in Aztec ceremonies; and flute players, Maya *ah chul,* Tarascan *orpinzacucha.* Bands of musicians played various instruments. In one type of band, many musicians played big, noisy instruments, such as trumpets, to accompany ceremonies, as seen in the Bonampak murals; in the other type, one or two players were themselves participants in the ritual. There are no representations of women as musicians in ritual contexts, probably because of religious prohibitions against female participation in many rites.

The instruments were accompanied by vocal music, generally sung by a chorus or the musician himself. From the days before birth until death, all important moments in the life of a Mesoamerican were accompanied by music and songs. There were songs for every religious activity—some very old, transmitted from one generation to another, and some new, changing yearly. The Aztec named them *teocuicatl,* or "divine song," and the Maya had sacred hymns, some of which are recorded in the *Book of Chilam Balam,* in the *Popol Vuh,* or in Colonial sources.

Because sacrifices were an important part of ceremonies, many hymns, such as the "Song of the Dance of the Bowman," were related to them. There were also war songs, which the Aztec called *yaocuicatl, cuauhcuicatl,* or *ocelocuicatl,* the last two meaning, respectively, "song of the eagle" and "song of the tiger," referring to the two Aztec warriors orders. These songs extolled the greatness and heroism of warriors and princes and recorded battles between nations and the conquest of land and cities. The

"songs of deprivation," *icnocuicatl,* speak philosophically about the brevity of existence or enigmas of destiny; *xochicuicatl,* or "songs of flowers," concern love, friendship, the beauty of flowers and nature, or sorrow and death. Lullabies and pleasure songs (Aztec *ahuicuicatl,* Maya *kay nicte*), more joyful and popular, complete the repertory.

Singing and the recitation of poetry are depicted in the Teotihuacan murals at Tepantitla and Tetitla. These show human, deity, or animal figures with ornamented scrolls emerging from their mouths or hands: such scrolls symbolize speech, but when they are ornamented with flowers, shells, or jade, they are associated specifically with songs and poetry. In Sahagún's *Florentine Codex,* the expression "his word is like jade" indicates someone who spoke well.

Songs were ways to communicate with supernatural powers, and people expected some result—victory, rain, or wealth, for example. Singers and musicians were also regarded as a channel to the spirit world, and as was the case in many cultures, persons of non-normative physical type were regarded as having a special relationship to beauty and holiness. In Bonampak's murals in Room 3, and in the *Florentine Codex,* crippled persons and dwarves play and sing in ceremonies or in homes of high-ranking individuals.

Dance complemented music and songs. Maya dictionaries show three classes of performances: dance *(okot),* theatrical representations *(baldzamil),* and illusionism *(ezyah).* Dances were essentially religious and, in general, participants fasted and abstained from sexual relations for days before the performance. Dances were so numerous that a sixteenth-century writer noted that there were more than a thousand kinds. The number of people who came to see or participate in these dances could also be remarkable: in one case, witnesses counted more than fifteen thousand people who came from villages as far as 400 kilometers distant.

Some dances mimicked sacrificial scenes, and the dancers' prime objective was to identify themselves with an animal or a god by the power of masks, special garments, colored feathers, or body painting. Magic and incantational power possessed dancers of the "Dance of Arrows and Deer Head," performed just before hunting in the Maya month of Zip. Before war, hundred of Maya, dancing with small banners and following the drumbeats with long steps, performed the dance *batel okot,* when the first day of the year was Muluc. There were also dances for

MUSICAL INSTRUMENTS OF ANCIENT MESOAMERICA.

	Aztec	Maya
PERCUSSION		
Rattle	*ayacachtli*	*zoot*
Drums		
Hand drum	*huehuetl*	*pax*
	panhuehuetl	*zacatán*
Played with stick	*teponaxtli*	*tunkul*
Tinkler	*kizmoc*	
Bell	*mazcab*	
Rasp	*omichicahuaztli*	*bohol che*
Tortoise shell	*ayotl*	*kayab*
Hollow stick	*chicahuaztli*	
WIND INSTRUMENTS		
Conch shell	*atecocolli*	*hub*
Trumpet		*hoin*
Whistle		*xob xix*
Ocarina	*huilacapiztli*	*chichi*
Flute	*tlapitzcalli*	*chul*

the principal times of the agricultural cycle, such as the beginning of the rainy season. The *baldzamil* dance had a more popular tone with much humor and many tricks; Colonial Maya dictionaries also give names for some "very indecent" dances. In the *ezyah,* people showed their talents as magicians, just as the Twin Heroes of the *Popol Vuh* did in front of the underworld gods; the Aztec called this kind of performance *cuexteca.*

In some feasts, men and women danced together; in others, only one sex danced, generally men. For the feast of the seventh month in Tenochtitlan, only women of all ages sang and danced in honor of the Salt Goddess. Clay figurines from the Tarascan area show women dancing around musicians, a common form of dance in all Mesoamerica; in some cases, the central figure is a tree or an ornamented post. One surviving example of this class of dance is the *volador* ("flier") performance in Papantla, Mexico. The *voladores* are four performers atop the pole; their feet are tied to a long, wound rope attached to a wheel on top of the pole. They descend as the ropes unwind, and meanwhile a musician on top of the pole plays a flute and beats a drum. In some dances, participants, joined hand in hand, moved like a snake around courtyards or temples.

Poetry was common. The Nahuatl word for poetry was *in xochitl in cuicatl,* which means "flower and song." Poems, like songs, spoke of rituals and daily life, love and hate, life and death, war and peace. Other subjects were flowers, birds, rain, and the arrows of sacrifice.

Composers were honored for their songs and poetry. Some Maya scribes and painters *(ah ts'ib)* signed their names and professions on the vases or mural paintings they produced. The most famous artistic name of pre-Hispanic times was Nezahualcoyotl, a fifteenth-century Aztec king of Texcoco, whose skills included poetry, architecture, law, garden design and horticulture, and philosophy. The names of artists that have been preserved are almost all masculine, in spite of the mentions in colonial writings of women as poets and songwriters, such as the Aztec noblewoman Macuilxochitzin (5 Flower, daughter of Tlacaelel, counselor of the kings of Tenochtitlan). It is worth noting that Nahuatl texts state that people born on the day 5 Flower were destined to be songmakers.

Pre-Hispanic people had special houses for teaching and learning music, dance, and theater. The Aztec *cuicalli,* or "house of the song," seems to have been very similar to the Maya *popolna.* The head of these houses (Maya, *ah hol pop*), themselves singers and musicians, had under their administration different kinds of teachers and personnel: there was the song teacher (*kayom* or *tlapiz-catzin*) who knew every song, the proper occasion for singing it, and how to perform it best; there was the person who taught dance or theater, and the one who was in charge of the costumes and masks of dancers and actors *(ah cuch tzublal).* Some musicians taught students how to play instruments and how to make them. Besides special buildings in towns, there were special places in the palaces where singers and musicians gathered: Sahagún gives the name Mixcoacalli, or House of the Cloud Serpent, for one of these in the palace of Aztec kings, where the artists waited for the orders of their lord to perform.

Musicians, singers, songmakers, and poets were well respected: nobles, warriors, priests and common people accepted them, and the elite themselves composed and performed. In the Toltec area, to be a good singer was a great distinction. In Bonampak murals, the spatial position of the musicians near the great nobles implies that a special rank was accorded to them. Some musicians were paid, and during an Aztec ceremony that took place every

M

year, the emperor offered them presents. A slave's value was enhanced by musical talent.

FURTHER READINGS

Acuña, R. 1978. *Farsas y representaciones escénicas de los mayas antiguos.* Centro de Estudios Mayas, Universidad Nacional Autónoma de México, Cuaderno 15. Mexico City.

Estrada, J. (ed.). 1984. *La Musica de Mexico.* Vol. 1, *Historia,* part 1, *Periodo Prehispanico.* Mexico City: Universidad Nacional Autónoma de México.

Franco C., J.-L. 1971. Musical Instruments from Central Veracruz in Classic Times. In *Ancient Art of Veracruz,* pp. 18–22. Los Angeles: Ethnic Arts Council of Los Angeles.

Marti, S. 1955. *Instrumentos Musicales Precortesianos.* Mexico City: Instituto Nacional de Antropología.

Marti, S., and G. P. Kurath. 1964. *Dances of Anahuac: The Choreography and Music of Precortesian Dances.* Chicago: Aldine.

Sophia Pincemin Dilberos

N

Nacascolo (Guanacaste, Costa Rica)

At this Greater Nicoya site on the northern side of the Bay of Culebra in a dry, tropical environment, subsistence was based on marine resources, hunting, gathering, collecting, and some agriculture. The site consists of extensive shell middens distributed across the entire valley floor. Habitation areas appear to have been concentrated around the oval-shaped adobe hearths/ovens. The site was occupied from 300 B.C. to A.D. 1520. Mortuary remains consist of multiple, secondary, and individual primary interments; Sapoa period (A.D. 800–1350) polychrome ceramics occur most frequently as grave goods; La Ceiba has comparable Sapoa period mortuary complex remains. Imported materials include a copper bell, probably from Honduras, and White-slipped ceramics from Pacific Nicaragua. The site has some associated stone sculpture, indicating a sculptural tradition shared with the lakes region of Nicaragua.

FURTHER READINGS

Accola, R. M. 1980. Sitio Nacascolo: Arqueología en un sitio saqueado. In *Memoria del Congreso sobre el Mundo Centroamericano de su Tiempo: V Centenario de Gonzalo Fernández de Oviedo*, pp. 167–174. San Jose: Editorial Texto.

Lange, F. W., and S. Abel-Vidor (eds.). 1980. Investigaciones arqueológicos en la zona de Bahía Culebra, Costa Rica (1973–1979). *Vínculos* 6(1–2):5–7.

Vazquez, L. R. 1986. Excavaciones de muestreo en el sitio Nacascolo: Un paso adelante dentro del Proyecto Arqueológico Bahía Culebra, Costa Rica. *Journal of the Steward Anthropological Society* 14:67–92.

Wallace, H., and R. M. Accola. 1980. Investigaciones arqueológicas preliminares de Nacascolo, Bahía Culebra, Costa Rica. *Vínculos* 6(2):51–65.

Frederick W. Lange

Naco (Cortés, Honduras)

This town in the middle Chamelecón valley in northwestern Honduras is described in sixteenth-century documents as a commercial center with ties to towns in Yucatán and the Gulf Coast region. Cortés visited Naco during his march across the Maya Lowlands to Honduras in 1524–1525. Naco was occupied at least periodically during the Late Formative and Classic periods, but it did not achieve even modest local prominence until late in the Early Postclassic period (c. A.D. 1100), the time of the construction of its small group of cobble-faced platforms for civic buildings. In the Late Postclassic period, after A.D. 1250, Naco grew explosively to about 150 hectares, and quantities of obsidian imported from highland Guatemala increased sharply. The simultaneous addition of many new artifact types, styles of pottery painting, housing styles, and dietary preferences to traditional repertoires suggests the arrival of a new group with ties to the north and west. A building in the central plaza with unusual quantities of painted pottery, incense burners, and possible musical instruments may be a combination temple and men's house. Nearby was a plastered columnar altar with an odd "cog-wheel" plan.

In the last century before the Spanish invasion, another set of changes—new styles of building decoration and of pottery painting, concentrated in the central part

N

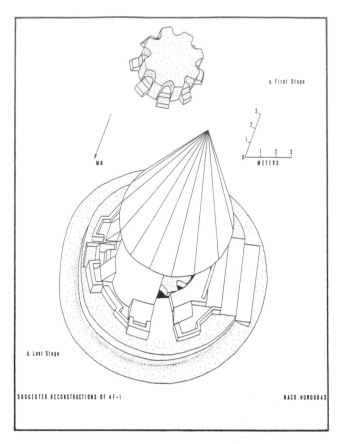

Drawing of suggested reconstruction of circular building at Naco, Honduras. Illustration courtesy of the author.

of the community—suggests the emergence of an elite group emphasizing foreign cultural affiliations. Several of the older central buildings were burned; the altar, enlarged and enclosed in a round building, and an I-shaped ball court built nearby, now formed the architectural focus of Naco's civic core. Obsidian imports continued to grow, and these represent the only archaeologically documented confirmation of Conquest period references to long-distance exchange, although bells, needles, and other copper artifacts in private collections are said to have been found at Naco.

FURTHER READINGS

Henderson, J. S., I. Sterns, A. Wonderley, and P. A. Urban. 1979. Archaeological Investigations in the Valle de Naco, Northwestern Honduras: A Preliminary Report. *Journal of Field Archaeology* 6:169–192.

Strong, W. D., A. V. Kidder II, and A. J. D. Paul, Jr. l938. Preliminary Report of the Smithsonian Institution–Harvard University Archeological Expedition to North-

western Honduras, 1936. Smithsonian Miscellaneous Collections, 97. Washington, D.C.

Wonderley, A. W. 1986. Materials Symbolic in Pre-Columbian Households: The Painted Pottery of Naco, Honduras. *Journal of Anthropological Research* 42:497–534.

John S. Henderson

SEE ALSO
Southeast Mesoamerica

Nadzcaan (Campeche, Mexico)

Extending over about 40 square kilometers in an area of small hills (up to 50 meters high) and extensive *bajos* (swampy areas), this site consists of dispersed architectural groups situated in the areas of highest elevation. It was occupied from at least 300 B.C. to at least A.D. 600, and its buildings conform to the style of sites in the Petén region. Just 15 kilometers north of Balamku, Nadzcaan is part of a chain of sites beginning in the central Petén of Guatemala and extending up to Edzna; no doubt many socio-cultural and economic ties linked this set of sites.

Two of Nadzcaan's largest buildings measure 40 to 50 meters high, with bases 65 to 180 meters long. There are two ball courts; numerous habitations and other structures are grouped around plazas, many of which have stairways made of large blocks of stone. Thirteen stelae and several round altars have been located.

Florentino García Cruz

SEE ALSO
Maya Lowlands: North

Naj Tunich (Petén, Guatemala)

This is one of the most important archaeological cave sites in Mesoamerica; its name means "stone house," and its discovery in 1980 was widely publicized. Three kilometers long, the cave served as a Maya religious shrine from about 250 B.C. to A.D. 800. The cave is notable for abundant man-made construction in the entrance, including masonry structures that may have served as tombs, and retaining walls that reshaped natural rock fall. Objects crafted from bone, shell, obsidian, flint, jade, and clay were recovered; among the last is an exceptional group of Protoclassic (c. 100 B.C.–A.D. 250) ceramics representing one of the most active periods of site use. Features typical of Maya cave artifactual assemblages include massive piles of pottery sherds and the deposition of pottery near water; a number of "shoe pots" were left near a pool in the cave's interior.

Naj Tunich is famous for its unique collection of eighty-nine wall paintings, created between A.D. 700 and 770 and exemplifying the highest form of Classic Maya calligraphic art. Rendered in a whiplike, dark line, their subject matter is restricted to human figures and hieroglyphic inscriptions. The latter, numbering around forty, are largely historical in nature (dates, emblem glyphs, personal names); they are valuable for reconstructing Late Classic Maya political history and seem to commemorate pilgrimages to the cave by elites from regional sites (e.g., Ixtutz, Sacul, and Caracol). The forty or so human figures are clad simply in loincloths and head scarves. Some are engaged in obvious ritual acts like bloodletting, offering copal incense, and dancing. Others, however, sit or stand with little indication of action or context. Presumably the figures represent the personages named in the inscriptions.

The paintings are concentrated mainly in easily accessible areas, with some isolated examples in the deepest recesses of the cave, such as the painting in a hidden ceiling-level chamber associated with a stone altar and smashed pottery, or the painted stalagmite at the bottom of a remote shaft. These are among the most deeply sequestered examples of cave art known in Mesoamerica. The paintings were the handiwork of court scribes who were also professional pottery painters, and who memorialized themselves by painting their own names and likenesses on the cave walls. Naj Tunich provides a remarkable picture of ritual cave use in the Maya Lowlands, and thus it is a tragedy that twenty-three of the paintings were destroyed by an act of vandalism in 1989.

FURTHER READINGS

Brady, J. E. 1991. New Vandalism at Naj Tunich Cave. *National Geographic Research and Exploration* 7(1): 114–115.

Stone, A. 1995. *Images from the Underworld: Naj Tunich and the Tradition of Maya Cava Painting.* Austin: University of Texas Press.

Stuart, G. E. 1981. Maya Art Treasures Discovered in Cave. *National Geographic* 160(2):220–235.

Andrea J. Stone

SEE ALSO

Caves; Maya Lowlands: North; Maya Lowlands: South

Names and Titles

Personal names among ancient Mesoamerican peoples were often drawn from the 260-day ritual calendar, or from animals, plants, or powerful natural forces, such as Lightning, Wind, and Earthquake. The Mixtec and Zapotec relied heavily on names taken from the 260-day calendar. Ideally, a child took the day-name of its birthday, but if that was an unlucky day, the parents consulted a diviner and chose a more auspicious day to name the child. Thus, not all 260 days are equally represented. Several historically known people had the same calendric name, and nicknames were used to distinguish between them. For example, the Mixtec ruler 8 Deer was nicknamed "Tiger Claw" to distinguish him from the 8 Deer who married his granddaughter.

Maya and Aztec nobles were not known by names drawn from the 260-day calendar; instead, animals such as felines and birds as well as precious objects were often combined to form their names; for example, "shield" was part of some rulers' names. The Aztec combined their word for "shield," *chimalli,* to form names such as Chimalpahin ("Swift-Running Shield"), Chimalpopoca ("Smoking Shield"), Chimalman ("Resting Shield"), and Chimalcuauhtli ("Eagle Shield"). Among the Maya nobles of Palenque, at least two have names using "shield" (*pacal*).

Sometimes among the Aztec and Maya, names were compounded of the names of animals and attributes of different objects, evoking fantastic creatures. For example, the Aztec ruler Itzcoatl ("Obsidian Serpent") had a name glyph depicting a snake with eleven obsidian pieces projecting from its back. Maya rulers at Tikal had composite names such as an animal skull plus a shield, or a jaguar paw plus a mandible; rulers of Yaxchilan had such composite names such as bat plus jaguar head, shield plus jaguar head, or bird plus jaguar head.

Some rulers changed their names (usually, their nicknames) during their lifetime. Thus, a royal Mixtec woman during the early years of her life was known as 6 Monkey "Serpent Blouse"; after she successfully defeated two rival lords in battle and had them sacrificed, she celebrated the victory by taking on a new nickname, "Warband Blouse." A similar situation obtained among the Maya, where hieroglyphic texts indicate that a lord acquired a new title, "Captor of X," after having taken "X" as his prisoner. The famous rulers at Yaxchilan took such titles as "Captor of Macaw" or "Captor of Jeweled Skull" as proof of their success in military ventures.

N

The titles held by Mesoamerican rulers were numerous, and some could be acquired during the span of their reigns as a result of claimed military successes and other deeds. Below the office of ruler were many other nobles who had important titles as well. Some titles first made their appearance around A.D. 300–600 and continued to be used until the seventeenth century A.D. in various parts of Mesoamerica. What is not yet clear is how their meaning or the duties associated with those positions changed.

FURTHER READINGS

Marcus, J. 1992. *Mesoamerican Writing Systems.* Princeton: Princeton University Press.

Joyce Marcus

SEE ALSO

Emblem Glyphs; Writing

Naranjal and Environs (Quintana Roo, Mexico)

Tumben-Naranjal is a medium-sized Maya center situated within the Yalahau wetland region, where there is evidence of landscape manipulation in the form of rock-alignment features that apparently functioned to control soil and water movement within the seasonally inundated portions of the wetlands. The site is organized around a north–south axis that follows the orientation of the large natural depression in which the site lies. Limited systematic survey and more extensive reconnaissance indicates that settlement at Tumben-Naranjal was concentrated around the wetland north of the site center.

The site is in an excellent state of preservation, with outstanding examples of the megalithic-style architecture generally attributed to the Late Formative and Early Classic periods; this is strikingly similar to the megalithic-style structures at sites such as Aké and Izamal, both on the western side of the Yucatán Peninsula. Naranjal's principal occupation was in the Late Formative through Early Classic, with little evidence for activities from the Late Classic through the Early Postclassic. There was a reoccupation during the Late Postclassic, with evidence of residential settlement as well as the construction of altars and shrines upon the older, ruined monumental architecture.

Two *sacbes* have been identified. One leads approximately 250 meters north from the outskirts of the site center to a pyramidal structure situated at the edge of a wetland. The second *sacbe* runs west from the periphery of Tumben-Naranjal for a distance of 3 kilometers, terminating at a small ancient center at the modern village of San Cosmó. Within the boundaries of the ancient site of Tumben-Naranjal is the modern village of Naranjal.

FURTHER READINGS

Fedick, S. L. 1998. Ancient Maya Use of Wetlands in Northern Quintana Roo, Mexico. In K. Bernick (ed.), *Hidden Dimensions: The Cultural Significance of Wetland Archaeology,* pp. 107–129. Vancouver: University of British Columbia Press.

Fedick, S. L., and K. A. Taube. 1995. *The View from Yalahau: 1993 Archaeological Investigations in Northern Quintana Roo, Mexico.* Latin American Studies Program, Field Report Series, 2. Riverside: University of California.

Scott L. Fedick

SEE ALSO

Maya Lowlands: North

Naranjo (Petén, Guatemala)

Naranjo ranks among the most important Late Classic city-level centers in the southern Maya Lowlands. The site core includes more than fifty major structures, several acropolis-like elevated plaza groups, a hieroglyphic stairway, and more than forty carved stelae and altars (most long ago carried off by looters or government authorities). The center is best known historically for two late seventh- to early eighth-century rulers, Lady Wac-Chanil-Ahau and her son, Lord K'ak'Til (literally "Fire-Tapir," also known incorrectly as "Smoking-Squirrel"), and for its early seventh-century conquest by Caracol, an event recorded in hieroglyphic texts at both sites. By the late seventh century, a resurgent Naranjo was itself subjugating such centers as Yaxha and Ucanal. Naranjo also was home to an outstanding school of Late Classic vase-painting, the Holmul Dancer style, and to the important late eighth-century royal-born painter, Ah-Maxam. Vessels from Naranjo have been excavated at Tikal and Buenavista del Cayo.

FURTHER READINGS

Morley, S. G. 1909. *The Inscriptions of Naranjo, Northern Guatemala.* Santa Fe: School of American Archaeology, Archaeological Institute of America, Papers, 9.

Joseph W. Ball

SEE ALSO
Maya Lowlands: South

Naranjos, Los (Cortés, Honduras)

Long recognized as one of the few primary chiefly centers in the central Honduran highlands during the Middle to Late Formative periods, Los Naranjos was occupied from 800 B.C. to A.D. 1200. It was probably a central node in a regional interaction sphere across the Central American isthmus, and it may have been one locus of early agricultural experimentation and adoption.

Situated within tropical forests on the northern shore of Lake Yojoa, a region where swidden farming of maize may have occurred by 3000 B.C., the site is surrounded by two concentric canals and spoil banks more than 2 kilometers long, presumably constructed by the Late Formative period. The core of the site is dominated by the Principal Group near the ancient lakeshore, with a central plaza containing several small mounds and stone sculpture, flanked by two Middle to Late Formative mounds as much as 19 meters tall. The total site area covers 4 square kilometers, with an estimated sustaining population of more than one thousand inhabitants by 400 B.C., and Late Classic and Postclassic populations extending across the rest of the northern margin of the lake.

Los Naranjos is known for its Late Classic polychrome ceramics and for its stone sculpture, some of it late Olmec in style. Limited quantities of obsidian, jade and jadeite, and marble were imported, as were shells from the Pacific and Caribbean coasts, and ceramics from the Sula and Comayagua valleys. Exotics indicate interaction with Maya sites as far away as the Guatemalan highlands, and with cultures on both Central American coasts, as well as within the Lenca heartland of the central Honduran highlands.

FURTHER READINGS

Baudez, C. 1976. Los Naranjos, Lagio Yojoa, Honduras. *Vínculos* 2(1):5–14.

Rue, D. 1987. Early Agriculture and Early Postclassic Maya Occupation in Western Honduras. *Nature* 326: 285–286.

———. 1989. Archaic Middle American Agriculture and Settlement: Recent Pollen Data from Honduras. *Journal of Field Archaeology* 16:177–184.

Strong, W. 1937. *Archaeological Explorations in Northwestern Honduras*. Washington, D.C.: Smithsonian Institution.

Strong, W., A. Kidder, and A. Paul. 1938. *Preliminary Report on the Smithsonian Institution–Harvard University Archaeological Expedition to Northwestern Honduras, 1936*. Washington, D.C.: Smithsonian Institution.

George Hasemann and Boyd Dixon

Nicaragua: North Central and Pacific Regions

The north central and northern Pacific coastal regions of Nicaragua form part of a land bridge, with depressions or low-elevation passages across the isthmus via the Nicaraguan Rift which have facilitated the movement of fauna, flora, material culture, people, and ideas. In addition, the extremely fertile volcanic soils of the Pacific Coast allowed for dense concentrations of indigenous settlement in pre-Hispanic times. The prehistory of these areas is rich, dynamic, and complex: extensive areas were sometimes integrated into the Greater Nicoya subarea, and the arrival of Mesoamerican groups, beginning around A.D. 800 (Chorotega groups, followed by Nahua-speaking Pipil and Nicarao), certainly caused displacements and disruptions as well as introducing new cultural institutions.

This archaeological region comprises two major ecological regions in Nicaragua: the Central Highlands and the Pacific Region. It does not include Lake Nicaragua or the southern sector of Lake Managua, the islands of Zapatera and Ometepe, and the Isthmus of Rivas, which are discussed in the article on Greater Nicoya (see "Nicoya, Greater, and Guanacaste Region").

Pre-Hispanic Nicaragua provided a vast array of wild resources that were used, and sometimes domesticated, by its early inhabitants. Coastal, riverine, lacustrine, and upland habitats all occur in the Pacific and north central regions. Agriculture, combined with fishing, hunting, and gathering when possible, was the main subsistence activity. Maize (*Zea mays*) as well as root crops, beans, calabashes, and peppers were cultivated. Important fruit trees included a number of *Spondias* species, mammees (*Mammea americana*), zapote (*Calocarpum sapota*), nance (*Byrsonima crassifolia*), papaya (*Carica papaya*), guava (*Psidium guajava*), guanabana (*Annona muricata*), and avocado (*Persea americana*).

Economically and/or ceremonially important crops included cotton, cacao, tobacco, and coca as well as copal incense, a variety of dye plants, the balsam tree (*Myroxylon balsamum*), the wild fig (*Ficus* spp.) and the kapok tree or ceiba (*Ceiba pentandra*). Only the mute dog and the

N

turkey were domesticated; important wild game animals included the white-tailed deer, tapir, a number of large cats, monkeys, the collared peccary, and the cottontail rabbit. Birds, fish, mollusks, crustaceans, reptiles (particularly the iguana), and amphibians were also abundant and utilized as food.

Northern Pacific Coast

It is unfortunate that little archaeological work has been conducted in the northern sector of the Pacific Coast region, because the whole of the Pacific Coast was part of the Greater Nicoya region and was integrated into the Mesoamerican system at various times. The Estero Real provided a natural transportation route, and this northern zone was one of the most densely settled at the time of the Conquest. There was probably pre-Columbian occupation in the Gulf of Fonseca area, which is strategically situated at an intersection of two natural corridors. The estuary environment of the Estero Real and the Pacific Coast from the Gulf of Fonseca to the modern port of Corinto might well have early sites, reflecting littoral and estuarine adaptations, which are now possibly buried by rising sea levels and shifting streams or ash layers.

In the Chinandega area, the known sites of Quebrada Seca, La Chanchera, Las Padillas, and Santa Marta all contain cultural layers buried by volcanic ash. At Las Padillas, a Mayan "venom jar" was found. The Santa Marta site exhibits cultural material dating to the Mesoamerican Classic period, with Usulutan-like sherds as the main diagnostic type, estimated to date prior to A.D. 300.

The results of neutron activation analysis of ceramics from the Greater Nicoya ceramic data base confirm the existence of north/south differences. Two distinct zones of production in the north are suggested; one is the northern Pacific coastal region, the area from Managua to the Gulf of Fonseca, which may have ceramic affinities with the northern zones.

North Central Region

In the Pueblo Nuevo–Río Estelí zone, thirty-one archaeological sites have been found, and fifty-nine sites are known in the Somoto–Río Coco zone. With the exception of one hilltop site, all were situated below 800 meters in elevation. Most sites in both zones appear to be habitational, as suggested by the general nature of the surface cultural remains, fragments of grinding stones (manos, metates, morteros), utilitarian ceramic sherds, and lithic debitage. Fragments of wattle and daub (bajareque) were also recovered from the test pits at one of the sites. Three

petroglyph sites were recorded, and no preceramic sites were located.

Sites vary from those lacking visible mounds to others with as many as 128 mounds. In general, these probable habitation mounds are slight elevations, circular to oval in shape. Based on mound numbers and variations, a four-level site hierarchy of sites was developed: hamlets, towns, nucleated towns, and regional centers. The largest sites were coeval, dating to c. A.D. 300–800 (Bagaces period, formerly Early Polychrome), with well-known diagnostic types such as Ulúa Polychromes. The site locations exhibit the familiar linear stream pattern characteristic of river basins not only in other areas of Nicaragua but also in the prehistory of Central America and Mesoamerica generally. Primary and secondary tributary streams were choice localities for small sites, probably hamlets and small villages of sedentary agriculturalists composed of lineage segments. The larger alluvial pockets on the second or third terraces of the Coco River, or at the confluences of several major tributary streams, were prime areas for the larger, nucleated settlements, which possibly represent local or regional centers.

This distribution is similar to the pattern found in the Comayagua Valley and along the length of the Sulaco River in Honduras. The regional centers have almost equidistant spacing; each center occupies a large pocket of alluvial soil along the river. A similar pattern obtains in the zone extending along the Coco River north of Somoto and along the adjacent land to one of its major tributaries, the Quebrada Somoto. The probable regional centers of Las Tapias, El Fraile, and Güiligüisca form a triangle, with each site almost an equal distance from the others. These three sites occupy strategic positions: each is situated at an entry point to the basin, with mountainous zones to the south, west, and east. Thus, their occupants could have monitored and controlled access to the basin, dominating economic, political, or military matters. This ranking or hierarchical pattern could be interpreted as the type of settlement formed by emerging or established elites who were controlling, via marriage alliances and solidified trading relationships, the lesser-ranking sites in their respective territories.

Because the chronology for northern Nicaragua is preliminary, the analysis for the period from 1000 B.C. to A.D. 500 is based mainly on cross-dating with established ceramic sequences from Honduras. The presence of ceramics related to the Usulutan tradition could indicate habitation in the area before 300 B.C., and perhaps north central Nicaragua's participation, along with Honduran societies, in the Uapala ceramic sphere. The sherds resemble the Muerdalo Orange and Bolo Orange types of Los Naranjos and of the El Cajón region of Honduras during the Yunque Tardia phase (A.D. 1–400) and the Sulaco Temprano phase (A.D. 400–600).

During this period relations with the Honduran regions seem to have intensified, as evidenced by the appearance in the northern zone of Cacauli Red on Orange pottery, with strong similarity to central Honduran types, especially with Early Sulaco from the Sulaco ceramic group. This type also appears stratigraphically before the diagnostic types of the period A.D. 500–800, such as sherds of some types of Ulua polychromes.

Increased contact with Honduras and El Salvador after A.D. 400–500 is evidenced by Ulua polychromes, such as Tenampua from the Comayagua Valley, and Delirio Red on White, a diagnostic from Quelepa (El Salvador) associated with the Lepa phase, A.D. 625–1000, which may have begun as early as A.D. 700. Comparative data from the area of Granada show a strong presence of Tenampua and Delirio Red on White, in addition to other ceramic evidence and iconography and form suggesting a Honduran origin. These data strongly support the existence of an interaction network extending to the south and the polities of lower Central America.

The socio-cultural development of the north central region after A.D. 1000 is difficult to interpret because it has not been possible to define a late period component for the ceramic sequence. White-slipped ceramics such as Papagayo Polychromes and Las Vegas Polychromes characterize this period in the Pacific zone elsewhere in Nicaragua (such as the Chontales and regions northwest of Lake Managua, adjacent to the north central zone); however, their presence in the north central zone is minimal, suggesting that the zone became isolated from the regions in Nicaragua and Honduras that produced the white-slipped types. The evidence suggests that this region may have suffered a decline in population and in socio-cultural complexity, resulting in a drastic reduction or even elimination of its role in macroregional systems. This may be related to the decline in the Honduran regions that occurred coevally with the disruption and decline of some Maya groups. It also appears that after about A.D. 1000 the region was not densely populated nor greatly affected by the arrivals of the migratory groups that disrupted life on the Pacific Coast and in other regions of Nicaragua.

Most lithic material from the north central zone is from surface collections; obsidian flakes, fine-grained basalt, chert, jasper, chalcedony, and opal flakes are all characteristic of the zone. Most of the obsidian artifacts are from other regions of Nicaragua, with few obsidian nodules large enough for efficient production of the typical Mesoamerican prismatic blade.

Central Zone

The Chontales is one of the regions in Nicaragua where monolithic statues with and without the "alter ego" motif are found. Recent surveys over 40 square kilometers have located ninety sites, with excavations at El Tamarindo, El Cobano, La Pachona, and San Jacinto. Five phases were established, documenting habitation from c. 500 B.C. to the Conquest. During the first three phases (Mayales I, 500–200 B.C.; Mayales II, 200 B.C.–A.D. 400; Cuisala, A.D. 400–800) population was sparse in the zone, with some interaction with the Pacific Coast of Nicaragua and central Costa Rica demonstrated by diagnostic ceramics and the presence of jade. During the Monota phase (A.D. 1200–1400), the abundance of Greater Nicoya ceramic types suggests that the region was well integrated into the Greater Nicoya sphere at that time. During the subsequent Cuapa phase, a rupture with the Greater Nicoya region is noted in the settlement patterns as well as the lithic industry.

For this time period, Chontales and north central region ceramic types and lithic assemblages show marked differences, with a notable absence of shared ceramic types and a differential use of obsidian between the two regions. The north central zone's abundant fine paste orange-slipped type is absent in the Chontales ceramic collections. In addition, Chontales shows an almost total absence of obsidian tools and debitage, with chert used as the preferred knapping material. There are several obsidian sources in the north, such as the recently discovered source at Guinope (Honduras), and possibly a source near El Espino (Nicaragua); these provided for the needs of the northern region, but obsidian was not included in an exchange system with Chontales.

The excavation of a midden at La Pachona revealed some of the earliest diagnostic ceramics for that period: Bocana Incised, Rosales Engraved, and Usulutan Negative Resist. However, La Pachona's most abundant cultural material dates from A.D. 1200–1520, and this is true of other sites as well, where we found numerous types of Greater Nicoya polychromes (Vallejo, Mombacho, Madeira, and Luna, as well as the continued importance of Papagayo Polychrome). For this time period, the cultural remains clearly reflect the presence of the Nicarao

N

ethnic group and the commercial relations they maintained with the Nicaros of Rivas and Ometepe.

The largest sites date to the post-Conquest period, A.D. 1520–1600. San Jacinto has 197 mounds, Site IV4 has 114, and Agua Buena possibly 300: these sites all exhibit planning, with large plaza areas and linearity in platform location. There is heterogeneity in mound area and height, with the largest mounds situated around a plaza-like central zone. La Candelaria, San Jacinto, and El Amparo have all been mapped. The settlement pattern, a development that went from small hamlets to medium-sized towns in the Cuisala, Potrero, and Monota phases, while experiencing increasing influence from the Greater Nicoya area, terminated in the Cuapa phase in substantially larger, better-organized sites. There is evidence of a rupture with the Greater Nicoya cultures, and a newly introduced group is believed to have been responsible for these changes.

This phase may correspond with an invasion of the Chontales area by a well-organized group, possibly Matagalpa-speakers, who were able to take advantage of the disruptions caused by the Spanish. In contrast to the preceding period, there is almost a complete absence of Greater Nicoya ceramic material, another marker of discontinuity. Differences in the lithic assemblages also reflect this change.

The locally known site of Garrobo Grande, in the Chontales area, appears to one of the few known sites with large standing masonry architecture and what may be a stepped pyramid structure. However, professional systematic archaeological work needs to be undertaken before the significance of this site can be understood.

The last region to be discussed, the Lake Managua basin, extends mostly to the north. In and around the city of Managua, many kinds of sites (habitation, funerary, etc.) have been explored over the years by archaeologists, looters, and local inhabitants. At the site of the footprints of Acahualinca, the Department of Archaeology of the Museo Nacional de Nicaragua is located. As yet there has been no synthesis of this region's culture history or its role in the larger cultural processes of the macroregion.

Because the lake basin region is extensive but archaeological data scarce, interpretation of the cultural material from the surveys and limited excavations is biased by the limited sample. The greater portion of the basin area remains to be explored. There are four survey zones: zones I and II along the length of the Río Viejo, and zones III and IV in the south basin of Lake Managua. The following review will cover only zones I and II, the Río Viejo area.

Fifty sites were located in the entire North Basin zone (la Cuenca Norte), most of them closely situated on river terraces at a maximum distance of 200 meters from the banks. Most sites are small, averaging 0.25 hectare; they probably represent satellite hamlets of larger, more important centers, of which three were located. Because of intense agricultural activities in the zone, especially the rice fields around Sebaco, only the sites of El Tamarindo and Mocuan have visible mounds. The following ceramic types have been identified for the region by Gorin's analysis: Usulutan Negative Resist, Chavez White on Red, Papagayo Polychrome, Sacasa Striated, Castillo Engraved, and Vallejo Polychrome, the majority diagnostic of the Greater Nicoya. Diagnostic types indicate habitation from 500 B.C. (Tempisque) to A.D. 1520 (Ometepe), with the twenty-two sites from the last pre-Columbian period, A.D. 1350–1520, exhibiting the greatest quantity of diagnostic cultural material.

This zone also shares cultural features with the north central zone—for example, the significant presence of the fine paste, orange-slipped ceramic type characteristic of north, and the use of obsidian, which appears to diminish in more southern zones. On the other hand, the zone displays a strong Greater Nicoya presence, which continues to the south. Recent work around Granada by Salgado confirms this.

Conclusions

Until recently, the northwestern and north central regions, and to some extent the central regions, of Nicaragua had not been the object of systematic archaeological research. Studies in the nineteenth and early twentieth centuries carried out by Squier, Bransford, Bovallius, Lothrop, and others focused on the lake zones, on the carved stone monuments, and on ceramic analysis, in preliminary attempts to establish regional chronologies. Later investigators continued in the same general area of Rivas, the lake areas, and the area east of the lakes in Chontales, as well as the Atlantic Coast.

Apart from the Atlantic Coast region, many of these zones were known to have been integrated into the Greater Nicoya subarea and at times participated in the Mesoamerican world system. Less is known about the degree to which some of the less-studied zones interacted within the local region or with Mesoamerica. A serious practical obstacle to expanding our knowledge is the difficulties and dangers of working in the war-torn northern zone in particular, where conditions have dissuaded archaeologists from conducting systematic explorations.

Owing to the lack of long-term, extensive archaeological studies in these areas, the reconstruction of settlement history and cultural processes is necessarily skewed by the biased database. As in much of Central America, sites have been destroyed by heavy looting, construction, agriculture, and—particularly in the north—recent guerrilla warfare and its impact on the landscape. Because more and more sites are being destroyed, there is an urgent need to gather basic data in order to establish chronologies for these areas and to assess the role of their interaction spheres and the extent of their contact with the Maya to the north and non-Maya groups to the south. It is also essential to understand past geological events; the region has active volcanoes and earthquakes, and their environmental impact—such as widespread ash falls and landslides—must be taken into account in research designs, fieldwork methodologies, and subsequent interpretations of the archaeological record.

FURTHER READINGS

Espinoza, E. P., L. Fletcher, and R. Salgado Galeano. 1996. *Arqueologia de las Segovias: Una secuencia cultural preliminar.* Managua: Instituto Nicaraguense de Cultural, Organizacion de Los Estados Americanos.

Espinoza, E. P., and R. Gonzalez Rivas. 1992–1993. Gran Nicoya y La Cuenca del Lago de Managua. *Vínculos* 18–19:157–172.

Fletcher, L., and R. Salgado Galeano. 1992–1993. Gran Nicoya y el Norte de Nicaragua. *Vínculos* 18–19: 173–189.

Fowler, W. R. 1989. *The Cultural Evolution of Ancient Nahua Civilizations: The Pipil-Nicarao of Central America.* Norman: University of Oklahoma Press.

Fowler, W. R. 1991. *The Formation of Complex Society in Southeastern Mesoamerica.* Boca Raton, Fla.: CRC Press.

Graham, M. M. (ed.). 1993. *Reinterpreting Prehistory of Central America.* Niwot: University Press of Colorado.

Lange, F. W. (ed.). 1996. *Descubriendo las huellas de nuestros antepasdados: El proyecto "Arqueologia de la Zona Metropolitana de Managua."* Managua: Alcaldia de Managua.

——— (ed.). 1996. *Pathways to Central American Prehistory.* Boulder: University of Colorado Press.

Lange, F., P. Sheets, A. Martinez, and S. Abel-Vidor. 1992. *The Archaeology of Pacific Nicaragua.* Albuquerque: University of New Mexico Press.

Newson, L. A. 1987. *Indian Survival in Colonial Nicaragua.* Norman: University of Oklahoma Press.

Vazueez, R. L., et al. 1992–1993. Hacia futuras investigaciones en Gran Nicoya. *Vínculos* 18:245–277.

Laraine Fletcher

SEE ALSO
Intermediate Area: Overview

Nicoya, Greater, and Guanacaste Region

The archaeological subarea called Greater Nicoya (Spanish, Gran Nicoya) comprises the northwestern region of Costa Rica and the Pacific region of Nicaragua. As I have written elsewhere, "Common cultural characteristics present throughout the region continue to make 'Greater Nicoya' as originally defined by Norweb (1961) a useful concept, but it is necessary to range north, south and southeast to place Greater Nicoya patterns in a systemic areal context" (1984:165). For example, "broader cultural implications can be, and have been, drawn which link the Greater Nicoya Archaeological Subarea with Mesoamerica in general and the Maya region in particular" (Healy 1980:154).

Greater Nicoya has been included as a subarea or region in several spatial and culture areas—Mesoamerica, the Intermediate Area, Central America, lower Central America, or Middle America—as scholars have attempted to characterize all or part of the geographical space between the areas occupied by the "high civilizations" of Mesoamerica and the South American Andes. In Norweb's original configuration, environment, geography, and ceramic types were the main variables. More recently, linguistic distributions and the selective distribution of other artifact categories, such as jade and obsidian, have acquired added importance.

Historically, the cultural development of Greater Nicoya and its various sectors has been interpreted in terms of cause-and-effect relationships with adjacent areas of Mesoamerica or South America rather than in terms of indigenous developments. Speculation has abounded about the source, direction, and nature of external influences, and archaeological research since the 1960s has provided some preliminary interpretations, seeing so-called elite cultural artifacts and traits as reflecting elite behavior, external influence, and even cultural/political dominance from external sources (the Maya, the Olmec, Teotihuacan, the Aztec, etc.).

More recently, scholars have reevaluated the Greater Nicoya concept and found it still useful, but most believe that the subarea was incorporated into the area of

Chibchan tradition from 4000 B.C. to A.D. 700, and was a subarea of Mesoamerica only in the period A.D. 700–1520. Linguistic and genetic data seem to support this model, proposed by Fonseca, but it remains to be tested archaeologically.

The division of Greater Nicoya into a southern sector and a northern sector is based at the most general level on the following differences: the northern sector (southern Pacific Nicaragua) has white-slipped ceramics, relative predominance of obsidian, and inland settlement patterns; the southern sector has tan-slipped ceramics, a relative predominance of jade, and coastal as well as inland settlement in the south.

Environment

Ecological homogeneity is often a defining characteristic of archaeological subareas. This region is comprised of coastal lowlands, delimited by the Gulf of Fonseca to the north and the Gulf of Nicoya to the south, and by the rising mountains of central Nicaragua and Costa Rica to the east, with their more temperate climate. Greater Nicoya is characterized by a seasonally wet and dry climate—wet or dry tropical in the Köppen classification. Prehistoric inhabitants enjoyed access to both coasts; in northwestern Costa Rica, nowhere is one coast more than one week's walk from the other, assuming that the weather is good and that one of the numerous natural passes between volcanoes is utilized. Along the Costa Rica/Nicaragua border, Lake Nicaragua and the San Juan River also offered a clearly defined and equally rapid route for interoceanic movement.

The relative ease of access is reflected in the distribution of clearly identifiable artifact classes. In Costa Rica, for example, the distribution of common forms and iconography of jade pendants from the Pacific, across the central cordillera, and on the Atlantic suggests that a shared ideology spanned the three ecological distinct areas. In both Nicaragua and Costa Rica, the distinctive white-slipped polychromes of the post–A.D. 800 era are found on both the Pacific and Atlantic watersheds, although in considerably greater quantities on the Pacific, their locus of production. The limited research into Caribbean-Pacific interaction has produced preliminary evidence of long-term, regular contacts, although the precise mechanisms and patterns of these contacts remain unclear. Finally, Greater Nicoya ceramics (primarily from the last two phases of the Middle Polychrome period) are found in other regions (Chontales in Nicaragua, the Cordillera of Guanacaste, the central Pacific Coast of

Costa Rica, Isla Cano, and the Central Valley and the Atlantic watershed of Costa Rica), but this does not call for these regions to be incorporated into the geographical-cultural sphere known as "Greater Nicoya."

Settlement History and Cultural Processes

Compared with those of adjacent Panama, the known cultural sequences from Greater Nicoya are relatively brief. Subarea cultural patterns characteristic of Greater Nicoya can be identified as early as 1000 B.C., marked initially by the presence of Bocana Incised Bichrome ceramics and subsequently by Rosales Zoned Engraved bichrome ceramics around 300 B.C.; these patterns continued until Spanish contact. Before this, peoples in the area participated in the more generalized "Northwest South American littoral tradition" (Willey 1971:263), or in what Fonseca has more recently labeled the "Area of Chibchan Tradition."

The earlier part of the regional sequence is perceived as part of more general hemispheric and Intermediate Area developmental patterns; see the entry "Intermediate Area: Overview" for an overview of the human occupation of Greater Nicoya from approximately 8000 to 1000 B.C. The integrity of the more detailed sequences provides strong support for an interpretation that the major features of cultural evolution were in situ rather than borrowed, diffused, or imposed. There were broad common trends and ongoing contacts and communication, but most important was a long tradition of subareal, subregional developmental independence.

For interpretation of cultural evolution and process, the rate and pattern of cultural development are as important as the length of the sequence. In the Intermediate Area, rates of development were much slower than those in Mesoamerica and the Andes. In Greater Nicoya, significant changes occurred during periods lasting three to four hundred years. This suggests much greater stability and a more peaceful existence for these peoples than for their more "civilized" neighbors.

Chronology

No Contact period sites have been definitely located or excavated, and this is one of the greatest gaps in our present knowledge. The prehistoric era in Greater Nicoya officially ended with the imposition of Spanish rule in 1522. The occasional use of 1550 as an end date for the Late Polychrome period was based on the possibility, not yet realized, of encountering relatively unaffected Contact-era indigenous activity. The Cuajiniquil conference proposed a slightly revised chronological sequence for Greater Nicoya, which here is integrated with the periodization for the final three periods of lower Central American prehistory.

There is very little evidence of sites from the early part of Period III (4000–1000 B.C.), but by its end there was sedentism and the use of ceramics throughout the subarea. Although there are general similarities among ceramic complexes, the overriding impression is one of local development from a common technological base, rather than technological and stylistic diffusion from a central source or direction. In Nicaragua, the Dinarte phase on Ometepe Island in Nicaragua had the first documented ceramics from the northern part of the area, dated to the middle part of the period, c. 2000 B.C. The Dinarte phase is important not only because it is relatively early and comparable with other regional ceramic complexes of the same approximate date, but also because it demonstrates—albeit indirectly—that efficient transportation in the form of rafting or sailing technology was well developed and in use by that time. The Tronadora site in the Lake Arenal area of the Cordillera of Guanacaste is also from this period (pre-2000 B.C.), although its locale is somewhat peripheral to the main Greater Nicoya subarea. Stylistic regionalism in ceramics paralleled and mirrored the regionalism of subsistence and settlement patterns that have been noted.

The development of a reliable subsistence base is a key variable in the accumulation of wealth, the emergence of elite personages or groups, and the evolution of hierarchical rankings of communities. Greater Nicoya had no single crop, such as maize, that was the staple for the entire area. Much of the area had access to coastal environments, and marine resources were certainly important; all investigators working in the area have reported mixed subsistence economies from all time periods, and trace element analyses of human skeletal remains from a broad time range also support this view of diversified prehistoric subsistence patterns.

Multiple food resources limited the ability of either individuals or communities to regulate subsistence, or to manipulate subsistence-related activities such as accumulation and redistribution. There is no evidence that cultigens and ceramics were introduced simultaneously as part of any broad-scale "Formative" expansion from either Mesoamerica or South America. In drawing a correlation between food specialization (maize) and the emergence of site hierarchies around 1000 B.C., it is important to emphasize that the hierarchical relationships were based

on advantageous locations and kinship-based redistribution systems, rather than on the emergence of centralized political-economic control. This model seems to be widely applicable throughout the area at this time and subsequently. The end of this period also marks the end of our ability to discuss almost all of the important sites in the course of this brief summary.

The next period (1000 B.C.–A.D. 500) saw a virtual explosion of sites and population, and while our discussions become much more generalized, we cannot draw more precise subareal boundaries. Greater Nicoya is flexible rather than rigid—a subarea with a core of cultural traits, but one that also contributed to, and received influences from, the material and intellectual cultures of surrounding areas. Only with such a flexible model can we incorporate the multiple linguistic groups and artifact distributions that we now see. This is also true of the northern and southern sector designations, as well as the southern Mesoamerican and Greater Nicoya designations.

Period IV (1000 B.C.–A.D. 500) includes parts of the Orosi phase (B.C. 1000–500), the Tempisque phase (500 B.C.–A.D. 300), and the Bagaces phase (A.D. 300–800). The earliest evidence for wealth, hierarchy, ranking, and ritual may have appeared around 1000 B.C. Sites with components from this period are found in all principal subdivisions of Greater Nicoya, except in the areas around the northern end of the Gulf of Nicoya: Ometepe Island and the Isthmus of Rivas in Nicaragua, and the Bay of Salinas, the Bay of Culebra, the Nosara Valley, the Tempisque River Valley, and the cordillera of Guanacaste in Costa Rica.

Around 500 B.C., jade and other greenstone artifacts became of widespread use and interest. In northern Costa Rica there developed a specialized funerary complex including various combinations of zoned bichrome ceramics, ceremonial stools or thrones, jade pendants, and mace heads. Based on recent evidence from the site of El Ostional, we now know that this special mortuary complex extends on the Nicaraguan side of the Bay of Salinas.

Relative to the situation in Parita Bay area of Panama, maize seems to have arrived late, at least in archaeologically detectable quantities, in Greater Nicoya. By the end of this period there is evidence of continuing human occupation (permanent villages and extensive cemeteries that may reflect clans, lineages, or other social units) in settings previously occupied but less permanent, as well as settlements in many additional places that appear to have been

N

previously uninhabited. Jade artifacts and ceramics of various styles (zoned engraved, Usulutan) validate interregional and intergroup contacts, although the specific mechanisms are still poorly understood; it is important to note that in the case of Usulutan we are documenting the distribution of a decorative technique, not of the finished ceramics themselves. In general, ceramic studies indicate that through the end of this period, ceramic production was locally controlled and directed.

Period V (A.D. 500–1000) includes parts of both the Bagaces (A.D. 300–800) and Sapoa (A.D. 800–1350) phases. The onset of Period V was a major time of change in Greater Nicoya, reflected in the archaeological record as shifts in settlement patterns and the introduction of new types or styles of artifacts. In the southern sector of Greater Nicoya there was a rapid buildup in coastal habitation, and white-slipped ceramics (such as the widely known Papagayo Polychrome) were developed shortly after A.D. 700. Because distinctions between site forms and sizes emerged in some adjacent areas during this period, it can be generalized that the larger sites were in the wetter central valleys and highlands on the Atlantic watersheds, while greater homogeneity continued to be the case in the drier Pacific lands of Greater Nicoya. Sites from this period are known from all major subdivisions of Greater Nicoya, as enumerated in the discussion of Period III, and also around the Gulf of Nicoya. The most extensively excavated sites include Ayala (Isthmus of Rivas), Los Angeles (Ometepe Island), Las Marias (Bay of Salinas), Vidor and Nacascolo (Bay of Culebra), and La Guinea and La Ceiba (Tempisque River Valley).

Period VI (A.D. 1000–1520) includes parts of the Sapoa (A.D. 800–1350) and Ometepe (A.D. 1350–1520) phases. This final period before the Spanish invasion is known to us from descriptions by Spaniards traveling in the region soon after Contact. They described chiefdoms in Panama and Colombia that were much larger than those in Costa Rica and Nicaragua in general, and in Greater Nicoya specifically. Sites from this period are known from most major subdivisions of Greater Nicoya, although the heaviest concentrations, based on current data, were in the upper Tempisque River Valley and around the Bay of Salinas. The most extensively excavated sites include Los Angeles (Ometepe Island), Las Marias (Bay of Salinas), Vidor (Bay of Culebra), and La Ceiba (Tempisque River Valley).

The area's broad diversity provided prehistoric populations with long-term cultural stability, in contrast to the cyclical upheaval and competition that characterized the centers of both highland and lowland Mesoamerican peoples, as well as Andean societies, and to a lesser degree the inhabitants of the Nicaraguan Pacific watershed.

Material and Ideological Resources

The accumulation of wealth, the emergence of ranked societies, and the evolution of economic/political (regional and extraregional) hierarchies have traditionally been identified as the consequences of mature, settled village life. Although such an evolutionary sequence is appropriate to the Andes, the Valley of Mexico, and the Maya Lowlands, the process was truncated at the less complex chiefdom level in some parts of Greater Nicoya, and at the tribal level in others.

Jade utilization was limited mostly to northwestern, central, and Atlantic coastal Costa Rica from approximately 300 B.C. to A.D. 700. In this context, the term "jade" includes all lithic materials (jadeite, quartz, serpentine, and others) used in the manufacture of earplugs, pendants, and beads. The closest presently known source of jadeite is outside the area, in the Motagua Valley of Guatemala. However, a group of artifacts that are also geologically and chemically jadeite but unrelated to Motagua or any other known source pose a tantalizing challenge to researchers. Although there has been extensive speculation regarding Olmec and or Maya influence on the Costa Rican jade-carving tradition, it is best to view the three archaeological cultures as having distinct carving traditions.

Obsidian from sources in Guatemala (Pixcaya and Ixtepeque) and Honduras (Guinope) is found more frequently at sites in the northern part of Greater Nicoya, but also at some sites in northern Costa Rica; most examples are from after A.D. 800. There is also a strong contrast between Pacific coastal sites in Nicaragua and Costa Rica, which more frequently have obsidian, and those sites in the central and Atlantic areas that tended to make more use of locally available raw materials.

The principal occurrences of gold in Central America, relative to Greater Nicoya, are the geographically peripheral Chontales region of Nicaragua and the more distant Diquis region of Costa Rica and western Panama. There was little gold produced in Greater Nicoya proper, although symbolism for gold is found on Sapoa and Ometepe phase ceramics.

Relatively few copper artifacts—all bells or earspools—have been found here. They are all thought to have been made in Honduras or Mexico and imported to Greater Nicoya during the Sapoa and Ometepe phases.

In this volcanically active area, erosional deposits of clays of variable quality are widely distributed, and most populations would have had access to ceramic-quality clays in their immediate vicinity. Eight major production areas (as opposed to specific sites) have been identified in the southern sector of Greater Nicoya in Costa Rica; a similar refinement awaits further research in the northern sector in Nicaragua.

Although samples of woods, fibers, drugs, plants, feathers, and skins are seldom recovered from archaeological contexts, depictions and symbolism on ceramics and stone statuary and in jade and gold figures indicate that they were important components of the cultural assemblage.

Interaction with Other Regions

Greater Nicoya has had the reputation of being little more than a transitional area, or the recipient of strong cultural influences from Mesoamerica, but the direct archaeological evidence of such incursions or passages is extremely limited and usually indirect. The degrees of Olmec influence on the jade-carving tradition, of Mesoamerican influence on the ceramic tradition, and of Mesoamerican elements in the subsistence system—especially in the northern part of the area—are still vigorously debated. Genetic data suggest significant population stability over the past several millennia, and there is no genetic evidence for any major population shifts.

The Usulutan technique, present from A.D. 200 to 500, and the Mexican symbolism on post–A.D. 800 ceramics are both indications of indirect, filtered influences. Another interesting data group is the Early Classic Maya belt celts, which have been recovered more frequently in Costa Rica than in the Maya area proper, and so far are absent from the geographically intermediate terrain of Honduras and Nicaragua.

Data Gaps and Interpretative Blanks

Scholars generally agree that a different model of cultural development and the evolution of social complexity is needed for the Intermediate Area in general and for Greater Nicoya specifically. The more traditional, idealized models developed for the highland and lowland Mesoamerican and South American Andean civilizations, or states, may be of limited, if any, applicability except as distinct contrasts for smaller regional patterns. To develop such a model, we need to focus attention on filling in the missing space-time gaps in clearly defined ecologically bounded basins, plains, and valleys. This is particularly urgent because of an unprecedented surge of site-destructive economic development in the area, combined with a sense of how many areas are still unknown. As these gaps in our knowledge continue to be filled and existing sequences become more detailed, we can address some high-priority regional themes for the Central American area, providing better understanding of regional trends in prehistoric nutrition, trade patterns, subsistence, settlement patterns, and other cultural patterns.

FURTHER READINGS

Barrantes, R., P. E. Smouse, H. Mohrenweiser, H. Gershowitz, J. Azofeifa, T. Arias, and J. V. Neel. 1990. Microevolution in Lower Central America: Genetic Characterization of the Chibcha Speaking Groups of Costa Rica and Panama, and a Consensus Taxonomy Based on Genetic and Linguistic Affinity. *Journal of Human Genetics* 46:63–84.

Bishop, R. L., F. W. Lange, and P. Lange. 1988. Ceramic Paste Compositional Patterns in Greater Nicoya Pottery. In F. W. Lange (ed.), *Costa Rican Art and Archaeology: Essays in Honor of Frederick R. Mayer,* pp. 11–44. Boulder: Johnson Books.

Bonilla V., L., M. Calvo M., J. V. Guerrero M., S. Salgado G., and F. W. Lange (eds.). 1990. *Tipos cerámicos y variedades de la Gran Nicoya. Vínculos* 13 (1–2). San José, Costa Rica: Imprenta Varitec.

Constenla U., A. 1991. *Las lenguas del Area Intermedia: Introducción a su estudio areal.* San José: Editorial de la Universidad de Costa Rica.

Fonseca Z., O. 1994. El concepto de area de tradicion chibchoide y su pertinencia para entender Gran Nicoya. *Vínculos* 18/19:209–227.

Haberland, W. 1959. A Pre-appraisal of Chiriquian Pottery Types. *Actas, 33rd International Congress of Americanists* 2:339–346.

Healy, P. F. 1980. *The Archaeology of the Rivas Region, Nicaragua.* Waterloo, Ontario: Wilfred Laurier University Press.

Hoopes, J. W. 1992. Early Formative cultures in the Intermediate Area: A Background to the Emergence of Social Complexity. In F. W. Lange (ed.), *Wealth and Hierarchy in the Intermediate Area,* pp. 43–83. Washington, D.C.: Dumbarton Oaks.

Lange, F. W. 1984. The Greater Nicoya Archaeological Subarea. In F. W. Lange and D. Z. Stone (eds.), *The Archaeology of Lower Central America,* pp. 165–194. Albuquerque: University of New Mexico Press.

———. (ed.). 1992. *Wealth and Hierarchy in the Intermediate Area.* Washington, D.C.: Dumbarton Oaks.

N

———. (ed.). 1993. *Precolumbian Jade: New Cultural and Geological Interpretations.* Salt Lake City: University of Utah Press.

———. (ed.). 1995. *Paths through Central American Prehistory.* Niwot: Univresity Press of Colorado.

Frederick W. Lange and Juan Vincente Guerrero

SEE ALSO

Intermediate Area: Overview

Nogalar

See San Antonio Nogalar

Nohmul (Orange Walk, Belize)

This large Maya site in northern Belize was first inhabited in early Middle Formative times (900–650 B.C.), though aceramic occupation dating back to 1500 B.C. is evident in adjacent wetlands. The ceremonial nucleus of Nohmul was founded in the Late Formative period (c. 400 B.C.) and underwent a major construction program during the Terminal Formative (A.D. 100–250), when the basic layout of the center was established, with the acropolis, a large plaza south of it, and a second plaza to the west. A 400-meter-long *sacbe* (causeway) leads to the West Group, which is dominated by a 20-meter pyramid and a small acropolis. Nohmul's Terminal Formative ceramics include one of the most extensive collections of vessels of Protoclassic or Holmul I early polychrome style.

During the late Early and Late Classic periods (A.D. 400–800), the population apparently declined. In the Terminal Classic and Early Postclassic Tecep phase (A.D. 800–1100), Nohmul rose again in importance and new construction was undertaken, influenced by northern Yucatán. Fragments of Late Postclassic incense burners found on the surface at Nohmul may indicate that the site's abandoned temples were visited by pilgrims.

The wetlands along the Río Hondo near Nohmul contain small zones of drained fields of Terminal Classic to Early Postclassic date; earlier wetland use, including aceramic occupation before 1500 B.C., has recently been detected.

FURTHER READINGS

Hammond, N. 1975. Maya Settlement Hierarchy in Northern Belize. *Contributions of the University of California Archaeological Research Facility* 27:40–55.

———. 1983. *Nohmul: A Prehistoric Maya Community in Belize; Excavations 1973–1983.* B. A. R. International Series, 250. Oxford.

Hammond, N., L. J. Kosakowsky, A. Pyburn, J. Rose, J. C. Staneko, S. Donaghey, M. Horton, C. Clark, C. Gleason, D. Muyskens, and T. Addyman. 1988. The Evolution of an Ancient Maya City: Nohmul. *National Geographic Research* 4:474–495.

Francisco Estrada Belli

SEE ALSO

Maya Lowlands: South

Northern Arid Zone

The northern frontier of Mesoamerica was traditionally defined by archaeologists according to economic criteria: south of the boundary lived Mesoamerican farmers, and north of it were hunters and gatherers, as Paul Kirchhoff noted in 1943. This northern region was called the "Gran Chichimeca" by Charles Di Peso in the 1970s, after the Chichimec nomads who lived there at the time of European contact, and who were thought to be barbarians by the civilized Aztecs of the Central Highlands of Mexico.

This northern frontier was a dynamic entity. Pedro Armillas observes that during the late Formative period, Mesoamerican farmers expanded into the region north of the Río Lerma, and that this northward movement peaked during the early Postclassic, then rapidly collapsed; the border then shifted back to the Río Lerma. He ascribed this northward pulse of Mesoamerican culture to a climatic shift to moister conditions, followed by desiccation. Beatriz Braniff refers to the region affected by this pulse as "Mesoamerica Septentrional," meaning "northern Mesoamerica," the southernmost region of the Northern Arid Zone.

The Northern Arid Zone does not form a coherent environmental, cultural, or research area, because archaeologists have defined the region largely in terms of what it is not—Mesoamerica—rather than on the basis of its own shared characteristics. Archaeologists working in the zone recognize four major regions: Baja California, Northeast Mexico, Mesoamerica Septentrional, and Southwest United States and Northwest Mexico.

Baja California is culturally and linguistically most like Southern California. Northeast Mexico is an immense area including all of the Mexican states of Coahuila and

Nuevo León, with portions of Durango, Zacatecas, San Luis Potosí, and Tamaulipas. The portion of the Mesoamerica Septentrional in the zone includes all of the state of Guanajuato, and portions of the states of San Luis Potosí and Tamaulipas. The Southwest United States and Northwest Mexico (hereafter, Southwest) region includes all of the states of New Mexico, Arizona, Sonora, and Chihuahua, as well as portions of Texas, Colorado, and Utah. Most anthropologists regard this as a culture area comparable to Mesoamerica, and one of the key issues for the zone is the nature and extent of interactions between the Southwest and Mesoamerica.

Environment

The one characteristic that unites all of the Northern Arid Zone is generally low precipitation. The entire area fits the technical definition of a desert as a region where the evaporation rate exceeds the precipitation rate. The two driest subregions, Baja California and Northeast Mexico, have few permanent streams, while in the Southwest and in Mesoamerica Septentrional, extant permanent streams depend on precipitation in the high mountains. Generally, throughout the region the environment becomes cooler and moister as elevation and/or latitude increase.

The zone is environmentally very diverse. In the north, in Arizona and New Mexico, the Southwest extends onto the Colorado Plateau and is bounded on the east by the Great Plains of the United States. To the south, the region ends in the grasslands of the Bajío area of Central Mexico. Within these boundaries, three physiographic provinces cover the region: the Sonoran Desert, the Sierra Madre, and the Chihuahuan Desert.

The Sonoran Desert is a low, hot, subtropical environment with the greatest species density and diversity of any desert in the Western Hemisphere. It is a cactus desert characterized by tall, columnar species such as the saguaro (Carnegiea gigantea). Temperatures routinely exceed 40° C in summer and only occasionally dip below 0° C in the winter. This desert covers most of Baja California, southern Arizona, and the western half of Sonora.

The Rocky Mountains in New Mexico and the Sierra Madre Occidental in Mexico form a sinuous mountainous backbone that splits the Northern Arid Zone in two. These mountains are rugged, steep, and high, with elevations up to 4,000 meters. At higher elevations, adequate moisture falls for temporal cultivation, but the growing season is too short for maize. The dominant vegetation type in the mountains is pine forest, with oak woodland at lower elevations. The lower Sierra Madre Oriental extends near the Gulf Coast.

The Chihuahuan Desert lies between the two mountain chains, extending south from New Mexico into San Luis Potosí. This is a high temperate desert covered primarily by grassland and scrubland, with xerophytes such as Yucca and Agave, and woody species such as mesquite (Prosopis), ocotillo (Fouquieria), and creosote bush (Larrea). There are few cacti present, mainly Opuntia. The hallucinogenic peyote cactus (Lophophora williamsii) occurs in the lower latitudes of this desert.

Paleoindian Period

The Paleoindian occupation of the Northern Arid Zone is poorly known and is interpreted largely on the basis of cultural traditions defined outside the region. There are some indications for a preprojectile stage occupation of the region, with evidence for a spatially limited fluted point tradition. The terminal Paleoindian occupation of much of the region seems to resemble traditions found in southern California.

The existence of a preprojectile tradition that precedes the fluted point, or Clovis, tradition is highly controversial, based on widely scattered and poorly dated remains such as pebble tools, choppers, crude unifaces, and occasional thinned bifaces. Many archaeologists believe that these are the remains not of this early stage but of functionally specialized activities of later, better-defined cultures. In the Northern Arid Zone archaeologists have inferred this occupation from surface remains in the most arid regions, and from the basal levels of cave excavations. The Malpais tradition has been defined based on heavily patinated surface finds in the Sonoran Desert and in the Chihuahuan Desert of trans-Pecos Texas. The earliest levels at San Isidro Cave in Nuevo León have been attributed to this tradition. The Diablo Complex at Diablo Cave in the Tamaulipas Mountains has been estimated to date to 28,000 B.C., and at Rancho La Amapola in northern San Luis Potosí, a single radiocarbon date on a hearth with a scraper yielded a range of 30,000 to 31,000 B.C.

Archaeologists have excavated Clovis (9500–9000 B.C.) mammoth kill sites in eastern New Mexico and southern Arizona. Scattered finds of fluted points have been made over much of Sonora and in southern Texas. However, no fluted points have been found in Northeast Mexico.

The San Dieguito tradition, originally defined in southern California and southwestern Arizona, is quite

N

distinct from the Clovis tradition. This tradition began around 6000 B.C. and continued into the Archaic; it features small, crudely made, triangular projectile points with tapering or rectangular stems. This assemblage extends into northern Baja California and Sonora. Artifacts from the earliest levels at La Calsada Cave in southern Nuevo León stylistically resemble this tradition.

Archaic Period

The appearance of ground stone artifacts marks the shift from the Paleoindian period to the Archaic in the Northern Arid Zone. Many archaeologists see the Archaic of the Northern Arid Zone as the southernmost extension of the desert culture of the western United States. In most of the zone, an Archaic adaption characterizes all of aboriginal history up to the Spanish conquest.

In Baja California, the earliest Archaic remains are a continuation of the San Dieguito tradition, and an Archaic lifeway continued until the Conquest. The Concepción tradition (5500–1000 B.C.) followed the San Dieguito; the shift is indicated by new projectile point styles and the appearance of grinding stones. The Concepción tradition appears to have been primarily a terrestrial adaptation, and the shift to the subsequent Coyote (1000 B.C.–A.D. 1000) is marked by the addition of a marine adaptation. This is also the time period during which rock rings, coastal shell middens, and abstract rock art began to appear. The best-defined and most extensively studied period is the Comond tradition (A.D. 1000–1540). In addition to shifts in projectile point styles, the appearance of basin *metates,* and cremation burial, the most dramatic characteristic of this tradition is large, brightly painted pictograph murals.

In Northwest Mexico, the major Archaic tradition across Sonora and Chihuahua is Cochise, originally defined in southern Arizona and dated from around 3500 B.C. to A.D. 100. During this time period, there was a progressive change from crude, small, triangular projectile points to distinctive, large, side-notched San Pedro points; grinding equipment was also elaborated from flat slab *metates* to well-made basin forms.

In Northeast Mexico archaeologists have defined two major Archaic traditions that originated around 5500 B.C. and continued to the Spanish conquest. The Coahuila complex has been defined primarily on the basis of materials from dry caves. In the rest of the region, the widespread Abasolo tradition, characterized by triangular and ovid projectile points, appeared around 3500 B.C. Between A.D. 800 and 1000, the projectile point styles of this tradition changed to small triangular points suitable for use with a bow and arrow.

Mesoamerica Septentrional (Northern Mesoamerica)

The earliest ceramic tradition north of the Río Lerma is the Chupícuaro, named after a cemetery site found on the Río Lerma in Guanajuato. This tradition dates from the Terminal Formative (300 B.C.–A.D. 300). Chupícuaro style has widespread distribution, appearing from Guanajuato south to Cuernavaca. Most of the excavated sites of this tradition are cemeteries, but remains of wattle-and-daub houses have been found, and archaeologists excavated a circular pyramid at the site of Chupícuaro.

During the Early Classic period (A.D. 300–600), Mesoamerican farming cultures expanded northward into San Luis Potosí. Two distinctive ceramic provinces appear: one is centered on the Tunal Grande in the north, and the other to the south on the Bajío. There is greater site differentiation, with farming hamlets and regional centers with civic-ceremonial architecture. Centers, such as Ibarrilla and Cañada de Alfaro, have as many as twenty-three mounds or platforms. The largest mound yet examined covered an area of 80 by 95 meters and had a sunken plaza within it.

In the Late Classic period the regional extent of these traditions remained stable, but there is evidence of greater population density and architectural elaboration. Cloisonné ceramics occasionally occur in local assemblages, and on rare occasions excavators find a few sherds of Thin Orange ware. Late Classic architecture is similar to earlier forms, but with more stone construction and larger, more architecturally complex centers with plazas, platforms, pyramids, and patios. Civic-ceremonial centers like Cañada de la Virgin tend to occur on hilltops surrounded by smaller farming hamlets.

The Early Postclassic (A.D. 900–1200) represented a continuation of Classic Period patterns, but with a decline in the extent and density of occupation north of the Río Lerma. Contact with Tula is evidenced by the appearance of Toltec ceramic types such as Plumbate ware. Some scholars think that Tula dominated the region militarily, and many sites have been interpreted as forts because of their defensible positions. Tula's collapse, c. A.D. 1200, coincided with the abandonment of Mesoamerica Septentrional by Mesoamerican farmers.

Southwest United States and Northwest Mexico

The first maize appeared in the Southwest about 1500 B.C., when local Archaic populations incorporated its cultivation into their foraging rounds. Small pit houses and pit storage features dated between 200 B.C. and A.D. 200 appear in a wide variety of environments, but sedentary life and ceramic production did not begin until at least A.D. 200–300. There is little regional differentiation in this early pattern, and it appears to be the northernmost extension of a Mesoamerican pattern that originated with the Chupícuaro tradition. Mesoamerican influences that archaeologists link to this economic and social change range from the basic (maize, pottery) to the subtle (highly stylized and altered iconographic elements).

Regional Traditions (A.D. 300–900)

Starting about A.D. 300, the Southwest traditions began to differentiate from societies to the south, and internally within the region. An Anasazi, or ancient Pueblo, tradition emerged on the Colorado Plateau, a Mogollon tradition in the mountains, and a Hohokam tradition in the Sonoran Desert. Each tradition is manifest in a relatively uniform pattern of ceramic style, architecture, subsistence, ritual, and social organization, spread over large areas of the Southwest. Later (A.D. 600–900), increasing regional differentiation created subdivisions in the existing traditions, as well as many smaller traditions.

The distribution of Black-on-White pottery with a distinct set of design styles defines the Anasazi tradition. Around A.D. 300 the Anasazi lived in deep, round, pit houses organized in widely scattered, sometimes stockaded settlements of from two to thirty-five pit houses. At the bigger villages, larger pit structures called "great kivas" are thought to have served as local ceremonial structures. After A.D. 600 the Anasazi began building rectangular surface rooms. By A.D. 900 a typical settlement consisted of several contiguous aboveground rectangular rooms with a circular subterranean kiva. Larger settlements consisted of a series of these units with as many as three hundred rooms.

The Mogollon tradition existed in the mountains south of the Anasazi, extending in a long arc into the Sierra Madre Occidental of Mexico. The people of this tradition made brownware pottery with red designs. By A.D. 900 many of the Mogollon had begun to build surface pueblos like those of the Anasazi and to make Black-on-White pottery. Most settlements consisted of only a few houses, but the larger villages had as many as fifty circular or square pit houses houses, with an associated great kiva.

The early farming tradition of the Sonoran Desert has traditionally been called Hohokam. From A.D. 300 to 700 the Hohokam in southern Arizona appear to have been the northernmost expression of a Sonoran tradition that stretched from the Río Fuerte in Sinaloa to central Arizona. The cultures of this Sonoran tradition shared domed brush houses built in shallow pits, a figurine style, and finely made brown to gray pottery. These peoples lived adjacent to major rivers and planted crops in the floodplains. This tradition developed a distinctive marine shell jewelry assemblage that is stylistically similar from northern Sinaloa to central Arizona.

Between A.D. 700 and 900 this tradition broke down into four major regional variants: Hohokam, Trincheras, Seri, and Huatabampo. The Hohokam tradition is distinguished from the others by large, oval ball courts, platform mounds, large-scale canal irrigation, cremation burial, censers, palettes, and the use of paddle and anvil pottery-making techniques to produce buffware pottery with red designs. Their villages had as many as two hundred houses.

The Trincheras tradition developed just to the south of the Hohokam; these people used coil-and-scrape pottery-making techniques to produce brownware painted in purple designs, and left cremation burials. Along the coast of central Sonora, a thin coil-and-scrape ware appears that is similar to the Trincheras and the Huatabampo but is associated with a hunting-and-gathering population ancestral to the Seri. At the far southern end of Sonora there appeared a distinctive Huatabampo tradition with shell-scraped redware pottery, domed and adobe houses, and inhumation burial. These people built villages with communal plazas and trash mounds, and they seem to have depended more on marine resources than on agriculture. The Hohokam, Trincheras, and Huatabampo peoples all continued to make very similar shell jewelry and to trade this jewelry to the north. These traditions show the earliest evidence of Mesoamerican contact, both stylistically and in the form of Mesoamerican trade items such as copper bells and macaws.

Regional Centers (A.D. 900–1200)

The years from A.D. 900 to 1200 saw the development and demise in each major tradition of elaborate regional centers that formed the core of larger, highly centralized regional systems. The three regional systems—Hohokam, Chaco, and Mimbres—were all quite large by Northwest standards: the Chaco regional system covered an area of about 75,000 square kilometers, the Hohokam regional system 100,000 square kilometers, and the Mimbres, 56,000 square kilometers. Each of these systems had a clear core or center with a surrounding peripheral area. The defining characteristics of each system—architectural features, ceramics, and site types—seem to have originated in its center, and the peripheries appear to have been linked to it. Most archaeologists think that these systems united multiple ethnic and cultural groups.

These centers were contemporaneous with the northernmost pulse of Mesoamerica Septentrional. The Guasave tradition replaced the Huatabampo in Sinaloa about A.D. 1000. On the other side of the Sierra Madre Occidental, the Chalchihuites tradition expanded northward into Durango.

The core of the Hohokam regional system lies in the Phoenix Basin. This area has large, internally differentiated sites, with as many as five hundred scattered houses, and often with ball courts, an important Mesoamerican culture trait. The largest and best-known of these sites is Snaketown. The settlement hierarchy consisted of multiple-ball-court villages, single-ball-court villages, and habitation settlements lacking ball courts. By A.D. 1100 the irrigation network extended to its maximum size and exceeded all others in Mesoamerica in size and complexity. There is little evidence for an overall political organization that united all of the basin. Ceramic styles, iconography, and aspects of material culture (such as ball courts, copper bells, and macaws) suggest indirect linkages to Mesoamerica. A social and ideological glue appears to have bound the system together, with ball courts being the physical focus of these relations. By the 1100s, the limits of the system were established by more than 165 sites with at least 206 ball courts. The Phoenix Basin Hohokam obtained marine shell from the Gulf of California, manufactured it into shell jewelry, and exchanged it over an area slightly larger than the range of the ball courts.

The core of the Chaco regional system lies in Chaco Canyon in northwestern New Mexico. In Chaco Canyon itself the ancient Pueblo people built communal dwellings of two to nine hundred rooms, which archaeologists call "great houses." The system was defined by a network of roads that linked the great houses in the canyon to others in the region. Mesoamerican objects and features (such as colonnades) appear as rare elements in the Chaco culture, in contrast to their integral role in the Hohokam pattern.

The Mimbres regional system was considerably smaller and less developed than the others, but still bigger than other local traditions, and possessed similar characteristics of centrality. The core of the Mimbres system is in south-western New Mexico, where pueblos of as many as three hundred rooms were built alongside irrigated fields. The most distinctive marker of the Mimbres system is a finely made Black-on-White pottery painted with fanciful zoomorphic and anthropomorphic designs. The Mimbres people trekked to the Gulf of California to gather marine shell, which they made into Sonoran-style jewelry.

These three highly centralized systems all collapsed in the middle of the twelfth century A.D. There was a major reorganization in the Hohokam about A.D. 1150, with a shift to aboveground architecture, a decline in the ball court ritual complex, changes in mortuary practices, and stylistic changes in artifacts. Chaco Canyon lost population in the late twelfth century and was abandoned by the early fourteenth. The major sites in the Mimbres Valley were deserted by the middle of the twelfth century.

Regional Networks (A.D. 1200–1450)

In the centuries following the demise of the regional centers, several extensive regional networks appeared in the Southwest, each associated with a distinctive ceramic style. The distributions of these ceramic styles crosscut earlier regional boundaries. These networks shared certain similarities: they were distinct from one another and from their antecedents; they entailed widespread population aggregation; their ceramics were widely traded outside their production centers; and a common set of design motifs cross-cuts the ceramic types.

The northern pulse of Mesoamerica Septentrional went into decline after A.D. 1200 and collapsed back into Mesoamerica by 1350. In the Southwest, the strongest evidence of Mesoamerican contacts shifts to the major regional center of Casas Grandes in northwestern Chihuahua. This center developed after 1200 and was abandoned by the late fifteenth century.

The largest of the regional networks, the Salado, appeared in the second half of the thirteenth century. This network was anchored on the west by the Classic period Hohokam of the Phoenix Basin, and on the east by Casas Grandes. The reorganized Phoenix Basin continued to grow, with a consolidation of the canal system, special administrative sites, and the concentration of population in more than forty villages, the largest of which contained thirty-five compounds spread over 2.5 square kilometers, and elite residences on platform mounds. A great arch of multistory pueblos and compound villages of as many as several hundred rooms stretched between the two regional centers. The network may have been a weakly linked system of exchange and elite intermarriage between smaller, independent regional polities, or perhaps it represented a shared religious cult. The material culture of the system included a shared polychrome pottery style and a distinctive set of elite goods—turquoise-on-shell mosaic, copper bells, macaws, *Strombus* shell trumpets, asbestos, and some types of shell beads. Utilitarian items like pottery, however, tended to vary between regions depending on cultural and environmental factors.

This network did not develop in a vacuum, but in relation to other networks of relations adjacent to it. To the north of the Salado network, the Little Colorado network extended from western New Mexico into Arizona along the Mogollon uplands. This network appears to have been similar to the Salado: a weakly linked system of exchange and religion that cross-cut different local polities and cultural boundaries. In what had been the southern peripheries of the Hohokam system and the Trincheras tradition, the O'odham network appeared, defined by the distribution of brownware pottery, terraced villages (Cerros de Trincheras), and a relatively uniform material culture inventory over the entire area. This network may represent an ethnogenesis as people who shared a common ethnic identity or language intensified these bonds in opposition to the power center of the Salado network.

We have only limited knowledge of what was happening in contemporary societies farther south. On either side of the Sierra Madre Occidental there were Mogollon-like local traditions—Río Sonora on the western slope and Loma San Gabriel on the east. Both these traditions consisted of scattered small settlements with unpainted brownware pottery. In both Sonora and Chihuahua, a gap of several hundred kilometers with no major regional centers separated the regional networks of the Northwest from the northernmost Mesoamerican regional centers.

The Pueblo world witnessed a dramatic series of population movements and reorganizations at the end of the thirteenth century. Sedentary agricultural populations moved off the Colorado Plateau and into the Rio Grande Valley, leaving only the Hopi and the Zuni in the west. Concurrently, the Katsina (or Katchina) religion appeared, crosscutting the various ethnic groups of the Pueblo world; this religion included a distinct set of symbols, beliefs, and rituals, many of Mesoamerican origin. New forms of social organization also appeared, and pueblos became quite large and similar in layout. Along the Río Grande in New Mexico, a regional network developed that linked different linguistic groups. These people built pueblos as large as a thousand rooms, consisting of multiple multistory apartment blocks organized around central plazas with one or two large kivas. Villages specialized in the production of glazeware pottery and traded it throughout the region. Each major village appears to have been politically independent from the others, but alliances between villages may have existed.

During the fifteenth century the face of the Southwest was once again transformed. The Salado network and the Little Colorado network both collapsed, and sedentary farmers abandoned these regions. The Classic period societies of the Phoenix Basin suffered severe population loss. In the late fifteenth century intruders razed Casas Grandes, and the survivors probably fled over the Sierra Madre Occidental. The O'odham in northern Sonora continued to live in the region, but there appears to have been a drop in the number and size of settlements. Farther south, the Loma San Gabriel populations probably became the Tarahumara. Only the Pueblo world continued to develop along the lines laid out in the previous period. Some archaeologists argue that these changes occurred as a result of the introduction of European diseases, about 100 years later than they have been traditionally dated.

Southwest-Mesoamerica Interactions

A great deal of the culture of the Southwest clearly derived from Mesoamerica. All the major agricultural crops (corn, beans, squash, and cotton), pottery, many details of architecture, and aspects of cosmology (a multitiered universe, and cyclic creation and destruction of the world), religious beliefs (Twins myths, Feathered Serpent), and ritual (masked dancers, New Fire ceremony) clearly originated in Mesoamerica. The people of the Southwest adopted these and many other things from Mesoamerica and thus transformed their cultures, but they did so in a uniquely Southwestern way. The social systems of Mesoamerica and the Southwest were analogous to two families of languages that have some cognate words but differ in deep structure.

Objects of Mesoamerican origin, including pseudo-cloisonné mirror backs, copper bells, ceramics, and macaws, have been found in some of the largest Southwest sites. The total number of such objects from all sites does not exceed 1,500. With the possible exception of the macaws, all these items originated from the northwestern frontier of Mesoamerica and from West Mexico. Southwestern turquoise has been found in both these regions and in the Central Highlands of Mexico.

It is clear that societies in Mesoamerica interacted with Southwest cultures, but archaeologists hotly debate to

N

what extent events and processes in the Southwest were determined by this interaction. Two extreme positions, known as "imperialist" and "isolationist," have characterized this debate. The imperialist position, advocated by archaeologists such as Charles Di Peso and J. Charles Kelley, basically sees the Southwest as simply an extension of Mesoamerica and not as a separate cultural area. These researchers propose that Mesoamerican societies actively dominated Southwest cultures through the use of traders like the Aztec *pochteca,* or through other agents. Many Southwest archaeologists, however, are isolationists who recognize the Mesoamerican origin of many traits but discount interactions with Mesoamerica as a significant force in Southwest developments. Recent archaeological research has tended to demonstrate that interactions between specific regions in each culture area were significant, but that these interactions did not drive the overall processes of cultural development in the Southwest.

FURTHER READINGS

Armillas, P. 1969. *The Arid Frontier of Mexican Civilization.* New York Academy of Sciences, Transactions (2nd series) 31:697–704.

Braniff, B. 1989. Oscilación de la frontera norte mesoamericana: Un nuevo ensayo. *Arqueología* 1:99–114.

Cordell, L. 1997. *Archaeology of the Southwest.* Orlando: Academic Press.

Foster, M. S., and P. C. Weigand. 1985. *The Archaeology of West and Northwest Mesoamerica.* Boulder: Westview Press.

García, C. (coord.). 1988. *La Antropología en México, Panorama Histórico 12. La Antropología–en el Norte de Mexico.* Mexico City: Instituto Nacional de Antropología e Historia.

Gumerman, G. J. 1994. *Themes in Southwest Prehistory.* Santa Fe: SAR Press.

Guzmán, A., and L. Martínez. 1991. *Querétaro prehispánico.* Mexico City: Instituto Nacional de Antropología e Historia.

MacMahon, J. A. 1985. *Deserts.* Alfred New York: Knopf.

Mathien, F. J., and R. H. McGuire (eds.). 1986. *Ripples in the Chichimec Sea: New Considerations of Southwestern—Mesoamerican Interactions.* Carbondale: Southern Illinois University.

Nance, R. 1992. *The Archaeology of La Calsada.* Austin: University of Texas Press.

Phillips, D. A. 1989. Prehistory of Chihuahua and Sonora, Mexico. *Journal of World Prehistory* 3:373–401.

Vargas, V. D. 1995. *Copper Bell Trade Patterns in the Prehispanic U. S. Southwest, and Northwest Mexico.* Arizona State Museum Archaeological Series, 187. Tucson.
Randall H. McGuire

Northern Mesoamerica (Mesoamerica Septentrional)

See Bajío Region; Northern Arid Zone; Northwestern Frontier

Northwestern Frontier

The Northwestern Frontier is defined as the region north of the Lerma-Santiago river system and west of the interior deserts, extending to northern Sinaloa and Durango. The rugged ranges of the Sierra Madre Occidental divide the interior plateau from the coastal lowlands, forming a significant but surmountable barrier to movement and trade. Rainfall, higher on the coastal side, generally increases from north to south. In the interior, major streams tend to flow from north to south, but they run from east to west on the coast. Much of the Northwestern Frontier is agriculturally marginal; piedmont pockets of alluvium and coastal deltas are the most productive agricultural lands, and farmers can make one crop annually on the interior side, but two or even three on the coast. The mountains receive slightly more precipitation than the interior, sustaining only a short growing season.

Vegetative cover has been affected profoundly by modern activities; contrasts among zones, however, are still informative. Traversing the mountains from the interior, one passes through a foothill zone of zacate grass, prickly pear cacti *(Opuntia),* and shrubs such as mesquite *(Prosopis)* and huizache. Stream bottoms tend to be relatively narrow and shallow. At higher elevations, pines and oaks appear, and the land surface is deeply dissected by canyons with patches of alluvial development. Between canyons are high remnant mesas, some forested and others open. Descending on the coastal side, grassland is succeeded by scrub oak and then dense, thorny vegetation dominated by scrub plants. Originally, much of this zone may have harbored tall tropical deciduous forest of trees such as higuera. Finally, a coastal plain varying from 1 to 35 kilometers in width is covered with mangrove swamps, which are separated by higher-lying deltas at intervals of 30 to 50 kilometers.

The culture history and processes of the Northwestern Frontier are unique enough that some archaeologists see

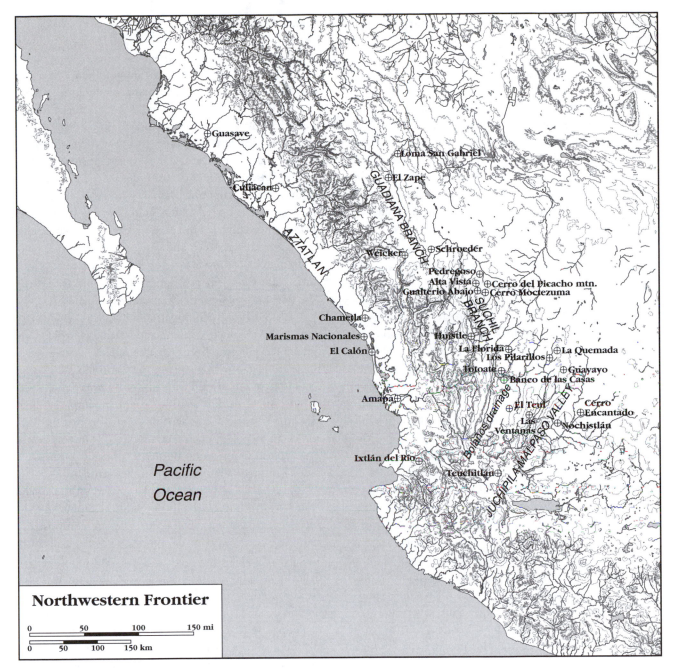

Northwestern Frontier. Map design by Mapping Specialists Limited, Madison, Wisconsin.

the region as outside Mesoamerica; a preferable position, however, is that the region is Mesoamerican because it affected, and was affected by, the stream of developments that produced the multiethnic Mesoamerican civilization. Northwestern sites bear some Mesoamerican hallmarks, such as human sacrifice, the ball game, astronomical concepts, and iconography, yet lack others such as hiero-glyphic writing and urban scale. Many changes lagged behind those of core Mesoamerica by centuries. Seden-tism appeared in the Northwest about A.D. 200–400 and later disappeared. The Spaniards, arriving in the late 1530s, found only nomadic peoples in some areas. On the other hand, the region may have been the source of such unquestionably Mesoamerican traditions as skull

N

racks and colonnaded halls, and Northwesterners were intermediaries for procuring exotic resources such as turquoise for Central Mexican and Maya peoples.

Early History

The earliest evidence of human presence, dated from the Early Paleoindian period, consists of fluted projectile points from Durango, Jalisco, and Sinaloa, as exemplified by the Weicker site (Durango). There are sporadic later Paleoindian, Early Archaic, and Middle Archaic sites. The scarcity of evidence from these periods probably reflects a paucity of archaeological work rather than an absence of early occupation.

An Archaic or Formative period anomaly, because of its unexpected monumentality at an early date, is El Calón, a coastal shell mound in the marshes of the Marismas Nacionales. The occupants built a steep-sided platform of unopened mollusk shells 25 meters in height and 7 by 10 meters in area at the summit. Radiocarbon dates from the shell average 1750 B.C., uncalibrated. The only mound-associated artifacts are clay figurines of Middle to Late Formative style; visitors may have deposited them ritually long after the mound was built. Although the surrounding area has been surveyed, it has not been possible to associate this mound definitively with any other settlements. If others existed, they may have been covered by later sediment accumulation.

The Formative period (1200 B.C.–A.D. 100) is otherwise almost unrepresented; apparently, mobile hunter-gatherers occupied the region while other Mesoamerican peoples were first settling into villages. The Northwestern Frontier also lacks very early ceramics, such as the Capacha, Pox, and Barra-Ocos traditions found farther south along the Pacific Coast. There is no Olmec presence, and the arc of shaft tombs that spans several states to the south is sharply bounded by the Santiago River, with the notable exception of the Bolaños drainage, which extends into the Northwestern Frontier. Examples of shaft tombs in the Bolaños, however, all seem to postdate A.D. 100. There is also little evidence of a Chupícuaro presence that would link this region to Formative developments in the neighboring Bajío region along the Lerma River. These patterns imply that most people in the region did not engage in Formative period experiments with economic intensification and hierarchical social organization taking place elsewhere in Mesoamerica.

Classic Period

Developments of the Classic and later periods are most conveniently described by subregion—interior or coastal—beginning in the north and moving clockwise. By A.D. 200–400, villages began to appear along the eastern side of the Sierra Madre Occidental. Archaeologists divide these early villages into two traditions, Loma San Gabriel and Chalchihuites, the latter probably representing an intrusive population. Loma sites consist of small, rectangular rooms, sometimes occurring in pairs and often surrounded by a compound wall. They tend to be on high spots, sometimes overlooking "gunsight" passes in ridges that have been bisected by a stream. Ceramics include olla-style jars as well as bowls and vases, which are either plain or decorated in simple red designs on the brown paste. Burials are found in association with some residences. The best-known sites are Weicker and Gualterio Abajo.

The Chalchihuites occupation is divided into southern and northern branches, Suchil and Guadiana, which have different settlement histories. The Suchil occupation of the south began with people of the Cañutillo phase, who seem to have intermixed with the local Loma San Gabriel population. Cañutillo ceramic designs are simple geometric patterns, incised-engraved or painted in Red on Buff, and occur on plates, open bowls, or tripod-support bowls. The typical architectural unit is a series of rooms on a raised banquette surrounding a sunken patio.

Alta Vista was the ceremonial center of the Suchil branch and was presumably its political capital. By the Alta Vista phase (A.D. 750–900), the site comprised at least three oversized patio complexes, a possible ball court, and perhaps 0.3 square kilometer of surrounding residences. Its highly distinctive public architecture included an astronomical observatory, a large colonnaded hall, a merlon-capped palace, a row of low stone columns depicting a serpent, and a temple-pyramid–altar complex, all oriented to a sacred landscape consisting of natural peaks and constructed elements such as a roadway.

Suchil people developed specialized knowledge, long-distance trade, and intensive economic activity. Local astronomers knew of the solstices and equinoxes and marked their occurrence in architecture and ceremony; today thousands come to watch a beam of light penetrate the core of the Alta Vista observatory at the summer solstice sunrise. Ancient traders brought rare minerals such as turquoise from as far away as New Mexico; evidence for jewelry-making includes finished pieces as well as manufacturing debris. Specialized potters made technically sophisticated vessels of incised-engraved, Red-on-Buff, and pseudo-cloisonné wares. Chemical and mineralogical analyses indicate that certain potters in particular villages concentrated on the production of Suchil Red-on-Buff wares.

Chalchihuites miners dug approximately 8,000 hectares of subsurface mines, removing several million cubic meters of spoil. Working by the light of torches, they used split-handled mauls to loosen conglomerate deposits beneath a hard layer of *caliche* (calcified soil), opening shafts up to a kilometer long with numerous side chambers. The materials were initially sorted inside, then hauled out to the light for disposal or further processing. The target minerals were apparently several varieties of soft white and green stone such as weathered chert, which was carved into pendants and other ornaments. Radiocarbon dates (uncalibrated) suggest that mining may have begun as early as A.D. 300, though most of it appears to have occurred during the Alta Vista phase, A.D. 700–850.

As elsewhere along the interior foothills, hundreds of sacrificial victims were displayed and deposited according to complex mortuary customs. In the Temple of the Skulls, Alta Vista residents hung the skulls and long bones of at least twenty-one people, while in the Hall of Columns they buried a decapitated Tezcatlipoca impersonator, along with an offering of special ceramics and a flute, beneath a pile of skulls and long bones. Honored individuals were placed in a crypt inside the main pyramid, and others, defleshed and disarticulated, were heaped outside the main hall. Such practices suggest ritualized warfare and sacrifice; the overwhelming majority of these deceased were young to middle-aged males. Similar deposits are found at other ceremonial centers, such as La Quemada, Los Pilarillos, Cerro del Huistle, and El Teul de González Ortega. Ordinary inhabitants, by contrast, were buried beneath the floors of rooms in smaller villages.

In deciding where to settle, Suchil people took agriculture, mining, defensibility, and cosmology into consideration. Habitation sites tended to be built closer to the mines as mining activity intensified. Some, such as Cerro Moctezuma and Cerro de los Bueyes, were located on hilltops, possibly to facilitate defense. Many villages were distributed along a roadway running northeast from Alta Vista toward Cerro del Picacho, where the summer solstice sunrise aligns with a feature in Alta Vista's observatory.

North of the Suchil branch, the Guadiana branch occupation began much later, overlapping with the last century of occupation in the Suchil branch. Something precipitated a northward migration of some Suchil population and the founding of Schroeder, Navacoyan, and other Guadiana branch settlements in the vicinity of Durango City. In this more arid terrain, major sites were located on prominences, some of which were surrounded by cliffs. The Red-on-Buff ceramic tradition continued to evolve, incorporating elements of the west coast Aztatlán tradition, especially at Cañon del Molino. Objects of copper and bronze were imported, either from the west coast or Michoacán. Pyramids apparently were no longer constructed, but the quadrilateral arrangement of rooms around patios was preserved. This occupation seems to have ended about A.D. 1300–1400. Although it was in part contemporaneous with the northern center of Casas Grandes (Paquimé), there is very little evidence of interaction with that population. The Loma San Gabriel occupation, which was prior to any Chalchihuites presence, continued throughout.

La Quemada, situated in the Malpaso Valley, was partly contemporaneous with Alta Vista. Radiocarbon dates indicate that the site was occupied from A.D. 500 to 900 and was used thereafter as a shrine. The absence or extremely low frequency of several Postclassic artifact types, such as spindle whorls, smoking pipes, and copper objects, is consistent with the apparent lack of a resident Postclassic population. This hilltop site in the Malpaso Valley covers an area of about 0.5 by 1 kilometer and includes at least three ball courts, a number of pyramids, a large hall of columns, and perhaps sixty patio-banquette complexes built atop massive artificial terraces. Various parts of the site are connected by grand staircases and causeways, some of which extend into the surrounding valley as roads. The occupants appear to have selected the location and designed the architecture to facilitate defense, since the terrace walls create steep ramparts passable only in a few places. Enclosure of the monumental core of the site is completed by natural cliffs and a masonry wall as much as 4 meters thick. Farmers grew maize and maguey in the valley, terracing some areas for soil retention.

The people of La Quemada, unlike those of Alta Vista, do not appear to have engaged in extensive mining, mineral exchange, or other specialized economic activity. Turquoise and iron pyrites have been recovered from the site, but only as 2 by 2-mm beveled pieces that were fitted into mosaics. There are no mines, workshop areas, or caches of raw materials. Obsidian is also rare; that which has been chemically identified comes from sources in northern and western Mexico, not from the more southerly Mesoamerican obsidian exchange networks. Prismatic blades are exceedingly rare. Mineral and chemical characterization of clays and ceramics shows that pottery was used and discarded in the same villages where it was made, demonstrating that ceramic production was at the household rather than workshop level. Similarly, within La Quemada different stages of chipped stone manufacturing are equally represented in different parts of the site, rather than disproportionately, as would be expected with specialization. Burials lack wealth items.

From these economic patterns, it appears that social power was based on something other than the accumulation of surplus or the acquisition of prestige goods. Internal and external social relations seem to have been founded largely on coercion and conflict; human remains are even more prevalent at La Quemada than at Alta Vista. Skulls and long bones representing perhaps four hundred individuals were heaped inside the Hall of Columns; 250 to 350 individuals were placed at the foot of a small pyramid in the Cuartel area of the site. Skulls and long bones were also hung from the ceiling of a temple, suspended in patios, and hung on exterior walls in at least one residential area. At the site of Los Pilarillos in the Malpaso Valley, a multiple burial of disarticulated bones was found in a plaza. Disarticulated human bones have turned up in virtually every excavated area at La Quemada. Ordinary inhumations, on the other hand, are found only in the smaller residential sites.

The settlement pattern around La Quemada includes an ancient road system. More than two hundred sites are known within an area of 10 by 12 kilometers, many connected directly to La Quemada by road. The sites form three clusters and are comprised of patio-banquette complexes; the largest, Los Pilarillos, is less than one-third La Quemada's size. Phase chronology is not well established. Some scholars have thought that La Quemada was a colonial outpost of the Toltecs; however, recently obtained radiocarbon dates indicate earlier growth and probable abandonment by the time the Toltec capital arose. Although it is reasonable to expect an early phase of occupation similar to Loma San Gabriel, the relevant sites have not yet been found.

La Quemada's occupation may have ended around A.D. 900. Some scholars suggest that the end was brought about by a calamitous attack and conflagration, citing burned floors and the skeletal evidence mentioned above as representing a final episode. Further support is found in a Huichol myth that describes the destruction of a tribute-collecting town situated atop a large rock and dominated by warriors. Stratigraphic evidence, however, shows that both burning and the deposition of human skeletal material were regular occurrences. The proposed episode may have been the last in a long series of hostile engagements.

La Quemada's social alliances apparently changed gradually. Up to perhaps A.D. 650, the pottery designs seem to have paralleled those of Chalchihuites. In the final century or two of occupation, a stylistic split occurred such that La Quemada ceramics came to resemble those of southern Zacatecas and the Altos region of Jalisco, and even the Bajío of Guanajuato. Some centers in southern Zacatecas, such as Las Ventanas, Nochistlan, and El Teul, were occupied later than La Quemada, and the Spaniards encountered sedentary peoples known as "Cazcanes" in these areas in the sixteenth century. The La Quemada and Chalchihuites areas, on the other hand, were occupied by nomadic Zacatecos and Guachichiles. Thus, political disintegration and dispersal created a vacuum in an area previously dotted with ceremonial centers and villages.

A social boundary marked by pronounced architectural differences apparently set off the Chalchihuites–La Quemada people from their neighbors south of the Santiago River. Following the pattern established by the Late Formative period with the shaft tomb complex, there is strong symbolic contrast between the rectangular patio complexes of the region described here and circular ones built by the Teuchitlan peoples to the south. Also following the Formative pattern, the Bolaños drainage represents an intrusion of the southern architectural pattern into the north, for instance at Totoate and La Florida.

On the coast, the developmental sequence was similar to that of the interior in being delayed relative to Mesoamerica as a whole, but it had its own patterns of material culture expression and timing. During the Classic period, coastal peoples built small villages that apparently consisted of thatched dwellings arranged in no particular order, as at Amapa and Culiacán. There was no monumental architecture. More grandiose Mesoamerican-style mound-and-plaza complexes, marking greater social differentiation, did not appear until the Epiclassic or possibly the Early Postclassic. In the Cerritos phase at Amapa, earthen mounds up to 110 meters long were built in groups around plazas as large as 50 by 75 meters in area. From a burial-associated clay model, it would appear that some mounds were capped by elaborate buildings. The model shows a truncated pyramid mound with an elevated central platform ascended by a staircase. Attributes of the staircase match adobe stairway fragments encountered during excavation. In the model, low colonnaded buildings on either side flank the higher central structure, probably a temple, which has a stela-like upright element in front of its doorway. Amapa's residents also built a ball court measuring 35 by 70 meters and consisting of a playing alley and end courts—the only example known in the coastal region of the Northwestern Frontier.

With the introduction of mounds, plazas, and the ball court came several technological developments. Potters had already been manufacturing fairly elaborate Red-on-Buff, polychrome, and engraved ceramics, but they now began to decorate their wares in the lively incised polychrome designs of the Aztatlán tradition. The predominant vessel form is an open bowl, sometimes with a ring base. Mold-made figurines, typical of the Early Postclassic period in Central Mexico, partially replaced the hand-modeled types of the earlier phases. Other ceramic objects include smoking pipes, whistles, spindle whorls, mirror backings, plaques, stamps, beads, earspools, and labrets. Most notably, people began to use metal artifacts. Copper and copper alloys were used to manufacture rings, bracelets, beads, tubes, bells, fishhooks, tweezers, awls, pins, and needles. Obsidian prismatic blades were found among the chipped stone remains.

During the Postclassic period, many of these material culture traditions continued. More mound-plaza complexes were added at Amapa, and ceramic decoration evolved into a style sometimes called Mixteca-Puebla. Chametla was abandoned, but Culiacán's occupation continued. A new center, representing the farthest extension of the Aztatlán tradition, was founded at Guasave in the Late Postclassic period. Motifs emphasized in Aztatlán ceramics include human faces, full human bodies in contorted positions with exaggerated heads, animals (costumed dancers?), and feather bundles. Geometric motifs such as chevrons, scrolls, stepped frets, and the "lazy S" are also common; shapes of decorated vessels include jars and tripod-support jars as well as the previously encountered open and ring-based bowls. Effigy vessels, though not common, are also present.

The economic basis of the coastal populations apparently included maize cultivation, since archaeologists find only two-handed manos and trough metates, though both are infrequent. A surprising aspect of subsistence is that some people who lived quite close to the coast apparently did not exploit the sea for food. At Amapa, all documented fish bones are of freshwater species, and no bones of the sea turtle, a tremendous food resource, are reported. A single whale bone almost certainly represents scavenging of a beached specimen. Other sites, however, reflect the intensive collection of oysters and other edible shellfish.

So far as is known, coastal people did not construct mines; their most specialized resource extraction may have been the collection of shells for trade. However, the presence of craft specialists, or least access to the specialists' products, is suggested by the abundance of fine items of ceramics, metal, and chipped stone. At Amapa, direct evidence of metallurgy includes seven pieces of slag that bear traces of copper. One can also imagine a role for specialists in the sacred knowledge that went into the construction and orientation of mounds, ball courts, and buildings.

Coastal burial patterns show evidence of warfare, but less so than in the interior. Complete skeletons accompanied by trophy skulls were found in the cemeteries, as well as decapitated individuals. A multiple burial was found at Chametla; its condition did not permit evaluation for defleshing or disarticulation. Coastal centers such as Chametla, Culiacán, and Guasave have urn burials, which by nature are indicative of disarticulation, given the difficulty of inserting a whole body into the typical 30-cm orifice of the vessel. At Amapa, a layer of cremated remains and trophy skulls was found in the upper levels of a small mound. Mortuary treatment does not seem to have been used to mark elevated social status. Although a range of burial accompaniments has been found, no sharp distinction for any individual or class has been observed. The apparent contrast between this and the architectural evidence suggests the presence of political hierarchy, but not its strong development.

Interregional and External Interactions

The northward spread of Mesoamerican lifeways was a product of social interactions and relations. Were the northern centers colonies or dependencies of larger states in Central Mexico? Probably not, since most florescences in the Northwest Frontier occurred when Teotihuacan, the most likely sponsor of any distant colonial enterprise, was in decline. Alta Vista, founded in the Classic, is an exception, but even Alta Vista grew vigorously after A.D. 600. History and linguistics reveal that at the time of European contact, the coastal and interior populations were politically independent from one another and from the Aztecs and Tarascans. Two separate polities controlled the coast; several other less sedentary groups held the sierra and the interior foothills. For the ancient past, architectural and artifactual patterns suggest several different coastal and interior populations interacting while maintaining traditions distinctly their own.

In the interior, the strongest expressions of Mesoamericanization occurred in the Classic and Epiclassic periods with the formation of the Chalchihuites and La Quemada polities. Archaeologists continue to investigate the possibility that mining at Chalchihuites developed to meet demands for mineral resources by elites in Central Mexico. The strongest stylistic ties in the interior, however, are to populations in areas such as the Altos, Malpaso-Juchipila, and Bajío regions, not to Central Mexico. On the coast, the strongest links are to nearby river populations such as Ixtlán del Río, and across the Sierra Madre, to the Guadiana branch of Chalchihuites. Some archaeologists also recognize stylistic resemblances to the southern Pacific Coast. The coastal region exhibited its greatest links to the rest of Mesoamerica in the Postclassic period. Of the three waves of West Mexican–South American interaction, represented by early ceramics, shaft tombs, and metallurgy, the coastal Northwestern Frontier participated only in the last. This exchange pattern perhaps indicates a northward shift in a network that once had ended at the Santiago River.

People of the Northwestern Frontier also interacted with groups farther north, in the U.S. Southwest, through trade and communication routes along both sides of the sierra. Archaeologists and chemists have demonstrated several patterns of movement, including those of copper, turquoise, and shell. Objects of these materials undoubtedly had social and sacred connotations associated with the remote places from which they were obtained.

When Nuño de Guzmán arrived in 1530, native towns were strung along rivers such as the Santiago, Acoponeta, Chametla, Piaxtla, and Culiacán. The Spaniards, noting that many people lived on artificial mounds, declared the food to be abundant and the population dense. Chametla had at least twenty subject villages, Culiacán perhaps two hundred. The sizes and internal political structure of these polities are unclear in the documents; however, they fielded several thousand warriors. Despite the explorers' known penchant for exaggeration, corroborative evidence makes the accounts plausible. The coastal population numbered a few hundred thousand. It was catastrophically reduced in two years as the Spaniards systematically attacked, sacked, and burned village after village, bringing

to an end a native history stretching back at least to the mound of El Calón, built more than three thousand years earlier.

FURTHER READINGS

Armillas, P. 1969. The Arid Frontier of Mexican Civilization. *Transactions of the New York Academy of Sciences* (2nd series)31:697–704.

Braniff, B., and M.-A. Hers. 1998. Herencias Chichimecas. *Arqueologia* (2nd series)19: 55–80.

Ekholm, G. 1942. *Excavations at Guasave, Sinaloa.* American Museum of Natural History, Anthropological Papers, 38, part 2. New York.

Foster, M. 1985. The Loma San Gabriel Occupation of Zacatecas and Durango, Mexico. In M. S. Foster and P. C. Weigand (eds.), *The Archaeology of North and West Mesoamerica,* pp. 327–351. Boulder: Westview Press.

Hers, M.-A. 1989. *Los Toltecas en Tierras Chichimecas.* Mexico City: Universidad Nacional Autónoma de México.

Holien, T., and R. B. Pickering. 1978. Analogues in a Chalchihuites Culture Sacrificial Burial to Late Mesoamerican Ceremonialism. In E. Pasztory (ed.), *Middle Classic Mesoamerica: A.D. 400–700,* pp. 145–157. New York: Columbia University Press.

Hosler, D. 1994. *The Sounds and Colors of Power.* Cambridge, Mass.: MIT Press.

Kelley, J. 1971. Archaeology of the Northern Frontier: Zacatecas and Durango. In G. F. Ekholm and I. Bernal (eds.), *Handbook of Middle American Indians,* vol. 11, *Archaeology of Northern Mesoamerica,* part 2, pp. 768–804. Austin: University of Texas Press.

Kelly, I. 1945. Excavations at Culiacán, Sinaloa. *Iberoamericana* 25.

Meighan, C. (ed.). 1976. *The Archaeology of Amapa, Nayarit.* Monumenta Archaeológica 2. Los Angeles: Institute of Archaeology, University of California.

Nelson, B., J. Darling, and D. Kice. 1992. Mortuary Practices and the Social Order at La Quemada, Zacatecas. *Latin American Antiquity* 3:298–315.

Scott, S. 1999. The Marismas Nacionales Project, Sinaloa and Nayarit, Mexico. In M. Blake (ed.), *Pacific Latin America in Prehistory: The Evolution of Archaic and Formative Cultures,* pp. 13–24. Pullman: Washington State University Press.

Trombold, C. 1991. Causeways in the Context of Strategic Planning in the La Quemada Region, Zacatecas, Mexico. In C. Trombold (ed.), *Ancient Road Networks* and *Settlement Hierarchies in the New World,* pp. 145–168. Cambridge: Cambridge University Press.

Weigand, P., and G. Harbottle. 1992. Turquoise in Pre-Columbian America. *Scientific American* 266:78–85.

Ben A. Nelson

SEE ALSO

Northern Arid Zone; Quemada, La

Nosara (Guanacaste, Costa Rica)

In the dry, tropical environment of the Nosara Valley, aboriginal occupation consists of habitation sites and cemeteries dating from 300 B.C. to A.D. 1350. The cemeteries are primarily from the Bagaces period, A.D. 300–800, and are situated on the surrounding hilltops and slopes, in concentrated groups of 50 to 100 or more, in individual locations. Skeletal preservation was poor; grave goods included ceramics, jade pendants (jadeite source unknown), carved stone, and mace heads.

Other artifacts from the region are ceramics (including White-slipped ceramics from Pacific Nicaragua) and carved stone stools *(metates).* Similar Bagaces period sites exist in the general area and on the foothills along the Pacific Coast.

FURTHER READINGS

Guerrero, J. V. 1986. Recientes investigaciones en el Valle de Nosara. *Journal of the Steward Anthropological Society* 14(1982–1983):171–188.

Lange, F. W. 1977. Estudios arqueológicos en el Valle de Nosara, Costa Rica. *Vínculos* 3:27–36.

Lange, F. W., D. J. Bernstein, M. Siegel, and D. Tase. 1974. Preliminary Archaeological Research in the Nosara Valley. *Folk* 18:47–60.

Frederick W. Lange

SEE ALSO

Huacas, Las

Oaxaca and Tehuantepec Region

The Valley of Oaxaca and Tehuantepec are part of an environmentally diverse area, now the state of Oaxaca (Mexico), where human occupation dates back to Paleoindian times. Later in prehistory Oaxaca's most notable indigenous peoples, the Zapotec and Mixtec, are credited with some of Mesoamerica's greatest cultural achievements. Better known is the Zapotec civilization, which arose in the Oaxaca Valley. Tehuantepec became the seat of the Zapotec domain after the paramount ruler and many of his followers, under Mixtec pressure, migrated there from the Oaxaca Valley toward the end of the fifteenth century.

Environment

Although the entire area lies within the tropics, the 1,500-meter elevation of the Oaxaca Valley ameliorates the torrid temperatures of the adjacent coastal lowland. Both regions have a distinct summer rainy season extending from May through October, during which almost all appreciable precipitation occurs.

Physiographically, the Oaxaca Valley is part of the Mesa del Sur, the rugged, east–west-trending mountains within the Southern Mexican Highlands. It embraces a broad expanse of 1,200 square kilometers of open farmland in an area of otherwise narrow, deeply cut valleys. The Atoyac River and its tributary, the Salado, cut through the three arms of the Y-shaped valley, providing alluvial soils with good agricultural potential; however, with annual precipitation ranging from a scant 300 mm to rarely over 1,000 mm, small-scale irrigation has been employed for more than 1,500 years to expand the farming area beyond the riverine zone. Where the three arms

of the valley intersect, there are several low peaks, one of which, Monte Albán, is the site of the ancient capital of the Zapotec state.

In the past, tropical evergreen forests flourished along the rivers of the Oaxaca Valley, while farther back, where the water table is lower, mesquite and other deciduous trees dominated. Agave *(maguey),* organ cacti, and other xerophytic plants typified the thorny vegetation of the drier piedmont fringes. The surrounding mountains, rising 3,000 meters above sea level, were once blanketed by pine-oak woodland, with cloud forest at higher elevations. Today much of this cover has been lost to harvesting and agricultural clearance.

About 150 kilometers southeast of the Oaxaca Valley, the Mesa del Sur downfaults to the Isthmus of Tehuantepec, a narrow depression separating the mountains of southern Mexico from their southeastern extension into Central America. At the isthmus, a distance of only 200 kilometers separates the Pacific and Gulf coasts, and at the divide between the two watersheds the altitude is a mere 250 meters. On the Pacific side, referred to here as the Tehuantepec region, soils are fertile. Although 500 to 1,700 mm of rain fall each summer, severe evapotranspiration from high temperatures (averaging over 38° C at the onset of the rainy season) and an almost unrelenting north wind create a mean annual moisture deficit. Today canal irrigation extends the agricultural growing season beyond the rainy months, but the time depth of this practice is uncertain.

Between the more verdant piedmont and the coastal lagoon and estuarine zone, the broad plains of Tehuantepec, where uncleared for agriculture, support a low, thorny deciduous forest, dotted with columnar cactus,

O

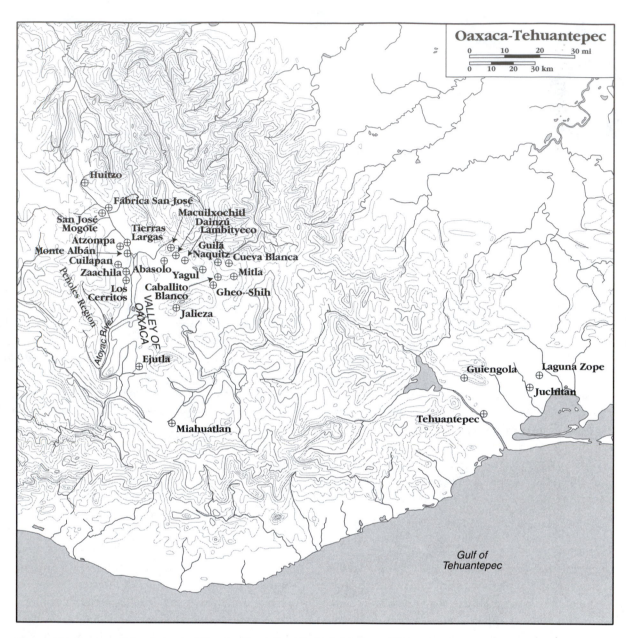

Oaxaca-Tehuantepec. Map design by Mapping Specialists Limited, Madison, Wisconsin.

other succulents, and the occasional guanacaste (*Entero-lobium*) tree. Along the coast, subsistence potential was enhanced by the abundant seafood and waterfowl. Farther inland, white-tailed and brocket deer, peccary, and a host of smaller animals were hunted in pre-Columbian times.

Early Occupation

The Oaxaca area was first settled during the last Ice Age by a small number of mobile hunters and wild-food gatherers. The initial time of late Pleistocene colonization is unknown, but the lowest stratigraphic levels of excavations at Cueva Blanca, a cliffside cave site near Mitla, in the eastern (Tlacolula) arm of the Oaxaca Valley, indicate occupation by 10,000 B.C., if not earlier. From these levels archaeologists have recovered bones of tortoise, fox, antelope, rabbit, deer, and various birds, apparently burned and broken by the human inhabitants of the cave in the course of food preparation. No stone tools or other artifacts accompanied the faunal remains, but on the valley floor not far away was a fragment of a fluted spear point resembling the Clovis type that was widely distributed in

North America 12,000 years ago. The cave appears to have been occupied seasonally by a "microband" of perhaps four to eight related individuals. The valley was sparsely populated, probably by fewer than 150 people at a density of no more than one person per 9 square kilometers.

At Guilá Naquitz, another rock shelter near Cueva Blanca, occupational levels define a subsequent Naquitz phase dated from about 8900 to 6700 B.C. The Naquitz phase marks the beginning of a period, referred to as the Archaic in Mesoamerica, when people began to abandon the Late Paleoinidan hunting-and-gathering lifestyle for one that ultimately led to settled village life based on an agricultural economy. Lithic technology remained simple, producing mainly unstandardized flake tools, but also cobblestone *metates* and one-handed *manos,* implements for grinding seeds and other plant foods. Wild plant foods included acorns, supplemented by other nuts, mesquite seeds and pods, maguey hearts, prickly-pear leaves and fruits, hackberries, onions, and runner beans; these furnished an important dietary component for the small family bands occupying the rock shelter during fall seasons. Squash seeds and stalks and fragments of bottle gourds may be evidence of early experiments with plant domestication—for food, the other for use as water containers. Agave and yucca fibers were used to make knotted nets and coiled baskets; wood fragments reveal the manufacture of firedrills, roasting skewers, and possibly *atlatl* (spear-thrower) dart shafts. Considering the abundant bone remains of cottontail rabbits, mud turtles, collared peccary, raccoons, various birds, and other small animals, the use of traps could account for the apparent dearth of projectile points.

Spear and *atlatl* dart points, most commonly of the short-stemmed Pedernales type, are more abundant at Gheo-Shih, a 1.5-hectare open-air camp in the Tlacolula arm. At Gheo-Shih, type site for the Jácaras phase, tentatively dated at 5000–4000 B.C., about twenty-five related persons are thought to have joined to form a temporary "macroband" when the rainy season made more food available. Oval patterns of rocks on the ground may mark the foundations of crude temporary shelters. A particularly intriguing architectural feature consists of two parallel lines of boulders, about 20 meters from end to end, spaced 7 meters apart, enclosing an area that had been swept clean of the stone tools and other discarded artifacts that elsewhere littered the site. The enclosure is said to resemble the ceremonial "dance grounds" built by historic period hunter-gatherers of the North American Great

Basin. Maize or teosinte pollen recovered during excavations at Gheo-Shih suggests further tentative steps toward plant cultivation.

The two final phase of the Oaxaca Valley Archaic—Blanca, dated approximately 3300–2800 B.C., and Martínez, ending about 2200 B.C.—show a proliferation of food-processing tools and botanical remains, further evidence of the transition from foraging to agriculture. By the Blanca phase, domesticated maize was widely cultivated in the valley, as elsewhere in highland Mesoamerica.

No evidence of Paleoindian or Archaic period habitation has yet been recovered from Tehuantepec, a fact attributable to the deep alluvial stratigraphy and poor organic preservation in the coastal lowlands. Archaic period sites are found just to the southeast along the Chiapas coast and on the Gulf side of the isthmus, so there is reason to suppose that Tehuantepec too was occupied by this time. Indeed, there is evidence that the rich biodiversity of the coastal habitat may have supported some of Mesoamerica's earliest permanent settlements, predating the development of agriculture. While the Archaic foragers in places such as the Oaxaca Valley had to schedule a series of annual movements within the patchy highland habitat to take advantage of the seasonal availability of wild plants and animals, their contemporaries in coastal locations such as Tehuantepec, with ample food near at hand, could easily have established year-round settlements.

Formative Period

Archaeologists debate whether the initial transformation to an agricultural economy in Mesoamerica was a highland phenomenon, necessitated because wild food resources proved insufficient in the face of population growth and/or post-Pleistocene environmental change, or whether it developed because highland foragers wanted better to manage unpredictable plant food availability in the face of variable annual rainfall. Alternatively, agriculture might have originated in the Lowlands when already sedentary wild-food collectors sought to enhance their prestige through the production and exchange of food surpluses. An independent lowland development of agriculture, if it occurred at all, may have been based on a different set of cultigens, particularly starchy root crops, which would have supplemented the protein-rich seafood resources of the coast. Whatever the explanation (or explanations), it is indisputable that by the end of the Archaic period, about 2000 B.C., domesticated plants, especially maize, beans, and squash, had become the mainstay of the Mesoamerican diet in both highlands and lowlands.

O

The Early Formative period is distinguished by the appearance of agriculturally supported permanent villages, the development of ceramic technology, and the widespread growth of long-distance exchange networks. Extending from about 2000 to 1100 B.C., it was also a time when regional cultural diversity proliferated. In the Oaxaca Valley, pottery found at the villages of Tierras Largas and San José Mogote rivals Tehuacan's Purron ceramic complex as Mesoamerica's very earliest. Designated the Esperidión ceramic complex and dated to 1900–1400 B.C., the pottery consists mainly of undecorated, press-molded *ollas* (low-necked jars) and hemispherical bowls, seemingly modeled after gourds. A crude figurine head in the form of a feline is the Valley's oldest example of ceramic art.

Small wattle-and-daub houses at San José Mogote and Tierras Largas, with associated burials, storage pits, ovens, and other features, are typical of the eighteen to twenty settlements that had sprung up in the Oaxaca Valley by the Tierras Largas phase (1400–1150 B.C.). Most of the settlements were little more than 3-hectare hamlets, each composed of several households. An important exception was San José Mogote, which had grown to 7 or 8 hectares, with a population approaching 150. One wattle-and-daub Tierras Largas phase structure at San José Mogote is called Oaxaca's first known "public building" because of its large size, lime plaster floor and wall surfacing, altarlike interior structure, orientation to 8° west of north, and other features prefiguring those of later civic or ceremonial buildings in the valley. San José Mogote may have become the ritual and economic center of the valley's Etla arm.

Tierras Largas phase pottery shares elements of a horizon style that extends over much of Early Formative central and southern Mesoamerica. The most common Oaxaca Valley vessel forms continued to be hemispherical bowls and ollas, although flat-bottomed bowls with outslanting walls, *tecomates* (pumpkin-shaped jars), and bottles were also produced. Red slip, stripes, or rim bands, rocker or dentate stamping, and gadroon decorate the otherwise buff, burnished exteriors. Long-distance trade for exotic items, such as ornamental seashells from the Pacific Coast, expanded as the demand for status-marking and ritual preciosities increased.

Far less is known about Tehuantepec during the Early Formative. Lagunita, the first established cultural phase, dated at 1500–1100 B.C., was identified from excavations at Laguna Zope, a small hamlet at the time but destined to become the region's largest and most important Formative period settlement. Laguna Zope is situated 1 kilometer east of the Río de los Perros, at a point about 10 kilometers upstream from where the river empties into the lagoons that separate the mainland from the open Pacific Ocean. It was almost surely just one of a number of Lagunita phase villages situated along the eight small rivers that cut across the semiarid coastal plain.

No direct evidence of maize agriculture dating to this early phase has been recovered, equivalent to the maize, beans, squash, chile pepper, and other plant remains found in the Oaxaca Valley, although contemporaneous remains of domesticated maize are known from just down the coast in Chiapas. Small obsidian flakes, imported from quarries 400 to 500 kilometers away in highland Central Mexico and Guatemala, suggest to some researchers that these flakes served as the teeth of graters, similar to those used in South America for processing domesticated manioc. Hunting, trapping, and fishing are well documented by the abundant bone remains recovered at Laguna Zope, including bones of white-tailed deer, rabbit, armadillo, iguana, rat, and various birds. Evidence of catfish, snapper, jack, mullet, shark, and freshwater mussels indicates that fish and shellfish also contributed substantially to the diet.

Lagunita phase pottery was very well made, most closely resembling that of neighboring regions along the Pacific coast of Chiapas and Guatemala, but with enough similarity in design to indicate communication with the Oaxaca Valley as well. Flat-bottomed bowls, bottles, *tecomates,* and *ollas* were typical, many with highly burnished, brushed, or wiped buff-colored clay exteriors, some covered with a white slip, others black-smudged or with specular red-painted rims and zones of linear decoration. One or two circumferential lines were commonly incised on the exterior rims of *tecomates,* and straight or curvilinear lines embellished the exterior walls, often enclosing zones of red painting, brushing, rocker-stamping, gadroon, and other forms of plastic decoration. We also find one of Mesoamerica's earliest manifestations of a technically sophisticated differential firing technique, which produced white-rimmed bowls with black exteriors and/or interiors.

The centuries between about 1100 and 800 B.C. were a time of enormous change in the Oaxaca Valley and Tehuantepec, as elsewhere in Mesoamerica. Subsistence almost everywhere by this time was increasingly rooted in agriculture, as more productive varieties were developed. The agricultural economy probably promoted a concept of land ownership or usufruct, since the labor investment in cultivating crops militated against the rights of others to share the harvest. Cultivation of a storable grain such as maize enabled much larger populations to live together and to weather times of poor harvest. Individual differences in wealth and power would have widened as a limited number of landholding farmers gained control over the production and distribution of food supplies.

San José Mogote and Laguna Zope

Facilitated by agriculture's economic potential, in both the Oaxaca Valley and Tehuantepec one community remained many orders of magnitude larger than its neighbors. While most San José phase settlements in the valley ranged from 1 to 3 hectares, San José Mogote had grown to more than 70 hectares, with an estimated population as high as seven hundred; similarly, Golfo phase Laguna Zope, at more than 40 hectares, had grown sixfold to a population of perhaps four hundred. The principal settlements in both the Oaxaca Valley and Tehuantepec grew not only in size but also in social complexity, a probable result of their serving as centers of regional craft production, interregional trade, and ceremonialism. In these settlements high-status individuals were treated to more elaborate burials, accompanied by jade ornaments and other precious goods. Some of the fancy pottery associated with elite households was decorated with the jaguar paw-wing, fire serpent, and other motifs recognized as status markers throughout much of early Middle Formative Mesoamerica.

The elite lived in larger, more ornate houses and had greater access to the procurement and local distribution of imported products, such as obsidian from Central Mexico and Guatemala, just as they controlled the production and disposition of locally made luxury goods. The elite of San José Mogote, for example, possessed larger amounts of ornamental seashells from faraway coastal sites such as Laguna Zope, and in turn they governed the local manufacture and export of decorative iron-ore mirrors. Increasingly, access to luxury goods became a symbol of high status in Middle Formative Mesoamerica. The elites of San José Mogote and Laguna Zope typified a widespread Mesoamerican phenomenon that saw the inhabitants of previously egalitarian communities become segregated into socially if not economically differentiated ranks, creating societies similar in structure to ethnographically known chiefdoms. Religion probably chartered the special status of upper-rank individuals, who may have claimed descent from a tribal deity.

Through the later centuries of the Middle Formative, ending around 500 B.C., rapid development continued in both the Oaxaca Valley and Tehuantepec. Having expanded to 60 or 70 hectares and an estimated population of one thousand during the Guadalupe and Rosario phases (850–500 B.C.), San José Mogote retained its place as the principal settlement in the Oaxaca Valley, and its Etla territory remained the most populous. By then a few minor centers had appeared, marked by mound construction and a size somewhat larger than the 1 to 3 hectares typical of the more than seventy or eighty other farming hamlets allied hierarchically to them. Small-scale irrigation, drawing on shallow wells, was introduced early in this period to increase agricultural production. Important residential and public buildings were being constructed of stucco-covered adobe bricks. Of all the construction, none rivaled that at San José Mogote, where limestone blocks—some weighing more than a ton—were hauled 5 kilometers to transform a natural hill into a monumental central acropolis.

That the developing hierarchy of prestige and power among valley communities may not have been achieved without conflict is indicated by a large, flat stone set into the floor of a narrow passageway connecting two buildings on the San José Mogote acropolis. Carved on the face of the monolith is the stylized image of a naked, prostrate man, blood spewing from a wound in his chest. The placement of the stone on the passageway floor suggests an attempt to debase the individual depicted by having his image trod upon by passers-by. Further humiliation was achieved by the nudity, a sign of indignity in ancient Mesoamerican culture. Archaeologists interpret this stone carving as ancestral to the later "Danzantes" of Monte Albán. Many see it as a representation of a captive leader or sacrificial victim from a rival valley community. Between the man's legs are two engraved hieroglyphs depicting the date "1 Earthquake," probably his birthday in the 260-day Mesoamerican ritual calendar. (Dates in this calendrical system were calculated by cycling the numbers 1 through 13 against twenty named days; birthdates typically served as a person's name.) The inscription is the earliest known example in Mesoamerica of the use of the ritual calendar.

A somewhat different pattern of settlement evolved during the corresponding years of the later Middle Formative in the Tehuantepec region. There, no secondary centers grew to challenge Ríos phase Laguna Zope, which between 800 and 400 B.C. had expanded to an estimated 90 hectares in size, its maximum spatial extent. Not only was Laguna Zope Tehuantepec's unrivaled center for the export of locally obtained ornamental seashell; it had also

O

become an important node in the extensive long-distance exchange network for other exotic goods, such as obsidian from Central Mexico and highland Guatemala. This long-distance exchange had its counterpart in a widespread sharing of ceramic styles. Best known of these horizon styles is the so-called double-line-break, a decorative motif consisting of two circumferential lines, one continuous and the other broken, typically incised just below the inner lip of white-slipped, flat-bottomed, outslanting-wall bowls. Buff-colored wares of various forms continued to be employed for utilitarian purposes, along with other longstanding local types, most notably differentially fired black-and-white ware.

Monte Albán

Around 500 B.C., an event of unprecedented significance in the Oaxaca Valley occurred with the founding of Monte Albán as the capital of a confederation of the region's rival, chiefdom-level Zapotec polities. Perched high above the valley floor at the summit of a steep-sided, previously uninhabited hill, Monte Albán was probably selected for its defensibility, locational centrality at the juncture of the three valley arms, and political neutrality, and possibly for its importance as a religious shrine. Once established, it replaced San José Mogote as the valley's principal settlement, growing within one century into a civic-religious center with an estimated population of as many as five thousand people, mostly drawn from surrounding communities.

The creation of the Monte Albán confederacy may not have been entirely consensual. Most archaeologists subscribe to the hypothesis that the gallery of more than three hundred "Danzantes" carved on stone slabs originally set into the wall of a building on Monte Albán's main plaza reflects interpolity strife. Dating to period Monte Albán I, the earliest phase of occupation at the center, the "Danzantes" are variously construed as dancers, swimmers, royal ancestors, castrated priests, men in religious trance, or shamans. The most widely accepted interpretation is that the nude figures—in twisted poses, eyes closed in death, some with blood spouting from their genitals—represent slain captives or sacrificial victims. They could have served as visual propaganda aimed at striking fear into those within or outside the valley who might have questioned the authority of the Monte Albán polity.

The initial success of the Zapotec confederation was marked by explosive population growth. Nearly half of the forty thousand inhabitants of the Oaxaca Valley at 200–100 B.C., the end of the period Monte Albán I,

resided at Monte Albán, which had developed into a densely settled urban center. A multitiered hierarchy of subsidiary centers was also expanded to administer the hinterland population, funneling surplus food and other products into Monte Albán and regulating the movement of goods produced by rural farmers and craft specialists.

Beginning with the period Monte Albán II, an ambitious project was undertaken to level the entire Monte Albán hilltop, creating a gigantic, stucco-paved Main Plaza. Among the structures built on and around the plaza was the first of seven I-shaped ball courts. At the base of the hill, construction of a defensive wall, begun during the previous period, was completed; this suggests problems attendant on the rapid Zapotec expansion and its aggressive efforts to procure goods needed to nurture its burgeoning bureaucracy. A 19 percent decline in valley population during the four to five centuries of Monte Albán II has been attributed to an outward movement to colonize adjacent regions.

The nature of the Terminal Formative unrest may be better understood through an examination of approximately fifty "conquest slabs" displayed on the walls of arrowhead-shaped Building J at the south center of Monte Albán's Main Plaza. Carved on each of the stone slabs is a hieroglyphic "hill sign," below an identifying place glyph or glyphs, with an inverted human head sometimes depicted below. It is believed that these stone carvings record places outside the Oaxaca Valley subjugated by a growing Zapotec state. Not all the places named on the slabs may actually have been forcefully conquered; some may have been more peacefully colonized, and others may merely have been targets of Zapotec economic exploitation. The Zapotecs appear to have decided that their appetite for exotic goods could, where feasible, be more effectively satisfied by commanding tribute than through reciprocal trade.

Some archaeologists disagree with the idea that there was an imperialistic Zapotec state at 200 B.C.–A.D. 300. Instead, they posit state formation much later, during the Classic period, attributing signs of Monte Albán II conflict to localized strife between valley chiefdoms competing for scarce agricultural land. Under this interpretation, Terminal Formative Monte Albán would have been just another Oaxaca Valley chiefdom, albeit the largest and most successful.

Tehuantepec in the Late Formative Period

Tehuantepec was never a victim of Zapotec imperialism during the period Monte Albán II, although it remained a source of goods for the Oaxaca Valley elite. Zapotec efforts at conquest or colonization seem rarely to have been directed beyond a distance of about 150 kilometers from Monte Albán imperialism, or to areas where they encountered militarily strong polities. Notwithstanding its political autonomy, Tehuantepec maintained cultural as well as economic ties with the Zapotec state, as evidenced by the adoption of a burnished grayware ceramic tradition, unmistakably related to the pottery of Monte Albán. The new Tehuantepec styles replaced the eastward-looking Usulutan ware and Maya-related lustrous-waxy slipped tradition of the previous Goma phase (400–200 B.C.).

Tehuantepec's economic importance to the Zapotec state was based in part on its role as a major source of the ornamental seashell that had come to serve as a status marker throughout much of Mesoamerica. At Laguna Zope during the final Kuak and Niti phases of occupation (200 B.C.–A.D. 1, A.D. 1–300), even the procurement of seashell and the production of shell ornaments appears to have been limited exclusively to the elite. Significantly, shell species such as *Spondylus, Ostrea, Strumbus, Oliva, Olivella,* and others collected by the high-ranking inhabitants of Laguna Zope are identical to those found at Ejutla, a settlement just south of the Oaxaca Valley, whose role seems to have been that of a gateway for Zapotec importation of seashell and perhaps other exotic goods from the coastal lowlands.

For reasons not yet understood, Laguna Zope was abandoned around A.D. 300. After almost two millennia as Tehuantepec's principal center, it was replaced by a settlement a few kilometers to the east, alongside the Río de los Perros, on the outskirts of the present-day town of Juchitán. At an area of 68 hectares, the new Saltillo center during the Early Classic Xuku phase (A.D. 300–600) was slightly smaller than the Laguna Zope settlement it supplanted, although population in the Tehuantepec region as a whole appears to have increased with the establishment of a number of new communities. Grayware was replaced by a local tradition of fine-paste kaolin pottery decorated with incised or red-painted lines and resist designs of geometric and avian forms, suggesting that cultural and economic ties to the Oaxaca Valley were less important. Also ended was the more than thirteen-century tradition of differentially fired black-and-white ware in Tehuantepec. A completely oxidized coarse whiteware took its place.

Classic Period in the Oaxaca Valley
The Early Classic was a time when many regions of Mesoamerica fell under the cultural and economic influence of the powerful central Mexican civilization at Teotihuacan, but Tehuantepec appears to have been excluded. Despite its location along the main route from Teotihuacan to important obsidian and cacao sources in Guatemala, there is no evidence that Tehuantepec developed any significant exchange relationship with Teotihuacan. Indirectly, however, Teotihuacan's rise to power may have been responsible for the diminished relationship between Tehuantepec and Monte Albán, as the latter responded to Teotihuacan dominance by withdrawing from outlying zones and consolidating its hegemony at home, leaving places like Tehuantepec to pursue their own courses.

The two great civilizations, Monte Albán and Teotihuacan, appear to have maintained a cordial if wary relationship. One barrio at Teotihuacan housed a group probably composed of Zapotec merchants from the Oaxaca Valley, while images of Teotihuacan dignitaries appear on stone monuments at Monte Albán. Other stone monuments at Monte Albán depict royal Zapotec personages, a shift from the previous militaristic emphasis on subjugation.

In the Oaxaca Valley Monte Albán III period (A.D. 300–750), growth continued unabated, concentrated for the first couple of centuries at and around subsidiary centers such as Dainzú, Jalieza, Macuilxochitl, and Tlacochahuaya, which began to approach Monte Albán in size. During the second half of the period, the situation reversed as development shifted back to the area around Monte Albán, apparently the consequence of a failed agricultural expansion into the peripheral piedmont zones of the valley. By the end of Monte Albán III, almost twenty-five thousand of the valley's eighty thousand inhabitants lived at the Zapotec civic and religious capital. Construction of the main plaza was completed, its perimeter ringed by stone masonry palaces, two-room temples, royal tombs, and other structures, effectively limiting access to all but Monte Albán's upper-class residents.

At the north and south ends of the Main Plaza, monumental platform complexes were built; the northern complex probably served as the residence of the supreme Zapotec ruler. Aside from the ruler and a limited number of the elite, most of Monte Albán's residents lived below the Main Plaza area on many terraces cut into the steep hillside. Most were farmers and craftspeople. The pottery they manufactured was produced in a limited number of standardized but poorly made forms. In other parts of the valley, local centers also served as pottery producers for their sustaining areas.

O

By A.D. 750, the beginning of period Monte Albán IV, the Zapotec metropolis and its integrative role in the Oaxaca Valley had begun to deteriorate. Over the next 250 years the Main Plaza fell into disrepair, and population dwindled to fewer than four thousand as the inhabitants of the former capital abandoned it for settlements in other parts of the Valley. Instead of a single sovereign power, Zapotec political control shifted to a number of smaller centers, some located with an eye to defensibility. Of these, Jalieza was the largest, with a population of sixteen thousand.

The cause for Monte Albán's collapse is uncertain, but it is likely to have been related, at least in part, to the concurrent disintegration of Teotihuacan. Without the menace of Teotihuacan to the north, the valley's inhabitants may no longer have considered it worthwhile to remain united under an expensive centralized polity. Hieroglyphic writing, previously limited to Monte Albán, began to appear at other major settlements throughout the valley. Inscriptions carved on small stone "genealogical registers" in royal tombs at these settlements describe marriage alliances and other events aimed at integrating the otherwise competing valley centers.

Classic Period in Tehuantepec

No such political upheaval occurred in the Tehuantepec region during the Late Classic Tixum phase (A.D. 600–900). New communities were established, but the primary population center continued to be Saltillo, which had grown to about 150 hectares, an area nearly twice the size of Formative period Laguna Zope at its largest. Little evidence is found to indicate political or economic ties to the Zapotec civilization, whose power and influence no longer extended much beyond the Oaxaca Valley. Maintaining an affiliation established in the Early Classic, Tehuantepec's principal cultural relationship was with the Gulf Coast, with which it shared a tradition of kaolin and white-slipped pottery decorated with resist-painted images of feathered serpents, monkeys, and other zoomorphic and geometric designs. The relationship is also discernible in Tehuantepec's obsidian procurement, which was mainly from Zaragoza (Puebla) and Altotonga (Veracruz), sources adjacent to the Gulf Coast. Indicative of the northern and southern extent of this Gulf Coast affiliation are finds in Tehuantepec of an El Tajín-style votive stone *hacha* in the form of a stylized human head, and polychrome pottery imported from the Maya Lowlands. Although no formal ball courts have yet been identified, ballplayer figurines, a

stela carved in the image of the scroll-jaguar sun god, and the ceremonial interment of multiple decapitated heads at Late Classic Saltillo all suggest that Tehuantepec's leaders participated in the sacrificial ball game cult that swept Mesoamerica's coastal lowlands at this time.

Independence and prosperity were sustained in the Tehuantepec region throughout the Early Postclassic. During the Aguadas phase (A.D. 900–1300), the region's highest pre-Hispanic settlement density was achieved. The bulk of this population remained around Saltillo, which had grown to cover an area of some 267 hectares, spread over both banks of the Río de los Perros. Numerous low platform mounds capped by plaster-floored buildings mark the many house sites of the estimated six thousand inhabitants of the regional center. Taller, centrally located mounds probably served a civic-religious function or, as earlier at Laguna Zope, elevated the residences of high-status families.

Postclassic Period

The Ulam phase, beginning around A.D. 1300, comprises the last two centuries of Tehuantepec's pre-Hispanic era. It was a time of foreign interference and turbulent population dislocation that resulted first from the Zapotec invasion of the region and finally from the Spanish conquest. After more than a thousand years of occupation, Saltillo was abandoned, and its indigenous inhabitants, along with those of the region's other settlements, dispersed into small hamlets and family homesteads. Intruding were Oaxaca Valley Zapotecs, settling land newly conquered by their ruler. The political center of the region shifted to its western border, around the terminus of the Tehuantepec River route of travel down from the highland Oaxaca Valley. There, in the barrios of the Late Postclassic town of Tehuantepec, an estimated twenty-five thousand Zapotec inhabitants resided under the governance of the Zaachila royal family. A massive fortified mountaintop administrative and religious center was constructed at nearby Guiengola, overlooking the riverine gateway from the highlands. To understand the motivation for this late but decisive subjugation of Tehuantepec, one must recognize the state of affairs at the time in the Oaxaca Valley.

After the decline of Monte Albán, no single polity dominated the Oaxaca Valley until the early sixteenth-century arrival of the Spanish. Rather, the region during period Monte Albán V, its lengthy final pre-Hispanic phase, beginning A.D. 1300, was partitioned into a checkerboard of about twenty contentious petty states, of which Zaachila was perhaps the most important. Despite this unstable political environment, the valley's population rose to a record 160,000. One integrating element was the continued growth of the regional market system based on community specialization in the production of pottery and other goods. The quality of production was high, including some of the finest polychrome pottery ever produced in the valley. Extensive foreign trade supplemented local products.

A disturbingly disruptive factor, however, was the inward movement of Mixtec-speaking peoples, the traditional inhabitants of the mountainous Mixteca Alta to the north and west. The Mixtec expansion into the valley was probably stimulated by a growing shortage of agricultural land in their mountainous home territory. The perpetually quarrelling Zapotecs probably regarded the irascible Mixtecs with dread and, in an effort to turn the situation to their advantage, sought strategic alliances with them, sealed through royal marriages and gifts of farmland.

Once ensconced in the valley, the Mixtecs proliferated, collaborating or feuding impartially with rival Zapotec or Mixtec groups. From an archaeological perspective, the intermarriage and sharing of material culture between the twenty-odd Late Postclassic ethnic groups of the Oaxaca Valley makes it difficult and perhaps meaningless to sort out which settlements were Zapotec and which were Mixtec, at least at the level of royalty. At many sites, Mixteca-Puebla polychrome pottery is found alongside the traditional Zapotec graywares. Tomb 7 at Monte Albán, a reused Classic period Zapotec burial vault, served as the resting place of one Mixtec ruler. Accompanying the dead king were the sacrificed bodies of his servants, along with an immense hoard of burial goods fashioned from gold, silver, amber, coral, pearl, turquoise, carved jaguar bone, and other precious materials. Mitla, in the Tlacolula arm of the valley, is renowned for the intricate *greca*-patterned stone mosaic façades on its buildings; it is thought to have been home to a group of Zapotec high priests as well as a burial place for royalty. Along with several other Tlacolula centers, it was apparently subordinate to the ruling dynasty at Zaachila. Zaachila itself incorporated considerable Mixtec material culture in its art and architecture. On more than one occasion, Mixtec military might served to thwart Aztec efforts to gain control of the trade route through the Oaxaca Valley to Tehuantepec and the Soconusco.

Mixtec expansion into the Oaxaca Valley was un-doubtedly a critical factor in the late fifteenth-century decision of the ruler of Zaachila, Cociyopij, to transfer his court to Tehuantepec—a move that may have begun with the establishment of a Zapotec colony in the region a century or more earlier. The relocation resulted in a significant population decline in the Tlacolula arm of the Oaxaca Valley, while the town of Tehuantepec saw its numbers swell to more than twenty-five thousand. A consequence of the Zapotec takeover of Tehuantepec was the marginalizing of the ethnic groups occupying the Tehuantepec region at the time. The region's major ethnic group, the Zoque, was pushed to the extreme eastern edge of the region, while the Chontal (Tequistlatec) and Mixe withdrew to the mountain fringes to the west and northwest. The Huave (Mareños) were driven to the formerly uninhabited lagoon shores and desolate barrier beaches adjacent to the coast, where they may have supplemented a livelihood based on fishing and subsistence farming by aiding Aztec merchants in their travels along the waterway route to the rich cacao sources of the Soconusco.

Having wrested control of Tehuantepec from its local inhabitants, the Zapotec ruler was still faced with hindering periodic Aztec efforts to conquer the region. In a particularly protracted battle late in the fifteenth century, the Zapotecs withdrew to their fortified mountaintop center at Guiengola, where, with Mixtec military support from below, they successfully withstood a seven-month Aztec siege, an engagement somewhat fancifully recounted by the Spanish chronicler Burgoa. As part of the armistice agreement, the Aztec emperor offered one of his daughters in marriage to Cosijojueza, who had succeeded his father as head of the Tehuantepec Zapotec dynasty.

Clearly, the Aztec emperor Ahuizotl and his successor Moctezuma II hoped to use the princess as a source of intelligence in furthering their imperialistic objectives. But in a case of love triumphing over politics, Pelaxilla, as she was called in Zapotec, remained faithful to her husband, even foiling an Aztec plot to have him assassinated. Eventually her firstborn son succeeded his father as heir to the territory of Tehuantepec. By that time, despite the best efforts of the Zapotec and Mixtec military, the Aztecs had succeeded in bringing most of the Oaxaca Valley and some key towns in Tehuantepec into tributary status. Allying himself with Hernán Cortés in 1521, the young ruler naively saw Spanish sovereignty as preferable to the burden of Aztec domination. His baptism in 1527 as Don Juan Cortés marked a prophetic endpoint to the area's pre-Hispanic development.

O

FURTHER READINGS

Blanton, R. E. 1978. *Monte Albán: Settlement Patterns at the Ancient Zapotec Capital.* New York: Academic Press.

Caso, A., I. Bernal, and J. R. Acosta. 1967. *La cerámica de Monte Albán.* Memorias del Instituto Nacional de Antropología e Historia, 13. Mexico City.

Drennan, R. D. 1976. *Fábrica San Jose and Middle Formative Society in the valley of Oaxaca.* Museum of Anthropology, University of Michigan, Memoir 8. Ann Arbor.

Feinman, G. M., and L. M. Nicholas. 1990. At the Margins of the Monte Albán State: Settlement Patterns in the Ejutla Valley, Oaxaca, Mexico. *Latin American Antiquity* 1:216–246.

Flannery, K. V. (ed.). 1986. *Guilá Naquitz: Archaic Foraging and Early Agriculture in Oaxaca, Mexico.* New York: Academic Press.

Flannery, K. V., and J. Marcus (eds.). 1983. *The Cloud People: Divergent Evolution of the Zapotec and Mixtec Civilizations.* New York: Academic Press.

———, ———. 1994. *Early Formative Pottery of the Valley of Oaxaca, Mexico.* With technical ceramic analysis by W. O. Payne. Museum of Anthropology, University of Michigan, Memoir 27. Ann Arbor.

Marcus, J. 1989. Zapotec Chiefdoms and the Nature of Formative Religions. In R. J. Sharer and D. C. Grove (eds.), *Regional Perspectives on the Olmec,* pp. 148–197. Cambridge: Cambridge University Press.

Sanders, W. T., and D. L. Nichols. 1988. Ecological Theory and Cultural Evolution in the valley of Oaxaca. *Current Anthropology* 29:33–80.

Stark, B., and B. Voorhies. 1978. *Prehistoric Coastal Adaptations: The Economy and Ecology of Maritime Middle America.* New York: Academic Press.

Zeitlin, J. F. 1994. Precolumbian Barrio Organization in Tehuantepec, Mexico. In J. Marcus and J. F. Francis (eds.), *Caciques and Their People: A Volume in Honor of Ronald Spores,* pp. 275–300. Museum of Anthropology, University of Michigan, Anthropological Papers, 89. Ann Arbor.

Zeitlin, R. N. 1990. The Isthmus and the valley of Oaxaca: Questions about Zapotec Imperialism in Formative Period Mesoamerica. *American Antiquity* 55:250–261.

———. 1993. Pacific Coastal Laguna Zope: A Regional Center in the Terminal Formative Hinterlands of Monte Albán. *Ancient Mesoamerica* 4:85–101.

———. 1994. Accounting for the Prehistoric Long-Distance Movement of Goods with a Measure of Style. *World Archaeology* 26:208–234.

Robert N. Zeitlin

SEE ALSO
Monte Albán

Obsidian: Properties and Sources

Obtaining primary mineral materials for tool-making was one of the most important economic activities in ancient Mesoamerica. The physical characteristics of obsidian, a volcanic glass, made it a prime material for a wide range of tools, weapons, and ornaments. It has a glassy luster and a hardness of 5 to 5.5 on the Mohs' scale, with specific weight of 2.31 to 2.75. It breaks with perfect concoid fractures that permit accuracy in the direction and placement of fractures in the course of stoneworking (knapping) in order to make chipped stone tools. Furthermore, it offers a combination of transparency and diverse colors: black to gray, green to brown, red, and purple. Its properties made it fundamental for many productive processes in pre-Hispanic cultures.

The process of obtaining, distributing, and using obsidian began at natural occurrences of volcanic glass close to the surface of the earth, many of which bear archaeological evidence of exploitation through time. Each source possesses particular geological, spatial, topographical, stratigraphic, petrographic, and chemical characteristics, and these determine the occurrence and quality of obsidian and how it was extracted and used.

Obsidian is a natural glass, formed by the rapid cooling of lava in volcanic zones of rhyolitic composition, rich in silica oxides. Two volcanic processes can form obsidian, both extrusive magma expulsions; one as flowing lava, and the other as pyroclastic (fractured) materials.

In Mesoamerica there exist numerous obsidian sources, principally in two broad volcanic regions. One region, in Mexico, is constituted by the Neovolcanic Axis and the Sierra Madre Occidental, an area extending from east to west, from the north central Gulf Lowlands across the center of Mexico to the Pacific coast in West Mexico and the Northwestern Frontier region. In Central America, about 900 kilometers south of the Neovolcanic Axis, is another zone that runs from east to west, from the extreme west of Honduras to the Pacific coasts of Guatemala and El Salvador.

Major obsidian sites in Mexico and Central America. In Mexico: Hidalgo (1–3); Querétaro (4–8); Guanajuato (9–10); Jalisco (11–15); Durango (16, 17); Zacatecas (18); Michoacán (19–21); Puebla (22–26); Veracruz (27, 28); México (29); Sonora (30); Baja California (31); Nayarit (32). In Guatemala (33–39); in El Salvador (40–42); in Honduras (43–44). Illustration courtesy of the author.

Lava Sources

Obsidian formation in most sources is due to the development of rhyolitic domes, as in the Otumba (México) and Guadalupe Victoria-Tlanalapa (Puebla) sources. The morphological expression of the sources depends on the grade of erosion and the volcanic events posterior to the evolution of the rhyolitic dome. In general, lava sources can concentrate huge volumes of obsidian in specific zones where mineral exploitation is very productive.

Ignimbritic Sources

An ignimbrite is a deposit or cap formed by eruptions of incandescent pyroclastic materials, enveloped in a mass of gases at high temperature, which flow quickly over great distances, covering and filling the existing topography with large mounds of various depths. During the deposit of these materials, lithostatic pressure fuses particles of ash, and rapid cooling forms this material into obsidian at the base of the deposit. The internal stratigraphy presents variations in grade of density and texture: the upper part is less compact and principally composed of vitreous materials, crystals and fragments of rock; with depth, the rock becomes more compact and glassy until it becomes obsidian, first in the form of lenses. The lenses can become larger with greater depth, forming massive strata of obsidian.

Owing to the low degree of compaction in the upper deposits, erosion uncovers glassy strata relatively rapidly. When erosion has been very intense, these sources are reduced to low, isolated mounds composed of tufa of different grades of compaction. Here we find some sectors in which obsidian nodules are conglomerated in a matrix of tufa, and much obsidian with cortex on the periphery, as in the sources of Zacatlán (Puebla) and Altotonga (Veracruz).

O

Neovolcanic Axis

Sierra de las Navajas–Pachuca (Hidalgo, Mexico), the most studied source in Mexico, forms part of the Sierra de Pachuca. Flows include the Cruz de Milagro–Cerro de los Pelados–Cerro Pelón, Barranca de Izatla, Peña de las Aguilas, Ococingo, Cerro Piñal, La Esperanza, and San Lorenzo Zembo. The obsidian may be green, transparent or translucent, golden, or a mottled, reddish-brown type commonly called _meca_. The mine entrances are circular openings into the soil, from 0.8 to 1.2 meters in diameter, which continue vertically for 8 to 10 meters until they reach small rooms of irregular form, about 2 meters in diameter, where horizontal tunnels meet. The workshops have debitage from making three kinds of tools: rasps, bifaces, and prismatic cores. This source supplied green obsidian to Teotihuacán, the Toltecs, and the Aztecs, continuing into the early Colonial period. Obsidian from this source was most widely distributed during the Postclassic period.

Zacualtipán (Hidalgo), in the Sierra de Zacualtipán, has not been completely studied; flows are identified as Metzquititlan, Tuzampa, El Durazno, and Zacualtipán. The obsidian occurs as nodules and blocks that vary in size, exposed in road cuts and on the surface. The obsidian may be dark green, black, opaque black, red, or blue. It was extracted from open surface trenches, and blades, cores, and debitage are found associated with production of prismatic cores. We know little of its distribution and use; artifacts from this obsidian have been found in Late Classic and Postclassic contexts in Oaxaca, Chiapas, Morelos, and Guatemala.

Tulancingo (Hidalgo) consists of an extensive zone of surface nodules and flows, identified at Santiago Tulatepec, Valle de Agua Bendita, Rancho Tenango, and Tulancingo-Pizarrín. The best-studied flow is Tulancingo-Pizarrín, situated in a natural pass in the valley, its material exposed in the adjacent hillsides and on the valley surface. The most common color is green-brown, although there are also red, brown, gray, black, and _meca_. Though not of the highest quality for making tools, obsidian from this source is very accessible and extensive. In addition to using surface obsidian, people dug mines into the sides of adjacent Cerro Tecolote, with trenches 0.5 meter wide cutting into a deposit of compacted volcanic ash _(tepetate)_ and excavating vertical shafts about a meter in diameter. Debitage found at the source indicates reduction of blocks for the production of prismatic cores, rasps, bifaces, and projectile points.

El Paredón–Tecocomulco (Hidalgo and Puebla) consists of a series of flows and discontinuous concentrations of irregular nodules, exposed in the walls of _barrancas_ and in hillsides over a total area of about 1.2 square kilometers. Flow areas occur at Tres Cabezas, Paredón, and Coyaco. The obsidian is gray, varying from transparent to translucent or banded, and _meca_ varieties colored yellow, brown, and red-brown in a gray matrix. Obsidian was collected from the surface as nodules and extracted from flows by means of shallow surface trenches. Mine shafts are about 3 meters wide and 1 meter deep where deposits of nodules and blocks of obsidian were removed. Debitage indicates reduction of blocks to forms suitable to produce cores and blades.

Otumba (Mexico) covers an area of about 40 square kilometers. The rhyolitic dome and its flows form two complexes: one located northeast of the Cuello volcano, and the other formed by the Soltepec volcano, Barranca de los Ixtetes, and Barranca del Muerto. Flows include the Barranca de Santa María, Barranca de los Ixtetes, Barranca de las Navajas–del Muerto, Salto de las Peñas, and Cerro Olivares. Obsidian is exposed on the surface and was exploited on the sides of the Soltepec volcano in Barrancas de los Ixtetes, and in Barranca del Muerto. Obsidian strata flowed to the ground surface in sections a meter wide, with interspersed layers of _meca_ obsidian. Nodules were also found as intrusions in conglomerate of low compaction. The color is gray-black with translucent, transparent, banded, and _meca_ varieties. Pits from 5 to 15 meters wide and 1 to 2 meters deep evidence pre-Hispanic exploitation, as do tunnels 3 meters in diameter and 5 meters deep. Debitage from tool manufacture indicates production of prismatic blades, rasps, projectile points, and bifaces.

At Pico de Orizaba (Veracruz) obsidian is found on the west side of the volcano; it was formed as part of a rhyolitic dome, partially exposed and surrounded by andesite rocks, with no direct relation to the formation of the Pico de Orizaba volcano itself. The obsidian was amply exposed on the surface in a slightly sloping vertical cut, about 70 meters high, with the upper part presenting about 30 meters of rhyolitic tubes, little compacted, overlying a great sector of flowing rhyolite, becoming vitreous with greater depth, until a stratum of obsidian occurs around 8 meters from the base of the escarpment. The obsidian is dark gray with transparent and _meca_ varieties; it cleanly fractures concoidally. The mines are at the foot of the cut and exhibit a homogeneous pattern. Extraction was begun with the excavation of the mine opening over the base of the obsidian stratum, enabling principal fractures in a vertical position. The miners excavated sloping tunnels descending 3 to 5 meters in depth, following the major fractures, where they opened rooms of greater size with various excavations in different directions to detect obsidian strata. Only five separate flows here have yet been reported, and only two have been studied: the mines of the Valle de Ixtetal (Veracruz) and the deposits located in the barranca near the city of Guadalupe Victoria (Puebla). Evidence of prismatic blade and biface production has been found. This source was among the most exploited during the Formative period, but its period of most intense use was the Late Postclassic. Orizaba obsidian was distributed along the coastal lowlands of the Gulf of Mexico, including the Olmec area and part of the Isthmus of Tehuantepec.

The Eastern Basin (Puebla, Veracruz) comprises the mountainous boundary between the states of Puebla and Veracruz; sources there originated in the ignimbritic eruption of Xaltipan, which provoked the collapse of the Caldera de los Humeros; later various rhyolitic domes erupted along the length of the fractures that limit the caldera. Most of the flows of rhyolitic lava have crystalline structures, but the Caltonac flow does not, and its vitreous parts constitute the principal obsidian source of the zone. In addition, obsidian blocks from Xaltipan present good characteristics for working, although they are small (less than 15 cm). Caltonac obsidian is lustrous black and clear gray.

The Xaltipan Ignimbrite source area (Veracruz, Puebla) represents the surface of an ignimbritic eruption including flows at Altotonga (Veracruz), Zacatlan (Puebla), and Tezuitlan (Puebla). The Altotonga source, nodules in a *barranca,* was important for central and southern Mesoamerica from the Formative through the Classic and Postclassic periods. A source at Zaragoza (Puebla, near the Veracruz border) consists of a series of flows, but no mines or workshops have been encountered; it is thought to have been important for southern Mesoamerica from the Formative period until the Postclassic. The Caltonac-Cerro Oyameles (Puebla) source consists of outcroppings of obsidian, plus rhyolitic domes, at Las Durrumbadas, Pizarro, and Los Aguilas. A flow of varying depth is exposed in the sides of a *barranca.* Various mines are detectable, with pits between 3 and 7 meters deep. Associated workshops produced prismatic blades and bifaces. Exploitation began in the Formative, reached its height in the Classic, and continued until the Late Postclassic.

Guadalupe Victoria (Puebla) is an extensive zone of nodules exposed in *barrancas* along the western base and sides of Pico de Orizaba. There is also a system of flows near the town of Tlanalapa (Puebla), 16 kilometers to the southeast.

The Caldera de los Azufres area (Michoacán) is a geological area of numerous rhyolitic lava domes around the city of Hidalgo. It includes two reported sources and numerous outcroppings, which some authors call the Zinapécuro-Ucaréo complex, formed by two geologic events and having petrographic and chemical differences: Zinapécuro is associated with the development of a rhyolitic dome, and Ucaréo with a great lava eruption. The obsidian of Zinapécuro is gray-green with some crystallization, while that of Ucaréo is clearer, with only a few crystals, oriented in the direction of the flow.

The Zináparo-Prieto-Zacapu (Michoacán) source is of lava origin and is situated in front of outpourings from the Cerro Zináparo volcano. The outcroppings of obsidian consist of large pieces and nodules formed as part of conglomerates. One of these, Cerro Prieto, is a rhyolitic dome that developed into andesite and comprised nodules that eroded out onto the surface. The obsidian is of good quality, although inclusions are present; colors include black, gray, gray-blue, and red-brown.

North of the Neovolcanic Axis

Sources in Querétaro present an advanced state of erosion, with obsidian in the form of blocks sometimes 20 centimeters in diameter and covered with cortex. Such obsidian can be collected from the surface near the sources. Only at Cerro de la Bola and Cerro el Raptor is there evidence of horizontal extraction, where differential erosion revealed various strata and isolated lenses of obsidian in a matrix of rhyolite. The obsidian is of poor quality and was used to make scraping tools and projectile points. Exploitation was discontinuous, and associated ceramics indicate use from 500 B.C. to A.D. 1, A.D. 400–800, and A.D. 1300–1500.

At El Paraíso–Rancho Navajas (Querétaro, Mexico), located 25 kilometers east of Querétaro, the Paraíso source is on a ranch called Rancho Navajas, northeast of the community of El Paraíso. Obsidian flows and nodules are exposed on the surface over an area of about one square kilometer.

At Fuentezuela (Querétaro, Mexico), obsidian is found in large nodules in a *barranca* about 48 kilometers east of the city of Querétaro and 20 kilometers northeast of San Juan del Río. No flows or mines have been found in the area, but it is possible that there exist systems of obsidian flows in the extensive area of rhyolitic formations found west of Fuentezuela.

Sources in Guanajuato exist only as eroded nodules and are similar to the sources found in Querétaro. There are only two known sources: Abasolo–La Caldera and Pénjamo. These areas consist of an extensive system of obsidian flows and deposits of nodules in matrices of volcanic ash. They cover an area roughly 15 by 20 kilometers near the towns of Pénjamo and Abasolo in southwest Guanajuato. Workshops are associated with the obsidian, but no evidence of mining has been found.

In Jalisco, the Caldera de la Primavera (Jalisco) area is located 10 kilometers west of the city of Guadalajara. The most important obsidian sources are Cañon de las Flores, Cerro el Pedernal, and Primavera.

Tequila-Magdalena (Jalisco) is near the settlement of Magdalena and the volcano Tequila. Local sources are La Mora–Teuchitlán, La Joya, Osotero, and Santa Teresa. They were exploited by open-air extraction from pits about 20 meters in diameter. In the same region, Weigand and Spence (1982) studied a mining complex and source at La Joya that was linked to the chronology of the Etzatlán-Teuchitlán-Tequila region and was an important resource for the local population from the Formative period until the Late Postclassic, when the source was subject to massive exploitation the local use and and long-distance trade.

Sierra Madre Occidental

This physiographic zone forms an immense volcanic area that extends more than 1,200 kilometers from Chihuahua in the north down to the Neovolcanic Axis. In a rhyolitic zone, Darling (1993) has found many obsidian deposits and by neutron activation has identified two possible source areas, Llano Grande–Cerro Navajas and Huitzila–La Lobera.

Huitzila–La Lobera is a source area of about 480 square kilometers with many outcrops, such as La Mina (Jalisco), La Lobera (Jalisco), Mesa Pedernal (Jalisco), Llano Grande (Jalisco, Las Parejas (Zacatecas), Mesa sin Nombre (Zacatecas), and Cerro Espinazo del Diablo (Zacatecas).

The Llano Grande–Cerro Navajis (Durango) source consists of surface-deposited nodules of good quality at Lagunitas and at Leonitas. Northern Mexico comprises a vast but little-investigated area, with sources located in Sonora, Nayarit, and Baja California Sur and Norte. In Baja California are obsidian flows and eroded nodules at the southwestern edge of the complex of the caldera of the Tres Vírgenes volcano. Preliminary studies show that this gray-black obsidian was collected as nodules then worked into scrapers and projectile points. In some areas of the Sierra del Pinacate are deposits of eroding gray-black obsidian nodules that hunter-foragers made into tools, including small projectile points. In Nayarit, in the Ixtlán region are deposits of eroded nodules of gray-black obsidian that, from the Late Classic period to the time of the Spanish conquest, was used to make prismatic blades, bifacially flaked tools, and scrapers.

Central American Sources

El Chayal (Guatemala) includes at least five outcrops in an area of about 110 square kilometers. The obsidian is gray to black (transparent, translucent, and variegated), and its surface is smooth and brilliant. During the Early Classic period almost all the Guatemalan obsidian found in the sites of the Maya lowlands came from El Chayal, and the source continued to be exploited until the Terminal Classic period. The El Chayal outcrop has nodules 25 to 30 centimeters in diameter. It seems to have been exploited during the Late Classic and Late Postclassic periods. The La Joya outcrop consists of a dome of obsidian where one finds nodules up to 15 centimeters in diameter; this outcrop was from the Formative period to the Classic period.

Ixtepeque (Guatemala) is the obsidian source near the Ixtepeque volcano. It occupies an area of about 300 square kilometers, including at least seven outcrops that were used in antiquity. The colors are browns and grays with transparent, translucent, and mottled varieties, with a smooth and brilliant surface. During the Terminal Classic period Ixtepeque obsidian appeared in great quantities in almost all Maya sites, but the source's major period of exploitation was the Postclassic.

San Martín Jilotepeque (Guatemala) has at least four outcrops in an area of about 60 kilometers. It appears in the literature as Río Pixcayá and Aldea Chatalun, names that refer to outcrops in those areas. The Aldea Chatalun is an obsidian flow with two outcrops bearing good quality obsidian that is translucent black and brown. The Pachay outcrop is an extensive slope covered by obsidian, including a source of *meca* obsidian. During the Middle Formative period most obsidian found in the Maya lowlands came from San Martín Jilotepeque. In the Late Formative, El Chayal was the most important source, although San Martín Jilotepeque obsidian was found in significant quantities.

Tajamulco (Guatemala) is an area of about 95 square kilometers with several outcrops associated with the Tajamulco volcano, such as Palo Gordo and San Lorenzo.

O

Amatitlán (Guatemala) is located near the south side of Lake Amatitlán, and the source consists of several outcrops, such as San Bartolomé Milpas Altas, a minor source for the Maya area.

Jalapa or Jalpa (Guatemala) consists of a rhyolitic flow of obsidian; it has not been systematically studied.

Media Cuesta (Guatemala), near Lake Ayarza, is a minor source of interest because of its varying chemical characteristics.

Santa Ana (El Salvador) consists of the dome known as Cerro Pacho or Cerro El Pedregal, located to the southwest of Lake Coatepeque near the Santa Ana volcano. Three outcrops have been detected, and obsidian from this source was made into blades.

Río Comalapa (El Salvador) is in the Comalapa River region and has several outcrops of gray-red obsidian.

Zaragoza–La Libertad (El Salvador) is an area between Zaragoza and La Libertad, with deposits of obsidian similar to those of Río Comalapa.

La Esperanza (Honduras) is in the southwestern Honduran highlands and consists of several outcrops not studied in detail. Near the mountain El Cedral is an outcrop of nodules between 1 and 30 cemtimeters in diameter. The Los Hoyos area has evidence of extraction during the Late Classic and Postclassic periods, with more than one hundred mines with vertical shafts descending to the level of the flows. Prismatic and bifacial blades were manufactured.

Guiñope (Honduras), approximately 35 kilometers southeast of Tegucigalpa, in the Cerro Grande, is a source that yields eroded blocks between 1 and 10 centimeters in diameter. Outcrops have not been located, and the obsidian in the region is apparently eroded from an ancient flow. During the Postclassic period the source was exploited, and unifacial blades produced.

When studying a determined source, one should consider the occurrence of geological, technical, and social characteristics. In general, obsidian sources are associated with broad volcanic zones of rhyolite composition, rich in SiO^2, where the extrusive events, expelling magma to the surface as lava flows or pyroclastic materials. Both processes could form obsidian, originating with special characteristics, topography, stratigraphy, petrography and different chemicals, which determined in large part the pre-Hispanic technique of exploitation, and the volume and quality of the obsidian exploited. Owing to the fact that obsidian is a natural glass, its occurrence within the Transmexican Neovolcanic Axis was a relatively common phenomenon, and doubtless, not all the obsidian outcrops were exploited.

FURTHER READINGS

Bové, F., S. Medrano, B. Lou, and B. Arroyo (eds.). 1993. La transición entre el Formativo Terminal y el Clásico Temprano en la Costa Pacífica de Guatemala. *Memorias en Arqueología Latinoamericana,* 6. Pittsburgh: University of Pittsburgh.

Charlton, T., and M. W. Spence. 1982. Obsidian Exploitation and Civilization in the Basin of Mexico. *Anthropology* 6:7–86.

Cobean, R. H., J. R. Vogt, M. D. Glascock, and T. L. Stocker. 1991. High-precision Trace-element Characterization of Major Mesoamerican Obsidian Sources and Further Analyses of Artifacts from San Lorenzo Tenochtitlan, Mexico. *Latin American Antiquity* 2: 69–91.

Darling, J. A. 1993. Notes on Obsidian Sources of the Southern Sierra Madre Occidental. *Ancient Mesoamerica* 4:245–253.

Darras, V. 1994. Les mines-ateliers d'obsidienne de la région de Zináparo-Prieto, Michoacán, Mexique. *Bulletin de la Société Préhistorique Française* 91:290–301.

Demant, A. 1983. Les gisements d'obsidienne de l'axe Transmexicain. *Bulletin Centre D'Études Mexicains el Centraméricaines* 5:23–36.

Ferriz, H. 1985. Caltonac, Prehispanic Obsidian-mining Center in Eastern Mexico: A Preliminary Report. *Journal of Field Archaeology* 12:363–370.

Nelson, F. 1985. Summary of the Results of Analysis of Obsidian Artifacts from the Maya Lowlands. *Scanning Electron Microscopy* 2:631–649.

Pastrana, A. 1987. El proceso de trabajo de la obsidiana de las minas de Pico de Orizaba. *Boletín de Antropología Americana* 13:132–145.

Sheets, P., K. Hirth, F. Lange, F. Stross, F. Asaro, and H. Michael. 1990. Obsidian Sources and Elemental Analyses of Artifacts in Southern Mesoamerica and the Northern Intermediate Area. *American Antiquity* 55: 144–158.

Weigand, P. C., and M. W. Spence. 1982. Obsidian mining complex at La Joya, Jalisco. In P. C. Weigand and G. Gwynne (eds.), *Mining and Mining Techniques in Ancient Mesoamerica,* pp. 175–188. *Anthropology* 6, special edition. Stony Brook: State University of New York.

Alejandro Pastrana and Ivonne Athie

SEE ALSO

Obsidian: Tools, Techniques, and Products

O

Obsidian: Tools, Techniques, and Products

Obsidian is a homogeneous, fine-grained, volcanic glass that lacks natural cleavage planes. Thus, it fractures conchoidally, like glass, in a predictable manner and can be shaped by chipping via a process analogous to sculpting. The controlled fracture of obsidian and other cryptocrystalline rocks such as chert and flint is called "knapping." Prehistoric artisans learned how to knap obsidian and fabricate a variety of exquisitely sharp cutting implements from it. Skill and patience were required to work obsidian because each blow had to be delivered at a precise point on the stone, and with the correct force, to shape it in the desired manner. Some knapping techniques require more skill than others. Evidence from documentary sources indicates that all of the specialized knapping in Mesoamerica was undertaken by adult males; less specialized knapping may have been performed by women and children as well as men.

Knapping Techniques

Several indigenous groups around the world still occasionally make and use chipped stone tools. Archaeologists rely on these documented examples of tool manufacture, as well as on descriptions from Spanish chroniclers, to determine how ancient Mesoamerican stone tools were made. Three basic knapping techniques were employed in Mesoamerica for making chipped obsidian tools; these are distinguished by the particular types of implements used to break the obsidian and the kind of force employed. Knapping techniques include direct percussion, indirect percussion, and pressure. Technologically, these procedures are all considered to be "reduction techniques" because knapping results in a continuous reduction of the mass of the original stone with each flake removal.

In direct percussion, the artisan used a stone cobble as a hammerstone, or a hardwood mallet as a baton, to strike the obsidian nodule directly and break off flakes. Greater control was possible with the use of an intermediate, chisel-like tool known as a "punch." The latter technique is considered indirect percussion because, instead of striking the obsidian nodule directly with a hammerstone or baton, the artisan placed the tip of the punch at a precise point on the core and then struck the other end of the punch with the hammerstone or baton with sufficient force to break a flake from the core, thereby indirectly transferring the force of the blow through the punch to the core. Punches were made of stone, antler, bone, and wood. Indirect percussion is analogous to sculpting with a hammer and chisel.

Like indirect percussion, pressure techniques required an intermediate pressure-flaking tool made of stone, bone, wood, or, most commonly, a tine of deer antler. Instead of striking the core directly or indirectly, with pressure techniques the artisan placed the tip of the pressure tool on the edge of the core and pushed off a flake of obsidian with the strength of his arms and upper torso. This technique allowed the artisan to exert greater control over the removal of material from the core. Pressure techniques provided at least two advances over direct and indirect percussion for the artisan: placement of the tool was much more precise, and the application of force was slower and more controlled.

Obsidian Tools

Archaeologists have identified a bewildering variety of obsidian tools that were made in Mesoamerica. The general framework of all stone tool typologies can be quickly grasped, however, by keeping in mind five general forms and the three knapping techniques mentioned.

The primary distinction is between cores and flakes. Flakes are pieces broken from a parent stone called a "core." Cutting and scraping tools were made from both flakes and cores. A blade is a specialized flake—an elongated, parallel-sided flake removed from a special core; blades are at least twice as long as they are wide.

Most of the everyday household tools used in Mesoamerica were made from flakes and blades. These can be further distinguished typologically by identifying the knapping technique used. For example, one can distinguish among direct percussion, indirect percussion, and pressure blades, and then subdivide each class of blade by size (macroblades, blades, and microblades) or by shape.

The other two major tool forms known from Mesoamerica are christened "bifaces" and "unifaces" by archaeologists. Bifaces are tools that have been knapped on two faces of a flake or core; such tools include spear points, arrowheads, and sacrificial knives. They were chipped from expended cores, flakes, or large blades, most commonly by direct percussion; pressure was often used for final finishing work.

Unifaces are flaked on only one face instead of two and were commonly made from large percussion flakes or macroblades. The most frequent unifacial tools found in Mesoamerica are scrapers; they were used to scrape wood, gourds, animal hides, maguey, and other fibrous plants. Both bifaces and unifaces were made either by percussion or pressure techniques. It is noteworthy that all of the types of tools mentioned can be produced sequentially, during the reduction sequence, from one nodule. Indeed, from the Middle Formative period to the Postclassic, such reduction schemes appear to have been the norm.

Manufacture and Use of Pressure Blades

Mesoamerican obsidian industries are best known for the fine, prismatically shaped pressure blades, known as "prismatic blades," that predominated there for the last two thousand years before Contact. The Spanish conquerors showed an understandably keen interest in the manufacture of these tools because they constituted the critical elements of the weapons used by the resisting natives. Segments of obsidian blades were inset along the margins of wooden broad swords and spears; these included the *tepuztepilli* (long spear), *tlacochtli* (short spear), *tlatzontectli* (pronged spear), and *macuahuitl* (broad sword). Blades provided these tools with razor-sharp edges capable of decapitating a horse, but the edges were also fragile and had to be replaced frequently.

The most common blade tools mentioned by the Spanish chroniclers are awls (*punzones*) and razors (*rasuraderas*). These were also traded to the far reaches of the Aztec Empire by *pochteca* merchants. Razors are described as double-edged knives, serviceable for a variety of tasks such as cutting hair "and things that are not very hard." Awls are pointed blades destined as implements for autosacrifice (self-bloodletting) from the ears, tongue, fleshy parts of the arms or legs, or penis. These were pious rites reminiscent of the mythic creation of humankind by the gods at Teotihuacan by means of autosacrifice onto figures made of ground maize.

Of all of the indigenous technologies observed by the Spanish, they were most amazed at the production of the obsidian "knives" (*navajas*) now called "prismatic blades." These knives are shaped like the barber's iron lancet known to the Spanish. Blades were produced from specially prepared, long, parallel-sided cores by means of a pressure technique and a long, leverlike pressure tool (c. 1.5 meters long) that had a hook at its working end. A blade-maker seated himself on the ground and then placed a prepared blade core between his bare feet. Flexing his legs to exert pressure, the artisan held the core immobile with his toes or the balls of his feet and then placed the hook part of the lancelike pressure tool on the edge of the core and levered off a prismatic blade by pulling back on the other end of the long handle. Eyewitness descriptions concur that the technique was marvelously clever, and that an artisan could produce more than a hundred nearly identical blades from one core in a very short time. Blades sold in the Aztec market were very cheap.

Distribution of Obsidian Tools

The first clear evidence of manufacture and use of formal tools in Mesoamerica dates to about 12,000 years ago. Paleolithic hunters fashioned spear points and various cutting and scraping implements from fine-grained cherts and obsidian. Lanceolate points used by the big-game hunters at the dawn of prehistory closely resemble the hafted knives used 11,000 years later by the Maya, Aztec, and other Mesoamericans for human sacrifice.

The transition from the Late Archaic to the Formative period was marked by a major shift in obsidian technology. The special toolkits characteristic of the Archaic period (flakes, bifacial knives and spear points, and scrapers) diminished in importance. Some bifaces continued to be made in the highlands of western Mesoamerica, but they were absent in eastern Mesoamerica. The rise of sedentary villages during the Early Formative period was paralleled by a shift to a simple, nonspecialized flake technology. Small obsidian flakes were struck by direct percussion from irregular chunks of obsidian imported to these village sites from highland sources in Guatemala and Mexico.

Bipolar percussion also became predominant at this time. This variant of direct percussion is analogous to cracking a nut between two stones and is the simplest of all knapping techniques. It is most appropriate for pieces of obsidian that are too small to hold in the hand and break with direct hammerstone blows. Instead, the flake or small chunk of obsidian is placed on a stone (which acts as an anvil) and struck with a hammerstone until the obsidian cleaves in two.

The obvious implication of the shift in fabrication techniques at the start of the Formative is that specialized techniques were replaced by simpler ones that could be performed by almost anyone over six years of age. One explanation for this shift is that the flexible toolkits and curated tools of the Archaic were no longer necessary because sedentary Formative farmers had little need to design lightweight tools, capable of multiple resharpenings, to minimize transport and travel costs. ("Curated" is an archaeological term referring to any item that the ancients kept track of very carefully—sometimes an item from another culture and time.)

Toward the end of the Early Formative (1200 B.C.), prismatic blades appeared for the first time in Mesoamerica.

O

Earlier blades are known for the Archaic period, but they were manufactured by percussion rather than by pressure. The popularity of prismatic blades increased during the Formative until they became the technology of choice for all of Mesoamerica by about 200 B.C. The dichotomous distribution of obsidian spear points and flaked knives continued as before, however, with obsidian bifaces occurring only in the Mexican highlands. Biface technology did become characteristic of the Maya Lowlands, but it relied on chert, the local substitute material, to make large, thick bifaces used as axes and hoes. Later, knives and spear points were also made.

The spread of blade technology throughout Formative Mesoamerica occurred in two significant episodes. Blades first appeared during the Early Formative and were exported from the obsidian quarries to major Olmec centers in the Gulf Coast lowlands. At this time specialist blade-makers performed their work near the sources of obsidian in highland Mexico and Guatemala. During the Middle and Late Formative (900–200 B.C.) patterns of production and exchange shifted, with large prepared blade cores rather than blades being the commodity exported from the quarries. This shift meant that each polity importing the prepared macrocores now had to support specialist blade-makers within its borders in order to produce blades. Macrocores were reduced in a two-step process at each importing community by indirect percussion and then by pressure, yielding both percussion and pressure blades. This process was further simplified in the Terminal Formative (200 B.C.–A.D. 250). At this time, and in all subsequent periods, more extensive core preparation was undertaken at the quarries, and the exported blade cores were ready to reduce by pressure techniques. From this time onward, prismatic blades became the predominant obsidian artifacts at most Mesoamerican sites.

During the Late Classic and Postclassic periods obsidian technology in Mesoamerica was technologically uniform, with the noted differences being those of quantity rather than quality. Two major innovations in the use of obsidian at this time appear to have been the adoption of the bow and arrow and the use of prismatic blades in lances, spears, and swords. Simple arrowheads were made from small sections of prismatic blades. Other blade sections appear to have been trimmed for use in lances and swords. Trimmed blade sections could be made rapidly and easily from prismatic blades, and damaged ones could be quickly replaced.

A remnant of the sophisticated blade technology of

Mesoamerica persists today among the Lacandón Maya of the tropical forests of Chiapas, Mexico. They continue to manufacture chert blades by means of indirect percussion from small blade cores previously roughed out by direct percussion. They use a small punch made of deer antler to strike blades from a core. The suitable blades are then retouched into arrowheads; the tool used for pressure is made from a section of an old machete. Use of indirect percussion to manufacture chert blades is mentioned in the Early Colonial sources from Yucatán.

FURTHER READINGS

Clark, J. E. 1982. Manufacture of Mesoamerican Prismatic Blades: An Alternative Technique. *American Antiquity* 47:355–376.

———. 1987. Politics, Prismatic Blades, and Mesoamerican Civilization. In J. K. Johnson (ed.), *The Organization of Core Technology*, 259–284. Boulder: Westview Press.

Crabtree, D. E. 1968. Mesoamerica Polyhedral Cores and Prismatic Blades. *American Antiquity* 33:446–478.

Gaxiola, M., and J. E. Clark (eds.). 1989. *La obsidiana en Mesoamerica*. Colección Científica, 176. Mexico City: Instituto Nacional de Antropología Historia.

Sheets, P. D. 1975. Behavioral Analysis and the Structure of a Prehistoric Industry. *Current Anthropology* 16:369–391.

Sullivan, T. D. 1972. The Arms and Insignia of the Mexica. *Estudios de Cultura Nahuatl* 10:155–193.

Tolstoy, P. 1971. Utilitarian Artifacts of Central Mexico. In G. F. Ekholm and I. Bernal (eds.), *Handbook of Middle American Indians*, vol. 10, pp. 270–296. Austin: University of Texas Press.

John E. Clark

SEE ALSO

Chipped Stone Tool Production and Products; Obsidian: Properties and Sources

Olmec Culture

"Olmec" is the name given to the Early and Middle Formative period (c. 1200–500 B.C.) archaeological culture of southern Mexico's tropical Gulf Lowlands region. Olmec culture is particularly notable for its massive and remarkably sophisticated stone monuments, the first created by any Mesoamerican society. Because for several centuries the Olmec were the only culture producing such carvings, that monumental art distinguishes them from other early Mesoamerican societies. The occurrence of their monuments within a limited area of the Gulf Coast also helps to demarcate the extent of the Olmec domain.

Olmec monuments have been found at nearly two dozen sites within a region bounded on the west by the Papaloapan River of southern Veracruz and in the east by the Chontalpa area of western Tabasco. However, more than 80 percent of the nearly two hundred known monuments occur at just three sites—La Venta, San Lorenzo, and Laguna de los Cerros; these are believed to have been major Olmec centers. Other sites, with only a few carvings each, may have been secondary centers. Tres Zapotes, often misclassified as a major center, is an example of the latter. Although monuments assist in identifying principal sites, the majority of Olmec settlements were simple farming hamlets that lacked such elite objects.

The three major centers are spaced nearly equidistantly across the Olmec domain and in different ecological settings. Commerce was important to the Olmec political economy, and each center had the potential to exploit, distribute, and control different resources important within the overall economy. The westernmost center, Laguna de los Cerros (Veracruz), is situated on an upland plain near the basalt-rich Tuxtla Mountains, and could have provided much of the stone utilized throughout the Olmec domain for both elite monuments and mundane utilitarian grinding tools. The middle center, San Lorenzo (or San Lorenzo Tenochtitlan), in Veracruz, overlooks a large expanse of riverine floodplains with multiple resources and was strategically positioned to control river trade. The eastern center, La Venta (Tabasco), on another major river, is also adjacent to the coast, with access to salt, tar, rich food resources from coastal estuaries, and coastal trade.

Archaeological knowledge of Olmec culture is based almost entirely on excavation data from the major centers of La Venta and San Lorenzo. Few small Olmec sites have been studied, and very little research has been conducted at Laguna de los Cerros.

Research on the Olmec began first at La Venta, a site characterized by massive platform mounds arranged around large plaza areas, dominated by a 32-meter-high earthen pyramid mound, one of the earliest such constructions in Mesoamerica. Those investigations, carried out in 1942–1943 by Matthew Stirling and Philip Drucker, focused on Complex A, a plaza extending northward from the base of the Great Pyramid. The excavations uncovered colored clay floors, caches of polished jade celts, and royal burials associated with jade figurines and jewelry. Further research in Complex A by Drucker,

Robert Heizer, and Robert Squier in 1955 provided the first radiocarbon dating for the Olmec: 1000–600 B.C.

The Complex A excavations obviously did not provide a comprehensive view of La Venta's prehistory nor of Olmec culture. No evidence was found of earlier periods of settlement at the site, and the antecedents to Olmec culture remained puzzling. Nevertheless, as the first researched site, La Venta's public architecture and the fabulous discoveries in Complex A were perceived as the archetype of Olmec culture for several decades. Although the site was extensively damaged by oil refinery construction following the 1955 research, renewed investigations there by Rebecca Gonzalez have rehabilitated key site areas; these have also discovered pre-Olmec (1750 B.C.) settlements on levees along old channels of the nearby Río Barí. Data indicate maize use at these small settlements, and in the centuries that followed throughout their domain, maize remained the basic Olmec food crop.

San Lorenzo is situated atop a large plateau overlooking the Coatzacoalcos River and its tributaries and floodplains. Several smaller associated sites—Tenochtitlan, Potrero Nuevo, and El Azuzul—each with a few monuments, are situated near the base of the plateau, closer to the rivers. Although San Lorenzo was briefly investigated in 1946 by Stirling and Drucker, its importance was brought to scholarly attention through major 1966–1968 excavations by Michael Coe and Richard Diehl. Their research there defined six Formative period phases: Ojochi (1500–1350 B.C.), Bajío (1350–1250 B.C.), Chicharras (1250–1150 B.C.), San Lorenzo (1150–900 B.C.), Nacaste (900–700 B.C.), and Palangana (600–400 B.C.). It provided the first archaeological evidence of the pre-Olmec peoples on the Gulf Coast (Ojochi, Bajío, and Chicharras phases) and documented in the stratigraphic record their evolution into Olmec culture (San Lorenzo, Nacaste, and Palangana phases). Data on the site's public and domestic architecture are being unearthed by a project begun in the 1990s by Ann Cyphers.

Evidence suggests that San Lorenzo's greatest importance was during the San Lorenzo phase (Early Formative period), and its public architecture is thus earlier than that of Middle Formative La Venta. Instead of platform mound–plaza arrangements and a central pyramid, Cyphers's investigations have uncovered large, houselike buildings constructed atop low, earthen platforms. The site's major monuments stood atop specially prepared clay floors, some perhaps within walled enclosures. An important feature at both San Lorenzo and La Venta is their buried network of stone "drain" lines, created from long

O

rectangular blocks of basalt carved into a U shape, laid end to end, and covered with capstones. Cyphers's research suggests that these systems were aqueducts used to provide drinking water to the different areas of the settlement. Several carvings specially associated with the aqueduct system imply that it had a sacred character as well.

The monuments found at the major Olmec sites provide archaeologists with information on the nature of Olmec ideology. Rulership is clearly a principal focus of the art, and rulers are portrayed in all four of the major classes of monuments: colossal heads, altars (or thrones), stelae, and statues. The colossal heads epitomize the rulership carvings; they are massive yet superb portraits of individual Olmec rulers, and each ruler seems to be particularly identified by the motif appearing in his headgear. These huge stone heads glorified the rulers while they were alive and commemorated them as revered ancestors after their death. Ten colossal heads are presently known at San Lorenzo and four at La Venta.

Huge monolithic rectangular "altars" are another major category of monuments; they appear to have been thrones for Olmec rulers. The front face of such an altar contains a carving of a ruler seated within a large niche that symbolizes a cave entrance to the supernatural powers of the underworld. Four altars have been found at La Venta, and two are known from San Lorenzo. Statues and stelae also bear depictions of rulers, but carvings of anthropomorphic and zoomorphic supernaturals are common as well in these monument types. Statues occur at both large and small Olmec centers.

Most Olmec monuments are found mutilated. Statues are usually missing their heads, faces are effaced from stelae, and massive fragments have been broken from the corners of altars. Only the colossal portrait heads are found relatively unharmed. For decades this damage was interpreted as the result of internal revolutions within Olmec society, or of external invaders, but most scholars now believe that the mutilation represents ritual or sacred destruction of the carvings by the Olmec themselves, perhaps at the death of the portrayed ruler. New evidence also indicates that some monuments were "recycled' by breaking them and recarving their pieces into new monuments.

Various other aspects of Olmec religious belief can be inferred from the iconographic motifs found on Early Formative pottery and Middle Formative greenstone objects from San Lorenzo and La Venta. Similar motifs are found on comparable artifacts in other areas of Mesoamerica as well, supplying evidence of a shared belief system common to many Formative period societies. Early scholars identified the major designs as representing felines and wrote of Olmec jaguar deities. More recent research interprets the highly abstract motifs as mainly symbolizing two supernatural creatures; a crocodilian supernatural related to the earth and earthly fertility, and a sharklike supernatural associated with water, blood, and ritual bloodletting. Actual feline symbolism is more evident in Middle Formative period art.

Springs and sources of clear water have always been sacred places to Mesoamerican societies, including the Olmec. This is confirmed by the surprising discoveries at El Manatí, a site on the floodplains of the Río Coatzacoalco, near San Lorenzo. There, archaeologists Carmen Rodriguez and Ponciano Ortiz have excavated remarkably preserved Olmec objects from the mud of an ancient spring. The objects, apparently ritually deposited in the spring, include more than two dozen wooden heads (or busts), jade axes and jewelry, and several rubber balls. The last indicate that the Olmec played a version of the Mesoamerican ball game.

Linguists believe that the Olmec spoke a language related to the present-day languages Mixe and Zoque, and it is clear that they had important trade relationships and social interactions with regions and societies whose peoples spoke other different and unrelated languages. The nature and impact of those relationships is a hotly debated issue; the available archaeological data can be interpreted in at least two different ways, and each has its vocal proponents. The standard viewpoint for decades has been that the Olmec were a civilization more advanced than other groups of their time period. That perspective considers the widespread similarities in Early Formative period artifact types and motifs as the result of Olmec influences, and likewise ascribes the cultural development of other Early Formative Mesoamerican societies to such influences. The Olmec are seen as the "mother culture" that singularly laid the foundations for later Mesoamerican civilizations.

The competing and equally prevalent school of thought has developed as the Formative period prehistory of other regions of Mesoamerica has become better known. This viewpoint argues that the similarities in art and artifacts are not due to Olmec influences, and that the archaeological evidence shows that social complexity in other regions evolved independently of the Gulf Coast, following ideological beliefs that did not require expression in monumental art. The societies in the regions are seen also to have contributed a legacy to later civilizations, as "sister cultures" with the Olmec. Confusing understanding of the situation is the fact that for more than fifty years the name "Olmec" has also been applied loosely to art, artifacts, and sites that are unrelated to the Olmec archaeological culture.

While the debate on Early Formative period Olmec "influences" continues, it is significant to note that during the Middle Formative period, monumental art executed to Olmec stylistic canons appears at a limited number of sites in west central Mexico (e.g., Chalcatzingo and Teopantecuanitlan) and on the Pacific slopes of southern Mesoamerica (e.g., Pijijiapan, Abaj Takalik, and Chalchuapa). Both sides of the debate recognize that those carvings attest to significant interactions between those distant centers and the Olmec, perhaps related to the procurement of raw materials.

Did Olmec culture cease around 500 B.C., or did it—as is more likely—evolve into the regional Late Formative culture seen at Tres Zapotes, and expressed in objects such as the Tuxtla Statuette and the La Mojarra Stela? The answer does not exist in the current archaeological data, but there is an Olmec legacy that continued to be important long after them, seen particularly in the stone monuments and commemoration of rulership by Classic period Maya civilization.

FURTHER READINGS

Benson, E. P. (ed.). 1968. *Dumbarton Oaks Conference on the Olmec*. Washington, D.C.: Dumbarton Oaks.

———. (ed.) 1981. *The Olmec and Their Neighbors*. Washington, D.C.: Dumbarton Oaks.

Benson, E. P., and G. G. Griffin (eds.). 1988. *Maya Iconography*. Princeton: Princeton University Press.

Bernal, I. 1969. *The Olmec World*. Los Angeles and Berkeley: University of California Press.

Coe, M. D. 1968. *America's First Civilization: Discovering the Olmec*. New York: American Heritage Publishing.

Coe, M. D., and R. D. Diehl. 1980. *In the Land of the Olmec*. Austin: University of Texas Press.

Coe, M. D., R. A. Diehl, and M. Stuiver. 1967. Olmec Civilization, Veracruz, Mexico: Dating of the San Lorenzo Phase. *Science* 155:1399–1401.

Drucker, P., R. F. Heizer, and R. J. Squier. 1959. *Excavations at La Venta, Tabasco, 1955. Bureau of American Ethnology Bulletin 170*. Washington, D.C.: Smithsonian Institution.

Grove, D. C. 1974. The Highland Olmec Manifestation: A Consideration of What It Is and Isn't. In N. Hammond (ed.), *Mesoamerican Archaeology*, pp. 109–128. Austin: University of Texas Press.

———. 1981. The Formative Period and the Evolution of Complex Culture. In J. Sabloff (ed.), *Supplement to the Handbook of Middle American Indians*, vol. 1, Archaeology, pp. 373–391. Austin: University of Texas Press.

Sharer, R. J., and D. C. Grove (eds.). 1987. *The Olmec and the Development of Mesoamerican Civilization*. Cambridge: Cambridge University Press.

———, ——— (eds.). 1991. *Regional Perspectives on the Olmec*. SAR Advanced Seminar Series. Santa Fe: School of America Research.

David C. Grove

SEE ALSO
Formative Period; Gulf Lowlands: South Region

Olmec-Guerrero Style

This geographically specific variant of the Olmec style is best known for polychrome murals in caves or rock shelters. The Olmec-Guerrero style flourished during in the Middle Formative period (900–400 B.C.) at sites centered on either side of the middle Balsas River in north central Guerrero, where it seems to have originated around six hundred years earlier. While forms and symbols from the Olmec heartland influenced the Olmec-Guerrero style, its vitality and craftsmanship sprang from local innovations, evidencing the significant contribution of regional cultures beyond the Gulf Coast Olmec "heartland" to pan-Mesoamerican Olmec style. The style's name is applied to objects (celts, spoons, figurines, earflares, and masks) made of clay, shell, wood, and stone.

Olmec-Guerrero-style art was created for chiefly rulers to use as ceremonial objects to validate publicly their access to supernatural and, hence, secular power. Sometime after 400 B.C., the Olmec-Guerrero style began to disappear, concomitant with the decline of the general Olmec style throughout Mesoamerica.

The Olmec-Guerrero style was distinctively expressed in polychrome paintings depicting humans with supernaturals; monolithic sculptures shaped like inverted Ts, bearing images of snarling, Olmec-style were-jaguars; and objects carved from the Pacific Coast pearl oyster shell (*Pinctada mazatlanica*). Architectural features that seem to have originated within the Olmec-Guerrero style include the earliest corbel vaults in Mesoamerica and stone-lined sunken courts. Splendid examples of both

O

these features have been recovered archaeologically at the site of Teopantecuanitlán. Iconographically, the Olmec-Guerrero style contributed the corn-curl headdress and the corn-kernel knot to the Olmec symbol corpus.

FURTHER READINGS

Grove, D. C. 1970. *The Olmec Paintings of Oxtotitlan Cave, Guerrero, Mexico.* Studies in Pre-Columbian Art and Archaeology, 6. Washington, D.C.: Dumbarton Oaks.

Martínez Donjuán, G. 1986. Teopantecuanitlán. In *Arqueología y ethnohistoria del Estado de Guerrero*, pp. 55–80. Mexico City: Instituto Nacional de Antropología e Historia/Gobierno del Estado de Guerrera.

Niederberger, C. 1996. *Olmec Horizon Guerrero: Olmec Art of Ancient Mexico.* Washington, D.C.: National Gallery of Art.

Paradis, L. I. 1995. Archaeology, History and Ethnography: The Precolumbian History of the Mezcala Region. In J. D. Amith (ed.), *The Amate Tradition: Innovation and Dissent in Mexican Art.* Chicago and Mexico City: Mexican Fine Arts Center and Las Casa de las Imagenes.

Rena Robles, R., and G. Martínez Donjuán. 1989. Hallazgos funerios de en Época Olmeca en Chilpancingo, Guerrero. *Arqueologia* 1:13–22.

F. Kent Reilly III

SEE ALSO
Caves of Guerrero; Guerrero Region; Olmec Culture

Opeño, El (Michoacán, Mexico)

This village site from the Early Formative (c. 1500 B.C.) has given its name to one of the earliest and most intriguing archaeological cultures in West Mexico. Its ties to other pre-Hispanic cultures in West and Central Mexico (Capacha in Colima, and Tlatilco in the Basin of Mexico) are evident. It is possible that cultural contacts between the El Opeño and Capacha peoples and other areas during the Formative period extended as far south as Ecuador, as evidenced by shared ceramic types and other common traits such as shaft tombs.

To date, only the tombs and the associated funerary objects pertaining to this culture are known. They are dated to around 1500 B.C., a period of considerable volcanic activity that buried in ash the site of tombs, and perhaps also nearby habitation areas, which have not yet been located.

These tombs could be the earliest antecedent for the shaft tombs typical of West Mexico. The El Opeño tombs are characterized by an underground passageway and a stairway sculpted in the hard subsoil, which lead to the funerary chambers. Nine tombs were discovered between 1938 and 1970, and an additional three in 1991. They could have functioned as family crypts with multiple burials. Some of the human crania evidence deliberate deformation, as well as trepanation, which was survived by the individuals operated upon.

Among the offerings found in the tombs are clay figurines that, because of their attire and dynamic postures, remind one of ballplayers and their companions: five standing men with a padded protective piece around one shin, holding a bat or club to strike the ball. This primitive ball game was probably practiced in West Mexico without ball courts; the earliest evidence for this architectonic feature in Jalisco dates from the sixth century B.C.

Other offerings found in the El Opeño tombs included artifacts made of clay, shell, obsidian, jade, and other greenstone; a 43-cm-long bat made of slate, which may have been used in the ball game; a little yoke made of stone, probably used to protect the hand of a ballplayer; and a small pectoral sculpted in basalt, shaped like a turtle shell and with holes for suspension.

Ceramics from this site include simple bowls and small *ollas* (jars), decorated with incised lines, indentations, and applications of the same clay, very similar to the pottery found at Tlatilco, which is more or less contemporaneous with El Opeño. Jars have negative resist-painted decoration (red or black), which may be the earliest precursor of Tarascan pottery decorated with this technique.

Materials pertaining to this archaeological complex have also been found on the coast of Michoacán, in the Tomatlán River basin, in Jalisco, and in the Etzatlan-Teuchitlan area of Jalisco.

FURTHER READINGS

Oliveros, A. 1989. Las tumbas más antiguas de Michoacán. In E. Florescano (ed.), *Historia general de Michoacán*, pp. 123–134. Morelia: Instituto de Cultura de Michoacán.

Eduardo Williams

SEE ALSO
West Mexico

Ostional, El (Rivas, Nicaragua)

Small habitation sites in the El Ostional area on the southern Pacific coast of Nicaragua revealed the first evidence outside Costa Rica of the late Tempisque period (500 B.C.-300 A.D.) mortuary pattern characteristic of the central highland and northwestern Costa Rica. It includes carved stone *metates* or ceremonial stools, jade pendants, mace heads, and Rosales Zoned Engraved ceramics. Shell midden sites also have extensive faunal and molluscan deposits and represent a range of occupation from 1000 B.C. to 1522 A.D.

Frederick W. Lange

Otomí Cultural Tradition

According to a historical tradition reported by Sahagún in the *Florentine Codex,* Central Mexico was settled by people from the east who had disembarked on the Gulf Coast. They lived for a time at Tamoanchan (location unknown), then built Teotihuacan and Chololan (Cholula), and eventually migrated toward the north. Some, who remained in the mountains, were known as "Otomí." The rest went farther north, later returning south to their area of origin. All these people who had been to the north were called "Chichimec," including the Toltec and all the groups that later moved southward after the fall of Tollan. Thus, "Chichimec" stands in contrast to other peoples—Olmec, Huixtotin, and Nonoalca—who had not moved north. According to Sahagún's informants, there were three kinds of Chichimec: Teochichimec (true Chichimec) were hunters and gatherers living north of Mesoamerica, sometimes found in areas such as Tlaxcallan; a second Chichimec group lived among and spoke the language of the Huaxtec, Nahua, or Otomí; and the third group, the Otomí, were described by Sahagún as typically Mesoamerican farmers and artisans, with permanent settlements, rulers and priests, temples, and men's houses.

Otomí traditions cite their origins in caves near Chiappan (Chapa de Mota, México), where the divine couple, Old Mother and Old Father, dwelt. Their ancestral home was this same highland area northwest of the Central Basin, the region of Xilotepec. The chronicles also place the Otomí in the nearby area of Tollan at the time of that city's decline.

Some Otomí or Otomí-speaking Chichimec may have been part of groups migrating from the Tollan region in the thirteenth century into the Basin of Mexico under Xolotl's leadership, moving into the Chololan area. The Tetzcocan chronicler Ixtlilxochitl considered Xolotl's people to be the major Chichimec group and referred to the Otomí as a separate people. Xolotl later welcomed into the Basin three groups with Toltec-type culture: the Otomí, the Acolhua, and the Tepanec. The Tepanec (with Otomí and Matlatzinca components in their population) settled in Azcapotzalco, and the Acolhua in Coatlinchan in the eastern part of the basin, which came to be known as Acolhuacan.

The Otomí founded the kingdom of Xaltocan, which is specifically identified as Otomí but which, like other Mesoamerican polities, probably included other ethnic elements. Xaltocan's polity comprised areas of the northern basin and adjacent zones to the east and north, including Otompan, Tollantzinco, Metztitlan, Tototepec, and Oxitipan, thus roughly coinciding with the sixteenth-century distribution of Otomí, with the exception of Xilotepec and environs, which remained independent. The Xaltocan kingdom was destroyed about A.D. 1400 by Azcapotzalco under the Tepanec ruler Tezozomoc. Its ruler fled to Metztitlan (which survived as a Nahua-Otomí kingdom, never conquered by the Tenochca Empire), and Otomí farmers found refuge in the Teotihuacan Valley, where the Acolhua ruler settled them around Otumba.

Shortly thereafter (c. 1428), the Azcapotzalco Tepanecs were defeated, and the Triple Alliance (Tenochtitlan, Tetzcoco, and Tlacopan) was established. The Otomí core area of Xilotepec and the Valley of Toluca entered into the Triple Alliance as part of the realm of Tlacopan, and Xilotepec was given a king of the Tenochca dynasty. The people of Xilotepec and the mountain area (Cuauhtlalpan) to the west of the Basin of Mexico participated in military expeditions and colonial settlements ordered by the Tenochca kings. Later in the fifteenth century, this region was more thoroughly subjugated by the Tenochca, and some of the native population—Otomí as well as Matlatzinca—left for Michoacán, where they settled as military colonists. Tlaxcallan also established Otomí along its borders against the Triple Alliance. The Otomí of Xilotepec had garrisons on their northern borders to fight the warring Chichimec; they also traded with the Chichimec in the area of Querétero.

Specific references to the Otomí in documentary sources describe the negative attitudes the Nahuas, and later the Spaniards, had toward them. According to Sahagún's informants, the Otomí were civilized people and had many good qualities, but they were also said to be

O

stupid, lazy, and oversexed. Although the men were known to be good farmers and fighters, and "Otomí" was the name given to one of the more respected military ranks, they were not considered fit to govern. The women were known to be excellent weavers, especially of maguey fiber, but were given to wearing too many ornaments and gaudy clothes. The Otomí were seen as improvident; for example, their taste for green corn led to eating their crops before they were fully ripe and thus having to hunt and gather wild plants in order to survive. Their less intensive agriculture and predilection for hunting can also be related to their more marginal environment and to their proximity to Chichimec groups in the north. The main areas of Otomí settlement were the cold, high-altitude areas of the basins of Mexico and Toluca, which contrast with the southern basin where most urban Nahuatl-speaking settlements were located. This social and political inferiority accords with the presence of Otomí in some areas only as immigrant farmers, and with the ruling of King Techotlalatzin of Tetzcoco that they should not settle in the cities. The kingdom of Xaltocan was never one of the most important in the Basin of Mexico, and although Otomí or Otomí-speaking peoples inhabited a very large area, most of them were peasants or military colonists in polities where other ethnic groups, such as the Nahuas, were dominant and urban. This contributed to the Nahuas' disdain. Spanish sources such as the *Relación de Querétero* (1582) also show a strongly negative attitude; remarks on Otomí drunkenness are found in the Spanish text of Sahagún's *Florentine Codex,* but not in the corresponding Nahuatl text.

Some widespread religious festivals (Xocotlhuetzi, Quecholli) were probably of Tepanec-Otomí origin. The patron god of the Otomí was Otonteuctli ("Otomí Lord") or Xocotl, also the patron of the Tepanec of Azcapotzalco and Coyoacan, a fact that emphasizes the presence of Otomí ethnic elements among the Tepanec. Otonteuctli can be identified with the warriors who died in battle, and as the war deity of the setting sun, complementary to Huitzilopochtli, the warrior god of the rising sun. Otonteuctli was also described as a fire god and as the patron of gemstone workers and goldsmiths. Other Otomí gods, such as the original couple, the rain god, and the wind, are equivalent to similar Nahua deities; the cult of the moon is also said to be typical of the Otomí. Sahagún names another Otomí god, Yocippa, without identifying him clearly; his feast was celebrated in the open fields. Probably this corresponds to Mixcoatl and the celebration of the month Quecholli, since in his

description of this month Sahagún names Mixcoatl as god of the Otomí. A major Otomí festival was dedicated to offering fruits of the earth to the mother goddess, and to holding military exercises.

Otomí was the major language after Nahuatl in highland Central Mexico at the time of European contact; its speakers lived in areas adjacent to various Chichimec groups north of the Mesoamerican cultural boundary. In the Central Highlands, Otomí speakers formed part of a number of Postclassic city-states; most of them were subject to the Triple Alliance, but some—such as Metztitlan, Tototepec, and Tlaxcallan—were independent. The main sources on Otomí culture are Sahagún's *Florentine Codex* (book 10, chap. 19), and the *Relación de Querétaro,* which describes the area of Xilotepec. Ixtlilxochitl, the *Annals of Cuauhtitlan,* and Durán give some idea of their role in pre-Spanish history.

Otomí is a language of the Otomanguean family, which also includes Matlatzinca and Mazahua (spoken by Mesoamerican peoples) as well as Pame and Jonaz (spoken north of the Mesoamerican border). Related to Mixtec and other Oaxacan languages, it belongs to one of the longest established Mesoamerican linguistic stocks, in contrast to Nahuatl, which seems to have been an intrusion from the north.

FURTHER READINGS

Acuña, R. (ed.). 1987. *Relaciones geográficas del siglo XVI: Michoacán.* Mexico City: Universidad Nacional Autónoma de México.

Bierhorst, J. 1992. *History and Mythology of the Aztecs: The Codex Chimalpopoca.* Tucson: University of Arizona Press.

Carrasco, P. 1950. *Los Otomies: Cultura e historia prehispánica de los pueblos Mesoamericanos de Habla Otomiana.* Publicacion del Instituto de Historia, 15. Mexico City: Universidad Nacional Autónoma de México.

Dow, J. 1986. *The Shaman's Touch: Otomi Indian Symbolic Healing.* Salt Lake City: University of Utah Press.

Guerrero, R. 1983. *Los Otomies del Valle de Mezquital.* Pachuca: Instituto Nacional de Antropología e Historia.

Lanks, H. C. 1938. Otomí Indians of Mezquital Valley, Hidalgo. *Economic Geography* 14:184–194.

Manrique, L. 1967. The Otomí. In E. Vogt (ed.), *Handbook of Middle American Indians,* vol. 8, pp. 682–722. Austin: University of Texas Press.

Sahagún, B. 1961. *General History of the Things of New Spain, Book 10: The People.* C. E. Dibble and

A. J. O. Anderson (transl.). Santa Fe: School of American Research and the University of Utah.

Salinas, J., and R. Bernard. 1978. *The Otomí*. Vol. 1. Albuquerque: University of New Mexico Press.

Soustelle, J. *La Famille Otomí-Pame de Mexique Central*. Université de Paris Institut d'Ethnologie, Travaux et Memoirs, 26. Paris.

Pedro Carrasco

SEE ALSO
Agave; Languages at the Time of Contact

Otumba (México, Mexico)

This provincial urban capital of the Aztec city-state of Otumba (Otompan), in the eastern Teotihuacan Valley in the Basin of Mexico, was first encountered by Cortés on 14 July 1520, at the Battle of Otumba. Its earliest occupation dates to the Early Postclassic period (after A.D. 900). Occupation in the city-state consists of hamlets, large and small dispersed and nucleated villages, and the urban center of Otumba. The city-state territory is astride the trade route to Calpulalpan and several other trade routes. Major obsidian sources (Otumba and Malpais) are nearby.

Survey and excavations in these settlements document low mounds composed of the stone foundations of commoner and elite residences with stone or adobe superstructures, and some pyramids preserved as higher mounds. Otumba's nucleated core has large, widely spaced elite residences and a spatially separate pyramid-plaza complex. Outside the core there is a more lightly occupied zone of smaller residences. Population estimates for Otumba (c. 2 square kilometers) range from 2,500 to 6,500 persons for the urban center, and from 19,000 to 75,000 for the entire city-state. Among archaeologically studied Aztec sites, the urban center of Otumba is unique for the number and intensity of craft specialties present. The industries include obsidian-based lapidary and core-blade production, cotton and maguey fiber spinning, ceramic manufacture (domestic pottery, figurines, incense burners, and spindle whorls), and basalt-working.

FURTHER READINGS

Charlton, T. H. 1973. Texcoco Region Archaeology and the *Códice Xolotl*. *American Antiquity* 38:412–413.

———. 1991. Land Tenure and Agricultural Production in the Otumba Region, 1785–1803. In H. R. Harvey (ed.), *Land and Politics in the Valley of Mexico*, pp. 223–263. Albuquerque: University of New Mexico Press.

———. 1994. Economic Heterogeneity and State Expansion: The Northeastern Basin of Mexico during the Late Postclassic Period. In M. G. Hodge and M. E. Smith (eds.), *Economics and Polities in the Aztec Realm*, pp. 221–256. Studies on Culture and Society, 6. Albany: Institute for Mesoamerican Studies, State University of New York.

Charlton, T. H., D. L. Nichols, and C. Otis Charlton. 1991. Aztec Craft Production and Specialization: Archaeological Evidence from the City-State of Otumba, Mexico. *World Archaeology* 23:98–114.

Otis Charlton, C., T. H. Charlton, and D. L. Nichols. 1993. Aztec Household-Based Craft Production: Archaeological Evidence from the City-State of Otumba. In R. Santley and K. Hirth (eds.), *Household, Compound, and Residence: Studies of pre-Hispanic Domestic Units in Western Mesoamerica*, pp. 147–171. Boca Raton, Fla.: CRC Press.

Thomas H. Charlton

SEE ALSO
Basin of Mexico; Cihuatecpan

Oxkintok (Yucatán, Mexico)

Situated on a plain about 50 kilometers south of present-day Mérida, Oxkintok was an important Maya city, similar in extent and construction to Edzna and even Uxmal. Architectural remains of limestone, frequently surmounted by the corbel vault characteristic of Maya civilization, cover an area of at least 30 square kilometers, though it is also possible that some of the structures pertaining to the city's periphery were elite residences or small dependent centers. Six large groups of structures, distributed along a north–south axis, have been identified. The site is mentioned by Spanish chroniclers of the Colonial era, and by John Lloyd Stephens, who surveyed it the mid-nineteenth century. It was investigated in the 1930s by H. E. D. Pollock, George Brainerd, and Ed Shook, and excavations undertaken by a Spanish team led by Miguel Rivera Dorado began in 1986 and continued for six years. These excavations located three principal groups in the city center, as well as an isolated structure known as the Satunsat or Laberinto; the researchers determined the first complete sequence of occupation for the site, discovered eleven tombs, and uncovered and reconstructed three pyramids and twenty other different buildings, including architectural and other evidence for widespread settlement in the area during the Early Classic (A.D. 300–550), a little-known period in the northern Yucatán Peninsula.

The occupation of Oxkintok continued without interruption from the Middle Formative (c. 500 B.C.) to the Early Postclassic (c. A.D. 1000). Early Classic remains include architecture of the Early Oxkintok style and hieroglyphic inscriptions and dates of the Initial Series, computed to fall in the second half of the fifth century A.D., the oldest encountered in Yucatán. The great ring of the ball court has been discovered, with another long hieroglyphic inscription mentioning a ruler named Walas, who governed the city in the early eighth century A.D. Oxkintok has a strategic position atop the Puuc Hills, permitting control of a fringe of land paralleling the Atlantic coast, through which merchants from the cities of the south traveled.

FURTHER READINGS

Rivera Dorado, M. (ed.). 1988–1992. *Oxkintok.* 4 vol. Madrid: Misión Arqueológica de España en México y Ministerio de Cultura.

———. 1991. *Oxkintok, una ciudad Maya de Yucatán.* Madrid: Comisión del Quinto Centenario.

Miguel Rivera Dorado

SEE ALSO

Maya Lowlands: North

P

Pachona, La (Chontales, Nicaragua)

Situated near the Mayales River, in a relatively arid zone of clay soils, this site extends over about 4 hectares, with thirty-six visible mounds of earth and river cobbles that have no discernible distribution pattern, except for a vacant space that may have functioned as a plaza. Two occupations have been documented: Mayales phases I and II, c. 400 B.C.–A.D. 500, and Monota, c. A.D. 1000–1400, with dating derived from cross-dating excavated ceramics with diagnostics from the Greater Nicoya subarea. The artifact repertoire includes incised and bichrome ceramics as well as white-slipped sherds. Ties to the Atlantic zone of Nicaragua as well as the early complexes of Costa Rica and Nicaragua are suggested.

During the Mayales I and II phases, the site appears to have been a small agricultural hamlet with infrequent interaction with outside groups. Abandoned c. A.D. 400, it was reoccupied during the Monota phase, with ties to the cultures of Pacific Nicaragua. Some statuary of the Chontales type was also found at the site.

Laraine Fletcher

Painting

Painting was essential to the visual culture of Mesoamerica. Images overlaid the surfaces of houses, temples, and tombs, as well as ceramics, manuscripts, textiles, and sculptures. Even human bodies bore the marks of painters. Today, the best-known paintings are those created for high-status individuals and settings. People of modest political and economic resources also consorted with painted imagery, but in Mesoamerica, social and economic status manifestly shaped one's visual activities. Simply put, certain people enjoyed access to a wealth of sophisticated images while others made do with far fewer.

The paintings known today represent but a fragment of what once existed. Numerous stone and ceramic objects have lost their color; other, more perishable articles have not survived, and many painted books and sculptures were destroyed both before and after the Spanish conquest.

Surviving paintings appear in a variety of media and styles. With fingers, pieces of cloth, brushes, and stylus-like objects of bone or wood, painters applied color to cloth, clay, animal hide, paper, stone, and human skin. In some cases, colored feathers were used in place of paint to create resplendent images (today called "feather paintings") on semiflexible supports. Mesoamerican painters practiced both resist techniques and direct application of pigment. Their palettes ranged widely, incorporating blacks, grays, and whites, along with reds, oranges, blue-greens, browns, and purples; not all colors appeared in every setting. Cultural, contextual, and individual discretion played a crucial role in the genesis of images.

In Mesoamerica, painting and glyphic writing were intimate allies. The Classic Maya used the verb *ts'ib* to speak of both arts, and a Nahua *tlacuilo* was both painter and scribe. Current evidence suggests that male painters typically crafted the most prestigious images. Among the Maya, Mixtec, and Aztec, painters were erudite men who were nobles or had close connections to ruling families. Their creations included images for palace settings, ritual performances, and diplomatic exchanges of gifts. Such paintings would have been charged with metaphysical

P

and political meaning; thus, adherence to convention and attentiveness to occasion were both expected and highly valued.

Whether paintings made by and for commoners were subject to similar expectations remains unclear. Certainly not all painters in Mesoamerica were privileged or male, nor was visual expression always subject to direction from higher authorities. At present, the visual practices among subaltern painters and these painters' identities and social sensibilities remain poorly understood. Scholars assume that much painting was completed in workshops serving local as well as regional needs; paintings—especially on ceramics—were also produced and consumed locally, perhaps by single villages, lineages, or families.

The diversity of painted media and of historical contexts in which painted objects circulated implies that painting bore no fixed meaning in Mesoamerica. Furthermore, painted images were rarely viewed or contemplated in isolation. Rather, painting filtered through and participated in complex, richly variegated visual settings.

Mural painting is the focus of another article in this volume. The present article focuses on two portable representational object-types: painted ceramics and manuscript paintings.

Ceramics

Ceramic painting can be traced over two thousand years in Mesoamerica, with pre-Hispanic iconographic traditions persisting well into the sixteenth century A.D. The finest painters excelled at wrapping complex images around the curved surfaces of pots and creating vibrant patterns on sculpted figures. Often ceramic painting delineates the features and forms of humans and their surroundings, yet rarely is this painting strictly a mimetic exercise. Abstract and geometric designs conspire in the semiotic mix to evoke both mundane and supernatural worlds. Mesoamerican painters also deployed color symbolically, often aligning particular hues with world directions and cosmological principles. Consequently, much ceramic painting depicts things that could be known (or imagined), but not necessarily observed in daily life.

Across Mesoamerica, people exchanged painted ceramics both locally and across long distances; they also used painted wares for daily eating and special-occasion feasts. They interred many of their most sophisticated ceramics in funerary and offertory caches. In burying painted pottery in significant quantities, Mesoamericans implied that, in certain contexts, paintings wielded metaphysical powers that extended well beyond mere visibility.

Standing male figure, Nayarit, Mexico, c. A.D. 200–400 (29.4 cm height). Photo courtesy Los Angeles Country Museum of Art.

Because ceramic painting follows regionally and temporally distinct conventions, four representative examples are discussed below. These traditions, taken together, offer insight into the ways pre-Hispanic people combined paint and clay to organize earthly and exalted experience.

West Mexico

Shaft tombs constructed from 200 B.C. to A.D. 500 held the bodies of multiple individuals and were well endowed with funerary offerings, especially painted ceramic sculptures. Among the most numerous of these ceramics are weapon-wielding males dressed in painted tunics, women and men adorned with elaborate jewelry, and narrative scenes representing houses, people, and animals. Working primarily on reddish clays with black, cream, yellow, and white pigments, painters relied on resist techniques and the direct application of color to create bold geometric patterns on sculpted figures and architectural structures.

Some scholars construe these painted figures as mimetic attempts to capture the West Mexican visual environment. Thus, painting is primarily descriptive: patterns on ceramic clothes and bodies are believed to mirror actual pre-Hispanic patterned cloth and skin markings. Others argue that the ceramic figures arose from sacred rather than mundane concerns. As mediators between human and supernatural worlds, these funerary ceramics bear sacrosanct and ritual connotations, and so does the logic of their painted marks. These two interpretations need not be mutually exclusive, however, for nowhere in Mesoamerica—even among people of similar class or political affiliation—do painted ceramics betray a single set of meanings.

Teotihuacán. In Central Mexico, Teotihuacán once housed the largest multiethnic population in the Americas. Here painters created a profusion of visual images. Brightly colored and iconographically complex paintings covered the walls of apartment complexes and façades of buildings along Teotihuacán's primary arteries. Between A.D. 250 and 750, people also fashioned a multitude of painted ceramics: cylindrical vessels, masks, sculpted figures, and censers. An apogee of Teotihuacán artistry

Stucco-painted tripod vessel with plumed serpent. Teotihuacán, Mexico c. A.D. 600–750 (35 cm diameter). Photo courtesy Cleveland Museum of Art.

appears in the painting of ceramic tripod vessels. To fashion these pots, painters applied green, red, orange, yellow, black, and white pigments to thin stucco layers affixed to the exterior surfaces of vessels. In this way they created fragile, fresco-like images. These paintings favor static poses over dynamic action, anonymity over individual identity. Many vessels feature geometric patterns, floral motifs, or masked beings with humanoid faces baring fangs. Others display plumed serpents, or figures garbed in goggle-eyed masks, enormous earrings, and extravagant feathered headdresses; still others evoke sublime combinations of speech, sound, and violence through the use of speech scrolls, obsidian blades, blood, and arrows.

Little is known of Teotihuacán painters or their workshops, but similarities in the imagery on ceramics, wooden boxes, and architectural surfaces point to a shared sphere of visual culture—for people of political, economic, and ritual power—wherein paintings in different media accrued meaning through mutual reference. Moreover, the iconography of Teotihuacán stucco-painted vessels may well refer to the religious, social, or political affiliations of the vessels' owners. The images on certain ceramics perhaps evoke, in highly conventionalized visual language, personal, lineal, or social identities.

Maya. The best-known Mesoamerican ceramic paintings are Classic period Maya wares (A.D. 250–850). Well before this, Maya painters composed monochrome and polychrome images, but their finest work embellishes the plates, cylindrical vessels, and bowls of this period. Regional conventions shaped Maya painting in choice of color, composition, and iconography; for instance, reds and oranges predominate, although, depending on place and time, cream, yellow, blue, black, pink, maroon, and brown augment the basic palette. Iconographically, Maya painters ranged widely: historical scenes, especially palace gatherings, presentations of tribute or prisoners of war, and ball games are prevalent; so, too, are animal images such as bats, fish, jaguars, turkeys, rabbits, and deer. Maya painters also depicted sacrificial events, otherworldly beings, and scenes from Xibalba (the *Popol Vuh* underworld). The most highly skilled painters executed fluid, graceful lines; they also modeled and shaded their figures, often situating them in shallow three-dimensional spaces. Rather than reproducing the world mimetically, however, Maya painters tended to present multiperspectival vantages or to combine frontal and profile views.

A distinctive feature of Maya pottery painting is glyphic writing. Hieroglyphs operate as a complementary

P

Maya cylindrical vessel with seated ruler and Primary Standard Sequence. Guatemala, c. A.D. 670–800 (16.3 cm height). Photo courtesy Museum of Fine Arts, Boston.

mode of expression on ceramics, overlapping but not fully describing the painted images. Stylistically, glyphs betray nuances that distinguish one painter from another. The texts themselves, however, address a limited inventory of themes. Glyphs may name the actors depicted or the pot's painter; frequently, the Primary Standard Sequence—a series of glyphs that dedicates the pot, identifies the vessel type, describes its contents, and, often, names its owner or patron—encircles the lips of Classic Maya vessels.

As elsewhere in Mesoamerica, Maya vase imagery resonated against and reinforced other forms of representation. Some vessels parallel Maya codices; others more closely mirror images carved into stone. Furthermore, painted vessels circulated through many social venues. As serving containers for meals in palaces and other imposing settings, as royal gifts, and as tomb offerings, finely painted wares both proclaimed and cemented the social and religious authority of those who owned and handled them.

Guanacaste-Nicoya. For centuries, people living in Guanacaste-Nicoya (in present-day Nicaragua and Costa Rica) created striking ceramic paintings on orange- or

white-based wares. These elaborately painted polychrome vessels point to ties with outsiders and long-distance exchange networks.

Although made locally for daily use and funerary offerings, these ceramics find strong parallels in pottery from the north, particularly Honduras, El Salvador, and Central Mexico. Around A.D. 800, for example, orange-red and black images set against white or cream backgrounds become integral to the Guanacaste-Nicoya repertoire. These ceramics feature local interpretations of imported iconographies: battles of humans and jaguars, plumed serpents, and goggle-eyed faces. Through reiteration and reinterpretation over generations, these northern iconographies accrued local meanings. The cultural appropriations and innovations in Guanacaste-Nicoya are unique in their specific forms and details, but the processes are detectable elsewhere in Mesoamerica. Certain paintings

Pedestal jar painted with stylized jaguar and plumed serpent motifs. Guanacaste-Nicoya, Costa Rica, A.D. 1000–1200 (23.2 cm height). Photo courtesy Museo del Jade, Lic. Fidel Tristan del Instituto Nacional de Seguros, San Jose, Costa Rica.

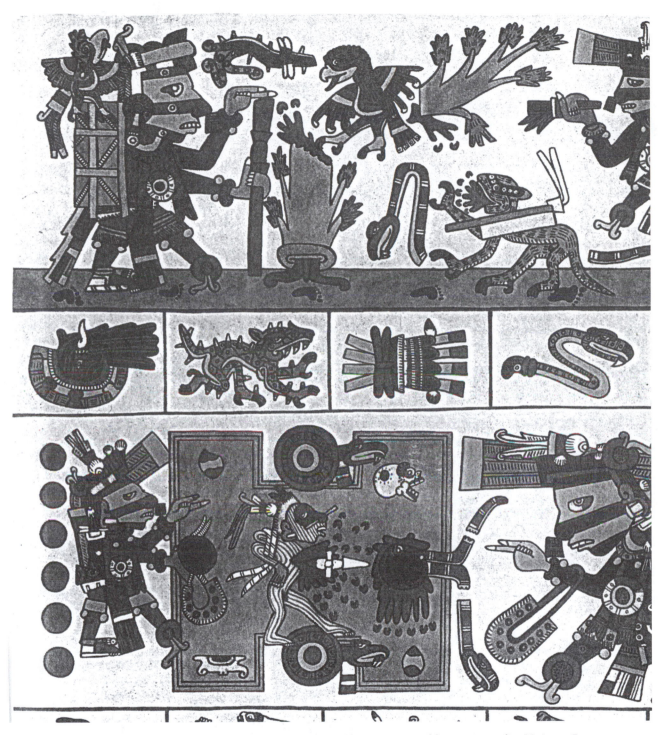

Codex Borgia (page 20). Mexico, c. A.D. 1250–1520 (27 × 26.5 cm). Photo courtesy Biblioteca Apostolica Vaticana, Rome.

P

and images were temporally and regionally distinct; others migrated across ethnic, linguistic, and political boundaries. Neither isolated nor self-contained, paintings could inherit and shed meaning as they moved from place to place and were replicated and renewed over time.

Manuscripts

In pre-Hispanic Mesoamerica, people created local and imperial histories, cosmologies, genealogies, prognostications, and census and tribute records, all in pictorial form. These records, known today as "manuscripts" or "codices," were stored in royal libraries, owned by high-status families, and kept by religious leaders. Nearly every group of Mesoamericans relied on painted records, yet only a small fraction actually trafficked in manuscripts.

Usually these were well-educated men: painters with intensive training, and readers or interpreters with expertise in the histories and rituals of their communities. Today about fifteen pre-Hispanic codices are known, all Postclassic in date (c. A.D. 1250–1520). Scores of post-Conquest pictorial manuscripts also exist, many of which draw upon pre-Hispanic graphic practices.

Mesoamerican manuscripts take numerous forms. Typical is the *tira*, a long, relatively narrow painting on strips of animal hide or paper glued together end to end. *Tiras* were rolled into bundles, or folded into accordion pleats to create booklike objects today called "screenfolds." When closed, a screenfold fits easily onto a person's lap; when opened fully, some extend more than 6 meters. *Lienzos* are large, rectangular paintings on cotton or

Codex Zouche-Nuttall (page 32). Mexico, A.D. 1250–1500 (19 × 25.5 cm). Photo courtesy British Museum, London.

maguey-fiber cloth which frequently depict community lands and histories. Shortly after the Spanish conquest, indigenous painters gained access to alphabetic writing and European paper, books, and images. After 1521, native painters worked for both indigenous and Spanish patrons, intertwining—in complex, multifaceted ways—graphic elements of pre-Hispanic and European origin in screenfolds, *lienzos,* maps, economic accounts, and European-style books, as well as elaborate murals for religious complexes in indigenous communities.

In most codices, especially pre-Hispanic works, pictorial elements and hieroglyphs dominate. Nonetheless, painted codices rarely formed complete records. Manuscripts provided frameworks for oral performances, public or semipublic occasions for recounting narratives or prognostications. Visual images were read much as musicians read scores: specific details of the narrative were fixed, while possibilities for interpretation remained more open. Unfortunately, the roles assigned to manuscript paintings remain poorly understood, but scholars believe that these works served as substantial sources of legitimacy for the rulers and priests who commissioned and owned them. Described below, through a few prime examples, are the basic visual qualities exhibited by Mesoamerican manuscripts and the social meanings invested in them.

Pre-Hispanic Manuscripts. All the pre-Hispanic manuscripts known today come from Mexico. Whether working on paper or animal skin, painters treated their surfaces before applying pigment; frequently they also placed images on both sides of these supports. The most skillful painters excelled at balancing firm black outlines with solid blocks of color, generally eschewing modeling, shading, and the intermingling of hues. No pre-Hispanic codex precisely replicates another in form, iconography, or style, but surviving manuscripts stress one of two themes: either ritual, divinatory, and calendrical information, or genealogical, historical, and political narratives.

Nine codices (four Maya and five Mixteca-Puebla screenfolds) focus on sacred, prognosticatory, and calendrical information. The oldest and most replete of the Maya screenfolds, the Dresden Codex, emphasizes the *tonalamatl*—the book of the 260–day sacred calendar. Its polychrome glyphs and images also record divinatory almanacs, farmers' almanacs, descriptions for New Year's ceremonies, and tables for charting astronomical phenomena. As with all pre-Hispanic manuscripts, the painters' names are no longer known, although stylistic analysis suggests that the Dresden Codex is not unusual in displaying the work of multiple hands. In short, the Dresden and other divinatory screenfolds, like the Mixteca-Puebla style Codex Borgia, use complex and densely painted images of deities, calendars, and esoteric themes to lend visual and physical form to concepts of time and cosmological principles.

In contrast, manuscripts from the Mixtec area of Oaxaca emphasize genealogical and historical memory. The Codex Zouche-Nuttall is a prime example: it represents one of the longest continuous dynastic records known from Mesoamerica (more than five centuries), along with tales of dynastic power and conflict. As is characteristic, painters enlisted a wealth of color—red, blue, purple, yellow, green, and orange—but confined these hues within firm black frame lines. Figures and forms are highly schematized, many appearing to float in space. In addition, human clothing, gesture, and pose receive more care than does anatomy; territory and physical settings are evoked through iconic and metaphoric signs rather than mimetic images. The painted narratives registered here would probably have been performed through chanting and recitation, perhaps for the benefit of guests who dined from painted ceramic vessels and wore garments decorated with images keyed to those in the manuscripts. In such contexts, codex paintings would have buttressed the socio-political, ritual, and economic relations of elite individuals and families.

Post-Conquest Manuscripts. After the Spanish conquest, painters rarely made codices representing pre-Hispanic rituals, cosmogonies, or calendars; those who did worked primarily for Europeans who desired records of (forbidden) native practices. Hundreds of paintings about history, territory, and economics were made, however, for indigenous and European patrons alike. Many of these works are faithful to pre-Hispanic traditions; others, especially after 1560, juxtapose pre-Conquest-style images with alphabetic writing, or, deriving inspiration from European models, disclose new commitments to mimetic representation. Among the most elaborate manuscripts produced in post-Conquest Mesoamerica are compilations and encyclopedic codices created in conjunction with, or for, friars and colonial officials working in Central Mexico. Crafted by indigenous artists and scribes on European paper, these documents take the form of European-style books and rely on both alphabetic texts and pictorial images. Paintings in the Florentine Codex and the Codex Mendoza typically evoke memories and narratives of the pre-Hispanic (especially Aztec) past

P

Codex Telleriano Remensis (Bibliotheque Nationale, Paris).

through ancient as well as sixteenth-century images and writings. The result is manuscripts of mixed ancestry that chronicle colonial no less than pre-Conquest practices.

Pictorial annals represent another key form of image-making. Before and after the Conquest, Mesoamericans maintained annalistic histories—accounts organized year by year, with one or two key events registered per year. In stressing temporality and momentous happenings, these codices feature royal accessions and deaths, military conquests, city foundings, and natural phenomena like floods, eclipses, and comets. Today only post-Conquest annals survive. In these, painters give few details; instead, year glyphs and iconic, metonymic signs (often pre-Hispanic in style) evoke the primary features of a complex series of events. As in other Mesoamerican manuscripts, these paintings do not stand alone as historical accounts; rather, readers were obliged to elaborate the narrative, to make the history replete (a role sometimes assumed by alphabetic glosses written near the pictorial signs. Recently, scholars have linked the annals form of manuscript painting to Aztec claims to power. If the connection holds, it suggests that the form of a Mesoamerican manuscript, and not just its iconography and style, sustained ethnic, political, and social potency.

Although early sixteenth-century accounts tell of impressive pre-Hispanic maps, no pre-Conquest examples survive; however, a characteristic form of Mesoamerican painting, the cartographic history, betrays strong pre-Hispanic affinities. These works, which include *lienzos* and range from less than 30 cm on a side to more than 2.5 meters in length, weave representations of territory together with prophetic moments and actors in the history of a region or community. Typically, the main town appears toward the center of the composition, and hill glyphs circle the perimeter, defining community boundaries. Sprinkled across the painting or set to one side are depictions of genealogies, conquests, land negotiations, and boundary markings. The "Mapa Pintado en Papel Europeo e Aforrado en el Indiano" (1530–1540) represents one of the earliest post-Conquest examples. True to cartographic history traditions, the "Mapa Pintado" is fully local in conception: its preoccupations are those of a single town and its leaders. In some Mexican towns today, *lienzos* remain critical community possessions and are kept hidden from public view. It is unclear whether such practices pre-date the Conquest, although it seems likely that the roles assigned to *lienzos* in the construction and maintenance of community identity have deep roots in the soil of Mesoamerican history.

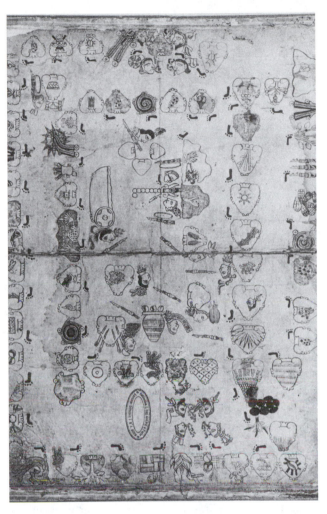

Mapa Pintado en Papel Europeo e Aforrado en el Indiano (Bibliotheque Nationale, Paris).

FURTHER READINGS

Berrin, K., and E. Pasztory. (eds.). 1993. *Teotihuacan: Art from the City of the Gods.* San Francisco: Fine Arts Museum of San Francisco.

Boone, E. H. 2000. *Stories in Black and Red: Pictorial Histories of the Aztecs and Mixtecs.* Austin: University of Texas Press.

Boone, E. H. and W. Mignolo. (eds.). 1994. *Writing Without Words: Alternative Literacies in Mesoamerica and the Andes.* Durham: Duke University Press.

Coe, M. D. 1978. *Lords of the Underworld: Masterpieces of Classic Maya Ceramics.* Princeton: Princeton University Press.

Glass, J. B. 1975. "A Survey of Native Middle American Pictorial Manuscripts." In Howard F. Cline (ed.), *Handbook of Middle American Indians,* vol. 14, pp. 3–80. Austin: University of Texas Press.

P

Kubler, G. 1984. *Art and Architecture of Ancient America.* Harmondsworth and Baltimore: Pelican Press.

Miller, M. E. 1996. *The Art of Mesoamerica: From Olmec to Aztec.* London: Thames and Hudson.

Reents-Budet, D. 1994. *Painting the Maya Universe: Royal Ceramics of the Classic Period.* Durham: Duke University Press.

Reyes-Valerio, C. 1993. *De Bonampak al Templo Mayor: el azul maya en Mesoamérica.* Mexico City: Siglo Veintiuno Editores.

Robertson, D. 1994. *Mexican Manuscript Painting of the Early Colonial Period: The Metropolitan Schools.* Forword by Elizabeth Hill Boone. Norman: University of Oklahoma Press.

Smith, M. E. 1973. *Picture Writing of Ancient Southern Mexico: Mixtec Place Signs and Maps.* Norman: University of Oklahoma.

Townsend, R. (ed.). 1998. *Ancient West Mexico: Art and Archaeology of the Unknown Past.* New York and Chicago: Thames and Hudson and Art Institute of Chicago.

Dana Leibsohn

SEE ALSO

Ethnohistorical Sources and Methods; Maps and Place-Names; Mural Painting

Pala Chica Cave (Sonora, Mexico)

This small cave is in the coastal plain near Guaymas on Sonora's Pacific coast. A narrow crevice runs upward at a steep angle, ending in a small chamber where six individuals were buried in a shallow, dry deposit. Wood and fiber artifacts were well preserved. Some are unique in the archaeological and ethnographic reports for the Sonora coast, Baja California, and the Greater Southwest. There were three extended burials—a male, aged 17 to 19, and two children, aged 10 to 14—with fragments of two young adults and one small child. The two teenage children had undergone removal of their maxillary central incisors before death. Artifacts included a wooden scoop or hand-shovel (for which the cave was named); a finely made, thin, ring-shaped shell ornament with tiny drilled decorative holes; a bracelet of thick disk beads looped on cordage shingle-fashion; loose shell and stone beads; and human hair and vegetal materials. The cave is near the territorial boundary of present-day Seri and Yaqui ethnic groups. Though not uniquely diagnostic of the Seri, Pala Chica's artifacts are consistent with their material culture. Incisor ablation was evidently practiced by the Seri in female puberty rites but was discontinued long ago. Extensive comparative analyses suggest attribution to the Seri culture and the minimum age as the late nineteenth century. This finding shows the persistence of Archaic culture for many millennia (more than 8,000 years) in the Northern Arid Zone.

FURTHER READINGS

Bowen, T. 1976. *Seri Prehistory: The Archaeology of the Central Coast of Sonora, Mexico.* Anthropological Papers, 27. Tucson: University of Arizona.

Dixon, K. A. 1990. *La Cueva de la Pala Chica: A Burial Cave in the Guaymas Region of Coastal Sonora, Mexico.* Publications in Anthropology, 38. Nashville, Tenn.: Vanderbilt University.

Keith A. Dixon

SEE ALSO

Northern Arid Zone

Palenque (Chiapas, Mexico)

Situated on the northwestern Maya periphery, Palenque was occupied from the Early Classic period (A.D. 200–600), becoming one of the major Maya centers in Late Classic times and continuing as such until its downfall about A.D. 800. Acknowledged as one of the most beautiful of all Maya sites, it sits in the foothills of the Sierra de Palenque, in a lush tropical jungle where annual rainfall is close to 3,000 mm, overlooking the alluvial plain stretching north to the Gulf of Mexico. With close proximity to Tabasco cacao cultivation areas and numerous waterways for travel, Palenque's location would have been ideal economically as well as ecologically. The city's layout is governed by the six rivers that run through it—the Otolum, Murcielagos, Balunte, Motiepa, Piedras Bolas, and Picota—making it literally "a city of rivers."

Palenque art is noted for its accuracy in portraying the human figure in stucco and stone. The iconographic sophistication of these works exceeds anything else in Mesoamerica. The piers on Houses A, D, C, and the Temple of the Inscriptions are all compositions of one, two, or three human figures in rounded relief sculpture that at times (as on House D) is almost three-dimensional. Body proportions and likenesses are accurate. The monumental architecture with mansard roofs and high delicate roofcombs of open fretwork and painted stucco sculpture is still a splendid sight, even if the paint is no longer visible.

Sarcophagus cover at Palenque. Illustration courtesy of the author.

P

The Temple of the Inscriptions, the most impressive monument dedicated to a single person in all of ancient America, houses the crypt and sarcophagus of Lord Pacal, Palenque's most prestigious king, who was born 9.8.9.13.0 8 Ahau 13 Pop (A.D. 603), became king in A.D. 615 at the age of twelve years, and ruled until his death on 9.12.11.5.18 6 Etz'nab 11 Yax (A.D. 683) after a sixty-eight-year reign (see table). The stone sarcophagus bears two carved portraits each of his mother, Lady Zac-Kuk, and his father, Kan-Bahlum-Mo', on the ends of the sarcophagus, and portraits of his ancestors Chaacal I, Chan-Bahlum I, Lady Kan-Ik, Pacal I, and Kan-Xul on the sides. They are all depicted emerging at waist level from the earth symbol and have various native fruits in their headdresses. The sarcophagus cover depicts Pacal falling into the underworld between the open jaws of a serpent, above the Underworld Sun Monster, whose cap is the Quadripartite Badge. Pacal's clubfoot is readily seen on the portrait. Behind him rises the world tree, across which undulates a double-headed serpent from whose open jaws on the west emerges God K, or Smoking Mirror; from the east head, the Jester God emerges. On top of the tree, the sacred ceiba, the Principal Bird Deity is perched. The cover is divided into the three Maya worlds: the underworld, the world of the living, and the heavens. The cover's edge is carved at the south end with Pacal's birthdate and with other information around the sides, ending with his death date. There is a psychoduct (a hollow passage) that starts with a hole in the top of the sarcophagus, crosses the stone next to it, and continues up the stairs within the tomb. Then, step by step, this square, hollow stone slab duct goes all the way to the top of the temple stairs and across the floor to the base of Pier C, where the mother of Pacal is depicted. This has a twofold meaning—

RULERS OF PALENQUE.

MYTHICAL GENEALOGY

GI, First Father	Birth: 3122 B.C.		
Ancestral Goddess	Birth: 3121 B.C.		
GI, Hunahpu	Birth: 2697 B.C.	1.18.5.3.2	9 Ik 15 Ceh
GIII, Xbalanque	Birth: 2697 B.C.	1.18.5.3.6	13 Cimi 19 Ceh
GII, God K	Birth: 2697 B.C.	1.18.5.4.0	1 Ahau 13 Mac
U-Kix-Chan	Birth: 994 B.C.	5.7.11.8.4	1 Kan 2 Cumku
O Pop	Accession: 967 B.C.	5.8.17.15.17	11 Caban

HISTORICAL GENEALOGY

Bahlum-Kuk (K'uk Balam)	Birth: A.D. 397	8.18.0.13.6	5 Cimi 14 Kayab
	Accession: A.D. 431	8.19.15.3.4	1 Kan 2 Kayab
"Casper"	Birth: A.D. 422	8.19.6.8.8	11 Lamat 6 Xul
	Accession: A.D. 435	8.19.19.11.17	2 Caban 10 Xul
Manik (Btuz' ah-Sak-Chik)	Birth: A.D. 459	9.1.4.5.0	12 Ahau 13 Zac
	Accession: A.D. 487	9.2.12.6.18	3 Etz'nab 11 Xul
Chaacal I (Akul-Anab I)	Birth: A.D. 465	9.1.10.0.0	5 Ahau 3 Tzec
	Accession: A.D. 501	9.3.6.7.17	5 Caban 0 Zotz'
	Death: A.D. 524	9.4.10.4.17	5 Caban 5 Mac
Kan-Xul I (K'an-Hok'-Chitam I)	Birth: A.D. 490	9.2.15.3.8	12 Lamat 6 Uo
	Accession: A.D. 529	9.4.14.10.4	5 Kan 12 Kayab
	Death: A.D. 565	9.6.11.0.16	7 Cib 4 Kayab

Historical Genealogy (*continued*)

Chaacal II (Akul-Anab II)	Birth: A.D. 523	9.4.9.0.4	7 Kan 17 Mol
	Accession: A.D. 565	9.6.11.5.1	11 Imix 4 Zip
	Death: A.D. 570	9.6.16.10.7	9 Manik 5 Yaxkin
Chan-Bahlum I (Kan-Balam I)	Birth: A.D. 524	9.4.10.1.5	11 Chicchan 13 Ch'en
	Accession: A.D. 572	9.6.18.5.12	10 Eb 0 Ou
	Death: A.D. 583	9.7.9.5.5	11 Chicchan 3 Kayab
Lady Kan-Ik (Lady Olnal)	Accession: A.D. 583	9.7.10.3.8	9 Lamat 1 Muan
	Death: A.D. 604	9.8.11.6.12	2 Eb 20 Ceh
Aach-Kan (Ah-Ne-Ol-Mat)	Birth: A.D. 605	9.8.11.9.10	8 Oc 18 Muan
	Death: A.D. 612	9.8.19.4.6	2 Cimi 14 Mol
Pacal I (Hanab Pacal)	Death: A.D. 612	9.8.18.14.11	3 Chuen 4 Uayeb
Kan-Bahlum-Mo' (Kan-Mo-Balam)	Death: A.D. 643	9.10.10.1.5	13 Cimi 4 Pax
Lady Zac-Kuk	Accession: A.D. 612	9.8.19.7.18	9 Etz'nab 6 Ceh
	Death: A.D. 640	9.10.7.13.5	4 Chicchan 13 Yax
Lady Ahpo-Hel (Lady Tz' ak-Ahaw)	Marriage A.D. 626	9.9.13.0.17	7 Caban 15 Pop
	Death: A.D. 672	9.12.0.6.18	5 Etz'nab 6 Kankin
Pacal II (Hanab Pacal)	Birth: A.D. 603	9.8.9.13.0	8 Ahau 13 Pop
	Accession: A.D. 615	9.9.2.4.8	5 Lamat 1 Mol
	Death: A.D. 683	9.12.11.5.18	6 Etz'nab 11 Yax
Chan-Bahlum II (Kan-Balam II)	Birth: A.D. 635	9.10.2.6.6	2 Cimi 19 Zotz'
	Heir Desig.: A.D. 641	9.10.8.9.3 9	Akbal 6 Xul
	Accession: A.D. 684	9.12.11.12.10	8 Oc 3 Kayab
	Death: A.D. 702	9.13.10.1.5	6 Chicchan 3 Pop
Kan-Xul II (K'an-Hok' Chitam II)	Birth: A.D. 644	9.10.11.17.0	11 Ahau 8 Mac
	Accession: A.D. 702	9.13.10.6.8	5 Lamat 6 Xul
	Captured: A.D. 711	9.13.19.13.3	
Xoc* (Ox Yohun; Ox Hun)	Birth: A.D. 650	9.10.17.6.0	1 Ahau 3 Uayeb
	Date of office: A.D. 720	9.14.8.14.15	9 Men 3 Yax
Chac-Zutz', a regent (Sahal)	Birth: A.D. 671	9.11.18.9.17	7 Caban 15 Kayab
	Death: A.D. 731	Post 9.15.0.0.0	4 Ahau 13 Yax
Chaacal III (Akul-Anab III)	Birth: A.D. 678	9.12.6.5.8	3 Lamat 7 Zac
	Accession: A.D. 722	9.14.10.4.2	9 Ik 5 Kayab
	Death: A.D. 723	Pre. 9.14.11.12.14	8 Ix 7 Yaxkin
Kuk II	Accession: A.D. 764	9.16.13.0.7	9 Manik 15 Uo
Cimi-Pacal (6–Kim'i-Hanab-Pacal)	Accession: A.D. 799	9.18.9.4.4	7 Kan 17 Muan

*Xoc was a regent who either oversaw the kingdom during the imprisonment of Kan Xul II (K'an-Hok' Chitam II) at Toniná, or after his death, or possibly a Toniná supervisor in the wake of war, a local puppet of Palenque's conquerors.

P

a connection to the umbilical cord, and bringing life breath to the deceased Pacal.

The next most important king of Palenque was Chan-Bahlum II, son of Pacal and Lady Ahpo-Hel, born in A.D. 635; he acceded to the throne in 684 and died in 702. He completed his father's monument, and for his own monument he built the three Cross Group temples—the Temple of the Cross, the Temple of the Sun, and the Temple of the Foliated Cross. Each of these structures has an inner sanctuary with a stone tablet depicting Chan-Bahlum and Pacal (or a younger Chan Bahlum) and a lengthy text proving Chan-Bahlum's legitimate right to the throne by showing his relationship to the First Mother (the ancestral goddess born in 3121 B.C.). The Temple of the Cross is dedicated to the birth of God GI of the Palenque Triad. The tablet is divided into two sections, the left panel relating mythological events, and the right panel, historical events. The mythological events lead up to the birth of "Lady Beastie," the ancestral goddess and mother of the Triad Gods. Her accession is recorded 915 years later, and then that of U-Kix-Chan. The birth of the First Father is recorded, and that of U-Kix-Chan at 993 B.C. On the right side of the tablet, U-Kix-Chan's accession in 968 B.C. is recorded along with all the legitimate kings of Palenque, thereby legitimizing Chan-Bahlum's birth by showing his descent from the First Mother to U-Kix-Chan and to Bahlum-Kuk, the first ruler of Palenque in historic times. The Temple of the Sun, the war temple, is dedicated to the birth of God GIII, or Xbalanque, the secondborn son of the First Mother. This tablet goes into the rite that took place when Chan-Bahlum was six years old, legitimizing him as heir to the throne. Bloodletting rituals are recorded, and the war shield centers the tablet. The Temple of the Foliated Cross is dedicated to God GII, the lastborn of the ancestral goddess; he is known as God K, or Smoking Mirror, because of the smoking mirror or celt in his forehead. This temple records life, death, and rebirth.

Palenque had two women rulers: Lady Kan-Ik, who ruled for twenty-one years, and Lady Zac-Kuk, mother of Pacal, who ruled only for three years before turning the throne over to her son. However, she continued living for twenty-five more years, during at least part of which time she probably acted as regent for her son. The last known ruler of Palenque was 6 Cimi Pacal, who acceded to the throne in A.D. 799. We know nothing about him, but Lord Kuk II, who ruled from A.D. 764 to sometime after A.D. 783, left us the beautiful Tablet of the 96 Hieroglyphs, which tells his history.

The Palace, situated on a large elevated platform just southeast of the Temple of the Inscriptions, consists of Houses E, B, C, A, D, A-D, F, G, H, I, J, K, the East Court, West Court, and Tower and Tower Court. This complex structure is ornately decorated on piers, walls, and roofs with brightly painted stucco. The sequence of stucco sculptured figures is here, and on the House A piers one can see how the sculptors formed a naked figure and how they made a taller figure by simply elongating the center portion of the body. Clothing was built up in stucco just as if one were dressing a person: underclothes first, then skirt, belt and finally ornaments, beads and buckles. Each piece of clothing was painted before the next piece of dress was added. The same was the rule for feathers; each feather was formed and overlapped, and each was painted before the next was laid over it. In all stucco sculpture at Palenque, all worldly things, including backgrounds and bodies, were painted red; all heavenly, divine, royal, or precious things were blue, and those pertaining to the underworld were yellow.

Other major groups include the Olvidado, 0.5 kilometer west of the main center. This is a small temple built along a steep escarpment, with a series of three-staired terrace platforms leading up to a final platform where the temple was built. The vaulting system is quite different from any other vaults at Palenque. Rather than sloping in a straight line toward the capstone, the Olvidado vaults form two separate curves. The lower portion sweeps in an arc of radius 120 cm, stopping at a point about 40 percent of the way to the capstone, and then another curve is formed above the 4.5-cm inverted step. At this time in Palenque's history, builders were striving for ever higher vaults and were trying this out here. The resulting room, however, is very narrow; the height of the vault is 3.5 times the width of the room, ending with a capstone only 9 cm wide. Peter Mathews has deciphered the inscription on the piers as giving the date 9.10.14.9.10 3 Oc 3 Pop, the name of Pacal and his dates, and the names of Kan-Bahlum Mo' and Lady Zac-Kuk. The parentage statement with the relationship is the most important part of the inscription. This is the earliest recorded date concerning Pacal after his accession thirty-one years earlier.

The visible portion of Palenque is completed by the North Group on the northern boundary of the civic center; the nearby Temple of the Count; Group Four, near the turn of the road as one enters the parking area today and where the Tablet of the Slaves was found; the Temple of the Jaguar, up the trail behind the Inscriptions Temple, along the Otolum river, and numerous smaller groups. Much of the city is still unmapped or unexcavated.

The major sculptured limestone tablets at Palenque are, first, the Sarcophagus cover; the Palace Tablet, found on the northern wall of House A-D; three sanctuary tablets from the Temple of the Cross, the Temple of the Sun, and the Temple of the Foliated Cross; the East Jamb and West Jamb of the Temple of the Cross; the Tablet of Temple XIV; the Tablet of the Slaves from Group IV; the Oval Palace Tablet from House E; the Tablet from Temple XXI; and the Tablet of the 96 Hieroglyphs, the Tablet of the Scribe, the Tablet of the Orator, and the Creation Stone, all from the Tower Court.

Recent excavations by Mexico's Instituto Nacional de Antropología e Historia, including restoration of the Temple of the Cross, have shown that this was not a man-made hill with a temple on top, but a natural mound of immense stone blocks. Temple XVII was uncovered, revealing the Tablet of Temple XVII, a large sanctuary tablet whose glyphs indicate that the event depicted took place during the reign of either Manik (Butz' ah-Sac-Chik) or Chaacal I (Akul-Anab I) during the fifth century. The birthdates of these two, just five years apart, indicate that they were probably brothers. The other figure is a seated, bound figure sculpted in much the same manner as the "cushion slaves" on the Tablet of the Slaves. The other recent important excavation was in Temple XIII, next to the Temple of the Inscription, where a stone sarcophagus was uncovered. The bones indicate that this was a woman of some noble status, because the inside of the sarcophagus was covered with cinnabar; there were no glyphs.

Palenque has five emblem glyphs, the "wavy bone" being the most prominent, with "Lady Beastie" also a favored glyph.

Early visitors and explorers to the site included Ramon Ordonez y Aguiar (1773), Jóse Calderón and the artist Antonio Bernasconi (1784–1785), Antonio del Rio (1786), Captain Guillermo Dupaix and the artist Jose Luciano Casteneda (1807), Jean Frédéric Maximilien, the Comte de Waldeck (1832), John Lloyd Stephens and Frederick Catherwood (1840), Juan Galindo (1832), Patrick Walker and John Herbert Caddy (1840), Désiré Charnay (1858), Captain Lindsay Prime (1869), Teobart Maler (1877), Leopold Batres (1888), Rio de la Losa and Romero (1892), William H. Holmes (1895), Marshall H. Seville (1897), Alfred Percival Maudslay (1890–1891), and Benito Lacroix (1898).

FURTHER READINGS

Berlin, H. 1965. The Inscription of the Temple of the Cross at Palenque. *American Antiquity* 30:330–342.

Berlin, H. 1968. The Tablet of the 96 Glyphs at Palenque, Chiapas, Mexico. *Middle American Research Institute, Publications* 26:135–149.

de la Fuente, B. 1965. *La Escultura de Palenque.* Mexico City: Estudios y Fuentes del Arte en México. Instituto de Investigaciones Estéticas, Universidad Nacional Autónoma de México.

Greene Robertson, M. 1983–1991. *The Sculpture of Palenque.* 4 vols. Princeton: Princeton University Press.

——— (eds.). 1973–1996. *The Palenque Round Table Conferences.* 10 vols. San Francisco: Pre-Columbian Art Research Institute.

Kelley, D. H. 1965. The Birth of the Gods at Palenque. *Estudios de Cultura Maya* 5:93–134.

Rands, R. L. 1974. The Ceramic Sequence at Palenque, Chiapas. In N. Hammond (ed.), *Mesoamerican Archaeology,* pp. 51–75. Austin: University of Texas Press.

Ruz Llhuillier, A. 1952, 1955, 1958, 1960. Exploraciones arqueológicas en Palenque:1952–1957. *Anales de INAH* 5:25–45; 6:79–110; 10:69–299; 14:35–90.

Schele, L. 1978–1996. *Notebooks for the Maya Hieroglyphic Workshops at Texas.* Austin: Institute of Latin American Studies, University of Texas.

Schele, L., and P. Mathews. 1979. *The Bodega of Palenque, Chiapas, Mexico.* Washington, D.C.: Dumbarton Oaks.

Schele, L., and M. E. Miller. 1986. *The Blood of Kings.* Fort Worth: Kimbell Art Museum.

Merle Greene Robertson

SEE ALSO

Maya Lowlands: South

Paleoindian Period

The vast area of Mexico and adjacent parts of Mesoamerica is characterized by a tremendous range of climates, vegetational patterns, and topography, from volcanic mountain ranges to jungle-covered coastal plains. For most of the past eight thousand years there has apparently been little major change in the overall environment, although rises in sea level, expansion of wetlands, dry cycles, and other local phenomena have been documented by palynologists (pollen researchers) and soil scientists.

P

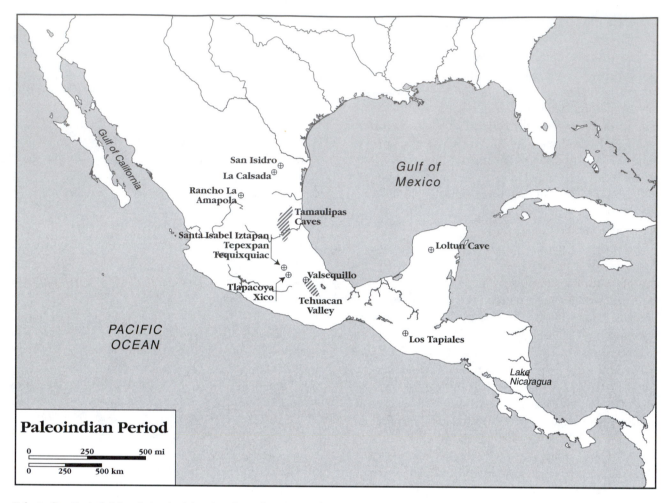

Paleoindian Period. Map design by Mapping Specialists Limited, Madison, Wisconsin.

The late Pleistocene (Ice Age) environment of Mesoamerica remains very poorly known. Glaciers diminished in size, and the runoff affected the development of the landscape in some regions. Some areas were certainly cooler and even drier, but others apparently experienced increased rainfall. Pollen records in some areas indicate more expansive forests that have retreated with the increasing aridity of certain regions in later times. The animals roaming the landscape, however, were clearly different, especially mammoth, mastodon, giant ground sloth, llama, horse, and glyptodont. Some of these fauna were clearly contemporary with humans, though others may have already been extinct by the time humans arrived. Indeed, some of the earliest evidence of human presence in Mesoamerica reflects the hunting of these now-extinct animals, especially mammoth.

Conservatively, we can place the first people in the region at 11,500 years ago, since Clovis points of the early Paleoindian period have been found scattered across Mexico, Guatemala, and Belize, and into Central America. Based on their form and technology, there is no reason to doubt that they are contemporary with the Llano Complex (11,200–11,500 years ago) of the American Southwest, or with broader Clovis patterns across North America.

Later Paleoindian cultural remains are harder to recognize, and some types have very limited distribution in Mesoamerica. For example, the distinctive Folsom points (c. 10,800 years ago) of North America occur in only a

P

couple of locales in northern Mexico (there are fluted points of the Fell's Cave style in Belize and Central America, but their age is uncertain). The parallel-sided middle and late Paleoindian points distinctive in the Southern Plains (e.g., Plainview, Golondrina, Scottsbluff, Angostura) are rare in Mesoamerica, found thus far only in the deserts of northeastern Mexico. Claims have been made for the occurrence of some of these types in Mesoamerica, but I find most of these either erroneous or unconvincing.

Pre-Clovis in Mesoamerica

Consideration must be given to "Pre-Clovis" sites (sometimes called the "Pre-Projectile Point stage"), prior to 11,500 years ago. The finds at Monte Verde in Chile have been widely accepted by New World archaeologists and could easily push Paleoindian chronology back to c. 18,000–20,000 years ago. Claims have been made for sites of this age, or of even greater antiquity, in Mesoamerica, but most fail to meet basic geological and archaeological standards of credibility.

One early argument for great antiquity of human cultures in Mesoamerica resulted from the discovery in 1870 of the sacrum of a Pleistocene camelid, found buried at 13 meters in the Becerra formation at Tequixquiac, northwest of Mexico City. The sacrum had been slightly carved to represent an animal, perhaps a coyote. The dating of this specimen, especially as to when it was "carved," is unclear, though a reanalysis by L. Aveleyra Arroyo de Anda in the 1950s convinced him of its authenticity. In the 1940s, a number of equivocal stone and bone objects were found in this fossil-rich deposit in the bed of old Lake Texcoco, but they have no significance in current research.

Despite assertions and chronologies put forth by several scholars, notably R. S. MacNeish, there is currently little solid evidence for Pre-Clovis occupations in Mesoamerica. This does not mean that such occupations will not eventually be found—just that the present data are insufficient. Among the localities claimed to be of Pre-Clovis age are Loltun Cave, Valsequillo, El Bosque, and Tlapacoya.

Loltun Cave (Yucatán) is perhaps the best candidate for such antiquity. There is a variety of late Pleistocene fauna, including mastodon and horse, along with modified stone and bone objects. There are no radiocarbon dates yet available, and the contexts remain unclear; however, these remains appear to be at the bottom of a stratigraphic column that contains ceramics and other artifacts in levels above it.

The Valsequillo Reservoir area near Puebla (México), was the scene of much research in the early 1960s. Five locales yielded late Pleistocene fauna and a number of lithic specimens. However, the Valsequillo data are far from clear; a wide range of dates has been claimed for the locales, either based either on geologic estimates or on experimental dating techniques.

Much has been made of a "chopper industry" claimed to be representative of Pre-Clovis sites, with an age of greater than thirty thousand years. For example, at El Bosque (Guatemala), the remains of horse, mastodon, and sloth were found with what were described as crudely flaked tools; but even MacNeish recognized only one of them as a primitive "chopper," and it, too, may not be an artifact.

At Tlapacoya (Mexico), Jose Luis Lorenzo and Lorena Mirambell found fossil bones, stone tools, and possible cooking areas, radiocarbon dated at 21,000–24,000 years ago on ancient Lake Chalco. While there is no doubt that the 2,500 lithics found at the site are artifacts, including imported obsidian, there has been dispute as to their association with these early dates. In a similar situation, the same excavators worked at the site of Rancho La Amapola in San Luis Potosí. Again a hearthlike feature was found, radiocarbon dated at more than 31,000 years ago. Only a few lithics and a possible worked horse bone were found, and their associations are also debated. The excavators claim that a scraper made of chalcedony came from a stratum radiocarbon dated at more than 33,000 years ago.

Thus, Mesoamerica has a number of localities that contribute to the emerging picture of Pre-Clovis peoples in the New World. Many of the localities noted here, especially Loltun Cave, and others that could not be discussed because of space limitations, need to be carefully evaluated by Paleoindian specialists.

Clovis Tradition

Clovis spear points are easily recognized by their shape and technology of manufacture, including distinctive flake patterning and the presence of short flutes at the base. In North America they have been found with mammoth kill sites in the Southwest, but they occur broadly across the United States and exhibit considerable variation in shape and size. In Mesoamerica, Clovis points are known from as far south as Belize and perhaps into Costa Rica. They have also been found in highland Guatemala, and in Mexico from Oaxaca, San Luis Potosí, Tlaxcala, Sonora, Durango,

P

and the northern desert areas. It is clear that peoples of Clovis age, or even Clovis tradition, were exploiting obsidian in Central Mexico, because a biface of El Paraíso (Querétaro) obsidian was found associated with a Clovis occupation at Kincaid Rockshelter in south central Texas, more than 1,000 kilometers from its geologic source (which was determined by neutron activation studies).

Most Mesoamerican Clovis points, however, are surface finds; none has been found in stratigraphic context, and none is associated with mammoth kills. The site of Los Tapiales (Guatemala) was shallow, but it yielded a Clovis base, spurred end scrapers reminiscent of North American early forms, and at least one radiocarbon date of Clovis age.

In contrast, the two reported mammoth kills from Mesoamerica, both at Santa Isabel Iztapan, yielded projectile points very unlike Clovis. Situated in Lake Texcoco lake sediments, 33 kilometers northeast of Mexico City, the two mammoth skeletons were excavated between 1945 and 1954. With the first, dug mainly in 1952, there were several stone tools, including a stemmed point with Paleoindian-style flaking; while it has a vague resemblance to the much later Scottsbluff type of North America, it cannot be placed in any known typological category. The other artifacts included an obsidian scraper, an obsidian prismatic blade, a trimmed chert blade, and a biface fragment. Although some have criticized the excavation methods and, thus, the association of these artifacts (especially the obsidian blade), it is now clear that blade technology was common in the Clovis tradition and likely in other lithic industries that were contemporary. The second mammoth was excavated in 1954, a little less than kilometer from the first. The skull and some of the bones showed evidence of damage during butchering, and three lanceolate points were in association. One has a pointed, contracting base and has been called "Lerma," while the other has a rectangular base and resembles in form the obsidian biface found with the Clovis occupation at Kincaid Rockshelter. The third specimen is fragmentary.

The "Tepexpan Man," found by Helmut de Terra in 1949 in the Valley of Mexico, may be linked to these early mammoth hunters. The skeleton (actually that of an adult female) was in the upper part of the Becerra formation and was originally thought to be perhaps ten thousand years old. There was much criticism of the excavation techniques and suggestions that the burial might be much more recent, with the grave pit intrusive into the Becerra. However, fluorine analyses have since shown that the burial may be contemporary with the late Pleistocene mammoth finds at Santa Isabel Iztapan, making it as much as eleven thousand years old. The mandible of a human infant from the site of Xico, found in 1890, may be of equal antiquity.

Other Fluted Points

Though poorly understood at the moment, so-called "fish-tail" fluted or Fell's Cave points have been found at least twice in Belize and in several instances in Panama. This suggests that the South American fluting tradition extended well to the north. Its age, with reference to the Clovis Tradition, remains unclear.

Late Paleoindian

Early Holocene cultural patterns dating between 8200 and 6800 B.C., common in the Southern Plains and throughout North America, are very difficult to recognize in Mesoamerica. Indeed, lanceolate forms of this type may not be present in Mesoamerica, where other, as yet undefined regional lithic traditions may have developed. Points resembling Plainview have been found in several locales as surface finds; recent typological revisions of Plainview indicate that these do not fall clearly into that type. Much better known is the Golondrina Complex (radiocarbon dated at 9,000 years ago in lower Pecos, Texas); an important surface site, San Isidro (Nuevo Léon), was found by J. F. Epstein on the coastal plain of northeastern Mexico. There are points called "Plainview" by MacNeish from the Tehuacan Valley, though they are clearly not part of that type as currently defined. His El Riego points, however, include some specimens closely resembling Golondrina.

The term "Lerma" has been widely, and poorly, used in Mesoamerica to describe all sorts of bipointed dart points reputedly of Paleoindian age. However, only the careful excavations of Roger Nance at La Calsada Rockshelter (Nuevo León) have yielded bipointed specimens in clear, early contexts, roughly 9550–10,600 years ago (based on radiocarbon dates from Unit 6 at the base of the site). MacNeish has found "Lerma" points in the Sierra de Tamaulipas as well as in the Tehuacan Valley and generally dates them around 9,000 years ago.

Summary

The contextual evidence for Paleoindian occupations in Mesoamerica is mostly ambiguous. Excavations often have not been carefully done, and attempts have been made to link established North American Paleoindian typology to inappropriate categories in Mexico and elsewhere. At present, there is little to offer in terms of reconstructing the cultural patterns, subsistence, settlement, or lithic technologies of the early sites—indeed, if we only knew which ones were clearly early!

There may well be Pre-Clovis sites in Mexico (prior to 11,500 years ago), and the many localities dug in Central Mexico may hold the clues to unraveling this issue. Fluted points, widely recognized in North America, occur with some frequency in Mesoamerica and into Central America, and while they are linked here to the Clovis Tradition (based on their technology of manufacture), they are surface finds. Fell's Cave fluted points have only recently been recognized as far north as Belize, and we do not yet know how to interpret these in terms of the early occupation of the region. Mammoth-hunting of the kind associated with Clovis in North America is known from Central Mexico, but with no evidence of Clovis involvement. A full reanalysis of the Santa Isabel Itzapan situation is needed. Archaeologists such as MacNeish and Nance have attempted environmental interpretations with excavated materials of Paleoindian age. Nance sees a drier, warmer epoch beginning in northeastern Mexico after 9500 B.C. This may be supported by the data from the Golondrina Complex of 9000 B.C., especially as it is known from excavated contexts at Baker Cave, Texas.

With the renewed interest in Pre-Clovis stimulated by the Monte Verde discoveries and with the advent of sophisticated geomorphological and paleoenvironmental studies, we can look forward to more and improved data on Paleoindian sites in Mesoamerica. Most of the time, archaeologists have either not been looking for such sites (given the emphasis on the study of Mesoamerican civilizations) or have not been looking in the right places (this is where geomorphological studies are critical). Analysts must view emerging Paleoindian patterns in this vast area in terms of regional developments and not seek to link them immediately with known North American Paleoindian patterns. Though there are clearly influences from North America (Clovis tradition) and probably South America (the Fell's Cave points), it is likely that the Paleoindian of Mesoamerica will prove to be much different, in almost every facet; the materials from Santa Isabel Itzapan are a good example.

FURTHER READINGS

Aveleyra Arroyo de Anda, L. 1964. The Primitive Hunters. In R. West (ed.), *Handbook of Middle American Indians,* vol. I, pp. 384–412. Austin: University of Texas Press.

Epstein, J. F. 1969. *The San Isidro Site.* Austin: Department of Anthropology, University of Texas.

Gruhn, R., and A. L. Bryan. 1977. Los Tapiales: A Paleo-Indian Campsite in the Guatemalan Highlands. *Proceedings of the American Philosophical Society* 121: 235–273.

Hester, T. R., et al. 1982. Observations on the Patination Process and the Context of Antiquity: A Fluted Projectile Point from Belize, Central America. *Lithic Technology* 11: 29–34.

———, et al. 1985. Trace Element Analysis of an Obsidian Paleo-Indian Projectile Point from Kincaid Rockshelter, Texas. *Bulletin of the Texas Archeological Society* 56:143–153.

Irwin-Williams, C. 1967. Associations of Early Man With Horse, Camel and Mastodon at Hueyatlaco, Valsequillo (Puebla, Mexico). In P. S. Martin and H. E. Wright, Jr. (eds.), *Pleistocene Extinctions,* pp. 337–347. New Haven: Yale University Press.

Lorenzo, J. L. 1964. Dos puntas acanaladas en la region de Chapala, Mexico. In *Boletin* 18, pp. 1–6. Mexico City: Instituto Nacional de Antropología e Historia.

MacNeish, R. S., A. Nelken-Terner, and I. W. Johnson. 19167. *The Prehistory of the Tehuacan Valley.* Vol. 3, *Nonceramic Artifacts.* Austin: University of Texas Press.

Nance, C. R. 1992. The Archaeology of La Calsada, a Rockshelter in the Sierra Madre Oriental, Mexico. Austin: University of Texas Press.

Wormington, H. M. 1957. *Ancient Man in North America.* 4th edn. Denver: Denver Museum of Natural History.

Zeitlin, R. N., and J. F. Zeitlin. In press. The Paleoindian and Archaic Cultures of Mesoamerica. In R. E. W. Adams and M. MacLeod (eds.), *Cambridge History of the Native Peoples of the Americas.* Cambridge: Cambridge University Press.

Thomas R. Hester

Palerm, Angel (1910–1980)

Born in Spain, Palerm emigrated to Mexico in 1939 after an active involvement in Republican militancy during the Spanish Civil War. He earned degrees in history (Universidad Nacional Autónoma de México, 1949) and anthropology (Escuela Nacional, 1951); he benefited from the influence of Pablo Martínez del Río, Pedro Armillas, and

Paul Kirchhoff. With his dissertation on hydraulic agriculture and irrigation in Mesoamerica, he began one of his main scientific endeavors. Scarcity of prospects in Mexico forced him to move to Washington, D.C., where he worked with the Pan American Organization (OEA) from 1952 to 1966. He also acquainted himself with the American social sciences, met Karl Wittfogel, and extended his scope of interest to social planning and agrarian reform processes. Returning to Mexico to carry out academic and research activities, Palerm exerted considerable influence on many Mexican anthropologists and played a key role in the diversification of anthropological institutions. With Gonzalo Aguirre Beltrán and Guillermo Bonfil, he founded the Centro de Investigaciones Superiores del Instituto Nacional de Antropología e Historia (CIESAS); he served as its first director. He also was director of the Instituto de Ciencias Sociales of the Jesuit-run Universidad Iberoamericana.

Palerm showed the importance of irrigation in Mesoamerica, suggesting its recognition as a definitional trait of the area. He promoted a revival of interest in ethnology in the professional training of anthropologists. He also contributed novel interpretations concerning colonial history and modes of production.

FURTHER READINGS

Kelly, I., and A. Palerm. 1952. *The Tajín Totonac, Part 1: History, Subsistence, Shelter and Technology.* Institute of Social Anthropology, Publication 13. Washington, D.C.: Smithsonian Institution.

Palerm, A. 1955. The Agricultural Basis of Urban Civilization in Mesoamerica. In *Irrigation Civilizations: A Comparative Study,* pp. 28–42. Social Science Monographs, 1. Washington, D.C.: Pan American Union.

———. 1973. *Obras hidráulicas prehispánicas en el sistema lacustre del Valle de México.* Mexico City: Instituto Nacional de Antropología e Historia.

Palerm, A., and E. Wolf. 1960. Ecological Potential and Cultural Development in Mesoamerica. *Social Science Monographs* 3:1–37. Washington, D.C.: Pan American Union.

Teresa Rojas Rabiela

Pánuco (Veracruz, Mexico)

This cluster of closely related sites in northern Veracruz has deep stratigraphic deposits and is significant as the first site complex in the North Gulf region from which a long culture chronology has been derived; this has broad regional applicability in northeastern Mesoamerica. It is situated on the south margin of the Pánuco River about 45 kilometers from the Gulf of Mexico (80 kilometers via river).

Although Pánuco was an important population center at the time of the Spanish conquest, as well as the location of an early Spanish settlement, the site's previous surface features have been extensively modified by the construction of the twentieth-century town on the same high ground. Pioneering excavations were carried out here in 1941–1942 by Ekholm at the Pavón and El Prisco sites in the center and southern reaches of the town. He divided the long, continuous cultural sequence into six periods, the first corresponding roughly with the Late Formative and the sixth with the Terminal Postclassic. In 1948–1949 MacNeish explored the eastern riverbank zone of the town, adding three earlier periods and extending the sequence back through the latter portion of the Early Formative. MacNeish renamed Ekholm's numerical divisions, providing the present nomenclature. The "periods" of both excavators, while in some instances corresponding temporally to standard Mesoamerican periods, are best considered "phases" in terms of current usage. Dating has been derived primarily from comparisons of the artifact corpus with others elsewhere in Mesoamerica.

Although the geographical scope of the cultures recorded at Pánuco is likely to be ample, the chronological sequence has been variously utilized, both accurately and incorrectly, as a temporal reference for extremely diverse portions of the Huasteca. In spite of the occasional presence of largely unrelated culture manifestations, such as the Late Formative Tancol Complex downstream, the chronology is clearly representative of most of the lower Pánuco drainage, and, during the Postclassic period, of much of the North Gulf Area. Modern urbanism increasingly threatens the upper levels of the archaeological sites at Pánuco.

FURTHER READINGS

Ekholm, G. F. 1944. Excavations at Tampico and Pánuco in the Huasteca, Mexico. *Anthropological Papers of the American Museum of Natural History* 38(5):320–512.

MacNeish, R. S. 1954. An Early Archaeological Site near Pánuco, Vera Cruz. *Transactions of the American Philosophical Society,* n.s. 44.

Wilkerson, S. J. K. 1997. Die Huaxteca: Ein mittelamerikanisches Grenzland. In *Präkolumbische Kulturen am Golf von Mexiko,* pp. 175–186. Zürich: Museum Rietberg Zürich.

S. Jeffrey K. Wilkerson

SEE ALSO
Gulf Lowlands: North Region

Papagayo (Guanacaste, Costa Rica)

This Greater Nicoya region architectural and shell midden site is on northern side of the Bay of Culebra, in a dry tropical environment. Subsistence was based on marine resources, gathering, collecting, hunting, and some agriculture. The span of occupation was A.D. 500–1520. Architectural remains consist of stone circles (unique for Greater Nicoya, and possibly ceremonial in function) and other occupation remains. Artifacts found included stone statuary, ceramics, lithics, worked bone, and archaeofauna. Burials occurred in a wide variety of positions (primary extended and flexed, multiple, and secondary), and some were accompanied by grave goods.

Interaction with other regions is evidenced by White-slipped ceramics from Pacific Nicaragua and obsidian from Honduras and Guatemala, as well as a sculptural tradition shared with the lakes region of Nicaragua.

FURTHER READINGS

Baudez, C. F., N. Borgnino, S. Laligant, and V. Lauthelin. 1992. *Papagayo: Un hameau précolombien du Costa Rica.* Paris: Editions Recherche sur les Civilisations.

Borgnino, N., S. Laligant, and V. Lauthelin. 1988. *Le site de Papagayo (Guanacaste, Costa Rica): Typologie et sequence céramique.* Reporte de D.E.A., Université de Paris, 1. Paris.

Frederick W. Lange

SEE ALSO
Intermediate Area: Overview

Paper

Manufactured and used throughout Mesoamerica at the time of Contact, paper was produced from felted mashed vegetable fibers, particularly agave leaves and the inner bark of fig (*Ficus*) trees. The Nahuatl word *amatl* refers both to the fig tree and to the finished paper. Striated stone beaters were probably used in this process; archaeological examples found on the Pacific coast of Guatemala date as far back as 1000 B.C. In addition to using paper for maps and screenfold books bearing ritual and historical information, the ancients used it as clothing to adorn priests and sacred statues, as ritual banners, and as a medium for ritual offerings of images, latex drops, and blood. Paper's ritual uses were so widespread that Spanish colonial law prohibited papermaking and ritual use, but the practices survive to this day among certain indigenous cultures of Mexico.

FURTHER READINGS

Lenz, H. 1973. *El papel indígena mexicano: Historia y supervivencia.* SepSetentas, 65. Mexico City: Secretaría de Educación Pública.

Sandstrom, A. R., and P. E. Sandstrom. 1986. *Traditional Papermaking and Paper Cult Figures of Mexico.* Norman: University of Oklahoma Press.

Seemann Conzatti, E. 1990. *Usos del papel en el calendario ritual mexica.* Mexico City: Instituto Nacional de Antropología e Historia.

Tolstoy, P. 1963. Cultural Parallels between Southeast Asia and Mesoamerica in the Manufacture of Bark Cloth. *Transactions of the New York Academy of Sciences,* series 2, 25:646–662.

Alan R. Sandstrom and Pamela Effrein Sandstrom

SEE ALSO
Ground Stone Tools

Paquimé

See Casas Grandes

Paso de la Amada (Chiapas, Mexico)

One of Mesoamerica's earliest villages, this site in the Mazatan region of Pacific coastal Chiapas was occupied continuously from 1550 to 850 B.C. (Mokaya tradition); at its peak, 1400–1250 B.C. (Locona phase), it covered 50 to 75 hectares. There are more than fifty low house mounds visible on the site's surface, and many more household remains are buried in the low-lying areas between them. One of the largest mounds, Mound 6, contained at least six superimposed structures that may have been elite residences. Structure 4 in the sequence sits on an apsidal earthen platform almost 1 meter high, 22 meters long, and 10 meters wide. It had standing clay walls, steps, porches, hearths, postholes, and a wide range of domestic trash scattered on the floor. Most other residences at the site are also apsidal but most are much smaller, ranging from 6 to 8 meters long, and lack platforms.

Mound 7, the largest mound at the site, contains Mesoamerica's earliest ball court. Open-ended, it consists of two parallel earthen mounds, each almost 2 meters

P

high and 80 meters long, separated by a 7-meter-wide court floor and flanked by low benches made of compact clay. Radiocarbon dates and ceramics show that the ball court was built early in the Locona phase and fell into disuse by the Cherla phase (c. 1100 B.C.).

Many human skeletal remains have been found outside the structures; all are similarly simple in mortuary treatment and show no clear signs of wealth or status differentiation. Paso de la Amada engaged in interregional trade, but there is little evidence of economic specialization. However, the Mokaya people may have begun to develop social and political structures characteristic of simple chiefdoms, as evidenced by large, elaborate residences such as Mound 6. The ball court suggests that, in addition to being the largest settlement in the region, this site was the center of a network of competing communities. Paso de la Amada provides a clear example of the Early Formative period roots of later Mesoamerican civilization.

FURTHER READINGS

Blake, M. 1991. An Emerging Early Formative Chiefdom at Paso de la Amada, Chiapas, Mexico. In W. L. Fowler, Jr. (ed.), *The Formation of Complex Society in Southeastern Mesoamerica*, pp. 27–46. Boca Raton: CRC Press.

Ceja T., J. F. 1985. *Paso de la Amada: An Early Preclassic Site in the Soconusco, Chiapas*. Papers of the New World Archaeological Foundation, 49. Provo: Brigham Young University.

Clark, J. E., and M. Blake. 1994. The Power of Prestige: Competitive Generosity and the Emergence of Rank Societies in Lowland Mesoamerica. In E. M. Brumfiel and J. W. Fox (eds.), *Factional Competition and Political Development in the New World*, pp. 17–30. Cambridge: Cambridge University Press.

Hill, W. D., M. Blake, and J. E. Clark. 1998. Ball Court Design Dates Back 3,400 Years. *Nature* 392:878–879.

Lesure, R. G. 1997. Early Formative Platforms at Paso de la Amada, Chiapas, Mexico. *Latin American Antiquity* 8:217–236.

Michael Blake

SEE ALSO

Mazatan Region; Soconusco–South Pacific Coast and Piedmont Region

Pavón (Veracruz, Mexico)

Hillside sites near the Pánuco River, on the land of Roberto Pavón, were excavated in 1941 by Gordon Ekholm. He used the figurines and ceramics recovered to define a sequence of six periods, from Period I (Chila phase), starting c. 400 B.C. to Period VI, ending at the time of Spanish conquest. Three earlier phases—Pavón (1500–1200 B.C.), Ponce (1200–800 B.C.), and Aguilar (800–400 B.C.)—were added by the 1948 excavation by Richard S. MacNeish. With one of the longest continuous sequences for the Huasteca region of the Gulf Lowlands of Mexico, Pavón has been occupied by Huastec Indians for almost three thousand years.

FURTHER READINGS

Ekholm, G. 1944. *Excavations at Tampico and Pánuco in the Huasteca, Mexico.* Anthropological papers of the American Museum of Natural History, 38. New York.

MacNeish, R. S. 1954. An Early Archaeological Site near Pánuco, Veracruz. *Transactions of the American Philosophical Society,* 95:5. Philadelphia.

Richard S. MacNeish

SEE ALSO

Gulf Lowlands: North Region; Pánuco

Paxil (Veracruz, Mexico)

Partially reconstructed, this medium-sized site is representative of many with El Tajín-like architecture in the humid central mountains of Veracruz. Located at 200 meters elevation by the Arroyo Paxil, an affluent of the Chapachapa tributary of the Nautla River, Morelos-Paxil (or Paxilila) is situated on a commanding rise. The urban center consists of twenty or more stone structures ranging from low platforms to multistory temples up to 12 meters high. Construction is of ashlar masonry, utilizing local limestone flags and thin stucco surfacing. Many buildings flank a north–south axial plaza more than 300 meters long, regionally characteristic of the Late Classic and Epiclassic periods. Paxil is likely to have been the major site of its time in the Misantla area.

Most exposed structures employ an architectural style with an elongated, steep *talud* terminating in a reduced "flying cornice" similar to late, but not terminal, El Tajín buildings. Constructions with niches, a pronounced *tablero* panel, or associated sculpture have not yet been found. At least one structure has a tunnel passage emerging in a stairway, as at Tajín Chico. The space between two prominent buildings (D, I) may be a ball court. Ceramics, mostly collected in the course of clearing operations, are largely from the Epiclassic period.

FURTHER READINGS

Garcia Payon, J. 1942. Conclusiones de mis exploraciones en el Totonacapan Meridional Temporada de 1939. *XXVII Congreso Internacional de Americanistas,* 2:88–96.

———. 1947. Exploraciones arqueológicas en el Totonacapan Meridional (Region de Misantla). *Anales del Instituto Nacional de Antropología e Historia* 2: 73–111.

S. Jeffrey K. Wilkerson

SEE ALSO
Gulf Lowlands: North Central Region

Peña Pintada, La (Jalisco, Mexico)

This rock art site is situated in the mountainous upper Tomatlan River Valley, about 45 kilometers from the Pacific coast. There are about two hundred red pictographs and four superimposed petroglyphs on the back wall and ceiling of a rock scar on the sheltered underside of a boulder perched on the western side of the river, 40 meters directly above the riverbed. The chronology of habitation sites in the Tomatlan River Basin suggests that the pictographs were painted during the last phase of pre-Hispanic cultural development in the Valley (A.D. 1000–1500).

Analysis of the pictograph designs, utilizing ethnographic analogy with the nearby Huichol Indians, suggests that the whole composition was a record of a system of astronomical observations that used the changing position of the sun along the eastern horizon to construct a wet season/dry season calendar. Most of the individual pictographs are physical manifestations of the prayers offered by shamans to obtain life-giving rain from the sun for the growth of the plants and animals the people depended on for sustenance.

FURTHER READINGS

Mountjoy, J. B. 1982. An Interpretation of the Pictographs at La Peña Pintada, Jalisco, Mexico. *American Antiquity* 47:119–126.

Joseph B. Mountjoy

SEE ALSO
West Mexico

Peñoles Region (Oaxaca, Mexico)

The Peñoles region in the Mixtec Sierra of Mexico's southern highlands evidences occupation in the Archaic period and possibly the Middle Formative period, and continuous and significant settlement from Late Formative through Late Postclassic times. In the Contact period, the heart of this region was the seat of the petty kingdom or *cacicazgo* known as Ixcuintepec. It may also contain parts of several adjacent late prehistoric kingdoms.

Two key features of the Peñoles region figure prominently in its settlement history and societal evolution: the region's agricultural marginality, and its pre-Hispanic role as a boundary zone between Zapotec and Mixtec groups. Good agricultural land is extremely limited, the risk of damaging frosts is high, and successful farming in many areas—especially hillslopes and the narrow river valleys—required a significant input of labor to construct and maintain terraces, field boundaries, and irrigation channels. But there were other abundant resources, including hardwood for fires and charcoal, pine for construction timber, orchard fruits, and probably many game animals.

As a boundary zone, the Peñoles region separated the Valley of Oaxaca to the east (largely Zapotec-speaking today) from the smaller valleys of the Mixteca Alta (predominantly Mixtec-speaking). In pre-Hispanic times, the linguistic, cultural, and social boundaries between the Zapotec and Mixtec languages and cultures emerged and were negotiated within the Peñoles region. The frontiers of larger centralized states, focused on capitals in adjacent valleys to east and west, were established and, no doubt, contested there. Principal communication routes linking the Valley of Oaxaca to the Mixteca Alta and to the Central Plateau passed through the mountains and were traveled by armies, traders, diplomats, and others.

The settlement history of the Peñoles region is known from a systemic regional survey, primarily of ridgetops, covering 1,000 square kilometers, as well as intensive investigation of one site. In large parts of the Peñoles region sites are totally undisturbed, so that architectural preservation of mounds, terraces, stone foundations, and other features is excellent. Architectural plans were made at more than one hundred such sites. More than five hundred sites were identified, ranging in age from the Archaic period to the Late Postclassic period.

Middle Formative settlements are concentrated in the southern part of the Peñoles region. It is distinguishable by the presence of Valley of Oaxaca diagnostic pottery types, both imported ware and as locally made imitations.

P

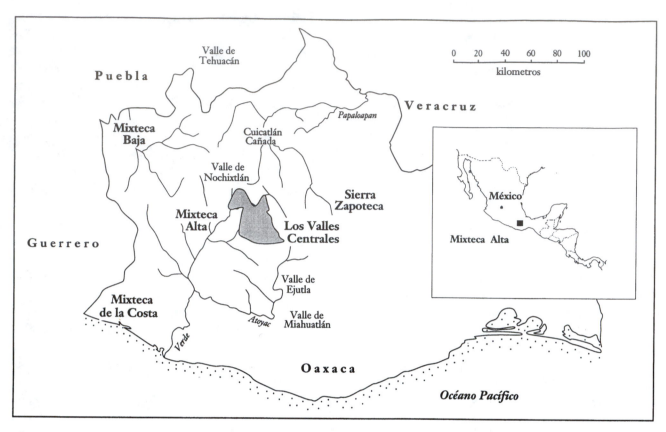

The Peñoles region in the Sierra Mixteca of Oaxaca, Mexico. Illustration courtesy of the author.

The distribution of one distinctive ceramic vessel form at Middle Formative sites suggests an autonomous system in the mountains, with links to the Valley of Oaxaca.

There are many more Late/Terminal Formative period sites. Virtually all diagnostic ceramics are Monte Albán I and/or II imports or local imitations. Pottery styles of the Nochixtlán Valley are extremely rare. The major concentration of settlements is in the south and reflects strong continuity from the Middle Formative. The other major area of settlement is along or near the Continental Divide, which forms the northern boundary of the Peñoles regional survey and was an important transportation corridor in pre-Hispanic times. Sites in this corridor area generally were not occupied earlier and tended to be abandoned at the end of the Terminal Formative. They appear to have been related to Monte Albán's well-documented expansionism in Monte Albán II.

Classic Period settlements are found throughout the Peñoles region, except for a block in the northeast that has never been inhabited, probably because of high eleva- tions, poor soils, and few springs. Fairly dense settlement in the eastern part, against the Valley of Oaxaca survey boundary, represents a direct continuation of Valley of Oaxaca settlement. The Peñoles region was a fortified frontier of Monte Albán in the Valley of Oaxaca during the Classic period, yet the western limit of Monte Albán's reach is not contained within it. The most common remains are the undecorated, conical bowls that are ubiq- uitous at Valley of Oaxaca Classic period sites, or local imitations. Nochixtlán-style pottery is very rare. Many major Classic sites had been previously occupied in the Formative period. A wide range in site sizes suggests a sys- tem of considerable complexity. Except for the smallest sites, settlements in the Peñoles region assume a linear aspect as they follow ridgelines, rarely spilling any signifi- cant distance down the steep sideslopes. The largest sites are more than 3.6 kilometers along their longest axes, and many others are 1.5 to 3 kilometers in extent. Residential terraces, stone foundations, mounds, platforms, and elab- orate strings of patio groups are common. At many sites,

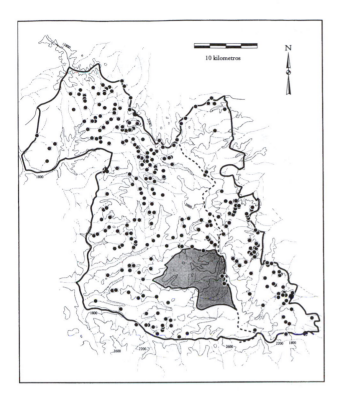

Postclassic Settlements in the Peñoles region. Illustration courtesy of the author.

gateway features are located at saddles or other direct accessways. Complete encircling walls are rare and tend to enclose only the most elaborate architecture.

Postclassic settlement is quite dense, except in the vacant zone of the northeast and at the highest elevations along the divide. The demographic center of gravity for the region falls around Ixcuintepec, the largest single site in the region, and the mountaintops in all directions above Santa María Peñoles have dense settlement. Many major Postclassic sites were also important centers in the Classic period, and the mountains around Peñoles and to the south show considerable settlement continuity from the Late Formative through the Late Postclassic.

FURTHER READINGS

Finsten, L. 1996. Frontier and Periphery in Southern Mexico: The Mixtec Sierra in Highland Oaxaca. In *Pre-Columbian World Systems*. Peter N. Peregine and Gary M. Feinman (eds.), pp. 77–95. Madison: Prehistory Press.

———. 1997. Archaeological Survey in the Mixtec Sierra. In *Research Frontiers in Anthropology*. M. Ember,

C. Ember and P. N. Peregrine (eds.). Englewood Cliffs: Prentice Hall. Volume 2, *Archaeology*, pp. 105–132.

Finsten, L., S. A. Kowalewski, C. A. Smith, R. D. Garvin, and M. D. Boland. 1996. Circular architecture and symbolic boundaries in the Mixtec Sierra, Oaxaca. In *Ancient Mesoamerica* 7:19–35.

Laura Finsten

SEE ALSO

Mixteca-Puebla Style; Oaxaca and Tehuantepec Region

Petexbatun Region (Petén, Guatemala)

The Petexbatun region lies in the southwestern portion of the Petén rainforest, centered on Lake Petexbatun and the surrounding rivers and swamps. The region is important for its evidence of Late Classic militarism and the collapse of Maya civilization in the eighth and ninth centuries A.D. Decipherment of hieroglyphic monuments showed that a single kingdom came to dominate this entire region through conquest and alliance. Archaeological evidence from many sites showed that after A.D. 761, conflicts turned to true siege-and-fortification warfare. The great centers and even small villages of the region experienced violent ends between A.D. 761 and 830. The Petexbatun witnessed one of the earliest and most dramatic manifestations of the so-called Classic Maya Collapse, leaving evidence that has led scholars to posit that endemic warfare was one of the major factors in the demise of Maya civilization in this region.

To the west of Lake Petexbatun an uneven, eroded limestone escarpment rises to over 200 meters, and on the edge of this high escarpment lie several major sites of the region: Tamarindito, Arroyo de Piedra, and Aguateca. As warfare became more intense in the eighth century, this uneven landscape provided natural defensive systems that were bolstered by the addition of walls and palisades. This karstic region has an abundance of cave systems; most of those investigated contained ancient ritual offerings. The caves were clearly an important part of the native sacred geography, since site placement and structure alignments often parallel subterranean corridors or entomb these sacred chthonic features.

The earliest evidence of occupation in the region consists of a few Mamom and some Xe phase monochrome ceramic sherds (c. 900–500 B.C.) found in cave deposits inland and in a few scattered surface deposits closer to Lake Petexbatun. The first substantial occupations are

P

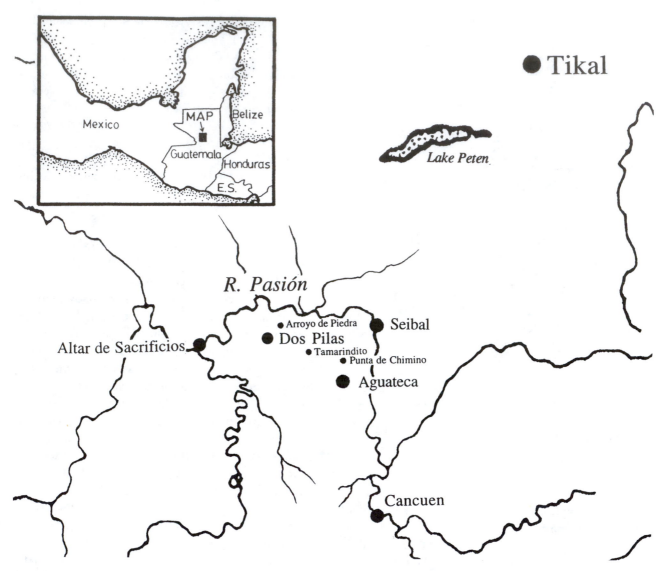

Map showing Petexbatun region and major sites. Illustration courtesy of the Petexbatun Project Vanderbilt University.

also along watercourses, at the sites of Punta de Chimino and Aguateca, dating to the Late Formative (Preclassic) period (c. 500 B.C.–A.D. 200). Settlement in these periods was sparse in the intersite areas. In the Early Classic period, two modest ceremonial centers and the first epigraphically identified kingdoms were centered on the sites of Tamarindito and Arroyo de Piedra. The small but well-constructed ceremonial centers and palaces were surrounded by light, scattered occupation that grew in the Late Classic period to substantial density.

Extraordinary developments in this region occurred after A.D. 600, when princes from Tikal established a kingdom at the site of Dos Pilas and began a program of

regional expansion. They rapidly constructed a ceremonial center at Dos Pilas, including ceremonial plazas, palaces, a ball court, and a massive presentation temple, as well as commoners' houses. Monuments there and at Seibal, Aguateca, Arroyo de Piedra, and Tamarindito have provided a hieroglyphic history from the mid-seventh century to the late eighth; recent excavations, artifact studies, and ecological researches have provided a detailed culture history for this important period.

The epigraphic history tells of a period of wars between the upstart cadet lineage of Dos Pilas and their relatives and rivals at Tikal. These wars may have been instigated by the great center of Calakmul, which had long been in conflict with Tikal. Calakmul's role is implied by references in the glyphs of a recently discovered hieroglyphic staircase at Dos Pilas, and in recent epigraphic studies scholars have proposed that in the sixth and seventh centuries there were attempts to create great alliances of warring centers under the sway of Calakmul or of Tikal. Dos Pilas appears to have been an ally of Calakmul in this series of wars against their more ancient and prestigious rival. The wars between Dos Pilas and Tikal ended in A.D. 678 with the defeat of Tikal and the death of its ruler.

After raising several monuments to celebrate this victory, subsequent Dos Pilas rulers did not dominate Tikal but turned their attention to regional consolidation within the Petexbatun itself. First, they gained control over the nearby kingdoms of Tamarindito and Arroyo de

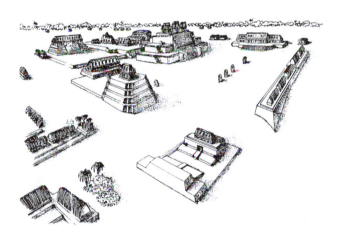

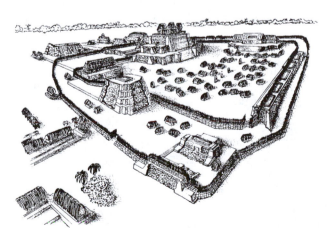

Artist's reconstruction of Dos Pilas main plaza before (above) and during siege in A.D. 761. Illustration courtesy of Petexbatun Project Vanderbilt University.

Piedra. Later, "Ruler 3" of Dos Pilas defeated the large, important, and strategically located site of Seibal on the Pasíon River. This victory was celebrated in several spectacular monuments at the sites of Dos Pilas and Aguateca, and at Seibal itself. Thus, through alliance, conquest, and marriage, the lords of Dos Pilas had created a polity by about A.D. 740 that controlled not only the entire Petexbatun region but also nearly all of the greater Pasíon River Valley, a major trade and transport artery of the Maya world. Perhaps to control this territory better, they had established a second royal seat at the highly defensible site of Aguateca.

The wealth from this expanded realm in the early eighth century is seen in the many rich caches, monuments, tombs, and especially the cave offerings of its capital center, Dos Pilas. Recent archaeological research has recovered new hieroglyphic stairways, palaces, caches, and royal tombs, all dating to this period of success, expansion, and tribute. The monumental art is almost redundant in its emphasis on martial themes. The architecture consists of beautiful façades over loose rubble cores, reflecting both the rapid construction and the lofty pretensions of this rising power. In 1990, the tomb of "Ruler 2" yielded rich grave goods, including beautiful polychrome ceramics that were probably tribute from sites as far away as the central Petén. The upstart kingdom's short-lived success is best reflected in the astonishing offerings that fill the cave systems beneath the Petexbatun sites; recent archaeological exploration has recovered more than 100,000 artifacts from offering deposits from all social strata of the population. Whole vessels, carved bone and wood, and even human sacrifices were found.

The unique importance of Petexbatun culture history is seen in events after A.D. 761, when its capital, Dos Pilas, fell to a siege by enemies led by one of its vassal sites, Tamarindito. Recent excavations at Tamarindito discovered the tomb of the ruler who defeated Dos Pilas, with a monumental stairway inscribed to record his victory over the former overlord. At Dos Pilas itself, recent excavations uncovered defensive walls, gateways, killing alleys, and other evidence of the last stand of the inhabitants. The desperate nature of the defense can be seen in the rapid construction of fortifications. Excavations revealed that hastily constructed stone walls surrounded the main palaces and temples in concentric circles. These walls were built of masonry ripped from the façades of the sacred structures themselves to support wooden palisades. Apparently the defense failed, since the site rapidly became depopulated after 761, and some principal

P

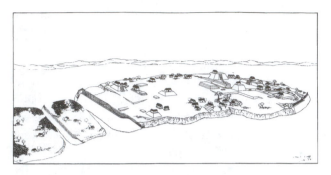

Reconstruction view of Punta de Chimino peninsula showing innermost moats, palisades, and protected field zone. Illustration courtesy of Petexbatun Project Vanderbilt University.

ceremonial structures and palaces show signs of deliberate destruction.

After the fall of Dos Pilas, its expansion state broke up into smaller warring polities—first two or three warring states, and then ever smaller units. During the subsequent decades, endemic warfare between centers changed all aspects of life in the Petexbatun. Many kilometers of defensive systems are found throughout the region, protecting site epicenters with limestone base walls supporting palisades. These were reinforced at some sites by moat systems, baffled gateways, and killing alleys. The nobles of Dos Pilas itself may have fled after its fall to Aguateca, their second royal capital situated on a naturally defensible location atop a great hill, with the site epicenter protected by high cliffs on one side and a 70-meter-deep chasm on the other. They enhanced these natural defenses with more than 5 kilometers of concentric wall systems, protected bridges, and walls extending to enclose water sources and terraces. Despite these elaborate defenses, Aguateca was overrun, burned, and abandoned by about A.D. 800.

Many other centers in the period of 761–830 invested in fortifications. One center, Punta de Chimino, had temples, monuments, and houses on a narrow peninsula within Lake Petexbatun. Recent excavations revealed a series of fortifications here that were among the most massive in the history of the region. At some point at the end of the eighth century or the beginning of the ninth, the entire peninsula was cut off from the mainland by the excavation of a deep defensive moat system. Three concentric moats and walls were constructed around the base of the Punta de Chimino peninsula, the innermost being more than 15 meters deep, cutting into the limestone

bedrock. The waters of Lake Petexbatun flowed through this moat, making the site an island fortress. The moat defenses were reinforced by some walls with postholes, indicating the presence of substantial palisades. The labor invested in the site's defensive system, if measured by volume of earth and rock moved, is several times greater than that invested in the architecture of the site itself. The terminal trajectory of warfare in the Petexbatun region is indicated by this massive investment of energy in protection from neighbors. Ongoing investigations at this site are exploring the impact of siege warfare and population concentrations on the thin soils of the surrounding area.

By the late eighth century and early ninth, siege-and-fortification warfare had redefined all aspects of life in the Petexbatun. Archaeological transects inland to the west of Aguateca explored, mapped, and excavated a dozen hilltop fortresses. Some of these were wall-and-palisade systems surrounding villages of eight or nine houses. Like the defenses of Punta de Chimino and the fortifications around agricultural fields, these tiny fortified villages are a measure of the degree of endemic warfare and political devolution in the last decades of Maya civilization in the Petexbatun. By the beginning of the Terminal Classic period, the Petexbatun region was largely abandoned. Intersite survey and many site excavations have identified only a few scattered households left in the region after A.D. 830. Only the Punta de Chimino island fortress has a concentrated, though small, population, with Fine Orange ceramics and other diagnostics of the Terminal Classic and Postclassic period.

The evidence from the Petexbatun region has led Demarest, Juan Antonio Váldes, and others to debate the role of warfare in the Classic Maya Collapse. Warfare was always a central factor in Classic Maya political, ritual, and economic life. The scale, frequency, and interregional involvements in warfare increased in the Late Classic period. In the Petexbatun, however, warfare by the mid-eighth century had become so intense and frequent that it profoundly affected settlement, economy, and probably ecology. This shift is seen in the great investment in extensive fortification systems around epicenters, villages, and even rural fields. Such warfare would lead to population concentration and a shift from the Classic Maya ecological adaptation and dispersed settlement systems. Indeed, ecological studies have shown that the Maya in this region had used a complex mixture of subsistence systems to mimic the biodiversity of the rainforest and to limit the destructive impact of erosion from fields. However, the hilltop and island fortresses and the defended fields of the late eighth century would have necessitated radical changes in settlement and subsistence strategy. Such change from a millennium of successful adaptation in the region apparently led to disaster: population dwindled by the mid-ninth century to less than 5 percent of previous levels, and all major centers had been virtually abandoned.

In overview, the Petexbatun is of particular interest because of its well-preserved evidence concerning political dynamics and warfare at the end of the Classic period. The collapse of Maya civilization here occurred fifty to one hundred years earlier than in other regions of the Classic Maya world. The correlation of this early collapse with the spread of endemic siege-and-fortification warfare suggests that changes in politics and intercenter conflict were among the many factors involved in the general collapse of Classic Maya civilization. At the least, for this one region, we can assert that Maya civilization collapsed in a state of endemic warfare. The degree to which such patterns are characteristic of the late Maya world as a whole will be a subject for future archaeological research.

FURTHER READINGS

Brady, J. E. 1997. Settlement Configuration and Cosmology: The Role of Caves at Dos Pilas. *American Anthropologist* 99:602–618.

Demarest, A. 1993. The Violent Saga of a Maya Kingdom. *National Geographic* 183. (2):94–111.

Dunning, N. P., and T. Beach. 1994. Soil Erosion, Slope Management, and Ancient Terracing in the Maya Lowlands. *Latin American Antiquity* 5:51–69.

Houston, S. D., and P. Mathews. 1985. *The Dynastic Sequence of Dos Pilas, Guatemala.* Pre-Columbian Art Research Institute, Monograph 1. San Francisco.

Mathews, P., and G. R. Willey. 1991. Prehistoric Polities of the Pasión Region: Hieroglyphic Texts and Their Archaeological Settings. In T. P. Culbert (ed.), *Classic Maya Political History: Hieroglyphic and Archaeological Evidence,* pp. 30–71. Cambridge: Cambridge University Press.

Arthur Demarest

SEE ALSO

Dos Pilas; Maya Lowlands: South

Piedras Negras (Petén, Guatemala)

Situated on the eastern bank of the Usumacinta River in heavily karstic terrain, this important Maya site had a strategic position with respect to well-drained soils, drainage, and east–west channels of communication. The river presumably provided fish and water, but its violent rapids limited its value for long-distance transport of goods and people. The city itself consists of several large groups of pyramids, of which the earliest are freestanding and the latest are shaped in part around bedrock outcroppings. Today, Piedras Negras is best known for its rich record of carved stelae and panels and for architectural reconstruction drawings by Proskouriakoff, who revolutionized Maya historiography with her visionary synthesis of the site's texts and monument position and dating. Proskouriakoff noticed periodic patterns in hieroglyphic inscriptions and deduced from these a set of royal biographies, thus revealing the historical content of Classic Maya texts.

Piedras Negras had a sequence of at least six rulers, who were linked to particular structures and who seem to have governed a political landscape encompassing subsidiary sites that were sometimes briefly and partially autonomous. Epigraphic evidence indicates overall dynastic isolation, with relatively few contacts between Piedras Negras and more distant centers of population.

Research at Piedras Negras undertaken by the University of Pennsylvania in the 1930s was of exceptional quality for its time; researchers excavated the site's central portion, produced an excellent map, documented architectural development to an unprecedented standard, and removed carvings for museum display and storage in Guatemala City and Philadelphia. Innovative methods used at the site included test-pitting, probing in more modest structures, and the detection of new building types, such as the monumental sweat baths that cluster near Piedras Negras' plazas and courtyards. Excavations by Brigham Young University in 1997 have built on earlier research, revealing a chronology going back to the Middle Formative period, and extensive buried architecture, some ritually terminated. Settlement evidence points to a large sustaining area extending 4 to 5 kilometers from the site. Future work will assist the Guatemalan National Park Service (CONAP) in guarding the site for later generations.

FURTHER READINGS

Coe, W. R. 1959. *Piedras Negras Archaeology: Artifacts, Caches, and Burials.* University Museum Monographs. Philadelphia: University of Pennsylvania.

Proskouriakoff, T. 1936. A Pyramid without Temple Ruins. In *Piedras Negras Preliminary Papers,* 5. Philadelphia: University Museum, University of Pennsylvania.

P

The Acropolis of Piedras Negras, Guatemala, in an illustration by Tatiana Proskouriakoff. Illustration reproduced from *An Album of Maya Architecture,* by Tatiana Proskouriakoff. Norman: University of Oklahoma Press, 1963, p. 17.

———. 1943–54. *Piedras Negras Archaeology: Architecture.* Parts 1–6. Philadelphia: University Museum, University of Pennsylvania.

———. 1960. Historical Implications of a Pattern of Dates at Piedras Negras, Guatemala. *American Antiquity* 25:454–475.

———. 1963. *An Album of Maya Architecture.* Norman: University of Oklahoma Press.

Satterthwaite, L. 1935. Palace Structures J-2 and J-6. In *Piedras Negras Preliminary Papers,* 3. Philadelphia: University Museum, University of Pennsylvania.

Stone, A. 1989. Disconnection, Foreign Insignia, and Political Expansion: Teotihuacán and the Warrior Stelae of Piedras Negras. In R. A. Diehl and J. C. Berlo (eds.), *Mesoamerica After the Decline of Teotihuacán A.D. 700–900,* pp. 153–172. Washington, D.C.: Dumbarton Oaks.

Stephen D. Houston

SEE ALSO

Bonampak; Classic Period; Maya Lowlands: South; Palenque; Yaxchilan

P

Pilar, El
See Belize River Region

Pilarillos, Los
See Northwestern Frontier

Pital, El (Veracruz, Mexico)

Situated at the apex of the Nautla River Delta just a few meters above sea level, El Pital is one of the largest archaeological sites in Veracruz. It was not readily visible until the late 1930s, when rainforest was replaced by plantations of fruit and sugarcane. Although it was originally thought to be a series of small and moderate-sized sites, survey and mapping revealed a single urban complex of huge proportions and early date. In spite of its humid location in the rainiest portion of the north central Gulf Coast, most of the buildings have thick burnt-earth coatings and were constructed with very little stone and stucco. The remains of at least 150 edifices—including massive earthen buildings up to 30 meters or more high, multistructure platforms, and ball courts—cover approximately 5 square kilometers between two waterways. Many additional building clusters are adjacent or connected by a probable causeway.

Unlike many Gulf Coast sites, El Pital's avenues or broad streets suggest a rough grid and rigorous urban layout throughout the life of the city. Stretching downstream from the metropolis, in proximity to former river channels, is a 100-square-kilometer region of satellite communities and house mounds associated with extensive canal systems and raised fields.

Initial dating of the site was based on comparative analysis of artifacts from surface reconnaissance and small test pits in the city, house mounds, and agricultural field systems. The ceramic materials from these contexts were found to be largely identical to those from Santa Luisa, about 35 kilometers to the north. The current evidence indicates a localized Middle Formative period presence in the delta region. This was followed by an explosive, and extensive, Late Formative occupation, suggesting both a sudden influx of people and rapid concentration of regional population. Many of the structures at El Pital, including some of the largest, appear to be associated with this period.

An extensive Protoclassic and Early Classic presence is manifest at the site and throughout the delta, but this is followed by an abrupt and pervasive decline in population.

At the end of the Postclassic, population again expanded, although it never approached the densities of the earlier apogee; many field systems were then rehabilitated, apparently for cacao production. At European contact, the urban focus was 2 kilometers to the east in a former suburb, where earlier buildings were refurbished in Terminal Postclassic architectural style. It is probable this was historical Nautlan, burned by Cortés's lieutenant Juan Escalante following his rout by an Aztec garrison. Colonial documentation indicates total depopulation of the delta by fifty years after the Conquest as a result of catastrophic epidemics, and a rapid reversion to rainforest.

El Pital is highly significant because it manifests early urbanism on a grand scale, with multiple ball courts, artifacts with "Classic Veracruz" styling, a dense population, and intensive agricultural systems, all at an earlier date than previously supposed for the northern Gulf Coast. In large part it pre-dates El Tajín, 60 kilometers away, and is contemporaneous with Teotihuacán. It may have had a multiethnic population, including early Nahua speakers. Its mid-Classic demise was related to the expansion of peoples associated with El Tajín, perhaps following a time of extreme climatic stress evidenced by extensive flooding in the region.

FURTHER READINGS

Wilkerson, S. J. K. 1993. Escalante's Entrada: The Lost Aztec Garrison of the Mar del Norte in New Spain. *National Geographic Research and Exploration* 9:12–31.

———. 1994a. The Garden City of El Pital. *National Geographic Research and Exploration* 10:56–71.

———. 1994b. Nahua Presence on the Mesoamerican Gulf Coast. In E. Quinones-Kerber (ed.), *Chipping Away on Earth*, pp. 177–186. Culber City: Labyrinthos Press.

S. Jeffrey K. Wilkerson

SEE ALSO
Gulf Lowlands: North Central Region

Planchón de las Figuras (Chiapas, Mexico)

Planchón de las Figuras, or simply Planchón, consists of a large natural shelf of relatively smooth limestone containing one of the greatest and most interesting concentrations of petroglyphs and low-relief rock art in Mesoamerica. The formation slopes gently out of the base of the left bank of the Lacantun River, just upstream from where that river enters the larger Usumacinta. It measures more than

Petroglyph carvings at Plachon de las Figures, Mexico. Illustration courtesy of the author.

160 meters long (parallel to the river), and averages 30 to 35 meters wide during the dry season (the shelf is seasonally submerged to varying levels). Most of the carvings are concentrated near the bank. Planchón holds sixty-eight known incised or low-relief images in varying states of preservation. These include *patolli* game "boards," human figures, fantastic animals, and geometric forms. Among the most interesting depictions are those of structures—ball courts, pyramids with staircases, and summit-structures with elaborate roofs. One large set of these appears to be a map showing buildings around an open area—it recalls the Great Plaza at Tikal—with the pyramids shown in front elevations, but depicted as if they had been pushed down flat on their backs (see figure).

George Stuart

SEE ALSO
Maps and Place-Names; Maya Lowlands: South; Rock Art

Playa de los Muertos (Yoro, Honduras)

Situated in the lower Ulúa Valley on an ancient levee of the Ulúa River and exposed by erosion by the modern river, this residential site of undetermined extent was occupied during the Middle Formative period (c. 900–200 B.C.). The site or similar river-cut deposits were sampled by excavators in 1894 and 1910; more extensive excavations in 1928, 1936, and 1975 revealed burials and a series of house floors, a hearth, and remains of wattle-and-daub walls. Excavations documented two occupation levels with hand-modeled figurines, lobed bottles, and everted-rim bowls carrying variants of the double-line-break motif. Sixteen buried individuals, including three juveniles, were accompanied by twenty-three complete ceramic vessels, ten strings of shell, bone, iron pyrite, jade beads, and other items. The use of jade, "Olmec" incised motifs on selected burial vessels, and the double-line-break motif all suggest participation in wide networks of

Plumbate ceramics existed in simple forms that included bowls and cylinders as well as in jars and pyriform vases with effigies or complex abstract incised decorations. Illustrations courtesy of the author.

material and ideological exchange. The range of variation in burials is continuous, an indication of ranking, with ascribed status suggested by the great elaboration of juvenile burials. Playa de los Muertos is in part contemporary with Yarumela, Los Naranjos, the Cuyamel Caves and early Copán, and Chalchuapa.

FURTHER READINGS

Popenoe, D. H. 1934. Some excavations at Playa de los Muertos, Ulúa River, Honduras. *Maya Research* 1: 62–86.

Strong, W. D., A. V. Kidder II, and A. J. D. Paul, Jr. 1938. *Preliminary Report on the Smithsonian Institution–Harvard University Archaeological Expedition to Northwestern Honduras, 1936.* Smithsonian Miscellaneous Collections 97(1). Washington, D.C.: Smithsonian Institution.

Vaillant, G. 1934. The Archaeological Setting of the Playa de los Muertos Culture. *Maya Research* 1:87–100.

Rosemary Joyce

SEE ALSO
Southeast Mesoamerica

Plumbate Ware

Plumbate ware is a key ceramic diagnostic of the Late Classic and Early Postclassic periods in southern Mesoamerica. Technological investigation by Anna O. Shepard demonstrated that the distinctive lustrous gray surface of Plumbate was not a lead glaze, as "plumbate" would imply and as was once thought; it is, instead, a high-alumina, high-iron slip that vitrifies at around 950° C in a reducing atmosphere.

P

Tohil Plumbate jars and pyriform vases with effigies or complex abstract incised decorations are distributed throughout Mesoamerica, from Nicaragua to Nayarit, with important occurrences at the major Early Postclassic centers of Chichén Itzá and Tula. Tohil's wide distribution and its frequent association with Fine Orange ceramics document widespread commercial interaction during Early Postclassic times. Tohil peaks in frequency in mortuary contexts in western highland Guatemala.

Simpler Plumbate forms, including bowls, composite silhouette vessels, and cylinders, are called "San Juan Plumbate." San Juan occurs only in southern Mesoamerica, most commonly along the Pacific coast between Chiapas and western El Salvador. Peak frequencies in sherd collections from the vicinity of the Mexico-Guatemala border indicate the probable source region. San Juan is assumed to date to the Late Classic period.

Petrographic analysis and chemical characterization of Plumbate define two compositional groups, one dominated by the widely distributed Tohil Plumbate and one dominated by simpler San Juan forms. Large jars once thought to constitute a distinct Plumbate class ("robles") are of San Juan composition. The San Juan group also includes pottery-making byproducts from the Pacific Guatemalan region identified as the probable source. Plumbate compositional diversity also peaks in this region: a highly localized third compositional group (Guayabal) is present, and substantial proportions of bowls and other simple vessels from this region are of Tohil composition. Based on the latter evidence, widely traded fancy Tohil vessels appear to represent a specialized offshoot of the "background" Plumbate tradition of Pacific coastal Guatemala.

FURTHER READINGS

Neff, H. 1991. The Theoretical and Methodological Lessons of Shepard's Research on Plumbate Ware. In R. L. Bishop and F. W. Lange (eds.), *Anna O. Shepard: A Ceramic Legacy,* Niwot: University Press of Colorado.

Neff, H., and R. L. Bishop. 1988. Plumbate Origins and Development. *American Antiquity* 53:505–522.

Shepard, A. O. 1948. *Plumbate: A Mesoamerican Tradeware.* Carnegie Institution of Washington, Publication 573. Washington, D.C.

Hector Neff

SEE ALSO
Ceramics; Pottery

Ports of Trade

Introduced by Anne C. Chapman for Mesoamerica, the term "port of trade" refers to long-distance, elite-administered trade. Chapman identified Late Postclassic (A.D. 1200–1500) Aztec and Maya coastal locations, including the Soconusco in Chiapas, Mexico, the Laguna de Terminos in the Gulf of Mexico, and Naco in the Gulf of Honduras. Chapman's concepts belong to the "substantivist" view of economies in ancient civilizations, which defines a separation between long-distance trade in elite valuables and local trade in subsistence goods for the general public. Ports of trade were located in politically neutral territory, where elites or their representatives exchanged goods at fixed values.

Finding the conditions of "ports of trade" too restrictive, particularly since nonelites had access to exotic goods, researchers use terms such as "transshipment center" and "trading port" to describe coastal trading sites from the Classic through Postclassic at strategic locations at river mouths or along the coast, or where goods were transshipped between land and water. Isla Cerritos was a coastal trading port for the inland center of Chichén Itzá during the Early Postclassic (A.D. 900–1200). Isla Cerritos had Mexican obsidian, Tohil Plumbate pottery, and other trade goods. Cozumel was a trading port controlled by an inland city during the Early Postclassic that became an independent "port of trade" in the Late Postclassic. The recovery of only a few exotic trade goods was attributed to merchants using their wealth in their businesses rather than displaying wealth as grave offerings. Wild Cane Cay (Belize) was a Classic (A.D. 300–900) to Postclassic Maya trading port situated on the southern terminus of the circum-Yucatán coastal canoe route. In contrast to commerce at Cozumel, abundant obsidian from six sources in Central Mexico, Guatemala, and Honduras, and other exotic goods (Tulum Red and Tohil Plumbate pottery, gold and copper artifacts) were traded to Wild Cane Cay. Ambergris Cay (Belize), midway along the canoe trade route, was linked to Wild Cane Cay and Isla Cerritos by obsidian from similar sources. Other ports of trade or trading ports include Naco in Honduras, Matacapan in Mexico, and in the Soconusco area.

FURTHER READINGS

Andrews, A. 1990. The Role of Trading Ports in Maya Civilization. In F. Clancey and P. Harrison (eds.), *Vision and Revision in Maya Studies,* pp. 159–167. Albuquerque: University of New Mexico Press.

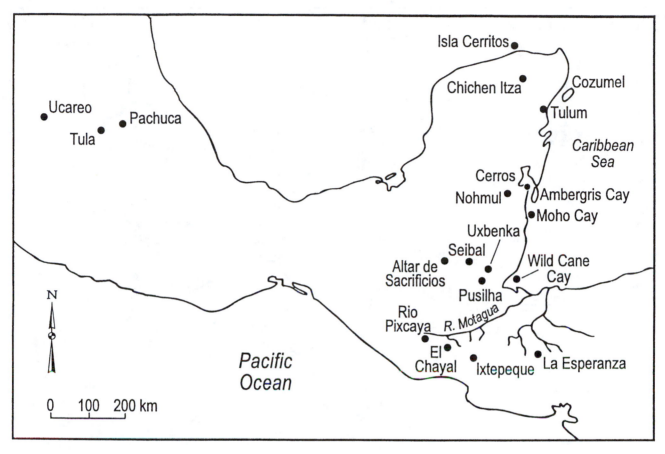

Map of Mesoamerica showing trading ports. Illustration by Mary Lee Egart, Louisiana State University.

Chapman, Anne C. 1957. Port of Trade Enclaves in Aztec and Maya Civilizations. In K. Polanyi, C. Arensberg, and H. Vearson (eds.), *Trade and Market in Early Empires,* pp. 114–153. Glencoe, Ill.: Free Press.

McKillop, H. 1996. Ancient Maya Trading Ports and the Integration of Long-Distance and Regional Economies: Wild Cane Cay in South Coastal Belize. *Ancient Mesoamerica* 7:49–62.

McKillop, H., and P. Healy (eds.). 1989. *Coastal Maya Trade.* Occasional Publications in Anthropology, 8. Peterborough, Ont.: Trent University.

Sabloff, J., and W. Rathje. 1975. *A Study of Changing Pre-Columbian Commercial Systems.* Monographs of the Peabody Museum, 3. Cambridge, Mass.: Harvard University.

Heather McKillop

SEE ALSO
Economic Organization

Postclassic Period

This term designates the time period between the fall of the Classic period cultures and the Spanish conquest, or approximately A.D. 900–1530. The term "Postclassic" was first used to designate a stage of cultural development during which supposedly warlike, secular, and less highly developed cultures replaced the peaceful, theocratic, artistically accomplished, and intellectually advanced Classic period civilizations of the Maya, Teotihuacán, and Monte Albán. These subjective judgments were later shown to be misleading, and concepts such as "Classic" and "Postclassic" are now applied to blocks of time, not to stages or types of cultures.

During the Postclassic period, systems of competing city-states arose in many regions to replace the larger states and empires of the Classic period. These small polities typically consisted of a central town or city and its surrounding hinterland of farmland and villages. They were ruled by kings aided by a small hereditary elite who

P

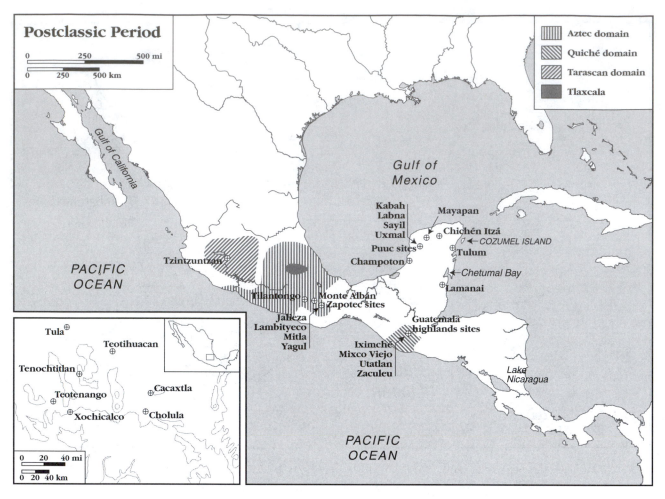

Postclassic Period. Map design by Mapping Specialists Limited, Madison, Wisconsin.

owned the land of the city-state and extracted tribute in the form of goods and labor from the commoners. Key institutions in these city-states were the palace of the ruler, a marketplace, and one or more modest temple-pyramids dedicated to the polity's patron gods. Postclassic temples and shrines in most areas were smaller than their Classic antecedents, suggesting changes in the social role of public religion in the smaller Postclassic polities. City-states did not develop in isolation; they were nearly always parts of regional systems of polities characterized by simultaneously antagonistic and friendly interactions.

The Postclassic period witnessed tremendous growth in the activities of merchants and marketplaces. Long-distance trade and stylistic interaction reached their height in Postclassic times, drawing many diverse cultures together into a single Mesoamerican world system based on economic and cultural links. Within this context of economically active and competitive city-states, several expansionist states (including the Aztec, Tarascan, and Quiché Maya) achieved military success at the expense of their fellow polities and forged tributary empires.

The ruling dynasties of Postclassic city-states and empires were greatly concerned with their history and legitimacy, and many local historical traditions have survived in painted manuscripts. Writing in Mesoamerica was concerned primarily with dynastic affairs. Two of Mesoamerica's five writing systems—the Mixtec and the Aztec—developed during the Postclassic period, and in Yucatán a simplified version of Maya writing survived from Classic into Postclassic times (other Mesoamerican writing systems were the Zapotec and Epi-Olmec scripts). Texts written on bark paper, cotton cloth, and animal skins provide an inside view of the ideas and actions of Postclassic rulers, nobles, and priests. Most of these painted manuscripts are from the Late Postclassic period, but a few survive from Early and Middle Postclassic times. Many Postclassic cultures also carved texts and images on stone monuments.

These native writings are only one type of ethnohistoric document with valuable information on Postclassic Mesoamerica. Accounts of the Spanish conquest by Hernando Cortés, Bernal Díaz del Castillo, and others contain firsthand descriptions of many cultures. After the Conquest, numerous chroniclers recorded a wide range of information on Late Postclassic cultures, including dynastic histories, religious practices and beliefs, economic and political organization, and social customs and institutions. Administrative documents from the Spanish imperial government also provide abundant material on Late Postclassic cultures; these include lawsuits, wills, deeds, census reports, records of meetings, and a variety of other reports. Most chronicles and administrative documents were recorded in Spanish, but numerous native-language documents were also produced. The applicability and relevance of the various ethnohistoric sources for understanding Postclassic cultures decline as one moves back in time from the Conquest, and the nature and extent of correlations between ethnohistory and archaeology is an important topic of research for the Postclassic period.

Epiclassic Period

The change in the meaning of "Postclassic" from an evolutionary stage to a period of time led to the definition of the Epiclassic Period (c. A.D. 700–900). It covers the interval between the fall of Teotihuacán (c. 700) and the Lowland Classic Maya collapse (c. 900). This period, called "Terminal Classic" in reference to the Maya Lowlands, witnessed the height of Classic Maya civilization. The Puuc Maya culture, separate from the Lowland Classic culture, was established around A.D. 800 in northern Yucatán. Sites such as Uxmal, Sayil, Labna, and Kabah exhibit the distinctive Puuc architectural style, in which buildings are adorned with elaborate stone mosaics of deities and geometric designs. The Puuc cultures were in contact with the Classic Maya to the south, but the nature of their interactions is not well understood. The collapse of the southern Maya cities had little effect on Puuc culture, which ushered in the Postclassic period in Yucatán. In the southern Maya Lowlands, communities in the Petén lakes region of Guatemala and the major center of Lamanai in Belize continued their occupation through the collapse, after which they established economic and political ties to northern Yucatán.

The Epiclassic period in Central Mexico was a time of warfare and conflict. The largest sites, such as Xochicalco, Cacaxtla, and Teotenango, are located on hilltops and have elaborate systems of defensive walls and ditches. Polychrome murals at Cacaxtla and carved stone monuments at Xochicalco emphasize themes of warfare, conquest, and sacrifice. There was still a sizable settlement at Teotihuacán in Epiclassic times, and one excavation there uncovered a workshop for obsidian arrowheads. In the Valley of Oaxaca, the period from A.D. 600 to 800 (formerly the Monte Albán IV phase, now the Xco phase) witnessed the continued importance of the large Classic period city of Monte Albán. Although this was the period of Monte Albán's maximum population size, political power became more dispersed as emergent Zapotec polities such as Lambityeco, Yagul, Mitla, and Jalieza rose to complement Monte Albán. This is the period when the greatest number of Zapotec inscriptions were created for funerary monuments.

Early Postclassic Period

The Early Postclassic period (c. A.D. 900–1150) is often called the "Toltec" period. Toltec civilization was based at the site of Tula, a large urban center with impressive public architecture. Although archaeologists agree that Tula was an important local polity, there is disagreement over the role of the Toltecs outside the Tula area. Toltec civilization figured prominently in later Aztec native history. To the Aztecs, the Toltecs were the great and wise inventors of much of Mesoamerican culture (from the calendar to various crafts), who ruled a vast empire from their luxurious capital city. The Toltec rulers were viewed by later cultures as semidivine, and dynasties throughout Mesoamerica drew their legitimacy from claims of descent (either real or invented) from the Toltec kings.

The results of excavations suggest that the Aztec portrayal of the Toltecs was highly exaggerated. Tula was not a particularly luxurious city; it was a far cry from both Teotihuacán and Tenochtitlán in size, architectural quality, and richness of material culture. There is no material evidence for a Toltec empire, and analyses of trade wares show that Tula was not a major participant in the extensive long-distance exchange networks of Early Postclassic Mesoamerica.

The possible role of the Toltecs at Chichén Itzá in Yucatán is another controversial issue. Chichén Itzá flourished as an important political center that controlled much of northern Yucatán between A.D. 1000 and 1250. Public architecture in one part of the site is in the Puuc

P

style, and buildings incorporate carved inscriptions with Maya glyphs. Several buildings and features in another sector of the site resemble the architecture of Tula. Some scholars cite Maya historical legends to argue that a group of Toltecs from Tula invaded Yucatán and set up a base at Chichén Itzá, where they built pyramids and other buildings in their native Central Mexican style. Other scholars believe that the so-called Toltec-style architecture at Chichén Itzá evolved gradually out of the Puuc style, and thus similarities with Tula must be explained by some form of two-way interaction and communication, not by Toltec conquest. A third model holds that an intermediary group of warlike traders known from ethnohistorical accounts as the Putun Maya brought Toltec-influenced cultural traits to Chichén Itzá. Unfortunately, the archaeological chronology of Chichén Itzá is not sufficiently refined to choose between these scenarios.

The Epiclassic and Early Postclassic periods witnessed a dramatic growth of trade and communication throughout coastal and peripheral Mesoamerica. Two of the most widely distributed trade goods were distinctive ceramic wares known as Fine Orange and Plumbate. Fine-paste orange ceramics were manufactured in several places in the eastern Maya and Gulf Coast areas, and high-fired Plumbate ceramics with a glazelike finish were made along the Soconusco area of the Pacific Coast. Obsidian from the Ucareo and Zinapécuaro sources of Michoacán was imported in large quantities to Xochicalco in Epiclassic times, and in the Early Postclassic period Zinapécuaro obsidian was exchanged as far away as Yucatán, where it was common at Chichén Itzá, Isla Cerritos, and other sites.

Many coastal regions of Mesoamerica developed traditions of painted ceramics in Early Postclassic times, and these shared a number of distinctive iconographic motifs such as step-frets, solar disks, and feathered serpents. This Postclassic Religious style, rarely found in highland or interior areas, provides additional evidence for intensive trade and communication throughout coastal and peripheral Mesoamerica. One result of the active maritime trade of the Early Postclassic period was the introduction of South American copper-bronze metallurgy into West Mexico through Pacific trade networks. West Mexican metallurgy began through the copying of techniques and styles of Ecuadorian metal-working, but artisans soon experimented with copper alloys containing varying amounts of tin and arsenic. This technology did not spread out of West Mexico until later times.

Middle Postclassic Period

In many areas of Mesoamerica, the Early and Late Postclassic periods are separated by the Middle Postclassic period (c. A.D. 1150–1350); in other areas, chronological refinement is insufficient to define a Middle period. In Central Mexico, the fall of Tula is dated in native historical accounts at around A.D. 1175. This coincided with the arrival of Nahuatl-speaking immigrants from semimythical Aztlan in northern Mexico. The Aztlan populations settled much of Central Mexico, where they forged a new culture: the Aztec. The final Aztlan group to arrive, the Mexica, were later to rise to prominence as lords of the Aztec Empire. During Middle Postclassic times the Aztecs organized themselves into many small, competing city-states, whose rulers set up new dynasties said to be descended from the Toltec kings. Although these city-states warred with one another constantly, they were unable to establish large, enduring tributary domains. Many regions developed distinctive local styles of painted ceramics, and these were widely traded through marketplaces and by professional merchants.

In the Middle Postclassic period, the Mixteca-Puebla region (southern Puebla and northeastern Oaxaca) rose to artistic prominence. The cultures of this region, particularly the city of Cholula, created the Mixteca-Puebla style out of the earlier Postclassic Religious style. The new style employed vivid colors in standardized and often geometric depictions of gods, ceremonies, and various religious symbols. The style appears on polychrome ceramics, murals, and painted manuscripts throughout the Mixteca-Puebla region.

Late Postclassic Period

The Late Postclassic period (c. A.D. 1350–1550) witnessed the continuation of earlier patterns of small polities engaged in active long-distance trade and stylistic interaction. In Yucatán, the collapse of Chichén Itzá around 1250 was followed by the rise to prominence of Mayapan as the dominant city and polity in the area. Warfare was endemic, and Mayapan consisted of closely packed residences surrounded by a defensive wall. Once Mayapan succumbed to military defeat in 1450, Yucatecan society broke apart into numerous small warring polities, which were loosely organized into regional provinces.

The prevalence of war and dynastic strife did not prevent the Maya towns from trading with one another, however. Commodities such as salt, obsidian, pottery, cacao, and slaves were exchanged throughout the Maya area in Late Postclassic times. In particular, the use of obsidian increased dramatically. Chemical characterization methods that permit the identification of the sources of obsidian artifacts have contributed greatly to our understanding of Late Postclassic Maya trade patterns. Volatile trade relationships among competitive polities were facilitated by the construction of new shrine/pilgrimage complexes that were integrated with key trading activities; these have been studied at Cozumel and in other areas.

The major trade routes followed the Caribbean coast, where canoes carried people and goods among sites such as Champoton, Cozumel Island, Tulum, Chetumal, and numerous small settlements on the Belize coast. Christopher Columbus encountered one of these Maya trade canoes on his fourth voyage in 1502; he noted that the merchants carried cotton textiles, obsidian blades and swords, copper-bronze axes and bells, and crucibles for smelting the metal.

In the Maya Highlands of Guatemala and southern Mexico, the Late Postclassic period was a time of warfare, unrest, and movements of peoples. The Quiché were a warlike people who moved into highland Guatemala from the Gulf Coast of Mexico, conquering many towns. They built an impressive capital city, Utatlan, in a defensible hilltop location (other fortified capital cities in this region included Mixco Viejo, capital of the Pokomam peoples, and Zaculeu, the Mam capital). Archaeological mapping has located zones that were probably inhabited by lineages which can be identified from ethnohistoric records. The Quiché established a modest empire and extracted tribute from surrounding peoples. In the late 1400s, the power of the Quiché began to erode. The Cakchiquel peoples broke away from Utatlan and established their own fortified hilltop center at Iximché. The Soconusco, the Pacific coastal region controlled by the Quiché, was taken over by the expanding Aztec Empire. This region was rich in lowland resources needed by both the Quiché and the Aztecs, including colorful feathers, animal skins, amber, and especially cacao.

Among the best-documented city-states of Postclassic Mesoamerica are the Mixtec kingdoms of highland Oaxaca. The Mixtecs devised a limited form of hieroglyphic writing and used it to record the exploits of their rulers in books such as the Nuttall Codex. These native histories covered several centuries of political and ritual events. One major topic was the life of the renowned ruler of Tilantongo, or 8 Deer Tiger Claw, in the eleventh century A.D. He conquered many towns, forged marriage alliances with others, and travelled to Tula (or perhaps a Toltec-affiliated foreign polity) to have his nose ceremonially pierced; this gave 8 Deer important foreign legitimation in his quest for the Tilantongo throne. Similar patterns of concurrent antagonistic and friendly interactions characterized the Mixtec city-states up through the Spanish conquest. The Mixtecs were accomplished goldsmiths, producing delicate jewelry using the lost wax technique. Some of the finest surviving examples are from Tomb 7 at Monte Albán, excavated by Alfonso Caso; other examples have been found at Tenochtitlán (Mexico City), where Mixtec goldsmiths worked for Aztec patrons. Recent research in the Mixteca region has located many of the archaeological sites that correspond to polities described in the codices.

In Central Mexico, the Late Postclassic period was a time of dramatic social change. After establishing dynasties, towns, and villages in the Middle Postclassic, the 150 to 200 Aztec city-states in the Basin of Mexico and surrounding valleys experienced rapid demographic and economic expansion in Late Postclassic times. Population grew to the highest level of any period before the mid-twentieth century; when the Spaniards arrived in 1519, there were more than one million people living in the Basin of Mexico. Farmers intensified their production to feed the growing population and to meet the increasing tribute demands of city-state elites. The changes in farming transformed the Central Mexican landscape: gently sloping hillsides were covered with stone terrace walls; gullies and ravines were filled in with check dams; flat alluvial lands were irrigated from dams and canals; and the swamps of the Basin of Mexico were transformed into productive farms by the construction of *chinampas,* or raised fields. Similar patterns of agricultural intensification characterized many other areas of Mesoamerica in the Late Postclassic period.

Ethnohistoric documents and archaeological excavations provide rich details on Aztec social organization. Many features of Aztec society were shared by other Late Postclassic cultures. City-states were ruled by kings who represented a small hereditary nobility (2 to 5 percent of the population). The nobles owned the land of the city-state and controlled the government. Marriage alliances between city-states were important parts of the political process and served to strengthen bonds within the elite class that transcended polity boundaries. Commoners paid tribute to nobles in the forms of labor, cotton textiles, food, and other goods. They lived in households ranging from simple nuclear families to complex multigenerational families. In many areas, commoner households were

P

organized into larger corporate groups such as villages or urban neighborhoods; among the Aztecs, these were called *calpulli*. Excavations of Aztec commoner houses in both rural and urban settings have turned up rich and diverse domestic artifact inventories that typically include abundant imported goods, such as foreign ceramics and obsidian.

The prominence of trade and markets in Postclassic Mesoamerica is nowhere so strongly documented as in Aztec Central Mexico. The Spanish conquerors were amazed at the huge, bustling marketplace in Tlatelolco, Tenochtitlán's adjacent sister city. Hernando Cortés stated that sixty thousand persons attended this market each day, and he provided a list of hundreds of goods and services that were offered. Each commodity was sold in its own section of the market, and the layout and operation were overseen by a group of *pochteca* merchants who served as administrators and judges. All Aztec cities and towns had marketplaces. The largest markets were open daily, and smaller markets were held every twenty days (the Aztec month). The most common category, however, were the intermediate-sized markets held at most cities and towns on a weekly basis (every five days, in line with the Aztec calendar of five-day weeks and twenty-day months).

Nearby towns typically held their markets on different days of the week, much like modern peasant markets in Mesoamerica. This allowed regional merchants to travel from market to market, offering a wide range of products. The professional long-distance merchants, the *pochteca,* also sold their exotic imports in the markets, and petty artisans set up stalls to sell their products. Commercial exchange was facilitated by the use of several kinds of money. Cacao beans were used for small purchases; one bean could buy a fresh tomato, five chili peppers, a cooked tamal, or a load of firewood. For larger transactions, standardized lengths of cotton cloth were used; most of these were worth between sixty-five and one hundred cacao beans each; twenty-five pieces of cloth would buy a gold lip plug, while a fine jade necklace could cost as much as six hundred cloths. Cacao beans had to be imported from distant lowland areas such as the Soconusco through channels of imperial tribute and independent merchant trade.

The Aztecs placed few restrictions on market purchases. Commoners could buy almost anything they wanted in the markets, and only a few types of special jewelry and clothing were restricted to the nobility. Commoners obtained not only exotic pottery and obsidian, but also jade beads, shell necklaces, and other luxury goods through the markets, and these items turn up in excavations of Aztec commoner houses. The relatively open and commercialized market economy of Late Postclassic times contrasted with earlier Mesoamerican exchange systems which restricted many luxury goods to members of the elite class. Mesoamerican commoners were much heavier participants in the exchange economy in Late Postclassic times than they had been in earlier cultures.

In the second half of the Late Postclassic period, the Aztec Empire expanded by conquering several hundred city-states in northern Mesoamerica. The empire was formed as a military alliance among the Mexica, the Acolhua, and the Tepanecs, but the Mexica of Tenochtitlan soon became the dominant force. They employed several strategies in the creation and operation of the empire. Within the Basin of Mexico, the Mexica began to reorganize conquered city-states in order to ensure their loyalty to the empire and to generate tribute payments. In the outer provinces, the empire instituted tribute payments and promoted markets and regional commerce. When the Aztecs came up against strong enemy states, they employed a frontier strategy of alliances with border polities to keep the enemies at bay.

The Aztec Empire's most serious competition came from the Tarascans of western Mexico. Although the Tarascans were unrelated to the Aztecs culturally or historically, the evolution of Tarascan culture in Middle and Late Postclassic times paralleled that of the Aztecs. The Tarascans too were recent immigrants into a large highland basin (the Pátzcuaro Basin), and their population grew rapidly once they had settled in. One of a number of competing city-states, Tzintzuntzan, succeeded in subjugating its neighbors and then began a program of imperial expansion out of the basin. By the Late Postclassic period, the Tarascans had perfected a variety of techniques for working copper into bronze, and metallurgy was under the control of the Tarascan state. One of the goals of imperial expansion was to acquire territory with deposits of copper, tin, and arsenic. Bronze metallurgy spread beyond the Tarascan realm, however, and an independent metal production zone was established in the Huastec area of the eastern Aztec Empire. In the 1470s, the expanding Tarascan and Aztec Empires came up against each other in battle. The Tarascans won an impressive victory in 1478, killing or wounding twenty thousand Aztec soldiers. After this, the two empires established a frontier of empty land guarded by local fortresses on each side, and they remained at a military standoff until the Spanish conquest.

Ethnohistoric sources mention marketplaces in virtually every part of Mesoamerica at the time of the Spanish conquest. Markets were closely integrated with long-distance exchange networks through the participation of merchants, including the Aztec *pochteca.* Excavations in many areas provide evidence for extensive trade in ceramics, obsidian, salt, bronze, jade, and other items, and ethnohistoric sources list hundreds of goods sold by merchants. Long-distance trade crossed political borders with ease. The *pochteca* traded both inside and outside the Aztec Empire, and commerce even crossed the hostile Aztec-Tarascan frontier; Tarascan bronze and obsidian have been found at Aztec sites, and Aztec obsidian at Tarascan sites.

Long-distance trade was not the only bond linking together widely separated groups in Late Postclassic Mesoamerica. Mural paintings with religious themes were executed in a single style throughout Mesoamerica, suggesting widespread ideological integration that transcended political boundaries. Called the International style, this Late Postclassic variant of the Mixteca-Puebla style was used on murals from Central Mexico to Yucatán to highland Guatemala. Particularly noteworthy examples survive at Tulum and Mitla.

Summary

The three major social trends in Postclassic Mesoamerica—the growth of city-states, the increase in trade and markets, and the expansion of empires—were not isolated processes. The rulers of city-states derived part of their power and prestige from exotic luxury goods obtained by merchants, and rulers tried to promote their local markets above those in other polities. Empires expanded in order to supplement trade with tribute payments from subjects, and they generally left conquered city-states alone to manage their affairs under imperial control. The Mexica promoted trade and marketing throughout the Aztec Empire as a deliberate strategy.

Long-distance trade and stylistic interaction went far beyond the boundaries of any single city-state, valley, or empire to link the entire region of Mesoamerica into a single dynamic economic and cultural system. This was an example of a preindustrial world system—a geographically extensive network of independent polities linked through a common division of labor. In the Mesoamerican case, stylistic interaction supplemented economic exchange as a force holding the world system together. The growth and interactions of city-states, markets and trade, and empires within the larger world system gave Late Postclassic Mesoamerican cultures a vibrancy and dynamism unequaled in earlier periods. This vigorous world system did not last very long, however; it was cut short by the Spanish conquest, starting in 1519.

FURTHER READINGS

Andrews, A. P. 1993. Late Postclassic Lowland Maya Archaeology. *Journal of World Prehistory* 7:35–69.

Blanton, R. E., S. A. Kowalewski, G. M. Feinman, and L. M. Finsten. 1993. *Ancient Mesoamerica: A Comparison of Change in Three Regions.* 2nd edn. New York: Cambridge University Press.

Byland, B. E., and J. D. Pohl. 1995. *In the Realm of 8 Deer: The Archaeology of the Mixtec Codices.* Norman: University of Oklahoma Press.

Carmack, R. M. 1981. *The Quiché Mayas of Utatlan: The Evolution of a Highland Guatemala Kingdom.* Norman: University of Oklahoma Press.

Chase, A. F., and P. M. Rice (eds.). 1985. *The Lowland Maya Postclassic.* Austin: University of Texas Press.

Diehl, R., and J. Berlo (eds.). 1989. *Mesoamerica after the Decline of Teotihuacán,* A.D. *700–900.* Washington, D.C.: Dumbarton Oaks.

Freidel, D. A., and J. A. Sabloff. 1984. *Cozumel: Late Maya Settlement Patterns.* New York: Academic Press.

Healan, D. M. (ed.). 1989. *Tula of the Toltecs: Excavations and Survey.* Iowa City: University of Iowa Press.

Hodge, M. G., and M. E. Smith (eds.). 1994. *Economies and Polities in the Aztec Realm.* Albany: Institute for Mesoamerican Studies.

Hosler, D. 1994. *The Sounds and Colors of Power: The Sacred Metallurgical Technology of Ancient West Mexico.* Cambridge, Mass.: MIT Press.

Pollard, H. P. 1993. *Tariacuri's Legacy: The pre-Hispanic Tarascan State.* Norman: University of Oklahoma Press.

Voorhies, B. (ed.). 1989. *Ancient Trade and Tribute: Economies of the Soconusco Region of Mesoamerica.* Salt Lake City: University of Utah Press.

Michael E. Smith

SEE ALSO

Aztec Culture and History; Classic Period; Colonial Period

Pottery

Pottery vessels constitute one of the most abundant artifact types encountered by archaeologists, and one of the most valuable for reconstructing the lives of pre-Hispanic

P

peoples. Following the introduction of ceramic technology into Mesoamerica by 2000 B.C., pottery vessels were quickly adopted as containers essential for a variety of tasks. In domestic contexts, pottery was utilized for the storage, preparation, and serving of food and beverages. In ritual contexts, distinctive ceramic vessels were used to burn incense and hold ritual fires, and as funerary effigy urns. Because the raw materials of pottery were inexpensive and widely available, pottery containers were employed by all segments of society, and because this medium is extremely plastic, variation in pottery reflects a broad array of functional, economic, and social factors. (For a glossary of terms used in this article, see Table 1.)

Origins

Pottery first appears in Central America's archaeological record between 3000 and 2000 B.C.; the oldest is Monagrillo pottery (2850–1300 B.C.) from the vicinity of Parita

TABLE 1. ANATOMY OF A CERAMIC VESSEL (AFTER RICE 1987).

Vessel Part	Definition
Orifice	The mouth or opening of a vessel.
Restricted	Orifice is less than maximum vessel diameter.
Unrestricted	Orifice is equal to or greater than maximum diameter.
Lip	The edge or margin of the orifice of a vessel; sometimes refers more specifically to a modification of the rim.
Rim	The area between the lip or margin and the side wall or neck of a vessel; sometimes used interchangeably with "lip," especially if there is no change of orientation between the lip and neck or wall.
Neck	The part of the vessel between the shoulder and the rim, typically characterized by a marked constriction of the maximum body diameter; where there is little constriction, the region is often called a "collar."
Throat	The base of a neck or collar on a vessel, or the point of maximum diameter restriction of a neck or collar.
Shoulder	The upper part of the body of a restricted vessel; that portion between the maximum diameter and the orifice or neck.
Body	That portion of a vessel between the orifice and the base that includes the maximum diameter of the vessel or the region of greatest enclosed volume.
Base	The underside of a vessel, or that part of a vessel in contact with the surface it rests on during normal use.
Wall	The side of the vessel, from lip to base, exclusive of appendages and supports.
Flange or Ridge	Band or projection that extends out from the vessel wall, typically running around the entire circumference. Placement can be labial (at the lip or rim), medial (along the wall), or basal (near the junction of wall and base).
Supports	Appendages attached to the lower vessel wall or base (including rings, pedestal, feet, or nubbins) that lift and/or stabilize vessel.
Handle	Appendage attached to the body, neck, or collar to facilitate carrying vessel.
Profile	The vertical cross-section of a ceramic vessel, showing wall thickness and details of lip, rim, and base configuration.
Simple	Smooth, uninterrupted straight or curved wall.
Composite/Complex	Profile consists of two or more straight or curved segments.

Bay, Central Panama. Simple vessel forms (hemispherical bowls and *tecomates*) predominate, and decoration is limited to red-painted bowl rims and simple incising. Manufacture is generally shoddy, with coils incompletely smoothed and still visible; vessels are poorly fired and friable.

In Mesoamerica, the earliest pottery so far identified comes from Puerto Marqués on the Pacific coast of Guerrero, with a carbon date of 2440 ± 140 B.C. This Pox pottery, named for the rough, pitted interior surfaces of sherds that contrast with well-smoothed exteriors, is in *tecomate* form, fiber tempered, and quite friable. A similar surface is found on the earliest pottery from the Tehuacan Valley. There, Purrón phase (2300–1500 B.C.) pottery is crude and crumbly, with a coarse, gravel-like temper. The *tecomate* is again the dominant form, but flat-bottomed bowls with low, flaring sides also appear. Both forms echo the shapes of stone vessels from the previous aceramic phase and may represent attempts to reproduce those vessels in a lighter medium. Alternatively, these earliest vessel forms may have been modeled after bottle gourds, which the occupants of the Tehuacan Valley had used as containers for thousands of years. The vessels themselves could have been produced by press-molding clay on the inside or outside a gourd container.

The early development of pottery in multiple areas at approximately the same time suggests that pottery was largely an indigenous development rather than a result of simple diffusion. However, the idea of ceramic technology may have come from cultures to the south, because potters at sites such as Valdivia, Ecuador, and Puerto Hormiga, Colombia, were producing sophisticated ceramics as early as 3000 B.C.

Classification and Analysis of Ceramic Variability

Although all pottery classification schemes document variation in paste, form, surface treatment, and decoration, a bewildering array of approaches and definitions is used by archaeologists to classify and interpret these dimensions of variability. One of the best known classification schemes is the Type-Variety system proposed by Smith, Willey, and Gifford, which has been widely applied within the Maya Lowlands. In this polythetic, hierarchical system, the smallest unit recognized is the variety, defined as a cluster of visually distinct ceramic attributes or characteristics such as a specific type of temper, method of firing, surface finish, form, and decoration. Varieties are subsumed within types based on a majority of shared attributes. In turn, one or more types may be subsumed within a ceramic group, usually on the basis of similar surface treatments, such as the presence and color of slip. The broad-scale application the type-variety system has permitted the spatial and temporal integration of material from different regions. Ceramic complexes from individual sites are identified as belonging to the same temporal horizon, based on shared ceramic traits. Such chronologically sensitive ceramic traits are termed "horizon markers." When a majority of dominant types and varieties are shared between complexes, the sites are said to belong to the same "ceramic sphere."

In other geographical areas, more rigid classification schemes are employed in which specific variables consistently define each level of the typological hierarchy. As in the case of Aztec ceramics, wares are frequently distinguished on the basis of general uniformity of paste and modal surface color and finish. Types are distinguished within each ware according to basic decorative traditions, including the presence and type of paint, incising, and specific motifs. Ceramic types are often combined with vessel forms to create single type-shape units. Decorative variants may be defined within each type-shape class on the basis of specific decorative patterns such as consistencies in the choice and execution of design motifs and in the spatial organization of the design.

Informal categories often emphasize broad differences in vessel appearance (slipped vs. unslipped, decorated vs. plain), function, or status, as judged from vessel form and physical characteristics. A common distinction is between serving vessels (vessels used for the serving and display of foods and beverages in domestic, feasting, and ritual contexts) and utilitarian vessels used for cooking and storage; the distinction recognizes the greater potential of the first class to communicate information on status or ethnicity.

To analyze variability in pottery, archaeologists use other kinds of typologies. Attribute analysis focuses on the presence or absence of specific attribute states, such as different types of lip modification (direct, everted, thickened, etc.) or temper. Design analysis concentrates on identifying decorative elements and motifs, their configuration in the design space, and their placement on the vessel. In contrast, morphometric analysis quantifies variability in vessel size and shape through detailed measurements of vessel dimensions and proportions. Functional analysis focuses on the range of vessel uses, as determined through historic data, ethnographic analogy,

P

or an assessment of use-related properties, including vessel capacity, stability, accessibility of contents, transportability, durability, weight, and closure (Rice 1987:225–226). Compositional analysis determines the mineralogical and chemical makeup of pottery. Mineralogical analyses frequently utilize microscopic examination of ceramic thin sections to identify the mineral constituents of aplastic inclusions from their crystalline structure, and to determine particle size and shape, abundance, and association. Chemical analyses employ techniques such as instrumental neutron activation analysis (INAA) or the electron microprobe to determine concentrations of minor and trace elements in pastes, slips, and paints.

Uses of Ceramic Data

Chronology remains one of the primary goals of ceramic analysis: establishing the contemporaneity of two assemblages based on shared ceramic types, vessel forms, or attributes, or determining the relative temporal order of assemblages through seriation. Beyond chronology, the range of functionally specific vessel forms sheds light on the range of activities performed at a site or feature, while differing degrees of elaboration or labor invested in ceramic vessels can be assessed as markers of differences in the socio-economic status of their owners. Overall similarity of shared design elements or other stylistic attributes reflects the relative intensity of social interaction among groups.

Compositional studies of ceramic pastes can identify ceramics produced from the same clay source or production center; the distribution of these products can then be mapped to model the organization of trade and exchange on local and interregional levels. The products of known manufacturing centers can be examined through attribute, morphometric, or compositional analyses to characterize aspects of craft production, including standardization and degree of product specialization—measures associated with the intensity and scale of production.

Ceramic Technology and Manufacture

The extreme plasticity of pottery presents the archaeologist with a complex, multidimensional challenge: each pot potentially varies in clay composition, vessel form, surface treatment, decoration, and firing. Sorting out the cultural significance of this variability requires an understanding of indigenous ceramic technology—the steps involved in clay preparation and vessel manufacture as practiced by native potters.

Ceramic Clays. The clay body (alternatively called "paste" or "fabric") of a ceramic pot consists of two main ingredients: clay, chiefly alumina-silicate minerals, formed by decomposition of rock to an extremely fine particle size, less than 0.002 mm in diameter; and aplastic inclusions, generally rock and mineral particles larger than the clay-size fraction, which give the paste its texture (Rice 1987). Aplastics (also termed "nonplastics") may be naturally occurring inclusions found in the clay bed or source, including minerals from the parent material and from rocks and sediments encountered during the erosion and redeposition of clay deposits. Excessive amounts of these natural inclusions were removed by potters through sorting, sieving, and/or levigation (mixing the clay with water and allowing the coarser particles to settle out). Alternatively, specific aplastic materials may have been added by the potter as temper to improve the workability and firing properties of the clay. Inorganic materials added as temper include quartz sand, crushed rock, volcanic ash, and grog (pulverized pottery). Organic tempering agents, including crushed shell and plant fibers, were less common; the use of plant materials such as reed fibers or cattail fluff is indicated by the fired casts of plant parts preserved in vessel walls. Because the proportion, size, and shape of aplastics (as well as their chemical composition) determine the strength and quality of pottery vessels, specific cultural "recipes" developed as an important part of ceramic technology. These distinctive combinations of clays and inclusions in turn provide the basis for many archaeological reconstructions of events in prehistoric times, from establishing the contemporaneity of ceramic assemblages to tracing trade contacts between distant groups.

Vessel Shape. New World pottery was formed by hand-modeling or in molds prior to European contact, when the potter's wheel was introduced. Techniques such as hand-modeling (in which the mass of clay is patted, pulled, and/or beaten into the desired shape), coiling (in which the vessel walls are built up from superimposed rolls of clay), and the extensive use of concave or convex molds made of ceramic, stone, or gourd were used individually or in combination.

Clay was shaped into the standard repertoire of cooking, serving, and storage vessels with local variations in profile and elaboration (Tables 1, 2). General shape classes widely recognized by archaeologists include plate, dish, bowl, jar, and vase, defined by the ratio of vessel

TABLE 2. DEFINITION OF COMMON VESSEL FORMS.

Morphological Classes		Functional Classes	
VESSEL	DEFINITION OF SHAPE	VESSEL	DESCRIPTION
Plate	A shallow vessel with unrestricted orifice, having a height less than one-fifth its maximum diameter.	Olla	A large, generally wide-mouthed jar for holding liquids.
Dish	A shallow vessel with unrestricted orifice, slightly deeper than a plate, with a height more than one-fifth but less than one-third of its maximum diameter.	Tecomate	A globular, neckless pot with restricted opening, sometimes called a "seed-pot."
		Cazuela	A casserole dish; i.e. a flat-bottomed, relatively shallow dish for serving food.
Bowl	Vessel with restricted or unrestricted orifice, with a height varying from one-third the maximum diameter of the vessel up to equal to the diameter. Bowls may have collars, but they do not have necks.	Comal	A flat griddle for cooking tortillas.
		Molcajete	A grater bowl in which the base has been slashed to create a rough surface for grating chiles and other condiments.
Jar	A necked vessel with its height greater than its maximum diameter.	Copa	A goblet with a pedestal base, and either a rounded or flaring cup.
Vase	A restricted or unrestricted vessel with a height greater than its maximum diameter.	Censer/ Incensario	A small globular vessel with perforated walls generally with a long, tubular handle; used for burning incense.
		Brazier/ Brasero	Large urn for burning incense or holding ritual fires, frequently in effigy form.

height to maximum diameter and by the kind or size of orifice. More functionally specific forms are recognized as well, including *olla, tecomate, cazuela, comal, molcajete,* and *copa* (Table 2). Ritual vessel forms include censers *(incensarios)* and braziers *(braseros).*

Surface Treatment. After forming, vessel surfaces were generally finished by wiping and smoothing the vessel wall to fill in cracks and depressions. The vessel surface could then be burnished with a polishing stone, bone, or piece of smooth wood. Burnishing compacts and reorients the fine clay particles to give the surface luster. Careless burnishing leaves a series of narrow linear tracks or facets, while complete burnishing yields a smooth, lustrous surface. Surface color and luster were often further improved by application of a slip, a fluid suspension of clay in water that coats the entire vessel surface; this was

generally burnished. Slips usually differ in color from the clay of the vessel wall, ranging through black, brown, red, orange, cream, and white. True glazes (vitrified clay paints requiring high firing temperatures) were not produced until after European contact.

Surface Decoration. A broad range of plastic and painted techniques were utilized to add decorative elements to the vessel's surface. In the repertoire of manipulative techniques, designs and patterns were created through incising to cut lines into the paste, or through excising, carving, or gouging to remove grooves or areas of clay. Alternatively, the wet clay could be impressed or stamped to achieve a variety of textures and patterns. Cord-marking (generated by a cord-wrapped paddle or stick) and rocker-stamping (produced by "walking" a shell edge back and forth to create a zigzag line) are two

P

distinctive imprinted textures shared by Formative Meso-america and contemporaneous cultures of the southeastern United States. Carved pottery stamps were widely used to press motifs into the clay. Modeled or molded adornments were added onto the vessel surface as appliqué decoration. In other cases, surface manipulation was more functional than esthetic: scored striations applied to the necks of water jars were not for decoration, but to roughen the surface and reduce the chance of slippage.

It is with painted decoration, however, that the potters of Mexico and Central America attained some of their greatest artistic achievements during Classic and Postclassic times. In addition to monochrome slips, elaborate designs and pictorial scenes were painted in bichrome (two-color) or polychrome (multicolor) schemes including black, brown, tan, orange, red, pink, and white pigments. Polychrome painted decoration was frequently applied over a white underslip to enhance the clarity of superimposed translucent slips and paints. A less common form of polychrome decoration involved a fresco technique: after firing, a coat of plaster was applied to the vessel and the colors were brushed in while the plaster was still wet. Another widespread painting technique was resist painting (incorrectly called "negative painting"), in which a temporary protective coating was applied over portions of the vessel surface to create the desired design, after which the entire vessel was slipped or painted. When the protective coating was removed (generally during firing), the design showed up in the basal color of the vessel. In contrast, in cloisonné, a layer of paint was applied to the entire surface; this paint was then cut out and removed from the design area and the hollow spaces filled in with another color.

Firing. Throughout the region, pottery appears to have been fired between 700° and 900° C, a temperature range easily attained even under primitive firing conditions. Pre-Hispanic pottery kilns have been identified in highland Mexico as well as in a few other areas; most date to after A.D. 500. These small kilns typically consist of a circular pit (1–2 meters in diameter) surrounded or enclosed by a low wall of rock and clay that contained both pottery and fuel. More elaborate indirect-firing kilns are known from the Valley of Oaxaca. One excellent example from Mitla (c. A.D. 1000–1300) consists of a pair of circular chambers each a meter in diameter, connected by a stone-lined tunnel or flue. One chamber held pottery, and the other held fuel, with heated air moving through the flue.

Earlier examples (c. 300–100 B.C.) were constructed as single pits 60–80 cm in diameter, divided by an adobe wall into a ware chamber and a firing chamber. However, the general scarcity of kilns in the archaeological record suggests that most pottery was fired in open bonfires or simple firing pits rather than in enclosed chambers. In this case, it is the presence of kiln wasters (misfired vessels marked by blistering or warping) that alerts the archaeologist to the presence of a ceramic production site.

Potters manipulated the firing atmosphere to achieve an oxidizing environment (having ample free oxygen) or a reducing environment (lacking free oxygen). Oxidation typically produces clear surface colors in the range of buff, orange, and red through complete combustion of hydrocarbons, while reduction tends to produce dark surface colors, including brown and gray. Smudging, produced through the introduction of additional carbon (such as fine manure or sawdust) late in the firing process, yields a black surface. Subterranean kilns maintained even temperatures and a controlled firing atmosphere; the more variable temperature and atmosphere conditions of bonfire firings led to irregular surface color and fireclouds, a darkened area of the vessel surface resulting from uneven firing.

Ceramic Traditions

Given these basic constraints, and from simple beginnings, a tremendously diverse pottery tradition developed in Mesoamerica and Central America. Among these ceramics, a few pottery attributes, types, and wares stand out so distinctly that they have become markers for specific timespans and/or particular cultures.

A cluster of distinctive traits characterizes the Early Formative period over large portions of Mesoamerica, from the Basin of Mexico and the Valley of Oaxaca, down to the Pacific Coast of Chiapas and Guatemala, and the Olmec heartland of Veracruz and Tabasco. These traits include rocker-stamping, plain, dentate, and zoned (in which patterned areas alternate with smooth areas), on *tecomates*; excised "Olmec" motifs, such as the wing-paw and flame brows; and differential firing to produce a white-rimmed black ware. The stirrup-spout jar, an unusual form having two hollow tubes that rise and join to form a single spout, first appears late in the Early Formative and continues through the Late Formative.

A similarly diagnostic trait of the Middle Formative from the central highlands of Mexico to coastal Guatemala is the double-line-break. This motif, consisting of two lines running parallel to the rim which then turn sharply or break toward the lip, was frequently incised on the interiors of white- or cream-slipped bowls and dishes.

In the Basin of Mexico, the ceramic hallmark of Classic Teotihuacán culture is Thin Orange ware, a fine-textured, thin-walled pottery with an unslipped but well-burnished surface. Its most common form is the simple hemispherical bowl with an annular base. Petrographic studies and archaeological investigations of workshops have identified the production source in southern Puebla, but Teotihuacán appears to have controlled its distribution, and it was widely traded throughout Mesoamerica. Equally characteristic of Teotihuacán is the cylindrical vase with three hollow, cylindrical supports or slab-shaped feet; decoration is commonly plano-relief carving (or *champ-levé*), with the cut-away areas painted vermilion. Other distinctive Classic forms include the *florero* (a "flower vase," a small jar form with a tall neck and flaring rim) and little two-holed *candeleros* presumably used as incense burners.

The Coyotlatelco Red-on-Buff style marks the rise of the Toltec; characteristic geometric motifs range from straight and curvilinear lines to checker-boards, ellipses, crosses, and dots painted on simple bowls and dishes with tripod supports. Wavy-line Mazapan Red-on-Buff reflects the period of Toltec dominance; in this type, matte buff-to-brown bowls and plates were painted with parallel wavy red lines applied by placing several brushes side by side in a holder. Tula Watercolored decorated in *blanco levantado* (an unburnished painted decoration of streaky, white transparent lines), is present at Tula, but not common, as is cloisonné: both are related to a West Mexican tradition. During the Late Postclassic, Aztec Black-on-Orange is associated with the rise of the Aztec Empire. This type features an orange paste with a well-burnished but unslipped surface; fine parallel black lines were painted around the rims of simple bowls, tripod plates, dishes, and *molcajetes* using a multiple-brush technique.

In the Valley of Oaxaca, a long tradition of burnished Oaxacan Grayware marks Monte Albán's hegemony from c. 500 B.C. through A.D. 950. Early forms include small effigy bottles and bowls incised with geometric motifs; Classic period vessels bear curvilinear pseudo-glyph carvings. Particularly distinctive is the bridgespout jar, in which a support bridges or links the spout to the vessel wall; these vessels are often decorated with modeled effigy forms. Zapotec urns—effigies of deceased ancestors or venerated rulers that were placed in elite tombs—are another well-known product of the Monte Albán people.

The later Postclassic saw the arrival of polychromes painted in the distinctive Mixteca-Puebla style, featuring precise, detailed figures in clear, vivid colors frequently likened to the Mixtec codices.

In the southern Maya Lowlands, waxy slips in red, black, and cream are hallmarks of the Formative, as is the presence of labial or medial flanges on plates. The Early Classic Tzakol period is marked by the appearance of Petén glossware types and true polychrome painting employing geometric designs and conventionalized depictions of humans and animals. The ring-base bowl with a basal flange and polychrome decoration is a well-known diagnostic, as are cylindrical vases with tripod slab supports. During the Late Classic Tepeu period, polychromes feature figure painting and glyph bands; flat-based cylindrical vases and tripod basal-ridged plates are characteristic forms. The tall, cylindrical vessels of San Juan Plumbate (a fine-textured ware with a high percentage of iron compounds that acquires a metallic iridescence on firing) indicate Late Classic trade with the Pacific coastal plain of Guatemala.

The Late Classic/Early Postclassic transition in the Lowlands is characterized by the appearance of distinctive fine-paste (temper-free) ceramics. A series of Fine Orange types that vary considerably in shape, method of decoration, and design were mass-produced in the southern Gulf Coast plain and widely traded. Tohil Plumbate, featuring effigies and complex abstract incised designs, indicates continued Postclassic trade with coastal Guatemala.

Along the southern periphery of Mesoamerica, Usulutan "resist" provides an important horizon marker for the Late Formative and is a sign of southern influence in the Maya area. Produced in Honduras and western El Salvador, the most striking and best-known version consists of parallel wavy lines of light color (pink to white) on a darker background (orange to pink), probably achieved through a resist technique. During the Early and Late Classic periods, El Salvador exported an even more important product to the Maya Lowlands—volcanic ash for tempering ceramics.

Several famous polychrome traditions emerged in the Intermediate Area. The Nicoya or Papagayo Polychrome of northwestern Costa Rica was traded as far west as Tula, Mexico. Polychromes of the early period (A.D. 100–800) utilized geometric designs boldly executed in black and partially filled with red, while later polychromes (A.D. 800–1200) featured a repeating pattern of fine linear and geometric designs that suggests woven textiles.

P

Coclé Polychrome from Sitio Conte and related sites in Coclé province of Panama spanned the period A.D. 500–1100; curvilinear representations of mammals, reptiles, birds, and insects were painted on the cream-colored interiors of plates, rectangular trays, and shallow bowls, using shades of red, brown, purple, and black.

FURTHER READINGS

Arnold, D. E. 1985. *Ceramic Theory and Cultural Process.* New York: Cambridge University Press.

Brush, C. F. 1965. Pox Pottery: Earliest Identified Mexican Ceramic. *Science* 149:194–195.

Caso, A., I. Bernal, and J. R. Acosta. 1967. *La Cerámica de Monte Albán.* Mexico City: Memorias del Instituto Nacional de Antropología e Historia, 13.

Flannery, K. V., and J. Marcus. 1983. *The Cloud People.* New York: Academic Press.

Foster, G. M. 1965. *Contemporary Pottery Techniques in Southern and Central Mexico.* Middle American Research Institute, Publication 22. New Orleans: Tulane University Press.

Lange, F. W., and D. Z. Stone (eds). 1984. *The Archaeology of Lower Central America.* Albuquerque: University of New Mexico Press.

Lothrop, S. K. 1937–1942. *Coclé: An Archaeological Study of Central Panama.* Memoirs of the Peabody Museum of Archaeology and Ethnology, 7, 8. Cambridge, Mass.: Harvard University Press.

———. 1966. Archaeology of Lower Central America. In G. F. Ekholm and G. R. Willey (eds.), *Handbook of Middle American Indians,* vol. 4, *Archaeological Frontiers and External Connections,* pp. 180–208. Austin: University of Texas Press.

Noguera, E. 1965. *La cerámica arqueológica de Mesoamerica.* Mexico City: Instituto de Investigaciones Históricas, Universidad Nacional Autónoma de México.

Rice, P. M. 1987. *Pottery Analysis: A Sourcebook.* Chicago: University of Chicago Press.

Shepherd, A. O. 1980. *Ceramics for the Archaeologist.* Carnegie Institution of Washington, Publication 609. Washington, D.C.

Smith, R. E., G. R. Willey, and J. C. Gifford. 1960. The Type-Variety Concept as a Basis for the Analysis of Maya Pottery. *American Antiquity* 25:330–340.

Smith, R. E., and J. C. Gifford. 1965. Pottery of the Maya Lowlands. In G. R. Willey (ed.), *Handbook of Middle American Indians,* vol. 2, *Archaeology of Southern Mesoamerica, Part I,* pp. 498–534. Austin: University of Texas Press.

Willey, G. R., and C. R. McGimsey. 1954. *The Monagrillo Culture of Panama.* Papers of the Peabody Museum, 54(2). Cambridge, Mass.: Harvard University Press.

Leah Minc

Proskouriakoff, Tatiana (1909–1985)

Tatiana Proskouriakoff was born on 23 January 1909 in Tomsk, Siberia, to Avenir Proskouriakoff, a chemist, and Alla Nekrassova, a physician. She and her older sister, Ksenia, were brought to the United States in 1916 when the tsar of Russia commissioned their father to inspect the munitions the United States was selling to the Russians during World War I.

Proskouriakoff and her sister entered grade school in Philadelphia. Years later, in 1930, she earned her B.S. in architecture at Pennsylvania State University. During the Depression of the 1930s few buildings were being built, and Proskouriakoff found it impossible to get a job that would allow her to design new structures.

Known especially for her pioneering work with Maya hieroglyphic writing and for her perspective drawings and architectural reconstructions of ancient Maya cities, Proskouriakoff established that Maya stone monuments such as stelae depicted actual rulers and that the texts actually recorded events in their lives—their dates of births, accession, and death. Before 1960, most Maya scholars regarded the figures on stelae as priests or astronomers, and the accompanying hieroglyphic texts as accounts of planetary phenomena and calculations of the lengths of astronomical cycles. In her breakthough article, based primarily on the carved stone monuments from the Maya city of Piedras Negras (Guatemala), Proskouriakoff opened the "door to history" for the ancient Maya civilization.

FURTHER READINGS

Marcus, J. 1988. Tatiana Proskouriakoff. In U. Gacs et al. (eds.), *Women Anthropologists: A Biographical Dictionary,* pp. 297–302. Westport, Conn.: Greenwood.

Proskouriakoff, T. 1950. *A Study of Maya Sculpture.* Carnegie Institution of Washington, Publication 593. Washington, D.C.

———. 1960. Historical Implications of a Pattern of Dates at Piedras Negras, Guatemala. *American Antiquity* 25:454–475.

———. 1963. *An Album of Maya Architecture.* Norman: University of Oklahoma Press.

Joyce Marcus

SEE ALSO
Stela Cult; Stelae; Writing

Puebla-Tlaxcala Region

The Puebla-Tlaxcala region lies in the southeastern corner of the central highlands of Mexico, astride important crossroads leading to the Basin of Mexico, the Gulf Coast, the Mixteca, Guerrero, and Morelos. The ancient cities and kingdoms at the region's core in the Puebla-Tlaxcala Valley created fine examples of monumental architecture, mural painting, and polychrome ceramics. The area was home to several ethnic groups, including Pinome (Popoloca), Otomí, Olmeca-Xicalanca, and Nahua (Tolteca-Chichimeca).

Environment

There is no precise geographical definition of the Puebla-Tlaxcala region. Its core, the Puebla-Tlaxcala Valley, extends into the adjacent valleys of Atlixco and Tepeaca and is surrounded by marginal upland plains to the east and a zone of increasingly irregular topography to the south that forms the transition to the Mixteca Baja. This central area is separated from the Basin of Mexico on the west by the Sierra Nevada, constituted primarily by two volcanos, Popocatepetl (5,452 meters) and Iztaccihuatl (5,286 meters), that are part of the Transverse Neo-Volcanic Axis; to the north, it is ringed by low hills that divide it from the plains of Apan in Hidalgo and the Sierra Norte de Puebla, or Eastern Sierra Madre. In the center of the Puebla-Tlaxcala Valley, the Malinche volcano

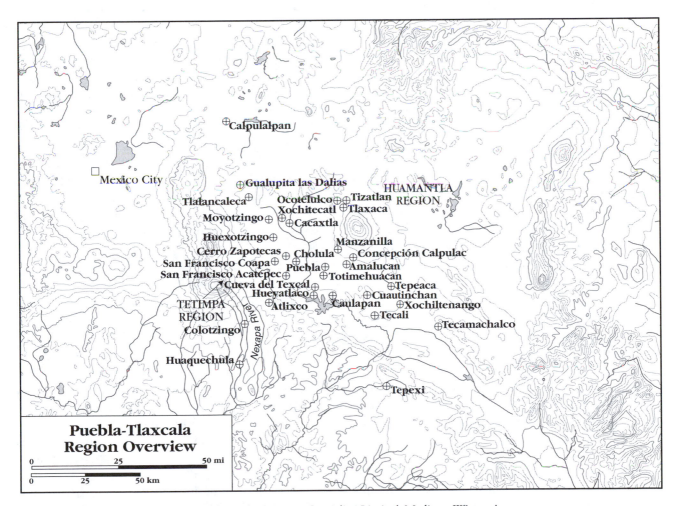

Puebla-Tlaxcala Region Overview. Map design by Mapping Specialists Limited, Madison, Wisconsin.

P

rises to an altitude of 4,461 meters and, along with the Sierra Nevada, plays an important role in local weather patterns.

Most of the core area has elevations between 2,000 and 2,600 meters, although the southern part of the Atlixco Valley and the Valsequillo Depression drop to below 1,800 meters. Valley floors are dotted with low limestone hills and extinct cinder cones that were often the focus of pre-Hispanic settlements, particularly in swampy areas with high water tables along the Atoyac and Zahuapan rivers.

Geologically, the core area consists of uplifted marine sediments ringed by some of the most important volcanoes of Mexico. These have deposited enormous amounts of volcanic ash and have created huge mudflows, or lahars, which have been eroded to form steep *barrancas* on their lower flanks. Soils on the Valley floors are predominantly chernozems, while on the slopes of the mountains they tend to be podzolic, ranging toward andosols in the higher elevations.

The Puebla-Tlaxcala Valley is a cool highland basin defined by two major tributaries of the Balsas River: the Atoyac, which originates in northern Tlaxcala and flows through the Valsequillo Depression, and the Nexapa, which drains the eastern slopes of the Sierra Nevada and continues through the Atlixco Valley. The climate is temperate subhumid, with a dry season (October–May) and a rainy season (June–September), although there is a good deal of local variation that is due largely to changes in elevation. In the core region, mean annual temperatures range from 14° to 22° C, with ten to twenty days of frost. Annual rainfall varies between 800 and 1200 mm. In general, the northern part of the region is cooler than the southern, and the eastern area is drier than the western.

Vegetation on the slopes of the volcanoes below the tree line (at 4,000 meters) consists of a pine forest that gradually incorporates evergreen oaks on the lower slopes. This region has been subjected to intensive cultivation for more than three thousand years, however, so most areas are open farmland or have highly disturbed secondary growth. Traditional pre-Hispanic domesticates such as maize, beans, squash, amaranth, chile, nopal, *maguey*, peanuts, guajes, guamuchil, zapote, and avocado are still the major crops of the Puebla-Tlaxcala region. Wild plants have always been important in native Mesoamerican diets, and in this area these consist of fruits, like capulin and *tejocote*, and various chenopods, including *huazontle* and *epazote*. The only domesticated animals

before European contact were turkeys and dogs, although the hunting of deer, rabbit, quail, and migratory waterfowl provided significant additional protein. The forested areas were home to coyote and mountain lion, but these are almost extinct today. Natural resources that were important in pre-Hispanic times include clays, building stone, stone for grinding implements, wood, charcoal, marble (*tecalli*), lime, cochineal, and *tzempazuchitl* flowers.

Throughout its history, the western part of the region has been affected by periodic activity from the Popocatepetl volcano, as evidenced in both the Tetimpa region and the Atlixco Valley. The entire area is subject to earthquakes, heavy frosts, and damaging hailstorms.

Paleoindian and Archaic Periods

The Valsequillo Depression has produced some of the earliest evidence for human occupation in the Americas at the sites of Caulapan, radiocarbon dated prior to 21,000 years ago, and Hueyatlaco. These data, however, have been the subject of much debate. Remains of mammoth and other megafauna are relatively common, although they have never been found in association with stone tools. A Clovis point was found at Chaucingo, Tlaxcala, and occasional surface finds of Hidalgo, Plainview-like, and La Mina points have been reported.

The Paleoindian period and the Archaic (see table, p. 614) are not well understood. Excavations at the cave of El Texcal in Valsequillo have produced sequences covering the period between 7000 and 2500 B.C. that include lithic materials similar to those of the Tehuacán Valley, but no plant remains were recovered that could document the beginnings of agriculture in this area.

Formative Period

Little extensive excavation has been undertaken at Formative settlements in the Puebla-Tlaxcala region. Sites that have provided radiocarbon dates and ceramics collections include Moyotzingo, Acatepec, Huejotzingo, Tlalancaleca, Gualupita las Dalias, Totimehuacan, Colotzingo, Tetimpa, Cholula, Xochitecatl, and Teteles de Ocotitla.

The earliest traces of settled life in the region are a few hamlets situated on hillsides near permanent water sources. These Tzompantepec phase (?–1200 B.C.) settlements have been identified by the presence of ceramics that show affinities with those of the Ajalpan phase in the Tehuacán Valley to the southeast.

The second half of the Early Formative, the Tlatempa phase (1200–800 B.C.), is better represented, with a significant increase in both number and size of settlements, most of which are on terraced hillslopes. Canals for erosion control have been reported in Tlaxcala. Both bell-shaped pits and maguey-roasting pits occur throughout the Formative sequence. Olmec or Olmecoid materials associated with this time period are more important in the western part of the area, at Moyotzingo and Colotzingo, where ceramics carved with Olmec motifs and C9 figurines have been reported. Las Bocas, just south of the core area, has produced important Olmec artifacts, including white-slipped, hollow, baby-face figurines. Interaction with the Basin of Mexico is reflected in the differentially fired black-and-tan wares and incised dark brown monochromes from the Atlixco Valley. Whitewares, both plain and incised, are also important. Early Formative figurines were common, with distinct types characterizing the northern area and the valleys to the south. The first evidence of occupation at Cholula dates to the final years of the Tlatempa phase.

The Middle Formative period, or Texoloc phase (800–400 B.C.), was marked by a dramatic increase in population, a clearly differentiated settlement hierarchy, and the appearance of ceremonial centers with stone architecture, which reflect the emergence of chiefdoms and civic-ceremonial centers throughout the area. Primary regional centers developed at Tlalancaleca, Coapa, Colotzingo, Xochiltenango, and Cerro Nogal. Fortified sites, such as Gualupita las Dalias, are reported toward the end of this phase. Irrigation systems and hillside terracing have been described. The ceramics of the Middle Formative include whitewares, often incised with double-line-breaks, white grater bowls, distinctive red-on-white bowls with incised rims, red-slipped ceramics, and dark brown to black wares, which become more common at the end of this phase. Figurine types include B, C10, E, and H; in the Atlixco Valley, C8 figurines like those of Chalcatzingo also occur. Spindle whorls, possibly used in making maguey-fiber cloth, are reported for Tlaxcala, but in the rest of the region these do not appear until the Classic period.

The Tezoquipan phase (400 B.C.–A.D. 100) covers the Late and Terminal Formative, a period characterized by continued population growth, the first monumental constructions at Cholula (known as "Proto-Cholula"), and the beginnings of urban life. Agricultural systems including canals, raised fields, and *chinampas* have been documented. Most regional centers of the Middle Formative continued as important settlements during Tezoquipan times, while new ceremonial centers emerged at Totimehuacan and Xochitecatl, where large pyramidal structures

were constructed. Common to Totimehuacan, Tlalancaleca, and Xochitecatl are large stone basins of unknown function, sometimes referred to as "sarcophagi." At Totimehuacan the stone basin was found inside one of the mounds at the bottom of a flight of steps in an underground chamber; the outer walls of the basin are carved with four frogs. Although the construction sequence at Cholula has not been well dated, ceramic evidence indicates that the earliest monumental architecture of the city dates to the Tezoquipan phase. The Templo Rojo below the Great Pyramid and a large temple platform under the sixteenth-century Franciscan monastery of San Gabriel belong to this time period.

One of the most important developments, the use of *talud-tablero* architecture for house and temple platforms, dates to the end of the Texoloc phase or the very beginning of the Tezoquipan, as evidenced at both Tlalancaleca and Tetimpa in the western Puebla-Tlaxcala Valley. At Capulac Concepción a huge ball court was constructed, and to the east of the core area, an urban center with several ball courts was being built at Cantona.

The whitewares of the Middle Formative disappear in the first years of the Tezoquipan phase, and variations in ceramic collections from surface surveys suggest the development of some stylistic regionalization. At Cholula and Coapa negative painting is a distinctive decorative technique, although the most common diagnostics for this period are pedestal bases, red-on-brown wares, composite silhouette tripod bowls, incised zig-zag lines, solid clay earspools, and E, H, and early Cholula figurines. White-on-red wares and Ticoman Polychromes are rare in the Puebla-Tlaxcala region, but Thin Orange ceramics from southern Puebla make their first appearance in the Tezoquipan phase, as do shoulder-break bowls. There is limited ceramic evidence for relations with West Mexico in Atlixco and Tlaxcala. Graywares also constitute part of the ceramic assemblages.

Classic Period

The Classic period belongs to the Tenanyecac phase in Tlaxcala, while at Cholula a separate sequence, tied directly to the old Teotihuacán chronology, is used. Proto-Cholula and Cholula I belong to the Terminal Formative, while the Classic begins with Cholula II, a time period characterized by striking stylistic similarities to Teotihuacán. Cholula was the major city of this region during the Early Classic (Cholula II, IIA, III), a time when most of the major construction of the Great Pyramid was undertaken; by A.D. 500 the city probably covered about 10 square kilometers.

P

CHRONOLOGY OF THE PUEBLA-TLAXCALA REGION.

Processes/Events	Chronology: Phases	Optional Chronology: Subregion Phases	Sites, Pottery Types
Spanish Conquest; Franciscan monasteries and open chapels; foundation of Spanish cities and towns.	Colonial (1519–1810)	Cholulteca IV (sixteenth century)	Tlaxcala; Cholula; Atlixco; Tepeaca; Puebla. Mayolicas; polished redwares; polychromes.
Alliance formation and warfare; partial conquest by Triple Alliance; flowery wars.	Late Postclassic Tlaxcala phase (1100–1519)	Cholulteca III (1325–1520)	Cholula; Tizatlan; Tepeaca; Cuauhquechollan. Codex style polychromes; black-on-red; miniature temples; biconical god figurines with handles.
Tolteca-Chichimeca conquest; Chichimec migrations.	Late Classic/Early Postclassic Texcalac phase (650–1100)	Cholulteca II (900–1325)	Cholula; Tizatlan; Atlixco; Tepeaca; Cuauhtinchan. Polychrome ceramics; black-on-orange; Plumbate; fine paste wares.
Reemergence of Cholula under Olmeca-Xicalanca.		Cholulteca I (800–900)	Cholula; Cacaxtla. Fine paste wares; black-on-orange.
Florescence of Olmeca-Xicalanca kingdoms.		Cholula IV (700–800)	Cacaxtla; Xochitecatl; Cerro Zapotecas. Stamped and zone punctate ceramics; geometric red-on-brown.
Decline of Cholula; rise of Olmeca-Xicalanca kingdoms.	Early/Middle Classic Tenanyecac phase (100–650)	Cholula IIIA (550–700)	Cacaxtla; Xochitecatl; Cerro Zapotecas; Cholula; Manzanilla; Atlixco; Tepeaca; Calpulalpan. Thin Orange; Teotihuacán figurines; monochromes.
Massive construction projects and population implosion at Cholula; Teotihuacán trade networks.		Cholula III (450–550) Cholula IIA (350–450) Cholula II (200–350)	Cholula; Manzanilla; Atlixco; Tepeaca; Calpulalpan; Thin Orange; Teotihuacán figurines; floreros; polished monochromes.
Beginnings of urban life and monumental architecture; volcanic activity.	Late/Terminal Formative (Preclassic) Tezoquipan phase (400 B.C.–A.D. 100)	Cholula I (0–A.D. 200) Proto-Cholula (200 B.C.–0)	Cholula; Tetimpa; Capulac Concepción. Resist decoration; shoulder-break bowls; ball courts.
Population growth; regionalization; *talud-tablero* architecture.			Coapa; Tlalancaleca; Colotzingo; Amalucan; Totimehuacan; Xochitecatl; Xochiltenango. Composite silohuette tripod bowls; E and H figurines; solid clay earspools.
Emergence of chiefdoms and temple towns.	Middle Preclassic Texoloc phase (400–800)		Tlalancaleca; Coapa; Colotzingo; Moyotzingo. White wares; double-line breaks.

Processes/Events	Chronology: Phases	Optional Chronology: Subregion Phases	Sites, Pottery Types
Initial ceramic; emergence of settlement hierarchies; Olmec influence.	Early Preclassic Tzompantepec (1600–1200) and Tlatempa (1200–800) phases		Colotzingo; Moyotzingo; Las Bocas. Carved and differential fired wares; Olmec motifs; C9 and D2 figurines.
Development of agriculture and settled life.	Archaic (7000–1600)		Cueva El Texcal.
Nomadic hunters and gatherers.	Paleoindian (22,000–7000)		Caulapan; Hueyatlaco; Chaucingo. Clovis, La Mina, and Plainview points.

Only one house of this period has been partially excavated, and consequently we know little about social organization and craft production. Classic period burials, like those of the Formative, are flexed and usually placed in shallow pits excavated into the tepetate, although tombs have been reported from Manzanilla, Los Teteles de Ocotitla, and Cholula. Cranial and dental modifications are rare during this period. Few ball courts have been located in the core area, although there are two at Manzanilla and another at Cerro Zapotecas; they also occur in the Atlixco Valley.

The Classic in Tlaxcala was characterized by population decline and cultural stagnation, perhaps a result of the rise of a large urban center at Cholula and increasing Teotihuacán intrusion into the northern part of the state, around Calpulalpan, to control trade routes toward Oaxaca and the Gulf Coast. The few remaining large sites appear to be the seats of chiefdoms built in defensive positions. Strong Teotihuacán influence can also be detected in the Atlixco and Tepeaca valleys by A.D. 400, and perhaps this was partially responsible for the decline of Cholula that began with the second part of the Classic, about A.D. 550. Many of the important ceramic markers of the Late Xolapan-Metepec phase at Teotihuacán (tripod cylinder vessels, semiconical and throned figurines, plano-relief vessels, decorated Thin Orange, candeleros, and elaborate appliqué incensarios) are absent or scarce at Cholula, although some of these items occur in other parts of the Puebla-Tlaxcala region.

By A.D. 600 most building activity ceased in Cholula, and it has been proposed that political unrest forced the population to take refuge on a nearby hilltop, Cerro Zapotecas. Defensive hilltop sites are characteristic of the period between A.D. 650 and 850 (the Early Texcalac phase), and it is generally thought that this phenomenon was related to a bid for power by the Olmeca-Xicalanca, an ethnic group with strong Gulf Coast ties who established their capitals at Cacaxtla and Xochitecatl at the beginning of the Texcalac phase as Teotihuacán power began to erode. Studies of the iconography of the Cacaxtla murals, which contain clear Mayan references and evidence of warfare and sacrifice, have been instrumental in our understanding of the post-Teotihuacán world in Central Mexico. Diagnostics include bowls with stamped or zoned punctate designs, "Balancan" Fine Orange wares, "host" figurines, and geometric red-on-brown wares.

Postclassic Period

The resurgence of Cholula began with the Olmeca-Xicalanca occupation between A.D. 800 and 900. It represented the start of the Early Postclassic in the Puebla-Tlaxcala region, a stage that includes the Cholulteca I and II phases and the latter part of Texcalac, and should probably be dated between A.D. 850 and 1200. Ceramic markers include the appearance of Black-on-Orange wares similar to Aztec I, polychromes, tripod grater bowls (often with stamped bottoms), cylindrical and zoomorphic supports, engraved decoration, high-rimmed *comals*, Plumbate wares, and imported fine-paste wares. There is much confusion about the chronology of the Early Postclassic, and this makes it difficult to address settlement pattern data, but it would appear to have been a time of important population movements of Mixtec, Otomí, and Huastec along the fringes of the region and of the abandonment or conquest of Olmeca-Xicalanca centers within the core itself.

The beginning of the Late Postclassic was marked by the arrival of the Tolteca-Chichimeca and other Chichimec

P

groups who established themselves at Cholula, Tlaxcala, Huejotzingo, Totimehuacan, Cuauhtinchan, and other centers in the region. Osteological studies at Cholula have established differences between the Classic and Postclassic populations of the city and support the historical source materials that document the arrival of new groups in the Postclassic; cranial deformation becomes common. The immigrants introduced gods of the Nahua pantheon: the tutelary Chichimec hunting god, Camaxtli (Mixcoatl)—often represented in his red-and-white striped body paint and black "Lone Ranger" mask, with his hunting basket slung around his neck—and Tezcatlipoca, god of warriors, sorcerers, and rulers. The major themes in the *Historia Tolteca-Chichimeca,* the best documentary source for this period, are alliance formation among the Chichimec kingdoms and continual warfare between these shifting alliances. Fortress sites, like Tepeji el Viejo and Cuthá, appeared in the Popoloca region between Tepeaca and Tehuacán.

Cholula emerged again as the primary economic and religious center of the region as the Tolteca-Chichimeca build a new ceremonial center at the site of the present-day Franciscan monastery of San Gabriel. The main temple was dedicated to Quetzalcoatl and served as the focal point of perhaps the most important pilgrimage center of Mesoamerica; tradition holds that rulers of surrounding areas were anointed here. Cholula was also an important market center whose merchants specialized in long-distance trade. It was one of several kingdoms that produced codex-style polychrome ceramics in a number of forms: frying-pan censers, goblets, tripod bowls with zoomorphic supports, plates, pedestal incense burners, and large basins. It is likely that the Codex Borgia, very similar in style to these painted wares, was produced in Cholula or Tlaxcala. The polychrome ceramics, codices, and mural paintings found at Ocotelulco and Tizatlan are all executed in the Mixteca-Puebla style that characterizes Late Postclassic Puebla and Tlaxcala.

In the second half of the fifteenth century, the Triple Alliance conquered the southern and eastern parts of the area from Cuauhquechollan—where an Aztec garrison was established—to Tecamachalco. Shortly thereafter, the Alliance initiated an institutionalized form of warfare, called *xochiyaoyotl,* or "flowery wars," with the remaining independent Chichimec kingdoms (Huejotzingo, Tlaxcala, and Cholula). These were often fought on the plains of the Atlixco Valley. Although the Aztecs claimed that these wars served to obtain sacrificial prisoners, the Chichimecs alleged that they were attempts by the Triple Alliance to conquer the remaining kingdoms of the Puebla-Tlaxcala region. As is to be expected, there are few Aztec III ceramics in the independent kingdoms, although they are often found in the conquered areas.

The Puebla-Tlaxcala region played a significant role in the Spanish conquest. Cortés formed an alliance with Xicotencatl and Maxixcatzin, the most important rulers of the Tlaxcalan military federation, who provided the Spaniards with the manpower and information necessary to complete the Conquest. Tlaxcala also served as a refuge after their defeat at Tenochtitlan. Because of its role in the Conquest, Tlaxcala was granted special privileges during the Colonial period. Cholula, on the other hand, was allied with the Aztecs by 1519 and, according to the Spaniards, set a trap for Cortés and his men on their way to Tenochtitlan. The ambush was discovered, and the Spaniards massacred a large number of Cholultecans in retaliation.

FURTHER READINGS

Foncerrada de Molina, M. 1993. Cacaxtla: La iconografía de los Olmeca-Xicalanca. Mexico City: Instituto de Investigaciones Estéticas, Universidad Nacional Autónoma de México.

Fowler, M. 1987. Early Water Management at Amalucan, State of Puebla, Mexico. *National Geographic Research* 3:52–68.

García Cook, A. 1981. The Historical Importance of Tlaxcala in the Cultural Development of the Central Highlands. In *Supplement to the Handbook of Middle American Indians,* vol. 1, pp. 244–276. Austin: University of Texas Press.

Gibson, C. 1967. Tlaxcala in the Sixteenth Century. Stanford: Stanford University Press.

Irwin-Williams, C. 1978. Archaeological Evidence from the Valsequillo Region, Puebla, Mexico. In D. Browman (ed.), *Cultural Continuity in Mesoamerica,* pp. 7–22. The Hague: Mouton.

Kirchhoff, P., L. Odena, and L. Reyes (eds. and trans.). 1988. *Historia Tolteca-Chichimeca.* 2nd edn. Mexico City: Ciesas, Gobierno del Estado de Puebla, Fondo de Cultura Económica.

Lind, M. 1994. The Obverse of the Codex of Cholula: Defining the Borders of the Kingdom of Cholula. In J. Marcus and J. F. Zeitlin (eds.), *Caciques and their People, A Volume in Honor of Ronald Spores,* pp. 87–100. Museum of Anthropology, University of Michigan, Anthropological Papers, 89. Ann Arbor.

Marquina, I. (coord.). 1970. *Proyecto Cholula.* Serie Investigaciones, 19. Mexico City: Instituto Nacional de Antropología e Historia.

Mountjoy, J. 1987. The Collapse of the Classic at Cholula as Seen from Cerro Zapotecas. *Notas Mesoamericanas* 10:119–151.

Nicholson, H. B., and E. Q. Keber (eds.). 1994. *Mixteca-Puebla: Discoveries and Research in Mesoamerican Art and Archaeology.* Culver City: Labyrinthos.

Plunket, P., and G. Uruñuela. 1994. The Impact of the Xochiyaoyotl in Southwestern Puebla. In M. Hodge and M. Smith (eds.), *Economies and Polities in the Aztec Realm,* pp. 433–446. Studies on Culture and Society, 6. Albany: Institute for Mesoamerican Studies, State University of New York.

———, ———. 1998. Appeasing the Volcano Gods. *Archaeology* 51(4):36–42.

———, ———. 1998. Preclassic Household Patterns Preserved under Volcanic Ash at Tetimpa, Puebla, Mexico. *Latin American Antiquity* 9:287–309.

Prem, H. J. 1988. Milpa y hacienda: Tenencia de la tierra indigena y española en la cuenca del Alto Atoyac, Puebla, Mexico, 1520–1650. Mexico City: CIESAS, Gobierno del Estado de Puebla and Fondo de Cultura Economica.

Snow, D. 1969. Ceramic Sequence and Settlement Location in pre-Hispanic Tlaxcala. *American Antiquity* 34:131–145.

Spranz, B. 1970. Las pirámides de Totimehuacan y el desarrollo de la pirámides preclásicas en Mesoamérica. Wiesbaden: Franz Steiner.

Uruñuela, G., P. Plunket, G. Hernandez, and J. Albaitero. 1997. Biconical God Figurines from Cholula and the Codex Borgia. *Latin American Antiquity* 8:63–70.

Patricia Plunket Nagoda and Gabriela Uruñela

Puerto Escondido (Cortés, Honduras)

This is one of a series of sites on the alluvial floor of the lower Ulúa River valley in northwestern Honduras that consist of extensive accumulations of architectural remains and associated domestic debris produced by clusters of households that evolved in place over many centuries. An Early Formative village at Puerto Escondido—the oldest known in Honduras—was among the earliest pottery-making communities in Mesoamerica, with ceramics contemporary with and very similar to Barra and Locona pottery from the Pacific Coast of Chiapas, Mexico. Beginning about 1100 B.C., Puerto Escondido was part of the interaction sphere that linked the Gulf Coast Olmec heartland with most of the rest of Mesoamerica. One building is substantially larger (5 by 8 meters) than would be expected for an ordinary residence and may represent a special-purpose community structure. Middle Formative householders deposited caches—including small pottery jars in the style of Playa de los Muertos and a stone celt—above this building. Later households, which appear to represent continuous occupation of the *lomas* through the Terminal Classic period, reflect economic prosperity and a rich domestic ceremonial life. Late Formative (Preclassic) and Early Classic villagers maintained a ceremonial precinct in which steam baths (among the earliest in Mesoamerica), remodeled and relocated many times, were the focus of rituals involving feasting and elaborate costumes (indicated by beads, spangles, and inedible animal parts such as jaguar paws). Concentrations of broken earspools suggest that these steam baths, like their ethnohistorical and ethnographic counterparts, were the focus of rituals marking transitions between stages of life. Burials in stone cists in this zone contrast with simple inhumations adjacent to houses elsewhere in the community. Elaborately painted local Ulúa polychrome pottery, along with exotic raw materials (greenstone, obsidian) and manufactured goods (polychrome vessels from the Petén region and vessels with stucco coatings painted in pastel colors, perhaps from as far away as Teotihuacan) testify to the prosperity of Classic period villagers and to the scope of the interaction networks in which they participated.

John S. Henderson

Pulltrouser Swamp (Orange Walk, Belize)

This wetland site produced evidence documenting the transition from the Archaic period to agriculture in the Maya Lowlands. Data from northern Belize confirm findings from Panama and Honduras that suggest parallel developments in experimentation with crops and the importation of maize, probably from West Mexico, that were occurring in both highlands and lowlands. Pollen from Pulltrouser and Cob Swamp demonstrates the presence of maize (*Zea mays*) and manioc (*Manihot* sp.) before 3000 B.C. A projectile point, as well as remains of fish (*Chiclasoma, Synbranchus, Ictalurus*) and turtle (*Staurotypus*), indicates that early farming occurred in the context of an indigenous mixed economy that included hunting and fishing.

Fluctuations in water levels resulted in the formation of organic soil, inducing farmers to compete for land and intensify cultivation at the swamp's edge, especially after 1300 B.C. A constricted uniface, similar to artifacts from

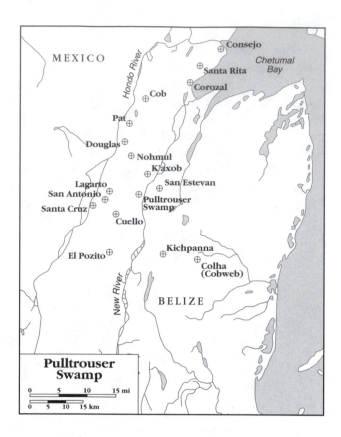

Pulltrouser Swamp

0   5   10   15 mi

0   5   10   15 km

the workshop site of Colhá, was probably used to chop wood. Additional crops included squash and bottle gourd. A continued rise in water forced farmers to drain their fields in some places (e.g., San Antonio and Cob Swamp) beginning around 1000 B.C. Reexamination of deposits at Pulltrouser Swamp failed to confirm construction of "raised fields"; nevertheless, investment in drainage in northern Belize may have contributed to the emergence of social inequality that became overt in the eastern Maya Lowlands after 1000 B.C. at sites such as Cuello, because farmers who had accomplished this would have been reluctant to move to escape an ambitious leader.

FURTHER READINGS

Piperno, D., and D. Pearsall. 1998. *The Origins of Agriculture in the Lowland Neotropics.* San Diego: Academic Press.

Pohl, M., K. Pope, J. Jones, J. Jacob, D. Piperno, S. deFrance, D. Lentz, J. Gifford, M. Danforth, and K. Josserand. 1996. Early Agriculture in the Maya Lowlands. *Latin American Antiquity* 7:355–372.

Pope, K., M. Pohl, and J. Jacob. 1996. Formation of Ancient Maya Wetland Fields: Natural and Anthropogenic Processes. In S. Fedick (ed.), *The Managed Mosaic. Ancient Maya Agriculture and Resource Use,* pp. 165–176. Salt Lake City: University of Utah Press.

Mary Pohl and Kevin Pope

SEE ALSO

Maya Lowlands: South

Purrón Dam (Puebla, Mexico)

The Purrón Dam is situated in Arroyo Lencho Diego, a major tributary *barranca* of the Tehuacán Valley. The climate here is arid, with rainfall averaging only 400–500 mm per year, and usable rainfall is even less because of severe evapotranspiration. All agriculture today requires irrigation, utilizing water that originates as rain in the high mountains to the east before entering the Valley through the arroyo.

In 1962, Richard S. MacNeish's Tehuacán Archaeological-Botanical Project discovered the Purrón Dam and a number of associated archaeological settlements. Further study of the dam determined that it had been built in four stages, beginning as a small structure built around 700 B.C. during the Early Santa María phase. The last stage brought the dam to truly monumental size: 400 meters long, 20 meters high, and 100 meters thick at the base; it has been calculated to have empounded a reservoir containing 2,640,000 cubic meters of water. The dam functioned until the end of the Early Palo Blanco phase (c. A.D. 250), when both it and the locality were abandoned.

Intensive archaeological research in Arroyo Lencho Diego has located a series of habitation sites contemporaneous with the dam. Spencer and Redmond were able to show that successive increases in the scale of the dam and reservoir were associated with a steadily growing human population, greater social differentiation, increasing economic specialization, and more complex political organization.

FURTHER READINGS

Redmond, E. 1979. A Terminal Formative Ceramic Workshop in the Tehuacán Valley. In R. D. Drennan (ed.), *Prehistoric Social, Political, and Economic Development in the Area of the Tehuacán Valley,* pp. 111–127. Technical Reports of the University of Michigan Museum of Anthropology, 11. Ann Arbor.

Spencer, C. 1979. Irrigation, Administration, and Society in Formative Tehuacán. In R. D. Drennan (ed.), *Prehistoric Social, Political, and Economic Development in the Area of the Tehuacán Valley,* pp. 13–109. Technical Reports of the University of Michigan Museum of Anthropology, 11. Ann Arbor.

Woodbury, R., and J. Neely. 1972. Water Control Systems of the Tehuacán Valley. In F. Johnson (ed.), *The Prehistory of the Tehuacán Valley,* vol. 4, *Chronology and Irrigation,* pp. 81–153. Austin: University of Texas Press.

Charles Spencer and Elsa Redmond

SEE ALSO

Tehuacán Region

Putun

J. Eric S. Thompson called this group of aggressive and enterprising Late Classic to Early Postclassic Maya the "Phoenicians of the New World," hypothesizing that their expanding presence throughout northern Yucatán signaled a "New Empire." The historical and archaeological identity of the Putun as being solely the Chontal Maya is debated. The word "Putun" appears either to be Yucatec Maya, referring to "serpents" or "those of the Tun," or Chol, meaning "peaceful." "Chontalli" is a Nahuat word meaning "stutterers," indicating people who spoke a foreign language. Most scholars agree that there is strong association between the name "Putun" and the Chontal Maya of sixteenth-century southwestern Campeche and eastern Tabasco. Scholes and Roys present strong evidence for Chontal Maya inhabiting the Candelaria River trade center of Acalan and the coastal wet lands of Campeche and Tabasco. Thompson proposed a unified Putun/Chontal maritime, pan-Yucatán Peninsula trade network at the time of the Conquest, resulting from aggressive Putun expansion from the Gulf Coast near the time of the Classic Maya Collapse. Other scholars suggest that Postclassic events may be more productively viewed as the result of gradual movements of groups of several related but competitive "Gulf Coast peoples" along the northern and western coasts of Yucatán.

FURTHER READINGS

Andrews, A. P., and F. Robles C. 1985. Chichén Itzá and Cobá: An Itzá-Maya Standoff in Early Postclassic Yucatán. In A. F. Chase and P. M. Rice (eds.), *The Lowland Maya Postclassic,* pp. 62–72. Austin: University of Texas Press, 1985.

Fox, J. W. 1987. *Maya Postclassic State Formation: Segmentary Lineage Migration in Advancing Frontiers.* Cambridge: Cambridge University Press.

Ray T. Matheny

SEE ALSO

Maya Lowlands: North; Maya Lowlands: South

Q

Quachilco (Oaxaca, Mexico)

This Late Formative town site in the central zone of the Tehuacán Valley was founded at the beginning of the Late Santa María phase (500–150 B.C.), on a dry plain at about 1,200 meters above sea level between the Río Salado and the Río Zapotitlán. The principal public or ceremonial architecture surrounded a plaza some 150 by 125 meters and formed the core of an occupation zone of more than 30 hectares, estimated to have had several hundred inhabitants. Occupation continued until perhaps the middle of the Early Palo Blanco phase (150 B.C.–250 A.D.). There is no evidence of fortification at this fairly dispersed community in a very indefensible location in the middle of the level valley floor. The town was sustained by irrigating the dry land through an extensive canal network that later became "fossilized" as a consequence of the high mineral content of the springwater that fed it. Outlying barrios of the Late Formative Quachilco community are unmistakably associated with this network. Quachilco was the largest community in the Tehuacán Valley during the Late Santa María phase, and the earliest indication of regionally centralized political or economic organization there, although it probably did not serve as a central place for the entire Tehuacán Valley but only for its central sector.

FURTHER READINGS

Alden, J. R. 1979. Systematic Surface Survey at Quachilco (Ts218). In R. D. Drennan (ed.), *Prehistoric Social, Political, and Economic Development in the Area of the Tehuacán Valley: Some Results of the Palo Blanco Project*, pp. 129–157. Museum of Anthropology, University of Michigan, Technical Reports, 11. Ann Arbor.

Drennan, R. D. 1978. *Excavations at Quachilco: A Report on the 1977 Season of the Palo Blanco Project in the Tehuacán Valley.* Museum of Anthropology, University of Michigan, Technical Reports, 7. Ann Arbor.

MacNeish, R. S., and F. A. Peterson. 1972. Excavations in the Ajalpan Locality in the Valley Center. In R. S. MacNeish (ed.), *The Prehistory of the Tehuacán Valley, Vol. 5: Excavations and Reconnaissance,* pp. 161–218. Austin: University of Texas Press.

Robert D. Drennan

SEE ALSO

Tehuacán Region

Quemada (Tuitlan), La (Zacatecas, Mexico)

This hilltop ceremonial center on the northern frontier of Mesoamerica was once interpreted as an outpost on the Toltec turquoise trail, but the site is now securely dated by more than forty radiocarbon samples at A.D. 500–900, placing it in the earlier Epiclassic period. The agriculturally marginal region receives about 500 mm of annual rainfall, but with radical fluctuations from year to year. Excavated plant remains and tools document significant dietary utilization of agave as well as maize. La Quemada covers about 0.5 square kilometer and is comprised of about sixty artificial terraces amid natural cliffs and an enclosing wall. Rectangular patio complexes, ball courts, pyramids, altars, staircases, and a large colonnaded hall are arrayed in conformity with the steeply sloping rock

Q

outcrops. A road system radiates from the site, linking it with numerous small villages in the Valley below.

Well-appointed burials are rare, but thousands of human bones have been found disarticulated, cut, broken, and burned in pits, in piles, and suspended from walls and ceilings, both indoors and out. Obsidian, which is the most significant trade item, is relatively rare and comes from sources in Northwestern rather than Central Mexico; single tesserae of iron pyrite and turquoise have also been found. The site is now considered an indigenous development rather than an imperial outpost, and investigation focuses on explaining its monumentality, its institutionalized violence, and the absence of wealth in the context of political disintegration in the Mesoamerican core.

FURTHER READINGS

Hers, M.-A. 1989. *Los Toltecas en tierras Chichimecas.* Mexico City: Instituto de Investigaciones Estéticas, Universidad Nacional Autónoma de México.

Jiménez Betts, P. 1989. Perspectivas sobre la arqueología de Zacatecas. *Arqueología* 5:7–50.

Nelson, B. A. 1990. Observaciones acerca de la presencia Tolteca en la Quemada, Zacatecas. In F. Sodi Miranda (ed.), *Mesoamerica y el norte de México, siglo IX–XII,* vol. 2, pp. 521–540. Mexico City: Instituto Nacional de Antropología e Historia.

Nelson, B. A., J. A. Darling, and D. A. Kice. 1992. Mortuary Practices and the Social Order at La Quemada, Zacatecas. *Latin American Antiquity* 3:298–315.

Trombold, C. D. 1991. Causeways in the Context of Strategic Planning in the La Quemada Region, Zacatecas, Mexico. In C. Trombold (ed.), *Ancient Road Networks and Settlement Hierarchies in the New World,* pp. 145–168. Cambridge: Cambridge University Press.

Ben A. Nelson

SEE ALSO
Northwestern Frontier

Quiahuiztlan (Veracruz, Mexico)

This fortified coastal site in Central Veracruz is noted for its miniature temple tombs and for historical events in the initial phase of the Spanish conquest of Mexico. Perched spectacularly on the flanks of a 300-meter-high volcanic mountain overlooking the beach, at the time of European contact Quiahuiztlan (or Cerro de los Metates) was subject to the Totonac metropolis of Zempoala about 30 kilometers to the south. Apart from functioning as a frontier post for Zempoala along the narrow, sea-level route around the central mountains of Veracruz, the location was strategic for the control of adjacent salt-producing lagoons. Its ritual center was the scene of the celebrated encounter among Spaniards, Aztec officials, and Totonac chiefs in which, with duplicitous intent, Hernan Cortés obliged the Totonacs to imprison the Aztecs, but then secretly freed one prisoner to attest to Spanish friendship. The site lies in steeply inclined brushy slopes and cattle pastures, 3 kilometers southwest of Villa Rica de Vera Cruz.

It is laid out on a series of natural and artificial terraces that straddle the lower slopes. On the southern flanks are a number of levels that may have served as both house locations and catchment fields. On the north is the ceremonial complex, which consists of a series of small, one- and two-story temple platforms, a ball court, and some narrow plazas. In this area there is a remarkable series of stucco and stone tombs in the form of miniature temples. Each contained one or more secondary burials placed in or adjacent to a terminal Postclassic ceramic vessel. Most of these tombs are situated on the borders of plazas dominated by temple structures, one or more of which may have been converted into a chapel by the Spaniards.

There has been some debate as to the pre-Columbian or Early Colonial identity of these unique tombs, of a type known only from a small region. García Payón's original analysis that these are Indian imitations of Spanish-style mausolea in the very first years of Contact is probably correct. Such structures may reflect the rapid death of the local Totonac elite in the first catastrophic epidemics of European diseases, which began with smallpox in this area in 1520. The tombs are found primarily at Quiahuiztlan; only a few neighboring sites, as far away as Zempoala, have similar constructions.

Although a surface reconnaissance and examination of the chronological placement of the tombs in a regional context were undertaken by Garcia Payon, excavations began with the explorations of Medellín Zenil in 1951–1953. This was followed by a reconstruction project in 1983–1985 and recent work by Arellanos. Most of these activities have focused on the tombs, adjacent temples, and a ball court.

FURTHER READINGS

Arellanos M., R., and L. Sanchez O. 1990. Proyecto Quiahuiztlan-Villa Rica. Boletin 13–15. Mexico City: Instituto Nacional de Antropología e Historia.

García Payón, J. 1945. *Mausolea in Central Veracruz.* Carnegie Institution of Washington, Notes on Middle American Archaeology, 59. Washington, D.C.

Medellín Zenil, A. 1960. *Ceramicas del Totonacan.* Jalapa: Universidad Veracruzana.

Wilkerson, S. J. K. 1983. So Green and Like a Garden: Intensive Agriculture in Ancient Veracruz. In J. P. Darch (ed.), *Drained Field Agriculture in Central and South America,* pp. 55–90. BAR International Series, 189. Oxford.

S. Jeffrey K. Wilkerson

SEE ALSO

Gulf Lowlands: North Central Region

Quiotepec

See Cuicatlán Canyon

Quiriguá (Izabal, Guatemala)

Situated in the Motagua Valley of the Maya Lowlands, about 100 kilometers from the Caribbean, Quiriguá is a Classic period (c. A.D. 250–900) site known for its monuments, the largest and among the most beautiful of any carved by the ancient Maya. The site extends over about 4 square kilometers on the floodplain and on terraces along the Valley margins. Maximum population size for the floodplain center during the Late Classic can be estimated at three thousand.

Today, only the largest structures and monuments on the floodplain rise above the 1 to 2 meters of alluvium deposited over the past thousand years, most of these in a site core of about 0.5 square kilometer in the center of the Valley. This is surrounded by satellite groups and buried residences. One outlier, Group A, sits on a hilltop 4 kilometers west of the site core. Monument 21 from this group provides the earliest known historical date at Quiriguá, A.D. 478. In 1978, Monument 26 (c. A.D. 493) was discovered beneath the alluvium in a satellite group near the site core; its text refers to Quiriguá's third and fourth rulers. There is evidence that from early in its history, Quiriguá was part of the large and powerful Classic Maya polity of Copán, which had its capital about 50 kilometers to the south. Quiriguá was probably an important dependency of Copán for much of its history, controlling the lucrative jade and obsidian trade that followed the Motagua Valley.

The site core is composed of an acropolis to the south and, on the north, the vast Great Plaza (300 by 150 meters), the setting for most of the carved stelae, altars, and boulder sculptures. These combine texts recording historical events and portraits of Quiriguá's rulers with symbols of authority that reinforced their claims to earthly and supernatural power. Most of the monuments date from the reign of Quiriguá's most important ruler, Cauac Sky (724–784). Buried beneath the northern portion of the Great Plaza is a massive platform supporting five stelae and two zoomorphs, all dedicated during the final twenty-four years of Cauac Sky's reign. Their texts record that he came to power under the aegis of Copán, but that in 737 he captured and sacrificed his former overlord, Copán's ruler, 18 Rabbit. After this event, Quiriguá achieved political and economic independence from Copán. The archaeological record shows clearly that for a century afterward, Quiriguá was the focus of unprecedented construction and prosperity.

Cauac Sky's death and the accession of his successor, Sky Xul, are recorded on Monument 7, which dates from 785. The next ruler, and Quiriguá's last known, Jade Sky, dedicated two monuments, dated to 800 and 805 and situated in the southern part of the Great Plaza. Both the historical and archaeological records fade away shortly thereafter, although there is evidence of a brief revitalization during the Terminal Classic period (A.D. 850–900).

The acropolis is an administrative and residential complex that was used by Quiriguá's rulers. Its six masonry buildings, built over earlier structures and placed around a central court, date to the reigns of Cauac Sky, Sky Xul, and Jade Sky. Most of these buildings were once adorned with elaborate painted stucco reliefs, now collapsed and destroyed. None retains its original masonry vaults, but Structure 1B-2, probably Cauac Sky's original palace, is decorated with exterior carved corner masks. One of three carved masks of the Maya sun deity, Kinich Ahau, survives on a wall that once overlooked the Motagua River along the western side of the complex. The largest palace at Quiriguá, Structure 1B-5, built around 800, was probably Jade Sky's residence. Carved texts on the southern acropolis building (Structure 1B-1) refer to a visit by the last known Copán ruler and provide the latest date at Quiriguá (810). Within a century of this date, Quiriguá was totally abandoned, to be forgotten for a thousand years. It has been investigated since the late nineteenth century, most recently (1974–1979) by the University of Pennsylvania Museum.

Q

FURTHER READINGS

Ashmore, W. (ed.). 1979. *Quiriguá Reports I*. University Museum, University of Pennsylvania, Monograph 37. Philadelphia.

————. 1986. Petén Cosmology in the Maya Southwest: An Analysis of Architecture and Settlement Patterns at Classic Quiriguá. In P. A. Urban and E. M. Schortman (eds.), *The Southeast Maya Periphery*, pp 114–137. Austin: University of Texas Press.

Hewitt, E. L. 1912. The Excavations at Quirigua in 1912. *Archaeological Institute of America Bulletin* 3:163–171.

Jones, C., and R. J. Sharer. 1986. Archaeological Investigations in the Site-core of Quiriguá. In P. A. Urban and E. M. Schortman (eds.), *The Southeast Maya Periphery*, pp. 27–34. Austin: University of Texas Press.

Maudslay, A. P. 1883. Explorations in Guatemala and Examination of the Newly Discovered Ruins of Quirigua, Tikal, and the Usumacinta. *Proceedings of the Royal Geographical Society* 5:185–204.

Sharer, R. J. 1978. Archaeology and History at Quiriguá, Guatemala. *Journal of Field Archaeology* 5:51–70.

————. 1987. *Quiriguá: A Classic Maya Center and Its Sculpture*. Durham: Carolina Academic Press.

Robert J. Sharer

SEE ALSO

Copán; Maya: Motagua Region

R

Remojadas (Veracruz, Mexico)

This small but chronologically important site in south central Veracruz is noted for its diverse and expressive figurines. Remojadas is situated in a dry rain shadow region and consists of a series of low mounds where secondary burials were placed beneath burnt clay floors. Many of these interments were accompanied by ceramic offerings, including both vessels and figurines. While numerous Late Formative period examples were encountered, a large percentage of the grave goods were of Protoclassic and Early Classic date. The excavated corpus included solid and hollow seated effigies, hollow hand-made figures, and finer mold-made specimens. Thick asphalt paint was common as decoration. Many of the figurines are related to specific regional cults that are diagnostic of the south central area.

At the time of the only explorations here—in 1949–1950, by Medellín Zenil—many of the recovered figurine types were novel, with unknown distribution patterns, and the regional chronologies were weak for comparative purposes. In subsequent years, the name "Remojadas" was applied indiscriminately in the literature to many non-Olmec, Formative artifacts from widely dispersed points in central Veracruz, to "smiling face figurines" of both contemporary and later date, and even to monumental statuary of much later date and of a type never found at the site. Attempts to apply the term "Remojadas culture" spatially to all of the central Gulf Coast, including the north central part, and temporally to all of the Formative (Lower Remojadas) and Classic (Upper Remojadas), have proved largely inaccurate in the light of subsequent research throughout this very large area.

The archaeological significance of Remojadas is in its evidence for the nature of the local artifact transition from Late Formative to Early Classic times, its contextual affirmation of the diversity and strength of the coastal figurine traditions, and its confirmation of the dynamic stylistic and manufacturing modifications of the Early Classic. There has been no follow-up stratigraphic exploration at the site or environs to define both initiating and ending occupations, as well as to extend knowledge of the chronological variation of the figurines of the immediate region, which except in Remojadas have predominantly been derived from uncontrolled contexts. Little is known of the settlement pattern of this specific zone of south central Veracruz, but many sites of similar and larger size are to be found in the vicinity. The site today remains much as it was when first explored, beneath agricultural fields at the edge of a small village of the same name.

FURTHER READINGS

Medellín Zenil, A. 1960. *Ceramicas del Totonacan*. Jalapa: Universidad Veracruzana.

———. 1983. *Obras Maestras del Museo de Xalapa*. Jalapa: Gobierno del Estado de Veracruz.

Wilkerson, S. J. K. 1988. Cultural Time and Space in Ancient Veracruz. In M. M. Goldstein (ed.), *Ceremonial Sculpture of Ancient Veracruz*, pp. 6–17. New York: Hillwood Art Gallery, Long Island University.

S. Jeffrey K. Wilkerson

SEE ALSO

Gulf Lowlands: North Central Region

R

Río Azul (Petén, Guatemala)

First settled around 800 B.C. by village farmers, this ancient Maya site was developing political and religious complexity by 400 B.C. The urban center of Río Azul was established by A.D. 200 and displays influence from Tikal and Teotihuacán through the Early Classic period, when its population was about 3,500. After a brief decline, it reached that level again in the middle to late Late Classic. In the late Classic it was overrun by northern Maya, who occupied it until its abandonment about A.D. 880.

The site extends over about 1.3 square kilometers on a leveled ridge. Three distinct zones can be defined: the urban zone, with massive and extensive construction; the riverine environment, with subsistence and transportation resources; and the zone of channelized *bajo* (swamp) agricultural fields. The site's orientation is toward temple structures and their associated palace buildings. Remains of cotton and cacao have been recovered from tomb contexts, while dog bones were identified from a Late Formative (c. A.D. 200) cache.

In the early 1980s Río Azul was severely looted, including several Classic period tombs. Although there are no skeletal remains from the looted tombs, fragments of greenstone have been recovered, indicating the use of mosaic funerary masks. A triangular fragment of an elaborately carved wooden bowl was also found from Tomb 1. Looted items from these tombs, including high-quality pottery, have been seen in private collections and occasionally on the art market

Unlooted tombs that were archaeologically excavated have provided detailed data on mortuary practices, particularly for the Early Classic. One example included preserved textile fragments used to wrap an individual who had been placed on a litter. Another fascinating find was the residue of cacao (chocolate), verified by chemists from the Hershey Corporation. These special excavations also located numerous ceramic vessels of local manufacture, as well as some demonstrating Teotihuacán influences. An Early Classic lock-top jar was among the rarer finds during tomb excavations here.

FURTHER READINGS

Adams, R. E. W. 1986. Río Azul: Lost City of the Maya. *National Geographic* 169:420–451.
Adams, R. E. W., and J. L. Gatling. 1964. Noreste del Petén: Nuevo sitio y un mapa arqueológico regional. *Estudios de Cultura Maya* 4:99–118.

R. E. W. Adams and Fred Valdez

SEE ALSO
Maya Lowlands: South

Río Claro (Colón, Honduras)

This site in northeastern Honduras by the Río Claro, a small tributary of the Aguan, is one of the largest known from this region. It was a major regional center, settled primarily in the Early Cocal period (A.D. 1000–1400) but continuing into the Late Cocal (1400–1530). Trade materials found included obsidian, traced to sources in western Honduras and highland Guatemala. However, Río Claro shows a distinctive local ceramic tradition, quite non-Mesoamerican in form and decoration. In addition, elaborate carved stone metates suggest possible cultural affiliations with lower Central America. Río Claro may well be the chiefdom center called Papayeca, which was described by Hernando Cortés from his exploration of the northern coast of Honduras in 1525.

Spreading across an elevated knoll for about 8.5 hectares, the site's rather congested but orderly center contains more than fifty quadrangular earthen mounds, some more than fifty meters long, and many faced by boulders and approached via unmortared stone ramps. Constructions tend to be either long, low habitation mounds, or taller, nonhabitational structures (possibly substructures for temple mounds), all arranged around plazas and courtyards of varying dimensions. The largest mound, centrally located, rises about 7 meters tall. The site may once have been surrounded by a palisade fortification. It is approached from three directions by separate walkways, marked by large, flat paving stones.

At least two-thirds of Río Claro is encircled by an artificial ditch or depression (1.8–2.5 meters deep today), and the rest of the site's perimeter seems to have held a small pond or lagoon, now dry. Excavations in 1975 produced abundant pottery, lithics, limited faunal remains, and radiocarbon samples. Cocal sherds are largely a distinctive incised line-and-punctation ware called the North Coast Applique style. Lithics included chipped stone (obsidian blades, scrapers, and flakes; basaltlike T-shaped axes) as well as ground stone—*manos* and *metates,* including fragments of the elaborate, carved, legged grinding stones that are a diagnostic feature of this region and time period. Other ground stone implements include bark beaters, celts, and polished, biconically drilled greenstone (serpentine) beads. No human remains or burials were unearthed. Secondary evidence (grinding stones) suggests a heavy local reliance on maize agriculture in the Cocal period.

FURTHER READINGS

Healy, P. F. 1978. Excavations at Río Claro, Northeast Honduras: Preliminary Report. *Journal of Field Archaeology* 5:15–28.

————. 1984. The Archaeology of Honduras. In F. W. Lange and D. Z. Stone (eds.), *The Archaeology of Lower Central America,* pp. 113–161. Albuquerque: University of New Mexico Press.

————. 1992. Ancient Honduras: Power, Wealth, and Rank in Early Chiefdoms. In F. W. Lange (ed.), *Power and Wealth in the Intermediate Area,* pp. 85–108. Washington, D.C.: Dumbarton Oaks.

Paul Healy

SEE ALSO

Intermediate Area: Overview

Río Verde Region (Oaxaca, Mexico)

The lower Río Verde Valley on the Pacific coast of Oaxaca was the location of the Postclassic (A.D. 800–1521) city-state of Tututepec. The region supported large populations and complex societies from the Late Formative period (400–100 B.C.) to the time of the Spanish conquest. By the Late Classic (A.D. 500–800) the urban center of Río Viejo was one of the largest sites on the Pacific coast of Mesoamerica. People in the lower Río Verde interacted with some of Mexico's most powerful pre-Hispanic centers, including Teotihuacán in the Basin of Mexico and Monte Albán in the Valley of Oaxaca. The valley's importance was undoubtedly related to its ecological characteristics: a broad coastal floodplain and marine, estuarine, and mountain habitats.

The region was only sporadically occupied until about 500 B.C. The late Middle Formative Charco phase (500–400 B.C.), shows clear evidence of sedentary villages.

Regional settlement and social complexity increased dramatically during the Late/Terminal Formative (400 B.C.–A.D. 250), with the largest increases occurring during the Late Formative Minizundo phase (400–100 B.C.) and the early Terminal Formative Miniyua phase (100 B.C.–A.D. 100). Over time, archaeologists observe increases in number of sites, site size, and internal complexity, suggesting a significant rise in social complexity.

By the Minizundo phase a two-tiered settlement hierarchy was in place, with Charco Redondo as the first-order center. The second-order village, Cerro de la Cruz, covered about 1.5 hectares, with an architectural complex comprising a possible high-status residence, three small storehouses, and a public building. The remains of forty-eight individuals, including forty-one adults, were interred under the clay floors of the public building, suggesting this structure's use as a communal mortuary. Mortuary and architectural data, as well as the distribution of wealth items, such as imported Oaxaca Valley pottery, suggest emerging status differences at this time.

Survey data suggest that a four-tiered settlement hierarchy emerged by the early Terminal Formative Miniyua phase (100 B.C.–A.D. 100), with Río Viejo as the first-order center at 200 hectares. The second largest site was Charco Redondo at 70 hectares, half of which was a 3–4-meter-high artificial platform supporting several structures. Third-order centers, covering 2 to 20 hectares, had mounded architecture; fourth-order sites of 0.1 to 10 hectares lacked mounds. Given Río Viejo's large size and the presence of a four-tiered settlement hierarchy, it appears that a complex chiefdom and perhaps a state had developed in the lower Verde by the Terminal Formative.

Anthropogenic changes in the Verde's drainage system may have triggered an increase in alluviation that expanded the floodplain and raised agricultural productivity. In addition to Río Viejo, other large floodplain sites like Charco Redondo and Yugue are dominated by impressive residential platforms that were probably adaptations to flooding.

Early Classic Coyuche phase (A.D. 250–500) political developments are difficult to define in the lower Verde. The number of sites in the region increased, but Río Viejo seems to have decreased significantly in size. Other large Formative sites (Charco Redondo, Yugue) also declined in size, and the regional settlement hierarchy was reduced to three levels. Interaction with Teotihuacán during the Early Classic is suggested by formal and decorative attributes of Coyuche phase ceramics and by obsidian from the Pachuca source controlled by Teotihuacán. The proportion of Pachuca obsidian from Early Classic contexts is the highest known for a region outside the Central Mexican highlands.

The lower Río Verde valley underwent a change in socio-political organization during the Late Classic Yuta Tiyoo phase (A.D. 500–800). Río Viejo expanded, perhaps

LOWER RIO VERDE VALLEY CERAMIC CHRONOLOGY

PERIOD		CERAMIC PHASE	DATE
			1522
			1400
			1300
POSTCLASSIC		YUCUDZAA	1200
			1100
			1000
			900
LATE CLASSIC		YUTA TIYOO	800
			700
			600
EARLY CLASSIC		COYUCHE	500
			400
			300
TERMINAL FORMATIVE		CHACAHUA	200
			100
		MINIYUA	A.D. 1
LATE FORMATIVE		MINIZUNDO	100 B.C.
			200
			300
MIDDLE FORMATIVE		CHARCO	400
			500
		?	600

at the expense of nearby communities, with fewer Late Classic sites recorded. Río Viejo appears to have been the first-order capital of a state polity, given its large size (250–300 hectares), monumental architecture, and numerous carved stone monuments. A four-tiered settlement hierarchy is suggested by the survey and regional reconnaissance data. Second-order sites, covering 30 to 50 hectares, have impressive monumental build-ings and carved stone monuments. Third-order sites (2–15 hectares) have mounds but lack carved stones. Fourth-order sites are generally a few hectares or less in extent and lack mounded architecture. All the platform mounds mapped at Río Viejo show Late Classic occupa-tions.

By the beginning of the Postclassic period Yucudzaa phase (A.D. 800–1521), the lower Verde region had expe-

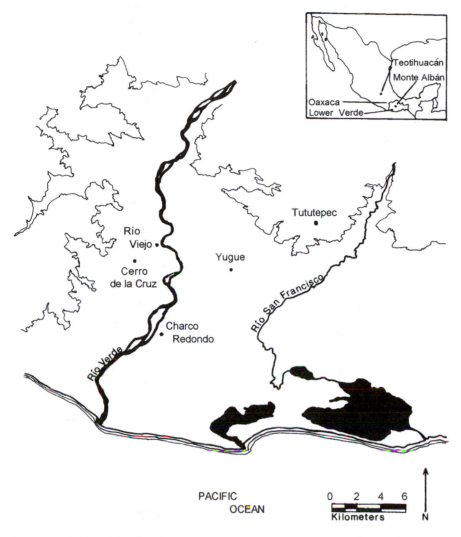

The Lower Río Verde Valley showing major sites. Illustration courtesy of the author.

rienced the type of political disruption noted for the Classic period collapse in much of Mesoamerica. Population declined and monumental building activities ceased at Río Viejo as well as at most other large Classic sites. There appears to have been a shift in settlement during the Postclassic, with people moving from the floodplain into the piedmont and secondary valleys. This change in settlement pattern may be related to the rise of the Tututepec polity, with its political center situated in the foothills approximately 16 kilometers east of Río Viejo. It is possible that the shift in settlement toward the piedmont resulted from defensive considerations, since the Mixtec codices record frequent episodes of warfare between Tututepec and other Postclassic polities.

FURTHER READINGS

Joyce, A. A. 1991. Formative Period Social Change in the Lower Río Verde Valley, Oaxaca, Mexico. *Latin American Antiquity* 2:126–150.

———. 1993. Interregional Interaction and Social Development on the Oaxaca Coast. *Ancient Mesoamerica* 4:67–84.

Joyce, A. A., and R. G. Mueller. 1992. The Social Impact of Anthropogenic Landscape Modification in the Río Verde Drainage Basin, Oaxaca, Mexico. *Geoarchaeology* 7:503–526.

Joyce, A. A., M. Winter, and R. G. Mueller. 1998. *Arqueología de la costa de Oaxaca: Asentamientos del periodo Formativo en el valle del Río Verde inferior.* Estudios de

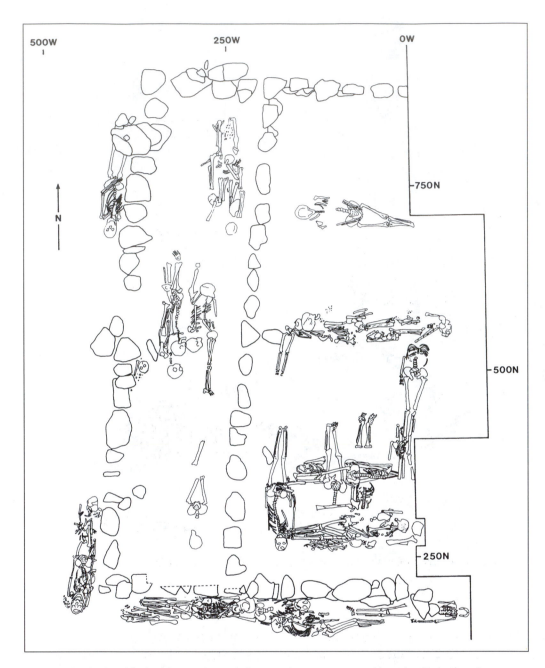

Minizundo Phase public building at Cerro de la Cruz showing associated burials. Illustration from *Journal of Field Archaeology,* vol. 21 (1994), p. 157.

Antropología e Historia, 40. Oaxaca: Centro Instituto Nacional de Antropología e Historia.

Urcid, J. 1993. The Pacific Coast of Oaxaca and Guerrero: The Westernmost Extent of Zapotec Script. *Ancient Mesoamerica* 4:141–165.

Arthur A. Joyce

SEE ALSO

Guerrero Region; Mixteca-Puebla Style; Río Viejo

Río Verde Region, San Luis Potisí

See Buenavista Huaxcama and Río Verde Region

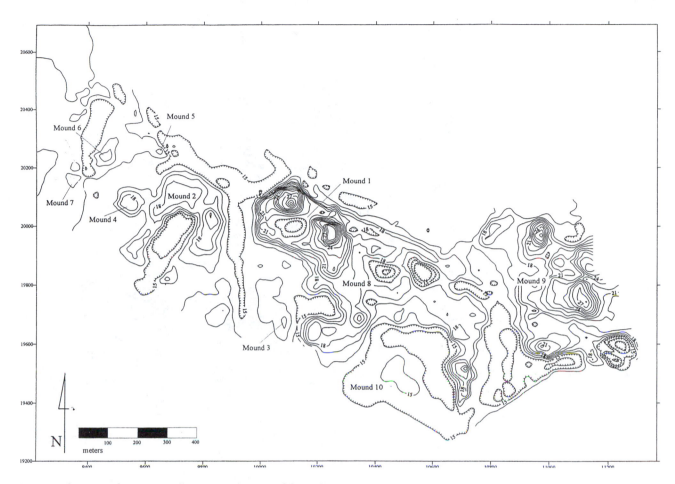

Topographic map of Río Viejo. Illustration courtesy of the author.

Río Viejo (Oaxaca, Mexico)

A pre-Columbian urban center in the lower Río Verde Valley, at 250 to 300 hectares Río Viejo is one of the largest sites on the Pacific coast of Mesoamerica. The site is dominated by approximately fifteen earthen platforms, the largest covering 16 hectares. Most of the platforms functioned to raise residences above the floodwaters of the Río Verde. Sixteen carved stone monuments have been recorded at Río Viejo; most depict probable Classic period (A.D. 250–800) rulers. Río Viejo was first occupied during the late Middle Formative (500–400 B.C.), with settlement increasing dramatically during the Terminal Formative (100 B.C.–A.D. 250), when large-scale mound-building began as the site became a small urban center, reaching about 225 hectares. Río Viejo contracted during the Early Classic, although imported obsidian suggests exchange ties with Teotihuacán in the Basin of Mexico.

By the Late Classic, Río Viejo was the capital of a state polity and covered 250 to 300 hectares. The Late Classic civic-ceremonial center of the site was defined by a huge acropolis (Mound 1) measuring 350 by 200 meters along its base, and supporting substructures reaching heights of 15 meters. About A.D. 800, Río Viejo collapsed. Settlement declined until the Late Postclassic (A.D. 1000–1520) when the site was completely abandoned.

FURTHER READINGS

Joyce, A. A. 1991. Formative Period Social Change in the Lower Río Verde Valley, Oaxaca, Mexico. *Latin American Antiquity* 2:126–150.

———. 1993. Interregional Interaction and Social Development on the Oaxaca Coast. *Ancient Mesoamerica* 4:67–84.

Arthur A. Joyce

R

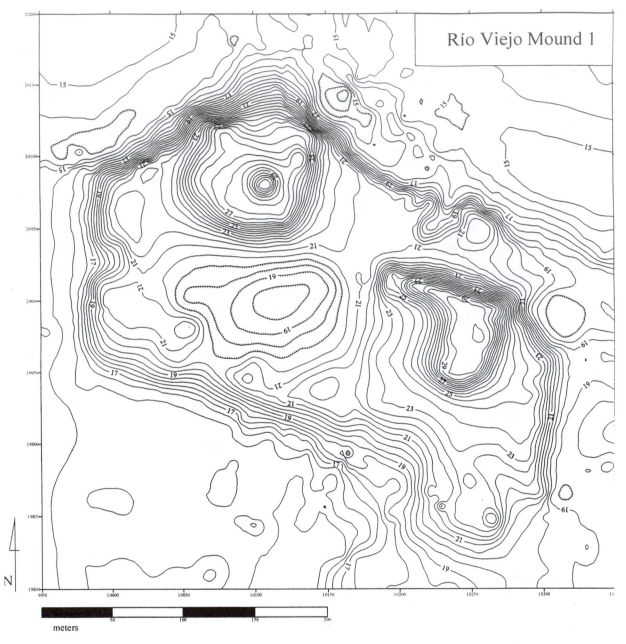

Plan of Mound 1 at Río Viejo. Illustration courtesy of the author.

SEE ALSO
Río Verde Region

Rivas (San José, Costa Rica)

Extensive, large-scale architectural remains mark Rivas as one of the largest and most complex late prehistoric sites in southern Costa Rica. It was an important ceremonial center and long-distance exchange node. Radiocarbon assays date the site to around A.D. 900–1200, during the Chiriquí phase. Situated in the General River Valley, 1,000 meters above sea level near a major pass to the Atlantic slopes, Rivas exploited varied resources, long-distance trade, and spiritual powers associated with high altitudes. Subsistence included fruits, grass seeds, maize, and probably deer and smaller animals. Remains include pottery, stone tools, and carbonized plants. Architecture

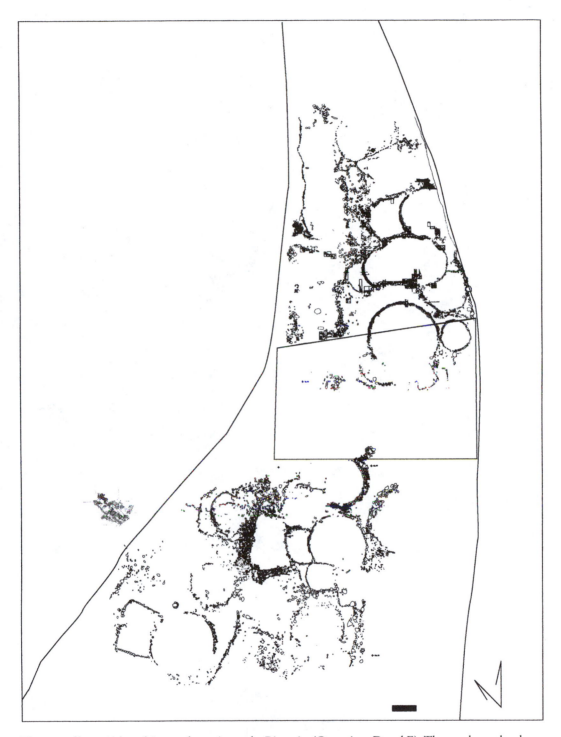

The area of large-scale architectural remains at the Rivas site (Operations D and E). The quadrangular shape indicates boundaries of a coffee field in which detailed mapping could not be carried out. Lines bordering most of the architecture denote terrace edges. Note similar plans of these larger structures to smaller dwelling in the following figure (scale = 10 meters; arrow: vertical = "grid north"; diagonal = magnetic north). Illustration courtesy of the author.

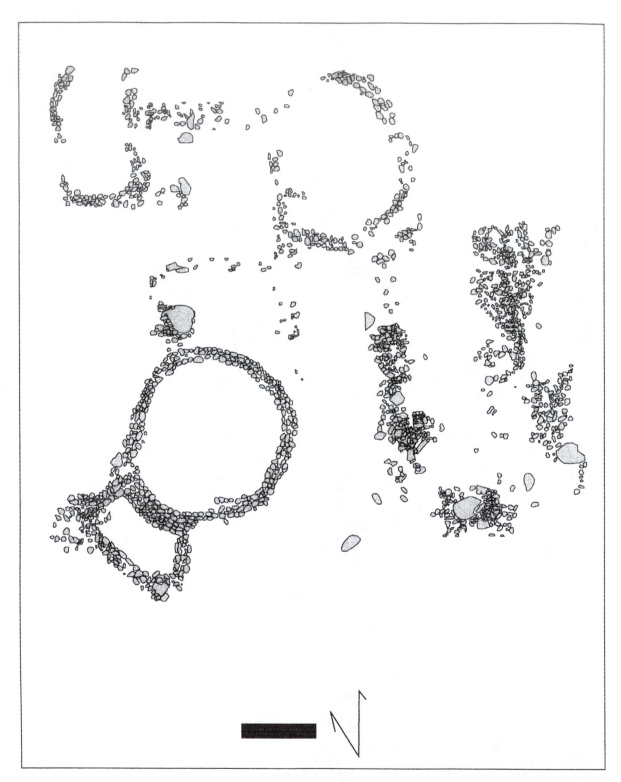

Small-scale architecture at the Rivas site (Operation A). Three stone rings indicate perimeters of former perishable structures, the best preserved of which is in the lower left-hand corner of the illustration. The four groups of cobbles to the right likely were work areas and refuse piles (scale = 5 meters; arrow: vertical = "grid north": diagonal = magnetic north). Illustration courtesy of the author.

ranges from "house rings," 10 meters in diameter, to interconnected complexes of large stone circles, ovals, causeways, and patios with mixed private and public spaces covering hundreds of square meters. The nearby, severely looted elite cemetery of the Panteón de La Reina held the remains of the residents of the large-scale Rivas buildings. At Rivas itself, nonelite cemeteries contained domestic pottery and an occasional stone tool. The social system appears to have consisted of a hierarchical social system of elites and commoners. Owing to tropical conditions, no well-preserved skeletal remains have been found. Excavations revealed artificial fill and at least two major construction periods at the site. Dense accumulations of ceramics were encountered outside the wall of a large plaza-like space; many were nearly complete vessels of Atlantic watershed or Central Valley styles. Long-distance exchange, ceremonial feasting, and subsequent destruction of exotic ceramics are in evidence. Rivas is contemporary with similar sites such as Guayabo, but it is the only site of its kind currently known in Costa Rica's Pacific region.

FURTHER READINGS

Quilter, J., and A. Blanco Vargas. 1995. Monumental Architecture and Social Organization at the Rivas Site, Costa Rica. *Journal of Field Archaeology* 22(2):203–221.

Jeffrey Quilter

SEE ALSO

Intermediate Area: Overview; Nicoya, Greater, and Guanacaste Region

Roads, Routes

See Transport

Rock Art

This term encompasses designs embellishing naturally formed rock surfaces such as boulders and cliff faces. Designs executed by pecking with stone tools are called "petroglyphs," and painted designs are called "pic-tographs." In Mesoamerica, pictographs are extremely rare in comparison with petroglyphs—perhaps only one of the former for every thousand of the latter—although this may be due in part to the much greater long-term preservability of petroglyphs. In Mesoamerica, Olmec culture provides the earliest secure cultural association for both petroglyphs and pictographs. From Olmec times up to the Spanish conquest, natural rock surfaces all over Mesoamerica were pecked or painted with designs.

Although there must have been some variation in the meaning of the designs depending on the culture that produced them, in some cases where careful and extensive analysis has been possible, the vast majority seem to be related to rain-making ceremonies performed to induce a deity such as the sun god to release rain for the benefit of the cultivated crops and the wild plants and animals on which the people depended for food. In this way, such glyphs served as a rudimentary system of writing intended to communicate certain human needs to supernatural beings. The association of rock art and rain-making ceremonies may explain the apparent high incidence of rock art in areas like the northern and southern frontiers of Mesoamerica where people were dependent on rainfall for their cultivated crops and wild foods, in contrast to its relative scarcity in areas like the Central Mexican highlands and the Maya Lowlands where extensive irrigation or wetland agriculture was practiced.

FURTHER READINGS

Gay, C. T. E. 1971. *Chalcatzingo.* Graz: Akademische Druck u. Verlagsanstalt.

Mountjoy, J. B. 1982. An Interpretation of the Pictographs at La Peña Pintada, Jalisco, Mexico. *American Antiquity* 47:110–126.

———. 1987. *Proyecto Tomatlán de salvamento arqueológico: El arte rupestre.* Colección Científica Arqueología, 163. Mexico: Instituto Nacional de Antropología y Historia.

Joseph B. Mountjoy

SEE ALSO

Caves

S

Sacred Places and Natural Phenomena

It has long been observed that Mesoamerican architecture displays an organic relationship with the landscape. At Chalcatzingo, Teotihuacan, Tikal, Tenochtitlan, and other major archaeological sites, broad plazas echo the wide valley basins and stepped pyramids mirror the shapes of the mountains. Architecture and the natural setting appear to live together in symbiosis, with architecture forming a mediating zone between people and landscape. Since the late 1970s, new inquiries by scholars have begun to explore these relationships in an effort to understand the deeper structures of visual expression and the patterns of thought and action they portray. These studies identify a principle, widely held in Mesoamerica and neighboring regions, that the arts were informed by an underlying order that derives from the way the land was perceived, used, and translated symbolically. In that mode of thought and perception, the placement of monuments, the layout of cities, and the great diversity of styles and systems of symbols all speak of an ancient idea that the organization and activities of human societies formed an integral part of the structure of the land and the progression of the seasons. Ritual drama and the visual arts played an active role in bonding the social and the natural orders, maintaining a vital exchange to bring about the seasonal cycle, the earth's renewal, and the economic and social renewal that followed.

Although these themes are expressed by the monumental constructions of complex societies that evolved during and after the first millennium B.C., they stem from much older ways of thought, spatial organization, and ritual activity. In Mesoamerica, where archaeology has concentrated on questions surrounding the beginnings of agriculture and sedentary life, and the socio-economic evolution of complex societies, little attention has been given to the symbolic domains of early hunting-and-gathering peoples. It is reasonable to speculate that here, as in other regions where bands gleaned their livelihood according to the seasonal availability of animals and plants, the habitat was being articulated with paths, places, and zones that were perceived to be charged with religious, historical, and economic significance. In the Southwest of the United States and northern Mexico, petroglyphic and pictographic systems attributed to Archaic desert hunter-gatherers are beginning to be charted to show how territories were symbolically appropriated and invested with cultural meaning. No people, however economically simple and rudimentary in social organization or geographically isolated, has lacked a way to account for the origins of the world, the organization and rhythms of the natural environment, and the place of human society within a larger cosmological system. The pragmatic business of obtaining food went hand in hand with the making of a culturally meaningful habitat, and a range of activities was regulated by a sense of periodicity and cyclic recurrence. Economy, religion, and history were fused in the perception and use of the landscape. From this standpoint, Mesoamerican monuments and sacred geographies are projections of intellectual and esthetic concerns transmitted from earlier inhabitants.

FURTHER READINGS

Aveni, A., and S. Gibbs. 1976. On the Orientation of Pre-Columbian Buildings in Central Mexico. *American Antiquity* 41:510–517.

Boone, E. 1987. *The Aztec Templo Mayor.* Washington, D.C.: Dumbarton Oaks.

Carrasco, D. (ed.). 1991. *To Change Place: Aztec Ceremonial Landscapes*. Boulder: University of Colorado Press.
Townsend, R. 1992. *The Ancient Americas: Art from Sacred Landscapes*. Chicago: Art Institute of Chicago.

Richard F. Townsend

Sacrifice

The term "sacrifice" comes from the combination of the Latin words *sacer* and *facere* and means "to set something apart in order to establish, maintain, or renew a relationship with the sacred." Throughout Mesoamerica, extensive ritual strategies were used to keep human beings in constant, renewing relationships with deities and the forces they symbolized. These strategies included the sacrifice of animals, humans, plants, and plant products—destructions that were pervasive ritual actions to assist in making and remaking the social and spiritual worlds. A number of rationales were developed, including the feeding of the sun, the payment of debts to the gods who had sacrificed themselves in order to create human life, the renewal of agriculture, the renewal of relationships with dead ancestors, the intimidation of enemy communities, and the revitalization of the cosmos at large. These practices are depicted on sculptural and architectural assemblages as well as in pre-Hispanic pictorial screenfolds and in sixteenth-century written and pictorial manuscripts.

Here we will review some of the major practices of sacrifice, including some of the human sacrifices that animated central Mexican religions, with a focus on the cosmological settings of sacrifice and some of the practices and paraphernalia of human sacrifice. The Maya, the Aztec, the Toltec, and other Mesoamericans experienced and related to their cosmos, their gods, and the powers of nature not only through poetry, art, and architecture but also in ritual bloodletting and the killing of animals, plants, and human beings.

Cosmology of Human Sacrifice

In various creation myths and sacred histories, the cosmos is shown to have a dynamic, unstable, and destructive nature. The cosmic setting of communities, cities, agricultural work, and the schedules of priests, kings, workers, and warriors is marked by sharp alterations between order and disorder, cosmic life and cosmic death. Sometimes these alterations are marked by the death and sacrifice of gods.

At least three major cosmogonic episodes contain paradigms for some of the practices of human sacrifice, and two important cosmic patterns came to influence the social world. First, the gods were involved in struggles that included a widening of the practice of sacrifice from killing a single deity to the sacrifice of masses of deities. Second, these cosmic sacrifices sometimes favor the gods of the "center" in episodes in which they conquer and sacrifice gods from the "periphery" of the cosmos.

A major cosmogonic episode related to human sacrifice is reported in Sahagún's *Florentine Codex*. After the universe has passed through the first four cosmogonic ages, the gods gather around a divine fire at Teotihuacan ("Abode of the Gods") to create the new sun. Following four days of penance and ritual, the god Nanahuatzin ("the Pimply One"), dressed in ceremonial garb, hurls himself into the fire, followed by a second deity, Tecuciztecatl ("Lord of Snails"). Immediately, an eagle and a jaguar rise from the flames. Then the dawn appeared, and the gods, led by Quetzalcoatl, look eastward: "When the sun came to rise, when he burst forth, he appeared to be red, he kept swaying from side to side." Because the sun is thus motionless, the gods decide to sacrifice themselves, and the wind god Ecatl (Ehecatl) "deals death" to the other gods by cutting their throats. But the sun only moves through the heavens when Ecatl exerts himself and blows mightily into the sky. It is important to note that the initial sacrifice of two gods unfolds into a massive sacrifice of gods in order for cosmic order to appear, and even then, it takes more than just killing to create cosmic motion.

The cosmic pattern of mass sacrifice to energize the sun is repeated when the god Mixcoatl ("Cloud Serpent") creates five human beings and four hundred Chichimec warriors to stir up discord and warfare. While the warriors pass their time hunting and drinking, the god sends the five human beings to slay them. In this account, war is created specifically to provide sacrificial victims for the gods.

There is a specific story about the massive sacrifice of human beings that ties gods, sacrifice, and warfare together in Aztec religion. Sahagún collected a *teotuicatl* ("divine song") of the birth of Huitzilopochtli, the Aztec war god, which illustrates the pattern of the conquest and ritual killing of warriors from the periphery of the state at the major temple in the heart of the capital. The story begins when the mother of the gods, Coatlicue ("Serpent Skirt"), becomes pregnant while sweeping out the temple at Coatepec ("Serpent Mountain"). When her daughter Coyolxauhqui hears of the pregnancy, she incites her 399 siblings to dress for war. Attired for war and driven into a berserk frenzy, the siblings travel through many towns, led by Coyolxauhqui, and charge up Serpent Mountain to kill Coatlicue. As they reach the top, Huitzilopochtli is born, fully dressed and attired for war. Attacking Coyolxauhqui, he cuts off her head and dismembers her. The text notes, "The body of Coyolxauhqui rolled down the slope; it fell apart in pieces; her hands, her legs, her torso fell in different places." Next, Huitzilopochtli attacks the other warriors, annihilating them and taking their prized emblems, which he "introduces . . . into his destiny." As in many instances in Mesoamerica, myth becomes embedded in stone and architecture.

As excavations of the Templo Mayor of Tenochtitlan have revealed, this mythic episode was replicated in the architecture and ritual action of the temple, which was dedicated to Huitzilopochtli and Tlaloc. The temple, called "Coatepec" or "Serpent Mountain," was arranged with Huitzilopochtli's shrine at the top of one of the great stairways and the round stone depicting the dismembered Coyolxauhqui at the bottom, in an architectural repetition of this mythic episode. Research has shown that the largest number of ceremonial sacrifices of enemy warriors from surrounding communities took place at this temple. In this case, the story may represent the daily sunrise (Huitzilopochtli) above the earth (Coatlicue) and its progressive slaying of the moon (Coyolxauhqui) and the stars (the four hundred siblings); but we also see both the increment in sacrifice and the killing of gods from the periphery by the supreme god of the center.

Practice and Paraphernalia of Human Sacrifice

It is important to emphasize that all sacrifices—especially human sacrifice—were carried out within a complex ceremonial system dedicated to a crowded and hungry pantheon. All was not sacrifice in central Mexican society, but the ritual transformation of objects through destruction was a pervasive fact of life. In addition, there was an intimate relationship among sacrifice, warfare, and (sometimes) the ingestion of parts of the sacrificed beings. Certain metaphors and symbols of sacrifice show us these relationships. Among the Nahua-speaking peoples, blood was called *chalchiuh-atl,* meaning "precious water." Human hearts were likened to fine burnished turquoise, and war was *teoatltlachinolli,* meaning "divine liquid" and "burnt things." War was the place "where the jaguars roar," where "feathered war bonnets heave about like foam in the waves." And death on the battlefield was called *xochimiquiztli,* "the flowery death."

Besides the theatrical ritual killings of many warriors and enemies, everyone in the Aztec and Maya world participated in some form of autosacrifice, or bloodletting. Bloodletting, either an offering or a penitential rite, involved pricking one's earlobes with maguey thorns or, in more severe cases, drawing strings through holes cut in the tongue, ears, genitals, or other fleshy parts of the body, practiced throughout Mesoamerica. We have a vivid and powerful image of autosacrifice from the Maya lintels of Yaxchilan. In several panels we see the figure of Lady Xoc, a member of the royal family, pulling a thorn-studded rope through her tongue while her blood is slowly collected in a basket filled with paper. This painful sacrifice results, in the next panel, in the emergence from the blood of a giant vision serpent out of whose mouth appears one of the royal ancestors of the Maya kings.

Though important variations of ritual killing were carried out at temples, schools, skull racks, and bath houses, the general pattern of human sacrifice was as follows. Abstracting from the Aztec case about which we have the most information, the sacrificial ritual began with a preparatory period of priestly fasting (*nezahualiztli*) which lasted four (or a multiple of four) days. An important exception was the year-long fast of a group of priests and priestesses. This preparatory period also involved nocturnal vigils and offerings of flowers, food, cloth, rubber, paper, and poles with streamers, as well as censing, the pouring of libations, and the flowery decoration of temples, statues, and ritual participants. Dramatic processions of elaborately costumed participants, moving to sacred songs played by musical ensembles, passed through the ceremonial precinct before arriving at the specific temple of sacrifice. The major ritual participants were deity impersonators. All important rituals involved a death sacrifice of either animals or human beings.

Sacrifices were carried out in many ceremonial centers throughout Central Mexico. Among the most impressive theaters for sacrificial festivals were the sacred precincts of Cholula, Tula, Xochicalco, Teotihuacan, Cacaxtla, and Malinalco. The surviving evidence reveals a wide range of sacrificial techniques, including decapitation (usually of women), shooting with darts or arrows, drowning, burning, hurling from heights, strangulation, entombment, starvation, and gladiatorial combat. Usually, the ceremony peaked when splendidly attired captors and captives sang and danced in procession to the temple, where they were escorted (sometimes willing) up the stairways to the sacrificial stone. The victim was quickly thrust on the sacrificial stone, and the temple priest cut through the chest wall with the ritual flint knife. The priest grasped the still-beating heart, called "precious eagle cactus fruit," tore it from the

S

chest, offered it to the sun for vitality and nourishment, and placed it in a carved circular vessel. In many cases, the body, now called "eagle man," was rolled down the temple steps to the bottom, where it was dismembered. The head was cut off and the brain taken out; after skinning, the body was placed on the *tzompantli,* a rack consisting of long poles laid horizontally and loaded with skulls. In many cases, the captor was decorated (for instance, with chalk and bird down) and given gifts. Sometimes the captor, together with his relatives, consumed a ritual meal. To each celebrant went a piece of the flesh of the captive.

Sacrifice, especially the public display of human sacrifice, was closely related to the intimidation of allied and enemy city-states as a means of acquiring massive tribute payments in the form of maize, beans, cloth, war service, and labor. An example of this use of geopolitical sacrifice among the Aztecs was the *xochiyayotl* ("flowery wars"), a series of scheduled battlefield confrontations staged primarily to provide sacrificial victims for ritual festivals and to keep the warriors in training. One Aztec political leader, Tlacael, compared the warrior going to the flowery wars with a merchant going to distant markets to purchase luxuries. The god and his army went to the battlefield to purchase blood and hearts, the luxuries of the temples. In fact, the flowery wars were true wars—political expressions aimed at intimidating allies and enemies into maintaining an inferior relationship with the great island capital in the lake.

Among the most remarkable festivals was "the feast of the flaying of men," during which a prisoner of war was taken by a priest and tied to a huge, round sacrificial stone, called *temalacatl,* which was placed flat on the ground. The captive was provided with a pine club and a feathered staff to protect himself against the attacks of four warriors armed with clubs of wood and obsidian blades. When he was defeated, he was taken off the stone, his heart was taken out, and he was flayed.

Still another remarkable ceremony was the New Fire Ceremony, also called the Binding of the Years, held only once every fifty-two years on the summit of the Hill of the Star outside Tenochtitlan. At midnight, when the star cluster called Tianquiztli (the Pleiades) passed through the zenith, marking the end of the fifty-two-year calendrical cycle, a captive warrior was sacrificed. In his chest cavity a new fire was started, marking the regeneration of the cosmos. The fire was then taken to the Templo Mayor and thence to all the cities and towns in the empire, providing the spark for new fires and the new fifty-two-year cycle.

A remarkable festival, celebrated on the first day of the month of Atlcahualo, involved the paying of debts to Tlaloc, the rain god. On this day, children with two cowlicks in their hair and favorable day-signs were dressed in costumes of various bright colors such as dark green, black striped with chili red, and light blue, and they were sacrificed in seven different locations. The flowing and falling of the tears of the children ensured the coming of rain.

Sacrifice and human sacrifice among Mesoamerican peoples have stimulated intense debates about the nature of religion, human beings, and culture. Reports have been wildly exaggerated, completely denied, and given specious explanations. It seems clear, nonetheless, that ritual sacrifice of gods, humans, animals, and plants pervaded Mesoamerican cultures, consciousness, and politics.

FURTHER READINGS

Boone, E. H. (ed.). 1984. *Ritual Human Sacrifice in Mesoamerica.* Washington, D.C.: Dumbarton Oaks.

Carrasco, D. 1991. The Sacrifice of Tezcatlipoca: To Change Place. In D. Carrasco (ed.), *To Change Place: Aztec Ceremonial Landscapes,* pp. 31–57. Niwot: University Press of Colorado.

———. 1995. Cosmic Jaws: We Eat the Gods and the Gods Eat Us. *Journal of the American Academy of Religion* 63:101–135.

———. 1995. Give Me Some Skin: The Charisma of the Aztec Warrior. *History of Religions* 35:1–26.

Ingham, J. M. 1984. Human Sacrifice at Tenochtitlan. *Comparative Studies in Society and History* 26:379–400.

Issac, B. L. 1983. The Aztec "Flowery War": A Geopolitical Explanation. *Journal of Anthropological Research* 39:415–432.

Nicholson, H. B. 1971. Religion in Pre-Hispanic Central Mexico. In Robert Wauchope (ed.), *Handbook of Middle American Indians,* vol. 10, *Archaeology of Northern Mesoamerica,* part 1, pp. 395–446. Austin: University of Texas Press.

Sahagún, B. 1950–1982. *Florentine Codex: General History of the Things of New Spain.* A. J. O. Anderson and C. E. Dibble (eds. and trans.). Santa Fe: School of American Research and University of Utah.

David Carrasco

SEE ALSO
Blood and Bloodletting; Warfare

Sahagún, Bernardino de (c. 1499–1590)

Born in Sahagún, Spain, and educated at the University of Salamanca, Fray Bernardino de Sahagún went to Mexico as a Franciscan missionary in 1529. Working primarily in Tlatelolco and Tepepulco, he spent most of his life (particularly the period 1547–1590) in producing his *General History of the Things of New Spain,* a monumental twelve-volume description of the life, society, language, history, arts, literature, and culture of the Aztecs. The scope and organization of this work owe much to the model of medieval encyclopedias, but the influences of the Renaissance and Franciscan millennialism give it a startlingly modern cast, and it is arguably both the first and the best ethnography ever written.

Largely composed in Nahuatl, the work was attacked by the Inquisition for its pro-Indian thrust and was suppressed for three hundred years. Various versions were scattered among European and American libraries: the Florentine Codex, Spanish and Nahuatl, illustrated, 1547–1577?; the Madrid Codices, Spanish and Nahuatl, 1560?–1565?; the Manuscript of Tolosa, Spanish, 1580?; and other writings, many still unpublished. The impact of Sahagún's work was thus delayed until modern times.

Sahagún was not himself a witness of the Spanish conquest of Mexico City, but many of his native informants were actual participants in the fighting and recorded in great detail the culture of Aztec Mexico and the epochal events that ended it. They did so, furthermore, in Nahuatl, and thus provide us with an unparalleled account of the confrontation of two worlds, almost as distant from each other culturally as if they had developed on different planets.

FURTHER READINGS

Cline, H. F. 1973. Sahagún Materials and Studies, 1948–1971. In H. F. Cline (ed.), *Handbook of Middle American Indians,* vol. 13, pp. 218–232. Austin: University of Texas Press.

Edmonson, Munro S. (ed.). *Sixteenth-Century México: The Work of Sahagún.* Albuquerque: University of New Mexico Press.

Nicolau d'Olwer, L., and H. F. Cline. 1973. Sahagún and His Works. In H. F. Cline (ed.), *Handbook of Middle American Indians,* vol. 13, pp. 186–207. Austin: University of Texas Press.

Sahagún, Fray Bernardino de. 1950–1963. *General History of the Things of New Spain (Florentine Codex).* A. Anderson and C. Dibble (eds. and trans.). 12 vols.

Santa Fe: School of American Research and the University of Utah.

———. 1974. *Primeros Memoriales.* W. J. Moreno (ed. and trans.). Colección Científica 16. Mexico City: Instituto Nacional de Antropología e Historia, Consejo de Historia.

Munro S. Edmonson

SEE ALSO

Colonial Period

Salinas la Blanca (Guatemala)

Salinas la Blanca is a Formative archaeological site on the left bank of the Río Naranjo near Ocos, Guatemala. The environmental setting is the Pacific coastal plain of extreme southwestern Guatemala, a region featuring lagoons, estuaries, mangrove swamps, savanna, and mixed tropical forest. Excavations in 1962 by Michael D. Coe and Kent V. Flannery revealed a small village of wattle-and-daub houses on low clay platforms, surrounded by large outdoor hearths and piles of discarded mollusk shells. The bulk of the deposits dated to the Cuadros and Jocotal phases (c. 1100–800 B.C.). During these periods the occupants of Salinas la Blanca grew maize, avocados, white zapotes, amd hog plum; they hunted deer, iguana, and turtle; they fished and collected crabs, oysters, mussels, marsh clams, and other invertebrates.

FURTHER READINGS

Coe, M. D., and K. V. Flannery. 1967. *Early Cultures and Human Ecology in South Coastal Guatemala.* Washington, D.C.: Smithsonian Press.

Kent V. Flannery

SEE ALSO

Soconusco–South Pacific Coast and Piedmont Region

Salitron Viejo (Honduras)

Situated by the Sulaco River in the El Cajón region of west central Honduras, this site represents the largest community in the region during the period A.D. 400–800, with a population of 1,000 to 1,500. It functioned as the center of a chiefdom-level polity. The community plan indicates organization into four distinct architectural groups. The South and West groups contained the bulk of the site's population. Small residential structures were

S

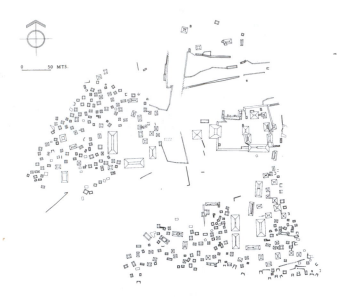

Plan of Salitron Viejo. Illustration courtesy of the author.

built on low mounds (0.2–1.0 meter high) around a large ceremonial plaza, defined by large range structures between 2 and 3 meters high. The ceremonial plaza and associated residential cluster was the basic organizational feature of communities throughout the El Cajón region and may correspond to a clan-level form of social organization.

On the east side of the site, the Iglesia Precinct is a large elite civic-ceremonial precinct; at its center is a large acropolis platform, 120 by 75 by 2.5 meters, on the summit of which large range structures define a ceremonial plaza and an elite residence group. Excavations within the Iglesia Precinct recovered 2,259 jade and marble artifacts that had been deposited in ritual caches associated with the construction, dedication, and desanctification of civic-ceremonial buildings.

The North Group, a ceremonial plaza linked to the rest of Salitron Viejo by a street or *sacbe,* is the largest ceremonial plaza in the region, but it was screened from other parts of the site by a small palisade or living hedge. The form and location of this group suggest that it was used as an assembly area on special ritual occasions when groups from throughout the region joined people at Salitron Viejo for mass celebrations.

FURTHER READINGS

Hirth, K. G. 1982. Excavaciones en Salitron Viejo: 1981. *Yaxkin* 5:5–21. Tegucigalpa.

———. 1988. Beyond the Maya Frontier: Cultural Interaction and Syncretism along the Central Honduran Corridor. In E. H. Boone and G. R. Willey (eds.), *The Southeast Classic Maya Zone,* pp. 297–334. Washington, D.C.: Dumbarton Oaks.

Kenneth G. Hirth

SEE ALSO

Cajón, El; Southeast Mesoamerica

Salt

Salt sources are found throughout Mesoamerica, though their uneven distribution, coupled with the high demand for dietary purposes, made salt a strategic trade commodity. The largest production areas are in the Central Mexican highlands and along the northern coast of the Yucatán Peninsula. Other production areas include the highlands and Pacific coasts of Guatemala, Chiapas, Oaxaca, and Guerrero, and the coasts of West Mexico and El Salvador. Pre-Hispanic production techniques included solar evaporation (*sal solar,* employed mostly in coastal areas) and cooking brine from coastal estuaries or highland brine springs, sometimes leached through salt-impregnated soils *(sal cocida).* Beginning in Late Formative times (c. 300 B.C.), trade networks originating from the main production areas supplied most of Mesoamerica with salt. The trade was a prominent part of the economy of the Classic and Postclassic states of Central Mexico and the Valley of Oaxaca; Yucatecan salt was exported throughout the Maya Lowlands and was a key economic factor in the growth of political complexity in their northern portion.

FURTHER READINGS

Andrews, A. P. 1983. *Maya Salt Production and Trade.* Tucson: University of Arizona Press.

———. 1991. Las salinas de El Salvador: Bosquejo histórico, etnográfico y arqueológico. *Mesoamerica* 21:71–93.

Ewald, U. 1985. *The Mexican Salt Industry, 1560–1980: A Study in Change.* Stuttgart and New York: Gustav Fischer.

Mendizábal, M. O. 1946. Influencia de la sal en la distribución geográfica de los grupos indígenas de México. In his *Obras Completas,* vol. 2, pp. 81–340. Mexico City: Imprenta del Museo Nacional de Arqueología, Historia y Etnografía.

Noguera, E. 1975. Identificación de una saladera. *Anales de Antropología* 12:117–151.

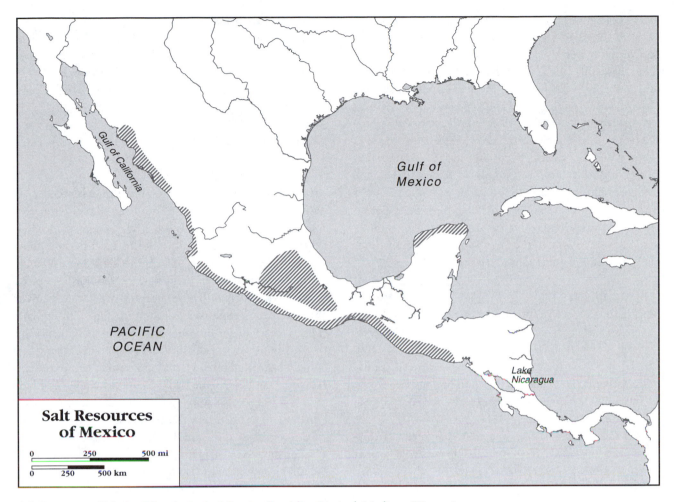

Salt Resources of Mexico. Map design by Mapping Specialists Limited, Madison, Wisconsin.

Parsons, J. R. 1989. Una etnografía arqueológica de la producción tradicional de sal en Nexquipayac, Estado de Mexico. *Arqueología* 2:69–80. Mexico City: Instituto Nacional de Antropología e Historia.

Anthony P. Andrews

SEE ALSO
Fábrica San José; Minerals, Ores, and Mining

San Antonio Nogalar (Tamaulipas, Mexico)

Sprawling down steep slopes to a narrow valley in mountainous central Tamaulipas, this 20-hectare expanse of more than two hundred predominantly round structures and crescent terraces constitutes the first large site of the northeastern Mesoamerican frontier to be excavated and mapped. Settled from the Late Formative through the Early Classic periods and reoccupied in the terminal Postclassic period, the site was a significant ancient population center in the northern Gulf borderlands. Apart from numerous low stone platforms for domestic structures, frequently on terraces, there are masonry bases for temples and other ceremonial or administrative constructions ranging up to 3.2 meters high, as well as a ball court about 20 meters long. The site may have been known as "Tamaholipa" in the mid-sixteenth century, when it was an important early Colonial town for which the present-day state is named.

Following localization by Meade in 1950, then brief testing and collecting by MacNeish during his area survey of 1953–1954, the site was explored by Stresser-Péan in 1968–1969 and 1973. He determined that the principal occupation dates to the Early Classic, and that Mesoamerican sedentary and agricultural patterns prevailed in

S

this remote peripheral region. The majority of the ceramics were found to be similar to or identical with those known to the north in the Sierra de Tamaulipas (Laguna, Eslabones, and initial La Salta phases); the remainder mirror the Pánuco region to the south, particularly the Pithaya, initial Zaquil, and Panuco phases. Lithic artifacts were largely within the Sierra corpus. Stresser-Pean's consideration of the archaeological evidence from the site, along with the extensive ethnohistorical data for the greater region, contributes amply to understanding the complex culture history of this rarely examined frontier zone. The lower elevations of San Antonio Nogalar, including most of the principal structures, have suffered in recent years owing to the expansion of the nearby modern village and its subsistence activities.

FURTHER READINGS

MacNeish, R. S. 1958. Preliminary Archaeological Investigations in the Sierra de Tamaulipas, Mexico. *Transactions of the American Philosophical Society* 48:1–209.

Meade, J. 1954. Identificación de las ruinas de Tamaholipa, pueblo que dio su nombre al Estado de Tamaulipas. *Boletin de la Sociedad Mexicana de Geografía y Estadística* 77:299–309.

Stresser-Pean, G. 1977. *San Antonio Nogalar.* Études Mesoaméricaines, 3. Mexico City: Mission Archéologique et Etnologique Française au Méxique.

S. Jeffrey K. Wilkerson

SEE ALSO

Gulf Lowlands: North Region

San Cristóbal (Managua, Nicaragua)

Extending over more than 20 hectares on the eastern edge of the Managua metropolitan area, this site formerly had twelve large mounds and many small ones, but all were leveled for cultivation. The site stratigraphy is separated by a distinct layer of volcanic tephra; the cultural levels above it are from A.D. 500 to 1520, and those below it from at least 1200 B.C. to A.D. 500. Test excavations have revealed extensive cemetery areas with shoe-shaped funerary urns, local and foreign ceramics (primarily Usulutan Negative); local chert, jasper, and chalcedony and imported obsidian lithic industries are also present. Ceramic beads, drilled potsherds, and carved turtle shell were utilized for personal adornment.

FURTHER READINGS

Lange, F. W., P. D. Sheets, A. Martinez, and S. Abel-Vidor. 1992. *The Archaeology of Pacific Nicaragua.* Albuquerque: University of New Mexico Press.

Frederick W. Lange

SEE ALSO

Intermediate Area: Overview

San Isidro and Environs (Chiapas, Mexico)

Although it was occupied from the Early Formative period to the Classic, San Isidro is best known as a Middle Formative center with strong ties to the Middle Olmec site of La Venta (Tabasco). San Isidro lies along the banks of the Grijalva River in the little-explored northern piedmont of the Chiapas Plateau, near the point were the river becomes impassable to canoe traffic. This wet, verdant region, separated from the dry interior of Chiapas by rugged limestone mountains and deep, narrow canyons, is on a historically known trade route that connected the Chiapas interior to the Gulf Coast lowlands. The San Isidro region is also suitable for the cultivation of cacao. The site appears to have been established to control a major access point in Middle Formative trade routes.

The ceremonial center features a C-group arrangement of a long mound and flanking pyramid, probably some kind of "astronomical commemoration" complex, and is similar to those known for the contemporaneous centers of Chiapa de Corzo and Mirador, situated upstream from San Isidro. Salvage operations at San Isidro in some of the principal earthen pyramids in 1966 recovered a series of Middle Formative cruciform axe offerings similar to those known from La Venta. Most of the "axes" at San Isidro, however, were actually pseudo-celts made of slate and softer stones. The site is now submerged by the Mal Paso Reservoir.

FURTHER READINGS

Lee, T. A. 1974. Middle Grijalva Regional Chronology and Ceramic Relations: A Preliminary Report. In N. Hammond (ed.), *Mesoamerica Archaeology: New Approaches,* pp. 1–20. London: Duckworth.

Lowe, G. W. 1981. Olmec Horizons Defined in Mound 20, San Isidro, Chiapas. In E. P. Benson (ed.), *The Olmec and Their Neighbors,* pp. 231–255. Washington, D.C.: Dumbarton Oaks.

Gareth W. Lowe

SEE ALSO
Chiapas Interior Plateau

San Jacinto (Nicaragua)

Situated on the outskirts of the village of Cuapa, on the bank of the Cuapa River in west central Nicaragua, this site extends over the river terrace, covering about 6 hectares. One hundred ninety-seven mounds constructed of earth and river cobble were counted, of round to elliptical shape. Most mounds are between 4 and 10 meters in height, but some measured 15 to 18 meters high. These larger mounds are arranged around what appears to be a central plaza area. Based on analysis of the ceramic diagnostics, the site was occupied during the Cuapa phase, A.D. 1400–1600.

The Cuapa phase has been interpreted as one in which the zone experienced a rapid migration that perhaps had connections with an area to the north, possibly the Matagalpas. Although this inference has yet to be conclusively demonstrated, the ceramic styles as well as the lithic technology characteristic of the San Jacinto site are completely different from the earlier ceramic traditions of the Chontales region.

Laraine Fletcher

SEE ALSO
Intermediate Area: Overview

San José Mogote (Oaxaca, Mexico)

This large and complex archaeological site, on a bend of the Atoyac River in the northern Valley of Oaxaca, is the oldest permanent village so far known for its region; it was the largest in the Valley prior to the founding of the city of Monte Albán. After Monte Albán had risen to prominence, San José Mogote became a second-order administrative center of regional significance.

Founded in the Espiridion phase, sometime between 1600 and 1400 B.C., San José Mogote grew to be a 7.8-hectare village during the Tierras Largas phase (1400–1150 B.C.). At that time it featured a series of small public buildings (thought to be men's houses) that are among the oldest in Mesoamerica. Between 1150 and 850 B.C., in the San José phase, San José Mogote became a chiefly center covering 60 or 70 hectares. Characterized by flamboyant pottery with pan-Mesoamerican motifs that feature Earth (Earthquake) and Sky (Lightning), the village

engaged in the craft production of magnetite mirrors, pearl oyster and spiny oyster ornaments, mica, polished celts, and other trade items. Its elite exchanged gifts with those of Morelos, Veracruz, Chiapas, and the Basin of Mexico.

In the Guadalupe phase (850–700 B.C.), the site had large public buildings on adobe platforms. Still larger stone masonry platforms appeared during the Rosario phase (700–500 B.C.), a period when chiefly individuals wore jade, deformed their skulls, practiced bloodletting with obsidian stilettos, lived in adobe houses with courtyards, and buried their dead in tombs. Toward the end of the Rosario phase, a carved stone monument with an early form of hieroglyphic writing appeared erected at the site.

San José Mogote was almost entirely abandoned around 500 B.C., presumably because its inhabitants participated in the founding of nearby Monte Albán. During Period II of Monte Albán (150 B.C.–A.D. 150), San José Mogote underwent a renaissance as a regional administrative center below Monte Albán. At the center of the 70-hectare site was the Main Plaza, with temples, palaces, a ball court, and tombs in Monte Albán II style. Among the offerings found below temple floors were jade statues, ritual scenes composed of ceramic sculptures, effigy incense burners, and sacrificed humans and animals.

FURTHER READINGS

Flannery, K. V. (ed.). 1976. *The Early Mesoamerican Village*. New York: Academic Press.

Flannery, K. V., and J. Marcus. 1994. *Early Formative Pottery of the Valley of Oaxaca, Mexico*. With technical ceramic analysis by William O. Payne. Ann Arbor: Museum of Anthropology, University of Michigan.

Kent V. Flannery and Joyce Marcus

SEE ALSO
Oaxaca and Tehuantepec Region

San Lorenzo Tenochtitlán (Veracruz, Mexico)

The archaeological site zone of San Lorenzo Tenochtitlán, the earliest Olmec regional center in the Olmec heartland of Mexico's Gulf Coast region, rose to prominence more than three thousand years ago. Over a period of three or four hundred years, it attained a degree of cultural complexity greater than any other contemporaneous site in Mesoamerica, possibly achieving incipient statehood. The

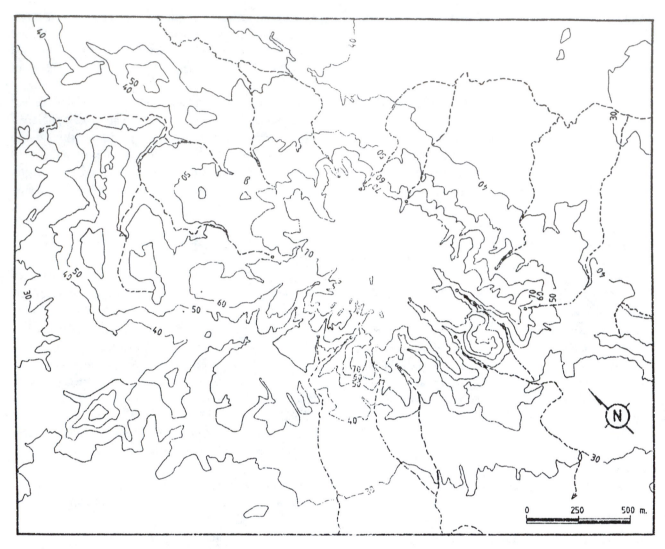

Topographic map of San Lorenzo. The Early Formative occupation extends to the 30-meter contour level. Illustration courtesy of the author.

pioneer Olmec archaeologist, Matthew Stirling, gave the name "San Lorenzo Tenochtitlán" to a complex of sites now differentiated as three separate sites: San Lorenzo, where the major Olmec occupation is found; Tenochtitlán, where an Olmec occupation of unknown magnitude is covered by a large Late Classic–Early Postclassic site; and the lands pertaining to the community of Potrero Nuevo. This article deals primarily with the Olmec site of San Lorenzo.

The earliest occupation at San Lorenzo dates to before 1500 B.C., and the latest ends about A.D. 1100. The site's apogee of occupation occurred during the Early Formative period (1200–900 B.C.), and it declined in size and importance during the Middle and Late Formative

(900–100 B.C.). No evidence of Early Classic period occupation has been found at the site, and it was not until around 900 A.D. that there was a significant though small Late Classic occupation that carried through the Early Postclassic (A.D. 1100).

The tropical lowlands of the Coatzacoalcos River drainage in the southern part of the state of Veracruz were the home of the San Lorenzo Olmec. Fed by the waters originating in the Sierra Atrevesada and its affluents, the lower reaches of the Coatzacoalcos River flow through a broad low plain that forms the widest part of the Gulf Coastal plain, approximately 60 kilometers wide, characterized by a complex pattern of ancient and recent oxbow lakes and meanders. Ancient geologic terraces, 40 to 80 meters above sea level and dating from the Miocene Epoch, emerge above the plain. Today, as in the past, people prefer the high ground for permanent habitation. The volcanic Tuxtla Mountains are visible about 60 kilometers to the northwest. Closer to San Lorenzo, and once sacred to the Olmec, are the high salt domes named Cerro el Mixe and Cerro el Manatí.

Studies of regional geomorphology show that the present-day landscape is considerably different from that of the Formative period. In ancient times San Lorenzo was surrounded by two branches of the Coatzacoalcos River that now do not exist as active rivers. These river courses have been dramatically altered as a result of the uplift of the Tuxtlas volcanic mass, known to have been active during the Early and Middle Formative periods. In a sense, the high ground of San Lorenzo was an island, similar to the location of La Venta in Tabasco. Dominating two or more important river confluences and an ample dendritic fluvial network, San Lorenzo held a strategic position to control communication, transportation, and trade.

The subsistence base of the ancient Olmec was principally the Mesoamerican triad of corn, beans, and squash, although they also relied heavily on wild resources such as fish, turtle, white-tailed deer, and white-lipped peccary. No ceramic griddles were found at the site, so it is possible that maize was consumed as tamales rather than tortillas. The domesticated dog was also a source of food, since its remains are often found in household debris.

The general pattern of monumental architecture in Mesoamerica can be characterized as a predefined pattern in which mounds or pyramids were built around plazas, but the Early Formative architecture of San Lorenzo is not typical of this later Mesoamerican pattern. At San Lorenzo, the Olmec created the desired spaces through the monumental modification of natural landforms. The San Lorenzo plateau was not a giant effigy mound, but it certainly was one of the largest works of monumental architecture in Early Formative Mesoamerica; originally a natural hill, it was modified by terraces, filling and cutting operations, and earth removal to shape a sacred and everyday space for the ancient inhabitants. Two or three levels of long, wide terraces provided areas usable for habitation and production. Thousands of cubic meters of earthen fill brought in from low-lying spots were used to level the land, and large retaining walls were built. The present form of the plateau is further distorted by human activity and erosion following the Olmec occupation, which have altered the original silhouette of this enormous earthen monument, possibly the first "sacred mountain" in

Discovery of the tenth colossal head from San Lorenzo in 1994. Colossal heads are portraits of ancient rulers of the site. Photograph courtesy of the author.

Mesoamerica. Other important architectural elements of the Early Formative period are low earthen platforms and causeways.

Surface remains extend from the heights of the San Lorenzo plateau to the 30-meter contour interval to cover approximately 690 hectares, or 7 square kilometers, of occupation during the Early Formative period. Because the Early Formative habitation is deeply buried, the presence of low mounds on the surface does not reflect population size and cannot be used for estimates. The levees, the floodplains, and the now-dissected uplands to the south and west were farmed.

At San Lorenzo the rulers, their families, and their attendants lived on the heights of the site, where the majority of sculptures are found. The extremely wealthy and powerful could afford to use basaltic stone, a scarce resource imported from the distant Tuxtla Mountains, for steps, columns, and aqueducts in dwellings.

San Lorenzo Tenochtitlán (Veracruz, Mexico) 647

S

These three sculptures from the Azuzul acropolis of the Loma del Zapote site form a scenic display of four monuments. Scenic display of sculptural ensembles was a means to re-create mythological and historical events used by the Olmec. Photograph courtesy of the author.

Below the heights on the terraced sides of the plateau, there were concentrations of less elaborate dwellings made of wattle and daub or mud brick. Floors were prepared with tamped dirt covered with a layer of irregularly shaped sedimentary stones, and the roofs were made of palm thatch. Dwellings in the household cluster tend to be large, covering more than 100 square meters, and vary in form, size, and function. Cooking areas, found outside the main dwellings, consist of hearths with firedogs or shaped clay hearths. The Olmec kept their structures quite clean and deposited their garbage in pits, in gullies as landfill, or downslope away from the dwellings.

Because Olmec culture was originally defined on the basis of its art, even today sites are often identified as Olmec because they have monumental or portable sculpture in that style. The Olmec style is distinctive in its sculptural technique and concepts, the most notable being colossal heads, monolithic thrones, and fantastic representations of animals and humans. But Olmec art

across the heartland of southern Veracruz and Tabasco is characterized by diversity, not uniformity; the sculpture is highly varied in form and theme even though a number of features are clearly held in common. Matthew Stirling and Beatriz de la Fuente both pointed out that the principal representation in Olmec art is the human form. In the elaborate Olmec belief system, symbols of status and power and animals were used to render tribute to the rulers and supernaturals. The central position of the feline in Olmec art has been repeatedly questioned; however, San Lorenzo possesses a large number of clear feline representations, establishing the feline as one of the most ancient Olmec symbols. After the decline of San Lorenzo, feline representations may have declined in popularity or may have been transformed.

Contextual data indicate that Olmec sculptures were not mere idols to be worshipped in sacred spaces, but rather were used in ensembles or groups to reenact mythological or historical events. The use of monuments to form scenic displays indicates that each Olmec sculpture constitutes an distinctive piece of a conceptual framework concerning the earth and the cosmos. Olmec scenic displays re-created mythological and historical events in conjunction with commemorative and/or cyclical festivities, thus confirming Olmec social identity, rulership, and cosmological principles.

San Lorenzo was the site of several large-scale craft production activities. During the apogee phase, agriculture and the importation of foodstuffs intensified in order to maintain an ever-increasing population of craftspeople and other non-food-producers. The largest craft activity found to date is the recycling and recarving of monuments and the fabrication of preforms, which was directly controlled by the elite. In another specialized workshop, more than six metric tons of ilmenite multi-drilled blocks were recovered; these are the exhausted or discarded pieces of a rotation technology used in drilling. Greenstone and obsidian working seem to have been conducted at the household level. The obsidian at San Lorenzo derives from three basic sources—Guadalupe Victoria (Puebla), Otumba (Central Mexico), and El Chayal (Guatemala).

Interregional trade in exotic resources and objects controlled by the San Lorenzo elite is well documented. Artifacts such as magnetite mirrors from Oaxaca and other sources and jade from the Motagua Valley were used only by the elite. Other resources—such as basalt from the Tuxtla Mountains, ilmenite from Chiapas and Oaxaca, mica, serpentine, schist, jasper, and other metamorphic rocks—were obtained through elite control of trade networks.

The population of San Lorenzo's hinterland increased during the apogee phase, creating a hierarchical settlement pattern in which San Lorenzo functioned as the regional center, surrounded by a complicated administrative hierarchy of small and large sites, each specialized according to its geographical position. Because it was situated in a strategic spot in the communication network, San Lorenzo was able to regulate the importation and exportation of local and regional products. The centralization of sites and the population increase coincided with intensive production specialization and the appearance of an exchange network regulated by the elite.

During this time, large monuments created in volcanic stone brought from the Tuxtla Mountains were dedicated. An efficient organization that controlled a large work force was necessary to conduct this extraordinary activity, in which stones as large as 25 metric tons were transported. We do not know if the monuments were brought as uncarved blocks and sculpted on the site or if they arrived already carved. Both land and water routes are feasible for the transport of stone, although it is obvious that land routes provided greater safety. The magnitude of the human force necessary to transport the stones places the Olmec on a plane of organization, technology, and organization truly exceptional for their time. The transportation of stones was an effort at least as monumental than the construction of great architectural works.

San Lorenzo constituted a well-developed and structured hierarchical society whose successful integration and development were founded on the adaptive strategies used to exploit its environment efficiently and to take advantage of its optimal geographical location. Once considered a fairly small, 53-hectare site, San Lorenzo actually occupies more than 690 hectares and shows significant internal differentiation, making it the largest and most complex Early Formative site in Mesoamerica. The rulers of San Lorenzo, portrayed in the site's ten colossal heads, achieved an extraordinary power that was legitimated and reinforced by complicated ceremonies and sumptuous monuments. The colossal heads and thrones were probably never transported to other communities because they were the most important symbols of Olmec leadership, which was centered on the capital.

The florescence of San Lorenzo lasted until 900 B.C., when the site suffered a significant decline and population loss. After San Lorenzo, La Venta rose in importance, but it is still not known if La Venta, or some other polity, was responsible for the decline of San Lorenzo. Various causes of its decadence have been proposed, including internal revolt, invasions, and a gradual loss of importance owing to internal problems in the functioning of the regional polity.

Another possible factor is environmental, based on regional evidence for tectonic activity emanating from the Tuxtla Mountains, which could have had repercussions in the San Lorenzo region. Gradual or sudden environmental disequilibrium may have caused internal problems of a social, political, and economic nature, such as disruptions in trade and communications and significant crop losses.

The Middle Formative settlement pattern changed and population diminished. Between 900 and 400 B.C. San Lorenzo's importance waned, but other Olmec sites utilized its legacy and achieved greatness.

FURTHER READINGS

Cobean, R. H., J. R. Vogt, M. D. Glascock, and T. L. Stocker. 1991. High-Precision Trace-Element Characterization of Major Mesoamerican Obsidian Sources and Further Analyses of Artifacts from San Lorenzo Tenochtitlán, Mexico. *Latin American Antiquity* 2: 69–91.

Coe, M. D., and R. A. Diehl. 1980. *In the Land of the Olmec.* Austin: University of Texas Press.

Cyphers, A. 1992. Investigaciones arqueológicas recientes en San Lorenzo Tenochtitlán, Veracruz: 1990–1992. *Anales de Antropología* 29:37–93.

———. 1994. Olmec Sculpture. *National Geographic Research and Exploration* 10:294–305.

———. 1994. San Lorenzo Tenochtitlán. In J. Clark (ed.), *Los Olmecas en Mesoamérica,* pp. 42–67. Mexico City: Ediciones el Equilibrista and Citibank.

———. 1995. *Descifrando los misterios de la cultura Olmeca.* Mexico City: Instituto de Investigaciones Antropológicas, Universidad Nacional Autónoma de México.

de la Fuente, B. 1981. Toward a Conception of Monumental Olmec Art. In E. Benson (ed.), *The Olmec and Their Neighbors,* pp. 83–94. Washington, D.C.: Dumbarton Oaks.

Stirling, M. W. 1955. Stone Monuments of the Río Chiquito, Veracruz, Mexico. *Bureau of American Ethnology Bulletin* 157:1–23.

Wing, E. 1980. Faunal Remains from San Lorenzo. In M. D. Coe and R. A. Diehl (eds.), *In the Land of the Olmec,* pp. 375–386. Austin: University of Texas Press.

Ann Cyphers

S

SEE ALSO
Gulf Lowlands: South Region; Olmec Culture

Santa Catarina (México, Mexico)

This hamlet, about 6 hectares in extent, on the Lake Chalco shore of the Ixtapalapa Peninsula in the Basin of Mexico, was occupied from c. 1000 B.C. (uncalibrated radiocarbon date) to Aztec times. The site retains unmixed deposits of late Manantial (1000 B.C.; uncalibrated radiocarbon date) and Bomba (900 B.C.; uncalibrated radiocarbon date) phases within twelve storage pits, some with high concentrations of maize pollen. The material from these illustrates the transition from Manantial to El Arbolillo in ceramics and includes macroremains of amaranth, sieva beans *(Phaseolus luratus),* and prickly pear. Unlike the earlier sites of Tlapacoya and El Terremote, Santa Catarina (Ix–EF–2) is situated somewhat above and away from the lakebed of Conquest times, on slopes that today are under extensive rainfall cultivation. The site was found by Richard E. Blanton in 1969 and partially excavated by Tolstoy in 1971 and 1972.

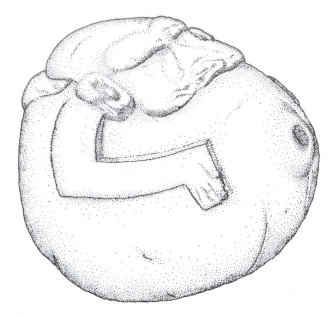

Monument 1, Santa Leticia. A pot-bellied styled monument, height 1.6 meters. Illustration courtesy of Middle American Research Institute, Tulane University.

FURTHER READINGS

Smith, C. E., and P. Tolstoy. 1981. Vegetation and Man in the Basin of Mexico. *Journal of Economic Botany* 35:415–433.

Tolstoy, P., S. K. Fish, M. W. Boksenbaum, K. B. Vaughn, and C. E. Smith. 1977. Early Sedentary Communities of the Basin of Mexico. *Journal of Field Archaeology* 4:91–107.

Paul Tolstoy

SEE ALSO
Basin of Mexico; Formative Period

Santa Leticia (Ahuachapan, El Salvador)

The site of Santa Leticia in the highlands of western El Salvador is important for addressing several issues pertinent to the Late Formative period and questions of highland influence on the origins of Maya civilization. The Santa Leticia ceremonial center was established above a humid cloud forest at about 1,400 meters elevation on the steep slope of the Cerro de Apaneca, an extinct volcano. The three enormous "pot-bellied" style monuments of the site were set atop a great earthen terrace construction facing outward to a spectacular view of the Pacific Ocean.

A number of scholars previously had suggested that the "pot-bellied" sculpture style and related boulder sculptures were antecedent to the Olmec sculpture style found on the Gulf Coast of Mexico and across Formative Mesoamerica. Some believed that boulder sculptures at sites like Santa Leticia, Monte Alto, and Abaj Takalik may have represented the origins of Olmec art. Archaeological excavations and artifact studies of the Santa Leticia project investigated the area around and below the monuments, recovering ceramic and carbon samples dating to the Late Formative period (c. 500–0 B.C.). Excavations also recovered a well-preserved ash-covered village of the same period, with the residences of the people who had raised the great terrace and massive monuments. Together these findings suggested a Late Formative, post-Olmec date for the "pot-bellied" style.

Other Santa Leticia research clarified the diverse nature of Formative subsistence, ceramic styles and dates, decorative techniques, and the definition of Formative patterns of interregional interaction. Such refinement of our understanding of the southeastern highland artifact complexes negated earlier theories that a migration from El Salvador was a major factor in the Protoclassic florescence of Lowland Maya civilization to the north.

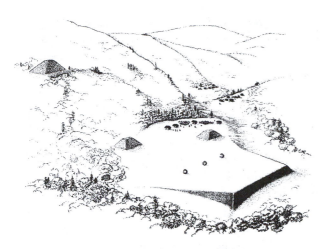

Reconstruction drawing of the Santa Leticia terrace, ceremonial center, and village at 100 B.C. Illustration courtesy of the Middle American Research Institute, Tulane University.

FURTHER READINGS

Demarest, A. A., R. Switsun, and R. Berger. 1982. The Dating and Cultural Association of the Pot-bellied Sculptural Style. *American Antiquity* 47:557–571.

————. 1986. *The Archaeology of Santa Leticia and the Rise of Maya Civilization.* Middle American Research Institute Publication 52. New Orleans: Tulane University.

Demarest, A. A., and R. J. Sharer. 1982. The Origins and Evolution of the Usulutan Ceramic Style. *American Antiquity* 47:810–822.

Demarest, A. A., and R. J. Sharer. 1986. Late PreClassic Ceramic Spheres, Culture Areas, and Cultural Evolution in the Southeastern Highlands of Mesoamerican. In P. A. Urban and E. M. Schortman (eds.), *The Southeast Maya Periphery,* pp. 194–223. Austin: University of Texas Press.

Arthur Demarest

SEE ALSO
Southeast Mesoamerica

Santa Luisa (Veracruz, Mexico)

This large, sprawling coastal site in the Tecolutla River delta of northern Veracruz is highly significant for a chronology spanning nearly eight thousand years that reflects a largely continuous occupation from the Early Archaic period to the present. The seventeen phases of the cultural sequence, most of which are bracketed by radiocarbon dates, appear to be valid for much of the north central Gulf lowlands. This chronology is currently the longest and oldest on the Mexican Gulf coast, and the Archaic presence is the most extensive known from the eastern lowlands. Throughout the Formative period this was the largest known settlement in the Tecolutla Valley. Because of its strategic location between El Pital and El Tajín, Santa Luisa reflects the rise and demise of both these metropolitan centers of the Classic Veracruz culture. The deep, extensive middens from the habitation zones, as well as the extensive raised field systems, cover at least 10 square kilometers.

Early Archaic through Middle Formative occupations were strategically situated on delta islands, convenient locations for the intensive exploitation of surrounding riverine, estuarine, and marine environments as well as the proximal forest and savanna zones. Nearby sites, such as La Conchita, which also has remains of extinct megafauna, appear to have been seasonal hunting locations (c. 5600 B.C.), dependent on island base camps.

Preceramic villages came into being during the Late Archaic, probably largely subsisting on a core diet of shellfish supplemented by hunting and, perhaps, manioc cultivation. Trade in obsidian from sources in distant Querétaro was important from midway through the Archaic. This lowland subsistence and settlement pattern, seemingly widespread in coastal Mesoamerica, has been called the Palo Hueco tradition after the Late Archaic phase at Santa Luisa.

Ceramics appeared and village densities increased in the Early Formative. After the initial phase there was a rapid diversification of ceramic forms and a gradual augmentation of grinding stones associated with maize preparation; concomitantly, obsidian chips, probably used for manioc grating, decreased. Sherd spindle whorls for the preparation of cotton thread were present by 1400 B.C. Artifacts increasingly reflected influence and direct contact with the southern Gulf Coast. By the final phase of the Early Formative there was much local imitation of Olmec ceramics, and some importation, but the region appears to have remained a frontier beyond direct Olmec domination. Carefully constructed burnt-clay floors and hearths, and probably platform-mound construction, began at this time.

The Middle Formative phases, beginning in 1000 B.C., demonstrate a strong and dynamic regionalism, setting apart the north central Gulf lowlands culturally from neighboring areas. Ceramic motifs include local glyphs as well as the standard line-break and hatch designs. Large villages with substantial structures, some containing massive, perhaps communal hearths, were present on the islands. Estuarine and riverine resources were still exploited but were decreasing in importance. Following catastrophic flooding that greatly modified the river channels and absorbed the older islands into the current river levee, an event perhaps corresponding to a prolonged weather abnormality or an extreme El Niño cycle, the Late Formative began with a massive population increase and demographic concentration. This was accompanied by rapid site growth and many new ceramics. Apart from the probable arrival of a distinct ethnic group, possibly Nahua, on the coast, this growth is likely to have been linked to the emergence and dominance of El Pital, a major, probably multiethnic city 35 kilometers to the southeast. Canal systems and raised fields for intensive agriculture may have existed toward the end of the period.

By the Protoclassic period, earthen temples were sealed with burnt clay or thin stucco surfaces and decorated with red-painted designs. Ceramics found are largely identical with those found at contemporary El Pital. Population continued to increase and the site expanded, particularly in the direction of the canal systems in back of the higher river terraces. By the end of this period, Santa Luisa was a major provincial town or even capital and an intensive food-production center, probably directly dominated by El Pital. The following Classic and Epiclassic periods represent the apogee of the site in terms of architecture, sculpture, intensive agriculture, and size.

During the Early Classic, large distributary canals were built in the field systems. Numerous small temples, and associated structures, were clustered together along the higher riverbank, many in a raised-platform acropolis. Although stairways, wall bases, and a few floor foundations had some stone, earth fill from massive midden borrow pits was the primary construction material. The upper walls of sanctuaries were of wood covered with clay and stucco. During subsequent refurbishing or new building, the earlier stucco surfaces, including murals, were broken up and utilized as backing for walls. Elite burials within these structures were sometimes accompanied by ball game accouterments such as yokes and *palmas,* and by sacrificed attendants. Toward the middle of the Classic there may been a decrease in construction and a shift in site affiliation. At this time or shortly thereafter, Santa Luisa almost certainly passed into the orbit of El Tajín, the regionally dominant power about 30 kilometers to the west.

By the Late Classic period, building resumed; it continued into the Epiclassic, utilizing thick, sandy stucco similar to that of El Tajín. A sandstone sculpture fragment with characteristic scrolls, reportedly from the site and very similar to those from the carved ball courts at El Tajín, suggests the presence of a vertical-wall ball court. Infant burials within water jars and accompanied by dogs, probably representing commemorative construction sacrifices, are associated with one structure of this period. Intensive agriculture continued to be of paramount importance at the site. The potential production of the field systems far exceeds the archaeologically verifiable population and suggests that a major portion of the considerable food production was destined for El Tajín. Canal systems reached their maximum extent, and even catchment terraces were constructed in the adjoining hills at this time. By the Epiclassic, *comal* griddles for tortilla preparation appeared in the ceramic corpus. Population, too, was noticeably denser, so that house structures directly abutted some temples.

Depopulation during the following Early Postclassic period was profound. Near-total abandonment—resulting from forcible population concentration elsewhere, or more probably from migrational exodus—left only a few houses, often built atop earlier temple structures. The associated ceramics are quite distinct, suggesting new inhabitants. By the end of the Postclassic, though, there was once more a large, growing settlement on the south end of the site, with artifacts very similar to those of the lower Huasteca, once again suggesting population displacement. The latter deposits are often associated with massive cemeteries that appear to mark the drastic Early Colonial epidemics of European diseases that depopulated the region, leaving it practically uninhabited by the early seventeenth century. Rain forest then dominated the region until Totonac hamlets were established nearby in following centuries. The present town of Gutierrez Zamora was established on the spot by Italian immigrants in the mid-nineteenth century.

Because of the extremely long chronology indicated by extensive stratigraphic deposits at Santa Luisa, its cultural sequence has broad regional implications. More than any other excavation in the north central Gulf area, it has anchored the time placement of El Tajín and El Pital, the principal Classic Veracruz metropolitan centers, in an evolutionary regional context. The site is also extremely important as the first point on the Mexican Gulf coast where major preceramic remains have been found, delineating the transition from hunting and gathering to sedentism.

S

FURTHER READINGS

Wilkerson, S. J. K. 1973. An Archaeological Sequence from Santa Luisa, Veracruz, Mexico. *Contributions of the University of California Archaeological Research Facility* 13:37–50.

———. 1975. Pre-agricultural Village Life: The Preceramic Period in Veracruz. *Contributions of the University of Califorma Archaeological Research Facility* 27: 111–122.

———. 1980. Man's Eighty Centuries in Veracruz. *National Geographic* 158:202–231.

———. 1981. The Northern Olmec and Pre-Olmec Frontier on the Gulf Coast. In E. Benson (ed.), *The Olmec and Their Neighbors,* pp. 181–194. Washington, D.C.: Dumbarton Oaks.

———. 1983. So Green and Like A Garden: Intensive Agriculture in Ancient Veracruz. In J. P. Darch (ed.), *Drained Field Agriculture in Central and South America,* pp. 55–90. BAR International Series, 189. Oxford.

S. Jeffrey K. Wilkerson

SEE ALSO

Gulf Lowlands: North Central Region

Santa María

See Cihuatán and Santa María

Santa Marta Cave (Chiapas, Mexico)

This cave, 70 meters wide and 13 meters deep, has a small permanent spring in its extreme northeastern section. Its occupation sequence extends from 9,400 years ago to the present and encompasses five preceramic phases, followed by five ceramic phases, which occupy the past three thousand years and are similar to phases Cotorra to Tuxtla in the Chiapa de Corzo sequence.

During the first preceramic phase, Santa Marta I (7400–7200 B.C.), the site was repeatedly occupied during the rainy season by small groups who foraged for small game and plants (some requiring grinding for their preparation, as inferred from the flat and rounded stones showing use wear like that resulting from grinding). Lithic remains are almost all made of local stone, manufactured principally by percussion and pressure-flaking; they include projectile points, unifaces, chopping tools, grating and abrading tools, denticulates, perforators, and many triangular knives, as well as flakes used as cutting tools. Bone tools are punches worked only on the extreme distal end, or over all the surface.

During Santa Marta II (7200–5200 B.C.), the site was occupied only occasionally for very short periods during the dry season, as indicated by a few hearths and associated remains of bird bones and some slabs of stone.

In Santa Marta III (5200–4600 B.C.), the site was sporadically occupied by small groups during the rainy season. The people hunted small game and gathered plants, including seeds that could be ground, and there are milling stones. Lithics are almost entirely local stone; forms include flakes, some of them retouched to serve as scrapers, and chopping tools made from cores; there are no projectile points.

Santa Marta IV (4600–4300 B.C.) saw continued occupation during the rainy season, but by considerably larger groups, foraging for a wider range of plants and animals. Lithic remains are also more varied, percussion-flaked from polyhedric or pyramidal prepared cores, including forms of previous phases, as well as projectile point types Almagre, Abasola, Nogales and Matamoros, artifacts that were retouched as much by percussion as by pressure. There are also bone punches and retouching tools.

The site does not appear to have been occupied between 4300 and 1300 B.C. It was then reoccupied (Santa Marta V, 1300–1000 B.C.), with the same range of plant foods and no evidence of cultivated plants; snails continued to be important, as did game animals. For this phase, MacNeish and Peterson report the presence of a few ceramic sherds of the Cotorro phase of the Chiapa de Corzo sequence, but subsequent excavations have not confirmed this.

FURTHER READINGS

García-Bárcena, J., and D. Santamaría. 1982. *La Cueva de Santa Marta, Ocozocoautla, Chiapas.* Colección Científica, 3. Mexico City: Instituto Nacional de Antropología e Historia.

García-Bárcena, J., D. Santamaría, T. Alvarez, M. Reyes, and F. Sánchez. 1976. *Excavaciones en el Abrigo de Santa Marta, Chis. (1974).* New World Archaeological Foundation Papers, 14. Provo: Brigham Young University.

MacNeish, R., and F. Peterson. 1962. *The Santa Marta Rock Shelter, Ocozocoautla, Chiapas, Mexico.* New World Archaeological Foundation Papers, 14. Provo: Brigham Young University.

Joaquin García-Bárcena

S

SEE ALSO
Chiapas Interior Plateau

SEE ALSO
Maya Lowlands: South

Santa Rita Corozal (Corozal District, Belize)

This Maya site on Corozal Bay has had continuous occupation from 1200 B.C. to the present and is best known for its Late Postclassic remains (A.D. 1300–1530). However, Early Classic period (A.D. 300–500) artifacts from burials and caches indicate a site well connected to the rest of Mesoamerica through trade. Population figures are difficult to determine because the houses were primarily perishable constructions; however, excavations suggest that the number of people at the site ranged from approximately 150 at 1200 B.C. to almost 7,000 at A.D. 1500. It is likely that the site was once called Chetumal and was the capital of the historic Maya province of the same name. Mural painting found by Thomas Gann late in the nineteenth century has been described by some as being of the Mixteca-Puebla style and by others as indicative of an internationalized pan-Mesoamerican Postclassic art style. The murals are, however, similar in style and content to other modeled artifacts from the site. Late Postclassic artifacts include metal objects, arrow points, effigy incense burners, and notched and modeled sherds; however, most characteristic of Santa Rita Corozal at this time are modeled and painted pottery effigy figures found in ritual cache deposits. These caches may reflect rites undertaken during the *uayeb,* or five unlucky days before the New Year, which are described by Bishop Landa in his *Relacion* and depicted in the Maya codices.

FURTHER READINGS

Chase, D. Z. 1981. The Maya Postclassic at Santa Rita Corozal. *Archaeology* 34:25–33.

———. 1990. The Invisible Maya: Population History and Archaeology at Santa Rita Corozal. In T. P. Culbert and D. S. Rice (eds.), *Precolumbian Population History in the Maya Lowlands,* pp. 199–213. Santa Fe: School of American Research.

Chase, D. Z., and A. F. Chase. 1988. *A Postclassic Perspective: Excavations at the Maya Site of Santa Rita Corozal, Belize.* Pre-Columbian Art Research Institute, Monograph 4. San Francisco.

Gann, T. 1900. Mounds in Northern Honduras. In *Bureau of American Ethnology, Nineteenth Annual Report, 1897–1898,* part 2, pp. 661–92. Washington, D.C.

Diane Z. Chase

Sayil and Chac (Yucatán, Mexico)

The "place of ants" is an important archaeological zone about 6 kilometers south of Kabah along the "Puuc Route" highway, where intensive research on settlement patterns has been under way since 1982. It is known for its elaborate ninety-four-room, three-story North Palace executed in the Puuc core-veneer architectural style. The site's major occupation dates to the Terminal Classic "florescent" period (A.D. 800–1000). The Mirador complex, a group of stone buildings and linear stone features interpreted as a central marketplace, is linked to the North Palace (approximately 500 meters north) by an internal causeway that continues a kilometer south to the site's ball court and the South Palace complex.

Mapping and excavation have documented more than 2,500 architectural features covering an area of 4.5 square kilometers, including more than three hundred *chultuns* (underground water storage cisterns), the main water supply for the site. The population of the site is estimated at ten thousand, and soil studies have shown that settlement was conditioned in part by the disposition of good agricultural soils. Archaeological surface collection and soil testing indicate that Sayil had decentralized elite neighborhoods, a major pottery-making barrio, and intensive urban garden agriculture.

The survey work at Sayil uncovered a causeway leading to a site called Chac II (after the Maya rain god), 1.7 kilometers to the northwest. This discovery and the known major architectural remains suggest that Chac was not a satellite of Sayil but an independent community dating to the Late Classic period (A.D. 600–800) or earlier. The main Chac group consisted of a three-story palace building with twenty rooms, a "red hands" mural, and an adjacent plaza; a large central acropolis with two temple pyramids and several multiroom range structures arranged in three distinct plaza groups; and a 20-meter-tall pyramid with an attached courtyard group to the south. The total settlement area of Chac II is now estimated to be around 3 square kilometers.

FURTHER READINGS

Sabloff, J. A., and G. Tourtellot. 1991. *The Ancient Maya City of Sayil: The Mapping of a Puuc Region Center.* Middle American Research Institute, Tulane University, Publication 60. New Orleans.

S

Smyth, M. P., C. D. Dore, and N. P. Dunning. 1995. Interpreting Prehistoric Settlement Patterns: Lessons From the Maya Center of Sayil, Yucatán. *Journal of Field Archaeology* 22:321–347.

Smyth, M. P., J. Ligorred P., D. Ortegon Z., and P. Farrell. 1998. An Early Classic Center in the Puuc Region: New Data from Chac II, Yucatán, Mexico. *Ancient Mesoamerica* 9:233–257.

Tourtellot, G., and J. A. Sabloff. 1994. Puuc Development as Seen from Sayil. In H. J. Prem (ed.), *Hidden Among the Hills: Maya Archaeology of the Northwest Yucatán Peninsula,* pp. 71–92. Mockmuhl: von Flemming.

Michael Smyth

SEE ALSO
Maya Lowlands: North

Schroeder Site (Durango, Mexico)

Numerous masonry structures in the form of courtyards with associated house platforms, sunken courtyards, a small pyramid, and a ball court are scattered across two hills and an intervening saddle overlooking the Tunal River south of the city of Durango. Investigations at the site in the early 1950s by J. Charles Kelley determined that the primary occupation extended from the Ayala phase into the Calera phase (A.D. 875–1350). An earlier Loma San Gabriel occupation was also identified. Clearly a large habitation site with public architecture and space, this is not a ceremonial center. It lacks the architectural and organizational complexity seen in earlier Suchil branch Chalchihuites sites in western Zacatecas. Found with local Chalchihuites ceramics, some of which have basket handles, are intrusive West Coast types, spindle whorls, and copper, indicating the expansion of the Aztatlán mercantile system into the highlands. This is the most extensively investigated site to date in the state of Durango.

FURTHER READINGS

Kelley, J. C. 1971. Archaeology of the Northern Frontier: Zacatecas and Durango. In G. F. Ekholm and I. Bernal (eds.), *Handbook of Middle American Indians,* vol. 11, *Archaeology of Northern Mesoamerica,* pp. 768–804. Austin: University of Texas Press.

———. 1986. The Mobile Merchants of Molino. In F. J. Mathien and R. H. McGuire (eds.), *Ripples in the Chichimec Sea,* pp. 81–104. Carbondale and Edwardsville: Southern Illinois University Press.

Kelley, J. C., and H. D. Winters. 1960. A Revision of the Archaeological Sequence in Sinaloa, Mexico. *American Antiquity* 25:547–561.

Michael Foster

SEE ALSO
Northwestern Frontier

Scribes

Writing was a hallmark of Mesoamerican culture, and scribes accordingly occupied important and esteemed roles in most areas and time periods. According to the *Relación de Tezcoco,* the Aztec nobility routinely dabbled in the arts and crafts, including the painting of manuscripts. The earliest direct evidence of scribes comes from the Classic Maya, but they surely existed far earlier—composing, for example, the Formative period inscriptions from the Valley of Oaxaca and the Gulf Coast. The Maya called a scribe *ah ts'ib* ("one who writes or paints"), and the title appears in several ancient texts. One documented scribe who resided at Naranjo was the son of the local king and queen, but he was apparently not in the direct line to inherit political office. He, like many other scribes, was also called *its'at* ("artisan, wise man"). Scribes were significant figures in Maya mythology, equated with Hun Bats' and Hun Chuwen, stepbrothers of the Hero Twins celebrated in the *Popol Vuh.* A unique statue of a supernatural "monkey-man" scribe from Copán is shown holding a paintbrush and cut conch-shell ink pot, the two basic tools of writing and painting. The great Maya deity, Itsamnah, was called a "scribe" and a "diviner." Mexica gods also had scribal connections, most notably Xochipilli, the "Flower Prince." According to the divination scheme of the 260–day calendar, children born on the day "Flower" were "to be painters, metal-workers, weavers, sculptors, carvers—that is to say, (workers in) all the arts that imitate nature."

FURTHER READINGS

Coe, M. D. 1974. *The Maya Scribe and His World.* New York: Grolier Club.

———. 1977. Supernatural Patrons of Maya Scribes and Artists. In N. Hammond (ed.), *Social Process in Maya Prehistory,* pp. 327–347. London: Academic Press.

Reents-Budet, D. 1994. *Painting the Maya Universe: Royal Ceramics of the Classic Period.* Durham: Duke University Press.

Webster, D. L. (ed.). 1989. *The House of the Bacabs, Copán, Honduras.* Studies in Pre-Columbian Art

S

and Archaeology, 29. Washington, D.C.: Dumbarton Oaks.

David Stuart

SEE ALSO
Writing

Sculpture

Stone-carving appeared in Mesoamerica during the Early Formative period with the freestanding sculptures of the Olmecs on the southern Gulf Coast. Two-dimensional art and architectural decoration predominated in the Classic period in most areas; the finest sculptors were relief carvers in the central Maya Lowlands. Sculpture in the round reappeared during the Postclassic in areas dominated by the "Toltecs" in Central Mexico and the Yucatán Peninsula, the later Aztecs in Central Mexico, the Tarascans in Michoacán, and the Huastecs in the northern Gulf Coast.

Mesoamerican carvers generally used local materials, although the Olmecs, of necessity, quarried stone many kilometers from the intended setting, transporting large pieces by raft over water and by rollers and ropes over land. They, like the inhabitants of all highland areas, worked hard volcanic stones—basalt and andesite. The people of the northern Gulf Coast used sandstone, and the Lowland Maya, limestone. The latter also created architectural reliefs from lime stucco. For the Olmecs, the acquisition of stone from the distant Tuxtla range was motivated by the desire for permanent materials and the powers inherent in a material of volcanic derivation. For the Aztecs, the acquisition of stone was also an act of domination over the people in whose territory the quarry was found. That magical properties were inherent in the stone itself is revealed in Colonial descriptions of the Aztec Calendar Stone. Priests performed sacrifices and rituals throughout the raw stone's extraction and conveyance to the city of Tenochtitlán. The stone itself spoke along the way, predicting the overthrow of the empire. Crashing through a bridge, it sank into the water and returned to the quarry, still covered with sacrificial materials.

Sculptures were worked with blades, chisels, hammers, saws, and drills, tools made from reed, stone, wood, or bone; strings and abrasive sand were also used for sawing. Surfaces received a final polish with pebbles, reeds, animal skins, and powdered obsidian. Stone quarries have been identified in all areas, and a monumental stone-carving workshop adjacent to a "palace" was excavated in recent years at the Olmec site of San Lorenzo. Similar palace workshops must have existed at other political centers, but even in late pre-Conquest times the powerful Aztec emperor in Tenochtitlán had to call carvers from the four quarters of the capital and other cities for large projects.

Although many Mesoamerican sculptures were painted in polychrome over a base color of white or red, this important dimension remains only in rare traces. The vivifying purpose of color is indicated by the fact that in some late Formative Maya temples, paint was scraped off before the burial of architectural "masks."

Monumental ceramic figures were a major tradition in southern Veracruz during the Classic period; Central Mexicans later adopted this tradition. Portable sculptures of jade resembling the monumental versions were transported to distant areas by the Olmecs and their contemporaries; a type of Maya plaque featuring a seated ruler is also found in both original Maya works and copies as far from the area of origin as the Basin of Mexico. Although only a few wooden sculptures have been preserved, they must have been common in many cultures of Mesoamerica.

Gulf Coast

Around 1200 B.C. the Olmecs began producing finely carved, large-scale stone sculptures. Four major sites in the modern states of Veracruz and Tabasco have monumental sculptures: San Lorenzo, La Venta, Laguna de los Cerros, and Tres Zapotes. San Lorenzo and La Venta were centers of craft production in the Early and Middle Formative, respectively. Most sculptures of the earlier period are figures, colossal heads, or thrones of Tuxtla basalt. Figures range from entirely human, to were-jaguar (jaguar-human), to jaguar in form. Many sculptures were mutilated and buried; some mutilations indicate ritual "killing," but others were the result of recycling the stone of defunct images. Olmec sculptures are difficult to place in original contexts because they stood free from the earthen architecture. At San Lorenzo, colossal heads, thrones, and figures were arranged in ensembles to create ritual spaces. Early Formative–style basalt sculptures are found at La Venta as well as in the San Lorenzo area. These coexisted with Middle Formative sculptures in different styles and stones. Relief carving became important and a new form, the freestanding stela with depictions of human personages, was invented. A buried cache with a group of jade figurines backed by a half-circle of incised, stela-like "celts" may model an arrangement once formed by monumental sculptures on the surface.

Babies are common in monumental sculptures, but women are absent; male figures are depicted presenting babies, usually with were-jaguar features. The sculptures were unpainted, color perhaps having been concentrated in plaza floors of colored sands and clays, relaid periodically. Monumental Olmec sculptures are rare outside the southern Veracruz-Tabasco heartland. Important exceptions are narrative reliefs at Chalcatzingo in Morelos and architectural reliefs at Teopantecuanitlán in Guerrero.

In the Late Formative, after the demise of Olmec society, the production of narrative stelae and other reliefs, now with hieroglyphs, continued at Tres Zapotes and elsewhere in the heartland. In contrast to the Early Formative, the quality of carving varies greatly from object to object, with the finest bearing evidence of professional artisans.

During the Classic Period, stone stelae representing single standing figures with hieroglyphic texts, in compositions reminiscent of contemporary Classic Maya art, represent the rulers of Cerro de las Mesas. There, at nearby El Zapotal, and elsewhere in the river drainage north of the former Olmec domain, monumental figural sculptures were fashioned from modeled slabs of clay rather than stone. Artisans throughout Veracruz made finely carved and elaborately decorated stone replicas of ball game equipment—*yugos, hachas,* and *palmas*—some of which have been found in burials.

Monumental, public relief carvings are seen only at El Tajín, the great trading city situated on the northern Gulf Coast plain. Columns in a palace called the Building of the Columns depict conquests by the ruler 13 Rabbit and his cohorts and the ensuing sacrifice of prisoners. Panels on the South Ballcourt feature the sacrifice of a ballplayer and his journey to the underworld to ask the gods for pulque, a ritual intoxicant. Reliefs at the site are framed by the same distinctive scrollwork found on the ball game equipment. Just north of El Tajín, the Huastecs carved freestanding figures throughout the Postclassic; the finest of these, like the "Tamuin Youth," are incised to represent skin and textile patterns.

Central Mexico

Monumental sculptural art began here during the Middle Formative with the Olmec-style reliefs at the site of Chalcatzingo and on rocks on the hill above. In the Valley of Mexico to the north, Olmec-style carvings are small stone

yuguitos, a distinctive Central Mexican form. The Classic period was dominated by the great city of Teotihuacan, where mural paintings were far commoner than sculptures. Nevertheless, a few colossal deity figures have survived. More common are stone masks representing human faces of a generic type, which are visually uninteresting without the mummy or deity bundles that they originally decorated. Found frequently in the plazas of domestic compounds at the site, roughly carved braziers supported by figures of bent old men identified as "Old Fire God" seemingly remain from communal cults. One major public program was displayed in early times on the *tableros* of the Feathered Serpent Pyramid in the form of feathered serpents carved in relief but with fully sculpted serpent heads on the front of each body and a sculpted headdress near the tail. Given the pyramid's location adjacent to a palace in a large plaza complex at the center of the city, these serpent images must have had political implications; however, political matters are embedded in natural and mythical images in ways difficult for modern observers to comprehend.

After the fall of Teotihuacan sometime between A.D. 600 and 700, Central Mexico was dominated by smaller polities, two of which left sculptural traditions impressive enough to influence the later Aztecs. At Xochicalco, a fortified hilltop site in Morelos, a major relief-covered pyramid and other freestanding reliefs are noteworthy for their dense patterned carvings, Maya-looking personages, and hieroglyphic inscriptions. Although the impetus to inscribe stone monuments came from southeastern Mesoamerica, the calendar in use at Xochicalco was ancestral to that of the Aztecs. The site is contemporary with Cacaxtla in Tlaxcala, where Maya traits are visible in monumental murals.

In contrast to Xochicalco's reliefs are the freestanding sculptures at Tula in Hidalgo, a site that the Aztecs called Tollan. Figures dressed as warriors served as architectural supports and furniture; atlanean figures supported roofs and tables, and there is a new form, the so-called *chac mool,* a recumbent human figure serving as a platform. Animals are also common, but these are carnivorous animals probably linked metaphorically with warrior groups. Sculptures are found in multiples, carved exactly alike and often uninteresting in surface details. However, traces of paint indicate that polychromy provided an important dimension now lost. In reliefs, hundreds of warriors march in processions along benches, and single figures decorate prismatic columns and stelae. These distinctive

S

forms of the early Postclassic are also common in other areas of Mesoamerica. Some are roughly contemporary with Tula—for instance, *chac mools* and "Toltec" animal and figural types in the Tarascan area of Michoacán, on the Gulf Coast, and on the Yucatán Peninsula. Others are later survivals and revivals, like those made by the Aztecs and their predecessors in Central Mexico.

In late Postclassic times, the Basin of Mexico was the center of Aztec sculptural production, particularly in the great metropolis of Tenochtitlán, founded by the Mexica Aztecs in the mid-fourteenth century and now beneath modern Mexico City. Aztec sculptors were organized in guildlike groups living in distinct civic districts or working under royal patronage. The Aztecs represented their principal deities in stone and wood, but few remain. Images of conquered gods are more common, in monumental representations of the defeated goddess Coyolxauhqui and in smaller representations around the sides of cylindrical sacrificial stones.

Among major sculptures excavated from beneath Mexico City since 1790 are three great sacrificial stones, called "Stones of the Sun," and one whole and several partial representations of Coyolxauhqui. All of these were set on low platforms. The great Coyolxauhqui Stone, found in 1978, is unique in being still in situ in front of the Templo Mayor at the base of the southern half, which was dedicated to her enemy-brother, the Aztec war god Huitzilopochtli. The great sacrificial stones all feature circular platforms with a huge image of the sun; these include the Ex-Arzobispado Stone from the reign of Motecuhzoma I, the Tizoc Stone from that king's time, and the Calendar Stone from the reign of Motecuhzoma II. In addition, the Aztecs made archaizing copies of ancient works found at Tula, Teotihuacan, and Xochicalco. They also studied natural forms and carved monumental plant, animal, and shell sculptures, as well as images in stone of functional objects like drums.

Early Aztec sculpture (before 1450) was roughly carved, then stuccoed and painted (e.g., the *chac mool* still on the Phase II platform of the temple). The fine, imperial sculpture style seems to have developed in a few decades after 1450, probably at a time when Aztec society and the city itself were being reorganized by Motecuhzoma I. The early masterpiece of this style, the great Coyolxauhqui Stone, was created around 1470. Later developments after 1490 were highly detailed surfaces, as in the last great sacrificial stone of the city, the Calendar Stone of about 1512. The Aztecs did not impose their distinctive style on conquered peoples, but at the colony site at Castillo de Teayo in northern Veracruz a distinctive provincial figural style flourished.

Oaxaca

Stone-carving in Oaxaca is of equal time depth, but most examples are rough in carving and composition. Middle Formative art at the Zapotec mountaintop site of Monte Albán took the form of 320 reliefs known as "Danzantes" ("dancers"), which actually represent dead prisoners of war; these were once incorporated into the walls and stairs of Building L. From the late Formative, victories are represented in hieroglyphic form on Structure J, where defeated polities take the form of heads hanging upside-down from place glyphs. At the coeval site of Dainzú in the valley bottom, the theme of conquest and defeat is presented on slabs facing the major mound, depicting fallen ballplayers. In the Classic period, the Zapotecs at Monte Albán imitated the Maya in carving stelae with leaders standing on hill glyphs and sometimes on captives. They imitated contemporary Central Mexican art in processional reliefs of Teotihuacanos, presumably journeying from the great northern metropolis to their city. After the decline of Monte Albán around A.D. 700, slabs were carved at valley sites such as Etla, Noriega, and Zaachila. These show a new concern for genealogy, depicting either married couples seated beneath a sky motif or a single enthroned figure.

Maya Region

During the Late Formative, distinctive sculptural styles rose in both the central and southern Maya regions. In the central Maya Lowlands, colossal architectural masks personifying the sun and Venus flanked pyramid stairways. In the south at Izapa, a stela and altar cult developed, with reliefs representing mythic events, some now interpreted as the adventures of the hero twins known from the *Popol Vuh*. At sites like El Baúl, stelae feature historic personages accompanied by inscriptions and dates in the Maya long count calendar.

By the Early Classic period, immigrants from the south brought this type of dynastic commemoration to the central lowlands, where stelae with single figures, lengthy texts, and altars lined the plazas at such important sites as Tikal and Uaxactun. Carved stucco roof combs and wooden lintels decorate the shrines on pyramids, many of which served as royal tombs. These Classic period relics, unlike sculptures of other places and times, focus on historic personages and their deeds and describe these in lengthy hieroglyphic inscriptions.

By the Late Classic, Maya cities in the peripheral areas to the north, west, and south rose to prominence, and each city had a distinctive regional style. Sculptors at Copán in Honduras, for instance, varied the classic stela-altar complex by making both forms larger and more three-dimensional, and covering them with extremely dense detail. In the west, sites on the Usumacinta River are notable for their reliefs. At Piedras Negras, series of stelae show a ruler seated frontally in a niche surrounded by a cosmic band and reached by a ladder. At Yaxchilan, stone lintels depict the relatives and dynastic rituals of the rulers Shield Jaguar and Bird Jaguar; distinctive of this style are the depth of the cut-out background, the finely detailed textiles, the variety of activities, and the presence of women.

The most spectacular and distinctive style of the area developed at Palenque, beginning in the reign of Lord Pacal (A.D. 615–683). His stone sarcophagus lid beneath the Temple of the Inscriptions explicitly depicts a king's cosmic fate. Pacal descends into the mouth of the underworld on the head of the dying sun. On the sides of the sarcophagus, his ancestors grow from the ground like trees, and on the piers of the temple above, his heir, the baby Chan Bahlum, is presented by other ancestor depictions. Palenque is notable for the extensive use of stucco, especially in palace decorations, and for a rare individualization in portraiture.

In the Puuc and Río Bec areas of the northern lowlands, sculptural production took the form of geometric mosaics on façades. As elsewhere in Mesoamerica, sculpture in the round was reintroduced in the Postclassic at Chichén Itzá, the site of sculptural forms very similar to those at Tula in Central Mexico, but carved in soft limestone with a more refined sense of surface and detail.

FURTHER READINGS

Benson, E., and B. de la Fuente (eds.). 1996. *Olmec Art of Ancient Mexico.* Washington, D.C.: National Gallery of Art.

Easby, E. K., and J. Scott. 1970. *Before Cortés: Sculpture of Middle America.* New York: Metropolitan Museum of Art.

Marcus, J. 1980. Zapotec Writing. *Scientific American* 242(2):51–64.

Schele, L., and M. E. Miller. 1986. *The Blood of Kings: Dynasty and Ritual in Maya Art.* Fort Worth: Kimbell Art Museum.

Umberger, E. 1996. Art and Imperial Strategy in Tenochtitlan. In F. Berdan et al., *Aztec Imperial Strategies,* pp. 85–106. Washington, D.C.: Dumbarton Oaks.

———. 1996. Aztec Presence and Material Remains in the Outer Provinces. In F. Berdan et al., *Aztec Imperial Strategies,* pp. 151–179. Washington, D.C.: Dumbarton Oaks.

Wilkerson, S. J. K. 1984. In Search of the Mountain of Foam: Human Sacrifice in Eastern Mesoamerica. In E. Boone (ed.), *Ritual Human Sacrifice in Mesoamerica,* pp. 101–132. Washington, D.C.: Dumbarton Oaks.

Emily Umberger

SEE ALSO
Art

Seibal (Petén, Guatemala)

The Lowland Maya center of Seibal is situated on the western bank of the Río Pasión in the south central Petén. Seibal attracted the attention of early archaeologists because of its abundant stelae—fifty-five in all, twenty-one of which are carved. Monumental buildings at the site core are situated on several steep hills and cover an area of about a square kilometer. Three large groups of structures are connected by artificial causeways. Major architectural elements include ceremonial platforms, temples, ball courts, and palaces, all built from the local limestone. Many of the smaller groups of structures interspersed among the major architecture represent modest residences. Many archaeologists visited, mapped, and briefly tested Seibal before 1964, when Harvard University initiated an intensive five-year project under Gordon Willey that provided most of the detailed information about the site.

The earliest occupation detected at Seibal dates to the Middle Formative period, Real phase (c. 900–600 B.C.). The local population increased steadily through the Protoclassic Cantutse phase (A.D. 1–270), when the site's first known ceremonial building was constructed. Like many other centers, Seibal experienced a decline in population size and construction activity during the Early Classic period (A.D. 270–650), and it may even have been largely abandoned between A.D. 500 and 650. Seibal recovered between A.D. 650 and 770, although during the latter part of this period it became entangled in wars with other polities of the region. In A.D. 735, the Seibal ruler Yich'ak Balam was captured by the king of nearby Dos Pilas, and Seibal seems to have been politically dominated by Dos Pilas for the next fifty years. Seibal eventually reached its

S

peak during the Terminal Classic Bayal phase (A.D. 830–930), a time when many other Classic centers were in decline. During Bayal times, "foreign" ceramic influences such as Fine Orange wares appeared, and some iconographers detect foreign elements on carved monuments as well, leading them to postulate an invasion of non-Petén Maya people to account for these new elements. Others, however, see no firm evidence for such a military intrusion. For whatever reasons, a process of abandonment occurred after A.D. 930.

FURTHER READINGS

Houston, S. 1993. *Hieroglyphs and History at Dos Pilas.* Austin: University of Texas Press.

Tourtellot, G. 1988. *Excavations at Seibal, Dept. of Peten, Guatemala,* Memoirs of the Peabody Museum, 14.3. Cambridge, Mass.: Harvard University.

Willey, G., (ed.). 1982. *Excavations at Seibal.* Vol. 15, nos. 1–2. Memoirs of the Peabody Museum, 15. 1–2. Cambridge, Mass.: Harvard University.

Willey, G., A. L. Smith, G. Tourtellot, and I. Graham. 1975. *Excavations at Seibal: No. 1, Introduction.* Memoirs of the Peabody Museum, 13. 1. Cambridge, Mass.: Harvard University.

David L. Webster

SEE ALSO

Maya Lowlands: South

Settlement Patterns and Settlement Systems

The concept of "settlement patterns," especially as the term has been used in archaeology, pertains to the way peoples dispose themselves over the landscape on which they live. It refers to dwellings, to their arrangement, and to the nature and disposition of other buildings pertaining to community life; and such a definition can be expanded to include all intentional modifications of the landscape—agricultural canals or terraces, roadways or highways, and extensive walls or other features relating to defense—as well as unintentional modifications brought about by human occupation, such as long-term depletion of forests and soil erosion. A settlement pattern is, by this definition, essentially a descriptive, static record of settlement and other cultural features of the landscape.

In contrast, the related term "settlement systems" refers to the way settlements function to promote the economic, social, and political welfare of the community. It has been formally defined as "the sites in a particular region during a particular period of time, and their social, economic, and political interrelations" (Webster, Evans, and Sanders 1993:20, 358). As such, a settlement system is the dynamic aspect of a settlement pattern.

The functioning of a settlement system may be perceived from a synchronic perspective, as the above definition's "during a particular period of time" implies, or from a diachronic or chronological perspective. That is, the patterning of the settlement in any given locale, region, or area may have changed through time, and these changes can be important in posing questions for the archaeologist as to how and why these changes occurred. As an example, a hypothetical "Period 1" settlement may have been that of a single small village which exploited nearby lands for simple farming. A succeeding "Period 2" settlement in the same locality may show a pattern of several villages which exploited more extensive lands through intensive farming techniques. This pattern, in turn, may be succeeded by one of a hypothetical "Period 3" in which the intensive cultivation features have fallen into disuse and the number of villages has been reduced. What were the factors that led to these changes? Were they brought about by over-cropping and soil exhaustion? Or were there other causes?

To turn to socio-political functions of a settlement system, a diachronic perspective of a region may reveal a Period 1, in which there were a few scattered villages throughout a region; a Period 2, in which there were more and larger communities, with convincing archaeological evidence of warlike competition among them; and a Period 3, in which it seems apparent that one large community has risen to dominate all the rest in the region. Do we have here an example of chiefdom or state formation? Other kinds of archaeological evidence must be examined in conjunction with these data to answer such a question, but the framework of settlement system changes through time establishes a firm framework to address such questions.

Mesoamerica: A General View

The basic unit or element of Mesoamerican settlement patterns and settlement systems is usually the village community (see Flannery 1976), or the isolated rural farmstead. As settlements, these villages are marked by houses for domestic living. Although the styles of the houses and the materials with which they were constructed vary considerably from region to region within Mesoamerica, these are generally relatively small structures, suitable for nuclear families or small extended families, with clearly evident facilities for cooking, storage, and other daily liv-

S

ing functions. It is assumed—and there is considerable archaeological evidence to support this—that such simple villages were the first settled, sedentary communities in pre-Columbian Mesoamerica. The best evidence for them comes from regions in which subsistence farming was established by about 2000 B.C. There is also some evidence from these same regions, as well as from others in Mesoamerica, that a degree of sedentism had been established even earlier on subsistence bases that relied more heavily on shellfish, fish, game, and uncultivated plants. However, by at least 1500 B.C., in southern and central Mesoamerica the simple sedentary village, supported by an agricultural economy, was the dominant settlement system in many regions.

After about 1500 B.C. Mesoamerican settlement became more complex. The basic village unit was incorporated into systems that included public buildings or constructions erected by community labor. These were mound structures of earth and stone and served as bases for temples or palace buildings. Such temples or palaces pertained to religious and political functions of the society; they were the centers where religious and political leaders were housed and where ceremonies, ritual, or other public events, involving to some degree all members of the society, were carried out under the direction of the leaders. The dwelling units for most of the population were grouped on the outskirts of these politico-religious centers. The form of these dwelling settlements varied from those where the houses of the commoner populations were closely concentrated to those in which the houses were more dispersed.

In Mesoamerica, this concentration or dispersal of dwelling residences correlates with the character of the natural terrain and with soil fertility. In regions where soils are exceptionally fertile and well suited to farming, or where intensive agricultural practices such as irrigation, raised field construction, or terracing were practical, dwelling units tended to be closely grouped around a center, producing an urban settlement effect. In contrast, in regions where arable soils are thinner or more easily exhausted, or where intensification techniques could not be employed, dwelling units were more widely dispersed and the politico-religious centers do not have the same urban appearance.

This basic dichotomy in Mesoamerican settlement patterns was noted more than fifty years ago by G. C. Vaillant. As examples, the relatively open regions of the uplands of Central Mexico supported, at various times in the pre-Columbian past, such densely settled urban cen-

ters as Teotihuacan, Tula, and Tenochtitlan. Here there were deep, fertile soils, and raised field, or *chinampa,* cultivation was possible in many places in and around the upland lakes. This contrasts with the Maya Lowlands of southern Mexico and adjacent Central America, where the landscape was heavily forested and where, in many places, the soils were thin and the rotation of cultivated fields, with long fallow periods between cropping, was a necessity. In this terrain, the dwelling settlements of farmers were widely dispersed through the forests rather than being clustered around the politico-religious centers.

Having established these two basic types of Mesoamerican settlement, we must note that there is a continuum between the two, and that these gradations reflect both specific regional natural environments and settlement changes that went on in individual regions through time. In general, upland terrain favored concentrated urban settlement, whereas that of the Lowlands favored a more dispersed pattern. However, there are degrees within and exceptions to this generalization, as the regional summaries in this volume indicate.

FURTHER READINGS
Flannery, K. V. (ed.). 1976. *The Early Mesoamerican Village.* New York: Academic Press.
Vaillant, G. C. 1940. Patterns in Middle American Archaeology. In *The Maya and Their Neighbors,* pp. 295–305. New York: Appleton-Century.
Webster, D. L., S. T. Evans and W. T. Sanders. 1993. *Out of the Past: An Introduction to Archaeology.* Mountain View: Mayfield.

Gordon R. Willey

Shaft Tombs

This mortuary tradition is associated with the Middle to Late Formative and Early Classic period cultures of West Mexico (c. 500 B.C.–A.D. 300). Although concentrated in the highlands of western Jalisco, Nayarit, and Colima, forming the so-called tomb arc, tombs also occur in nearby areas. Until recently, information was restricted to data from looted tombs; however, unlooted tombs have now been excavated at El Grillo, north of Guadalajara, and more recently at Huitzilapa in western Jalisco, and in the municipality of Puerto Vallarta.

Four general styles of tombs are known: subsurface rectangular vaults, bell-shaped vaults, vertical shafts with a single burial chamber, and vertical shafts with multiple burial chambers. Tombs with as many as five chambers

S

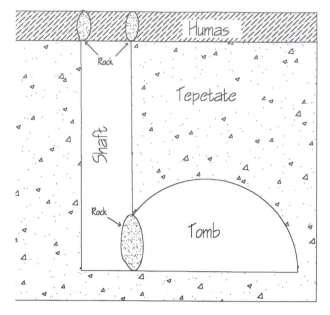

Cross-section of a shaft tomb. Illustration courtesy of the author.

have been reported, and some tomb shafts go directly into the burial vaults. Stone slabs or ceramic jars act as seals between shafts and chambers. Offerings are sometimes placed in the shafts. Tombs also vary in size and detail. Some chambers are only large enough to hold a single body, while others measure 5 by 6 meters and 2.5 meters high. A tomb at El Arenal in the Magdalena Lake Basin, west of Guadalajara, has a shaft 17 meters deep. Some tombs clearly represent a single burial event, while others appear to have been used over a long period of time, perhaps as much as two hundred years.

The origin of the shaft tomb tradition is unclear. El Opeño (Michoacán) provides possible antecedents of shaft tombs. These tombs are stylistically different, and earlier (1500 B.C.), than those to the west. Pottery from these tombs has affinities with both Tlatilco and the Capacha material from coastal Colima. Shaft tombs are also found in northwestern Argentina, Colombia, Peru, Ecuador, and along the west coast of Central America. Colombian tombs are similar to West Mexican tombs and may date as early as 500 B.C. Northwestern South America and West Mexico also share several other traits, but the nature and extent of pre-Columbian contact between the two regions is greatly debated.

Because of the lack of systematically collected data, the role of shaft tombs in West Mexican society is not well understood. Weigand, working in the Etzatlán Basin in western Jalisco, has suggested that the variation seen in shaft tomb architecture and contents reflects a multitiered society; he finds support for this argument in the association of shaft tombs with the circular architectural complexes of his postulated Teuchitlan tradition. More elaborate tombs are suggested to be associated with more complex architectural elements. However, many circular architectural complexes found outside the Teuchitlan core area lack shaft tombs. Mountjoy, working near Puerto Vallarta, has found no significant evidence to suggest an association between social status and the use of shaft tombs.

Another aspect of the tombs is their rich artifact assemblages. Most notable are the large, hollow figurines depicting humans, animals, and plants. Village scenes and house models are common in tombs from Nayarit, while Colima produces highly polished figurines, mostly redware. Bowls, jars, shell trumpets, perishable items, and food were also placed in the tombs.

FURTHER READINGS

Kan, M., C. Meighan, and H. B. Nicholson. 1989. *Sculpture of Ancient West Mexico.* Albuquerque: University of New Mexico Press.

Oliveros, J. A. 1971. Nuevas exploraciones en El Opeño, Michoacán. In B. B. Bell (ed.), *The Archaeology of West Mexico,* pp. 182–201. Ajijic: Sociedad de Estudios Avanzados del Occidente de México.

Ramos de la Vega, J., and M. L. Lopez Mestas Camberos. 1996. Datos preliminares sobre el descubrimiento de una tumba de tiro en el sitio de Huitzilapa, Jalisco. *Ancient Mesoamerica* 7:121–134.

Weigand, P. C. 1985. Evidence for Complex Societies during the Western Mesoamerican Classic Period. In M. S. Foster and P. C. Weigand (eds.), *The Archaeology of West and Northwest Mesoamerica,* pp. 47–92. Boulder: Westview Press.

Michael Foster

SEE ALSO
West Mexico

Sierra, La (Santa Barbara, Honduras)

La Sierra lies at 100 meters above sea level on the western bank of the Río Chamelecon, surrounded by fertile alluvial soils. Scattered, generally deeply buried remains from the Middle (800–400 B.C.) and Late Formative (400 B.C.–

A.D. 200) suggest a sparse early population residing in isolated homesteads. Early Classic (A.D. 200–600) remains are more prevalent and include platform clusters that served as nuclei for later structure groups.

In the Late Classic (A.D. 600–950), La Sierra was the capital of a small state; most of the 468 visible platforms, covering about 0.7 square kilometer, date to this period. The site core contains a ball court and its associated terraced hillside, elite residences, and temples among its thirty-seven structures. Surrounding the core are dense agglomerations of structures that served as elite and nonelite residences, ritual/sacred spaces, and workshops for obsidian, marine shell, textiles, and a wide variety of ceramic vessels, stamps, incensarios, figurines, and ocarinas. A 6-meter-diameter kiln north of the site core is encircled by staging areas for various steps in ceramic manufacture, and borrow pits for clay. Late Classic rulers apparently maintained power through local control over craft production, imports, exports, and some aspects of ritual life (ball game, ritual caching).

In the Terminal Classic (A.D. 950–1100), the site core was abandoned, but house construction and modification and craft production continued north and south of the epicenter. The last kiln firing dates to the Early Postclassic (A.D. 1100–1300), when most structures in all parts of the site were abandoned; there is no evidence of Late Postclassic (A.D. 1300–1500) occupation, and only faint suggestions of use. During the Classic, La Sierra was connected to surrounding areas (the middle Ulúa drainage, northern coastal plain, Mayan sites of Copán and Quirigua, and highland Guatemala) through exchanges involving marine shell, ceramics, and obsidian, the last derived from Honduran and Guatemalan sources.

Edward Schortman and Patricia Urban

Silex

"Silex" is a term used, especially in the older literature, to refer to a variety of cryptocrystalline rocks, especially chert (or "flint"). Luedtke (1992:5) defines "chert" as including "all sedimetary rocks composed primarily of microcrystalline quartz, including flint, chalcedony, agate, jasper, hornstone, novaculaite and several varieties of semiprecious gems." In archaeological reports from Mexico, the term *pedernal* is widely used to refer to chert or flint. There is much confusion among Mesoamerican archaeologists on the identification of siliceous raw materials; most common is the misidentification of chalcedony as chert. Chalcedony is generally fibrous rather than cryptocrystalline, has numerous flaws, and tends toward white, brown, gray, and tan colors. There are distinct deposits of chalcedony in northernmost Belize, in the Petén, and in the southern Yucatán; various Mexican sources (see below) also note chalcedony outside the Maya area.

Well-defined sources of chert are few, though the literature refers to occurrences of various types of this material in many parts of Mexico and Central America. The best-documented chert outcrop is the "chert-bearing zone" of northern Belize. This chert is fine grained and often banded, and with colors including tan, gray, and brown. It is easily distinguished visually from chalcedonies in the region and from coarser-grained cherts that occur in western Belize and the northern Petén. Neutron activation analysis has distinguished at least two distinct groups of chert, and further studies are ongoing. There are other distinctive outcrops of chert in the upper Belize River Valley and in the southern Puuc Hills of the Yucatán, and in the Becan area of Campeche, where chert nodules are exposed in solution pockets in the local limestone matrix. Cherts in Belize sometimes appear to be black, leading to misidentifications of "black chert." However, neutron activation studies have demonstrated that this is a result of chemical weathering, usually involving the dissolution of manganese within the chert. In addition, cherts in the region often weather to a white or yellow chalky texture through the patination process.

The archaeological literature in Mexico and Central America is uneven in its description of chert artifacts, and little is provided on the sources of cherts. Since obsidian is so widely used in much of the region, it is not surprising that so little attention has been given to siliceous materials.

For the Maya area, in addition to information on the Belize chert sources, we also have a very detailed raw materials analysis by Clark for the site of La Libertad, Chiapas. Clark's treatment of the "microcrystalline chipped stone industries" should serve as a model for other Mesoamerican projects. He describes and maps the stone sources, discusses manufacturing techniques, and present the results of experiments. There are also good descriptions of cherts in the central Petén Lakes region, where Aldenderfer characterizes the mineral as coming from outcrops in the Mancanche Basin and at Lake Yaxha, along with "float" chert in small nodules in the basins or *bajos* in the region. These cherts are of variable quality, mostly coarse grained, and are characterized by colors that include white, red to pink, and yellow; they

S

were used to produce flakes for casual use, some unifaces (perhaps scrapers), moderate to small bifaces, projectile points, and perforators. Aldenderfer also notes the occurrence of chalcedony in his study area. In the Tikal zone, chert is abundant in forms varying from small nodules up to boulders 60 cm across; it is of medium to coarse grain. These local materials were used to make flake tools, bifaces, points, and eccentrics; fine-grained stemmed blades were probably imports. At Río Azul in the northern Petén, cherts are coarse grained, generally gray to brown in color, and come in nodular form, selected from stream beds; at site BA20, biface workshops are present. Interestingly, much of the Río Azul chert appears to have been heat treated, probably to improve its chipping quality. At Copán, utilitarian tools were made largely of chalcedony, but also some chert from nodules procured from the Copán River. In the Petexbatun area, a "vast chert source and workshop" is reported by Demarest (1990:9) from a site near Sayaxche. This source is thought to have provided the raw material for many of the chert tools found in the area.

Finely flaked anthropomorphic eccentrics found in Copán caches are chipped from a high-quality brown chert of nonlocal origin; its source is unknown. In the San Agustín Aguacastlan area of Guatemala, Gary R. Walters reports chert workshops near jade workshops; he feels that the "chert" is actually a fine-grained brown chalcedony. At the Yerba Buena site in the Central Chiapas Highlands, chert was used to make projectile points. Clark and Bryant report that local cherts were processed at nearby sources and brought into the site as large chunks and spalls (much as the Lacandón do today); some nodules were also carried in, particularly yellow chert. In the Tabasco lowlands, Maya sites in the Río San Mártir region reflect the use of chert, rhyolite, jasper, chalcedony, and quartz. Some lithic workshops are reported for the Late Classic; bifaces and eccentrics were being made.

In the Valley of Oaxaca, Parry has described eight chert sources, with the cherts highly variable in color and texture; chalcedonies also occur. During the Formative era, these resources were used to make edge-modified flakes (the flakes derived from both bipolar and flake cores) and projectile points. In the Nochixtlan Valley of central Oaxaca, Spores reports a large chert quarry at Yucunudahui; we have seen formal end scrapers from this region but have no other data on the nature of the chert or other tools made from it. Elsewhere in the Valley of Oaxaca, Williams and Heizer have described the sources and geologic contexts of silicified materials used in making utilitarian tools; these include "silicified tuffs" and "chalcedonic flint." Scraper-planes from the sites of Mitla and Yagul are made of silicified tuff, rhyolitic ignimbrite, silicified ignimbrite, and andesite.

Another important study from the Valley of Oaxaca is the work of Whalen, which details the geologic sources of materials used in the chipped stone industries at Guila Naquitz. For example, he provides a summary of sources within 10, 25, and 44–55 kilometers (procurement of stone from the latter sources probably involved a two-day trip). The closest materials (within 10 kilometers) were ignimbrites; more distant (within 25 kilometers) were Cretaceous limestones with "mediocre" brownish-white cherts. At the greatest distance, in the Etla arm of the Valley, are better-quality cherts and chalcedonies that were extensively utilized. The Matadamas source is the most important, with white cherts and chalcedonies, often with blue, gray, and brown hues; the preceramic "Pedernales" points from Guila Naquitz are made of this material.

At the Cuevo de los Grifos in Chiapas, preceramic lithics are made of chert, jasper, and quartz (Santamaría and Garcia Bárcenas). Chert outcrops are found in the Valley where the cave is located, while the jasper comes from a source about 30 kilometers distant. Preceramic and Mesoamerican lithics in the Tehuacán Valley are reported by MacNeish et al. The raw material is described as "flint" and the sources as "pebbles or nodules." Brunet's geologic study of the area provides more detail on local cherts, quartz sandstone, basalt, silicified limestone, and quartz.

At Chalcatzingo, Central Mexico, Grove describes a small hill with a source of red chert; numerous cores were found there, and the material is distributed at other sites in the Valley. Some chert artifacts at Chalcatzingo are from this source, but others, of different color, are from unknown outcrops.

In the Teotihuacan Valley chert sources are essentially absent, and Iceland suggests import of cherts to the site of Teotihuacan from Puebla (where he notes many chert sources) or the Tula region. In the Merchant's Barrio at Teotihucan, Iceland reports fine-grained chocolate-brown chert bifaces, and fine-grained banded brown and gray cherts; these appear to have come from the Maya area.

Late Postclassic use of chert in Central Mexico is often seen in large to small bipointed bifaces. The Aztecs used ceremonial bipointed knives of brown chert and banded gray-white chalcedony at the Templo Mayor. These were often decorated to represent faces in profile and are sometimes found inserted into the mouth or nasal cavity of skulls. We are unaware of any studies on the source(s) of the raw materials used for making these artifacts, though Matos Moctezuma (1988:97) refers to them as "locally available."

FURTHER READINGS

Aldenderfer, M. 1991. The Structure of Late Classic Lithic Assemblages in the Central Petén Lakes Region, Guatemala. In T. R. Hester and H. J. Shafer (eds.), *Maya Stone Tools,* pp. 119–142. Madison: Prehistory Press.

Clark, J. E. 1988. *The Lithic Artifacts of La Libertad, Chiapas, Mexico: An Economic Perspective.* Papers of the New World Archaeological Foundation, 52. Provo: Brigham Young University.

Hester, T. R., and H. J. Shafer. 1984. Exploitation of Chert Resources by the Ancient Maya of Northern Belize, Central America. *World Archaeology* 16:157–173.

Luedtke, B. E. 1991. *An Archaeologist's Guide to Chert and Flint.* Archaeological Research Tools, 7. Los Angeles: Institute of Archaeology, University of California.

Matos Moctezuma, E. 1988. *The Great Temple of the Aztecs.* London: Thames and Hudson.

Moholy-Nagy, H. 1991. The Flaked Chert Industry of Tikal, Guatemala. In T. R. Hester and H. J. Shafer (eds.), *Maya Stone Tools,* pp. 189–203. Madison: Prehistory Press.

Parry, W. J. 1987. *Chipped Stone Tools in Formative Oaxaca, Mexico: Their Procurement, Production and Use.* Memoirs of the Museum of Anthropology, University of Michigan, 20. Ann Arbor.

Rovner, I. 1981. Maya Lowlands Chert: Variations in Local Industries and Regional Exchange Systems. *Revista Mexicana de Estudios Antropologicos* 27(2):167–176.

Spores, R. 1972. *An Archaeological Settlement Survey of the Nochixtlan Valley, Oaxaca.* Publications in Anthropology, l. Nashville: Vanderbilt University.

Tobey, M. H. 1986. *Trace Element Investigations of Maya Chert from Belize.* Papers of the Colha Project, 1. San Antonio: Center for Archaeological Research, University of Texas.

Whalen, M. E. 1986. Sources of the Guila Naquitz Chipped Stone. In K. V. Flannery (ed.), *Guila Naquitz. Archaic Foraging and Early Agriculture in Oaxaca, Mexico,* pp. 141–146. Orlando: Academic Press.

Williams, H., and R. F. Heizer. 1965. Geological Notes on the Ruins of Mitla and Other Oaxacan Sites, Mexico. In *Sources of Stone Used in Prehistoric Mesoamerican Sites,* pp. 41–54. Contributions of the University of California Archaeological Research Facility, 1. Berkeley.

Wright, A. C., et al. 1959. *Land Use in British Honduras.* Colonial Research Publication 24. London: HMSO.

Thomas R. Hester and Harry J. Shafer

SEE ALSO

Chipped Stone Tool Production and Products; Colha

Siteia (Southern Atlantic Autonomous Region, Nicaragua)

This shell midden site on a high bank on the southern side of the Pearl Lagoon is one of several sites comprising the Siteia complex (c. 200 B.C.–A.D. 400). Monochrome, polychrome, and incised ceramics, ground stone celts; utilized expedient chert flakes, legless *metate* fragments, *manos,* and a bone projectile point comprised the assemblage from this complex. This is the earliest known complex on the Atlantic Coast. Stirrup-spout forms were found, and the polychrome ceramics are from a distinctive Atlantic Coast tradition and are unrelated to the Pacific Coast polychrome traditions. Magnus believes that the Siteia complex was from a different tradition than the subsequent complexes of the region.

FURTHER READINGS

Magnus, R. 1976. The Costa Atlantica de Nicaragua. *Vínculos* 2(1):67–74.

Frederick W. Lange

SEE ALSO

Intermediate Area: Overview

Skeletal Analysis

The study of the hard tissue remains of humans—bone and teeth, recovered archaeologically—is often the best way to study directly what life was like in a particular past society and culture. Preserved on the skeleton is information about age at death, sex, diet, health, activity patterns, the risks of accidents and warfare, and biological relationships. Human osteologists (biological anthropologists specializing in skeletal analysis) have developed a variety of techniques to reconstruct personal information about a

S

skeleton. In ancient Mexico and Central America, skeletal remains are often encountered in archaeological excavation, but their state of preservation ranges from very good in the arid highlands to poor in the humid lowlands. Perhaps because of variable preservation, modern skeletal analyses stressing a population-based approach have only recently been applied to these skeletal populations.

Though often the only recoverable remains, human bone is not a very efficient source of information on health and mortality compared to rarely preserved soft tissue. Because of its importance to the support and protection of an organism, bone is involved in disease and stress primarily when the physiological resources of soft tissues are overwhelmed by an insult. Thus, many diseases and nutritional deficiencies are not preserved, and only those that are both severe and chronic, or long lasting, will be visible. The skeleton then presents an incomplete and biased record of health problems encountered by an individual during life, and often the cause of death is too acute and sudden to be recorded in the bone. In spite of these drawbacks, analyses that focus on the incidence of various skeletal pathologies and demographic characteristics in a population give insight into the ages at which individuals tended to die, diseases suffered, risk of accident or injury and death in warfare, the amount and kind of physical labor performed, and the presence of nutritional deficiencies. This information can be combined with other archaeological data to evaluate the quality of life in a past society.

In addition to observing actual bone, researchers can also employ bone in chemical and DNA analyses. DNA analysis is a very new technique that is still being pioneered on archaeological bone, but it promises to revolutionize the study of biological relationships. Chemical analysis is an established technique for studying diet because bone incorporates various chemical substances present in food an individual ate.

The most successful chemical analyses for ancient Mexico and Central America involve stable isotopes of carbon and nitrogen. Atmospheric ^{13}C is incorporated into plants differentially according to the carbon pathway used in photosynthesis. C_3 plants (the majority) discriminate against ^{13}C, while C_4 plants (tropical grasses such as maize) incorporate it more efficiently. Thus, by measuring the isotope, it is possible to determine when maize became an important staple and to calculate its percentage in the diet. Nitrogen isotopes are used to indicate the source of dietary protein—that is, terrestrial plants and animals versus marine—and the importance of legumes or beans. Both isotopes should be measured to characterize differences in diet through time and among different ages and genders.

FURTHER READINGS

Price, T. D. (ed.). 1989. *The Chemistry of Prehistoric Human Bone.* Oxford: SAR Advanced Seminar Series.

Steele, D. G., and C. Bramblett. 1990. *The Anatomy and Biology of the Human Skeleton.* College Station: Texas A&M University Press.

White, T. 1991. Human Osteology. Orlando: Academic Press.

Rebecca Storey

SEE ALSO

Cosmetic Alterations of the Face and Body; Demographic Trends; Diet and Nutrition

Smiling Face Figurines

Smiling Face figurines *(sonrientes),* hallmark of the Classic Period in south central Veracruz, are characterized by squinting, puffy cheeks, and sometimes by protruding tongues and caps. The expressions have often been mistaken for the European expression of laughter or mirth, but they probably portray inebriated participants in a regional *pulque* (agave beer) cult. They are found throughout much of the lowland zone between the Chiconquiaco Mountains of central Veracruz and the Tuxtla Mountains.

Ranging in size from approximately 15 to 40 cm in height, these clay figurines most often depict nude, youthful males with upraised hands and occasionally a pectoral band. Decoration, if present at all, tends to be on the forehead, bands, or skirts. Paint is rare, although some have tattoolike designs in negative paint. The heads, which normally are more anatomically detailed than the bodies, frequently illustrate fronto-occipital cranial deformation. A very few have articulated arms or legs, permitting multiple postures. Except in the earliest examples, the faces are mold-made and, sometimes, retouched before firing. While many of the finest have lifelike qualities, suggesting the portrayal of individuals, the latest examples are frequently mass-produced and crude.

Although these figurines have occasionally been assigned to the Totonacs, neither their geographic distribution nor their dating coincides with a verifiable Totonac presence. Present in large numbers in pre-Columbian collections, most are derived from looted sites in the rain shadow region of south central Veracruz. They have been found in excavated, salvage, or reconnaissance contexts at sites such as Cerro de las Mesas, Remojadas, Los Cerros, Dicha Tuerta, Nopiloa, Chachalacas, Isla de Sacrificios, and El Zapotal. Although they have been encountered in fill and ritual dumps, they are most frequently found as burial offerings. Some are functional whistles, suggesting their use in participatory rituals prior to interment. Produced in enormous quantities and decreasing quality over time, they represent one of the most popular cults in an area of many.

Other major figurine complexes reflecting specific cults include Nopiloa, depicting robed ritualists with outstretched arms, found primarily in dedicatory offering caches; Larios, generally large, hollow warriors, often helmeted with asphalt accouterments; Xipe, small, solid flayed victims, or their displayed skins on celebrants, frequently on sacrificial platforms; and Mayanoid, small, hollow, fine-paste elaborately dressed women, possibly impersonating a moon goddess. Each figurine type has distinctive characteristics of depiction as well as a separate, if overlapping, distribution during the Classic period.

These figures appear to increase in size with time but rarely exceed 60 cm. The largest examples should not be confused with the massive monumental clay statuary of the terminal Classic and Epiclassic, which were utilized primarily as construction or rite dedicatory offerings. The quality of craftsmanship of the best of the larger figures, however, clearly foreshadows that of the modeled and composite mold-made monumental clay statuary. There are many more significant figurine complexes to be defined in south central Veracruz, one of Mesoamerica's areas of greatest diversity in figurines.

FURTHER READINGS

Medellín Zenil, A. 1960. *Ceramicas del Totonacapan.* Jalapa: Universidad Veracruzana.

Medellín Zenil, A., and F. A. Peterson. 1954. A Smiling Head Complex from Central Veracruz, Mexico. *American Antiquity* 20:162–169.

Medellín Zenil, A., O. Paz, and F. Beverido. 1962. *La Magia de la Risa.* Mexico City.

Wilkerson, S. J. K. 1988. Cultural Time and Space in Ancient Veracruz. In M. M. Goldstein (ed.), *Ceremonial Sculpture of Ancient Veracruz,* pp. 6–17. New York: Hillwood Art Gallery, Long Island University.

S. Jeffrey K. Wilkerson

SEE ALSO

Figurines, Terracotta; Gulf Lowlands

Snaketown (Arizona, United States)

The largest and best-known Hohokam site in southern Arizona, Snaketown's initial occupation began about A.D. 450 and continued until about 1150. At its peak, between 750 and 1150, Snaketown covered an area of more than 250 hectares. At the center of the site is a large plaza, surrounded by sixty platform mounds ranging in height from 1 to 4 meters. The site contains two oval ball courts, the largest of which is 100 meters long. Surrounding this ceremonial-administrative core are hundreds of shallow pit houses. The inhabitants of the site practiced cremation burial, and these cremations have yielded some of the finest artifacts found for the Hohokam tradition. Among them were several dozen items of West Mexican origin, including copper bells, pseudo-cloisonné mirror backs, and macaws. Emil Haury directed the two major excavations at the site, the first in 1934–1935 and the second in 1964–1965. The first discovered ball courts, Mesoamerican items, and Mesoamerican iconography, sparking a major reevaluation of Mesoamerican–Southwestern relations. Before Snaketown's discovery, archaeologists had limited the Southwest to ancient Pueblo sites, and thought that Southwestern cultural developments, such as corn agriculture and ceramics, were independent of and even prior to similar developments in Mesoamerica. The Snaketown excavations helped to demonstrate that the Southwest culture area was greater than the Pueblos, and that it had been influenced by Mesoamerica in important ways.

FURTHER READINGS

Gladwin, H. S., E. W. Haury, E. B. Sayles, and N. Gladwin. 1965 [1938]. *Excavations at Snaketown: Material Culture.* Tucson: University of Arizona Press.

Haury, E. W. 1976. *The Hohokam: Desert Farmers and Craftsmen.* Tucson: University of Arizona Press.

Wilcox, D. R., T. R. McGuire, and C. Sternberg. 1981. *Snaketown Revisited.* Arizona State Museum Archaeological Series, 155. Tucson.

Randall H. McGuire

SEE ALSO

Northern Arid Zone

Soconusco–South Pacific Coast and Piedmont Region

The Pacific coastal plain and adjacent piedmont of the state of Chiapas, Mexico, and Guatemala are known as

S

the setting for the early emergence and development of ranked societies, and for cacao production in late prehistoric and colonial times. The region lies southwest of the Maya area. Its natives were akin to and interacted with the Maya, but they generally spoke languages of the Mixe-Zoquean family.

The region consists of a flat, relatively narrow plain flanked on its inland side by a steep mountain chain at the northern end and by a piedmont in the south. The Pacific Ocean forms the western boundary. The coastline generally is straight and unbroken by embayments or promontories. This means that the coast experiences the full onslaught of adverse marine conditions, including hurricanes. However, a barrier beach exists along most of the coast, behind which are protected waterways that were used for travel in ancient times.

The plain is formed of Quaternary alluvium on which deep, rich soils have developed, expecially on the older, landward surfaces. It is traversed by rivers that rush seaward from the mountains in relatively straight, unentrenched courses. In premodern times it was hazardous to cross the rivers during the rainy season. Rainfall varies greatly across the plain, ranging between 1,000 and 2,000 mm annually at the northwestern end (the Tonalá District) and between 2,000 and 3,000 mm in the southeast (the Soconusco and Suchitepeques districts). Significantly, rain occurs seasonally between the months of April and October, producing a pronounced dry season during the other months.

The natural biota of the region is tropical but varies depending upon the amount of moisture available. A xeriphytic flora is predominant in the Tonalá District; to the south, tropical evergreen and deciduous forests predominated, but now little of the forest remains because of its removal for modern agricultural and cattle-raising activities. A wide variety of tropical animals once inhabited the region. Land animals included deer, jaguar, peccary, and many smaller species; migratory waterfowl winter over in the coastal wetlands, and parrots and macaws are year-round residents. Fish are diverse and were once plentiful in the rivers, estuaries, and sheltered waters of the wetlands. Among the ancient domesticates of the region were corn, beans, gourds, avocados, and dogs, with other species probable but not yet documented archaeologically.

Settlement History

No Paleoindian remains have been found, probably because of poor recovery conditions rather than because no one lived in the area. Caves are scarce in the piedmont and early sites on the plain are deeply buried, which means that early sites with low archaeological profiles are difficult to find.

The earliest occupation known for the region is that of the Chantuto people, whose archeological site signatures consist of six high-profile shell mounds in the coastal wetlands and one inland site. This occupation in the Late Archaic period spanned the time between 4000 and 1600 B.C. Voorhies's interpretation of the evidence is that the Chantuto people were complex hunter-gatherers who had developed a semisedentary way of life. The shell mound sites (Islona Chantuto, Campón, Tlacuachero, Zapotillo, El Chorro, and Cerro de las Conchas) are places where clams, fish, and probably shrimp were procured in great quantities and sun-dried in order to deliver them to consuming populations at inland locations. One such inland location, Vuelta Limón, is situated upstream from the Chantuto site. It may be a base camp where some horticultural activities were carried on, as evidenced by heavy tools that could have been used to clear the forest. A concentration of trash is all that has been excavated.

The Chantuto people were replaced in the Early Formative period by the sedentary Mokaya, the first producers of pottery. Coe initially identified this occupation at the small coastal site of La Victoria. Later, at nearby Salinas La Blanca, Coe and Flannery expanded knowledge of the temporal, spatial, and ecological attributes of these people. The Mokaya occupied rich agricultural lands close to wetlands teeming with aquatic resources. The precise nature of their subsistence base is still being investigated, but it combined fish and game with early domesticates such as corn and beans. It is possible that the rich wild resource base of the area permitted larger and more sedentary populations in this region during the Early Formative than could exist other regions in Mesoamerica. The early Mokaya people made pottery jars simulating the forms of antecedent gourd containers; these vessels were used principally for storing liquids, rather than for cooking, and may be the material remains of ancient feasts that were hosted by emerging elites who were jockeying for power. At Paso de la Amada, leaders built large residences and possibly sponsored ritual ball games that were played in a large, clay ball court.

In the Middle Formative period, the Pacific coastal peoples were in contact with the great Olmec society based along the Gulf Coast, across the Isthmus of Tehuantepec. Archaeological indicators of contact consist of Olmec-style figurines, practices of head deformation, design motifs on pottery, portable sculptures of stone, and bas-reliefs on large boulders. Archaeologists debate the best way to interpret this evidence because it is not yet clear where these traits originated and in which direction the influences flowed.

Tzutzuculi was one major center of the Middle Formative period. It overlooks the Río Zanatenco and is now about 12 kilometers from the sea, within the modern town of Tonalá. The site is at least 35 hectares in extent and had a minimum of twenty-five platform mounds arranged around plazas. These mounds are earthen with cobble facings, a regionally typical construction technique because easily workable stone for masonry is very scarce. Carved monuments with Olmec motifs are present, as are ceramics with Olmec-associated designs.

La Blanca and Abaj Takalik are two other regional centers that rose to prominence during the Middle Formative in the region near the Mexican-Guatemalan border. Survey evidence indicates a spurt in regional population and the development of a multitiered settlement hierarchy. Both sites were large and had public architecture, characteristics that are viewed as hallmarks of a new developmental stage in community life. La Blanca is situated on the coastal plain near the Río Naranjo. It covers approximately 100 hectares and has at least forty-three residential platforms, which do not exhibit a formal layout. The largest mound, now destroyed, was 25 meters high, making it among the most impressive Mesoamerican constructions of its time. Sculpture with Olmec motifs was found at the site.

Abaj Takalik was situated on the upper reaches of the Río Tilapa, close to the foothills and approximately 40 kilometers from La Blanca. It is known principally for its sculpture; its size during the Middle Formative period has not been determined, but it is likely that public constructions were built during this time.

In Late Formative times the site of Izapa, near the Mexican-Guatemalan border, was the dominant social and political center. It almost certainly had been a regional center since the Middle Formative, but more is known about its Late Formative appearance. The archaeological site has eighty large platform mounds formally arranged around courtyards. More than 250 carved stone monuments with artistic resemblances to both earlier Olmec and later Maya art styles were carved and erected at the site.

Other primary Late Formative sites to the northwest of Izapa include La Perseverancia, Tonalá, and Horcones. La Perseverancia is situated on the plain near the foothills,

about 9 kilometers southeast of Tonalá. Said to be unrivaled for its time in Chiapas for the bulk and extent of its earthen mounds, it must have been the primary center of the northern end of the region during the Late Formative period. Oddly, no sculpture was found at the site during its exploratory and unpublished excavations.

The ancient site of Tonalá (or Iglesia Vieja) is on a hilltop, 13 kilometers northwest of modern Tonalá. Boasting masonry architecture and sculptured monuments, it was mapped and recorded by Ferdon during two field seasons in the 1930s and 1940s but has never been carefully excavated. Drucker collected ceramics there during his 1947 survey of the Chiapas coast; Pfeiffer dated these to the Late Formative through Late Classic. It is not certain when the construction activity was carried out, but Ferdon thought that a major occupation occurred midway through the Classic Period. Horcones appears to have had a similar occupational history, but it is situated in the lower foothills. It, too, has cut stone masonry, stone-paved causeways, and plaza complexes. A 3-meter-high stela of Tlaloc from the site is now in the Tonalá plaza, about 20 kilometers to the northwest. This site has not been investigated in detail.

Late Formative period sites to the southeast of Izapa include Sin Cabezas, El Balsamo, and Monte Alto. Sin Cabezas, in the Tiquisate region, covers 327 hectares and has nearly ninety surviving earthen platforms. These constructions are not as formally arranged as those at Izapa and many fewer stone monuments are present, so Sin Cabezas was apparently not as powerful a socio-political center as Izapa. Nevertheless, it was the primary center of a three-tiered regional settlement hierarchy during the Late Formative period.

El Bálsamo is situated on the interior coastal plain near the foothills, a location generally favored for the large Formative period centers. Shook and Hatch sketched sixteen mounds at the site, some of which delimited a long, narrow plaza. The major building activity occurred during the Late Formative period, but ceramics indicate a Middle Formative occupation as well. An artificial pond had been built on one mound, and some small stone sculpture was found at the site and its environs.

Only 10 kilometers east of El Bálsamo is Monte Alto, a contemporary site occupied from Middle Formative through Early Classic times. The approximately fifty mounds are not particularly impressive, but the site merits attention because of the anthropomorphic carvings on boulders, known as "pot-bellies." The pot-bellies are rotund, full-figure sculptures, and together with two

S

carvings of heads they may depict conquest victims similar to the Monte Albán "Danzantes."

Dominant centers during the Classic period include Abaj Takalik and Izapa, discussed above, Balberta, and Santa Lucia Cotzumalhuapa. Balberta is located in the Escuintla region of the Guatemalan coast. It must have been a regional center in Terminal Formative times, when explosive growth occurred here, as in other parts of the southern coast. The main complex consists of a low platform supporting twenty-four platform mounds and surrounded by a protective wall and ditch. This complex was built in Early Classic times, when earlier constructions were either destroyed or modified. There is no evidence of Teotihuacan cultural traits at the site, as might be expected given the prevalence of incense burners looted from the Escuintla area that bear strong resemblance to incense burners from Teotihuacan.

Three clusters of monumental architecture and carved stone monuments are present in the vicinity of Santa Lucia Cotzumalhuapa (Bilbao, El Baúl, El Castillo), also situated in the Escuintla area of the south coast. It is probable that occupational debris is continuous between the three centers and that they are best considered parts of a single archaeological site. Analysis of the stone monuments suggests that the three centers were built by three successive rulers, all of whom ruled during the Late Classic Period. However, the region was occupied for a long time, and Bilbao at least was inhabited and perhaps experienced massive construction during the Late Formative period as well.

Smaller Classic period sites were found across the Proyecto Soconusco survey area. One of these, Río Arriba, is near the inland edge of the coastal wetlands. Investigations revealed that it was a pottery-producing village in Classic times. Its products were elegant, thin-walled pots fired at high temperatures and destined for serving or display purposes rather than for ordinary cooking or storage.

During Late Classic times, one area within the region began mass-producing a distinctive pottery with a vitrified slip which eventually was traded widely throughout Mesoamerica. This popular Plumbate pottery, which was made in distinctly different styles throughout its history, was probably manufactured at various production centers on the western coastal plain of Guatemala. Production locations have not been found, but the chemical composition of Plumbate pottery matches that of clays from this area.

Knowledge about human lifeways during the Early Postclassic period is virtually absent, probably because no

archaeological investigations have focused on this time period and archaeologists cannot reliably recognize its occupations. Tohil Plumbate was manufactured and traded widely, but major occupation centers have not been identified.

Late Postclassic sites are not abundant, but written documents indicate that at the time of the Spanish conquest the region was heavily populated. It is possible that Postclassic period peoples invested much less energy in building large constructions than their ancestors did, and for this reason their archaeological signatures are less visible.

Acapetahua is a Late Postclassic site that was conquered by the Aztecs when they took over the Soconusco, perhaps in A.D. 1486. The Late Postclassic component at the site is centered on a long, narrow ridge that was artificially widened and leveled at that time or earlier. A series of courtyards delimited by platform mounds is strung along the ridgetop, and there are a pair of temple mounds and a ball court in this part of the site.

Many of the cooking and serving vessels used during the Late Postclassic period are strikingly similar to those made by traditional peoples in modern times. People also used large jars, presumably to store foodstuffs, and water-carrying vessels very similar in shape to those used today. Pottery colanders were used to rinse rehydrated corn kernels, and tortillas were baked on flat griddles, or *comales*. Grater bowls with scored interior bottoms were used with stone pestles to grind spices used in making sauces. Serving dishes with tall tripodal effigy supports and polychrome decoration were used for the presentation of ritual foods, as in contemporary Aztec society. Incense for ceremonial activities was burned in long-handled pans that resemble ladles.

Acapetahua was the head town of a relatively small, independent polity that was one of a series of such polities located along the Soconusco coast. After being conquered by the Aztecs, the former rulers of the independent polities paid tribute to the Aztec emperors and became integrated into the Aztec state bureaucracy. This arrangement lasted only a few decades, until the arrival of the Spaniards. The Quiché of highland Guatemala reached the southern coast of western Guatemala and similarly extracted tribute for a brief time before the Spanish conquest.

The first impact of the arrival of Europeans and Africans on the region was indirect but catastrophic. Epidemics swept through the area, resulting in great loss of life on the part of the natives, who had no immunity to foreign diseases; by 1570 the population of the Soconusco may have been 5 to 10 percent of its size at contact. Spaniards did not immediately attempt to settle the region and thus did not establish *encomiendas,* haciendas, or plantations. In the northwestern sector, cattle-ranching became established, and some indigo production for dye was carried out, primarily by non-Indian populations. In the southeast, aboriginal landowners were allowed to keep their cacao orchards but were taxed by the Spaniards even more heavily than they had been by the Aztecs. Since cacao was the primary export crop during early colonial times, this arrangement provided local Indian growers with some degree of economic independence.

The fate of one small town, Ocelocalco, occupied from the late sixteenth to the late eighteenth century, has been investigated through archival documents and archaeologically. This small, unimportant town was founded by 1572 and was elevated to the provincial *cabecera* (head town) in 1611. By 1680 it was displaced as the provincial capital and fell into decline until final abandonment in 1767. During its time as an administrative center, Ocelocalco reached its largest size and its residents were using goods imported from Central Mexico, Chiapas, Guatemala, Panama, Spain, and China. This wealth was generated by trade in cacao that linked this small town with distant consumers.

FURTHER READINGS

Coe, M. D. 1961. *La Victoria: An Early Site on the Pacific Coast of Guatemala.* Papers of the Peabody Museum, 53. Cambridge: Harvard University.

Coe, M. D., and K. V. Flannery. 1967. *Early Cultures and Human Ecology in South Coastal Guatemala.* Smithsonian Contributions to Anthropology, 3. Washington, D.C.: Smithsonian Institution.

Ferdon, E. N. 1953. *Tonalá, Mexico: An Archaeological Survey.* Monographs of the Schoool of American Research, 16. Santa Fe.

Love, M. W. 1990. La Blanca y el Preclásico Medio en la Costa del Pacífico. *Arqueología* 3:67–76.

Lowe, G. W., T. A. Lee, Jr., and E. Martínez. 1976. *Izapa: An Introduction to the Ruins and Monuments.* Papers of the New World Archaeological Foundation, 31. Provo: Brigham Young University.

McDonald, A. J. 1983. *Tzutzuculi: A Middle-Preclasssic Site on the Pacific Coast of Chiapas, Mexico.* Papers of the New World Archaeological Foundation, 47. Provo: Brigham Young University.

Parsons, L. A. 1967. *Bilbao, Guatemala: An Archaeological Study of the Pacific Coast Cotzumalhuapa Region.* Volume 1. Publications in Anthropology, 11. Milwaukee Public Museum.

Stark, B. L., L. Heller, F. W. Nelson, R. Bishop, D. M. Pearsall, D. S. Whitley, and H. Wells. 1985. El Bálsamo Residential Investigations: A Pilot Project and Research Issues. *American Anthropologist* 87:100–111.

Voorhies, B. (ed.). 1989. *Ancient Trade and Tribute: Economies of the Soconusco Region of Mesoamerica.* Salt Lake City: University of Utah Press.

Barbara Voorhies

Soul and Spirit Companion

The term "spirit companion" refers to an indigenous Mesoamerican concept difficult for outsiders to grasp: the notion that something not physically attached to one's body can be considered an intimate part of the self. The idea of a spirit companion—often referred to as a kind of soul—deals, in part, with the question of why people are different from one another. As Mendelson reports being told by Baltasar Ajcot of Santiago Atitlán, the spirit companion *(aljebal)* "is that which separates a man from other men." Similarly, the spirit companions of the people in the Maya communities of Chiapas rank them in a hierarchy of power.

One usually acquires a spirit companion at the moment of one's birth, since birth not only determines membership in particular kin and ethnic groups but also provides individual selves with their destinies. In Mesoamerica, destiny should be seen not as an outside force that makes one's personal character irrelevant to one's fortunes or misfortunes, but rather as a part of one's being, encompassing aptitudes, personality, and even physical characteristics. Defined by the movement of the sun, and in some areas even spoken of as a kind of bodily essence morphologically and semantically linked to the word for "sun," destiny provides individual selves with the spatio-temporal orientation necessary for social life. Thus, those who were born in the five days that lie outside the normal solar and ritual year (Nahuatl, *neomini;* Maya, *uayeb;* the period Motolinía calls *"sin año"* or "outside time") would not, according to Molina, have a destiny, and they would turn out to be ambiguous and incomplete beings. (Lincoln says that among the Ixil, boys born at this time would "be like girls," while Father Varea tells us in his early seventeenth-century Cakchiquel dictionary that these individuals would not grow, always remaining small.) Other creatures born at the same moment a human is born will have a similar spatio-temporal orientation, and such pairs are spoken

S

of as having a similar destiny, and in some cases a single "soul." Although they are of different orders, the shared destiny endows them with common physical traits and behavioral characteristics; they may even share a consciousness. The last usually occurs during nighttime dreams, which are said to be the experiences of one's companions. Most spirit companions are wild animals, which is consistent with the notion that one sees the world through one's companion's eyes during a dream, since wild animals are most active at night.

The animal one shares a destiny with is always marked in some way, indicating its status as something apart from other members of its species. It may walk on its hind legs, have human hands, or otherwise demonstrate its shared destiny with a human self. Likewise, humans sometimes display their shared identity with their spirit companions: men with hairy chests have jaguars as their companions, according to the Tzotzil and Tzeltal; those with hunched backs have turtles as their companions among the Huave. Spirit companions are not always animals. Pitt-Rivers reports that those with a twisting forelock are felt to have a whirlwind as a spirit companion.

In discussions by leading figures both in and outside the field of Mesoamerican studies, the spirit companion has been viewed by Daniel Brinton as the center of a nigromantic cult intent on overthrowing Spanish rule, by Marcel Mauss as an example of mana, by Toro as a personal totem, and by Elsie Clews Parsons as a bush soul. Foster attempts to distinguish between the spirit companion (which he called the *tonal*) and the transforming witch, or *nagual*. A continuing problem in discussions of this sort has been terminology: Foster's choice of Nahuatl words has created difficulties, since these may be used in non-Nahuatl-speaking areas in ways that do not reflect the meaning he has tried to give them, and a consistent etic vocabulary has not emerged. Thus, Dennis Tedlock tells us that among Quiché speakers, *nagual* refers to the spiritual essence of character of a person, animal, plant, stone, or place; and when used as a metonym for shamanic power, it refers to the ability to make these essences visible or audible by means of ritual. In any event, López Austin argues in favor of Foster's distinction, noting that among the Nahuas, the *ihiyotl,* an *entidad anímica* located in the liver, could be projected by gods, leaders, and witches into the body of an animal. As Musgrave-Portilla points out however, it is hard to reconcile this idea with accounts—such as one in the *Leyenda de Los Soles*—in which an individual and his or her companion are so independent that they can have conversations with each other. Moreover, in many indigenous languages, such as Mixtec, the distinction between "spirit companion" and "transforming witch" is one of degree, not kind. In other words, the spirit companion of a witch is a specific aspect of the more general phenomenon of the spirit companion. Thus, the transforming witch is a *tenuvi* or *ñanuvi* (male or female *nuvi*), while everyone possesses a *kiti nuvi* (animal *nuvi*). What distinguished the *tenuvi* is a special baptism they undergo, which imbues them with the power of rain and makes them into lightning bolts and animals associated with the sky. In other areas, a witch is simply a person with a spirit companion associated with birth on a particular day.

The problem may be that in many places the generic and specific levels are not readily distinguished. Ethnographic work has related the spirit companion to systems of social control, noting that illness is often attributed to divine retribution or vengeance worked against one's animal companion. Partly for this reason, the identity of one's companion is a matter of some concern. In the past, and today in places where the ancient Mesoamerican calendar survives, as among the Chontal (as reported by Carrasco), the identity of one's spirit companion could be determined by calendar specialists. In a variation on this, zodiac signs associated with the day of one's birth indicate the identity of one's spirit companion. Among the Amuzgo, Mixtec, Mixe, Popoluca, Zapotec, and Zoque, the spoor of an animal passing near a newborn child shows the identity of its spirit companion. The spirit companion can also be examined in light of the kinds of explanations it provides: like Azande witchcraft beliefs, it allows one to account for the unexpected (such as a sudden death) in a way that goes beyond simply calling it chance.

Evidence for the belief in spirit companions exists for nearly every period of Mesoamerican history. Houston and Stuart have recently deciphered a glyph meaning *wayel,* or "spirit companion," in Classic Maya writing. Chroniclers throughout the Colonial period and modern ethnographers too numerous to mention also document its existence. However, there is no evidence for spirit companions among the otherwise conservative Kekchi (as reported by Wilson), the northern Totonac (as reported by Ichon), and Nahua groups in Veracruz (as reported by Sandstrom). It is also clear that in the highly stratified indigenous societies of the pre-Conquest period, the spirit companion complex had a different configuration than in the relatively unstratified modern peasant communities studied by ethnographers.

FURTHER READINGS

Foster, G. 1944. Nagualism in Mexico and Guatemala. *Acta Americana* 2:85–103.

Holland, W. 1963. *Medicina Maya en los altos de Chiapas.* Mexico City: Instituto Nacional Indigenista.

López Austin, A. 1988. *The Human Body and Ideology: Concepts of the Ancient Nahuas.* 2 vols. T. and B. Ortiz de Montellano (trans.). Salt Lake City: University of Utah Press.

Musgrave-Portilla, L. M. 1982. The Nahualli or Transforming Wizard in Pre- and Postconquest Mesoamerica. *Journal of Latin American Lore* 8:3–62.

Saler, B. 1964. Nagual, Witch and Sorcerer in a Quiche Village. *Ethnology* 3:305–328.

John Monaghan

South America, Interaction of Mesoamerica with

Contact between Mesoamerican and South American cultures seems probable, given that the two continents are physically connected and that they share many cultigens, technologies, and social practices. Many of these perceived similarities are, however, very general: agriculture, ceramics, cannibalism, paved roads, wearing sandals, and so on can be shown to be due either to the common origin of all Native Americans or to independent invention. Specific evidence of contact after initial settlement is rare, but this has only encouraged the development of theories concerning direct contact between the two continents and what it might have meant in pre-Columbian culture history. If there was such contact, then there are three possible routes: overland on the Central American isthmus, by water along the eastern coast of Central America, and by coast and open sea along the western coasts of the continents.

The overland route is demonstrably the earliest (beginning perhaps in the early Formative period) and almost certainly involved only down-the-line trade until very late in prehistory. Lower Central America was culturally closely allied to northern and central Colombia, where there were specialist manufactures, organized markets, and professional traders. The extent of these traders' movements to the northwest is unknown. Demonstrated movements include those of useful cultigens such as manioc, tomatoes, and pineapples from south to north, and of maize (Mesoamerican varieties to northern Colombia in late prehistory); of recycled Maya belt celts to Costa Rica in the Classic; and of some Central American ornaments and ceramics.

Down-the-line exchange also accounts for the occasional Mesoamerican appearance of a "South American" motif, such as a double-headed serpent in Mixteca-Puebla ceramics or a *Strombus* monster on a West Mexican vessel. The only southern artifacts found in Mesoamerica—mainly Costa Rican or Colombian gold pieces found at Copán, Altun Há, and Chichén Itzá—are small and portable. Mesoamerican imports in Central America are rare and restricted largely to Honduras (a few Plumbate vessels reportedly have been found in Panama). No materials of Mesoamerican manufacture or Mesoamerican technologies have yet been discovered in South America.

The sea route along the eastern coast of Central America became important in the Late Classic with the increasing use of large dugout canoes for transporting goods along the protected shoreline of the Gulf Coast, the Yucatán Peninsula, and Honduras. Ethnohistoric accounts of colonies of possible Mexican traders, such as the Sigua of northern Panama, have not been documented archaeologically, though numerous port sites, including Naco (Honduras) and a series of sites along the coast of Belize, Yucatán, and the Gulf have been investigated in southern Mesoamerica. Colombia and lower Central America represent a continuous, single interaction sphere, but there is no indication of any Mesoamerican involvement.

The arrival of metallurgical techniques in Mesoamerica in the Late Classic to Early Postclassic may have been due either to increased contact with lower Central America or to changes in value systems seen in Postclassic cultures in general. Colombian forms of metallurgical tools and the forms of metal ornaments themselves suggest that there may have been some movement of technicians, but the specific origin of these technicians is unknown. It is evident that coastwise trade was important to the southern and eastern Mesoamerican cultures of the Postclassic, and Columbus's encounter with one of the large traders' canoes tells us that ordinary goods such as salt, ceramics, and textiles, as well as metal and pearls, formed part of this trade.

The Pacific route, which must involve both coastwise sailing and deep-sea navigation, has been the subject of much attention from archaeologists on both continents. In the sixteenth century, trade was known along the Ecuadorian coast south to far northern Peru, borne in balsa-wood rafts with cotton sails. There is no evidence for rafts before about A.D. 1100, when highly stylized depictions of *Spondylus* shell fishing from a raft appear in northern Peruvian art. Earlier art styles (e.g., Moche,

S

c. 200 B.C.–A.D. 500) show *Spondylus* being moved on llamas. In the Colonial period, the area served by raft traders expanded to the south, but there is no evidence that it ever went north of the Colombia-Ecuador border region. Ecuadorian and Colombian peoples had dugout canoes as well; the Peruvians were largely limited to reed and sealskin floats, reed boats, and net-and-gourd rafts, none of which was equal to a long voyage on the open sea.

The Ecuador trade was fueled by the Peruvians' growing need for *Spondylus* shell for rituals, something that can be demonstrated archaeologically and historically. It has been suggested that depletion of the Ecuadorian *Spondylus* beds resulted, and thus the rafters were forced to go north to the Guerrero coast to find trade goods. Similarly, it has been suggested that the appearance of iridescent painting on ceramics of the Guatemalan Ocos (c. A.D. 1500) culture is an Ecuadorian import; that the West Mexican metallurgical tradition came from Ecuador or Peru (or both); and that various vessel shapes, shirts, wrap skirts, and geometric textile patterns seen in West Mexican cultures, and found in their shaft and chamber tombs, all came via rafts from the south.

The predisposition to look for long sea voyages is fostered by the emphasis in American education on the deeds of the Vikings and the romance of the fifteenth- and sixteenth-century European voyages of exploration. Deep-sea travel is, however, rare and late in most of the world, and the majority of coastal cultures never developed the craft or the navigational skills to go far to sea. Any direct contact between Guatemala or West Mexico and western South America would have to involve such travel because the currents and winds necessitate sailing southwest to the Galapagos before one can get back to the coast of Ecuador and Peru. There is no pre-Columbian presence on the Galapagos; sherds claimed to be pre-Columbian are in fact Colonial.

Moreover, there is no evidence that Ecuadorian raft traders ever left sight of land willingly (the farthest offshore they are known to have ventured is La Plata Island, 20 kilometers from the mainland and visible from shore). The region in which rafts are known to have moved freely is also protected by offshore islands. North of Tumaco, the coast of Colombia and of Central America is open and dangerous, with strong currents and surf and unpredictable storms. Although there were many eastern coastal ports in Mesoamerica and Central America in the sixteenth century, there was only one port on the western coast: a small salt-making facility 20 kilometers north of the Guatemala–El Salvador border. Dugout canoes are known from Pacific Coast cultures at different times and places, and some short-haul local trade is evident. Rodrigo de Albornoz, writing to the king of Spain in 1525, refers to just such a local tradition (by then no more) in Colima, where sometime in the past there had been regular barter with people who came in canoes from "some islands to the south." There is no reason to identify these islands as Ecuador.

On the basis of current archaeological and historical evidence, it appears that contact between Mesoamerica and South America was indirect and involved peoples of many ethnicities and polities as well as various modes of transport. There is no need to postulate long sea voyages in a situation of known shorter voyages coupled with long-established overland routes in both areas. Regular, direct contact should leave some trace in the archaeological record. However, it is unlikely that such widespread traits as shaft and chamber tombs, stirrup bottles, wrap skirts, male shirts (not worn in Ecuador until Inca times), supplementary warp weaving, and simple geometric textile patterns were the result of any direct contact. As for the *Spondylus* depletion model, we lack any evidence concerning the size and productivity of either Ecuadorian or Mesoamerican *Spondylus* beds.

There remains, of course, the seemingly separate appearance of metallurgy in West Mexico, which cannot be linked definitely with any single time or culture in South America. Independent invention is still as unpopular as it was in 1929, when Erland Nordenskiold wrote "The American Indian as Inventor"; but it is possible that West Mexican metallurgy and Guatemalan iridescent painting are independent inventions. This is at least as likely as the possibility that a non-deep-sea sailing group suddenly took their craft north into the unknown, through perilous waters, to introduce a technology (metal-working) that had been in the hands of specialists (not traders) for centuries in their homeland, or that the same people, two thousand years earlier, had done the same to introduce a single ceramic decoration technique, iridescent painting, to a couple of fishing villages in Guatemala.

It is possible that the expansionist policies of both Mesoamerican and South American polities in the sixteenth century would eventually have led to an opening up of direct contact. However, the arrival of Europeans rapidly destroyed indigenous systems of exchange and, through slaving and consolidation of ethnic groups, led to the first significant direct contact between Mesoamerica and South America.

FURTHER READINGS

Bray, W. 1977. Maya Metalwork and Its External Connections. In N. Hammond (ed.), *Social Process in Maya Prehistory*, pp. 365–403. New York: Academic Press.

Bruhns, K. O. 1994. *Ancient South America*. Cambridge: Cambridge University Press.

Estrada, J. 1990. *La balsa en la historia de la navegación ecuatoriana*. Guayaquil: Instituto de Historia Maritima, Armada del Ecuador.

Hosler, D. 1988. Ancient West Mexican Metallurgy: South and Central American Origins and West Mexican Transformations. *American Anthropologist* 90:832–855.

Kelley, J. C., and C. L. Riley (eds.). 1969. *Precolumbian Contact within Nuclear America*. Mesoamerican Studies, Record Series, 69M4A. Carbondale: Southern Illinois University Museum.

Lothrop, S. K. 1942. The Sigua: Southernmost Aztec Outpost. *Proceedings of the 8th American Scientific Congress* 2:109–116.

Marcos, J. G., and P. Norton (eds.). 1982. *Primer simposio de correlaciones antropológicas andino-mesoamericana*. Guayaquil: Escuela Superior Politecna del Litoral (ESPOL).

Nordenskiold, E. 1929. The American Indian as Inventor. *Journal of the Royal Anthropological Institute of Great Britain and Ireland* 59:273–309.

Pollard, H. P. 1993. Merchant Colonies, Semi-Mesoamericans, and the Study of Cultural Contact: A Comment on Anawalt. *Latin American Antiquity* 4:383–385.

Karen Olsen Bruhns

SEE ALSO

Interregional Interactions

Southeast Mesoamerica

Southeast Mesoamerica comprises a broad transect stretching from the Caribbean coast of Honduras south to El Salvador's Pacific littoral. This area encompasses a poorly known mosaic of prehistoric cultures occupying an equally varied set of environments for at least of two millennia. Though the region was long ignored by archaeologists, work conducted here over the past three decades has begun to uncover the complex interplay of ecological, political, and cultural processes that combined in the creation of the region's rich prehistoric past.

This review concentrates on the varied patterns of demographic, cultural, and political change reconstructed for prehistoric Southeast Mesoamerica. Discussion of political shifts focuses on centralization processes, the concentration of power in the hands of a single faction. Political centralization is inferred from several kinds of evidence: as the appearance of monumental constructions (platforms 1.5 meters or higher) reflects privileged labor control; differential burial treatment mirrors status distinctions; and the complexity of site hierarchies expresses intrasocietal ranking of decision-makers. These features are emphasized because sufficient data are available to make comparative statements possible within and beyond Southeast Mesoamerica.

The region's environments contributed to its cultural diversity. A crucial ecological component for early populations is variation in agricultural potential, a factor strongly conditioned by the nature of soils, slope angles, and the amounts, seasonality, and reliability of rainfall. The northern coast, characterized by high year-round temperatures and precipitation, originally supported dense rain forests giving way to mangrove swamps near the shore. The Sula Plain and lower Aguan Valley comprise major southward extensions of the coastal zone. The Ulúa, Chamelecon, and Aguan rivers also seasonally replenish northern coastal soils with alluvium, making these some of the richest agricultural environments in Central America.

Farther south, in Honduras, the middle and upper reaches of these same rivers and their major tributaries cut fissures through steep escarpments that rise to over 2,000 meters above sea level. Temperatures here are somewhat cooler than on the coast, and rainfall is generally lighter, divided into clearer wet (May through November) and dry (December through April) seasons. Natural upland vegetation consists of deciduous and pine forests, the latter especially prevalent at higher elevations. Soils are generally poorer than those in the Sula Plain and lower Aguan valleys, being formed from heavily weathered parent materials on relatively steep slopes that are susceptible to erosion when cultivated. Underlying these generalizations, however, is a complex environmental mosaic. Timing and amounts of precipitation vary significantly over relatively short distances where high mountains form barriers to moisture-bearing clouds. Fertile alluvium deposited along major rivers and their affluents contrasts starkly with the thin, easily eroded sediments that mantle the adjoining slopes. The extent of relatively level terrain suitable for cultivation also varies consider-

S

Southeast Mesoamerica. Map design by Mapping Specialists Limited, Madison, Wisconsin.

ably, from the relatively large Comayagua Valley, covering 550 square kilometers, to small pockets of river terrace encompassing a few hundred square meters. In general, relatively large valleys tend to be found along the middle Chamelecon and the north–south fault linking Honduras's northern and southern coasts. More restricted areas of flat land lie within the middle drainages of the Ulúa and two of its principal tributaries, the Sulaco and Humuya. The heavily dissected nature of Honduras's rugged interior not only affected the zone's agricultural potential but also constrained contact among neighbor-

ing areas to a few passes cut by major streams. Covering 308 square kilometers, Lake Yojoa creates an almost unique highland environment rich in agricultural and aquatic resources.

Central Honduras's physical environment, therefore, offers a range of developmental possibilities. Differential access to arable land and communication routes presented opportunities and challenges for prehistoric populations. High mountains isolating settlements might frustrate efforts at political unification. Uneven resource distribution would also make some areas more attractive to early occupation than others and create conditions favorable for the concentration of wealth, power, and people.

These heavily dissected uplands give way on the south to El Salvador's volcanic ranges and extensive Pacific coastal plain. Soils here, primarily formed on recent volcanic deposits, exhibit fertility levels at least as high as those seen along the Caribbean littoral. The porosity of volcanic soils facilitates cultivation on even relatively steep slopes without significant erosion. With the exception of the Rio Lempa, southward-flowing rivers crossing this zone are relatively short and experience fluctuations in volume corresponding to seasonal rainfall. Nevertheless, precipitation is sufficient to sustain intensive cultivation on some of Central America's most productive soils. Such agricultural bounty helped to attract early settlers and sustained significant population growth throughout the prehistoric occupation sequence. The very source of this fertility, however, could also wreak destruction; volcanic eruptions caused tremendous environmental damage and loss of life at various times in El Salvador's past.

The region is not rich in mineral resources. Volcanic stones such as andesite and vesicular basalt (used in the manufacture of chipped and ground stone tools, respectively) are widely distributed, while cherts are occasionally found associated with limestone deposits. The La Esperanza obsidian flows lie within this area in the steep slopes defining the Ulúa's headwaters. Marine shell, used in ritual and ornament manufacture, is available from both coasts.

Environmental diversity may have encouraged the complex linguistic distributions recorded for Southeast Mesoamerica by sixteenth-century Spanish chroniclers. Language groups reconstructed for the area at this time include Cholan (Maya) in far western Honduras, Jicaque in the lower Ulúa and Chamelecon drainages, Paya on the coast along the lower Aguan River, and Lenca in the central Honduran mountains, possibly extending into eastern El Salvador. Nahua speakers are represented by the Pipil of western and central El Salvador, though even here enclaves of Pokomam (Maya) were recorded at the time of the Spanish conquest. Nahua was also spoken by small groups of apparent merchants scattered among trading centers in Honduras. The actual number of languages and relations among them remain poorly understood. It is clear, however, that Southeast Mesoamerica was culturally and linguistically dynamic when first encountered by the Spanish, and there is every reason to believe that this dynamism has a long history.

Archaeologists successfully ignored the possibilities for studying varied cultural patterns in Southeast Mesoamerica until the late 1960s. Surveys—supplemented, in a few cases, by limited test-pitting—span the nineteenth to mid-twentieth centuries. Throughout this period archaeological attention was fixed on the more impressive remains found at such Lowland Maya centers as Copán and Quirigua. Research in areas bordering these centers was devoted largely to establishing the limits of Lowland Maya civilization and to charting the diffusion of Mesoamerican traits across the zone. During the course of these investigations, Southeast Mesoamerica came to be seen as a periphery of "advanced" Mesoamerican civilizations, hardly a powerful incentive to systematic study.

The situation began to change with the intensive excavation of Chalchuapa in western El Salvador and of Los Naranjos, on Lake Yojoa's northern shore, in the late 1960s. The 1970s and 1980s saw intensive study of the La Venta and Florida valleys (grouped together here as the La Entrada area) and the Naco Valley along the Chamelecon River, the Sula Plain, the lower Aguan Valley, the middle drainages of the Ulúa, Sulaco, and Humuya rivers in Honduras, and of Quelepa, Cihuatan, the Zapotitán Valley, Santa Leticia, and the Cerron Grande area of El Salvador. Much of this work is recently completed or still in progress. Earlier neglect has meant that recent investigations must focus on constructing chronologies and describing local sequences of events. Cognizant of developments in archaeological method and theory, researchers have recently combined extensive regional surveys with excavations at sites of all sizes and complexity levels to write comprehensive accounts of past developments. Attention has also turned to broader issues of cultural process; questions of human/land relations are being addressed in several areas, as is the impact of intersocietal contacts on local developments. Part of the excitement and frustration of Southeast Mesoamerican archaeology is the rapid pace of research. Given this situation, where today's facts are tomorrow's quaint anachronisms, much of the following discussion must be viewed as reasonable hypotheses rather than unassailable truths.

Formative Period

Very little is known of human occupation in this area prior to 1200 B.C. The La Esperanza obsidian flows near the Ulúa's headwaters were probably visited by nomadic hunters and gatherers sometime between 4000 and 1200 B.C. Systematic study of this early span is just beginning, and we have much to learn about the timing, speed,

S

and nature of early settlement. It was near the end of this interval that the first clearly identified occupations in western El Salvador (at Chalchuapa) and Honduras (possibly in the Naco Valley) occurred. In the first case, the migrants seem to have derived from the Pacific coast of Guatemala and/or Chiapas; the source of early Honduran populations is less clear. The earliest known Southeast Mesoamerican cultures were based on agriculture and possessed sophisticated technologies for manufacturing ceramics.

Materials dating to the Mesoamerican Early and Middle Formative are found throughout northern and central Honduras. Population increased gradually during this long span, concentrated primarily along major streams. These early settlers practiced a mixed economy—hunting, gathering, fishing, and agriculture—exploiting fertile alluvial and volcanic soils. Maize seems to have been among the early cultigens. The subsistence regime begun now persisted throughout Southeast Mesoamerican prehistory, though agriculture undoubtedly assumed greater importance with time. Preference for settlement in low-lying areas within easy reach of alluvial and/or volcanic soils also remained important in ancient regional cultural patterns. Indications of increasing cultural and political complexity began to appear by 1000 B.C. in the form of two-tiered site hierarchies, topped by centers with monumental constructions, and differential burial treatment. The clearest manifestation of this trend is seen at Chalchuapa, where Structure E3-1-2nd, a conical, stone-faced earthen platform, was raised at least 20 meters above the surrounding terrain. Large-scale earthen platforms rising 2 to 20 meters also dominate the early centers of Yarumela in the Comayagua Valley and Los Naranjos on Lake Yojoa. A ditch 1,300 meters long, 15–20 meters wide, and 7 meters deep may also have been built at this time in an effort to bolster Los Naranjos' defenses. In Naco, three settlements dating to this span each possess a single large earthen construction 2–3 meters high. A fourth Middle Formative center contains five extensive stone-faced platforms, 0.45–1.66 meters high, roughly arranged around a central patio. Available evidence suggests a gradual shift throughout Naco's Middle Formative from the use of single large edifices as community foci to a wider range of substantial but smaller buildings centered on an open plaza.

Most of the population everywhere apparently lived in dispersed hamlets composed of perishable dwellings. A few interments accompanied by highly valued objects are associated with both monumental edifices (at Los Naran-

jos) and more humble constructions (at Playa de los Muertos in the Sula Plain). A child at the latter site was interred with belts and necklaces of shell and jadeite, elaborate ceramic vessels, and two figurines; the individual's youth suggests that these prerogatives were inherited and not earned during an illustrious life. The La Entrada area and lower Aguan Valley exhibit no signs of political centralization. Early and Middle Formative ceramics from the Cuyamel Caves overlooking the lower Aguan are associated with large quantities of redeposited skeletal remains. These containers are not clearly tied to specific individuals, however, and there are no status distinctions preserved in this ossuary.

Material culture styles, especially in ceramics, are generally similar throughout the area, though each segment is characterized by its own repertoire of designs and decorative techniques. Lower Central American and southern Mesoamerican affinities can be noted in Honduran ceramics at this time. Certain pieces incorporate motifs that define the "Olmec" horizon centered on the Gulf Coast, pointing to participation in this broad interaction sphere. The most obvious similarities are evident in sculpture, figurines, and ceramics from Middle Formative Chalchuapa. Some poorly dated Los Naranjos sculpture may also be linked with this horizon. Evidence for long-distance transactions is limited to jadeite ornaments and marble vessels recovered from Yarumela, Los Naranjos, and Playa de los Muertos. These exotics were probably the possessions of an emerging elite with whom the goods were often interred.

Southeast Mesoamerican societies apparently participated in demographic and political processes paralleling those noted in the better-studied portions of southern Mesoamerica with which they were in contact. Population growth and political change were variably expressed in different areas; the large, fertile interior valleys of Honduras and western El Salvador's rich volcanic soils supported the most precocious of these developments.

Cultural trends diverged markedly during the Late Formative. Small highland valleys along the middle Ulúa, Sulaco, and Humuya rivers were pioneered, while population growth continued unabated in the Sula Plain, Comayagua Valley, around Chalchuapa, and possibly on Lake Yojoa's northern shore. Settlement hierarchies composed of two to three levels are now found in the Comayagua Valley, middle Ulúa drainage, Sula Plain, and on Lake Yojoa. The most pronounced expression of elite power is seen, once again, at Chalchuapa. Here, a century-long hiatus in monumental construction (c. 500–400

B.C.) was succeeded by intensified building efforts that eventually produced the massive El Trapiche complex, covering half a square kilometer. This acceleration in the tempo of construction implies a concomitant population increase. Smaller centers, such as Santa Leticia, were raised in nearby areas.

Monumental centers were integrative foci for dispersed populations resident in small hamlets. Communal rituals performed by social leaders atop tall earthen platforms may well have played a larger role in consolidating Late Formative societies than did any economic or military power wielded by elites. Los Naranjos and Chalchuapa are possible exceptions. An even larger ditch, roughly 5 kilometers long, may have been built now around Los Naranjos to enhance its defenses. Chalchuapa seems to have been an important node linking exchange networks that extended from highland Guatemala through El Salvador and Honduras.

Marked population declines occurred in the La Entrada area and lower Aguan Valley, neither of which supported hierarchically organized polities at this time. Naco experienced a demographic fall-off, though the site of Santo Domingo achieved political importance during the first centuries A.D. Quelepa, a major eastern Salvadoran site, may also have been initially occupied at this time.

Material culture styles continued to be widely shared within the area, though there was an apparent trend toward increased regionalization at the period's end. Pottery in the Usulutan tradition (fine-paste serving bowls decorated with linear and blobby negative-painted designs) was widely distributed among Southeast Mesoamerican societies. This distinctive ware originated in western El Salvador and was traded to the north, where it inspired local imitations. Styles of ceramics and sculpture, and the arrangement of monumental platforms show their closest connections with southeast Highland Maya societies, especially that centered on Chalchuapa. Chalchuapa may have been a conduit through which ideas derived from such highland Guatemalan centers as Kaminaljuyú were disseminated over large portions of Southeast Mesoamerica. Few similarities can be noted with contemporary Lowland Maya material culture. Sourced obsidian samples point to varied procurement systems drawing on flows in Honduras (La Esperanza) and Guatemala (El Chayal, Ixtepeque, and San Martin Jilotepeque). Valued exotics, especially jadeite, marble vessels, and marine shell, become more prevalent now in elite contexts within the Comayagua Valley and are recov-

ered to a more limited extent at Chalchuapa; their presence is not clearly indicated for other areas.

Some Southeast Mesoamerican societies, therefore, seem to have experienced demographic and political processes paralleling, on a smaller scale, those in the Maya Highlands and Lowlands. These developments were not uniform, however, and at least some areas that had supported earlier occupation seem to have suffered declining fortunes. Environmental variables are not clearly implicated in these divergent trajectories, nor can perturbations generated by external contacts be specified as causes of observed variation.

Classic Period

The Early Classic was marked by quickening population growth in most areas. Political changes did not necessarily correlate directly with demographic increases. La Florida in the La Entrada area underwent an explosive period of growth and came to dominate a two-tiered site hierarchy. Levels of political complexity seem to have held more or less steady at Los Naranjos and in the middle Ulúa drainage. Power in the latter area, however, shifted from the residents of the Baide site to Gualjoquito, about 12 kilometers to the north. The Yarumela and Santo Domingo polities fragmented, giving rise to decentralized political fields even as population continued to increase. Comayagua remained divided among as many as five polities throughout the Late Classic. Population is once more attested in the lower Aguan, but diagnostics of political complexity are absent.

Quelepa, in eastern El Salvador, underwent a significant, sustained period of growth; large constructions were raised along the margins of sizable artificial terraces. This distinctive site form does not replicate the patio focus of most Mesoamerican centers, suggesting that portions of eastern El Salvador may have been more closely tied to developments in lower Central America than to events transpiring to the west.

The third-century A.D. eruption of Ilopongo spread searing ash over much of western El Salvador, truncating developments at Chalchuapa and in neighboring areas. Some populations may have weathered this catastrophe by cultivating hillslopes where ashfall was minimal and soon cleared by erosion. There is no doubt, however, that massive loss of life, out-migration, and burial of some of the most fertile soils beneath volcanic ejecta disrupted socio-political processes throughout Early Classic western El Salvador.

S

The situation in the Sula Plain and along the middle Sulaco and Humuya is unclear. The recovery of more than five hundred pieces of jade and jadeite artifacts from Salitron Viejo on the Sulaco strongly suggests the presence of a well-connected elite capable of acquiring valued exotics in large quantities over great distances. The nature and extent of the settlement hierarchy focused on this center is still being reconstructed.

Shared ceramic styles suggest diffuse, wide-ranging ties among all of the studied areas save the lower Aguan. Usulutan decorated wares are found in most of the collections from this period, but red-painted decorations now may supplement resist designs (the former are designated Chilanga Usulutan). Chilanga containers are found throughout the zone, except in the middle Sulaco, Humuya, and lower Aguan drainages. Polychrome-painted vessels of the Ulúa tradition make their first clear appearance now, especially in the Sula Plain. Evidence for Lowland Maya ties to Southeast Mesoamerican ceramics is not strong, though some Ulúa designs may have been inspired by motifs drawn from that area. Sculpture from the middle Sulaco, Humuya, and La Entrada zones reflects ties with lower Central America, not with the developing stoneworking traditions of the neighboring Maya Lowlands. At least some of the jade found at Salitron Viejo derives from quarries in the middle Motagua drainage in eastern Guatemala; stylistic analyses of these pieces point to diverse sources of inspiration, including Kaminaljuyú in highland Guatemala and lower Central America. A few pieces of green obsidian and examples of *talud/tablero* architecture, the latter associated with Teotihuacan, at Salitron Viejo also argue for Central Mexican contacts, possibly mediated through Kaminaljuyú. Material culture from the lower Aguan Valley gives little evidence of contact with other portions of Honduras or Mesoamerica.

Southeast Mesoamerican societies in general experienced demographic and political florescences that paralleled those witnessed in the Maya Lowlands. The concentration of political centers in agriculturally productive zones strategically situated to monitor intersocietal exchanges implies that successful acquisition of power depended on local factions gaining control over both regional and extraregional sources of goods. The distinctive nature of local material culture, influenced but not dominated by foreign styles, combines with evidence of diverse developmental trajectories to indicate that cultural and political changes in any one area must be explained by the complex interplay of local and external processes. While societies in eastern El Salvador may have taken part in similar demographic upsurges and sociopolitical changes, those west of the Lempa River were laid low beneath the Ilopongo ash.

The Late Classic was a period of maximum population density and political complexity in all of the studied areas except the lower Aguan and Comayagua valleys. Recolonization of previously blighted fields is evident throughout western El Salvador, where new political centers—such as Tazamul within the Chalchuapa site zone, and Campana-San Andres in the adjoining Zapotitán Valley—became capitals of sizable polities. The burial of Cerén, a moderate-sized settlement in the Zapotitán Valley, by ash from a localized volcanic eruption in the seventh century A.D. was a powerful reminder of the perils incurred by living in such a volcanically active area.

Agriculturally marginal hillslopes were intensively settled for the first time in this period, in many areas strongly suggesting that increasing populations had exceeded the capacity of the favored alluvial fields to accommodate new settlers. Demographic growth rates were so steep over most of Southeast Mesoamerica that natural population increase must have been supplemented by immigration. The latter process was almost certainly stimulated by the growing power of local elites who attempted to attract and hold ever larger numbers of clients. Increased population densities undoubtedly encouraged intensified agricultural production throughout the area, though terraces and irrigation canals are rarely recorded.

Evidence of these more powerful magnates is also found in increasingly extensive and complex settlement hierarchies (three to five tiers) dominated by capitals containing as many as five hundred structures. Such paramount centers were foci of ritual, economic, and administrative activities that were overseen by elites; these leaders resided within monumental cores delimited by large stone-faced platforms arranged with varying degrees of rectilinearity around formal plazas. Elite monopolies of the long-distance exchange through which prized items such as jadeite, obsidian, and marine shell were acquired combined with privileged control over local ideological and material resources to create socio-political hierarchies. These polities were linked through complex ideological and material exchanges that are reflected in the movement of such goods as obsidian and pottery vessels and ceramic and architectural designs. The southern La Entrada area may have been incorporated within the Copán state from A.D. 628 to 738, but there is no evidence that this hegemony extended farther into Southeast Mesoamerica.

Ceramic styles continue to reflect wide-ranging connections across the region. Distinct interaction systems that linked neighboring zones and within which contacts were concentrated may now have appeared, however. Usulutan wares gradually vanish from assemblages, replaced by elaborately decorated polychromes remarkable for their diversity. Ulúa polychromes—characterized by complex combinations of human, animal, and geometric figures, sometimes associated with "false glyphs" set in sublabial bands—are widely distributed and may have been inspired by Lowland Maya prototypes. Sulaco polychromes, distinguished by geometric designs (formerly called Bold Geometric), evidence eastern Honduran influences. The latter vessels are especially common in the Sula Plain and may have been manufactured along the middle Humuya and Sulaco. Few ceramics were directly imported from the Maya Lowlands; Copador polychromes, fabricated in the Copán Valley, were distributed in varying amounts throughout the area, especially in western El Salvador. Obsidian exchange networks remained diverse, with the Ixtepeque flows being particularly well represented along the Chamelecon River and in the Chalchuapa site zone; La Esperanza material is the most commonly reported source in the middle Humuya and Sulaco drainages. Distinctive Ulúa Marble vessels, decorated on the exterior with complexly carved volutes, are found in the Sula Plain and along the middle Sulaco and Humuya, and were traded to the Maya Lowlands as well.

Political and demographic growth was sustained by local agricultural resources, with each polity's core incorporating fertile alluvial soils. Late Classic Southeast Mesoamerican societies were also integrated within diverse interaction networks that were not focused on or controlled by a single major polity. Regional elites dealt with each other on a more or less equal footing, and these contacts led to the spread of goods and ideas. Power centers, therefore, appeared in areas strategically situated to control external transactions. Southeastern rulers, outside the southern La Entrada area, were largely impervious to Lowland Maya elite culture. Though some components of this complex were adopted by local paramounts, especially the ball court, expressions of hierarchy remained rooted in local traditions.

Postclassic Period

The Terminal Classic and Early Postclassic saw dramatic change throughout the zone. At varying times during this span, population dropped in all areas except the lower Aguan and western El Salvador. The decline was especially precipitous along the middle Humuya and Sulaco and in the La Entrada area, all of which seem to have been abandoned by A.D. 1000. More gradual diminutions are recorded elsewhere. Population may have held steady in the middle Ulúa drainage, though people formerly concentrated near Gualjoquito dispersed to other portions of the zone after that center's fall. Dwindling populations accompanied political decentralization, as realms fragmented and were replaced by simpler political forms.

There were brief reversals of this trend, however. Cerro Palenque, with more than five hundred structures, became a major center in the Sula Plain, controlling a territory of unknown size. Political centralization here was short-lived, extending from A.D. 850 to 1000, when the site was abandoned. Tenampua, a fortified hilltop center, may have been the capital of a newly revitalized Comayagua polity dating to A.D. 900–1100. This political unit was possibly created by, or in reaction to, intrusive bands of Quiché- and/or Nahua-speaking warriors thriving in the unstable political environment created by the fall of Teotihuacan and Lowland Maya polities. Comparable fortified centers are not recorded elsewhere in northern and central Honduras. Comayagua's strategic position on the north–south fault linking the Pacific and Atlantic coasts may have made it a particularly attractive target for these putative marauders. Las Vegas, on the valley flats, is the sole successor to the hilltop centers; it administered a Comayagua polity of uncertain size.

Cihuatan, whose nine hundred structures overlook the middle Lempa drainage in central Honduras from a significant elevation, is one of the largest successors to Tazumal and Campana-San Andres. Like Cerro Palenque, Cihuatan was occupied for a relatively short span, meeting a violent end in the early eleventh century A.D. Architectural, ceramic, and sculptural patterns throughout all of Early Postclassic El Salvador bespeak close economic and ideological ties with such distinctive central and southern Mexican forms as *chac mool* (reclining) sculptures, Tlaloc braziers, and *talud/tablero* (slope-and-panel) architecture; these similarities are at least partly the result of migrations. The best-known of these peregrinations brought Nahua-speaking Pipiles into El Salvador sometime between A.D. 800 and 1350.

Polychrome pottery decreases in variety and frequency throughout the southeast. By A.D. 1100, Las Vegas Polychrome, distinguished by red and black geometric and zoomorphic designs on a cream slip, appears to be the sole

S

example of this class. Las Vegas Polychrome was possibly manufactured in the Comayagua Valley but is rare elsewhere. Southeast Mesoamerican ceramics, in general, underwent processes of simplification and regionalization that continued up to the Historic era.

External ties dwindled throughout this span in most areas. Fine-paste orange ceramics, some of which are closely related to the Altar Fine Orange group of the Boca Ceramic sphere in the southwestern Maya Lowlands, are common components of Sula Plain collections and are found in El Salvador in contexts from roughly A.D. 850 to 1000. Such pottery links both areas with surviving Lowland Maya centers. Examples of this taxon are not commonly found in the mountainous interior. Tohil and San Juan Plumbate ceramics, green obsidian (presumably from the Central Mexican Pachuca flows), copper bells, Las Vegas Polychrome motifs, Mixteca-Puebla polychromes (presumably from Central or East Mexico), and elaborately carved grinding stones tie portions of Honduras's rugged interior and El Salvador, with exchange networks stretching from Tula to lower Central America from A.D. 1100 to 1300. Surviving centers such as Cihuatan and Las Vegas may have been nodes of long-distance exchange, judging by the quantities of foreign goods found in them. The Quimistan Bell Cave near Naco, from which Blackiston recovered eight hundred copper bells in the early twentieth century, is another locus of imported goods. These find spots contrast starkly with most other areas, which seem to have been largely isolated from extensive interaction systems.

The changes noted above were generally contemporary with and paralleled the so-called Maya Collapse. The simultaneity of these events suggests that they were somehow related, though the precise connections and processes remain to be determined. The varying pace, timing, and severity of demographic and political declines across Southeast Mesoamerica strongly indicate that the observed changes must be explained on a case-by-case basis, taking into account local and exogenous forces. Interestingly, even in the areas where population declines were the most severe, there is no clear evidence that environmental degradation precipitated by human action played a significant role in the reconstructed events. This interpretation contrasts markedly with data from Lowland Maya centers as close as Copán that point to a causative role for such ecological processes in population and political changes.

The Late Postclassic remains one of the least-known intervals in Southeast Mesoamerican prehistory. The tendency of Historic period towns to be built over late prehistoric centers, coupled with problems in recognizing sites of this period on survey, frustrates efforts to reconstruct demographic and political trends. Available data, including scanty Conquest period documents, indicate that population levels in the middle Ulúa, Naco, and Sula valleys held steady or rose slightly over Early Postclassic levels, while Comayagua may have continued to experience a gradual decline. The Honduran political landscape in most areas was divided among diminutive, competitive, internally ranked chiefdoms whose hereditary leaders ruled dispersed populations from central towns containing no more than a few thousand people. Such centers frequently controlled optimal agricultural land along major rivers. Fortified refuges, or *penoles,* were occasionally part of these realms, reflecting the severity of endemic warfare. Several polities may have been linked by intermarriage and/or alliance to form larger units, the stability of which is uncertain. There is relatively little evidence of exotic ties; each polity was more or less autonomous both politically and economically.

Developments in Naco contrast with this simple picture. The sites of Naco and its contemporary, Viejo Brisas del Valle, were sizable political centers containing substantial populations. Naco covers about 160 hectares and is reported by early Spanish chroniclers to have been densely settled, while Brisas contains 343 constructions covering half a square kilometer. Each has a site core composed of moderately large earthen platforms with plastered surfaces, organized around formal plazas. Centers on this scale had not been seen in Naco since La Sierra, and their appearance suggests a resurgence of centralization processes. Naco was well known in the sixteenth century as a trading emporium integrated within long-distance exchange networks that extended from lower Central America well into Mesoamerica. Archaeological evidence of these extensive contacts is found in traded goods at both centers, including obsidian (from the La Esperanza and Ixtepeque flows) and some copper, as well as exotic ceramic and architectural styles. Distinctive circular structures found in the Naco and Brisas cores are almost unknown in Late Postclassic Honduras and may well have been inspired by Central Mexican models. Some of the few painted wares known for the period, the Nolasco and Victoria Bichromes, derive primarily from these centers and may represent syntheses of foreign and local ideas. These taxa are characterized by red-painted geometric and avian images on white-slipped bowls. An enclave of "mexicanized" traders, possibly the Nahua speakers alluded to in early Spanish accounts of Naco, may have been the source of these exotic styles and goods. Naco and Brisas seem to represent late efforts at political centralization within the Naco Valley, fueled in part by the extensive foreign ties their residents enjoyed.

El Salvador was now divided among relatively small, competitive states, many ruled by descendants of Pipil immigrants. Segments of these populations were involved in long-distance trade with Mesoamerican societies to the west and north. They also took advantage of the fully recovered volcanic soils to grow such highly valued and widely exchanged crops as cacao.

Throughout the Terminal Classic and Postclassic, lower Aguan populations maintained only weak ties with areas to the west and continued to experience both demographic and political florescence. Large fortified sites such as Río Claro, containing stone-faced earthen platforms up to 7 meters tall, appeared now as capitals of polities of unknown size. Their ceramic and sculptural styles reflect close ties with lower Central American societies, while Mesoamerican trading connections are suggested by finds of Plumbate ware, copper bells, and obsidian. Lower Aguan residents may well have profited from the flourishing coastal trade linking lower Central America and Mesoamerica, which is described in early Spanish reports. Wealth derived from these transactions probably underwrote cultural developments in northeastern Honduras, resulting in a trajectory that seems more closely to parallel developments in El Salvador than those observed elsewhere in Honduras. Gradually accumulating data from the low-lying portions of the Sico, Paulaya, and Platano drainages east of the Aguan support this interpretation. Major centers—for example, Las Crucitas, with more than two hundred structures, including monumental platforms arranged around plazas—may have been capitals of thriving late prehistoric polities. Dense stands of cacao found growing in the environs of the above sites tentatively suggest that commercial cultivation and exchange of this valued crop contributed to the power exercised by late rulers in northeastern Honduras, as was the case in Postclassic El Salvador.

The Spanish conquest of Southeast Mesoamerica dragged on through much of the early to middle sixteenth century. The rugged terrain, the large number of autonomous polities to be subdued, dogged indigenous resistance, and fighting among Spanish factions all contributed to the protracted struggle. The demographic and cultural outcomes of the conflict were devastating. The diseases, slaving, and warfare that so adversely affected the larger, more densely settled populations farther north and west nearly destroyed their Southeast Mesoamerican counterparts. Agents of Spanish ecclesiastical and administrative institutions attempted to convert and control an ever-dwindling native population that had essentially disappeared by the early nineteenth century in Honduras and about a century later in El Salvador.

FURTHER READINGS

Ashmore, W., P. Urban, E. Schortman, J. Benyo, and S. Smith. 1986. Ancient Society in Santa Barbara, Honduras. *National Geographic Research* 3:232–254.

Baudez, C., and P. Becquelin. 1973. *Archéologie de Los Naranjos, Honduras.* Mission d'Archéologie et Ethnologie Française au Méxique, vol. 2. Mexico City: Études Américaines.

Boone, E., and G. Willey (eds.). 1988. *The Southeast Classic Maya Zone.* Washington, D.C.: Dumbarton Oaks.

Dixon, B. 1992. Prehistoric Political Change on the Southeast Mesoamerican Periphery. *Ancient Mesoamerica* 3:11–25.

Fowler, W. R. 1989. *The Cultural Evolution of Ancient Nahua Civilizations: The Pipil-Nicarao of Central America.* Norman: University of Oklahoma Press.

Healy, P. 1984. The Archaeology of Honduras. In F. W. Lange and D. Stone (eds.), *The Archaeology of Lower Central America,* pp. 113–161. Albuquerque: University of New Mexico Press.

Hirth, K., G. L. Pinto, and G. Hasemann (eds.). 1989. *Archaeological Research in the El Cajón Region.* Vol. 1. Pittsburgh and Tegucigalpa: University of Pittsburgh, Department of Anthropology, and Instituto Hondureno de Antropología e Historia.

Joyce, R. 1991. *Cerro Palenque: Power and Identity on the Maya Periphery.* Austin: University of Texas Press.

Pinto, G. L. 1991. Sociopolitical Organization in Central and Southwest Honduras at the Time of the Conquest: A Model for the Formation of Complex Society. In W. Fowler (ed.), *The Formation of Complex Society in Southeastern Mesoamerica,* pp. 215–235. Boca Raton: CRC Press.

Robinson, E. (ed.). 1987. *Interregional Interaction on the Southeast Mesoamerican Periphery: Honduras and El Salvador.* British Archaeological Reports Series, 327, Oxford.

Schortman, E., and P. Urban. 1991. Patterns of Late Preclassic Interaction and the Formation of Complex Society in the Southeast Maya Periphery. In W. Fowler

S

(ed.), *The Formation of Complex Society in Southeastern Mesoamerica*, pp. 121–142. Boca Raton: CRC Press.

Sharer, R. J. (ed.). 1978. *The Prehistory of Chalchuapa, El Salvador.* 3 vols. University Museum Monograph 36. Philadelphia: University of Pennsylvania Press.

Sheets, P. (ed.). 1983. *Archaeology and Volcanism in Central America: The Zapotitán Valley of El Salvador.* Austin: University of Texas Press.

———. 1992. *The Cerén Site: A Prehistoric Village Buried by Volcanic Ash in Central America.* Fort Worth: Harcourt Brace Jovanovich.

Urban, P., and E. Schortman (eds.). 1986. *The Southeast Maya Periphery.* Austin: University of Texas Press.

Wonderley, A. 1985. The Land of Ulúa: Postclassic Research in the Naco and Sula Valleys, Honduras. In A. F. Chase and D. Z. Chase (eds.), *The Lowland Maya Postclassic,* pp. 254–269. Austin: University of Texas Press.

———. 1991. The Late Preclassic Sula Plain, Honduras: Regional Antecedents to Social Complexity and Interregional Convergence in Ceramic Style. In W. Fowler (ed.), *The Formation of Complex Society in Southeastern Mesoamerica,* pp. 143–169. Boca Raton: CRC Press.

Edward Schortman and Patricia Urban

Spinden, Herbert Joseph (1879–1967)

Born in South Dakota Territory and educated at Harvard University (A.B., 1905; Ph.D., 1909), Spinden was appointed assistant curator at the American Museum of Natural History. He revised and expanded his Ph.D. dissertation into *A Study of Maya Art* (1913), a precocious and important work in which he studied the evolution of stylistic traits. Working from Manuel Gamio's stratigraphic excavations at Azcapotzalco and his own observations elsewhere in Mesoamerica, he developed his Archaic Hypothesis (1917), pioneering in the Americas the use of objective data to establish a broad culture historical formulation. His next article (1916) argued for the representation of living people in Maya sculpture, and for name-glyphs referring to them. In 1920 Spinden was appointed to the Peabody Museum (Harvard University), primarily to study the correlation between the Maya and Christian calendars. Initially, his correlation was accepted, but within five years newly interpreted Maya notations of astronomical observations practically eliminated it. In 1926 Spinden moved to the Buffalo Museum of Science, where he produced a new edition of his handbook, including a chronological development chart for the Americas that was remarkable for its time. He moved in 1929 to the Brooklyn Museum, where he remained until his retirement in 1951. He served as president of the American Anthropological Association (1936–1937). He traveled widely, making surveys in Central America although he never excavated, and wrote on many topics.

FURTHER READINGS

Spinden, H. J. 1917. The Origin and Distribution of Agriculture. In *Proceedings of the Nineteenth International Congress of Americanists,* pp. 268–276. Washington, D.C.

———. 1928. *Ancient Civilizations of Mexico and Central America.* American Museum of Natural History Handbook Series, 3. New York.

———. 1975. *A Study of Maya Art.* New York: New York.

Willey, G. R. 1981. Spinden's Archaic Hypothesis. In J. D. Evans et al. (eds.), *Antiquity and Man: Essays in Honour of Glyn Daniel,* pp. 35–42. London: Thames and Hudson.

Ian Graham

Stann Creek District (Belize)

This area of approximately 2,600 square kilometers in east central Belize is best known for Protoclassic to Early Classic (A.D. 100–300) carved jades with glyphic inscriptions, recovered from tombs at the sites of Pomona and Kendal. Coastal sites corroborate florescence at this time, with abundant evidence of maritime activity and exchange. Sites in the district are architecturally distinctive; the dearth of limestone, the typical Maya building material, meant that local inhabitants used slate, granite, quartzite, and various clays for buildings, platforms, construction cores, and floors. The profusion of building techniques provides a strong sense of the great cultural variety in the Maya Lowlands that remains to be described.

The major environmental zones are the Maya Mountains in the western portion of the district, the coastal plain extending from the foothills to the sea, a fringe of coastal mangrove swamps, and offshore coral sand cays. Rivers and creeks drain the mountains, traverse the coastal plain from west to east, and empty into the Caribbean. Although transport and travel by canoe or raft connected communities along a given river valley, north–south communication between the watershed systems was overland or by sea.

We assume that weather patterns in the past were similar to those of today. Mean annual rainfall in the district increases from 280 centimeters in the north to 380 centimeters in the south. October is the rainiest month; the dry period typically lasts from March to mid-May, with a short dry spell in August. People in the past planted crops in the dry season and hoped for the regular arrival of the rains to water their fields. Hurricanes then, as now, brought disaster.

Cultivable soils border the rivers and creeks and have determined the distribution of human settlement, but these acidic soils provide growing conditions quite different from the limestone-derived, relatively alkaline soils of much of the Maya Lowlands; they are not as inherently fertile as limestone soils. On the other hand, the weathering of siliceous rocks produces extensive deposits of clays which were used by the ancient Maya in ceramic and slip manufacture, and these clays or their products were almost certainly exchanged for needed resources that originated outside the district.

The known pre-Columbian settlement history of the district covers a considerable timespan, from the Middle Formative period (beginning about 600 B.C.) to the Late Postclassic (A.D. 1350–1500). Details of occupation remain elusive, despite archaeological investigation, because the preservation of ceramics and other artifacts at inland sites is poor. Nonetheless, it is clear that Pomona (North Stann Creek Valley) and Kendal (Sittee River Valley) were flourishing settlements in Protoclassic–Early Classic times. Occupation and utilization of coastal sites at Colson Point, just north of the North Stann Creek Valley and not far from Pomona, began by at least 50 B.C.–A.D. 100, with evidence of intensive maritime resource procurement and exchange dating to about A.D. 1–300; some activity continued until the end of the Early Classic period (A.D. 450). The Colson Point sites, Kakalche and Watson's Island, are distinctive for the abundance of basal-flange polychrome pottery in shell midden deposits. This regionally produced pottery was accumulated at coastal locations for transport upriver and/or farther along the coast.

Occupation of coastal sites continued after the Early Classic period, but Late Classic use (A.D. 600–800) does not seem to have focused on pottery transport. Intensive activity included salt processing, maritime resource procurement, and the burning of shells for lime. By Postclassic times the situation had changed again, and evi-

dence of light occupation and trade continues until about A.D. 1450.

Smaller sites along other rivers and creeks are farther upriver than Pomona and Kendal and represent a different settlement type. A strong local flavor is apparent in techniques of construction. At Maintzunun and Mayflower, along Silk Grass Creek, sandstone, granite, and slate were used for terrace faces, and sand and pulverized granite as core. Even in nondomestic buildings, floors were often made of thick clay, perhaps deliberately burned. Although Mayflower produced fairly well preserved Mars Orange ware bowls from Middle Formative times, and Maintzunun was probably established during the Classic, the bulk of architectural remains from Silk Grass date to the Terminal Classic period (ninth century A.D.). Early to Late Postclassic pottery was also recovered from this area, but sherds are few and poorly preserved. Fragments of slate game boards for playing *patolli* were found on the surface and in post-abandonment soil accumulation along North Stann Creek, Silk Grass Creek, and the Sittee, along with ceramic and architectural evidence. All indicate that a significant change in cultural practices took place in the ninth or early tenth century A.D.

The Stann Creek District boasts almost no limestone, and no chert deposits at all. Although materials other than limestone could be mustered for construction, lime was imported or manufactured from shells, and chert for stone tools came from sources to the south. Exchanged in return were probably clays that could be used for slips, since the district has many fine clay deposits. The polychrome pottery from Colson Point may have been manufactured in the district, but it was almost certainly manufactured somewhere in the clay-rich zone around the Maya Mountains. Minerals such as hematite and pyrite from the Maya Mountains were almost certainly exported and used as colorants in pottery and textile manufacture; these mineral pigments were also important in rituals. Granite was exported for use in the manufacture of grinding stones. A wide variety of perishable items such as fruits, vegetables, and tree and root crops were probably also exchanged; the district's distinctive soils support a range of crops that flourish only in acid soils, such as cacao and cashew.

The most ubiquitous exotic found at Stann Creek District sites is obsidian from sources in highland Guatemala. It is more abundant along the coast. The origin of the jade found at Pomona and Kendal is unknown, but no jade sources exist in Belize. The ceramics tell us that communities in the district were in close contact with sites in the

S

Belize Valley and the Petén during the Classic period, but that the orientation changed in the Postclassic, when we begin to see pottery that is stylistically closer to northern Belize and Yucatán. The Middle Formative Mars Orange ware is very close to Belize Valley examples, but there is enigmatic pottery from coastal sites in the southern part of the district that has no parallels in the lowlands and is more like Formative period pottery from coastal Guatemala. Goods exchanged in trade passed up and down the coast, from Placencia in the south to the Colson Point sites in the north. The main overland corridor ran through the North Stann Creek Valley, over the Maya Mountains through Hummingbird Gap to the Sibun Valley, and from there to the Belize Valley and the Petén. This corridor was used throughout the prehistoric period, and also during Spanish Colonial times, when marine products were transported to the Belize Valley. In modern times, travel through the gap has been facilitated by the presence of a paved road.

FURTHER READINGS

Graham, E. 1985. Facets of Terminal Classic to Postclassic Activity in the Stann Creek District, Belize. In A. F. Chase and P. M. Rice (eds.), *The Lowland Maya Postclassic*, pp. 215–229. Austin: University of Texas Press.

———. 1987. Resource Diversity in Belize and Its Implications for Models of Lowland Trade. *American Antiquity* 54:753–767.

———. 1994. *The Highlands of the Lowlands: Environment and Archaeology in the Stann Creek District, Belize, Central America.* Monographs in World Archaeology, 19. Madison: Prehistory Press and Royal Ontario Museum.

MacKinnon, J. J. 1985. The Point Placencia Archaeological Project, 1984–85 Fieldwork. *Mexicon* 7:80–83.

———. 1989. Coastal Maya Trade Routes in Southern Belize. In H. McKillop and P. F. Healy (eds.), *Coastal Maya Trade,* pp. 111–122. Occasional Papers in Anthropology, 8. Peterborough, Ont.: Trent University.

———. 1990. Tobacco Range, South Water Cay, Placencia Cay and Maya Sea Trade Routes in Belize. *Mexicon* 12:75–78.

———. 1991. A Reconnaissance of the Quebrada de Oro Site: Implications for a Regional Model of Maya Civilization in Southern Belize. *Mexicon* 8: 87–92.

MacKinnon, J. J., and S. M. Kepecs. 1989. Pre-Hispanic Saltmaking in Belize: New Evidence. *American Antiquity* 54:522–533.

Elizabeth Graham

SEE ALSO

Maya Lowlands: South

Stela Cult

This complex of elite ceremonialism centered on the erection of stelae in association with dynastic and calendrical rites of passage. The stela cult was largely a phenomenon of complex societies in Southern Mesoamerica, including the Olmec, Pacific Slope, and Classic Maya. The cult originated in the Middle Formative Olmec civilization at La Venta. Spreading south along the Pacific slope, the cult flourished during the Late Formative at highland sites such as Izapa, Abaj Takalik, and Kaminaljuyú, and in the Maya Lowlands at Nakbe and El Mirador. The cult persisted in the Lowlands until A.D. 909, when the last stela was erected at Tonina. It was closely linked to the ideology of rulership, and its origins, development, and collapse parallel the trajectory of centralized authority among the Maya and their Formative predecessors.

In its most specific sense, the term defines the Classic Maya practice of erecting stelae in association with royal accessions and the completion of temporal cycles, such as the completion of the *katun* (twenty-year long count period). Iconographic themes on stelae include elite blood sacrifice, supernatural apparitions, and mythological elements related to cosmic order, fertility and rebirth. Stela dedication rites were highly specialized, systematic, and widespread throughout the southern Lowlands, with sacred dances, sacrifices, and visionary rites performed by Maya lords. Stelae were often erected atop foundation vaults with cached offerings, such as ceramic containers for maize, cacao, or blood, small flaked flint or obsidian blades, and even fragments of stalactites. Stelae were sometimes deliberately broken or defaced, apparently as part of "termination rituals."

Stela dedication vanished from the southern Lowlands in the tenth century, but related practices continued into the Postclassic and Colonial periods among northern Yucatecan Maya. Among these was the erection of directional markers at town entries during New Year preparation rites. Colonial sources describe the Postclassic Maya anointing these with sacrificial blood and addressing them as gods.

FURTHER READINGS

Schele, L. 1985. The Hauberg Stela: Bloodletting and the Mythos of Maya Rulership. In M. G. Robertson and V. M. Fields (eds.), *Fifth Palenque Round Table, 1983, Vol. VII,* pp. 135–149. San Francisco: Precolumbian Art Research Institute.

Schele, L., and D. Freidel. 1990. *A Forest of Kings: The Untold Story of the Ancient Maya.* New York: William Morrow and Company.

Tozzer, A. M. 1941. *Landa's Relación de las Cosas de Yucatán: A Translation.* Papers of the Peabody Museum, 18. Cambridge: Mass.: Harvard University.

Elizabeth Newsome

SEE ALSO

Calendrics; Maya Culture and History; Sacrifice; Stelae

Stelae

A stela is an upright stone slab embedded into a horizontal surface, often covered with sculpture and hieroglyphic texts. Stelae are distributed throughout ancient Mexico and Central America; they have been found in Central Mexico, coastal Veracruz, Costa Rica (as thin, decorated slabs resembling grinding stones), and especially in the Yucatán Peninsula and adjacent regions. The earliest known examples were made in Mexico during the first half of the first millennium B.C.

In fusing historical portraiture and sacred imagery, these sculptures clearly developed within Olmec traditions of massive, freestanding sculpture, although with increased emphasis on standing figures holding regalia. The majority of stelae are found in the Maya area, where the earliest sculptures of this sort display mythological beings within apparent mythological narratives (e.g., at Izapa, Mexico, and Nakbe, Guatemala). When adorned, later sculptures emphasize dynastic persons of the Classic period (for unknown reasons, the Maya left some stelae plain). Artistic composition is static, although iconography and texts confirm the thematic prominence of dance. For ritual reasons, the Maya often positioned stone altars in front of stelae. Archaeologists sometimes find deposits underneath, along with evidence of quarrying nearby.

Sculptors favored limestone but imported and used other, more difficult materials such as slate. Recent decipherments reveal Maya terms for stelae ("large stones" or "banner stones") as well as descriptions of their placement ("drive into the ground"). By the Postclassic period, stelae as historical monuments were no longer being erected, and depictions of deities displaced the historical content of earlier monuments.

FURTHER READINGS

Stuart, D., and S. D. Houston. 1994. *Classic Maya Place Names.* Dumbarton Oaks Studies in Pre-Columbian Art and Archaeology, 33, Washington, D.C.

Stephen D. Houston

SEE ALSO

Maya Culture and History; Sculpture; Stela Cult; Writing

Stephens, John Lloyd (1805–1852) and Frederick Catherwood (1799–1854)

Born in New York City and educated in the law, Stephens gained early fame for his travel accounts of Europe and the Middle East in the 1820s and early 1830s. In the mid-1830s he met the English architect Frederick Catherwood, who had attracted considerable notice for his drawings and paintings, particularly a huge panorama of the city of Jerusalem, which was exhibited in London and New York.

Between October 1839 and July 1842, Stephens and Catherwood made two arduous overland journeys through Central America and southeastern Mexico. The results of their collaboration, published under Stephens's name, appeared in 1841 and 1843. The vivid and informative narrative, combined with four hundred engravings made from Catherwood's field drawings, revealed for the first time the extent and nature of the ruined cities of the ancient Maya. For most scholars it represents a beginning point of the scientific pursuit of Maya archaeology.

Many of Stephens's speculations on the Maya ruins have held up for more than 150 years, including his ideas that ancestors of the living Maya built them, and that the figures depicted in the art were rulers of the places. Catherwood's illustrations, including a magnificent folio of lithographs he published in 1844, created new standards of accuracy in archaeological draftsmanship.

Stephens died in Panama, where he was serving as president of the Panama Railroad. Catherwood was lost at sea in the sinking of the SS *Arctic* in the North Atlantic.

FURTHER READINGS

Brunhouse, R. L. 1973. *In Search of the Maya: The First Archaeologists.* Albuquerque: University of New Mexico Press.

S

Stephens, J. L. 1950. *Frederick Catherwood, Arch'*. New York: Oxford University Press.

———. 1963 [1843]. *Incidents of Travel in Yucatán*. 2 vols. New York: Dover.

———. 1969 [1841]. *Incidents of Travel in Central America, Chiapas and Yucatan*. 2 vols. New York: Dover.

von Hagen, V. W. 1947. *Maya Explorer: John Lloyd Stephens and the Lost Cities of Central America and Yucatán*. Norman: University of Oklahoma Press.

George Stuart

Stirling, Matthew Williams (1896–1975)

Stirling's research in Mexico represents the first scientific investigations of the Olmec culture, in the eight successive archaeological expeditions he led to southern Mexico (1938–1946). He found that the Olmec had sculpted huge blocks of stone into colossal heads weighing 25 tons, as well as making small, well-polished masterpieces of carved jade. His interest in Olmec culture dated to 1920, when he saw a blue jade "crying baby" maskette in Berlin. In 1928 he was appointed chief of the Bureau of American Ethnology at the Smithsonian Institution.

After a visit to Tres Zapotes in 1938, Stirling proposed research at Olmec sites, which was funded by the National Geographic Society. In 1939 and 1940, he worked at Tres Zapotes, finding Stela C with its bar-and-dot date of 31 B.C. This caused considerable controversy, especially among Mayanists, who could not accept the greater age of Olmec culture. Stirling's findings were in accord with those of the brilliant artist and ethnographer Miguel Covarrubias, and of Alfonso Caso, who in 1942 was the first to apply the term "Mother Culture" to the Olmec.

In the 1940s Stirling worked at Cerro de las Mesas, La Venta, and San Lorenzo, finding dated stelae, jade caches, and colossal heads; at La Venta he discovered a columnar basalt tomb, deeply buried stylized jaguar masks of polished green serpentine blocks, altars, and rich caches of jade ornaments and figurines. In the 1940s, 1950s, and 1960s, the National Geographic Society sponsored his expeditions to Panama and Costa Rica. Stirling's encouragement of his colleagues and assistants ensured the continuity of research into Olmec and other cultures.

FURTHER READINGS

Benson, E. P. (ed.). 1968. *Dumbarton Oaks Conference on the Olmec*. Washington, D.C.

Coe, M. D. 1976. Matthew Williams Stirling. *American Antiquity*. 41:67–73.

Marion Stirling Pugh

SEE ALSO

Olmec Culture

Stone, Doris Zemurray (1909–1994)

Stone's thirty-five years of archaeological publications defined many of the themes that were, and in many cases continue to be, the foci of research in Costa Rica and in Central America. In regard to the nature and extent of Mesoamerican influence, while she tended to see somewhat more direct diffusion than did many of the following generation of researchers, she kept an open mind for integrating new data with her established views, and she joined the ongoing debate with vigor and interest. She established the tripartite subdivision that has been the established research framework in Costa Rica for more than four decades. She emphasized an ethnohistorical and ethnoarchaeological approach to elements of the database, such as southern Costa Rican cult symbols, and the importance of the technological relationship between tool assemblages and subsistence practices, especially the role of maize in pre-Columbian Costa Rica. In 1948, she encouraged President Jose Figueres Ferrer to allow her and her associates to convert the Bellavista fortress, a central location in the 1948 revolution (Costa Rica's last), into the permanent site of the National Museum of Costa Rica.

It is a reflection of the breadth, intensity, and longevity of Stone's interests (and of her accessibility to younger scholars) that her earlier work is extensively referenced in scholarly publications in her subject, as well as in relevant theses and dissertations from Costa Rican, Central American, and European and North American universities.

Frederick W. Lange and E. Wyllys Andrews V

SEE ALSO

Intermediate Area: Overview

Sweat Baths

Enclosed chambers heated with rocks were used for hygiene and curing in ancient and modern indigenous communities throughout Mesoamerica, North America, and, probably, ancient highland South America. Although the basic design includes a sweating room (some-

The Aztec bath house, used for hygiene and curing, is illustrated in the Codex Magliabechiano (c. 1550), 77 recto. The bath house attendant is in the lower left, and the idol over the door is identified in an accompanying gloss as the deity Tezcatlipoca. Water streams through the bottom of the bath house, and the same iconographic symbol indicates that water is in the bowl held by the woman in the lower right. Illustration courtesy of the author.

times of perishable materials), an oven, and exhaust openings and flues, and drains, Mesoamerican sweat baths vary enormously in terms of layout and construction. Some are improvised, but many are permanently integrated into house compounds.

The Aztecs and other central highlands peoples called the sweat bath "a *temazcal,* which means 'bath house with fire,' made up of *tletl,* 'fire,' and *mozcoa,* 'to bathe'" and *calli,* "house" (Durán 1971 [1579]:269). According to Durán, *temazcales* were "heated with fire and are like small, low huts" with a "low and narrow" entrance; they were "used commonly by the Indians, both healthy and ill.

After having perspired thoroughly there, they wash themselves with cold water outside the bathhouse so that the fiery bath will not remain in their bones. . . . There were male and female fanners in the wards as bringers or health . . . [believing] that fanning . . . blew away illness, strengthened the flesh, and gave health and strength to the sick. . . . The noblemen possessed appointed people . . . men and women [who] accompanied them to the bathhouse to wash them. Most . . . were dwarfs or male and female hunchbacks" (269–270). Aztec sweat baths have been excavated in Tenochtitlan (Mexico City), at the site of Motecuhzoma II's palace, and at rural Cihuatecpan.

S

Sweat baths were known among the Quiché Maya as *tuj*. Hieroglyphic records at Palenque provide a rich terminology for sweat baths: *kun*, "oven," *pibna*, "house for steaming," and *chitin*, "oven," but in a symbolic setting. Triadic structures at Palenque known as the "Cross Group" evidently served as the symbolic sweat baths of local gods, and texts within the group emphasize connections with godly birth. The Maya elite would have used monumental sweat baths such as those excavated at Classic period Piedras Negras; other Maya examples are from San Antonio (Chiapas) and Cerén (El Salvador).

FURTHER READINGS

Agrinier, P. 1964. La casa de baños de vapor de San Antonio, Chiapas. *Boletín de Instituto Nacional de Antropología e Historia* 25:27–32.

Alcina Franch, J., A. Ciudad Ruiz, and J. Iglesias Ponce de León. 1980. El 'temazcal' en Mesoamérica: Evolución, forma y función. *Revista Española de Antropología Americana* 10:93–132.

Cresson, F. M. 1938. Maya and Mexican Sweat Houses. *American Anthropologist* 40:88–104.

Durán, D. 1971. *Book of the Gods and Rites and the Ancient Calendar.* F. Horcasitas and D. Heyden (trans. and eds.). Norman: University of Oklahoma Press.

López Austin, A. 1988. *The Human Body and Ideology: Concepts of the Ancient Nahuas.* 2 vols. T. and B. Ortiz de Montellano (trans.). Salt Lake City: University of Utah Press.

Pihó, V. 1989. El use del temazcal en la Altiplanicie Mexicana. In R. García Moll and A. García Cook (coords.), *Homenaje a Román Piña Chán,* Mexico City: Instituto Nacional de Antropología e Historia.

Satterthwaite, L. 1952. *Piedras Negras Archaeology: Architecture: Part V: Sweathouses.* Philadelphia: University Museum.

Sheets, P. 1992. *The Cerén Site: A Prehistoric Village Buried by Volcanic Ash in Central America.* Fort Worth: Harcourt Brace Jovanovich.

Stephen D. Houston and Susan Toby Evans

SEE ALSO

Architecture: Vernacular-Mundane; Disease, Illness, and Curing

T

Tabachines (Jalisco, Mexico)

This site on the northern outskirts of Guadalajara in the Atemajac Valley is relatively close to El Grillo, and the two may have been related. Construction in the 1970s exposed twenty-one shaft tombs and twenty-seven box tombs; these were salvage excavated by Galván and Schöndube. The shaft tombs included a wide variety of offerings; Galván has analyzed the relationship of artifacts to social status, resulting in the definition of the Tabachines phase. Galván argued that on the basis of quantity of offerings and elaboration of the tombs, there were wealthier and poorer classes, and that this disparity in wealth declined as the neighboring Tequila Valley societies began to grow in socio-political complexity. Aronson later studied the production, distribution and use of Tabachines materials and provided a wealth of additional detail. Obsidian hydration dates from the tombs range from 750 B.C. to A.D. 460, and their relative order has allowed a seriation of the tomb lots.

The small box tombs include seated and flexed single burials, with an artifact assemblage completely distinct from that found in the shaft tombs. Ceramics include miniature cups and ollas, trays, and molcajete grater bowls, utilizing a wide range of pseudo-cloisonné, fugitive paint, paint-filled incision, and resist types of decoration. These materials were used to define the El Grillo phase. Aronson's materials analyses indicate that production methods differed considerably from those in the shaft tombs.

FURTHER READINGS

Aronson, M. 1996. Technological Change: Ceramic Mortuary Technology in the Valley of Atemajac from the Late Formative to the Classic Periods. *Ancient Mesoamerica* 7:163–169.

Galván Villegas, L. J. 1991. Las Tumbas de Tiro del Valle de Atemajac, Jalisco. Serie Arqueológica. Mexico City: Instituto Nacional de Antropología e Historia.

Schöndube Baumbach, O., and L. J. Galván Villegas. 1978. Salvage Archaeology at El Grillo-Tabachines, Zapopan, Jalisco, Mexico. In C. L. Riley and B. C. Hedrick (eds.), *Across the Chichimec Sea: Papers in Honor of J. Charles Kelley,* pp. 144–164. Carbondale: Southern Illinois University.

Christopher S. Beekman and Luís Javier Galván Villegas

SEE ALSO

West Mexico

Tajín, El (Veracruz, Mexico)

Situated in the Gulf Coast lowlands between two streams, this important Classic Veracruz center had a series of occupation stages—preurban, urban, decadent, and post-abandonment; in the last, the city was reused as a necropolis. It flourished during the Classic period, when its population may have exceeded twenty thousand. The central part of the site, which constitutes the present-day archaeological zone open to the public, has 168 public-scale buildings distributed over 196 hectares and five barrios, and spatially arranged according to several orientations, including 20° northeast and 45° northeast. The principal structure is the Pyramid of the Niches; other buildings include temples, ball courts, and palaces. The central portion of the city was divided into three areas: first, the lower valley with large buildings dedicated to

T

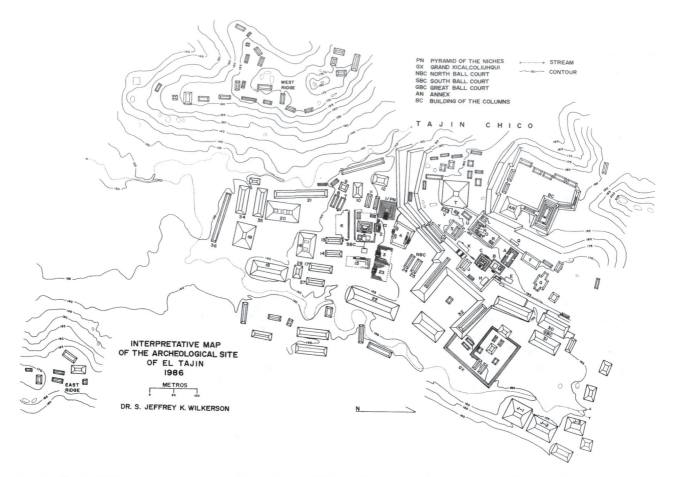

INTERPRETATIVE MAP
OF THE ARCHEOLOGICAL SITE
OF EL TAJIN
1986

METROS

DR. S. JEFFREY K. WILKERSON

PN PYRAMID OF THE NICHES
GX GRAND XICALCOLIUHQUI
NBC NORTH BALL COURT
SBC SOUTH BALL COURT
GBC GREAT BALL COURT
AN ANNEX
BC BUILDING OF THE COLUMNS

→ STREAM
— CONTOUR

TAJIN CHICO

WEST RIDGE

EAST RIDGE

Dr. S. Jeffrey K. Wilkerson's map of the archaeological site of El Tajín. Illustration courtesy of Dr. S. Jeffrey K. Wilkerson.

cults and administration; then "Tajín Chico" with elite residences; and finally, at the top, the Building of the Columns, the palace complex of Tajín's rulers. Beyond the two streams were large-terraced areas where the bulk of the urban population lived. Houses were clustered into domestic compounds separated by garden plots. Wattle-and-daub houses with thatched roofs and other perishable components were built on low platforms, similar to present-day structures in native style.

Tajín was first reported in 1785 and was visited or mentioned by such pioneering traveler-antiquarians as Father Marques, Alexander von Humboldt, Karl Nebel, Teobert Maler, don Francisco del Paso y Troncoso, and the artist José Mariá Velasco. The first sculptural interpretations were in the early 1930s by Ellen Spinden, then Enrique Palacios and Enrique Meyer. Later that decade Agustín de la Vega cleared the site to catalogue structures and sculpture and to begin consolidation of the Pyramid of the Niches. From 1939 to the 1970s, José García Payon explored, consolidated, and restored eleven buildings (1, 3, 4, 5, 15, 23, A, B, C, D, and K), trying to infer chronology from architectural stratigraphy, ethnohistoric sources, and stylistic comparisons with other cities, principally Teotihuacan. Ceramic studies initiated by Wilfrido Du Solier in 1939 were continued by Krotser in the 1970s. Further research by the Instituto Nacional de Antropología e Historia and the Universidad Veracruzana began in 1984.

FURTHER READINGS

Brueggemann, J. K. 1991. *Proyecto Tajín.* 3 vols. Mexico City: Instituto Nacional de Antropología e Historia.

García Payón, J. 1971. Archaeology of Central Veracruz. In *Handbook of Middle American Indians,* vol. 5, part 2, pp. 505–542. Austin: University of Texas Press.

Juergen K. Brueggemann and Patricia J. Sarro

Tajín, El: Architecture and Murals

Architecture at El Tajín is distinguished by the profile of its buildings, the widespread use of ornamental niches, and the utilization of novel construction techniques and materials. The innovations include true second stories, concrete ceilings, and asphalt sealants. Stepped pyramid bases of earth or rubble were faced with cut stone and placed around mostly rectangular plazas. Some functioned as open platforms, and others as temples, elite residences, or administrative structures. Parallel structures enclose numerous ball courts.

At El Tajín an upper, triangular "flying cornice" is added to the Mesoamerican system of *talud-tablero* (slope-and-panel) walls. The *tablero* may have fret designs, or deep niches of stone slabs, or stucco over stone armatures, features also found at satellite and regional sites. Building facings, primarily of limestone, were sealed with cement and then painted. Staircases at times cover complete sides of platforms. The balustrades are occasionally decorated, sometimes with modeled frets. Many staircases have central, altarlike projections that may mimic the building's profile and decoration; these probably had a ritual function in access to the sanctuaries or residences above. Large buttresses, some ornamented with niches, reinforced sagging walls, terrace *taluds,* and even stairways. Ball courts, mostly restricted to the valley floor, have both sloping and vertical profiles but no known marker rings.

Tajín Chico, a terraced and greatly modified natural rise, has the largest concentration of elite residences and administrative structures. Buildings there exhibit the greatest technological and engineering innovation. Massive concrete roofs, a few arched, were poured in layers up to a meter thick. Some surfaces, as elsewhere in the city, were sealed with asphalt. Pillars and columns supported roofs and, in at least one case, a superimposed second story.

Murals and color were used extensively to ornament buildings throughout El Tajín. Most were monochrome, usually red but occasionally blue or yellow. Contrasting colors were also utilized to accentuate geometric designs or recesses. The red-painted Pyramid of the Niches had black niches and, probably, blue balustrades. Polychrome murals adorned interior and exterior walls and some staircases. True fresco and dry plaster painting techniques were utilized, at times even combined in a single work. Subjects included geometric forms such as stepped frets and scrolls, as well as both narrative and formal depictions of human or mythical personages.

The majority of the known murals are from the interiors of the elite structures in Tajín Chico. The intimate scale and diverse subject matter of these elaborate, finely painted compositions reflect the buildings' restrictive nature. Some fragments depict ritual processions with figures holding military or ceremonial regalia such as banner poles and spears. The most complete mural suite known here is from Building J, where a central U-shaped room, perhaps used for elite gatherings, is ringed by a painted bench in the city's standard architectural profile. Pairs of formally presented supernatural beings wearing elaborate feathered headdresses alternate with masked deity impersonators framed in cruciform cartouches. Typical of El Tajín, despite the static portrayal these figures gesture and appear animated. Fewer murals are known from the city's public sectors. The most complete are large-scale exterior presentations that are thematically related to architectural decoration. One is a row of stepped frets nearly a meter high on a sanctuary *talud.* In red and pink against a blue background, the geometric design is composed of interlacing scrolls and eyes that suggest supernatural faces, a pattern also seen in relief sculpture.

FURTHER READINGS

García Payon, J. 1957. *El Tajín, Official Guide.* Mexico City: Instituto Nacional de Antropología e Historia.

———. 1971. Archaeology of Central Veracruz. In R. Wauchope (ed.), *Handbook of Middle American Indians,* vol. 11, pp. 505–542. Austin: University of Texas Press.

Ladron de Guevara, S. 1992. Pintura y escultura. In *Tajín,* pp. 99–132. Mexico City: Citibank.

Wilkerson, S. J. K. 1990. El Tajín, Great Center of the Northeast. In *Mexico: Splendors of Thirty Centuries,* pp. 155–181. New York: Metropolitan Museum of Art.

Patricia J. Sarro

Tajín, El: Art and Artifacts

The art of El Tajín is expressed in a dynamic variant of the Classic Veracruz style. Depictions in paint, stone, or clay tend to be in double outline and, in the case of stone and clay, in low relief. Scrolls, curvilinear devices, grotesques, and plumes are common in costume accouterments, furniture, depictions of plants and animals, and even on structures. Scenes are frequently narrative or depict richly attired protagonists, often as deity impersonators. Many sculptures were probably polychromed. The large

T

sculptural corpus of the city is the greatest known from any Classic period site of the Gulf Lowlands.

The context for most stone sculpture is architectural. Two ball courts (North Ball Court, South Ball Court) have ample, sequential narrative scenes carved directly into the huge, vertical flagstone walls bordering the playing area. Large stone drum columns from the portico of the massive Building of the Columns depict, in a series of registers separated by bands of grotesques, sacrificial rituals celebrating the ruler 13 Rabbit. The sanctuary of the Pyramid of the Niches had a considerable concentration of carved tablets depicting an ancestral ruler in an array of rites and deity impersonations. Individual tablets and altars have been found in or about other sanctuaries, reused as building blocks, or even dragged a considerable distance away. A unique example is a carved natural basalt column found broken at the base of a temple stairway where it had been thrown. Freestanding sculptures reminiscent of Maya sites such as Toniná, carved in the round and deep relief, were encountered at the base of the Pyramid of the Niches. Various ball courts have associated freestanding or embedded deep relief sculpture. A large, three-dimensional lunar cult rabbit, seemingly associated with small Postclassic structures, was unearthed by bulldozers.

Portable stone sculpture, common at many sites with El Tajín cultural attributes, is rare in the city. Only one plain yoke, an important item of ball game rituals, has been found in building debris. This dearth of examples is certainly due to the lack of excavated elite burials at the site. Stucco sculpture, usually on thin stone armatures, is known primarily from Tajín Chico. It appears as reticulate designs and as wall-backed or freestanding three-dimensional anthropomorphic or zoomorphic presentations. Sanctuaries sometimes have small stucco representations of plants. Much stone or stucco sculpture, particularly that from sanctuaries, from elite palaces, or once freestanding on temple platforms, appears to have been deliberately smashed in antiquity. Perishable items have not been found, but there are direct basket and leaf impressions in poured cement. The former may have been used for the transport of earth or cement and the latter as food wrapping, as for tamales.

Ceramic artifacts include a few figurines—small, solid figures of probable early date and later mold-made examples, as well as fragments of hollow modeled effigies. Blackwares tend to be in early deposits, as are cylindrical tripod vessels and candeleros. Common throughout are flat-bottomed outflaring bowls in polished black, orange,

or red. Very common, and found across the greater region of El Tajín culture, are large domestic jars (ollas) with roughened or scraped bottoms, pinched fillet divider ridge, and painted, polished shoulders. Large, flat-bottomed tubs with rough exteriors and red-orange or unpainted interiors are frequent in later centuries. So too are comals, suggesting a change in diet to include tortillas. Fine-paste globular tripod vessels also occur in elite circumstances, as do vessels with carved exteriors, in some cases depicting ritual processions with number or name glyphs. Postclassic ceramics include many fine-paste types, often shallow, open bowls with red-painted surfaces and black decoration. Terminal Postclassic vessels frequently are open bowls with black or red-on-cream decoration, a format common in the greater Huasteca region.

S. Jeffrey K. Wilkerson

FURTHER READINGS

Du Solier, W. 1945. La cerámica arqueológica de El Tajín. *Anales del Museo Nacional de Arqueológia, Historia y Etnografia* 3:147–192.

Kampen, M. 1972. *The Sculptures of El Tajín, Veracruz, Mexico.* Gainesville: University of Florida Press.

Proskouriakoff, T. 1954. *Varieties of Classic Veracruz Sculpture.* Contributions to American Anthropology and History, 58. Carnegie Institution of Washington, Pub. 606. Washington, D.C.

Wilkerson, S. J. K. 1984. In Search of the Mountain of Foam: Human Sacrifice in Eastern Mesoamerica. In E. H. Boone (ed.), *Ritual Human Sacnfice in Mesoamerica,* pp. 101–131. Washington, D.C.: Dumbarton Oaks.

Tajín, El: Chronology

El Tajín has a very long occupational history that is much obscured by the extensive construction activity in the city's final centuries. The disparate chronological data from the site are greatly reinforced by the regional stratigraphic evidence. Occupation began with a small Late Formative or Protoclassic settlement that urbanized and grew throughout the Early Classic, expanded rapidly during the Middle Classic, and achieved a possibly double florescence during the Late Classic and Epiclassic. There followed rapid depopulation characterized by the movement of monuments and the destruction of many significant buildings. At the end of the Postclassic, there was once again a growing settlement on the southern margins of the site, and some reuse of earlier structures.

The temporal analysis of El Tajín has long been hindered by the enormous earth-moving activities of the Late Classic and Epiclassic periods, when most previously undisturbed midden deposits were utilized as fill for extensive construction. Early buildings are buried in the interiors of some structures on the valley floor and under some of the lower portions of Tajín Chico. To date there has been very little systematic exploration of building interiors, so there is scant knowledge of sealed fill or direct architectural sequences. A recent interpretation by Bruggemann, stemming from a reconstruction project, would place the entire city in the centuries from A.D. 800 to 1150. Although these dates bracket the time of maximal earth movement and the apogee of construction, they are simply not compatible with the strong regional data from many points that indicate roughly a millennium's duration for the Tajín version of Classic Veracruz culture. From the first attempts at stratigraphic excavations in the late 1930s, summarized by Du Solier, it has been apparent that the chronological framework of the city would have to be confirmed initially from the examination of the greater region.

In spite of these hindrances, temporal evidence from various contexts and different locations in the city is discernible: structural fill in the central portion of Tajín proper suggests midden debris from at least the Protoclassic if not the terminal Late Formative. Test trenches, largely in fill, on the mid-terrace levels of Tajín Chico produced Early Classic pottery. Base deposits in the elite West Ridge have an associated radiocarbon date from the Middle Classic. Abundant pottery fragments, used as binding aggregates in thick concrete roofs in Tajín Chico, are frequently from the Late Classic and Epiclassic periods. Late, and particularly Terminal, Postclassic ceramics are found scattered about the city and are especially associated with a substantial settlement on the site periphery. Corroboration comes from the proximate region, particularly at Santa Luisa, where explorations in the late 1960s were undertaken expressly to place El Tajín in a regional chronology. The resulting 8,000-year sequence, with radiocarbon dating for many phases, permits the confident placement of El Tajín in the areal context. At Santa Luisa, the ceramics also found at El Tajín are encountered in deep stratigraphic deposits and associated with small temples. The time placement is directly parallel to that now suggested by the aggregate of the evidence at El Tajín. Other explorations and surface reconnaissance have shown that the same ceramics are widely situated across the lowland portions of the north central area and even up to the edges of the eastern highlands, essentially the sphere of El Tajín influence where its architectural and sculptural attributes are also found. Many of these ceramics are encountered at El Pital, suggesting that important aspects of El Tajín's material culture may have been heavily

Southern corner of the Xicalcoliuhqui Plaza, El Tajín. Illustration courtesy of Jurgen K. Bruggemann.

T

View of Building "Y" from the North Ball Court, El Tajín. Illustration courtesy of Jurgen K. Bruggemann.

influenced, if not directly derived, from this earlier major city.

FURTHER READINGS

Bruggemann, J. K. 1993. El Problema Cronologico del Tajín. *Arqueológia* 9–10:61–72.

Du Solier, W. 1945. La cerámica arqueológica de El Tajín. *Anales del Museo Nacional de Arqueológia, Historia y Etnografia* 3:147–192.

García Payon, J. 1971. Archaeology of Central Veracruz. In R. Wauchope (ed.), *Handbook of Middle American Indians,* vol. 11, pp. 505–542. Austin: University of Texas Press.

Wilkerson, S. J. K. 1980. Man's Eighty Centuries in Veracruz. *National Geographic* 158:202–231.

———. 1987. *El Tajín, A Guide for Visitors.* Jalapa: Government of Veracruz.

———. 1997. El Tajín und der Hohepunkt der Klassischen Veracruz-Kultur. In *Präkolumbische Kulturen am Golf von Mexiko,* pp. 61–76. Zürich: Museum Rietberg.

S. Jeffrey K. Wilkerson

SEE ALSO

Santa Luisa

Tajín, El: Religion and Ideology

The religion and ideology of El Tajín—the principal metropolitan center of Classic Veracruz culture at its apogee—is unintelligible without consideration of the ball game cult. The ball game, along with a group of closely associated rites, constituted a virtual obsession to the elite of the city and the surrounding region. The gamelike ritual was conducted in several forms with varying numbers of participants. It is manifest architecturally in at least thirteen vertical or sloping-walled stone courts at El Tajín, as well as dozens of others throughout the immediate hinterland. The broad geographical acceptance of the cult focus, as well as the intensity of its celebration, is further emphasized by the hundreds of portable sculptures known as *yokes, palmas,* and *hachas* that have been encountered throughout the north central Gulf Lowlands and beyond. Through the ritual of the ball game, rulership, lineage, conquest, astrological cycles,

T

access to the gods, and cosmology were expressed. The rite was clearly central to the worldview of El Tajín and an integral part of the dynamic impact of Classic Veracruz culture on its contemporaries. Distant elites, perhaps as far away as the American Southeast, were influenced by the concepts, symbolism, and paraphernalia of El Tajín ball game ritualism.

The nature of the ball game cult is vividly illustrated in the well-preserved sculptures of the South Ball Court (SBC). A series of six dramatic narrative panels, carved in the vertical walls of the Late Classic period court, presents a sequence of acts in which mortals and gods interact in the context of the ritual. Depicted are (1) preparation for warfare and prisoner capture; (2) an hallucinogenic vision session prior to the game, in which the deity identified with the planet Venus appears; (3) the face-off on the court itself, with the protagonist symbolically brandishing a large sacrificial knife; (4) the protagonist beheading a player at the termination of the game in the presence of the descending Venus deity; (5) the sacrificed player, now in the underworld realm of the rain and wind deities, soliciting *pulque* from a temple vat at the mythical source called the "mountain of foam"; and (6) the rain god performing genital autosacrifice to refill the depleted vat in the presence of the wind deity and the moon goddess. The last two panels are overlain by a bifurcated version of the *pulque* deity.

Convergent cults and rites are embedded in the matrix of the ball game. Panels 1 to 4 are consistent with the Venus cult, in which warfare, prisoner capture, and sacrifice were dictated by the appearances and disappearances of the planet in its 584-day cycle. All panels have *pulque* (agave sap beer) vats in the principal scenes or adjacent to them, indicating that procurement of the drink through divine intervention was one of the principal aims of the ritual. The gods themselves participate in the rites through their patronization of different aspects and their ultimate self-sacrifice, to bring the ritual cycle full circle. The ruler-protagonist reaffirms his position and martial stature by the capture and sacrifice of another elite player-prisoner in the ball game. The sacrificed player, an offering himself, through death becomes a messenger to the underworld gods who control the availability of the sacred drink. Because both gods and men were considered participants in this complex of interwoven rituals, the courts themselves became access ways to the deities. Approached through visions or death, the gods confirmed rulership, abundance, and ritual well-being. The cosmology of El Tajín was centered on the continua of divine-

profane, life-death, and sacrifice-abundance that were embodied in the ball game cult.

Ball game symbolism is omnipresent in the city. Even buildings, such as palace A in Tajín Chico, have stairways that emerge in miniature courts, implying symbolic passageways to sacred premises. Lineage succession or affirmation rites are also depicted being undertaken in the presence of various ball game symbols, including a marker (*tlaxmalacatl*) formed by intertwined serpents. One elegant carved tablet, found by Building 4 but probably from the sanctuary of the Pyramid of the Niches, contains a possible succession ceremony in the presence of a serpent marker and a pulque vat. Ascension seating scenes in front of a marker may be depicted in the fragmentary panels of the North Ball Court, probably of similar Middle Classic date. Columns show an Epiclassic ruler sacrificing elite prisoners in or about courts.

Many of the courts at El Tajín may have been constructed by successive rulers who situated them with other buildings and plazas refurbished or constructed during their rule. A major example is the assemblage composed of the SBC, Temple 5, (audience) Building 15, and Court 13–14, all likely to be associated with the protagonist of the SBC panels. The Great Ball Court, at the base of Tajín Chico, may be linked with the named ruler 13 Rabbit and the massive fortified compound of the Building of the Columns. The North Ball Court, with its carved sequence of ritual acts by still another ruler, may be grouped with Building 4 and the Pyramid of the Niches. Court 34–35 was associated with Building 19 and the Arroyo Group, refurbished during the last apogee of the city. Unlike so many Mesoamerican cities that have only one or two courts, usually added in adjunct manner, the El Tajín courts are both urban and religious focal points. The essential role of the ball game cult for rulership, cosmological perspective, and religious ideology required constant reaffirmation which was expressed in construction. Only one other major Gulf Coast city, El Pital, which largely precedes El Tajín, may have had a similar number of courts or such an intense ball game cult emphasis.

The exceptional strength of the El Tajín ritual focus throughout the immediate region and the Gulf Lowlands is amply demonstrated by the great number of portable ball game sculptures. These stone objects tend to be found as grave goods in elite burials. Their presence symbolizes the prerogative of the deceased to participate in the ritual and to take the symbols of that status to the afterlife. *Yokes* appear to represent elaborations of the wooden waist protectors used in the game. Frequently these have depictions of the female earth monster, associated with the entranceway to the underworld and the threshold of death. *Hachas* often depict severed heads, and *palmas* reflect secondary deities and sacrificial aspects of the ritual. Although of much greater antiquity than El Tajín, the ball game evolved into the core ritual expression of its worldview, achieving a participatory intensity and cult preeminence rarely seen in Mesoamerica.

FURTHER READINGS

Garcia Payón, J. 1973. Chacmol en el apoteosis del pulque. In *Los enigmas de El Tajín,* pp. 31–54. Collección Científica, 3. Mexico City: Instituto Nacional de Antropología e Historia.

Wilkerson, S. J. K. 1984. In Search of the Mountain of Foam: Human Sacrifice in Eastern Mesoamerica. In E. H. Boone (ed.), *Ritual Human Sacrifice In Mesoamerica,* pp. 101–131. Washington, D.C.: Dumbarton Oaks.

———. 1991. And They Were Sacrificed: The Ritual Ballgame of Northeastern Mesoamerica through Time and Space. In V. L. Scarborough and D. R. Wilcox (eds.), *The Mesoamerican Ballgame,* pp. 45–72. Tucson: University of Arizona Press.

S. Jeffrey K. Wilkerson

SEE ALSO

Ball Game; Gulf Lowlands: North Central Region

Talamanca de Tibas

See Tibas, Talamanca de

Tamuín-Tantoc (San Luis Potosí, Mexico)

These two large sites on the Tampaón tributary of the Pánuco River are significant for their architectural features, murals, and sculptural remains. Situated just east of the Sierra Abra Tanchipa escarpment, both are on high points along the southern riverbank, surrounded by low country susceptible to major flooding. They are approximately 7 kilometers apart and 110 kilometers west of the Gulf of Mexico (190 kilometers by water). Although forested until the middle of this century, the region is today a savanna with sugar cane plantations and cattle. At the time of the Spanish conquest there was an important Huastec population in the vicinity.

Tamuín (or El Consuelo) has a series of platforms that support structural groupings. One, which has been cleared, is surmounted by temples, palaces, vats, and low benchlike "altars." Both round and (predominantly) rectangular buildings have veneer masonry, often with cut stone, and a cement covering. A famous Huastec sculpture, "The Adolescent," a nude, tattooed male carrying an infant on his back, was found here in 1918. Du Solier in 1946 excavated an "altar" decorated with black and red paint, depicting an elaborate processional scene. Although earlier occupations are probably present, the time placement of most of the currently visible features can be situated in the Postclassic period. The Instituto Nacional de Antropología e Historia (INAH) resumed reconstruction here in the mid-1990s.

Tantoc (also spelled Tamtok, Tantoque, or Tantocob) is a more extensive site within a great loop of the river. Brought to scientific attention in the 1930s, principally by Joaquin Meade, it has the largest structures and plazas known from the Huasteca region. Major earthen buildings, some of which may partially utilize natural heights, stretch for a kilometer. The two highest structures rise to just over 30 meters above their facing plazas. Smaller rectangular and round structures with veneer masonry are also present. Fragments of large slab sculptures, some with scrolls reminiscent of central Veracruz, have been found here, including the Castrillón Stela, encountered about 1939 and now in the National Museum of Anthropology. Although ceramics from excavations initiated by Stresser-Pean in 1962 suggest a strong Postclassic occupation, it would appear on both architectural and sculptural grounds that parts of the site date to at least the Early Classic. In the mid-1990s Patricio Davila Cabrera reinitiated excavations here for INAH. Tantoc is likely to have a longer and more complex chronology than Tamuín.

FURTHER READINGS

Du Solier, W. 1946. Primer fresco mural Huasteco. *Cuadernos Americanos.* 6:151–159.

Meade, J. 1948. *Arqueología de San Lus Potosí.* Mexico City: Sociedad Mexicana de Geografía y Estadística.

Stresser-Pean, G. 1964. Première campagne de fouilles à Tamtok près de Tamuín, Huasteca. *XXXV Congreso Internacional de Americanistas 1962* 1:387–394.

Wilkerson, S. J. K. 1997. Die Huaxteca: Ein mittelamerikanisches Grenzland. In *Präkolumbische Kulturen am Golf von Mexiko,* pp. 175–186. Zürich: Museum Rietberg.

S. Jeffrey K. Wilkerson

Tancol (Tamaulipas, Mexico)

Occupied in two widely separated periods, Tancol is the type site for a still ill-defined, Formative period cultural manifestation found in the coastal reaches of the northern Gulf Lowlands. Just to the northwest of modern Tampico City, it is situated on a low rise by La Vega Escondida Lagoon (Chairel Lagoon), near where the Tamesi and Pánuco rivers merge. The highest elevation once had a series of twelve round and rectangular mounds, 2 to 6 meters in height, surrounding a plaza or (less probably) a ball court. Some of these buildings had typical Postclassic period plaster coverings. An earthen reservoirlike feature, bordered by a dam or dike, was placed between the structures and the lagoon edge. Ekholm undertook a series of stratigraphic excavations along the northern margins of the site in 1941, locating Postclassic (Las Flores phase) middens similar to those at Pánuco and nearby Las Flores, as well as significant Late Formative deposits contemporary with the El Prisco phase at Pánuco.

The earlier occupation has a strikingly distinct artifact corpus called the Tancol complex. Ceramics include unpolished black and red wares with wide-grooved, incised exterior designs. The marked contrast with the materials from concurrent regional sites, including nearby Isla de Pithaya, suggests a complex multicultural settlement pattern. In recent decades Tancol, and especially its structures, have been greatly affected by the construction of a large water-pumping station, expansive government fish tanks, and a city bypass highway. Today it is further threatened by housing sprawl as metropolitan Tampico absorbs the environs of the Tancol village and site.

FURTHER READINGS

Ekholm, G. F. 1944. Excavations at Tampico and Pánuco in the Huasteca, Mexico. *Anthropological Papers of the American Museum of Natural History*, 38, part 5: 320–512.

S. Jeffrey K. Wilkerson

SEE ALSO

Gulf Lowlands: North Region

Tapias, Las (northwestern Nicaragua)

This site is on an ample expanse of level ground at a bend in the Coco River, occupying both the first and second river terraces. It measures about 7 hectares, with 128 mounds counted; many more were probably destroyed by agricultural activities, especially on the first river terrace.

A hierarchy of mound sizes and heights was noted, with at least one main plaza area and what appears to be a causeway. Despite the site's size, the surface scatter of cultural material was light; a polychrome vase was found at the site by a local farmer.

The span of occupation may have been c. A.D. 300–800, based on the cross-dating of ceramic material. Las Tapias, El Fraile, and Guiliguisca, to the west and southwest, respectively, formed three regional centers that were coeval during at least some of the span A.D. 300–800.

Laraine Fletcher

Tarascan Culture and Religion

In 1522 the Tarascan king ruled over a domain of more than 75,000 square kilometers between the Lerma and Balsas basins in the west central highlands of Mexico. The Tarascan Empire was at that time the second largest empire in Mesoamerica. It was ethnically dominated by a population the Spaniards called "Tarascan," who spoke the language of Michoacán, also called "Tarascan." Their modern descendants refer to themselves as either "Tarascan" or *purépecha* ("commoners" in the native language).

Environment

The Tarascan domain spanned the lands between two of Mexico's greatest rivers, the Lerma-Santiago to the north and the Balsas to the south. The Tarascans controlled four major geographic regions and an enormous variety of resources. The first region, the Tarascan Central Plateau, is a volcanic area above 2000 meters in elevation that constitutes the western extension of the Central Mexican Mesa Central. Human occupation of this region has been focused on the lake basins, such as Pátzcuaro, and the marshes, such as Zacapú.

Second, the semitropical rims contain volcanic mountains and plains decreasing in elevation from 2000 meters to 1200 meters, to the north and south of the Central Plateau. The northern rim includes the Lerma River Basin, Lake Chapala, Lake Cuitzeo, and Lake Yuríria. In the northeast and northwest are thermal springs, obsidian flows (Zinapécuaro-Ucareo in the northeast and Zináparo in the northwest), and, in the northeast, small deposits of silver and gold.

Directly south of the Central Plateau is the third region, the Balsas Depression, including the middle and lower Balsas Basin and the tributary Tepalcatepec Basin, both below 500 meters. Resources of particular value to human occupation include marble deposits in the southwestern Tepalcatepec Basin, and copper, gold, silver, iron pyrites, and lead deposits in the eastern and central Balsas Basin.

The final major region of the Tarascan domain is the southern Sierra Madre, largely located southwest of the Tepalcatepec basin. Deposits of copper, gold, and silver are found in the southeastern part of this region near Huetamo and in the southwestern part near Coalcomán.

Legendary and Historic Expansion

In the legendary history of the Tarascans recounted in the *Relación de Michoacán* (1541), the culture hero Taríacuri established himself as lord of Pátzcuaro (see table), and his two nephews, Hiripan and Tangáxoan, as lords of Ihuatzio and Tzintzuntzan, respectively. Between A.D. 1250 and 1350, this elite lineage under Taríacuri, the *uacúsecha*, effectively dominated political interaction within the Pátzcuaro Basin. By 1350 Taríacuri, with his lineage in control of the largest and richest parts of the basin (Pátzcuaro, Ihuatzio, and Tzintzuntzan), joined with his allies in Urichu, Erongarícuaro, and Pechátaro and began to lead his followers on a series of military campaigns within and outside the Pátzcuaro Basin. The rationale for these conquests is presented in a mystical dream in which Taríacuri foresaw the cosmic mission of creating a state. Beginning with the southwestern corner of the basin itself, the conquests moved to encircle the basin. At this point Taríacuri died, and under Hiripan, based in Ihuatzio, the people moved out to the Lake Cuitzeo Basin. These territories were the most densely settled at contact, and they greatly enriched the *uacúsecha* elite who led these campaigns. However, it is quite clear that at this point the military expansion was little more than a series of raids for booty, made by a war leader, Taríacuri, and later by Hiripan, on behalf of a state that was merely an amalgam of distinct polities, with a series of "capitals" that were residences of the highest-ranking members of the ruling lineages. The booty of military conquest was still being divided among the participating lords, and the conquests themselves were patchy.

Sometime around A.D. 1440, first under Hiripan and later under Tangáxoan, the first steps were made to institutionalize the military conquests and produce a tributary state. This involved the creation of an administrative bureaucracy and the allocation of conquered territories to members of the nobility. By the 1460s, the Tarascans had taken the province of Zacatula, on the Pacific Coast at the mouth of the Balsas; they had advanced their northeastern frontier into the Toluca Basin, established centers north of the Lerma River, and moved north of Lake Chapala in the west. Despite some later losses of territory when the Tarascan King ceded Irechecua Tzintzuntzani ("the Kingdom of Tzintuntzan") to the Spanish crown, they effectively controlled the 75,000 square kilometers between the Lerma and Balsas river systems, from the modern Michoacán-Mexico border to the Sayula Basin in the west.

Structure of Authority

The central administration of the state was located in the capital, Tzintzuntzan. There the Tarascan king, or *irecha*, held his court, administered justice and received emissaries from within and outside his territory. The court included members of the Tarascan nobility in a series of hierarchically organized offices, including the *irecha* (the head of the *uacúsecha* lineage; the king or *cazonci*), *angatacuri* (governor or prime minister), captain (military leader in warfare), *petámuti* (chief priest), tribute minister (steward in charge of the tribute collectors), *carachacapacha* (governors of the four quarters of the state), and *achaecha* (other members of the nobility acting as advisors).

Below the court was a large bureaucracy composed of members of the nobility and of commoners. This included *quangariecha* (captains of the military units in wartime), *ocámbecha* (tribute collectors), *mayordomos* (heads of units that stored and distributed tribute, produced crafts, and served within the palace), priests (a hierarchy of ten levels below the chief priest serving in temples dedicated to the state religion), and *angámecha* (leaders of towns and villages).

All positions appear to have been hereditary from father to son, with preference given to sons of senior wives. However, in most positions the Tarascan king had final approval of the officeholder. Local leaders were chosen by the king from among a number of candidates; they could be replaced and their decisions overruled by the king. In some instances, ties between the central dynasty and a local leader were reinforced by marriage to one of the king's daughters.

Economic Structure

This flow of authority from the center to the village was supported by the fundamental system of land and resource ownership. All land titles within the Tarascan domain were legitimized by having come from the king. This included even agricultural lands, fishing rights, min-

GENEALOGY OF THE TARASCAN KINGS.

Ruler	Seat of Power	Reign
COLONIAL		
Don Antonio Huitziméngari	Governor of Michoacán	1545–1562
Don Francisco Taríacuri	Governor of Michoacán	1543–1545
Don Pedro de Arellano[1]	Corregidor of Michoacán	1530–1543
PROTOHISTORIC		
Tangáxuan II (Tzintzicha Don Francisco)	Tzintzuntzan	1520–1530
Zuangua	Tzintzuntzan	1479–1520
Tzitzispandáquare	Tzintzuntzan	1454–1479
LATE POSTCLASSIC		
Tangáxuan I	Tzintzuntzan	?–1454
Hirepan	Ihuatzio	
Hiquingaje (younger son)	Pátzcuaro	c. 1350–?
Taríacuri	Pátzcuaro	c. 1300–1350[2]
Pauacume II	Pátzcuaro	
EARLY POSTCLASSIC		
Uapeani II	Uayameo	
Curatame I	Uayameo	
Uapeani I	Uayameo	
Pauacume I	Uayameo	
Sicuirancha	Uayameo	
Thicatame (Hireti-ticatame)	Zacapú, then Zichaxuquaro	

[1]Arellano assumed control after the execution of Tangáxuan II and acted as regent for the king's sons.
[2]Interrupted by brief rule by Curatame II, his older son.

eral resources, and hunting territories within the Pátzcuaro Basin.

There were four categories of land tenure: patrimonial lands of the royal dynasty (*uacúsecha*); fiscal lands of the state, on which tributary goods were produced; lands allotted to local lords; and lands of the commoners. In addition, the state controlled usufruct rights for hunting, fishing, and lumber, state mines, and the long-distance merchants.

Labor to work the state lands was recruited from among the commoners (*purépecha)*, with additional lands worked by slaves. The slaves (*teruparacua-euaecha*) included war captives, criminals, those who sold themselves into slavery, and others bought in the market. In addition, there were *acípecha,* who appear to have been servants of the nobility. Finally, each son of the ruling king was granted lands that were maintained by his mother's family.

Within the Tarascan Empire there were several channels through which goods circulated. Those under the direct control of the state included the state long-distance merchants, the tribute system, and various categories of

T

land and water resources allocated by the royal dynasty. In addition, there were regional and local markets, which appear to have had overlapping territories and which crossed the borders of the state itself.

Social Structure

Most of our evidence about Tarascan culture comes from Tzintzuntzan, the settlement that was ceded to the Spaniards in 1522. It had flourished during the Proto-historic period (A.D. 1450–1520) as the imperial capital, and before that as the largest center of the Tarascan state (1350–1450). Other large Tarascan sites that have been studied archaeologically include Ihuatzio and Urichu in the Pátzcuaro Basin, El Palacio and Milpillas in the Zacapú Basin, Huandacareo, Tres Cerritos, and Zinapécuaro in the Cuitzeo Basin, and Acámbaro on the Lerma.

All persons living within the same house were considered a family. This sometimes included extended family, but some households comprised, for example, only a married couple or a mother and son. The average family size for the Tarascan region was five to six persons. The recognized forms of marriage are described in some detail in the *Relación de Michoacán* (1541): monogamy and several forms of polygamy, including mother-and-daughter polygamy. There is mention of one king who had at least sixteen wives, seven of whom were buried with him. It is likely that polygamous households were concentrated among the elite, since references to polygamy always refer to the nobility. Sororate and levirate marriages were also practiced. Residence was generally virilocal, although since it was on land provided by the husband's father, it might be termed patrilocal. Kin groups, probably patrilineages, had some role in regulating marriage and descent, at least among the upper class; however, the kinship terminology and the ethnohistorical documents offer no evidence for strong matrilineal or patrilineal institutions.

There is considerable evidence for the presence of wards or barrios within Tzintzuntzan, and these territorial units appear to have had marriage-regulating and religious and ceremonial functions in the center. For both upper- and lower-class residents, marriage was officially recognized only if it took place within the same ward. Tzintzuntzan had fifteen or more endogamous, territorial units with ceremonial functions. Occupational specialists may have resided in separate wards. However, within Tzintzuntzan these wards had no land-regulating func-

tion; that was done on a settlement-wide basis. There was a second level of territorial grouping within the settlement; this unit consisted of twenty-five households and was used for tribute collection, labor for public works, and taking censuses. An official of the government, the *ocámbecha*, was appointed to oversee each of these units.

In the ethnohistoric documents four social classes are distinguished: the king (*irecha, cazonci*) and lords (*señores*); the nobles (*principales*); the commoners (*la gente baja, purépecha*); and slaves. Each class was distinguished by dress, household structure, marriage, wealth, responsibilities and privileges, and access to occupations; there was minimal movement between these classes.

State Religion

The basic Tarascan conception of the world shared fundamental principles with all Mesoamerican societies. The universe was believed to be made up of three parts: the sky (*arandaro*), associated with eagles, hawks, and falcons; the earth (*echerendo*), viewed as a goddess with four quarters; and the underworld (*cumiechucuaro*), or the place of death, associated with mice, gophers, moles, snakes, and caves. The four quarters of the earth were associated with the cardinal directions, plus the center, and with particular colors: black (*turis*) with the south, white (*urauras*) with the west, red (*charapequa*) with the east, yellow (*tsipambequa*) with the north, and blue (*chupiqua*) with the center. The north and south were also referred to as the right and left, respectively, based on their direction seen from the vantage of the rising sun. Not surprisingly, given the geography of Michoacán, the west was also associated with the god of the sea, and the east with the earth goddess, Cuerauáperi—east was the direction from which she brought the rains.

There are a number of Central Mexican traits, associated with basic belief systems, that have no counterparts in the Tarascan intellectual tradition. Perhaps most significant is the relative paucity of major religious cults, and the (unsuccessful) attempt on the part of the Tarascans to relate the major deities in a divine "family." There is no clear indication of dualism as a fundamental principle of Tarascan ordering, and few of the deities have clear counterparts of the opposite gender. The major deities, whether male or female, controlled multiple forces of nature. Major Central Mexican deities either were not worshiped at all or may have had a Tarascan counterpart in a minor (usually regional) deity. Thus, there was no Tarascan Tlaloc; rain was the province of the earth goddess, Cuerauáperi. There was no Quetzalcoatl, although Hurendecuavecara (Tiripeme Cuarencha) may have aspects that recall Quetzalcoatl.

Among the many deities known, it is Cuerauáperi, Curicaueri, and Xarátanga who are mentioned most often, to whom the greatest number of temples seem to have been dedicated, and who were linked most directly with the Tarascan state. The earth was conceived of as the body of the great creator goddess, Cuerauáperi, who represented the forces that controlled fertility, including rain, birth, and death. She was the mother of all the gods and was actively venerated throughout Tarascan territory. The sky forces were associated with major celestial bodies, including the sun, moon, and stars. The sun was embodied in Curita Caheri or Curicaueri, the great burning god and the god of fire. He was both the messenger of the sun (the sun's rays), connecting the earth and sky, and the warmth of the hearth. As a sky force, he was referred to by different terms for the rising, noon, and setting sun; as an earth force, these phases of the sun were related to directions. As the original patron god of the Tarascan royal dynasty, he was a warrior and the god of the hunt. The moon goddess, Xarátanga, was the daughter of the earth creator and wife of the sun, and was associated with childbirth and fertility.

There were, broadly speaking, two types of major rituals represented by the monthly feasts. The first acknowledged the yearly cycle of birth and death in an agrarian society: the rebirth in spring, the fall harvest, and the return of migratory animals. These festivals were devoted primarily to Cuerauáperi, Xarátanga, or one of the related fertility deities. The second type had as its main focus the glorification of the state and the legitimation of the king. Thus, the "great gathering" (ecuata conscuaro) was the scene of the retelling of official state history; the "imprisoning of rebels" (hanciuanscuaro) allowed communities to publicly renew their loyalty to the state; and the "initiation of warriors" (purecatacuaro) gave social and moral prestige to the military power of the empire. Not surprisingly, these festivals were devoted to the Tarascan patron deity, Curicaueri, and to other sky gods associated with warfare.

The Tarascans divided time into parts of the day, days of the month, and months of the solar year. The basic calendar was the huriyata miuqua, or sun count. This solar year (uexurini) was divided into eighteen months of twenty days. The month was the cutsi miuqua, or moon count, with five extra days. Within the month, units of five or ten days were recognized, and often delimited the length of festivals. The day itself was a solar unit, huriatequa, and was divided into four parts based on the movement of the sun; the night was divided into four corresponding parts. The calendar adopted by the Tarascan state has been reconstructed and was similar to the Protohistoric Matlatzinca and Aztec solar calendars.

Tarascan public architecture associated with the state religion was characterized by large artificial platforms on which one or more stepped pyramids were built. The platforms and pyramids were constructed of a rubble core of volcanic stone, faced with dressed stone. Whenever possible, the natural slope of a hill was terraced to produce platforms with minimal building effort, but the aim was a size (up to 300 meters or more wide) that when faced with dressed stone and viewed from below would be monumental in impact. Examples exist in Tzintzuntzan, Pátzcuaro, Acámbaro, Zinapécuaro, and Huandacareo. A specialized pyramid form, the keyhole-shaped yacata, was constructed at major religious centers associated with the Tarascan sun god Curicaueri. Wooden temples were built on top of these platforms.

A number of stone sculptures have been found adjacent to the major temples. These include three chac mool forms and a coyote from the site of Ihuatzio; the coyote represented the goddess Xarátanga, one of the deities to whom the center was dedicated. Other large sculptures, including sacrificial altars and depictions of Curicaueri, were located at Tzintzuntzan and were destroyed by the Spaniards. Although there was no ball court at the Tarascan capital, there were ball courts in other Tarascan centers, continuing a tradition known in Michoacán from at least the late Classic period. Within the Pátzcuaro Basin, a ball court existed at Ihuatzio.

Tarascan-Aztec Relations

The Tarascans are generally considered to have been the foremost enemy of the Aztecs. From the 1450s until the Spanish conquest, these two powers were continually engaged in offensive or defensive military actions. In response to repeated Aztec aggression along their eastern frontier, the Tarascans established a series of fortified, strategically placed settlements at the major passes from the Lerma River in the north to the Balsas River in the south. These were generally staffed by non-Tarascans, but they often included Tarascan colonists, and all were controlled directly by Tarascan administrators from Tzintzuntzan.

T

It is clear that both the Tarascans and the Aztecs had economic interests in portions of the disputed territory. The middle Balsas is a zone of metamorphic rock with copper, tin, silver, and gold deposits, greenstone, and localized salt production. The northern border region was also of great value to the Tarascans, containing major obsidian deposits and sacred thermal springs. In a larger framework, the most active sections of the border controlled access to the Lerma and Balsas river systems, with the Tarascans preventing Aztec penetration of either. This effectively blocked further Aztec expansion to the west and northwest along major trade routes.

The Tarascan frontier with the Aztecs was clearly a closed border. Although it was only 160 kilometers from the border settlement of Taximaroa to Tenochtitlan, and messengers could move between the two capitals (Tzintzuntzan and Tenochtitlan) within four days of travel, clearly movement was strongly restricted. Aztec messengers had to present themselves at the official "ports of entry" and await permission to pass into the Tarascan domain, under Tarascan escort. Safety was clearly the enforcing principle, and the continuing hostilities along the border bred distrust of spies, who might precede raids or major campaigns. The movement of Tarascans within Aztec territory was probably also difficult, since Tarascan culture was clearly distinct from Aztec, and Tarascans would have had to undergo deliberate cultural (including linguistic) transformation to pass. On both sides, one solution was to use Otomí or Matlatzinca messengers and spies, but this meant that communication between the elites of these states was indirect and intermittent.

The available ethnohistoric and archaeological data indicate that the primary type of economic interaction between the Tarascan and Aztec domains included goods acquired by long-distance traders of both empires. Tarascan long-distance merchants traveled to the borders of the Tarascan state—to Zacatula on the Pacific coast and Taximaroa on the frontier with the Aztecs—to acquire materials utilized by the elite of Tzintzuntzan. These included green obsidian from Central Mexico and the Cerro Tequila sources, and a range of raw materials that would have come from Central and Southern Mexico, including jade, onyx, serpentine, pyrites, and copal. There is, however, no indication that Tarascan long-distance merchants went beyond the borders of the Tarascan domain, nor that Aztec merchants (*pochteca*) entered Tarascan territory. Exchanges made at frontier settlements like Taximaroa may have been directly between Tarascan and Aztec mer-chants, or Tarascan merchants may have dealt with Matlatzinca or Otomí traders at these places.

Tarascan–West Mexican Relations

The Tarascans were able to incorporate the uncentralized polities on their eastern frontier into their empire relatively rapidly, but they were not so successful in the north and west, where they faced a variety of small states. While the relative weakness of these political systems made conquest easier, it also made incorporation into the empire more difficult. During the 1460s, major campaigns were launched into the Lake Chapala Basin and to the southwest to Zacatula (Zacatollan). In the following two decades, much of the territory gained from what is now Jalisco and Colima was lost. The inability of the Tarascans to hold territory west or north of Lake Chapala was probably due to three factors: the politically factional nature of this region, where rebellion was a constant threat; the diversion of Tarascan military strength to the eastern portions of their empire; and the general difficulties that pre-Hispanic states had in holding hostile territory beyond a distance of five or six days' travel from political capitals.

The Tarascan military expansion to the west was clearly motivated by the desire of the royal dynasty to control specific raw materials. Once conquered, the western region supplied silver, gold, copper, and salt through the state tribute system. However, there were a number of other scarce raw materials found in Jalisco and Nayarit that were used by the Tarascan elite and probably obtained by long-distance merchants: tin, marine shell, chrysocolla, malachite, azurite, hematite, cinnabar, pyrites, lead, specular iron, opal, quartz crystals, and gourds. In addition, the presence of the term *peyote* in the *Diccionario Grande* of the Tarascan language, without a Tarascan name, suggests that it was imported from Nahuat-speaking peoples; the most likely sources would have been populations to the west and north of the empire. Finally, it is likely that Tarascans obtained turquoise through trade networks operating beyond their northwestern border.

Summary

Apart from specific, unique traits, Tarascan culture was characterized by the following traits: an administrative capital, with only weakly developed urbanism elsewhere; full-time craft specialists who were associated with the royal palace; household and workshop production serving local and regional markets; a geopolitical core that was spatially and demographically small relative to the territory under control, yet dependent on territorial tribute for basic resources; an ethnically homogeneous economic heartland surrounded by multiethnic communities along the military frontiers; and an extremely high degree of centralization of administrative and judicial functions, reinforced by the interweaving of state and religious authority.

FURTHER READINGS

Gorenstein, S. 1985. Settlements of the Protohistoric Tarascan Core. In M. Foster and P. Weigand (eds.), *The Archaeology of West and Northwest Mesoamerica,* pp. 117–130. Boulder: Westview Press.

Gorenstein, S., and H. P. Pollard. 1983. *The Tarascan Civilization: A Late Prehispanic Cultural System.* Vanderbilt University Publications in Anthropology, 28. Nashville, Tenn.

Pollard, H. P. 1993. *Taríacuri's Legacy: The Prehispanic Tarascan State.* Norman: University of Oklahoma Press.

Helen Perlstein Pollard

SEE ALSO

Michoacán Region; Postclassic Period; Tzintzuntzan

Tayasal (Petén, Guatemala)

Centered on Lake Petén along the densely occupied spine of the Tayasal Peninsula, the larger Tayasal-Paxcaman zone includes the sites of Tayasal, Cenote, and Paxcaman. Smaller sites and largely perishable housing once dotted the shoreline and intermediate areas. There is evidence for continuous occupation of the zone beginning during the Middle Formative period (750–250 B.C.) and continuing through the present.

The archaeological site of Tayasal probably is not identical with the historic capital of the same name. Several alternative locations for the Maya provincial capital of Tayasal have been suggested, including the archaeological site of Topoxte in nearby Lake Yaxha and the modern island of Flores in Lake Petén. Archaeological remains from the Tayasal-Paxcaman zone and Flores largely predate the Late Postclassic to historic period time that would be expected for a historic regional capital. Remains dating to the Early and Middle Postclassic periods (A.D. 950–1350), however, are relatively common at Tayasal, Flores, and other lakeshore settings around Lake Petén. The largest population in the peninsular zone dates to the earlier Late Classic and Terminal Classic periods (A.D. 550–

950), when the entire zone is estimated to have had a population of between 21,000 and 34,000 people.

FURTHER READINGS

Chase, A. F. 1976. Topoxte and Tayasal: Ethnohistory in Archaeology. *American Antiquity* 41:154–168.

———. 1982. Con manos arriba: Archaeology and Tayasal. *American Antiquity* 47:167–171.

———. 1985. Archaeology in the Maya Heartland: The Tayasal-Paxcaman Zone, Lake Petén, Guatemala. *Archaeology* 38:32–39.

———. 1990. Maya Archaeology and Population Estimates in the Tayasal-Paxcaman Zone, Petén, Guatemala. In T. P. Culbert and D. S. Rice (eds.), *Precolumbian Population History in the Maya Lowlands,* pp. 149–165. Albuquerque: University of New Mexico Press.

Arlen F. Chase

SEE ALSO

Maya Lowlands: South

Tazumal

See Chalchuapa

Tehuacán Region

The Tehuacán region is a basin about 115 kilometers long and 50 kilometers wide in the south central part of the Mexican highlands, encompassing the southern part of Puebla and northernmost Oaxaca. Along its eastern border, the Sierra Madre Oriental shields the region from the Gulf Coast rains, and annual rainfall is less than 300 mm.

The region is comprised of seven micro-environments, or ecozones. Below the eastern flanking rain forest zone at the top of the Sierra Madre Oriental lie the alluvial eastern slopes of the Tehuacán Valley. The main vegetation is thorn forest, but lusher gallery forest occurs at the edge of the Salado River and along some southwest-trending arroyos. As one ascends the flanks of the mountains, the thorn forest gradually includes more pines and oaks. Although statistical data show that most of this region has the same limited rainfall (less than 300 mm) as the rest of the valley, where it occurs only in the rainy season, rainfall is much greater (as much as 800 mm) and of longer duration in the mountains; some of this flows down into the arroyos of the eastern zone, providing a water supply during all but the driest part of the dry season.

In the southeastern portion of the Tehuacán Valley are

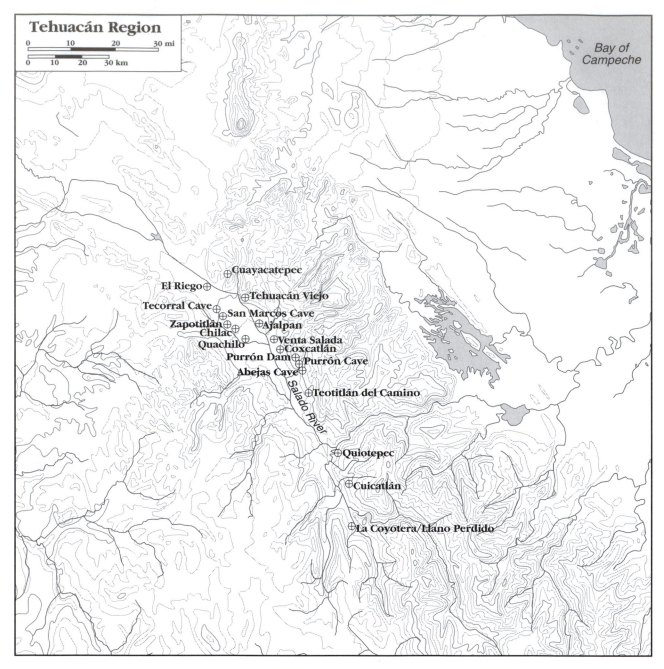

Tehuacán Region. Map design by Mapping Specialists Limited, Madison, Wisconsin.

the canyon bottoms and dissected alluvial slopes, where animals congregate during the dry season. Water can be obtained throughout the year by damming.

To the west is the valley steppe, the major ecozone running the length of the Tehuacán Valley from north to south as well as through the major east–west river valley of the Zapotitlán to the west. This ecozone is characterized by travertine-impregnated salty soils with a predominance of short-grass vegetation, except along the flanks of hills or terraces and the main waterways (the Zapotitlán, Salado, Calapilla, and Xiquila), where gallery forest occurs along the humid river bottoms. Though it is uninviting as a whole, parts of this ecozone can be exploited relatively successfully by irrigation, and seeps in saline deposits can be worked to obtain salt.

The western travertine slopes of the Tehuacán Valley

and the northeastern travertine slopes and canyons of the Zapotitlán Valley form an even more inhospitable zone, with a Sonoran desert type of vegetation, few springs, and little rain; shallow soils cover limestone or travertine beds. This ecozone has salt and limited game, and edible plants appear in some profusion during the rainy season. Similar are the canyons eroded into the travertine slopes, but these have deeper alluvial soils.

The most inviting area is the El Riego Oasis, a lush patch with permanent springs, rich in plants and animals. Its relatively small area can accommodate only a small human population.

Few environmental changes appear to have taken place in the Tehuacán region since the Pleistocene, when valley floor grassland zones were larger and the oak-pine forest of the highlands crept down to squeeze out the thorn forest. Thirty-five years (1960–1995) of research have uncovered nine cultural phases in the Tehuacán region.

Ajuereado Phase

Ajuereado, (30,000 ± 10,000–8650 B.C.) was characterized by small, nomadic families or microbands who moved their camps three or four times a year. These people, living in the so-called big-game hunting stage or mammoth-hunting period, were far from being the large-game hunters they are often supposed to have been. For subsistence they collected wild plants and hunted and trapped animals. During the earliest part of the phase, they hunted such animals as horses and antelope of now-extinct species, but even then most of their meat came from smaller game, such as jackrabbits, giant turtles, birds, gophers, rats, and other small mammals. In the later part of the phase, only species that exist today were available for trapping.

Tools manufactured were not numerous, and all were made by chipping flint. They include a series of bifacially chipped leaf-shaped knives and projectile points, keeled and ovoid end scrapers, flake and bifacial choppers, side scrapers, gravers, and crude prismatic blades struck from even cruder polyhedral cores. No ground stone was utilized, and few perishable remains were recovered.

El Riego Phase

Ajuereado gradually evolved into El Riego, (c. 8650–5700 B.C.). Like their predecessors, these people were seasonally nomadic and depended on plant collecting and animal trapping, supplemented by some hunting, for their subsistence. A definite increase in population and some changes in the settlement pattern seem to have taken place. El Riego sites are almost equally divided between very small camps of family groups or microbands and much larger sites that probably represent macroband camps.

During the dry season, apparently, people still hunted and trapped in small groups and probably suffered famine, but when the spring came, and later the rains, a number of microbands seem to have come together in macrobands to live off the lusher vegetation. The evidence suggests that they were collecting a large variety of plants, and it may have been in this period that they realized that if one dropped a seed in the ground, a plant came up—a concept basic to the beginning of agriculture. Among plants that later became domesticated, the El Riego people were eating one variety of squash (*Cucurbita mixta*), chile, and avocado. It is possible that they were also gathering and consuming wild maize.

The tools recovered give considerable evidence about the industries these people pursued. They finely chipped a variety of contracting-stemmed and concave-based projectile points, which were probably used to tip atlatl darts used in the hunt. Large plano-convex scrapers and choppers chipped from pebbles or nodules of flint were even more prevalent. These tools could have been used for preparing skins, but it seems more probable that they were used for preparing various plants. Some blades, burins, and end scrapers of types found in the Ajuereado phase continued to be made and used. Mortars and pestles were particularly numerous and became characteristic of the Archaic. Such ground stone tools were probably used to grind plant and animal foods into some sort of palatable stew.

El Riego also yielded the first evidence of weaving and wood-working: knotted nets, a few small fragments of twined baskets and coiled baskets, fragments of dart shafts, and pieces of traps. One of the most surprising findings was evidence of relatively elaborate multiple burials, which suggest the possibility of complex beliefs and ceremonies. The ceremonialism that is so characteristic of the later Mexican periods may thus have begun at this time.

The El Riego phase seems to be related to early cultures of northern Mexico, the U.S. Southwest, and the Great Basin, areas which have been classified as belonging to the Desert Culture tradition. However, the later preceramic phases that follow El Riego in the Tehuacán Valley are difficult to classify in this tradition because they have

T

incipient agriculture and they developed distinctive types of grinding tools, baskets, nets, projectile points, blades, and other implements that are all unlike artifacts found in the Desert Culture manifestations.

Coxcatlán Phase

The phase developing out of El Riego, Coxcatlán, has been dated by twelve radiocarbon determinations indicating that it lasted from c. 5700 to 3825 B.C. The way of life may have been much the same as during El Riego, with people living in nomadic microbands in the dry season and macrobands in the wet season. The macrobands, however, seem to have been larger than those of the earlier phase, and they seem to have stayed in one place for longer periods—perhaps because of their rather different subsistence pattern.

Although the Coxcatlán people were still basically plant collectors who did a little animal trapping and hunting, all through this period they acquired more and more domesticated plants. Early in the phase they began using domesticated maize, chile, avocados, and gourds. By the middle of the phase they had acquired amaranth, tepary beans, yellow zapotes, and squash (*Cucurbita moschata),* and by the end they may have had black and white zapotes. Apparently, microbands still came together at some favorite collecting spot in the spring, and it may be that while they were there they planted some of their domesticates. This action would have given them food so they could continue living at that camp after they had consumed the wild foods. As the numbers of domesticates increased, the group could stay together as a macroband for longer and longer periods. With the onset of the dry season and the depletion of their agricultural surpluses, they probably broke up again into nomadic microbands.

Coxcatlán industries differed little from those of El Riego. Some different types of tanged projectile points were manufactured, blades were more delicately made, scrapers and choppers were of new types, and true metates with manos were replacing mortars, pestles, and milling stones. Some minor improvements were also made in the manufacture of nets, coiled baskets, bags, and blankets.

The most distinctive aspect of the Coxcatlán phase is its incipient agriculture, yet Tehuacán was not the only early center of plant domestication. In fact, the accruing archaeological data on the beginnings of New World plant domestication seem to indicate that there was no single center; rather, domesticates had multiple origins over a wide area of Nuclear America and the southern United States.

Abejas Phase

On the basis of eight radiocarbon determinations, the Abejas phase probably lasted from 3825 to 2600 B.C. The settlement pattern seems to have changed significantly during this period. Ten of the known cave occupations were hunting (dry-season) camps of macrobands, while eight of the macroband settlements appear to have been larger (five to ten pit houses), some of them perhaps occupied year round, on river terraces in the valley. This more sedentary way of life was made possible by more efficient food production based on plants already known and on newer species—domesticated *canavalia* (jack beans) and perhaps pumpkins *(C. pepo)* and common beans, as well as some varieties of hybrid maize with teosinte introgression. Even with this increase in domesticates, botanical studies and studies of feces reveal that more than 70 percent of the people's foods still came from wild plants and animals.

Many of the older techniques of artifact manufacture continued, though the types made were a little different. Some of the types that carried over into much later times originated during this period: split-stitch basketry, stone bowls and *ollas,* oval *metates* and large plano-convex *manos,* and obsidian blades made from long cylindrical cores.

If this phase provides evidence of a Marxian "Neolithic revolution," it must be noted that the revolution came long after the first plant domestications; the population showed no sudden increase in size, and the artifacts were little better than those of the preceding phase. In fact, Abejas was part of a Neolithic evolution, not a revolution.

Purrón Phase

Six radiocarbon determinations place Purrón between 2600 and 1600 B.C. The least clearly understood Tehuacán phase in the sequence, it was represented by only two floors in excavation. Excavated materials included a few plant remains, early tripsacoid maize cobs, *manos, metates,* scrapers, fine obsidian blades, and a number of very crude, crumbly pieces of broken pottery—the earliest yet found in Mesoamerica. This pottery is made in the same vessel forms as the Abejas stone bowls and *ollas.* It may not be the first to be modeled in Mexico, but rather an imitation of still earlier pottery (as yet unfound) in some other area.

Ajalpan Phase

Ajalpan, dated by eighteen radiocarbon determinations between 1600 and 900 B.C., is much better understood. Seventeen floors were found in excavation and two open sites were found during survey. The Ajalpan people were full-time agriculturists; they planted early hybrid maize, mixta, moschata and pepo squashes, gourds, amaranth, beans, chile, avocado, zapotes, and cotton. They seem to have lived in small wattle-and-daub villages of one to three hundred inhabitants. Whether they built religious structures is not yet known, but their figurines, mainly female, attest to a complex religious life.

Many stone tools of the older types were still made, but one of the more notable industries of this period was pottery-making. The well-made pottery was usually unpainted, although a few examples of monochrome specular-hematite redware occurred. A limited number of forms were modeled; the *tecomate,* or small-mouthed seed jar, is the dominant type of receptacle. The pottery, large figurines (often hollow), and rocker-dentate stamp decoration are like those found in the earliest cultural manifestations in lowland Mesoamerica—Veracruz, Chiapas, Pacific lowland Guatemala, and the Pacific coast of Oaxaca. This similarity does not, however, mean there was a migration, diffusion, or relationship only from the coast to the highlands, since remains from periods of comparable age occur throughout the highlands.

Santa María Phase

Some pottery of the Santa Mariá period resembles pottery of the Veracruz coast, but other resemblances are to the earliest ceramic remains in Monte Albán, the Valley of Mexico, and other highland regions. These similarities provide good evidence for correlating a number of sequences from several areas, not only with Santa Mariá but also with one another. Cross-dating indicates that the Santa Mariá period lasted from just before 900 to about 200 B.C. During this time the people lived in small wattle-and-daub houses in villages oriented around a single larger village that had ceremonial structures.

The Santa Mariá people were full-time farmers, using all the plants previously known, many of which had been developed into much more productive hybrids. Excavation at various sites around Purrón Dam indicates that this is when irrigation was first used. Further, this study shows how a group of inhabitants at the foot of the dam gained control of other hamlets downstream. In subsequent early Palo Blanco times, when Purrón Dam was a huge structure, the descendants of these people became the rulers of a large hilltop town that controlled various villages and hamlets downstream. Santa Mariá thus marks the gradual rise of a ranking system and a shift from the sacred to the secular in terms of power.

It is in this period that the great coastal Olmec sites rose, but their influence was not great in the Tehuacán Valley. Trade with them and with other cultures grew in importance. Trade in graywares was intense with Oaxaca, which was beginning to pull ahead of Tehuacán, and Tehuacán was part of the Orizaba obsidian trade network; in fact, obsidian became an indicator of upper-class status.

Palo Blanco Phase

People of the Palo Blanco period, dated between 200 B.C. and A.D. 700, were full-time agriculturists who systematically used irrigation. To known domesticates, they had added tomatoes, peanuts, lima beans, guavas, and turkeys. They lived in villages or hamlets in wattle-and-daub houses, either oriented toward or adjacent to large hilltop ceremonial centers that had the elaborate stone pyramids, plazas, ball courts, and other massive structures typical of Mesoamerican urban culture. Some of these centers covered whole mountaintops and, in terms of population, might be considered cities.

Palo Blanco manufactured products were varied and more elaborate than those of previous phases. Particularly distinctive were the fine gray and orange pottery, worked obsidian, bark cloth, and elaborately woven cotton fabrics.

Trade ties with other regions became stronger. Palo Blanco seems to have been an extension of the Monte Albán III (and IV?) cultures of central Oaxaca, but it was also heavily influenced by the Mixteca Alta to the west, from which it imported numerous Thin Orange bowls. Tehuacán was also part of the obsidian trade network; the numerous salt-producing sites in the valley suggest that some of this output was processed for export.

Some sort of chiefdom may have developed in Tehuacán during the Palo Blanco phase. Elsewhere—in Oaxaca and the Valley of Mexico—true city-states evolved at this time.

Venta Salada Phase

The final period in the Tehuacán Valley falls between A.D. 700 and 1540. The people were full-time agriculturists who used irrigation and supplemented their economy by commerce with other regions. Local salt-making and cotton-processing industries made products for export. Other manufactured articles included such distinctive items as polychrome pottery, a wide variety of cotton fabrics, bark cloth, chipped stone tools, and arrowpoints. More than fifty occupations of this final phase have been

T

excavated, and about two hundred sites have been found in surface surveys, providing a great deal of information about the social organization of Venta Salada. Politically, the valley seems to have been divided up into a series of little kingdoms, each of which had urban centers with surrounding hamlets. The excavation of Tehuacán Viejo, a hilltop city-state capital, revealed a mural with hieroglyphs in the style of the Codex Borgia; it therefore seems that the codices in this group pertain to the peoples of Tehuacán. Furthermore, ethnohistorical studies reveal that at about this time the Nonoalco from Tula invaded the valley and became rulers of at least three city-states—Teotitlán del Camino, Coxcatlán, and Tehuacán. Further studies of this realm and more intensive excavation of Tehuacán Viejo should yield a rich body of information about this final pre-Hispanic occupation of the Tehuacán Valley.

FURTHER READINGS

Drennan, R. D., P. T. Fitzgibbons, and H. Dehn. 1990. Imports and Exports in Classic Mesoamerican Political Economy: The Tehuacán Valley and the Teotihuacan Obsidian Industry. *Research in Economic Anthropology* 12:176–199.

Johnson, F. (ed.). 1972. *Chronology and Irrigation.* Vol. 4 of (R. MacNeish, ed.) *The Prehistory of the Tehuacán Valley.* Austin: University of Texas Press.

MacNeish, R. S., F. Peterson, and K. V. Flannery. 1970. *Ceramics.* Vol. 3 of *The Prehistory of the Tehuacán Valley.* Austin: University of Texas Press.

MacNeish, R. S., M. L. Fowler, A. Garcia-Cook, F. A. Peterson, A. Nelken-Turner, and J. A. Neeley. 1975. *Excavation and Reconnaissance.* Vol. 5 of *The Prehistory of the Tehuacán Valley.* Austin: University of Texas Press.

Sisson, Edward B. 1973. *First Annual Report of the Coxcatlan Project.* Andover: Robert S. Peabody Foundation for Archaeology.

Smith, C. 1967. Plant Remains. In D. Byers (ed.), *The Prehistory of the Tehuacán Valley,* vol. 1, pp. 220–255. Austin: University of Texas Press.

Smith, C., and T. Kerr. 1968. Pre-Conquest Plant Fibers from the Tehuacán Valley, Mexico. *Economic Geography* 22:354–358.

Richard S. MacNeish

Temesco (México, Mexico)

Temesco is a small civic-ceremonial center on the eastern side of the Valley of Mexico, situated on a sloping plain below Cerro Portezuelo. Pottery fragments and stone implements from within the four ceremonial structures and from surrounding stratigraphic excavations are consistent with the Terminal Late Formative types of the valley, dating from the first century B.C., as confirmed by radiocarbon and obsidian hydration analysis.

Trenches excavated in two mounds to analyze the wall profiles showed that each structure was covered with fill and rebuilt three times during a relatively short period. Structure sides were faced with stones set in mud mortar over fill, usually forming a sloping wall *(talud)* divided by a narrow offset. Variations suggest experimentation with building techniques and organization by simultaneous work crews. Each structure probably supported a room built of perishable materials. Small, shallow, clay-lined basins were carved into the hard soil (tepetate) underlying the structures; their function is not known.

The Temesco evidence suggests an alternative interpretation of regional culture change processes. Temesco may have been a small independent polity, supported by surrounding villagers until Teotihuacan became dominant in the Basin of Mexico.

FURTHER READINGS

Dixon, K. A. 1966. Obsidian Dates from Temesco, Valley of Mexico. *American Antiquity* 31:640–643.

———. 1969. A Comparison of Radiocarbon and Obsidian Hydration Dating as Applied to Ceremonial Architecture at Temesco, Valley of Mexico. *Katunob* 7(2):9–16.

Keith A. Dixon

SEE ALSO

Basin of Mexico; Cerro Portezuelo

Tenam Rosario and Environs (Chiapas, Mexico)

Tenam Rosario was the largest and most complex of the Late Classic *tenam,* or fortified hilltop sites, of Chiapas. The site lies atop a 100-meter-high limestone mesa in the semiarid thorn forest at the northwestern edge of the Upper Tributaries region of the Grijalva River Basin, an area of relatively thin and rocky soils that favor surface visibility of the sites and thousands of individual house foundations. Tenam Rosario was founded about A.D. 650, possibly by immigrants from Yaxchilan; it endured until about 1000, when the entire region was virtually abandoned. Tenam Rosario was but one of nineteen coeval polities or kingdoms known for this densely populated region during the Late Classic period.

The main ceremonial center covers the 4 hectares of the mesa top; the sides of the mesa bear impressive habitational terraces and some fortification walls, bringing the total occupied area to 17.5 hectares. The most unusual feature of the fortified center is its ten plazas and seven ball courts; the latter appear to correspond to ball courts found at secondary centers within the Rosario Valley, leading de Montmollin to suggest that the center was a microcosm of the Rosario polity itself. All mounds are constructed of stone rubble with carefully finished and fitted small stones for veneer. Unlike its contemporaneous capital centers, Tenam Rosario has one known carved stela with a long count date and seven carved ball court markers. The large ball court disks depict warriors, some in mexicanized style and others in clear Maya style, with atlatls and darts.

FURTHER READINGS

de Montmollin, O. 1989. *The Archaeology of Political Structure.* Cambridge: Cambridge University Press.

———. 1995. *Settlement and Politics in Three Classic Maya Polities.* Monographs in World Archaeology, 24. Madison: Prehistory Press.

John E. Clark

SEE ALSO

Chiapas Interior Plateau

Tenampua (Comayagua, Honduras)

The Terminal Classic site of Tenampua, occupied from around A.D. 900 to 1000, has a commanding view of the Comayagua Valley 250 meters below. It is situated on a high precipice overlooking this major pre-Hispanic cultural corridor between the Caribbean and Pacific coasts. Tenampua was constructed during a period of apparent military tension, judging from its impressive fortifications and defensive location. While the town's inhabitants were probably Lenca speakers, the name "Tenampua" appears to be of Nahua origin and to refer to the presence of the large walls for which the site is known today.

During its occupation, Tenampua contained more than four hundred residential structures, as well as a small ball court, a possible elite residential and/or administra-

tive complex, two water entrapment reservoirs, three modified caves, probable planting areas, several petroglyphs, and three defensive wall networks surrounding much of the town. The tallest of these walls, extending over 290 meters in length, measured approximately 3 meters tall by 2 meters wide, with interior parapet and access stairways. The site has been badly looted in the past seventy-five years for its distinctive polychrome ceramics, but plans are under consideration by the Honduran government to construct an archaeological interpretive park at the site in the near future.

FURTHER READINGS

Dixon, B. 1987. Conflict along the Southeast Mesoamerican Periphery: A Defensive Wall System at the Site of Tenampua. *British Archaeological Reports* 327(i): 142–153.

———. 1989. A Preliminary Settlement Pattern Study of a Prehistoric Cultural Corridor: The Comayagua Valley, Honduras. *Journal of Field Archaeology* 4:257–272.

———. 1992. Prehistoric Political Variability on the Southeast Mesoamerican Periphery. *Ancient Mesoamerica* 3:11–25.

Lothrop, S. 1927. *Indian Notes.* Vol. 4. New York: Museum of the American Indian.

Popenoe, D. 1935. The Ruins of Tenampua, Honduras. In *Annual Report,* pp. 559–572, Washington, D.C.: Smithsonian Institution.

Boyd Dixon

Tenayuca (México, Mexico)

Tenayuca was part of of the domain of Tlacopán (Tacuba) prior to the Spanish conquest. The Codex Xolotl relates that Tenayuca was founded in about A.D. 1200 by Xolotl, the leader of a group of Chichimecs who arrived in México and established themselves in the caves of the Cerro del Tenayo. The Chichimecs wore animal skins, lived in caves, and did not farm, but time and interaction with Toltec peoples brought about adoption of Toltec customs, and the establishment of the Chichimeca capital in Tenayuca.

The pyramid of Tenayuca was erected after the fall of Tula (c. A.D. 1200). It has a quadrilateral plan with a staircase oriented to the west and divided into two sides, to ascend to twin temples for the simultaneous veneration of two deities, an idea expressed later in the Templo Mayor of Tenochtitlán. The pyramid of Tenayuca underwent several stages of construction; in the last, the Coatepantli,

T

or Serpent Wall, consisting of a line of serpents sculpted from stone, was erected on a platform around three sides of the base of the pyramid. North and south of the pyramid are small adoratorio altars, as well as a depiction of a *xiuhcoatl* (fire serpent), its head crested with points indicating a relation to the cult of the sun, the renewal ensuing from the New Fire Ceremony, and the periodic cycle of fifty-two years.

FURTHER READINGS

León Portilla, M. 1967. El proceso de aculturación de los Chichimecas de Xólotl. *Estudios de Cultura Náhuatl* 7:59–86.

Marquina, I. 1935. Tenayuca, estudio arqueológico de la pirámide de *Este Lugar*. Talleres Gráficos del Museo Nacional de Arqueología, Historia y Ethnografia, 35. Mexico City: Departamento de Monumentos de La Secretaria de Educación Publica.

Zúñiga Bárcenas, B. 1992. *Tenayuca Miniguía.* Mexico City: Instituto Nacional de Antropología e Historia.

Beatriz Zúñiga Bárcenas

SEE ALSO

Aztec Culture and History

Tenochtitlán: Ceremonial Center

At the heart of Tenochtitlán stood one of the most prominent ritual spaces in all Mesoamerican history, the center *par excellence* for divine propitiation and the quintessence of the Nahua worldview. The ceremonial center of Tenochtitlán was, in a religious sense, the architectonic image of the cosmic order. It was also the divine model in the world of humans, because at that place high, medium, and low elevations intersected with the four directions of the universe, which were represented by the city's four principal causeways. In the economic and political sense, the ceremonial center was the materialization of centralized power. Around it revolved, like satellites, the multi-ethnic populations of the city itself, of the surrounding productive centers, and of the tributary regions of the periphery that periodically sent raw materials and manufactured goods to Tenochtitlán.

The history of the ceremonial center of Tenochtitlán begins with the foundation of the city on an island in Lake Texcoco. According to several myths, this event took place in the year 2 House (A.D. 1325), when a divine vision—of an eagle perched on a nopal cactus, or of a miraculous spring of red and blue waters—revealed to the Mexica the location where they should settle and end their wanderings. The Mexica raised their temple in that spot, which represented the threshold of the opening that communicated between the world of humans and the world where gods dwelt. This portal was represented by either an anthill, a sabine tree (Juniperus mexicana), a double cave, or a double spring. These binary elements, along with the colors red and blue, would later determine the principal characteristics of the main pyramid dedicated to Huitzilopochtli (god of war, a solar deity) and to Tlaloc (god of rain, an earth-related deity), two gods who played opposite but complementary roles.

Thirteen years later, around A.D. 1337, a group of discontented Mexica broke away from the rest and founded a new city on a nearby island known as Tlatelolco. So situated, the two Mexica settlements formed one dual entity of complementary symbolic character. The Tenochca, the southern of the two communities, used the celestial figure of an eagle with one of the toponomic glyphs, holding a sacred bundle with the sticks used to make fire. The Tlatelolcans, on the other hand, used the terrestrial figure of the jaguar with a toponomic glyph and a sacred bundle that enclosed a green stone, an aquatic symbol. In a manner similar to that of the Tenochca, the Tlatelolcans built their ceremonial center in the location marked by the miraculous appearance of a whirlwind that connected earth with heaven. From then on, the antagonism and competitiveness that prevailed between the twin cities of Mexico—Tenochtitlán and Tlatelolco—would be clearly reflected in the growth of their respective ceremonial centers. It can be said that the construction, continuous remodeling, and final destruction of these two architectural complexes occurred in parallel.

After the Spanish conquest in August 1521, Cortés made the historic decision to level the two cities in order to build the first houses for the conquerors, using the materials obtained from the demolished temples. Mexico City, the capital of New Spain and, since 1821, of the Mexican Republic, was erected over the ruins of Tenochtitlán and Tlatelolco. Obviously, the Colonial and modern buildings represent a huge obstacle for the archaeologists. Until recently, it had been possible to unearth only very small sections of the ancient cities, and always under exceptional circumstances and in specific areas.

For centuries, the only reliable sources of knowledge about the ceremonial centers of Tenochtitlán and Tlatelolco were the accounts written by the conquerors

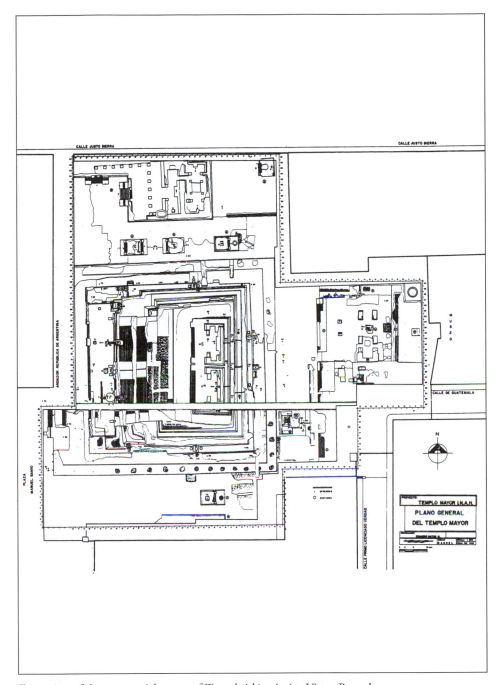

Illustration of the ceremonial center of Tenochtitlán. Artist: Victor Rangel.

themselves, who actually saw them still functioning (Hernán Cortés, Bernal Díaz del Castillo, Andrés de Tapia), and the detailed narratives of the natives compiled by the Spanish friars Bernardino de Sahagún, Diego Durán, Motolinía, and others. In these sources, the name Huey Teocalli or Templo Mayor (Great Temple) is applied indiscriminately to the large precinct and to the main pyramid that was inside this sacred space, causing numerous misunderstandings. There are also a few sixteenth-century drawings that show the ceremonial center of Tenochtitlán, such as plate 269r from Sahagún's *Primeros Memoriales* and the 1524 map, ascribed to Cortés, that was included in the Latin translation of his *Second Letter to King Charles V.*

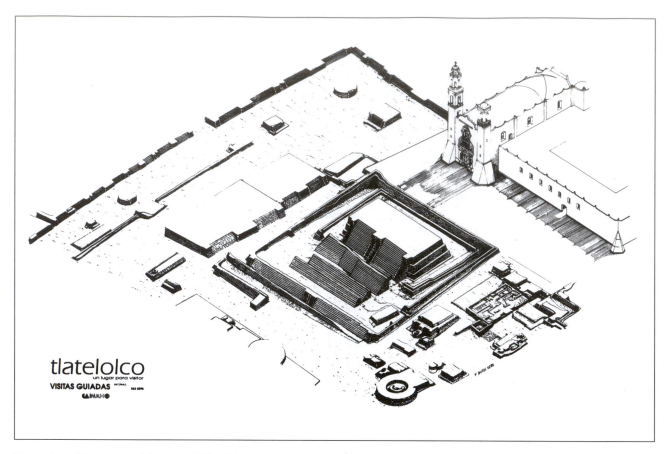

Illustration of the ceremonial center of Tlatelolco. Artist: Fernando Botas Vera.

Since 1790, this invaluable historic information has been enriched with frequent archaeological dicoveries of buildings and monoliths that once stood inside the ceremonial centers. Major archaeological projects started with the arrival of the twentieth century, aimed at a systematic search for the most important buildings of the two pre-Hispanic cities. In the center of Tenochtitlán the most notable were excavations undertaken by Leopoldo Batres (1900), Manuel Gamio (1913), Jordi Gussinyer (1968–1970), and Constanza Vega (1975–1976). The most important projects in Tlatelolco were those coordinated by Pablo Martínez del Río, Antonieta Espejo and Robert H. Barlow (1944–1948), Francisco González Rul, Alberto Ruz and Eduardo Contreras (1960–1968), and Eduardo Matos (1987–1993).

The most ambitious exploration yet has been the Templo Mayor Project, coordinated by Eduardo Matos (1978–1989), and by Matos and Leonardo López Luján (1991–1997). Among the most remarkable discoveries made by this project in five field seasons are the main pyramid of Tenochtitlán and fourteen adjacent buildings, 136 buried offerings, thousands of artifacts, and numerous sculptures and mural paintings. The extensive excavation covered an area of 1.29 hectares behind the Metropolitan Cathedral. This amounts to only 10 percent of the area occupied by the ceremonial center of Tenochtitlán (estimated at 12.96 hectares), and approximately 0.1 percent of the total extent of the two cities (estimated by several authors as 13.5 square kilometers).

After two centuries of historic and archaeological studies, our knowledge of the ceremonial centers of Tenochtitlán and Tlatelolco has improved substantially. Nevertheless, the various hypothetical recreations of the ceremonial center of Tenochtitlán—all of them derived from the pioneer work of Ignacio Marquina—still offer an idealized image of the reality, particularly regarding its dimensions and symmetry.

Nowadays there is no doubt that the ceremonial centers of Tenochtitlán and Tlatelolco were constructed and remodeled following the same archetypal pattern. Both sacred precincts were similar in form and dimensions. It is very probable that the precinct of Tlatelolco measured 303 meters from north to south, and that of Tenochtitlán around 360 meters in the same orientation. In both cases, the sacred space was demarcated by a wide platform. Its façades were characterized by a series of vertical walls, balustrades, and staircases. It has been estimated that the limits of the *tenochca* ceremonial center were the present-day streets of San Ildefonso and González Obregón to the north; the National Palace courtyards to the south; the streets of Licenciado Verdad to the east, and Monte de Piedad and Brasil, to the west. The platform had three or four openings or gates that gave access to the ceremonial center.

Likewise, several of the buildings known from Tenochtitlán and Tlatelolco have almost identical form and dimensions; they maintained the same spatial distribution inside their precincts, and they were dedicated to the same deities. For instance, a distinctly Teotihuacán-style temple is situated to the southeast of the main pyramid in Tenochtitlán as well as in Tlatelolco. The same is true of the principal temples of the two cities: both are at the heads of their respective ceremonial centers; they are stepped pyramids with two flights of stairs oriented toward the west, leading to double temples on top dedicated to the cult of Huitzilopochtli (southern half) and Tlaloc (northern half).

Each pyramid underwent seven total enlargements or stages. Moreover, the second enlargements (Stage II) of the pyramids of Tenochtitlán, Tlatelolco, and Tenayuca all have the same dimensions. This fact suggests that the pyramids of the island cities were built at the same time as the one in Tenayuca, and therefore the dates of their construction are much older than those recorded in the official history of the Mexica.

There is much discussion regarding the number, characteristics, and location of the other buildings inside the ceremonial center of Tenochtitlán. The map presumably drawn by Cortés shows eight buildings, a bordering wall, and four entrances, while Sahagún's map shows nine buildings, the bordering wall, and three entrances. This reduced number of buildings contradicts Sahagún's own text, since he mentions seventy-eight buildings inside the sacred precinct. Among them were the Coatepec or Great Temple (Huitzilopochtli-Tlaloc), the temples dedicated to Chicomecoatl, Mixcoatl, Xiuhtecuhtli, Xipe Totec, and Cinteotl, several *calmecac* (temple schools for the nobility), ball game courts, *tzompantli*s (wooden racks where the skulls of the sacrificial victims were displayed), the

Coacalco (a temple used to keep the divine images of the conquered towns), the Teutlalpan (an enclosure which contained a re-creation of arid land), and the sacred springs called Tezcaapan and Tozpalatl. Durán also mentions the temple of Quetzalcoatl, of circular plan, and the temple of Tezcatlipoca, with spatious chambers at its base.

Several authors speculate that Sahagún included not only the religious buildings of the ceremonial center but also those scattered throughout the city. However, Sahagún's list does not seem so large if we consider that more than thirty buildings, including large temples, small shrines, and platforms, have been exhumed to date. Among the excavated buildings, the most remarkable is the main pyramid or Great Temple. Its last-stage platform, decorated with serpent heads (*coatepantli*), measures 84 meters from east to west and 77.2 meters from north to south. The pyramid had between 100 and 130 steps, which would give it a height of 30 meters. If we add the two sanctuaries that were on the top, the Great Temple would have risen to a total height of 45 meters.

Another very interesting structure is the House of Eagles, with beautiful polychromed benches that decorate the rooms inside the building. These benches, which depict processions of armed warriors, are a magnificent example of the Mexicas' habit of imitating the artistic styles of past civilizations. In this case, we can see a revival of the Palacio Quemado, one of the many buildings that the Mexica excavated among the ruins of Tula. Other archaizing structures recently excavated are four small shrines known as the Red Temples, which combine features from the Mexica and the Teotihuacán styles in perfect harmony.

When the Spanish arrived at Tenochtitlán, this city was the most powerful capital of Mesoamerica. This is evident not only in the high quality of the last enlargements of the Great Temple but also in the richness of its offerings. About 80 percent of the objects that were offered in the pyramid of Huitzilopochtli and Tlaloc were imported brought from the various tributary provinces of the Triple Alliance (Tenochtitlán, Texcoco, and Tlacopan). The most abundant offering items found are animal remains; researchers have identified more than two hundred species from the temperate ecosystems of the Central Plateau, as well as from tropical rainforests, coral reefs, salt marshes, and coastal lagoons. In contrast, there are very few minerals and plant remains: minerals include sea sand, fragments of jet, turquoise, and various kinds of greenstone; among plants, *maguey*, copal, conifer wood, and rubber remains were identified.

T

Human remains are also represented among the offering items. Some of these are bones that belonged to high-ranking individuals who were ritually buried after their bodies were cremated, but the great majority belonged to sacrificial victims who were decapitated. Notable among the recovered artifacts are the imported goods that came to Tenochtitlán either as tribute paid by conquered regions, through commerce, or as gifts, or even pillaged by the Mexica themselves: obsidian artifacts from Sierra de las Navajas, Mixtec-style sculptures, urn vessels from Veracruz, ceramic and stone objects from the Puebla-Tlaxcala region, and a great number of copper bells and greenstone ornaments of yet undetermined origin.

There are also several artworks from ancient cultures that were looted from their tombs and offering caches during the fifteenth century: a stone mask and several fragments of Olmec sculptures, hundreds of stone masks and figurines from the Mezcala culture, dozens of stone and ceramic artifacts from Teotihuacán, and a Plumbate ceramic vessel from southern Mesoamerica. Surprisingly, Mexica manufactures were the least abundant of all the recovered offerings.

In a religious sense, all the objects that constituted an offering followed a purposeful order. The gifts were placed according to clear patterns of spatial composition. As in verbal language, each gift functioned as a sign or a symbol, transmitting information only when it was combined with other gifts. A considerable number of the offerings recovered by the Templo Mayor Project were tiny scale models of a section or of the whole universe, as it was conceived by the Nahua. Following a strict liturgy, the Mexica priests carefully re-created with artifacts, animals, and plants the surface of the earth and, sometimes, even the heavens and the levels of the underworld. Thus, it can be said that during the ritual ceremonies they made cosmograms, repeating the primordial actions of the gods.

FURTHER READINGS

Academia Mexicana de la Historia. 1944–1956. *Tlatelolco a través de los tiempos.* 12 vols. Mexico City: Academia Mexicana de la Historia.

Boone, E. H. (ed.). 1987. *The Aztec Templo Mayor.* Washington, D.C.: Dumbarton Oaks.

Broda, J., D. Carrasco, and E. Matos Moctezuma. 1987. *The Great Temple of Tenochtitlan: Center and Periphery in the Aztec World.* Berkeley: University of California Press.

Dahlgren, B., E. Pérez Rocha, L. Suárez Díez, and P. Valle. 1982. *Corazón de Cópil: El Templo Mayor y el Recino Sagrado de Mexico–Tenochtitlan según fuentes del siglo XVI.* Mexico City: Instituto Nacional de Antropología e Historia.

González Rul, Francisco. 1998. *Urbanismo y arquitectura en Tlatelolco,* México: Instituto Nacional de Antropología e Historia.

Graulich, Michel. 1987. Les incertitudes du Grand Temple. In *Lez aztèques: Trésors du Mexique Ancien.* vol. 2, pp. 121–131. Wiesbaden: Roemer-und Pelizaeus-Museum, Hildesheim.

Gutiérrez Solana, Nelly. 1989. Diez años de estudios sobre el Templo Mayor de Tenochtitlan (1978–1988), *Anales del Instituto de Investigaciones Estéticas,* v. 60, pp. 7–31.

León-Portilla, M. 1978. *Mexico–Tenochtitlan: Su espacio y tiempo sagrados.* Mexico City: Instituto Nacional de Antropología e Historia.

López Luján, L. 1994. *The Offerings of the Templo Mayor of Tenochtitlan.* B. Ortiz de Montellano (trans.). Boulder: University of Colorado Press.

———. 1999. Water and Fire: Archaeology in the Capital of the Mexica Empire. In *The Archaeology of Mesoamerica. Mexican and European Perspectives,* W. Bray and L. Manzanilla (eds.), pp. 32–49. London: British Museum Press.

———. In press. *La Casa de las aguilas: un ejemplo de arquitectura sacra mexica,* 2 vols. México: Instituto Nacional de Antropología e Historia/Princeton University/Mexican Fine Arts Museum Center.

Marquina, I. 1960. *El Templo Mayor de México.* Mexico City: Instituto Nacional de Antropología e Historia.

Matos Moctezuma, Eduardo. 1979. *Trabajos arquelógicos en el Centro de la Ciudad de México (Antología),* México: SEP/Instituto Nacional de Antropología e Historia.

———. 1982. *El Tempo Mayor: excavaciones y estudios,* E. Matos Moctezuma (coord.), México: Instituto Nacional de Antropología e Historia.

———. 1988. *The Great Temple of the Aztecs: Treasures of Tenochtitlan.* London: Thames and Hudson.

———. 1999. *Excavaciones en la Catedral y el Sagrario metropolitanos. Programa de Arqueología Urbana,* México: Instituto Nacional de Antropología e Historia.

Seler, Eduard. 1960. Die Ausgrabungen am Orte des Hauptempels in Mexico. In *Gesammelte Abhandlungen zur Amerikanischen Sprach-und Altertumskunde,* vol. 2, pp. 767–904. Graz: ADV, v. II.

Vega Sosa, Constanza (coord.). 1979. *El Recinto Sagrado de Mexico-Tenochtitlan. Excavaciones 1968–69 y 1975–76.* México: Instituto Nacional de Antropología e Historia.

Leonardo López Luján

Tenochtitlán: Imperial Ritual Landscape

As the tribute empires of Tenochtitlán, Texcoco, and Tlacopan developed during the fifteenth century, Aztec policy called for the construction of ceremonial centers. The great public religious festivals had powerful emotional and imaginative appeal, bringing different groups together through common experiences and beliefs and a shared vocabulary of visual symbols. The ceremonial centers and activities provided a vehicle for social cohesion among all segments of the heterogeneous, highly stratified, and increasingly specialized population.

Following long-standing tradition, the island capital, Tenochtitlán, was designed according to a cosmological plan. Four roadways led to the cardinal directions from the central ritual precinct. Royal palaces stood close by this central enclosure, surrounded in turn by the grid of residential districts and peripheral *chinampa* plantations. Causeways linked the capitol with the mainland on the north, west, and south; on the east was a landing place to the lake.

Within the central ritual precinct, the Main Pyramid rose as an *axis mundi,* marking the center of the city and of the Aztec world. The building was aligned with the equinoctial path of the sun, and with distant springs high on Mount Tlaloc on the eastern side of the Basin of Mexico. The South Temple was devoted to the legendary, deified tribal hero Huitzilopochtli, patron of kings and god of war. The North temple enshrined the deity Tlaloc, associated with rain, mountains, and agricultural fertility. The dual pyramid represented a conflation of two symbolic mountains: the mythic Coatepetl, or "Serpent Mountain," site of Huitzilopochtli's magical birth and victorious battle with his rival Coatlicue; and Tlaloc's rain-mountain, Tonacatepetl, the archetypal "Mountain of Sustenance." War and agriculture, the two bases of Aztec economy, were thus acknowledged by Tenochtitlán's dominant monument. Thousands of offerings recovered from the pyramid foundations feature anaimals and plants from near and far, including the Gulf and Pacific Ocean. The building was a representation of the Aztec universe.

The Main Pyramid and other city temples were linked by lines of sight and routes of pilgrimage to a system of shrines and sacred places on mountains, in caves, at springs and on lakes, and overlooking agricultural districts; many of these sites were used before their incorporation into Aztec sacred geography. The primary Temple of Tlaloc, on the summit of Mount Tlaloc, was visited annually by kings of the allied Aztec cities. A long, narrow processional way led to the temple quadrangle, where a houselike structure housed the effigy of the deity and other images representing neighboring mountains. In microcosm this was a symbolic landscape, and the form of the whole architectural enclosure symbolized the womb of the earth. At the height of the dry season, the kings entered to offer sacrifices to summon rain, ensuring the change from the time of death to the time of rebirth and renewal. The concluding act of this royal pilgrimage took place at Pantitlan in Lake Texcoco, where the kings reassembled in canoes at a sinkhole (or spring) to offer another sacrifice to Chalchihuitlicue, "She of the Jade Skirt," the deity of groundwater. The lake and the sea were ritually denominated *tonan huey atl,* "mother great water," in honor of their life-giving properties. Soon after the rites, rain clouds would form on the mountains, and the fruits of the earth would soon be given. The kings' long journey to the earth-and-rain temple and the lake shrine during the time of drought, the offerings, and their return to the city bringing a gift of life suggest the enactment of a mythic event in the time of creation.

Mount Huixachtlán was another key site of Aztec sacred geography, the location of an ancient cult devoted to Huehueteotl, the "Old God" of fire. Huixachtlán rises between the central and southern sections of the Basin of Mexico. A special procession was made to this mountain shrine every fifty-two years to enact a rite ushering in the new cycle of time. As darkness descended on the last evening of the old period, a procession of fire priests and men masked as gods departed from Tenochtitlán across the southern causeway. Silence was everywhere observed, all fires were extinguished, and the three stones of domestic hearths were cast into water. All watched the Pleiades rise to the zenith transit of the celestial meridian, directly above the fire temple. At the moment of transit new fire was kindled, and a human sacrifice was made and cast into a pyre, as the assembly of gods stood in witness. Torch-bearers carrying the flame ran down to the waiting temples of towns and cities. In Tenochtitlán, the first place to receive new fire was the Temple of Huitzilopochtli,

T

followed by the Fire Temple and the local ward temples, whence it was carried to relight the home hearths. Sunrise heralded a day of feasting. This ritual drama reenacted a myth of solar and lunar creation, said by the Aztecs to have been originally performed when "the council of gods met there at Teotihuacan."

A third rite connecting the city and its surroundings was the annual festival of Panquetzalitztli in honor of Huitzilopochtli. November ushered in the dry season and the time of war. The twenty-day festival began with dances and songs below the Main Pyramid. On the ninth day, captives and slaves destined for sacrifice were bathed and adorned. There followed many days of processions and ceremonies featuring these victims, including their presentation on the Main Pyramid. A priest carrying the effigy of Paynal, the "substitute" of Huitzilopochtli, descended from the high platform to perform sacrifices in the ball court nearby. The effigy was then borne by the priestly runner on a large circuit leading across the causeways from Tenochtitlán to towns and sacred places on the north, west, and south. Sacrifices were made at these sites as the procession hastened around and back toward the city. Meanwhile, a mock battle was staged before the Main Pyramid, and the sacrificial victims were paraded around the monument. As this was completed, a great red-feathered fire serpent was seen to descend as a symbol of Huitzilopochtli's power. This was the signal for the final sacrifice. Brought to the summit, the captives were killed, and their bodies were rolled down the pyramid steps to lie on a sculpture of Coyolxauhqui, the antagonist defeated by Huitzilopochtli in the mythic battle on the hill Coatepetl. The rite recalled specific aspects of this mythic event, while the ceremonial circuit symbolically extended Huitzilopochtli's warlike dominion—and Aztec rule—around the perimeter of the world. In Aztec sacred geography, the empire itself was defined in cosmological terms.

These are but some of the principal places of Aztec sacred geography where the renewal of time, the rebirth of the sun, the renewal of vegetation, and the renewal of the empire were expressed. Elsewhere, to the north of Tenochtitlán, was the temple of Tonantzin ("Our Honored Mother"), the earth deity, today the site of the shrine of the Virgin of Guadalupe. To the south, the temple Zacatepetl was also dedicated to the earth goddess, and here hunting rites were also performed in commemoration of earlier Aztec history. At Chapultepec to the west and Texcotzingo in the east, hills were transformed as rit-

ual centers with architecture, sculpture, and processional pathways. The immensely complex, interrelated ceremonial organization of the Aztecs and their neighbors in the Basin of Mexico involved dozens of sacred locations, where the cults of the deities, socio-political aims, and economic activities were linked with historical memories and myths. An inherited principle underlying these concerns held that rulers and nobles, warriors and priests, and architects, artisans, traders and farmers were all bound in a system of reciprocal, vital exchange with the eternal forms of their land and the changing seasonal elements.

FURTHER READINGS

Aveni, A. F. 1992. Moctezuma's Sky: Aztec Astronomy and Ritual. In D. Carrasco and E. Matos M. (eds.), *Moctezuma's Mexico: Visions of the Aztec World,* pp. 149–158. Niwot: University Press of Colorado.

Townsend, R. F. 1979. *State and Cosmos in the Art of Tenochtitlán.* Studies in Pre-Columbian Art and Archaeology, 20. Washington, D.C.: Dumbarton Oaks.

———. 1991. The Mt. Tlaloc Project. In D. Carrasco (ed.), *To Change Place: Aztec Ceremonial Landscapes,* pp. 26–30. Niwot: University Press of Colorado.

Richard F. Townsend

SEE ALSO

Aztec Culture and History; Basin of Mexico; Postclassic Period

Tenochtitlán: Palaces

In 1519 and 1520, Cortés and his men lived in Tenochtitlán as guests of Motecuhzoma II, who lodged them in one of his palaces. The Aztec word for palace, *tecpan calli,* means "lord-place-house," and referred to different kinds of palaces: the large main administrative-residential palaces, and also pleasure palaces. In Tenochtitlán there were least two large residential and administrative palaces: "Montezuma's New Palace," built during Motecuhzoma II's reign, and thus sometime after 1502, at the location now occupied by Mexico's Palacio Nacional; and the palaces Motecuhzoma II inherited as ruler, which were called "Axayacatl's Palace" (also known as Ahuizotl's Palace, Montezuma's Old Palace, and the Palace of Montezuma the Elder).

Much of Tenochtitlán was leveled during the Conquest, and the Spaniards immediately built the new capital of New Spain directly over the wreck of the indigenous city. Thus, the Cathedral was situated in the old Aztec Templo Mayor precinct, and the wreckage of Motecuhzoma II's *tecpan calli* was claimed by Cortés himself. In the 1560s the site passed to the Colonial government, and since then it has been occupied by the national palace. Because of this overbuilding, systematic archaeological investigation is unlikely, so the form and the functions of this palace must be reconstructed from ethnohistoric sources, particularly Cortés's *Letters,* Durán's *History,* and Díaz's *True History of the Conquest of Mexico.*

They describe Motecuhzoma II's main *tecpan calli,* which covered about 200 by 200 meters, as consisting of courtyards surrounded by suites of rooms. The main courtyard opened onto Tenochtitlán's (and Mexico City's) main plaza, the Zócalo. Across the courtyard from the plaza, in a dais room, the ruler held court. Cortés wrote that every day six hundred men of rank visited the court, with their attendants, and were fed by Motecuhzoma.

The rooms around the main entry courtyard were used for smaller congregations of lords and for judicial deliberations. There were armories and music halls, guest rooms and gardens, kitchens, sweat baths, and suites of residential rooms for Motecuhzoma's many wives, their children, and their attendants.

The pleasure palaces included elaborate dynastic monuments; for the Tenochtitlán dynasty, this was Chapultepec Park, and for the Texcoco dynasty, Texcotzingo. The lords also had palaces at their horticultural gardens (Huaxtepec, for example) and at their game reserves. Cortés and his comrades had visited all these locales while they were "guests" of Motecuhzoma II and must have decided to try to acquire them as spoils of conquest, so quickly did they claim these properties and their palaces. Many passed into their hands, but several exceptions followed a culturally syncretic pattern. The zoological gardens were claimed by the Order of St. Francis, and Chapultepec became the property of the Colonial government, with a new palace built immediately over the old. Just as it was five hundred years ago, Chapultepec is today the most important park in the largest city in the New World.

FURTHER READINGS

Evans, S. T. 1998. Sexual Politics in the Aztec Palace: Public, Private, and Profane. *RES* 33:165–183.

———. [1999]. Aztec Palaces. In S. T. Evans and J. Pillsbury (eds.), *Palaces of the Ancient New World.* Washington, D.C.: Dumbarton Oaks.

Lombardo de Ruiz, S. 1973. Desarrollo urbano de México-Tenochtitlan segun las fuentes históricas. Mexico City: Instituto Nacional de Antropología e Historia.

Palacio Nacional. 1976. *Palacio Nacional.* Mexico City: Secretaría de Obras Públicas.

Villalobos Pérez, A. 1985. Consideraciones sobre un plano reconstructivo del recinto sagrado de México-Tenochtitlan. *Cuadernos de Arquitectura Mesoamérica* 4:57–63.

Susan Toby Evans

Tenochtitlán-Tlatelolco (Federal District, Mexico)

Tenochtitlán and its adjacent sister city, Tlatelolco, were the capitals of the Mexica Aztecs, and Tenochtitlán at the time of the Spanish conquest (A.D. 1521) was the capital of the Aztec Empire. Following the conquest, Tenochtitlán-Tlatelolco became the capital of New Spain; during the sixteenth century its new name, Ciudad de México, began to be used. Today Mexico City is one of the world's largest cities. Its site has a continuous history of occupation going back nearly a thousand years to its origins as a fishing camp. Significant amounts of ceramics dating from the early Postclassic (beginning c. A.D. 950) have been recovered in excavations under the Metropolitan Cathedral. Tenochtitlán was established as a Mexica community during the early 1300s.

Material Remains

Archaeological strata dating back to c. A.D. 1000 and encompassing Aztec period occupation now underlie the heart of the modern city at depths ranging from about 1.5 meters to 12 meters or more in some districts. Surface architecture was largely destroyed during the siege to capture the city in 1521. The first systematically conducted excavations commenced in about 1900 but were on a very small scale. The remains of the Great Temple (Templo Mayor) and adjoining religious structures in both Tenochtitlán and Tlatelolco have been exposed and consolidated at various times in the twentieth century. The results of these excavations, salvage archeology, and accidental discoveries are a continuing source of new information.

Ethnohistorical Sources

An unusually detailed record of city-building and urban life was preserved in Aztec pictorial manuscripts (codices), eyewitness accounts of the conquest, chronicles, post-Conquest

T

ethnographic works, and early Colonial period archival records. A great deal of historical information recorded in now-lost pictorial manuscripts and oral texts was transcribed after the Conquest in European cursive script, recording Nahuatl (Aztec) and Spanish texts. The correlation of ethnohistorical sources with archaeological evidence has always been a major research objective.

Span of Occupation

Tenochtitlán was established on a set of marshy islands near the western shore of Lake Texcoco in the Basin of Mexico. The Mexica Aztecs had arrived in the Basin of Mexico from the northwest about A.D. 1250. They made several abortive attempts to found permanent settlements on the mainland before occupying an unclaimed marshy zone in western Lake Texcoco. According to most accounts, Tenochtitlán was founded in 1325, and Tlatelolco, by a dissident faction, in 1337. Other sources reverse the order of settlement, while citing alternative founding dates ranging from 1318 to 1366. The local ceramic sequence, though still poorly understood, is most compatible with foundation dates in the earlier part of this range. No currently accepted chronological framework allows the city a period of development longer than two hundred years before the time of the Spanish invasion, though the islands show traces of ephemeral occupation as early as A.D. 1000.

Environmental Setting

Lake Texcoco was shallow, saline, and landlocked. Its salt marshes, less than ideal for agriculture, supported numerous species of small fish, edible larvae, migratory game birds, and other resources. Freshwater springs existed on patches of dry land. Settlers gradually transformed the marshlands by constructing packed-earth platforms for residential use, along with artificial raised-field garden plots called *chinampas*. The most common building materials, including wood, stone, and adobe, were available only on the mainland.

The most serious disadvantage of this location was the constant threat of severe inundation. Devastating floods destroyed *chinampas* and resulted in severe damage to residential platforms in 1382–1385, 1450, and 1499. Flooding did not cease with the Conquest: the city suffered periodic inundations well into the nineteenth century. Massive hydraulic works, including dikes, causeways, and feeder-drainage canals, were built in the fifteenth century, in part to control changes in lake level, as well as for transport and provisioning. During the period of Aztec impe-rialist expansion (1428–1519), these works were built and maintained with labor and material resources from conquered city-states.

In spite of the threat of flooding, the island location admirably situated Tenochtitlán and Tlatelolco to profit from participation in regional trade networks, in which canoes provided the most rapid and inexpensive vehicle for the transportation of bulk goods. By the end of the fourteenth century, market trade and craft production were well established as the principal alternatives to risky reliance on *chinampa* agriculture.

Historical Development

Once established, Tenochtitlán and Tlatelolco were quickly absorbed into the rapidly expanding Tepanec Empire, with its capital at nearby Azcapotzalco. Tributary cities provided goods and military contingents for Azcapotzalco's wars. The Tepanecs permitted Tenochtitlán to establish its own dynasty in 1367 or 1376. These rulers in turn negotiated more favorable political and economic arrangements, while at the same time forming close marital alliances with the Tepanec lords.

Azcapotzalco emerged as the dominant power in the Basin of Mexico with the conquest of Texcoco in 1418. By this time the Mexica were receiving a generous share of the spoils of war, while quietly increasing their own prosperity and military strength. Tenochtitlán had greatly outstripped Tlatelolco this respect by the 1420s. In 1427 Tenochtitlán headed a major rebellion against Azcapotzalco, emerging victorious in the following year. Tlatelolco, while clearly subordinate to its more powerful neighbor, retained nominal independence for a time but was conquered and annexed in 1473. The two cities, both singly and combined, almost certainly comprised the largest and most populous Mesoamerican polity by the middle of the fifteenth century, and its greatest city since Teotihuacán's collapse in the eighth century A.D.

City Plan, Settlement Pattern, and Demography

The area of the combined cities on the eve of the Conquest was approximately 12 square kilometers, and the boundary canal between them was crossed by a half-dozen streets and bridges. The long period of political independence preceding 1473 was reflected in the existence of separate monumental religious precincts, each with its own Templo Mayor, royal palaces, and large market plaza. The great market at Tlatelolco was the most important commercial center in Central Mexico, both before and after the city's conquest.

Tenochtitlán was divided into great quarters by avenues extending from the gates of its ceremonial precinct; after 1473, Tlatelolco comprised a fifth "quarter." The quarters were subdivided into smaller districts which are usually called "barrios" in Spanish and English. The great quarters and barrios had their own patron deities, temples, military leaders, and administrative functionaries. Territorial organization in Tlatelolco included a division into fifteen to twenty great barrios; these were subdivided into minor barrios, some consisting of no more than a row of houses on one side of a single street.

A large core area extending through the central districts of both cities was characterized by exceptionally dense house-to-house occupation. The underlying packed-earth residential platforms had for the most part been joined together as a continuous mass. The urban core was surrounded by neighborhoods in which most residential sites were adjoined by two or more small *chinampa* gardens. The most common arrangements were dwelling units, patio space, and *chinampas* (where present). Residential compounds enclosing two to six dwelling units were usually closed off from the outside by adobe walls, or, in the poorest neighborhoods, by fences constructed with marsh reeds or maize stalks. The layout of compounds was much the same, whether or not *chinampas* were present.

As a rule, each compound housed a bilateral joint family including elderly couples and their married offspring. Each couple commonly occupied a single one or two-room dwelling unit, or a single floor in a two-story house. Adobe was the most commonly used building material; large wooden beams supported a flat roof. Individual houses, except in neighborhoods occupied by the nobility or especially prosperous citizens, were usually small, reflecting the costs involved in purchasing and transporting basic construction materials from the mainland. (A description of palace sites appears in the following article.)

Total population, based on early Spanish reports as well as on estimates derived from settlement pattern analysis, fell somewhere between about 150,000 and 225,000 inhabitants. This places Tenochtitlán-Tlatelolco in a category distinct from all other known population centers in ancient Mesoamerica, with the single exception of Teotihuacan. The demographic composition of this population was still more unusual, since more than 75 percent—possibly more than 90 percent—of the city's inhabitants were dependent on full-time nonagricultural occupational specializations. The corresponding figure for Teotihuacan is believed to have been no higher than about 40 percent.

Internal Organization

Tenochtitlán-Tlatelolco was a strongly centralized city-state ruled by hereditary dynastic elites. These were headed by a sacred king, elected from among the sons and grandsons of previous rulers by an assembly of nobles, elders, and adult men of military age. The king appointed nobles, who were usually close kin, to a ruling council charged with primary administrative responsibilities involving both city and empire. Civic authority was channeled downward to a host of officials and minor functionaries in the great quarters and barrios of Tenochtitlán, and in the large and small barrios in Tlatelolco. Religion and ceremonial life were controlled by a parallel hierarchy of priests headed by two high priests who presided from the paired shrines of the gods Huitzilopochtli and Tlaloc at the Templo Mayor (see Tenochtitlán Ceremonial Centers, below).

Social status within the urban milieu was determined by birth, by occupation, and, for adult males, by military achievement. The division between hereditary nobles (*pipiltin*) and commoners (*macehualtin*) was sharply defined, but it could be partially bridged by personal wealth or especially, by valorous battlefield performance. Hereditary occupational specializations were closely linked to the barrio system, functioning in a manner somewhat analogous to medieval European craft guilds. Professional merchants, feather-workers, goldsmiths, stonemasons, lapidaries, and many other groups lived in their own barrios, worshipped their own deities, and were led by their own barrio headmen and priests. The barrios maintained schools for their young men (*telpochcalli*, "young-men's house"), where they were trained in religion and warfare, and where most of them lived from the age of about twelve until marriage. The nobility and semi-elite merchant and craft groups were more likely to place their male offspring in a school for priests, the *calmecac,* where they might learn the art of government as well as religion and military skills.

The urban population also included a host of menial specialists, including porters, water vendors, domestic servants, prostitutes, weavers, and numerous others. An indeterminately large stratum of urban poor is mentioned from time to time in the chronicles, but with little supporting detail. Some light was shed on their conditions of life when a maze of densely clustered slumlike dwellings was revealed by salvage archaeology in eastern Tlatelolco in 1977.

T

FURTHER READINGS

Calnek, E. E. 1972. Settlement Pattern and Chinampa Agriculture at Tenochtitlan. *American Antiquity* 37: 104–115.

———. 1973. The Localization of the Sixteenth Century Map Called the Maguey Plan. *American Antiquity* 38:190–195.

———. 1976. The Internal Structure of Tenochtitlan. In E. R. Wolf (ed.), *The Valley of Mexico: Studies in Pre-Hispanic Ecology and Society,* pp. 287–302. Albuquerque: University of New Mexico Press.

Caso, A. 1956. Los barrios antiguos de Tenochtitlan y Tlatelolco. *Memorias de la Academia Mexicana de la Historia* 15:7–62.

Cervantes de Salazar, F. 1953 [1554]. *Life in the Imperial and Loyal City of Mexico in New Spain.* Austin: University of Texas Press.

Rojas, José Luis de. 1986. *México Tenochtitlan: Economía y sociedad en el siglo XVI.* Mexico City: Fondo de Cultura Económica.

Vega Sosa, C. (ed.). 1979. *El recinto sagrado de México-Tenochtitlan: Excavaciónes 1968–69 y 1975–76.* Mexico City: Instituto Nacional de Antropología e Historia.

Edward Calnek

Teopantecuanitlán (Guerrero, Mexico)

A Formative period archaeological site at the confluence of the Amacuzac and Balsas rivers in northeastern Guerrero, Teopantecuanitlán is noteworthy for its extremely early architectural and hydraulic innovations. The site's corbel vaulting, ball court, and extensive system of irrigation canals are the oldest known in Mesoamerica. The site's ceremonial precinct was occupied as early as 1400 B.C. and later developed in four major construction phases, ending in 500 B.C. Clay architectural construction may have been in place as early as 1300 B.C. However, during Phase II (1000–800 B.C.) the large stone-lined sunken court was constructed, surmounted by four inverted T-shaped monumental sculptures bearing Olmec-style zoomorphic representations. The site core was built on a series of stone terraces surrounded by an extensive residential area (160 hectares); beginning in 1983, Guadalupe Martínez Donjuán conducted excavations in this area. The discovery of Teopantecuanitlán clearly demonstrates that cultures of incontestable social complexity developed early in Formative period Guerrero, and that during this period the region was linked to the rest of Mesoamerica through an extensive network of material and ideological exchange.

FURTHER READINGS

Martínez Donjuán, G. 1985. Sitio de Teopantecuanitlán en Guerrero. *Anales de Antropología.* 22:215–226.

———. 1986. Teopantecuanitlán. In *Arqueología y ethnohistoria del Estado de Guerrero,* pp. 55–80. Mexico City.

Niederberger, C. 1996. Olmec Horizon Guerrero. In E. P. Benson and B. de la Fuente (eds.), *Olmec Art of Ancient Mexico,* pp. 95–105. Washington, D.C.: National Gallery of Art.

Paradis, L. I. 1995. Archaeology, History and Ethnography: The Precolumbian History of the Mezcala Region. In *The Amate Tradition: Innovation and Dissent in Mexican Art,* pp. 113–128. Chicago and Mexico City: Mexican Fine Arts Center Museum.

F. Kent Reilly III

SEE ALSO

Guerrero Region; Tlacozotitlán

Teopanzolco

See Cuauhnahuac and Teopanzolco

Teotenango

See Toluca Region

Teotihuacán (México, Mexico)

The city of Teotihuacán flourished in highland Central Mexico between about 150 B.C. and A.D. 650 to 750. It covered 20 square kilometers, with one hundred thousand or more inhabitants. It was one of the largest and most imposing cities in the world in its day. Besides its scale, the city was exceptional in other ways. From about A.D. 300 onward, most inhabitants lived in substantial plaster-and-concrete compounds composed of multiple apartments. War was important and armed figures are represented in art, but references to conquest and vanquished enemies have not been found. This contrasts sharply with the Classic Lowland Maya, whose monuments name rulers, celebrate their victories, and proclaim their exalted pedigrees. At Teotihuacán, representations of hierarchical relations among humans are unknown and individual rulers are hard to identify.

The present drab, horizontal ruins give a misleading impression of the city in its prime. Horizontality was characteristic of the *talud-tablero* architectural style of sloping aprons under wide vertical panels, but only foundations survive. Mural paintings show that the temples had ornate roof decorations, and in the central city the outer walls were colorful.

Our knowledge of Teotihuacán is limited. A comprehensive surface survey was directed by René Millon, but less than 3 percent of the city has been excavated. Ethnohistory is problematic: aspects of the culture perished or changed drastically, and Aztec traditions about Teotihuacán's importance are sketchy and shaped by mythic and political purposes. Nevertheless, there is enough continuity to make later sources valuable, and it would be as foolish to neglect them as to use them uncritically. There are too few radiocarbon or other absolute dates for Teotihuacán, and the accepted chronology may be inaccurate by a century or more.

The language the Teotihuacános spoke is unknown. It may have been Nahua, but evidence suggests that Nahua speakers were not influential in Central Mexico before about A.D. 500. Standardized graphic signs were used, but no phonetic or syntactic elements have yet been recognized.

Environment

The city is on a semiarid broad plain in the northeastern part of the Basin of Mexico, about 2,300 meters above sea level. Rainfall is highly seasonal, mostly during June to October, averaging around 600 mm per year but varying greatly from year to year. Rainfall alone sometimes allows a fair maize harvest, but irrigation makes yields larger and more secure. There are no large streams, and floodwater irrigation is feasible in only part of the valley. Winter frosts are common, and unseasonal frost can destroy crops. Irrigation from permanent year-round springs near the southwestern margin of the city is more reliable than floodwater irrigation and permits earlier planting, which reduces the frost hazard. However, the spring flow is not large: it irrigated 3,650 hectares in 1954. In 1922 the flow was nearly twice as much, but this may not mean that twice the area was ever irrigated, since a limit is set by the area reachable by gravity flow. Intensive *chinampa*-like agriculture is practiced today on 100 hectares of swampy land just downstream from the main springs. It is virtually certain that drainage, spring-fed canals, and floodwater irrigation were all in use several centuries before the beginning of Teotihuacán.

Crops included maize, amaranth, agave, cactus (nopal, or prickly pear), and others. Cotton does not grow in the Basin of Mexico and must have been imported from Morelos and/or the Gulf Coast. Other nearby resources include building stone, hard stone for maize grinding and other uses, obsidian, and (near Tula) limestone.

Before 150 B.C.

The Ticoman phase spans about 500 to 150 B.C. in the Basin of Mexico; its local manifestation is called Cuanalan. There were towns with respectable ceremonial centers in the southern basin, notably Cuicuilco, which may have had a population of five to ten thousand; however, the Teotihuacán Valley was marginal. It held a number of villages, including a sizable settlement that covered 15 to 30 hectares, with a population of one or two thousand living near the year-round springs, well situated for irrigated agriculture.

150 B.C.–A.D. 150

This interval includes the Patlachique and Tzacualli phases. Ceramics developed primarily from Cuanalan and do not suggest massive population replacement. Cuicuilco reached its maximal size early, with pyramids as large as 80 meters in diameter and a population of around twenty thousand. A nearby volcano erupted sometime during this period and its lava flow seriously damaged Cuicuilco, but the community may have survived as a small regional center as late as A.D. 200.

The poorly understood Tezoyuca ceramic complex may date to the beginning of this period. The defensible locations of Tezoyuca sites suggest that warfare was important. Probably several political units within the basin contended for control with increasing intensity. Perhaps Cuicuilco and Teotihuacán defeated all others and became rivals for dominance, and then Cuicuilco was crippled by lava.

At Teotihuacán, there was an abrupt shift from the Cuanalan phase settlement near the springs. From a new center a kilometer west of the Moon Pyramid the city grew explosively until it covered 20 square kilometers by the end of this period. Proximity to the best irrigated land was no longer the main consideration, since the new center was 2 kilometers farther from the springs than was the Cuanalan village. There is no obvious defensive advantage, but the new location contains numerous caves. Probably religion, connected in part with caves, was significant in the city's location and rapid growth.

Around A.D. 1, almost the entire population of the Basin of Mexico seems to have moved into the city. By A.D. 150 it held sixty to eighty thousand people. The commercial and sacred significance of Teotihuacán must

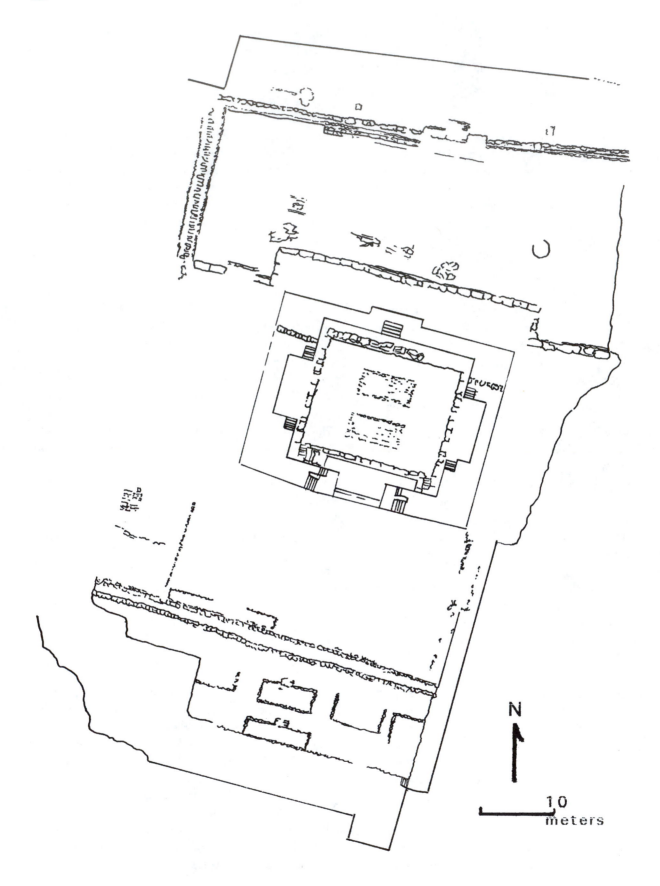

Teopantecuanitlan's sunken courtyard was the site's ceremonial focus *(left)*. The plan shows the northern and southern platforms enclosing the central feature, the sunken courtyard with its miniature ball court. The walls of the sunken courtyard are decorated with four massive Olmec-style sculptures, and the drawing *(above)* depicts one of these, Monument 1, measuring about 1 meter high. Plan drawn by Susan Toby Evans from Martinez Donjuan 1986; monument drawn by Susan Toby Evans.

have offered many attractions, but relocation of most of the basin's farmers would have put them uneconomically far from much of the basin's good land. Almost surely, strong coercion was required to effect the shift.

The Sun Pyramid was begun about the same time as the population movement; doubtless the events were related. By A.D. 150 the pyramid reached nearly its final volume of around one million cubic meters, one of the largest pre-Hispanic structures in the New World. It was built above a cave whose sacred significance, probably related to origin myths, was the reason for the pyramid's

location. About twenty other pyramid groups, mostly three-temple complexes, probably existed this early, as did at least the northern 1.5 kilometers of the Avenue of the Dead, which runs south from the Moon Pyramid and passes west of the Sun Pyramid. There were structures where the Ciudadela now stands, but little is known of them. Teotihuacán was already majestic, awe-inspiring in the size of individual temples and the scale of the overall layout. Distances between major structures and their orientation (15.5° east of true north) probably related to astronomical and calendric phenomena of religious significance.

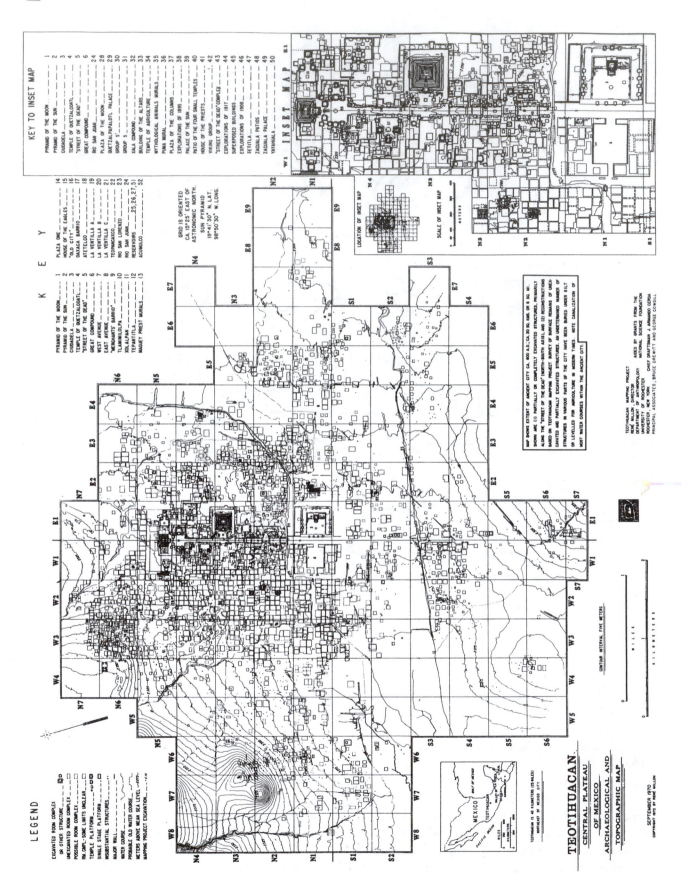

LEGEND

EXCAVATED ROOM COMPLEX
OR OTHER STRUCTURE
UNEXCAVATED ROOM COMPLEX
POSSIBLE ROOM COMPLEX
RM.CMPL-SOME LIMITS UNCLEAR
TEMPLE PLATFORM
SINGLE STAGE PLATFORM
INSUBSTANTIAL STRUCTURES
MAJOR WALL
WATER COURSE
PROBABLE OLD WATER COURSE
METERS ABOVE MEAN SEA LEVEL
MAPPING PROJECT EXCAVATION

KEY

PYRAMID OF THE MOON	1	PLAZA ONE	14
PYRAMID OF THE SUN	2	HOUSE OF THE EAGLES	15
CIUDADELA	3	"OLD CITY"	16
TEMPLE OF QUETZALCOATL	4	OAXACA BARRIO	17
"STREET OF THE DEAD"	5	ATETELCO	18
GREAT COMPOUND	6	LA VENTILLA A	19
WEST AVENUE	7	LA VENTILLA B	20
EAST AVENUE	8	LA VENTILLA C	21
"MERCHANTS' BARRIO"	9	TEOPANCAXCO	22
TLAMIMILOLPA	10	RIO SAN LORENZO	23
XOLALPAN	11	RIO SAN JUAN	24
TEPANTITLA	12	RESERVOIRS	25,26,27,51
MAGUEY PRIEST MURALS	13	ACOMULCO	52

KEY TO INSET MAP

PYRAMID OF THE MOON	1
PYRAMID OF THE SUN	2
CIUDADELA	3
TEMPLE OF QUETZALCOATL	4
"STREET OF THE DEAD"	5
GREAT COMPOUND	6
RIO SAN JUAN	24
PLAZA OF THE MOON	28
QUETZALPAPALOTL PALACE	29
GROUP 5	30
GROUP 5'	31
XALA COMPOUND	32
TEMPLE OF AGRICULTURE	34
MYTHOLOGICAL ANIMALS MURALS	35
PUMA MURAL	36
PLAZA OF THE COLUMNS	37
EXPLORATIONS OF 1895	38
PALACE OF THE SUN	39
PATIO OF THE FOUR SMALL TEMPLES	40
HOUSE OF THE PRIESTS	41
VIKING GROUP	42
"STREET OF THE DEAD" COMPLEX	43
EXPLORATIONS OF 1917	44
SUPERPOSED BUILDINGS	45
EXPLORATIONS OF 1908	46
PERITLA	47
ZACUALA PATIOS	48
ZACUALA PALACE	49
YAYAHUALA	50

GRID IS ORIENTED
CA. 15°25' EAST OF
ASTRONOMIC NORTH.
SUN PYRAMID
19°41'30" N. LAT.
98°50'30" W. LONG.

MAP SHOWS EXTENT OF ANCIENT CITY CA. 600 A.D., CA. 20 SQ. KMS. OR 8 SQ. MI.
SHOWN ARE (1) PARTIALLY OR COMPLETELY EXCAVATED STRUCTURES, PRIMARILY
ALONG THE "STREET OF THE DEAD" (NORTH-SOUTH AXIS), AND (2) RECONSTRUCTIONS
BASED ON TEOTIHUACAN MAPPING PROJECT SURVEY OF SURFACE REMAINS OF UNEX-
CAVATED AND PARTIALLY EXCAVATED STRUCTURES. AN UNDETERMINED NUMBER OF
STRUCTURES IN VARIOUS PARTS OF THE CITY HAVE BEEN BURIED UNDER SILT
OR LEVELLED FOR AGRICULTURE IN MODERN TIMES. NOTE CANALIZATION OF
MOST WATER COURSES WITHIN THE ANCIENT CITY.

TEOTIHUACAN MAPPING PROJECT
RENÉ MILLON, DIRECTOR
DEPARTMENT OF ANTHROPOLOGY
UNIVERSITY OF ROCHESTER
ROCHESTER, NEW YORK
PRINCIPAL ASSOCIATES, BRUCE DREWITT AND GEORGE COWGILL.

AIDED BY GRANTS FROM THE
NATIONAL SCIENCE FOUNDATION

CHIEF DRAFTSMAN J. ARMANDO CERDA

LOCATION OF INSET MAP

SCALE OF INSET MAP

TEOTIHUACAN
CENTRAL PLATEAU
OF MEXICO
ARCHAEOLOGICAL AND
TOPOGRAPHIC MAP

CONTOUR INTERVAL FIVE METERS

SEPTEMBER 1970
COPYRIGHT 1973 BY RENÉ MILLON

TEOTIHUACAN IS 40 KILOMETERS (25 MILES)
NORTHEAST OF MEXICO CITY

Possibly a single integrated master plan governed the overall spatial organization. There is no evidence from this time for *talud-tablero* architecture (possibly already used in Puebla), nor for apartment compounds.

Thin Orange ware, made in southern Puebla about 160 kilometers away, was imported in small amounts. A few sherds of Lowland Maya waxy wares, probably Chicanel, have been found, implying interaction (possibly indirect) with the Maya Lowlands.

By this time Teotihuacán exercised tight political control over the entire basin, but it is unclear how much farther its power extended. Specialized production of obsidian may have begun, but commerce was only one factor contributing to Teotihuacán's rise. Warfare was highly sacralized. Teotihuacán's explosive growth was probably effected by leaders who used an astute combination of violence and religiously based legitimate authority.

A.D. 150–300

This interval spans the Miccaotli and Early Tlamimilolpa phases. The most notable new building was the Ciudadela, an enclosure bounded by platforms 400 meters long, 80 meters wide, and 8 meters high. It contains the Temple of Quetzalcoatl, or Feathered Serpent Pyramid, famed for the feathered rattlesnakes carved in massive blocks of stone on its façades, 65 by 65 meters at its base and 20 meters high, the third largest in the city. The pyramid is flanked on the north and south by large apartment compounds, probably residences of Teotihuacán rulers. The serpents are related to the Aztec Quetzalcoatl, but we cannot project the whole Aztec complex back to Teotihuacán.

A second entity in these carvings is called "Tlaloc" but has few traits in common with the storm god. It is probably a headdress, perhaps associated with Feathered Serpent, or perhaps pertaining to the fire serpent. The symbolism is probably related to rulership, sacred war, and a Venus cult.

The construction of the Ciudadela suggests some change in ideological emphasis but no great discontinuity. Additions were made to the Sun Pyramid, still a major religious focus. West of the Ciudadela, across the Avenue of the Dead, an even larger but much lower pair of platforms, the Great Compound, was built. Its plaza may have been a major marketplace. Structures on its broad platforms may have been used for state purposes. Wide eastern and western avenues may also be this early. Their axis crosses the Avenue of the Dead at the midpoint of the mega-complex formed by the Ciudadela and the Great Compound. Urban settlement now extended considerably south and east of the Ciudadela, although the city's growth rate was much slower than before.

Approximately two hundred victims were sacrificed when the Feathered Serpent Pyramid was built. Most were richly attired, and most were bound. Possibly they were enemy prisoners or low-status impersonators of elites, but they may have been Teotihuacános who held the ranks indicated by the grave goods. If they were high-status Teotihuacános in good standing, their sacrifice implies a strong, perhaps despotic, central authority, whether they were slain to accompany a dead ruler or dedicated to a nonhuman deity. The burials fall into four or five well-defined ranked categories. Many were associated with weapons and military symbolism; others suggest a wider range of activities. Three large pits were looted long ago, probably by Teotihuacános; they may have held one or more rulers, but the extent of the looting means we cannot be sure.

These finds show that hierarchy was already symbolized by differences in costume. Early Teotihuacán was not egalitarian. In recognizing status differences, it resembled other early states. What was unusual was the apparent degree to which individuality was suppressed. Teotihuacán art is stiff, distant, and formalized; individuals are often nearly invisible under elaborate but standardized costumes and insignia, very unlike the naturalism and individuality of Classic Maya art. Multiplicity and replication are already conspicuous in the hundreds of repeated elements in the Feathered Serpent friezes and in the standardization of costumes and offerings in the associated sacrificial burials. In the next period these characteristics are seen in mural paintings showing sets of figures all dressed alike and in identical poses. The message seems to be that everyone has many interchangeable counterparts. This outlook seems to have been well developed by the time of the Feathered Serpent Pyramid and to have continued after the social and political changes that characterized the next period.

The Teotihuacános probably drew on stylistic traditions that had deep roots in Central Mexico and, at least at first, they were not intentionally different in their art. However, in contrast to the eclecticism of later sites such as Cacaxtla and Xochicalco, they were uninterested in copying from their neighbors, except, early on, those in the Gulf Coast, with whom they probably had close connections.

Ollas and other utilitarian ceramics changed gradually. Flat-bottomed outcurving bowls and everted-rim vases, both with solid nubbin supports, are now common.

Much scarcer are *floreros* (small vase-shaped vessels) and "Tlaloc" vessels, which represent a goggle-eyed individual. Fine straight-line incising on blackware, in hard clay, often with cross-hatching and triangles, is shared with Veracruz, Chiapas, and other regions, though vessel shapes are different. Broader line curvilinear incising in soft clay is rare until late in this period. A few vessels have red slip, sometimes with flecks of specular hematite. Coarse Matte censers with hourglass bodies are predecessors of the elaborate composite censers of the following period. Figurines are handmade, often with slit eyes and prognathous profiles.

Absent are cylinder vases, rectangular supports, *candeleros* of all kinds, and elaborate composite censers. It is unlikely that cylinder vases were developed locally, and it should not be assumed that every cylinder vase in Mesoamerica was tied to Teotihuacán. "Lustrous ware" imports include sherds probably from cylindrical vases, apparently produced in Veracruz significantly earlier than at Teotihuacán. Thin Orange ware was imported in slightly higher proportions than before, reaching 3 to 4 percent of some collections. Graywares, probably from southern Puebla and Oaxaca, appear in small quantities.

Ceramic connections with Veracruz do not include utility wares, and massive population movement is unlikely. Interlocking scroll motifs in Teotihuacán sculpture and murals are probably from Veracruz, and some may pertain to this period.

In Oaxaca, a few ceramics from the Monte Albán II-IIIA transition phase are so similar to Teotihuacán examples that they suggest significant contact this early. Oaxaca-related ceramics appear in a Teotihuacán enclave by the end of this period.

At Altun Há, a Maya site in Belize, numerous green obsidian objects in an offering closely resemble objects from the Feathered Serpent Pyramid and were surely made by Teotihuacán artisans. The ceramics in the offering were not made at Teotihuacán, but they are similar to Teotihuacán forms of this period. Cylinder vases are absent. Pendergast suggests a date around A.D. 200–275, which agrees with the Teotihuacán chronology. This deposit reflects contact on an elite level. Strangely, nothing else like it has been found in the Maya area.

Later Maya elites adopted some Teotihuacán symbols, mostly associated with war. These were probably not imposed by Teotihuacán, but adopted by independent groups for their own ends. Nothing would have so effectively imbued Teotihuacán military symbolism with potency as the memory of great victories. Widespread

Teotihuacán influences are supposedly not much earlier than A.D. 400; however, it is unlikely that after drastically altering societies throughout the Basin of Mexico and building the great monuments of their city by A.D. 200, Teotihuacános waited another two centuries to make their power felt much beyond their core area. Perhaps early rulers of Teotihuacán campaigned beyond the Basin of Mexico and overwhelmed many of their neighbors, but it is unlikely that they created any large, long-lived empire. Their most enduring effect, like that of Alexander or Napoleon, was probably the memory of dazzling successes.

A.D. 300–650/750

This period comprises the Late Tlamimilolpa, Xolalpan, and Metepec phases. It was the heyday of Teotihuacán influence abroad, but most of the excitement within the city seems to have been over. There was great material prosperity, perhaps tapering off in the last century. Population was on the order of one hundred thousand or more for most of this period. The large stone and concrete apartment compounds that now housed most of the city's population were built and frequently rebuilt. Temples and other civic structures already in existence were renovated and enlarged, but nothing was undertaken that compares with the mind-boggling achievements of the period between about A.D. 50 and 250. There may have been episodes experienced by the Teotihuacános as times of crisis, uncertainty, and struggles for power, but there was no disruption large enough to leave gross archaeological signs, except that the locus of active political management may have shifted from the Ciudadela to the "Avenue of the Dead" macro-complex. Nothing suggests major incursions of outsiders, although infiltration from various sources was probably chronic. Possibly the number of Nahua speakers was increasing significantly.

Such a long period of comparative stability is unusual, and it demands explanation. Perhaps rulers in the preceding period committed excesses, including the mass sacrifices at the Feathered Serpent Pyramid, that led to an elite reaction. René Millon suggests that a new ethic of collective leadership and institutionalized restraint on personal power was adopted around A.D. 300 and remained effective for the next several centuries. However, the change may have been less drastic and may have involved differences in the personalities of rulers more than radical institutional changes. Formality, impersonality, and multiplicity are pervasive, but these traits were present earlier. The relation between Teotihuacáno representations and their concrete social actions remains puzzling.

A distinctive kind of apartment compound now housed nearly the entire urban population. Many were around 60 meters on a side, but they vary greatly in size and layout and are much less uniform than often thought. Nevertheless, the state may have been involved in their construction. Most were large enough to house several extended families, and many probably held sixty or more individuals. A compound's occupants were probably related in part by descent and marriage, but perhaps also by other principles. They probably formed a social unit above the extended family/household level but below the "barrio" or neighborhood level. Such units would have been a distinctive factor in the constitution of Teotihuacán society.

Cylindrical tripod vases began to be made at Teotihuacán around A.D. 300, with both circular and slab supports. Small, cream-pitcher-like vessels (copas) occur; similar vessels have been found in sites in Veracruz and Chiapas and as far away as Kaminaljuyú. Small, crudely made incense burners resembling candle-holders, called candeleros, appear; at first some have only a single chamber, but soon nearly all are twin chambered. Larger, coarse ware censers with flowerpot bodies continue from before, but now in elaborate composite "theater" forms; intricate arrays of mold-made elements are attached to a hand-modeled framework extending up from the lid.

Cooking, storage, transport, and serving vessels continue from the previous period without dramatic changes. Most were probably made in local workshops for neighborhood consumption. Midway in the period, a distinctive utility ware, San Martín Orange, was developed and produced in great quantities in two standard forms—amphoras and large open craters. It was fired at a higher temperature than most Teotihuacán ceramics, and specialists produced it for distribution throughout the city.

Figurine types developed out of those of the previous period, but molds were used, at first for heads attached to featureless, hand-modeled nude bodies (often in active poses) that had perishable clothing and ornaments. Molds were later used for bodies as well, often with elaborate costumes. Most known Teotihuacán murals and perhaps most stone carvings pertain to this period.

There were at least two localized residential concentrations with outside connections. One was a long-lasting enclave with strong Oaxacan ties near the western outskirts. The other was the so-called Merchants' Barrio, which has significant amounts of pottery imported from various parts of the Gulf Coast and lesser amounts from the Maya Lowlands.

Teotihuacán remained a primate city, by far the largest settlement in the Basin of Mexico, although small settlements seem to have become more numerous. Isolated rural households may have been missed by the Valley of Mexico survey, but medium-sized settlements were very scarce relative to pre- and post-Teotihuacán times. There were, however, a few good-sized regional centers, such as Atzcapotzalco and Cerro Portezuelo.

The region politically controlled by Teotihuacán extended beyond the Basin of Mexico, but its core area was probably only 25,000 to 50,000 square kilometers, with a population perhaps around one-half million to one million—far fewer than the Aztec state controlled. There is a strong Teotihuacán presence in the Tula region, and a major center at Chingú. Control may have been strong in the Valley of Toluca, but it probably did not extend much farther north or west. There are tenuous iconographic connections as far west as Jalisco. Influence in Zacatecas and Durango seems weak. Drastic settlement pattern changes in eastern Morelos were probably due to Teotihuacán intervention, and it was very likely part of the Teotihuacán polity. Influence in western Morelos was perhaps not so strong, although it certainly extended into Guerrero.

The situation in Puebla-Tlaxcala is unclear. Some sites were culturally close to the city and probably under its control, and apparently corridors of Teotihuacán-related sites traversed the region. Cholula was an important Teotihuacán-related settlement, but its political status is a puzzle. Perhaps Teotihuacán politically controlled producers of Thin Orange ware near Tepeji de Rodríguez, in south central Puebla. Teotihuacán imported this ware in huge quantities; it forms up to 10 percent of ceramic collections from this period.

The picture in the Gulf Coast is also obscure. Besides ceramics imported from Veracruz, there are shared styles and vessel forms, but the Gulf Coast may have been more donor than recipient. Possibly there was an especially direct relationship with the area near and south of El Tajín, the coastal section closest to Teotihuacán. Tres Zapotes has some Teotihuacán ties. Sculptural evidence of Teotihuacán connections at Cerro de las Mesas is slight, but elsewhere a few Gulf monuments have marked Teotihuacán affinities, notably a figure from Soyoltepec with flaming bundle torches and other symbols associated with war and political authority at Teotihuacán. Matacapan had some sort of connection, although its nature has been misunderstood and its intensity exaggerated. Especially questionable is a supposed Teotihuacán enclave. Few, if any, cylinder vases are of specifically Teotihuacán subtypes; however, some Matacapan objects are strongly linked to Teotihuacán, notably twin-chambered candeleros. These were presumably used in household ritual, yet their abrupt disappearance after the destruction of Teotihuacán suggests a close tie with the state. Matacapan figurines also show some resemblances to those of Teotihuacán.

Development of rival centers in Central Mexico was probably inhibited for several centuries, even without political control. Probably Teotihuacán armies could squelch any society that threatened serious competition. The rise of Xochicalco, Cacaxtla, and other centers marks the decline of this dominance, probably not long after A.D. 650, and perhaps earlier. Possibly they rose when Teotihuacán was already in ruins, but they may have overlapped with the Metepec phase, during which Teotihuacán maintained a show of prosperity in spite of weakening power. Population of the city probably declined somewhat in its last century, mainly by shrinkage around the edges; Metepec ceramics are especially abundant near the center.

The Monte Albán state in Oaxaca was independent (though in communication with Teotihuacán), but Teotihuacán may have inhibited its expansion. Teotihuacán-related manifestations are stronger in highland Guatemala. At Kaminaljuyú these include *talud-tablero* pyramids, rich burials with some elite ceramics and other objects imported from Teotihuacán, and locally made elite materials in Teotihuacán style. Persistence of local styles of utility wares suggests continuity of the local population. Locally made ceramics of Teotihuacán inspiration—notably composite censers—are found elsewhere in the highlands and Pacific slopes. The nature of this presence remains controversial. It is hard to believe that any part of Guatemala was politically controlled from Teotihuacán; nevertheless, the large Teotihuacán-style pyramids at Kaminaljuyú, with rich burials and costly offerings laden with symbolism of the state religion, suggest more than a trading colony. Perhaps adventurers from Teotihuacán set up a local state that replicated the elite religion and culture of the metropolis. The later Cotzumalhuapa style is not closely connected with Teotihuacán, and Teotihuacán probably had no lasting impact on highland Guatemala.

Teotihuacán influences are also evident in the Maya Lowlands. Their nature is poorly understood, but they can scarcely have involved political control by Teotihuacán or high-volume commerce. Elites exchanged precious objects. Possibly persons with Teotihuacán connections played important roles in Maya politics for a time, and possibly some new techniques and aims of warfare were inspired by Teotihuacán. At any rate, symbols shared with Teotihuacán became important in the Maya iconography of rulership.

Trade was important for the Teotihuacán state and society, but its significance has been exaggerated at the expense of other factors, such as warfare and religion. Teotihuacán controlled production of the highly valued green obsidian from the Pachuca source (about 55 kilometers away), as well as the much closer source near Otumba, and Pachuca obsidian appears in sites over much of Mesoamerica at this time. However, most of what spread beyond Teotihuacán's political sphere was ideational and symbolic, together with some manufactured goods that embodied these ideas (often on an elite level). Probably Teotihuacán traded green obsidian extensively because Mesoamericans appreciated its superior properties, and it was perhaps the only raw material controlled by Teotihuacános that could be offered in exchange for imports. It is unlikely that Teotihuacános controlled the production or distribution of obsidian from sources outside Central Mexico. We have no evidence about perishable materials that Teotihuacános may also have traded, such as textiles spun from imported cotton.

Decline, Fiery Destruction, and Aftermath

Perhaps around A.D. 750, but possibly a century or more earlier, the principal temples and many elite residences in the central part of Teotihuacán were burned and the carved figures were smashed; most residences outside the center were abandoned without burning. It was evidently necessary to destroy the objects and settings of state-related ritual in order permanently to disable Teotihuacán as a political force. The agents of destruction may have been insiders, outsiders, or some combination; but only a decline in the system that had worked so well for Teotihuacán could have made the city vulnerable. What ended was not just a dynasty—it was the belief system that had supported the state. There were marked changes in material remains on both elite and ordinary levels. The *talud-tablero* style for temples and the "apartment compound" residences disappear, and many ceramic forms vanish, including cylindrical vases, Thin Orange ware, candeleros, composite censers (replaced by ladle censers), and San Martín Orange ware. Ollas and other cooking and storage vessels assume quite different shapes. Some distinctive figurine types, such as "portraits," disappear, although there are continuities in some other figurine forms. The city may have been briefly abandoned; a poorly understood "Oxtoticpac" complex may represent peoples who lived in and near the city.

Briefly abandoned or not, Teotihuacán soon was a large settlement again. In the Xometla phase (related to Coyotlatelco), settlement covered around 8 square kilometers and population was around forty thousand. Locations of highest sherd concentrations change markedly, in the greatest spatial shift since the onset of the Patlachique phase many centuries earlier. The abruptness and intensity of changes suggest a considerable in-migration of ethnically different people, who may have been Nahua-speakers.

In the ensuing Mazapan phase the city remained quite large, probably around thirty thousand. Mazapan ceramics are quite different from Coyotlatelco. They may be a Central Mexican innovation, or they may represent more newcomers.

FURTHER READINGS

Berlo, J. C. (ed.). 1992. *Art, Ideology, and the City of Teotihuacan.* Washington, D.C.: Dumbarton Oaks.

Berrin, K. (ed.). 1988. *Feathered Serpents and Flowering Trees: Reconstructing the Murals of Teotihuacan.* San Francisco: Fine Arts Museums of San Francisco.

Berrin, K., and E. Pasztory (eds.). 1993. *Teotihuacan: Art from the City of the Gods.* New York: Thames and Hudson.

Cowgill, G. L. 1992. Toward a Political History of Teotihuacán. In A. Demarest and G. Conrad (eds.), *Ideology and Precolumbian Civilizations*, pp. 87–114. Santa Fe: School of American Research Press.

Langley, J. C. 1986. *Symbolic Notation of Teotihuacan: Elements of Writing in a Mesoamerican Culture of the Classic Period.* British Archaeological Reports, International Series, 313. Oxford.

McClung de Tapia, E., and E. C. Rattray (eds.). 1987. *Teotihuacan: Nuevos datos, nuevas síntesis y nuevos problemas.* Mexico City: Universidad Nacional Autónoma de México.

Millon, C. 1973. Painting, Writing, and Polity in Teotihuacan, Mexico. *American Antiquity* 38:294–314.

Millon, R. 1973. *The Teotihuacan Map. Part One: Text.* Austin: University of Texas Press.

———. 1981. Teotihuacan: City, State, and Civilization. In J. Sabloff (ed.), *Supplement to the Handbook of Middle American Indians*, vol. 1, pp. 198–243. Austin: University of Texas Press.

———. 1988. The Last Years of Teotihuacan Dominance. In N. Yoffee and G. L. Cowgill (eds.), *The Collapse of Ancient States and Civilizations*, pp. 102–164. Tucson: University of Arizona Press.

Millon, R., B. Drewitt, and G. Cowgill. 1973. *Urbanization at Teotihuacan, Mexico: The Teotihuacan Map.* Austin: University of Texas Press.

Sempowski, M. L., and M. W. Spence. 1994. *Mortuary Practices and Skeletal Remains at Teotihuacan.* With an addendum by R. Storey. Salt Lake City: University of Utah Press.

Storey, R. 1992. *Life and Death in the Ancient City of Teotihuacan: A Paleodemographic Synthesis.* Tuscaloosa: University of Alabama Press.

von Winning, H. 1987. *La iconografía de Teotihuacan: Los dioses y los signos.* 2 vols. Mexico City: Universidad Nacional Autónoma de México.

George L. Cowgill

SEE ALSO
Basin of Mexico; Classic Period

Teotihuacán: Religion and Deities

Its massive pyramids, highly organized plan, and complex iconography indicate clearly that Teotihuacán was driven by powerful religious belief; however, our understanding of its rites, gods, and mythology remains elusive. This is due in part to the antiquity of the site, which was destroyed more than eight hundred years before the Spanish conquest. For this reason, early colonial documents tend to be of limited use for the study of Teotihuacán religion. In addition, writing—even in the form of calendrical notation—is extremely limited at the site, despite the fact that Teotihuacán was in direct contact with the highly literate Maya and Zapotec. In addition, the bold art style of Teotihuacán tends to be highly abstract and static, with little attempt at narrative scenes.

Although the elucidation of Teotihuacán religion is a difficult task, it is by no means insurmountable or unproductive. Contemporary research frequently combines a number of fruitful approaches to interpret Teotihuacán religion. There is contextual information provided by archaeological excavations at Teotihuacán, which can offer vital clues into such ritual practices as sacrifice, burial, and the offering of incense. In addition, the rich archaeological remains, including architecture, murals, and ceramic vessels and figurines, provide a wonderfully complex and detailed array of information.

Aside from the internal study of Teotihuacán artifacts, there are also data provided by contemporary Classic period cultures, such as the Zapotec and, especially, the Maya. In their graphic art and highly developed writing, the Classic Maya made many direct allusions to Teotihuacán, including deities and ritual regalia. Teotihuacán also had a profound impact on later cultures of highland Mexico, including the Postclassic Toltec and later Aztec. The careful use of these more recent and better understood Postclassic traditions can offer important insights into Teotihuacán ritual practices and belief. In addition, early Colonial period Aztec accounts provide tantalizing clues concerning some of the more fundamental concepts of Teotihuacán religion, including fire symbolism and the Teotihuacán cult of war.

Perhaps the most impressive statements of Teotihuacán religion occur in its monumental architecture. The massive Pyramid of the Sun and Pyramid of the Moon dominate the site and can be seen from many kilometers distant. Like other Mesoamerican pyramids, these structures are probably representations of sacred mountains and thus constitute a form of mountain worship. This concern with sacred mountains is also reflected by the orientation of the Pyramid of the Moon, which is backed by the massive, looming mountain known as Cerro Gordo. The Pyramid of the Sun lies directly atop a cave that passes to the virtual center of the pyramid. Although recent investigations reveal that this was a quarried, artificial cave, this does not detract from its obviously sacred nature. It quite possibly symbolized the cave of emergence, the womb and birthplace of mankind. Other artificial caves recently found at Teotihuacán contain altars and vertical shafts, presumably for solar calendrical sightings. Aside from the two massive pyramids, there are many other pyramidal buildings, including the richly ornamented Temple of Quetzalcoatl and the three-temple complexes found in many portions of the city. In addition, altars in the form of miniature temples typically occur in principal patios of apartment compounds, as if replicating the much larger public pyramids on a more private, domestic level.

Like the Pyramid of the Moon, which it abuts, the Street of the Dead is oriented directly toward Cerro Gordo. It has been suggested that the directional placement of this avenue, 15° 20' east of true north, is related to the crossing of the Pleiades, a constellation commonly identified with agricultural events in many parts of the world. Aside from its possible astronomical orientation, the great avenue was surely used for ceremonial pro-

The Teotihuacán Tlaloc grasping a water jar and lightning bolt with clouds, Stela 3, Los Horcones, Chiapas (after figs. 3–5 of Carlos Navarrete, The Sculptural Complex at Cerro Bernal on the Coast of Chiapas, *Notes of the New World Archaeological Foundation*, no. 1).

cessions, which are commonly represented in the mural paintings at Teotihuacán.

Among Teotihuacán deities there is a strong tendency toward anthropomorphization, a common trait of Mesoamerican gods. Among the more readily recognizable beings is the Teotihuacán Tlaloc, who typically appears with goggle-eyes and a jaguar maw from which a waterlily plant emerges. Like his well-known Postclassic counterpart, the Teotihuacán Tlaloc commonly appears with thunderbolts and water jars as signs of his rain and lighting powers (see figure). His circular eye elements resemble the shell goggles worn by warriors at Teotihuacán and other regions of Classic Mesoamerica and probably label this powerful entity as a warlike being, perhaps even a war god. Another common Teotihuacán deity is a quetzal-plumed serpent, clearly an ancestral form of the Postclassic Quetzalcoatl; however, in contrast to Postclassic depictions, this being rarely appears in human form. Instead, it usually occurs as an undulating, plumed rattlesnake, frequently with water spewing from its mouth, and sometimes with rain cascading from the body. Still another Teotihuacán deity is the Old Fire God, known as Huehueteotl or "Old God" among the Postclassic Aztec. In Teotihuacán stone sculpture, this wizened being commonly sits cross-legged while supporting a censer bowl on his stooped shoulders.

As among the Postclassic Aztec, female deities are quite prevalent at Teotihuacán. These female goddesses can be most readily identified by their costume, which typically includes a skirt and an upper garment equivalent to the Postclassic *quechquemitl* overblouse. Although the term "Great Goddess" is frequently applied to female divinities at Teotihuacán, it is probably too inclusive; rather, a number of distinct goddesses probably existed there. One can be identified by her nose pendant, formed of a horizontal bar atop a series of upper teeth; this being appears to be identified with the earth, divination, spiders, and warfare, and may be related to the Aztec Toci as well as to Spider Grandmother of the contemporary American Southwest. A number of Teotihuacán figurines depict a female figure with a coiffure resembling a tasseled ear of maize; this may well be a maize goddess, analogous to the Aztec maize goddess known as Xilonen or Chicomecoatl (see figure).

Mural paintings and the great Street of the Dead suggest that ceremonial processions were an important aspect of ritual life at Teotihuacán. Art depicts striding figures scattering streams of objects from their hands, suggesting the offering of jade, water, incense, or other sacred items. Many of these figures have elaborate speech scrolls, probably representing ritual speech and song. Though in the static style of Teotihuacán, striding figures tend to have their feet planted firmly on the ground; many are probably dancing.

As in other regions of Mesoamerica, fire offerings were of great importance. Along with the stone Huehueteotl braziers, complex ceramic censers, or *incensarios*, are com-

A possible portrayal of the Teotihuacán Maize Goddess (after Lám55 of Lourette Séjourné. 1966. *El lenguage de las formas en Teotihuacan.* Gabriel Mancera 65, Mexico City).

mon at the site, and they may have been an important component of the ceremonies performed at the patio altars within apartment compounds. Many of the motifs found on these censers, including flowers, butterflies, maize, and squash, suggest that these fire offerings at least partly concerned agricultural fertility and abundance.

Much of the more recognizable iconography at Teotihuacán—Tlaloc, the plumed serpent, rain, rivers, shells and maize—is clearly related to water and agriculture. However, it is becoming increasingly apparent that human sacrifice and warfare were also extremely important components of Teotihuacán religion. Many scenes depict bleeding hearts impaled on curving obsidian blades. In addition, archaeological excavations have revealed groups of severed heads as well as the dedicatory offering of infants and children. By far the most striking case of human sacrifice at Teotihuacán was revealed by the recent excavations at the Temple of Quetzalcoatl (also known as the Pyramid of the Plumed Serpent). It is estimated that

T

more than two hundred adults were deposited in mass graves for the dedication of this pyramid around A.D. 200. The majority of the individuals are dressed as warriors, wearing shell collars imitating human teeth and upper jaws. With their series of false maxillae, these macabre necklaces may mark particularly exalted warriors, with each jaw perhaps referring to a single coup or kill.

Along with the abundant evidence for human sacrifice, there was a highly developed cult of war at Teotihuacán. The sculpted façade of the Temple of Quetzalcoatl portrays an entity which I have termed the War Serpent, known as *waxaklahun uba chan* ("eighteen its image snake") in Classic Maya inscriptions. The temple façade examples appear as shell platelet helmets, complete with warrior goggles on the brow. Known archaeologically from both Teotihuacán and the Maya area, these helmets are worn by many Teotihuacán warrior figurines. In most cases, these figurines appear to depict warrior mortuary bundles like those documented for the Postclassic Aztec. The Aztec burned these bundles in funerary rites, and there are archaeological indications of similar ceremonies at Teotihuacán. In both Teotihuacán and later Aztec thought, butterflies are closely identified with both fire and the soul of the dead warrior. Fire appears to have been considered as the transforming force that metamorphoses the chrysalis-like mortuary bundle into the butterfly warrior. The early colonial *Florentine Codex* describes Aztec conceptions of rebirth at Teotihuacán: "And so they named the place Teotihuacán, because it was the burial place of the rulers. For it was said: When we die, we are resurrected . . . In this manner they spoke to the dead when one died; . . . 'Awaken! It hath reddened; the dawn hath set in. Already singeth the flame-colored cock, the flame-colored swallow; already flieth the flame-colored butterfly'" (Sahagun 1950–1963, book 10:192).

According to Aztec mythology, the most important resurrection at Teotihuacán was the rebirth of the sun and moon out of a sacrificial pyre. It is noteworthy that the eagle and jaguar—avatars of the two great military orders—also emerged from this fiery place. Thus, the Aztec attributed much of their own cult of war to the ancient city of Teotihuacán.

FURTHER READINGS

Berlo, J. C. (ed.). 1992. *Art, Ideology, and the City of Teotihuacan*. Washington, D.C.: Dumbarton Oaks.

Berrin, K., and E. Pasztory (eds.). 1993. *Teotihuacan: Art from the City of the Gods*. London: Thames and Hudson.

Sahagún, Bernardino de. 1950–1963. *General History of the Things of New Spain (Florentine Codex)*. A. Anderson and C. Dibble (trans.). Santa Fe: School of American Research and University of Utah.

Taube, K. 1992. The Temple of Quetzalcoatl and the Cult of Sacred War at Teotihuacan. *RES: Anthropology and Aesthetics* 21:53–87.

Karl Taube

SEE ALSO

Central Mexican Religion

Teotihuacán: Sacred Landscape

In the first century A.D., an agglomeration of agricultural villages in the northeastern Valley of Mexico was given coherence by the layout of a 3-kilometer-long ritual way, now known as the Street of the Dead. This north–south axis visually connects Cerro Gordo—the mountain to the north—to the city in the center, and the agricultural zone and its springs in the south. Set with pyramids, precincts, and seats of rulership, the line drawn by the Ritual Way governed the regular plan of the residential grid and the orientation of agricultural fields across a broad highland district. At Teotihuacán the buildings are not so much in the land, but of it; buildings enhance the setting, responding on an almost geological scale to the formal and symbolic possibilities presented by the location. The city itself became an icon, a civic metaphor of the natural world. In imagination and scale, this architectural achievement was unprecedented in Mesoamerica. The urban design of Teotihuacán was a major invention, yet the architects were transforming old principles into fresh solutions as they created a new esthetic and symbolic vocabulary to suit new historical and cultural circumstances.

The political and economic power of Teotihuacán was legitimized by the network of religious connections that joined the urban plan to topographic and celestial features. At the northern extremity of the processional way, the Moon Pyramid stands framed by Cerro Gordo. The Nahuatl name for this mountain, Tenan ("mother rock"), suggests that it was regarded as a natural icon of the earth. The denomination "Moon Pyramid" is almost certainly a misnomer, because the position of the monument in relation to the mountain points to its function in the long tradition of worshipping mountains as containers of water and embodiments of the earth's regenerative power. Teotihuacán religion concentrated on two principal deities—a god of rainstorms and lightning, and a "Great Goddess" of the earth and fertility; but which was enshrined at the Moon or Sun pyramids is presently unknown.

The processional way continues past the forecourt of the colossal Sun Pyramid. The east–west orientation of the building corresponds to the path of the sun at zenith passage, indicating a religious function of the building in marking this pivotal time of the year. Another key feature of the building is a long cave that extends underground from the base of the west façade stairway to a chamber approximately below the summit. This cave has been interpreted as a place for communion with chthonic forces, and it was probably seen by the Teotihuacános as a mythic place of emergence, where (according to a widespread Amerindian mythic theme) the first human beings came forth from the earth in the time of creation. If correct, this supposition would indicate that the pyramid was an *axis mundi,* marking the center of the Teotihuacán world. A network of underground man-made and natural tunnels and chambers are now being explored; one has been found to contain a spring presided over by the storm god, with vessels full of seeds.

Sometime after A.D. 200, the processional way was extended south as other impressive constructions were built. The first group of apartment compounds and temple platforms is thought to have functioned as an administrative-residential center. A "pecked cross" marker on a floor in this complex is aligned with a similar marker on a distant hill on the western horizon. The line of sight points to the place where the Pleiades set on the night of their zenith transit of the celestial meridian. In later centuries, the Aztecs observed this astronomical event to determine the New Fire ceremony, initiating a new fifty-two-year calendric cycle.

The Ciudadela was among the last great public constructions to be carried out, around A.D. 250. The spacious courtyard is contained by an elevated quadrangular platform on which individual temple-platforms were symmetrically placed. In the center and to the east, the Temple of the Feathered Serpent stands flanked by twin apartment complexes. The tiers of this platform are adorned with repetitive sculptured panels featuring a serpent head projecting from an undulating feathered body with a headdress-like mask on the tail. Although designated as a temple, the building is unlikely to have been a place of cult activity; rather, it appears to have been the seat of Teotihuacán's theocratic rulership. The plumed serpent image, a beneficent and powerful sky symbol

identified with seasonal windstorms, rain, and the forces of renewal, is qualified by the headdress mask as a sign of royal office. In later centuries the name "Quetzalcoatl" ("quetzal-feather serpent") could denote either a nature deity or a title of royal or priestly office. Excavations below the platform foundations have revealed the remains of about two hundred sacrificed victims, mostly in military attire.

Opposite the Ciudadela to the west lies an equally large marketplace quadrangle. Two roadways converge on these complexes from the west and east, respectively. To the south, the city gives way to the agricultural district. The market and the place of government thus stood in the middle of the urban-agricultural continuum.

Considered as a whole, the layout of Teotihuacán constitutes a cosmogram. Although the processional way does not form precise 90° angles with the approximate east–west alignments of the Sun Pyramid, the Pleiades Marker, or the roadways leading to the Ciudadela and market, the designers' intention was to incorporate diverse topographical and celestial reference points in a plan that was visually and intellectually understood as an integrated, coherent diagram.

Richard F. Townsend

Tepeapulco (México, Mexico)

This name refers to two distinct sites at the northern end of the Plains of Apan in the Basin of Mexico, approximately 30 kilometers northeast of Teotihuacán: a provincial center of the Teotihuacán period, and an urban capital of the Aztec city-state known as Tepeapulco (Tepepolco), with post-Conquest occupation continuing to the present. Numerous communication routes converge on the Tepeapulco area from the north, northeast, southeast, and southwest, creating a critical communications juncture.

Teotihuacán-period Tepeapulco is situated in a small valley between low hills on the gently sloping piedmont and the lowermost steep western slopes of Cerro Jihuingo, north of the Aztec, colonial, and contemporary urban center of Tepeapulco. Ceramics from the site and adjacent areas indicate a regional occupation from the early Terminal Formative period to the end of the Classic period (300 B.C.–A.D. 650/750), with Tepeapulco's occupation starting slightly later (late Terminal Formative, Tzacualli phase, 100 B.C.–A.D. 150). Regional population was concentrated there to the exclusion of other sites from A.D. 150 to 650/750. Tepeapulco was compact and nucleated, covering about 60 hectares, and had an estimated population of 1,500 to 2,000, with concentrations of low mounds that were probably the remains of apartment compound residences. There is a partially reconstructed pyramid/plaza complex with some architectural similarities to the small platform mounds on the enclosing quadrangle platforms of the Ciudadela at Teotihuacán, with a well-defined ceremonial avenue (Calzada de los Vientos) originating at the pyramid/plaza complex. This avenue is about 40 to 50 meters in width, situated between low, long, parallel mounds that mark the edges; it extends to the northwest with a total length of approximately 300 to 350 meters. The orientation of the ceremonial avenue running along the northeastern edge of the site deviates substantially from the 15° east of north orientation of the Calzada de los Muertos (Street of the Dead) at Teotihuacán. Also unlike Teotihuacán, the Tepeapulco ceremonial avenue does not seem to be part of any obvious overall site grid plan. Evidence for specialized craft production centers on obsidian core-blade production using obsidian from several sources, including Otumba and/or Malpais, Pachuca, and Tecocomulco.

On the lower piedmont of Cerro Santa Ana above the alluvial plain is the Late Postclassic provincial urban capital of the Aztec city-state of Tepeapulco. It covered an estimated 2.5 to 3 square kilometers, with a population estimated between three and ten thousand. Ceramics from Tepeapulco and other sites in the city-state show only traces of Aztec II (Early Aztec, A.D. 1200–1400) occupation, an almost exclusively Aztec III (Late Aztec, A.D. 1300–1521+) occupation, and a declining Aztec III/IV (Early Colonial, A.D. 1521–1620) occupation. Much of the Aztec *cabecera,* or capital, including a suspected nucleated core, is obscured by the Colonial, Republican, and contemporary occupations in the same area.

Occupation in the Aztec city-state consisted of aceramic obsidian-carrying sites, hamlets, large and small dispersed and nucleated villages, and the urban center of Tepeapulco. Most of the city-state's settlements were situated within a radius of about 4 kilometers from Tepeapulco, with a total population of about fifty thousand.

FURTHER READINGS

Charlton, T. H. 1991. The Influence and Legacy of Teotihuacán on Regional Routes and Urban Planning. In C. D. Trombold (ed.), *Ancient Road Networks and Settlement Hierarchies in the New World,* pp. 186– 197. Cambridge: Cambridge University Press.

———. 1994. Economic Heterogeneity and State Expansion: The Northeastern Basin of Mexico during the Late Postclassic period. In M. G. Hodge and M. E. Smith (eds.), *Economics and Polities in the Aztec Realm,* pp. 221–256. Studies on Culture and Society, 6. Albany: Institute for Mesoamerican Studies, State University of New York.

Matos Moctezuma, E., M. T. Garcia Garcia, F. Lopez Aguilar, and I. Rodriguez Garcia. 1981. Proyecto Tepeapulco: Resumen preliminar de las actividades realizadas en la primera temporada de trabajo. In E. C. Rattray et al. (eds.), *Interaccion cultural en Mexico Central,* pp. 113–148. Instituto de Investigaciones Antropologicas, (Arqueológia), Serie Antropologica, 41. Mexico City: Universidad Nacional Autónoma de México.

Nicholson, H. B. 1974. Tepepolco, the Locale of the First Stage of Fr. Bernardino de Sahagún's Great Ethnographic Project: Historical and Cultural Notes. In Norman Hammond (ed.), *Mesoamerican Archaeology: New Approaches,* pp. 145–164. Austin: University of Texas Press.

Thomas H. Charlton

SEE ALSO
Basin of Mexico

Tepexi el Viejo (Puebla, Mexico)

Tepexi el Viejo is a Postclassic fortified site in the Mixteca-Puebla region of Mesoamerica. The site was the center of a city-state with tributaries and, in that way is typical of the Mixtec area, where small city-states were connected culturally but were political rivals. It was occupied from about A.D. 1300 to the Conquest; the dates are based primarily on ceramic cross-dating. At an altitude of 1700 meters above sea level, Tepexi is in the *tierra templada* climatic zone. The soil is thin; within less than 30 cm of the surface an indurated laminar horizon of nearly pure carbonate, a lime accumulation known as caliche, locally called *tepetate* and used as the major building material. To judge from an existing tribute list, products of the agricultural subsistence base were primarily cotton, maize, pumpkins, and hot peppers.

The site stands on a hill that is surrounded on three sides by deep canyons. The main precinct is completely enclosed by a series of massive outer walls. Within it, as well as within the subsite to the northwest, are monumental architectural constructions, including pyramidal mounds and building complexes. About forty ceramic groups were identified and used to devise three chronological periods. Lithic artifacts consist primarily of chert and obsidian points and blade implements. Tepexi was conquered by the Mexica in 1503 and by Cortés in 1520.

FURTHER READINGS

Gorenstein, S. 1973. *Tepexi el Viejo: A Postclassic Fortified Site in the Mixteca-Puebla Region of Mexico.* American Philosophical Society, Transactions, 63, Part 1. Philadelphia.

Shirley Gorenstein

SEE ALSO

Puebla-Tlaxcala Region

Tepoztlán (Morelos, Mexico)

The Postclassic period city-state of Tepoztlán is situated at 1,600 meters elevation overlooking the Valley of Morelos, in a warm, subhumid climate. Originally occupied in the Formative period (300 B.C.), it was inhabited during the Middle and Late Postclassic period by the Tlahuica, Xochimilca, and Mexica ethnic groups. The local economy was based on agriculture and production of cotton, paper made of the bark of fig trees *(Amate),* and agave *(maguey)* products. In the mountains above the site are cave paintings and the Late Postclassic Tepozteco temple, dedicated to the gods of *pulque* (agave sap beer).

FURTHER READINGS

Carrasco, P. 1964. Family Structure of Sixteenth Century Tepoztlan. In R. A. Manners (ed.), *Process and Pattern in Culture: Essays in Honor of Julian H. Steward,* pp. 185–210. Chicago: Aldine.

Lewis, O. 1960. *Tepoztlán, Village in Mexico.* New York: Holt, Rinehart, and Winston.

Maldonado Jiménez, D. 1990. *Cuauhnáhuac y Huaxtepec (Tlalhuicas y Xochimilcas en el Morelos prehispánico).* Cuernavaca: Universidad Nacional Autónoma de México, Centro Regional de Investigaciones Multidisciplinarias.

Octavio Rocha Herrera

SEE ALSO

Morelos Region

Terremote, El (D.F., Mexico)

This hamlet has two low house mounds (two others were probably leveled by plowing) and refuse of the Ayotla to Manantial phases (1100–1000 B.C.) over 1.7 hectares on the bed of Lake Xochimilco. Parsons found the site, and Tolstoy partially excavated it in 1972. The mounds contain layers of black mud, yellow clay, and matted vegetal material, as well as retaining walls of rocks brought from higher ground. One mound bore a rectangular platform (c. 5 by 10 meters) oriented north–south, with a mud-plastered talus faced with pieces of compacted volcanic ash, perhaps a dwelling foundation. The situation and recovered maize and beans suggest Early Horizon use of permanently humid soil at the lake's edge. Ceramics and figurines resemble those of Ayotla, which is similarly situated. Aztec refuse occurs but is not associated with these features. Mounds of Ticoman date nearby (Xo–LF–2) have been excavated by Mari Carmen Serra Puche.

FURTHER READINGS

Parsons, J. R., E. Brumfiel, M. H. Parsons, and D. J. Wilson. 1982. *Prehispanic Settlement Patterns in the Southern Valley of Mexico.* Memoirs of the Museum of Anthropology, University of Michigan, 14.

Smith, C. E., and P. Tolstoy. 1981. Vegetation and Man in the Basin of Mexico. *Journal of Economic Botany* 35:415–433.

Tolstoy, P., S. K. Fish, M. W. Boksenbaum, K. B. Vaughn, and C. E. Smith. 1977. Early Sedentary Communities of the Basin of Mexico. *Journal of Field Archaeology,* 4:91–107.

Paul Tolstoy

SEE ALSO

Basin of Mexico; Formative Period

Tetimpa Region (Puebla, Mexico)

The northeastern flank of the Popocatepetl volcano in western Puebla, around the modern towns of San Buenaventura Nealtican, San Nicolás de los Ranchos, and San Andrés Calpan, has been subject to intense and destructive volcanic activity since the Terminal Formative period; it is still one of the highest-risk areas in the region. Between A.D. 50 and 100 the villages of Tetimpa were abruptly buried by an airfall deposit of yellow pumice that protected and preserved the buildings and activity areas at the same time that it devastated the settlements and made the region uninhabitable for generations to come. It is probable that this violent eruption had an important ideological impact on the developing urban center at Cholula, 15 kilometers to the east.

T

The Formative occupation of the Tetimpa region has been radiocarbon dated to between 700 B.C. and A.D. 100. This can be divided into the Early (700–200 B.C.) and Late (50 B.C.–A.D. 100) Tetimpa phases, which are separated by a short period of abandonment.

The region lies between 2300 and 2400 meters elevation in what was originally a pine and evergreen oak forest with higher rainfall than most of the Puebla-Tlaxcala region; owing to its situation on the slopes of the volcano, it is also subject to frequent storms and frosts. The primary natural resources are stone for *manos* and *metates*, andesite slabs for construction, and wood for building and charcoal.

Excavations in the Tetimpa region have uncovered intact agricultural fields with handmade furrows, interspersed with houses consisting of two or three rooms placed on low stone platforms with *talud-tablero* profiles, situated around a central patio that has a shrine, usually a carved stone head, in the center. In one Late Tetimpa house, the shrine appears to have been a representation of the smoking volcano that overshadows the settlements; the central platform of this unit is decorated with modeled and painted mud faces, set on top of intertwined cords, and placed in a recessed U-shaped *tablero*. Superstructures are made of wattle-and-daub, and there is evidence for the use of corner columns on the main façades. Room sizes vary between 6 and 15 square meters. In the Early Tetimpa phase, kitchens form part of each individual house, while in the Late Tetimpa phase kitchens are separated from the household units, perhaps reflecting a change to communal food preparation and eating patterns.

Burials, flexed and sometimes covered with stone slabs, have been recovered for the Early Tetimpa phase. Grave goods consist of bark beaters and small vessels, sometimes with geometric incised decoration; the most frequent forms are chamfered pedestal-base bowls and composite silhouette tripods. It appears that Late Tetimpa represents a recolonization of the area after a brief hiatus; the occupation was cut short by the volcanic eruption. No human remains associated with the Late Tetimpa phase have been found, and it is assumed that the population had time to escape.

Research has included the application of resistivity and ground-penetrating radar prospection. In both cases, excellent results were achieved.

FURTHER READINGS

Plunket, P., and G. Urunuela. 1998. Preclassic Household Patterns Preserved Under Volcanic Ash at Tetimpa, Puebla, Mexico. *Latin American Antiquity* 9.

Seele, E. 1973. Restos de milpas y poblaciones prehispánicas cerca de San Buenaventura Nealtican, Puebla. *Comunicaciones Proyecto Puebla-Tlaxcala* 7:77–86.

Patricia Plunket Nagoda and Gabriela Uruñela

SEE ALSO

Puebla-Tlaxcala Region

Teuchitlan Tradition

The Teuchitlan tradition represents West Mexico's first experiment in civilization, and a previously unknown hearth for complex societies within early Mesoamerica. It spanned the middle Formative period through the Classic, until its collapse during or at the end of the Epiclassic period.

The core of this tradition is in the highland valleys of west central Jalisco, with sites in the municipalities of Teuchitlan, Tala Ahualulco, Magdalena, San Juanito, Etzatlan, Tequila, Amititan, and Arenal, an area that encircles the dominant geological feature of the region, the Volcán de Tequila. The core is characterized by rich alluvial and volcanic ash soils, many lakes and swamps, mineral and obsidian sources, a diagnostic type of monumental circular architecture, and large habitation zones.

By the San Felipe phase (c. 1000–300 B.C.), surface architecture accompanied tombs. Circular or oval, the platforms average 28 to 30 meters in diameter and 2 meters high. Flat figurines, often with two heads (as found in Tlatilco, Basin of Mexico), were common offerings. The red-on-cream/white wares that remained characteristic of the area till the end of the Classic period began during this time.

The El Arenal phase (300 B.C.–A.D. 200) is characterized by extremely rich shaft tombs, some of which are truly monumental (as deep as 18 meters, with three interior chambers), and by the concentric circular ceremonial buildings typical of the tradition. At Huitzilapa, a rare unlooted tomb was recently explored by López and Ramos; a wealth of hollow figurines, carved stone objects (including blue-gray jade), fine vessels, pseudo-cloisonné objects, and food offerings accompanied six adults in two chambers at the base of an 8-meter shaft. Rare architectural figurines occasionally are included as tomb furniture and offer important insights into the organization of space and building details. With this phase, the differential socio-cultural evolution of the core began, and the surrounding valleys underwent a slow process of depopulation as they were gradually converted into a hinterland.

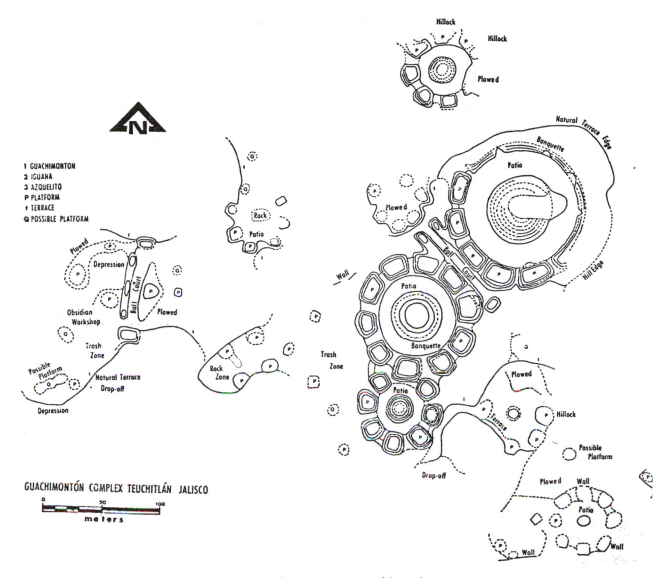

Map of the Guachimontón Complex at Teuchitlán. Illustration courtesy of the author.

During the Ahualulco phase (A.D. 200–400), the sociological differentiation between the core and the hinterland grew, as did complexity within the core. The circular precincts were becoming monumental, and the shaft tombs slowly were deemphasized. Many of these elite burials are still very elegant, however, though the figurines are far less naturalistic than the apparent portraits often found among offerings from the El Arenal phase; the later figurines appear far more standardized. The circular architecture achieved its final refinement in geometry during this period, and many structures are obviously the results of formal design. The precincts are composed of circular, terraced, and truncated pyramids, surrounded by elevated circular patios, which in turn are surrounded by circular banquettes, atop which are eight to twelve square or rectangular platforms. These concentric elements are families of circles utilizing a radical center. Strict rules for proportionality and symmetry govern the grammar of design.

During the Teuchitlan I phase (A.D. 400–700), the architecture reached its maximum expression in monumentality and complexity. Some circles are grouped (as many as eight at Guachimontón, with two ball courts), and the largest achieved a diameter of more than 125

T

meters, or 400 meters in circumference. The largest precincts are 400 by 250 meters, and, while not huge volumetrically, they represent building design of a sophistication not seen elsewhere in ancient Mesoamerica. There are four monumental precincts (Guachimontón, Ahualulco, Santa Quiteria, and San Juan de los Arcos), and many others that were clearly of less importance. This hierarchy of ceremonial precincts is reflected exactly in a hierarchy of ball courts and rectangular palacelike buildings. The greatest ball court is at Santa Quiteria, atop an elongated platform; it measures more than 130 meters in length. The largest palacelike structure is at the Arroyo de las Chivas and constitutes a block of 85 by 50 meters.

The lesser circular precincts are grouped in two tiers and may represent barrios within the overall habitation zones. The largest such zone extends from Ahualulco in the west to San Juan de los Arcos in the east, including the Guachimontón and Teuchitlan area. Within this zone are thirty-eight circular precincts and thousands of residential compounds. Although this habitation zone covers about 24,000 hectares, it is not very nucleated. Even in the densest residential areas, there is an average distance of 100 meters between compounds, and most areas are even less nucleated. It is certainly a semidispersed habitation zone, far more reminiscent of Mayan centers than of typical Central Mexico. While the processes of urbanization seem to have been under way, the habitation zone per se probably never achieved actual urban status. Population has been estimated at 25,000–40,000 for this habitation zone.

Obsidian workshops follow an apparent hierarchical organization. Craft specialization was very well developed in obsidian, mold-made pseudo-cloisonné ceramics, shell work, and fine lapidary arts. During this phase, many of the pseudo-cloisonné vessels appear to have complex ideographic designs that may represent an early codical system. Motifs that are identified as glyphs elsewhere in Mesoamerica are present on these vessels. Apparently, lists of priests or rulers, toponyms, numbers, and gods (especially prominent are the depictions of Ehecatl) are represented. Some of the individuals appear to be named.

Obsidian mining areas are common at the best-quality outcrops. Approximately 3,200 hectares of formal *chinampas* have been identified within the swamps and lakes of the region, and these are closely associated with Teuchitlan I phase sites. Some of the garden blocks are very impressive and highly geometric in layout. In one area, large canals appear to interconnect different subbasins. In the piedmont, canals and terraces are also evident.

During the Teuchitlan I phase, the subcultural patterns within the region were quite diverse. Each major site area has relatively distinct ceramic and figurine styles. Some differences in burial ceremonialism also occur, especially at the nonelite level. Box burials became more common during this period, even for the elite. As grave goods, miniature ceramic vessels slowly replaced full-sized vessels, and even figurines, as this period progressed.

The Teuchitlan II phase (A.D. 700–900) was a period of dramatic socio-cultural change. The huge habitation zones began to disband, and the nearby valleys recovered a large part of their former populations. No new circular buildings were started, and those that were remodeled were often done so at the expense of their symmetry. Rectangular architecture, especially open U-shaped buildings, replaced the circles as elite ceremonial or administrative centers. The large center at Santa Cruz de Barcenas dates from this period. Ceramic types changed, and Huistla polychrome tripod molcajetes (as at Eztatlan) became popular. The reasons for this collapse are not clear, but they apparently reflect pan-Mesoamerican changes. Metallurgy started at this time in West Mexico, and the new trade and procurement patterns for this technology may have adversely affected the Teuchitlan tradition. It seems certain that outsiders were somehow involved in ending West Mexico's first experiment in civilization.

FURTHER READINGS

Bell, B. 1971. Archaeology of Nayarit, Jalisco, and Colima. In *Handbook of Middle American Indians,* vol. 11, part 2, pp. 694–753. Austin: University of Texas Press.

Corona Nuñez, J. 1955. *Tumba de El Arenal, Etzatlán, Jalisco.* Dirección de Monumentos Prehispánicos, 3. Mexico City: Instituto Nacional de Antropología e Historia.

Galvan V., J. 1991. *Las tumbas de tiro del Valle de Atemajac, Jalisco.* Colección Científica. Mexico City: Instituto Nacional de Antropología e Historia.

López Mestas Camberos, L., and Ramos de la Vega. 1998. Excavating the Tomb at Huitzilapa. In R. Townsend (ed.), *Ancient West Mexico.* Chicago: The Art Institute of Chicago, pp. 52–69.

Oliveros, A. 1989. Las tumbas mas antiguas de Michoacán. In *Historia General de Michoacán,* vol. 1, pp. 121–133. Morelia: Gobierno del Estado de Michoacán.

Weigand, P. C. 1974. The Ahualulco Site and the Shaft-Tomb Complex of the Etzatlán Area. In B. Bell (ed.),

The Archaeology of West Mexico, pp. 120–131. Ajijic: West Mexican Society for Advanced Study.

———. 1985. Evidence for Complex Societies during the Western Mesoamerican Classic period. In M. Foster and P. Weigand (eds.), *The Archaeology of West and Northwest Mesoamerica,* pp. 47–91. Boulder: Westview Press.

———. 1994. Large Scale Hydraulic Works in Prehispanic Western Mesoamerica. In V. Scarborough and B. Isaac, (eds.), *Research in Economic Anthropology,* suppl. 7, pp. 223–262. Greenwich, Conn.: JAI Press.

von Winning, H., and O. Hammer. 1972. *Anecdotal Sculpture of Ancient West Mexico.* Los Angeles: Ethnic Arts Council of Los Angeles.

Phil C. Weigand

SEE ALSO
West Mexico

Teúl, El (Zacatecas, Mexico)

This site lies atop an isolated hill adjacent to the modern village of Teúl de Gonzalez Ortega. The Cerro de Teúl rises 2,000 to 2,100 meters above sea level, or 250 meters above the floor of the Tlaltenango Valley, on the eastern flank of the southern Sierra Madre Occidental. Perennial springs and limited access make this site an advantageous and easily defended location in the semiarid landscape. El Teúl covers about 1 square kilometer of surface area and is known for its masonry architecture, including platforms, rectangular patios, and an I-shaped ball court, as well as numerous

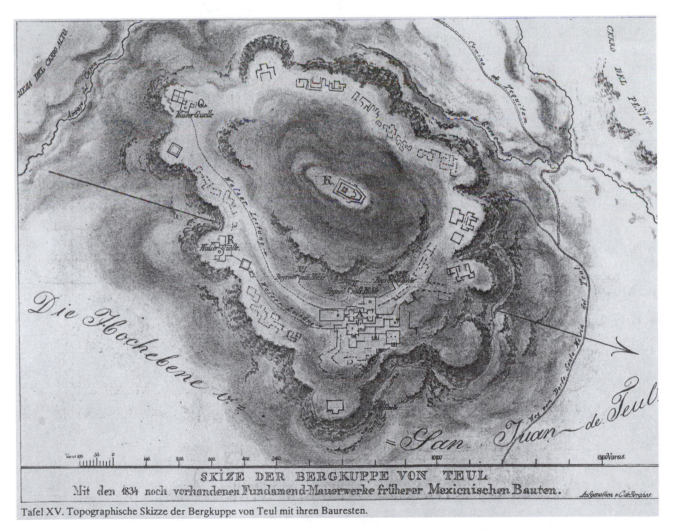

Tafel XV. Topographische Skizze der Bergkuppe von Teul mit ihren Bauresten.

Nineteenth-century topographic map of Teúl. Illustration from Berghes (1990), courtesy of the author.

T

shaft tombs. Although the site's role as a central place reaches back into prehistory, El Teúl is best known as a historic civic-ceremonial center for the Cazcan culture. In the absence of absolute dates, artifactual evidence suggests an occupation from c. A.D. 1 until Spanish contact in the sixteenth century, marked by early West Mexican influence and later occupation tied to Postclassic Mesoamerica. Artifacts of note include hollow figurines found in shaft tombs, abundant obsidian from local sources, imported obsidian blades from Jalisco, and copper or bronze artifacts. Brief explorations beginning in the nineteenth century were conducted by Carl de Berghes, who mapped the site, as well as by Guillemin Tarayre, Aleš Hrdlička, and Franz Boas. Recent work has included shaft tomb salvage excavation by José Corona Nuñez in the 1950s and by Darling and García in 1993, and limited surface reconnaissance by Darling (1991–1994), performed in connection with regional surveys in the Tlaltenango Valley.

FURTHER READINGS

Darling, J. A. 1993. Notes on Obsidian Sources of the Southern Sierra Madre Occidental. *Ancient Mesoamerica* 4:245–53.

Hrdlička, A. 1903. The Region of the Ancient "Chichimecs," with Notes on the Tepecanos and the ruin of La Quemada, Mexico. *American Anthropologist* 5:385–440.

Kelley, J. C. 1971. Archaeology of the Northern Frontier: Zacatecas and Durango. In G. F. Eckholm and I. Bernal (eds.), *Handbook of Middle American Indians,* vol. 11, *Archaeology of Northern Mesoamerica, Part Two,* pp. 768–801. Austin: University of Texas Press.

J. Andrew Darling

SEE ALSO
West Mexico

Texcoco (México, Mexico)

One of the principal cities of Late Postclassic Mexico, Texcoco was capital of the kingdom of Acolhuacan, and a partner with Tlacopan (Tacuba) and Tenochtitlan (Mexico City) in the Empire of the Triple Alliance, or Aztec Empire. After the Spanish conquest Texcoco was rebuilt on a grid plan, with the center of the modern city occupying the same ground as the center of the pre-Hispanic city.

Historical acounts indicate that the city of Texcoco (Nahuatl, Texcoco) was established by King Quinatzin (r. c. 1272–1330), and it served as the headquarters city for all succeeding kings of Acolhuacan. It was conquered by the Tepanec of Azcapotzalco around the beginning of the fifteenth century, but in 1428 the Tepanec were overthrown by Acolhua forces led by Prince Nezahualcoyotl, allied with King Itzcoatl of Tenochtitlan. Shortly thereafter, Nezahualcoyotl was installed as king of Texcoco, and he and Itzcoatl collaborated in planning and rebuilding their respective cities, which as a consequence shared many features.

Nezahualcoyotl ruled until 1472 and was succeeded by his son Nezahualpilli, who died in 1515. A dynastic struggle ensued which lasted until the Spanish conquest. When Cortés reached Central Mexico, he formed an alliance with one faction.

The center of Aztec Texcoco was formed by the palaces and associated structures built by kings Nezahualcoyotl and Nezahualpilli. Sixteenth-century sources describe Nezahualcoyotl's palace as occupying about 1 square kilometer, and that of Nezahualpilli as slightly smaller. Included as parts of these palaces were council chambers, armories, storehouses, guest accomodations, a ball court, and a market plaza—indeed, most of the civic center of the city. There was also a temple area, dominated by the twin temples of Huitzilopochtli and Tlaloc, set atop a single pyramidal platform. The older temple of Tezcatlipoca is said to have been even larger, but it was somewhat more distant from the palace. It was the custom for each new ruler in Aztec Mexico to build a new palace once he had attained sufficient military merit to legitimize such an undertaking; the palace of his predecessor was presumably left for that king's surviving wives and other kin and dependents.

Because the pre-Hispanic city is overlain by the modern city, there has been very limited archaeological excavation. Near the center are the ruins known as Los Melones, consisting of three conjoined mounds constructed of adobe brick and rock rubble, with façades of finished stone and stucco. Although never systematically excavated, the complex appears to include broad platforms on several levels, with rooms on the lower levels. Associated ceramics are Late Postclassic, and the site is presumed to have been part of the Aztec-period civic center, possibly the palace of Nezahualpilli.

There was a tightly nucleated zone around the royal palaces, but the city in the political sense extended well beyond that to include an area of just under 80 square kilometers, with more than 100,000 people, mostly in numerous small clusters of houses. Settlement pattern

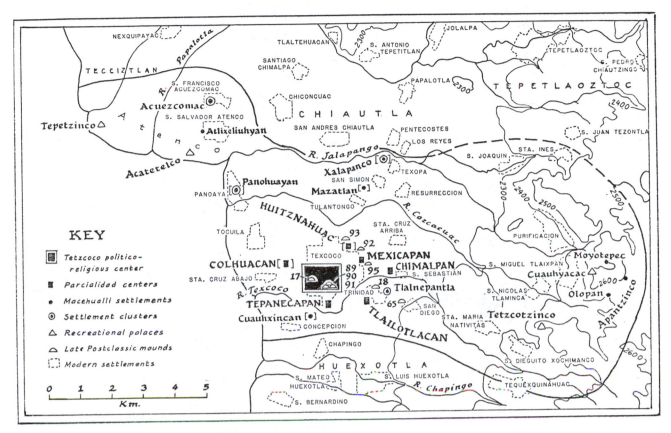

The city of Texcoco at the time of the Spanish conquest. Locations within brackets are approximate locations, probably correct within 2 km. From Hicks, Texcoco in the Early 16th Century. *American Ethnologist* (1982) 9(2): 232.

surveys have revealed many small settlements throughout this area, most of them in the piedmont zone east of the present city. Documentary sources have provided the names of about forty-five of these small villages, hamlets, or noble establishments; again, many of those that can be located are in the piedmont zone. The city center, in Aztec times as today, is on the plain, close to the former lakeshore. Documentary sources tell of a canal or waterway of some sort linking Nezahualpilli's palace with the lake.

The city was divided into six sections (generally called *parcialidades* in the Spanish sources), called Chimalpan, Tlailotlacan, Mexicapan, Colhuacan, Huitznahuac, and Tepanecapan. These names are based on dynastic or "ethnic" names that can be found throughout Central Mexico. Apparently each of these groups had its own nobility with its headquarters palaces in the city, and some of the small communities are known to have served the nobles of one or another of these six major sections. Archaeological surveys appear to confirm this, because six principal

ceremonial-civic clusters have been located within the general area of central Texcoco.

By the beginning of the sixteenth century, the kingdom of Acolhuacan was made up of fourteen subordinate kingdoms, as well as extensive outlying areas subject directly to Texcoco. Within this area, many lands and communities were assigned to support the royal palace or other institutions with agricultural produce and the labor of their people for certain portions of each year. In addition, Texcoco was a junior partner in the Aztec Empire, which by 1519 had come to dominate much of Central and Southern Mexico. Texcoco thus received tribute from various regions, such as Chalco and Cuernavaca, in addition to what it got from Acolhuacan. It was the wealth received from these regions, and the extensive bureaucracy and service personnel needed to administer them, that enabled Texcoco to become the second-largest city in Central Mexico, and possibly in all of Mesoamerica, by the time of the Spanish conquest.

T

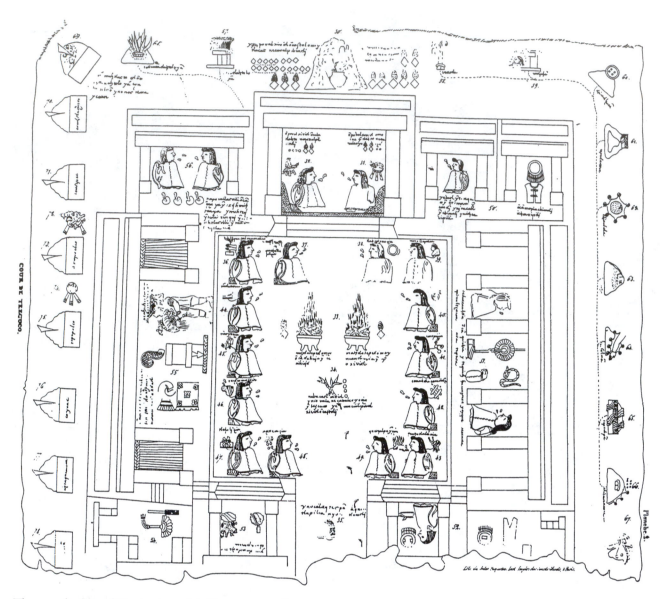

The central palace of Nezahualcoyotl, in Texcoco, according to a sixteenth-century manuscript (the Mapa Quinatzin). East is at the top. In the central room, Nezahualcoyotl and his successor Nezahualpilli sit facing each other. Other rooms around the courtyard represent the sites of other administrative functions. Seated in the courtyard are rulers of the fourteen Acolhua kingdoms subject to Texcoco, and around the periphery outside the palace are the glyphs representing the towns of Acolhuacan that had various obligations to the palace. Illustration from Robertson, *Mexican Manuscript Painting of the Early Colonial Period*. Norman: University of Oklahoma Press, 1994.

FURTHER READINGS

Hicks, F. 1982. Texcoco in the Early 16th Century: The State, the City, and the Calpolli. *American Ethnologist* 9:230–249.

———. 1984. Rotational Labor and Urban Development in Prehispanic Texcoco. In H. R. Harvey and Hanns J. Prem (eds.), *Explorations in Ethnohistory*. Albuquerque: University of New Mexico Press.

Offner, J. A. 1983. *Law and Politics in Aztec Texcoco*. Cambridge: Cambridge University Press.

Parsons, J. R. 1971. *Prehistoric Settlement Patterns in the Texcoco Region, Mexico*. Memoirs of the Museum of Anthropology, University of Michigan, 3, Ann Arbor.

Frederic Hicks

SEE ALSO

Basin of Mexico; Postclassic Period

Texcotzingo (México, Mexico)

A hill near San Nicolás Tlaminca, 6 kilometers east of Texcoco, was made into a recreational garden and retreat by King Nezahualcoyotl of Texcoco (r. 1431–1472). Encircling the hill is a walkway, sometimes built up and sometimes cut into the hill, about 55 meters from the summit. The walkway leads past four baths or shallow basins that are carved from the bedrock and supplied with water through an aqueduct from a reservoir on an adjacent hill. There are lookout points, the remains of relief and freestanding sculptures, and traces of a possible temple on the summit. A series of steps cut into the bedrock lead past one of the baths down to a series of chambers, which may be the remains of the villa and gardens of Nezahualcoyotl. Historical accounts indicate that a pictorial history of Nezahualcoyotl's achievements had been carved on the mountain, but it was destroyed in early Colonial times. The site commands an excellent view over the eastern Valley of Mexico. Archaeological reconnaissance indicates no significant permanent settle-ment and confirms historical accounts that the site was strictly recreational.

FURTHER READINGS

Nuttall, Z. 1923. The Gardens of Ancient Mexico. In *Annual Report of the Board of Regents of the Smithsonian Institution, 1923,* pp. 453–464. Washington, D.C.

Parsons, J. R. 1971. *Prehistoric Settlement Patterns in the Texcoco Region, Mexico.* Memoirs of the Museum of Anthropology, University of Michigan, 3. Ann Arbor.

Townsend, R. F. 1982. Pyramid and Sacred Mountain. In A. F. Aveni and G. Urton (eds.), *Ethnoastronomy and Archaeoastronomy in the American Tropics,* pp. 37–62. Annals of the New York Academy of Sciences, 385. New York.

Frederic Hicks

SEE ALSO

Aztec Culture and History; Basin of Mexico; Gardens

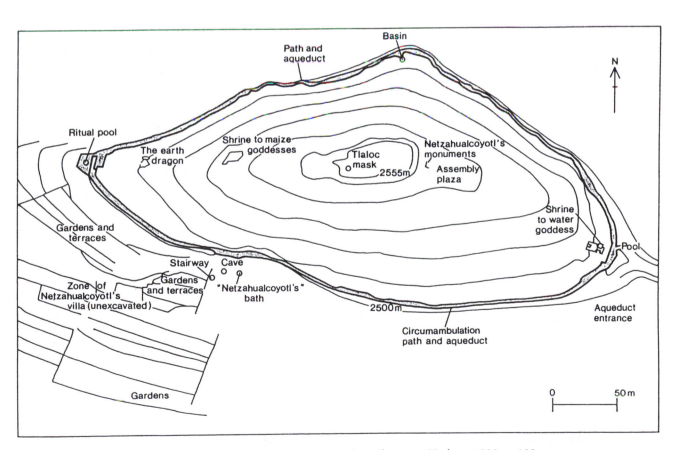

The hill of Texcotzingo. From Richard F. Townsend, *The Aztecs.* London: Thames & Hudson, 1992, p. 139.

T

Thin Orange Ware

Thin Orange is a widely distributed ceramic ware of Classic period Mesoamerica. It was an extraordinary achievement for the ancient potters: its appearance and finish are close to perfect; at the same time, it is strong, durable, and lightweight, qualities that contributed to its becoming one of Mesoamerica's most important trade wares. It is closely identified with the large urban center of Teotihuacán from about A.D. 300 to 650.

Contributing to its popularity was the distinctive style that encompassed both domestic and ceremonial types. Bright orange annular-based bowls that were used in households and sometimes burials make up the bulk of the shapes; tripod cylindrical vases and human and animal effigies were inextricably linked with burial and religious customs. The utilitarian amphoras *(cántaros)*, excellent carrying and storage vessels (perhaps for *pulque*, the fermented *maguey* beverage), made up a good proportion of the Thin Orange trade carried to Teotihuacán in the Classic period.

During systematic surface surveys in the Tepexi de Rodriquez (Puebla) region, about 300 kilometers southeast of Teotihuacán, archaeologists found sites littered with potsherds indicative of ceramic workshops. Exploratory excavations confirmed that they were the ancient pottery-making centers for Thin Orange ware. By A.D. 300 the potters were producing for an export market, with Teotihuacán as the major consumer and distributor.

Among the most notable finds of Thin Orange ware are those from the burials at Monte Albán (Oaxaca), Kaminaljuyú (Guatemala) Copán (Honduras), and sites in West Mexico (in the states of Colima and Michoacán). Besides serving as a "time marker," Thin Orange has great potential as an aid to reconstructing Teotihuacán's contacts throughout Mesoamerica.

FURTHER READINGS

Kolb, C. C. 1986. Commercial Aspects of Classic Teotihuacán Period "Thin Orange" Wares. *Research in Economic Anthropology,* Supplement 2, pp. 155–205. Greenwich, Conn.: JAI Press.

Lackey, L. M. 1986. "Thick" Thin Orange Amphorae: Problems of Provenience and Usage. Research in Economic Anthropology, Supplement 2, pp. 207–219. Greenwich, Conn.: JAI Press.

Rattray, E. C. 1990. New Findings on the Origins of Thin Orange Ceramics. *Ancient Mesoamerica* 1:181–195.

Rattray, E. C., and G. Harbottle. 1992. Neutron Activation Analysis and Numerical Taxonomy of Thin Orange Ceramics from the Manufacturing Sites of Rio Carnero, Puebla, Mexico. In *Chemical Characterization of Ceramic Pastes in Archaeology.* Monographs in World Archaeology, 7. Prehistory Press.

Evelyn Rattray

SEE ALSO
Ceramics; Teotihuacán

Thompson, J. Eric S. (1898–1975)

Sir John Eric Sidney Thompson was an archaeologist, ethnologist, and epigrapher active from 1926 to 1975. He was the author of five important books and numerous professional articles and reports for the Carnegie Institution, from a 1927 essay on the correlation of Maya and Christian calendars to his 1972 study, *The Dresden Codex. Maya Archaeologist* (1963) is his autobiography. The most influential student of Maya hieroglyphic writing of the mid-twentieth century, he disagreed with theories of its phonetic basis and historical content proposed by Yuri Knorosov and Tatiana Proskouriakoff, although he accepted the latter's version after 1960. After field work in British Honduras (now Belize) at Lubaantun and Pusilha (1927), Cayo District (1928–1929), and San José (1930–1936), he dedicated himself to decipherment of the noncalendric Maya hieroglyphs, using a wide range of ethnohistoric and ethnographic reference.

FURTHER READINGS

Obituary: Sir J. Eric S. Thompson. 1977. *American Antiquity* 42:180–190.

Thompson, J. E. S. 1950. *Maya Hieroglyphic Writing.* Carnegie Institution of Washington, Publication 589. Washington, D.C.

———. 1963. *Maya Archaeologist.* Norman: University of Oklahoma Press.

———. 1966. *The Rise and Fall of Maya Civilization.* Norman: University of Oklahoma Press.

———. 1970. *Maya History and Religion.* Norman: University of Oklahoma Press.

Norman Hammond

SEE ALSO
Maya Lowlands: North; Maya Lowlands: South

Thrones and Benches

Thrones and benches are common interior architectural features of rooms in Mesoamerican residential, civic, and religious structures. Ancient Mesoamericans did not use furniture in the conventional Western sense. Instead, room interiors were furnished with various kinds of hangings, mats, cushions, and low stools, and sometimes low, movable beds. Benches, along with built-in niches or shelves, are among the few permanent features commonly found inside rooms. Benches are raised platforms that take up much of the interior space, typically along the rear and side walls. How benches were constructed depended on the function and quality of the room. In small, commoner residential structures, such as at Maya Cerén (El Salvador) and Aztec Cihuatecpan, the benches are typically low platforms of adobe or uncut stone only a few centimeters high. In elite residences, the benches are often almost a meter high, built of fine masonry and expertly plastered and painted. In either case, their presence defines domiciles in the strict sense—household spaces for sitting, socializing, and sleeping.

Large interior benches are also found in rooms in structures that had more general civic or religious functions, such as men's houses, council houses, and temples. Benchlike features associated with Maya summit temple rooms were probably used as altars. Major civic ceremonial halls at such Mesoamerican centers as Tula and Tenochtitlan had carved and painted benchlike features in their principal rooms.

Particular kinds of seats were powerfully symbolic of leadership in Mesoamerica. In many cultures, woven reed mats symbolized political authority, and the word for "mat" occurred in some political titles, as in *ah pop* ("he of the mat") of the Postclassic Maya. Thrones were more elaborate seats of power. Thrones are essentially grandiose benches or seats built in rooms of particular political or religious importance. They are sometimes found associated with obvious elite residences, and they often display elaborate carving, painting, and inscribed glyphs. Such thrones were not restricted to Mesoamerican kings but were used by some lesser elites as well. Some of the best evidence for how thrones were used comes from highly representational scenes painted on Maya ceramic vessels. Scenes of palace interiors show kings, lords, and gods sitting on elaborately carved and painted thrones that are often covered with fine fabrics, mats, cushions, and skins.

Although thrones are usually interior features, some large carved monuments were set up in plazas or other outdoor places as more public seats for powerful individuals, beginning as early as 1200 B.C. Many of the "altars" found in the royal centers of the Olmec, Maya, and later Mesoamerican cultures were apparently used as thrones.

FURTHER READINGS

Kerr, J. 1989–94. *The Maya Vase Books.* 4 vols. New York: Kerr Associates.

Pollock, H. E. D. 1965. Architecture of the Maya Lowlands. In G. R. Willey (ed.), *Handbook of Middle American Indians,* vol. 2, pp. 378–440. Austin: University of Texas Press.

Proskouriakoff, T. 1978. *An Album of Maya Architecture.* Norman: University of Oklahoma Press.

David L. Webster

SEE ALSO

Architecture: Civic-Ceremonial

Tibas, Talamanca de (San José, Costa Rica)

Found near the bank of a small creek during housing construction, this site yielded a disturbed artifact assemblage consisting of numerous fragments of carved stone *metates,* as well as greenstone beads, pendants, and mace heads that were looted before the National Museum of Costa Rica was notified. Scientific excavations by that institution recovered a tomb whose central feature was an individual eighteen to twenty-five years of age who had been interred in an extended position over the surfaces of three "metate" ceremonial stools. The most spectacular artifact accompanying the interment was a carved jade pendant in the form of a clamshell, 22 cm long, which according to Snarskis was produced during Middle to Late Formative times in southern Mesoamerica; stylistically, it represents a transition from Olmec to Izapa style, with a combination of human, feline, and insect symbolism. The interment was accompanied by additional greenstone pendants and beads, and ceramic offerings dated from 200 B.C. to A.D. 400 that were brought from both the Atlantic and Pacific watersheds of Costa Rica. The combination of dated objects and styles suggests that the carved clamshell arrived in Costa Rica as an heirloom item.

FURTHER READINGS

Snarskis, M. J. 1979. El jade de Talamanca de Tibas. *Vínculos* 5:89–107.

———. 1992. Wealth and Hierarchy in the Archaeology of Eastern and Central Costa Rica. In F. W. Lange

T

(ed.), *Wealth and Hierarchy in the Intermediate Area*, pp. 141–164. Washington, D.C.: Dumbarton Oaks.

Frederick W. Lange

SEE ALSO
Intermediate Area: Overview

Ticoman (D.F., Mexico)

This village site of moderate extent (c. 20 hectares) lies at the southern base of the Guadalupe Hills, on the northwestern edge of Mexico City; it was occupied c. 500–50 B.C. It is on a promontory jutting out into the former lake, 0.5 kilometer southeast of El Arbolillo. It was noted by Franz Boas in 1911 and partially excavated in 1929–1930 by George C. Vaillant, who distinguished three successive phases, today referred to as Ticoman or Cuicuilco 1, 2, and 3. Some authors believe a Cuicuilco 4 phase is merged here with 3 but represented by unmixed deposits elsewhere (e.g., at Atlamica). Vaillant exposed retaining walls of habitation terraces similar to those at Zacatenco. The fifty-eight burials are relatively poor, but rank inequalities seem more pronounced than at El Arbolillo. Figurines are still abundant, but a stone figure is thought to represent the Old Fire God, Huehueteotl, of later mythology.

FURTHER READINGS

McBride, H. W. 1974. *Formative Ceramics and Prehistoric Settlement Patterns in the Cuauhtitlán Region, Mexico.* Ph.D. dissertation, University of California, Los Angeles.

Tolstoy, P. 1978. Western Mesoamerica before A.D. 900. In R. E. Taylor and C. W. Meighan (eds.), *Chronologies in New World Archaeology*, pp. 241–284. New York: Academic Press.

Vaillant, G. C. 1931. *Excavations at Ticoman.* Anthropological Papers of the American Museum of Natural History, 32, part 2.

Paul Tolstoy

SEE ALSO
Basin of Mexico

Tikal (Petén, Guatemala)

The ancient Maya site of Tikal is in the central Petén region of Guatemala. The large areal extent of the site, its architectural style, and cultural history within the Maya Lowlands earn it the classification of regional capital, one of several such capitals in the Lowlands.

Tikal was first occupied during the Middle Formative ceramic phase, around 800 B.C., and continued until around A.D. 900. The peak of site development in terms of both architectural achievement and political power occurred between A.D. 682 and 800, coinciding with the rule of three dynastic kings. The physical setting on the crown of a drainage divide probably accounts for its choice for settlement. With water routes nearby that connected to the Usumacinta in the west and the Río Hondo and Caribbean Sea in the east, the location was ideal for trade control. Locally, the site comprises a series of hills and ridges flanked to the east and west by poorly drained wetlands.

There is visual evidence, as yet unexplored, that these wetlands were exploited agriculturally by the Maya of Tikal. Although agriculturally based, the large population was supported by a variety of food sources. In addition to basic *milpa* food production and the intensive exploitation of the adjacent swamps, other suggested food sources include root crops, ramón nuts, wild game, salt fish fillets (obtained by trade); the people also grew numerous useful wild plants in kitchen gardens. The average annual rainfall in this part of the Petén is 1,762 mm, which falls in the usual rain forest cycles of dry and wet seasons. The well-drained uplands at Tikal are fertile and suitable for *milpa* agriculture. The impermeable clays of the adjacent wetlands also support crops even without manipulation of the water supply. Severe variation in rainfall can cause drought, a major hazard if it should continue for more than one wet season, and a factor that has been postulated as one probable cause of the Maya Collapse. The mapped core of the ceremonial center measures 16 square kilometers, while the extent of known settlement covers an area of 265 square kilometers. The boundaries of settlement have an irregular shape, terminating on the east and west at the high-water borders of the wetlands. The northern boundary appears to be marked by a defensive wall-and-ditch combination, extending from swamp to swamp and separating Tikal from the settlement zone of its nearest neighbor, Uaxactun to the north. An unoccupied no-man's-zone lies immediately north of this defense before the outlying southern occupation of Uaxactun is encountered. This defense was constructed during the Early Classic period at Tikal; another defensive wall lies to the south, but little is known about either its extent or date.

As seen today, the site is focused on the Great Plaza, surrounded by major architectural features: the North

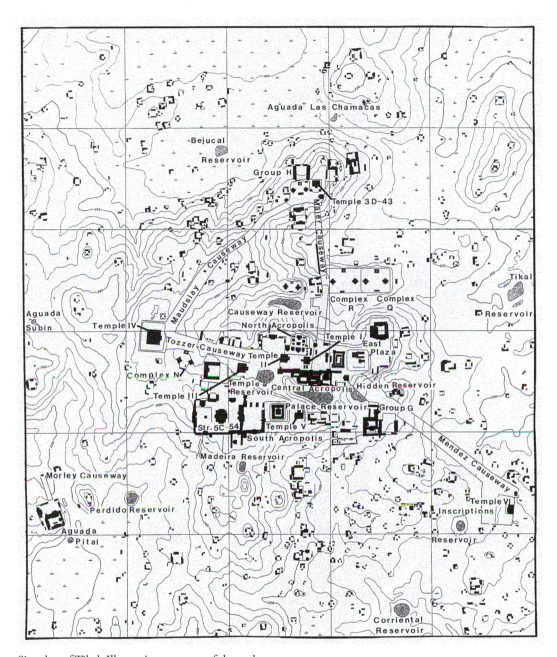

Site plan of Tikal. Illustration courtesy of the author.

Acropolis, Temple I, Temple II, and the Central Acropolis. Other major features that delineate the core are the North Group, Temple IV to the west, and Temple VI to the south and east of the Great Plaza. These features are connected by a series of ancient causeways, known as *sacbes*. Additional outstanding architectural features that define the site are Temple III, the South Acropolis, Temple V, the East Plaza and a monumental feature known as the "Lost World Pyramid" (Structure 5C-54).

As new information was gained, researchers over the years have estimated Tikal's population at levels from 10,000 to 100,000 and higher. Always rising, such estimates are based on increasing understanding of the site—its numbers of structures, and its potential for economic

Temple I at Tikal. Photograph courtesy of the author.

To the west lie Temple III and Temple IV, the tallest of the great temples at over 70 meters in height. To the north is the H Group, including a significant temple, Structure 3C-43, and Complex P, one of several twin-pyramid groups. The Great Plaza, Temple IV, and the H Group are connected by three causeways that form a rough right triangle; these are named the Tozzer, Maudslay, and Maler causeways. A fourth, the Mendez Causeway, connects the East Plaza to Temple VI, also known as the Temple of the Inscriptions, southeast of the Great Plaza. This causeway passes by two palace groups: Group G on the south side, probably raised as a royal residence during the Late Classic, and Group F, due north of Group G, another residential palace group.

On the south side of the Great Plaza and the Tozzer Causeway are Temple V, the South Acropolis, the Plaza of the Seven Temples, and the Lost World Pyramid group with 5C-54, the pyramid itself. Twin-pyramid complexes are a feature of Tikal architecture, very rarely found elsewhere. This complex consists of identical four-staired, flat-topped pyramids on the east and west sides of a defined plaza. On the north is an enclosure with a pair of monuments, stela and altar. On the south is a small seven-doored "palace." Five such groups prominently survive: Complex P, already mentioned, is part of Group H in the north; Complex O is immediately west of the Maler Causeway; complexes R and Q are along the east side of the same causeway and adjacent to each other; finally, Complex N lies near the foot of Temple IV on the immediate south side of the Tozzer Causeway. These are the major architectural components of the site are open to visitors.

Art and Texts

Apart from portable objects retrieved from burials and refuse dumps, the major sources of art at Tikal are the carved monuments and lintels. Monuments include stelae and altars, which are often paired to commemorate either important time period endings or dedication of a major structure. When preserved, the accompanying hieroglyphic texts have been a source for the identification of rulers, their achievements, and their dynastic relationships. Carved wooden lintels have survived in part from Temples I, II, III, and IV, and from a palace structure (5D-52, or the Five-Storied Palace) in the Central Acropolis. A very long inscription is partially preserved on the back of the roof comb of Temple VI, also known as the Temple of the Inscriptions. This extraordinary text covers a timespan from 1139 B.C. until A.D. 766, speculated to be the period from initial occupation of the site until the

bases. Excavation was accomplished by two major field projects: the University of Pennsylvania from 1955 to 1969, and a Guatemala government project, Proyecto Nacional Tikal, from 1979 to 1989. Further investigation has been conducted by numerous epigraphers, who have made great strides in revealing the history of the site. All three sources are drawn on for the following discussion.

Architectural Features and Groups

The Great Plaza is the focal point of the site and is surrounded by the North Acropolis, Temples I and II to the east and west sides of the Plaza , and the Central Acropolis on the south. The last complex of palaces evolved from the Late Formative through the Late Classic periods. The East Plaza contains a configuration of structures interpreted as a marketplace and a ball court, as well as a number of other palace structures. South of Temple II is Structure 5D-73, a pyramid without surmounting temple that covered Burial 196, an important royal tomb.

The clan house of the Jaguar Claw clan, built around A.D. 350. Photograph courtesy of the author.

time of the ruler who placed the inscription on Temple VI. Inscriptions from Tikal, as well as from other sites, aid in reconstruction of its dynastic history. The earliest contemporary inscription is from Stela 29 at A.D. 292, while the last occurs on Stela 11 at A.D. 869, a span of 577 years. During this span there is a 125-year hiatus of inscriptions between the Early and Late Classic periods, now interpreted to mean that during this period Tikal fell under the domination of another city, possibly Caracol in Belize.

In terms of art and architecture, the city of Tikal was a major center of innovation, establishing styles and practices that were both its own and imitated elsewhere. Because of the monumentality of the site, it is often thought of as the capital of the Maya world; however, text translations indicate that, while central, Tikal was but one of the cities that played a principal role in the history of the Maya Lowlands.

Development and History

Occupation and construction activity in the North Acropolis span nearly the entire occupation of Tikal from 800 B.C. until A.D. 700. Use of the North Acropolis certainly continued until the cultural collapse of the site. The Acropolis was used as a place of royal burial almost throughout its history, and the central north–south axis held special sanctity in the cosmic formation of the Great Plaza. The place of royal burial once shifted briefly to the area around the Lost World Pyramid, probably in response to a temporary shift in location of the royal clan house.

Pure deposits of ceramics are used as indicators of settlement patterns of growth within the city, especially for the early stages. These deposits show settlement during the Middle Formative (800–250 B.C.) in four locations: two on the edge of the eastern wetland (Bajo Santa Fé), one on the hilltop that was to become the North Acropolis, and one adjacent the Lost World Pyramid.

During the Late Formative period (250 B.C.–250 A.D.) there was both continuity and spread of occupation, documented in sixteen unmixed ceramic deposits. The continuity included increased use of the area of the North Acropolis, the area of the Lost World Pyramid—including the pyramid itself—and two loci adjacent to the

Tikal (Petén, Guatemala) 751

T wetland borders. New settlement locations included a zone southwest of the G Group palace complex, and adjacent Temple VI.

By the end of the Formative an architectural style had been achieved, as well as ceremonialism and burial patterns. It is extremely difficult to make realistic population estimates for any period prior to the Late Classic, when adequate data are available as a basis for such an estimate. By the end of the Formative there were two main centers of ceremonial growth, around the Great Plaza and in the Lost World group.

The Early Classic period at Tikal (A.D. 250–550) saw great growth and expansion of the site, evident in the monumental architecture as well as in residential refuse dumps in outlying parts of the greater site. This was a period of major development in the North Acropolis and Central Acropolis. All of the present structures on the North Acropolis and most of the temples fronting the North Terrace were built during this period, serving as tombs for the kings of Tikal as well as functioning temples. Briefly, the burial function shifted to the area of the Lost World group during the Early Classic, but it returned to the North Acropolis before the period ended.

Apart from the North Acropolis and the Lost World Pyramid, most of the rest of Tikal as we know it was constructed during the Late Classic period (A.D. 550–850). Developments for the Classic period as a whole are best presented in the form of the known king list, together with their associated achievements, where known. Because of the sheer size of the city and the length of its development, excavation and epigraphic studies have revealed only a fraction of the city's history. Many data have been lost through intentional destruction, a major feature of the site, whether through internal ritual renewal or by external hostile attack; Tikal was subjected to both forms of destruction, with concomitant loss of texts as well as archaeological data.

Dynastic Progressions

Translation of the Maya texts is a study both in progress and in flux at this time. In many cases the Maya name for a ruler is known, but the English translation is uncertain. In other cases, the glyph is known but neither the Maya nor English orthography is. In such cases, an English descriptive phrase is used. One feature of Tikal's dynastic name sequence is the reuse of names through time, possibly in admiration or recognition of the great deeds of an ancestor. Since the Maya of Tikal did not distinguish in any way the ordinal sequence of such reused names, it is necessary for us to impose such designation for the sake of clarity.

The founder of the Tikal dynasty is referred to frequently with reference to the number of succession for many of the subsequent rulers. His name in Maya was Yax-Moch-Xoc. Jones has argued that Burial 125 in the North Acropolis was his spartan burial, devoid of grave goods. He was ruling around A.D. 270. The ceramics of this period already show an influence from Teotihuacán in the Mexican highlands. There are known to have been thirty-one successors after Yax-Moch-Xoc, before the collapse, but they are not all identified.

Scroll Jaguar (Foliated Jaguar). This ruler's name has no Maya translation as yet; he is associated with Stela 29 at A.D. 292. His number of succession is not known, but he was probably third or fourth.

Chak-To-Ich'ak. This name had recurring use throughout Tikal's history. The name glyph is associated with a jaguar paw with extended claws, and the English translation has been variously "Jaguar Paw" and "Jaguar Claw." Stela 31, from a later date, records part of the story of Jaguar Claw I. He was in power by A.D. 317, and several references to this name over the next fifty-eight years do not make clear whether one or two different rulers of the name existed. During this period, Structure 5D-46 in the Central Acropolis was constructed as the clan house of Jaguar Claw the Great, who lists himself as the ninth ruler in succession. This apparently sacred building persisted unmolested until the collapse of the site.

Zero Moon Bird. This personage held a position of some importance in Tikal during the same period as Chac-To-Ich'ak. He is recorded as seated as king in A.D. 320, and the meaning of this overlap is not resolved. He may have been a regent for the young Chac-To-Ich'ak or a collateral ruler of different title.

Nu Yax-Ain. This ruler's name has been published as "Curl Nose" and "Curl Snout." The glyphic image actually represents the American crocodile, whose presence was not recognized in Central America until recent years. He was the tenth ruler in succession from the founder, successor to Great Jaguar Claw (I or II). A skeleton of a crocodile was included in Yax-Ain's tomb (Burial 10) under the temple Structure 5D-34 on the North Terrace of the Great Plaza. His accession to power is recorded on Stela 31 in A.D. 379. An ambiguous, possibly collateral ruler known as Smoking Frog died in A.D. 402, at which time Yax-Ain succeeded to the title of *chacte,* or supreme ruler of Tikal. According to an inscription at the site of El Zapote, Yax-Ain died in A.D. 420. His successor (Stormy Sky) had acceded to the title of *ahaw* of Tikal in A.D. 411 (or possibly 416), some years prior to Yax-Ain's death. The contents of Burial 10 show that influence from Teotihuacán reached a peak at Tikal during Yax-Ain's reign of forty-one years.

Stormy Sky (Sian Kan K'awil). Stormy Sky was the eleventh successor and a son of Yax-Ain. It is this ruler's portrait that appears on the very important Stela 31; the text is the longest genealogical record found at Tikal. Stormy Sky came to power in either A.D. 411 or 416, according to different texts, as *ahaw* of Tikal, and as *chacte* (supreme ruler) in 426. Burial 48 in the North Acropolis is believed to be his tomb, dated at A.D. 456 by an inscription painted on its walls. His rule lasted at least thirty years. The main figure of the tomb lacks both head and hands, suggesting defeat in battle and a ransomed body buried devoutly by his family.

K'an Boar (K'an Ak). This ruler is mentioned on both Stelae 9 and 13 and is thought to be the son of Stormy Sky, probably the twelfth ruler of Tikal. He is known to have been ruling at A.D. 475, but no other dates are secure. He may be the individual in Burial 160 from the far southeast region of the site. He is associated with a woman known as "Woman of Tikal," or Ix Cuchil, who appears on Stelae 23 and 25 near the tomb.

Mah K'ina Bird Skull. This individual is little known. He is suggested to have been a younger brother of K'an Boar and possibly the missing thirteenth ruler. Mention comes from a text on a looted, unprovenienced vessel.

Chac-To-Ich'ak (III). Once called "Jaguar Paw Skull I," this ruler is known to be the son of K'an Boar and the fourteenth ruler in the succession. His record appears on Stelae 3, 7, 15, and 27 and his period of rule extended from A.D. 488 until 495. He is now known as Great Jaguar Claw III. A series of unnamed rulers follows him, possibly all his brothers. The "Stela 8 Ruler" was in power in A.D. 497, and the "Stela 6 Ruler" in 514. One ruler, at least, is missing from this sequence.

Curl Head. Known from Stela 10 and 12, his only known date is his accession in A.D. 527.

Chac-To-Ich'ak (IV). Clearly a popular name, Great Jaguar Claw appears once again on Stelae 26 and 17 (also published as Jaguar Paw Skull II). He is firmly established as the twentieth successor; his death occurred in A.D. 537.

Double Bird. This person is reported on Stela 17 as the twenty-first ruler of Tikal, with an accession date of A.D. 537, following the demise of Jaguar Claw IV, who is recorded as his father. No translation yet exists, but he may be identical with Yax K'uk Mo', the founder of the Copán dynasty, an alliance city of Tikal; the glyph for both is a double bird.

Lord Animal Head. The twenty-second ruler has been identified from Burial 195 under Temple 5D-32 on the North Terrace of the Great Plaza. He succeeded sometime after Double Bird's death (A.D. 567). His death date is suggested to be A.D. 593, close to the formal end of the Early Classic period.

Tentative identifications for Rulers 23 and 24 have been made from looted vessels. This is a murky time in Tikal history because there are no inscriptions at the site. The first name is Black Jaguar, and the second is Bird Head. We know nothing about these individuals other than their names and an association with this time period.

Shield Skull (Nu-U-Bak). Knowledge of this ruler, the twenty-fifth, derives from texts made by his son, Hasaw Kan K'awil. His rule fell within the "hiatus," but he was important as the father of that great ruler. In A.D. 672, this man waged successful war against Dos Pilas. His death is presumed to have occurred in 682, just prior to the accession of his son. His interment under Temple 5D-33-1st, in Burial 23, was conducted with great ceremony and reverence, including the ritual redeposition of Stela 31. His conquest of Dos Pilas was part of an ongoing feud between Tikal and the great capital city of Calakmul to the north, which had become the target of a number of its nearest neighbors in a long-term war reflected by the 125-year hiatus.

Hasaw Kan K'awil (Ruler A; Ah Cacao; Hasaw Chan K'awil). This personage stands out as the "great man" of Tikal, in terms of effecting the greatest achievements in the history of its fluctuating fortunes. His accession as the twenty-sixth ruler took place in A.D. 682. His first act was construction of Structure 5D-33-1st, in which he created a new style of architecture that came to epitomize the city: tall, vertical in proportion, with a single-doored temple at the summit. Other contributions to the architecture of Tikal include Temple I, where his tomb, Burial 116, is located and carved Lintels 2 and 3 give details of his conquests; Temple II, dedicated to the memory of his deceased wife, Lady Twelve Macaw; the twin-pyramid Group N (Stela 16 and Altar 5); and Complex O, another

T

twin-pyramid group. In A.D. 695 he defeated the king of Calakmul, whose name was Chac-To-Ich'ak like those of many kings of Tikal. This defeat ended a major campaign being waged against Tikal. Hasaw Kan K'awil restored glory to the city after 125 years of darkness. He is assumed to have died in A.D. 734, with elaborate burial under Temple I.

Yik'in Kan K'awil (Ruler B; Yaxkin Kan Chac; Yik'in Chan K'awil). Yik'in acceded as *chacte* of Tikal, the twenty-sixth ruler, in A.D. 734, presumably on the death of his father, Hasaw Kan K'awil. Temple IV, the tallest of the city, and Structure 5D-52 (Central Acropolis) were both constructed in 743; both have carved lintels. Lintels in Temple IV tell of his conquest of the cities of El Peru, west of Tikal, and Naranjo to the east, thus reestablishing Tikal as a dominant regional force. Temple VI, which has a lengthy inscription dealing with the life of Yik'in, was probably built by him. Complex P, a twin-pyramid group, was built in 751 adjacent to Group H, the North Group. Stela 20 and Altar 8 there mark the beginning of the sixteenth *katun*. His death date is understood to be 766, but his burial place is unresolved.

Twenty-Eighth Ruler. Very little is known about this ruler. He may have been Yik'in's younger brother and may be the personage in Burial 196 under Structure 5D-73. Some argue that this burial is that of Yik'in himself, but its identity remains unresolved.

Yax-Ain (Ruler C; Chitam; Ak). Known to be the son of Yik'in, Yax-Ain II has been referred to by many names. The glyph, originally thought to be a peccary, is in fact a crocodile and repeats the name of his distant ancestor in Burial 10. He was the twenty-ninth ruler, acceding in A.D. 768. His major known constructions are two twin-pyramid groups built twenty years apart. Complex Q, built in 771, lies due east of his grandfather's Complex O. Twenty years later (790), Complex R was built immediately adjacent the earlier twin-pyramid and hard against the Maler Causeway. Speculation based on stratigraphy in the Central Acropolis and on construction style suggests that Yax-Ain was also responsible for Temple V and Structure 5D-65 (Maler's Palace), a major construction in the Central Acropolis. Similar speculations attribute the palace Group F to Yax-Ain, and the palace Group G to his father, Yik'in. The death date of Yax-Ain is not known but is estimated at around 800. His burial place is not known.

Last Rulers. Only two texts aid in the identification of the last rulers of Tikal. These are on Stela 24 and its accompanying Altar 7, which stand before Temple 3. Lintel 2 in the great temple shows a portly ruler whose name has been read as Nu-Bak-Chak, which would make him Shield Skull II. The date on the stela is A.D. 810, suggesting that this must be the thirtieth ruler in succession.

Finally, Stela 11 (with Altar 11) is dated at A.D. 869, about fifty-nine years after the date on Stela 24. The ruler is identified as Hasaw Kan K'awil, who should be the thirty-first and last known ruler of Tikal, bearing the same name as Tikal's "great man," who had died 135 years earlier.

Summary

Art in the form of portable objects, recovered largely from tombs around the Great Plaza and the environs of the Lost World pyramid, represents many of the finest works created by the ancient Maya in the Lowlands. That Tikal was a prominent center of trade is obvious, and perhaps the reason for this great city's being the target of so much neighborly hostility. The peak of the city's glory and political power occurred during the reign of three patrilineal rulers—Hasaw Kan K'awil I, Yik'in Kan K'awil, and Yax-Ain II—over a mere 118 years. Archaeological evidence shows that Tikal's collapse was a slow process, lasting between fifty and a hundred years; this means that the approximate length of Tikal's existence was 1,700 years, from which its people left some of the finest remains of the Maya culture.

FURTHER READINGS

Carr, R. F., and J. E. Hazard. 1961. *Map of the Ruins of Tikal, El Petén, Guatemala.* University Museum, University of Pennsylvania, Tikal Reports, 11. Philadelphia.

Coe, W. R. 1990. *Excavations in the Great Plaza, North Terrace, and North Acropolis of Tikal.* 5 vols. University Museum, University of Pennsylvania, Tikal Reports, 14. Philadelphia.

Coe, W. R., and W. A. Haviland. 1982. *Introduction to the Archaeology of Tikal, Guatemala.* University Museum, University of Pennsylvania, Tikal Reports, 12. Philadelphia.

Coe, W. R., E. M. Shook and L. Satterthwaite. 1961. The Carved Wooden Lintels of Tikal. University Museum, University of Pennsylvania, Tikal Reports, 6, pp. 115–112. Philadelphia.

Haviland, W. A. 1967. Stature at Tikal, Guatemala: Implications for Ancient Maya Demography and Social Organization. *American Antiquity* 32:316–325.

———. 1970. Tikal, Guatemala, and Mesoamerican Urbanism. *World Archaeology* 2:186–198.

———. 1974. Occupational Specialization at Tikal, Guatemala: Stoneworking–Monument Carving. *American Antiquity* 39:494–496.

———. 1977. Dynastic Genealogies from Tikal, Guatemala: Implications for Descent and Political Organization. *American Antiquity* 42:61–67.

———. 1985. *Excavations in Small Residential Groups of Tikal: Groups 4F1 and 4F2.* University Museum, University of Pennsylvania, Tikal Reports, 19. Philadelphia.

Jones, C., and L. Satterthwaite. 1982. *The Monuments and Inscriptions of Tikal: The Carved Monuments.* University Museum, University of Pennsylvania, Tikal Reports, 33. Philadelphia.

Maudslay, A. P. 1883. Explorations in Guatemala and Examination of the Newly Discovered Ruins of Quirigua, Tikal, and the Usumacinta. *Proceedings of the Royal Geographical Society* 5:185–204.

Puleston, D. E. 1983. *The Settlement Survey of Tikal.* University Museum, University of Pennsylvania, Tikal Reports, 13. Philadelphia.

Puleston, D. E., and D. W. Callender. 1967. Defensive Earthworks at Tikal. *Expedition* 9(3):40–48.

Peter D. Harrison

SEE ALSO

Maya Lowlands: South

Tilantongo (Oaxaca, Mexico)

Tilantongo lies adjacent to the southern end of the Nochixtlán Valley in the heart of the Mixteca Alta. The region was first dominated by a single large ceremonial center at Monte Negro throughout much of the Formative period Ramos phase. During the Classic, or Las Flores, period, a new focus of elite power emerged with citadels like Yucu Yoco, Huachino, and Mogote del Cacique situated on Tilantongo's eastern perimeter. Around A.D. 1000, political centralization finally shifted to the location of the present-day community center of Tilantongo itself; this continued to dominate throughout the Postclassic, or the Natividad phase.

At the time of the Spanish conquest, Tilantongo was reputed to have been the residence of the highest-ranked Mixtec royal line. The origins of these claims are documented in surviving pre-Columbian-style pictographic books, the Mixtec codices. A full-coverage survey of the Tilantongo Valley was made by Byland and Pohl in 1985. Using the codices as maps, supplemented by a rich tradition of local oral history and legends, their team was able to correlate the Terminal Classic abandonment of the

mountaintop citadels with a legendary factional struggle called the "War of Heaven." The subsequent establishment of Tilantongo's Postclassic paramountcy is recorded in the epic saga of a twelfth-century warlord known as Lord 8 Deer, from whom nearly twenty generations of Tilantongo's nobility claimed descent.

FURTHER READINGS

Byland, B. E., and J. M. D. Pohl. 1994. *In the Realm of 8 Deer: The Archaeology of the Mixtec Codices.* Norman: University of Oklahoma Press.

Caso, A. 1949. El Mapa de Teozacoalco. *Cuadernos Americanos* 8(5):145–181.

Pohl, J. M. D. 1994. *The Politics of Symbolism in the Mixtec Codices.* Vanderbilt University Publications in Anthropology, 46. Nashville, Tenn.

John M. D. Pohl

SEE ALSO

Coixtlahuaca; Mixtec History, Culture, and Religion; Yanhuitlán

Tingambato (Michoacán, Mexico)

The site of Tinganio, in the municipality of Tingambato, Michoacán, had two periods of occupation: A.D. 400–600, and A.D. 600–900. In the latter period, an architectural style was introduced that has been interpreted as Teotihuacán-derived. The site's geographical location was chosen not only because of its ample vegetation and water, but also because it is a strategic point between the Lowlands and highlands of Michoacán; the town served as a link between the peoples of these areas, just as it did during Colonial times. Among the items that were traded are conch shells and other types of marine shells from the Pacific Ocean, turquoise, pyrites, jade, and other raw materials.

The site has a religious area with courtyards, pyramids, temples, and a ball court, the last including a circular stone marker that is unique in West Mexico. There is a civil area with residential structures and a tomb, where the remains of more than thirty-two individuals were found during excavation, together with many offerings: ceramic vessels, braziers, anthropomorphic figurines, zoomorphic musical instruments (whistles), conch-shell trumpets, other marine shells, and small stone sculptures.

FURTHER READINGS

Piña Chan, R., and K. Oi. 1982. Exploraciones arqueológicas en Tingambato, Michoacán. Mexico City: Instituto Nacional de Antropología e Historia.

Eduardo Williams

T

SEE ALSO
Michoacán Region

Tizatlán (Tlaxcala, Mexico)

This Postclassic settlement in the center of the present-day state of Tlaxcala formed, together with Tepeticpan, Ocotelulco, and Quiahuiztlán, the four-part Tlaxcaltecan capital (the "Cuatro Señorios") of a confederation of about twenty city-states (señorios) at the time of the arrival of the Spaniards. When Hernán Cortés arrived in Tlaxcala in 1519, the Tizatlán ruler, Xicotencatl, received him in his palace. At that time Tizatlán had a population of about five thousand. It is situated on the lower slopes of a hill, on the the Zahuapan River. Its economy was based on agriculture and tribute. Houses were built on artificial terraces and platforms, and temples were constructed of *tepetate,* stone, adobe, and fired brick. Fired brick was relatively rare in pre-Columbian Mesoamerican architecture but was much used in Tlaxcala.

Two altars were found (1.9 and 1.8 meters long; 1.12 and 0.37 meters high), covered with a thick layer of stucco and decorated with polychrome paintings on three sides. The north sides feature semicircular columns. On the south sides are represented animals and deities in the style of the Codex Borgia: a jaguar, an eagle, and the deities Tezcatlipoca, Xolotl, and Mayahuel, among others. To the sides are hieroglyphs of scorpions, skulls, shields, hands, hearts, stylized *maguey* spines, and other elements. Because of their proportions and decoration, it is thought that the altars were for human sacrifice. Other finds included ceramic figures with handles on the back, molded and polychromed, representing people and deities.

FURTHER READINGS

Caso, A. 1927. *Las Ruinas de Tizatlán.* Revista Mexicana de Estudios Históricos, 4. Mexico City.

García Cook, A., and B. L. Merino Carrión. 1996. *Antología de Tizatlán.* Mexico City: Instituto Nacional de Antropología e Historia.

Angel García Cook

SEE ALSO
Postclassic Period; Puebla-Tlaxcala Region

Tlacozotitlán (Guerrero, Mexico)

As part of the Teopantecuanitlán-Lomeríos Zone, Tlacozotitlán was the name first given to the major Formative period archaeological site of Teopantecuanitlán located at the confluence of the Amacuzac and Balsas rivers in northeastern Guerrero. Currently, Tlacozotitán is a label commonly applied to a specific residential quarter (Site 5/6 of the Lomeríos zone) of that site. Christine Niederberger conducted excavations in 1984, revealing that by Teopantecuanitlán Phase II (1000–800 B.C.) domestic units in the Lomeríos Zone consisted of several rectangular houses grouped around a courtyard. These houses were built on stone foundations but constructed of perishable materials. Niederberger's excavations uncovered traces of subsistence activities, fragments of figurines incised with Olmec-style motifs, and evidence of specialized craft production involving the working of imported materials such as obsidian and shell. The Lomeríos Zone excavations further demonstrate that Teopantecuanitlán was linked to the rest of Formative period Mesoamerica through an extensive exchange network and that the complexity of this site may have had a great deal to do with its access to and working of highly prized Pacific Coast shell.

FURTHER READINGS

Niederberger, C. 1986. Excavación de un área de habitación doméstica en la capital "olmeca" de Tlacozotitlán. In *Arqueología y ethnohistoria del Estado de Guerrero,* pp. 83–103, Mexico City.

———. 1996. Olmec Horizon Guerrero. In *Olmec Art of Ancient Mexico,* pp. 95–105. Washington, D.C.: National Gallery of Art.

Paradis, L. I. 1995. Archaeology, History and Ethnography: The Precolumbian History of the Mezcala Region. In *The Amate Tradition: Innovation and Dissent in Mexican Art,* pp. 113–128. Chicago and Mexico City: Mexican Fine Arts Center Museum.

F. Kent Reilly III

SEE ALSO
Guerrero Region; Olmec-Guerrero Style; Teopantecuanitlán

Tlalancaleca (Puebla, Mexico)

This Formative period city in the central highlands controlled a large part of the Puebla-Tlaxcala Valley during the Middle and Late Formative. It was occupied from the Early Formative until the Protoclassic, reaching its apogee

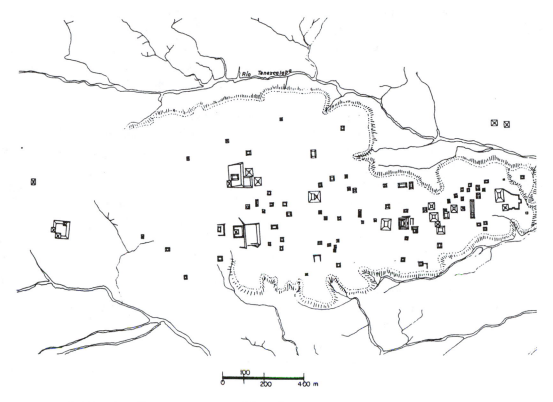

Site map of Tlalancalea. Illustration courtesy of the author.

between 600 and 300 B.C. (chronology based on radiocarbon dates), with a population of about ten thousand. It was contemporaneous with Cuicuilco and Tlapacoya in the Basin of Mexico, and with Coapa, Amozoc, Amalucan, and Formative Cholula in the Puebla-Tlaxcala Valley. It is situated on a lava flow, an elongated slope 3,000 meters long to 650 meters wide, bounded by two *barrancas* and elevated on three sides over the surrounding plain.

Architecture included ceremonial platforms, pyramids of two or three levels, wide balustrades on the staircases, and *talud-tablero* style construction. Stucco was used abundantly. Networks of walls were built of adobe and filled with stones and earth, compacted for the construction of platforms and pyramids. There were sculptures, "sarcophagi" of stone, and "calendric" elements. Two stelae were found, one smooth and the other carved with a representation of Xolotl or Tlahuizcalpantecuhtli. These stelae, the ceremonial plazas, the pyramids, and representations of deities such as Tlaloc, Huehueteotl, and Xolotl all indicate the conduct of rituals in the city.

The city interacted with and contributed cultural elements to adjacent regions such as the Basin of Mexico and the Puebla Valley, as well as having contacts with the more distant valleys of Tehuacán and Oaxaca, and the Chiapas region. The site plan is based on an aerial photograph and on twenty-two test trenches. There have been no major investigations.

FURTHER READINGS

García Cook, A. 1973. Algunos descubrimientos en Tlalancaleca, Estado de Puebla. *Comunicaciones* 9. F. A. I. C., Mexico City.

———. 1981. The Historical Importance of Tlaxcala in the Cultural Development of the Central Highlands. In J. A. Sabloff (ed.), *Supplement to the Handbook of Middle American Indians,* vol. 1, pp. 244–276. Austin: University of Texas Press.

Angel García Cook

SEE ALSO
Puebla-Tlaxcala Region

Tlapacoya (México, Mexico)

This area of archaeological remains at the base (2240 meters elevation) of the cone of Tlapacoya volcano, an island in pre-Columbian Lake Chalco in the southern

Basin of Mexico, contains extensive Formative materials, along with an earlier preceramic occupation (referred to as Zohapilco) and an isolated Late Aztec residence. The modern town of Tlapacoya extends over the northern edge of the Formative site; looting and earth-moving have disturbed the southern part of the area.

Stratified deposits contain architectural remains, features, and artifacts from nearly the entire Formative period, beginning at 1500 B.C., and possibly as early as 1700–1500 B.C. (Initial Ceramic period). Radiocarbon dates ranging from 1675 ± 140 B.C. to 830 ± 100 B.C. support the ceramic cross-dating of the Early Formative deposits. The Ayotla phase occupation, dating from the Early (1500–1050 B.C.) and Middle Formative (1050–650 B.C.), is one of the earliest examples of a sedentary agricultural settlement in the basin; the Tlapacoya phase occupation covers the Late (650–300 B.C.) and Terminal (300 B.C.–A.D. 100) Formative site.

Ayotla is situated on the southwestern edge of Tlapacoya Island; its northern extension overlaps the later Tlapacoya site. During the Early and Middle Formative phases the occupation consisted of a village with an estimated population of 90 to 225 persons, maize agriculturalists who intensively exploited lacustrine resources (e.g., waterfowl and turtle) and hunted deer and rabbit. Pottery and figurine styles are similar to those found at other early Formative sites in the central highlands (e.g., Tlatilco and Chacaltzingo) and thus suggest that Ayotla was part of an early regional culture that included Morelos and the Basin of Mexico. Hereditary ranking may have begun to develop, and the presence of Olmec-like motifs on some pottery suggests that Ayotla participated in interregional exchange systems of prestige items; Ayotla is strategically situated for the movement of goods to and from the Basin of Mexico, Puebla, and Morelos.

The focus of settlement on the island shifted slightly north in the Late and Terminal Formative phases, to Tlapacoya, which developed into a tightly nucleated regional center covering 37 hectares, with an estimated population of 925 to 1,850 persons. Political and economic stratification are evidenced by a large (4 meters high by 24 by 26 meters) platform mound, constructed in three stages and containing three high-status tombs with elaborate grave goods in the fill of the platform. A residential zone contains terraces and mounds, a second large platform mound (2 meters high by 25 by 35 meters), and non-tomb burials with few grave goods. Agricultural terracing probably was expanded in the early Terminal Formative phase to accommodate an increase in population on the lakeshore opposite Tlapacoya; the nucleation was most likely for defensive reasons. Tlapacoya was abandoned by the start of the late Terminal Formative (Tzacualli phase, 100 B.C.–A.D. 100) as part of the aggregation of population at Teotihuacan.

FURTHER READINGS

Barba de Pina Chan, B. 1956. Tlapacoya: Un Sitio Preclassico de Transicion. *Acta Antropológica*, ser. 2, 1(1): 1–205.

Niederberger, C. 1979. Early Sedentary Economy in the Basin of Mexico. *Science* 203:131–142.

Tolstoy, P., S. K. Fish, M. W. Boksenbaum, K. B. Vaughn, and C. E. Smith. 1977. Early Sedentary Communities in the Basin of Mexico. *Journal of Field Archaeology* 4:91–106.

Tolstoy, P., and L. I. Paradis. 1971. Early and Middle Preclassic Culture in the Basin of Mexico. *Science* 167: 344–351.

Deborah L. Nichols

SEE ALSO

Ayotla-Zohapilco; Basin of Mexico

Tlatilco (México, Mexico)

This village site of moderate extent (c. 20 hectares) is situated on a small alluvial plain west of modern Mexico City. Discovered in 1936 by brick-diggers, it was brought to public attention by the Mexican artist Miguel Covarrubias. Excavations by Mexico's Instituto Nacional de Antropología e Historia (1942, 1947–1951, 1955, 1962–1969) brought to light hundreds of burials dating from c. 1200–950 B.C. These contained pottery, figurines, seals, masks, tools of stone and bone, musical instruments, and personal ornaments. They suggest a ranked society, perhaps divided into two moieties. Four periods are recognizable; the earliest is contemporaneous with Coapexco, and the latest with Manantial of Tlapacoya. Later domestic refuse (800–500 B.C.) also occurs. Olmec (San Lorenzo complex) attributes are evident in the earliest graves, but these are outnumbered and eventually replaced by the "Tlatilco style," with links to the West Coast and, through it, perhaps with South America.

FURTHER READINGS

García Moll, R., D. Juárez C., C. Pijoan A., M. E. Salas C., and M. Salas C. 1991. San Luís Tlatilco, México, Catálogo de entierros, Temporada IV.

Piña Chan, R. 1958. *Tlatilco I.* Instituto Nacional de Antropología e Historia, Investigaciones, 1. Mexico City.

Porter, M. N. 1953. *Tlatilco and the Pre-Classic Cultures of the New World.* Viking Fund Publications in Anthropology, 19. New York.

Tolstoy, P. 1989. Coapexco and Tlatilco: Sites with Olmec Materials in the Basin of Mexico. In R. J. Sharer and D. C. Grove (eds.), *Regional Perspectives on the Olmec,* pp. 85–121. Cambridge: Cambridge University Press.

Paul Tolstoy

SEE ALSO

Basin of Mexico

Tollan

Tollan (Nahuatl, "place of reeds") was the legendary capital of the Toltecs ("people of Tollan"), who preceded the Aztecs in Central Mexico. Tollan was supposedly founded around A.D. 900 by nomadic Chichimecs from northwestern Mexico and by the Nonoalca, a Gulf Coast people reputed to be skilled artisans. Its rulers are said to have included the legendary god-king Quetzalcoatl. Tollan was supposedly destroyed around A.D. 1200 by other Chichimec tribes, who may have been related to the Aztecs. Hyperbolic Aztec accounts of Tollan's grandeur led some scholars to doubt that the city actually existed, and the Aztec habit of referring to any large city as "Tollan" created additional confusion surrounding its true identity. Recent ethnohistorical and archaeological research has provided cogent evidence that the site of Tula, Hidalgo, constitutes the ruins of ancient Tollan.

FURTHER READINGS

Davies, N. 1977. *The Toltecs until the Fall of Tula.* Norman: University of Oklahoma Press.

Jiménez-Moreno, W. 1941. Tula y los Toltecas según las fuentes históricas. *Revista Mexicana de Estudios Antropológicas* 5:79–83.

Kirchhoff, P. (ed.). *Historia Tolteca Chichimeca.* Mexico City: Instituto Nacional de Antropología e Historia.

Dan M. Healan

SEE ALSO

Teotihuacán; Toltec Culture; Tula de Hidalgo; Tula Region

Toltec Culture

In the indigenous Mesoamerican chronicles and codices that survived the sixteenth century Spanish conquest or were written shortly after it, the Nahuatl word "Toltec" has so many distinct meanings and is used in such varied cultural, ethnic, and geographic contexts that superficially it would seem to be almost meaningless. The uses of "Toltec" in these texts, however, when they are analyzed in specific narrative contexts—as Jiminez Moreno (1941), Nicholson (1957), Carmack (1968), and others have done—generally fall into groups of related meanings which appear to have cultural and historical significance. Among other meanings, "Toltec" is used to refer to skilled artists and learned, highly civilized persons; persons who lived in cities (urban people); sometimes, specifically the people who lived in the legendary Central Mexican city of Tollan or Tula during the ninth through twelfth centuries A.D.; the ancestors of the people of Tula, who came originally from the northern Mesoamerican periphery ("Tolteca-Chichimeca"); and descendants of the people of Tula, especially later Mesoamerican royal dynasties whose kings claimed to have Toltec blood. During the past 150 years, historians, archaeologists, and art historians have also used the term "Toltec" to describe or classify specific archaeological sites, ancient monumental buildings, and pre-Hispanic art styles. The academic literature interpreting Toltec culture is vast: key studies include Jimenez Moreno (1941), Acosta (1956–1957), Kirchhoff (1976), Nicholson (1957), Davies (1977), Diehl (1983), and Healan (1989).

Here we will limit the discussion of "Toltec culture" to peoples and cultural processes that formed part of the Early Postclassic state (A.D. 900–1200) centered on the ancient city of Tula, Hidalgo, which most scholars consider to be identical with Tollan, the Toltec capital mentioned in indigenous Central Mexican chronicles.

During the Early Postclassic, Tula's cultural influence extended over an area that was considerably larger than its empire. After the fall of Teotihuacan in the seventh or eighth century A.D., Tula was the first state to integrate large areas of Mexico and Central America into a new cultural system. Many aspects of Nahua civilization, which would reach its apogee in the Aztec Empire, began nearly five centuries earlier with the Toltecs. The transformation of key aspects of Mesoamerica by the Toltecs involved at least four interrelated processes: (1) the expansion of Toltec populations speaking Nahuatl (and sometimes Otomí) into religions outside Central Mexico; (2) the founding in different areas of Mexico and Central America of royal dynasties that claimed Toltec origins; (3) the consolidation of a great system of trade networks (partially centered on Tula) that extended from Costa Rica to the present states of New Mexico and Arizona; and (4) important changes in the religion and ideology of many Mesoamerican peoples, including the introduction of some Nahua gods among non-Nahua groups and the incorporation of the epic cycle concerning the man-god Quetzalcoatl into the mythology of key peoples in Central Mexico, Yucatán, highland Guatemala, and some other areas.

During Tula's apogee between the tenth and twelfth centuries A.D., it was one of the largest cities in Mesoamerica, and its cultural and economic influence extended for hundreds of kilometers. The political and ethnic structure of the Toltec Empire was probably the direct antecedent for Aztec imperial institutions, but it is unlikely that the Toltecs conquered as many provinces as did the Mexica, even though evidence exists that the Toltecs dominated some regions that Tenochtitlan never managed to subjugate. On the basis of archaeological research and indigenous chronicles, it appears that Tula controlled much of Central Mexico, along with some important zones in the Bajío, the Gulf Coast, Yucatán, and possibly the Soconusco on the Pacific coast of Chiapas and Guatemala (Mastache and Cobean 1985). It is possible that the Toltecs conquered some areas of the Huasteca and Michoacán that the Aztecs never subjugated, and the extraordinary Toltec presence at Chichén Itzá has no Mexica analog in Yucatán.

Coincident with Tula's conquests of different provinces, there apparently were important movements of Nahua-speaking populations that may have been directed by the Toltec state. In areas of the Huasteca that probably were dominated by Tollan, the names of many key centers are Nahuatl. Various scholars have proposed that the Pipiles, Nahua groups who occupied extensive areas on the Pacific coasts of Chiapas and Central America during the sixteenth century A.D., were descendants of the Toltecs. Some Early Postclassic Pipil sites in El Salvador have so many similarities with Tula in terms of architecture, sculpture, ceramics, figurines, and other elements that they may well have been Toltec colonies (Fowler 1989). The Soconusco was probably the most important Pipil province of the Toltec state. Centuries later, the Aztecs also conquered the Soconusco, which possesses the best land for cacao cultivation in Mesoamerica. Cacao probably functioned as money and as a high-status drink among the Toltecs, as it

did during the Late Postclassic. Potters in the Early Postclassic Soconusco also produced the fine trade ceramics Plumbate ware, which were imported in great quantities by Tula.

There were various types of Toltec penetration and influence on the Gulf Coast. In the south, Maya groups like the Chontal or Putún of Tabasco and Campeche maintained strong trading and cultural relations with Central Mexican Nahua groups and probably helped the Toltecs invade Yucatán (Thompson 1970). Cultures of Early Postclassic north central Veracruz possessed strong Toltec influences in architecture and ceramics, and some key centers—such as Castillo de Teayo and Xiutetelco (on the Veracruz-Puebla border)—may have been founded by Toltecs.

In the Bajío and the northern Mesoamerican periphery there is a series of sites located on key trade routes—for example, Carabino, Guanajuato, and Villa de Reyes, San Luis Potosí—that possess most of the diagnostic Tollan phase pottery types found at Tula, along with Toltec-style architecture. The people of these sites probably participated in trade networks that extended northward beyond Mesoamerica and supplied the Toltec state with turquoise and other luxury products. In the southern Bajío, the important obsidian mines at Ucareo, Michoacán, may have been exploited by the Toltec state. During the first stages of urban expansion at Tula (ninth–tenth centuries A.D.), Ucareo was the major source for the city's obsidian tools (Healan 1989). During the early sixteenth century A.D., the Ucareo region formed part of the Tarascan Empire, but its population was ethnic Otomí. These Otomís may have been Toltec descendants, because it is probable that Otomís and Nahuas were the two major population groups at Tula and many other Toltec centers in highland Mexico (Mastache and Cobean 1985).

Tula and Chichén Itzá

Archaeologists and historians have studied the relationship between Tula and Chichén Itzá for more than a century. The similarity between the art and architecture of these two centers was first identified in Charnay (1885). Most investigators who have analyzed the Toltec presence in Yucatán propose that Chichén Itzá probably was conquered by Toltecs under a Quetzalcoatl-like leader, Kukulcan, as some sixteenth-century Maya chronicles state. These chronicles, however, are quite ambiguous, and the chronologies of both cities (especially Chichén Itzá) are too inexact to prove directly the specific events described in the indigenous histories. Kubler (1961) published a famous essay contending that Chichén Itzá (and not Tula) was the center where Toltec culture originated; his proposals have been variously criticized and supported by scholars, and recently his interpretation of a Toltec Chichén Itzá has received backing from several Mayanists.

Obviously the relations between Mayas and Toltecs at Chichén Itzá were very complex, involving strong mutual influences and cultural transformations: Mayas transformed by Toltecs, and Toltecs by Mayas. Recent analyses of elite personages represented in the sculptures and murals of Chichén Itzá propose that its ruling class consisted of a cosmopolitan group (Kristan-Graham 1989) of nobles from several peoples: Yucatec Mayas, Toltecs and Itzás (probably Chontal Mayas). Studies of the glyphs associated with elite figures depicted on the architectural columns at Chichén Itzá and Tula suggest that some of the same noble lineages or dynasties were present at both centers.

In our opinion, the majority of the so-called Toltec elements in the art of Chichén Itzá, such as *chac mools,* atlanteans, feathered serpents, skull racks (*tzompantli*), and "Toltec warriors" on columns and murals, probably had their origins in the Tula region. Recent investigations by Mexico's Instituto Nacional de Antropología e Historia (INAH) in the Tula area have found clear antecedents for major types of Toltec architecture and sculpture in centers of the Coyotlatelco culture dating around A.D. 700, which is nearly two centuries before the first Toltec elements appear at Chichén Itzá.

Toltec Dynasties

The kings of Tula probably strengthened their political influence in regions beyond the frontiers of their empire through formal political alliances that often were based on marriages between Toltec nobles and members of the royal families of other states. These royal marriages seem to have been a key cultural tradition; five centuries after Tula's apogee, the royal dynasties of many Mesoamerican peoples, including the Aztec emperors, claimed to be direct descendants of Tula's kings and expressed great pride in their Toltec ancestry. Tula's kings apparently functioned as arbiters of political power and prestige among Mesoamerican peoples, somewhat as France's Louis XIV did in seventeenth- and early eighteenth-century Europe. The Mixtec codices of the dynasty of Tilantongo, which narrate the life of the eleventh-century A.D. military hero and king 8 Deer, recount that he had the honor of traveling to Tula, where he took part in a ceremony probably organized as a Toltec recognition of his status as supreme leader of the Mixtecs.

Sixteenth-century chronicles of the Quiché Mayas of highland Guatemala state that their kings were descendants of the Toltecs, who arrived in their land centuries before under the leadership of King Gucumatz ("Plumed Serpent," or Quetzalcoatl). Carmack (1968) analyzed the Quiché Maya descriptions of these "Toltecs," especially in terms of mentioned place names, plants, and languages, and concluded that these invaders came from somewhere in the southern Gulf Coast of Mexico or the Maya Lowlands. It is probable that royal dynasties founded by Toltecs from Tula in some regions of Mesoamerica subsequently founded new "Toltec dynasties" in other areas.

Many of the late Postclassic royal dynasties in Central Mexico cities probably possessed direct kinship ties with Tula's kings. Acamapichtli, the first king of Tenochtitlan, was chosen by the Aztecs specifically because he had Toltec blood from the royal dynasty of Culhuacan, one of the principal cities founded by the Toltecs in the Basin of Mexico.

Toltec Trade

The scope of Tula's economic interaction with peoples from within and beyond Mesoamerica can be crudely measured by considering the great variety of foreign goods used by the city's inahbitants. In the excavations of three nonelite residential groups in the northeastern sector of Tula, the University of Missouri project (Healan 1989) recovered complete vessels of Nicoya Polychrome from Costa Rica or Nicaragua, several wholes Plumbate vases from the Soconusco along with several hundred fragments of this ware, and small quantities of pottery from the Huasteca, central Veracruz (probably) Campeche, and the northern Mesoamerican periphery (probably Zacatecas and Jalisco). Also found were fragments of serpentine and jade (probably from Guerrero and Guatemala), onyx (perhaps from Puebla), a few tiny plaques of turquoise from New Mexico or Arizona, marine shells from both the Pacific and Gulf coasts, and thousands of flakes and tools made from obsidian. Chemical analyses indicated that almost 90 percent of the obsidian came from the Sierra de Pachuca quarries, 70 kilometers east of Tula, but there was also obsidian from Michoacan, the Huasteca, Puebla, and the Basin of Mexico. The fact that nonelite "common people" in Tula possessed exotic goods from so many regions suggests that the Toltec state's trade and tribute systems had great geographic extension and considerable institutional complexity.

T

Excavations by Jorge Acosta and others in Tula's main plaza recovered luxury products from many different areas: ceramics from Central Veracruz, the Huasteca and probably Guatemala; carved jades from Oaxaca and some Maya areas; and damaged offerings of wood covered by turquoise mosaics. A recent INAH project excavated two offerings in the Palacio Quemado which contained a mosaic disk composed of more than two thousand turquoise fragments and an elaborate ceremonial breast-plate made of more than 1,200 carved *Spondylus* shell plaques. The turquoise mosaic disk has four serpents as its main iconographic theme and is very similar to a turquoise disk found in the Temple of the Warriors at Chichén Itzá. Acosta also identified luxury goods represented in Tula's sculptures, especially quetzal feathers from Guatemala and gold jewelry from West Mexico or Central America. Toltec elites probably consumed perishable imported commodities such as cotton clothing from lowland areas, cacao from the Gulf Coast and the Soconusco, and skins of tropical jungle animals.

Tula surely received some foreign products as tribute from its provinces, but many goods from distant zones probably were obtained by professional merchants who may have been the prototype for the Aztec *pochteca*. Images of the *pochteca* god Yiacatecuhtli have been identified on Tula's Early Postclassic sculptures. Several archaeological projects have found evidence for Toltec merchant colonies in areas as distant as central El Salvador and Chihuahua. Tools made from Sierra de Pachuca green obsidian probably constituted an important export of Tula's merchants to other regions. During the tenth and eleventh centuries A.D., Pachuca green obsidian tools were used at a number of Maya centers and other regions in Central America, where local people probably traded with the Toltecs.

The Toltec Ideological Heritage

On the basis of archaeological investigations and interpretations of indigenous chronicles, it appears that the expansion of Toltec culture in the ninth through eleventh centuries produced important changes in the ideology and religion of many Mesoamerican peoples. The Toltecs introduced some Nahua gods among Maya groups and other Central American peoples: the most important of these was Quetzalcoatl, but during the Early Postclassic, Toltec-style images of Xipe Totec, Mictlantecuhtli (the god of death), and other Mexican gods also appeared in southern Mesoamerica. In the north, the gods and rites at Toltec Tula probably provided the direct antecedents of

Aztec religion. Tezcatlipoca, the god who supposedly defeated Quetzalcoatl at Tula, was the prototype for Huitzilopochtli, the paramount Aztec deity.

Quetzalcoatl and Tezcatlipoca symbolized the cultural transformation of many Mesoamerican peoples who were inspired by the Toltecs. The eventual predominance of Tezcatlipoca's followers at Tula and in the Toltec Empire increased the emphasis on human sacrifice and warfare among many Mesoamerican peoples who had contacts with the Toltecs, but the heritage of Quetzalcoatl in some ways surpassed the influence of the Tezcatlipoca war sacrifice cults. The epic cycle of Topiltzin Quetzalcoatl, and of his variants such as Kukulkan and Gucumatz among Maya groups, became one of the central legends of Mesoamerican civilizations. Centuries after the Toltec era, the ancient Mexicans were still waiting for Quetzalcoatl's return when the Spanish conquest destroyed their world.

FURTHER READINGS

Acosta, J. R. 1956–1957. Interpretación de algunos datos obtenidos en Tula relativos a la epoca tolteca. *Revista Mexicana de Estudios Antropológicos* 14:75–110.

Carmack, R. M. 1968. Toltec Influence on the Postclassic Culture History of Highland Guatemala. In *Tulane University Middle American Research Institute, Publication 26*, pp. 49–92.

Charnay, D. 1885. *Les anciennes villes du Nouveau Monde.* Paris.

Davies, N. 1977. *The Toltecs until the Fall of Tula.* Norman: University of Oklahoma Press.

Diehl, R. A. 1983. *Tula, the Toltec Capital of Ancient Mexico.* New York: Thames and Hudson.

Fowler, W. R. 1989. *The Cultural Evolution of Ancient Nahua Civilizations: The Pipil-Nicarao of Central America.* Norman: University of Oklahoma Press.

Healan, D. M. (ed.). 1989. *Tula of the Toltecs: Excavations and Survey.* Iowa City: University of Iowa Press.

Jimenez Moreno, W. 1941. Tula y los Toltecas según las fuentes históricas. *Revista Mexicana de Estudios Antropológicos* 5:79–83.

Kirchhoff, P. (ed.). 1976. *Historia Tolteca Chichimeca.* Mexico City: Instituto Nacional de Antropología e Historia.

Kristan-Graham, C. 1989. *Art, Rulership and the Mesoamerican Body Politic at Tula and Chichén Itzá.* Ph.D. dissertation, University of California at Los Angeles.

Kubler, G. 1961. Chichén-Itzá Tula. *Estudios e Cultura Maya* 1:47–80.

Mastache, A. G., and R. H. Cobean. 1985. "Tula." In J. Mojarás-Ruiz et al. (eds.), *Mesoamerica Centro de México* pp. 273–307. Mexico City: Instituto Nacional de Antropología e Historia.

Nicholson, H. B. 1957. *Topiltzin Quetzalcoatl of Tollan: A Problem in Mesoamerican Ethnohistory.* Ph.D. dissertation, Harvard University.

Thompson, J. E. S. 1970. *Maya History and Religion.* Norman: University of Oklahoma Press.

Alba Guadalupe Mastache Flores and Robert H. Cobean

SEE ALSO

Chichén Itzá; Tollan; Tula de Hidalgo; Tula Region

Toluca Region

The Valley of Toluca has three basic landforms: first, an alluvial plain and residual lacustrine deposits, in the zone between 2,580 and 2,700 meters elevation; second, surrounding the alluvial plain, a zone with a series of low hills with moderate slopes, between 2,600 and 2,700 meters elevation; and third, a mountainous zone higher than 2,750 meters, with abrupt slopes and deep *barrancas*. The valley was strongly shaped by vulcanism, but lacustrine sedimentation and alluvial deposits were also important elements in its formation.

The highest valley in Mexico, the Valley of Toluca has a colder and less varied climate than other regions. There are two basic climatic zones: the alluvial plain is a sub-humid temperate zone with c.1,000 mm of rain each year, primarily falling in summer (Köppen classification C (w2)(w)); and the mountains have a subhumid semi-cold climate with rain in summer (Köppen classification C(E)(w2)(w)).

The region has three marshes—Cienega de Chignahuapan, Chimapiapan, and Chiconahuapan—and a stretch of the Lerma River, which originates in Almoloya del Río on the southeast side of the valley. The marshes are fed by the abundant waters of many large springs along the western foot of the Cruces and Ajusco ranges and by several rivers descending from the surrounding mountains. Major springs exist on the eastern margin of the valley, with some in the western and central portions and still others in the high mountains.

Cultural Development

So far, there is no direct archaeological evidence for human presence in the region before the Early Formative, although there are fossil remains of extinct big game ani-mals from the Pleistocene. Mammoth remains have been found at the former Hacienda of San Mateo Atenco, at San Miguel Yustepec, and San Miguel Almoloyan, but none were associated with evidence of human activities.

The oldest archaeological evidence of human settlement in the valley dates to the Early Formative. By probably 1500 B.C., a few small settlements were located along the Lerma River and some of its affluents. The ceramic style closely resembles some of the materials of the Ayotla phase of the neighboring Basin of Mexico, implying that these early colonizers of the Valley of Toluca probably came from that area. From the Formative period until the Spanish conquest, these two regions maintained a very close cultural, social, and political relationship. The subsistence of the early inhabitants was based on incipient agriculture, though complemented to a substantial degree by gathering, fishing, and hunting of natural biotic resources, especially in the lacustrine environment.

Around 1200 B.C., so-called Olmec-style ceramics appeared in the valley. These were identified at a very small number of habitational sites, located on hilltops or slopes above 2650 meters elevation in broken topography, in an area that is neither appropriate for agriculture nor near the rich lacustrine environment. Most of the sites of this time period are limited to the center of the valley, around the Sierrita de Toluca, although there is some evidence that this ceramic style was also present in Tenango del Valle, toward the valley's southern edge.

During the subsequent phase, equivalent to that of Manantial in the Valley of Mexico (1000–800 B.C.), the number of settlements increased, spreading toward the east central and south central parts of the region, especially around the present town of Metepec. There is no direct evidence for clear hierarchical differences among these sites, but within each settlement there is some evidence for social inequality. By this time, agriculture had been gradually gaining in importance as the subsistence base, especially the cultivation of grains such as maize and amaranth, although hunting and gathering still played a substantial role in the economy. The crops were probably stored in the conical formations (*tronco-conico*) found at several sites—Metepec, Ocotitlán, and San Lorenzo Cuauhtenco, all near the city of Toluca. The close ties between the Basin of Mexico and the Valley of Toluca were clearly manifested in ceramic materials with similar forms, techniques, and decorative motifs.

The marginal character of the Valley of Toluca persisted during the Middle Formative (800–400 B.C.), accompanied by slow socio-political development. Although the

T

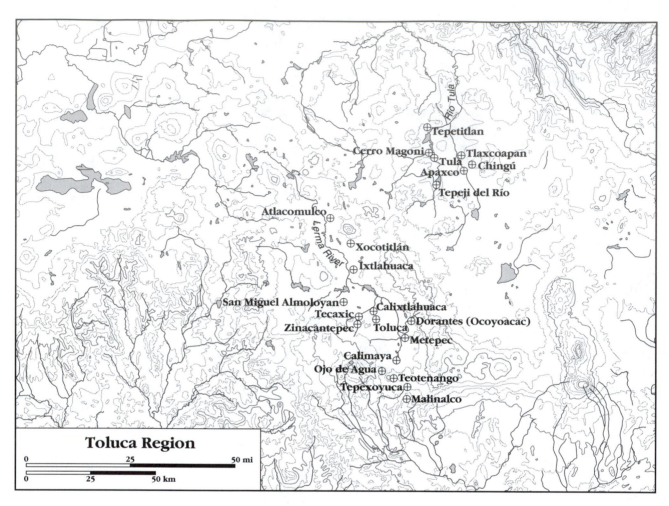

Toluca Region. Map design by Mapping Specialists Limited, Madison, Wisconsin.

population increased, reflected in the density (one per 14 square kilometers) and extent of the sites, no clear hierarchical differences between sites is apparent, except in the size of the settlements. The settlement pattern is defined by groups of four or five sites, but none emerged as a center with monumental structures. New areas were colonized: the central zone of the plain, the northwestern portion of the valley, the basin of the Dolores River, and the mountain area near Xonacatlan. In ceramics and figurines, the region continued to share many features with the Basin of Mexico, in a progression characterized by the gradual disappearance of the Olmec heritage and the appearance of new forms, and by the fusion of the two traditions.

The Late Formative period (400–200 B.C.) marked drastic changes not only in the settlement pattern but also in the ceramic tradition. First, these changes are evident in the rapid, drastic reduction of the number (half that of the former periods) and size of the settlements. Several areas occupied since the Middle Formative were entirely abandoned, especially in the southern and east central portions of the valley. At the same time, new zones (north and northeast) were colonized. All the new sites are on hilltops, with rugged topography and difficult access, far from the valley's core area. Toward the end of the Terminal Formative (200–50 B.C.), the population decline accelerated so much that the Valley of Toluca appears to have become depopulated. The causes of these changes are yet to be deciphered. These events are reflected in the material culture; for example, the ceramics are coarse and thick and of poor quality, with less varied forms and hardly any decoration.

When a strong state emerged in the Valley of Teotihuacán, imposing its cultural, social, and political patterns on the people of neighboring regions of the central highlands, the Valley of Toluca came under the sway of the Teotihuacán system. The influence of the so-called supraregional center was present in all the dimensions of society: the social complexity manifested by funerary treatment and architectural patterns; the development of the material culture tradition, especially in ceramics, figurines, lithics, and other artistic objects; settlement location; and subsistence pattern. All of these indicate strong influence from Teotihuacán. The impact of Teotihuacán on the region is clearly apparent in the Tlamimilolpa phase (A.D. 300–500), although there are some remote indication from the Miccaotli (A.D. 150–300) phase.

The recolonization of the valley was directed principally toward the fertile region, particularly in the south with its abundant water sources and in the southwest, where a piedmont extends with very gentle slopes, providing well-drained soil. There were also new settlements in the central zone around the natural corridor connecting the Valley of Toluca with the Valley of Mexico, where the most important site is Santa María Azcapotzaltongo. Toward the end of the Tlamimolpa phase, there were nearly thirty sites, distributed principally in the alluvial plain. The inhabitants, who immigrated to the Toluca region at this time, brought with them a cultural tradition intimately related to that of Teotihuacán. Social complexity is clearly apparent in both intrasite contexts and intersite relationships.

During the Xolalpan phase (A.D. 450–650) the population of the valley increased steadily, reflected in both the number and the extent of sites. The focal zone was the same as that of the former phase, principally in the fertile zone of the valley. By this time, clear hierarchical differences existed between sites; numerous small rural settlements were scattered around cultivable land, and there were a few small centers with low mounds, many of them situated at connecting points of routes. Still fewer sites can be classified as major centers, such as Ojo de Agua (Tenango), Dorantes (Ocoyoacac), and Santa Cruz Azcapotzaltongo (Toluca); these too are at strategic points. Although the extent of these focal sites was considerably smaller, the population was more nucleated and the sites represent more functions than do others. Internal social complexity is increasingly evident. Material culture remains show definite influence from Teotihuacán, especially in ceramics, figurines and lithic objects. Authentic Thin Orange ceramics were imported; green obsidian from Pachuca was widely used; slateware, painted with red and used as offerings, was probably introduced from the Tierra Caliente.

Finally, during the Metepec phase, the supremacy of Teotihuacán declined and the Teotihuacán system fell apart. In the Valley of Toluca this change is manifested by the appearance of local styles of ceramic decoration. The decline of Teotihuacán's dominion is also reflected in a rapid increase in number of settlements. Although settlements were distributed almost throughout the region, with the exception of the northwestern portion where poor environmental conditions exist, this phase's major concentration of sites is in the southern half of the valley. The major centers already mentioned continued functioning as administrative focal points, although some small centers of the former phase grew into major ones in various strategic locations; an example is La Campana-Tepozoco of Santa Cruz Atizapan, on the northeastern shore of the Lake of Lerma. Local variation and modification are quite noticeable in the ceramic assemblages, though on the whole the ceramics of the Toluca region are still closely related to the Teotihuacán tradition of the Valley of Mexico.

The disintegration of Teotihuacán ushered in a new historical stage, the Epiclassic period. The Valley of Toluca now experienced a remarkable increase in population. The demographic movement toward this region observed during the Metepec phase was of considerable magnitude, but its scale is not comparable to that of Epiclassic times in terms of either number or size of settlements. The number of known sites doubled, and the area occupied by the sites increased; these trends cannot be explained without positing a massive population movement out of the Valley of Mexico, probably from Teotihuacán and the Guadalupe Range.

The Valley of Toluca's Epiclassic settlement pattern shows a clear hierarchical differentiation between sites; some of the major centers already functioning from the Classic time, such as La Campana-Tepozoco and Ojo de Agua, became regional centers. Others sites, like Santa María Azcapotzaltongo, disappeared, and yet other new centers appeared in the hilltop zone, especially in the northeastern valley along the Toluca-Azcapotzalco corridor. To the south, Teotenango became the most important center of the valley, controlling the interaction between Toluca and the Tierra Caliente. Around these centers clustered a considerable number of lower-level sites, forming six groups separated by unoccupied land. Seen from a regional perspective, the southern half, especially the southwestern portion of the valley, continued to be the focal zone, with a high density of sites. During this period the occupation area was expanded to hilltops and zones of medium to steep slopes with sharp topography, suggesting that the defensible character of these places was one of the most important attributes in the selection of sites. By this time, a process of gradual saturation of the ecologically optimal region began to push the new settlers toward the northwestern valley, where the thin soils are susceptible to erosion.

The new emigrants seem to have brought with them the Coyotlatelco ceramic complex. In contrast to the Metepec phase, when certain local characteristics were developing and modifying the basic patterns of Teotihuacán ceramics, the Epiclassic in the Toluca region was characterized by the rapid spread of Coyotlatelco wares, which were very similar to those of the Valley of Mexico.

A certain degree of cultural homogeneity during the Epiclassic period disappeared in the Postclassic Horizon, when cultural regionalism flourished. To the west was the Matlatzinca culture, characterized by the Matlatzinca red-on-brown ceramic complex; to the east, the Otomí culture, represented by a utilitarian ceramic complex with inclusions of mica, consisting basically of jars (ollas), bowls, tecomate-style jars, and griddles (comals). Also to the west we find a ceramic tradition probably related to that of the Mazahua ethnic group from the northern part of the state of México, such as the Valley of Ixtlahuaca and Temazcalcingo-Acambay.

For the Late Postclassic, as the result of the Aztec conquest in A.D. 1473, Aztec III and III–IV ceramic complexes are found virtually everywhere in the Valley of Toluca. Naturally, in some areas, these unmistakable orange and black-on-orange vessels are associated with other Postclassic materials.

In the political and economic sphere, the Matlatzinca ethnic group, which originally occupied the fertile western portion of the valley, consolidated its power. During the Early and Middle Postclassic their domain expanded, incorporating regions far beyond the Valley of Toluca. Among the clearest evidence for Matlatzinca predominance is the development of regional centers with religious and administrative characteristics, such as the strategically located centers, Calixtlahuaca and Teotenango. These, and probably other centers destroyed in the course of history, controlled the circulation of a variety of products not only in the Valley of Toluca but also between this region and its neighbors such as the Valley of Mexico and the Tierra Caliente of Guerrero and Michoacán.

Probably in the process of the political consolidation, the Matlatzinca pushed other ethnic groups to the marginal areas. As a result, the majority of Otomís were dispersed in the eastern mountainous region, where environmental conditions were not optimal, and the Mazahuas were pushed toward the western and northwestern parts of the valley.

FURTHER READINGS

García Payon, J. 1942. *Matlatzincas ó Pirindas*. Mexico City: Ediciones Encuadernables El Nacional.

Piña Chan, R. 1983. *El Estado de México antes de la Conquista*. Toluca: Universidad Autónoma del Estado de México.

Yoko Sugiura

SEE ALSO
Coyotlatelco

Tonalá (Chiapas, Mexico)

An imposing site on the little-explored western Chiapas coast, Tonalá consists of massive stone-faced platforms built on top of a ridge at an elevation of 600 meters. The area and site are known primarily from a mapping project by Ferdon and several test pits excavated by Philip Drucker. Ferdon believed the site to have been occupied principally in the Late to Terminal Formative and Middle Classic periods, but Tonalá's cultural relationships and chronology are still basically unresolved.

The site is near the southern end of the Isthmus of Tehuantepec, an important communication route connecting the Mexican Gulf Coast with the Pacific Corridor. This region is identified as the Peripheral Coastal Lowlands, a key link between the Mexican highlands and the Maya Lowlands; here cultural and stylistic relationships were apparently maintained throughout Mesoamerican prehistory.

Several monuments supposedly from Tonalá have Cotzumalguapa stylistic characteristics. Another monument is reported to be similar to the Late Formative "potbelly" style of Guatemala's Pacific coast. The Cotzumalguapa-style stelae from Tonalá and one other reportedly from the vicinity have traits associated with the ball game, an important and common motif found on many monuments in the Cotzumalguapa heartland in the central Guatemalan piedmont. The fact that possible Late Classic Cotzumalguapa style sculpture and Late Formative potbellies are found as far from the central Cotzumalguapa zone as Tonalá is supportive of the Peripheral Coastal Lowlands concept.

Some confusion exists in regard to the identification of Tonalá. McDonald identified Ferdon's Tonalá site as Iglesia Vieja, and it is shown as such on recent maps. Nevertheless, the Tonalá district is a center of abundant archaeological remains, and early explorers treated the site and district as synonymous. Further confusing the issue are newly reported sites in the region: Los Horcones, a large Middle Classic complex of four to five ball courts and four stelae in Teotihuacan style; the Tzutzuculi site, approximately 14 kilometers from Tonalá, with Olmec-style monuments; and Pijijiapan, a nearby location with Olmec-style petroglphs.

FURTHER READINGS

Ferdon, E. N. 1953. *Tonalá, Mexico: An Archaeological Survey.* Monographs of the School of American Research, 16. Santa Fe.

Navarette, C. 1959. *A Brief Reconnaissance in the Region of Tonalá, Chiapas, Mexico.* Papers of the New World Archaeological Foundation, 4. Provo, Utah.

Parsons, L. A. 1978. The Peripheral Coastal Lowlands and the Middle Classic Period. In E. Pasztory (ed.), *Middle Classic Mesoamerica: A.D. 400–700,* pp. 25–34. New York: Columbia University Press.

Frederick J. Bové

SEE ALSO

Cotzumalhuapa Style; Soconusco–South Pacific Coast and Piedmont Region

Toniná (Chiapas, Mexico)

Overlooking the extensive and fertile Ocosingo Valley, Toniná is the region's most important Classic Maya site; it is surrounded by dozens of other sites. The Ocosingo Valley has been occupied, apparently continuously, since at least 300 B.C. Toniná has been known to Europeans since the end of the seventeenth century. It was excavated by French archaeologists in the 1970s and early 1980s, and since the mid-1980s by Mexican archaeologists.

Toniná's main section overlies a series of human-modified terraces. Some temples rose 70 meters above the plaza and remain in a good state of preservation, as does a palace complex built on several levels with interconnecting stairways.

Toniná is most famous for its sculpture. About three hundred stone sculptures and fragments are known,

including statues of standing rulers carved in the round, panels displaying captives, and hieroglyphic panels. Stucco reliefs included modeled captive figures and a frieze more than 20 meters long, showing a sacrificial scene. Martial inscriptions and iconography document successful wars against centers in the Usumacinta drainage to the east and against Palenque to the north, particularly the capture of Palenque's king K'an-Hok'-Chitam, in A.D. 711 by Toniná's king, K'inich Baknal-Chak.

At least seven Toniná rulers can be identified from inscriptions. One monument bears a hieroglyphic date equivalent to A.D. 909—one of the two last Classic Maya hieroglyphic texts.

FURTHER READINGS

Becquelin, P., and C. F. Baudez. 1973. *Toniná: Une Cité Maya de Chiapas.* 3 vols. Mexico City: Mission Archéologique et Ethnologique Française au Mexique.

Graham, I., et al. 1975. *Corpus of Maya Hieroglyphic Inscriptions.* Cambridge, Mass.: Peabody Museum of Archaeology and Ethnology, Harvard University.

Lothrop, S. K. (ed.). 1961. *Essays in Pre-Columbian Art and Archaeology.* Cambridge, Mass.: Harvard University Press.

Mayer, K. H., and B. Riese. 1983. Monument 134 aus Toniná, Chiapas. *Mexicon* 5:87–90.

Peter Mathews

SEE ALSO

Chiapas Interior Plateau

Transport

Transportation efficiency fundamentally structures societies, patterning the nature and extent of political, economic, and social integration as well as the size and spacing of cities. It dictates the size of the area within which a community can trade commodities, import food to sustain the population, and otherwise interact. Transport was severely constrained in ancient Mesoamerica by the absence of wheels (except on small figurines) and draft animals. Consequently, all land transportation was limited to foot traffic. Log rollers were used to move very large objects (such as massive worked stone) over short distances and elite persons were sometimes carried in palanquins or litters; the occasional post-Conquest practice of individual porters carrying an individual for short distances in relays was probably also a pre-Columbian practice. Otherwise, everything moved by foot, carried by porters, or *tlamemes*

T

(Nahuatl, sing. *tlamemeh*, pl. *tlamemeque*; called *tamemes* by the Spaniards).

Foot traffic is much less efficient than draft animals and wheeled vehicles, but humans on foot can cross obstacles that more complex means of transport cannot. The pattern of roads in Mesoamerica emphasized directness rather than accommodation to the intervening terrain, whether mountains, ravines, or other transportationally difficult landforms. The result of this was a network of roads that was not well suited to post-Conquest forms of transportation.

Although individual producers doubtless served as their own porters, there were also professional *tlamemes*, trained from the age of five to carry burdens, who inherited their fathers' occupations. Although the demand for transport within a polity could be met with this system, going beyond political boundaries was often a problem. Only empires could guarantee significant transport continuity, and the *tlameme* system was expanded in the wake of Aztec conquests as part of their tribute demands, although this occupational shift may also have been spurred by dispossession following the loss of lands in tribute.

Professional *tlamemes* were organized by town and were available for hire. An individual customarily carried goods for a stage of five leagues (between thirteen and sixteen miles), a distance that reflects one day's journey; the actual linear distance depended on terrain and other factors. After a day's journey, the *tlamemes* returned to their home town and another relay of *tlamemes* from the next town carried the loads on the next day. Thus, long-distance transport entailed a relay of porters between towns, with each carrying a relatively modest load, averaging about 23 kilograms (50 pounds) per *tlameme*, using a packframe and tumpline. This relative inefficiency hindered the movement of all but the most costly goods over significant distances.

Navigable bodies of water offered access to the only truly efficient form of transportation in Mesoamerica—canoes. Canoe transport was prevalent along the coasts and in the lowlands, but elsewhere rugged terrain prevented long-distance river transport. Lakes, however, permitted the integration of large areas by canoe, as in the Valley of Mexico, in the Lake Pátzcuaro region, and around Lake Atitlan.

Square-bow, shallow-draft dugout canoes ranging from 3.5 to 30 meters in length, with correspondingly large cargo capacities, dominated these lakes. Canoes were poled or paddled, sails were unknown, and a single man could pole a one-ton cargo at the same speed as a walking man, making canoes forty times more efficient than porters in the limited areas in which they competed. In the Valley of Mexico, canoers were professionally organized on a level comparable to *tlamemes*. Within lacustrine areas, efficient canoe transport could link distant towns into a unified or semiunified economic region by transporting goods at significantly lower cost than foot transport. Canoes were more efficient in volume moved rather than in speed, so their primary advantage was in trade linkages.

Canoes and rafts were also used in the Gulf of Mexico and the Caribbean, and their best speeds here probably matched the inland canoes. Here too their role was limited primarily to trade, but with enough efficiency that such bulky and relatively inexpensive goods as salt were traded in coastal shipping over hundreds of miles. The net effect of the transportation limitations in Mesoamerica was to foster cities that controlled relatively small economic hinterlands, unless they had access to navigable waterways.

FURTHER READINGS

Drennan, R. 1984. Long Distance Transport Costs in Pre-Hispanic America. *American Anthropologist* 86: 105–112.

Hassig, R. 1985. *Trade, Tribute, and Transportation*. Norman: University of Oklahoma Press.

Trombold, C. D. (ed.). 1992. *Ancient Road Networks and Settlement Hierarchies in the New World*. Cambridge: Cambridge University Press.

Ross Hassig

SEE ALSO

Economic Organization; Transport

Trapiche

See Chalchuapa

Travesía (Cortés, Honduras)

Travesía is one of a number of equally large and complex Classic period (c. A.D. 500–950) centers in the Ulúa Valley of Honduras. Deposits at the site show evidence of repeated episodes of flooding from the ancient river course that abutted the site. Stratigraphic excavations documented as many as five components, which were assigned relative dates from Early to Terminal Classic on the basis of pottery. A map of the central architecture, covering an area of approximately 125 by 125 meters, shows buildings oriented east of north around three rectangular courtyards, with a ball court adjacent on the southwest. Early reports claimed there were more than fifty-six mounds in the center, but no complete map was made before the site was destroyed. Post-destruction foot and air-photo surveys showed evidence of occupation concentrated in a 25-hectare core and dispersed throughout another 100 hectares.

A series of stone sculptures, probably architectural ornaments, in a style also known from Cerro Palenque farther south in the valley, were recovered from the monumental core. Architectural caches from the same zone included a bowl containing jade, pottery, and feline tooth beads, *Spondylus* shells containing a piece of jade, and a complete jaguar skeleton. Small platforms aligned with major buildings were preferred sites for caches. One such platform supported a small stela with remains of painted plaster designs. Carved stone Ulúa Marble vases have also been reported from informal excavations at the site. Excavation of nonmonumental areas of the site produced evidence of obsidian blade production and a possible pottery kiln.

FURTHER READINGS

Joyce, R. 1987. Intraregional Ceramic Variation and Social Class: Developmental Trajectories of Classic Period Ceramic Complexes from the Ulúa Valley. In E. J. Robinson (ed.), *Interaction on the Southeast Mesoamerican Frontier: Prehistoric and Historic Honduras and El Salvador*, pp. 267–279. BAR International Series, 327 (ii). Oxford.

Stone, D. 1941. *Archaeology of the North Coast of Honduras*. Memoirs of the Peabody Museum 9, Part 1. Cambridge, Mass.: Harvard University.

Rosemary Joyce

SEE ALSO

Southeast Mesoamerica

Tres Zapotes (Veracruz, Mexico)

An important center of the Olmec, Epi-Olmec, and Classic Veracruz cultures in southern Veracruz state, Tres Zapotes is most significant for its long sequence of occupation—which stretches from the Early Formative period (c. 1500–900 B.C.) into the Early Postclassic (A.D. 900–1200)—for its prominent role in the history of Olmec studies, and for its large corpus of Olmec and Epi-Olmec stone monuments. The most famous Epi-Olmec monument from Tres Zapotes is Stela C, a plano-relief carving that bears a date in the long count calendar corresponding to 31 B.C., the second earliest recorded date in Mesoamerica. Olmec monuments found at the site include two colossal heads, one of which was the first such monument to be discovered. Consequently, Tres Zapotes is frequently identified with San Lorenzo, La Venta, and Laguna de los Cerros as a principal Olmec site, although the extent of its Early and Middle Formative occupations is currently unknown.

Tres Zapotes is situated at a prominent bend in the Arroyo Hueyapan, just north of the village of the same name. In contrast to the riverine settings of the eastern Olmec centers of La Venta and San Lorenzo, Tres Zapotes sits amid dissected sedimentary uplands between the volcanoes of the Sierra de los Tuxtlas and the broad deltaic plain of the Papaloapan and San Juan rivers. The tropical rain forest that originally flourished in the hot, humid climate has long since been cleared for pastureland and cultivated fields of sugar cane and maize. The site contains more than fifty mounds, most of which occupy an area of about 2 square kilometers on the floodplain and alluvial terrace on the western bank of the arroyo. Three principal mound groups arranged around irregular plazas share this zone of major construction with clusters of smaller, presumably residential mounds. A fourth, isolated mound group lies about 2 kilometers northwest of the site center, and a few scattered mounds occupy the eastern bank of the arroyo. The mounds, which range in height from less than a meter to 18 meters, are constructed mainly of earth and clay; stone construction is confined to the occasional use of sandstone slabs for steps, facing stones, and pavements.

Tres Zapotes holds a prominent place in the archaeological literature as the first major Olmec site to be seriously investigated. In 1869 José M. Melgar described a colossal stone head that had been discovered prior to 1862 by a laborer on the Hacienda Hueyapam [sic]. The "Cabeza Colosal de Hueyapan," later designated Tres Zapotes Monument A by Matthew W. Stirling, was the first of these characteristic Olmec monuments to be reported. Other early visitors to the site included Eduard Seler and Caecilie Seler-Sachs, in 1906–1907, and A. Weyerstall, in 1925–1926. Inspired by Weyerstall's report, Stirling initiated modern Olmec field studies in 1938 with a reconnaissance of Tres Zapotes and the surrounding region. Supported by the Smithsonian Institution and the

T

National Geographic Society, Stirling returned to Tres Zapotes in the winter of 1938–1939 with his assistant, C. W. Weiant, to excavate nonstratigraphic exploratory trenches in mounds and to clear monuments. Stirling continued field work in the winter of 1939–1940 with the assistance of Philip Drucker, excavating additional nonstratigraphic test pits and mound cuts as well as five stratigraphic trenches. Weiant described the ceramics from the 1938–1939 season and suggested a ceramic chronology, but it was Drucker's stratigraphic excavations that provided the first well-documented ceramic sequence from the Olmec heartland. Since 1940, field work at Tres Zapotes has been infrequent and sporadic. In the early 1970s, Ponciano Ortiz Ceballos excavated a stratigraphic pit to sample Formative period deposits, and in 1978 workers from the Instituto Nacional de Antropología e Historia discovered a basalt column enclosure during salvage operations for the construction of a gas pipeline.

Stirling's discovery of Stela C in 1939 provided the first strong indication that the Olmec art style pre-dated the Classic period. When Stirling discovered it, the upper half of the monument was missing, and with it the crucial *baktun* coefficient of its long count date. He and Marion Stirling reconstructed the date as (7).16.6.16.18 (3 September 31 B.C.), for which they were roundly criticized by Mayan scholars, led by J. Eric S. Thompson, who regarded Olmec culture as a Classic period offshoot of Maya civilization. The date was, however, accepted by the Mexican scholars Alfonso Caso, Miguel Covarrubias, and Roman Piña Chan, who argued that the Olmec represented the earliest civilization in Mesoamerica. Radiocarbon samples collected at La Venta and San Lorenzo in the 1950s and 1960s ultimately demonstrated a much earlier placement of Olmec culture, prior to 400 B.C. The denouement of the controversy over Stela C came in 1969 when Esteban Santo, a local farmer, discovered the stela's upper half, which bears the missing coefficient of seven predicted by the Stirlings.

With the exception of the Stela C inscription, the only absolute date from Tres Zapotes is a clearly erroneous radiocarbon date of 9000 B.C. on wood charcoal that was later found to be contaminated by asphalt. Current understanding of the chronology of Tres Zapotes therefore relies on stratigraphy, stylistic features of ceramics and monuments, and cross-dating of the ceramic and sculptural sequences with those from better-dated sites. Drucker's stratigraphic excavations revealed the existence of early deposits on the valley floor that had been sealed by a layer of volcanic ash. Above the volcanic ash lay 1.8

meters of brown alluvium containing few sherds. Another 2 meters of culturally sterile yellow-brown alluvium lay above the brown alluvium. Most of the mounds excavated by Stirling and his associates appear to have been constructed after the deposition of the volcanic ash, which appears to have been rapidly eroded from the adjoining alluvial terrace.

The ceramic chronology of Tres Zapotes has been revised several times over the years. In 1943, Weiant published his typological analysis of the ceramics from the nonstratigraphic 1938–1939 excavations and suggested a ceramic sequence, but this was immediately superseded by Drucker's more detailed and complete chronology, derived from his stratigraphic excavations. Drucker distinguished a Formative period Lower phase comprising the ceramics from the deposits under the volcanic ash; he divided the later ceramics into a transitional Middle phase, a Classic period Upper phase, and a Postclassic Soncautla complex, which he considered intrusive. In 1965 Coe proposed a revision of Drucker's sequence based on typological comparisons with sites in the Olmec heartland and elsewhere. Coe defined five phases, numbered I through V in Roman numerals. The most significant contribution of Coe's revision was its division of Drucker's Upper phase into an Early Classic component, Tres Zapotes III, and a Late Classic component, Tres Zapotes IV. Drucker's Lower and Middle phases and his Soncautla complex were assigned to Coe's phases I, II, and V, respectively.

The age of the sub-ash deposits at Tres Zapotes has evoked considerable debate. Both Drucker and Coe assigned them to the Late Formative period, but Ignacio Bernal suggested they were pre-Olmec. In the early 1970s, Ortiz Ceballos helped to resolve this confusion by excavating a pit adjacent to Drucker's Trench 26 in the bank of the Arroyo Hueyapan. The lowest levels in his excavation yielded a handful of sherds corresponding to the pre-Olmec Ojochí horizon (1500–1350 B.C.). Ortiz Ceballos divided the remaining levels below the volcanic ash into three phases, which he named Tres Zapotes, Hueyapan, and Nextepetl. He assigned the Tres Zapotes phase to the end of the Early Formative period and the Middle Formative period (c. 1000–300 B.C.), and the Hueyapan phase to the Late Formative period (300 B.C.–A.D. 100). The Protoclassic Nextepetl phase (A.D. 100–300) witnessed the addition of fine-paste Classic period types to the Formative period ceramic tradition; in this respect, it corresponds to Coe's Tres Zapotes II and Drucker's Middle Tres Zapotes, both of which were defined on the basis of post-ashfall assemblages. This correspondence of assemblages above and below the ash deposit suggests placement of the volcanic eruption sometime in the Protoclassic period (but see Lowe for an earlier placement of the Hueyapan and Nextepetl phases).

To date, more than forty stone monuments have been found at Tres Zapotes. Most of them were carved from basalt found on the nearby Cerro el Vigía and in other parts of the Sierra de los Tuxtlas. The dating of these monuments has proved even more problematic than establishing a ceramic chronology because of clear evidence that many of the monuments were reused long after they were carved. The colossal heads (Monuments A and Q) are clearly Olmec. Although Beatriz de la Fuente has argued on the basis of their formal qualities that the Tres Zapotes heads are late, most scholars agree that such monuments date to the Early Formative period. Other probable Olmec sculptures include Monument H, a head in Olmec style though not of the colossal type; Monument M, a head and torso with the arms and legs missing; and Monuments I and J, the lower fragments of sculptures of seated individuals.

Some of the Late Formative sculptures from Tres Zapotes exhibit elements that are derived from Olmec precursors. Several scholars have also identified resemblances to the Izapan style of Chiapas and Guatemala, although this position has recently been challenged by John Graham and James Porter. Stela D, which depicts three figures in a niche formed by the open mouth of a feline or "earth monster," is strikingly similar in conception to Monument 2 from Izapa. Stela A has a similar arrangement of three figures in a niche below a stylized "monster" mask, one of whom carries a trophy head, as does a figure on Stela 21 at Izapa. Both of these also recall earlier Olmec stelae such as La Venta Stela 3 and El Viejón Monument 1, as well as Pijijiapan Monument 1 from the Pacific Coast. Izapan influence is also frequently claimed for Monument C, an elaborately carved stone box, and for the carving on the reverse of Stela C. The latter consists of a stylized feline mask of Olmec derivation surmounted by a glyphic element that calls to mind the Aztec *ollin* sign for "motion," and a human head in profile against a background of undulating bands.

In conclusion, disputes over the ceramic and sculptural chronology of Tres Zapotes will undoubtedly continue until adequate chronometric dates are recovered from the site. Nevertheless, the following sequence of events appears best to fit the current evidence. The initial occupation of the site may be as early as the Ojochí phase at

San Lorenzo (1500–1350 B.C.). By the close of the Early Formative period (1200–900 B.C.), Tres Zapotes appears to have achieved some prominence, as indicated by the two colossal heads recovered from the site. Occupation continued into the Late Formative (400 B.C.–A.D. 100), when the greater part of the sculptural corpus at the site (including Stela C) was carved in a style that combined Olmec and Izapan elements. At some point in the Protoclassic the site suffered a volcanic eruption, which may have caused flooding of the Arroyo Hueyapan Valley. The eruption, however, does not appear to have severely affected the course of occupation at the site, since little typological discontinuity is observed in the substantial Protoclassic occupation (A.D. 100–300), when earlier ceramic styles were modified and elaborated. During the Early and Middle Classic periods (A.D. 300–700), the ceramic assemblage was influenced by Teotihuacán styles, possibly via a Teotihuacán enclave at Matacapan. In Coe's opinion, Tres Zapotes experienced an intensive occupation in the Late Classic period (A.D. 700–1000) that was responsible for the major mound-building occupation of the site. Later, during the Early Postclassic (A.D. 1000–1200), an intrusive Soncautla complex appears at the site in association with cremated burials.

FURTHER READINGS

Coe, M. D. 1965. Archaeological Synthesis of Southern Veracruz and Tabasco. In G. R. Willey (ed.), *Handbook of Middle American Indians*, vol. 3, *Archaeology of Southern Mesoamerica, Part 2*, pp. 679–715. Austin: University of Texas Press.

de la Fuente, B. 1973. *Escultura Monumental Olmeca*. Mexico City: Universidad Nacional Autónoma de México.

Drucker, P. 1943. *Ceramic Sequences at Tres Zapotes, Veracruz, Mexico*. Smithsonian Institution, Bureau of American Ethnology, Bulletin 140. Washington, D.C.

Hester, T. R., R. F. Heizer, and R. N. Jack. 1971. The Obsidian of Tres Zapotes. In *Papers on Olmec and Maya Archaeology*, pp. 65–133. Contributions of the University of California Archaeological Research Facility, 13. Berkeley.

Lowe, G. W. 1989. The Heartland Olmec: Evolution of Material Culture. In R. J. Sharer and D. C. Grove (eds.), *Regional Perspectives on the Olmec*, pp. 33–67. Cambridge: Cambridge University Press.

Melgar, J. M. 1869. Antiguedades Mexicanos. *Boletín de la Sociedad Mexicana de Geografía y Estadística*, ser. 2, 1:292–297.

T

Stirling, M. W. 1940. An Initial Series from Tres Zapotes, Vera Cruz, Mexico. National Geographic Society Contributed Technical Papers, 1(1). Washington, D.C.

———. 1940. 1943. *Stone Monuments of Southern Mexico.* Smithsonian Institution, Bureau of American Ethnology, Bulletin 138. Washington, D.C.

Weiant, C. W. 1943. *An Introduction to the Ceramics of Tres Zapotes, Veracruz, Mexico.* Bureau of American Ethnology, Bulletin 139. Washington, D.C.

Williams, H., and R. F. Heizer. 1965. *Sources of Rocks Used in Olmec Monuments.* Contributions of the University of California Archaeological Research Facility, 1. Berkeley.

Christopher A. Pool

SEE ALSO

Gulf Lowlands: South Region; Olmec Culture

Tribute

Tribute is defined as payment in goods and/or services by a conquered population to its overlords. While the citizens of a state or empire may pay taxes (usually individually), products or labor demanded of conquered peoples (usually collectively) are labeled "tribute" in recognition of both the physical assessment and the symbolism of subservience. In Mesoamerica as elsewhere in the ancient world, imperial states arose which demanded substantial and varied tributes from subjugated peoples. Tribute was surely an economic reality among such early Mesoamerican civilizations as Teotihuacán, the Toltecs, and the many Mayan states. However, ethnohistorical information on tribute is particularly abundant and revealing for the later Aztec Empire, and its patterns will be presented as a specific case as we look at general patterns of tribute assessments and payments.

An understanding of late Postclassic (in this case, Aztec) tribute relies most heavily on written documentation from both native and Spanish sources. Empire-wide tribute assessments are pictorially recorded in the Matrícula de Tributos and the second part of the Codex Mendoza. These documents are so similar that it is hard to avoid the conclusion that they are somehow related (the Mendoza copied from the Matrícula, or both from yet another codex). Both are annotated—the Matrícula in Nahuatl and the Mendoza in Spanish—so that they tend to function as a "Rosetta Stone." Added to this is a Spanish document composed in 1554 that describes imperial tribute demands of nearly the same collection of provinces as in the Matrícula and Mendoza; it was surely based on a pre-Hispanic pictorial prototype (Scholes and Adams 1957).

These codices were composed by native scribes, the Matricula most likely in pre-Spanish times and the Mendoza in the early 1540s. Other written documentation is available in the form of chronicles and histories composed, especially, by Spanish friars or native chroniclers later in the sixteenth century. These include works by the Franciscan friar Bernardino de Sahagún, the Dominican friar Diego Durán, and the native noblemen Fernando de Alvarado Tezozomoc and Fernando de Alva Ixtlilxochitl. Each of these writers provides valuable details about types and quantities of tribute payments, the structure of tribute collection, and the uses to which tributes were put.

Imperial tribute payments and patterns can also be inferred from archaeological finds. Excavations in and around the Aztec Templo Mayor have revealed physical remains of items possibly paid in tribute, and archaeological analyses of less grandiose sites (for example, in Morelos and the Teotihuacán Valley) suggest production activities geared toward the payment of tribute.

Details of localized tribute systems are also available from a wide array of source materials, both pictorial and textual. These date exclusively from the Spanish Colonial period and typically describe Colonial tribute impositions on either native lords or Spanish *encomenderos;* or, like the *Relaciones Geográficas,* they describe pre-Conquest conditions. These documents reflect, to some extent, the type of tribute obligations present at non-imperial levels in pre-Hispanic times.

Aztec empirewide tribute, as outlined in the Matrícula de Tributos and Codex Mendoza, encompassed thirty-eight geographically distinct provinces. These provinces consisted of one to twenty-six city-states *(altepetl)* conquered by the Mexica of Tenochtitlan. In many cases, such conquest was undertaken with the aid of the Mexica's military allies in the Basin of Mexico, particularly the Acolhua of Texcoco and the Tepaneca of Tlacopan. Although it appears that this documented tribute was paid to the Mexica ruler alone, other sources suggest that various tribute payments were shared among the three allies, with Tenochtitlan and Texcoco sharing equally and Tlacopan receiving a lesser portion. In addition, the Mexica were not the only military overlords in Central Mexico. Their neighbors the Acolhua and the Tepaneca, for instance, boasted their own conquered lands from which they drew tribute. Similar patterns pertained in present-day Morelos and Oaxaca south of the Basin of Mexico. Conquest by the Mexica basically added another layer of political subservience and tribute payments to the existing hierarchical order. Thus, the inhabitants of a single community or city-state may have had several tribute obligations to satisfy: to a local lord, to the lord of a conquest state, and to a yet more powerful imperial overlord.

Tribute collection, imperial or otherwise, was in the hands of specialized political officials. Little is known about how tribute was allocated or collected at an individual or household level, but records indicate that the yields of some agricultural fields were designated for tribute payment. Undoubtedly labor on such fields was distributed among obligated households and communities, much as corvée labor on bridges, roads, and other public constructions was allocated. At the imperial level, tribute collectors (*calpixque*, sing. *calpixqui*) were stationed in important communities throughout the empire and were responsible for assembling the levies and delivering them to the imperial capital(s). In Tenochtitlan, a *petlacalcatl* was in charge of accounting, warehousing, and distributing the vast quantities of goods acquired through tribute.

Specific payments in kind or service varied from province to province, depending on the ability of the conquered peoples to pay, the availability of particular raw materials and finished goods, the province's geopolitical location, and the needs of the conquerors. Immediately upon conquest, tribute in specific goods was demanded of the defeated city-state. This initial tribute was often top-heavy with textiles, which were produced by women, and would have reflected an imbalance in the gender ratio at places where men had been disproportionately killed on the battlefield or taken as prisoners. As time went on and the gender balance evened out, tribute demands tended to diversify to draw more on goods produced by both men and women. Thus, the ability to pay particular types of tribute changed over time.

It is often stated that a province (or city-state) was required to pay tribute in readily available goods. This included raw materials and finished goods directly produced by the conquered peoples. But demands were also made for goods that were not naturally available in a conquered realm but rather entered that polity through ancient trading and market channels. Thus, the conquest of a city-state allowed the conquerers not only economic control over the conquered area itself but also economic access to resources beyond the imperial boundaries. Under these arrangements, a vast array of raw materials and manufactured products flowed into Tenochtitlan and its urban neighbors, as illustrated by the Matrícula de Tributos and Codex Mendoza. This tribute was paid on a

regular schedule—every eighty days, biannually, or annually—thus ensuring a predictable, steady supply of products for the imperial capitals.

From nearby provinces came bins of staple foodstuffs, predominantly maize and beans but also chia and amaranth. Other foodstuffs were sent by provinces near or far which excelled in such production: chiles from the eastern Sierra, cacao from the Pacific and Gulf lowlands, maguey honey from the northwest, bees' honey from south of the Basin of Mexico, and salt from the west. Warriors' costumes and shields, intricately fashioned of feathers and following specified styles, were sent by all but nine of the Mendoza's thirty-eight provinces and totaled some 665 ensembles; the bulk of this martial attire was sent by provinces in relatively close proximity to the imperial capital.

Textiles (capes, loincloths, women's tunics, and women's skirts) comprised the bulk of tribute goods and were delivered by all but two of the Mendoza's tributary provinces, mounting to nearly 300,000 items annually. Most were made of cotton, but some were woven of maguey and yucca fibers. Some were plain white items (which could be used as a medium of exchange as well as an item of clothing); others were elaborately decorated and clearly fit for kings and high-ranking nobles. Provinces paid decorated cloth based to a great extent on their own design traditions, rather than on styles imposed by the imperial rulers.

Some provinces were especially noted or renowned for the availability or production of specialized goods, and the conquerors took advantage of such specializations in their tribute assessments. Thus, individual provinces paid such products as wood for building and firewood, cochineal for dyeing, canes for spears, paper for writing and rituals, rubber for games and rites, and a host of other goods, including copal, liquidambar, deerskins, live eagles, and seashells. As might be expected, there was an emphasis on goods exclusive to the nobility; the most distant (and most recently conquered) provinces paid opulent tributes in precious stones (greenstone and turquoise), gold adornments, copper axes and bells, amber, jaguar skins, and shimmering tropical feathers.

Overall, there is a predominance of manufactured goods over raw materials, although the Tenochtitlan feather-workers were especially well supplied with thousands of feathers annually. It is also notable that little in the way of armament was delivered in tribute, although warrior costumes and canes were sent, and one province provided captive warriors as part of its annual tribute obligation. By way of military obligation, some communities fulfilled their tribute duties by provisioning a local garrison, by serving as warriors on imperial military campaigns, or by supplying armies on the march.

Geopolitical location had some effect on a conquered people's relationship with its conquerors. Many city-states strategically located along hostile borderlands or astride active commercial routes were folded into the empire on a somewhat different tributary basis. Many such city-states do not appear on the Matrícula or Mendoza tribute rolls at all; their subservient ties to the empire are described in other sources. The particular value of such strategically located city-states lay in their ability to secure trade routes or hold tense borderlands with fairly constant, low-level warfare. Their tribute obligations are most frequently described as "gifts" rather than tribute, and they were at times reciprocated by the imperial ruler.

The needs of the imperial powers changed over time, and this is reflected in changing tribute demands. In particular, the growing sumptuary needs of an expanding nobility had to be met. As the empire expanded, it moved more and more into regions able to provide exquisite luxury items in tribute: plush jaguar skins, luxurious tropical feathers, elegant gold ornaments, beads and mosaics of fine stones. Nobility and other high achievers (especially warriors) were recipients of tribute payments in the form of gifts and commissions. Other tribute was applied to the ruler's extravagant lifestyle, to administrative and military needs, to underwriting foreign trade, and to subsidizing artisans. Foodstuffs were distributed to the urban populace at specific ceremonies and were stockpiled against the likelihood of drought and famine. Tribute was also collected for special events, such as the dedication of a temple or the coronation or funeral of a ruler. This special-purpose tribute was in addition to the regularly assessed tribute. Many of the offerings deposited around Tenochtitlan's Templo Mayor, such as greenstone beads, marine fauna, and stone masks, may have been the result of special-purpose demands.

Tribute represented political and economic control over conquered regions and provided a regular and periodic flow of raw materials and finished goods to the burgeoning imperial capitals. It was not sufficient, however, to provide all the material needs of the Basin of Mexico urban centers; local production, long-distance trade, and lively markets likewise moved goods from producers to consumers. Of these exchange mechanisms, tribute was the most closely entwined with the political and military goals of the empire.

FURTHER READINGS

Anderson, E., and R. H. Barlow. 1943. The Maize Tribute of Moctezuma's empire. *Annals of the Missouri Botanical Garden* 30:413–418.

Barlow, R. H. 1943. *The Periods of Tribute Collection in Moctezuma's Empire*. Notes on Middle American Archaeology and Ethnology, 23. Washington, D.C.: Carnegie Institution.

Barrera Rubio, A. 1984. *El modo de producción tributario en Mesoamérica*. Analté 3, Escuela de Ciencias Antropológicas. Mérida: Ediciones de la Universidad de Yucatán.

Berdan, F. F., and P. R. Anawalt. 1992. *The Codex Mendoza*. 4 vols. Berkeley: University of California Press.

Berdan, F. F., R. E. Blanton, E. H. Boone, M. G. Hodge, M. E. Smith, and E. Umberger. 1995. *Aztec Imperial Strategies*. Washington, D.C.: Dumbarton Oaks.

Berdan, F. F., and J. de Durand-Forest (eds.). 1980. *Matrícula de Tributos*. Graz: Akademische Druck u. Verlagsanstalt.

Carrasco, P. 1962. Tres libros de tributos del Museo Nacional de México y su importancia para los estudios demográficos. *Congreso Internacional de Americanistas, Actas y memorias* 111:373–378. Mexico City.

Scholes, F. V., and E. B. Adams. 1957. *Información sobre los tributos que los indios pagaban a Moctezuma, año de 1554*. Vol. 4 of *Documentos para la historia del Mexico colonial*. Mexico City: José Porrua.

Frances F. Berdan

SEE ALSO
Economic Organization

Tuitlán

See Quemada, La

Tula de Hidalgo (Hidalgo, Mexico)

Tula is a Central Mexican site in southwestern Hidalgo, about 50 kilometers northwest of Mexico City. The site extends over a series of alluvial valleys and adjacent uplands that form the confluence of the Tula and Rosas rivers, incorporating the modern town of Tula de Allende. Tula is believed to be the ruins of Tollan, legendary capital of the Toltec Empire, which ethnohistorical sources traditionally date to the Early Postclassic period (A.D. 900–1200).

Tula is situated on the Central Mexican Plateau, a volcanic upland broken by numerous localized basins and

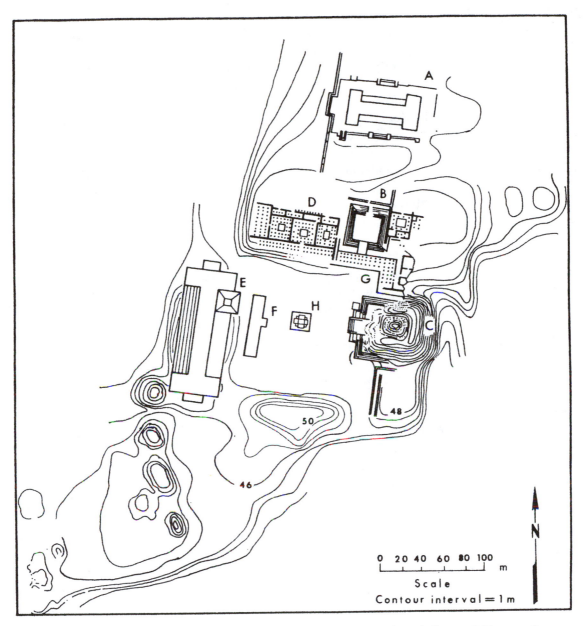

Plan of Tula Grande. A. ball court; B. pyramid; C. pyramid; D. Palacio Quemado; E. ball court; F. Tzompantli; G. vestibule; H. Adoratiro. Illustration from Diehl, 1983.

valleys, the largest of which, the Basin of Mexico, is the site of the preceding Teotihuacan and subsequent Aztec civilizations and present-day Mexico City. Much of the Tula region lies within the rain shadow of the eastern Sierra Madre, occupying the southwestern corner of a semiarid region known as the Valle del Mezquital. Annual precipitation at Tula (c. 612 mm) occurs mostly during April through October. The principal plant communities found in the Valle del Mezquital include shrub thicket

and subhumid grassland. Except for localized alluvial deposits, the soil of the region is generally thin and calcareous, with an indurated B horizon (caliche) often exposed to the surface. The extensive erosion and generally marginal character of the region today can be traced to human-induced practices of deforestation and overcultivation that began in pre-Hispanic times.

The earliest published accounts of archaeological investigations at Tula deal with Charnay's partial excavation of two large, apparently residential structures and his exploration of a small platform located in the center of the site's main ceremonial center, known today as Tula Grande. In 1940, Jorge Acosta of the Instituto Nacional de Antropología e Historia (INAH) began a thirteen-season program of investigations at Tula that included restoration of much of Tula Grande's distinctive ceremonial architecture and sculptural elements—colonnades, columned halls flanked by wall benches, warrior caryatids, and bas-relief depictions of human and animal processions. Investigations conducted since 1970 by INAH, the University of Missouri, and Tulane University included systematic intrasite surface survey, regional survey, and excavation of a number of localities at Tula and at other sites in the region.

The earliest well-defined occupation of the Tula region began in the Late Formative period (c. 400–200 B.C.) with the appearance of small hamlets and several larger settlements. The Early Classic period (c. A.D. 300–750) was marked by the abrupt appearance of numerous settlements in the region, though no occupation has been identified at Tula itself. Many of these sites possess a ceramic complex virtually identical to that of Teotihuacan, the urban capital of a major Early Classic empire situated about 80 kilometers to the southeast. Several settlements cover more than 100 hectares; one, Chingú, measures nearly 250 hectares, with layout, orientation, and ceremonial and residential architecture apparently modeled after those of Teotihuacan. The rapid appearance in the region of settlements with strong external cultural ties is believed to represent colonization by Teotihuacanos or others with strong ties to that city. Many of these sites were abandoned around the time of the demise of Teotihuacan, around A.D. 750.

The earliest (Prado phase) occupation at Tula is dated to the Epiclassic period (c. A.D. 700–850), during which a small community existed in the northern portion of the site. This early settlement appears to have been centered on Tula Chico, a small mound/plaza complex believed to have been the prototype for Tula Grande, the politico-religious center of the subsequent city. Though most ceramics are associated with the Coyotlatelco ceramic complex of the Late Classic to Epiclassic period, many ceramics recovered from Prado phase deposits in excavations at Tula Chico show ties to the Bajío region of Guanajuato and Querétaro, and thus lend credence to ethnohistorical accounts that associate Tula's founding with the intrusion of Tolteca-Chichimeca peoples from the northwest. In subsequent periods, Tula underwent a

program of growth characterized initially by a southward shift in settlement and a concomitant relocation of the principal politico-religious center to Tula Grande. This period of initial growth was also characterized by the appearance of Mazapa Red-on-Brown, which, though common to sites in the Basin of Mexico, is a relatively minor ceramic type at Tula that peaks in popularity before Tula's urban florescence. The association of Mazapa pottery with settlement near the southern and eastern extremes of the site, including areas where obsidian-working was carried on, suggests its possible association with immigrants from the Basin of Mexico.

During the Tollan phase (c. A.D. 900–1200), Tula attained its maximum size of about 13 square kilometers, with a population estimated as high as sixty thousand. The Tollan phase city incorporates remarkably diverse terrain, including hills and slopes, adjoining alluvial valleys, and a brackish reed marsh (El Salitre). Within this area occur hundreds of mounds and terraces and a dense surface cover of artifact debris. Excavations at twelve separate localities within the city each uncovered complex configurations of residential structures indicative of a dense, highly structured settlement. A common residential pattern is the house group, a closed configuration of single- or multiple-family houses arranged around a central, open courtyard. Evidence of planning at the neighborhood level includes the use of a common orientation scheme and the presence of closed alleys, passageways, and paved thoroughfares connecting juxtaposed house groups. Three schemes of structural orientation are evident among extant surface remains and excavated structures; each scheme may represent a specific, citywide policy of structural alignment followed at one particular time in the city's history.

The numerous rural settlements that existed in Tula's hinterland indicate that the city was supported by a substantial rural population who farmed the alluvial valleys and uplands, and there is evidence of specialized production of various nonfood items within the city itself. Excavation within an extensive area of obsidian surface debris discovered near the city's eastern limits exposed a workshop where obsidian imported from sources near Pachuca (Hidalgo) and Zinapécuaro (Michoacán) was made into the prismatic cores and blades that were ubiquitous as household items as well as weaponry. The uniformity of ceramic assemblages among urban and rural households suggests centralized systems of ceramic production and distribution; evidence of other specialized production activities include manufacture of mold-made ceramic figurines, fired ceramic tubes used in drainage and water control systems, and the manufacture of onyx *(tecalli)* vessels. Other exotic items indicative of long-distance exchange include Pacific and Gulf Coast shell and exotic pottery vessels, such as Plumbate pottery from Guatemala and polychrome vessels from Central America.

During its Tollan phase apogee, Tula is believed to have controlled a sphere of influence that minimally included much of the Basin of Mexico. Its principal rival appears to have been Cholula in the Puebla Valley to the southeast. The presence of similar architectural and sculptural elements at Chichén Itzá in northern Yucatán has been cited as corroborating evidence for ethnohistorical accounts of colonization of that Maya site by Toltec invaders from Tula. Though there is no real archaeological evidence for this, the architectural similarities and other evidence, including a reliance on the Pachuca and Zinapécuaro sources of obsidian, suggest significant interaction between the two sites.

The end of the Tollan phase was marked by the apparent collapse and depopulation of Tula. During subsequent Late Postclassic Aztec times (c. A.D. 1200–1520), the Tula region appears to have attained its maximum pre-Hispanic population size. There is evidence of Aztec settlement at Tula, though this does not appear to have been as extensive as the Tollan phase settlement. Acosta encountered large amounts of the Aztec II ceramic complex at Tula Grande, which he associated with its destruction, though this complex is generally rare elsewhere in the city and in the region as a whole. The most abundant Late Postclassic ceramics in the region are Aztec III, but their widespread, low-density distribution suggests a correspondingly low-density occupation. Thus, the Tollan phase appears to have been the only pre-Hispanic period during which there was a city at Tula.

FURTHER READINGS

Charnay, D. 1887. *Ancient Cities of the New World.* New York: Harper and Brothers.

Cook, S. F. 1949. The Historical Demography and Ecology of the Teotlalpan. *Ibero-Americana* 33 (entire volume). Berkeley.

Diaz Oyarzabal, C. 1980. Chingú, un sitio clásico del area de Tula, Hgo. Colección Científica, Arqueología, 90. Mexico City: Instituto Nacional de Antropología e Historia.

Healan, D. M. 1989. *Tula of the Toltecs: Excavations and Survey.* Iowa City: University of Iowa Press.

Matos Moctezuma, E. (coord.). 1974. *Proyecto Tula.* Part 1. Colección Científica, 15. Mexico City: Instituto Nacional de Antropología e Historia, Departamento de Monumentos Prehispánicos.

Dan M. Healan

SEE ALSO
Tollan; Toltec Culture; Tula Region

Tula Region

Tula was one of the largest and most complex pre-Hispanic cities of the central highlands of Mexico, covering nearly 16 square kilometers during its apogee between A.D. 950 and 1200. The Tula region lies 60 kilometers north of Mexico City in the modern state of Hidalgo, constituting a well-defined geographic unit bordered by a series of natural barriers, such as mountain ranges with some passes or natural accesses that connect it with other regions—especially, the Basin of Mexico to the south and the Mezquital Valley (pre-Hispanic Teotlalpan) to the north. Even though it is partially separated from the Basin of Mexico, the Tula region can be considered as a northern prolongation of the basin, sharing with it the advantages of access to a wide variety of important economic resources, and a central location with respect to trade routes and natural passes to other regions of Mesoamerica, especially in the central highlands, the northern Mesoamerican periphery, and West Mexico.

The Tula region covers approximately 1,000 square kilometers, small enough that it would have been possible to travel on foot from the ancient city to any settlement in the area in less than a day. Important contemporary towns included Mizquiahuala and Tepetitlan in the north, Heroes de Carranza and Jilotepec in the west, Tlahuelilpan, Atitalaquia, and Atotonilco Tula in the east, and Tepeji del Río in the south.

The Tula area possesses three permanently flowing rivers of considerable size, along with an extensive alluvial valley and diverse zones of potentially irrigated and nonirrigated agriculture. The Tula area, like some zones in the Basin of Mexico, the Puebla-Tlaxcala Valley, and the Valley of Morelos, was one of the most important areas for pre-Hispanic irrigation in the central highlands. Some of its irrigation systems probably were first constructed during the Classic period.

The regional studies done in the Tula area provide a good overview of the processes that formed this city and its social, economic, and political structure, a picture derived through identifying the specific kinds of settlements and resource exploitation systems of the area

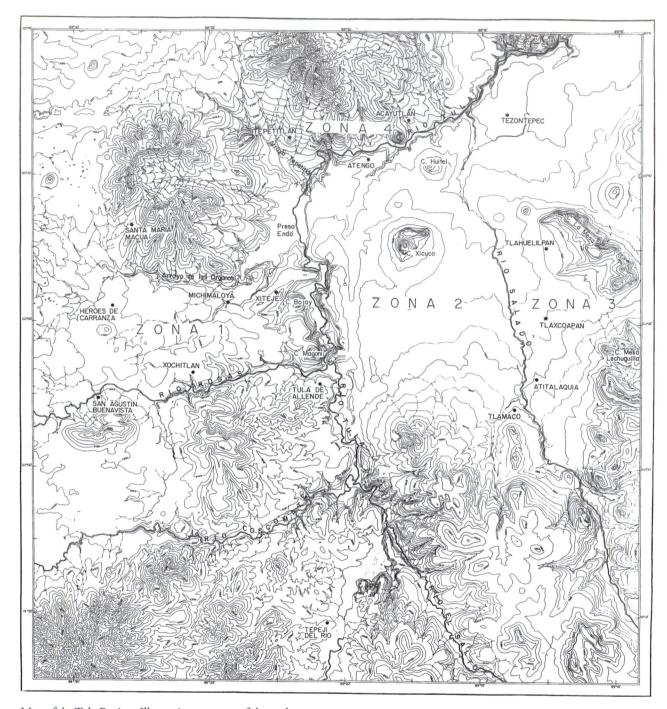

Map of the Tula Region. Illustration courtesy of the authors.

during different periods. Settlement pattern investigations have generally followed the methodology and objectives of previous research by Sanders and his collaborators for the Teotihuacan Valley, because the central goals of their project were similar to those of the Tula project and the ecological conditions of both areas are similar. The Tula investigation was based mainly on surface surveys of approximately 1,000 square kilometers.

Subsequent investigations addressed contemporary settlement patterns and soil exploitation; a study of traditional and modern irrigation systems obtained information about types of agriculture and cultivation. Regional pollen studies were done, as well as a geological study which identified major rock formations and exploitable deposits of limestone, basalt, rhyolite, and chert.

Formative Period

In the area where the ancient city of Tula eventually emerged, the earliest settlement dates to the Formative period. A few hamlet-sized sites probably existed during the Middle Formative (c. 800–600 B.C.). Two diagnostic Middle Formative potsherds were recovered from excavations of a present-day water-pipe ditch in the main plaza of the modern town of Tula de Allende. The earliest occupations with well-defined settlements date to the Late Formative period (c. 400–200 B.C.) and contain nearly pure Ticoman III ceramics, along with some Chupícuaro pottery and figurines.

Classic Period

The Early Classic sites coeval with Teotihuacan's Late Tlamimilolpa through Metepec phases (c. A.D. 300–750) are much more numerous and much larger than the Formative sites. Mastache and Crespo propose that many of these Classic sites are the result of extensive colonization of the Tula region by people who either came from Teotihuacan or had close ties to that city. This occupation appears to have been a gradual process which reached its peak in Late Tlamimilolpa times.

A number of the Early Classic settlements are situated in lime-producing areas, which their inhabitants may have exploited for Teotihuacan. Most Early Classic sites have total areas of around 10 hectares, but there are two centers approaching 100 hectares, and Chingú, 10 kilometers east of Tula, covers nearly 250 hectares and has a large Ciudadela-like plaza and numerous groups of apartment compounds. This site probably functioned as Teotihuacan's provincial center for the entire region. An important aspect of Chingú is that it is surrounded by lands that were potentially irrigated by the largest pre-Hispanic irrigation system yet identified in the Tula region. Surveys elsewhere in the region have found a number of other Early Classic sites near the same irrigation canal system.

Most sites of this period have ceramic complexes nearly identical to those of Teotihuacan, especially Late Tlamimilolpa and Metepec types, besides local pottery, particularly jars (ollas). Corresponding to this period are two settlements near Tepeji del Río that were occupied by people who used pottery very similar to types from Teotihuacan's Oaxaca Barrio, associated with pure Teotihuacan pottery types.

The settlement pattern surveys indicate that the Tula region was part of the direct economic and political orbit of the Teotihuacan state. The irrigation systems and the lime exploitation zones in this region probably played important economic roles in the succeeding Toltec state.

Coyotlatelco Culture

In contrast to the Basin of Mexico, in the Tula area there is notable discontinuity in settlement pattern between the Teotihuacan-related population and the Late Classic Coyotlatelco population (c. A.D. 700–900), suggesting that at least some of the Coyotlatelco people were new arrivals to the region. The major Coyotlatelco sites are generally in different environmental zones from the previous sites; in particular, the high hilltops were occupied for the first time during this period.

These sites have one or more open ceremonial plazas and extensive systems of residential and agricultural terraces. One of the largest settlements is on top of Cerro Magoni immediately west of Tula; it has two large ceremonial plazas and at least 4 square kilometers of residential occupation associated with extensive artificial terraces.

The first large occupation of Tula's urban zone was by Coyotlatelco people who founded a major center at Tula Chico, a mound-plaza complex situated 1.5 kilometers northeast of the principal ceremonial center of the Early Postclassic city. The settled zone surrounding Tula Chico covered about 5 square kilometers and constituted the initial nucleus of the ancient city.

Early Postclassic (A.D. 900–1200)

During the Early Postclassic (which marks the apogee of Tula's city), the area was the heartland of a major state. The complexity of the associated social, economic, and political institutions is manifested both in the size and complicated structure of the ancient city and in the distribution and specific settlement characteristics of the rural population in the city's direct sustaining area. During this period, the city and its rural hinterland formed the economic and political entity that constituted the Toltec state; the cultural processes in the city cannot be explained without investigating the area, and vice versa.

The ancient city is situated in an elevated zone at the confluence of two of the three most important rivers in the region, dominating the alluvial valley and adjacent to extensive irrigated lands; thus, it held a geographic position favorable for military defense and agricultural exploitation. Some sectors of the city—such as the main plaza, which was surrounded by high terraces and platforms bordering cliffs above the river—possessed especially strategic defensive locations.

The city's form, size, and limits varied through time. During its initial stages (the Prado and Corral phases), the main urban nucleus was located on the central hill above the river confluence, especially around the precinct now called Tula Chico. In the Tollan phase apogee, various nearby settlements were incorporated into the urban zone as the city grew. At its height, Tula covered almost 16 square kilometers, with a very nonhomogeneous, irregular topography including large hills, extensive slopes, and lowlands, varying in elevation between 2,005 and 2,060 meters.

Even though the city was not surrounded by a wall or other delimiting structures or topographic formations, its urban limits are quite clear because there are zones without pre-Hispanic occupation, 1 to 3 kilometers wide, adjacent to the city. These zones constitute a kind of frontier between the city and its rural hinterland, and between the urban community and the rural population.

It is interesting that the pre-Hispanic city is situated in the extreme western sector of its rural hinterland. Most zones in the area west of the city have eroded mountainous topography and were essentially unoccupied during the pre-Hispanic era. Most Early Postclassic settlements are in the eastern sector of the area, especially in the extensive alluvial valley northeast of the ancient city. With the city's Tollan phase apogee, there was a notable increase in occupation density in its sustaining area in comparison to the total population and number of sites during the Classic. The Tollan phase rural population extended to zones that had been only partially occupied previously and also colonized new areas and ecological niches for the first time.

The definition of Early Postclassic sites was a difficult problem because some zones during this period have almost uninterrupted occupations, with no clear limits between different settlements. It is clear that the population distribution, and the specific forms of structuring and grouping of sites, express distinct levels of social integration and reflect the area's socio-economic organization. In defining sites, Cobean and Mastache attempted to identify these different levels of social integration, postulating that the defined settlement types really represent some kind of territorial unit or entity that had meaning within the economic and social structure of the Toltec state.

The Tollan phase sites were defined principally on the basis of habitational structures, using as key criteria the distances between these structures and the zones of dispersed archaeological material surrounding them. Fourteen different site types were defined for this period, ranging from concentrated sites with or without ceremonial architecture to various forms of dispersed occupation, which consists of isolated habitational structures or small groups of them. Not surprisingly, dispersed occupations constituted most of the sites in the area during this period; this is a very common kind of rural settlement, and it has been considered the optimal living relationship between the agricultural family unit and its cultivation lands.

The western extreme of the area was sparsely occupied during this period. This zone is covered mainly by ranges of hills (serranías) with altitudes between 2,650 and 2,300 meters. Sites occur principally on the eastern slopes west of the Endí Dam and in the serranía Magoni-Bojay, located to the west and north of the ancient city in zones with thin, poor soils on steep slopes.

Some sites are zones of dispersed archaeological material in small valleys among the hills where there are intermittent or permanent sources of water and strips of land with relatively deep soils. It is significant that various zones of dispersed material are directly associated with canals, such as the Zanja San Miguel and Zanja Xitejí, which were parts of the extensive irrigation system controlled by the town of Xochitlan; during the sixteenth century this system served seven communities, including Tula.

Most of the region's Early Postclassic occupation existed in the alluvial valley northeast of the ancient city. This zone possesses both deep and shallow soils adequate for dry farming, along with strips of deep soils that are potentially irrigable. It was extensively occupied, with numerous settlements surrounding Cerro Xicuco and almost uninterrupted occupation to the north and west up to the Río Tula.

In the southwestern sector of the area, which is almost entirely covered by hills from 2,200 to 2,500 meters high and has eroded shallow soils, the settlements are principally on the lower edges of hills, on slopes, and on summits of low hills. Some sites are near intermittent water sources, and others are next to the Tula and El Salto rivers. The most common sites are small concentrated settlements alternating with zones of dispersed material. To the south and the east of the ancient city of Tula, there are sites near lands that could be irrigated by the old canal systems of La Romera and Zanja Nueva, which are several kilometers long and originate in the Río Tepeji in the extreme south of the Tula region. The settlements in the small valley of the Río El Salto are near land that could be irrigated by the Zanja de El Salto.

The zone east of the Río Salado (which is bordered on the west by a mountain range with altitudes up to 2,800 meters) contains extensive flat areas, especially toward the north where the Valle del Mezquital begins, between the towns of Tlahuelilpan, Atitalaquia, and Tlaxcoapan. Occupations in the extreme north, to the east of the town of Tezontepec, are very dispersed; to the south, on the lower slopes of Cerro la Mesa, there are concentrated settlements associated with deep soils. Also in the south, on the slopes of Mesa Lechugilla, there is a zone of dense occupation extending to the banks of the Río Salado and near intermittent streams. Many of these occupations are near soils suitable for dry farming; near the Río Salado, there are strips of high-quality soils that can be irrigated by traditional canal systems originating in this river.

In the extreme north of the Tula region, on the lower edges of the mountain range that constitutes the northern limit of the area studied, there are many zones of concentrated and dispersed occupation on the lower slopes north of the town of Tepetitlan, between 2,000 and 2,200 meters elevation. The densest occupations in this sector are along an arroyo fed by the *manantial* (artesian spring) El Sabino, which supplies a traditional irrigation system that probably dates to pre-Hispanic times. Small, concentrated sites alternating with dispersed occupations are found on the banks of the Tula and in zones near the confluence of the Tula and Salado rivers.

As part of an excavation program begun in 1984, a habitational structure was excavated at a rural site in the extreme north of the ancient city's support area. This settlement, which is coeval with Tula's Early Postclassic apogee, is situated along the El Sabino *manantial* on the lower edges of the Sierra Taxhuada, which forms the northwestern limit of the Tula region north of the modern town of Tepetitlan. In terms of its internal planning, room distribution, architecture, and dimensions, the excavated habitation is very similar to the residences in the city of Tula that Healan calls "house groups." These buildings consist of a sunken central patio surrounded by domestic structures, each of which corresponds to an individual house having several rooms of different dimensions. Surely these compounds, like the house groups in the ancient city, were occupied by several related nuclear families who lived in the individual houses.

The well-preserved state of the excavated structure made possible the identification of numerous primary contexts and activity areas, most of which involved the preparation and consumption of food. Many plant remains were preserved, including amaranth, different races of maize, various types of beans (*Phaseolus*), agaves (especially *maguey*), nopal, and chile. Even though it is difficult to use the single excavated structure at Tepetitlan to generalize about rural Tollan phase habitation units, the excavations recovered much information concerning the production and consumption of different classes of artifacts by its inhabitants, and also concerning similarities with and differences from Tula's urban population.

Diverse production areas were identified in the region's settlements, almost always associated with habitational structures. To the northwest of the urban zone in the area of Daxthí, a site was located whose inhabitants specialized in the production of ground stone implements (*manos, metates,* and *mortars*), using basalt from nearby outcrops. Apparently these ground stone tools were distributed around the area, as were the chert bifaces produced in a site near the Río Salado on the eastern boundary of the area. Even though the latter site was not excavated, the surface data show that knapping debitage from chert bifaces extends over much of the settlement, suggesting that many individuals worked at this activity.

Estimates of the Tollan phase population in the ancient city's support area, though approximate and tentative, suggest that as much as 70 percent of the total population in the Tula area during this period lived in the city, and that the dispersed and concentrated rural sites contained only about 30 to 40 percent of the area's inhabitants.

Studies of the potential for irrigation in the region have produced two different estimates: a very conservative calculation of potentially irrigated land is approximately 3,000 hectares; another calculation, based on the maximum capacity for irrigation in the area using preindustrial technology, projects an area as large as 10,000 hectares. Resolving the difference is crucial for determining the type of agriculture that constituted the subsistence base for the city and rural sites during the Early Postclassic. A realistic estimate of irrigated lands in the region during the city's apogee is probably between 5,000 and 6,000 hectares, which would have supported approximately half the regional population, with the rest depending on dry farming.

It is important to emphasize that these estimates of agricultural potential fundamentally take into account the production capacity for grains in the case of both irrigation and dry farming. It is probable that both systems (especially dry farming) were more complex in terms of variety of crops. Above all, we must take into account that medium- and poor-quality soils predominate in the region; these are not optimal for maize farming but are adequate for plants that are more resistant to drought, frost, and shallow soils, such as amaranth and *maguey*, which have high nutritional value.

It is probable that the exploitation of *maguey* as a source of drink and perhaps of food may have begun here in the Coyotlatelco occupation, before the emergence of Tula as a densely populated urban center; in subsequent periods the cultivation of this *maguey* was very important. The investigations of Jeffrey and Mary Parsons emphasize the high nutritional value and diverse uses of *maguey*, along with its potential importance in pre-Hispanic times as a complementary and alternative food, above all during times of drought. The importance of amaranth in the Tula region during the Early Postclassic is evidenced by plant remains in both rural and urban archaeological contexts and by pollen analyses.

Population estimates for city and region, specific patterns of site distribution, and the locations of distinct soil classes and potentially irrigated lands suggest that besides the rural population, at least one-third of the city's inhabitants were involved in the production of food. Even though the direct interaction area of the city ought to have constituted the subsistence base for the urban inhabitants, it is probable that during its apogee its growing population required supplementary resources from neighboring regions, such as the northern Basin of Mexico, and from other zones that were subject to Tula or constituted integral parts of the Toltec state. This broad area thus formed a second ring of sustaining lands for the production of food and the other resources.

Late Postclassic (A.D. 1200–1520)

The nature of the transition between the Tollan phase occupation in the region and the initial Aztec occupations is unclear. Tula's Early Postclassic city probably collapsed toward the end of twelfth century A.D. Acosta attributes the destruction of the Toltec city to people using Aztec II pottery because he found great quantities of Aztec II sherds associated with burning and looting in his excavations of the main plaza. However, there are no important Aztec II occupations in the rest of urban zone or in the Tula region.

The first significant Aztec occupation in the region and in Tula itself is Aztec III; these sites are much more numerous, varied, and extensive in terms of settlement pattern than those of any preceding period. Zones were occupied that had not been inhabited previously, especially in the mountainous western sector. The main Aztec III center for the region was Tula, which probably constituted a small city during this period. By the fourteenth century, the Tula area was controlled by the Tepanecs of Azcapotzalco; with the defeat of that center by the Mexica, the region was divided among the Aztec provinces of Jilotepec, Atotonilco, and Ajacuba.

FURTHER READINGS

Acosta, J. R. 1956–57. Interpretación de algunos datos obtenidos en Tula relativos a la epoca Tolteca. *Revista Mexicana de Estudios Antropológicos* 14:75–110.

Cobean, R. H., and A. G. Mastache. 1989. The Late Classic and Early Postclassic Chronology of the Tula Region. In D. M. Healan (ed.), *Tula of the Toltecs: Excavations and Survey*, pp. 34–48. Iowa City: University of Iowa Press.

Crespo, A. M., and A. G. Mastache. 1981. La presencia en el area de Tula, Hgo. de grupos relacionados con el Barrio de Oaxaca en Teotihuacan. In E. C. Rattray et al. (eds.), *Interacción cultural en México Central*, pp. 99–106. Mexico City: Universidad Nacional Autónoma de México.

Díaz O., C. L. 1980. *Chingú: Un sitio clásico del área de Tula*. Colección Científica, 90. Mexico City: Instituto Nacional de Antropología e Historia.

Healan, D. M. (ed.). 1989. *Tula of the Toltecs: Excavations and Survey*. Iowa City: University of Iowa Press.

Mastache, A. G. 1976. Sistemas de riego en el area de Tula, Hgo. In *Proyecto Tula, Part 2*. Colección Científica, 33. Mexico City: Instituto Nacional de Antropología e Historia.

Mastache, A. G., and A. M. Crespo. 1974. La ocupación prehispánica en el area de Tula, Hgo. In *Proyecto Tula, Part 1*, pp. 71–103. Colección Científica, 15. Mexico City: Instituto Nacional de Antropología e Historia.

———, ———. 1982. Análisis sobre la traza general de Tula, Hgo. In *Estudios sobre la antigua ciudad de Tula*, pp. 11–38. Colección Científica, 121. Mexico City: Instituto Nacional de Antropología e Historia.

Parsons, J. R., and M. H. Parsons. 1990. *Maguey Utilization in Highland Central Mexico*. Anthropological Papers, Museum of Anthropology, no. 82. Ann Arbor: University of Michigan.

Porter, M. N. 1956. *Excavations at Chupícuaro, Guanajuato, Mexico.* Transactions of the American Philosophical Society, 46. Philadelphia.

Vaillant, G. C. 1931. *Excavations at Ticoman.* Anthropological Papers of the American Museum of Natural History, 32. 2. New York.

Alba Guadalupe Mastache Flores and Robert H. Cobean

SEE ALSO

Tollan; Toltec Culture; Tula Region

Tulum (Quintana Roo, Mexico)

The Postclassic Maya center of Tulum overlooks the Caribbean Sea from a clifftop on the eastern coast of the Yucatán Peninsula. First occupied about A.D. 1200, Tulum was probably founded as a port for coastal trade. It is protected by a system of high stone walls on its landward sides, which enclose an area of about 6.4 hectares. Seagoing canoes could approach Tulum through a breach in the barrier reef and pull ashore on the undefended beach. Within the walls are a permanent water source and crudely built palaces and temples. Two of these, the Palace of the Frescos and the Temple of the Diving God, are decorated with murals and stucco reliefs, some dating to the late fifteenth century. Tulum may have been one of the inhabited towns seen by the first Spanish explorers of Yucatán as their ships sailed up this coast in 1518.

FURTHER READINGS

Lothrop, S. K. 1924. *Tulum: An Archaeological Study of the East Coast of Yucatán.* Carnegie Institution of Washington, Publication 335. Washington, D.C.

Miller, A. G. 1982. *On the Edge of the Sea: Mural Painting at Tancah-Tulum, Quintana Roo, Mexico.* Washington, D.C.: Dumbarton Oaks.

Sanders, W. T. 1960. Prehistoric Ceramics and Settlement Patterns in Quintana Roo, Mexico. Carnegie Institution of Washington, Publication 606; *Contributions to American Anthropology and History* 60:155–264. Washington, D.C.

Vargas P., E. 1984. Consideraciones generales sobre las fortificaciones militares en Tulúm, Quintana Roo, Mexico. *Estudios de Cultura Maya* 15:29–54.

David L. Webster

SEE ALSO

Maya Lowlands: North

Tumben-Naranjal

See Naranjal and Environs

Turkeys

Two species of turkey are native to Mesoamerica. One is the ocellated turkey of the tropical Lowland Maya region. The other is the common wild turkey, whose range extends from forested North America south to Central Mexico. The ocellated turkey seems never to have been domesticated, but the common wild turkey was domesticated by the Indians of both North America and Mesoamerica; unfortunately, we still do not know when, or in how many separate regions, this first took place.

Turkey bones occur at Formative sites in the Basin of Mexico, but it is not known whether they were wild or domestic. Our first solid evidence for domestic turkey comes from areas such as the Valley of Tehuacán (Puebla) and the Valley of Oaxaca, which were apparently outside the natural range of the wild turkey. In both valleys, remains of domestic turkeys appear between 150 B.C. and A.D. 150 and increase in number over time. At the time of the Spanish conquest, domestic turkeys were used as a meat source, as a source of eggs and feathers, and as an animal for sacrifice.

Kent V. Flannery

SEE ALSO

Fauna

Tututepec del Sur (Oaxaca, Mexico)

Tututepec (called Yucudzaa in Mixtec) was a powerful Postclassic period (A.D. 800–1521) city-state in the Mixteca de la Costa region. Most of what is known about Tututepec comes from the Mixtec codices and early Colonial documents. Archaeological survey suggests that Tututepec was first occupied during the Late Formative (400–100 B.C.) but remained a small settlement until the Postclassic. The codices record that the famous Mixtec ruler 8 Deer "Jaguar Claw" resided at Tututepec during the late eleventh century. While 8 Deer's role at Tututepec has been debated, his arrival on the coast from his birthplace of Tilantongo may have been related to the Mixtec expansion into the coastal region and the rise of the Postclassic Tututepec Empire. The ethnohistoric record indicates that the Tututepec domain covered an area of 25,000 square kilometers, including much of the southwestern coast of Oaxaca. Although Tututepec was apparently ruled by

T

Mixtec nobles, its domain included Mixtec, Chatino, Zapotec, Chontal, and probably Nahuatl speakers. The codices show that the rulers of Tututepec attempted to expand against nearby polities, attacking towns as distant as Achiutla in the Mixteca Alta and Zaachila in the Valley of Oaxaca. Like many Postclassic Mixtec centers, Tututepec has only a single monumental building: a large platform on which the Colonial church was built. Twelve carved stones have been placed on this structure, including the well-documented Monument 6.

FURTHER READINGS

O'Mack, S. 1990. Reconocimiento arqueológico en Tututepec, Oaxaca. *Notas Mesoamericanas* 12:19–38.

Smith, M. E. 1973. *Picture Writing from Ancient Southern Mexico: Mixtec Place Signs and Maps.* Norman: University of Oklahoma Press.

Spores, R. 1993. Tututepec: A Postclassic-Period Mixtec Conquest State. *Ancient Mesoamerica* 4:167–174.

Arthur A. Joyce

SEE ALSO
Mixteca-Puebla Style

Tuxtla Region
See Matacapan and the Tuxtla Region

Tuxtla Statuette

The Tuxtla Statuette, an 18-cm-tall figurine of green nephrite, came to light in 1902 when it was turned up during plowing of a farm field near San Andres Tuxtla in southeastern Veracruz state, Mexico. It is presently part of the collection of the National Museum of Natural History, Smithsonian Institution. The object represents what appears to be a human in the guise of a duck, with bill and wings, and bears sixty-four hieroglyphs engraved on its front, sides, and back. The Tuxtla Statuette has proven to be of great importance for the history of writing and calendrics in Mesoamerica, and also for its apparent implications for rulership and shamanism in the Late Formative period.

The "Epi-Olmec" hieroglyphic inscription on the Tuxtla Statuette is in the same script as that on La Mojarra Stela 1, and analyses by Winfield Capitaine and Justeson and Kaufman indicate close relationships between the two objects in terms of both chronology and content. The Tuxtla Statuette bears a long count date of 8.6.2.4.17 (equated to March 14, A.D. 162, in the Gregorian calen-

dar), represented solely by bar-and-dot numbers for the five periods, as is typical of calendrical notations of the La Mojarra stela and others of this general time and region.

FURTHER READINGS

Justeson, J. S., and T. Kaufman. 1993. A Decipherment of Epi-Olmec Hieroglyphic Writing. *Science* 259:1665–1796.

Winfield Capitaine, F. 1987. *La Estela 1 de La Mojarra, Veracruz, Mexico.* Research Reports in Ancient Maya Writing, 16. Washington, D.C.: Center for Maya Research.

George Stuart

SEE ALSO
Gulf Lowlands: South Region; Mojarra, La

Tzintzuntzan (Michoacán, Mexico)

Tzintzuntzan was the capital of the Tarascan Empire, which controlled a large portion of West Mexico at the time of Spanish contact. The Tarascans are generally considered to have been the foremost enemy of the Aztecs, and, like that of the Aztecs, their civilization emerged after A.D. 1350. The capital is known to us primarily from archaeological, ethnohistoric, and historic sources dating to the last century before the Conquest (A.D. 1450–1520), when the empire was dominated by a hereditary dynasty ruling from Tzintzuntzan. In the primary sixteenth-century document that describes Tarascan society, the *Relación de Michoacán* (written in 1541 in the Tarascan capital), the creation of the Tarascan state is attributed to the legendary culture-hero Taríacuri. To the modern observer, Taríacuri's and the empire's most visible legacy is the capital city, Tzintzuntzan, "place of the hummingbird." It is situated in the Lake Pátzcuaro Basin and is now a zona arqueológica under the supervision of the Mexican Instituto Nacional de Antropología e Historia (INAH).

Although present-day Tzintzuntzan is a small town (famous for its greenware pottery), archaeological survey and excavation since 1930 have revealed that in 1522, when the first Spaniards arrived, it was a thriving city of 25,000 to 35,000 people, who inhabited almost seven square kilometers of land along the lakeshore and the lower slopes of two large volcanic hills. Within the city were distinct residential zones for the royal dynasty and upper nobility, the lower levels of the nobility, and the commoners. There were specialized workshops for the production both of goods used by most households in the city and of highly valued objects used only by the nobility or in state ritual. While there is evidence of small temple complexes within commoner barrios, the primary public ritual of the city was focused on the main ceremonial platform, now the Zona Arqueológica de Tzintzuntzan.

The earliest modern description of this main ceremonial complex was published by Nicolás León in 1888. The largest platform (450 by 250 meters) exhibits the basic characteristics of Tarascan architecture, which is characterized by large artificial platforms on which were built one or more stepped pyramids. The platforms and pyramids were constructed of rubble-core volcanic stone and faced with dressed stone. Whenever possible, the natural slope of a hill was terraced to produce platforms with minimal building effort but maximal size—in this case, more than 450 meters wide; when faced with dressed stone and viewed from below, these constructions were monumental in impact. From the center front of the platform a ramp extends in a series of sloping terraces toward the northwest. Several small structures were located at the top of the ramp. Five specialized, keyhole-shaped pyramid platforms, called *yácata* in the Tarascan language (or *purépecha*), were constructed along the east side of the platform surface. The *yácatas* were faced with dressed basalt and often covered with petroglyphs. They were dedicated to the Tarascan sun god, Curicaueri (a deity similar to the Aztec patron, Huitzilopochtli), and his four brothers, the Tiripeme. Temples of wood were constructed on top of these platforms. Over time the pyramids were enlarged; four, or perhaps five, superpositions are visible on Yácata 5, one of the four pyramids reconstructed by INAH.

The main platform contains evidence of several elite burial chambers (fifty-eight to sixty-one burials have been excavated), a room complex (Edificio B) believed to have housed the high priests, storehouses, and treasuries. Illustrations in the *Relación de Michoacán* indicate that most buildings were of wood, often with stone foundations, and had roofs of wood or straw. Temples and elite residences included carved wooden lintels and posts and painted posts and walls. The documents indicate that a skull rack and large sacrificial stones were also erected on the platform. An ossuary was located just off the northeast side of the platform; long bones (femurs) and skull fragments excavated there show evidence of holes for stringing, indicating that more than just the skulls of sacrificial victims were placed on display.

At the neighboring site of Ihuatzio, a number of stone sculptures have been found. These include three *chac mool* forms and an animal sculpture (53 cm high) generally interpreted as a coyote (Ihuatzio means "place of the coyote"). These basalt sculptures are stiff and formal, with little detail indicated. Sculptures similar to these were largely destroyed by the Spaniards in the first years of contact because of their association with native ritual, including human sacrifice. Like the temple architecture, they are simple but powerful expressions of the patron gods, especially the earthly representative of Curicaueri, the Tarascan king. Unlike Ihuatzio, however, there is no evidence of ball courts in the Tarascan capital, although the ball game (*querehta*) survived in some Sierra Tarasca communities until this century, and many other ball courts (*querétaros*) are known from other Tarascan centers.

The Tarascan capital was both the primary settlement which received large quantities of tributary goods from communities throughout the empire and a center of specialized craft production and market exchange. Within the city, imperial tribute was collected and deposited in granaries, in chests in the palace, and in the residences of special deputies. Goods were redistributed by the king (*cazonci*) and his administration in the form of religious offerings, support for the army, major feasts, gifts to foreign emissaries, and support for his household. However, the primary services produced in the settlement were activities of the functionaries of the state: members of the state bureaucracy, priests of the patron deities, doctors, herbalists, custodians of the palace, storytellers, merchants, spies, messengers, and couriers.

Much of our knowledge of Tarascan society in the capital comes from the material remains of smaller objects associated with households, burials, and public architecture. Small objects—ear and lip plugs, beads, and pendants—of carved and polished obsidian (red, green, gray, and striated), turquoise, quartz crystal, bone, marine shell, opal, serpentine, jadeite, and pyrite were used for personal adornment by members of high social status. They were also used as offerings and ritual paraphernalia in public celebrations of the state religion. Common designs included nonrepresentational lines, spirals, and dots, similar to those found on decorated pottery, but a number of animal effigies and human masks were also made. Rare and precious stones were also used as inlay and mosaics in metal and wooden objects.

Gold, silver, copper, and bronze alloys were made into bells, beads, pendants, pins, disks, animal effigies, masks, figurines, and a variety of tools (such as needles, awls, tweezers, axes, punches, and fishhooks). Ores were smelted and both cold-hammered and cast using the lost wax process. Decoration was produced by gilding, embossing, soldering, and (probably false) filigreeing. In style and form, Tarascan metalwork was different from that of contemporary Central and Southern Mexico, reflecting both the long West Mexican metallurgical tradition and specific Tarascan design canons.

Much of Tarascan art was on perishable materials that have rarely survived. Our knowledge of them is limited largely to descriptions and illustrations in early historic documents. Thus, relatively little can be said about their techniques of manufacture, design elements or their social meaning. While our greatest information pertains to woodwork, featherwork, and textiles, tribute lists include carved gourds, basketry, leatherwork, and rare animal skins. Large carved and painted gourds were carried on the backs of high priests during major rituals.

Tarascans utilized wood as the primary building material, unlike the peoples to the east and south, who relied on wattle-and-daub, adobe brick, and stone. Wood was also used for furniture, house posts, canoes, weapons, ceremonial drums, and figurines. Illustrations in the *Relación de Michoacán* indicate that furniture—especially stools and storage chests—and house posts were painted and carved. House posts are shown painted in geometric patterns of alternating bands of red, white, yellow, and blue. The Tarascan king, chief minister, and major priests carried carved and painted staffs adorned with feathers and stone spearpoints. From Spanish tribute lists and occasional archaeological preservation, it is known that objects of wood were inlaid with precious stones, and that lacquer decoration was also used.

Feather-working was a highly specialized and prestigious occupation. Feathers of both local and exotic tropical birds were used to decorate costumes, shields, standards, and spears of noble warriors. Feathered capes and headdresses were worn by the royal rulers for major public rituals, and standards carried into battle by units of Tarascan warriors representing different wards or villages were uniform in design, bearing alternating red and white bands. Shields were decorated with bull's-eye designs in alternating circles of white and red. Elite warriors may have carried shields with specific symbols, but the sixteenth-century illustrations are not clear enough to tell.

Tarascan textiles were made of woven *maguey* fiber and cotton. Like all Mesoamerican cloth, these were woven on backstrap looms in varying widths, depending on the nature of the garment or blanket being produced. Pottery spindle whorls are common artifacts at Tarascan sites and in elite female burials, suggesting that women, both commoner and elite, produced most of the cloth. Most fabric shown in the *Relación* illustrations is either colored in alternating bands of red, blue, yellow, or white, or (for some ceremonial robes) woven in a stepped fret or checkerboard pattern. In two illustrations of robes worn by a Tarascan leader, a large red circle is shown on the upper back; each has a central red dot and red lines or triangles radiating from the red circle. Small remnants of cotton cloth, which were preserved because of their contact with copper bells sewn to the cloth, indicate that elite and ritual garments were probably embellished with metalwork, stone beads and pendants, and featherwork.

The most abundant medium for the expression of Tarascan beliefs and styles was fired clay. Pottery vessels, tobacco pipes, spindle whorls, beads and pendants, figurines, and musical instruments were among the objects made of clay. Pottery vessels included a range of bowls, plates, and jars that were common in Postclassic Mesoamerica. Certain forms were restricted to the elite, were used for ritual offerings, or were part of major religious and political ceremonies; these are highly decorated, finely finished, and particularly characteristic of Protohistoric Tarascan art. Of note are miniature bowls with tripod supports (3–6 cm in diameter), miniature jars, modeled jars in animal and plant forms, spouted vessels with solid or hollow handles (with or without supports), and spouted vessels in animal (often bird) form. The variety of form and decorative treatment characteristic of pottery is also found among clay pipes, which were used by priests and other members of the nobility in association with religious ceremonies; large quantities of pipe fragments have been found near the main ceremonial platform at Tzintzuntzan.

Unlike that of other prehistoric Mexican cities, the initial growth of Tzintzuntzan appears to have been stimulated by political/religious rather than economic factors. It was an administrative city in which political and religious functions were central, and economic activity was embedded within or peripheral to the basic power structure. The distribution of population within the city, the location of major public buildings, and the choice of buildings to receive significant investment of labor and materials all reflect the centrality of political, not economic, activities. The most prominent archaeological features of the settlement, the two large artificial platforms, were associated with these two powerful components of the city—the king's palace on the Santa Ana platform, and the temples of Curicaueri on the main platform. Their significance was clearly recognized by the Spanish, who first occupied the priests' residences on the main platform in 1522 and built the first Catholic chapel (Santa Ana) on the palace platform in 1525.

To this administrative city whose political and economic power depended on the flow of imperial tribute, the Spanish conquest, with its usurpation of tribute and labor outside Michoacán, was a major blow. When Archbishop Vasco de Quiroga moved the seat of regional administrative and religious power to Pátzcuaro in 1540, most of the remaining craft specialists and members of the Tarascan nobility abandoned Tzintzuntzan. After 1580, when the ascendant Spanish elite moved the regional capital to Morelia (then called Valladolid), the entire Pátzcuaro Basin became increasingly marginalized. Only the archaeological remains, historic documents, and twentieth-century reestablishment as a *municipio cabecera* are left to proclaim the imperial status Tzintzuntzan held in 1522.

FURTHER READINGS

Cabrera Castro, R. 1987. Tzintzuntzan: Décima temporada de excavaciones. In *Homenaje a Román Piña Chan,* pp. 531–565. Universidad Nacional Autónoma de México, Instituto de Investigaciones Antropológicas, Serie Antropológica, 79. Mexico City.

Castro-Leal, M., C. L. Díaz, and M. T. García. 1989. Los Tarascos. In E. Florescano (ed.), *Historia General de Michoacán,* vol. 1, pp. 193–304. Morelia: Gobierno del Estado de Michoacán.

Miranda, F. (ed.). 1980 [1541]. *La Relación de Michoacán.* Morelia: Estudios Michoacános V. Fimax.

Pollard, H. P. 1993. *Tariacuri's Legacy: The Prehispanic Tarascan State.* Norman: University of Oklahoma Press.

Warren, J. B. 1985. *The Conquest of Michcacan.* Norman: University of Oklahoma Press.

Helen Perlstein Pollard

SEE ALSO

Michoacán Region; Tarascan Culture and Religion

U

Uaxactun (Petén, Guatemala)

This Maya center, situated 24 kilometers north of Tikal, was first reported by Sylvanus G. Morley in 1916; he gave it the Maya name Uaxactun ("8 stone") because of the discovery of Stela 9, which records a date in the eighth cycle of the Maya calendar. The site was occupied from the Middle Formative to the end of Late Classic times and consists of a series of of architectural groups situated on five low hills or ridges, surrounded by a dense scatter of house platforms.

Investigations of the site between 1926 and 1937 by researchers from the Carnegie Institution concentrated principally on Groups A, B, and E. It was determined that Group E had an astronomical alignment that corresponded to observations of the solstices and equinoxes. An earlier substructure in this group (E-VII-sub), dating to the Late Formative, has a stairway on each of its four sides; flanking both sides of each stairway are large stuccoed masks (sixteen in all) that depict a cosmological being. Investigations in groups A and B exposed a complex of temples, palaces, and monuments. One interior room of Structure B-XIII has a painted mural depicting a royal visit. The extensive excavations during the period 1983–1985 in Group H revealed an important Formative structure, also decorated with large modeled stucco masks.

The Formative period at Uaxactun is divided into two phases, Mamom (500–250 B.C.) and Chicanel (250 B.C.–A.D. 250). The occupation began with the Mamom phase, when small plaforms were constructed to support simple houses; well-made ceramics and adornments of shell, bone, and stone were in use, and people were interred in simple burials. In the succeeding Chicanel phase, wealth and differences in status increased and ceremonial life became more elaborate. Large pyramidal platforms were constructed, some with façades decorated with large stucco masks and elaborate friezes, such as exist in Groups E and H. The astronomical complex in Group E was in use.

The Classic period is divided into two main phases that are broken down into subdivisions: Tzakol 1, 2 and 3 (A.D. 250–600), and Tepeu 1, 2, and 3 (A.D. 600–800). By Early Classic Tzakol times, Uaxactun was a major center with sculpted monuments, temples, palaces, and a ball court. Elaborate burials indicate the growing importance of the elite. The tomb offerings included costly jade ornaments, fine polychrome vessels, and ritual objects. However, the hieroglyphic texts of stelae 5 and 22 indicate that in A.D. 378 Uaxactun was taken over by the ruler of Tikal, whose name is read as "Smoking Frog." Some controversy exists over whether this event was actually a conquest; if it was, it provides the earliest evidence of forced takeover by an expansionist power in the Maya area. Whether by conquest, marriage, or other means, Uaxactun clearly came under the control of Tikal for the rest of the Early Classic period.

The dynastic sequence at Uaxactun during the Late Classic is not entirely clear, owing to the almost total absence of royal tombs and the poor preservation of carved monuments. A cessation in the practice of erecting dedicatory monuments to rulers at the site is apparent at the beginning of Late Classic, between A.D. 554 and 711. However, construction of buildings and religious ceremonies continued. The burials of important people are no longer associated with such lavish offerings and funerary rites as was the case during the Early Classic, probably an indication of reduced prestige and rank.

U

By the middle of Late Classic there was new vigor at Uaxactun, evident in population increase, new construction, and remodeling of old structures. More residential areas sprang up in the outlying zones, and much effort went into new plaza groups and buildings throughout the site. The fine quality of architecture and the number of sculpted monuments concentrated in groups A and B indicate that a new elite governing body was in residence, exercised centralized authority, and controlled local economic and political activity.

The end of the Late Classic period was a time of marked decline in population throughout Uaxactun. Only a few, relatively exclusive burials have been found, these in Structure A-V. Stela 5, the last inscribed monument at the site, indicates that the local elite maintained their power until A.D. 889, and that they had close ties with Tikal. Following this Uaxactun was virtually abandoned, although a few burials in collapsed buildings indicate that some people remained in residence in groups A and B into Early Postclassic times.

A site map and extensive excavations were financed by the Carnegie Institution of Washington between 1926 and 1937. Among those who participated were Frans Blom, Tatiana Proskouriakoff, Oliver Ricketson, Edwin M. Shook, A. Ledyard Smith, Robert E. Smith, and Robert Wauchope. The cultural chronology and the names of the archaeological phases were worked out at this time, based on the calendrical inscriptions, pottery sequence, and architectural development. This sequence became the basic framework for Maya sites in the Petén area. Between 1983 and 1985, the Guatemalan Instituto de Antropología e Historia sponsored a program of further research and consolidation of the ruins at Uaxactun under the direction of Juan Antonio Valdés.

FURTHER READINGS

Adams, R. E. W. 1974. A Trial Estimation of Classic Maya Palace Populations at Uaxactun. In N. Hammond (ed.), *Mesoamerican Archaeology*, pp. 285–296. Austin: University of Texas Press.

Kidder, A. V. 1947. *The Artifacts of Uaxactun, Guatemala.* Carnegie Institution of Washington, Publication 576. Washington, D.C.

Proskouriakoff, T. 1946. *An Album of Maya Architecture.* Carnegie Institution of Washington, Publication 558. Washington, D.C.

———. 1950. *A Study of Classic Maya Sculpture.* Carnegie Institution of Washington, Publication 593. Washington, D.C.

Puleston, D. E. 1974. Intersite Areas in the Vicinity of Tikal and Uaxactun. In N. Hammond (ed.), *Mesoamerican Archaeology*, pp. 303–311. Austin: University of Texas Press.

Ricketson, O. G., E. B. Ricketson et al. 1937. *Uaxactun, Guatemala: Group E, 1926–1931.* Carnegie Institution of Washington, Publication 477. Washington, D.C.

Smith, A. L. 1937. *Structure A-XVIII, Uaxactun.* Carnegie Institution of Washington, Publication 483, Contribution 20. Washington, D.C.

———. 1950. *Uaxactun, Guatemala: Excavations of 1931–1937.* Carnegie Institution of Washington, Publication 588. Washington, D.C.

———. 1965. *Ceramic Sequence at Uaxactun, Guatemala.* 2 vols. Middle American Research Institute Publications, 20. New Orleans: Tulane University.

Smith, R. E., and J. C. Gifford. 1966. *Maya Ceramic Varieties, Types, and Wares at Uaxactun.* Supplement to *Ceramic Sequence at Uaxactun, Guatemala.* Middle American Research Institute Publication 28. New Orleans: Tulane University.

Valdés, J. A. 1988. Breve historia de la arquitectura de Uaxactun a la luz de nuevas investigaciones. *Journal de la Société des Américanistes* 74:7–23.

Wauchope, Robert. 1934. House Mounds of Uaxactun, Guatemala. *Carnegie Institution of Washington, Contributions to American Archaeology* 2(7):107–160.

Marion Popenoe de Hatch

SEE ALSO
Maya Lowlands: South

Underworld

Caves had multiple functions and meanings for pre-Hispanic peoples: shelters, living sites, ritual places associated with lineage and passage rites, solar observatories, quarries, dwellings of the gods of water and those of death, mouth or womb of the earth, underworld, or fantastic space. Creation myths related caves to sun, moon, foodstuffs, and the emergence of human groups. Caves were entrances to the underworld (and therefore, funerary chambers), but also an access to the womb of the earth, and thus a place where fertility rites took place. Water petition ceremonies for good harvests were conducted in caves, where water spirits dwelt.

The sixteenth-century Maya spoke of a subterranean place called Mitnal or Xibalbá. Many difficult passages were encountered by those who descended to it. For the Maya, "the ballcourts themselves opened into the Otherworld . . . Thus the ball court was not only a place of sacrifice; it was an entry portal to the time and space of the last Creation" (Freidel, Schele, and Parker 1993:350, 352). Similarly, the entrance of 8 Deer to the Mixtec underworld, house of One Death, was said to have begun in the ball court, continuing past violent watercourses, a curved mountain, a building in fire, and a fight with strange beings. The underworld of the Maya, and probably also of Formative and Early Classic Mesoamerica in general, was a watery place; the presence of aquatic plants, turtles, and frogs suggests clear, slow-moving water.

The Nahua of the central highlands of Mexico and elsewhere identified three aspects of the underworld: Mictlan, Tlillan, and Tlalocan. Mictlan was situated to the north and was guarded by a divine couple, Mictlantecuhtli and Mictecacíhuatl. The Nahua thought that the sun entered Mictlan during the first month of its zenith passage, Tóxcatl (in May), a prelude to the rainy season; the observatories in Building P at Monte Albán, Xochicalco, and the "Astronomical Cave" at Teotihuacan were used to observe these zenith passages. The underworld of Tlillan was an artificial cave, home of the goddess Cihuacóatl, an old goddess of the earth and also the rain god Tlaloc's wife.

The underworld of Tlalocan was conceptualized in various ways among the Nahua of Central Mexico, according to Anderson. In the Florentine Codex, it is depicted as a place of no suffering, great wealth, and abundant maize, squash, amaranth, chile, and flowers; the "Prayer to Tlaloc" says that sustenance has not disappeared, but rather the gods have hidden it in Tlalocan. In several examples of Nahuatl poetry, it is portrayed as a place of beauty, where birds with lovely feathers sing on top of pyramids of jade. It is also described as a building consisting of four rooms around a patio, with four containers filled with water; one is good, and the other three are associated with frosts, sterility, and drought. Durán mentions that this Tlalocan was represented on Mount Tlaloc, in the eastern fringe of the Basin of Mexico, as a walled enclosure with a patio and a figure representing Tlaloc, around which were placed smaller figures representing the lesser mountains. Finally, Tlalocan was thought of as an underground space filled with water which connected the mountains with the sea—a place where rivers originated. Durán and Tezozómoc mention that Tlalocan and Cincalco could be the same concept: one enters them through a cave.

FURTHER READINGS

Anderson, A. J. O. 1988. A Look into Tlalocan. In J. K. Josserand and K. Dakin (eds.), *Smoke and Mist. Mesoamerican Studies in Memory of Thelma D. Sullivan,* pp. 151–159. BAR International Series, 402. Oxford.

Broda, J. 1982. Astronomy, *Cosmovisión,* and Ideology in Pre-Hispanic Mesoamerica. In A. F. Aveni and G. Urton (eds.), *Ethnoastronomy and Archaeo-astronomy in the American Tropics* (*Annals of the New York Academy of Science* 385), pp. 81–110. New York.

Durán, D. 1994 [1581]. *The History of the Indies of New Spain.* D. Heyden (trans. and ed.). Norman: University of Oklahoma Press.

Freidel, D., L. Schele, and J. Parker. 1993. *Maya Cosmos: Three Thousand Years on the Shaman's Path.* New York: William Morrow.

Graulich, M. 1987. *Mythes et rituels du Mexique ancien préhispanique.* Mémoires de la Classe des Lettres, Colléction in-8, 2nd series, vol. 67, fasc. 3. Brussels: Palais des Académies.

Heyden, D. 1981. Caves, Gods, and Myths: World Views and Planning in Teotihuacan. In E. P. Benson (ed.), *Mesoamerican Sites and World Views,* pp. 1–39. Washington, D.C.: Dumbarton Oaks.

Sullivan, T. D. 1965. A Prayer to Tláloc. *Estudios de Cultura Náhuatl* 5:39–55.

Linda Manzanilla

Usumacinta River Dams Project

One of the greatest dangers to the archaeological sites along the Usumacinta River of Guatemala and Mexico is the recurrent proposal to build a series of huge hydroelectric dams on this international border. No other single construction project in the Lacandón Forest or the Petén region has had such potentially far-reaching archaeological consequences.

First proposed in Mexico during the 1960s, the project had by the mid-1980s been subject to formal binational feasibility studies that were notably devoid of archaeological impact assessments or consultation, but which resulted in the plan to establish as much as 1,315 square kilometers of reservoirs behind live dams along a 525-kilometer portion of the Usumacinta River system (see map). About two-thirds of this immense flood zone is in Guatemala, and one-third in Mexico.

The project would affect hundreds of small and largely uncharted sites as well as many large ones, including

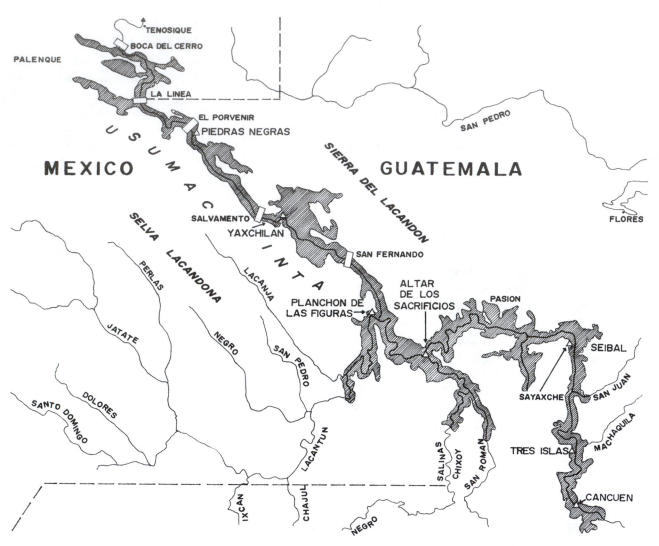

Proposed dam locations and basins on the Usumacinta River, showing relation to important archaeological sites. Illustration after Wilkerson 1991.

Piedras Negras, Yaxchilan, Altar de Sacrificios, Aguas Calientes, Tres Islas, Cancuen, and to some extent Seibal. Potentially more damaging, not only to the threatened riverbank sites but also to many others situated away from waterways, would be secondary effects ensuing from construction, such as the proliferation of access roads, encroachment by numerous new population centers, wholesale forest clearing, and the inevitable acceleration of looting. The proposal has been revived by each Mexican administration and sporadically opposed by national environmental and some international scientific groups. It is bound to be a contentious issue for years to come.

FURTHER READINGS

Wilkerson, S. J. K. 1985. The Usumacinta River: Troubles on a Wild Frontier, *National Geographic Magazine* 168: 514–543.

S. Jeffrey K. Wilkerson

SEE ALSO

Maya Lowlands: South

Utatlán (Quiché, Guatemala)

This site holds the remains of the capital of the Quiché Maya kingdom, built up about A.D. 1400 during the rule of Feathered Serpent (Q'ukumatz), one of the Quiché's most famous kings. Utatlán is the site's Nahua name; its meaning, "place of the reeds," is very similar to that of its Quiché Mayan name, Q'umarkaaj. The site extends for about 7 square kilometers over several adjacent plateaus in the central highlands of Guatemala. Architectural remains consist largely of lineage council houses, temple mounds and shrines, and elite residences ("palaces"). Traces of elaborate painted murals have been found on the buried palace walls. Correlations between the archaeological remains and documentary sources, such as those in the Temple of Tohil and the palace of the ruling lineage, make it possible to identify many of the buildings with specific lineages, kings, and classes of people. The extent to which the settlement was a true "city" continues to be debated, but even if the actual inhabitants numbered only a few thousand, they clearly were socially diverse and cosmopolitan in outlook. In 1524 Spaniards entered the settlement and subsequently had it burned. For a few years after the Spanish conquest it continued to be occupied by the natives, and it remains to this day an important offertory shrine for local Quiché Maya priest-shamans.

FURTHER READINGS

Carmack, R. M. 1981. *The Quiché Mayas of Utatlán: The Evolution of a Highland Guatemala Kingdom.* Norman: University of Oklahoma Press.

Carmack, R. M., and J. Weeks. 1981. Archaeology and Ethnohistory of Utatlán: A Conjunctive Approach. *American Antiquity* 46:323–341.

Fox, J. W. 1978. *Quiché Conquest: Centralism and Regionalism in Highland Guatemalan State Development.* Albuquerque: University of New Mexico Press.

Robert M. Carmack

SEE ALSO
Guatemala Highlands Region

Uxmal (Yucatán, Mexico)

The site of Uxmal ("Thrice Built" or "Place of Three Harvests") was one of the great urban centers of ancient Mexico. Believed to be the largest Puuc regional center during the Terminal Classic period (A.D. 800–1000) and classified as a Rank One center by the *Atlas Arqueológico,* Uxmal covers at least 10 square kilometers, according to a provisional estimate; the site has not undergone a complete settlement survey. Situated south of the Puuc Hills, the low range from which the region takes it name, Uxmal lies within a relatively flat, bowl-shaped basin of deep, rich agricultural soils, flanked on the southwest by five clay-filled sinkholes, or *aguadas,* which provided a vital source of water in this semiarid tropical environment.

The urban core of Uxmal contains the bulk of the large monumental architecture at the site and has been the main focus of research and tourism. Surrounded by a stone wall enclosing an area of about 16.5 hectares are a number of massive buildings executed in the Puuc style, perhaps the most highly developed architectural style in the pre-Columbian Americas. This style is characterized by veneer stones cemented onto a concrete core (core/veneer masonry), stone roofs with corbeled vaulting, and intricately decorated façades of geometric and mosaic stone veneers. Unlike those of most Maya centers, Uxmal's site plan is notable because its layout and building orientations appear to defy the natural topography, perhaps representing a self-conscious effort to transcend nature and construct a built environment conforming to the ideals and wishes of man.

Except for its Terminal Classic florescence, Uxmal's occupation history is not clearly understood. Although the site seems to have been initially occupied during the Middle Formative period (600–300 B.C.), there has not been any targeted research program to investigate Uxmal's origins. The earliest building groups are believed to be the North Group and the Temple of the Old Woman to the southeast; both contain large temple-pyramids incorporated into small acropolises.

The Pyramid of the Magician, defining the eastern zone of the central precinct, is elliptical in plan and over 30 meters high. The structure consists of five distinct superimpositions; the latest is the uppermost today, called Temple V. Two staircases on the east and west partially cover earlier temples, including Temple I, which bears a Tlaloc mask with a Mexican year sign in the headdress, implying Mexican influence, and which has been controversially radiocarbon dated to the late sixth century A.D. The western stairway leads to Temple IV's doorway, decorated as an earth monster mask in a manner typical of the Chenes style from Maya sites to the south. The same staircase is associated with a small courtyard (the Birds Group), where recent restorations have the revealed bird sculptures and feather motifs on the upper façades of two range structures with multiple-column entryways located on the south and west sides of the courtyard.

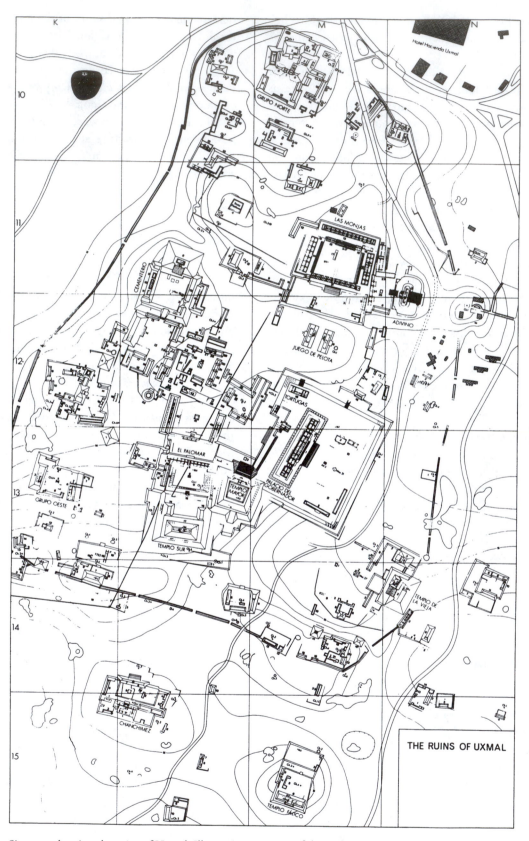

Site map showing the ruins of Uxmal. Illustration courtesy of the author.

Farther west is the Nunnery Quadrangle, a rectangular plaza enclosed by four large range structures with elaborately decorated façades. Kowalski has argued that the number of entryways for each building and their relative elevations, cardinal directionality, and complex decorative symbolism embody the quadripartite horizontal organization of the Maya universe, although this complex continues to elude functional explanation.

Aligned with a portal vault running south through the center of the Quadrangle's south structure is the largest known plaza at the site. Here one of the site's two ball courts is found, with the remains of ball rings and feathered serpent sculptures. Behind the ball court is a massive basal platform reaching a height of 14 meters above the central plaza and covering an area greater than two football fields. It provides a base for the House of the Turtles, which takes its name from exquisitely carved turtle sculptures on the upper façade, and for the regal Palace of the Governor, thought to be the finest and one of the largest palace buildings ever erected in ancient America. Set on a high building platform, the Governor's Palace contains twenty separate rooms and measures 95 meters long, 11 meters wide, and nearly 9 meters tall; it is actually three separate buildings connected by two large portal vaults. The upper façade is beautifully decorated with elaborate geometric designs, step frets, lattice patterns, human figures, and mask mosaics of Chac, the Maya rain god. Recent epigraphic research suggests that the Governor's Palace and many of the magnificent buildings one sees today were commissioned by Lord Chac, one of the last and greatest rulers at Uxmal. Archaeological and ethnographic data suggest that the Governor's Palace functioned as a political administrative structure and also as Lord Chac's royal residence. The building is also associated with the cult of Venus, as indicated by "Venus symbols" on mask panels and by its alignment corresponding to the azimuth of the maximum southern rise of Venus.

To the southwest is the Great Pyramid, a truncated pyramid with stepped sides, a broad northern stairway leading to a multichambered range-type building, and single-room structures on the east, west, and south sides. It is the single largest building mass at Uxmal, displaying elaborate Chac masks and a huge step-mask on the interior of the range structure. Farther west is the Acropolis Group, the second-largest and most complex building group at Uxmal, which comprises the South Temple—the highest point at the site—its plaza space to the north, another lower plaza surface with east and west flanking multiroom range structures, the House of the Doves building with its gigantic roof comb and lower-level plaza, and still another sunken plaza level surrounded by two additional range-type buildings.

To the west is the Round Structure, which is comparable to the Caracol building at Chichén Itzá; it was excavated by INAH's Centro Regional de Yucatán. Although the stone masonry and associated Cehpech ceramics place its construction and use in the Terminal Classic period, a cached offering of six whole Tohil Plumbate vessels deposited after the structure had begun to collapse suggests a late occupation at Uxmal by people who had trade contacts with Chichén Itzá. The presence of a few small-scale, poorly built buildings, now being investigated, suggests that any chronological overlap between Uxmal and Chichén Itzá was only partial, with the later center continuing after the Puuc sites had declined.

Continuing to the north, we encounter the densest settlement zone at Uxmal, largely unexcavated and associated with the Cemetery Group. This acropolis complex contains an early-style building and remains of a roof comb set atop a high western platform, a temple-pyramid to the north, and four platforms within the plaza decorated with skull-and-crossbones motifs and death imagery (tzompantli), showing further indications of Central Mexican influence at the site. A short distance north is a platform where seventeen stelae have been recovered; although several are providing important historical information on Uxmal, many are badly weathered and their inscriptions are sadly unreadable.

Recent research suggests that Uxmal became the regional capital of a confederacy of Maya city-states relatively late in the Terminal Classic period. In the late ninth and early tenth centuries, it experienced a building boom; at this time many of the largest structures were erected, including the Palace of the Governor, the Nunnery Quadrangle, and the principal ball court.

Uxmal is at the northwestern terminus of an intersite system of causeways (sacbeob) stretching 18 kilometers to the southeast. This causeway passes through the large site of Nohpat and eventually arrives at Kabah. At Nohpat there is little of the late-style architecture characteristic of Uxmal, suggesting that Uxmal became the dominant member of this political triad at the expense of its southern neighbor, perhaps by political and economic coercion or outright military force. The charismatic leader, Lord Chac, is associated with this late period of Uxmal history, is mentioned and represented prominently on several late monuments recently deciphered by Nicholas Grube. Kowalski argues that Lord Chac is depicted as the cosmic

U

ruler in a sculptural figure over the central doorway of the Palace of the Governor.

Uxmal's relationship with Chichén Itzá at this time is a controversial subject and has been postulated as either competitive or cooperative. Although evidence can be marshaled to support either view, there may in fact have been a changing relationship that was initially collaborative but over time became confrontational and eventually contributed to the demise of Uxmal and the Puuc cities by 1000 A.D. Unfortunately, at present scholars do not understand the political and economic processes and events that shaped the fall of these large Classic Maya polities.

The story of Uxmal does not end with the Classic period, however. Native chronicles such as the *Books of Chilam Balam* of Chumayel and Mani mention Uxmal as one of three members (along with Mayapan and Chichén Itzá) of the League of Mayapan. Although current archaeological evidence suggest that Uxmal was abandoned long before Mayapan became an important center, it is possible that Uxmal was reoccupied by the Xiu dynasty, an important Postclassic Maya lineage claiming Mexican descent who figured prominently in the history of Mayapan and later allied themselves with the Spanish during the conquest of Yucatán.

Unlike many other Maya sites, Uxmal never really became a lost city; there are references to it in various documents shortly after the Spanish conquest. The history of serious research at the site, however, began with John Lloyd Stephens in 1841 and 1843. Since Stephens, especially during the first half of the twentieth century, there have been numerous studies by such scholars as Edward Seler, Frans Blom, and Sylvanus Morley. Marta Foncerrada de Molina's 1965 work provided an important synthesis of the archaeology, architecture, and iconography of Uxmal. Harry Pollock's and George Andrews's surveys of Uxmal architecture and Jeff Kowalski's study of the Palace of the Governor, with his interpretations regarding iconography and epigraphy, are providing new information on Uxmal's dominant position in the region's political hierarchy. An important series of reconnaissances, excavations, and restoration projects has been undertaken by a number of Mexican archaeologists over the years and remains ongoing under the direction of Alfredo Barrera Rubio and Jose Huchim Herrera of INAH's Centro Regional de Yucatán (CRY). Today Uxmal is one of the most rewarding and popular tourist destinations in Mexico.

FURTHER READINGS

Andrews, G. 1995. *Architecture of the Puuc Region and Northern Plains Areas.* Vol. 1 of *Pyramids and Palaces, Monsters, and Masks: The Golden Age of Maya Architecture.* Culver City: Labyrinthos.

Barrera Rubio, A., and J. Huchim Herrera. 1990. *Restauración arquitectónica en Uxmal, 1986–1987.* University of Pittsburgh Latin American Archaeology Reports, 1. Pittsburgh.

Blom, F. 1930. Uxmal: The Great capital of the Xiu Dynasty of the Maya. *Art and Archaeology* 30:199–209.

Dunning, N. P., and J. K. Kowalski. 1994. Lords of the Hills: Classic Maya Settlement Patterns and Political Iconography in the Puuc Region, Mexico. *Ancient Mesoamerica* 5:63–95.

Foncerrada de Molina, M. 1968. *Uxmal: La ciudad del dios de la lluvia.* Mexico City: Fonda de Cultura Económica.

Graham, I. 1992. *Uxmal.* Vol. 4, part 2 of *Corpus of Maya Hieroglyphic Inscriptions.* Cambridge, Mass.: Peabody Museum, Harvard University.

Kowalski, J. K. 1987. *The House of the Governor: A Maya Palace at Uxmal, Yucatán, Mexico.* Norman: University of Oklahoma Press.

Michael Smyth

SEE ALSO

Maya Lowlands: North; Stephens, John Lloyd, and Frederick Catherwood

Vaillant, George Clapp (1901–1945)

Born in Boston and educated at Phillips Academy (Andover) and Harvard University (A.B., 1922; Ph.D., 1927), Vaillant was one of the outstanding Mesoamerican archaeologists of his generation. He began his career with major contributions to the study of Maya ceramics. He later carried out a decade of important excavations in the Basin of Mexico that resulted in precise definitions of a cultural chronology for that region (1941). He was on the staff of the American Museum of Natural History from 1927 until 1941, and was director of the University Museum (Philadelphia) from 1941 until his death.

FURTHER READINGS

Vaillant, G. C. 1940. Patterns in Middle American Archaeology. In *The Maya and Their Neighbors,* pp. 295–305. New York: Appleton-Century.

———. 1966. *Aztecs of Mexico.* Baltimore: Penguin Books.

———. 1973. *Artists and Craftsmen in Ancient Central America.* American Museum of Natural History Guide 88. New York.

Willey, G. R. 1988. *Portraits in American Archaeology.* Albuquerque: University of New Mexico Press.

Gordon R. Willey

SEE ALSO

Basin of Mexico

Vega de la Peña and Cuajilotes (Veracruz, Mexico)

Both of these important sites are situated in a narrow mountain canyon, just over 2 kilometers apart on the rocky upper reaches of the Nautla (Bobos, Gavilanes) River where it descends along the northern flank of the mountains of central Veracruz. The choice of location was certainly a function of ancient trade routes and corridors of highland-lowland contact as well as conquest. In recent years either or both of these sites, as well as the canyon locality, have sometimes been referred to by the geographically incorrect name "Filobobos."

Vega de la Peña is the smaller, downstream site. Although it may once have been a Classic period satellite of its much larger neighbor, it was a historically significant settlement in the terminal Postclassic period. The powerful Aztec garrison that controlled much of the northern Gulf Coast for the Triple Alliance was very likely placed here. Nearby, a large punitive expedition of Spaniards and Totonacs, led by Cortés's captain, Juan Escalante, was utterly routed by the Aztecs.

The major buildings are a 14-meter-high twin temple, a long vertical-walled ball court with monolithic rings, and low platforms topped with small rooms that may have served as warehouses, perhaps for tribute storage. There are also smaller temples, palaces, and numerous minor platforms. Surviving stucco decoration on one structure has a stepped fret *(xaicoliuhqui)* design. A number of the buildings of medium and small size have platforms with the sloping base walls *(taluds)* and extended cornices that are associated with the culture of El Tajín during the Middle and Late Classic. These structures appear to have been refurbished for use at the end of the

Postclassic. Situated on the bank of the river, Vega de la Peña has been repeatedly damaged by flooding and has probably lost much of its original western extent.

Cuajilotes (Guajilotes, El Cuapiote) is the much larger, upstream site in a wider part of the valley. It is likely to have a very long chronology, beginning at least by the Early Classic if not in the Protoclassic or even Late Formative. Its apogee, however, appears to have been largely after the zenith of El Tajín, or perhaps contemporary with its last Epiclassic florescence. Its primary architectural focus is a 380-meter-long rectangular plaza surrounded by elongated, multistory temple platforms as high as 21 meters, some with multiple stairways and two or even three sanctuaries.

A large sloping-walled ball court seals one end of the mammoth plaza, and a massive temple with multiple stairways the other. The western side of the system is buttressed by large sloping walls *(taluds)*, which, along with other walls and small platforms that link the various temples, convert the complex into a protected, limited-access compound. Additional plazas, building groups, and possible ball courts were constructed, for the most part, on a much smaller scale. A number of these, such as the Ranch and Corral groups, are likely to be of earlier date. Along the upper slopes of the valley downstream from the city there may be terraces for domestic structures. The western reaches of the city have been damaged by the changing river course.

Sites in this valley came slowly to the attention of archaeologists following road and dam construction in the region from 1920 to 1950. The first formal explorations were at Vega de la Peña in 1950 by Medellín Zenil. These were followed by a surface examination of the sites preparatory to a project proposal by Wilkerson in 1990–1991, and an INAH project focusing on reconstruction in 1993–1994. Access to both sites can be difficult in bad weather.

FURTHER READINGS

Medellín Zenil, A. 1960. *Cerámicas del Totonacapan.* Jalapa: Universidad Veracruzana.

Wilkerson, S. J. K. 1994. Escalante's Entrada. *National Geographic Research and Exploration* 9:12–31.

———. 1994. Nahua Presence on the Mesoamerican Gulf Coast. In E. Quiñones Keber (ed.), *Chipping Away on Earth: Studies in Prehispanic and Colonial Mexico in Honor of Arthur J. O. Anderson and Charles E. Dibble,* pp. 177–186. Lancaster, Calif.: Labyrinthos.

S. Jeffrey K. Wilkerson

SEE ALSO
Gulf Lowlands: North Central Region

Venta, La (Tabasco, Mexico)

The archaeological site at La Venta in southeastern Mexico is a key feature in the history of ancient Mesoamerica. Its monumental architecture and sculpture define it as one of the most important cities of the Olmec civilization, and one of the clearest examples of complex societies in Middle America during the first millennium before the common era.

La Venta is situated in the northwestern corner of the state of Tabasco in the municipality of Huimanguillo. The climate is humid tropical, with an average rainfall of more than 2,000 mm and a mean temperature of 27° C. This ancient Olmec city was constructed on a natural elevation of Miocene origin with an average elevation of 20 meters above sea level. It is surrounded by lowlands, less than 10 meters above sea level, which form part of Mexico's largest alluvial coastal plain. As recent as forty years ago, one could find marshlands, mangroves, and semideciduous and tropical rain forest within walking distance.

The natural elevation on which La Venta was constructed is surrounded by a complex and dynamic hydrological system. The nearest major river system is the Tonalá, which today runs 4 kilometers west of the site and drains directly into the Gulf of Mexico. Two of its tributaries, the Chicozapote and Blasillo rivers, are respectively north and south of the site. Various coastal and freshwater lagoons dot the terrain, and 15 kilometers north of La Venta is the coastline. The richness and diversity in land and water ecosystems have important implications for our understanding of the ancient La Venta Olmec subsistence base, since varied terrestrial and aquatic fauna and flora were readily available food resources.

Recent geomorphological studies indicate that the La Venta riverine system was, and continues to be, extremely

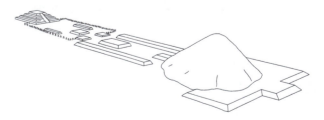

Perspective drawing of La Venta's Great Pyramid and Complex A, from Diehl and Coe, *Olmec* (1996).

dynamic. The abundance of abandoned courses and meanders on today's surface attest to this. In 1943, Matthew Stirling reported an ancient river course found approximately 1 kilometer north of La Venta, locally known as the Palma River. On its banks, two kinds of settlements dot the landscape: some are moundless, and some exhibit a central mound. Most of these sites are contemporary with La Venta's occupation (1200–400 B.C.), but some have been dated as far back as 1750 B.C., and others show continued occupation up to the present day. It is assumed that their location along the river bank is related to its utility as a communication route, as well as to the adjacent rich alluvial soils, which could provide three agricultural crops per year. Excavations at these sites have recovered remains of corn, beans, palm nuts, deer, crocodile, turtle, dog, and a variety of fish bones and mollusks, offering a glimpse of the subsistence base of the ancient Olmec.

The original extent of the ancient Olmec city at La Venta is estimated to have been approximately 200 hectares. Today only about one-half of its earthen architectural vestiges remain, owing to recent urban and industrial blight. La Venta's edifices are composed of earthen platforms and mounds. It is assumed that on them were perishable structures with wooden posts, wattle-and-daub walls, packed earthen floors, and thatched roofs. The earthen mass of the platforms and mounds consists of a highly compacted mixture of local clays and sands. A few mounds were built of sun-dried adobe. Because there are no stone sources near the site, stone was used minimally in the architecture. Basalt and andesite blocks were utilized to delimit the foundation of some buildings, while limestone slabs were used as internal buttresses in other cases. La Venta's site map reveals the layout of one of the earliest examples of planned monumental architecture in ancient Mexico. Its edifices are oriented on a north–south axis, forming avenuelike areas and plazas. The organization of its various spaces probably reflects their uses. For example, Complex A, a ceremonial precinct including subterranean features, was highly restricted in access by a series of architectural barriers, including a 30-meter-tall pyramidal structure south of it and a basalt column fence. Other areas were probably intended for public use, such as the 4-hectare plaza south of Complex C, the principal pyramidal structure at the site.

Most of La Venta's edifices have not been subject to archaeological excavation, making it difficult to know their precise functions. Based on the sheer size of the platforms that form complexes B, D, G, and H, it is likely that they were civic-administrative in function. Excavations on the Stirling "Acropolis" revealed the presence of a water distribution and/or drainage system formed by troughs carved in the shape of an elongated "U," joined together with tar, covered with stone slabs and associated with large stone basins. Concentrations of sculpture fragments may also indicate the presence of stone-carving workshops on the Stirling "Acropolis." Evidence of domestic architecture and occupation has been found in complexes E and I, as well as beyond these in areas now occupied by the town of Villa la Venta. The excavated house structures presented packed earthen floors, post molds, and trash pits. Activity areas have been defined, indicating hearths and domestic-scale working of obsidian and greenstones.

Thus far, a large part of our information on La Venta derives from the excavations in Complex A, the ceremonial precinct, conducted in 1942, 1943, and 1955 under the auspices of the Smithsonian Institution. This architectural unit is composed of two courtyards with its edifices arranged symmetrically. The northern courtyard is delimited on its east and west sides by a basalt column fence, by a 4-meter-high earthen mound (A-2) on the north, and by two mounds on the south, constructed of sun-dried adobe bricks (A-1-d and A-1-e). Within mound A-2, a basalt column funerary chamber was found containing the remains of two young individuals and a rich assortment of exquisitely carved jade objects, all covered with cinnabar. In close proximity to this tomb was a sandstone coffer; its exterior walls were carved in low relief representing the figure of a supernatural being. Although no skeletal remains were found, the coffer has been interpreted as a burial because of the disposition of the objects, such as jade jewelry and figurines.

The two sun-dried adobe mounds on the south were constructed on top of a unique subterranean offering known as "Massive Offerings." These consisted of a 4-meter-deep pit within which a platform of unworked serpentine stones was built. On its surface an abstract mosaic was laid, made up of more than four hundred carefully shaped serpentine blocks. These mosaics were not intended for public viewing, since they were covered by a thick layer of clay and sand on which the adobe platforms were built. In addition to these two Massive Offerings, three others have been found, less sophisticated in construction but equally impressive in terms of the enormous quantity of imported stone utilized. Their ritual function is unknown, though they might have been offerings to Mother Earth.

V

In La Venta's ceremonial precinct more than fifty offerings were found. Most of these consisted of caches of ceramic vessels, concave magnetite mirrors, and more than one hundred votive celts and axes. One of the most remarkable offerings excavated in this precinct consisted of a group of sixteen figurines and reworked votive celts, carved in jade, serpentine, and sandstone. This assemblage is important because the figurines were found arranged in a semicircle, indicating that their creators meant to represent a significant scene.

As a result of the investigations in Complex A, a four-phase architectural chronological sequence was proposed, covering the time period 1000–600 B.C. This sequence has been subject to controversy and should be used with caution; one of its weaknesses is that most of the radiocarbon dating derives from charcoal found in construction fills.

La Venta has produced the largest and most thematically diverse corpus of Olmec monumental sculpture. Because there is no evidence of a written language for the Olmec civilization, there are no texts to help explain the meaning of the themes depicted in its sculptural art. For the most part, Olmec sculptures have been studied divorced from their architectural contexts and in isolation from one another. However, recent research at La Venta indicates that monumental sculptures had a specific function and were associated with particular kinds of edifices. Examples are the three colossal heads found at the northern edge of the site, as well as three monumental representations of supernatural beings found at the southern edge; these may have marked two of the primary entries to the principal part of this ancient city, or they may have marked the southern and northern boundaries of the ancient city. Another example is the pairing of "altars," specifically Altars 2 and 3, as well as Altars 4 and 5. In both cases, the objects repeat themes that suggest they are meant to be "read" as pairs. It is also significant that altars representing a seated human figure holding on its lap the limp body of an infant were placed facing pyramidal structures, suggesting that the infants were objects of offering. A third example is a group of six stela-like sculptures distributed along the southern base of the main pyramid. Four of these, carved in low relief, share the theme of representations of supernatural beings. The fifth sculpture depicts a scene of historic or mythological import, while the sixth is a "plain" stela with no carving, but probably originally painted. This group of sculptures underscores the relationship between the supernatural beings and the main pyramidal edifice.

While the historical or mythic scene is important, it plays a secondary role. These sculptures constitute one of the earliest examples in ancient Mexico of large-scale ideological communication through the interaction of architecture and sculpture.

The La Venta Olmec traveled great distances to procure the raw materials for their stone objects. These include an ample range of products: monumental and portable sculptures, stone-working tools, grinding implements, jewelry, luxury items, and architectural elements such as columns, blocks, and slabs. The most prevalent materials employed were basalt, andesite, limestone, sandstone, schist, gneiss, serpentine, chert, obsidian, and jade. The sources for these raw materials are in present-day Veracruz, Hidalgo, Chiapas, and Oaxaca in Mexico, and in Guatemala. The distances covered ranged from a minimum of 60 kilometers to more than 400 kilometers. The incredibly impressive technological feat involved in the transportation of blocks of stone weighing over 30 tons—the weight of some of the monumental sculptures—is something yet to be explained.

The socio-political organization of the La Venta Olmec has not been clearly defined. It is apparent that this society comprised an elite sector, a wide range of specialists—farmers, fishermen, sculptors, architects, and engineers—and a large labor force. Based on the sculptural art, we can propose that the supernatural world played an important role among the ruling sector.

The range of raw materials utilized by La Venta's inhabitants indicates that they had contact with a wide spectrum of distant neighbors. This contact surely entailed the mutual borrowing and adaptation of cultural traits. La Venta's influence has been detected throughout ancient Mesoamerica, primarily in the presence of low-relief carvings stylistically similar to those of La Venta; examples occur at Chalcatzingo in Morelos and Chalchuapa in El Salvador. The nature of contact between the La Venta Olmecs and contemporary civilizations is not entirely clear, but it seems to have been limited to the elite sectors of the societies, and it may have combined economic transactions with exchanges of ideology.

The archaeological remains at La Venta provide irrefutable evidence of the sophistication and complexity of the Olmec civilization. La Venta represents the culmination of a long-term cultural manifestation that crystallized and consolidated a cultural substratum that was adapted and adopted by contemporary and subsequent civilizations in ancient Middle America.

FURTHER READINGS

de la Fuente, B. 1973. *Escultura monumental olmeca.* Mexico City: Instituto de Investigaciones Estéticas. Universidad Nacional Autonoma de Mexico.

Drucker, P. 1952. *La Venta, Tabasco: A Study of Olmec Ceramics and Art.* Bureau of American Ethnology, Bulletin 153. Washington, D.C.: Smithsonian Institution.

Drucker, P., R. F. Heizer, and R. J. Squire. 1959. *Excavations at La Venta, Tabasco, 1955.* Bureau of American Ethnology, Bulletin 170. Washington, D.C.: Smithsonian Institution.

González Lauck, R. B. 1996. La Venta: An Olmec Capital. In E. Benson and B. de la Fuente (eds.), *Olmec Art of Ancient Mexico,* pp. 73–81. Washington, D.C.: National Gallery of Art.

———. 1997. Acerca de pirámides de tierra y seres sobrenaturales: Observaciones preliminares en torno al edificio C-1 de La Venta, Tabasco. *Arqueológia,* ser. 2, 17:79–97.

Heizer, R. F., P. Drucker, and J. A. Graham. 1968. Investigations at La Venta, 1967. *Contributions of the University of California Archaeological Research Facility* 5:1–34.

Heizer, R. F., P. Drucker, and L. K. Napton. 1968. The 1968 Investigations at La Venta. *Contributions of the University of California Archaeological Research Facility* 5:101–203.

Jimenez Salas, O. H. 1990. Geomorfologia de la region de La Venta, Tabasco: Un sistema fluvio-lagunar costero del Cuaternario. *Arqueológia,* ser. 2, 3:5–16.

Rust, W., and R. J. Sharer. 1988. Olmec Settlement Data from La Venta, Tabasco, Mexico. *Science* 242:102–104.

Stirling, M. W. 1943. *Stone Monuments of Southern Mexico.* Bureau of American Ethnology, Bulletin 138. Washington, D.C.: Smithsonian Institution.

West, R. C., N. P. Psuty, and B. G. Thom. 1969. *The Tabasco Lowlands of Southeastern Mexico.* Coastal Studies Institute, Technical Report 70. Baton Rouge: Lousiana State University.

Williams, H., and R. F. Heizer. 1965. Sources of Rocks Used in Olmec Monuments. *Contributions of the University of California Archaeological Research Facility* 1:1–39.

Rebecca González Lauck

SEE ALSO

Gulf Lowlands: South Region

Veracruz
See Villa Rica de Veracruz

Victorias, Las (Ahuachapan, El Salvador)

This Formative period site in the highlands of western El Salvador consists of four bas-relief petroglyphs in clear Olmec style on a great stone boulder, with some poorly associated ceramic deposits. The four figures of the Las Victorias monument are each over a meter high; they wear helmets, capes, and other elements of elaborate costume. Three of the figures bear large objects variously identified as ceremonial scepters or torches. The helmets, downturned mouths, flat faces, and elements of costume are in pure Olmec style, similar to boulder sculptures and cave paintings found in Chiapas, Central Mexico, and West Mexico from the period 1000–600 B.C. Boggs, who defined the site in 1950, attributed these monuments to that period and considered them to be evidence of contact with the Early to Middle Formative Olmec civilization of the Gulf Coast of Mexico.

Subsequent extensive excavations were carried out here and throughout the surrounding valley by the University of Pennsylvania Chalchuapa Project, directed by Robert Sharer. Analysis of the monuments by Dana Anderson and study of nearby ceramic deposits by Sharer supported Boggs's hypothesis of Olmec style and Middle Formative date for the monument (c. 900–500 B.C.). Sharer hypothesized that the monument and other evidence indicated the presence of Olmec traders here, perhaps utilizing the Río La Paz as a trade route to the jade sources of the Motagua Valley to the east.

FURTHER READINGS

Anderson, D. 1978. Monuments. In R. J. Sharer (ed.), *The Prehistory of Chalchuapa, El Salvador,* vol. 1, pp. 155–180. Philadelphia: University of Pennsylvania Press.

Boggs, S. H. 1950. *Olmec Pictographs in the Las Victorias Group, Chalchuapa Archaeological Zone, El Salvador.* Carnegie Institution of Washington Notes of Middle American Archaeology and Ethnology, 99. Washington, D.C.

Sharer, R. J. (ed.). 1978. *The Prehistory of Chalchuapa, El Salvador.* Philadelphia: University of Pennsylvania Press.

Arthur A. Demarest

SEE ALSO

Olmec Culture; Soconusco–South Pacific Coast and Piedmont Region

Vidor (Guanacaste, Costa Rica)

This large shell midden complex on the south side of the Bay of Culebra (Greater Nicoya region) was occupied from 800 B.C. to A.D. 1520. It consists of more than thirty shell middens organized around informal "plaza" areas. Mortuary remains included more than 190 individuals, primarily from the Bagaces period (A.D. 300–800); some had associated grave goods, and there was a significant number of fetal/infant burials in inverted monochrome jars.

Interaction with other regions is indicated by obsidian from southern Honduras (flakes) and Guatemala (mostly blades), White-slipped ceramics from Pacific Nicaragua, Delirio Red-on-White ceramics from El Salvador, and fragments of Ulúa Marble vases. Other sites in Greater Nicoya have similar post-300 A.D. components. Las Marías on the Bay of Salinas, Chahuite Escondido, and Nacascolo are similar shell midden complexes. These people lived on marine resources and other foods they hunted or collected, and practiced some agriculture. They may have exported marine products to adjacent interior areas.

FURTHER READINGS

Abel-Vidor, S. 1980 Dos hornos precolombinos en el sitio Vidor, Bahía Culebra, Guanacaste. *Vínculos* 6(2): 43–50.

Kerbis, J. 1980. The Analysis of Faunal Remains from the Vidor Site. *Vínculos* 6(1–2):125–140.

Lange, F. W., and S. Abel-Vidor. 1980 Investigaciones arqueológicos en la zona de Bahía Culebra, Costa Rica (1973–1979). *Vínculos* 6(1–2):5–7.

Vázquez, R., and D. S. Weaver. 1980. Un análisis osteológico para el reconocimiento de las condiciones de vida en el sitio Vidor. *Vínculos* 6(1–2):97–105.

Frederick W. Lange

SEE ALSO
Intermediate Area: Overview

Viejon, El (Veracruz, Mexico)

Strategically situated at the narrowest point of the coastal plain of central Veracruz, and thus astride the only sea-level route for north–south trade, this modest site has important Middle Formative and Classic period occupations. The discovery by a local farmer of a massive basalt slab stela among low mounds brought archaeological recognition. Carved in full Olmec Intermediate period style and depicting two confronting figures, each with a cornstalk scepter, this stela is the northernmost example of such early monumental sculpture known from the Gulf Lowlands. Recovered ceramics also reflect a direct Olmec presence. The site may have served as both an Olmec frontier outpost and a control point for commerce with the upper coast. Late Formative ceramics and burials, including one mutilated primary interment lacking both hands and feet, have been recovered.

An extensive Classic presence expanded earlier constructions and site size. A plain yoke and *hacha* offering was found with one of the numerous burials within the structures of this period, and several yoke fragments were found in mixed fill. A light, dispersed terminal Postclassic occupation is evidenced by surface components. Starting in 1951, the site was briefly explored by Alfonso Medellín, who placed a number of test trenches in mounds. It was also surface-collected and stratigraphically tested, but not analyzed, during the examination of the central coast in the early 1960s by James Ford, Alfonso Medellín, and Matthew Walrath. El Viejón is situated on the Gulf of Mexico near the mouth of a seasonal stream that traverses a steep mountain valley. In proximity to salt-producing lagoons and adjacent to the Laguna Verde nuclear power plant, much of the site is today covered by a village and *ejido* (communally held lands).

FURTHER READINGS

Medellín Zenil, A. 1960. *Cerámicas del Totonacapan*. Jalapa: Universidad Veracruzana.

S. Jeffrey K. Wilkerson

SEE ALSO
Gulf Lowlands: North Central Region

Villa Rica de Veracruz (Veracruz, Mexico)

Although it is of considerable historical importance, this small site atop sand dunes on the central Veracruz coast has received only sporadic archaeological attention. Founded by the expedition led by Hernan Cortés in the spring of 1519, it overlooks a small embayment in the lee of a rocky point. The logistical base for the initiation of the conquest of Mexico, the first formally constituted Spanish town on the Mexican mainland was situated close to Totonac Quiahuiztlán. Here Cortés scuttled his fleet and began the subjugation of the Totonacs before marching to the Aztec capital of Tenochtitlan. Villa Rica was also the starting point for the disastrous Spanish-led attack on the Aztec garrison in the Nautla River Valley. By the mid-1520s, both the town and port were abandoned in favor of a new settlement and less exposed anchorage at the Antigua River mouth, about 45 kilometers to the south.

Although there were earlier recorded visits to the site, the initial archaeological exploration was by Alfonso Medellín Zenil in his 1951 examination of the foundations of the small fortress at the northern end of the promontory. Later, two INAH projects in the 1980s and early 1990s exposed other building bases, a lime kiln, and Spanish burials. European artifacts—principally sherds, nails, and metal armatures—were encountered, as well as indigenous (Postclassic) ceramics. Most structures had stone underpinnings and perishable wood superstructures. This is the only Contact phase Spanish site in Veracruz to have received sustained exploration. Because the chronological and historical parameters are known, the site is an invaluable resource for understanding the abrupt transition to the Colonial period in eastern lowland Mexico. Although preserved by isolation into the 1970s, Villa Rica is currently threatened by modern houses and a growing vacation village.

FURTHER READINGS

Hernandez Aranda, J. 1989. Excavaciones recientes en Villa Rica de Ia Veracruz. *Arqueológia* 5:217–244.

Medellín Zenil, A. 1960. *Ceramicas del Totonacapan.* Jalapa: Universidad Veracruzana.

Wilkerson, S. J. K. 1994. Escalante's Entrada. *National Geographic Research and Exploration* 9:12–31.

S. Jeffrey K. Wilkerson

SEE ALSO
Gulf Lowlands: North Central Region

Villa Tiscapa (Managua, Nicaragua)

This site in the Managua metropolitan area is larger than 20 hectares in extent, but its limits are undefined. The site has ceramics similar to those from the Ocos and Barra phases on the coast of Guatemala, and of the Tronadora phase in the cordillera of Guanacaste in Costa Rica. The site was occupied from approximately 1400 B.C. until the Spanish invasion of Nicaragua. At least three major episodes of site abandonment resulting from volcanic eruption and tephra deposition occurred during the prehistoric occupation. Early architectural remains (stone wall bases and a plastered floor) date to A.D. 70. Obsidian from either Honduras or Guatemala was present by 1200 B.C. There was utilization of locally available chert, jasper, chalcedony, and andesite lithic sources. After 800 A.D. the ceramic assemblages reflects the well-known Greater Nicoya White-slipped polychrome ceramic tradition.

FURTHER READINGS

Espinoza, E. 1995. La cerámica temprana de Managua y sus vínculos regionales. In F. W. Lange (ed.), *Descubriendo Las Huellas de Nuestras Antepasadas: El Proyecto "Arqueológia de la Zona Metropolitana de Managua,"* pp. 17–24. Managua: Alcaldia of Managua.

Frederick W. Lange

SEE ALSO
Intermediate Area: Overview

Warfare

Warfare is organized and sanctioned armed conflict, carried out by groups whose members share common interests and are prepared to fight for them. In pursuit of these interests, combatants engage in violent confrontations that they realize may result in deliberate killing, with the intent of maintaining the status quo or, more often, bringing about a shift of power relations. Conflict may involve separate, autonomous communities or societies, or interest groups within a society. So defined, warfare was a conspicuous feature of the Mesoamerican cultural tradition, beginning at least with the first complex societies of Early Preclassic times (1200–900 B.C.). Warfare probably had its roots in the feuds and raids of even earlier, egalitarian hunter-gatherer and farming peoples, and clearly war evolved in its scale, complexity, purposes, and motivations.

Evidence of Warfare

Some of the best information about how and why warfare was conducted derives from participant accounts of conflicts between the Spanish and native Mesoamericans. As early as 1517, Spanish expeditions encountered the bellicose Lowland Maya, and the last independent Maya kingdom was not subdued until 1697. Between 1519 and 1522 the forces of Hernan Cortés fought many Central Mexican peoples, most notably the Mexica (Aztecs) of Tenochtitlan and their allies. Subsequent accounts compiled in the sixteenth century preserve information not only about the conquest itself, but also, utilizing native books and oral histories, about pre-Conquest military institutions and events, and personages associated with them. The pre-Conquest books of the Mixtecs are particularly abundant and well preserved, providing details of political rivalries and wars that date back to the tenth century.

When books or oral accounts are absent, as they are for most of pre-Conquest Mesoamerica, evidence for war comes from dates and inscriptions on stelae, buildings, or portable objects. These are often associated with artistic depictions, and the combination of art, dates, and inscriptions is particularly informative about warfare in the Classic and Postclassic Maya Lowlands (A.D. 300–1500). More indirect evidence concerning war and conflict derives from fortifications, settlement patterns, artifacts (particularly weapons), and human skeletal remains, which may show signs of war-related trauma.

Brief Culture History of Mesoamerican War

What are plausibly military motifs and symbols appear in Olmec art in the Gulf Coast lowlands after 1050 B.C., and also in Olmec-related depictions elsewhere in Mesoamerica during the Middle Preclassic. According to some interpretations, one of the earliest lengthy texts (A.D. 159), on the La Mojarra stela from Veracruz, includes a reference to a military victory by the ruler portrayed on the monument. Late Preclassic mass burials at Cuello in Belize and Chalchuapa in El Salvador appear to be those of sacrificed young males of military age, and the massive Maya fortifications at Becan, Campeche, were probably built around A.D. 150, at the very end of the Formative period.

Some of the most convincing evidence for early warfare comes from the Valley of Oaxaca. The three hundred "Danzante" reliefs at Monte Albán's Building L, carved around 450 B.C., are thought to portray mutilated and sacrificed war captives and include glyphlike symbols that may be personal names. A nearby set of reliefs with accompanying inscriptions on Building J was carved several centuries later and seems to record the conquest of a series of named places by the expansive Monte Albán state. Fortifications were erected around the lower slopes of Monte Albán itself sometime about 150 B.C.

There may have been active hostility between Teotihuacan and Cuicuilco around 200–100 B.C., as these two emergent regional centers contended for supremacy in the Basin of Mexico, although this interpretation derives from settlement data rather than art and inscriptions. After A.D. 250, military themes, including heart sacrifice, are conspicuous in Teotihuacan art. Scores of apparently sacrificed males dressed in military regalia (as well as some female victims) have recently been unearthed at the Temple of the Feathered Serpent in the Cuidadela. Dating to around A.D. 200–250, these burials indicate a stronger role for war and militarism at Classic Teotihuacan than previously suspected. Although the dating is uncertain, massive destruction of religious and other structures along the Street of the Dead around A.D. 600–700 strongly suggests that internal violence, possibly civil war, was a factor in the decline of Teotihuacan.

Although the Classic Maya were long characterized as unusually peaceful, several lines of evidence have radically changed this perspective. Tikal was fortified by a system of earthworks at the very beginning of the Classic period. Although war-related inscriptions are rare before A.D. 650, military themes are conspicuous in Early Classic (A.D. 300–600) Maya art. During the Late Classic (A.D. 600–900) such themes are very pronounced, and many conflicts are epigraphically recorded as historical events involving specific centers or polities, along with their elite protagonists—usually rulers. Maya kings derived great prestige by portraying themselves on their public monuments as successful warriors, boasting particularly of the capture and sacrifice of illustrious enemies. The many alliances and royal marriages recorded in Classic inscriptions were in large part dictated by warfare.

In some regions inscriptions are complete enough to show that both the rise and the fall of Classic Maya kingdoms were associated with warfare. The best such evidence comes from the Petexbatun region in the southwestern Maya Lowlands, where four successive Dos Pilas kings, through alliance and warfare, patched together a sizable polity in the early seventh century; however, they were unable to prevent it from unraveling in a welter of conflict little more than a century later.

The decline of the great Classic cultures of Teotihuacan, the Lowland Maya, and Monte Albán ushered in new episodes of strife. Central Mexican Epiclassic (A.D. 700–900) centers exhibit strong evidence of warfare, such as the fortifications at Xochicalco and the murals of Cacaxtla. Military themes are strong in the art of Tula, the great city that replaced Teotihuacan as the dominant center in the Basin of Mexico after A.D. 900. Farther to the south, codices abundantly document the wars of emergent Mixtec royal dynasties as Monte Albán's power withered away in Oaxaca. Some of the Puuc centers that emerged in northern Yucatán around A.D. 750–1000 are fortified, and both Maya books and oral accounts show that warfare, perhaps including intrusions of non-Maya peoples, was associated with the rise of Chichén Itzá and later of the walled capital of Mayapan. The especially well documented warfare patterns of Mesoamerican peoples on the eve of the Spanish conquest are discussed below.

Technology and Logistics of Warfare

Mesoamerican warfare was constrained throughout its history by two factors: technological simplicity, and poorly developed logistical capability. Both offensive and defensive weaponry certainly changed as the character of conflict evolved, but wood, stone, and fiber always provided the raw materials for darts, arrows, spears, clubs, swords, shields, and defensive armor. Some West Mexican peoples, such as the Tarascans, made limited use of copper and copper-alloy weapons in the form of axes and points, but effective metal weapons or armor of bronze, iron, or steel were never developed. Gunpowder was not used to fire projectiles; horses were not available to bear cavalry, nor were large, highly specialized vessels used for naval combat. A consequence of such simple technology is that one side in a conflict rarely suffered from a serious disparity in weaponry, as was often the case in the Old World. In addition, Mesoamerican elites lacked privileged access to costly, highly specialized and effective weaponry that required special skills to use, as was the case in many Old World societies. Military technology thus contributed little in a direct sense to the development and maintenance of social stratification.

Energetic constraints imposed severe logistical limitations on warfare. Mesoamericans lacked the large domestic animals that served as beasts of burden or traction in the Old World, and they had no wheeled vehicles or well-developed road systems. Movement of goods of all kinds thus depended on the comparatively inefficient muscle power of human porters. Water transport was possible in some regions, but even it depended on human paddlers because sails were not used. Armies were thus usually limited to fairly slow foot travel, strung out along narrow paths, and they could operate for only short periods of time and over short distances if they depended on supplies carried with them. This logistical limitation might be overcome when armies moved through friendly territory, where they could acquire provisions along the way. Elsewhere, however, long campaigns often made it necessary to depend on food seized from enemy fields and storehouses.

Mesoamerican military forces were accordingly quite small, moved slowly, and did not operate for long far from secure home bases. In the Maya region the quick, sharp raid involving relatively few warriors was probably in part an adaptation to logistical constraints. Timing of military campaigns was strongly dictated by the agricultural cycle, especially where wet and dry season contrasts were pronounced. During the wet season it was difficult and costly to detach males from agricultural tasks for military service, and movement of armies was impeded by muddy trails and swollen rivers. The best time for campaigning was at or just after the harvest, when there was plenty of food to be looted in enemy territory. Even so, protracted field operations were difficult, and long sieges of fortified positions were virtually impossible to carry out against determined, well-provisioned defenders.

Most Mesoamerican centers were unfortified, though often situated in defensible positions. Lack of fortifications does not mean lack of warfare, however. The Aztecs and their enemies usually fought outside settlements, and if the local army lost, the city usually surrendered swiftly. Some formal fortifications did exist in Mesoamerica, protecting either settlements or special refuges. They typically consisted of enclosed precincts, often on hilltops, protected by ditches, earthworks, stone or timber walls, or sometimes even hedges of spiny plants. Occasionally settlements were built on islands, such as the Aztec capital of Tenochtitlan, and thus protected by water barriers. Despite their general lack of sophistication, such fortifications were quite serviceable once properly manned because of the difficulty of sieges and the lack of artillery that could breach even flimsy walls. Poorly developed military technology also helps to explain the lack of fortifications, since determined soldiers could defend massive public building complexes, such as walled temple enclosures, in the centers of their communities. Although such last-ditch defense was probably rare, Central Mexican hieroglyphs symbolize conquest with the image of a burning temple.

Military Organization

Almost everything we know about the organizational features of Mesoamerican warfare derives from ethnohistoric accounts of the Postclassic and Conquest periods. Military organization was quite varied, as we would expect for a region in which polities ranged from highly centralized, expansive empires to tiny city-states. One issue is professionalism. Some Old World societies developed true professional armies—bodies of permanently mobilized, strategically stationed men of all ranks, especially trained and equipped in the use of specialized weapons, strategy, and tactics, organized into separate units with their own command structure, and supported by the state or ruler. Such professional soldiers were often hired mercenaries.

Professionalism of this kind existed only to a very limited degree among even the most warlike Mesoamerican societies. For example, most Aztec elite males were trained for war and expected to participate in it, but apart from some frontier garrisons there was no permanently mobilized army. The Aztec military meritocracy richly rewarded successful warriors, including a few talented commoners, with land, serfs, and other status symbols commensurate with their achievements on the battlefield. High-status warriors were trained in special schools, belonged to prestigious military societies, attended the ruler's court as military advisors and retainers, and held high military offices.

Because hereditary noble males formed such small segments of Mesoamerican stratified societies, they did not by themselves constitute effective armed forces. For major campaigns it was necessary to mobilize large numbers of less rigorously trained and less experienced commoners. One of the obligations of commoners to the Aztec state was military service. Contingents of free commoners were raised by their *calpulli* leaders and armed with weapons from state armories. Impressive rituals preceded campaigns and followed their successful conclusions. Warriors, elite or otherwise, were seen as consecrated to the service of the patron deity Huitzilopochtli, and their success as essential to the preservation of the cosmos. Capture and dedication of sacrificial victims was a major object of war.

The early sixteenth-century Maya of northern Yucatán present a rather different picture. There were sixteen political "provinces," ranging from large, centralized polities with populations on the order of sixty thousand to loose confederations of towns allied for defensive purposes. Warfare between and even within provinces was frequent. Spanish accounts of early battles with the Maya in 1517–1519 clearly distinguish between elite and commoner warriors. Forces of thousands of warriors were quickly mustered, so people of widely varied status obviously took part. Commoners appear to have kept their arms in their own homes. Maya elite males were much less identified with war as a primary pursuit than were Aztec males. There were some prestigious "professional" warriors called *holcans* and *nacoms,* although they seem to have been activated only situationally, and their overbearing presence in Yucatecan towns was apparently regarded as a mixed blessing. So far as we can tell, there were no military societies or system of rewards for military success comparable to those of the Aztecs, nor was war so integral to religion and ritual.

This contrast brings us to a useful distinction. Although both the Aztec and Maya were warlike, Aztec society was far more militaristic, in the sense that warfare was more highly institutionalized, celebrated, and conventionally used as an extension of politics. A military ethos pervaded all levels of Aztec society, and the ideology of the state religion emphasized not only the necessity of conflict but its moral and cosmological imperatives as well.

Why Wars Were Fought

Many kinds of incidents served as pretexts for Mesoamerican wars: murder, trespass, theft of property or women, abuse of ambassadors or traders, refusal to trade, and all manner of real or imagined slights among rulers and elites, such as failure to reciprocate adequately in gift exchanges. Such incidents could set in motion a graded series of conflicts, beginning with very local, small-scale ones, which might, depending on circumstances, escalate through several phases of intensity into massive campaigns and hostile confrontations that could last for generations. The important thing is that the process of warfare could be curtailed at any level, depending on the interests and circumstances of the combatants. Military campaigns were costly and frequently risky. It was not always prudent to go to war, no matter what the provocation, or to let war escalate beyond a certain level of intensity. In fact, the military capabilities of many Mesoamerican societies were probably intended as much for intimidation as for actual use.

Regardless of what precipitated wars, from at least Late Preclassic times on, virtually all warfare was an elite and especially royal enterprise. War was initiated by elites, organized by elites, led in the field by elites, celebrated in elite symbols and rituals, and fought largely for elite inter-

ests. Sometimes material gain was the primary motive—victors acquired land, raw materials, labor, slaves, booty, and tribute. Some commoners were tangibly enriched by warfare, but the bulk of the acquired wealth most directly benefited elites. Campaigns against other polities were also carried out for strategic reasons: to neutralize an enemy, to gain access to or defend trade routes, or to manipulate royal succession in advantageous ways.

Although material and strategic considerations were probably foremost, there were unquestionably powerful religious and ideological imperatives to Mesoamerican warfare as well; these were strongly motivated individuals in psychological terms, and sometimes they were seen as essential to the maintenance of world order. Much Mesoamerican war has a ritualistic quality, not only for these reasons but also because wars were frequently fought between polities or factions that were ethnically and culturally similar. For example, most of the opponents of the Aztecs in the Central Highlands of Mexico also spoke the Nahua language, shared similar religious beliefs and traditions of common origin, and had the same basic political, social, and economic institutions. Often the royal and elite families of warring polities were related by marriage, which partly accounts for the many recorded elaborate exchanges of etiquette even between enemies. Such cultural commonalities and relationships served to regulate and conventionalize warfare, to limit its destructiveness, and to facilitate the reestablishment of peaceful conditions. Most Maya war also occurred among culturally similar groups. War between culturally dissimilar peoples, such as the long standoff between the Aztecs and the Tarascans on their western frontier, could be much more violent, and the conflicts difficult or impossible to resolve.

The status rivalry associated with the strongly hierarchical and politically centralized polities that had emerged by the Late Preclassic precipitated new forms of dynastic war. As such polities grew and spread, increasingly large numbers of highly ranked individuals and the factions that supported them competed for important and prestigious offices and titles, which in turn had associated tangible rewards of privilege, wealth, and political influence. Ambiguities of descent and inheritance, as well as the differing ambitions and capabilities of claimants, fueled conflict not only between polities but within them. Usurpation, assassination, and rebellion were common. Situational alliances and marriages between dynasties were made to strengthen royal rule, but in the long run they also intensified status rivalry. Status rivalry warfare is most evident when detailed native histories are preserved, as for the Aztecs and Mixtecs, but it probably characterized most complex societies of the Classic period and earlier.

In summary, warfare was an important process in the structure and evolution of Mesoamerican cultures from the earliest times. Mesoamerica had its own highly distinctive traditions of warfare for unique logistical, technological, historical, and ideological reasons. But in a larger sense, Mesoamerican wars, like wars elsewhere, were fought for very familiar goals—titles, offices, wealth, power, security, glory, and prestige.

FURTHER READINGS

Byland, B. E., and J. M. D. Pohl. 1994. *In the Realm of 8 Deer.* Norman: University of Oklahoma Press.

Culbert, T. P. (ed.). 1991. *Classic Maya Political History.* New York: Cambridge University Press.

Hassig, R. 1988. *Aztec Warfare: Imperial Expansion and Political Control.* Norman: University of Oklahoma Press.

———. 1992. *War and Society in Ancient Mesoamerica.* Berkeley: University of California Press.

———. 1994. *Mexico and the Spanish Conquest.* London and New York: Longman.

Houston, S. 1993. *Hieroglyphs and History at Dos Pilas.* Austin: University of Texas Press.

Marcus, J. 1992. Political Fluctuations in Mesoamerica. *National Geographic Research and Exploration* 8:392–411.

Webster, D. 1976. Lowland Maya Fortifications. *Proceedings of the American Philosophical Society* 120:361–371.

———. 1993. The Study of Maya Warfare: What It Tells Us about the Maya and about Maya Archaeology. In J. Sabloff and J. S. Henderson (eds.), *Lowland Maya Civilization in the Eighth Century A.D.,* pp. 415–444. Washington, D.C.: Dumbarton Oaks.

David L. Webster

SEE ALSO

Fortifications; Weaponry

Weaponry

Weapons are customarily divided into projectiles—such as bows and arrows, spears, atlatls and darts, and slings—and shock weapons, such as swords, maces, and staff weapons. Projectiles often have utilitarian as well as military purposes, whereas shock weapons are more often specialized and dedicated specifically to war. Before gunpowder, projectiles were typically secondary to shock weapons in complex warfare.

Little is known about arms in Mesoamerica before the Middle Formative period, although tools were probably turned to military uses, including hand-held spears and atlatl-thrown darts. The first complex warfare in Mesoamerica began as early as 1150 B.C. with the Olmecs, who supplemented their fire-hardened spears with the first professional weapons, stone-pointed spears, which were presumably used as slashing staff weapons rather than as projectiles. Clubs and maces depicted on sculpture were designed for hand-to-hand combat and required specialized training rather than simply being hunting tools turned to military purposes. Atlatls and darts, though present, do not appear to have been used in war; they were not suited to the hand-to-hand combat of the day. After 900 B.C., this complex of shock weapons and short-range projectiles was augmented by the introduction of the sling. Woven from maguey fiber, slings gave soldiers the ability to strike at distances in excess of 200 meters, using hand-shaped, spherical stones or fired clay pellets rather than randomly selected stones.

Offensive arms are depicted in Olmec art, but defensive arms are not, which probably reflects the actual armaments used at that time. The absence of armor is also suggested by the general prevalence of maces at this time. In the Near East, maces declined with the advent of helmets and armor, which undercut their effectiveness, and a similar inverse relationship is likely in Mesoamerica. This functional relationship is further supported by the subsequent decline of maces following the late Formative adoption of large rectangular shields that protected much of the body. The only examples of protection are the helmets on Olmec giant heads, although this interpretation is probably mistaken, since similar "helmets" do not appear in media where full expression is not limited by the material.

In Classic Teotihuacan, weaponry as depicted in murals and sculpture fell into two major clusters: atlatlists with large rectangular shields held by a grip at the top rear and, at least since A.D. 600, spearmen with bucklers (the latter perhaps borrowed from the Zapotecs). Made of wood, the atlatl is approximately 0.6 meter long, with a central groove ending with a hook at the distal end, and finished with fingergrips almost a third of the way from the proximal end. The atlatl was used as an arm extension to throw short spears, or darts; the projectiles were made of reeds and fletched and had oak foreshafts mounting stone, bone, or fire-hardened points. For warfare, points were typically barbed. Atlatls provide almost 60 percent more thrust than hand-throwing spears and have an effective range of nearly 60 meters; however, because only four or five darts were carried in combat and they were quickly exhausted, their use as general weapons was limited and an alternative role is indicated. Coupled with shock-weapons troops, atlatlists could pour effective massed fire into opposing formations, disrupting and scattering them, which suggests the presence of complementary units of atlatlists who provided projectile fire and spearman who engaged in hand-to-hand combat.

Quilted cotton helmets were adopted as early as A.D. 300 at Teotihuacan, and quilted cotton body armor around A.D. 450. With armor now providing considerable protection, shields were reduced in size. Body armor grew longer over time until some examples covered the arms and reached the ground, at which point the protective benefits were outweighed by the restriction of mobility.

Though not represented in works of art, slings doubtless continued in use at Teotihuacan, but probably as weapons for commoners. Axes were used as well, but mostly as executioners' weapons; they would have played only a secondary role in combat, as did knives. Although unhafted examples were used, Teotihuacan knives were also hafted. Adding handles significantly increased knives' efficiency by reducing the size of the blades by half without reducing the edges that could be brought to bear, producing significantly lighter but equally effective knives. Blowguns that shot clay pellets were used at Teotihuacan but had no military role, since neither darts nor poison were used in them.

The relative uniformity of arms depicted at Teotihuacan suggests state control of the armory, formal training, rehearsed group tactics, and a chain of command. By contrast, weapons in the Maya area were quite varied and eclectic, indicating that each warrior armed himself and suggesting little state control of the army. Among the weapons common to the Maya region were axes, clubs, maces, and throwing spears. The latter were also used as fire spears against structures. The atlatl, though introduced by the Teotihuacanos, was not used, nor was the sling, though it too was known. Armor was not used by the Classic Maya, but shields and sometimes helmets were, at least in the Late Classic.

At that time, the next major weapon innovation, the bladed spear, developed in this area. Spears with small stone points may have been thrown, although doing so disarms the user. Instead, spears were more typically and effectively used as staff weapons, to slash and to puncture.

However, their role as staff weapons was limited by the length of their cutting surfaces, which in turn depended on the size and weight of the stone point: the larger the point, the heavier and more fragile the weapon. This bottleneck was breached after A.D. 600, when the Maya began setting stone blades into the handle below a relatively small point. This innovation produced a spear that could still puncture yet also had much longer cutting surfaces behind the point, all of which was achieved at a minimal increase in weight. Body armor did not develop to meet this new weapon, but shields proliferated. In addition to rectangular, round, and keyhole-shaped shields and bucklers, the Maya also used flexible shields that could be rolled up, perhaps for easier passage through jungle growth.

Spears with inset blades reached Central Mexico (at Cacaxtla) by A.D. 700, where spearmen complemented atlatlists. Round shields secured by a central strap on the forearm appeared, presumably having spread from the Maya area as well. Carrying the shield on the arm freed the left hand, so a knife could be used without compromising the main weapon. No helmets or armor are evident, which suggests the intrusion of Maya combat styles. However, this absence could also indicate an increased reliance on speed and mobility in combat. It may also have been a result of the post-Teotihuacan regional disintegration, in that cotton and other materials were no longer widely available; armor persisted in the cotton-producing areas of the Gulf Coast.

Cacaxtla's innovations in arms do not appear to have affected other centers at this time. Arms and armor at El Tajín remain those typical of Classic Central Mexico—armor, spears, clubs, atlatls, and knives, unhafted in this case. Similarly, Xochicalco retained primary reliance on atlatls and rectangular shields, but the Cacaxtla innovations foreshadowed the main lines of weapons development in Central Mexico.

The next major shift in weapons, improving troop mobility, accompanied the Toltecs after A.D. 900. The primary innovation was an offensive shock weapon, the short sword, mislabeled a "fending stick" because it was thought to have been used defensively to bat away darts at Chichén Itzá. Moreover, it is depicted being used in human sacrifice and was clearly bladed, as were similar, later weapons. Unlike the development in the Old World, in which metal knives became longer and longer until they became swords, Mesoamerican swords were based on a wooden form with obsidian blades glued into grooves along the edges. But like Old World swords, this combination produced a light weapon, approximately half a meter long, with a continuous cutting surface that relied on speed and sharpness for effect, rather than weight and the crushing power of mass impact. For the first time, a slashing weapon's size and weight allowed the same soldier to carry both an atlatl and a short sword simultaneously. Thus equipped, soldiers could throw darts with their atlatls and shift to swords for hand-to-hand combat once they closed with the enemy. This combination effectively doubled the offensive power of the army over the previous pattern of complementary projectile- and shock-weapon units. This use of dual weapons occupied both hands, but the addition of cotton armor to the left arm minimized the need to carry a separate shield, and the short sword could also be used to parry blows. Hafted knives were also used, carried in the armband when not needed.

This Toltec complex of arms and armor spread into northern Yucatán in the tenth century and altered Maya combat accordingly. But there were two other military innovations in Yucatán for which there is no evidence elsewhere at this time. The first is naval warfare, with both canoes and rafts being used as platforms from which darts were cast. The second is the fire tower, a scaffold with elevated platforms as high as 20 meters. This vantage point helped to compensate for the short range of atlatls and allowed soldiers to provide covering fire for those attacking defended temples and other structures. Although naval warfare persisted through the Spanish conquest, the introduction of bows and arrows, with their greater range, rendered fire towers obsolete.

The bow reached Central Mexico from the north around A.D. 1100. Measuring up to 1.5 meters long, the wooden bows were simple rather than compound. Sinew and hide bowstrings were common in Central Mexico, but henequen was also used among the Maya. Arrows produced for military purposes were made of straightened reeds with oak foreshafts; they were bound with *maguey* fiber to prevent splitting, and fletched, with barbed stone (or sometimes copper) points glued and tied in place. They were constructed to standard, uniform sizes. These and other state-controlled arms were stored in public arsenals in the central precincts. With a probable range of 90 to 180 meters, bows and arrows quickly displaced atlatls in smaller armies, although swordsmen retained atlatls in large armies for use while closing with the enemy because the latter's great punching power at close range could disrupt the opposing formation.

Two other innovations appeared during the Aztec era: fully bladed thrusting spears and broadswords. Although thrusting spears had been in use for well over a thousand years, at this time stone points were dropped entirely and replaced by an ovoid wooden head 10 cm across at its widest, with close-set stone blades glued into grooves running the entire length. The entire thrusting spear was 1.8 to 2.2 meters long, with the head measuring about 0.3 meter long, producing a two-handed staff weapon with enormous slashing capability. The second innovation, the broadsword, displaced the short sword as the premier hand-to-hand weapon. More than 0.8 meter long, the oak broadsword was armed with close-set obsidian blades glued into grooves running along either side; it boasted a cutting surface of almost 0.6 meter on each side. These more efficient and deadlier weapons encouraged the retention of round shields which, in Aztec times, were made of fire-hardened cane tied with maguey fiber and backed with heavy cotton or leather; they measured 0.75 meter in diameter and carried hanging feather fringes that would have obscured the opponents' view and could probably have deflected spent projectiles. Better armor was adopted as well. Quilted cotton armor 5 to 8 cm thick was used to protect the torso, but it did not cover arms or legs, presumably because mobility was more important than protection. There is no evidence that this armor was strengthened by being soaked in salt brine, and the report that it was is probably a misunderstanding. In a few areas where cotton was unavailable, body armor was also made from *maguey*, although its longer, straighter fiber must have been noticeably inferior to the shorter, springier cotton fiber.

The Aztecs also used canoes in warfare, not simply for troop transport and logistical support but as offensive weapons. The *chimalacalli,* or shield canoe, was a military canoe armored with thick planks to withstand hostile fire. Unconventional arms also played a role. Chile fires were occasionally used to gas defenders, although this tactic was useful only against stationary targets, such as towns, and depended on favorable winds. Wasp nests were sometimes lobbed over city walls. Poison, and therefore poisoned arrows, were not used in Mesoamerican warfare, but fire arrows were employed against wooden structures.

The sequence of weapons development in Mesoamerica involved much borrowing and numerous changes in arms and armor. Much of this evolution reflects the famous offensive/defensive cycle, a deadly dialectic in which developments in offensive or defensive arms stimulate counterdevelopments. Combat death was most frequently the result of wounds to the stomach, chest, and head. Punctures to vital organs prior to modern medicine meant death. Slashing wounds were far less serious, and the history of Mesoamerican arms development mirrors this. Weapons became increasingly efficient, featuring more and more cutting surface with less and less weight, while armor generally grew better and focused increasingly on the vulnerable trunk area.

However, a significant part of the history of arms development and/or adoption in Mesoamerica reflects differences in social and political organization. Even though Mesoamerican arms and armor became more efficient over time, they were not uniformly adopted throughout Mesoamerica as soon as they were invented. Rather, the main developments were initiated (or adopted) by expansionary groups—especially empires—because greater combat effectiveness was important to their success. Adopting technologically superior arms and armor was of less interest to those city-states where warfare was used primarily to bolster the ruler's claims to office. There, military concerns were largely internal, combat efficiency was not pivotal, and innovations that might disrupt the existing social system were ignored.

FURTHER READINGS

Bandelier, A. F. 1880. On the Art of War and Mode of Warfare of the Ancient Mexicans. *Reports of the Peabody Museum of American Archaeology and Ethnology* 2:95–161.

Cook de Leonard, C. 1956 Dos atlatl de la época Teotihuacana. In *Estudios antropológicos publicados en homenaje al doctor Manuel Gamio.* Mexico City: Dirección General de Publicaciones.

Follett, P. H. F. 1932. *War and Weapons of the Maya.* Middle American Research Series, Publication, 4.

Hassig, R. 1988. *Aztec Warfare: Imperial Expansion and Political Control.* Norman: University of Oklahoma Press.

———. 1992. *War and Society in Ancient Mesoamerica.* Berkeley: University of California Press.

Ross Hassig

SEE ALSO

Fortifications; Militarism and Conflict; Warfare

Weaving and Textiles

"Fabric" (from Latin *fabricare,* "to make, to build, to fabricate") is the generic term for all fibrous constructions; "textile" (from Latin *texere,* "to weave") specifically denotes woven—interlaced, warp-weft—fabrics. The be-

ginning of fabric craft occurred in the Old World in the middle of the Upper Paleolithic, 20,000 to 30,000 years ago, when a genius discovered the principle of twisting handfuls of short, weak plant fibers into long, strong string. Suddenly it was possible to catch, to hold, and to carry. Elizabeth Barber sees simple string as taming the world to human will and ingenuity, serving as the unseen weapon that allowed the human race to conquer the earth, to move out into every econiche on the globe. Indeed, the oldest fabrics known in the New World reflect this "string revolution."

The earliest extant Mesoamerican fabric fragments were found at the preceramic cave site of Guila Naquitz (Oaxaca). These fragments, produced by methods that did not require looms, included coiled basketry, cordage, and knotted netting. Mary Elizabeth King suggests that these techniques may have been brought across the Bering Strait into the Americas by early hunter-gatherer migrants. All these ancient pieces were made of non-cotton plant fiber around 8000 B.C. Similar fragments from the Great Basin and Peru have comparable dates. The earliest evidence in Mesoamerica of unspun cotton comes from before 5000 B.C. and was found in Coxcatlan Cave in the Tehuacán Valley of southern Puebla.

Fibers

In Peru, camelid "wool" from llama, alpaca, and vicuña was used, but Mesoamericans had no knowledge of animal fibers until the Spanish introduced sheep. In pre-Hispanic Middle America, plants were the basis for all cloth. Bark cloth or paper was made by soaking and then pounding the treated inner bark of the native fig (*Ficus* spp.), the mulberry *(Morus niger),* or *maguey,* a fleshy-leaved *Agave.* These pounded fabrics were used for ritual banners, deity-impersonator attire, votive offerings, and pictorial screenfold manuscripts. Plant fibers were also made up into woven cloth. For these fibers—or any fabrics—the key qualities desired in raw materials are length and flexibility. Since little in nature is intrinsically long, strong, and flexible enough, all the Middle American textile plants had to be processed. Some required more work than others.

Spinning

Thousands of years ago, after early peoples realized that plant fibers could be twisted together into firm, coarse string, they discovered the benefits of spinning. The direction of the spin can be either S-twist or Z-twist. Later, when the potential value of softer textile fibers was

Wife of the married youth

Fig. 1. An Aztec woman spinning cotton thread from a fillet of prepared fibers. *Codex Mendoza* 1992: Vol.4:folio 68r.

realized, they were twisted—either S or Z—and then retwisted in the opposite direction into plies, the joining together of two or more single threads. All of this was, and still is, accomplished by attaching prepared fibers to a smooth, straight wooden stick with tapered ends: a spindle. This implement is weighted with a disk-shaped object, known as a whorl, made of wood, bone, shell, horn, baked clay, or stone, sometimes carved and ornamented. The whorl acts both as a weight and a flywheel, helping to maintain the motion of the spindle as it rotates within a small, shallow bowl set on the floor or ground (see Figure 1). As the spindle "dances," it twists the prepared fibers into a thread of desired thickness. In Middle America, spindle whorls still are called by their Nahuatl name, *malacate*.

A correlation exists between the weight and diameter of the spindle whorl, the length of fiber spun, and the thickness of thread produced. This relationship enables archaeologists to use measurements of whorls—weight, hole diameter, and total diameter—to deduce the raw material and thickness of the yarn that was produced at sites where spindle whorls are found. Large, heavy spindles are best for thick yarns spun from long-staple fibers such as *maguey*, whereas small, light spindles are used for thin thread spun from cotton, a short-staple fiber.

In the Late Postclassic (A.D. 1250–1519)—the best-documented pre-Hispanic period—a garment's fiber served as a social marker. The majority of the population wore clothing made of a strong, woody bast fiber obtained from nettles or, more often, from the phloem of such long-leafed plants as yucca, palm, or *maguey*; the last was the source of the common peoples' *ixtle* cloth. All these coarse plant fibers required laborious processing: the

leaves had to be roasted, soaked, and rotted to aid in the removal of the pulpy plant tissue from its long fibers. These fibers then had to be scraped, washed, combed, and treated with maize water before they could be spun and woven. Occasionally certain of the whiter, more delicate *maguey* fibers were used unspun, carefully woven into fine cloth that had a silk-like sheen.

The Mesoamerican status fiber *par excellence* was cotton, principally the white strain *(Gossypium hirsutum)*, although the tawny *coyuchi* cotton—known as *coyoichcatl* ("coyote-colored") in Nahuatl—was also used. The preparation of cotton for spinning first necessitated the removal from the boll of all seeds and impurities. The cleaned fibers were then placed on a mat or deerskin cushion and beaten with special sticks until the cotton was fluffy and even enough to be formed into a fillet from which fibers could be drawn out and spun into thread.

Weaving

In the far distant past, after the softer textile fibers started to be spun, it was discovered that the strength of these softer plied yarns could be better utilized when they were further combined into a fabric structure. Weaving, the interlacing of two sets of yarn elements, the warp and weft, is an example of such a structure. But because thread is very flexible—as opposed to the stiff materials from which mats and baskets are made—it is almost impossible to weave one set of threads through the other unless one group is held tightly in place. It is the warp threads that are put under tension; the device that holds the warp firm and fast is known as a loom.

The back-strap loom—named for the strap that encircles the weaver's hips (Figure 2)—has been Mesoamerica's

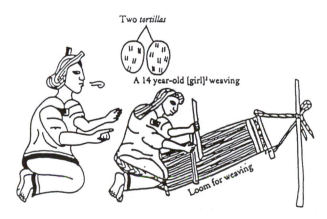
Two *tortillas*

A 14 year-old [girl][1] weaving

Loom for weaving

Fig. 2. An Aztec mother teaching her daughter to weave. *Codex Mendoza* 1992: Vol.4:folio 60r.

ubiquitous weaving tool from ancient times to the present. An outstanding feature of this loom is its ability to produce textiles with four completely finished edges. As a result, no further processing is necessary if the textile is to be worn as a narrow garment (e.g., loincloth or cape); wider clothing can be created by simply seaming together the sides of one or more webs of cloth. The finished edge of a textile is known as the selvage: each time the weft proceeds from one row to the next it binds the edge—the "self edge" or "selvedge"—thus keeping the finished work from slipping out of place. The selvages at the top and bottom of a textile are created in a different manner, reflecting the way in which the warp threads are attached to the loom.

Until a back-strap loom is set up with its warps under tension, it is literally just a bunch of sticks, as Figure 3 illustrates. The pointed stick shown at the top of the bundle is the batten, or weaving sword, used to tap down the newly inserted wefts. The two sticks below are the warp beam and the cloth beam, each notched so as to receive, respectively, the cord that attaches the loom to an upright post or tree and the backstrap that secures the loom to the weaver's body (see Figure 2). It is to these two beams that the warps are attached.

The thread that will become the warp is first measured out on a warping frame (Figure 4, arrow at right) to establish the length of the planned textile and the number of warp threads needed to form its width, which cannot exceed the weaver's reach. The warp is wound on the frame in a figure-eight configuration, creating a cross, or lease, that gives each warp its proper sequential position on the loom and also serves to form the alternating openings in the warp—the sheds—through which the weft will pass.

After the thread is removed from the frame with the cross securely tied (see Figure 4, arrow at left), a piece of hemp string is slipped through each end of the looped warp. It is these two strings, not the warps themselves, that are attached with spiral binding to the warp and cloth beams (Figure 5, b and n) respectively. As a result, the warps themselves need not be cut when the textile is removed from the loom; this results in finished selvages at the top and bottom.

The weaving of a textile proceeds from the cloth-breast beam up toward the warp beam. However, first the loom has to be reversed so that a narrow band can be woven at the warp-beam end to create a heading strip (Figure 5, z) that spaces and stabilizes the warps; the loom is then returned to its proper position. As the weaving proceeds, the cloth beam and the rolling stick are used to roll up the already-woven section of the textile, bringing the unwoven threads closer to the weaver (see Figure 5, l). When the space between the almost-completed textile and the heading begins to narrow, it is necessary to put the last wefts through with a needle.

Aside from child-rearing and food preparation, the life of a Mesoamerican woman from birth to death centered around the production of beautiful, well-made textiles. A newborn baby girl, at her bathing ceremony, was pre-

Fig. 3 Female accouterments: A spindle and unspun fibers; work basket; unassembled loom sticks; shallow bowl in which the spindle twirls; a *huipil* (blouse). *Florentine Codex* Sahagún 1979: Book 6:folio 170v.

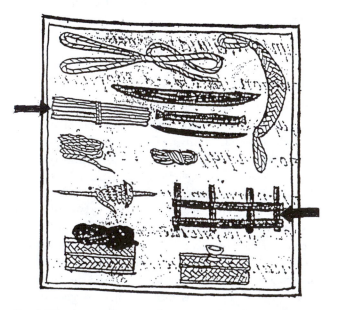

Fig. 4. Weaving equipment. *Florentine Codex* Sahagún 1979: Book 8:folio 31v.

sented all the equipment of women: "the spinning whorl, the batten, the reed basket, the spinning bowl, the skeins, the shuttle, her little skirt, her little blouse," according to Sahagún (see Figure 3). When a woman died, her weaving equipment was burned with her in the funeral pyre to make it available to her in the afterworld.

One of a mother's principal obligations was to teach her daughter how to spin and weave properly; this social emphasis appears repeatedly in the sixteenth-century Spanish chronicles. A woman who was a bad weaver was held in the lowest esteem; such a female was described as lazy, indolent, nonchalant, sullen, and a deceiver. A textile with a crooked hem was said to denote a selfish weaver. One text implies that such a woman was good for nothing but sacrifice. Obviously, in Mesoamerica there was strong pressure to be a competent weaver!

The social importance of weaving is further reflected in iconographic and ritual symbolism. Weaving apparatus was part of certain Aztec deity costumes. The fertility goddess Tlazolteotl is often shown with spindles filled with thread stuck in the unspun fillet of cotton that encircles her head; the deity Xochiquetzal, patroness of weaving, is sometimes depicted in association with looms, spindles, and weaving.

Textiles

The earliest extant indication of Mesoamerican weaving comes from the Tehuacán Valley of Puebla, in the form of a plain-weave impressed sherd dating from between 1500 and 900 B.C. Loom weaving may have begun in South America during the Early Formative period (1700–1000 B.C.) and traveled north to the Mexican plateau with early migrants. Such migrations might also have influenced the increasing numbers of garments depicted on Formative period Mexican ceramic figurines, clothing that appears to reflect outside influence. Unfortunately, information derived from actual ancient textiles is very sparse.

Climatic conditions have a great effect on the preservation of cloth over time. Unfortunately, the dampness and humidity of Middle America have destroyed all but occasional woven fragments, although some important textile techniques have been preserved owing to contact of cloth with copper. Fortunately, small pieces of pre-Hispanic cloth have also been found preserved in dry caves, such as those at Chiptic (Chiapas), the Mixteca Alta region (Oaxaca), and Tehuacán (Puebla).

Some Mesoamerican textile fragments have survived in the oxygen-deprived environment of Yucatán's Sacred Cenote, a deep sinkhole in limestone with a pool at the

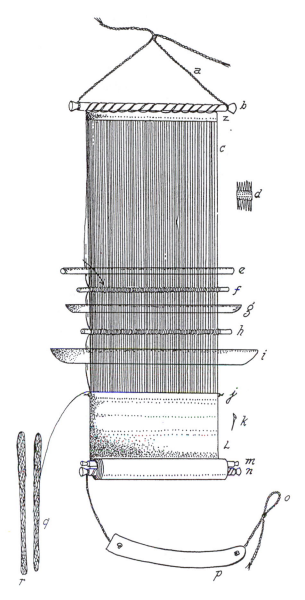

Fig. 5. Backstrap loom (after Cordry and Cordry 1968: 35). A. cord fastened to a tree or post after the heading (z) is finished; b. warp beam; c. warp threads; d. comb; e. shed roll or shed stick; f. headle or heald rods; g. small batten; h. headle or heald rods; i. large batten; j. tenter; k. thorn used to fasten tenter to web; l. woven cloth or web; m. rolling stick; n. cloth beam; o. cord fastened to backstrap; p. backstrap (mecapa); q. bobbins; r. bobbins; z. heading.

bottom that had a millennium of ceremonial use at the Maya site of Chichén Itzá. In 1904–1905, dredging was carried out at the Sacred Cenote and more than six hundred blackened textile fragments were recovered; close examination has revealed a substantial variety of weaving techniques. In addition to three types of plain weave (i.e., the wefts pass alternately over and then under the warps; see Figure 6, there are examples of more complex techniques: supplementary weft brocade, in which extra, decorative, nonstructural wefts are added during the weaving process; warp floats, also known as supplementary warps, in which extra, decorative, nonstructural warp threads sit atop and float at the back of the essential ground cloth; gauze, an open, lacelike weave achieved by crossing and recrossing two adjoining warps that are held in place by a passage of the weft; looped pile, in which supplementary, nonstructural threads are knotted to the warps as the fabric is being woven and subsequently are trimmed to create a plush surface; twill, in which one set of threads skips at regular intervals over and under another set, creating floats that progress forward to create the characteristic diagonal ribs or ridges on the face and reverse of twill fabrics; and bound open work, in which supplementary yarns float in the warp direction on the reverse side of the fabric and then are turned and used as wefts, or binding threads, to create diamond shapes or openwork bands. Virtually all of the Cenote textiles are made with Z-spun and S-plied cotton yarns. Unfortunately, the geometric designs used on these fragments are too generalized to serve as indicators of date or cultural affiliation.

King, analyzing a range of Mesoamerican fragments from the Oaxaca Valley, the Tehuacán Valley, and several other Middle American areas, has demonstrated that by the Postclassic period (A.D. 900–1521), weaving techniques also included twill doublecloth, in which the warp and/or the weft is composed of two series of threads, each having its own distinct set. On completion, one group of threads appears on one side of the textile, the second occurs on the reverse. Another technique she identified is

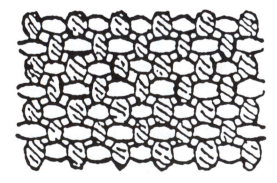

Fig. 6. Plain weave: The wefts pass alternately over and then under the warps (Barber 1994: 40).

slit tapestry, in which the weft—although essential to the structure of the cloth itself—is discontinuous, interlacing with the warp where a particular block of color is required by the design and creating a slit parallel to the warp where the adjacent wefts begin and end.

In the years since King's article was published, some impressive additional textile finds have been made. A few of the more important techniques include end-to-end warp lock, twined weft fringe, weft-twined cross bar, and warp-and-weft interlocking. Two of these newly discovered techniques—weft-wrap open work and shaped weaving—have never been found in Peru.

Embroidery, the application of decorative thread with a needle to already-woven fabric, was also a common technique to enhance cloth. One highly prized yarn used for the embroidering of textiles incorporated the soft underbelly fur of rabbits. When spun, this downy fiber produced an embroidery thread called *tochomitl,* famous not only for its ability to dye to rich hues but also for its lasting color and silklike sheen. There also is evidence that in certain regions of Mesoamerica, the filament of a wild silk—the cocoons of caterpillars feeding on the leaves of the *madroño* (red oak tree)—was used in small quantities for decorative purposes. The costly, bright colored feathers of tropical birds were either interwoven or carefully sewn onto high-status textiles. Other decorative materials applied to cloth were sea and snail shells, stones of different qualities and colors, and objects of copper, gold, or silver.

Pre-Hispanic textiles were also enhanced by painting or dyeing. Three methods of dyeing were employed: either the fiber was dyed before spinning, the thread was soaked in dye after spinning, or the cloth was dyed after weaving. A range of resist-dye techniques was known: ikat involved tying off ("reserving") portions of thread and dyeing it before the cloth was woven; plangi created small round or square patterns on an already-woven textile by tying off sections of the cloth and then dyeing it; bound-resist involved rolling and binding cloth prior to dyeing to create a series of dyed and undyed stripes; and batik utilized a waxy substance applied to specific areas of woven cloth to reserve those sections from the dye bath.

Dyeing materials were of vegetable, animal, and mineral origin. Mordants such as alum and copperas (ferrous sulfate) were used to fix or modify the colors of dyes. Vegetable dyes came from flowers, leaves, stems, roots, wood, bark, and fruit. Colors of animal origin included the famous caracol, a light purple shellfish dye *(Purpura patula pansa),* and the carmine-red cochineal *grana,* made from crushed, dried bodies of the female insect *(Dactylopius coccus)* that lives on the nopal *(Opuntia* or prickly pear) cactus. Mineral dyes from certain earths and oxides were also utilized.

Roles of Textiles

The socio-economic importance of the Mesoamerican textiles cannot be overestimated. In addition to their role in trade and tribute, one specific type of textile, the *quachtli* ("large cotton mantle"), even served as a standard of value in the Aztec economy. These long, plain white cloths may have been made of a heavy, utilitarian fabric similar to sailcloth or canvas. *Quachtli* served—along with cacao beans, the source of chocolate—as a primary medium of economic exchange. *Quachtli* were employed as restitution for theft, credit from merchants, and ransom for stolen property. Many goods, including slaves, are recorded by the early chroniclers as being valued in terms of *quachtli.*

Weaving was the domain of women, and each household appears to have been responsible for meeting its own needs as well as whatever cloth was required for tribute payment. Aside from the palace and the temples, which had resident groups of weavers producing the specialized fabrics needed by those institutions—elite clothing, high-level gift exchanges, decorative hangings, deity and priestly attire—no evidence has been found for the existence of organized weaving workshops. It was the wives and daughters of each family who wove the great bulk of Meso-american textiles, both utility cloth—family clothing, carrying cloths, tortilla covers, bedding, swaddling clothes, awnings, mummy wrappings—and the highly decorated fabrics exhibiting an impressive array of long-established regional patterns that so dazzled the Conquistadors.

Conclusion

The archaeological record indicates that Mesoamerican textile crafts were older than pottery and agriculture; ethnographic analogs suggest that the making of cloth may have consumed more hours of labor per year than ceramic and food production combined. As Barber notes, it was the late eighteenth-century Industrial Revolution, with its power looms, cotton gins, spinning jennys, and great cloth mills, that freed the modern Western world from dependence on handmade fabric. By now, we have forgotten the tremendous effort involved in such an enterprise, but not so long ago textile production was humankind's single most time-consuming labor. This certainly was true throughout pre-Hispanic Mesoamerica, an

exotic world of magnificent cloth and clothing, and a culture that truly excelled in the textile arts.

FURTHER READINGS

Anawalt, P. R. 1981. *Indian Clothing before Cortés: Meso-american Costumes from the Codices.* Norman: University of Oklahoma Press.

———. 1992. A Comparative Analysis of the Costumes and Accoutrements of Codex Mendoza. In *Codex Mendoza* vol. 1, pp. 103–150. Berkeley: University of California Press.

Barber, E. W. 1994. *Woman's Work: The First 20,000 Years.* New York: W. W. Norton.

Cordry, D., and D. Cordry. 1968. *Mexican Indian Costumes.* Austin: University of Texas Press.

Emery, I. 1966. The Primary Structures of Fabrics: An Illustrated Classification. Washington, D.C.: Textile Museum.

Hicks, F. 1994. Cloth in the Political Economy of the Aztec State. In M. Hodge and M. Smith (eds.), *Economies and Politics in the Aztec Realm,* pp. 89–111. Albany: State University of New York.

Johnson, I. W. 1967. Textiles. In *The Prehistory of the Tehuacán Valley,* vol. 2, pp. 191–226. Austin: University of Texas Press.

Kelly, I. T. 1944–1945. Ixtle Weaving at Chiquilistan, Jalisco. *Carnegie Institute of Washington, Notes on Middle American Archaeology and Ethnology* 2:106–112.

King, M. E. 1979. The Prehistoric Textile Industry of Mesoamerica. In *The Junius B. Bird Pre-Columbian Textile Conference,* pp. 265–278. Washington, D.C.: Textile Museum and Dumbarton Oaks.

Mahler Lothrup, J. 1992. Textiles. In C. C. Coggins (ed.), *Artifacts from the Cenote of Sacrifice: Chichén Itzá, Yucatán,* pp. 33–90. Cambridge, Mass.: Harvard University Press.

Parsons, J., and M. H. Parsons. 1990. *Maguey Utilization in Highland Central Mexico: An Archaeological Ethnography.* Museum of Anthropology, University of Michigan, Anthropological Papers, no. 82. Ann Arbor.

Sahagún, B. de. 1950–1982. *Florentine Codex: General History of the Things of New Spain.* A. J. O. Anderson and C. E. Dibble (trans. and eds.) Monographs of the School of American Research, 14, parts 2–13. Santa Fe: University of Utah Press.

Patricia Rieff Anawalt

Weicker Site
See Northwestern Frontier

West Mexico

Until recently, the archaeology of West Mexico has not received the professional attention that has been devoted to Mesoamerica's other regions. This vast zone has been left to looters and art historians, and many of the formulations concerning its archaeology were, and are, phrased in negative terms. Traditionally, the designation "West Mexico" has included the states of Jalisco, Nayarit, and Colima. Although it is somewhat artificial to discuss the archaeology of this great region in terms of contemporary administrative districts, there is nonetheless a need to subdivide the region for the purpose of discussion.

Jalisco

The archaeology of Jalisco has been characterized until recently by an exclusive focus on its spectacular shaft tombs and figurines. Contextualizations for these tombs were seldom sought because of a series of negative presuppositions concerning the nature of ancient society in West

Mexico which turned out to be inaccurate when field work oriented toward settlement patterns and architecture was finally undertaken.

The earliest phases of human activity in Jalisco are very poorly understood. A few Palaeoindian Clovis projectile points have been found in northernmost Jalisco and the general Zacoalco area. Sites from the Archaic have been discovered in the Autlán-Grullo and Etzatlán areas; the latter finds are characterized by Lerma-type projectile points dating to c. 5000 B.C. The transition to an agricultural economy has not been explored in detail, except in a preliminary study from the Zapotlán el Grande zone. The appropriate botanical foundation existed; for example, undomesticated diploid varieties of *Zea mays* can still be found in the Sierra de Manantlán area.

Our understanding of the Early Formative cultures is little better. Three sites in Jalisco (Citala, Teuchitlán, and San Juanito) have shaft tombs of the El Opeño variety found in Michoacán. They are less monumental than those at El Opeño itself but nonetheless have all the defining characteristics, including stairway access, oval chambers, and solid and small figurines. These tombs, dated to c. 1500 B.C., constitute the first indications of sociocultural complexity in the region. Apparently contemporary with these tombs are sites that have ceramics characteristic of the Capacha phase of Colima. One small platform, found near San Pedro, covered a pit bearing Capacha ceramics and human long bones. In addition, Capacha ceramics have been found near Tomatlán and Puerto Vallarta, along Jalisco's Pacific coast.

The Middle Formative San Felipe phase is represented by circular platforms averaging 28 meters in diameter and 2 meters high. These platforms contain burials, mostly simple pits but a few elegant shaft tombs. These shaft tombs have modest, partial stairways that represent an obvious carryover from the El Opeño period. Figurines are flat and show some relationships with Tlatilco varieties from Central Mexico. The platforms were constructed at fairly regular intervals around the upper shores of the lake basins of western Jalisco. Very few residential areas have been identified from this time period.

The Late Formative period (c. 300 B.C.–200 A.D.) gave Jalisco its fame in world archaeology, with spectacular hollow, portrait-style figurines that have been sought by collectors and museums for more than a century. The tombs in which these figurines were found are of four basic types: (1) simple pits, which have the widest distribution throughout Jalisco; (2) shallow shaft tombs with shafts c. 2 meters deep and one simple chamber—also widely distributed; (3) deep (to 10 meters) shaft tombs with one or two chambers; and (4) monumental shaft tombs with shafts to 18–22 meters deep, often with three chambers. The latter two varieties are found only in the Teuchitlán-Etzatlán region, which, by this period, formed the nucleus of an emerging regional civilization. The offerings in the greatest tombs are spectacular, including jade, turquoise, shell, pseudo-cloisonné, hollow ceramic figurines, and obsidian. Only one such tomb, at Huitzilapa, has been professionally excavated; it was a two-chamber, 8-meter-deep shaft tomb with *in situ* grave goods, including perishable food offerings and mats in which the bodies had been wrapped. In the Atemajac, Bolaños, and Sayula valleys, many tombs of the smaller varieties have been professionally excavated recently.

Associated with the shaft tombs in the Teuchitlán-Etzatlán region are small circular compounds, each composed of a circular altar that is surrounded by a circular patio, which in turn is surrounded by a circular banquette. Atop this banquette are either four or eight platforms. These small structures served as the vernacular models for the monumental, formal circular buildings of the following Classic period (A.D. 200–700).

The Classic period buildings are impressive and very symmetrical. This architectural format, based on concentric circles planned from a radical center, is found nowhere else in Mesoamerica or indeed in the world. The largest circles have diameters exceeding 120 meters or 400 meters or more in circumference. They are often grouped in precincts that have six to eight such structures, along with monumental ball courts (the largest, 135 meters long), and elite residential compounds. The greatest and best-preserved precincts are at Teuchitlán, Loma Alta, Mesa Alta, and Santa Quitería. The precincts at San Juan de los Arcos and Ahualulco, while also monumental, are very badly damaged by quarrying, land leveling, and plowing.

Accompanying these buildings are very large but fairly dispersed habitation zones that often cover thousands of hectares of terraced countryside. This concentration of monumental architecture and habitation zones does not occur in other areas in Jalisco; thus, it marks the presence within the overall zone of a nuclear area surrounded, at regular intervals or at passes, by hilltop fortifications. The presence of very large populations is indicated by the size of the habitation zones. The pseudo-cloisonné ceramic vessels may indicate the existence of an early glyph-based recording system.

Wetland drained-field features of the *chinampa* variety have been discovered at a number of localities within the nuclear region. Approximately 32 square kilometers of these features have been documented to date. Large concentrations of obsidian mines (1,265 mines and quarries at La Joya, more than 800 at Primavera, and around 150 at San Juan de los Arcos), malachite and azurite mines, and crystal quarries are found in the mountain uplands. The Classic period in this area was clearly a time of regional civilization.

The Valle de las Banderas (the hinterland of Puerto Vallarta) is another zone of complex development during the Classic period. A small, Teuchitlán-type circle has been located, along with a series of fairly simple shaft tombs. At Ixtapa there are a rectangular pyramid complex and a section of a large irrigation or drainage ditch. In the Sayula Valley, a number of sites show that salt procurement became an important economic specialization during the Classic period. The Ixtépete and El Grillo sites, just outside Guadalajara, began their architectural elaboration at this time. The format, however, is rectangular. The relationship of these buildings to the cemetery complex at nearby Tabachines is unclear.

The Epiclassic and early Postclassic periods (A.D. 700–900 and 900–1250) were a time of dramatic change throughout all of Mesoamerica, including Jalisco. The first experiment of civilization in Jalisco collapsed during the Epiclassic. Square and rectangular platforms and pyramids completely replaced the circular format both in the nuclear area and throughout the rest of Jalisco. Santa Cruz de Bárcenas, Tabaquero, and Portezuelo became the most important sites in the Teuchitlán zone. Ceramic types include polychrome *molcajetes* (grinders) with mold-made supports. Figurine art is largely mold-made, too, and of rather low quality. The Aztatlán complex, still poorly understood, spread throughout much of the region, especially along the coast. This complex is defined largely from elaborate and beautiful polychrome ceramic art styles; its social import is the subject of continuing debate.

Sites from southern Jalisco, such as those in the Autlán, Tuxcacuesco, Tamazula, Tuxpan, and Sayula areas, have received professional attention since the 1940s, when they were studied by the pioneer archaeologist Isabel Kelly. Many of these sites show some degree of Classic period occupation, but most activity post-dates c. A.D. 700. No Postclassic site or area shows the degree of elaboration seen in the Teuchitlán-Etzatlán nuclear region during the Classic period, though. For the last phases (beginning c. 1400), the Purepécha (Tarascans) from Michoacán started a predatory expansion into large segments of southern and central Jalisco. Certain contact sites from the late Postclassic (1250 to the Spanish conquest), such as Ocomo (Oconahua), Guaxacate (Magdalena), and Etzatlán, have received some attention. The structure at Ocomo is particularly notable: it forms a 125-meter-square block with an interior plazuela and high surrounding platforms of monumental proportions, very similar to the palace illustrated in the Codice Quinatzín from Texcoco.

The Spanish encountered a series of fairly small-scale states in much of Jalisco on their arrival in the mid-1520s and 1530s. This situation was due to the area's conversion into a military march, caught between the expansion of the Tarascans from the south and the Caxcanes from the north. The Spaniards' initial observations were made as the first wave of European epidemic diseases was beginning and thus do not report an entirely pristine situation. However, it is a mistake to characterize all ancient society in Jalisco only from the perspective of this last phase. The late Formative and Classic periods were times of very complex developments, constituting another region of civilization within Mesoamerica by the time of Christ.

Nayarit

Like those of Jalisco and Colima, the ceramic figurines from Nayarit are known throughout the world. The major difference is that the Nayarit area is much more thoroughly contextualized in archaeological studies, although looting, agricultural damage, urbanization, and official indifference still plague the area's pre-Hispanic heritage. Nayarit, though a small state, has a multiplicity of major ecological zones. The piedmont, southern highlands, and coastal plains were the focal zones for the most complex ancient activity. The area is extremely well watered, with several extensive estuary zones.

Unfortunately, political considerations have engendered a school of archaeological interpretation for the area. The tourist development of Mexcaltitán has restimulated the stale notion that this site was the legendary Aztec homeland, Aztlan. Much effort and scarce resources are being expended trying to publicize this Aztec link rather than exploring Nayarit's heritage on its own terms.

No Paleoindian remains have yet been documented for the area, though several private collections in the Ixtlán del Río area have Lerma-like projectile points. The Archaic period is represented by shell middens, especially those at Matanchén (in the San Blas region, dated to c. 2000 B.C.), and probably in the Marismas.

Formative developments are better documented. The earliest material is related, in ways yet to be determined, to the Capacha ceramics of Colima (and Jalisco), and has been found in the San Blas region. The suggested dates for this material range from 1200 to 1000 B.C. Relatively modest shaft tombs have been found throughout the state; those from the southern part were the most elaborate. These tombs date from the Late Formative (c. 300 B.C.–300 A.D.) and represent a broad range of architectural designs.

Ceramic architectural models probably date from this time period, as well. They have been found in small quantities by looters in the south central piedmont and highlands, extending through the Ixtlán del Río area into westernmost Jalisco. These architectural figurines provide an array of ethnographic information: ceremonial scenes, daily life, architectural detail, costume, musical instruments, domesticated animals, cooking and eating scenes, and so on. The survey for Formative period architectural sites, both habitational and ceremonial, though largely confined to west central Jalisco, has confirmed the accuracy of the ceramic models.

Other ceramic figurine types from the same general area are also notable. The "Chinesco" variety has attracted the most attention, but the realistic portrayals of individuals from the Ixtlán del Río area are also well known. Some Chinesco figurines are very large and are attempts to portray individuals in nearly lifelike scale. Only a few shaft tombs have been professionally studied in Nayarit, those at Maizal and El Ranchito being the best examples.

Late Formative period surface architecture is poorly understood, despite the ceramic figurines. The Teuchitlán-like concentric circular buildings that have been located to date probably belong to this period, as well as to the early Classic. Thus, influences from west central Jalisco appear to have been important. These circles have been located near Guaynamota, Santa María del Oro, and San Pedro Lagunillas. The latter two sites are in the heart of Nayarit's shaft tomb and figurine area. The earliest part of the Amapa sequence belongs to this general time frame.

The Cerro el Calón site, in the Sinaloa sector of the Marismas Nacionales adjoining Nayarit, is still the subject of much debate. El Calón's huge pyramid is about 80 by 100 meters at the base and over 20 meters high. Much of the fill is composed of unopened blocks of shellfish, and there is no buildup of any other type of organic material. It was constructed at some point during the Formative;

radiocarbon dates from shell samples ranged from 1500 B.C. to A.D. 1. The type of shellfish used in the construction, along with its location on the ancient beach system, also point to an early date for the structure. Of the more than six hundred shell mounds and ridges that exist in the Marismas, this is one of the largest. Many archaeologists assert that it is a midden, not a pyramid, but its rectangular and truncated shape, along with the construction details, argue for a planned structure. If the Calón structure were situated anywhere else in Mesoamerica, it would automatically have been classified as religious or corporate architecture of some sort. Most of the other shell mounds in the Marismas date to A.D. 700 and after, and belong to the phase of development of the estuary and beach system that exists today.

For the Classic period, by far the best sequences for ceramics and architecture belong to the Amapa and Ixtlán del Río zones. Although both these sites, and their site areas, have important Epiclassic and Postclassic overlays, it is obvious that during the Classic period complex societies were forming in a variety of regional configurations. The extant evidence strongly indicates continuity from the late Formative period rather than any sharp breaks, though linguistic evidence suggests that Uto-Aztecan languages were spreading through this area at this time.

The dates for the Cerritos phase from the Amapa area are still being disputed, but it was apparently under way by c. A.D. 700 or just afterward. A series of impressive polychrome ceramics characterize the period. The Iguanas/Roblitos style, in particular, was traded over a wide area. It is so plentiful in the Etzatlán area (Jalisco) that it represents one of the major wares; high-quality obsidian prismatic blades were exchanged for it.

The one hundred or more platforms found at Amapa appear to date predominantly from the period between A.D. 700 and the fifteenth century. Many of the platforms are lineal and arranged around what are probably plazas. Only a few are over 5 meters high. Several had cut stone stairways. One I-shaped ball court was excavated. The nearby sites of Peñitas and Coamiles also have platform architecture. At Peñitas, a number of well-preserved ceramic kilns were discovered. The developmental sequence for copper metallurgy in the Amapa-Peñitas region is the best yet described for all of Mesoamerica. Recent analytical work has strongly suggested a South American origin for much of this technology, though most certainly it came into an area that was prepared to accept it because of prior experimentation in the medium.

Gold and silver are reported from the Spanish contact period, but very few artifacts made of these metals have been professionally recovered. Like Colima, coastal and piedmont Nayarit seems to have been a focal point for early metallurgy.

In the highlands, Ixtlán del Río is the best-understood site, and one of the few archaeological parks in all of West Mexico. As in the Amapa area, most of the surface architecture appears to be fairly late, after A.D. 700, though there is excellent evidence for both Formative and Classic period occupations in the immediate region. The area of the major concentration of architecture is a little over a square kilometer. Within that area there are about one hundred platforms, several cemeteries, terraces, and an obsidian workshop. Platforms 31 and 32 probably form an open-I-shaped ball court. A 50-meter-diameter circular platform was obviously the central feature of the main concentration of buildings. Called the Quetzalcoatl Temple, it has been over-restored, but originally it was terraced and flat-topped. Some of the stone decorative elements undoubtedly belong to this structure, but their placement in the restoration has been rather fanciful. The rectangular platforms are most often arranged around courtyards. Courtyards of open U, L, and I shapes predominate. Several courts have small altars. The platforms served as the bases for large rooms with columned entrances above stairway accesses. These structures, both roomy and graceful, belong primarily to the Ixtlán Medio phase, c. A.D. 700–1200.

At some point toward the end of the Epiclassic period (c. A.D. 850–900), and certainly within the Ixtlán Medio phase, the Aztatlán horizon is thought to have begun. This horizon style, postulated to be of Mixteca-Puebla inspiration, is distributed over a very large area in West Mexico but is best expressed in Nayarit and Sinaloa. It is defined largely from ceramic motifs, some of which are clearly in the stylistic tradition of codices. A wide assortment of suggestions has been put forth to explain its appearance and distribution. These ideas range from a *pochteca*-like mercantile impulse sweeping through the region, ultimately linking the U.S. Southwest with Central Mexico, to the gradual diffusion of compatible art styles into a region that already had a highly evolved polychrome ceramic tradition.

The late Postclassic period is best defined from the general Amapa area, where several sites have levels that probably show Spanish contact. The Spanish found a series of small but highly territorial, stratified states, focused on a few major centers along the coast and in the southern highlands. As throughout West Mexico, European epidemic diseases devastated the native populations, leaving fewer than 10 percent surviving by the end of the sixteenth century.

Colima

Ceramic figurines from Colima have been a mainstay of collections representing the archaeological art of West Mexico since the beginning of the twentieth century. The finest are remarkable sculptures representing a wide range of human physical types and activities, as well as plants and animals. In the latter category, the dogs have captured the most attention. Red, burnished, and highly fired, these ceramic sculptures merit their fame in the repertoire of Mesoamerican high art. Most of these figurines are thought to date from the late Formative and/or early Classic periods (c. A.D. 1–500), though very few of them have actual site proveniences or firm dates.

Colima is a land of remarkable environmental contrasts. For example, in 100 kilometers one goes from the 4,250-meter peak of the active Volcán de Colima, near the northeastern corner of the state, to the beaches of the Pacific Ocean in the south, from alpine zone to tropical forest. The rivers are mostly permanent, and there are large, productive estuaries along much of the coast.

As in Jalisco, the archaeology of Colima has been characterized largely from the perspective of ceramic studies. Until recently, very little attention has been paid to architecture or settlement patterns. Nothing is known concerning the Palaeoindian or Archaic phases of the area, nor is there any current research to remedy this lack. Some of the extensive shell middens from the Barra de Navidad and Laguna Cuyutlán areas may have remains from the Archaic. The Capacha phase is the earliest fairly well documented period, with dates from the early Formative. Two radiocarbon dates suggest that it might begin as early as 1800 B.C., though these dates have found little support among archaeologists. Most accept 1400 to 1000 B.C. as more likely, though there are very few dates to support this revision. There is no known surface architecture associated directly with this phase, perhaps because survey for architectural features has been neither widespread nor systematic.

The ceramics of the Capacha phase are usually found with burials. Although these burials have been called "shaft tombs," in reality they are relatively simple pits, usually less than 2 meters deep. The elegant ceramics are obviously based on gourd prototypes. Composite vessels

are very elaborate, and stirrup and effigy vessels occur. The incised and punctate vessels have complex decorative panels that are often complemented by polychrome painting. The colors include red, brown, black, orange, and dull purple. The incising usually is hatching or the "sunburst" motif, and these designs are occasionally emphasized with raised ribs or other modeling elements.

Later Formative phases, Ortices and Comala, are not well understood. Their radiocarbon dates seem to overlap, though both ceramic typology and stratigraphy in excavation strongly suggest that Ortices is the earlier phase. Both phases have been characterized as Formative, though the Comala period, discussed below, is certainly far more complex. Some architecture dates from the latter part of these two phases (roughly, 400 B.C.–A.D. 500). At the site of Comala itself, two concentric circular structures have been found. Compared to the monumental circles of the same design found in the Teuchitlán-Etzatlán zone of Jalisco, these structures are not very impressive, but they evidence interaction with the Teuchitlán area. Thus, Colima can be said to have a Classic period, or perhaps better, to have participated in the Classic period with the societies of the Teuchitlán area. Other buildings from the Comala site, dating from the same phase, have rectangular formats and sunken patios. As survey for architecture is finally under way in Colima, more buildings and building complexes from the Comala phase are being registered.

The figurines from the Ortices phase are fairly simple. They are usually solid and sometimes depict action; occasionally, hollow figurines are attributed to this phase. Comala figurines obviously developed from their Ortices forerunners. Deep, strong shades of red were the favorite colors of this period. Effigy tripod feet occur on some vessels. The Comala phase is the apparent apogee of the realistic hollow effigy style discussed above, though there were antecedents in the Ortices phase and possible carryovers after the Comala period.

The shaft tombs of the Comala phase are simple when compared to the monumental ones of the same date, or slightly earlier, from west central Jalisco. When they have chambers, these are also relatively unelaborated. Since the origin for the shaft tombs of West Mexico is often postulated to be South American, one might expect to see more complexity in this area, rather than in the highlands fairly far to the north. Indeed, the argument for South American origins of the shaft tomb complex is so seriously flawed on chronological and distributional grounds, as well as from the perspective of architectural morphology, that it should probably be put to rest. At least with the Comala phase, we have other characteristics by which to define a period, the Teuchitlán-style circular compounds being perhaps one of the most important and fundamental traits.

The Morett site is one of the best documented, dating from c. A.D. 1–800. A large number of radiocarbon dates and a good ceramic sequence were recovered. The ceramics from this site allowed systematic cross-comparisons with sites in southern Jalisco, especially those with Tuxcacuesco affinities. A Thin Orange vessel (an obvious Teotihuacan trade piece), found near Chanchopa, dates from this time, but the other contents of the tomb in which it was found are more problematic.

The Colima and Armería phases, too, are defined almost exclusively from ceramic styles. The Armería phase may date toward the end of the Epiclassic period (c. A.D. 700–900), because Mazapan style figurines were associated with Armería-like material at a number of sites. Some of the fine stone sculptures from the state may date from these phases. Shaft tombs were no longer in style by this time.

The Postclassic phases are characterized by metal artifacts, including gold. Some of the metalwork is very sophisticated and artistically as attractive as any found elsewhere in Mesoamerica. As with shaft tombs, the case has been made for South American contacts influencing the presence and nature of metallurgy in West Mexico. Unlike the former argument, this theory seems to have a good foundation. Certainly West Mexicans were experimenting with the use of metals before the Postclassic, but the similarities in artifact morphology with those from South America seem too many to explain by coincidence. Colima was a possible point of entry for ideas from South America at this time. Certainly by the time the Spanish had arrived, much of ancient Colima's trade wealth and status-marking was related to metallurgy and beautiful metal artifacts.

Salt was another important industry, with much of the product being exported to inland areas. The Laguna de Cuyutlán was the focus for most of this activity; most of it appears to date from the Postclassic periods, but it may have begun far earlier. Surface architecture (though still largely unmapped and undescribed in the literature) is abundant at many sites throughout the state for the Postclassic period. The few building complexes that have been described are rectangular or square in format, with platforms and pyramids arranged around plazas. These plazas, as at the Alima site, are often found in very large groups.

The group at Alima prompted Carl Sauer to use the term "urban." This site extends for kilometer after kilometer on both sides of the Alima River. Most of the stone sculptures that portray glyphs probably date from the Postclassic, and some are described as having been part of architectural ornamentation, including stairways.

Sections of Colima were invaded, or at least raided, by the expansive Purépecha (Tarascans) from the state of Michoacán. How much of the area was incorporated into their empire, and for how long, remains an active issue in the historiography of the region. The Spanish became interested in Colima almost immediately after their conquest of Michoacán. Precious metals were among the major incentives for the early conquest of the area. Colima is one of the few areas of West Mexico that has a good early Colonial descriptive document, the *Relación Sumaria,* written by Lebrón de Quíones (1551–1554).

FURTHER READINGS

Bell, B. 1971. Archaeology of Nayarit, Jalisco, and Colima. In G. Ekholm and I. Bernal (eds.), *Handbook of Middle American Indians,* vol. 11, pp. 694–753. Austin: University of Texas Press.

Galván, J. L. 1991. *Las Tumbas de Tiro del Valle de Atemajac, Jalisco.* Colección Científica. Mexico City: Instituto Nacional de Antropología e Historia.

Kelly, I. 1980. *Ceramic Sequence in Colima: Capacha, an Early Phase.* Anthropological Papers of the University of Arizona Press, 37. Tucson.

Meighan, C. (ed.). 1972. *The Archaeology of Amapa, Nayarit.* University of California, Institute of Archaeology, Monumenta Archaeologica, 2. Los Angeles.

Meighan, C., et al. 1972. *Archaeology of the Morett Site, Colima.* University of California Publications in Anthropology, 7. Los Angeles.

Sauer, C. O. 1948. *Colima of New Spain in the Sixteenth Century.* Ibero-Americana, 29. Berkeley: University of California Press.

Scott, S. 1985. Core vs. Marginal America: A Coastal West Mexican Perspective. In M. Foster and P. Weigand (eds.), *The Archaeology of West and Northwest Mesoamerica,* pp. 181–191. Denver: Westview Press.

Weigand, P. C. 1993. *Evolución de una civilización prehispánica: Arqueología de Jalisco.* Zamora: Colegio de Michoacán.

Weigand, P. C., and A. García de Weigand. 1996. *Tenamaxtli y Guaxicar: Las raíces profundas de la rebelión de Nueva Galicia.* Zamora: Colegio de Michoacán, and the Secretaría de Cultura del Estado de Jalisco.

von Winning, H. 1969. *The Shaft Tomb Figurines of West Mexico.* Southwestern Museum Papers, 24. Los Angeles.

von Winning, H., and O. Hammer. 1972. *Anecdotal Sculpture of Ancient West Mexico.* Los Angeles: Ethnic Arts Council of Los Angeles.

Zepeda, G. 1994. *Ixtlán: Ciudad del Viento.* Tepic: Grupo ICA and the Instituto Nacional de Antropología e Historia.

Phil C. Weigand

Wood: Tools and Products

The use of wood in Mesoamerican cultures is difficult to chronicle because archaeological preservation is poor in tropical climates. What is known comes primarily from written accounts by the Spaniards at the time of the conquest and some remarkable archaeological remains. Wood preserves best in environments that are inhospitable to wood-metabolizing microbes—ideally, very wet soils with low oxygen transport, or very dry soils. There are only a few localities that fit this description in Mesoamerica: cenotes or wells, swamps, and dry caves. Occasionally, wood artifacts can be preserved by burning and carbonization.

Pre-Hispanic techniques of wood-working are poorly known. Even Sahagún provides very little information on this craft, and with the introduction of metal by the Spaniards, many indigenous tools and techniques were replaced. Today there are local native traditions of woodworking that have been revitalized by the interest of tourists, such as the fantastic animal figures of Oaxacan wood-carvers and the bows and arrows of the Lacandón Maya.

We know from indigenous documents and chroniclers at the time of the Spanish conquest that the pre-Hispanic peoples used wood for a variety of functional and ritual items; Aztec tribute lists, such as the Codex Mendoza, describe wooden offerings. The island city of Tenochtitlan was connected to the mainland by a series of bridges and by canoe traffic. Extensive irrigated lands in Central Mexico were no doubt aided by wooden dams. Houses and temples utilized wood in construction. Smaller items included tools and armaments, particularly the atlatl. Ritual items included wooden idols, masks, and musical instruments, like the *teponaztli* (horizontal drum) and the *huehuetl* (vertical drum).

Two spectacular archaeological finds of Mesoamerican wooden objects also demonstrate the widespread, long-standing tradition of wood-working. Early Formative sculptures were excavated from the swampy Gulf Coast region in the Río Coatzacoalcos Basin at the Olmec site of El Manatí. More than thirty-five intact sculptures have been reported to date; eighteen were found in their original context as ritual offerings, together with jade *hachas,* rubber balls, shark teeth, and bones. The sculptures are busts of males and females with slit eyes and large downturned mouths. These skillfully carved pieces foreshadow subsequent Maya figure carvings, two of which have survived to the present.

The Cenote of Sacrifice (Chichén Itzá) was dredged numerous times between 1904 and 1923. The anaerobic muck at the bottom was ideal for the preservation of organic materials, although some artifacts were broken during the dredging. Coggins notes more than three hundred pieces, two hundred identified, from the collections made by Edward H. Thompson. Unfortunately, there was no stratigraphy discernible in the muck, nor any possibility of controlling where items came from; therefore, the dates of the objects were based on style and ranged from A.D. 771 to 1480.

Many types of objects were recovered. Utilitarian items included spindle whorls and a sicklelike tool with a flat, curved tip and a straight shaft. Coggins speculates that these are early counterparts of the modern *coa* used by the Yucatec Maya for weeding. Among the armaments recovered were grooved sticks—noted in Terminal Classic/Early Postclassic depictions of warriors in place of shields—carved clubs, and handles used to hold stone bifaces. Carved scepters depict a number of images, including serpentine designs, kneeling figures, and a diving figure. Finally, there were a number of idols similar to those shown carried by gods in the Madrid Codex; these crudely carved objects have block heads with slashes for eyes and mouth, and generally stand about 18–20 cm in height.

FURTHER READINGS

Anawalt, P., R. Berger, and C. W. Clewlow. 1976. *Notes on a Maya Wood Carving.* Los Angeles: Institute of Archaeology, University of California.

Barbash, S. 1993. *Oaxacan Woodcarving: The Magic in the Trees.* San Francisco: Chronicle Books.

Coggins, C. (ed.). 1992. *Artifacts from the Cenote of Sacrifice, Chichén Itzá, Yucatán.* Memoirs of the Peabody Museum, 10. 3. Cambridge, Mass.: Harvard University.

Ekholm, G. 1964. *A Maya Sculpture in Wood.* New York: Museum of Primitive Art.

Saville, M. 1925. *The Wood-Carver's Art in Ancient Mexico.* Contributions of the Museum of the American Indian, 9. New York: Heye Foundation.

Mary Pye

SEE ALSO

Architecture: Civic-Ceremonial; Architecture: Vernacular-Mundane

Writing

Definitions of writing vary from broad ("a form of communication," or "a system of human communication by means of conventional visible marks") to restrictive ("a set of elements that shows some correspondence to speech or language"). Broad definitions make it impossible to distinguish writing from art; we would mistakenly classify the art of the Kwakiutl, Olmec, or Chavín as "writing." That error would, in turn, mask important differences between societies with writing and societies without writing. Restrictive definitions are more useful because they stress four factors: the degree of correspondence of writing to a given language; the linear format of texts (columns and rows); the order of reading (top to bottom, right to left, left to right); and the frequency and rules by which signs combine (grammar).

Scholars differ on the degree to which a given writing system corresponds to a spoken language. When we see long columns or rows of signs, there is no disagreement that we are dealing with a writing system. In the earliest stages of some writing systems, however, we see single, isolated signs, or signs that have a strong pictorial character; with such early systems, scholars are often divided as to whether the definition of writing has been met. Most agree, however, that items such as potters' marks, clay tokens, and individual motifs should not be labeled "writing."

Some anthropologists focus on how and why writing developed, and on how it has changed through time in its form, content, and function. Others focus on the way writing affects, and is affected by, other aspects of society.

Appearance of Writing

Writing was invented several times, in places as distant from each other as Asia and Mexico. The New World had fewer indigenous writing systems than the Old World, and all were confined to Mesoamerica (modern Mexico, Guatemala, Belize, Honduras, and El Salvador). The four principal writing systems were Zapotec (c. 650 B.C.), Maya (c. A.D. 100–200), Mixtec (c. A.D. 250–500), and Aztec, or Nahuatl (c. A.D. 1200–1500). A fifth and poorly known system, possibly Zoque, appeared around 100 B.C. and is considered a forerunner of the Maya system.

The Zapotec produced the earliest writing, but Maya writing was by far the most complex and showed the greatest correspondence to the spoken language. The Mixtec and Aztec used simpler systems in which pictures conveyed much of the information. All four major Mesoamerican systems combined pictographic, logographic, and syllabic elements. The only kind of writing not present in Mesoamerica was the alphabetic system, a development that occurred only in the Old World.

Early texts in southern Mesoamerica (Zapotec, Maya) contained political and genealogical data that were used to legitimize rulership. Rulers and their scribes were concerned with validating and sanctifying rulers, even when a particular ruler was not in direct line to rule.

The earliest signs identified in the texts of Mesoamerica are proper nouns (names of places and individuals) and calendric signs (day names, in particular). Early texts include short assertions about individuals taken captive in a raid, an individual's relationship to an ancestor, or an individual's position in a genealogical sequence; these kinds of information could be used to legitimize a leader about to take office. In fact, taking office and staying there were important motivations in the commissioning of texts.

Although the appearance of writing was once considered the hallmark of the state and linked exclusively to civilization, we know now that writing sometimes predated the emergence of the state. Some pre-state "chiefdoms" used limited forms of writing. For example, among the pre-state Zapotec, who occupied southern Mexico between 600 and 200 B.C., early writing was used to record the names of sacrificed elites taken captive in raids. Apparently, endemic competition among chiefs constituted the appropriate context for the emergence of writing in this part of the world. Later Mesoamerican states (Maya, Aztec) continued this pattern whereby individuals claimed military success as a way of enhancing their right to rule.

Since not all ancient states developed (or even borrowed) writing, it would be a mistake for us to include writing as a criterion for defining civilizations or states. Highly bureaucratic states such as the Inca, who maintained an empire extending 3,000 kilometers from north to south, flourished without writing.

Functions of Writing

Clues to the purposes of writing exist in several forms: the subject matter; the material, permanent or perishable, on which a text is written; the location where it is displayed, or where it is stored or hidden; its visibility and accessibility; and its intended audience. When the subject matter is royal politics and state propaganda, texts are often written on stone and displayed in public places. The purposes of writing are also revealed by associated art and architecture, so these factors must also be taken into account. In Mesoamerica, writing and art were combined to transmit a unified message. As an example, on the same carved stone, conquest could be conveyed in two complementary ways—by depicting a tiny prisoner whose hair is held in the grasp of a larger ruler, and in a written text carved alongside. The events might or might not be accurately depicted, but once they were recorded in stone such claims reinforced the ruler's prestige and became official state propaganda.

Although the purposes of early writing appear to have been limited to a restricted range of themes, its functions often expanded as the state saw new uses for it. Early Mesoamerican writing dealt mainly with rulers' political and military accomplishments, but the Aztecs (A.D. 1400–1600) expanded it into the realm of economics with painted tribute lists such as the Codex Mendoza. Maya, Mixtec, and Zapotec lords are depicted on pottery, in deerhide books, and on stone monuments in the act of receiving specific goods, but none of those items is quantified in the text.

Why All States Did Not Have Writing

Some ancient states, like the Incas and Tarascans, were extremely powerful and efficient without writing. Their success suggests that we may have overemphasized the role of writing and underestimated the roles of mnemonic devices, oral tradition, and memorization. Inventions such as the Andean *kipu* were used for accounting and record-keeping and are alternatives to writing. Some civilizations used monumental sculpture and mural painting to convey political propaganda. Even states whose neighbors had long-established writing systems did not always borrow them. Not only are there alternatives to writing; many ancient states even saw literacy as undesirable.

Literacy

Modern governments proudly announce high literacy rates because they equate literacy with civilization. The goal of such modern societies is to achieve 100 percent literacy; they attempt this by opening libraries, schools, and outreach programs to teach writing to all adults and children.

The goals of many ancient governments were the opposite. Their writing schools were private, their libraries were closed archives, and access to literacy skills was restricted to the elite. In Mesoamerica, for example, the ability to write was one of the behaviors that set nobles apart from commoners. Writing was a form of esoteric knowledge, not to be shared with the general populace.

Summary

Writing has arisen independently in many cultures, for many different reasons. It appeared first in ancient societies for which universal literacy was not a goal, and in which writing was a skill restricted to the elite. All texts from these ancient societies, whether political, military, or genealogical, cannot be read as unbiased history. Elites who controlled writing used it as a tool of the state, and its power and propaganda content were high.

FURTHER READINGS

Marcus, J. 1976. The Origins of Mesoamerican Writing. *Annual Review of Anthropology* 5:35–67.

———. 1992. *Mesoamerican Writing Systems.* Princeton: Princeton University Press.

Joyce Marcus

Xaltocan (México, Mexico)

This is a Middle and Late Postclassic site on Lake Xaltocan in the northern Basin of Mexico. Most of the site lies on the island of Xaltocan, but isolated mounds extend onto the surrounding lakebed. The site covers a total of 68 hectares.

Xaltocan rises about 5 meters above the level of the lakebed. Its surface is very irregular, marked by mound and depressions. Excavation reveals that the island is composed entirely of artificial fill and occupational refuse; there appears to be no natural basis for its elevation. Excavations reveal deeply stratified deposits covering six hundred years of occupation. Black-on-Orange I and Chalco-Cholula Polychrome pottery occur at the deepest levels, yielding calibrated radiocarbon dates of A.D. 900–1150. Above these levels, a phase of mixed Black-on-Orange I and Black-on-Orange II pottery is associated with calibrated dates of A.D. 1150–1350. Next, deposits of Black-on-Orange II and Black-and-White-on-Red pottery yield calibrated dates of A.D. 1350–1420. In the highest strata, Black-on-Orange III pottery occurs, associated with a calibrated date of A.D. 1410. Test pits on isolated mounds surrounding the island revealed shallow, single-component occupations, almost always associated with Black-on-Orange II and III ceramics.

Both on the mounds and on the island, excavations yielded the remains of domestic activity: potsherds, obsidian tools and waste flakes, grinding stones, ceramic spindle whorls, figurines, disks, animal bone, ash and carbonized plant materials, and the remains of structure, including clay and adobe bricks, postmolds, hearths, and pits. *Maguey*-processing tools rarely occur. The debris from a specialized obsidian biface-working locale and a prismatic blade workshop was encountered in the course of intensive, systematic surface collection. Waterfowl, dog, and rabbit bones were most common in the excavated debris; turkey and deer were relatively rare. Fabric-marked pottery, associated with salt production, is plentiful at Xaltocan during the last two phases of occupation. A unique type of T-shaped obsidian lip plug was manufactured at Xaltocan, and it may have served as a symbol of ethnicity. An excavation 100 meters east of the modern town center revealed two civic-ceremonial cobblestone platforms as well as the fragments of painted murals.

Some silted-in ridged features were found on the lakebed to the southeast of Xaltocan. These are probably prehistoric ridged fields or *chinampas*, the presence of which at Xaltocan is mentioned by the Colonial historian Alvarado Tezozomoc.

Xaltocan is frequently mentioned in the native histories from the Basin of Mexico. Before 1395, it was an important regional center. According to Alva Ixtilxochitl, it was the capital of Otomí-speaking peoples in southern Hidalgo and the northern Basin of Mexico. In 1428, Xaltocan fell under the rule of the Triple Alliance; the Aztecs installed a military ruler, and Xaltocan paid tribute to the rulers of both Texcoco and Tenochtitlan.

FURTHER READINGS

Brumfiel, E. M. 1991. Tribute and Commerce in Imperial Cities: The Case of Xaltocan, Mexico. In H. J. M. Claessen and P. van de Velde (eds.), *Early State Economics,* pp. 177–198. New Brunswick: Transaction.

Nichols, D. L., and C. D. Frederick. 1993. Irrigation Canals and Chinampas: Recent Research in the Northern Basin of Mexico. *Research in Economic Anthropology*, supplement 7:123–150.

Parsons, J. R., E. M. Brumfiel, and M. Hodge. 1996. Developmental Implications of Earlier Dates for Early Aztec in the Basin of Mexico. *Ancient Mesoamerica* 7:217–230.

Elizabeth M. Brumfiel

SEE ALSO

Basin of Mexico; Otomí Cultural Tradition

Xicalango (Campeche, Mexico)

Xicalango was a trade center of considerable importance to the coastal and inland Maya and the Aztec during the first quarter of the sixteenth century. Salt, cotton cloth, cacao, copper, obsidian, gold, feathers, honey, slaves, and finished products passed through this trade town. The exact location of the site is not known, but various sources place it on the Xicalango Peninsula of western Campeche, Mexico. In any case, the town was within the Chontal Maya territory of the Laguna de Terminos, the inland brackish lagoons, and the meandering Palizada River. It is thought that this trade center had an international atmosphere of several languages and cultures where ideas came together. The only archaeological sites in the area that might qualify as the Xicalango center are Atasta and El Aguacatal, both on the peninsula and possessing large Late Postclassic components, and Punta de Cedro, at the mouth of the Chumpan River on the shore of the Laguna de Terminos.

FURTHER READINGS

Matheny, R. T. 1970. *The Ceramics of Aguacatal, Campeche, Mexico*. Papers of the New World Archaeological Foundation, 27. Provo, Utah.

Scholes, F. V., and R. L. Roys. 1968. *The Maya Chontal Indians of Acalan-Tixchel: A Contribution to the History and Ethnography of the Yucatán Peninsula*. Norman: University of Oklahoma Press.

Ray T. Matheny

SEE ALSO

Maya Lowlands: South

Xico (México, Mexico)

Xico is a volcanic cone in the southeastern Basin of Mexico which was, in pre-Hispanic times, surrounded by the waters of Lake Chalco. The site of small Terminal Forma-

tive and Classic occupations, Xico grew to be a regional center. Early Toltec occupation at the site covers an area of 102 hectares along the northern end of the island. Late Toltec occupation covers 54 hectares, also at the northern end. Prehistoric occupation is also evident on an elevated, irregular, 24-hectare area just east of the island. This area rises 2 to 3 meters above the level of the surrounding lakebed. Excavations by Parsons and Parsons suggest that this elevated area is composed entirely of artificial fill and midden, with Early Postclassic and even Classic occupations underlying at least portions of it. The surface of this area is irregular and marked by at least 139 unexcavated mounds. Surface pottery is equally divided between Early Aztec (Black-on-Orange I) and Late Aztec pottery (Black-on-Orange III). Redwares are rare at Postclassic Xico, as are *maguey*-working tools.

FURTHER READINGS

Brumfiel, E. M. 1986. The Division of Labor at Xico: The Chipped Stone Industry. In B. L. Issac (ed.), *Economic Aspects of pre-Hispanic Highland Mexico*, pp. 245–279. *Research in Economic Anthropology*, Supplement 2. Greenwich, Conn.: JAI Press.

———. 1991. Agricultural Development and Class Stratification in the Southern Valley of Mexico. In H. R. Harvey (ed.), *Land and Politics in the Valley of Mexico*, pp. 43–62. Albuquerque: University of New Mexico Press.

Parsons, J. R., E. M. Brumfiel, M. H. Parsons, and D. J. Wilson. 1982. *Prehispanic Settlement Patterns in the Southern Valley of Mexico: The Chalco-Xochimilco Region*. University of Michigan Museum of Anthropology, Memoir 14. Ann Arbor.

Elizabeth M. Brumfiel

SEE ALSO

Basin of Mexico

Xochicalco (Morelos, Mexico)

This important site lies 25 kilometers southwest of modern Cuernavaca, on the top and sides of a group of five hills, of which the central one is known as Cerro Xochicalco. Civic-ceremonial architecture exists on the upper summit of Cerro Xochicalco, and residential terraces spread over the sides and onto the plain below. Xochicalco means "place of the house of flowers," after the highly decorated Pyramid of the Plumed Serpents on the summit.

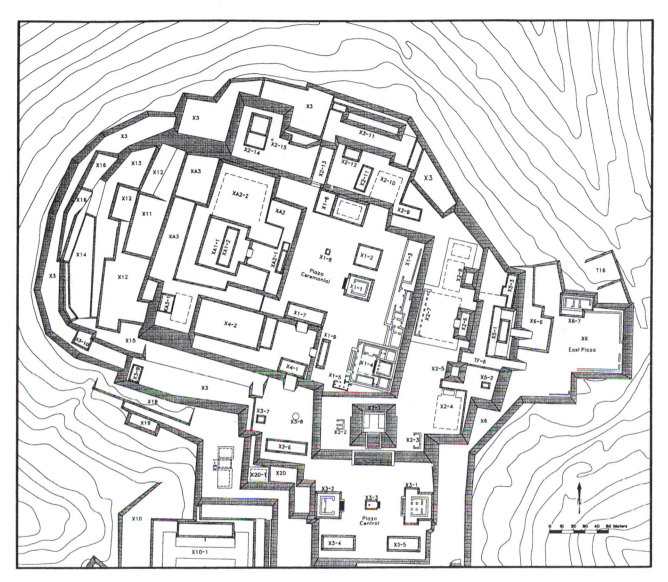

Civic-ceremonial structures on the summit of the North Hill of Cerro Xochicalco. Sloping surfaces are shaded. (Fig. 5.5, Hirth 2000.)

The site grew rapidly around A.D. 650, becoming one of the largest and most influential centers in Central Mexico during the Epiclassic period (A.D. 650–900), contemporaneous with Cacaxtla (Puebla-Tlaxcala Basin), Teotenango (Valley of Toluca), and Teotihuacan (Basin of Mexico) in its declining but still important Coyotlatelco phase occupation. Around A.D. 900, Xochicalco was catastrophically destroyed and rapidly abandoned as the result of a local revolt or military conquest. Public buildings in the upper ceremonial zone were burned and sacked; residences on the slopes below were destroyed and abandoned.

Xochicalco is situated at the interface of the rich agricultural Miacatlan-Coatetelco Basin and the arid, infertile upland plain stretching north to Cuentepec, Morelos. The presence of a large number of grinding and milling stones in all households, together with the recovery of carbonized remains of maize in stratigraphic contexts, indicates that groups at Xochicalco followed a traditional Mesoamerican subsistence pattern based on maize agriculture during the Epiclassic. Faunal remains recovered from household refuse indicate that domesticated turkey and wild deer were the primary sources of animal protein in the diet.

The selection of this locale for the development of a major center may have been due to the natural protection that Xochicalco's group of hills provided for local residents, who constructed ramparts, ditches, and defensive moats around the base of Cerro Xochicalco and adjacent hills to strengthen their defensive perimeters against possible outside attack. Large residential terraces on the slopes of Cerro Xochicalco were an important part of its overall defensive plan, creating a series of nested defensive perimeters inside the outer defenses; internal defensive perimeters were also fortified with walls, ramparts, and dry moats. Access into Xochicalco was restricted to a few points along roads entering the site, which were protected by guard platforms that could easily be sealed or barricaded during an attack.

Intensive reconnaissance and mapping of surface features revealed extraordinarily well preserved civic-ceremonial and domestic architecture dating to the Epiclassic on the summit and slopes of Cerro Xochicalco. The location of the site outside the best agricultural areas of Morelos meant that it attracted only limited population after its abrupt Epiclassic abandonment.

Limited disturbance by pre-Columbian and Colonial populations, together with the protection afforded by the establishment of the site as an archaeological zone in 1922, gave Xochicalco one of the longest traditions of site protection in Mesoamerica. Stratigraphic excavations have identified *in situ* domestic assemblages on the floors of Epiclassic households reflecting the rapidity of site abandonment around A.D. 900.

Xochicalco was a medium-sized urban center with a total population of between ten and fifteen thousand persons. Residential densities on the slopes range from 80 to 120 persons per hectare, comparable with other pre-Columbian urban centers in the highlands, such as Teotihuacan, Tula, and Tenochtitlan. The majority of the population resided in small residential compounds that contained between two and six nuclear families. Residents lived in adjoining rooms arranged around one or more interior patios. Individuals within these compounds were probably related by kinship or marriage and, together with their dependents, formed extended or conjoint households. Houses ranged from well-planned rectangular structures to clusters of platforms distributed across the slopes of Cerro Xochicalco. Excavation revealed that food was stored, prepared, and shared by individuals residing in structures sharing a common patio. Food and other resources were stored in small rooms that formed part of the patio compound, and also in small caves or rock shelters cut into bedrock adjacent to residential buildings.

Examination of the urban architecture on Cerro Xochicalco reveals internal divisions within the city and suggests that its population was subdivided into twelve to fourteen small wards or barrios. These barrios had internally stratified populations; elite residences and/or civic-ceremonial structures occur alongside nonelite residences in thirteen of the fourteen wards identified to date. These wards ranged from one hundred to three hundred persons in size and compare favorably with small *calpulli* or *chinamitl* ward divisions found in cities at the time of the Spanish conquest.

Evidence for craft activity has been identified in the city, but it is limited in both type and scope. Five obsidian workshop areas have been identified and excavated; they supplied obsidian tools for the site as well as the surrounding region. Four of these production workshops were in or near residence areas; the last was in a small plaza on the south side of Cerro Xochicalco that appears to have functioned as a marketplace. Excavations by Mexican archaeologists have also recovered production debitage from a lapidary workshop which produced wealth items from slate and marble in the acropolis area of the upper ceremonial zone. The majority of locally manufactured ceramic and ground stone tools, however, appear to have been produced outside the main site area, probably in regional workshops closer to sources of raw material.

The role of Xochicalco as an important regional center is reflected by the large quantity of long-distance trade goods recovered from the site. Trade goods include shells from the Atlantic and Pacific coasts, ball court paraphernalia from the Gulf Coast, marble vessels from the state of Puebla, obsidian from Michoacán and Hidalgo, carved stone and jadeite figures from Guerrero and possibly Oaxaca, and imported ceramics from the states of México and Guerrero. The available evidence suggests that Xochicalco actively participated in broad interregional exchange networks extending throughout Mesoamerica. Its location in western Morelos was favorable for controlling trade moving from the Pacific Coast up the Balsas corridor into Central Mexico.

A large quantity of monumental art has also been recovered from Xochicalco; it provides insight into the social, political, and religious structure during the Epiclassic period. The best-known monument is the Pyramid of the Plumed Serpents, a small temple on a platform mound constructed with *talud-tablero* architectural conventions. The exterior façades of both the temple building and *talud-tablero* platform are covered with richly carved bas-reliefs. The structure derives its name from the representation of large undulating plumed serpents on the platform's *talud*. Seated figures carved in Maya style and glyphs appear in the curves of the serpent. Small groups of glyphs on the west side of the platform depict the alignment of two Mesoamerican calendars and may record a royal marriage and/or political alliance.

The *tablero* on the Pyramid of the Plumed Serpents depicts the names of conquered towns that regularly paid tribute to Xochicalco during the Epiclassic. Additional military themes are depicted on the upper temple, where eighteen seated warriors are shown holding shields, three darts, and a spear-thrower. A sculpture depicting heart sacrifice of a decapitated human figure was recovered near the Pyramid of the Plumed Serpents in the late nineteenth century. The presence of this sculpture adjacent to the pyramid suggests that human sacrifice had become important in political and religious life during the Epiclassic.

Carved monuments at Xochicalco also record the names of three of the earliest known kings in Central Mexico. Their names appear on three carved stelae that depict each ruler's portrait, names, and titles, and information about his birth, death, coronation, and military conquests. Stelae are uncommon in Central Mexico as an artistic medium prior to the Epiclassic period and appear to have been borrowed from either the Zapotec or Maya region as a means of recording kingly histories. They are part of Xochicalco's eclectic Epiclassic art style, which borrowed glyphs, artistic motifs, and architectural forms from many different areas and peoples, including the Zapotecs, the Mixtecs, the Gulf Coast, and the distant Maya. This eclecticism seems to have been an intentional part of the artistic program and probably coincided with the emergence of new elites and their search for new media to express their status, sovereignty, and legitimacy. This eclecticism had two functions. First, the adoption of foreign motifs into the artistic program linked new elites with prestigious groups in distant lands. Second, it seems to represent an intentional rejection of traditional artistic canons emanating from the older center of Teotihuacan, from which they were expressing their independence.

Although Cerro Xochicalco has the greatest amount of defensive architecture at the site, six other fortified precincts are located in the Epiclassic city within a 1,000-meter radius of Cerro Xochicalco. The presence of multiple defensive precincts as part of the site's normal defense is important because it implies a degree of independence and segmentation in the defense and governance of the city's population. Moreover, three of these precincts lack any clear evidence of ongoing habitation and may have been redoubts or fortified strongholds used by populations from outside Xochicalco during times of strife. The pattern of clustered defensive precincts at Xochicalco suggests that several socially autonomous communities acted together for their mutual defense; it may reflect a political organization in which Xochicalco was the dominant community within a regional confederacy.

Important changes occurred in Xochicalco's sociopolitical structure during the Epiclassic. Militarism became the dominant theme, not only with respect to competition between political centers but also as a basis for the internal structure of society. Moreover, during this period we see the close association between military conquest and the development of tribute empires, the emergence of knight societies, and the appearance of human sacrifice.

Analysis of ceramic and architectural remains suggests that a large portion of western Morelos was under Xochicalco's political and economic control. The names of thirty towns are listed on the *tablero* of the Pyramid of the Plumed Serpents as paying tribute to Xochicalco. This, together with references to conquest and tribute events on the site's three carved stelae, underscores the role of militarism in creating a conquest empire during the Epiclassic. The presence of knight societies is better documented at the contemporaneous site of Cacaxtla than at Xochicalco; nevertheless, the prominence of warriors in Xochicalco's public art and the presence of human skeletal trophies in domestic contexts suggests that warrior or knight societies were present at Xochicalco, as they were elsewhere in Central Mexico during the Epiclassic.

Evidence for the existence of human sacrifice is supported by two monuments. The first is the large, realistic human sculpture recovered near the Pyramid of the Plumed Serpents. This monument's figure is portrayed with his rib cage cut open for removal of his heart and without his head, perhaps symbolizing decapitation in order to mount the head on a *tzompantli* (skull rack). The presence of a decorative emblem on the shoulder of the sacrificial victim may identify him as a war captive. The second monument commemorates the New Fire Ceremony, beginning a new fifty-two-year calendar cycle. Though not directly depicting human sacrifice, this monument documents that groups at Xochicalco shared with the later Aztec culture views about renewable time and the unstable nature of the universe—ideas that provided

X

the religious rationale for warfare, human sacrifice, and the Mesoamerican god-nourishment complex.

FURTHER READINGS

Gonzalez Crespo, N., S. Garza Tarazona, H. de Vega Nova, P. Mayer Guala, and G. Canto Aguilar. 1995. Archaeological Investigations at Xochicalco, Morelos: 1984 and 1986. *Ancient Mesoamerica* 6:223–236.

Hirth, K. G. 1984. Xochicalco: Urban Growth and State Formation in Central Mexico. *Science* 225:579–586.

———. 1989. Militarism and Social Organization at Xochicalco, Morelos. In R. Diehl and J. Berlo (eds.), *Mesoamerica after the Collapse of Teotihuacan, A.D. 700–900,* pp. 69–81. Washington, D.C.: Dumbarton Oaks.

———. 1995. Urbanism, Militarism and Architectural Design: An Analysis of Epiclassic Sociopolitical Structure at Xochicalco. *Ancient Mesoamerica* 6:237–250.

Hirth, K. G., and A. Cyphers Guillen. 1988. *Tiempo y asentamiento en Xochicalco.* Mexico City: Universidad Nacional Autónoma de México.

Litvak King, J. 1970. Xochicalco en la caída del clásico, una hipótesis. *Anales de Antropología* 7:131–144.

Piña Chan, R. 1977. *Quetzalcoatl serpiente emplumada.* Mexico City: Fondo de Cultura Economica.

Kenneth G. Hirth

SEE ALSO

Morelos Region

Xochipala Style

This pre-Columbian, Formative period, archaeologically unprovenienced art style is characterized by highly naturalistic ceramic figurines and skillfully executed stone bowls, which may presage the Mezcala lapidary tradition. Xochipala-style objects originated in a series of small sites near the village of Xochipala in north central Guerrero. First recognized in private collections in the late 1960s, Xochipala-style objects appear to be the product of a geographically restricted local tradition. However, the presence of Olmec-style motifs on some objects indicates that the Xochipala area had at least limited outside contacts within the extensive Formative period exchange network. The Xochipala tradition in many ways resembles the style said to originate at the site of Las Bocas. Unfortunately, like Las Bocas, most Xochipala objects are looted, and therefore little can be said about the origin, use, or dating of this material.

FURTHER READINGS

Gay, C. 1972. Xochipala: The Beginnings of Olmec Art. Princeton: University Art Museum.

F. Kent Reilly III

SEE ALSO

Bocas, Las; Lapidary Industry; Olmec Culture

Xochitécatl (Tlaxcala, Mexico)

East of the Cacaxtla archaeological zone is the hill of Xochitécatl, crowned by a civic-ceremonial complex that served the inhabitants of Cacaxtla as a focus for a female deity cult. Recent interdisciplinary research at Xochitécatl has revealed a great central plaza with stepped platforms on terraces at different levels.

The largest is the Pyramid of the Flowers, rich in cultural remains from a full system of burials, with abundant offerings of female figurines, and two huge monolithic tubes at the foot of its central staircase. The Building of the Spiral (with a circular plan), and the Building of the Serpent occupy the west and south sides of the plaza, respectively; they were probably built in the Late Formative period (400 B.C.–A.D. 200). The Platform of the Volcanoes, at the center of the plaza, was built at the end of the Classic period.

Xochitécatl has a strategic location between the valleys of Puebla and Tlaxcala, at the intersection of long-distance exchange routes between the Gulf Lowlands and Oaxaca. The region was the center of a large population which based its subsistence on agriculture in the surrounding valleys. Preliminary conclusions estimate a large occupation during the Middle and Late Formative, and a reoccupation from the Epiclassic until the Postclassic.

The reforestation of the hill of Xochitécatl, carried out after an earlier study of the original flora of the region, permitted the establishment of an archaeological-ecological park.

FURTHER READINGS

Serra Puche, M. C., and L. Beutelspacher. 1993. Xochitécatl, Tlaxcala. In *Arqueología, Imagen e Identidad,* pp. 48–67. Mexico City: Grupo Editorial Azabache.

———, ———. 1994. *Xochitécatl.* Mexico City: Guía INAH-Salvat.

———, ———. 1994. Xochitécatl. *Arqueología Mexicana* 2(10):66–69.

Spranz, B., D. E. Dumond, and P. P. Hilbert. 1978. *Las pirámides del Cerro Xochitecatl, Tlaxcala (México).* Wiesbaden: Franz Steiner.

Mari Carmen Serra

Xpuhil
See Maya Lowlands: North

Xunantunich (Cayo, Belize)

This ridgetop Maya site in west central Belize experienced its principal occupation in the Late and Terminal Classic periods (A.D. 650–1000). Emerging late as a center within a well-established regional hierarchy, Xunantunich was locally unique in political assertiveness and in the public veneration of rulers through sculptural and architectural monuments, at a time when the largest Maya Lowlands centers (e.g., Tikal) were collapsing.

Three carved stelae are known, all post-dating A.D. 800. The Castillo (Structure A-6) is one of the largest Maya constructions in Belize, towering more than 40 meters above adjacent plazas. The Castillo's penultimate version bore a now-famous stucco frieze exterior to the vaulted roof; the iconography of the frieze glorified Xunantunich's rulers. The final construction included a building with columns on an appended western platform, suggesting elite contact with Yucatán, from Becan northward.

Causeways and access points, along with three ball courts, served to integrate formally sectors of the site and populace. The site overlooks the Mopan River, and in pre-Columbian times it probably controlled riverine transport routes and good agricultural (especially alluvial) lands in this part of the valley. Abundant terracing on nearby hillslopes suggests a need for agricultural intensification by Late Classic times, but forms of terracing and domestic architecture indicate a relatively decentralized socio-economic system, probably with much autonomy at the hamlet or lineage level.

Wendy Ashmore and Richard Leventhal

Y

Yagul (Oaxaca, Mexico)

At Yagul, perhaps more than at any other pre-Hispanic site, one appreciates the integration of the social organization and architectural vision of its early inhabitants. Its fortress overlooks the site, the core of which consists of two large platforms occupied by the chiefs and nobility. The political-administrative center covers the highest level, with religious and ceremonial structures, such as temples and a ball court, slightly below. Commoners lived on the lower slopes or near adjacent cropland.

By the time of the Conquest the religious and administrative portions of the site were no longer used, but people continued to occupy the dwellings and fields of the commoners. Early in the Colonial period the surviving population was resettled at nearby Tlacolula. This removal inadvertently helped to protect the old site, and it also explains the historical memory in Tlacolula, which continues to refer to Yagul as the "old town." Ignacio Bernal and Lorenzo Gamio note that "Yagul" means "old tree" in Zapotec. Unlike Mitla a few miles to the east, where the modern community surrounds and invades the archaeological site, Yagul is still largely free from residential encroachment, although tourist services are beginning to appear within a few hundred meters of the site.

Yagul occupies a rocky ridge and slope on the north side of the Tlacolula Valley about 35 kilometers east of the city of Oaxaca. A paved road of about 1.5 kilometers connects it to the Pan-American Highway. The location is part of a series of outcroppings rising 60 to 150 meters above the surrounding valley. The fortress occupies one of the highest of these (about 1,700 meters above sea level) and commands a view of the eastern half of the Tlacolula Valley to the south. On the north side, the outcroppings merge into the foothills of the Sierra Juarez. The soft rock provides numerous small caves and overhanging shelters. The climate is essentially hot steppe and semiarid. Rainfall averages 508 mm annually, falling mainly as summer showers. Native vegetation reflects semidesert conditions.

Site History

Caves and shelters in nearby hills contain remains of human habitation dating back at least five thousand years. Caballito Blanco, a smaller outcrop about a kilometer from Yagul, has wall paintings and petroglyphs attributed to early hunter-gatherers who sheltered in the caves and overhangs. By 200 B.C., a structure similar to the building known as the "Observatory" at Monte Albán had been built on Caballito Blanco, but it appears that Yagul's fortunes as a minor urban center waxed and waned until Monte Albán went into decline after A.D. 700. Then Yagul emerged as an autonomous city-state, and construction began on the structures that are the most distinctive elements of the site. The fortress crowning the heights above the main platforms suggests that threats from other city-states or from invaders were a significant concern. Bernal and Gamio believe the last of the major ceremonial buildings was abandoned in the century before the Conquest, although the local population remained until they were concentrated in Tlacolula in the mid-sixteenth century.

Site Description

The layout of the city demonstrates attention both to its physical characteristics and to the prevailing social organization. Builders took advantage of the gradient of the slope to define the different areas of the community, but

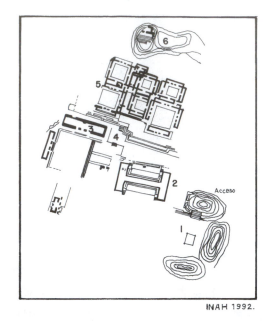

Zona Arqueologica de Yagul, Oax.
Archaeological zone of Yagul, Oax.

1.– Patio 4	1.–Patio 4
2.–_ Juego de Pelota.	2.–Ball Court.
3.– Sala del Consejo.	3.–Hall of the Council.
4.– Calle decorada con grecas.	4.–Street with greca decoration.
5.–Palacio de los Seis Patios.	5.–Palace of the six patios.
6.–Edificio V.	6.–Building V.

INAH 1992.

The archaeological zone of Yagul, Oaxaca, Mexico. Illustration courtesy of the author.

they also organized considerable labor to construct platforms, remove stone outcroppings, and fill uneven ground. The core of the site extends across c. 2.4 hectares, although minor structures, house sites, and other features cover a much larger area.

Reached by an unimproved and difficult trail northeast of the main site, the fortress demonstrates ways in which its builders sought to maximize the natural advantages of steep, broken terrain by adding massive walls of cut stone in strategic locations. Although the fortress could have offered some protection to the complex of civic and administration structures immediately below it, it more likely served as a highly defensible protected space.

The ball court is the second largest in Mesoamerica (only the court at Chichén Itzá, Yucatán, is larger); it has the traditional I-shaped construction, with well-defined elements and access. Although it is not known how the ball game became established in the Oaxaca Valley, evidence suggests that the court was built between A.D. 500 and 700, and enlarged somewhat later.

The Palace of the Six Patios is one of the most complex archaeological structures in Oaxaca. It received extensive attention from Bernal and Gamio and is the subject of a book by them. It is a labyrinth of rooms and corridors arranged around six open patios. Built in the form of an irregular rectangle with outside dimensions of approximately 68 by 50 meters, it includes a bewildering array of rooms that are reached only by passing through a series of other rooms, offset access passages, dead-end corridors, and other unusual features. It was built of local stone, which was then plastered, apparently as a single massive project rather than a series of small units with additions and remodeling. Some of the six patios—e.g., patios D and F—were readily accessible from outside and probably had public functions; Patio B, by contrast, has only a single doorway reached by a narrow access corridor. Materials found during excavation show that some of the patios were residences, a conclusion reinforced by subfloor burials, a common practice in pre-Hispanic Mesoamerica. The architectural design and construction found here are direct antecedents of the monumental structures built in Mitla somewhat later.

The south and east sides of the site are bounded by three large open spaces designated Patios Three, Four, and Five. Only Patio Four is enclosed by structures—four mounds probably once topped by temples or other religious buildings. Patio Four includes an unusual triple tomb, or, more accurately, three tombs with a common entrance, organized as a single unit. The facing of the principal tomb is decorated with friezework carved into the stone, as well as with small heads having human features. The style is Mixtec, and the offerings and ceramics associated with the tomb are Mixtec or Mixtec-influenced as well. A second distinctive feature of Patio Four is an enormous stone frog with a cavity or depression in its back. Given the scarcity of water at this rocky hillside site, one interpretation is that the frog played some part in rituals celebrated within this patio.

Across a narrow street from and aligned with the east–west axis of the Palace of the Six Patios, the Council Hall is so named because it displays characteristics that are neither those of a residence nor those of a structure with religious significance. Approximately 30 meters long and 10 meters wide, it opens through three doorways onto Patio One, an arrangement which suggests that it served administrative functions or was a focal point for public ceremony. The wall facing the Palace of the Six Patios was decorated with a stonework design commonly associated with Mitla. The configuration of this structure suggests that it served as a model for the Hall of the Columns at Mitla.

Social Organization

As a minor urban center, Yagul came under the influence of Monte Albán and paid tribute to it until Monte Albán began to lose its hegemonic position in the Oaxaca Valley after A.D. 700. Yagul established itself as one of a series of city-states—with Dainzú or Lambityeco—which emerged as Monte Albán's population migrated to the valley floor. Its social and religious life no longer revolved around a great ceremonial center but took on a more autonomous quality. Available evidence suggests that the population consisted of commoners, priests, and a military nobility. Recurring conflict with other city-states gave primacy to military chieftains, shifting alliances, and fortifications. Excavation to date suggests spatial differentiation among social classes. Although it flourished for two or three centuries, after A.D. 1000 Yagul itself began to slide into decline, to be replaced in time by Mitla as the primary urban center in the Tlacolula Valley.

FURTHER READINGS

Bernal, I., and L. Gamio. 1974. *Yagul: El Palacio de los Seis Patios.* Mexico City: Universidad Nacional Autónoma de México.

Paddock, J. 1966. *Ancient Oaxaca.* Stanford: Stanford University Press.

Robles Garcia, N. M., and R. Zarate Moran. 1992. *Yagul: Guia de la Zona Arqueológica.* Mexico City: Instituto Nacional de Antropología e Historia.

Whitecotton, J. W. 1977. *The Zapotecs.* Norman: University of Oklahoma Press.

Winter, M. 1992. *Oaxaca, the Archaeological Record.* Mexico City: Editorial Minutiae Mexicana.

Nelly M. Robles García

SEE ALSO

Fortifications; Oaxaca and Tehuantepec Region

Yanhuitlán (Oaxaca, Mexico)

Yanhuitlán's name means "new town," and an investigation of a cacique's palace by Ronald Spores suggests that it was constructed around the time of the Spanish conquest. Indications from both Spores's large-scale survey of the Nochixtlan Valley and a study of the Mixtec codices suggests that Yanhuitlán's royal family traced its descent to earlier Postclassic sites a few kilometers to the southeast, such as Suchixtlan, Andua, Chindua, Tillo, and ultimately the expansive Classic citadel of Cerro Jasmín. Despite frequent clashes with the Aztec Empire of the Triple Alliance, by A.D. 1500 Yanhuitlán had succeeded in expanding its network of control south through the Nochixtlán Valley to the Valley of Oaxaca and Cuilapan. Spanish charges of idolatry against Yanhuitlán's indigenous nobility in the 1540s resulted in a series of invaluable records of pre-Columbian Mixtec political organization and religious practices.

FURTHER READINGS

Caso, A. 1966. The Lords of Yanhuitlán. In J. Paddock (ed.), *Ancient Oaxaca*, pp. 313–335. Stanford: Stanford University Press.

Spores, R. 1967. *The Mixtec Kings and Their People.* Norman: University of Oklahoma Press.

———. 1984. *The Mixtecs in Ancient and Colonial Times.* Norman: University of Oklahoma Press.

John M. D. Pohl

SEE ALSO

Mixtec History, Culture, and Religion; Tilantongo

Yarumela (La Paz, Honduras)

The Formative period site of Yarumela lies in the geographical center of the 550-square-kilometer Comayagua Valley at 600 meters elevation, on the western bank of the Humuya River, which flows into the Caribbean via the Ulúa River drainage system. Yarumela may have been inhabited by Proto-Lenca speakers and was occupied from approximately 1000 B.C. until A.D. 200, after which time it was the locus of only sporadic Late and Postclassic period burials and settlement. The site occupies more than 30 hectares within an ancient river channel and today consists of fifteen mounds, the largest of which

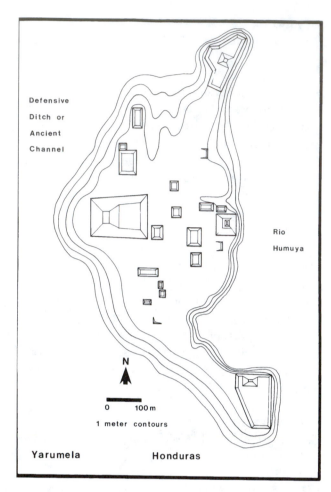

Site plan of Yarumela, Honduras. Illustration courtesy of the author.

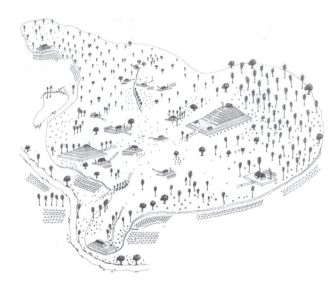

Drawing of the Yarumela site. Illustration courtesy of the author.

measures 19 meters tall and covers more than 7,000 square meters at its base.

Yarumela is presumed to have begun as a small farming hamlet around the end of the Early Formative period. It grew to become the primary center in the valley, in part because of its exploitation of both local and interregional exchange along this major cultural corridor. Evidence of this exchange has been found during excavation in the form of jade from Guatemala, Pacific and Caribbean marine shell ornaments, central highland obsidian, marble bowl fragments, and nonlocal botanical remains.

In addition to the erection of the 19-meter-tall "El Cerrito" mound during the Middle Formative period, four smaller mounds under 6 meters tall were constructed, enclosing a central plaza space containing rudimentary sculpture. By the site's abandonment at the end of the Late Formative period, these mounds had been enlarged and several more added to the site core, creating a village rivaled in size only by Los Naranjos (Honduras) and Chalchuapa (El Salvador) during this time.

FURTHER READINGS

Colby, S. 1988. An Analysis of Faunal Remains from Yarumela, Honduras. *Journal of New World Archaeology* 7(23):71–94.

Dixon, B., L. R. V. Joesink-Mandeville, N. Hasebe, M. Mucio, W. Vincent, D. James, and K. Petersen. 1994. Formative-Period Architecture at the Site of Yarumela, Central Honduras. *Latin American Antiquity* 5(1):70–87.

Joesink-Mandeville, L. R. V. 1987. Yarumela, Honduras: Formative period Cultural Conservatism and Diffusion. In E. Robinson (ed.), *Interaction on the Southeast Mesoamerican Frontier,* pp. 196–214. BAR International Series, 327(i). Oxford: British Archaeological Reports.

Boyd Dixon

SEE ALSO

Chalchuapa; Naranjos, Los; Southeast Mesoamerica

Yautépec (Morelos, Mexico)

A Postclassic urban center in the Morelos region, Yautépec was the capital of a small conquest state, drawing tribute from four subject city-states. It is one of the most intensively studied Aztec cities; surface surveys and excavations have revealed houses, a palace, and burials. Occupation of the area began with a hilltop site in the Epiclassic. The Aztec city was established along the Yautépec River during the Middle Postclassic (A.D. 1150–1350), with occupation continuing through the Late Postclassic (1350–1520) into the Colonial and modern periods. Yautépec's 2 square kilometers of settlement are nucleated around the palace and its surrounding neighborhood of affluent houses; the total population was about thirteen thousand. Architecture at Yautépec utilized adobe bricks on stone wall bases, with wide variation in building size and quality. The finest buildings were built on platforms and had painted lime-plaster floors and walls, while more modest houses were smaller, with earthen floors. The royal palace (the only extant example of an Aztec city-state capital palace) is situated on a platform 65 by 95 meters, with many passages and rooms, some with elaborate polychrome murals.

Other excavations at Yautépec located numerous small commoner houses and one large elite residence. Middens associated with these houses revealed a variety of craft activities, including cotton textile production at every house, and the manufacture of obsidian blades, bark paper, and ceramic figurines at some houses. Imported ceramics and obsidian were abundant at these urban households.

The region is agriculturally rich, with abundant rainfall and no threat of frost. Fields were probably irrigated by canals from the Yautépec River. Cotton-growing and textile production were important to the local economy, as was the production of obsidian tools and ornaments, bark-cloth paper, and ceramic figurines. These industries appear to have been household based. Artifact assemblages from residences include imported and local ceramic vessels for domestic and ritual purposes, abundant chipped stone tools of Pachuca obsidian and some of chert, and ground stone tools of basalt. Tools of copper and bronze, imported from Michoacán or West Mexico, are found in many domestic contexts.

Ritual activities took place in houses, as evidenced by incense burners and clay figurines. No public ceremonial structures have been located, but a small temple may have existed close to the palace. A number of burials of adults, juveniles, and infants have been excavated near houses. One adult burial included dismembered body parts from a possible sacrifice of retainers.

Imported ceramics and obsidian items indicate a high level of interaction with other communities in Morelos and in the Basin of Mexico. Other imports are from the Toluca and Puebla regions.

FURTHER READINGS

Carrasco, P. 1972. La casa y la hacienda de un señor Tlahuica. *Estudios de Cultura Nahuatl* 10:225–244.

———. 1976. The Joint Family in Ancient Mexico: The Case of Molotla. In H. C. Nutini et al. (eds.), *Essays on Mexican Kinship,* pp. 45–64. Pittsburgh: University of Pittsburgh Press.

Michael E. Smith

SEE ALSO
Morelos Region

Yaxchilan (Chiapas, Mexico)

Yaxchilan, a Classic Maya site overlooking the Usumacinta River, has the good fortune to have been well documented by the turn of the twentieth century, to have suffered relatively little depredation, and to have been the subject of more than fifteen years of archaeological excavation. As a result, its buildings are well known, and its 130 or more well-preserved stone monuments have provided epigraphers, iconographers, and political anthropologists with fertile ground for important discoveries and interpretations.

Yaxchilan is best known for its graphic narrative bas-relief scenes of women ritually perforating their tongues, kings offering genital blood on period endings, kings and warriors capturing enemies, kings and their allies, and rituals involving a floating serpent called Na Chan. The city's glyphs and images contain more representations of women than any other body of Maya art: as wives of kings and mothers of heirs, and as ritual assistants, holding sacred objects and participating in sacrificial bloodletting. It is less well known that nearly every building exterior was once decorated with high- and low-relief stucco sculpture, and that several interiors were also richly painted. The cornucopia of ritual imagery on more than sixty carved lintels and thirty-five stelae led to several important iconographic interpretations. The images of Yaxchilan were instrumental in the identification of dotted scrolls as royal blood, of bloodletting equipment and royal bundles, and of lunar and solar cartouches as frames for royal ancestors. They permitted the recognition that often a candidate of the royal bloodline had to defeat "supernaturals" in the ball game, produce an heir, and take important captives in order to be eligible for rulership; and they evidence the importance of Central Mexican symbols in the war complex of the Maya Lowlands.

Y

The glyphs of Yaxchilan provided data for the advancement of Tatiana Proskouriakoff's hypothesis that Maya inscriptions were historical in nature, and she identified the major Late Classic rulers and many events in the inscriptions. The act of capture, parentage statements, temple dedication ceremonies, bloodletting rituals, death, sculptor's signatures, ritual dance, building dedication ceremonies, summer solstice as the time when a ruler "stands up" the sky, have all been identified through clues in Yaxchilan's unique combination of text and image.

The large number of dated monuments also provided fertile ground for the study of artists, scribes, and workshops. At least twelve different hands wrote the glyphs on the approximately fifty-two monuments commissioned by Bird Jaguar IV during his twenty-year reign, pointing to a significant number of literate, elite men in scribal service. One workshop including three artists produced sculptures over a thirteen-year period. These artists specialized in certain types of representations: one rendered textiles and knots, and one invented the three-quarter view for the Maya and did dynamic compositions.

Dates in the hieroglyphic inscriptions range from A.D. 454 to 808, but the site was probably occupied prior to the inception of written documents. During the Late Classic, the city's rulers and warriors engaged in numerous battles to support the fragile web of political alliances and enmities that stretched across the southern Lowlands. Approximately sixteen individuals are documented as having ruled Yaxchilan; the best-known of them are Bird Jaguar III (r. A.D. 629–c. 681), his son Shield Jaguar I (r. 681–742), and his son Bird Jaguar IV (r. 752–c. 771). Currently, dating relies on hieroglyphic records, until publication of stratigraphic and ceramic evidence recorded by the Instituto Nacional de Antropología of Mexico under the direction of Roberto Garcia Moll.

Yaxchilan's political ties with Bonampak were close until about A.D. 620. Some scholars contend that the city was subordinate to Piedras Negras between 658 and 751 (dates 9.11.5.0.0., and about 9.16.0.0.0, as interpreted by Miller). An attack by Shield Skull of Tikal on a Shield Jaguar of Yaxchilan on 9.11.5.16.11 is documented on the Hieroglyphic Stairs at Palenque House C (Schele and Mathews 1993). Late in his life, Shield Jaguar I allied himself with the powerful Calakmul–Dos Pilas network by marrying a Calakmul woman, Lady Evening Star. During the reign of its last rulers, Shield Jaguar II and Mah K'ina Moon Skull IV, Yaxchilan again was closely involved with the royal dynasty of Bonampak.

The more than ninety stone buildings and large plazas which comprise the city are situated on a 100-meter-wide plain paralleling the river and on several hilly promontories which elevate groups of buildings. The location is well protected: the broad, swift river bends around the east, north, and west sides, while the neck of land connecting this peninsula to the rest of Chiapas is choked by steep hills.

Buildings from all eras define the northeastern and southwestern edges of the 1,200-meter-long Main Plaza, on the plain overlooking the river. As is customary in Mesoamerica, the ball courts occupy this lower portion of the site. The Main Plaza is subdivided by perpendicularly sited Structure 8 into two ritual spaces. The more central area contains the monuments erected (and some possibly re-erected) by Bird Jaguar IV at the foot of the great stair which leads to his accession building. Stela 1, located here, is like most other stelae at Yaxchilan in that it commemorates the capture of a foreign noble by the ruler on its river-facing façade, while the façade facing the associated temple notes the subsequent period ending (in this case, 9.16.10.0.0.) and accompanying ritual bloodletting. On the sides of Stela 1, Bird Jaguar IV's parents are carved in life-size bas-relief. Flanking the elevated stela are several low three-dimensional sculptures, one representing a cayman and one a jaguar, and fragments of carved thrones. Twelve of the structures along the Main Plaza and two farther southeast contain carved lintels. The earliest lintels found thus far were reset in Structure 22. Seven early lintels dating to (or possibly representing later references to) the reign of Ruler 10 (acceded A.D. 526) were found in Structure 12. With one exception, these early lintels are purely glyphic. The three lintels depicting women perforating their tongues in sacrificial rites were discovered in three buildings along the southwest side of the Main Plaza. One of these is part of a set of three lintels depicting Lady K'abal Xoc, a distant cousin and wife of Shield Jaguar I, with him on his accession day (A.D. 681, 9.12.9.8.1), on the 4 *katun* anniversary of his father's accession during a stationary conjunction of Jupiter and Saturn, and on several summer solstice and anniversary ceremonies.

Two terraces rise toward the Central Acropolis. Both support standing stone buildings with several preserved and/or consolidated corbel vaults. The 5.75-meter-high roof comb on Structure 33, the principal building on the Central Acropolis, is visible from the plaza below, while the 7-meter body of the building is obscured by the steep incline of the broad stairway lining the ascent of approximately 30 meters. Rebuilt several times, the final phase of

Structure 33 is a monument to the accession of Bird Jaguar IV. Associated monuments include a series of thirteen carved stair risers, describing the supernatural ball game events of this and prior kings; three carved stone lintels depicting Bird Jaguar IV and several allies, including his wife, Lady Great Skull, and their son; a stalactite stela showing a bloodletting; an over-life-size, three-dimensional seated figure of the ruler; and several carved pedestals.

The South Acropolis, at the highest part of the site, includes three structures, all associated with carved stelae. Structure 41 overlooks five stelae erected by Shield Jaguar I and nine uncarved stalactites. The interior of Structure 40 was once entirely decorated with mural paintings of great refinement.

On the West Acropolis, twelve buildings surround a central courtyard. However, the northernmost structures, including Structures 42 and 44 with their carved lintels, face the river rather than the adjacent plaza. In front of Structure 44, the lintels and stairs of which document the war deeds of Shield Jaguar I and several predecessors, several generations of rulers erected stelae. This group includes the second-earliest stela at the city, dated A.D. 523 (9.4.8.8.15), as well as one dated A.D. 788.

Structure 33, 40, and 41, all associated with stelae commemorating the war and period ending sacrifices of the rulers, face the summer solstice sunrise. A number of buildings on the Main Plaza contain historical references to ancestral rulers and women and face the winter solstice sunrise.

Although Yaxchilan may have been seen by Europeans as early as 1696, the first definite publication about the site was made by Edwin Rockstroh of Guatemala in 1881. A. P. Maudslay and D. Charnay arrived at Yaxchilan within two days of each other in 1882. Maudslay published nineteen lintels, a stela, and a preliminary map (1889–1902), and arranged for several lintels to be removed from the buildings and taken to the British Museum. Teobert Maler located and photographed more monuments, devised the nomenclature for monuments and buildings and the name of the site still in use, and documented the remains of paint and stucco on the buildings (Maler 1901). Sylvanus Morley published the calendric portion of some inscriptions (1937–1938), as well as the map by John Bolles that still serves today, and devised some misleading dates based on the erroneous assumption that all the monuments he considered beautiful belonged to a single period. Although many monuments are still *in situ,* eighteen are in the Museo Nacional de Antropología, and seven in the British Museum; one was destroyed in Berlin in World War II.

FURTHER READINGS

Carrasco V., R. 1991. The Structure 8 Tablet and Development of the Great Plaza at Yaxchilan. In V. M. Fields (ed.), *Sixth Palenque Round Table, 1986,* pp. 110–117. Palenque Round Table Series, 8. Norman: University of Oklahoma Press.

Graham, I. 1977, 1979, 1982. *Yaxchilan.* Corpus of Maya Hieroglyphic Inscriptions, 3, parts 1, 2, and 3. Cambridge, Mass.: Peabody Museum of Archaeology and Ethnology.

Grube, N. 1996. Palenque in the Maya World. In M. Macri (ed.), *Eighth Palenque Round Table, 1993,* Palenque Round Table Series, 9. San Francisco: Pre-Columbian Art Research Institute.

Maler, T. 1901. *Researches in the Central Portion of the Usumacinta Valley.* Memoirs of the Peabody Museum, 2. 1. Cambridge, Mass.: Harvard University.

Maudslay, A. P. 1889–1902. *Biologia Centrali-Americana,* vol. 2, *Archaeology.* London: Dulen.

Morley, S. G. 1937–1938. *The Inscriptions of Petén.* Carnegie Institute of Washington Yearbook, Publication 437, 2 and 5. Washington, D.C.

Proskouriakoff, T. 1963–1964. Historical Data in the Inscriptions of Yaxchilan, Part 1. *Estudios de Cultura Maya* 3:149–167; 4:177–201.

Schele, L., and M. Miller. 1986. *The Blood of Kings: Dynasty and Ritual in Maya Art.* Fort Worth: Kimbell Art Museum.

Tate, C. E. 1992. *Yaxchilan: The Design of a Maya Ceremonial City.* Austin: University of Texas Press.

Carolyn Tate

SEE ALSO

Blood and Bloodletting; Maya Lowlands: South; Proskouriakoff, Tatiana

Yaxhá (Petén, Guatemala)

The archaeological site of Yaxhá lies on the northern shore of Lake Yaxhá, which shares a large fault-fracture depression with Lake Sacnab to its east, the two being separated by a narrow isthmus. There was Maya occupation in these basins as early as the early Middle Formative period (c. 800 B.C.), and the site of Yaxhá was the major

Y

civic-ceremonial center in the basins from Late Formative (300 B.C.–A.D. 250) through Late Classic (A.D. 500–900) times. The site was abandoned in the tenth century, but there was Postclassic (A.D. 900–1697) occupation within the basins, particularly on the Topoxté Islands in Lake Yaxhá.

Don S. Rice

SEE ALSO

Maya Lowlands: South

Yaxuna (Yucatán, Mexico)

Yaxuna is the name given to the pre-Columbian ruin of a Maya settlement called "Cetelac" in the Conquest period *Chilam Balam* books. Research shows that this small city has been continuously occupied for more than 2,500 years.

Yaxuna was founded as a ceremonial center and community by 500 B.C., at the end of the Middle Formative period, and at that time its first large pyramids were built. Yaxuna expanded as a major community through the Late Formative and Early Classic periods, when most of the great plazas and pyramids were built. The center of ancient Yaxuna covers more than 0.75 square kilometer and contains four major concentrations of public buildings: the Northern Acropolis, the Eastern Acropolis, the Central Acropolis with its E-Group, and the Southern Group, which consists of three distinct clusters of buildings in close proximity. The center is laid out on a formal north–south axis defined by stone roads leading south from the Northern Acropolis and north from the Structure 5E-19 Group. There is a secondary east–west axis, also defined by stone causeways. This east–west axis has a major expression in the E-Group adjacent to the Central Acropolis and a second expression in a causeway passing through the densest settlement zone to the south of the Central Acropolis. The pre-Columbian settlement of Yaxuna has a dense core of residential platforms, pyramids, temples, and ground-level structures covering at least 2 square kilometers. The ancient community probably extended over a much larger area, perhaps as great as 6 square kilometers.

The discovery of two Early Classic royal tomb burials in pyramids of the Northern Acropolis confirms that the city was a royal capital in this period. Archaeologically, the Yaxuna tombs are the best evidence to date that some northern Maya Lowlands Early Classic governments were ruled by kings comparable to those documented for southern Lowlands governments.

During the Late Classic and Terminal Classic periods, population remained significant, as revealed through ceramic analysis of test excavation lots from residential features. This was true despite the evidence for demographic decline in the ninth century elsewhere in the Lowlands. Yaxuna was linked to Cobá by a 100-kilometer stone causeway in the Late Classic period. War symbolism on buildings, fortification of acropolises, and destruction events all suggest that it was a strategic center in military struggles between the great states of the northern Lowlands during the Late Classic to Terminal Classic periods. The Postclassic population was evidently that of a small village.

Archaeologists of the Carnegie Institution of Washington, interested in tying in the Chichén Itzá research to that of Cobá, a southern Lowlands-style site, carried out preliminary survey and test excavations at Yaxuna in 1932 and 1942. In fact, while Chichén Itzá was no doubt a larger city in antiquity, the major pyramidal structures at Yaxuna are as large as those at the more famous site. The Selz Foundation Yaxuna Project carried out systematic survey, test excavation in buildings of every size, extensive excavations in selected public and residential buildings, and consolidation work.

FURTHER READINGS

Suhler, C., and D. Freidel. 1998. Life and Death in a Maya War Zone. *Archaeology* 51:28–34.

David A. Freidel

SEE ALSO

Cobá; Maya Lowlands: North

Yohualinchan (Veracruz, Mexico)

Perched on a narrow ridge at 600 meters elevation in the Sierra Madre Oriental, this small but architecturally significant site is strongly linked to lowland El Tajín. Multistory temple platforms were constructed with the flying cornices, recessed niches, and stucco composition that are the hallmarks of El Tajín. Some niches are reported to have retained red paint. Also present is a vertical-walled ball court, approximately 80 meters long, without carved panels. The principal structures, including one with five levels, face onto a rectangular plaza just north of the ball court, which is on a rise. Natural terracing was exploited to enhance the visual perspectives of buildings, and locally procured limestone flags were the primary building materials. The construction quality, however, does not equal that of the finer structures at El Tajín.

Although the full chronology of Yohualinchan is unknown, it is clear that its architectural apogee probably occurred during the Middle to Late Classic. The function of the site, less than 50 kilometers in a direct line from El Tajín and situated on rugged high ground midway between two of the upper affluents of the Tecolulta River, was probably as an outpost for trade with the highlands as well as a gateway community controlling access to the El Tajín hinterland below.

Situated near the mountain town of Cuetzalan, an important modern market center for Nahuas and Totonacs of the Sierra Norte de Puebla, Yohualinchan received notice and visits starting at least by the 1920s. The first detailed examination, to determine the feasibility of restoration, was initiated by García Payon in 1953. Reconstruction efforts were undertaken by INAH in the 1980s and 1990s. A small modern village of the same name covers part of the site.

FURTHER READINGS

Marquina, I. 1964. *Arquitectura Prehispánica.* 2d ed. Memorias del Instituto Nacional de Antropología e Historia, 1. Mexico City.

Palacios, E. J. 1926. *Yohualinchan y El Tajín.* Mexico City: Dirección de Arqueología.

S. Jeffrey K. Wilkerson

SEE ALSO

Gulf Lowlands: North Central Region

Yucudzaa

See Tututepec del Sur

Z

Zacatenco (D.F., Mexico)

This village site of moderate extent (c. 15 hectares) is situated at the southern base of the Guadalupe Hills, on the northwestern edge of Mexico City, and dates to c. 900–50 B.C. (uncalibrated radiocarbon date). It was first noted by Franz Boas. George C. Vaillant's Trench D at Zacatenco provided the first stratigraphy within the Formative period for the Basin of Mexico, parts of which were later confirmed by him at El Arbolillo and Ticoman. As at El Arbolillo, farmers here had access to both lakeside and piedmont resources. Remains of habitation terraces are present. Fourteen flexed and extended burials (all but one seemingly pre-Ticoman) had no associated offerings. Pacific shell and greenstone objects suggest contacts westward. Abundant clay figurines in refuse suggest their transient value and use in domestic rituals.

FURTHER READINGS

Tolstoy, P. 1978. Western Mesoamerica before A.D. 900. In R. E. Taylor and C. W. Meighan (eds.), *Chronologies in New World Archaeology,* pp. 241–284. New York: Academic Press.

Vaillant, G. C. 1930. *Excavations at Zacatenco.* Anthropological Papers of the American Museum of Natural History, 32, part 1.

Paul Tolstoy

SEE ALSO

Basin of Mexico

Zaculeu (Huehuetenango, Guatemala)

In the seventeenth century, Fuentes y Guzmán recounted the 1525 Spanish conquest of Zaculeu, a major center of Mayan speakers of the Mam dialect. Scant documentary evidence indicates that it had been previously conquered by the Quiché of Utatlán, but eventually regained much of its autonomy as the chief center in the northwestern Guatemalan highlands.

Situated on the bank of the Selegua River (1,900 meters elevation), a main affluent of the Grijalva, and at the foot of the 3,500-meter-high Cuchumatanes range, the site is surrounded on three sides by ravines. Like other Late Postclassic sites in the area, it stands in a naturally defensible location. Its extensive history began with a major stage of occupation during the Early Classic, whose remains included an elaborate chamber tomb excavated in the subsoil, containing a multiple burial with abundant offerings.

Postclassic architecture featured terraced pyramid temples and elongated buildings around square plazas with elaborate median altars, as well as a large I-shaped ball court. Several buildings displayed porticoes with round or rectangular columns. Adobe was a common material, but late buildings were faced with well-shaped stone slabs and stucco. Excavations also produced one of the largest samples of human skeletal remains from the Maya area. Two hundred forty-nine individuals were recovered from 108 graves of many types—vaulted chambers, crypts, cists, urns, simple graves, and cremations. Most were found in the axis of major buildings; no research was carried out in commoner dwelling areas.

Z

FURTHER READINGS

Fuentes y Guzmán, F. A. de. 1933. *Recordación florida, discurso historial y demostración natural, material, militar y política del reyno de Guatemala.* 3 vols. Guatemala City: Sociedad de Geografía e Historia.

Smith, A. L. 1955. *Archaeological Reconnaissance in Central Guatemala.* Carnegie Institution, Publication 608. Washington D.C.

Woodbury, R. B., and A. S. Trik. 1953. *The Ruins of Zaculeu, Guatemala.* 2 vols. Richmond: United Fruit Company.

Oswaldo Chinchilla Mazariegos

SEE ALSO

Guatemala Highlands Region

Zapotec Culture and Religion

At the time of the Spanish conquest there were at least 350,000 speakers of the Zapotec language in Oaxaca, and their culture could be observed and described at first hand by the Spaniards. On the basis of sixteenth-century documents written in Spanish, we know that Zapotec society was divided into two strata kept separate by class endogamy, the custom of marrying within one's stratum.

The upper stratum, the hereditary nobility, was headed by a male ruler, the *coqui,* and his wife, the *xonaxi.* Within the upper stratum were many ranks or levels of nobility; however, since nobles of all levels could intermarry, these ranks were not truly separate social strata. The Spaniards saw parallels between Zapotec nobility and their own European ranking of princes, dukes, earls, barons, and so forth.

The Zapotec ranked lineages as *tija coqui,* those of the greatest hereditary nobles; *tija joana,* lineages of lesser nobles, also in the upper stratum; and *tija peniqueche,* lineages of the commoners (literally, "townspeople"). Within the lower stratum there were many levels, too: free commoners, landholding commoners, landless commoners, and slaves. There is no evidence for a middle class, if by that term we mean a third endogamous stratum. There were, of course, many people within the upper and lower strata who achieved different levels of wealth and prestige; for example, a wealthy commoner might have more wealth than a minor noble. The key differences between noblemen and commoners were hereditary privileges; nobles, for example, could wear feather garments or jade earplugs, and eat deer meat.

From the accounts of Spaniards we know that the Zapotec lord was head not only of the state but also of the church. To prepare himself for the latter office, he underwent religious training for a year to supplement his other education. Religion and state were closely linked in most Mesoamerican societies. Many of the highest-ranking priests were close relatives of the Zapotec ruler. The high priest was aided by a hierarchy of priests who performed a wide range of services, rituals, and sacrifices on behalf of the townspeople; lesser priests could be drawn from the stratum of commoners.

Zapotec religion was animistic. They recognized a supreme being "who created everything but was not himself created"; no images were made of him, and no one could come into direct contact with him. The principal supernatural being with whom the Zapotec could interact was Lightning (Cociyo); his companions were Wind (Pee, Pi), Clouds (Zaa), Hail (Quiezabi), and Rain (Nica). Lightning was the angry and jagged face of Sky, one of the great divisions of the Zapotec cosmos. The other great division was Earth, whose angry face was Earthquake (Xoo).

In Zapotec cosmology, everything that moved was worthy of reverence and respect and was considered alive. Living things were distinguished from inanimate matter through their possession of a "vital force" called *pee* or *pi* ("wind," "breath," or "spirit"). Since *pee* made all things move, such movement proved that they were alive. Some things considered alive by the Zapotec were a bolt of lightning, clouds sweeping across the sky, earth moving beneath one's feet, wind lifting one's hair, and even the foam on a cup of chocolate beverage.

Even time was considered to be alive. The Zapotec, like other Indians of Mesoamerica, believed that time was cyclic rather than linear and that given days returned over and over again. To keep track of the days, the Zapotec had two calendars—one ritual, and the other solar. The ritual calendar *(piye)* had twenty-day signs that combined with thirteen numbers from 1 to 13 to produce a cycle of 260 days. From its name *(piye)* we can see that this ritual calendar had *pi* and was thus considered to be alive. The solar calendar had eighteen units of twenty days each (360 days), with five extra days to equal a year of 365 days.

Each Zapotec was supposed to be named for the day of the 260-day calendar on which he or she was born. Names such as 8 Deer or 12 Jaguar are examples; some nobles also had nicknames such as "Lightning Creator" or "Great Eagle."

One aspect of Zapotec religion that was poorly understood by the Spaniards was royal ancestor worship. After Zapotec lords (or royal married couples) died, they were venerated as beings who could intercede on behalf of their people with supernatural forces such as Lightning. Indeed, deceased rulers were thought to metamorphose into clouds that flew above their descendants. The Spaniards recorded dozens of alleged "gods" in sixteenth-century communities, but when we translate these Zapotec names we discover that they were the names of actual rulers and their wives, and not the names of gods: many have names taken from the 260-day calendar, and some names include the titles *coqui* and *xonaxi*. Furthermore, there is almost no overlap between the lists of "gods" from town to town, which suggests that each town was actually venerating its own deceased rulers.

FURTHER READINGS

Marcus, J. 1978. Archaeology and Religion: A Comparison of the Zapotec and Maya. *World Archaeology* 10:172–191.

———. 1983. Zapotec religion. In K. V. Flannery and J. Marcus (eds.), *The Cloud People*, pp. 345–351. New York: Academic Press.

———. 1992. *Mesoamerican Writing Systems.* Princeton: Princeton University Press.

Marcus, J., and K. V. Flannery. 1994. Ancient Zapotec Ritual and Religion: An Application of the Direct Historical Approach. In C. Renfrew and E. B. W. Zubrow (eds.), *The Ancient Mind: Elements of Cognitive Archaeology,* pp. 55–74. Cambridge: Cambridge University Press.

———, ———. 1996. *Zapotec Civilization.* London: Thames and Hudson.

Whitecotton, J. 1977. *The Zapotecs.* Norman: University of Oklahoma Press.

Joyce Marcus

SEE ALSO

Oaxaca and Tehuantepec Region

Zapotec Mortuary Practices

Several hundred burials have been excavated from various archaeological sites in the central valleys of Oaxaca, allowing us to trace changes in mortuary practices through time. Between 1500 and 500 B.C., when the Zapotec lived in agricultural villages, in some communities the dead were buried in domestic contexts, but others had cemeteries, a practice that was apparently abandoned from the inception of urban life to the time of the Spanish conquest (500 B.C.–A.D. 1521).

Well-documented burial deposits from Monte Albán and several satellite communities provide insights into mortuary practices at the height of Zapotec civilization (A.D. 600–800). For example, by the eighth century people were buried under houses, although at some sites a few adult burials have been found in temples and other public contexts. Within a single household unit we may find different mortuary treatments, with a clear distinction made between burials placed inside subterranean tombs and those placed in simple graves.

The tombs contained multiple, usually mixed, remains of adults of both sexes, and seem to have been burial places reserved for several generations of household heads, or cohorts by marriage. Other individuals, apparently family members, were buried in simple graves. Comparison of burials in tombs and graves reveals a greater quantity and diversity of offerings with tomb interments; however, some children buried in single graves at elite residences have finer grave goods than adults interred in tombs from nonelite households.

Architecturally, wealthy tombs are integral masonry features of houses, usually built under the east room. Façades, entrances, and interior walls were decorated with painted, sculpted, or carved iconographic and epigraphic programs of a genealogical nature. Elite dead were buried with clothes and personal ornaments like earplugs and bracelets. Wrapped in a mat, the body was then laid to rest in an extended dorsal position with the head toward the east. Other funerary offerings included pottery serving vessels, miniature objects, hand-held incense burners, young dogs and small birds, and, most characteristic, ceramic effigy vessels portraying human figures with elaborate paraphernalia.

The remains placed inside the tombs were the focus of continuous rituals, suggesting that ancestor veneration may have been at the core of Zapotec notions of death. Rich and poor propitiated their ancestors to cope with crises and rites of passage, thus constantly engaging the dead, reopening the tombs for new interments or to seek the intervention of the ancestors. When tombs were opened, perishable and nonperishable offerings were deposited and bones were rearranged, painted red, and sometimes retrieved to serve as symbols of power.

FURTHER READINGS

Caso, A. 1933. Las tumbas de Monte Albán. *Anales del Museo Nacional de Antropología* 8:641–647.

Lind, M., and J. Urcid. 1983. The Lords of Lambityeco and Their Nearest Neighbors. *Notas Mesoamericanas* 9:71–111.

Whalen, M. 1983. Reconstructing Early Village Organization in Oaxaca, Mexico. *American Antiquity* 48: 17–43.

Javier Urcid

SEE ALSO

Zapotec Culture and Religion

Zapotitan Region (El Salvador)

The Zapotitan Valley is a broad, fertile drainage in the southeastern periphery of Mesoamerica, in what is now El Salvador. The interaction of people with an active volcanic landscape, including the processes of natural and human recovery from volcanic disasters, has been a feature of life here for the past few thousand years. Ringed by volcanoes with peaks above 2,000 meters, the valley encompasses an area of 546 square kilometers. It is broad and basinlike but constricted to the north, where it is drained by the Río Sucio to the Río Lempa and eventually to the Pacific Ocean. The central part of the valley contained a shallow lake in prehistoric times, ringed by marshes and agriculturally fertile land at about 450 meters elevation. The lake existed until the mid-1960s, when it was drained to extend the agricultural zone. Most settlements in the valley were below 700 meters in elevation, and very few sites were found above 1,000 meters.

The climate is tropical, with a strong division of precipitation into dry and wet seasons—often called a "tropical monsoon" climate. Most meteorological stations in the valley report mean annual precipitation between 1,500 and 2,000 mm, with standard deviations of about 300 mm. Thus, years with near-average precipitation are excellent for nonirrigated agriculture, but unusually wet or dry years create problems. The natural flora was largely tropical deciduous trees, shrubs, vines, and grasses, with gallery evergreen forests along watercourses or where groundwater is close to the surface. Only a few remnants of the natural vegetation remain. The most common trees are ceiba, conacaste, amate, ramon, balsam, madre cacao, and cedar. That natural forest gave way to a predominantly pine-oak forest at elevations over 1,000 meters, but most of that forest has now been converted to coffee and other crops. Fauna were diverse, with abundant herbivores, birds, and insects, and some carnivores. Soils, developed from volcanic ash deposits or lava flows, were very fertile where sufficient weathering had occurred. Temperatures are warm at lower elevations: the mean annual temperature at San Andres, near the center of the valley, is 24°C, with a low in December of 22°C, and a high in April of 26°C. The daytime-nighttime variation in temperature usually exceeds the annual variation.

The valley and its environs comprise one of the most volcanically active areas in Mesoamerica, with frequent explosive and effusive eruptions in the Pliocene, Pleistocene, and Recent times. The earliest such event that may have affected human populations was the massive explosive eruption of Coatepeque, sometime between 10,000 and 40,000 years ago. It deposited a thick mantle of ash over the countryside which weathered into the highly fertile soil that supported the dense agrarian populations of the Formative and later periods. Although El Salvador is known to have been occupied during the Paleoindian, Archaic, and Early Formative periods, the earliest sites known in the Zapotitan Valley date to the Middle and Late Formative. Earlier sites presumably are deeply buried by later eruptive materials.

Lava flows have often affected the landscape in and around the valley. A few hundred years ago, Cerro Chinto spewed lava that covered 15 square kilometers. Playon buried about 20 square kilometers under lava in 1658–1659, shortly followed by San Marcelino in 1722, which buried about 15 square kilometers. The most recent outpouring was the large flow from the north side of San Salvador volcano in 1917, burying approximately 20 square kilometers. On the northwest side of the valley, Izalco grew from nothing to a major volcano 1,900 meters in elevation in two centuries, from 1770 to 1965.

Physiographically, the Zapotitan Valley can be divided into four units. The eastern and the southern mountains are rugged and highly dissected, and have few areas suitable for habitation. They supported few settlements during any period of the archaeological past and continue to be sparsely inhabited today. Our survey of them found few artifacts other than small projectile points made from prismatic blade segments, probably evidence of hunting with bows and arrows during the Late Classic and Postclassic periods. The western mountains are topographically more gentle, with low hills, small flat valleys, and some plateaus that supported numerous prehistoric settlements from the Classic period through the Postclassic. The western mountains supported the highest number of sites per unit area during these two periods, but the sites tend to be small. The large area of flat to gently sloping land around Laguna Zapotitan, in the basin province, supported the most dense populations at all times,

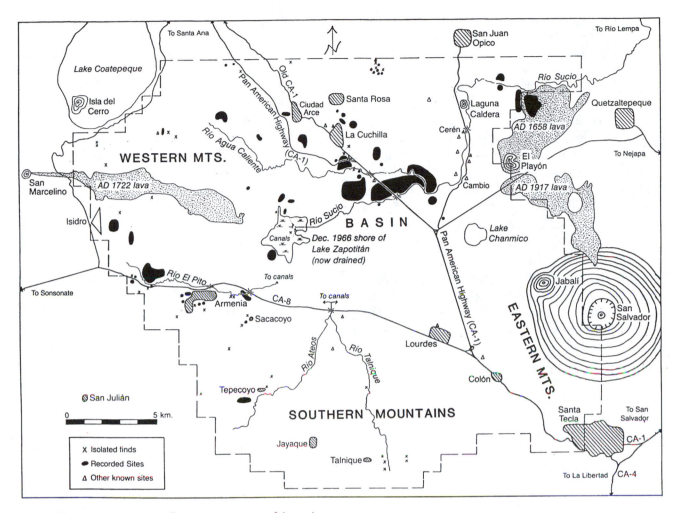

Map of the Zapotitan region. Illustration courtesy of the author.

including the present. The basin sites were much larger, and the population density of the basin is estimated to have been about two hundred people per square kilometer in the Late Classic—about three times the density of the western mountains at the same time. The soils are the most fertile, the water table is higher, and the climate is conducive to high crop productivity.

By the Late Formative, a hierarchical settlement system had developed, probably indicating a chiefdom (ranked society) with authority centalized at Campaña San Andres. Smaller settlements dotted the landscape around the lake that occupied the center of the valley, but population density was relatively low, particularly in areas more than a few kilometers from the lakeshore.

About A.D. 200 a vent opened under Lake Ilopango, around 50 kilometers to the east, and a cataclysmic volcanic eruption occurred that caused a regional natural disaster. One to two meters of white, acidic volcanic ash were deposited throughout the Zapotitan Valley, which caused its abandonment for about two centuries. Following weathering and soil formation, and vegetative and faunal recovery, people began to reoccupy the valley. San Andres was reoccupied and Cerén was founded. By the Late Classic period, the lower areas of the valley were densely populated with a hierarchical settlement system consisting of one primary regional center, a few secondary regional centers, and numerous villages of various sizes down to tiny hamlets. San Andres, with a large pyramid-plaza complex in its center, continued as the valley's primary regional center. It was a powerful chiefdom or a small state during the Late Classic. San Andres probably organized the import of Ixtepeque obsidian from

Z

Guatemala, pigments such as hematite cylinders and refined cinnabar (HgS) in miniature ceramic vessels, and shells and salt from the Pacific. The principal polychrome ceramic ware, Copador, was shared with Copán. The loci of manufacture and the system of distribution are unknown; however, Copador hemispherical and cylinder vessels from Copán and the Zapotitan Valley are very similar in materials, technology, and style. An elaborate flaked chert eccentric, in the mannikin scepter style with human profiles, was found recently at San Andres, and is further evidence of close connections with Copán and the Maya area to the north.

The Loma Caldera volcanic eruption that deeply buried Cerén was not a regional disaster, because it negatively affected only a few score square kilometers in the northwestern portion of the valley. Two later eruptions affected valleywide populations more than the Loma Caldera eruption, depositing ash throughout the valley. One of these recent eruptions was from Boqueron (San Salvador Volcano), and the most recent was from Playon. The Boqueron eruption probably occurred sometime between A.D. 800 and 1200, and it particularly affected the eastern half of the valley. The Playon eruption, well dated to A.D. 1658–1659, affected the northeastern edge of the valley by damming the river, creating a lake that flooded low-lying areas of the valley, and by depositing volcanic ash that negatively affected agriculture.

The nature of the settlement hierarchy, from primary and secondary regional centers through large and small villages, is reflected in the dynamics of obsidian implement production and distribution. As the obsidian prismatic blades reached smaller settlements, their cutting edge per unit weight increased, probably indicating increased transportation and distribution costs. Manufacturers were able to "stretch" the obsidian by making thinner blades at smaller settlements away from the San Andres. In contrast, knappers at San Andres made thicker prismatic blades that would have been more durable. Evidently San Andres controlled the access to Ixtepeque obsidian, but it did not control the manufacture of implements in the valley. Clear evidence of blade manufacture was found at hamlets and villages of all sizes, in the form of discarded exhausted cores, thus demonstrating that San Andres did not centralize manufacture of blades within its boundaries. The error rate, quantified as the hinge fracture frequency, was quite low in the larger settlements, probably indicating skill and some occupational specialization. However, the error rate of resident knappers increased in the smaller settlements. The smallest of settlements, hamlets, evidently were too small to support their own lithic specialists and had to rely on specialists from larger settlements.

The Classic to Postclassic transition in the valley was not marked by the dramatic disjunctures of the central Maya Lowlands. Most settlements continued to be occupied, but a few of the higher-elevation sites of the Classic period in the western mountains were abandoned. Valley population density declined only slightly from the Classic into the Early Postclassic. The Postclassic was a time of influx of Pipil peoples into the valley, originally from Central Mexico, probably via Salvadoran sites such as Cihuatan. San Andres continued to be occupied throughout the Postclassic. However, many Early Postclassic sites were abandoned by the beginning of the Late Postclassic. The overall valley population declined dramatically by the end of the Postclassic, to approximately half of what it had been during its Late Classic peak. Many of the contemporary towns in the valley are built atop their Late Postclassic antecedents, including Armenia, Sacacoyo, Ateos, Talnique, and San Juan Opico.

FURTHER READINGS

Fowler, W. 1989. *The Cultural Evolution of Ancient Nahua Civilizations: The Pipil-Nicarao of Central America*. Norman: University of Oklahoma Press.

Sheets, P. (ed.). 1983. *Archaeology and Volcanism in Central America: The Zapotitan Valley of El Salvador*. Austin: University of Texas Press.

———. 1984. The Prehistory of El Salvador: An Interpretive Summary. In F. W. Lange and D. Stone (eds.), *The Archaeology of Lower Central America*, pp. 85–112. Albuquerque: University of New Mexico Press.

———. 1992. *The Cerén Site: A Prehistoric Village Buried by Volcanic Ash in Central America*. Fort Worth: Harcourt Brace Jovanovich.

Payson Sheets

SEE ALSO
Southeast Mesoamerica

Zempoala (Veracruz, Mexico)

Zempoala (or Cempoala, Cempoalan), the major metropolitan center of the coastal Totonacs at the end of the Postclassic period, is the largest and most historically significant of a complex of important sites near the mouth of the Actopan (or Chachakicas) River. Situated in a dry region very near the upper limit of south central Veracruz, it was called "Sevilla" by the Spaniards, who in 1519 were astonished by its huge population (c. 80,000), its burnished white buildings, and its green irrigated fields. It was the most populous city of its day on the Gulf Coast, and hence its principal temple compound was the setting for a number of momentous events in the first year of the Conquest. Subsequent catastrophic epidemics of European diseases devastated the city, leaving it deserted by the early seventeenth century.

The urban center, stretching back from the northern bank of the river, is characterized by large, irregularly shaped plaza-temple compounds, some bordered by a platform wall with stepped merlons (*coatipantli*, "snake wall"). In general, the cults, temple forms, urban design, and art of the city reflect the norms of the Central Mexican highlands, a general Terminal Postclassic tendency reinforced by the late fifteenth-century Aztec dominance of the region. Major buildings are constructed of large river cobbles and thickly sealed with cement. Many have platforms with multiple stories of low height and vertical profile. Most temples are rectangular with broad stairways; some have screening structures at their base, and a few have round backs. Roofs were of thatch and, in a few instances, of masonry. Sanctuaries have glyphic polychrome designs on a white background. Ceramics reflect both regional fine-paste styles and more distant highland preferences, including a local, high-quality version of Cholula-Puebla polychrome.

Surrounding the city were extensive canal systems for water distribution to fields. These diverted water from the main river channels, themselves apparently altered in some sections. Such large-scale hydraulic engineering was crucial to sustaining a large population in the dry rain shadow zone stretching southward from the central mountains of Veracruz. A number of these artificial waterways are likely to be considerably older than Zempoala itself.

The explorations led by Francisco del Paso y Troncoso in 1891 confirmed the site as the location of the historical city, cleared temple structures, and produced a useful map, published by Galindo. During 1905 Fewkes photographed and described some major structures. From the late 1930s until the early 1970s, Garcia Payon undertook both stratigraphic excavations and reconstruction in and about Zempoala. His pioneering work was particularly important because it was the first attempt on the Gulf Coast to examine a major site in its regional context. It led to the recognition of a long

local chronology linking neighboring and satellite sites to the city. From 1979 to 1981 an Instituto Nacional de Antropología e Historia project resulted in further reconstruction in the temple compounds and an examination of the greater urban area. Zempoala has been much affected by the growth of the modern town of the same name (formerly Agostadero) and by intensive sugar cane production.

The temporal and spatial significance of Zempoala is greatly enhanced by information from the following nearby sites in the complex (distances are given from the main plaza).

Trapiche (El Trapiche, Mata Verde; 2 kilometers south), a large, low mound explored by Garcia Payon in 1942 and 1951 following flood exposure, was situated on a waterway by the field systems. The excavations here demonstrated that there were occupations within the complex dating at least as far back as the end of the Early Formative.

Chalahuite (Chalahuite Viejo, El Chalahuite; 3 kilometers northeast), characterized on the surface by a series of large earthen mounds, up to 20 meters high and containing a few stone walls of river cobbles, was initially explored stratigraphically by Garcia Payon in 1951 and 1959. The major settlement of the region during the Late Formative and Protoclassic times, Chalahuite is situated on the south side of Arroyo Frío (Agua Fría); this functions as a deltaic distributory channel of the Actopan River but is probably, in large part, an artificial waterway of early date. The first canal systems in the greater region may well be associated with this center. Later stratigraphic work was undertaken here by James Ford and Alfonso Medellín in the early 1960s and by an INAH project in 1981.

Chachalacas (Barra de Chachalacas; 8 kilometers southeast), situated on the south bank of the Actopan River two kilometers upstream from its mouth, was explored stratigraphically in 1949 by Garcia Payon. The site was found to have had a long occupation beginning in the Late Formative and lasting through the Classic, with a terminal Postclassic reoccupation.

Limoncito (El Limoncito, 3 kilometers southeast), situated on the southern bank of the Actopan, was probed inconclusively by Ford and Medellín in the 1960s in an effort to find materials of similar date to Trapiche.

FURTHER READINGS

Fewkes, J. W. 1907. Certain Antiquities of Eastern Mexico. In *Twenty-Fifth Annual Report, Bureau of American Ethnology*, pp. 221–296. Washington, D.C.

Z

Galindo y Villa, J. 1912. *Las ruinas de Cempoala y del templo del Tajín.* Anales del Museo Nacional de Arqueológia, Historia y Etnografia. Mexico City.

Garcia Payon, J. 1960. *Zempoala, Guia Oficial.* Mexico City: Instituto Nacional de Antropología e Historia.

Wilkerson, S. J. K. 1983. So Green and Like a Garden: Intensive Agriculture in Ancient Veracruz. In J. P. Darch (ed.), *Drained Field Agriculture in Central and South America,* pp. 55–90. BAR International Series, 189. Oxford: British Archaeological Reports.

———. 1984a. In Search of the Mountain of Foam: Human Sacrifice in Eastern Mesoamerica. In E. H. Boone (ed.), *Ritual Human Sacnfice in Mesoamerica,* pp. 101–132. Washington, D.C.: Dumbarton Oaks.

———. 1984b. Following Cortés, Path to Conquest. *National Geographic* 166:420–459.

S. Jeffrey K. Wilkerson

SEE ALSO

Gulf Lowlands: North Central Region

Zinapécuaro (Michoacán, Mexico)

Zinapécuaro had been incorporated into the Tarascan Empire by A.D. 1440. At the time of the Spanish conquest, however, apparently few of its inhabitants belonged to this ethnic group; they were Chichimecs, Matlatzincas, and Otomís. Zinapécuaro was an important religious place, associated with the Tarascan goddess Cuerauáperi, deity of rain and creation, whose cult developed around the thermal springs found in this place.

The name "Zinapécuaro" derives from the Tarascan word *tzinapu,* which means "knife" and refers to the abundant obsidian in this area. Both the capital of the Tarascans and the sites on the eastern frontier were supplied with obsidian primarily from this source.

Between 80 and 90 percent of the obsidian used in Tzintzuntzan, the Tarascan capital, came from Zinapécuaro. This site is in the Lake Cuitzeo Basin, in an area with elevated mountain valleys, forests, and abundant mineral resources—basalt and rhyolite as well as obsidian.

Pre-Hispanic exploitation of obsidian in the area is evidenced by three types of mines: Type I, the most common, is a shallow pit surrounded by a mound of earth, ash and flaking debris, made to extract obsidian from superficial flows. Type II is similar but much bigger in scale, with wider, deeper pits; and the surrounding mounds measure up to 3 or 4 meters. Type III consists of a long, wide trench with access ramps and artificial terraces built with refuse material from the mining activities.

FURTHER READINGS

Healan, D. M. 1994. Producción y uso instrumental de la obsidiana en el área Tarasca. In B. Boehm (ed.), *El Michoacán antiguo: Estado y sociedad Tarascos en la época prehispánica,* pp. 271–276. Morelia: Colegio de Michoacán.

Pollard, H. P., and T. A. Vogel. 1994. Implicaciones políticas y económicas del intercambio de obsidiana dentro del estado Tarasco. In E. Williams and R. Novella (eds.), *Arqueología del Occidente de México: Nuevas aportaciones,* pp. 159–182. Morelia: Colegio de Michoacán.

Eduardo Williams

SEE ALSO

Michoacán Region

Zohapilco

See Ayotla-Zohapilco

Zorita, Alonso de (1512–1585)

As a historian, this royal judge (*oidor*) belonged to the second generation of Spanish writers interested in the New World and its inhabitants. In writing his major work, the *Relación de las cosas notables de la nueva España y de la conquista* (1585), Zorita had at his disposal the accounts of conquerors, first settlers, missionaries, court historians, and other cultured Europeans. For his ethnographic writing this first bibliographer of works on the Indies drew primarily on his nineteen years of experience and observation in the royal tribunals (*audiencias*) of Santo Domingo, Guatemala, and Mexico, on his period of service in New Granada (present Colombia) as investigating judge (*juez de residencia*), and on the invaluable treatises of scholarly friars like Toribio de Motolinía and Bartolomé de las Casas. Indian elders and lords also supplied Zorita with accounts of pre-Conquest society.

As a royal judge, Zorita defended the Indians of America and was a pro-Indian reformer, like Bartolomé de las Casas. His writings reveal his deep piety, a familiarity with Greco-Roman literature and ancient history, and an acquaintance with the works of Sir Thomas More and Erasmus of Rotterdam. Like the Stoics, Zorita believed in the unity and brotherhood of mankind. His ardent defense of the Indians against the charge that they were savages included a relativist line of argument that anticipated Michel de Montaigne's celebrated comment, "Everyone calls barbarian what is not his own usage." The source of this idea is found in the ideal state of Zeno and in St. Paul's words, "There are diversities of gifts, but the same Spirit."

FURTHER READINGS

Vigil, R. H. 1987. *Alonso de Zorita: Royal Judge and Christian Humanist, 1512–1585.* Norman: University of Oklahoma Press.

Zorita, A. de. 1994. *Life and Labor in Ancient Mexico: The Brief and Summary Relation of the Lords of New Spain.* B. Keen (trans. and ed.). Norman: University of Oklahoma Press.

Ralph H. Vigil

SEE ALSO
Colonial Period; Ethnohistorical Sources and Methods

Zumpango del Río
See Tula Region

INDEX

Page numbers in **boldface** indicate article titles.

Agua Buena, 516
Aguacatal, El, 828
Aguacatecas, 309
Aguadulce Shelter, 483
Aguas Calientes, 792
Aguateca, 587, 588, 589, 590
Aguirre Beltrán, Gonzalo, 582
Aguná, 186
Ahal Puh (deity), 218
Ahal Zana (deity), 218
Ahav Xik (deity), 218
Ah Cacao. *See* Hasaw Kan K'awil I
Ah-Maxam (painter), 512
ahuacamolli (guacamole), 276
Ahualulco (Jalisco, Mexico), **15–16**, 819
Ahualulco circles, 15
ahuehuetl tree, 287
Ahuelican (Guerrero, Mexico), 315, 318
ahuianime (pleasure women), 288, 290
Ahuináhuac, 317, 319. *See also* Mezcala
 Lapidary style
Ahuitzotl (Mexica ruler), 62, 185, 320, 545
Ahuizotl's Palace (Tenochtitlán), 718
Ajalpan phase, 708–709
Ajcot, Baltasar, 671
Ajuereado phase, 707
Ak. *See* Yax-Ain II
Ake, 34, 435, 438, 512
Alajuela, Lake, 360
albatross, 257
Albion Island, 14, 355
albite, 381
Albornoz, Rodrigo de, 674
alcaldes mayores, 165
alcohol. *See* intoxicants and intoxication;
 pulque
Aldenderfer, M., 663, 664
alegría, 275
alidade optical mapping instrument, 28
Alima, 823
alkaloids, 374
allometry, skeletal, 25
alloys, 72, 457
All Saints Day, 20
All Souls Day, 20
almanacs, 91, 569
alphabetic writing, 569
Altamira, 90, 452
Altar de Sacrificios (Petén, Guatemala),
 17–19
 ceramics record, 18
 figurines, 269
 interregional interactions, 367

Maya Lowlands: South, 445
 Usumacinta dams, 792
Altares, Los, 160
Altar of the Carved Skulls (Cholula), 140
altars
 Chalcatzingo, 118
 El Tajín, 694
 La Venta, 118
 San Lorenzo, 118
 Tarascan, 703
 Tenayuca, 712
 West Mexico, 819, 821
 Zaculeu, 845
Alta Verapaz region, **16**
 Guatemala Highlands and, 306, 307, 310
Alta Vista de Chalchihuites (Zacatecas,
 Mexico), **16–17**, 351, 494
 Northwestern Frontier and, 530, 531, 532,
 533
 observatory, 120
Altun Há (Belize, Belize), **19**
 chipped stone artifacts, 136
 interaction with South America, 673
 Teotihuacán and, 728
Alva Ixtlilxochitl, Fernando de, 772, 827
Alvarado, Pedro de, 163
Alvarado Tezozomoc, Fernando de, 772, 827
Amacuitlapilco, 488
Amalucan (Puebla, Mexico), **19–20**
 Tlalancaleca and, 757
 water-management system, 20, 353
Amanita muscaria, 374
Amapa (Nayarit, Mexico), **20**, 305, 407,
 455
 Northwestern Frontier and, 532, 533
 West Mexico and, 821
amaranth, 32
 in Basin of Mexico, 75
 domesticated varieties of, 10
 Don Martín and, 222
 economic uses, 229
 as food, 213, 275
 medicinal use, 218
 Santa Catarina and, 650
 Tehuacán region and, 708, 709
 Teotihuacán and, 723
 Toluca region and, 763
 as tribute, 773
 Tula region and, 781, 782
 underworld association, 791
Amaranthus. See amaranth
Ambergris Cay (Belize), 596
Amblemidae, 264

American Anthropological Association, 684
"American as Inventor, The" (Nordenskiold),
 674
American Museum of Natural History (New
 York City), 684, 797
amino acids, 214
Amistad Basin, 373
Amozoc, 757
Amparo, El, 516
amphibians, 258–259
AMS technique (Accelerator Mass Spectrom-
 etry), 409
Amuco Abelino (Guerrero, Mexico), 315,
 318
Amuzgo, 672
Anadenanthera Peregrina, 372, 374
Anahlonin, 374
analytical methods. *See* archaeology; analyti-
 cal methods; dating methods
Anasazis, 525
Anawalt, P., 238
ancestor veneration, **20–21**
 Caracol and, 96
 carved images and, 42–43, 44, 46
 Maya, 450
Ancestral Goddess (Palenque mythical ruler),
 574
Ancient Calendar, The (Duran), 223
Anderson, A. J. O., 791
Anderson, Dana, 801
Andrews, A. P., 161
Andrews, E. Wyllys IV, 80, 227, 228
Andrews, George, 796
Andua, 837
anemia, 214
Angulo, Jorge, 117
animals. *See* fauna
Animas, Las, 422
animism, 216, 448
annalistic histories, 571
Annals of Cuauhtitlan, 560
Annals of the Cakchiquels, 309, 377
Annular category. *See* Orbiculor (Annular)
 category (head-shaping)
anteaters, 256
anthropology, 366, 368
anthropomorphism, 53, 105
Antigua, 336, 340
Antigua Basin, 186
Antilles ball court, 69
ants, 265
Apantipan, 317, 319
Aparicio, 327, 345

apartment compounds (Teotihuacán), 38–39,
40, 46, 49, 131, 722, 727, 728, 729,
730, 732, 253
Apatzingán region (Michoacán, Mexico), **21**
aplastics, 606
Apoala, 479
apparel. *See* clothing
apple snails, 264
aquatic mammals, 257
aqueducts, 13, 215, 353
Aquiles Serdan, 452
Arana, Raul, 117
Arboleda-Balsas, La (Guerrero, Mexico), 315,
318, 319
Arbolillo, El (D.F., Mexico), **21–22**, 748
ceramic sequence, 21, 57
figurines, 268
and Zacatenco, 845
archaeoastronomy. *See* astronomy, archaeoastronomy, and astrology; underworld
archaeofaunal analysis, 24–25
Archaeology (reference text), 418
archaeology: analytical methods, **22–26**
x-ray diffraction, 23, 24
ceramic chronological data, 605–606
ceramic production site indication, 608
chemical, 22, 606
and contamination, 22
coprolite, 25
dating methods, 9, 27, 143, 202–208
demographic trends, 208–209, 210–211
faunal, 24–25
for jadeitites, 383–384
macrofloral, 24
neutron activation, 23
for overlapping areas, 364
petrographic, 23
pollen study, 8–9, 19, 24. *See also* pollen
soil chemistry, 22
spectroscopic techniques, 23, 409
statistical, 25
and surface residues, 26–27
See also archaeology: research design and
field methods; artifacts and industries;
skeletal analysis
archaeology: research design and field
methods, **26–30**
caretaker institution (by country), 26
excavation methods and techniques,
28–30
mapping of sites, 28
reconnaissance techniques, 26–27
recording of observations, 29

site identification and assessment techniques, 27–28
vertical and horizontal positioning, 28, 29
See also archaeology: analytical methods;
dating methods; settlement patterns and
settlement systems; settlement studies
Archaic Hypothesis, 684
Archaic period (c. 8000–2000 B.C.), 3, 29,
30–33
agriculture and domestication, 9, 213
Chiapas interior plateau, 125
Chihuahua, West Central, 133–134, 134
chipped stone tools, 136
coprolite analysis, 25
Corralitos, 180
demographic analysis, 209, 212
diet indications, 213
family and household, 252
Guatemala Highlands, 308
Gulf Lowlands: North, 325
Gulf Lowlands: North Central, 325, 329
Gulf Lowlands: South Central, 336
hunter–gatherers, 31
Matanchén, 416
Maya Lowlands: North, 433
Mazatan region, 451
Michoacán region, 459
minerals, ores, and mining, 471
Morelos region, 487
Northern Arid Zone, 524
Northwestern Frontier, 530
Oaxaca and Tehuantepec region, 539
obsidian: tools, techniques, and products,
553, 554
Pala Chica Cave, 572
Peñoles region, 585
Puebla-Tlaxcala region, 612
Pulltrouser Swamp, 617
sacred places, 637
Santa Luisa, 651
Tehuacán region, 707
West Mexico, 818, 820, 822
Zapotitan region, 848
See also Early Archaic period; Late Archaic
period; Middle Archaic period
architecture: civic-ceremonial, **33–37**
Atlantean figure, 56
Aztatlan complex, 58
Aztec. *See* Tenochtitlán *subheadings below*
basic elements/characteristics of, 33
Basin of Mexico, 75–76
Calixtlahuaca, 92
Cantona, 94

cave construction beneath, 101
cave representations, 101
Cerén, 37, 110–112
Cerro del Huistle, 351
Cerro de Trincheras, 113
Cerro Palenque, 114
Cerros, 115, 116
Chaco Canyon great houses, 116–117
Chalchihuites culture, 120
Chalcotzingo, 117, 118
Chiapas interior plateau, 125
Chichén Itzá, 36, 127, 128–131, 129
Cholula, 139, 140–141
Cihuatan, 143, 144
Cihuatecpan, 145
civic-ceremonial center, 145–147
Cobá, 160
Colha, 162
Colonial period, 164
Comala, 166
Comalcalco, 167
Copán, 169, 171–176
Copán region, 178
Cotzumalhuapa, 186
Cotzumalhuapa style, 186
Cuauhnahuac, 195
Cuayucatepec, 195
Cuello, 196
Dainzú, 201
dating method, 204
divination and, 221
Dos Pilas, 222
Dzibilchaltún, 227
economic organization and, 233
Edzna, 235
El Grillo, 300
El Pital, 593
El Tajín, 35, 691, 693, 694
El Tajín innovations, 693
El Teúl, 741, 742
ethnicity and, 239
Etlatongo, 248
family and household and, 252
Feathered Serpent iconography, 266
Formative period, 280, 281, 282
gender roles and, 291
ground stone tools and, 301
Gualjoquito, 303
Gualupita Las Dalias, 304
Guasave, 305
Guatemala Highlands, 308, 310
Guayabo de Turrialba, 311
Guerrero, 315, 317

and Huatusco, 349
and Huaxtepec, 350
and Huexotla, 350
human ritual sacrifices, 93–94, 104, 106,
    107, 216, 258, 466, 639, 640
hydrology, 353
hygiene and sanitation, 215
instability of universe of, 103–104
interregional interactions, 366, 368, 370
intoxicants, 278, 371–372, 373, 374
and Ixtlan del Río, 378
jaguar iconography and symbolism, 385,
    386
language at Contact, 395–397, 399
lapidary industry, 400
leadership, 401
life expectancy, 215
and Malinalco, 410
maps and place-names, 411
market systems, 412, 413
mathematics, 416
and Maya deities and religion, 448, 449,
    431
medicinal plants, 219, 220
merchants, 63
metal tools, techniques, and products, 457
and Michoacán region, 458, 463, 464
militarism and warfare, 63, 104, 105, 107,
    465–467, 468, 807, 808, 809
minerals, ores, and mining, 470, 471
mirrors, 473
and Mitla, 474
and Mixtec, 478, 479
Mixteca-Puebla style, 481
and Morelos region, 489, 490
mural painting, 492, 494
museum ethnographic materials on, 495
music, dance, theater, and poetry, 505,
    506, 507–508
and Nahua, 652
names and titles, 511
and Northern Arid Zone, 522, 528
and Northwestern Frontier, 533
and Oaxaca and Tehuantepec region, 545
obsidian tools, techniques, and products,
    548, 553
and Otomí cultural tradition, 559, 560
and Otumba, 561
painted manuscripts, 571
painters, 563–564
personal hygiene, 215
pochteca. See long-distance trade
polygyny practice, 253

ports of trade, 596
Postclassic period, 598–603
pottery, 605, 609
and Puebla-Tlaxcala region, 615, 616
Quiahuiztlan, 622
religion and deities, 63, 102–108, 145,
    218, 266, 289–290, 717–718
resources of conquered areas, 64
sacred geography of, 717–718
sacred history of, 104
sacrifice. *See subhead* human ritual
    sacrifices *above*
Sahagún, 641
Santa Catarina, 650
scribes, 655
sculpture, 656, 657, 658
silex blades, 664
social organization of cities, 63
and Soconusco region, 670, 671
Spanish conquest of, 163, 213, 216, 805
spirit companion belief, 672
sweat baths, 689
Tarascan relations, 702, 703–704
and Teotihuacán, 723, 727, 729
and Teotihuacán religion, 732, 733, 734
and Teotihuacán sacred landscape, 735
and Tepeapulco, 735, 736
and Texcoco, 742, 743
and Texcotzingo, 745
thrones and benches, 747
and Tlapacoya, 758
and Tollan, 759
and Toltec culture, 759, 760, 761, 762
and Toluca region, 766
transport forms, 768
treatment of conquered peoples, 63
and Tres Zapotes, 771
tributary provinces, 63–64, 466
and tribute, 63–64, 275, 466, 772, 773,
    774, 826
and Tula de Hidalgo, 775, 777
and Tula region, 782
and Tzintzuntzan, 784, 785
underworld beliefs, 218, 791
and Vega de la Peña and Cuajilotes, 797
and Villa Rica, 802, 803
warfare ideology, 63. *See also subhead* mili-
    tarism and warfare *above*
weaponry, 811
weaving and textiles, 813, 815, 817
and West Mexico, 820
wood uses, 824
wound treatments, 219–220

writing system, 825, 826
and Xaltocan, 827
and Xicalango, 828
and Xico, 828
and Xochicalco, 831
and Yanhuitlán, 837
and Yautépec, 838, 839
and Zempoala, 851
See also Mexica; Tenochtitlán: ceremonial
    center; Tenochtitlán: imperial ritual
    landscape; Tenochtitlán: palaces;
    Tenochtitlán-Tlatelolco
Aztecs Under Spanish Rule, The (Gibson), 299
Aztlan, 60, 600, 820
Azuzul, El, 555

B

backstrap loom, 814–815
badgers, 256
Bahlum-Kuk (Palenque ruler), 574, 576
Baide, 679
Bajío region (Guanajuato and adjacent
    states), **65–66**
    Acámbaro-Cerro el Chivo, 2, 66
    and Cantona, 94
    ceramic artifacts, 65
    and Coyotlatelco, 188, 189
    Northern Arid Zone and, 523, 524
    Northwestern Frontier and, 532, 534
    and Toltec culture, 65, 760
    and Tula de Hidalgo, 776
    See also Chupícuaro
bajos (natural depressions), 13–14, 355
Baker Cave, Texas, 581
Baktun 8 stela, 491
Balamkú (Campeche, Mexico), **66**, 435, 510
Balankanche Cave, 301, 439
Balberta, 186, 670
balché (alcoholic drink), 278, 371, 373
Balcón de Montezuma (Tamaulipas, Mexico),
    66–67
ball courts. *See* ball game
ball game, **67–71**
    Ahualulco court, 16
    art associated with, 49
    Aztec version of, 67
    Buenavista Huaxcama and the Río Verde
        region, 85
    Cantona, 94
    Casas Grandes courts, 97
    Cerro de las Mesas court, 112

burial practices (*cont.*)
    Southeast Mesoamerica, 675, 678
    Stirling's discovery, 688
    Tabachines, 691
    Tehuacán region, 707
    Tenochtitlán-Tlatelolco, 107
    Teotihuacán, 4, 727, 730, 731, 734
    Tetimpa region, 738
    Teuchitlan tradition, 738, 739
    textiles and, 815
    Thin Orange ware and, 746
    Tibas, 747
    Ticoman, 748
    Tikal, 750, 751, 752, 753, 754
    Tingambato, 755
    Tlalancaleca, 757
    Tlapacoya, 758
    Tlatilco, 102, 758
    Toluca region, 765
    Tres Zapotes, 771
    tribute and, 774
    Tzintzuntzan, 785, 786
    Uaxactum, 789, 790
    Uxmal, 795
    Vidor, 802
    warfare and, 805, 806
    West Mexico, 818, 821, 822
    Xochitécatl, 832
    Yagul, 836
    Yarumela, 837
    Yautépec, 839
    Zacatenco, 845
    Zaculeu, 845
    Zapotec, 20, 847
    See also shaft tombs; tombs
burins, 707
butchering patterns, 25
Butz Chan (Copán ruler), 421
Byland, B. E., 477, 755

C

Caacal II (Palenque rule), 574
Caballo Pintado, 82
"Cabeza Colosal de Hueyapan" (sculpture),
    769
cabildo (municipal council), 165
Cabrera Castro, Ruben, 463
Cacahuatenco, 329
Cacahuaziqui (Guerrero, Mexico)
    cave art, 101
    mural painting, 492

cacao. *See* chocolate and cacao
Cacaxtla (Tlaxcala, Mexico), **87**, 94
    art style of, 50
    Cerro Zapotecas and, 115
    ethnicity, 493
    figurines, 268
    fortification, 468
    gender roles in, 291
    migrations and, 367
    mural painting, 87, 108, 367, 468, 492,
        493, 615, 806
    Postclassic period and, 599
    religious activity, 102, 107, 108
    sacrifice practices, 639
    sculpture, 657
    Teotihuacán and, 727, 730
    warfare and, 468, 806
    weaponry of, 810
    Xochicalco and, 829, 831
    Xochitécatl and, 832
caches, 45, **87–88**
    at Caracol, 96
    See also bundles
cactus, 25
    peyote, 371, 373–374
Caddy, John Herbert, 577
Cahn Muan II (Maya ruler), 493
Cajón, El (Honduras), **88**
    jades excavated from, 382
    and Salitron Viejo, 641–642
Cakchiquel
    and Iximché, 377, 430, 601
    warfare, 309, 367
Calakmul (Campeche, Mexico), **88–90**,
    435
    Classic period, 89–90, 147
    and Copán, 89, 169
    emblem glyph, 89, 236
    fortifications, 283
    and La Milpa, 470
    Maya culture and, 88, 89, 428, 429
    and Maya Lowlands: South, 89, 445, 446
    monumental architecture of, 35, 89, 435
    Petexbatun region and, 588–589
    raised roads, 89
    as regional capital, 89
    reservoirs, 89
    royal tombs at, 90
    sites in area of, 90
    structures at, 89
    Tikal feud with, 753, 754
    Yaxchilan and, 840
Calderón, Jóse, 577

Calendar Round, 90, 91, 130–131, 398
    and Maya religion, 450
Calendar Stone, 103, 107, 656, 658
calendrics, **90–92**
    all-Mesoamerica system, 90
    as personal name source, 511
    astronomical observation and, 53–54
    Aztec cosmology and, 104
    Aztec ritual and, 107
    and Central Mexican sacrificial ceremonies,
        107
    codices, 569
    dating technique, 204
    52–year, 450
    Formative period, 282
    Gregorian calendar, 92, 202, 208, 242, 784
    in Gulf Lowlands: South Central, 337
    interpretation as dating method, 205,
        207–208
    languages at Contact and, 398
    La Peña Pintada, 585
    long count, 91–92, 208, 428, 450, 482,
        711, 769, 770, 784
    Maya, 49, 53, 90, 91–92, 130, 208,
        427–428, 430, 448, 450, 569, 684, 746
    and naming of days, 91
    and New Fire Ceremony, 91
    Oaxacan development of, 49, 541
    and origins of 260–day calendar, 91
    as painted manuscript theme, 569
    personal names drawn from, 511
    as personal name source, 511
    prediction making and, 91
    Sacred Round, 90, 91
    and sculpture, 103, 107, 657, 658
    short count concept in, 207–208
    solar, 91, 703
    Spinden correlation, 208, 684
    and spirit companion determination, 672
    stela cult, 686
    Tarascan, 703
    Teotihuacán and, 725, 731, 732, 735
    Thompson correlation, 746
    365–day calendar, 90, 91, 107, 450
    Tlalancaleca and, 757
    Tuxtla Statuette, 784
    260–day calendar, 90, 91, 107, 450, 511,
        569
    two concurrent cycles of, 90
    Uaxactum and, 789
    writing and, 208, 825
    Xochicalco and, 831
    Yaxchilan and, 841

Zapotec, 846

See also astronomy, archaeoastronomy, and astrology

Calentura, La, 452, 471

Calichal phase, 17

Calixtlahuaca (Toluca, Mexico), **92–93**, 766. *See also* Tilantongo; Yanhuitlan

Calmecac (Calixtlahuaca), 92

calmil (home garden), 11

Calón, El. *See* Northwestern Frontier

Calpulalpan, 615

calpulli (residential groupings), 253

Calsada Cave, La, 31, 32, 524, 580

Camaxtli. *See* Mixcoatl

Cambridge University, 417, 418

Camino Real, 127

Campaña San Andres, 680, 681, 849, 850

Campana-Tepozoco, La, 765

Campbell, L., 396, 398

Campeche, Mexico, 663, 828

  Balamkú, 66, 435, 510

  Becan, 80, 90, 367

  Calakmul, 35, 88–90, 435

  Hochob, 346, 436

  Jaina, 269, 373, 375, 386, 438

  Nadzcaan, 510

  Toltec culture, 760, 761

  Xicalongo, 342, 828

CAM plants, 23

Cañada de Alfaro, 524

Cañada de Virgin, 524

Canajasté (Chiapas, Mexico), **93**, 126

canals, 352, 353, 354, 355

  agricultural, 13, 15, 353, 354

  Amalucan, 20

  Cerros, 115

  Classic period, 151

  Edzna, 234–235, 435

  El Pital, 593

  Gulf Lowlands: North Central, 327, 328

  Kaminaljuyu, 388, 389

  Las Higueras, 345

  Los Naranjos, 513

  Maya Lowlands: North, 434

  Oaxaca and Tehuantepec region, 13, 537

  Puebla-Tlaxcala region, 613

  and reservoirs, 89, 353

  Santa Luisa, 652

  and settlement patterns, 660

  Tenochtitlán-Tlatelolco, 62, 717, 720

  Teuchitlan, 740

  Texcoco, 743

  Tula region, 779, 780, 781

Yautépec, 839

Zempoala, 851

See also chinampa system

Cañas-Liberia project area, 454

Cancuen, 792

Candelaria Cave, La, 224, 516

cannibalism, **93–94**, 276

canoes, 132, 768, 811, 824

  Tenochtitlán-Tlatelolco, 717, 720

  trade route, 596

Cañon del Molino, 531

canons, 811

Cantona (Puebla, Mexico), **94**, 326, 613

Cañutillo phase, 16, 17, 530

Capacha (Colima, Mexico), **95–96**

  funerary pottery, 95–96

  shaft tombs, 662

Capachas, 558

capes and cloaks, 153, 156, 158, 159

  Cholula decorated, 139

  cotton, 184–185

  as exchange media, 231, 250, 817

Capilco, 39, 195, 489

Captain Feathered Serpent (Chichén Itzá), 130

Captain Sun Disc (Chichén Itzá), 130

Capulac Concepción, 613

capybara, 257

Carabino, 65, 760

Caracol (Cayo District, Belize), **96–97**

  Maya culture, 429

  Naranjo and, 512

  terrace systems, 12, 96

  Tikal and, 96, 751

caracol dye, 816

Carapan, 461

carbon–14 dating. *See* radiocarbon dating

carbonates, 22

carbonic acid, 22

carbonization, 9, 10, 23

Cárdenas, Efraín, 463

Caribs, 399

Carmack, Robert M., 309, 475

  and Toltec culture, 759, 761

Carnegie Institution

  and Becan, 80

  and Bonampak, 83

  and Chichén Itzá, 128, 491

  and Copán, 169, 172

  and Guatemala Highlands, 308

  and Kaminaljuyu, 389

  and Maya: Motagua region, 419

  and Mayapan, 451

Thompson articles and reports for, 746

  and Uaxactum, 789, 790

  and Yaxuna, 842

Carrasco, V. R., 387

carvings

  ceramic stamps, 110, 606

  Chalcotzingo, 118

  Dainzú stone reliefs, 201

  El Tajín religion, 694, 697

  Izapa style, 380

  jade, 381, 382, 384, 471, 656, 688

  La Venta, 799, 800

  Maudslay study of, 418

  Monte Albán stone relief, 103, 484, 541, 542, 658, 670, 805

  petroglyph. *See* petroglyphs as separate listing

  scribes and, 655

  Seibal, 660

  Soconusco region, 669

  stone writing and, 610, 826

  Teotihuacán, 727, 729, 730

  Tututepec, 784

  Uxmal, 795

  of warfare records, 806

  wood, 824. *See also* wood: tools and products *as separate listing*

  Xochicalco, 830, 831

  Yagul, 836

  Yaxchilan, 839, 840

  Zapotec mortuary practices, 847

  See also inscriptions; sculpture; stela cult; stelae

Casas, Bartolomé de las. *See* Las Casas, Bartolomé de

Casas Grandes (Chihuahua, Mexico), **97**, 133, 134

  ball courts, 97

  largest prehistoric pueblo, 97

  Northern Arid Zone, 526, 527

  Northwestern Frontier, 531

  site plan, 97, 526

  and Tarascan, 463

  water system, 354

Casitas, 328

Caso, Alfonso

  and Monte Albán, 81, 484, 486, 601

  and Monte Negro, 486

  on Olmec "Mother Culture," 688

  and Tres Zapotes, 770

"Casper" (Palenque ruler), 574

cassiterite deposits, 456

castas (castes), 165

Puebla-Tlaxcala region, 611
San José Mogote, 645
sculpture, 657
Teotihuacán, 723, 729
Tepoztlán, 490, 737
Tlapacoya, 758
Tula region, 777
Xochicalco, 828–832
Yautépec, 489, 838–839
Morett (Colima, Mexico), **490–491**, 823
Morgadal Grande, 327, 329
Morgan, Lewis Henry, 240
Morley, Sylvanus Griswold, 82, **491**, 789, 796
Altar de Sacrificios site description, 18
and Yaxchilan, 841
morning-glory seeds, 221, 372, 373, 374
mortality rate
Colonial period epidemic effects, 216
determination of, 211, 212
infant and child, 211, 215, 216
See also life expectancy
mortars and pestles, 707, 708
mortuary practices. *See* burial practices
Motagua River Valley, 382–384. *See also* Maya: Motagua region
Motecuhzoma Ilhuicamina (Motecuhzoma I) (Aztec ruler), 62, 320, 349, 489
sculpture of, 658
Motecuhzoma Xocoyotzin (Motecuhzoma II) (Aztec ruler), 62, 141, 216, 545
banquet of, 275
Cortés as guest of, 718
palace, 718, 719
sculpture of, 658
sweat baths of, 689
Mother Goddess cult, 288, 290
motmots, 258
Motolinía, Toribio de, 141, 289, 713, 852
"Mountain of Sustenance" (Tonacatepetl), 717
mountain sheep, 257
Mountjoy, J., 139, 491, 662
Mount Tlaloc, 106, 791, 717
Moxviquil, 126
Moyotzingo, 612, 613
Muir (geologist), 334
Mula-West, La, 360, 362
mulberry (*Morus niger*), 812
Mulchic, 493
mullets, 259
Mulucbacob, 160
mumps epidemics, 216

Muna, 438
mundane architecture. *See* architecture: vernacular-mundane
Muñeca, La, 90
municipios, 165
Munsell Soil Color Charts, 29
Munson Williams Proctor Institute, Museum of Art (Utica, New York), 119
mural painting, 50, **491–494**
as alternative to writing, 826
Bonampak, 82–85, 385, 492, 493
Cacaxtla, 87, 108, 367, 468, 492, 493, 615, 806
cave art, 46, 48, 101
caves of Guerrero, 101
Chichén Itzá, 129, 130, 284, 493
clothing depictions, 152, 157
El Tajín, 493, 693
fortifications depictions, 284
gender-role depictions, 291
geometric-type designs in, 417
Guerrero, 315, 492
Gulf Lowlands: North Central, 327, 329
interregional interactions, 367
Iximché, 377
jaguar symbolism, 385
Las Higueras, 345–346
Maya Lowlands: North, 440
Mixtec, 478
Mixteca-Puebla style, 481
music and dance depictions, 504, 507
Naj Tunich, 511
Northern Arid Zone, 524
Olmec-Guerrero style, 557
Postclassic period, 599, 600, 603
Puebla-Tlaxcala region, 611, 615, 616
Santa Luisa, 652
Santa Rita Corozal, 654
Sayil and Chac, 654
Tamuín-Tantoc, 698
techniques, 492
Tehuacán region, 710
Teotihuacán, 46, 49, 107, 372, 491, 492, 493, 494, 657, 723, 727, 728, 729, 731, 732, 733
themes and styles, 492–494
"Tlalocan" mural, 372
Toltec culture, 761
Tulum, 783
Uaxactum, 789
Utatlán, 793
warfare depiction, 806
Xaltocan, 827

Yagul, 835
Yautépec, 839
Murdock, G. P., 251
Muscovy duck, 276
Museo de Antropología (Jalapa), 345
Museo del Hombre (Panama City), 26
Museo Nacional (San Salvador), 26
Museo Nacional de Antropología (Mexico City), 83, 98, 106, 463, 495, 698, 841
Museo Nacional de Costa Rica (San José), 26, 72, 285, 688, 747
Museo Nacional de Nicaragua (Managua), 26
Department of Archaeology, 516
Museum für Völkerkunde (Berlin), 185
museums, archives, and libraries, **494–504**
listing of, 495–504
Musgrave-Portilla, L. M., 672
mushroom hallucinogens, 221, 372, 373
music, dance, theater, and poetry, **504–508**
ceramic instruments, 109, 332
figurines and, 266, 268, 269, 373
Guasave and, 304, 306
La Sierra and, 663
Naco and, 509
Northwestern Frontier and, 531, 533
Oaxaca and Tehuantepec region and, 542
percussion instruments, 504–505, 507
as sacrifice accompaniment, 639
sculpture of, 504, 658
Smiling Face figurines and, 667
stela cult and, 686
stelae and, 687
Teotihuacán religion and, 733
Tingambato and, 755
Tlatilco and, 758
Tzintzuntzan and, 786
vocal music, 506
West Mexico, 820
wind instruments, 109, 505, 507
wooden instruments, 824
Yaxchilan and, 840
mustelids, 256
Mutelidae, 264

N

Naachtun, 90
Nacascolo (Guanacaste, Costa Rica), 376, **509**, 520, 802
Na Chen (Yaxchilan ritual object), 839

Quiriguá (Izabal, Guatemala) (*cont.*)
    and Maya: Motagua region, 418–424
    and Southeast Mesoamerica, 677
Quiroga, Vasco de, 787
Q'ukumatz. *See* Quetzalcoatl

R

rabbits, 213, 257, 565, 816
raccoons, 256
radar, 27
radiocarbon dating, 9, 143, 202, 203, 204,
    206
    El Tajín, 695
    Etlatongo, 248
    and GMT long count correlation, 208
    Gualjoquito, 303
    Guasave, 305
    Guerrero, 315, 319, 605
    Gulf Lowlands: South Central, 336
    Ixtapa, 377
    Laguna Zope, 393
    Lambityeco, 394
    La Quemada, 621
    La Venta, 800
    Morett, 491
    Northwestern Frontier, 530, 531, 532
    Olmec culture, 555
    Paleoindian period, 579, 580
    Paso de la Amada, 584
    of peyote, 373
    of pottery, 605
    Puebla-Tlaxcala region, 612
    Río Claro, 626
    Rivas, 632
    Santa Luisa, 651
    Tehuacán region, 708
    Temesco, 710
    Teotihuacán, 723
    Tetimpa region, 738
    Tlapacoya, 758
    Tres Zapotes, 770
    Uxmal, 793
    West Mexico, 821, 822, 823
    Xaltocan, 827
    Zacatenco, 845
rails, 258
Rain (deity). *See* Nica
rainfall, 8, 266, 402, 748
    Tehuacán region, 705
    Tehuantepec region, 537
rain god. *See* Tlaloc

rain-making ceremonies, 635
Ramírez, José Fernando, 223
ramón, 10, 214
Ramos de la Vega (archaeologist), 740
Rana, 70
Ranchito, El, 820
Ranchoapan, 415
Rancho La Amapola, 579
Ranere, Anthony J., 360, 362
Raramuri, 371
rasping instrument, 505, 507
Rathje, William L., 191
rats, 257
rattles, 506, 507
rattlesnake, 259
Rattray, E. C., 188, 189
Ravesloot, J. C., 134
Rayón, 333
razors, 553
Recent era, 848
reconnaissance techniques. *See* archeology:
    research design and field methods
Reconquista, 165
reconstruction. *See* activity areas and
    assemblages; *specific sites*
Redmond, E., 618
Red-on-Buff pottery, 304, 531, 609
Red-Rim Decorated ceramics, 304
Red Temple (Cacaxtla), 493
Red Temples (Tenochtitlán), 715
Red Tezcatolipoca (deity), 103
reducción, 164
reincarnation, 450
Relación de las cosas de Yucatán (Landa), 395,
    431, 654
*Relación de las cosas notables de la nueva
    España y de la conquista* (Zorita), 852
Relación de Michoacán, 158, 462, 463, 464,
    700
    on Tarascan marriage forms, 702
    on Tzintzuntzan, 784, 785, 786
Relación de Querétero, 560
Relación de Tezcoco, 655
Relación geográfica (Bautista de Pomar),
    473
Relación geográfica (Rojas), 141, 240
    maps and place-names, 411
Relación geográficas, 490, 772
Relación Sumaria (Lebrón de Quíones), 823
relative dating methods, 202–203, 204–205
religion
    ancestor veneration, 20–21
    artwork and, 42, 44–45

Aztec, 63, 102–108, 145, 218, 266,
    289–290
Aztec creation myth, 270
as Aztec sacrifice basis, 104, 108, 216
blood and bloodletting rites, 81–82
caves' importance to, 99–100, 101, 103
Central Mexican. *See* Central Mexican
    religion
Cerén complex, 112
Cholula center, 102, 103, 139, 141
Cihuatecpan, 145
civic-ceremonial center, 145–147
Cobá, 161
Colonial period, 165
Cozumel, 189–190
Cuello, 196
disease relationship, 216–219
divination, 220–221
Dzibilchaltún, 227
El Manatí, 410
El Tajín, 691, 697
ethnographical sources on, 245
family and household and, 253
fauna and, 257, 258–259, 264, 265
food tributes and, 275, 276, 277
gender roles and, 289–290
ground stone tools and, 301
Gulf Lowlands: North, 332
Gulf Lowlands: North Central, 328
Huatusco, 349
Izapa style, 380
jade uses, 382
jaguar symbol, 257
languages at Contact and, 398
lapidary industry and, 400
La Quemada, 621
La Sierra, 663
La Venta, 800
Lecandón, Maya, 392
Lubaantún, 405
Malinalco, 410
market systems and, 412, 413
Maya, 429, 448–451
Maya Lowlands: North, 434, 437
Maya Lowlands: South, 444, 446
Mexica, 63, 716, 717–718
Mixteca-Puebla, 481
Monte Albán, 485
Morelos region, 488
mural painting and, 493
music, dance, theater, and poetry, 506
Naco, 509, 510
Nadzcaan, 510

theater. *See* music, dance, theater, and poetry

theodolite, 28

thermoluminescent dating, 202, 203, 205, 207

Thiaridae, 264

Thicatame (Tarascan ruler), 701

Thin Orange ware, 16, 18, 609, **746**, 765, 823

    Cerro Palenque, 114

    Southeast Mesoamerica, 682

    Teotihuacán, 609, 745

13 Rabbit (El Tajín ruler), 657, 694, 697

Thompson, Edward H., 391, 824

Thompson, J. Eric S., 99, 208, 619, **746**

    and Cotzumalhuapa sites, 185

    and Tres Zapotes, 770

thread. *See* weaving and textiles

thrones and benches, 4, **747**

    Chichén Itzá, 132

    Tenochtitlán, 715

Tibas, Talamanca de (San José, Costa Rica), **747–748**

Ticoman (D.F., Mexico), 268, **748**, 845

Tierra Caliente region, 320, 765, 766

Tierras Largas phase, 251, 540

"Tiger Claw" (Mixtec ruler). *See* 8 Deer

Tikal (Petén, Guatemala), **748–755**

    architectural features and groups, 34, 35, 750

    art and texts, 750–751, 754

    caches, 88

    and Calakmul's emblem glyph, 89–90

    Caracol conquest of, 96, 751

    carved bones at, 48

    ceramics, 18, 748, 751, 752

    civic-ceremonial center, 146

    Classic period, 147, 150, 428

    and Copán, 169

    dating method, 208

    demographic trends, 209, 748, 752

    development and history, 751–752

    and Dos Pilas, 222

    dynastic progressions, 752–754

    and El Mirador, 473

    emblem glyphs, 236

    ethnicity, 238

    family and household, 252

    fortifications, 283

    interregional interactions, 366

    and La Milpa, 470

    Maudslay visits to, 417, 418

    and Maya culture, 425, 427, 428, 429, 748–755

    and Maya Lowlands: South, 445, 446

    multiple ball courts, 70

    and Naranjo, 512

    and Petexbatun region, 588, 589

    and Planchón de las Figuras, 594

    reservoir system, 354–355

    and Río Azul, 626

    sacred places, 637

    sculpture, 658

    silex, 664

    site plan of, 749

    stelae, 48, 750, 751, 752, 753, 754

    stone monument inscriptions, 428

    and Uaxactum, 428, 748, 789, 790

    warfare, 428, 806

    and Yaxchilan, 840

Tilantongo (Oaxaca, Mexico), 478, 601, **755**, 761, 783

Tillo, 837

tilmatli (cloak), 153

tin, 456, 457, 704

tinamous, 258

Tingambato (Michoacán, Mexico), 460, 461, **755–756**

Tinganio, 755

tinklers, 506, 507

Tintal, 89

tinto tree, 14

Tintzunzan, 455

Tira de la Peregrinación, 240

Tiripeme (deities), 785

Tiristarán, 461

titles. *See* leadership and rulership; names and titles

Título Totonicapán (Maya epic), 309

Tizatlán (Tlaxcala, Mexico), 481, 494, 616, **756**

Tizoc (Aztec ruler), 62, 320, 467

Tizoc Stone, 291, 658

Tlacael (Aztec leader), 640

Tlachihualtepetl (Great Pyramid), 139, 140–141, 372

Tlacochahuaya, 543

Tlacolula, 835, 837

Tlacopán, 62, 711

    tribute, 772

    and Triple Alliance Empire, 78, 715, 717, 742

Tlacozotitlán (Guerrero, Mexico), **756**

Tlahuicas, 195, 320, 350, 489, 737

Tlahuizcalpantecuhtli. *See* Xolotl

Tlalancaleca (Puebla, Mexico), 222, 612, 613, **756–757**

Tláloc (deity)

    as disease cause, 217, 218

    and egret feathers, 258

    and fauna, 256

    fertility-rain association, 63, 106

    figures of, 98, 145

    flowers and, 272, 273

    gender and, 289–290

    interregional interactions and, 367

    and Maya Lowlands: North, 439

    mural painting at shrine of, 494

    nonrepresentation in Tarascan religion, 702

    relief sculpture of, 50

    sacrifice and, 639, 640

    shrine to, 106, 639, 712, 715, 717, 721

    Soconusco region and, 669

    Teotihuacán and, 727, 728, 732–733

    Texcoco and, 742

    Tlalancaleca and, 757

    underworld and, 791

    Uxmal and, 793

    War Serpent imagery of, 266

Tlaloc Group (Calixtlahuaca), 92

Tlapacoya (México, Mexico), **757–758**

    Archaic period, 31, 32

    Ayotla-Zohapilco and, 57

    Don Martín and, 222

    evidence of pre-agricultural society at, 75

    figurines, 266, 267, 268

    maize, 409

    Paleoindian period, 579

    Santa Catarina and, 650

    Tlalancaleca and, 757

    Tlatilco and, 758

    Zohapilco site, 75

Tlappa, 481

Tlatelolco. *See* Tenochtitlán-Tlatelolco

Tlatilco (México, Mexico), 34, **758–759**

    Capacha pottery similarities with, 95–96

    clothing, 152, 156

    Cuyamel Caves, 199

    demographic analysis, 212

    El Opeño and, 558

    figurines, 102

    funerary practices, 102

    Gualupita and, 304

    Guerrero and, 317

    Morelos region and, 487

    religious activity, 102, 103, 107

    shaft tombs, 662

Tlaxcala in the Sixteenth Century (Gibson), 299

hammers, 656
hoes, 554
in Intermediate area, 360
in Kaminaljuyu, 388
knives, 6, 553, 554, 810
in La Conchita, 168
lapidary industry, 400
in La Quemada, 621
in La Venta, 800
lime and limestone, 403
Maya, 443, 427
metal, 455
minerals for, 471
in Oaxaca and Tehuantepec region, 538, 539
obsidian, 552–554
Paleoindian period, 579, 580
punches, 552
razors, 553
residue analysis, 22
Santa Marta Cave, 653
saws, 656
scrapers, 6, 550, 552, 579, 580, 653, 664, 707, 708
in Soconusco region, 668
in Tehuacán region, 707, 708, 709
in Temesco, 710
in Tlatilco, 758
Toltec, 762
in Tzintzuntzan, 785
weaponry, 809
wood, 824
in Xochicalco, 830
in Yautépec, 839
See also blades; metal tools, techniques, and products; obsidian: tools, techniques, and products; silex; spindle whorls
Topiltzin-Quetzalcoatl (Mexican deity-king), 104, 762. See also Quetzalcoatl
Topoxte (Péten, Guatemala), 705
Topoxte Cave, 101
Toro (archaeologist), 672
tortillas, 275, 276, 694
tortoise shell (as musical instrument), 507
Totimehuacan, 612, 613, 616
Totoate, 532
Totonac, 184, 622, 672
Isla de Sacrificios, 375
language, 395, 397, 398
maps and place-names, 411
Santa Luisa, 652
Smiling Face figurines, 666

Vega de la Peña and Cuajilotes, 797
Villa Rica, 802
Zempoala, 850
Tototepec, 559, 560
toucans, 258
Tourtellot, G., 253, 470
Tovar, Juan de, 223
Tozpalatl (Tenochtitlán sacred spring), 715
Tozzer, Alfred M., 187, 395, 491
Tozzer Causeway (Tikal), 750
trade. See economic organization; exchange media; long-distance trade; market systems; ports of trade
trance-inducing agents, 221
transit optical mapping instrument, 28
transport, 767–768
Cobá, 160
craft production and, 193, 194
economic organization and, 229, 230, 232
food shortages and, 255
interaction with South America, 673, 674
La Quemada, 622
Northwestern Frontier, 532
Piedras Negras, 591
San Lorenzo Tenochtitlán, 647, 649
of sculpture materials, 656
Stann Creek, 684
Tenochtitlán-Tlatelolco canoes, 717, 720
tribute and, 773
warfare and, 806–807, 811
Xochicalco, 830
Xunantunich, 833
Yaxuna, 842
Zapotitan region, 850
Trapiche. See Chalchuapa
trash heaps
activity areas and assemblages, 3
agave flesh indications, 5
carbonized remains, 9
Don Martín, 222
figurine remains in, 268
ground stone tool remains in, 301
Kaminaljuyu, 388
Lagartero, 392
La Venta, 799
Loma Torremote, 404
Matacapan, 416
mineral and ore indications in, 471
Northern Arid Zone, 525
Smiling Face figurine remains in, 667
Soconusco region, 668
Tikal, 750, 752
Tlatilco, 758

Xaltocan, 827
Xochicalco, 829
Zacatenco, 845
Tratado (Ruiz de Alarcón), 373
Travesía (Cortés, Honduras), **768–769**
tree cultivation, 10–11
tree-ring dating (dendrochronology), 202, 203, 204, 206
trenches, 29
Tres Cerritos, 460, 463, 702
Tres Cerros, 423
Tres Islas, 792
Tres Zapotes (Veracruz, Mexico), **769–772**
clothing, 153
Gulf Lowlands: South and, 343
Gulf Lowlands: South Central and, 336, 338, 339
monumental workshop, 44
Olmec Colossal Heads found in, 34
Olmec culture, 554–557, 769–771
religious activity, 103
sculpture, 34, 656, 657
stelae, 49
Stirling visit to, 688
Teotihuacán and, 729
tribute, **772–774**
Aztec imperial conquests and, 63–64, 275, 466, 772, 773, 774
Aztec painted lists of, 826
bundles, 86
cotton as, 184, 773
foods as, 275, 773
painted records of, 568, 826
seeds as, 275
Spanish system of, 164
Tarascan and, 701, 705
Tenochtitlán, 715, 716, 722, 723, 724
textiles as, 817
Tzintzuntzan and, 785, 787
Vega de la Peña and Cuajilotes and, 797
warfare and, 808
Xochicalco and, 831
Yagul and, 837
Yautépec and, 838
trincheras (rock-water spreaders), 354
Trincheras tradition. See Cerro de Trincheras
Triple Alliance Empire. See Aztec culture and history; Mexica; Tenochtitlán-Tlatelolco; Texcoco; Tlacopan
Tronadora, 361, 519
tropical forests, 9
Tropic of Cancer, 16
trousers, 164